THE GROVE
BOOK OF
OPERA
SINGERS

THE GROVE
BOOK OF
OPERA
SINGERS

Edited by
LAURA MACY

OXFORD
UNIVERSITY PRESS

OXFORD
UNIVERSITY PRESS

Oxford University Press, Inc., publishes works that further Oxford University's
objective of excellence in research, scholarship, and education.

Oxford New York

Auckland Cape Town Dar es Salaam Hong Kong Karachi
Kuala Lumpur Madrid Melbourne Mexico City Nairobi
New Delhi Shanghai Taipei Toronto

With offices in

Argentina Austria Brazil Chile Czech Republic France Greece
Guatemala Hungary Italy Japan Poland Portugal Singapore
South Korea Switzerland Thailand Turkey Ukraine Vietnam

Copyright © 2008 by Oxford University Press

Published by Oxford University Press, Inc.
198 Madison Avenue, New York, NY 10016
www.oup.com

Oxford is a registered trademark of Oxford University Press

Library of Congress Cataloging-in-Publication Data

The Grove book of opera singers/edited by Laura Macy.
p. cm.
Includes indexes.
ISBN-13: 978-0-19-533765-5 (hardcover: alk. paper) 1. Singers—Biography—Dictionaries.
2. Opera—Biography—Dictionaries. 3. Operas—Characters—Dictionaries.
I. Macy, Laura Williams.
ML102.O6G76 2008
782.1092'2--dc22

2008017065

Contents

Preface

The Grove Book of Opera Singers is a collection of biographies of over 1500 opera singers. Most of these are based on entries in either *The New Grove Dictionary of Opera* (1992), or *The New Grove Dictionary of Music and Musicians*, second edition (2001). The book also includes about 100 articles that have not appeared before in print.

It may be helpful to explain the selection process for these articles. *Grove Music Online* includes over 3000 articles on singers in the classical tradition. Our first decision, therefore, was to limit the coverage here to singers of opera. We have been generous with this definition, including people who may have been better known as concert or even musical theatre singers if they also made a significant contribution to opera. Having decided to focus on opera, it seemed sensible to be guided by *The Grove Book of Operas*, second edition, which includes the synopses of 270 of the best-known operas in the repertory. That book includes extensive information on the singers who sang premières of the works, and we began our list of proposed contents with a list of singers mentioned in that context. It is our hope, therefore, that this book will serve as a companion to the other. A reader of *The Grove Book of Operas*, seeing that Victor Maurel was Verdi's first Falstaff, can turn to the *Book of Opera Singers* to learn more about Maurel.

Starting with figures who sang important premières works well for opera before 1900, but in the 20th and 21st centuries, where new works make up only a small fraction of the current repertory, many of the most important singers do not have premières on their résumés. For singers since 1900, therefore, we compiled a list of those included in *Grove Music Online*, and with the help of our advisor, Richard Wigmore, we chose the best known of those and added some new articles on figures who were missing. I am very grateful to Richard Wigmore for his advice and for writing many of these new articles for us.

Reading through these articles brings into focus the webs of professional relationships among singers in any given place and time. We have assisted the reader by adding cross references to singers who had a particularly important professional or personal relationship.

It remains to explain a few aspects of Grove editorial policy. Authors are given at the end of each article. A comma between two names means that the article was jointly authored; a backslash indicates a revision by the second author of an article originally written by the first. Small in-house revisions are indicated with the letter R. A book on singers necessarily refers to a great number of opera roles, and in the interest of brevity, Grove adopts a shorthand for the best known of these, referring to the role without reference to the opera (as in 'She sang Gilda at Covent Garden'). A consultation of the index of roles at the end of the book will enlighten readers unfamiliar with the role mentioned.

Choosing illustrations for this book was a pleasure and, as with the *Grove Book of Operas*, second edition, I have once again to thank Catriona Hopton for her astute and careful work in this area. We are also grateful to the Lebrecht Photo Library for their help in finding and obtaining the illustrations.

Laura Macy
April 2008

Illustration Acknowledgments

The publishers would like to thank the following individuals and institutions who have kindly provided the illustrations for this book.

Colour plate numbers are indicated in **bold**, black and white illustrations by page number.

© Alvaro Yanez/Lebrecht Music & Arts: 241
© B. Rafferty/Lebrecht Music & Arts: **13**
© Bildarchiv Preussischer Kulturbesitz/Art Resource, NY: **10**, 121
By courtesy of Lord Langford: **2**
© David Farrell/Lebrecht Music & Arts: 288
© Decca/Lebrecht Music & Arts: 99, 159, 163
© Eric Lessing/Art Resource, NY: **3, 6**
© Fayer/Lebrecht Music & Arts: **9**, 194
© Federico Patellani/Lebrecht Music & Arts: 70
© G. MacDomnic/Lebrecht Music & Arts: 24
George Grantham Bain Collection, Library of Congress, Prints and Photographs Division, LC-B2-3000-1: 193
George Grantham Bain Collection, Library of Congress, Prints and Photographs Division, LC-B2-2547-5: 226
George Grantham Bain Collection, Library of Congress, Prints and Photographs Division, LC-B2-1219-2: 306
© J. Massey Stewart/Lebrecht Music & Arts: 71
© James Heffernan/Lebrecht Music & Arts: 454
© Kurt Weill Foundation/Lebrecht Music & Arts: 278
© L. Birnbaum/Lebrecht Music & Arts: 221
© Lebrecht Music & Arts: 34, 37, 45, 78, 83, 104, 122, 135, 175, 263, 266, 274, 283, 317, 373, 376, 401, 430, 435, 448, 467, 468, 509, 549
© Lebrecht Music & Arts/Colourise: 438
Library of Congress, Prints and Photographs Division, LC-USZ62-54007: 140
Library of Congress, Prints and Photographs Division, LC-USZ62-89479: 168
Library of Congress, Prints and Photographs Division, LC-USZ62-64092: 179
Library of Congress, Prints and Photographs Division, LC-USZ62-109387: 343
© Metropolitan Opera Archives/Lebrecht Music & Arts: 442
© M.P. Leemage/Lebrecht Music & Arts: **11**
© National Portrait Gallery, Smithsonian Institution/Art Resource, NY: **15**, 79
© Nigel Luckhurst/Lebrecht Music & Arts: **9**, 489
© NYPL Performing Arts/Lebrecht Music & Arts: 157
© Peter Mares/Lebrecht Music & Arts: 230
© Private Collection/Lebrecht Music & Arts: 52, 67, 145, 177, 247, 293, 314, 315, 388, 469, 471, 487, 493, 495, 499, 519
© Ravenna Leemage/Lebrecht Music & Arts: **1**
© Reserved; Library of Congress, Prints and Photographs Division, LC-USZ62-83096: 153
© Réunion des Musées Nationaux/Art Resource, NY: 434
© Richard Haughton/Lebrecht Music & Arts: 127
Rights Reserved/OUP: 202, 529
© Royal Academy of Music/Lebrecht Music & Arts: 57, 369
© S. Lauterwasser/Lebrecht Music & Arts: 77, 347, 372, 391, 421
© Sabine Toepffer/Deutsches Theater/Lebrecht Music & Arts: 161, 184, 228, 290, 335, 526
© Scala/Art Resource, NY: **12**
© Scala/Piccagliani/Lebrecht Music & Arts: 477
© T.P./Lebrecht Music & Arts: 238, 336
© The Metropolitan Museum of Art/Art Resource, NY: 208
© Tristram Kenton/Lebrecht Music & Arts: **4, 5, 7, 8, 14**

Abbreviations Used in the Book

BBC	British Broadcasting Corporation	OBE	Officer of the Order of the British Empire
CBE	Commander of the Order of the British Empire	ON	Opera News
DBE	Dame Commander of the Order of the British Empire	OQ	Opera Quarterly
		PO	Philharmonic Orchestra
DTÖ	Denkmäler der Tonkunst in Österreich	RAI	Royal Audizioni Italiane
		RAM	Royal Academy of Music, London
ENO	English National Opera	RCM	Royal College of Music, London
GSM	Guildhall School of Music, London (to 1934)	RMCM	Royal Manchester College of Music
GSMD	Guildhall School of Music and Drama, London (1935–)	RNCM	Royal Northern College of Music, Manchester
HMV	His Master's Voice	RSFSR	Russian Soviet Federated Soviet Republic
MS	Manuscript		
MusAm	Musical America		
New York PO	New York Philharmonic Orchestra	SO	Symphony Orchestra
		WNO	Welsh National Opera

THE GROVE
BOOK OF
OPERA
SINGERS

A

Abbadia, Luigia

(*b* Genoa, 1821; *d* Milan, 1896). Italian mezzo-soprano. She studied with her father, the composer and teacher Natale Abbadia, making her début in 1836 at Sassari. In Vienna she sang Corilla in Gaetano Donizetti's *Le convenienze ed inconvenienze teatrali* (1840). At La Scala she created Giulietta in Giuseppe Verdi's *Un giorno di regno* (1840) and Ines in Donizetti's *Maria Padilla* (1841) and sang Marie (*La fille du régiment*). Her roles included Elvira (*Ernani*), Emilia (Mercadante's *La vestale*) and Giovanni Pacini's Sappho. After retiring from the stage, she taught in Milan. She had a fine voice, secure technique and a strong temperament.

Elizabeth Forbes

Achenbach, Max.

See ALVARY, MAX(IMILIAN).

Adam, Theo(dor)

(*b* Dresden, 1 Aug 1926). German bass-baritone. As a boy he was a member of the Dresden Kreuzchor, and he studied in that city and at Weimar before making his début at the Dresden Staatsoper in 1949. He joined the Berlin Staatsoper in 1952. That year he made his début in a small role at Bayreuth, graduating to King Henry in 1954 and to Wotan in 1963; his later roles there included the Dutchman, Amfortas and Hans Sachs. At the Salzburg Festival he was heard as Ochs (1969) and Wozzeck (1972), and at the Vienna Staatsoper he sang the title role in a new production of *Don Giovanni* in 1972. Also in Vienna he sang a memorable Pizarro in the Beethoven bicentenary production of *Fidelio* at the Theater an der Wien in 1970, conducted by Leonard Bernstein. He created the role of Prospero in Luciano Berio's *Un re in ascolto* (Salzburg, 1984). His other roles included Philip II, King Mark and La Roche (*Capriccio*). He made his débuts at Covent Garden as Wotan in 1967 and at the Metropolitan Opera as Hans Sachs in 1969. A leading member of the Dresden Staatsoper during the 1970s and 1980s, Adam was also a notable Bach singer and a fine Elijah. All his interpretations displayed an understanding of dramatic situation allied to an intelligently used, if not always totally ingratiating,

voice. His Sachs, Dutchman, Pizarro and, later in his career, Alberich, were all considerable readings; all are preserved on disc, as is his classic Elijah. He wrote two books about his life, work and views on opera, '*Seht, hier ist Tinte, Feder, Papier …*': *Aus der Werkstatt eines Sängers* (Berlin, 1980) and *Die hundertste Rolle, oder, Ich mache einen neuen Adam* (Munich, 1987).

Alan Blyth/R

Adamberger, (Josef) Valentin

(*b* Rohr, nr Rothenburg, Bavaria, 22 Feb 1740, or Munich, 6 July 1743; *d* Vienna, 24 Aug 1804). German tenor. In 1755 he studied singing with GIOVANNI VALESI while at the Domus Gregoriana, a Jesuit institution in Munich. In 1760 he joined the Kapelle of Duke Clemens and on Clemens's death in 1770 was taken into the elector's Hofkapelle. After making his début at Munich in 1772, he sang leading tenor roles in *opere serie* at Modena, Venice, Florence, Pisa and Rome (taking the italianized stage name Valentino Adamonti) from 1775 to 1777, then at the King's Theatre in London until 1779. Following appearances at Florence and Milan, he joined the Singspiel company of the Burgtheater, Vienna, where he made his début on 21 August 1780 and where he sang in a number of Gluck revivals, including Orestes in a German version of *Iphigénie en Tauride* in 1781. In the same year he married the Viennese actress Marie Anne Jacquet (1753–1804). On the dissolution of the Singspiel company in 1783 Adamberger was kept on for the Italian company that replaced it, and he sang in a revival of Joseph Haydn's *Il ritorno di Tobia* in 1784. When the Singspiel company was revived in 1785, alongside the Italian, he again became its leading tenor, and when it was disbanded for the second time, in 1789, he returned to the Italian company. He retired from the stage in 1793 but continued as a member of the imperial Hofkapelle and as an eminent singing teacher.

Adamberger's voice was universally admired for its pliancy, agility and precision, although C.F. Schubart and Richard Mount Edgcumbe also remarked on its nasal quality in the higher notes. Charles Burney, generally a harsh critic of singers, remarked that 'with a better voice [he] would have been a good singer'. W.A. Mozart wrote the part of Belmonte in *Die Entführung* (1782) and Vogelsang in *Der Schauspieldirektor* (1786) for him, as well as several arias (к420 and к431) and the cantata *Die Maurerfreude* (к471).

Before coming to Vienna, Adamberger created leading tenor parts in serious operas by J.C. Bach, Giuseppe Sarti, Pietro Guglielmi, Antonio Sacchini, Ferdinando Bertoni, Pasquale Anfossi and others. The arias they wrote for his voice reveal a fondness for moderate tempos, B♭ major, obbligato clarinets and expressive chromatic inflections. At Vienna, Mozart (*Die Entführung*), Ignaz Umlauf (the role of Alwin in *Das Irrlicht*) and Carl Ditters von Dittersdorf (the role of Captain Sturmwald in *Doktor und Apotheker*) perpetuated these features, which made Adamberger 'the favourite singer of softer hearts', according to a local journalist.

P. Clive: *Mozart and his Circle* (London, 1993), 9–10
D. Link: *The National Court Theatre in Mozart's Vienna: Sources and Documents 1783–1792* (Oxford, 1998)

Thomas Bauman (with Paul Corneilson)/R

Adamonti, Valentino.

See ADAMBERGER, (JOSEF) VALENTIN.

Adams, Charles R. [Adami, Carl]

(*b* Charlestown, MA, 9 Feb 1834; *d* West Harwich, MA, 4 July 1900). American tenor. He studied singing in Boston and in 1856 was soloist in the Handel and Haydn Society's performance of *The Creation*. In 1861 he made concert and opera appearances in the West Indies and Holland. He studied in Vienna with Carlo Barbieri, was engaged for three years by the Berlin Royal Opera, then for nine (1867–76), except for one year, as principal tenor of the Vienna Hofoper. He also sang at La Scala and Covent Garden. In 1877 he returned to the USA and during the 1877–8 season sang the title role in the first American production of Richard Wagner's *Rienzi*. An excellent singer and fine actor, he had a commanding stage presence. Tannhäuser, Lohengrin, Manrico and Rienzi were his most celebrated parts. From 1879 he lived in Boston as a successful singing teacher; MELBA and EAMES were among his pupils.

O. Thompson: *The American Singer* (New York, 1937/R), 85–9

H. Wiley Hitchcock/June C. Ottenberg

Adams, Donald

(*b* Bristol, 20 Dec 1928; *d* Norwich, 8 April 1996). English bass. He was a chorister at Worcester Cathedral and later became an actor. After singing in the D'Oyly Carte Opera chorus, from 1953 to 1969 he was principal bass of the company. In 1963 he co-founded 'G&S for All', with whom he toured extensively in Australia and the USA. In 1983 he sang the Mikado in Chicago, returning for Baron Mirko Zeta and the Theatre Director/Banker (*Lulu*). He made his Covent Garden début in 1983 as a Frontier Guard (*Boris Godunov*), and later sang Quince and Frank. For the ENO (1985–92) he sang Dikoj (*Kát'a Kabanová*), W.A. Mozart's Bartolo and Pooh-Bah; for the WNO (1985–7) his roles included Monterone and Gioachino Rossini's Bartolo. He also appeared at Glyndebourne (Dikoj, Quince and Swallow), Amsterdam, Los Angeles, San Francisco and Geneva. In 1991 he sang Schigolch in *Lulu* for the Canadian Opera. A superb comic actor with an imposing presence, meticulous diction and a resonant voice, he made a magnificent Ochs in *Der Rosenkavalier* for the WNO in 1990.

Elizabeth Forbes

Adini, Ada [Chapman, Adele]

(*b* Boston, 1855; *d* Dieppe, Feb 1924). American soprano. She studied with PAULINE VIARDOT and GIOVANNI SBRIGLIA in Paris. Her début role was Giacomo Meyerbeer's Dinorah, at Varese in 1876. She appeared with the Mapleson Company in New York and after returning to Europe sang at the Opéra from 1887, notably in the 1890 première of Ascanio by Camille Saint-Saëns. At Covent Garden she was heard as Donna Anna (1894, 1897). She was successful in the Wagnerian repertory and sang Brünnhilde in the Italian première of *Die Walküre* (1893, La Scala). Her second husband was Paul Milliet, the librettist of Jules Massenet's *Hérodiade*.

David Cummings

Affré, Agustarello

(*b* St Chinian, 23 Oct 1858; *d* Cagnes-sur-Mer, 27 Dec 1931). French tenor. For 20 years he was a principal lyric-heroic tenor at the Opéra in Paris. Its director, PIERRE GAILHARD, had heard him in the provinces and arranged for lessons with Victor Duvernoy. Affré's house début as Edgardo in 1890 coincided with MELBA's in *Lucia di Lammermoor*. He developed a large repertory, appearing in C.W. Gluck's *Armide* and also in the first performances at the Opéra of *Entführung* and *Pagliacci*. In 1891 he sang in the première of *Le mage* by Jules Massenet, who found his voice 'vibrant as pure crystal'. At Covent Garden in 1909 his roles were Faust and Camille Saint-Saëns's Samson. He went to the USA in 1911, appearing at San Francisco and New Orleans, where in 1913 he became director of the Opera. He was a prolific recording artist and sang Romeo in one of the earliest complete operatic recordings (1912), the firmness and power of his tone showing why he was often described as the French TAMAGNO.

Mrs Vellacott and J. Dennis: 'Gustarello Affré', *Record Collector*, iii (1948), 84–8, 131–3
M. Scott: *The Record of Singing*, i (London, 1977), 71

J.B. Steane

Agache, Alexandru

(*b* Cluj, 16 Aug 1955). Romanian baritone. After studying in Cluj, he made his début there in 1979 as Silvano (*Ballo in maschera*), followed in 1980 by Sharpless. During the next decade he sang Don Giovanni, Malatesta, Germont, Luna, Posa (*Don Carlos*), the title role of *Nabucco* and Schaunard at Cluj. He also appeared at Budapest, Dresden, Ankara and the Deutsche Staatsoper, Berlin, with which company he toured Japan in 1987 as W.A. Mozart's Almaviva. Agache made a notable Covent Garden début in 1988 as Renato in *Ballo*, later singing Enrico Ashton, Boccanegra, Rigoletto and Amonasro. He made his début at La Scala in 1989 as Belcore in *L'elisir d'amore*. Other roles include Escamillo and Charles Gounod's Méphistophélès. His powerful, flexible voice and imposing stage presence make him an ideal interpreter of Giuseppe Verdi's baritone roles.

Elizabeth Forbes

Agnew, Paul

(*b* Baillieston, nr Glasgow, 11 April 1964). Scottish tenor. He won a choral scholarship to Magdalen College, Oxford, where he read music. After singing in consorts and professional choirs, he quickly established a reputation in the early music field, where his agile, elegant tenor has been particularly admired in the French *haute-contre* repertory. Agnew has worked frequently with leading conductors in the field, including John Eliot Gardiner, Philippe Herreweghe, Ton Koopman, Paul McCreesh, Trevor Pinnock and Christopher Hogwood. He also sings regularly with William Christie and Les Arts Florissants, with whom he has performed many works by Jean-Philippe Rameau and his contemporaries (including the title role in *Hippolyte et Aricie* at the Palais Garnier, Paris) and other works such as G.F. Handel's *L'Allegro* (which he sang at the Proms in 2001). In 2001 Agnew appeared in Rameau's *Platée* at the Opéra Bastille, and in Hector Berlioz's *Les Troyens* at the Edinburgh Festival. His other non-Baroque roles include the Male Chorus in *The Rape of Lucretia*, which he has sung for the Opéra de Caen. Another speciality is English lute song: with the lutenist Christopher Wilson he has appeared in recital in London, Paris, Montreux and Vienna, and he has made a number of recordings praised for their grace and verbal acuity. Among Agnew's other recordings are many works by J.S. Bach (including a series of cantata recordings with Koopman), G.F. Handel and Rameau, Claudio Monteverdi's Vespers, Henry Purcell's *Timon of Athens* and Berlioz's *L'enfance du Christ*, in addition to Beethoven lieder and Sally Beamish's *In Dreaming*.

Richard Wigmore

Agthe, Rosa.

See MILDE-AGTHE, ROSA VON.

Ahlersmeyer, Matthieu

(*b* Cologne, 29 June 1896; *d* Garmisch-Partenkirchen, 23 July 1979). German baritone. He studied with Karl Niemann in Cologne and made his début at Mönchengladbach in 1929 as Wolfram. He sang at the Kroll Oper, Berlin (1930–31), at the Hamburg Staatsoper (1931–3 and 1946–61), and at the Dresden Staatsoper (1934–44), where he created the role of Schneidebart in *Die schweigsame Frau*. In 1938 he created the title role in Werner Egk's *Peer Gynt* at the Berlin Staatsoper. He appeared at Covent Garden in 1936 with the Dresden Staatsoper as Don Giovanni and Count Almaviva, and at the Edinburgh Festival with the Hamburg Staatsoper in 1952 as Paul Hindemith's Mathis. In 1947 he shared the title role in *Dantons Tod* with PAUL SCHÖFFLER at the Salzburg Festival, and in 1963 he created Count Almaviva in Giselher Klebe's *Figaro lässt sich scheiden* at Hamburg. He retired in 1973.

Harold Rosenthal/R

Ahnsjö, Claes Håkan

(*b* Stockholm, 1 Aug 1942). Swedish tenor. He studied at the Stockholm Opera School with Erik Saedén, Aksel Schiøtz and Max Lorenz. From 1969 he has appeared at the Royal Opera, Stockholm, notably in works by W.A. Mozart and Gioachino Rossini (début as Tamino). At Drottningholm he has sung in many revivals of Baroque operas. He left Stockholm in 1973 and has since been engaged at the Staatsoper in Munich, where he sang in *Lulu*, *Mathis der Maler* and the premières of Heinrich

Sutermeister's *Le roi Bérenger* (1985) and Krzysztof Penderecki's *Ubu Rex* (1991). Joseph Haydn's *Orlando paladino*, *La vera costanza* and *L'infedeltà delusa* are among his recordings.

David Cummings

Ainsley, John Mark

(*b* Crewe, 9 July 1963). English tenor. He studied music at Oxford University and with Diane Forlano. After early engagements with Gothic Voices and other groups he made his first operatic appearance in Alessandro Scarlatti's *Gli equivoci nel sembiante* at Innsbruck's Early Music Festival (1988). He made his American début in 1990 with concerts in Boston and New York, and has sung with the ENO (début in *Il ritorno d'Ulisse in patria*, 1989), the WNO (Idamantes), Scottish Opera (Fenton), and at the Aix-en-Provence and Glyndebourne festivals (Don Ottavio). He made his San Francisco début in 1995 as Don Ottavio (a role he has recorded with Roger Norrington) and his Netherlands Opera début as Claudio Monteverdi's Orfeo in 1996. More recent roles have included Lensky, David in Carl Nielsen's *Saul og David*, and Jupiter in *Semele*, which he performed to acclaim at the ENO in 1999. A supple lyric tenor in the English tradition, Ainsley has an extensive discography ranging from Monteverdi to Benjamin Britten. Among his recordings are Britten's *Serenade* for tenor, horn and strings, lieder by W.A. Mozart and Franz Schubert, songs by Roger Quilter, Peter Warlock and Herbert Howells, several Handel oratorios and the title role in *Orfeo*. In 1992 he created the tenor part in John Tavener's *We shall see Him as He is*.

James Jolly

Alagna, Roberto

(*b* Clichy-sous-Bois, 7 June 1963). French tenor. Born of Sicilian parents, Alagna began his career as a cabaret singer in Paris, accompanying himself on the guitar while studying with Raphael Ruiz, a Cuban émigré. After winning the Pavarotti International Voice Competition in Philadelphia in 1988 and receiving encouragement from PAVAROTTI himself, he began his career singing Alfredo Germont with Glyndebourne Touring Opera the same year. He repeated this role, and sang Rodolfo in *La bohème*, at the Monte Carlo Opera the following season, when he also appeared as Nemorino at Toulouse. Alagna made his début at La Scala as Alfredo, with Riccardo Muti conducting, in 1990, a performance issued on video and CD; he has subsequently sung the Duke of Mantua and Macduff at La Scala. In 1992 he sang

the title role in *Roberto Devereux* at Monte Carlo and Rodolfo and Alfredo in Barcelona, and made his much-lauded Covent Garden début as Rodolfo, following it with an equally admired Romeo in Charles Gounod's opera (1994) and, in 1996, Don Carlos and Alfredo. He appeared in Paris as Edgardo (*Lucia di Lammermoor*) at the Opéra Bastille in 1995 and Don Carlos at the Châtelet the following year. He made his Metropolitan début in 1996 as Rodolfo, followed with Nemorino (*L'elisir d'amore*), a role he recorded on video at the Lyons Opéra with his wife, ANGELA GHEORGHIU, as Adina. The pair appeared at Monte Carlo in Pietro Mascagni's *L'amico Fritz* in 1999 and in Gounod's *Roméo et Juliette* at Covent Garden in 2000. Later the same year Alagna returned to Covent Garden as Cavaradossi in *Tosca* and sang Don José (*Carmen*) at the Metropolitan Opera. In 2001 he performed Manrico (*Il trovatore*) in Monte Carlo and Florence. A film of *Tosca*, in which Alagna stars alongside Gheorghiu, received its première at the Venice Film Festival in September 2001. He has recorded discs of solos (including a *Gramophone* award-winning recital of French arias) and duets (the latter with Gheorghiu). These and his recordings of *Roméo et Juliette*, Jules Massenet's *Werther* and *Manon* and Giacomo Puccini's *La rondine* (all with Gheorghiu) capture the plangent lyricism of Alagna's tone and the appealing ardour and inner fire of his style.

A. Blyth: 'Roberto Alagna', *Opera*, xlviii (1997), 1403–8

Alan Blyth

Alaimo, Simone

(*b* Villabate, 3 Feb 1950). Italian bass-baritone. He studied in Palermo and Milan, making his début in 1977 at Pavia as Don Pasquale, then taking part in Carlo Evasio Soliva's *La testa di bronzo* at the Piccola Scala (1980). He has appeared throughout Italy, singing in Rome, Naples, Bologna, Turin and many other cities. A Rossini specialist, he sings a wide range of comic and serious roles, among them Selim, Dandini, Alidoro, Polidoro (*Zelmira*), Mustafà (on his US and British débuts at Chicago in 1987 and Covent Garden in 1988) and Mahomet. Alaimo's other roles include Count Robinson (*Il matrimonio segreto*), Dulcamara, Belcore, Henry VIII (*Anna Bolena*), Nottingham (*Roberto Devereux*) and Rodolfo (*Sonnambula*). He returned to the Covent Garden company as Don Basilio, Pharoah (*Mosè in Egitto*) and Don Magnifico. His many recordings include Giuseppe Apolloni's *L'ebreo*, in which he sings Issachar. A superb comic actor, he is equally convincing in tragic opera, while the exceptional range of his keenly focussed and flexible voice enables him to sing Verdi baritone roles such as Miller, as well as the *basso buffo* characters at which he excels.

Elizabeth Forbes/R

Alan, Hervey

(*b* Whitstable, 22 Feb 1910; *d* Croydon, 12 Jan 1982). English bass. After studying with ROY HENDERSON, he was engaged at Sadler's Wells Opera (1947–52), singing Colline, Don Basilio, Zuniga, Simone (*Gianni Schicchi*), Alfio, the Grand Inquisitor, the Commendatore, and Cancian (*I quatro rusteghi*). At Glyndebourne (1949–59) he sang Tom (*Un ballo in maschera*), Alidoro (*La Cenerentola*), Trulove and Padre Guardiano. He created Mr Redburn in *Billy Budd* at Covent Garden (1951). For the WNO (1952–61) he sang Sparafucile, Procida, Barbarossa (Giuseppe Verdi's *La battaglia di Legnano*), Melcthal (*Guillaume Tell*) and Méphistophélès (Charles Gounod and Arrigo Boito). He had a dark-toned, resonant voice, especially effective as Zaccaria in *Nabucco*.

Elizabeth Forbes

Alarie, Pierrette (Marguerite)

(*b* Montreal, 9 Nov 1921). Canadian soprano. She studied in Montreal with Salvator Issaurel and Jeanne Maubourg and in Philadelphia with ELISABETH SCHUMANN. She made her début in 1938 in Montreal with the Variétés Lyriques, later singing in *La fille du régiment*, *Il barbiere di Siviglia*, *La traviata* and *Mireille*. In 1943 she sang W.A. Mozart's Barbarina under Thomas Beecham. She made her Metropolitan Opera début in 1945 in *Un ballo in maschera* under Bruno Walter after winning the Auditions of the Air. In 1949 she made her début at the Paris Opéra-Comique as Olympia in *Les contes d'Hoffmann*; remaining in Paris for several seasons, she appeared frequently with the tenor LÉOPOLD SIMONEA, whom she had married in 1946. At the 1953 Aix-en-Provence Festival she sang for the first time *Chanson* and *Romance du comte Olinos*, two concert arias written for her by Werner Egk. She appeared at the 1959 Salzburg Festival in *Die schweigsame Frau*. For some years she taught in Montreal before moving to San Francisco in 1972. She taught at Banff from 1972 to 1978, and she moved to Victoria, British Columbia, in 1982, where she founded and directed Canada Opera Piccola with her husband. She was made an Officer of the Order of Canada in 1967 and received the honorary doctorate at McGill University in 1994.

Gilles Potvin

Albanese, Licia

(*b* Bari, 22 July 1913). American soprano of Italian birth. She studied with Giuseppina Baldassare-Tedeschi, and began her career at the Teatro Lirico, Milan, where in 1934 she was an emergency replacement for an indisposed Butterfly in the second half of the opera. The same opera, always closely identified with her, occasioned her formal début at Parma (1935) and her début at the Metropolitan (1940). During her career she made more than 1000 appearances in 48 roles, in the lyric or *lirico spinto* repertory, including W.A. Mozart (Donna Anna, Zerlina, Susanna) and French opera (Micaëla, Manon, Charles Gounod's Marguerite) as well as the obvious Italian challenges; her speciality was the Puccini heroines. A singer of extraordinary technical skill and emotional intensity, she was the Violetta and Mimì in Arturo Toscanini's recorded NBC broadcasts. She is perhaps best represented by the excerpts from her tragic Butterfly and her 1938 recording of Mimì in a complete *La bohème* from La Scala. Active in the movement to save the old Metropolitan Opera House, she never rejoined the company at Lincoln Center. In later years she taught, and sang sporadically in concert and in roles the Metropolitan had, perhaps wisely, denied her, such as Aida and Santuzza.

J. Hines: *Great Singers on Great Singing* (Garden City, NY, 1982), 19–24

L. Green: 'Licìa Albanese and Verismo: "I always Tell the Truth"', *OQ*, vii/4 (1990–91), 53–107 [with discography]

Martin Bernheimer/R

Albani [Lajeunesse], Dame Emma (Marie Louise Cécile)

(*b* Chambly, nr Montreal, 1 Nov 1847; *d* London, 3 April 1930). Canadian soprano. Her father was a professor of the harp, piano and organ. She was educated at the Couvent du Sacré-Coeur at Montreal. She gave concerts in some Quebec towns before her family moved to Albany, New York, in 1864; there she became a soloist at St Joseph's Church, and the Albany bishop and others advised Lajeunesse that his daughter should adopt a musical career. She went to Paris in 1868 where she was taught by DUPREZ. Later she studied with Francesco Lamperti in Milan. In 1870 she made her début at Messina as Amina in Vincenzo Bellini's *La sonnambula*, adopting, as suggested by her elocution teacher, the name of Albani, borrowed from an old Italian family. She then sang successfully at Malta and Florence.

On 2 April 1872 she made her London début at Covent Garden as Amina. The beautiful qualities of her voice and the charm of her appearance were at once appreciated. She sang nearly every season there until 1896, in a great variety of parts, notably as Elsa (1875) and Elisabeth (1876) in the first London performances of *Lohengrin* and *Tannhäuser*. In 1878 she married Ernest Gye, who became lessee of Covent Garden on his father's death. Later she was very successful as Eva (*Die Meistersinger*) and Desdemona (she sang in the first Covent Garden and Metropolitan productions of *Otello*). The last and greatest triumph of her career was on 26 June 1896, as Isolde to the Tristan of JEAN DE RESZKE and the King Mark of EDOUARD DE RESZKE.

Albani was for many years a great favourite at the Handel and provincial festivals and sang in many new works, notably in those of Charles Gounod, Arthur Sullivan, Alexander Mackenzie, Frederick Cowen, Antonín Dvořák, Edward Elgar (*The Apostles*), and in 1886 in *St Elizabeth* on the occasion of Franz Liszt's farewell visit to England. She also sang in opera and concerts in Paris, Brussels, Germany, the USA, Mexico and Canada, and later on tour in India, Australia and South Africa. Her voice was a rich soprano of remarkably sympathetic quality. The higher registers were of exceptional beauty, and she had perfected the art of singing *mezza voce*.

On 14 October 1911 she gave a farewell concert at the Royal Albert Hall, afterwards devoting herself to teaching the Lamperti method. In June 1925 she was created DBE.

E. Albani: *Forty Years of Song* (London, 1911/*R*)
N.A. Ridley: 'Emma Albani', *Record Collector*, xii (1958–60), 76–101 [with discography by W.R. Moran]; addenda, xii (1958–60), 197–8; xiv (1961–2); 236 only C.E. MacDonald: *Emma Albani: Victorian Diva* (Toronto, 1984)

Alexis Chitty/Gilles Potvin

Albertarelli, Francesco

(*fl* 1782–99). Italian bass. He spent the early part of his career mainly in Rome. For the 1788–9 season he was a member of the *opera buffa* company in Vienna. He made his début on 4 April 1788 as Biscroma in Antonio Salieri's *Axur, re d'Ormus*, sang the title role in the first Vienna performance of W.A. Mozart's *Don Giovanni* on 7 May 1788, and created the role of the Marchese in Thaddäus Weigl's *Il pazzo per forza*. Mozart contributed an aria for him (K541) in his role of Don Pompeo for the 1788 version of Pasquale Anfossi's *Le gelosie fortunate*. Albertarelli's final role in Vienna was Brunetto in Lorenzo Da Ponte's pasticcio *L'ape musicale* in March 1789. Later that year he appeared in Milan and Monza. The remainder of his career was centred in Italy, but he also sang in London (1791), Madrid (1792)

and St Petersburg (1799). According to Benedetto Frizzi, Albertarelli was well suited in appearance to a *buffo caricato*. His acting was polished and expressive and his singing and recitative were stylish. He made up for a lack of formal musical training through hard work and good judgment.

D. Link: *The National Court Theatre in Mozart's Vienna: Sources and Documents 1783–1792* (Oxford, 1998)

Dorothea Link

Albertini, Giuliano

(*fl* 1699–1738). Italian alto castrato. His first known appearance was in Livorno in 1699. Probably from Florence, he had a long career there, singing in 24 operas, including works by G.M. Orlandini, Francesco Gasparini and Tomaso Albinoni, from 1701 to 1738. He was employed by the Cardinal and later the Grand Duchess of Tuscany. He sang in Venice in 1705, 1709 (the premières of two operas by Antonio Lotti and G.F. Handel's *Agrippina*) and 1718–19, in Naples in 1707–9 (four operas, including the première of Alessandro Scarlatti's *Teodosio*), Bologna in 1711, Modena in 1716 and Rome in 1729. In *Agrippina* he played the freedman Narcissus, a part that makes no slight demands on range and skill; its compass is *a* to *d"*.

Winton Dean

Alboni, Marietta [Maria Anna Marzia]

(*b* Città di Castello, 6 March 1826; *d* Ville d'Avray, 23 June 1894). Italian contralto. She studied at the Liceo Musicale, Bologna, with Alessandro Mombelli. Gioachino Rossini coached her in the principal contralto roles in his operas. She made her début at Bologna in 1842 as Clymene in Andrea Pacini's *Saffo*, and then sang Maffio Orsini in *Lucrezia Borgia*. In the same year she first appeared at La Scala, as Néocle in *Le siège de Corinthe*; during that season and the next she also sang Rizzardo in M.A. Marliani's *Ildegonda*, Léonore in *La favorite*, Adalgisa, and Pierotto in *Linda di Chamounix*. She created Mirza in Salvi's *Lara* (1843) and Berenice in Giovanni Pacini's *L'ebrea* (1844). She made a very successful Vienna début in 1843 as Pierotto, and spent the winter of 1844–5 in St Petersburg, where she sang Pierotto, Maffio Orsini, Gondi in Gaetano Donizetti's *Maria di Rohan* and Arsace in *Semiramide*. During the next two years she toured Germany and eastern Europe, appearing as Tancredi in Berlin and as Anziletto in the first performance of G.B. Gordigiani's *Consuelo* in Prague (1846). She made her London début on 6 April 1847, as Arsace in the performance of *Semiramide* that opened the first season of the Royal Italian Opera at Covent Garden, and scored an immense personal triumph. She also sang Smeton (*Anna Bolena*), Malcolm (*La donna del lago*), Pierotto, Maffio Orsini, Cherubino, Rosina (*Il barbiere*), Isabella (*L'italiana in Algeri*), Don Carlo (the baritone role) in *Ernani* and Romeo (contralto version) in Vincenzo Bellini's *I Capuleti e I Montecchi*. She returned to Covent Garden in 1848 to sing Urbain in *Les Huguenots* (transposed from soprano to contralto for her by Giacomo Meyerbeer; see illustration in VIARDOT, PAULINE), Cenerentola and Tancredi, then in 1849 she moved to Her Majesty's Theatre, where she continued to sing until 1858.

Alboni made her Paris début at the Théâtre Italien on 2 December 1847, again as Arsace, and then sang the title role of *La Cenerentola*. In 1849 she sang in Brussels and in 1850 she made a tour through the French provinces, singing in Donizetti's *La fille du régiment*, *La favorite* and Fromental Halévy's *La reine de Chypre*. On her return to Paris she appeared at the Opéra for the first time, as Fidès in Meyerbeer's *Le prophète*, returning in 1851 as Zerline in the first performance of Daniel-François-Esprit Auber's *Zerline, ou La corbeille d'oranges*. She next made a tour of Spain and from June 1852 undertook a very successful year-long tour of the USA. Later, she married and settled in Paris. She sang a duet from Gioachino Rossini's *Stabat mater* with ADELINA PATTI at the composer's funeral in 1868. She toured with his *Petite messe solennelle* through France, Belgium and the Netherlands, giving the first of 64 performances on 24 February 1869 in Paris, and singing the work in London in 1871. Her final appearance was at the Théâtre Italien in 1872, as Fidalma in Domenico Cimarosa's *Il matrimonio segreto*.

Alboni's voice was considered a true contralto, powerful, flexible and rich and even from *g* to *c'''*, though she also sang several soprano roles, including Anna Bolena, Norina in *Don Pasquale* and Amina in *La sonnambula*. One of several singers during the early and middle 19th century who specialized in masculine roles, her singing was thought by some to lack fire; nevertheless, the beauty of her voice and the perfection of her technique made her one of the great representatives of classical Italian bel canto.

Elizabeth Forbes/R

Alcaide, Tomáz (de Aquino Carmelo)

(*b* Estremoz, 16 Feb 1901; *d* Lisbon, 9 Nov 1967). Portuguese tenor. He studied at the University of Coimbra, at the same time taking singing lessons in Lisbon, and in Milan (1925), where he made his début in 1926 as Wilhelm Meister (*Mignon*) at the

Teatro Carcano. He sang in various Italian cities, then made his début at La Scala in 1930 as Mascarillo in Felice Lattuada's *Le preziose ridicole*, followed in 1931 by M. le Bleau (Wolf-Ferrari's *La vedova scaltra*) and the King's Son (*Königskinder*). In 1931 he also sang Edgardo (*Lucia di Lammermoor*), the Duke of Mantua and Pinkerton at Monte Carlo; Alfredo (*Traviata*) in Rome; and Ernesto (*Don Pasquale*) at Salzburg. He sang Rodolfo and Cavaradossi at the Opéra-Comique, Paris (1936), and appeared at the Théâtre de la Monnaie (1937–8). His French roles included Werther, Des Grieux (*Manon*), Nadir and Faust. His final stage appearance was as Gioachino Rossini's Almaviva at São Paulo in 1948. A distinguished actor, he had a beautiful lyric voice, with easy top notes and excellent breath control. His memoirs, *Um cantor no palco e na vida*, were published in Lisbon in 1961.

Elizabeth Forbes

Alchevs'ky, Ivan [Jean] Olexiyovych

(*b* Kharkiv, 15/27 Dec 1876; *d* Baku, 27 April/10 May 1917). Ukrainian tenor. He studied in St Petersburg and from 1901 to 1905 was a soloist at the Mariinsky Theatre there. In 1906 he sang in London, as Lensky in the first performance there of *Yevgeny Onegin*; he later appeared in the Beecham season of Russian opera, 1913–14. At the Paris Opéra (1908–10) he sang Shuysky in the local première of *Boris Godunov* as well as French roles (Charles Gounod's Romeo, Faust, Raoul). He returned to Russia to sing at the Bol'shoy, Moscow (1910–14). Among his other roles were Lohengrin, Siegfried and Radames; he was also active in the promotion of Ukrainian music and he directed Gulak-Artemovsky's *Zaporozhets za Dunayem* ('Cossack beyond the Danube') at the Bol'shoy in 1915 and in Odessa the next year.

Virko Baley

Aldighieri, Gottardo

(*b* Lazise, Lake Garda, 6 Jan 1824; *d* Verona, 11 May 1906). Italian baritone. He studied in Verona and Milan, making his début in 1858 at Novara as Germont. For the next 20 years he sang at all the leading Italian theatres, including S Carlo, where he created Raoul in Gaetano Donizetti's posthumously performed *Gabriella di Vergy* (1869), and La Scala, where he sang Barnaba in the first performance of Amilcare Ponchielli's *La Gioconda* (1876). His other roles included Don Giovanni and William Tell. He had a powerful but flexible voice of attractive timbre.

Elizabeth Forbes

Alexander, John

(*b* Meridian, MS, 21 Oct 1923; *d* Meridian, 8 Dec 1990). American tenor. He trained at the Cincinnati Conservatory and made his début as Faust with the Cincinnati Opera in 1952. He joined the New York City Opera as Alfredo five years later and made his Metropolitan début as Ferrando in 1961. Important European engagements found him singing in Erich Korngold's *Die tote Stadt* at the Vienna Volksoper (1967), *La bohème* at the Vienna Staatsoper (1968), and Pollione at Covent Garden (1970). The Bellini opera became one of his specialities, and he sang it in a single season opposite the three most celebrated Normas of the time, SUTHERLAND, CABALLÉ and SILLS; he recorded the opera, and Gioachino Rossini's *Semiramide* (singing Idreno) with Sutherland. In May 1973 he sang the title role in the American première of the original French version of *Don Carlos*, staged by the Boston Opera. Alexander's value to leading American opera companies rested partly with his remarkable versatility and reliability in an enormous repertory, spanning bel canto at one extreme and such Germanic roles as Bacchus and Walther von Stolzing at the other. Although his acting sometimes lacked ardour and his singing was not invariably notable for dynamic finesse, he made the most of taste, fervour, stamina and a voice that commanded an exceptionally brilliant ring at the top.

J. Hines: *Great Singers on Great Singing* (Garden City, NY, 1982), 25–9

Martin Bernheimer

Alexander, Roberta (Lee)

(*b* Lynchburg, VA, 3 March 1949). American soprano. She graduated in voice studies at the University of Michigan and continued her training at the Royal Conservatory, The Hague (with Herman Woltman), and the Netherlands Opera Studio, with which she made her début in *La cambiale di matrimonio* (Gioachino Rossini). Making her home in Amsterdam, she sang a variety of roles with the Netherlands Opera, one of them in the première of Viktor Ullmann's *Der Kaiser von Atlantis* (1975). Her European engagements also included performances in both East and West Berlin. She made her American operatic début at Houston in 1980 as Pamina; she sang Richard Strauss's Daphne at Santa Fe (1981) and Zerlina at the Metropolitan Opera (1983), where she later sang Bess (George Gershwin), Jenůfa and Mimì. Her British operatic début was at Covent Garden as Mimì (1984), and her Viennese début (1985) as Cleopatra (*Giulio Cesare*) at the Theater an der Wien; she later appeared as Donna Elvira at the Staatsoper (1986). She sang a

highly acclaimed Jenůfa at Glyndebourne in 1989. Alexander is an accomplished actress with a smoothly produced soprano of wide expressive range. Her operatic recordings include W.A. Mozart's Elvira (1990, with Nikolaus Harnoncourt) and Electra (1991, with Colin Davis), the title role in Berthold Goldschmidt's *Beatrice Cenci* and Stella in his *Der gewaltige Hahnrei* (1994–5). She also has a flourishing concert career and is a notable interpreter of Gustav Mahler and various American composers. She has recorded discs of Ives and Bernstein songs and works for soprano and orchestra by Gershwin and Samuel Barber.

Noël Goodwin

Alizard, Adolphe-Joseph-Louis

(*b* Paris, 29 Dec 1814; *d* Marseilles, 23 Jan 1850). French bass-baritone. He began his career as a violinist, studying under Chrétien Urhan, but switched to singing in 1834, enrolling at the Paris Conservatoire. After earning first prize there in 1836, he made his début the following year as Saint-Bris (*Les Huguenots*). Alizard was associated with the Opéra, primarily in minor roles, until 1842, when he accepted a two-year appointment in Brussels. A throat problem, possibly induced by higher baritone roles, forced him to take leave from 1844 to 1846. Following a short recuperative sojourn in Italy, he enjoyed a brief second success in Paris from 1846 to 1848, when he created Roger at the première of *Jérusalem* (1847). A recurrence of his ailment necessitated his permanent retirement to the balmier climate of Marseilles, where he died. Contemporary critics described his voice as powerful and of a flattering timbre. His short and overly muscular stature, however, compromised his popularity with the public.

Laurie C. Shulman

Allen, Sir Thomas (Boaz)

(*b* Seaham Harbour, Co. Durham, 10 Sept 1944). English baritone. He studied at the RCM, 1964–8, with HERVEY ALAN (singing) and Harold Darke (organ). Early experience with the WNO (début as Marchese d'Obigny, *La traviata*, 1969) and in the Glyndebourne Festival Chorus led to important leading roles with WNO, among them Gioachino Rossini's Figaro and W.A. Mozart's Count Almaviva, and thence to a Covent Garden début (Donald, *Billy Budd*, 1971). In this first phase of his career Allen undertook an unusual variety of musical styles, from Purcell, Rameau and Gluck to Tippett and Thea Musgrave (the Count in the première of *The Voice of Ariadne*, Aldeburgh, 1974), while making a particular mark in the title role of *Billy Budd* and in Mozart works; but almost every appearance seemed to be stamped by his conjoining of striking appearance, magnetic command of the stage, and warm, naturally produced, vibrant lyric baritone of easy emission and wide range. At his peak Allen's Don Giovanni (which has been encountered in most of the world's leading theatres) was unrivalled for its compelling blend of comedy and menace, charm and cruelty, manly authority and sinuous elegance; many other successes – as Wolfram, Posa, Ambroise Thomas' Hamlet, Marcello, Eisenstein, Busoni's Faust, and Ulysses in Hans Werner Henze's Monteverdi arrangement – have convincingly demonstrated his powers. In later years has come a move toward 'mature' roles (Don Alfonso, Giorgio Germont, Sharpless, Beckmesser and Leoš Janáček's Forester among them), in which the deepening and refining of his art of characterization is everywhere in evidence.

In concert Allen's range has proved no less wide. A devoted but (measured by the highest standards) perhaps not exceptionally original exponent of lieder and *mélodies*, he has consistently championed the less familiar English composers of song (George Butterworth, Peter Warlock, Ivor Gurney, Gerald Finzi), colouring their words and phrases freshly and imaginatively, filling each note with a peculiar vigour of projection and intensity of communication. Allen's career is well documented on recordings: these include issues of Schubert, Schumann, Wolf and Mahler lieder, Brahms (lieder and *German Requiem*), the *War Requiem* (under Simon Rattle), and songs from British and American musicals (with VALERIE MASTERSON); and, of course, representation of many operatic roles, among them Gioachino Rossini's Figaro, Gaetano Donizetti's Malatesta, Benjamin Britten's Balstrode, and two versions each of C.W. Gluck's Orestes (under John Eliot Gardiner and Riccardo Muti) and Mozart's *Figaro* (the Count under Georg Solti, the title role under Muti) and Don Giovanni (under Bernard Haitink and Neville Marriner). His Billy Budd is preserved in the video of the 1988 ENO production. He is the author of *Foreign Parts: a Singer's Journal* (London, 1993). He was made a CBE in 1989 and knighted in 1999.

M. Loppert: 'Thomas Allen', *Opera*, xxix (1978), 671–7

Max Loppert

Allin, Norman

(*b* Ashton-under-Lyne, 19 Nov 1884; *d* Hereford, 27 Oct 1973). English bass. He studied at the RMCM (1906–10), intending to become a teacher, but after marrying the mezzo-soprano Edith Clegg, took up performing. He made his concert début in Manchester and his stage début in 1916 with the

Sir Thomas Allen, 1996

Beecham Opera Company at the Aldwych Theatre, London, as the Old Hebrew in *Samson et Dalila*; he later sang Dosifey when *Khovanshchina* was first given in English at Drury Lane. At Covent Garden in 1919 he appeared as Khan Konchak and Boris, and as Gurnemanz won particular praise for the beauty of his singing and the dignity of his acting. In 1922 he became a director and principal bass of the newly formed British National Opera Company, and added Méphistophélès, King Mark, Osmin and Sarastro to his notable roles. He took part in the international seasons from 1926 to 1933, sang W.A. Mozart's Bartolo at the first Glyndebourne season in 1934 and then appeared with the Carl Rosa Company from 1942 to 1949. His extensive concert repertory ranged from Henry Purcell to Modest Petrovich Musorgsky. A leading British bass of his day, he had a voice of comparative rarity, a true, voluminous bass capable of considerable agility and vitality. His singing, most notably of G.F. Handel and Richard Wagner, is preserved on a number of discs.

J.B. Richards and J. Fryer: 'Norman Allin', *Record Collector*, x (1955–6), 101–42 [with discography by Richards]

Alan Blyth

Alliot-Lugaz, Colette

(*b* Notre-Dame-de-Bellecombe, 20 July 1947). French soprano. She studied in Bonneville and then Geneva, where she graduated from the Centre Lyrique. She made her début at the Opéra-Studio in Paris as Pamina in 1976, and then joined the Lyons Opéra, where she remained a member of the company until 1983. Her roles there included Jonathas in Marc-Antoine Charpentier's *David et Jonathas* and Mélisande. She made her first appearance at Glyndebourne in 1981 as Cherubino, returning for Ninetta in *The Love for Three Oranges* in 1982. In 1983 Alliot-Lugaz created the role of the Page in Philippe Boesmans's *La passion de Gilles* at La Monnaie in Brussels. Her repertory also includes André Messager's *Véronique*, C.W. Gluck's *Alcestis*, Ascanius in *Les Troyens* (which she sang at the opening of the Opéra Bastille, Paris, in 1990) and Eurydice in Luciano Berio's *Opera*, while her many recordings include Claudio Monteverdi's *Orfeo*, Jean-Baptiste Lully's *Alceste*, André Campra's *Tancrède*, Jacques Offenbach's *Les brigands*, Messager's *Fortunio* and Maurice Ravel's *L'enfant et les sortilèges*. She also has a notable career as a concert singer and has recorded such works as Hector Berlioz's *Nuits d'été* and Ernest Chausson's *Poème de l'amour et de la mer*.

Patrick O'Connor

Althouse, Paul (Shearer)

(*b* Reading, PA, 2 Dec 1899; *d* New York, 6 Feb 1954). American tenor. Educated at Bucknell University, he studied with P.D. Aldrich in Philadelphia and Oscar Saenger and P.R. Stevens in New York. The first American tenor without European experience to sing at the Metropolitan Opera, he made his début there as Grigory in the American première of *Boris Godunov* under Artuto Toscanini (1913); between then and 1920 he participated in its first productions of Umberto Giordano's *Madame Sans-Gêne*, Victor Herbert's *Madeleine*, Reginald De Koven's *Canterbury Pilgrims*, Charles Wakefield Cadman's *Shanewis* and Joseph Carl Breil's *The Legend*. His voice was described as a 'lyric tenor of the more robust Italian type'. During part of the 1920s he devoted himself exclusively to concerts, but after a visit to Bayreuth, he decided to retrain as a Heldentenor. In 1933 he sang Tristan in San Francisco, and returned to the Metropolitan as Siegmund, a role he repeated in 1935 at KIRSTEN FLAGSTAD's début. Until the 1939–40 season he shared the principal Wagner roles at the Metropolitan with LAURITZ MELCHIOR. After a final appearance as Loge in 1941, he devoted himself to teaching; among his pupils were RICHARD TUCKER, ELEANOR STEBER, LÉOPOLD SIMONEAU and Irene Dalis.

Philip Lieson Miller

Altmeyer, Jeannine (Theresa)

(*b* La Habra, CA, 2 May 1948). American soprano. She studied with LOTTE LEHMANN in Santa Barbara and later at Salzburg. After winning the Illinois Opera Guild Auditions in 1971, she made her début at the Metropolitan as the Heavenly Voice in Giuseppe Verdi's *Don Carlos*. She sang Freia at the Chicago Lyric Opera (1972), Salzburg (1973) and Covent Garden (1975). After several seasons at Stuttgart (1975–9) she sang Sieglinde in Patrice Chéreau's production of the *Ring* (1976) at Bayreuth, where she also sang Isolde (1986). Apart from her Wagnerian roles (which include Elsa, Eva, Elisabeth, Gutrune and Brünnhilde), Altmeyer sings Agathe (*Der Freischütz*), Richard Strauss's Salome and Chrysothemis, Lisa (*The Queen of Spades*) and Leonore, which she sang at La Scala in 1990. The radiant tone of her voice and the intensity of her expression make her a particularly fine interpreter of Wagner and Strauss. Her recordings include Brünnhilde in a complete *Ring* under Marek Janowski.

Elizabeth Forbes

Alva, Luigi [Alva Talledo, Luis Ernesto]

(*b* Lima, 10 April 1927). Peruvian tenor. He studied in Lima with Rosa Morales and in Milan with Emilio Ghirardini and Ettore Campogalliani. He made his début in 1949 in *Luisa Fernanda* at Lima, where he sang Beppe (*Pagliacci*) the following year. His European début was at the Teatro Nuovo, Milan, in 1954 as Alfredo. He sang Paolino in *Il matrimonio segreto* to open the Piccola Scala in 1955, repeating the role in Edinburgh in 1957. At La Scala in 1956 he sang Almaviva, a role in which his highly developed sense of comedy and lack of exaggeration were to win him widespread admiration. He sang regularly in Milan (where he appeared in the premières of Luciano Chailly's *Una domanda di matrimonio* and Riccardo Malipiero's *La donna è mobile*), at Covent Garden (1960–77), at Chicago (1961–77) and at the Metropolitan (1964–76), where he made his début as Fenton and later sang Ernesto, Lindoro and Tamino. He appeared at the festivals of Aix-en-Provence and Salzburg and sang Nemorino at Glyndebourne in 1961. His elegant and refined style was specially suited to W.A. Mozart and Gioachino Rossini, and he continued to sing Paolino, at Naples (1978), the Piccola Scala (1979) and Bordeaux (1980). He recorded Fenton as well as Ferrando and Almaviva. He taught in Lima from 1982 and retired as a singer in 1989.

Harold Rosenthal/R

Alvares de Rocafuerte, Marguerite.

See D'ALVAREZ, MARGUERITE.

Alvarez, Albert [Gourron, Raymond]

(*b* nr Bordeaux, 16 Jan 1861; *d* Nice, 26 Feb 1933). French tenor. He studied in Paris and made his début in 1886 at Ghent as Charles Gounod's Faust. From 1892 until 1906 he was engaged at the Opéra, where he created Nicias in Jules Massenet's *Thais* (1894) and roles in Augusta Holmès' *La montagne noire* (1895), Victor Duvernoy's *Hellé* (1896), Alfred Bruneau's *Messidor* (1897), Paul Vidal's *La burgonde* (1898), Xavier Leroux's *Astarte* (1901), Camille Erlanger's *Le fils de l'étoile* (1904) and Ernest Guiraud's *Frédégonde* (1905). At Covent Garden he sang Leicester in the first performance of Isidore De Lara's *Amy Robsart* (1893) and created Araquil in Jules Massenet's *La navarraise* (1894). In Monte Carlo he sang Paris in the first performance of Camille Saint-Saëns's *Hélène* (1904). His large repertory included Romeo, Samson, Don José, Fernand (*La favorite*), Raoul (*Les Huguenots*), John of Leyden (*Le prophète*), Rodrigue (*Le Cid*), Mathô (*Salammbô*), Hoffmann, Hector Berlioz's Faust, Ernest Reyer's Sigurd, Radames, Canio and Otello, as well as Lohengrin, Tannhäuser, Walther, Siegmund and Tristan. A stylish singer, he excelled in heroic French roles.

Elizabeth Forbes

Álvarez, Marcello

(*b* Córdoba, 1963). Argentine tenor. After leaving school he took an economics degree and worked in the family firm of furniture builders while taking singing lessons. In 1993 he sang for GIUSEPPE DI STEFANO, who encouraged him to go to Italy to pursue a singing career. In 1995 he won a singing competition in Milan, and later the same year made his professional début, as Elvino (*La sonnambula*) at La Fenice, Venice. His success led to immediate invitations from several other Italian opera houses, including the Teatro Comunale Giuseppe Verdi in Trieste, where he sang his first Duke in *Rigoletto* in 1996. The following year Álvarez made his French début, in Toulouse, in the same role, and scored triumphs as Werther at the Teatro Carlo Felice in Genoa and as Arturo (*I puritani*) at the Teatro Comunale in Bologna.

Within two years of his arrival in Europe, Álvarez had established a reputation as an outstanding Italianate lyric tenor, with a warm, clear, easily produced voice and an elegant sense of style. In 1998 he made several triumphant débuts: as Alfredo (*La traviata*) with the Royal Opera House company at the Royal Albert Hall, the Metropolitan Opera, and the Vienna Staatsoper, and as Carlo (*Linda di Chamounix*) at La Scala. He has since returned to the Metropolitan as Alfredo and the Italian Tenor (*Der Rosenkavalier*). As Hoffmann for the Royal Opera at Covent Garden in 2000 he was acclaimed for his vivid acting as well as his virile and sensuous singing. Subsequent appearances at Covent Garden have included the Duke in *Rigoletto* (2001 and 2005),

Edgardo (*Lucia di Lammermoor*, 2003), Rodolfo (*Luisa Miller*, 2003), Werther (2004) and Riccardo in *Un ballo in maschera* (2005). In 2001 Álvarez made his début at the Opéra Bastille, as Des Grieux in *Manon* (a performance recorded on CD), returning as Rodolfo (*La bohème*) in 2003. His other roles include Nemorino (which he first performed in Toulouse in 2001), Fenton, Faust and Charles Gounod's Romeo, which he sang at the Staatsoper in Munich in 2004. Álvarez has recorded French and Italian arias, tangos by Carlos Gardel and a disc of popular romantic duets with the tenor Salvatore Licitra.

Richard Wigmore

Alvary [Achenbach], Max(imilian)

(*b* Düsseldorf, 3 May 1856; *d* Grosstabarz, Thuringia, 7 Nov 1898). German tenor. He pursued his singing career over the initial objections of his father, the painter Andreas Achenbach, and studied in Frankfurt with Julius Stockhausen and in Milan with Francesco Lamperti. He made his début (1879) in Weimar, under the name of Max Anders, singing the title role of Friedrich Flotow's *Alessandro Stradella*, and remained at the Weimar Opera until 1885 enjoying the favour of the grand duke. He had great success at the Metropolitan in New York, making his début there on 25 November 1885 singing Don José in German. He was the USA's first Siegfried (in *Siegfried*), his most celebrated role, in 1887; other important roles of his four years at the Metropolitan included Adolar in *Euryanthe* (1887), Alvar in Gaspare Spontini's *Fernand Cortez* (1888) and Loge in *Das Rheingold* (1889). In 1890 he was engaged by the Munich Hofoper and in 1891 by the Hamburg Stadttheater. He sang Tristan and Tannhäuser at Bayreuth in 1891, and in the following year he made his London début singing Siegfried (in *Siegfried*) at Covent Garden with Mahler conducting. He returned to London in 1893 and 1894 and was heard as Max in *Der Freischütz*, Florestan, Tannhäuser, Lohengrin, Loge, Siegmund and Tristan. In October 1894 he was seriously injured in a fall while rehearsing *Siegfried* at Mannheim and never fully recovered; he retired from the stage in 1897. He was the outstanding Wagnerian tenor of his time for dramatic force and refined interpretation, and the first to break tradition by performing Tristan and the other heroic parts without a beard.

Harold Rosenthal

Amato, Pasquale

(*b* Naples, 21 March 1878; *d* Jackson Heights, NY, 12 Aug 1942). Italian baritone. He studied in Naples and made his début there in 1900 as Germont. Soon in much demand, he sang at Covent Garden (1904) and at La Scala with Arturo Toscanini (1907–8), where he was the first Italian Golaud and also premièred the role of Folco in Francesco Cilea's *Gloria* (1907), before making his début at the Metropolitan Opera as Germont in *La traviata* on 20 November 1908. He quickly established himself there and remained a member of the company until 1921, singing all the principal roles of the Italian repertory, as well as Valentin, Escamillo and many other French parts, and Kurwenal and Amfortas in German. He often sang with Caruso; they appeared together in the 1910 première of Giacomo Puccini's *La fanciulla del West*, in which Amato sang Jack Rance. He also created the title role in Walter Damrosch's *Cyrano de Bergerac* (1913) and Napoleon in Umberto Giordano's *Madame Sans-Gêne* (1915). His voice was of fine quality and extensive range, with brilliant resonance in the upper register; he made himself into a reliable and complete artist in every respect. His qualities are well shown in a long series of recordings, at first for the Italian firm of Fonotipia (1907–10) and subsequently for Victor (1911–15) and Homocord (1924); the Victor series, made in Amato's prime, includes some notable Verdi duets with Caruso, Gadski and Hempel.

P. Kenyon and C. Williams: 'Pasquale Amato', *Record Collector*, xxi (1973–4), 3–47, 76, 95, 128–32 [with discography]

Desmond Shawe-Taylor/R

Ameling, Elly (Sara)

(*b* Rotterdam, 8 Feb 1933). Dutch soprano. Her principal teachers were Jo Bollekamp and Jacoba Dresden-Dhont in Rotterdam and Pierre Bernac in Paris. In 1958 she won first prize at the International Music Competition at Geneva and embarked on a career devoted almost entirely to recital work and oratorio. Her first concerts had been given in Rotterdam as early as 1953, and she subsequently sang throughout the world in a career which lasted for more than 40 years. Her reputation spread early through recordings, particularly of Bach cantatas and Schubert lieder. In 1959 she sang in the première of Frank Martin's *Mystère de la nativité* and was the soloist in Mahler's Fourth Symphony at Salzburg. She made her British début in 1966 and her American début in New York in 1968. Although she appeared with leading orchestras and conductors, Ameling sang only one role in opera, that of Ilia in *Idomeneo*, with the Netherlands Opera in 1973 and in Washington, DC, the fol-

lowing year. Her recital programmes broadened to include songs of many nations, but *mélodies* and lieder were always at the centre of her repertory. The expressiveness of her singing increased over the years, but its special pleasure owed much to the purity and freshness of her tone and to her reliability in all aspects of her musical work. She has won many awards, including a knighthood presented in 1971 by the Queen of the Netherlands for services to music. In later years she has taught, both privately and in public masterclasses. Her legacy of recordings is one of the largest among singers, encompassing a wide repertory, not the least delightful part of it being a stylish and totally unexpected collection of American popular songs called *After Hours*.

J.B. Steane: *Singers of the Century*, ii (London, 1998)

J.B. Steane

Amicis, Anna Lucia de.

See De amicis, anna lucia.

Ancona, Mario

(*b* Livorno, 28 Feb 1860; *d* Florence, 23 Feb 1931). Italian baritone. Having made his début in 1889 at Trieste as Scindia in Jules Massenet's *Le roi de Lahore*, in 1890 he sang the King (*Le Cid*) at La Scala, his only appearance there. He created Silvio in *Pagliacci* at the Teatro Dal Verme, Milan, in 1892 and the same year sang Alphonse (*La favorite*) at the New Olympic Theatre, London. He made his Covent Garden début as Tonio in the British première of *Pagliacci* in May 1893, singing the same role in his Metropolitan début later that year. He sang Riccardo (*I puritani*) at the Manhattan Opera House on its opening night, 3 December 1906. Ancona appeared all over Europe and the USA, in a wide repertory embracing W.A. Mozart (Don Giovanni, Figaro), Giuseppe Verdi (Germont, Rigoletto, Renato, Amonasro, Iago, Don Carlo in *Ernani*), Richard Wagner (Wolfram, Telramund, Hans Sachs), Giacomo Puccini (Lescaut, Marcello), Pietro Mascagni (Alfio, David in *L'amico Fritz*) and many French roles, including Nevers (*Les Huguenots*), Escamillo and Valentin (*Faust*). He retired in 1916. An elegant, stylish singer, he possessed a voluminous, dark-toned voice sustained by an impeccable technique, which can be heard to advantage on his recordings of 'Eri tu', Iago's Credo and the Prologue to *Pagliacci*.

Elizabeth Forbes

Anders, Max

See ALVARY, MAX(IMILIAN)

Anders, Peter

(*b* Essen, 1 July 1908; *d* Hamburg, 10 Sept 1954). German tenor. He studied under LULA MYSZ-MEINER in Berlin. In 1931 he appeared in *La belle Hélène*, making his solo début the following year at Heidelberg. In the following years he sang with the opera companies of Cologne, Hanover and Munich, joining the Berlin Staatsoper in 1936. He was then a lyric tenor, acclaimed in such roles as Tamino, which he also sang at the Salzburg Festival of 1943. From 1938 to 1940 he was at the Munich State Opera where he sang in the première of Richard Strauss's *Friedenstag* (1938). He then returned to Berlin where he remained at the State Opera till 1948. His roles at this time included Belmonte, Cavaradossi and Leukippos in *Daphne*, but from 1948, when he joined the Hamburg Opera, he added such heroic roles as Lohengrin, Florestan and Otello to his repertory. He appeared at the Edinburgh Festival of 1950 as Bacchus in *Ariadne auf Naxos* and at Covent Garden (1951) as Florestan and Walther in *Die Meistersinger*. He died after a car accident. Anders left many records, impressive for fine tone and technique, conviction in his operatic works, intelligence in lieder and charm in operetta.

A.G. Ross: 'Peter Anders', *Record News* [Toronto], iii/1 (1958–9), 3–16 [with discography]
F.W. Pauli: *Peter Anders* (Berlin, 1963)

J.B. Steane/R

Anderson, June

(*b* Boston, 30 Dec 1952). American soprano. She studied at Yale University and made her début in 1978 as the Queen of Night at the New York City Opera, where she also sang Rosina, Gilda, Olympia (*Les contes d'Hoffmann*) and Lora (*Die Feen*). In 1982 she made her European début at the Rome Opera in *Semiramide*. She has sung at La Scala and in many other European cities. In the USA she has sung in Chicago and San Francisco, and first appeared at the Metropolitan Opera in 1989, as Gilda. She made her British début in 1984 with the WNO as Violetta, disclosing her dramatic talents, and first sang at Covent Garden in 1986 in a concert performance of *Semiramide*, returning as Lucia, Gilda and Elvira (*I puritani*, 1992), roles that are peculiarly well suited to her vocal gifts of plangent tone and technical flexibility, and her sincere and eloquent acting. She is also perfectly suited to Isabelle in *Robert le diable*, which she sang at the Paris Opéra in 1985. Concentrating on the bel canto repertory, she has sung

Gioachino Rossini's Desdemona, Anna (*Maometto II*), Zoraid and Armida; Vincenzo Bellini's Amina, Juliet, Elvira and Beatrice; Gaetano Donizetti's Marie (*La fille du régiment*), Giuseppe Verdi's Lida (*La battaglia di Legnano*) and Gulnara (*Il corsaro*). Her recordings chronicle her skills in the French repertory: Georges Bizet's Catherine (*La jolie fille de Perth*), Ambroise Thomas' Ophélie, Rachel (Fromental Halévy's *La Juive*) and L'Ensoleillad (*Chérubin*).

Elizabeth Forbes/Alan Blyth

Anderson, Marian

(*b* Philadelphia, 27 Feb 1897; *d* Portland, OR, 8 April 1993). American contralto (see colour plate 15). After graduating from South Philadelphia High School, she studied in her native city with Giuseppe Boghetti but, as an African American, was refused entry to the Philadelphia Music Academy on racial grounds. Having won first prize in a competition sponsored by the New York PO, she appeared as a soloist with the orchestra at Lewisohn Stadium on 27 August 1925. After further study with Frank La Forge, she made a number of concert appearances in the USA, and her European début took place at the Wigmore Hall, London, in 1930. She was subsequently lionized throughout Europe, winning from Arturo Toscanini the reported tribute: 'A voice like yours is heard only once in a hundred years'. By then a mature artist, Anderson gained high critical acclaim for her first appearance at Town Hall in New York (1935) and then undertook further tours, across the USA and in Europe. Because of a lack of stage experience – and therefore confidence – she refused offers to sing in opera, but such discs as Delilah's 'Softly awakes my heart' show what might have been, and became bestsellers. In 1939 she was denied the use of Constitution Hall in Washington, DC, for a concert; with the support of Eleanor Roosevelt and other prominent Americans, she gave a concert at the Lincoln Memorial (9 April 1939), which drew an audience of some 75,000 people. At the invitation of Rudolf Bing, she made a belated début in opera at the Metropolitan Opera in New York as Ulrica in *Un ballo in maschera* in 1955. Although her voice was no longer at its best and she was understandably affected by the emotion of the moment, as the first black singer on the company's roster she paved the way for others.

After leaving the Metropolitan in 1956, Anderson continued her concert career, making a farewell tour in 1965. Her voice was a rich, vibrant contralto of intrinsic beauty. She left recordings covering every aspect of her repertory. Her lieder, though hardly idiomatic, are deeply felt, while in spirituals she is compelling. Her autobiography, *My Lord, What a Morning*, was published in New York in 1956.

K. Vehanen: *Marian Anderson: a Portrait* (New York, 1941/*R*)
J.L. Sims: *Marian Anderson: an Annotated Bibliography and Discography* (Westport, CT, 1981)
N.M. Westlake and O.E. Albrecht: *Marian Anderson: a Catalogue of the Collection at the University of Pennsylvania* (Philadelphia, 1982)

Max De Schauensee/Alan Blyth

Andrade, Francisco d'.

See D'ANDRADE, FRANCISCO.

Andrioli, Vincenzo.

See STAGNO, ROBERTO.

Angel, Marie

(*b* Pinnaroo, South Australia, 30 July 1953). Australian soprano. After appearing in Australia she joined Opera Factory Zürich, with whom she made her London début in 1980 as Galatea. With Opera Factory London (1982–92) she has sung Pretty Polly (*Punch and Judy*), Lucy (*The Beggar's Opera*), Denise (*The Knot Garden*), Juno and Callisto, C.W. Gluck's Iphigenia, Fiordiligi, Donna Anna, Countess Almaviva and Poppaea, and took part in the première of Nigel Osborne's *Hell's Angels* (1986). For ENO she sang Claudio Monteverdi's Eurydice and Hope (1983) and Queen Tye (*Akhnaten*), which she had already sung at Houston and for New York City Opera (1984), and created Oracle of the Dead/Hecate in Harrison Birtwistle's *The Mask of Orpheus* (1986). She sang the Queen of Night for WNO (1986), Musetta for Opera North (1988) and Jo Ann in Michael Tippett's *New Year* for Glyndebourne Touring Opera (1990), as well as creating Morgan le Fay in Birtwistle's *Gawain* at Covent Garden in 1991. The tonal purity, accuracy and flexibility of her voice are as admirable in 18th-century music as they are in that of the 20th century.

Elizabeth Forbes

Angelis, Nazzareno de.

See DE ANGELIS, NAZZARENO.

Angeri, Anna D'.

See D'ANGERI, ANNA.

Annibali, Domenico [Dominichino]

(*b* Macerata, *c*1705; *d* ?Rome, 1779 or later). Italian alto castrato. After appearances in Rome (Porpora's *Germanico*, 1725) and Venice (1727 and 1729), he was engaged in 1729 for the Saxon court at Dresden at a salary of 792 thaler. He sang there in Johann Adolf Hasse's *Cleofide* (1731) and *Cajo Fabricio* (1734), but was given frequent leave to take outside engagements: at Rome in 1730, 1732 and 1739, at Vienna in 1731, when his performance in Antonio Caldara's *Demetrio* won the approval of Pietro Metastasio, and from October 1736 to June 1737 as a member of G.F. Handel's company in London. He made his London stage début at Covent Garden in a revival of *Poro* on 8 December, when he introduced two arias by Giovanni Alberto Ristori and one by Leonardo Vinci (one of only two occasions on which Handel is known to have allowed this practice in his own operas). Annibali was in the first performances of Handel's *Arminio* (title role, 1737), *Giustino* (title role, 1737) and *Berenice* (Demetrio, 1737), revivals of *Partenope* and *Esther* (in Italian), the pasticcio *Didone*, and probably the rewritten *Il trionfo del tempo*.

While Annibali was in London the Saxon envoy offered him an increased salary of 1500 thaler (raised to 2000 at the end of 1739), and he returned to Dresden. He is listed among the court and theatre musicians there until 1756, and left in 1764 with a pension of 1200 thaler and the title of *Kammermusikus*. He was living in his native town in 1776, and three years later moved to Rome. In Dresden Annibali was particularly associated with the operas of Hasse, appearing in *Tito Vespasiano*, *Demetrio*, *Lucio Papirio*, *Arminio*, *Semiramide*, *Demofoonte*, *Attilio Regolo* (title role, 1750) and *Adriano in Siria* between 1738 and 1752.

According to Charles Burney, 'his abilities during his stay in England seem to have made no deep impression', but Mrs Pendarves wrote that he had 'the best part of Senesino's voice and Caristini's, with a prodigious fine taste and good action'. This is confirmed by the compass of the parts Handel wrote for him, Justin, Arminius and Demetrius (*Berenice*), which is *a* to *g″* (Hasse took him down to *g* in *Demofoonte*, 1748). Other accounts emphasized his brilliant and flexible coloratura, though some found his acting wooden. Anton Raphael Mengs made two portraits of Annibali.

Winton Dean

Anselmi, Giuseppe

(*b* Nicolosi, nr Catania, 6 Oct 1876; *d* Zoagli, nr Rapallo, 27 May 1929). Italian tenor. He first appeared at the age of 13 as a violinist in his native city. After some experience in operetta he made his operatic début, by his own account, at Patras, Greece (*c*1896–8), singing various leading Italian roles. Serious studies with the conductor Luigi

Mancinelli led to appearances in Genoa (1900) and soon afterwards at the S Carlo, Naples. In 1901 (and again in 1904 and 1909) he sang at Covent Garden; his success was still greater in Buenos Aires, Warsaw, Moscow and St Petersburg, and greatest of all in Spain. His warm, beautiful timbre and impassioned delivery (clearly evident in his many Fonotipia records made between 1907 and 1910) were helped by vivid enunciation as well as by a romantic appearance. He retired in 1918 and made his final public appearance, once more as a violinist, at Rapallo in 1926. Also a composer, he wrote songs, chamber music and a *Poema sinfonico* for orchestra.

D. Shawe-Taylor: 'Giuseppe Anselmi', *Opera*, vii (1956), pp. 146–51

L. Lustig, C. Williams and T. Kaufman: 'Giuseppe Anselmi', *Record Collector*, xxxii (1987), pp. 51–109 [with discography]

Desmond Shawe-Taylor

Anthony, Charles [Caruso, Calogero Antonio]

(*b* New Orleans, 15 July 1929). American tenor. He studied at New Orleans and in Rome, making his début in 1954 as the Holy Fool (*Boris Godunov*) at the Metropolitan, where he sang for 30 years in a wide variety of lyric and character roles. They included Almaviva, Ernesto, Nemorino, Beppe (*Pagliacci*), David (*Die Meistersinger*) and the four comic tenor roles in *Les contes d'Hoffmann*. He also sang at Boston, Dallas and Santa Fe. A reliable singer and a good actor, he had a sweet-toned though not very large voice.

Elizabeth Forbes

Antier, Marie

(*b* Lyons, 1687; *d* Paris, 3 Dec 1747). French soprano. Trained as a singer and actress by MARIE LE ROCHOIS, she made her début at the Opéra in the 1711 revival of Michel de la Barre's *La vénitienne* (1705). For the next 30 years she sang major roles in up to five productions each season, and she retired with a generous pension at Easter 1741. After her début she was immediately given important roles in new productions beginning with André Campra's *Idomenée* (1712) and Joseph-François Salomon's *Médée et Jason* (1713); 23 years later she sang the same role, Cléone, in a revival of the Salomon opera and was warmly praised by the *Mercure* (Dec 1736). Antier appeared in almost two dozen Lully revivals; at one performance of the 1713–14 revival of *Armide* (1686) she had the honour of presenting the victorious Marshal of Villars with a laurel crown. In 1720 she became *première actrice* of the Académie Royale de Musique and in the following year she was appointed a *musicienne de la chambre du roi*, a post that required her to sing at Versailles, Marly and Fontainebleau.

In the early 1720s Antier sang at the Château des Tuileries in private performances of *opéras-ballets*, in which Louis XV loved to dance, and later in the 'concerts chez la Reine'. She became *maîtresse en titre* to the Prince of Carignan and on her marriage in 1726 to Jean Duval, a Parisian *inspecteur du grenier à sel*, she received lavish gifts from the royal family. A love affair in 1727 with Le Riche de La Pouplinière caused him to be temporarily banished from Paris. Antier herself was installed for a time in the Convent of Chaillot while apparently continuing her career at the Opéra. Beginning in 1725, she frequently served as a soloist in motets by Destouches and Lalande performed at the Concert Spirituel; in 1727–9 she was the soloist in cantatas at the Concert Français, but her career had passed its zenith: major roles at the Opéra were increasingly given to her younger colleagues, and Destouches wrote somewhat disparagingly about her in a letter of 8 February 1728. Nevertheless, she took roles in such important new productions as Michel Pignolet de Montéclair's *Jephté* (1732), Jean-Philippe Rameau's *Hippolyte et Aricie* (1733), *Les Indes galantes* (1735) and *Castor et Pollux* (1737). Her last appearances were in revivals of works in which she had sung earlier in her career; she retired in 1741. After maintaining a lavish residence at 47 rue d'Auteuil from 1715 until 1729, she spent her last years living rent-free in accommodation attached to the Opéra; she was survived by her husband (*d* 1755). Her younger sister sang in the chorus of the Opéra from 1719 until 1743. She was the mother of the soprano Mlle de Maiz.

Julie Anne Sadie

Aprile, Giuseppe [Scirolo, Sciroletto, Scirolino]

(*b* Martina Franca, Taranto, 28 Oct 1732; *d* Martina Franca, 11 Jan 1813). Italian soprano castrato and composer. His early musical training from his father, Fortunato (a notary and church singer), was followed when he was 19 by study with Gregorio Sciroli in Naples (thus his nickname). He made his début in Sciroli's *Il barone deluso* (1752, Rome). Until 1757 he sang in Naples (in the royal chapel, 1752–6, though librettos continue to list him in the service of the court until 1758), Turin and Rome (where in 1754–5 he became primo uomo); during the next few years he travelled, visiting Venice, Madrid and Stuttgart. After returning briefly to Italy, he was appointed primo uomo in Stuttgart for the period 1762–9 (with one Italian interlude), appearing in Niccolò Jommelli's *Didone abbandonata* (1763), *Demofoonte* (1764) and *Fetonte* (Phaethon, 1768), among other works, and enjoying a salary comparable to Jommelli's own. His brother Raffaele, a violinist, was also engaged at court. The depletion of the duke's *cappella* provoked his departure; he left behind him considerable debts. In 1770 Charles Burney heard him in Naples; W.A. Mozart heard him there, in Bologna and Milan, remarking that 'Aprile, first man, sings well and has a beautiful, even voice', which was 'unsurpassed'. In Naples Aprile again collaborated with Jommelli on several operas and in 1783 replaced CAFFARELLI as first soprano in the royal chapel. From 1774 to 1780 his operatic appearances were primarily in Florence, Turin and Rome. His last known performance was in 1785 in Naples, where he was pensioned in 1798. Aprile was well known as a teacher (his students included MICHAEL KELLY, Domenico Cimarosa and the younger Manuel Garcia). His 1791 vocal method – published in English, as *The Modern Italian Method of Singing* – reprints his 36 *solfeggi*, found in many other contemporary sources. Its prefatory rules and 'progressive examples' are copied from Giusto Ferdinando Tenducci's *Instruction…to his Scholars* (1782), which in turn reflects ideas espoused early in the century by Pier Francesco Tosi. Aprile wrote a great deal of music (though no operas), as did many singers of his day, most very simple duets in thirds, possibly as pedagogical tools. He possessed an agile voice, with a wide range and diversity of expression, and he was a good actor. C.F. Schubart, writing in Stuttgart, praised his manner of varying arias and noted his great importance to Jommelli.

Dale E. Monson

Aragall (y Garriga), Giacomo [Jaume]

(*b* Barcelona, 6 June 1939). Spanish tenor. He studied in Barcelona and Milan. In 1963 he won the Verdi Busseto competition, made his début at La Fenice as Gaston in *Jérusalem* and was offered a three-year contract at La Scala, making his first appearance in the title role of *L'amico Fritz*. He then sang in Barcelona, Munich, Vienna, Verona and Covent Garden, where he made his début (1966) as the Duke (*Rigoletto*), returning for Edgardo, Rodolfo, Cavaradossi, Werther and Riccardo (*Ballo in maschera*, 1988). The Duke was also his début role at the Metropolitan (1968) and at San Francisco (1972). His repertory includes Romeo (*I Capuleti e i Montecchi*, in the adaptation of the role prepared by Claudio Abbado in 1966), Gerardo (*Caterina*

Cornaro), Fernand (*La favorite*), Charles Gounod's Faust, Alfredo, Don Carlos which he sang in 1990 at Orange and Maurizio (*Adriana Lecouvreur*). A stylish singer, he had an open, keen-edged voice which he used with sensitivity, though some of the roles he undertook in the latter part of his career strained his naturally lyric timbre. His many recordings include Gennaro (*Lucrezia Borgia*), Roland (*Esclarmonde*) and Gabriele Adorno (*Simon Boccanegra*).

Alan Blyth/R

Araiza, Francisco

(*b* Mexico City, 4 Oct 1950). Mexican tenor. He began singing with a university choir, and became a pupil of the Mexican soprano Irma González at the Conservatorio Nacional de Música. His début as the First Prisoner in *Fidelio* (1970) was followed in 1973 by appearances as Des Grieux (Jules Massenet) and Rodolfo. He went to Europe in 1974 and studied in Munich with RICHARD HOLM and Erik Werba; he then took a two-year contract at Karlsruhe, where he made his European début as Ferrando in 1975 and sang other lyric roles in Mozart and Italian operas. He sang the Steersman in *Der fliegende Holländer* at Bayreuth (1978), and appeared at the Vienna Staatsoper as Tamino, a role he recorded with Herbert von Karajan. His British début was as Ernesto (*Don Pasquale*) at Covent Garden in 1983; his American début the next year was at San Francisco in *La Cenerentola*, and he appeared as Belmonte at the Metropolitan Opera later the same year. He sang Charles Gounod's Romeo at Zürich, Lohengrin in Venice (1990) and Titus at Salzburg (1991). A lyric tenor whose voice has developed with experience (though heavier roles have at times taken their toll), he now takes leading Verdi and Puccini roles and also sings Werther, Faust, Hoffmann, Lohengrin and Walther von Stolzing. He has made notable recordings of *Faust* (1987), Alfredo Catalani's *La Wally* (1990), Gaspare Spontini's *La vestale* (1991), Giuseppe Verdi's *Alzira* and Mozart and Rossini operas.

S. von Buchau: 'Conquistador', *ON*, xlviii/14 (1983–4), 30–32

A. Stewart: 'Blessed with bel canto', *Opera Now* (1994), May, 35 only

Noël Goodwin

Arbell, Lucy [Wallace, Georgette]

(*b* Paris, Sept 1882; *d* Paris, 1947). French mezzo-soprano. She made her début in 1903 at the Paris Opéra as Delilah, then sang Amneris, Maddalena (*Rigoletto*), Uta (*Sigurd*) and Fricka (*Walküre*). In

1906 she sang Persephone in *Ariane*, the first of six roles that she created in operas by Jules Massenet, and in which she made a great impression. The others were the title role of *Thérèse* (1907, Monte Carlo), a role perfectly suited to her strong, vibrant mezzo-contralto and vivacious personality, Queen Amahelli in *Bacchus* (1909, Opéra), Dulcinée in *Don Quichotte* (1910, Monte Carlo), Postumia in *Roma* (1912, Monte Carlo) and Colombe in *Panurge* (1913, Gaîté, Paris). She was renowned for her interpretation of Charlotte (*Werther*) at the Opéra-Comique, where in 1924 she appeared as Dulcinée for the last time. Her warm, clear voice and sparkling personality inspired Massenet to continue composing operas in the last years of his life, but according to eye-witnesses, her demands on the composer tested even his infatuation, and after his death in 1912 she pursued his widow and his publishers with lawsuits over exclusive rights to his posthumous oeuvre, delaying the premières of *Cléopâtre* (1914) and *Amadis* (1922). The term mezzo-contralto, indicating an affinity with both the mezzo-soprano and the contralto, was applied to her voice with its wide range and weight of tone.

Elizabeth Forbes/R

Argenta, Nancy (Maureen Herbison)

(*b* Nelson, BC, 17 Jan 1957). Canadian soprano. She studied at the University of Western Ontario (1978–80), then privately in Düsseldorf and London. Her teachers included PETER PEARS, GÉRARD SOUZAY and Vera Rózsa. As a concert singer she rapidly gained recognition throughout Europe and America, her light, clear voice making her much sought after in a wide variety of Baroque and Classical repertory. She made her operatic début in Jean-Philippe Rameau's *Hippolyte et Aricie* (doubling as the High Priestess and Huntress) at the 1983 Aix-en-Provence Festival, and returned to the festival in 1990 in Henry Purcell's *The Fairy-Queen*. At Lyons in 1985 she sang Asteria in G.F. Handel's *Tamerlano* and Susanna in *Figaro*. She has also appeared as Claudio Monteverdi's Poppaea (1988, Queen Elizabeth Hall), Vespina in Joseph Haydn's *L'indeltà delusa* (1990, Antwerp; she also recorded the role) and Purcell's Dido (1991, Hämeenlinna Festival). Argenta has recorded extensively music by J.S. Bach, Handel, Haydn and W.A. Mozart, including a notable Zerlina in Roger Norrington's *Don Giovanni*. A recital of solo music by Purcell won her particular acclaim for its vocal refinement and naturalness of expression – qualities that inform all her work.

Alan Blyth/R

Ariè [Arie], Raffaele [Rafael, Raphael]

(*b* Sofia, 22 Aug 1922; *d* Switzerland, 17 March 1988). Bulgarian bass. He studied the violin in Sofia, then turned to singing, making a concert début in 1939. He joined the National Opera in Sofia in 1945, and the next year won first prize in the Geneva International Competition. This led to further studies in Italy with RICCARDO STRACCIARI, APOLLO GRANFORTE and CARLO TAGLIABUE, and to his début at La Scala as the King in *The Love for Three Oranges*. At Venice in 1951 he created Trulove in *The Rake's Progress*, and after appearing as the Commendatore at the Salzburg Festival in 1953, he developed a career in Europe and America. He recorded Raimondo (*Lucia*) with CALLAS. His deep, easily produced and fine-textured voice came to be widely admired in the role of Boris and other bass parts of the Russian and Italian repertories.

Noël Goodwin

Arimondi, Vittorio

(*b* Saluzzo, 3 June 1861; *d* Chicago, 15 April 1928). Italian bass. Gifted with a commanding stage presence and a sonorous voice, he studied singing while training for business. After his début at Varese in Carlos Gomes's *Il Guarany* in 1883 he sang in the provinces, going to La Scala in 1893, first as Sparafucile in *Rigoletto* and then as Pistol in the première of *Falstaff*; he also sang Geronte in the revised version of *Manon Lescaut* (1894). His international career dates from 1894, when he sang Don Basilio to PATTI's Rosina at Covent Garden, with a New York début at the Metropolitan in 1896. From 1905 he spent most of his time in the USA, having sung in Russia, Poland and Austria. He joined Oscar Hammerstein's Manhattan Opera Company, singing Arkel in the American première of *Pelléas et Mélisande*, and at the Metropolitan appeared as Nero, originally a tenor role, in Jean Nouguès's *Quo vadis?* His greatest personal success remained Méphistophélès in *Faust*. He joined the Chicago Opera Company in 1910 and later taught at the Chicago Music College. His few recordings suggest a voice more remarkable for bulk than beauty, though he was described in his prime as a graceful singer.

J.B. Steane

Arkhipova, Irina (Konstantinovna)

(*b* Moscow, 2 Dec 1925). Russian mezzo-soprano. She graduated in 1948 from the Moscow Institute of Architecture, where she learned singing in N. Malïsheva's group, and in 1953 from L. Savransky's class at the Moscow Conservatory. She sang with the Sverdlovsk Opera (1954–6) and made her Bol'shoy début as Carmen in 1956. Her voice, of wide range, was remarkable for its emotional warmth and variety of tone-colour. Her roles included Lyubasha (*Tsar's Bride*), Pauline and Lyubov' (*Queen of Spades* and *Mazepa*), Amneris and Eboli, and Jules Massenet's Charlotte. She participated in many Bol'shoy first performances, including Tikhon Khrennikov's *Mat'* ('Mother'; Nilovna, 1957), Sergey Prokofiev's *War and Peace* (Hélène, 1959) and *Story of a Real Man* (Klavdiya, 1960), Rodion Shchedrin's *Ne tol'ko lyubov'* ('Not for Love Alone'; Varvara, 1961) and A.K. Kholminov's *Optimisticheskaya tragediya* ('An Optimistic Tragedy'; Commissar, 1965). She sang throughout Eastern Europe and in the USA, Japan, Austria and Scandinavia. After appearances in Naples in 1960, as Carmen, she sang Hélène with the Bol'shoy at La Scala in 1964, returning as Marfa (1967 and 1971) and Marina (1968). She scored a great success as Azucena at Orange in 1972, and this led to her Covent Garden début in the same role in 1975. She subsequently sang Ulrica at Covent Garden (1988) and appeared as the Countess (*Queen of Spades*) in performances by the Kirov Opera in New York in 1992.

I.M. Yampol'sky/R

Arnould [Arnoult], (Magdeleine) [Madeleine] Sophie

(*b* Paris, 13 Feb 1740; *d* Paris, 22 Oct 1802). French soprano. A precocious child, she studied Latin and Italian and received a solid general education. Her performance in sacred music impressed the royal family and Mme de Pompadour, and she was appointed to the Opéra, studying declamation with the actress Mlle Clairon and singing with MARIE FEL. Her voice was sweet and expressive, not powerful, supported by fine diction and acting. She was the leading Opéra soprano from 1757 (début in Jean-Joseph Mouret's *Les amours des dieux*) to 1778. She sang over 30 roles, by Jean-Baptiste Lully, Jean-Philippe Rameau, Jean-Jacques Rousseau (*Le devin du village*) and others; several she created, but her greatest success was as Telaira in the revival of Rameau's *Castor et Pollux* (1764). She adapted to Italian-influenced music such as Pierre-Alexandre Monsigny's *Aline*, and the climax of her career was in *Iphigénie en Aulide* (1774, at Fontainebleau as late as 1777. Less successful as Eurydice, which she created for the French première of C.W. Gluck's *Orphée et Eurydice* (1774), she was mortified by Gluck's choice of ROSALIE LEVASSEUR for *Alceste*. The Dorothy Parker of her day, she entertained the *philosophes* while alienating colleagues; she bore three

illegitimate children to the Count of Lauraguais. Her colourful career inspired several biographies, two comedies and an opera by Gabriel Pierné (*Sophie Arnould*, 1927).

Julian Rushton/R

Arroyo, Martina

(*b* New York, 2 Feb 1937). American soprano. She studied at Hunter College, New York, and (with GRACE BUMBRY) won the 1958 Metropolitan Opera Auditions. That year she sang in the American première of Ildebrando Pizzetti's *L'assassinio nella cattedrale* at Carnegie Hall. After taking minor roles at the Metropolitan, she went to Europe for major roles at Vienna, Düsseldorf, Berlin, Frankfurt and Zürich (where she was under contract from 1963 to 1968). In 1965 she was a substitute Aida for BIRGIT NILSSON at the Metropolitan; she played there all the major Verdi parts that formed the basis of her repertory, as well as Donna Anna, Cio-Cio-San, Liù, Santuzza, Gioconda and Elsa. She made her London début as Valentine at a concert performance of *Les Huguenots* in 1968 – the year of her first Covent Garden appearance, as Aida. Her rich, powerfully projected voice, heard to greatest advantage in the Verdi *spinto* roles, was flexible enough for W.A. Mozart (she recorded Donna Elvira with Karl Böhm and Donna Anna with Colin Davis). In the USA she has often sung in oratorio and recital – she was the first performer of Samuel Barber's concert scena, *Andromache's Farewell* (April 1963). Arroyo's most admired recordings include Hélène (*Les vêpres siciliennes*), Amelia (*Un ballo in maschera*), Leonora (*La forza del destino*) and Aida.

J.B. Steane: *The Grand Tradition* (London, 1974/R), 413 ff

Alan Blyth

Artôt, (Marguerite-Joséphine) Désirée (Montagney)

(*b* Paris, 21 July 1835; *d* Berlin, 3 April 1907). Belgian mezzo-soprano, later soprano. She was the daughter of Jean Désiré Montagney Artôt, horn player and professor at the Brussels Conservatory. She studied with PAULINE VIARDOT in London and Paris, making her first concert appearances in Brussels and London in 1857. On Giacomo Meyerbeer's recommendation she was engaged for the Paris Opéra in 1858, making her début as Fidès in *Le prophète*. In spite of the praise lavished on her by many critics, she asked to be released from her contract following some intrigues and, deciding to concentrate on the Italian repertory, she toured the south of France and Belgium. Her vocal range had extended itself in both directions, allowing her to add soprano roles to her repertory. In 1859 she sang in Italy, and at the end of the year in Berlin, with Lorini's Italian company at the opening of the Victoria-Theater, where she won great acclaim as Rosina, Angelina (*La Cenerentola*), Leonora (*Il trovatore*) and even as Maddalena (*Rigoletto*). Thereafter the greater part of her career was spent in Germany, in both Italian and German opera.

During the 1859–60 season she appeared with great success in concerts in London, and in 1863 she sang with the Royal Italian Opera as Maria in *La figlia del reggimento*. In the same year she sang Adalgisa to the Norma of Therese Tietjens and Violetta. In spite of the great impression she invariably made in London, her appearances at Covent Garden in 1864 and 1866 were her last in England. In 1868 she went to Russia where, after a brief friendship, P.I. Tchaikovsky proposed marriage to her. Without a word of explanation, however, she married the Spanish baritone MARIANO PADILLA Y RAMOS at Sèvres in September 1869; she sang with him in Italian opera in Germany, Austria and Russia until her retirement. On 22 March 1887 they appeared together in a scene from *Don Giovanni*, performed for the kaiser's birthday at the Imperial Palace in Berlin. She taught singing in that city until 1889, when she and her husband went to live in Paris.

Harold Rosenthal

Artôt de Padilla, Lola [Dolores de Padilla]

(*b* Sèvres, 5 Oct 1876; *d* Berlin, 12 April 1933). Soprano. Daughter of DÉSIRÉE ARTOT and the baritone MARIANO PADILLA Y RAMOS. She made her operatic début in Paris in 1904 and subsequently sang in Berlin at the Komische Oper (1905–8), where on 21 Feb 1907 she sang in the première of Frederick Delius's *A Village Romeo and Juliet*, and at the Hofoper (1909–27). In 1911 she was the first Octavian heard in Berlin. Her other successful roles included Zerlina, Countess Almaviva, Oscar and Micaëla.

Harold Rosenthal/R

Aruhn, Britt-Marie

(*b* Motala, 11 Nov 1943). Swedish soprano. She studied in Stockholm, making her début there at the Royal Opera in 1974 as Olympia. Later roles included Violetta, Gilda, Sophie, Norina and Adina. In 1978 she made her Covent Garden début

as Zerbinetta, and in Stockholm she created the Chief of Secret Police in Ligeti's *Le Grand Macabre*, repeating the role at the Paris Opéra (1981), where she also sang Zdenka (*Arabella*). At the Théâtre de la Monnaie she has sung the Fairy Godmother (*Cendrillon*), Musetta, Mélisande, Susanna, Cinna (*Lucio Silla*), Adele (*Die Fledermaus*) and Sandrina (*La finta giardiniera*). In 1987 she sang Helen in C.W. Gluck's *Paride e Elena* at Drottningholm. Her voice is light and very flexible.

Elizabeth Forbes

Atlantov, Vladimir (Andreyevich)

(*b* Leningrad [now St Petersburg], 19 Feb 1939). Russian tenor. The son of an opera singer, he graduated from N. Bolotina's class at the Leningrad Conservatory in 1963, and had further training as a student-artist (1963–5) at La Scala opera school. He won the 1966 Tchaikovsky and the 1967 Sofia international competitions. In 1963 he made his début at the Kirov Theatre, and in 1967 he joined the Bol'shoy. His voice is full and ample, but capable of great beauty and delicacy; he has a strong temperament and a gift for character portrayal. His roles include Hermann, Vladimir (*Prince Igor*), Alfredo and Don José. He has toured in Europe, Canada and Japan, and was made People's Artist of the RSFSR in 1972. He made his Covent Garden début in *Otello*, one of his most famous roles, in 1987, and sang Canio there in 1989. Atlantov made his US début, as Canio, at San Francisco in 1990. He has also toured extensively as a concert singer. His recordings include Hermann, Lensky, Andrey Khovansky (*Khovanshchina*) and Canio.

I.M. Yampol'sky/R

Aubry, Marie

(*b* *c*1656; *d* Paris, 1704). French singer. She sang at a young age in the musical establishment of Philip, Duke of Orléans, and first appeared on stage as Diana in *Les amours de Diane et d'Endymion* by Jean de Granouilhet at Versailles (1671). Her performance impressed Robert Cambert, who cast her as Phyllis in his pastorale *Les peines et les plaisirs de l'amour* (1671). She created six leading roles in Jean-Baptiste Lully's operas: Aeglé in *Thésée* (1675), Sangaride in *Atys* (1676), Io in *Isis* (1677), Philonoé in *Bellérophon* (1679), the title role in *Proserpine* (1680) and Andromeda in *Persée* (1682). She assumed such a 'prodigious size' that she retired in 1684 because 'she could not walk and appeared *toute ronde*' (F. Parfaict: *Histoire de l'Académie royale de musique*, unpublished).

Aubry fanned the antagonism between Lully and the librettist Henry Guichard, her former lover. She told Lully that Guichard had plotted his murder by asking her brother to mix arsenic in Lully's tobacco. There followed a bitter trial lasting nearly three years.

James R. Anthony

Augér, Arleen

(b Long Beach, CA, 13 Sept 1939; d Leusden, The Netherlands, 10 June 1993). American soprano. As a girl she sang in a church choir and studied the piano and violin. She studied singing and the violin at the University of California, later took singing lessons in Chicago with Ralph Errolle, and won a scholarship to Vienna in 1967. At her audition she so impressed the conductor Josef Krips that he engaged her for the Staatsoper, with the role of the Queen of Night in Die Zauberflöte for her début. Another powerful admirer at this time was Karl Böhm, with whom she sang, and also recorded, a notable Konstanze in Die Entführung aus dem Serail. Appearances at the Vienna Volksoper included Marie in Gaetano Donizetti's La fille du régiment. Her reputation as a coloratura soprano grew with débuts at the New York City Opera (1969) and Salzburg (1970), both as the Queen of Night.

With her move to Frankfurt in 1974 Augér turned more to lyric roles in opera and to the development of her career as a concert singer. She toured Japan in programmes of J.S. Bach and G.F. Handel and worked extensively with the pianist Irwin Gage in the lieder repertory. In 1975 she sang as Fire in L'enfant et les sortilèges at La Scala, and in 1978 made her début at the Metropolitan Opera as Marzelline in Fidelio. She was greatly admired in Britain, where she gave many recitals and sang in memorable performances of Alcina and L'incoronazione di Poppea (both of which she recorded) at Spitalfields in the City of London Festival. In 1986 her singing of W.A. Mozart's Exsultate, jubilate at the wedding of Prince Andrew and Sarah Ferguson in Westminster Abbey was heard by millions worldwide on television. Augér's many recordings show her as a delightful singer of Bach, Haydn, W.A. Mozart, Schubert and Richard Strauss, to whose Vier letzte Lieder she brought a fresh voice and mature understanding in a performance with André Previn. Among her last recordings were a distinguished contribution to Graham Johnson's Complete Schubert Song Edition and Sonnets from the Portuguese, written for her by Libby Larsen. Her voice was of a gentle character with impressive reserves of power: her singing was unfailingly musi-

cal, her professional life refreshingly independent, and her death, after operations for a brain tumour, was deeply mourned.

J.B. Steane: Singers of the Century (London, 1996), 181–5

J.B. Steane

Austral [Fawaz, Wilson], Florence

(b Melbourne, 26 April 1894; d Newcastle, NSW, 15 or 16 May 1968). Australian soprano. Her real name was Wilson, but she was also known by that of her stepfather, Fawaz, before she adopted her familiar professional name. Having studied at Melbourne University Conservatorium and in New York, she is said to have been offered a contract with the Metropolitan Opera, but preferred to make her career in England. In 1923 she appeared at Covent Garden with the British National Opera Company as Brünnhilde in the complete Ring cycle, and this role was to remain her most famous; she was also successful as Isolde and Aida. Less forceful and more lyrical than many Wagnerian dramatic sopranos, she maintained a consistent beauty and evenness of tone through these arduous parts, which she also sang in the international Covent Garden seasons of 1924 and later. She married the flautist John Amadio and toured widely with him in Australia and America. Her many admirable recordings for HMV include the pioneer late-acoustic English-language series of excerpts from the Ring; in the early-electric German-language series, as at Covent Garden, she shared the role with FRIDA LEIDER.

D. White: 'Florence Austral', Record Collector, xiv (1961–2), 4–29, 168–9, [with discography by W. Hogarth and D. White]

Desmond Shawe-Taylor

Avdeyeva, Larisa (Ivanovna)

(b Moscow, 21 June 1925). Russian mezzo-soprano. She studied singing and dramatic art at the Stanislavsky Opera Studio (1945–6). From 1947 she was a soloist at the Stanislavsky Music Theatre, Moscow, where she sang Suzuki, La Périchole, Kosova and Varvara (respectively in Tikon Khrennikov's V buryu, 1952, and Frol Skobeyev, 1950 première) and Mistress of the Copper Mountain at the première of K.V. Molchanov's Kamenniy tsvetok ('The Stone Flower') in 1951. In 1952 she moved to the Bol'shoy Theatre, where she sang the leading Rimsky-Korsakov and Musorgsky mezzo roles, P.I. Tchaikovsky's Enchantress, Alexander Borodin's Konchakovna, Akhrosimova in War and Peace and the Commissar (A.N. Kholminov's *Optimisticheskaya tragediya*). She married the conductor Yevgeny Svetlanov. She toured widely, in the USA, Canada, Japan and Europe, and was made People's Artist of the RSFSR in 1964.

I.M. Yampol'sky/R

Aylmer, Jennifer

(*b* Oceanside, NY, 21 June 1972). American soprano. After graduating from the Eastman School of Music she studied at the Juilliard Opera Center. She then joined the Houston Grand Opera Studio, where she sang the role of Amy in the world première of Mark Adamo's *Little Women* in 1998. She has subsequently sung a wide range of lyric soprano roles, including W.A. Mozart's Susanna and Pamina, Norina (*Don Pasquale*), Sophie (*Der Rosenkavalier*), Helena (*A Midsummer Night's Dream*) and the Governess (*The Turn of the Screw*), in companies throughout the USA. With Austin Lyric Opera, Aylmer has performed Gilda in *Rigoletto* and Stella in André Previn's *A Streetcar Named Desire*. She sang Cynthia Read in the world première of Bernard Rands's *Belladonna* at Aspen in 1999, and in 2005 created the role of Bella in Tobias Picker's *An American Tragedy* in her Metropolitan Opera début. She returned to the Metropolitan, as Papagena, the following season. In 2001 she made her New York recital debut in the Alice Tully Hall. Aylmer's bright, silvery timbre has also been admired in Baroque repertory, including G.F. Handel's *Orlando*, *Flavio* and *Acis and Galatea*, and on the concert platform in works such as Mozart's *Exsultate, jubilate* and Gustav Mahler's Fourth Symphony.

Richard Wigmore

B

Baccaloni, Salvatore

(*b* Rome, 14 April 1900; *d* New York, 31 Dec 1969). Italian bass. He studied with Giuseppe Kaschmann and made his début at the Teatro Adriano, Rome, in 1922 as Dr Bartolo. In 1926 he was engaged at La Scala, where he sang regularly until 1940, first in serious roles and then, on Arturo Toscanini's advice, specializing in roles like Dulcamara, the two Bartolos and the *buffo* roles in Ermanno Wolf-Ferrari's operas. During this period he contributed significantly to several complete opera recordings by the La Scala company. He appeared at Covent Garden (1928–9) and at Glyndebourne (1936–9), where his Leporello, Dr Bartolo and especially Don Pasquale set a standard of excellence. He made his North American début in Chicago in 1930 as Melitone and sang at the Teatro Colón (1931–41, 1947). In 1940 he joined the Metropolitan, and sang there regularly until 1962, giving 297 performances, mostly in the Italian *buffo* repertory. He sang Falstaff at San Francisco (1944) and made numerous tours of the USA. Portly in build and good-humoured, Baccaloni had a communicative gift for comedy and was noted for his musicianship; in his early years he displayed a rare vocal quality in his *buffo* roles.

Francis D. Perkins/Alan Blyth

Bacquier, Gabriel (-Augustin-Raymond-Théodore-Louis)

(*b* Béziers, 17 May 1924). French baritone. Having gained a *premier prix* and two opera prizes at the Paris Conservatoire he began his career in Beckman's Compagnie Lyrique (1950–52). After three years at La Monnaie, Brussels (début as Gioachino Rossini's Figaro), he joined the Opéra-Comique (1956), singing Sharpless, Alfio, Albert (*Werther*), Zurga, Ourrias, Yevgeny Onegin and Gianni Schicchi. At the Opéra (1958–81) his roles included Germont, Rigoletto, Valentin, Escamillo, Boris, Boccanegra and Leporello; at Aix-en-Provence (1960–89) he sang Don Giovanni, Don Alfonso, Golaud, Falstaff, Don Pasquale and the King of Clubs. In 1962 he made his British début at Glyndebourne as W.A. Mozart's Count Almaviva and in 1964 sang Riccardo in *I puritani* at Covent Garden and the High Priest in *Samson et Dalila* at the Metropolitan, where his later roles (until 1981) included Melitone, the E.T.A. Hoffmann villains, Jules Massenet's Lescaut,

and Iago. His voice became richer and firmer during the early 1970s, his command of vocal and dramatic nuance increasingly skilful. His Scarpia was the more formidable for being sophisticated, his Dr Bartolo the more humorous for being stripped of buffoonery; his Don Alfonso, if suave, was also dominating. During the 1980s he sang Sancho Panza, the Father (*Louise*) and the Viceroy (*La Périchole*) with great success. In 1990 he returned to Covent Garden as Gioachino Rossini's Dr Bartolo. Among his many recordings, his Dulcamara, Don Giovanni, William Tell, Iago, Sancho Panza and Golaud vividly reveal his native wit and skilled vocal acting. He was made a Chevalier of the Légion d'Honneur in 1975.

S. Segalini: 'Gabriel Bacquier', *Opera*, xxxiii (1982), 577–81)

André Tubeuf, Elizabeth Forbes/R

Bada, Angelo

(*b* Novara, 27 May 1876; *d* Novara, 23 March 1941). Italian tenor. He made his début in 1898 in Italy and sang there for a decade. In 1908 he went to New York, where he made his Metropolitan début as the Messenger in *Aida*. He remained as chief comprimario at the Metropolitan for 30 years, creating roles in Giacomo Puccini's *Fanciulla del West* (1910), *Il tabarro* (1918, Tinca) and *Gianni Schicchi* (1918, Gherardo) and taking part in many New York first performances. In 1928–9 he sang at Covent Garden as Shuysky (*Boris Godunov*) and in 1935 appeared at the Salzburg Festival as Dr Caius (*Falstaff*). He made his last appearance at the Metropolitan in 1938 at Giovanni Martinelli's silver jubilee concert.

Elizabeth Forbes

Baglioni, Antonio

(*fl* 1780s–90s). Italian tenor and singing teacher. He may have been related to FRANCESCO BAGLIONI. He sang in productions of comic opera, particularly in Venice during the late 1780s and early 90s, and of serious opera. Two of his most important roles were Don Ottavio in the first production of W.A. Mozart's *Don Giovanni* (1787, Prague) and Titus in *La clemenza di Tito* (1791, Prague). He also sang the title role in the première of Giuseppe Gazzaniga's *Don Giovanni* in Venice in 1787. His range encompassed *e* to *b b'*. He was said to have had a well-trained, pure and expressive voice. As a singing teacher, he taught, among others, Giulietta da Ponte, the niece of Mozart's librettist Lorenzo Da Ponte, who claimed that Baglioni was 'a man of perfect taste and great musical knowledge who had trained the most celebrated singers in Italy'. Baglioni published a set of vocal exercises (Milan, n.d.) and a duet *Sommo ciel* (Venice, n.d.); his only other extant works are an *Ave regina* for three voices and an aria, *Come aboro fu deciso*.

J.A. Rice: *W.A. Mozart: La clemenza di Tito* (Cambridge, 1991)

Sven Hansell/Barbara D. Mackenzie

Baglioni, Clementina.

Soprano, daughter of FRANCESCO BAGLIONI. She created the role of Rosina in W.A. Mozart's *La finta semplice*.

Baglioni, Francesco [Carnace]

(*fl* 1729–62). Italian bass and impresario. He was one of the most popular comic opera singers of his day and a particularly important figure in the development and dissemination of the genre in the middle of the century. He performed in at least 100 productions beginning in the late 1720s, when he sang intermezzos in Foligno and Pesaro. He launched his comic opera career in Rome in 1738 with Gaetano Latilla's *La finta cameriera* and *Madama Ciana* and Rinaldo di Capua's *La commedia in commedia*. Productions throughout northern Italy of these operas along with another first performed in Rome, Rinaldo's *La libertà nociva* (1740), dominated Baglioni's career for the next decade. In 1749 he appeared in the *dramma giocoso L'Arcadia in Brenta* in Venice, the first collaboration between Baldassare Galuppi and Carlo Goldoni, and for the remainder of his career he primarily sang texts written by Goldoni, in cities along the axis from Venice to Turin. His range encompassed *B* to *f'* and music written for him is predominantly syllabic and laden with comic effects. Baglioni sang in the opera troupes of at least three well-known impresarios: Angelo Mingotti, Eustachio Bambini and Girolamo Medebach. Evidence that he worked as an impresario himself includes a payment record from 1744 indicating his fee of 155 lire for duties as impresario in Venice's San Cassiano for the autumn and carnival seasons. Three of his daughters appeared in productions with him: Giovanna from 1752, CLEMENTINA from 1754 (she later created the role of Rosina

in W.A. Mozart's *La finta semplice*) and Vincenza from 1757. His other children include the singers Costanza, Rosina and perhaps ANTONIO BAGLIONI (who created both Don Ottavio in Mozart's *Don Giovanni* and Tito in Mozart's *La clemenza di Tito*).

Barbara D. Mackenzie

Bahr-Mildenburg [née Mildenburg von Bellschau], Anna

(*b* Vienna, 29 Nov 1872; *d* Vienna, 27 Jan 1947). Austrian soprano. Having studied with Rosa Papier, she sang in 1895 to the Hamburg impresario Pollini, including in a formidable audition programme Vincenzo Bellini's 'Casta diva', Carl Maria von Weber's 'Ozean, du Ungeheuer', Ortrud's curse, Brünnhilde's battle-cry and arias of Donna Anna and the Queen of Night. Pollini immediately engaged her, and presented her as Brünnhilde in *Die Walküre* on 12 September 1895 in a performance conducted by Gustav Mahler. This was the beginning of a relationship between the young singer and Mahler which was personally emotional and somewhat tempestuous, but artistically harmonious and fruitful. Though greatly admired in Hamburg, she soon followed Mahler to Vienna, where she remained a much valued member of the company from 1898 until 1916, returning as a guest in 1920 and 1921. She excelled in all the great Wagner roles (including Kundry, which she often sang at Bayreuth between 1897 and 1914) and as the heroines of *Fidelio*, *Oberon* and *Don Giovanni* (Donna Anna); she also appeared successfully as Norma and in other Italian parts. In 1906 she was seen at Covent Garden as Isolde and Elisabeth; she made a still greater impression in the Beecham seasons of spring and winter 1910, and in 1913, especially for her masterly study of Richard Strauss's Clytemnestra. With such demands placed on it, her voice began to show signs of deterioration, and she gradually relinquished the heavier roles in favour of less vocally strenuous parts. As an intimate friend of the Wagner family, she assisted Cosima in her work at Bayreuth and later undertook similar duties with the Munich Opera. In 1922 and 1925 she appeared as an actress at the Salzburg Festival, and in 1927 she gave an operatic recital there at the Mozarteum. Her one recording, made in 1904, is of the recitative only of Weber's 'Ozean' aria, and gives a good, though tantalizing, impression of her brilliant voice and commanding style. In 1909 she married the Viennese author Hermann Bahr (1863–1934).

Desmond Shawe-Taylor

Bailey, Norman (Stanley)

(*b* Birmingham, 23 March 1933). English bass-baritone. He studied at Rhodes University, South Africa, and at the Vienna Music Academy, making his début with the Vienna Chamber Opera as Tobias Mill in Gioachino Rossini's *La cambiale di matrimonio* in 1959. He sang at Linz (1960–63) and in Germany (1963–7), where his roles included Rigoletto, Boccanegra, Nabucco and Renato. He joined the Sadler's Wells Opera (later the ENO) in 1967, making his British début in Manchester as W.A. Mozart's Count Almaviva; he celebrated his 25th anniversary with the company in 1992 as Sharpless. His London début, as Hans Sachs under Reginald Goodall (1968), established him as a Wagnerian of more than local importance, and he later undertook the role at Covent Garden, in Hamburg, Brussels and Munich, and at Bayreuth. He was an equally impressive Wotan (in a new production of the *Ring* at the London Coliseum, 1970–73), while at Bayreuth (Gunther, Amfortas) and elsewhere he expanded his Heldenbariton repertory. In 1972, starting with Luna at the Coliseum, he resumed the big Italian roles of his early days in Germany. At the Coliseum Bailey sang Pizarro, Kutuzov (*War and Peace*), the Forester and Prince Gremin. His La Scala début

was in 1967 as Luigi Dallapiccola's Job. In 1975 he sang Hans Sachs with the New York City Opera and in 1976 made his début with the Metropolitan in the same role. In 1985 at Duisburg he created Johann Matthys in Goehr's *Behold the Sun*. Later roles included Oroveso (1993) and Landgrave Herrmann in *Tannhäuser* (1997) for Opera North. In 1996 he made his Glyndebourne début, as Schigolch (*Lulu*). He was made a CBE in 1977. His timbre was definite, individual, firm, not rich or romantic in an italianate manner. Clarity, incisiveness and high musical intelligence distinguished his interpretations, as can be heard in his authoritative recordings of Wotan and Hans Sachs. His command of musical gesture, his vivid projection and his 'three-dimensional' presentation of a character have given his performances at once romance and uncommon dramatic power.

E. Forbes: 'Norman Bailey', *Opera*, xxiv, 1973, 774–80

Andrew Porter

Baker, Dame Janet (Abbott)

(*b* Hatfield, Yorks., 21 Aug 1933). English mezzo-soprano. She studied in London with Helene Isepp and Meriel St Clair, making her début in 1956 as

Dame Janet Baker with the conductor Raymond Leppard

Miss Róza in *The Secret* (Oxford University Opera Club). In 1959 she sang Eduige in the Handel Opera Society's *Rodelinda*; other Handel roles included Ariodante (1964) and Orlando (1966), which she sang to great acclaim at the Barber Institute, Birmingham. With the English Opera Group at Aldeburgh she sang Henry Purcell's Dido (1962), Polly (Benjamin Britten's version of *The Beggar's Opera*) and Lucretia (1966). At Glyndebourne she appeared again as Dido (1966) and as Diana/Jupiter (*Calisto*) and Penelope (*Il ritorno d'Ulisse*). For Scottish Opera she sang Dorabella, Dido (*Les Troyens*), Octavian, the Composer and C.W. Gluck's Orpheus. At Covent Garden she made her début in 1966 as Hermia, and later sang Hector Berlioz's Dido, Kate in *Owen Wingrave* (the role she created in its original television version in 1971), W.A. Mozart's Vitellia and Idamantes, William Walton's Cressida (1976; the composer transposed the soprano role to enable her to sing it) and, for her farewell performances, C.W. Gluck's Alcestis (1981). For the ENO she sang Poppaea, Mary Stuart, Charlotte (*Werther*) and G.F. Handel's Julius Caesar. In 1982 she retired from opera after singing Mary Stuart at the ENO and Gluck's Orpheus at Glyndebourne. She described her final opera season and her career in *Full Circle* (London, 1982). Complete emotional identification with her roles, many of which she recorded, and a rich, expressive and flexible voice enabled her to excel in florid as well as dramatic music.

Baker divided her time between the stage and the concert platform. Perhaps her greatest single success as a song recitalist was at her début in Town Hall, New York, on 2 December 1966; on that occasion her personal magnetism and sense of communication won her an entirely new audience. In her recital programmes she penetrated far beyond the normal confines of Schubert lieder, becoming a devoted exponent of French and English song. She gave the première (1975, Minneapolis) of Dominick Argento's song cycle *From the Diary of Virginia Woolf*, which won the Pulitzer Prize. Benjamin Britten wrote his dramatic cantata *Phaedra* for her in 1975 (first performance, Aldeburgh Festival, 1976), and André Previn wrote his *Five Songs* for her, to words by Philip Larkin (1977). She was also a noble interpreter of Gustav Mahler (all the great song cycles) and Edward Elgar, and a Bach singer of peculiar eloquence and technical accomplishment. Everything she sang was imbued with an innate feeling for the meaning and emotional import of the text. Many discs document fully all facets of her career. Her recordings include *Maria Stuarda* (1983) and *Giulio Cesare in Egitto* (1985) with the ENO conducted by Charles Mackerras, and Phaedra in the earliest near-complete recording of *Hippolyte*

et Aricie conducted by Anthony Lewis, following a production at Birmingham University in 1965. Numerous honours have been awarded her, including the Hamburg Shakespeare Prize (1971) and honorary degrees from the universities of London, Birmingham and Oxford. She was made a CBE in 1970 and a DBE in 1976.

A. Blyth: *Janet Baker* (London, 1973) [with discography by M. Walker]
J.B. Steane: *The Grand Tradition* (London, 1974), 500 ff
'The Singer and the Art of Communication', *RSA Journal*, no. 5468 (1996), 53–60

Alan Blyth

Baklanov [Bakkis], Georgy (Andreyevich)

(*b* Riga, 23 Dec 1880/4 Jan 1881; *d* Basle, 6 Dec 1938). Russian baritone of Latvian birth. He studied in Kiev and Milan, and with IPPOLIT PETROVICH PRYANISHNIKOV in St Petersburg. He made his début (1903, Kiev) as Anton Rubinstein's Demon, sang with the Zimin Private Opera in Moscow and was engaged in 1905 by the Bol'shoy, creating the Baron in Serge Rachmaninoff's *The Miserly Knight* (1906) and remaining until 1909, when he sang Barnaba (*La Gioconda*) at the inaugural performance of the Boston Opera House. At Covent Garden he appeared as Rigoletto (début, 1910), Scarpia and Amonasro, repeating the first two roles at the Komische Oper, Berlin in 1911. He sang in Boston (1915–18), then with Chicago Opera (1917–26), and in New York, where he later became a mainstay of the Russian Opera Company. Baklanov's repertory included Yevgeny Onegin, Hamlet, Boris, Méphistophélès (*Faust*), the Father (*Louise*), Golaud (*Pelléas et Mélisande*), Telramund and Wotan. He was greatly admired for his dramatic talents, and his voice was rich and vibrant, particularly in the middle and upper registers. Between 1910 and 1930 he made a number of recordings.

Harold Barnes, Katherine K. Preston

Baldassari, Benedetto [Benedetti]

(*fl* 1708–25). Italian soprano castrato. He was in the service of the Elector Palatine at Düsseldorf (*c*1708–14), where he sang a female part in Agostino Steffani's *Tassilone* in 1709. In 1710–11 he was at the Berlin court as the agent of the elector and Steffani in an attempt to convert the King and Queen of Prussia to Catholicism. G.F. Handel travelled to Düsseldorf in 1711 to secure him for the London opera, where he went in 1712 and sang in revivals of Francesco Mancini's *Idaspe fedele* and Francesco Gasparini's *Antioco* at the Queen's Theatre, playing a female part in the latter, and in the pasticcio *Ercole*. He was much applauded, again in a female role, in Gasparini's *Lucio Papirio* in Rome in 1714, and sang in operas by C.F. Pollarolo and Giuseppe Maria Orlandini in Venice in 1718. Returning to London in 1719, he sang as an original member of the Royal Academy company, in Giovanni Porta's *Numitore*, Handel's *Radamisto* (where he demanded to be elevated from a captain of the guard to a princely lover) and Thomas Roseingrave's adaptation of Domenico Scarlatti's *Narciso* in 1720, and in original productions of Handel's *Floridante* (1721) and Giovanni Bononcini's *Crispo* and *Griselda* (1722). In the autumn of 1725 he was singing in Dublin.

The two parts Handel wrote for him, Fraarte in *Radamisto* and Timante in *Floridante*, show that he was a high soprano with a compass from e' to a'' but the two leading male roles in *Radamisto* were allotted to women, implying that Handel did not rate him as a front-rank castrato. His portrait was painted by Antonio Belucci and engraved by George Vertue.

Winton Dean

Baltsa, Agnes

(*b* Lefkas, 19 Nov 1944). Greek mezzo-soprano. She studied in Athens, Munich and Frankfurt, where she made her début in 1968 as Cherubino. In 1969 she sang Octavian at the Vienna Staatsoper and the following year appeared at the Deutsche Oper, Berlin, and the Salzburg Festival. Baltsa made her American début in 1971 at Houston as Carmen, and first sang at La Scala in 1974 as Dorabella. She made her Covent Garden début in 1976 as Cherubino and first sang at the Metropolitan in 1979 as Octavian, returning as Carmen. Her repertory includes Orpheus, Sextus, Rosina, Cenerentola, Isabella (*L'italiana in Algeri*), Romeo (*I Capuleti e i Montecchi*), Eboli, Adalgisa, Azucena, Dido (*Les Troyens*), the Composer (*Ariadne auf Naxos*), Herodias (*Salome*), Delilah, Charlotte and Giulietta (*Les contes d'Hoffmann*). A powerful singing actress, Baltsa has sometimes sacrificed beauty of tone to dramatic effect; but she has brought a rare visceral excitement to a role like Carmen. She is also an admired interpreter of the mezzo part in Giuseppe Verdi's Requiem, which she recorded with both Herbert von Karajan and Ricardo Muti.

N. Goodwin: 'Agnes Baltsa', *Opera*, xxxvi (1985), 483–8

Elizabeth Forbes

Bampton, Rose (Elizabeth)

(*b* Lakewood, nr Cleveland, OH, 28 Nov 1908; *d* Bryn Mawr, PA, 21 Aug 2007). American mezzo-soprano, later soprano. She studied at the Curtis Institute, made her début in 1929 at Chatauqua as Siébel (*Faust*), and then sang secondary roles with the Philadelphia Grand Opera. She made her Metropolitan début in 1932 as Laura (*La Gioconda*), and sang as a mezzo until 1937, when she made her soprano début as Leonora (*Il trovatore*); other roles included Aida and Amneris (in the same season), Donna Anna, Alcestis, Elisabeth, Elsa, Sieglinde and Kundry. She appeared at Covent Garden (1937) as Amneris; in Chicago (1937–46), where her roles included Maddalena de Coigny; at the Teatro Colón, Buenos Aires (1942–8), where she sang the Marschallin, and Daphne in the South American première of Richard Strauss's opera; and in San Francisco (1949). She retired in 1950. Bampton had a strong, though not particularly individual, voice, and her sovereign musicianship was admired by Arturo Toscanini, for whom she recorded Leonore in *Fidelio*. Many of her Metropolitan broadcasts are preserved on disc, notably an exciting Donna Anna under Bruno Walter in 1942 (see P. Jackson: *Saturday Afternoons at the Old Met*, New York, 1992), as is a performance of *Gurrelieder* with Leopold Stokowski.

Max De Schauensee/Alan Blyth

Banse, Juliane

(*b* Tettnang, 10 July 1969). German soprano. She studied at the training school of the Zürich Opera, then in Munich with BRIGITTE FASSBAENDER and Daphne Evangelatos. She made her stage début at the Komische Oper, Berlin, in 1989 as Pamina, and followed that role with Ilia and Susanna at the same house. Since then she has appeared as Sophie at the Salzburg Festival, as Zerlina at Glyndebourne (the controversial Warner staging of 1994), at the Deutsche Oper Berlin as Pamina, Sophie and Manon, and at the Vienna Staatsoper as Susanna, Pamina, Marzelline, Sophie and Zdenka. In 1998 Banse was much praised for her assumption of the title part in the première of Heinz Holliger's opera *Schneewittchen* at Zürich. In 1999 she sang Ighino in a new production of *Palestrina* at the Vienna Staatsoper and made her début, as Pamina, at the Staatsoper in Munich. She has a wide concert repertory ranging from Haydn (she has performed *The Creation* under Simon Rattle with the Berlin PO and under Andrew Davis at the Proms) to Gustav Mahler and Alban Berg, and is a leading exponent of lieder, giving frequent recital tours in Germany and elsewhere and appearing regularly at the

Schubertiade in Feldkirch. She made her début with the Vienna PO under Claudio Abbado in 1994, singing Berg's *Lulu* Suite, and the following year made her US début, with the St Louis SO, in Mahler's Symphony No. 2. Her recordings of, among others, W.A. Mozart, Robert Schumann and Mahler have been much admired for her innate sincerity of purpose allied to a communicative manner, a pleasing timbre and a scrupulous care for the text.

Alan Blyth

Bär, Olaf

(*b* Dresden, 19 Dec 1957). German baritone. At the age of ten he joined the Dresden Kreuzchor and thereafter studied at the Musikhochschule in his native city, where he sang Nardo (*La finta giardiniera*) and created the title role of *Meister Mateh* by his fellow student, Jan Trieder. After winning the Walter Grüner Lieder Competition in London, he embarked on a career as a recitalist, quickly achieving a reputation for intelligence and sensitivity in his readings of lieder. In 1985 he joined the Dresden Staatsoper, singing Kilian in *Der Freischütz* at the reopening of the Semper Oper and creating the Marquis in Siegfried Matthus's *Die Weise von Liebe und Tod des Cornets Christoph Rilke*. The same year he made his Covent Garden début as Harlequin in *Ariadne auf Naxos*, a role he repeated at Aix-en-Provence in 1986. In 1986 he sang Papageno, probably his best role, at both the Vienna Staatsoper and La Scala, subsequently recording the part with Neville Marriner. Bär made his Glyndebourne début as the Count in *Capriccio* (1987) and returned as Don Giovanni (1991). He has appeared at Frankfurt, Vienna and Berlin in a repertory that includes Count Almaviva, Guglielmo, Silvio (*Pagliacci*) and Wolfram. In 1989 he created Hoffmann in Eckehard Mayer's *Der goldene Topf* at Dresden. His US opera début came in 1996, when he sang Papageno in Chicago. As a recitalist he has appeared at all the major festivals in Europe, including Salzburg and Hohenems, and has been a regular visitor to London's Wigmore Hall since the outset of his career. His other recordings include several choral works (notably Johannes Brahms's *German Requiem*), the major song cycles of Franz Schubert and Robert Schumann, and many of the songs of Hugo Wolf, all of which reveal his attractive, soft-grained tone (occasionally lacking an ideal body) and sympathy for the shaping of music and text.

Alan Blyth

Barbieri, Fedora

(*b* Trieste, 4 June 1920; *d* Florence, 4 March 2003). Italian mezzo-soprano. She studied at

Trieste with Luigi Toffolo and at the school of the Teatro Comunale, Florence, with Giulia Tess. She made her début at Florence in 1940 as Fidalma in Cimarosa's *Il matrimonio segreto*. In 1941 she created Dariola in Franco Alfano's *Don Juan de Manara* at the Florence Maggio Musicale, and also appeared in Monteverdi revivals. She sang regularly at La Scala from 1942, and at the Metropolitan from 1950 until the 1970s, making her début there as Eboli in *Don Carlos* on the opening night of Rudolf Bing's régime. She first visited England with the Scala company in 1950, when she was heard as Mistress Quickly and in Giuseppe Verdi's Requiem; she returned to Covent Garden in 1957–8 and in 1964. She later appeared in a number of comprimario roles, singing until she was well into her sixties. Her voice, of fine quality and considerable power, was well suited to the dramatic mezzo-soprano parts of Verdi and was also capable of majestic calm in the works of Claudio Monteverdi, Giovanni Battista Pergolesi and C.W. Gluck. Among many recorded roles, Amneris, Ulrica, Azucena and Mistress Quickly represent her at her best.

Desmond Shawe-Taylor/Alan Blyth

Barbieri-Nini, Marianna

(*b* Florence, 18 Feb 1818; *d* Florence, 27 Nov 1887). Italian soprano. After study with Luigi Barbieri, Giuditta Pasta and Nicola Vaccai, in 1840 she made a disastrous first appearance at La Scala in Gaetano Donizetti's *Belisario*. Shortly afterwards she broke her contract with the impresario Bartolomeo Merelli and joined Alessandro Lanari's troupe in Florence. Here she made a second, and this time triumphant, début in Donizetti's *Lucrezia Borgia*. For the next 15 years she sang with great success throughout Italy and in Barcelona, Madrid and Paris. She was a highly dramatic singer with a powerful voice, particularly effective in the title roles of Donizetti's *Anna Bolena* and Gioachino Rossini's *Semiramide*. She appeared in the first performances of three Verdi operas, singing Lucrezia in *I due Foscari* (1844, Rome), Lady Macbeth (1847, Florence), and Gulnara in *Il corsaro* (1848, Trieste). Her voice was powerful enough, especially in the middle register, to penetrate Giuseppe Verdi's orchestration, yet flexible enough to cope with *fioritura*. She retired in 1856.

Elizabeth Forbes/R

Barbot, Joseph-Théodore-Désiré

(*b* Toulouse, 12 April 1824; *d* Paris, 1 Jan 1879). French tenor. He studied with the younger Manuel Garcia in Paris, where he made his début at the Opéra in 1848. For a decade he toured Italy, singing at Bologna, Turin, Rome, Milan and Naples. In 1859 he returned to Paris and created the title role of Charles Gounod's *Faust* at the Théâtre Lyrique. Then he continued touring in Italy and Russia with his wife, the soprano CAROLINE BARBOT-DOUVRY, who sang Leonora at the first performance of *La forza del destino* in St Petersburg (1862). After retiring from the stage, Barbot taught in Paris.

Elizabeth Forbes

Barbot-Douvry, Caroline

(*b* Paris, 27 April 1830; *d* after 1875). She studied with JOSEPH-THÉODORE-DÉSIRÉ BARBOT, whom she later married. She made her début in 1858, then toured Italy and Russia with her husband, and sang *Les vêpres sicilienne* in Paris, where she impressed Giuseppe Verdi. He cast her as Leonore in the première, in St Petersburg, of *La forza del destino* (1862).

Barroilhet, Paul(-Bernard) [Paulo]

(*b* Bayonne, 22 Sept 1810; *d* Paris, April 1871). French baritone. After studying at the Paris Conservatoire, he went in 1830 to Italy, where he sang in Milan, Genoa, Verona, Trieste, Turin, Palermo and Rome. Engaged at S Carlo, he created roles in Gaetano Donizetti's *L'assedio di Calais* (1836, Eustachio) and *Roberto Devereux* (1837, Nottingham) and in Saverio Mercadante's *Elena da Feltre* (1838) and *La vestale* (1840). On returning to Paris he was engaged at the Opéra, where he sang in the first performances of Donizetti's *La favorite* (1840, Alphonse XI) and *Dom Sébastien* (1843, Camoëns); Fromental Halévy's *La reine de Chypre* (1841, Jacques de Lusignan) and *Charles VI* (1843); and Adolphe Adam's *Richard en Palestine* (1843, title role). His other roles included Don Giovanni, William Tell, Donizetti's Torquato Tasso, Enrico Ashton and Belisarius, and many others in the Italian and French repertories. In 1847 he left the Opéra and, apart from appearances in Madrid (1851–2) where he sang Don Carlo in *Ernani*, retired from the stage. His voice was beautiful in timbre, flexible and expressive.

J.-L. Tamvaco: 'Paul-Bernard Barroilhet', *Donizetti Society Journal*, ii (1975), 130–42

Elizabeth Forbes

Barstow, Dame Josephine (Clare)

(*b* Sheffield, 27 Sept 1940). English soprano. She studied in Birmingham and London, then sang with Opera for All. In 1967 she joined Sadler's Wells, singing the Second Lady, Cherubino, C.W. Gluck's Eurydice and Violetta, her début role with the WNO, for whom she sang Countess Almaviva, Fiordiligi, Mimì, Amelia (*Boccanegra*), Elisabeth de Valois, Lisa, Jenůfa, Ellen Orford and Tatyana. Having made her Covent Garden début in 1969 as a Niece (*Peter Grimes*), she created Denise in Michael Tippett's *The Knot Garden* (1970), Young Woman in H.W. Henze's *We Come to the River* (1976) and Gayle in Tippett's *The Ice Break* (1977), also singing Mrs Ford, Santuzza, Odabella (*Attila*) and Lady Macbeth, which she recorded on video for Glyndebourne. She has appeared in Paris, Berlin, Munich, San Francisco, Chicago, Boston and at the Metropolitan, where she made her début in 1977 as Musetta. For Sadler's Wells, later the ENO, she created Marguerite in Gordon Crosse's *The Story of Vasco* (1974); she sang Jeanne with them in Krzysztof Penderecki's *The Devils of Loudun* (1973) and Autonoe with the New Opera Company in Henze's *The Bassarids* (1974), both British stage premières. Her repertory at the ENO includes Natasha, Leonore, Salome, Octavian, the Marschallin, Arabella, Leonora (*La forza del destino*), Aida, Sieglinde, Emilia Marty, Katerina Izmaylova, Kostelni'ka, the Old Prioress (*Dialogues des Carmélites*) and Ellen Orford. Her roles for Opera North include Luigi Cherubini's Medea and a much-acclaimed Gloriana. In 1986 at Salzburg she created Benigna in Penderecki's *Schwarze Maske*, then sang Tosca and Amelia (*Ballo in maschera*), recording the latter role with Herbert von Karajan. An unusually intense actress with a vibrant, flexible voice of highly individual timbre, capable of expressing the strongest emotions, she excels in portraying troubled and distraught characters. She was made a CBE in 1985 and DBE in 1996.

E. Forbes: 'Josephine Barstow', *Opera*, xxv (1974), 859–64

Alan Blyth

Bartl, Robert.

See BURG, ROBERT.

Bartoli, Cecilia

(*b* Rome, 4 June 1966). Italian mezzo-soprano. She sang the Shepherd-Boy in *Tosca* as a child, and studied in Rome at the Accademia di S Cecilia. She made her professional opera début at Verona in 1987 and in 1988 undertook Rosina at Cologne, the Schwetzingen Festival and the Zürich Opera, an interpretation that delighted all who saw it. Following her La Scala début as Isolier (*Le Comte Ory*) in 1991, she quickly acquired a reputation as one of the world's leading Rossini singers, acclaimed both for her vocal accomplishments and her lively, quick-witted stage personality. She has also been admired in several Mozartian roles, including Cherubino (the role of her début at the Opéra Bastille in 1990), Idamantes (which she first sang at Hamburg in 1990), Zerlina, Susanna (a contoversial interpretation, emphasizing vulgarity rather than charm), Dorabella and Despina (the role of her Metropolitan début in 1996). In 2000 she triumphed in another Mozart soprano role, Donna Elvira, at the Deutsche Oper, Berlin. In 2001 she made a long-awaited Covent Garden début, taking the roles of Euridice and the Genio in the London stage première of Joseph Haydn's *L'anima del filosofo*. Much of her reputation has been built on her recording career, nurtured by the producer Christopher Raeburn. In addition to notable recitals of Mozart, Gluck, Vivaldi and Rossini arias and Italian and French song, Bartoli has been the central attraction in sets of *Rinaldo*, Haydn's *Armida* (taken from concert performances in Zürich in 2000) and *L'anima del filosofo*, *Il barbiere di Siviglia*, *La Cenerentola* and *Il turco in Italia*. These all reveal her warm, rounded tone, her wide vocal range, her extreme flexibility in *fioriture* (although she is inclined to aspirate runs) and above all, her infectious zest in projecting character.

M. Loppert: 'Cecilia Bartoli', *Opera* , xlviii (1997) 1152–60
K. Chernin and R. Stendhal: *Cecilia Bartoli: the Passion of Song* (London, 1998)
M. Hoelterhoff: *Backstage with Cecilia Bartoli* (London, 1998)

Alan Blyth

Basiola, Mario

(*b* Annico, nr Cremona, 12 July 1892; *d* Annico, 3 Jan 1965). Italian baritone. He studied with Antonio Cotogni in Rome, where he made his début in 1918. Appearances in Florence and Barcelona led to an engagement with the S Carlo company, which toured America in 1923, and this in turn brought him to the Metropolitan in 1925. His roles there included Amonasro, Escamillo and Count di Luna. In 1930 he appeared in the American première of Felice Lattuada's *Le preziose ridicole* and in that of Italo Montemezzi's *La notte di Zoraima* the following year. He was also the Venetian in the first Metropolitan production of *Sadko* (1930). In 1933 he returned to Italy, where for many years he was a leading baritone in Milan and Rome. The enthusiastic reports of his work there were not entirely borne out when, after a serious illness, he came to Covent Garden (as Iago, Amonasro and Germont) in 1939; nor are they well supported by the recordings he made of *Pagliacci* and *Madama Butterfly* with Gigli. In 1946 he joined a company

touring Australia, and in 1951 he returned there as a teacher. His earlier recordings show the full-bodied tone and flowing style which earned him a high reputation among the singers of his time. His son, Mario Basiola jr (*b* Highland Park, IL, 1 Sept 1935), was also a successful baritone, singing in many leading houses including La Scala and the Vienna Staatsoper; his repertory included the title role in *Wozzeck*.

J.B. Steane

Bassi, Amedeo

(*b* Montespertoli, nr Florence, 29 July 1874; *d* Florence, 15 Jan 1949). Italian tenor. He trained in Florence, making his début at Castelfiorentino in Filippo Marchetti's *Ruy Blas* in 1897. After travelling widely in Italy he sang with great success in South America, where he performed regularly until 1912. He joined the Manhattan Opera Company in 1906 and made his Covent Garden début the following year; he returned in 1911 for the British première of *La fanciulla del West*, in which he also sang at the first performances in Rome and Chicago. At Monte Carlo in 1905 he participated in the première of Pietro Mascagni's *Amica* and in Naples the following year that of Frédéric d'Erlanger's *Tess*; he was also in the first American performance of Ermanno Wolf-Ferrari's *I gioielli della Madonna* (1912). In the 1920s at La Scala he began a second career, as an admired Wagnerian tenor. He taught in Florence where FERRUCCIO TAGLIAVINI was among his pupils. Early recordings show a powerful voice produced in the typical *verismo* style.

M. Scott: *The Record of Singing*, i (London, 1977), 136

J.B. Steane

Bassi, Luigi

(*b* Pesaro, 4 Sept 1766; *d* ?Dresden, 1825). Italian baritone. He studied in Senigallia with Pietro Morandi and appeared on the stage at the age of 13. He completed his studies with FILIPPO LASCHI in Florence, where he appeared at the Pergola Theatre. In 1784 he joined PASQUALE BONDINI's company in Prague and in 1786 sang Count Almaviva in the first Prague performance of *Le nozze di Figaro*; the next year he created the title role in *Don Giovanni* (1787). He is said to have asked W.A. Mozart to write him another air in place of 'Fin ch'han dal vino' and to have induced Mozart to rewrite 'Là ci darem' five times. In later years he stressed that no two performances were the same and that Mozart had specifically wished that he should improvise as long as he paid attention to the orchestra.

Bassi was praised in the *Gothaer Taschenkalendar* (1793):

This rewarding singer was from the start the ornament of the company and he still is. His voice is as melodious as his acting is masterly. Immediately he comes on, joy and cheerfulness pervade the whole audience and he never leaves the theatre without unequivocal and loud applause.

In 1793 Bassi sang Papageno in Italian at Leipzig. But by 1800 his voice had deteriorated, although his histrionic ability remained unimpaired. According to the *Allgemeine musikalische Zeitung* (1800):

Bassi was an excellent singer before he lost his voice, and he still knows very well how to use what remains. It lies between tenor and bass, and though it sounds somewhat hollow, it is still very flexible, full and pleasant. Herr Bassi is furthermore a very skilled actor in tragedy with no trace of burlesque, and with no vulgarity or tastelessness in comedy. In his truly artful and droll way he can parody the faults of the other singers so subtly that only the audience notices and they themselves are unaware of it. His best roles are Axur, Don Giovanni, Teodoro, the Notary in *La molinara*, the Count in *Figaro* and others.

In 1806 Bassi left Prague because of the war and relied on the patronage of Prince Lobkowitz, making occasional appearances in Vienna. In 1814 he returned to Prague, where Weber consulted him about *Don Giovanni*. In the autumn he was engaged for the Italian company in Dresden; and in 1815 he was made director. He still appeared in Mozart's operas; in 1816 he sang Count Almaviva, although he could no longer encompass the role vocally, but in 1817 he was well received as Guglielmo. He no longer performed Don Giovanni but sang Masetto, for which he was criticized because his figure was unsuited to the part. His contract with the Dresden company continued until his death; in his last years he also appeared in Florence, but only to sing in oratorio.

Christopher Raeburn

Bassini, Achille de.

See DE BASSINI, ACHILLE.

Bastianini, Ettore

(*b* Siena, 24 Sept 1922; *d* Sirmione, 25 Jan 1967). Italian baritone. He studied with Flamio Contini in Florence and made his début in 1945, as a bass, singing Colline at Ravenna. He also sang Tiresias (*Oedipus rex*) at La Scala in 1948. After further study he made a second début in 1951, as a baritone, at Bologna as Germont. In 1953 he sang Andrey in the Western première of *War and Peace* at Florence and made his Metropolitan début as Germont, later singing Gérard, Marcello, Posa, Enrico Ashton, Scarpia and Amonasro. He returned to La Scala in 1954 as Yevgeny Onegin and continued to sing there until 1964. His only Covent Garden appearance was in 1962 as Renato. He was specially distinguished in Verdi roles, many of which he recorded; he sang Posa and Luna in Vienna and Salzburg under Karajan. At the peak of his short career his voice was rich and warm, his phrasing both musical and aristocratic.

Harold Rosenthal/R

Bastin, Jules

(*b* Brussels, 18 March 1933; *d* Brussels, 2 Dec 1996). Belgian bass. He studied in Brussels, making his début there at La Monnaie in 1960 as Charon in Claudio Monteverdi's *Orfeo*. He sang throughout Europe and in North and South America, in a repertory ranging from Rameau's *Hippolyte et Aricie*, through W.A. Mozart (notably Osmin and Dr Bartolo) and Gioachino Rossini, to roles such as Titurel, Varlaam, Graumann (*Der ferne Klang*), King Dodon (*The Golden Cockerel*), Arkel, Le Bailli (*Werther*), Würfl (*The Excursions of Mr Brouček*), the King of Clubs and the Cook (*The Love for Three Oranges*) and the Theatre Director and the Banker (*Lulu*). In 1993 he took part in the first performance of Claude Debussy's *Rodrigue et Chimène* at Lyons. Bastin's ample, sonorous voice, jovial presence and gift for comedy made him a memorable Baron Ochs; but he was perhaps at his finest in French repertory, as can be heard in his vivid recordings of such roles as Méphistophélès (*La damnation de Faust*), Balducci (*Benvenuto Cellini*), Somarone (*Béatrice et Bénédict*) and Pandolfe (*Cendrillon*).

Elizabeth Forbes

Battistini, Mattia

(*b* Rome, 27 Feb 1856; *d* Colle Baccaro, nr Rieti, 7 Nov 1928). Italian baritone. After a brief period of study with Venceslao Persichini and Eugenio Terziana, Battistini seized a sudden chance to sing the leading role of Alfonso XI in Gaetano Donizetti's *La favorite* at the Teatro Argentina in Rome on 11 December 1878, when his immediate success inaugurated a career of nearly 50 years. His early London appearances, in 1883 and 1887, attracted no special attention; his major English triumphs came at Covent Garden in 1905 and 1906, when he was heard in several of his leading roles, including Rigoletto, Germont, Amonasro and Yevgeny Onegin. In 1902 Jules Massenet adapted the tenor title role of *Werther* for him, and he sang other French parts, including Nélusko (*L'Africaine*) and Ambrose Thomas' Hamlet, as well as Don Carlo (*Ernani*), Rigoletto, Boccanegra, Scarpia and Valentin. By that time Battistini had established himself throughout Europe, and especially in Russia, as a baritone almost without rival in the older repertory and scarcely less famous in later and widely varied roles. The Russian aristocracy and imperial family treated him as an equal; the tsar loaded him with honours; on one occasion his personal intervention is said to have secured the release of a man condemned to death. In Germany and Austria, Poland and Spain, he was equally idolized; and his adoring compatriots saluted him with such fanciful titles as 'Il re dei baritoni' and 'La gloria d'Italia'. He never sang in North America and was doubtless the most important singer of his day to have resisted the pull of the Metropolitan – owing, it is said, to his dread of the Atlantic crossing. His vocal powers were almost undimmed by age. When, after a lapse of 16 years, he made a series of concert appearances at the Queen's Hall, London, in 1922 and the two following years, his unimpaired tone and technique astonished his audiences.

Battistini's voice was an unusually high baritone, verging on the range of a tenor, with some corresponding weakness in the lowest register. The quality was noble: clear, strong, vibrant, capable also of a deliberately 'villainous' harshness when required, even of a kind of scornful snarl that could prove dramatically telling; then suddenly melting into the extremes of tenderness and delicacy. He was a meticulous stylist with a superb florid technique. He had fabulous agility and breath control, and could spin out long phrases in the smoothest legato or execute the most flamboyant of flourishes, all with a natural instinct for the grand manner. His Mozart singing, as recorded, seems too wilful for modern taste; but his majestic style is clearly perceptible even in the delivery of a single line of recitative, such as the simple and lapidary 'Povero Lionello!' which precedes Plunkett's 'Il mio Lionel' in Friedrich Flotow's *Marta*. This is one of the best of some 100 recordings that he made between 1903 and 1924. Noteworthy, too, is a group of 1907 recordings from *Ernani*, including a 'Vieni meco, sol di rose' of surpassing delicacy and a finely modulated 'Eri tu' from *Un ballo in maschera* made during the same recording session.

J. Dennis: 'Mattia Battistini', *Record Collector*, viii (1953), 245–65 [with discography]
D. Shawe-Taylor: 'Mattia Battistini', *Opera*, viii (1957), 283–9
A. Kelly, J.F. Perkins and J. Ward: 'Mattia Battistini (1856–1928): a Discography', *Recorded Sound*, no.65 (1977), 652–6

Desmond Shawe-Taylor/R

Battle, Kathleen

(*b* Portsmouth, OH, 13 Aug 1948). American soprano. She studied with Franklin Bens at the Cincinnati College-Conservatory, and in the early 1970s she was engaged by James Levine for both the Ravinia Festival and the Metropolitan Opera. She made her début in 1976 as Susanna with New York City Opera. In 1977 she sang Oscar at San Francisco, then made her Metropolitan début as the Shepherd in *Tannhäuser*, subsequently singing Rosina, Despina, Zerlina, Blonde, Pamina, Zdenka, Richard Strauss's and Jules Massenet's Sophie and G.F. Handel's Cleopatra. She made her British début in 1979 at Glyndebourne as Nerina (Joseph Haydn's *La fedeltà premiata*) and sang Adina at Zürich in 1980. At Salzburg she has sung Despina, Susanna and Zerlina. She made her Covent Garden début in 1985 as Zerbinetta, returning as Norina in 1990. In 1993 she sang Marie (*La fille du régiment*) at San Francisco. A notoriously temperamental artist (she has been banned from appearing at the Metropolitan), Battle is gifted with a high, sweet soprano of considerable charm, which she governs with technical finesse; she also has an attractive and vivacious stage presence, and her work is skilful and stylish, if not always highly individual. Her numerous recordings include Zerlina, Blonde and Zerbinetta, Gabriel Fauré's Requiem and Johannes Brahms's *German Requiem*, and an admired interpretation of Handel's Semele. In February 1994 Joseph Volpe, general manager of the Metropolitan Opera, dropped Battle from a production of Gaetano Donizetti's *La fille du régiment*, citing unprofessional behaviour. This effectively ended her career in opera, though she has continued to record and perform in the concert hall with great success.

Richard Dyer, Elizabeth Forbes/R

Battu, Marie

(*b* Paris, 1838; *d* Paris, 1888). French soprano. After appearing as a child in Jacques Offenbach's *Pépito* at the Théâtre des Variétés, Paris, she made her début in 1860 at the Théâtre Italien as Amina (*La sonnambula*). She sang Oscar in the first Paris performance of *Un ballo in maschera*. Transferring to the Opéra, in 1865 she created Inès in Giacomo Meyerbeer's *L'Africaine* (1865) and sang Mathilde in the 500th performance of *Guillaume Tell* (1868). She made her Covent Garden début in 1862 as Gilda (*Rigoletto*) and also sang Elvire (*La muette de Portici*), Marguerite de Valois and Alice (*Robert le diable*). She retired in 1873. Her singing combined superb technique with faultless intonation.

Elizabeth Forbes

Baugé, André

(*b* Toulouse, 4 Jan 1892; *d* Paris, 22 May 1966). French baritone. His mother was the soprano Anna Tariol-Baugé and his father, Alphonse, was a teacher of singing. His studies with them led to his début with the Opéra-Comique in 1917 as Frédéric in *Lakmé*. Other roles with the company included Don Giovanni and Pelléas, with the Rossini Figaro as his tour de force. At the Opéra in 1925 he sang Germont in *La traviata* and the title role in Henri Rabaud's *Mârouf*. He appeared at Monte Carlo as Escamillo in 1924. His career took a new turn when at the Marigny Theatre in Paris he sang the title role in the French première of André Messager's *Monsieur Beaucaire* in 1925, and from then onwards he became increasingly associated with operetta, enjoying a special success in Franz Lehár's *Paganini*. He also appeared in some early French musical films and after World War II taught at the Ecole Normale. His recordings show a light, high baritone, firmly placed if somewhat dry-toned, better suited to Messager than to Rossini.

J.B. Steane

Bausewein, Kaspar

(*b* Aub, nr Ochsenfurt, 15 Nov 1838; *d* Munich, 18 Nov 1903). German bass. He studied in Munich, making his début there in 1854 at the Hofoper, where he was engaged for 46 years. A fine actor, equally gifted for comic and serious opera, he was a true bass with a wide repertory ranging from W.A. Mozart's Figaro and Leporello and Gioachino Rossini's Don Basilio to Caspar (*Der Freischütz*) and the three Wagner roles that he created: Pogner in *Die Meistersinger* (1868), Fafner in *Das Rheingold* (1869) and Hunding in *Die Walküre* (1870). He retired in 1900 after a farewell performance as Lord Cockburn in *Fra Diavolo*.

Elizabeth Forbes

Baxevanos, Peter

(*b* Salonika, 29 Sept 1908; *d* Vienna, 24 June 1982). Greek tenor. He studied in Vienna and made his début in 1934 at the Vienna Volksoper in Ermanno

Wolf-Ferrari's *Sly*. At the Zürich Opera, where he sang until the outbreak of war, he sang Alwa in the first (incomplete) performance of Alban Berg's *Lulu* (1937) and was the Cardinal in the delayed première of Paul Hindemith's *Mathis der Maler* (1938). He returned to Vienna in 1940 and until his retirement was successful there and in Italy as Florestan, Manrico, Don Carlos, Don José and Cavaradossi.

David Cummings

Bayo, Maria

(*b* Fitero, 28 May 1962). Spanish soprano. She studied at the Conservatorio Pablo Sarasate in Pamplona and the Hochschule für Musik in Detmold. After winning a series of international competitions, she quickly established herself in the major European opera houses, making débuts at La Scala, Milan, in 1991 as Musetta, at the Opéra Bastille, Paris, the same year as W.A. Mozart's Susanna and at Covent Garden in 1994 as L'Ensoleillad in Jules Massenet's *Chérubin*. With her pure, finely focussed soprano and versatile musicianship, Bayo is equally adept at conveying the minx-like qualities of G.F. Handel's Cleopatra and the innocent charm of Mélisande. Her other roles include Ilia (*Idomeneo*), Adina, Francesco Cavalli's Calisto and Oscar in *Un ballo in maschera*, the last two of which she has recorded.

Andrew Clark

Beard, John

(*b c*1717; *d* Hampton, 5 Feb 1791). English tenor. Trained by Bernard Gates at the Chapel Royal, he sang while still a boy in G.F. Handel's *Esther* (staged at the Crown and Anchor in February 1732). He won immediate success on his operatic début as Silvio in *Il pastor fido* with G.F. Handel's Covent Garden company (1734), and the same year Handel adapted the role of Alcestes for him at the revival of *Arianna in Creta*. This was the beginning of a long association with the composer from the late 1730s up to the 1750s. He sang more Handel parts under the composer than any other singer, appearing in ten operas, and created roles in *Oreste* (Pylades, 1734), *Ariodante* (Lurcanio, 1735), *Alcina* (Oronte, 1735), *Atalanta* (Aminta, 1736), *Arminio* (Varus, 1737), *Giustino* (Vitalian, 1737), *Berenice* (Fabio, 1737) and *Semele* (Jupiter, 1744). He was most known as an operatic singer, taking a leading role in every one of Handel's English oratorios, odes and musical dramas except *The Choice of Hercules* (which has no tenor part), including many first performances. He sang regularly in Handel's *Messiah* performances at the Foundling Hospital (refusing a fee), for Musicians

Fund benefits and other charities, and at provincial festivals (Oxford, Birmingham, Three Choirs).

Beard was not exclusively a Handel singer; from 1736, when he sang in J.E. Galliard's *The Royal Chace* at Covent Garden, he appeared in numerous ballad operas, pantomimes, burlesques and more serious pieces, and was a member of the Drury Lane company (1737–43, 1748–59) and at Covent Garden (1743–8, 1759–67). From 1737 he was a popular Macheath in *The Beggar's Opera* and appeared in J.C. Smith's *Rosalinda* (1740), *The Fairies* (1755) and *The Tempest* (1756). He also sang in many works by J.F. Lampe, William Boyce (Damon in *The Chaplet*, 1749 and Momus in *The Secular Masque*, 1750), and especially Thomas Arne, including *Comus*, *Rosamond*, *The Judgment of Paris*, *Thomas and Sally* (Squire, 1760), *Alfred*, *Artaxerxes* (Artabanes, 1762) and *Love in a Village* (Farmer Hawthorne, 1762), in which he made his last appearance in 1767.

In 1739 Beard married Lady Henrietta Herbert – a union which met with obloquy from the bride's family and scatalogical comment from the aristocracy. After his first wife's death in 1753, Beard in 1759 married Charlotte Rich, daughter of the proprietor of Covent Garden, whom Beard succeeded in the management from 1761 until his retirement with the onset of deafness in 1767, when he sold the Covent Garden patent for £60,000. For many years, before and after his retirement from the theatre, he held the post of 'vocal performer to his Majesty' with a salary of £100 a year, and he sang occasionally at the Chapel Royal. Charles Burney said he 'constantly possessed the favour of the public by his superior conduct, knowledge of Music, and intelligence as an actor'. Charles Dibdin considered him the finest English singer of the age. The heroic parts Handel composed for him, especially Samson, Judas (from *Judas Maccabeus*) and Jeptha, established the importance of the tenor voice at a time when leading male roles were still often taken by castratos or women, but many of the finest airs call for expressiveness and a firm *mezza voce* rather than agility. The extreme compass of his Handel parts is B to a', but they seldom go below d.

Winton Dean

Bechi, Gino

(*b* Florence, 16 Oct 1913; *d* Florence, 2 Feb 1993). Italian baritone. He studied in Florence with Raul Frazzi and Di Giorgi and made his début at Empoli in 1936 as Germont. He sang regularly in Rome (1938–52), and at La Scala (1939–53), where he sang the title role of *Nabucco* at the reopening of the theatre in 1946. He established himself as the leading Italian dramatic baritone of the day, especially in the Verdi repertory; his roles also included Gérard, Scarpia, Jack Rance, Tonio and Ambroise Thomas' Hamlet. In London he appeared with the Scala company at Covent Garden in 1950 as Iago and Falstaff, and at Drury Lane as William Tell in 1958. He sang in the premières of Lodovico Rocca's *Monte Ivnor* (1939, Rome) and Franco Alfano's *Don Juan de Manara* (1941, Florence). Bechi continued to sing until 1961, when he appeared as Antonio Salieri's Falstaff at Siena and in *Il barbiere di Siviglia* at Adria. His recordings reveal a powerful, dramatic voice of striking individuality, incisive in both tone and diction, and a 'growl' reminiscent of TITTA RUFFO.

A. Blyth: Obituary, *Opera*, xliv (1993), 425 only

Harold Rosenthal/Alan Blyth

Beck, Karl

(*b* Vienna, 1814; *d* Vienna, 4 March 1879). Austrian tenor. After studying with Joseph Staudigl, he began his career in Prague in 1838. He subsequently had great success in St Petersburg, where he was dubbed 'the king of tenors'. In 1848 Beck was engaged at the Hoftheater in Weimar, where he created the title role in Richard Wagner's *Lohengrin* (1850). By the mid-1850s his voice had deteriorated, perhaps as a long-term consequence of a serious throat infection contracted in St Petersburg. He retired shortly after unsuccessful appearances at the Estates Theatre in Prague in 1856.

Richard Wigmore

Bedini, Domenico

(*b* ?Fossombrone, *c*1745; *d* after 1795). Italian soprano castrato. His career began intermittently in comic opera at Pesaro (1762) and Rome (1764), and as secondo uomo in *opera seria* at Venice (1768). In 1770–71 he was secondo uomo in five Italian houses and then entered the service of the Munich court, resuming his career in Italy in 1776 and soon becoming primo uomo in leading houses. He is mostly remembered as the first Sextus in W.A. Mozart's *La clemenza di Tito* (1791, Prague). He retired after singing at Florence in Carnival 1792 and by 1795 was in the *cappella* of the Santa Casa of Loreto in his native region.

Dennis Libby

Behrens, Hildegard

(*b* Varel, nr Oldenburg, 9 Feb 1937). German soprano. She studied in Freiburg, making her début there in

Gemma Bellincioni

1971 as W.A. Mozart's Countess. She then sang at Düsseldorf and Frankfurt in roles including Fiordiligi, Agathe, Elsa, Eva, Kát'a, and Marie (*Wozzeck*). In 1976 she made her début at Covent Garden as Leonore (*Fidelio*) and at the Metropolitan as Giorgetta (*Il tabarro*). She sang Salome at Salzburg (1977) and Brünnhilde at Bayreuth (1983–6). Her repertory also includes Electra (*Idomeneo*), Tosca, Senta, Isolde, Donna Anna and Richard Strauss's Electra, which she first sang at the Paris Opéra (1986). Behrens sang Emilia Marty (*The Makropulos Affair*) at Munich (1988) and Senta at Savonlinna (1989) and the Metropolitan (1992). At the Vienna Staatsoper (1992–3) she sang Brünnhilde in a *Ring* cycle and Katerina Izmaylova (*Lady Macbeth of the Mtsensk District*), a role she repeated at Munich in 1994. She later added Kundry to her repertory, singing the role (in concert) in Cologne in 1998 and on stage in Dresden in 2000–01. A charismatic, highly imaginative singer with a rich, warm-toned voice, she excels in Wagner and Strauss. Her extensive discography includes an impassioned Isolde with Leonard Bernstein, Salome with Herbert von Karajan, Strauss's Electra with Seiji Ozawa, Marie (*Wozzeck*) with Claudio Abbado and Brünnhilde in the complete *Ring* under James Levine.

A. Blyth: 'Hildegard Behrens', *Opera*, xlii (1991), 502–8

Elizabeth Forbes

Bellincioni, Gemma (Cesira Matilda)

(*b* Como, 18 Aug 1864; *d* Naples, 23 April 1950). Italian soprano. She was taught by her father, a professional bass, and later by the famous tenor ROBERTO STAGNO, whom she first met in 1886 and subsequently married. Their daughter, Bianca Stagno-Bellincioni (1888–1980), was also a singer. Except in the role of Violetta (in which she was praised by Giuseppe Verdi), she was rarely at her best in the older type of opera. Her voice was powerful, and possessed with the dramatic conviction well suited to the late-19th-century *verismo* school; the great event of her life was her sensational portrayal of Santuzza in the première of *Cavalleria rusticana* (1890, Rome), with Stagno as Turiddu. Though very successful in the principal European opera houses and in South America, she failed to establish herself at Covent Garden, where she appeared in 1895 amidst a company that was exceptionally strong in soprano talent; even her Santuzza, like her Carmen, was overshadowed by the immense popularity of CALVÉ. She created many other roles in *verismo* operas, among them Giordano's Fedora (1898, Milan), with the then unknown CARUSO as Loris, and Cristina in Giordano's *Mala vita* (1892, Rome), a work which launched a 'Neapolitan' brand of operatic *verismo*. She also created the title role in Nicolò Massa's *Salammbô* (1886, Milan), Nicola Spinelli's *Labilia* (1890, Rome), and the leading role in Antonio Smareglia's *Nozze istriane* (1894, Trieste). According to Alfred Loewenberg, Giacomo Setaccioli's *La sorella di Mark* (1896, Rome) was written for Bellincioni.

The last phase of her career was dominated by *Salome*; she appeared in the first Italian performance of the opera (1906, Turin) under Richard Strauss, who much admired her interpretation, and she sang the role over 100 times. After World War I she spent some years as a teacher of singing in the Netherlands, and in 1924 reappeared as Santuzza, Tosca and Carmen at The Hague, Rotterdam and Amsterdam. Her 14 early recordings (1903–5), though dramatic, lend support to the view that sheer voice was not her strongest suit; they show, beside marked agility and individuality of style, a shrillness and excess of vibrato that cannot wholly be ascribed to the date of recording.

J.B. Richards: 'Gemma Bellincioni', *Record Collector*, xvi (1964–6), 196–219 [incl. discography]; xviii (1968–9), 139–40

Desmond Shawe-Taylor/R

Belloc-Giorgi [Bellochi; Giorgi-Belloc; née Trombetta], (Maria) Teresa

(*b* San Benigno Canavese, nr Turin, 2 July 1784; *d* San Giorgio Canavese, 13 May 1855). Italian contralto. She made her début in 1801 at Turin. Engagements in Parma and Trieste followed and in 1803 she appeared in Paris, singing the title roles of Giovanni Paisiello's *Nina* and Ferdinando Paer's *Griselda*. In the following year she sang *Nina* at La Scala, where she continued to appear during the next 20 years. It was here that she sang the title role in the revival of Simon Mayr's *Medea in Corinto* (1823), for which the composer thoroughly revised the score. From 1812, when she sang Isabella in the first performance of *L'inganno felice* in Venice, until her retirement in 1828, she specialized in Rossini roles. She created Ninetta, a soprano part, in *La gazza ladra* at La Scala (1817), but the contralto roles of Tancredi, Cenerentola and Isabella in *L'italiana in Algeri* were the most successful in her repertory. She appeared in London in 1819 under the name of Bellochi. After her début as Isabella in the British première of *L'italiana in Algeri*, the *Times* critic wrote that she had 'an agreeable and flexible voice … it is of the class called mezzo-soprano, but combines in a remarkable degree many of the peculiar qualities and facilities of the soprano'.

Elizabeth Forbes/R

Beňačková(-Cap), Gabriela

(*b* Bratislava, 23 March 1944). Slovak soprano. She studied in Bratislava, making her début in 1970 at the National Theatre, Prague, as Natasha (*War and Peace*). In 1975 she first sang Jenůfa, a role she has repeated many times in Europe and the USA. She sang Kát'a in Amsterdam (1976) and at Carnegie Hall, New York, in 1979, the year she made her Covent Garden début as Tatyana (*Yevgeny Onegin*), returning as Leonore (*Fidelio*). She made her Metropolitan début in 1991 as Kát'a followed by Mimì, Jenůfa, Leonore and Rusalka. Her repertory also includes such roles as Desdemona, Maddalena (*Andrea Chénier*), Mařenka, Manon Lescaut, Marguerite (Charles Gounod's *Faust*), Aida, Elsa, Ariadne and Bedřich Smetana's Libuše, which she sang at the reopening of the Prague National Theatre in 1983. Beňačková has a beautiful, vibrant voice and sings with great involvement, especially in Czech music. She has recorded several of her major operatic roles (notably Kát'a and Jenůfa, considered by many to be definitive interpretations) and is an admired soloist on disc in works such as Antonín Dvořák's Requiem and *Stabat mater*, Leoš Janáček's *Glagolitic Mass* and Ludwig van Beethoven's Ninth Symphony.

Elizabeth Forbes

Bendazzi, Luigia

(*b* Ravenna, 1827/8; *d* Nice, 5 March 1901). Italian soprano. The child of illiterate parents, she studied in Milan with Antonio Piacenti and in 1850 was apprenticed to the Bolognese composer Federico Dallara; with him (and his wife) she lived for nine years in what seems to have been at first a relationship of total, possibly sexual, dependence. She made her début in 1850 at Venice as Elvira in *Ernani*; after scoring a notable success at the San Carlo, Naples, in 1851, she sang in all the major Italian houses. Giuseppe Verdi objected to her in 1853 as a possible Violetta because she was too much the powerful dramatic soprano, but he exploited her resources in 1857 when she created Amelia in *Simon Boccanegra*; she was also successful as Amelia (*Un ballo in maschera*), Lady Macbeth, and Valentine in *Les Huguenots*. After appearances at the Liceo in Barcelona in 1869–70, where she sang Paolina (Gaetano Donizetti's *Poliuto*) and the title role in Errico Petrella's *Jone*, her career faded. Her voice was a classic *soprano d'agilità*, but she evidently possessed sufficient reserves of power to make a convincing Lady Macbeth. She married the composer Benedetto Secchi; their daughter Ernestina Bendazzi (1864–1931), also a soprano, married the tenor Alfonso Garulli.

J. Budden: *The Operas of Verdi* (London, 1973–81)
J. Rosselli: *Singers of Italian Opera* (Cambridge, 1992)

John Rosselli

Bender, Paul

(*b* Driedorf, nr Wetzlar, 28 July 1875; *d* Munich, 25 Nov 1947). German bass. A pupil of Louise Ress and Baptist Hoffmann, he made his official stage début as Sarastro in 1900 at Breslau. In 1903 he was engaged by the Munich Opera, and continued as their first bass for 30 years; his last performance, as Gioachino Rossini's Don Basilio, took place there only seven days before his death. Bender made his Covent Garden début in 1914 as Amfortas in the British stage première of *Parsifal*; although the role was described as being rather high for his fine *basso cantante*, he made a profound impression. His other roles during this German winter season were Hunding, Sachs and Jacob in Etienne-Nicolas Méhul's *Joseph*. When German performances resumed at Covent Garden in 1924 and 1927, Bender showed his outstanding gifts as a comedian in the parts of Osmin and Baron Ochs, but was again much admired in his Wagner roles, especially as Hagen. He created the role of Pope Pius IV at the première of Hans Pfitzner's *Palestrina* in Munich in 1917, and sang all the leading bass roles of the

German repertory at the Metropolitan (1922–7), where some of his performances were described as 'ponderous'. This is the very opposite of the impression he made, during the same period, on visitors to the Munich and Salzburg festivals. Bender was a fine actor, and his great stature contributed to an imposing stage presence. He became famous also as a lieder singer, especially in the songs and ballads of Carl Loewe. Among his many recordings, the most valuable are those of Loewe ballads made in 1930 and 1933, which reveal a gripping dramatic power, a distinctness of enunciation and a quiet humour that are in sum delightful. His students included JOSEF GREINDL and HANS HOPF.

J. Dennis: 'Paul Bender', *Record Collector*, xvii (1966–8), 244–56; xviii (1968–9), 4–6 [incl. discography]

Desmond Shawe-Taylor/R

Benedetti, Michele

(*b* Loreto, 17 Oct 1778; *d* after 1828). Italian bass. He made his début in 1805 and, after singing at Venice, Reggio Emilia and other cities, appeared in 1811 in Gaspare Spontini's *La vestale* at S Carlo. There he created the following roles in operas by Gioachino Rossini: Elmiro in *Otello* (1816); Idraote in *Armida* (1817); the title role in *Mosè in Egitto* and Ircano in *Ricciardo e Zoraide* (1818); Phoenicius in *Ermione* and Douglas in *La donna del lago* (1819); and Leucippo in *Zelmira* (1822). He also sang Atkins in the first performance of Gaetano Donizetti's *Alfredo il grande* (1823), Clemente in the première of Vincenzo Bellini's *Bianca e Gernando* (1826) and the King in the first performance of Donizetti's *Gianni di Calais* (1828), the last named at the Teatro del Fondo. He visited London in 1822. Nothing is known of his later career or the circumstances of his death.

Elizabeth Forbes

Benningsen, Lilian

(*b* Vienna, 17 July 1924). Austrian contralto. After studying with ANNA BAHR-MILDENBURG and Elisabeth Rado, she won first prize in the singing competition held by the Gesellschaft der Musikfreunde in 1947. The following year she made her professional début, at the Salzburg Landestheater. After a triumphant appearance as Eboli (*Don Carlos*) at the Munich Staatsoper in 1951, she became a long-standing member of the company, singing roles such as Fricka, Carmen, Amneris, Octavian and Dorabella. Benningsen sang in the British première, at Covent Garden, of Richard Strauss's *Die Liebe der Danaë* (1953), and the world première of Werner

Egk's *Irische Legende* (1955, Salzburg Festival). At the Schwetzingen Festival in 1961 she created the role of Carolina Gräfin von Kirch-stetten, in H.W. Henze's *Elegy for Young Lovers*. She also had a notable career as a concert singer and recitalist.

Richard Wigmore

Benucci, Francesco

(*b c*1745; *d* Florence, 5 April 1824). Italian bass. He sang at Pistoia in 1769, then more widely in Italy, appearing as the leading character *buffo* in Venice (1778–9), and singing in Milan (1779–82) with great success and in Rome (1783–4). He first appeared in Vienna in 1783 and became the leading member of the celebrated *opera buffa* company there, creating Rosmondo in Stephen Storace's *Gli sposi malcontenti* (1785), Tita in Martín y Soler's *Una cosa rara* (1786) and four Salieri roles including Blasio (La scuola de' gelosi, 1783), Trofonio (La grotta di Trofonio, 1785) and the title role in *Axur* (1788). Described by W.A. Mozart as 'particularly good' (letter of 7 May 1783), he sang Figaro at the première of *Le nozze di Figaro* (1786), Leporello in the first Vienna performance of *Don Giovanni* (1788), when Mozart composed an extra duet for him, and Guglielmo in the première of *Così fan tutte* (1790). Mozart also intended him to sing the role of Bocconio in the unfinished *Lo sposo deluso*. In 1789 he went to London, where he sang Bartolo in Giovanni Paisiello's *Il barbiere di Siviglia* and appeared in Giuseppe Gazzaniga's *La vendemmia* opposite NANCY STORACE, with whom he had sung in Vienna. They introduced the first piece from any Mozart opera to be heard on the London stage, the duet 'Crudel! perchè finora' from *Figaro*. Benucci returned to Vienna later in 1789, remaining until 1795. He helped establish the success of Paisello's *La molinara* in Vienna when he sang the role of Pistofolo in 1790. His last great triumph was to create Count Robinson in Domenico Cimarosa's *Il matrimonio segreto* in 1792. He had a round, beautifully full voice, more bass than baritone; probably he was the finest artist for whom Mozart wrote, and as a *buffo* he outshone his contemporaries as singer and actor.

Christopher Raeburn/R

Berbié, Jane [Bergougne, Jeanne Marie Louise]

(*b* Villefranche-de-Lauragais, nr Toulouse, 6 May 1934). French mezzo-soprano. She studied at the Toulouse Conservatory and in 1958 made her operatic début at La Scala in *L'enfant et les sortilèges* (Teapot, Squirrel). She appeared as the Second Lady in *Die Zauberflöte* at the Aix-en-Provence Festival in 1959, the year she joined the Opéra (her début was as Mercédès). Among the many parts she has played in Paris are Concepcion, Zerlina, Despina, Ascanio, Annina, Dorabella, Emilia (*Otello*), Aunt Lavinia (Damase's *L'héritière*), Grandmother Buryjovka, Auntie (*Peter Grimes*) and Marcellina (notably in the 1973 *Figaro* inaugurating Rolf Liebermann's administration). With a repertory ranging from Claudio Monteverdi to the 20th century, she is particularly delightful on stage in travesty, *ingénue* or soubrette roles. She sang Maffio Orsini in the Carnegie Hall concert performance of *Lucrezia Borgia* in which CABALLÉ made her American début (1965). She first appeared at Glyndebourne in 1967 (as Mirinda in *L'Ormindo*), returning as Despina (1969, 1971, 1984); as the latter, and as Rosina at La Scala and Covent Garden (début, June 1971). She has also sung at Marseilles, Florence, Bologna, Cologne, Barcelona and Geneva where she created Oulita in Rolf Liebermann's *Le forêt* (1987). She sang La Marquise de Berkenfeld (*La fille du régiment*) in Lisbon (1990). Her rich-toned, agile voice is combined with a warm personality and a very strong sense of humour.

André Tubeuf, Elizabeth Forbes

Berchtenbreitner, Marie.

See OLSZEWSKA, MARIA.

Berenstadt, (Sebastiano) Gaetano

(*b* Florence, 7 June 1687; bur. Florence, 9 Dec 1734). Italian alto castrato. His German father, Giorgio, was timpanist to the Grand Duke of Tuscany. Gaetano apparently sang in 55 dramatic works, 33 of which were freshly composed, during his 27-year career. Since 'Gaetano Beynstetter' first appears in Giuseppe Vignola's revision of *Le regine di Macedonia* (1708, Naples), he might have originally studied at a Neapolitan conservatory. He also studied with PISTOCCHI in Bologna, and his next known appearances were at the feast honouring St Gaudentius in Novara (1711), where Pistocchi was the leading alto castrato, and in Luca Antonio Predieri's new opera *La virtù in trionfo, o sia La Griselda* (1711, Bologna). After appearing in two pasticcios at Florence during Carnival 1712, he obtained a post at the court of the Palatine elector in Düsseldorf, where he presumably sang cantatas and serenatas as well as roles in Johann Hugo von Wilderer's new *Amalasunta* (1713) and in the anonymous *Annibale pacificatore* (1715). After the elector, Johann Wilhelm, died in June 1716,

From left: Gaetano Berenstadt with Francesca Cuzzoni and Senesino in a scene probably from 'Flavio' (Handel), King's Theatre, London, 1723. Engraving after John Vanderbank.

Berenstadt went to London, where he performed in four operas during the first half of 1717: Argante in *Rinaldo* (a Handel revival for which three new arias were written for Berenstadt), Nicola Haym's adaptation of Alessandro Scarlatti's *Pyrrhus and Demetrius*, the pasticcio *Vincislao, re di Polonia* and *Tito Manlio* (a new work by Attilio Ariosti). During this London trip Berenstadt wrote the first of his 42 extant letters (1717–33) to Giacomo Zamboni, a Florentine merchant and diplomat who lived in London. Berenstadt's correspondence (especially his letter of 1724 to 'maestro' Pistocchi) reveals his great love of books and the visual arts. He bought and sold many rare books and unique works of art in order to earn money, and assembled a fine library including many incunabula. In 1718 Apostolo Zeno recommended him as a 'worthy professor of music' who had 'an excellent knowledge of our best authors and superb taste in the realms of Italian poetry and eloquence'.

No Italian operas were performed in London between June 1717 and April 1720, and Berenstadt moved in September 1717 to the court of the elector of Saxony, Friedrich August I (King August II of Poland). During his year there he sang in Antonio Lotti's new *Ascanio, ovvero Gli odi delusi dal sangue* at Dresden and was handsomely paid 600 louis d'or plus living expenses. In 1719 he performed during Carnival at Rome in Francesco Gasparini's new *Lucio Vero* and *Astianatte*, during spring at Bologna in two revivals, then in August at Brescia in an unidentified work. At Bologna he was admitted to the Accademia Filarmonica on 3 July 1719. In 1720 he sang at Rome during Carnival in Gasparini's new *Amore e maestà* and *Faramondo*, then at Florence in his *Lucio Vero*. In 1721 he was at Milan during Carnival for two revivals, then at Padua for a summer production of Fortunato Chelleri's new *Temistocle*. His only appearances in Venice were for three newly written scores of 1721–2: Antonio Pollarolo's *Plautilla*, G.M. Capelli's *Giulio Flavio Crispo* and a collaboration (*Venceslao*) between these two composers and Giovanni Porta.

Berenstadt then returned to London for two seasons with the Royal Academy of Music, where he sang Timante in a revival of Handel's *Floridante* (1722). In 1722–4 he performed in new works by three composers: Adalberto and the title role in Handel's *Ottone, re di Germania* (1723), Guido and the title role in *Flavio, re di Longobardi* (1723) and Ptolemy in *Giulio Cesare in Egitto* (1724); Ariosti's *Caio Marzio, Coriolano, Vespasiano* and *Aquilio consolo*; and his friend Giovanni Bononcini's *Erminia, Farnace* and *Calfurnia*. In summer 1724 he and four other singers from the Royal Academy performed Handel's *Ottone* and *Giulio Cesare* in Paris. His main operatic role throughout his career was that of a

powerful man whose insidious machinations keep young lovers scurrying suspensefully until the happy ending. Pietro Metastasio affirmed this in a letter of 1732, when he said that the downright detestable Learco in his new *Issipile* would be a fine part for Berenstadt. He never portrayed a woman, perhaps because he had a 'huge, unwieldy figure' (Burney), which is clearly visible in John Vanderbank's engraving of June 1723 (see illustration) and in Pier Leone Ghezzi's caricature of 17 May 1725. His arias are usually blustery, filled with jagged leaps and with melismas of only moderate length. Languishing solos and stepwise passagework are avoided. His range is usually an 11th (*a* to *d''*) and rarely a 13th (*g* to *e''*). In Italy he sang from four to eight solos or duets in each opera, while at London in 1722–4 he usually performed only three solos.

After a 'sabbatical' in 1725, he began to sing music by the best-known *galant* composers. At Rome in 1726 he sang in three new works: Leonardo Vinci's *Didone abbandonata* and Domenico Sarri's *Valdemaro* and *Il sacrificio di Jefte*. During the rest of 1726 and Carnival 1727 he appeared in four new works at Naples: Johann Adolf Hasse's *Il Sesostrate* and *L'Astarto*, Vinci's *Ernelinda* and Sarri's *Siroe re di Persia*. During Carnival 1728 he sang at Florence in two revivals of Vinci scores. The following year he once again sang in new works at Rome: Pietro Auletta's *Ezio* and Vinci's *Semiramide riconosciuta*. Since his father had died, he and one of his sisters moved to Naples in mid-1728; but there he failed to obtain a court appointment and by 1730 he was back in Florence, where during Carnival 1730 he sang in one pasticcio and in Porta's new *Il Gran Tamerlano*. Between October 1730 and Carnival 1731 he sang in three revivals at Livorno. At Rome during Carnival 1732 he sang in the revival of the *Didone abbandonata* he had helped to create in 1726 and in G.A. Giai's new *Demetrio*. His final two productions were revivals at Florence during Carnival 1734. He suffered increasingly from rheumatism during his last years.

W. Dean and J.M. Knapp: *Handel's Operas, 1704–1726* (Oxford, 1987, 2/1996)

L. Lindgren: 'Musicians and Librettists in the Correspondence of Gio. Giacomo Zamboni (Oxford, Bodleian Library, MSS Rawlinson Letters 116–138)', *RMARC*, no.24 (1991) [whole issue]

Lowell Lindgren

Berganza (Vargas), Teresa

(*b* Madrid, 16 March 1935). Spanish mezzo-soprano. She studied in Madrid with Lola Rodriguez Aragon, a pupil of ELISABETH SCHUMANN. She made her début in 1957 as Dorabella at Aix-en-Provence, returning as Rosina, Henry Purcell's Dido, Cherubino,

Octavia (*L'incoronazione di Poppea*) and Ruggiero (*Alcina*). In 1958 she sang Isolier (*Le comte Ory*) at the Piccola Scala and Cherubino at Glyndebourne, and made her American début at Dallas as Isabella (*L'italiana in Algeri*). She first appeared at Covent Garden in 1960 as Rosina, then sang Cherubino and, during La Scala's 1976 visit, the title role of *La Cenerentola*. She sang at Chicago, the Metropolitan (1967–8), Vienna, Paris and Salzburg; her roles included Antonio Cesti's Orontea, W.A. Mozart's Sextus and Luigi Cherubini's Neris (*Médée*). Her rich, creamy voice with its great agility, perfect for the Rossini mezzo-soprano roles, developed a heavier tone and a more dramatic style appropriate to Carmen, which she sang at Edinburgh (1977–8) and repeated at Hamburg, San Francisco, Covent Garden and Paris; and to Charlotte, which she sang at Zürich (1979). She appeared as Zerlina in Joseph Losey's film of *Don Giovanni* (1979). In the 1980s she sang mainly in concerts, and in 1992 she took part in the gala ceremonies in the Olympic Games in Barcelona. Among her many recordings are memorable interpretations of Sextus (*La clemenza di Tito*), Carmen, Rosina and Cenerentola, operas by Manuel de Falla and a delightful recital of Spanish song. A volume of memoirs, *Flor de soledad y silencio: meditaciones de una cantante*, was published in Madrid in 1984.

K. Loveland: 'Teresa Berganza', *Audio & Record Review*, iii/5 (1963–4), 16–23 [with discography by F.F. Clough and G.J. Cuming]

J.B. Steane: *The Grand Tradition* (London, 1974/*R*), 395–7

Harold Rosenthal/R

Berger, Erna

(*b* Cossebaude, nr Dresden, 19 Oct 1900; *d* Essen, 14 June 1990). German soprano. After studying in Dresden, she was engaged by the Dresden Staatsoper in 1925, making her début as First Boy (*Die Zauberflöte*) and in the same year singing in the première of Ferruccio Busoni's *Doktor Faust*. She sang at Bayreuth (1929–33) as the Shepherd in *Tannhäuser*, the First Flowermaiden and the Woodbird. Her first Salzburg appearance (1932) was as Blonde, her last (1953–4) as Zerlina. She made her Covent Garden début in 1934 as Marzelline, returning in 1935 and 1938, when she sang Queen of Night, Konstanze and Sophie. She sang again in London in 1949, and in that year made her Metropolitan début as Sophie (performance preserved on disc). In 1941, during the occupation of Paris, she sang Konstanze with the Berlin Staatsoper at the Opéra. She continued to appear in Germany and Austria until the end of the 1954–5 season. On her retirement from the stage

she devoted herself to lieder, giving her final public recital in Munich in 1968. Berger's voice retained its youthful freshness throughout her career; her Queen of Night and Konstanze were considered peerless, and her purely sung, innocent Gilda was one of the best of its day. Among her recordings are the Queen of Night, Gilda and Zerlina (on film, 1954); she also made many notable recordings of lieder.

A. Blyth: Obituary, *Opera*, xli (1990), 934–5

Harold Rosenthal/Alan Blyth/R

Bergonzi, Carlo

(*b* Vidalenzo, nr Cremona, 13 July 1924). Italian tenor. He studied at the Parma Conservatory, making his début as a baritone at Lecce in 1948 as Gioachino Rossini's Figaro. After studying the tenor repertory he made a second début as Chénier at Bari in 1951. That year he was engaged by Italian radio to take part in performances to mark the 50th anniversary of Giuseppe Verdi's death. He first sang at La Scala in 1953, creating the title role of Jacopo Napoli's *Mas'Aniello*, and appeared there for the next 20 years. He made his London début at the Stoll Theatre in 1953 as Don Alvaro, the role in which he first appeared at Covent Garden (1962); he returned as Manrico, Riccardo, Radames, Cavaradossi, Nemorino, Rodolfo (*Luisa Miller*) and Edgardo. He gave farewell recitals at Covent Garden (1992) and Carnegie Hall (1994), but continued to give occasional concerts in Italy. He made his American début in Chicago in 1955 in a double bill as Luigi (*Il tabarro*) and Turiddu, and sang regularly at the Metropolitan from 1956 for 30 years, making his last appearance there in 1988 as Rodolfo (*Luisa Miller*). In addition to the Verdi tenor repertory Bergonzi sang more than 40 roles, including Pollione, Enzo, Arrigo Boito's Faust and Canio. His voice was of beautiful quality, well modulated and well defined; he used it with taste, discretion and an elegant sense of line. These qualities can be heard in his many recordings, most notably of Verdi. He continued to give recitals well into his 70s. In May 2000, at the age of 75, he returned to New York to sing his first Otello, abandoning the performance after showing evident signs of strain in the first act.

G. Gualerzi: 'Carlo Bergonzi', *Opera*, xxix (1978), 257–62

Harold Rosenthal/Alan Blyth

Bernacchi, Antonio Maria

(*b* Bologna, 23 June 1685; *d* Bologna, 1 March 1756). Italian alto castrato. He was a pupil of Pɪsᴛᴏᴄᴄʜɪ and G.A. Ricieri, and studied counterpoint with

G.A. Bernabei at Munich. He made his Italian operatic début at Genoa in 1703 and appeared in Vienna in 1709 and Venice in 1709–10, 1717–19, 1721–4, 1731–2 and 1735, singing in at least 22 operas there. During the same period he sang in many other Italian cities including Novara (1711), Bologna (1710, 1712–13, 1722, 1727, 1731), Florence (1712–15), Parma (1714, 1728–9, 1736–7), Pesaro (1719), Reggio nell'Emilia (1718, and 1719, in Gasparini's *Bajazet*), Milan (1719), Rome (1712, 1721, in the first performance of Alessandro Scarlatti's *Griselda*, and 1731), Turin (1726–7), Naples (1728–9) and Modena (1728–9, 1735–6). Following his success in Giuseppe Orlandini's *Carlo, re d'Alemagna* at Parma in 1714, he was appointed virtuoso to Prince Antonio Farnese. His fame spread throughout Europe and he sang in operas by all the leading composers of the age, from Carlo Pallavicino and Alessandro Scarlatti to Johann Adolf Hasse, Leonardo Vinci and Leonardo Leo. In 1720 he was engaged by the Elector of Bavaria for Munich and sang there frequently until 1727, remaining nominally in his service until 1735. In 1729 Owen Swiney described him as 'the very best singer in the world'.

Bernacchi made his London début at the King's Theatre in Scarlatti's *Pirro e Demetrio* in 1716 (when G.F. Handel composed three extra arias for him) and also sang in the pasticcio *Clearte*. In 1717 he appeared in Handel's *Rinaldo* and *Amadigi*. In 1729 Handel engaged him as leading man for the second Royal Academy and he sang in the first performances of *Lotario* (Lotario, 1729) and *Partenope* (Arsace, 1730), revivals of *Giulio Cesare* and *Tolomeo* (1730), and the pasticcio *Ormisda*. Though English audiences preferred SENESINO, Bernacchi was accepted on the score of his European reputation; Charles Burney described him as 'past his meridian', but paid tribute to his taste and intelligence. He retired from the stage in 1738, apart from an unsuccessful reappearance in Florence, 1741–2, and founded a famous singing school at Bologna; among his many distinguished pupils were Tommaso Guarducci, RAAFF and Giovanni Amadori Tedeschi. Bernacchi had been a member of the Accademia Filarmonica, Bologna, since 1722 and its president in 1748–9, and he sang in churches and private concerts in the city. He was also a composer; some arias, duets and church music survive.

The range of Bernacchi's voice was slightly higher than that of Senesino. The two parts Handel composed for Bernacchi – Lotario and Arsace – have a compass of *a* to *f'''*. Though his natural musical gifts were not exceptional, he was renowned for technical virtuosity, especially in ornaments and cadenzas. He was sometimes accused of sacrificing expression to execution and adopting an instrumental style; his old master Pistocchi is said to have exclaimed: 'I taught you to sing, and you want to play'. FARINELLI studied under him briefly in 1727.

Winton Dean

Bernardi, Franceso.

See SENESINO.

Bernasconi [Wagele], Antonia

(*b* Stuttgart, *c*1741; *d* ?Vienna, ?1803). German soprano. She was the daughter of a valet of the Duke of Württemberg. By her widowed mother's second marriage in 1743, she became the stepdaughter of the composer Andrea Bernasconi, who instructed her in singing. Her successful début followed on 21 January 1762 as Aspasia in her father's *Temistocle* in Munich. In Vienna from about 1765–6 she first performed in *opere buffe* by Niccolò Piccinni and Antonio Sacchini and in 1767 was highly successful as Alceste in the première of C.W. Gluck's opera. J.A. Hiller gave a detailed account of her in the *Wöchentlichen Nachrichten* of 24 October 1768. In December 1770 she sang Aspasia in the première of W.A. Mozart's *Mitridate*; it is also possible that the part of Ninetta in his *La finta semplice* was composed for her. In 1771–2 she sang in Cesena, Milan and at the Teatro S Benedetto in Venice, in 1772–3 and 1774–5 at the Teatro di S Carlo in Naples. From November 1778 to May 1780 she was a member of the Italian opera company at the King's Theatre, London, and in the summer of 1781, supposedly at Gluck's request, she returned to the Vienna Burgtheater to sing in three Gluck operas that were specially mounted for the Grand Duke Paul of Russia. Mozart's letters are severely critical of her intonation and German declamation, although he said he would have trusted her with a part in the German performance of *Idomeneo* that he was planning. She was retained for the *opera buffa* company that was created in April 1783, but was released four months later, probably because, as Mozart had said (29 August 1781), she really sang well only in serious operas. In 1786 she appeared in Piacenza and Lucca. She is supposed to have married, under the name of Rieler.

D. Link: *The National Court Theatre in Mozart's Vienna: Sources and Documents 1783–1792* (Oxford, 1998)

Robert Münster

Berry, Walter

(*b* Vienna, 8 April 1929; *d* Vienna, 27 Oct 2000). Austrian bass-baritone. After study with Hermann

Gallos at the Vienna Music Academy he joined the Staatsoper in 1950. His first big success was as the Count in *Le nozze di Figaro*, and in very few years he built up a sizable repertory and an enviable international reputation, appearing in the leading German houses and in North and South America. His Metropolitan début was as Barak in *Die Frau ohne Schatten* in 1966. From 1952 he was a regular soloist at the Salzburg Festival, creating roles in such modern operas as Gottfried von Einem's *Der Prozess* (1953), Rolf Liebermann's *Penelope* (1954), Werner Egk's *Irische Legende* (1955), and singing the standard bass-baritone repertory. From 1957 to 1971 he was married to, and frequently appeared on stage with, the mezzo-soprano CHRISTA LUDWIG. On 31 December 1960 he sang Orlofsky in a celebrated production of *Die Fledermaus* at the Vienna Staatsoper, conducted by Herbert von Karajan. Apart from his Mozart roles (Masetto and Leporello, Guglielmo and Don Alfonso, Papageno, the Count and, later, Figaro) he won acclaim in a wide variety of parts: Wozzeck, Ochs, Escamillo, Pizarro, Telramund and subsequently Barak (*Die Frau ohne Schatten*), in which role he made his Covent Garden début in 1976, Wotan and Béla Bartók's Bluebeard. He returned to Covent Garden in 1986, singing Waldner in *Arabella*. He also appeared frequently in the concert hall, and recorded the Bach Passions and Haydn oratorios, lieder and numerous choral works. His operatic recordings, for which he was especially noted, include leading roles in operas by Bartók, Richard Strauss (Barak and Ochs), Alban Berg (Wozzeck) and W.A. Mozart (Masetto, Leporello, Figaro and Papageno).

P. Lorenz: *Christa Ludwig, Walter Berry* (Vienna, 1968)

Peter Branscombe

Berselli, Matteo

(*fl* 1708–21). Italian soprano castrato. He was apparently Venetian; he sang in six operas in Venice (1708–9), including works by Francesco Gasparini and Tomaso Albinoni, in Bologna (1712), Reggio nell'Emilia (1713 and 1719), Rome (1714 Gasparini's *Lucio Papirio* and 1716), Florence (1715), Milan (1715) and in three operas at Naples, including the première of Alessandro Scarlatti's *La virtù trionfante* (1716). He was engaged at Dresden (1717–20) at a salary of 4500 thaler (and the use of a carriage), and appeared in Antonio Lotti's *Giove in Argo*, *Ascanio* and *Teofane* and Ristori's *Cleonice*. Handel negotiated with him in Dresden in 1719, but he did not reach London until September 1720, when he sang for one season with the Royal Academy at the King's Theatre. He made his début in Giovanni Bononcini's *Astarto* (1720) in a female role, and appeared in G.F. Handel's *Radamisto*, the pasticcios *Arsace* (*Amor e Maestà*) and *Ciro* (*Odio ed Amore*) and the composite *Muzio Scevola* (1721). Handel composed three new arias for him in *Radamisto* and a duet and aria in *Muzio Scevola*, of which Charles Burney remarked that 'this singer must have been high in the composer's favour for taste, as he is left to himself in no less than six *ad libitums* and adagios, which he had to embellish'. Berselli's voice was a high soprano with a compass from *e'* to *b"*; in Handel, though according to J.J. Quantz, who thought his tone pleasing but rather thin, he could sing from *c'* to *f"*.

Winton Dean

Berthelier, Jean-François (Philibert)

(*b* Panissières, 14 Dec 1830; *d* Paris, 29 Sept 1888). French tenor. He made his début in Poitiers in 1849 as Fernand in Gaetano Donizetti's *La favorite*, but when the theatre closed he took to singing in local *cafés-concerts*. In 1855 he was engaged by Jacques Offenbach to be a member of the first company at the Bouffes-Parisiens, and was a great success in the opening performance, creating Giraffier in Offenbach's *Les deux aveugles*; later he created several additional Offenbach roles, including Paimpol in *Une nuit blanche* and Kokikako in *Ba-ta-clan*. He was then engaged for the Opéra-Comique, where he created 12 roles, including those of Simplet in Eugène Gautier's *Le mariage extravagant*, Aignelet in François Bazin's *Maître Pathelin* and Xailoun in Offenbach's *Barkouf*.

Berthelier was credited with the discovery of HORTENSE SCHNEIDER, who became Offenbach's greatest female interpreter, and with whom he appeared at the Palais-Royal in *Jeune poule et vieux coq* (1858). He later appeared at the Variétés, Renaissance, Nouveautés and Gaîté theatres in many roles, including Zappoli in *La tzigane*, one of the earliest French versions of Johann Strauss's *Die Fledermaus*. Among his most famous numbers was 'Ah! Que c'est comme un bouquet de fleurs' from *Le petit ébéniste*, and his particular facility for wearing headgear led him to give a lecture on hats at the Variétés in 1874.

Patrick O'Connor

Bertolli, Francesca

(*b* Rome; *d* Bologna, 9 Jan 1767). Italian contralto or mezzo-soprano. In 1728 she was in the service of the Grand Duchess of Tuscany and sang in two operas in Bologna and two in Livorno. G.F. Handel engaged her for the second Royal Academy at the King's Theatre (1729–33); she appeared in 15 or 16 of his operas, including revivals of *Tolomeo* (1728), *Scipione* (1730), *Tamerlano* (1731) and *Rinaldo* (1731), as well as in Attilio Ariosti's *Coriolano*, Leonardo Leo's *Catone* and two pasticcios. She took part in Handel's first London performances of oratorio, singing in *Esther* and the bilingual *Acis and Galatea* (1732), and in the following year in *Deborah*. From 1733 to 1736 she sang with the Opera of the Nobility in 12 operas, including Dionysus in Nicolò Porpora's *Arianna in Nasso* (1733), F.M. Veracini's *Adriano*, and revivals of Giovanni Bononcini's *Astarto* and Handel's *Ottone*. She returned to Handel (1736–7) and sang in four or five of his operas, and in a pasticcio based on Leonardo Vinci's *Didone*. She sang in the first performances of Leo's *Achille in Sciro* and Baldassare Galuppi's *Adriano in Siria* in Turin (1740), in Vicenza (1740), Venice (three operas in 1740–41) and Genoa (1742). She retired soon after, but appeared with BERNACCHI in a private concert at Bologna in February 1746. She was married to one Vincenzo Corrazza.

No singer except STRADA and SENESINO appeared in so many of Handel's operas. The nine parts he composed for her, Idelberto in *Lotario* (1729), Armindo in *Partenope* (1730), Gandartes in *Poro* (1731), Honoria in *Ezio* (1732), Melo in *Sosarme* (1732), Medoro in *Orlando* (1733), Ramisa in *Arminio* (1737), Leocasta in *Giustino* (1737) and Selene in *Berenice* (1737), indicate a voice of limited range and capacity; her regular compass was *b* to *e''*. She specialized in male roles, as the above list suggests. Mrs Pendarves, who was contemptuous of her voice, ear and manner, described her as 'a perfect beauty, quite a Cleopatra'. In 1733 she was courted (unsuccessfully) by the Prince of Wales.

Winton Dean/R

Besanzoni, Gabriella

(*b* Rome, 20 Sept 1888; *d* Rome, 8 July 1962). Italian mezzo-soprano. She studied in Rome, making her début (as a soprano) as Adalgisa at Viterbo in 1911. After further study she became a mezzo-soprano, singing Ulrica in Rome and appearing throughout Italy. She first sang at the Teatro Colón, Buenos Aires, in 1918, returning there frequently; she also visited Rio de Janeiro and, in 1919, Mexico City, where she sang Ulrica, Delilah, Nancy (*Martha*), Carmen and Amneris, all with ENRICO CARUSO as principal tenor. Engaged at the Metropolitan (1919–20), she made her début as Amneris, then sang Isabella in the Metropolitan première of *L'italiana in Algeri*, as well as Delilah and Preziosilla (*Forza del destino*) with Caruso. Besanzoni's repertory also included

Laura (*La Gioconda*) and Santuzza, which she sang at performances of *Cavalleria rusticana* conducted by Pietro Mascagni himself. At La Scala (1923–4) she sang C.W. Gluck's Orpheus under Toscanini, and also appeared as Mignon and Carmen, the role of her farewell in 1939 at the Baths of Caracalla, Rome. Her voice was rich, powerful, smoothly produced and notably flexible.

Elizabeth Forbes

Best, Matthew

(*b* Farnborough, Kent, 6 Feb 1957). English bass-baritone and conductor. He studied at Cambridge and at the National Opera Studio in London, then made his début at Aldeburgh in 1980 as Snout (*A Midsummer Night's Dream*). In 1982 he won the Decca-Ferrier Award. Engaged at Covent Garden (1980–86), he sang a wide variety of roles, including Timur, Colline, Fiorello, the Monk/Charles V (*Don Carlos*), Masetto, the Doctor (*Macbeth* and *Pelléas et Mélisande*), the Police Commissioner (*Lulu*), Hans Foltz (*Die Meistersinger*) and Lamoral (*Arabella*); he took part in the British première of Luciano Berio's *Un re in ascolto* (1989). He has also sung frequently with Opera North, Scottish Opera (notably as Amfortas in 2000), WNO, Glyndebourne Touring Opera and Nederlandse Opera. In 1995 he toured with John Eliot Gardiner, singing Pizarro in his production of Ludwig van Beethoven's *Leonore*, which was also recorded. In the same year he sang the High Priest in *Alceste* at Glyndebourne, and was praised for the dignity of his voice and his commanding presence. He is perhaps less favourably heard on recordings, which expose a certain roughness of production and where his more valued contribution has been as conductor of the Corydon Singers, founded by him in 1973. Particularly fine have been their Beethoven and Bruckner recordings; but their repertory is large and the standard of performance invariably high. Best has also worked with orchestras in Britain and Europe, being appointed principal conductor of the Hanover Band in 1998.

J.B. Steane

Bettendorf, Emmy

(*b* Frankfurt, 16 July 1895; *d* Berlin, 20 Oct 1963). German soprano. She made her début in 1914 at Frankfurt in Conradin Kreutzer's *Nachtlager in Granada*. After two years with the company at Schwerin and an appearance in Vienna as Agathe in *Freischütz* she joined the Berlin Staatsoper, where her roles included Eva, Elsa and Desdemona; she also sang Ariadne and the Marschallin in performances conducted by Richard Strauss. During the 1920s she undertook much concert work and appeared in opera with an impressive German company touring Spain and the Netherlands. Increasingly important in her career were broadcasts and recordings, through which she became one of the most popular singers of her time. She retired in 1934, but toured the eastern front singing to troops in wartime, and from 1947 to 1952 taught at the Städtisches Konservatorium, Berlin. Recordings reveal her exceptionally pure and mellow voice, the style sometimes lacking in vitality but well suited to the quieter and more relaxed parts of her extensive repertory.

D. White: 'Emmy Bettendorf', *Record Collector*, xv (1963–4), 149–68 [incl. discography]

J.B. Steane

Betz, Franz

(*b* Mainz, 19 March 1835; *d* Berlin, 11 Aug 1900). German baritone. He studied in Karlsruhe and made his début at Hanover in 1856 as Heinrich in *Lohengrin*. In 1859 he sang Don Carlos in Giuseppe Verdi's *Ernani* at the Berlin Hofoper and was immediately engaged there, remaining until his retirement in 1897. He sang Valentin in the first Berlin performance of Charles Gounod's *Faust* (given as *Margarethe*) in 1863. At the Munich Hofoper he sang Telramund in *Lohengrin* (1863) and Hans Sachs in the première of *Die Meistersinger* (1868), repeating the role in the first Berlin performance (1870). He was also Berlin's first Amonasro in *Aida* (1874) and King Mark in *Tristan und Isolde* (1876), and in 1875 he created the role of Judas in the première in Berlin of Anton Rubinstein's *Die Maccabäer*.

Having sung in Ludwig van Beethoven's Ninth Symphony at the ceremony for laying the foundation stone of the Festspielhaus (1872), Betz sang Wotan at Bayreuth in the first complete *Ring* cycle in August 1876 (during which he created the Wanderer in *Siegfried*). He took part in a gala performance of Gaspare Spontini's *Olympie* in Berlin (1879) and visited London in 1882 to sing at the Crystal Palace and at a concert conducted by Hans Richter. Returning to Bayreuth in 1889, he alternated as Kurwenal and King Mark in *Tristan*, and also sang Hans Sachs. He made guest appearances in Vienna and other cities in Austria and Germany. His vast repertory included the Dutchman, Wolfram in *Tannhäuser*, Pizarro in *Fidelio*, Hans Heiling (title role in Heinrich Marschner's opera), Don Giovanni and Falstaff, which he sang at the first Berlin performance in German of Verdi's opera (1894), but his favourite role was Hans Sachs, which he sang

over 100 times in Berlin alone; it perfectly displayed the strength, evenness and warmth of his generous voice, and the humanity of his dramatic style.

Elizabeth Forbes

Bianchi [Tozzi], Marianna

(*b* ?Venice, *c*1735; *d* after 1790). Italian soprano. She made her *opera seria* début as *ultima parte* at Parma in 1753 and sang mostly secondary roles, sometimes appearing in *opera buffa*, before going to Vienna as prima donna in 1762, where she created Eurydice in C.W. Gluck's *Orfeo ed Euridice*. She then sang as prima donna in Italy and with her husband, the composer Antonio Tozzi, was engaged at Brunswick (1765–8), singing in *Andromaca*, and Munich (1773–5), where she sang in *Zenobia*, both by Tozzi; her Italian career then declined to secondary theatres and, after 1780, to *opera buffa*, ending in 1790. According to Charles Burney, she had 'a sweet and elegant toned voice, always perfectly in tune, with an admirable *portamento*; I never heard any one sing with more ease, or in a manner so totally free from affectation'.

Dennis Libby

Biancolini(-Rodriguez), Marietta

(*b* Fermo, Ascoli Piceno, 20 Sept 1846; *d* Florence, 31 May 1905). Italian mezzo-soprano. She made her début in 1864 as Vincenzo Bellini's Romeo at Novara, then appeared in Florence, Genoa, Naples, Lisbon, Buenos Aires and at La Scala, where she created Laura (*La Gioconda*) in 1876 and sang Fidès (*Le prophète*) in 1885. The flexibility of her voice enabled her to sing Gioachino Rossini's coloratura mezzo-soprano and contralto roles, including Rosina, Angelina, Isabella and Arsace, with special success.

Elizabeth Forbes

Bible, Frances (L.)

(*b* Sackets Harbor, NY, 26 Jan 1919; *d* Hernet, CA, 29 Jan 2001). American mezzo-soprano. After studying with Belle Julie Soudant and Queena Mario at the Juilliard School, she made her début as the Shepherd-boy (*Tosca*) in 1948 at the New York City Opera, where she remained a leading artist until 1977. She was particularly noted for her Cenerentola and her interpretations of trouser roles such as Cherubino, Hänsel, Nicklausse, Siébel and Octavian. In 1961 she created the role of Elizabeth Proctor in Robert Ward's *The Crucible*. She made her British début in 1955 at Glyndebourne as Cherubino, returning in 1962 as Claudio Monteverdi's Octavia. She sang Augusta Tabor in the second performance of Douglas Moore's *The Ballad of Baby Doe* (1956) at Central City, Colorado, and also appeared at San Francisco, Houston, Boston, Miami and other American cities, her repertory including Laura (*La Gioconda*), Cornelia (*Giulio Cesare*) and Marina (*Boris Godunov*). Bible's voice was warm, her technique assured; in her early career she was a lively and charming presence on stage, and later she excelled in roles demanding authority. Her qualities made her a prominent and well-loved figure in the American theatre.

Elizabeth Forbes/R

Bigonzi, Giuseppe

(*b* Rome; *fl* 1707–?33). Italian alto castrato. He sang intermittently in Venice (1707–23), appearing in five operas, including works by Tomaso Albinoni and Michelangelo and Francesco Gasparini, and in Florence (1718–19) in Antonio Predieri's *Partenope*. He was probably the 'Biganzo' who according to the Ruspoli account books sang in the Roman Chiesa degl'Agonizanti in June 1715. About 1723, also in Rome, he took the title role in Antonio Caldara's oratorio *Santo Stefano*. Engaged for the London season of 1723–4, he arrived on 7 October and made his début in Attilio Ariosti's *Vespasiano* at the King's Theatre on 14 January 1724. He sang small parts in G.F. Handel's *Giulio Cesare* (Nirenus) and G.M. Bononcini's *Calfurnia*, but made little mark. He sang in Paris later in 1724, and probably in Macerata in 1730 and Camerino in 1733. A caricature by A.M. Zanetti in the Cini collection may represent him as Megabise in M. Gasparini's *Arsace* (Venice, 1718). Another Bigonzi, Giovanni Battista, also an alto, sang at Senigallia in 1709.

Winton Dean

Bispham, David (Scull)

(*b* Philadelphia, 5 Jan 1857; *d* New York, 2 Oct 1921). American baritone. He studied in Milan (1886–9) with Luigi Vannuccini and Francesco Lamperti and then in London with the tenor William Shakespeare and Alberto Randegger. He made his operatic début in 1891 as Longueville in André Messager's *La basoche* at the English Opera House, where his comic acting ability and singing brought him immediate success. He sang Kurwenal the following year at Drury Lane, and later sang at Covent Garden as well. He made his début at the Metropolitan Opera as Beckmesser in 1896 and remained with the company until 1903. Much in demand in England and the USA in opera and ora-

torio and on the recital stage for several decades, he excelled in the Wagnerian roles, of which he considered Kurwenal and Beckmesser to be his best. He sang at the première of Walter Damrosch's *The Scarlet Letter* (1896, Boston), and his repertory also included Masetto, Pizarro, Escamillo, Alfio, Peter (*Hänsel und Gretel*), Iago, Falstaff and Urok in Ignacy Jan Paderewski's *Manru*. His voice was powerful and of fine quality, though with a tendency to excessive nasal resonance.

Bispham was ardently in favour of using the English language in operas and songs, and to this end helped to form the Society of American Singers in 1917, which presented comic operas in English using American casts; he toured with the troupe for several years both as singer and administrator. He also developed lecture-recital programmes, in which he promoted the works of English and American composers. The American Opera Society of Chicago awards the David Bispham Medal to motivate the composition and performance of American opera.

A highly skilled actor and a forceful delineator of character, Bispham appeared as Ludwig van Beethoven in Hugo Müller's play *Adelaide* (1898) in both England and America. In his later years he developed a repertory of monologues of poetry and prose which he performed to musical accompaniment, often provided by famous groups of the day. From 1902 he was also an influential teacher in Philadelphia. Bispham's musical memorabilia are in the New York Public Library.

D. Bispham: *A Quaker Singer's Recollections* (New York, 1921/*R*)

Obituary, *MusAm*, xxxiv/24 (1921), I

O. Thompson: 'David Bispham', *The American Singer* (New York, 1937/*R*), 204

J. Dennis: 'David Bispham', *Record Collector*, vi (1951), 5 [with discography]

Richard Aldrich/Dee Baily/R

Björling, Jussi [Johan] (Jonaton)

(*b* Stora Tuna, 5 Feb 1911; *d* Stockholm, 9 Sept 1960). Swedish tenor. He was first taught by his father, David Björling (1873–1926), a professional tenor, and from 1916 made many concert tours with his father and two brothers as a treble in the Björling Male Quartet, which made a few commercial recordings in the USA in 1920. In 1928 he entered the Stockholm Conservatory, where he studied with JOSEPH HISLOP and JOHN FORSELL. After a preliminary appearance at the Royal Swedish Opera as the Lamplighter in *Manon Lescaut* (21 July 1930), he made his recognized début there on 20 August 1930 as Don Ottavio, shortly afterwards singing Arnold in

Jussi Björling in the title role of 'Faust' (Gounod)

Guillaume Tell and Jonathan in Carl Nielsen's *Saul og David*. Until 1938 he was a regular member of the Stockholm Opera, and always maintained his connection with that house. He was soon in general demand in the leading European operatic centres (Vienna début as Radames, 1936); and his international status was confirmed by his successful débuts at Chicago in *Rigoletto* (8 December 1937), in New York in *La bohème* (24 November 1938), at Covent Garden in *Il trovatore* (12 May 1939) and at San Francisco in *La bohème* (18 October 1940). Covent Garden had to wait until the last year of his life for another chance to hear him (in *La bohème*), whereas in America he became an indispensable favourite, returning regularly to the Metropolitan and other houses except during the war years of 1941–5, which he spent in Sweden.

Although Björling's repertory had by this time become almost entirely Italian, his appearances were infrequent in Italy itself, where the purity and restraint of his style may perhaps have disconcerted a public used to a more overt and impassioned display. His voice was a true tenor of velvety smoothness, though capable also of ringing high notes; admirably schooled, it showed remarkable consistency from top to bottom of his register and throughout the 30 years of his career. To the end, the glowing tone and impeccable musicianship provided ample compensation for a stage presence that was rather a matter of deportment than of acting. His smooth legato and plangent tone were particularly well suited to Charles Gounod's Faust and Romeo; but the centre of his repertory consisted of Giuseppe Verdi's Manrico, Riccardo and Don Carlos and Giacomo Puccini's Rodolfo, Cavaradossi and Des Grieux. He was also a notable soloist in Verdi's Requiem, of which he made three recordings (the finest is with Arturo Toscanini at Carnegie Hall in 1940) and an appreciable interpreter of songs, especially those of Richard Strauss. Having a voice ideally adapted to the gramophone, he made a large number of delightful and valuable records, including many complete operas, among which his Rodolfo in the famous Beecham set of *La bohème* well illustrates the distinction of his tone and phrasing. Björling can also be heard on several live recordings from the Metropolitan and the Royal Opera in Stockholm. He published a volume of memoirs, *Med bagaget i strupen* [Travels with my larynx] (Stockholm, 1945).

E.S. Lund and H. Rosenberg: *Jussi Björling: a Record List* (Copenhagen, 1969)

J.W. Porter and H. Henrysson: *A Jussi Björling Discography* (Indianapolis, 1982)

A. Blyth: Jussi Björling', *Opera*, xxxvi (1985), 994–7

A.-L. Björling and A.Farkas: *Jussi* (Portland, OR, 1996)

A.-L. Björling and A.Farkas: 'Jussi Björling's Début at the Met', *OQ*, xiii/2 (1996–7), 78–88

Desmond Shawe-Taylor/Alan Blyth

Blachut, Beno

(*b* Ostrava-Vítkovice, 14 June 1913; *d* Prague, 10 Jan 1985). Czech tenor. He came from a poor mining family and at 14 worked in the iron works. He sang in a church choir, and in the Ostrava opera chorus. He studied at the Prague Conservatory under Louis Kadeřábek (1935–9) and made his début as Jeník with the Olomouc Opera in 1939. Under the director, Karel Nedbal, he studied 18 parts, notably Laca in *Jenůfa* and the Prince in *Rusalka*. He joined the Prague National Theatre in 1941 and was soon given Heldentenor roles; an excellent performance of *Dalibor* in 1945 made his name as the leading Czech tenor, whose Smetana roles, Laca in *Jenůfa* and later Ondřej in Eugen Suchoň's *The Whirlpool* were regarded as models. He was also in demand for concerts, in which he sang tenor parts in cantatas and oratorios (including Hector Berlioz's *La damnation de Faust*, Antonín Dvořák's *Stabat mater* and *The Spectre's Bride*, and Leoš Janáček's *Glagolitic Mass*), and songs. His recording of Janáček's *The Diary of One who Disappeared* achieved renown.

Blachut's voice, balanced in all registers, did not lose its lyric character even in Heldentenor parts. He was notable for his beautiful cantilena, a brilliantly mastered *mezza voce*, exemplary enunciation and pleasant dark vocal colouring. At dramatic moments he made use of a careful gradation and expressive accentuation, never at the expense of true vocal line, and always keeping his natural dignity. Towards the end of his career he took *buffo* roles, notably an excellently sung and acted Matěj Brouček in Janáček's opera. He sang with the National Theatre on tours to Moscow, Berlin, Brussels and Edinburgh and as a guest in Vienna, Amsterdam and Helsinki. His many operatic recordings include a classic portrayal of Boris in *Kát'a Kabanová*.

Alena Němcová

Black, Mrs Morris.

See CAHIER, MME CHARLES.

Blake, Rockwell

(*b* Plattsburgh, NY, 10 Jan 1951). American tenor. While still at school he began his studies with Renata Carisio Booth, who remained his principal teacher. After apprenticeships with the Goldovsky and Wolf Trap opera companies, he made his début with the Washington Opera in 1976 as Lindoro in *L'italiana in Algeri*. In 1978 he was the first winner of the Richard Tucker Foundation Award. The following year he made his New York City Opera début in *Le comte Ory*, and he has subsequently sung widely in Europe and the USA. His Metropolitan Opera début was in 1981, again as Lindoro, and since 1983 he has appeared regularly at the Rossini Festival at Pesaro. His repertory includes some 30 roles, mostly by Vincenzo Bellini, Gaetano Donizetti, W.A. Mozart and Gioachino Rossini. Although the range (extending to f''') and prodigious flexibility of his voice are widely acknowledged, its penetrating timbre, and his unusually muscular approach to this repertory, have provoked controversy.

Cori Ellison

Blamauer, Karoline Wilhelmine.

See LENYA, LOTTE.

Blanc, Ernest

(*b* Sanary-sur-Mer, 1 Nov 1923). French baritone. A student at the conservatories in Toulon and Paris, he made his début in Marseilles as Tonio (1950). At the Paris Opéra (1954–80) he sang a wide variety of roles including Rigoletto, Theogène (which he sang in the première of Henry Barraud's *Numance*, 1955), Valentin, Amonasro, Germont, Renato, Wolfram, Enrico Ashton, Michele (*Il tabarro*) and Andrey Shchelkalov. His large, well-focussed, sensuous voice was soon heard in Milan, Vienna and London, but the turning-point of his career came in 1958, when he sang a remarkable Telramund at Bayreuth (a recording of the occasion reveals that his German declamation was as clear and determined as his French). He made his American début in 1959 at Chicago as Escamillo (a role he recorded, in aptly swaggering fashion, for Beecham) and his British début in 1960 as Riccardo (*I puritani*) at Glyndebourne, where he also sang Don Giovanni. He sang Rigoletto at Covent Garden (1961) and appeared in Milan, Vienna, Brussels and throughout France in a repertory that included Zurga, Scarpia, Luna, Jules Massenet's Herod, Ourrias (Charles Gounod's *Mireille*), the Father (*Louise*), Golaud, Jacques Offenbach's Bluebeard and the Count des Grieux. Besides his Telramund and Escamillo, his recordings include Zurga, a sturdy Valentin and High Priest (*Samson et Dalila*), and a resplendent Dapertutto (*Les contes d'Hoffmann*). He could have had a longer international career, had he not preferred to stay in France.

André Tubeuf/Alan Blyth

Blaze, Robin

(*b* Manchester, 11 Jan 1971). English countertenor. He read music at Magdalen College, Oxford, and won a postgraduate scholarship to the RCM, studying with MICHAEL CHANCE and, subsequently, Ashley Stafford. With his clear, sweet tone, refined sense of style and verbal sensitivity, he quickly made a name in the Baroque concert repertory. He has worked in Europe (including the Saintes, Beaune and Utrecht festivals), North and South America, Australia and Japan, with such conductors as Harry Christophers, Philippe Herreweghe, Christopher Hogwood, Robert King, Gustav Leonhardt and Paul McCreesh.

Blaze made his début at the Göttingen Handel Festival, as Bertarido in *Rodelinda*, in 2000, repeating the role for Glyndebourne Touring Opera in 2001. His ENO début, as Arsamenes (*Serse*) came in 2002, the year of his Covent Garden début, as Athamas (*Semele*). He has since returned to the ENO as Benjamin Britten's Oberon, Athamas (both 2004) and Hamor in *Jephtha* (2005). In 2003 he was much admired for his subtle, touching portrayal of Didymus (*Theodora*) in the Glyndebourne Festival. His other roles include Narciso in *Agrippina* (which he has sung at the Karlsruhe Festival) and Anfinomo

(*Il ritorno d'Ulisse in patria*). Blaze's numerous recordings include Didymus, Unolfo (*Rodelinda*), William Byrd songs, odes and sacred works by Henry Purcell, G.F. Handel's *The Choice of Hercules*, and many J.S. Bach cantatas in the complete recorded cycle conducted by Masaaki Suzuki.

Richard Wigmore

Blegen, Judith

(*b* Missoula, MT, 27 April 1941). American soprano. She studied singing with Euphemia Gregory at the Curtis Institute from 1959. After an apprenticeship at the Santa Fe Opera Festival (to which she later returned as a principal), she was engaged for concerts at Spoleto in 1963. She studied further in Italy and in 1964 went to Nuremberg, where during two years she sang such varied roles as Lucia, Susanna and Zerbinetta. Engagements followed in Vienna, Salzburg and the major American houses; her début role of Papagena at the Metropolitan (1970) led to performances as Marcellina, Mélisande, Ascanius and Sophie in *Werther*. She made her Covent Garden début in 1975, as Despina, and her début at the Opéra in 1977, as Sophie in *Der Rosenkavalier*. Her singing, notable for its intelligence, charm and polish, is preserved on recordings of oratorio and lieder, and in her Susanna in *Le nozze di Figaro*. She avoids soubrette clichés and makes the most of a voice that is exceptionally pure and sweet if not particularly large or colourful. She has both sung and creditably played the violin in Gian Carlo Menotti's *Help, Help, the Globolinks* and *Die Fledermaus* (as Adele).

Martin Bernheimer/R

Blochwitz, Hans Peter

(*b* Garmisch-Partenkirchen, 28 Sept 1949). German tenor. He studied in Mainz and Frankfurt. After developing a successful career as a concert and lieder singer, he made his operatic début in 1984 at Frankfurt as Lensky (*Yevgeny Onegin*). He sang the Evangelist in stagings of the *St Matthew Passion* at La Scala, Milan (1985), and the *St John Passion* at the Théâtre des Champs-Elysées, Paris (1986). At Aix-en-Provence he has sung Belmonte, Ferrando and Tamino. Blochwitz made his Covent Garden début in 1989 as Ferrando, returning as Don Ottavio, the role of his Metropolitan début in 1990. In addition to his four major Mozart roles, his repertory includes Claudio Monteverdi's Nero and Wilhelm in Hans Werner Henze's *Der junge Lord*, which he sang at Munich in 1995. A very stylish singer, with superb diction, he has a firm-toned lyrical voice perfectly adapted to J.S. Bach and W.A. Mozart. His recordings include Ferrando, Don Ottavio and Tamino, and several admired discs of lieder.

Elizabeth Forbes

Blume, Heinrich

(*b* Berlin, 25 April 1788; *d* Berlin, 2 Nov 1856). German bass-baritone. He studied in Berlin, where he made his début in 1808 at the Hofoper in Peter Winter's *Das unterbrochene Opferfest*. He took part in the Berlin première of Gaspare Spontini's *Olympie* (1821) and, at the Berlin Schauspielhaus, created Huldbrant in E. T. A. Hoffmann's *Undine* (1816) and Caspar in *Der Freischütz* (1821). A famous Don Giovanni, he also sang Masetto and the Commendatore. His powerful voice had a wide range and he was able to sing both baritone and bass roles.

Elizabeth Forbes

Boccabadati, Luigia

(*b* Modena, 1800; *d* Turin, 12 Oct 1850). Italian soprano. She made her début in 1817 at Parma, then sang in Venice, Rome and at La Scala, where in 1826 she sang Nicola Vaccai's Giulietta and the title role in Giacomo Meyerbeer's *Marguerite d'Anjou*. At Naples she sang in five Donizetti premières: Amelia in *Elisabetta, o Il castello di Kenilworth* (S Carlo) in 1829; Cristina in *I pazzi per progetto* (Fondo) and Sela in *Il diluvio universale* (S Carlo) in 1830; La Contessa in *Francesca di Foix* (S Carlo) and Chiarina in *La romanziera e l'uomo nero* (Fondo) in 1831. She sang the title role in Gioachino Rossini's *Matilde di Shabran* at the Théâtre Italien, Paris (1832), and Angelina (*La Cenerentola*) at the King's Theatre, London (1833). Her other roles included Rosina, Vincenzo Bellini's Giulietta, Imogene, Elvira, Amina and Norma as well as Gaetano Donizetti's Zoraide, Eleanora (*Il furioso all'isola di San Domingo*), and the title roles in *Maria di Rohan*, *Gemma di Vergy* and *Lucrezia Borgia*. She retired in 1844. Her powerful, flexible voice was perfectly suited to Semiramis, her finest role. Her daughter, the soprano Virginia Boccabadati (*b* 29 April 1828; *d* Turin, 6 Aug 1922), made her début in 1847 at Palermo as Linda di Chamounix, then sang at Florence, Rome, Bologna and Paris in a repertory including Amina, Norina, Gilda and Violetta. She took part in the first performance of Filippo Marchetti's *La demente* at Turin (1856). Her voice, lighter than her mother's, was equally flexible.

Elizabeth Forbes

Boccabadati, Virginia.

Soprano, daughter of LUIGIA BOCCABADATI.

Böhme, Kurt

(*b* Dresden, 5 May 1908; *d* nr Munich, 20 Dec 1989). German bass. He studied with Kluge at the Dresden Conservatory, and made his début in 1929 as Caspar at Bautzen. He sang at the Dresden Staatsoper (1930–50), and in 1950 joined the Staatsoper in Munich. In Dresden he appeared in the premières of *Arabella* (Count Dominik, 1933), *Die schweigsame Frau* (Vanuzzi, 1935), *Daphne* (Peneios, 1938), Heinrich Sutermeister's *Romeo und Julia* (Capulet, 1940) and Sutermeister's *Die Zauberinsel* (Prospero, 1942). At Salzburg he created Ulysses in Rolf Liebermann's *Penelope* (1954) and Aleel in Werner Egk's *Irische Legende* (1955). Böhme first sang at Covent Garden with the Dresden company in 1936, and then regularly (1956–60) as Hunding, Hagen and Ochs; he last appeared there in 1972 with the Munich company as Sir Morosus. He made his début at Bayreuth in 1952 as Pogner, where he also sang Fafner and Titurel, and at the Metropolitan in 1954, also as Pogner; he also sang at La Scala. His most famous role was Ochs, which he first sang in 1942 and repeated more than 500 times; in this role his rich voice and even richer sense of humour had full play, as can be heard in his recordings under Rudolf Kempe and Karl Böhm. He also recorded Rocco, Caspar and his Wagnerian roles.

A. Blyth: Obituary, *Opera*, xlix (1990), 295–6

Harold Rosenthal/Alan Blyth

Boin, Henry Alphonse.

See DALMORÈS, CHARLES.

Bokor, Margit

(*b* Budapest, 1905; *d* New York, 9 Nov 1949). Hungarian soprano. She studied in Vienna and in Budapest, where she made her debut in 1928. Two years later she appeared in Berlin and then joined the Dresden Staatsoper, singing Zdenka in the world première of *Arabella* in 1933. She also sang this role the following year in the London première and, according to Richard Capell, 'could hardly have been better' (*Daily Telegraph*, May 1934). In the same year she sang in the première of Franz Léhar's *Giuditta* in Vienna. At Salzburg her parts included Octavian in *Der Rosenkavalier* and Zerlina in *Don Giovanni*. In 1939 she left Europe for the USA and appeared in Chicago, San Francisco and elsewhere, usually in light roles such as Susanna, Sophie and Adele in *Die Fledermaus*. She was engaged by the New York City Opera in 1947 but died within two years. Recordings preserve her voice in a duet from *Arabella* with VIORICA URSULEAC, and a transcript of *Don Giovanni*, broadcast from Salzburg, reveals the charm and accomplishment of her Zerlina.

J.B. Steane

Bonci, Alessandro

(*b* Cesena, nr Rimini, 10 Feb 1870; *d* Viserba, nr Rimini, 9 Aug 1940). Italian tenor. After study with Carlo Pedrotti and Felice Coen in Pesaro, and with ENRICO DELLE SEDIE in Paris, he made his début in Parma (1896) as Fenton in *Falstaff*. In the early years of the new century he was for some time regarded as CARUSO's only serious rival, excelling in roles demanding lightness, agility and elegance rather than in the heavier and more dramatic parts. After some appearances at Covent Garden, where he was part of the cast that first established *La bohème* in the repertory of the Royal Opera (1899), he scored a great success in New York in 1906, singing in *I puritani* at the opening of Oscar Hammerstein's new Manhattan Opera House; but for the next three seasons he transferred his activities to the Metropolitan, where he sang 65 performances of 14 roles. He performed in South America, singing at the première of *Il sogno di Alma* by Carlos López Buchardo in Buenos Aires in 1914. In World War I he served with the Italian Air Force; he made only sporadic appearances thereafter, devoting most of his time to teaching in Milan. In the older repertory he excelled by virtue of the sweetness of his tone and the finish of his phrasing, qualities that are especially evident in his earlier recordings.

T. Hutchinson: 'Alessandro Bonci', *Record Collector*, xi (1957), 148–62, 234–5 [incl. discography]

Desmond Shawe-Taylor

Bondini(-Saporiti), Caterina

(fl. 1786–88). Italian soprano, sister of THERESA SAPORITI. Her husband was the impresario PASQUALE BONDINI, and Caterina was a popular soprano in her husband's company in the mid-1780s. She sang Susanna in the first Prague production of *Figaro* in early December 1786, and on 14 December a performance was given for her benefit; her praises were sung in poems distributed in the theatre. She created the role of Zerlina in *Don Giovanni* (1787); from the rehearsals dates the anecdote that Mozart taught her to scream effectively during the abduction scene in the finale of Act 1 by grabbing her unexpectedly round the waist.

The Bondinis' daughter Marianna (1780–1813) sang Susanna in the French première of *Figaro* and often appeared with her husband, the bass Luigi Barilli, who was later manager of the Théâtre de l'Odéon in Paris.

Peter Branscombe/R

Bondini, Pasquale

(*b* ?Bonn, ?1737; *d* Bruneck, Tyrol, 30/31 Oct 1789). Italian impresario and bass. He is first mentioned as a *buffo* bass in Cajetan Molinari's opera company at Prague in the 1762–3 season. He was later a prominent member of Giuseppe Bustelli's company in Prague and Dresden. In 1777 he became director of the Elector of Saxony's new company at Dresden where he obtained the right to present the Churfürstlich Sächsische Hofcomödianten; he also assumed responsibility for Leipzig. Under J.C. Brandes and later J.F. Reinecke as heads of drama the company's repertory also included plays by William Shakespeare, Gotthold Ephraim Lessing and Friedrich Schiller. Operas performed included works by virtually all the leading Italian composers of the day. In 1781 Bondini also took over direction of the theatre at Count Thun's palace in Prague and shortly afterwards Count Nostitz's theatre. His company performed at Leipzig mainly in the summer, where a merchant-dominated audience could still be found, and gave *Die Entführung* there at Michaelmas 1783 and at Dresden on 12 January 1785. But because he and his personnel were so heavily extended by his many activities, Bondini was obliged to engage other troupes and managers. His most important assistant was Domenico Guardasoni, who in 1787 became his co-director and in 1788 or 1789 his successor as impresario of the operatic side of his companies. Johann Joseph Strobach became musical director in 1785, and though the opera ensemble was small, it was highly regarded and very popular.

In December 1786 Bondini mounted *Figaro*, and in January he invited W.A. Mozart and his wife to Prague to share in the triumph the opera was enjoying; during his stay Mozart conducted a performance. Before returning to Vienna in February he had been commissioned by Bondini to write *Don Giovanni*; after delays due to illness in the company, the work was first performed on 29 October 1787 with Mozart conducting. Mozart's letter to Gottfried von Jacquin of 15–25 October contains valuable but tantalizingly brief comments on Bondini's ensemble and on the preparations for the work. Within a year of the première Bondini's fortunes had waned;

ill-health led him to make Franz Seconda responsible for the drama company, and in summer 1789 he handed over his remaining assets before setting off for a visit to Italy. He died at Bruneck on the way.

Bondini's wife, CATERINA BONDINI, was a popular soprano in her husband's company in the mid-1780s.

The Bondinis' daughter Marianna (1780–1813) sang Susanna in the French première of *Figaro* and often appeared with her husband, the bass Luigi Barilli, who was later manager of the Théâtre de l'Odéon in Paris.

Peter Branscombe

Bonfigli, Lorenzo

(*b* Lucca, c1800; *d* Lucca, Jan 1876). Italian tenor. The year after his début in 1827 he created the title roles in Luigi Ricci's Ulisse in Itaca and Giuseppe Magagnini's Osmano Pascià d'Egitto at the Teatro S Carlo, Naples. In 1829 he sang in the premières of Giuseppe Persiani's Eufemio di Messina (Teodoto) and Constantino in Arles (title role), and the following year created Tebaldo in Vincenzo Bellini's *I Capuleti e i Montecchi* at La Fenice, Venice. His arrogant nature, which on occasion offended Saverio Mercadante and Gaetano Donizetti, nearly provoked a duel with Bellini, to whom Bonfigli complained about the specially written 'È serbato questo acciaro'. He did, however, apologise to the composer following the cavatina's considerable success.

In 1831 Bonfigli created the Duke in Donizetti's *Francesca di Foix* and Nerestano in Mercadante's *Zaira*. He also sang in the premières of Mercadante's *Francesca Donato* (1835) and operas by Antonio Granara, Ruggero Manna, Pietro Combi and Federico Ricci. His repertory also included Gioachino Rossini's *Il barbiere di Siviglia* (Almaviva), *Otello* (title role) and *Bianco e Falliero* (Contareno), Bellini's *La sonnambula* (Elvino) and *Norma* (Pollione), Donizetti's *Gemma di Vergy* and works by the young Giuseppe Verdi. His vocalism was florid and agile, but within a central tessitura suited to heroic parts. Initially a *tenore di forza*, he was among those (like Domenico Donizelli and Giovanni Basadonna) who catalyzed the transition to the modern tenor voice. His career continued successfully until about 1847.

Riccardo La Spina

Bonisolli, Franco

(*b* Rovereto, 25 May 1937; *d* Vienna, 30 Oct 2003). Italian tenor. He won first prize in a competition at Spoleto in 1961 and made his début at the festival there in 1962 as Ruggero (*La rondine*), later singing

the Prince in *The Love for Three Oranges*. Further engagements for leading roles in Verdi and the *verismo* repertory quickly followed. He made his Vienna Staatsoper début in 1968 and his American début as Alfredo at San Francisco in 1969; later he appeared at the Metropolitan Opera as Almaviva (1971). He was first heard at Covent Garden in 1981 as Vasco de Gama (*L'Africaine*); this was followed by Calaf, a role which, together with Don José, he also sang on the Royal Opera's Far East tour in 1986. At Verona (1988–9) he sang Enzo and Radames. His recordings include Ruggero Leoncavallo's *La bohème*, Georges Bizet's *Djamileh* and C.W. Gluck's *Iphigénie en Tauride* and *Paride ed Elena*; he also appeared in a film of *La traviata*. Bonisolli was a *tenore robusto* whose performance could be excitingly dramatic but also ill-disciplined in vocal style.

Noël Goodwin

Bonney, Barbara

(*b* Montclair, NJ, 14 April 1956). American soprano. She studied at the University of New Hampshire, then in Salzburg, where she sang with several choirs. In 1979 she joined Darmstadt Opera, making her début as Anne Page (*Die lustigen Weiber von Windsor*), also singing Blonde, Cherubino, Adina, Gretel, Gilda, Ilia, Jules Massenet's Manon, and Natalie (Henze's *Prinz von Homburg*). At Frankfurt (1983–4) she sang Aennchen (*Der Freischütz*), Norina, Marzelline and Papagena. In 1984 she made her débuts in Munich and at Covent Garden as Sophie (*Der Rosenkavalier*), a role she has also sung at the Vienna State Opera (1994). She sang Pamina at La Scala (1985) and in Zürich (1986), where she returned in 1989 as Susanna. Meanwhile, Bonney made her Metropolitan début in 1988 as Naiad (*Ariadne auf Naxos*), followed by Adele (*Die Fledermaus*), Sophie, Nannetta (*Falstaff*) and Susanna. She sang Despina at San Diego (1991), Eurydice (Gluck's *Orfeo*) at Geneva (1995) and Alphise in Rameau's *Les Boréades* at the Salzburg Festival and the Proms (1999). As a concert singer she has appeared in works such as Johannes Brahms's *German Requiem*, Joseph Haydn's *Creation*, G.F. Handel's *Acis and Galatea* and Gustav Mahler's Fourth Symphony. She is also a fine lieder singer and has recorded songs by Henry Purcell, W.A. Mozart, Felix Mendelssohn, Hugo Wolf, Richard Strauss, Edvard Grieg and Alexander Zemlinsky. Born with perfect pitch, she has a beautiful, pure-toned voice, a charming personality and an assured sense of style.

J. Allison: 'Barbara Bonny', *Opera*, l (1999), 905–14

Elizabeth Forbes

Bordoni [Hasse; Bordon Hasse], Faustina

(*b* Venice, 30 March 1697; *d* Venice, 4 Nov 1781). Italian mezzo-soprano. She was brought up under the protection of the brothers Alessandro and Benedetto Marcello and taught by Michelangelo Gasparini. For many years she was in the service of the Elector Palatine. She made her operatic début in 1716 in C.F. Pollarolo's *Ariodante* in Venice, where she sang until 1725 in operas by Tomaso Giovanni Albinoni, Antonio Lotti, Michelangelo and Francesco Gasparini, Carlo Francesco and Antonio Pollarolo, Giuseppe Maria Orlandini, Geminiano Giacomelli, Leonardo Vinci and others. She appeared at Reggio nell'Emilia in 1717, 1719 (F. Gasparini's *Bajazet*, in which she created the part of Irene) and 1720, Milan in 1719, Modena in 1720, Bologna in 1721–2, Naples in 1721–3 (seven operas, including Leonardo Leo's *Bajazete*), Florence (1723) and Parma (1724–5, including Vinci's *Il trionfo di Camilla*). She made her German début in 1723 at Munich in Pietro Torri's *Griselda*, and enjoyed great success there during the 1720s; she was also a favourite at Vienna (1725–6), appearing in operas by Antonio Caldara, Johann Joseph Fux, Giuseppe Porsile and others.

Faustina (as she was commonly known), was brought to London by the impresario Owen Swiny, and made her London début as Roxana in G.F. Handel's *Alessandro* at the King's Theatre in 1726, with FRANCESCA CUZZONI and SENESINO in the other leading roles. In the next two seasons (1727–8) she created four other Handel parts – Alcestis in *Admeto* (1727), Pulcheria in *Riccardo Primo* (1727), Emira in *Siroe* (1728) and Elisa in *Tolomeo* (1728) – and sang in Attilio Ariosti's *Lucio Vero* and *Teuzzone*, Giovanni Bononcini's *Astianatte* (in which she created Hermione in 1727) and Handel's *Radamisto*. Her rivalry with Cuzzoni, professional and personal, was notorious, and culminated in an exchange of blows on stage at a performance of *Astianatte* (6 June 1727), but despite this scandal they were both engaged for the following season. She sang at Florence, Parma, Turin, Milan, Rome, Naples and frequently at Venice in 1728–32; the operas included Orlandini's *Adelaide*, two by Giacomelli, and Johann Adolf Hasse's *Dalisa* (1730), *Arminio* (1730), *Demetrio* (in which she created Cleonice in 1732) and *Euristeo*. From her marriage to Hasse in 1730 she was associated chiefly with his music, and in 1731 both were summoned to the Saxon court at Dresden, where she enjoyed great success in his *Cleofide*. Hasse was Kapellmeister there for more than 30 years, and Faustina sang in at least 15 of his numerous operas between *Caio Fabricio* (1734) and *Ciro riconosciuto* (1751), but also paid many long visits to Italy, singing in Naples, Venice, Pesaro and other cities in operas by Vinci, Giovanni Battista Pergolesi and Nicola Porpora as well as Hasse. In all she sang in more than 30 operas in Venice. After retiring from the theatre in 1751 she kept her salary and her rank as *virtuosa da camera* until 1763. She and Hasse lived in Vienna until 1773, then in Venice; their two daughters were both trained as singers.

Faustina was universally ranked among the greatest singers of her age. Johann Quantz described her voice as a mezzo-soprano, 'less clear than penetrating', with a compass of *b* to *g″* (about a tone lower than Cuzzoni's range). In her Handel parts it is *c′* to *a″*. She was a very dramatic singer, with equal power and flexibility, and a fine actress. Esteban de Arteaga spoke of 'a matchless facility and rapidity in her execution…exquisite shake [and] new and brilliant passages of embellishment'. P.F. Tosi contrasted her pre-eminence in lively arias with Cuzzoni's gift for the pathetic, and considered the virtues of the two complementary.

An observer in 1721 remarked that Faustina 'always sang the first part of an aria exactly as the composer had written it but at the da capo repeat introduced all kinds of *doublements* and *maniere* without taking the smallest liberties with the rhythm of the accompaniment'. Burney emphasized her perfect intonation and exceptional breath control. His statement that 'E was a remarkably powerful note in this singer's voice, and we find most of her capital songs in sharp keys', is confirmed by the fact that half the arias Handel composed for her are in A or E, major or minor. Johann Quantz (translated by Charles Burney in *A General History of Music from the Earliest Ages to the Present Period* (London, 1776–89)) gives perhaps the clearest account of Faustina's quality:

> Her execution was articulate and brilliant. She had a fluent tongue for pronouncing words rapidly and distinctly, and a flexible throat for divisions, with so beautiful and quick a shake, that she could put it in motion upon short notice, just when she would. The passages might be smooth, or by leaps, or consist of iterations of the same tone, their execution was equally easy to her…She sung *adagios* with great passion and expression, but not equally well, if such deep sorrow were to be impressed on the hearer, as might require dragging, sliding, or notes of syncopation and *tempo rubato*. She had a very happy memory, in arbitrary changes and embellishments, and a clear and quick judgment in giving to words their full power and expression. In her action she was very happy; and as she perfectly possessed that flexibility of muscles and features, which

constitutes face-playing, she succeeded equally well in furious, amorous, and tender parts; in short, she was born for singing and for acting.

Pietro Metastasio described her and Hasse in 1744 as 'truly an exquisite couple'.

Winton Dean

Borg, Kim

(*b* Helsinki, 7 Aug 1919; *d* Copenhagen, 28 April 2000). Finnish bass-baritone and composer. He studied at the Sibelius Academy, Helsinki, and later in several cities abroad including Vienna, Rome and New York. He confined himself to concert work for three years and then made his operatic début in 1952 at Århus, Denmark, as Colline in *La bohème*. An international career opened up in 1956 when he sang at Salzburg and Glyndebourne, his roles there being Don Giovanni, Pizarro (1959) and Prince Gremin in *Yevgeny Onegin* (1968). He made his Metropolitan début in 1959 as Count Almaviva. From 1960 he was a member of the Swedish Royal Opera, also singing regularly in Hamburg where in 1966 he appeared in the world

Giuseppe Borgatti in the title role of 'Parsifal' (Wagner)

première of Gunther Schuller's *The Visitation*. His repertory included Boris and Pimen (sung in 1977 at Tel-Aviv), Baron Ochs, Méphistophélès and Osmin; he also sang Fafner and Hagen in the 1971 Stockholm *Ring*. Borg retired from the stage in 1980. From 1972 to 1989 he was professor of singing at the Copenhagen Conservatory. A fine linguist and a cultivated musician, he can be heard in many recordings from the 1950s and 60s (including Edward Elgar's *The Dream of Gerontius* with John Barbirolli) when his firm, full-bodied voice was in its prime. Borg also composed a number of orchestral works (including two symphonies, and concertos for trombone and double bass), chamber music, songs and a setting of the *Stabat mater*.

J.B. Steane/R

Borgatti, Giuseppe

(*b* Cento, Ferrara, 17 March 1871; *d* Reno di Leggiuno, Varese, 18 Oct 1950). Italian tenor. Of humble origin, he studied with Alessandro Busi at Bologna, and made his début in Charles Gounod's *Faust* at Castelfranco Veneto in 1892. During the following years he sang in Turin, Madrid and St Petersburg; at La Scala in 1896 he took the part of Andrea Chénier with great success in the opera's first performance. Over the next ten years he appeared in the leading Italian theatres and in Spain, Portugal and Argentina, most notably as Des Grieux in Giacomo Puccini's *Manon Lescaut* and as Cavaradossi, a role he sang in the Milan première of *Tosca* in 1900. From 1906 he devoted himself to Richard Wagner (having already sung Siegfried and Tristan at La Scala in 1899 and 1900 under Arturo Toscanini) with exceptional results. In 1914, after appearing in the Italian première of *Parsifal* (see illustration) at Bologna and La Scala, he was forced by glaucoma to retire from the stage, and in 1923 he became completely blind. He performed for the last time at a concert in Bologna in 1927, and subsequently devoted himself to teaching. His autobiography, *La mia vita d'artista*, was published in Bologna in 1927.

Borgatti's voice was large, robust and of beautiful timbre; he could also, especially in his early years, sing with delicacy and sweetness. Driven, perhaps, by his intensely dramatic temperament, he was the first tenor to introduce into the performance of *verismo* operas a forcefully emphatic delivery and an incisive, vehement declamatory manner. This was in contrast to the lyrical approach and virtuosity still frequently shown by the tenors of the preceding generation, such as ROBERTO STAGNO and FERNANDO DE LUCIA. These qualities, together with a strong physique, vigorous acting and remarkable insight into the character of his roles, made him an exceptional Heldentenor who did much to further the cause of Wagner's operas in Italy.

M. Scott: *The Record of Singing*, i: *To 1914* (London, 1977) 133–4

Rodolfo Celletti/Valeria Pregliasco Gualerzi

Borghi-Mamo [née Borghi], Adelaide

(*b* Bologna, 9 Aug 1826; *d* Bologna, 29 Sept 1901). Italian mezzo-soprano. She studied in Milan and made her début in 1843 at Urbino in Saverio Mercadante's *Il giuramento*. She sang in Italy and Vienna, then appeared in Paris at the Théâtre Italien as Azucena in the first performance in France of *Il trovatore* (1854) and at the Opéra as Léonore in *La favorite* (1856). She made her London début in 1860 at Her Majesty's Theatre, in the same two roles. She had a full-toned, vibrant voice and a passionate temperament. Her daughter Erminia Borghi-Mamo (1855–1941), a soprano, sang Margherita and Helen of Troy in Bologna in the successful revised version of Arrigo Boito's *Mefistofele* (1875).

Elizabeth Forbes

Borghi-Mamo, Erminia.

Soprano, daughter of ADELAIDE BORGHI-MAMO.

Borgioli, Dino

(*b* Florence, 15 Feb 1891; *d* Florence, 12 Sept 1960). Italian tenor. He studied with Eugenio Giachetti and made his début in 1914 as Arturo in *I puritani* at the Teatro Corso, Milan. More significantly he sang Fernand in *La favorite* under Tullio Serafin at Milan's Teatro Dal Verme in 1917. He was soon in demand for the lighter roles in other Italian theatres, and in 1918 began a long association with La Scala. His voice, of clear timbre but limited volume, was highly trained and well produced, and his elegant style made him a favourite in England, where he sang at Covent Garden (first in 1925, in *Lucia* and *Il barbiere di Siviglia* with TOTI DAL MONTE and in *Rigoletto* with EIDE NORENA; then in other roles, notably as Don Ramiro to the Cenerentola of CONCHITA SUPERVIA in 1934–5) and also at Glyndebourne (Don Ottavio 1937–9, Ernesto in *Don Pasquale* 1938). Borgioli also made some appearances in the USA, but settled in London as a teacher of singing, and acted as artistic director and producer to the Jay Pomeroy opera seasons of 1946–8 at the Cambridge Theatre. His recordings, which include complete versions of *Il barbiere di Siviglia* and *Rigoletto*, support his claim to be considered the best light tenor of his day after SCHIPA.

Desmond Shawe-Taylor

Borkh, Inge [Simon, Ingeborg]

(*b* Mannheim, 26 May 1917). Swiss soprano. She began her career as an actress, before studying singing in Milan and making her début in 1940 at Lucerne as Czipra (*Der Zigeunerbaron*), followed by Agathe. She appeared in Zürich, Munich, Berlin, Stuttgart, Vienna and Basle, where she sang Magda in the first German-language performance of *The Consul* (1951). She sang Freia and Sieglinde at Bayreuth (1952) and made her American début in 1953 at San Francisco as Richard Strauss's Electra, returning for Giuseppe Verdi's Lady Macbeth. In 1954 she sang Eglantine (*Euryanthe*) at Florence and in 1955 created Cathleen in Werner Egk's *Irische Legende* at Salzburg. She took part in the American première of Benjamin Britten's *Gloriana* (1956, Cincinnati) and made her débuts at the Metropolitan (1958) and at Covent Garden (1959) as Salome. A notable exponent of 20th-century opera, she counted Turandot, Carl Orff's Antigone and Ernest Bloch's Lady Macbeth among her roles, as well as the Dyer's Wife (*Die Frau ohne Schatten*). Her voice, bright and incisive, was capable of great dramatic intensity. Her Turandot, Salome and Antigone are preserved on disc. In 1977 she returned to straight acting.

Alan Blyth

Borodina, Olga

(*b* Leningrad, 29 July 1963). Russian mezzo-soprano. In 1987, while still a student at the Leningrad Conservatory, she joined the Kirov Opera, where her first role was Siebel. She quickly became one of the company's leading members, and television relays of *Boris Godunov* and *War and Peace*, allied to early success in international competitions, brought her to attention in the West. Modest Petrovich Musorgsky's Marina was also the role of her Paris (1992), Salzburg and Metropolitan Opera (both 1997) débuts; she has recorded the part, along with such roles as Marfa (*Khovanshchina*), Hélène Bezukhova (*War and Peace*), Konchakovna (*Prince Igor*), Olga and Preziosilla (in the original version of *La forza del destino*), mostly with the Kirov. Further Russian parts include Lyubasha (*The Tsar's Bride*), Laura (*The Stone Guest*) and the title role of Musorgsky's *Salammbô* (in concert). She is admired in French repertory; since making her Covent Garden début in 1992 as Dalila she has sung the part widely and recorded it. Carmen is another of Borodina's signature roles (she sang it to acclaim at the Metropolitan in the 2000–01 season), and she has also sung Marguerite in *La damnation de Faust*. She sang Angelina (*La Cenerentola*) at Covent Garden (1994) and San Francisco (her début there, 1995), recorded Eboli, and undertook her first Amneris on stage in Vienna in 1998, repeating the role at the Metropolitan in the 2000–01 season. She is also a regular on the recital platform (making her Wigmore Hall début in 2000) and has recorded an admired disc of Tchaikovsky songs and a disc of solos and duets (with DMITRY HVOROSTOVSKY) by Gioachino Rossini, Gaetano Donizetti, Camille Saint-Saëns and Nikolay Andreyevich Rimsky-Korsakov. While she is not always specific in her characterizations, her rich, liquid tone makes her one of the most sought-after Russian singers of her generation.

John Allison

Borosini [Boresini, Borosino], **Antonio**

(*b* Venice or Modena, *c*1655; *d* Vienna, after 1721). Italian tenor, father of FRANCESCO BOROSINI. He sang at S Marco, Venice, 1679–87, then moved to the ducal chapel at Modena, singing in oratorios and at the Teatro Fontanelli (1690, Giovanni Legrenzi's *Eteocle e Polinice*) and in Parma and Reggio nell'Emilia. In 1688 he was released at the request of the Elector of Hanover to sing in the première of Agostino Steffani's *Henrico Leone* (30 January 1689); he returned to Hanover for Carnival 1696. He was appointed to the imperial court at Vienna in 1692 and retired in 1711 (or 1721, according to J.G. Walther's *Musicalisches Lexicon*, Leipzig, 1732). He sang at the S Bartolomeo, Naples (1700, 1706–7), in Turin (1698, 1702), in Venice (1704–7, in serenatas and operas by C.F. Pollarolo and Antonio Caldara), in Genoa (1691, 1705, Caldara's *Arminio*) and at Pratolino (1707, G.A. Perti's *Dionisio*). His last theatrical appearance may have been in Vienna, in F.B. Conti's *Alba Cornelia* (1714). He was usually cast as heroic and solemn characters such as kings or military leaders. He was also a composer; some arias are extant.

Carlo Vitali

Borosini [Borseni], **Francesco**

(*b* Modena, *c*1690; *d* after 1747). Tenor, son of ANTONIO BOROSINI. A pupil of his father, he probably made his début in Antonio Lotti's *Il vincitor generoso* at Venice in 1709. He was engaged for the imperial court at Vienna from 1712 to 1731, and sang there in 11 oratorios by Antonio Caldara and a number

of operas by Johann Joseph Fux, the first (*Orfeo ed Euridice*) in 1715, and Franceso Bartolomeo Conti; he also created the title role in Porsile's *Spartaco* (1726). He was in the famous production of Fux's *Costanza e Fortezza* in Prague (1723), and was for a time co-director of the Kärntnertortheater in Vienna. He sang the title role in Francesco Gasparini's *Bajazet* (1719, Reggio nell'Emilia); the libretto was extensively rewritten for this production, and Borosini provided the inspiration for the revised finale. He also appeared at Modena (1720) and Parma (1729). He made his London début as Bajazet in G.F. Handel's *Tamerlano* at the King's Theatre (1724); he collaborated in Handel's treatment of this subject, and the part was rewritten for him before performance. Borosini sang Sextus (a soprano part rewritten with new music) in *Giulio Cesare* and was the original Grimoaldo in *Rodelinda* (1725); he also appeared in Attilio Ariosti's *Artaserse* and *Dario* and the Vinci-Orlandini *Elpidia*. He returned in 1747 to sing in Domenico Paradies's *Fetonte* and Domènech Miguel Bernabé Terradellas's *Bellerofonte*. A collection of *One Hundred Cantici in Italian after the Manner of English Canons and Catches* by 'Signor Borosini', published in London about this time, is attributed to him.

Borosini was the first great Italian tenor to sing in London. Johann Quantz called him a splendid singer and a fine actor, with a voice 'extraordinarily supple and lively' ('ausserordentlich biegsam und lebhaft'). The parts Handel composed for him were of exceptional quality and prominence, especially Bajazet, which has a compass of two octaves (*A* to *a'*) and requires a wide range of expression and dramatic power. Gasparini's parts for him extend down to *G*; Fux's are notated in the bass clef. He excelled in a forceful style of singing, with wide leaps and energetic declamation. He was married to the soprano ROSA BOROSINI.

Winton Dean

Borosini [née d'Ambreville], **Rosa**

(*b* Modena, *c*1693; *d* after 1740). Italian soprano, wife of FRANCESCO BOROSINI. She was the daughter of the second *maestro di cappella* at Modena, and probably married Borosini in 1722. She sang in opera at Modena (1713–14, 1717 and 1720), Venice (1715–16), Mantua (1718) and Turin (1719). On 1 March 1721 she was engaged for Vienna at a salary of 1800 florins, retiring on a pension in 1740. She sang in a number of oratorios by Caldara and in the première of Johann Joseph Fux's *Costanza e Fortezza* at Prague in August 1723. Her sister Anna (wife of the cellist Giovanni Perroni) sang at Bologna (1711), Modena (1713), Venice (1714 and 1726) and

Milan (1728). She was engaged for Vienna at the same time as Rosa, but at a lower salary. Both singers sang in Antonio Vivaldi's operatic undertakings in Venice and Mantua. Eleonora Borosini, a singer active at Innsbruck, Düsseldorf and Mannheim (1714–23), was not related to Rosa and Anna, but may have been related to Rosa's father-in-law, ANTONIO BOROSINI.

Winton Dean

Boschi, Giuseppe Maria

(*b* Viterbo; *fl* 1698–1744). Italian bass. He married the contralto FRANCESCA VANINI, probably in 1698, but does not appear in cast lists until 1703, when he sang the role of Oronte in Francesco Gasparini's *Il più fedel fra i vassali* at Casale Monferrato. He appeared in Venice in four operas by Francesco Gasparini and two by Lotti in 1707, and was re-engaged there in 1708–9 and 1713–14, singing in five further operas by Antonio Lotti and others by Antonio Caldara, G.F. Handel (*Agrippina*, 1709) and C.F. Pollarolo. He sang at Vicenza in 1707, Ferrara and Vienna in 1708, Bologna in 1709, 1717 and 1719, Verona in 1715, and Genoa in 1717. He made his London début with the Queen's Theatre company in Mancini's *Idaspe fedele* (1710), sang in Giovanni Bononcini's *Etearco* and created Argante in Handel's *Rinaldo* (1711). From 1714 he was a member of the choir at S Marco, Venice, but was allowed frequent leaves of absence. He was at Dresden from 1717 to 1720, singing in Lotti's *Giove in Argo* (1717), *Ascanio* (1718) and *Teofane* (1719). Handel engaged him from 1720 to 1728 in London, where he sang in all 32 operas produced by the Royal Academy. Among his Handel premières at the Royal Academy were Emireno in *Ottone* (1723), Achillas in *Giulio Cesare in Egitto* (1724), Leo in *Tamerlano* (1724), Garibaldo in *Rodelinda* (1725), Clitus in *Alessandro* (1726), Ernando in *Scipione* (1726), Hercules in *Admeto* (1727), Isaac in *Riccardo Primo* (1727) and Araspe in *Tolomeo* (1728). He also sang in seven operas each by Giovanni Bononcini and Attilio Ariosti. He reappeared in Venice in 1728–9 in three operas, two by Porpora, and was still living there in 1744.

Boschi's voice had a compass of *G* to *g'* and the tessitura of a high baritone. James Miller's line 'And Boschi-like be always in a rage' points to the style in which he excelled. He usually played villains or tyrants, and the power and agility of his voice encouraged Handel to accompany many of his arias with energetic counterpoint, though the voice is often doubled by the instrumental bass. In 15 operas Handel scarcely ever allowed him a slow aria. Lotti wrote very similarly for him in *Teofane*.

Winton Dean

Bostridge, Ian (Charles)

(*b* London, 25 Dec 1964). English tenor. He read history and philosophy at both Oxford and Cambridge (and later published a work on witchcraft in the 18th century) before he embarked on singing studies with various teachers, at the Britten-Pears School at Aldeburgh, and finally with DIETRICH FISCHER-DIESKAU. Bostridge made his recital début at the Wigmore Hall in London in 1993, and his opera début at Covent Garden as the Fourth Jew in *Salome* (1995). He sang a much acclaimed Peter Quint with the Royal Opera at the Barbican Theatre in 1997, made his ENO début, as Tamino, in 1996, and returned to the Royal Opera as Vašek (*The Bartered Bride*) in 1998. In 2001 he sang the title role in *Idomeneo* at the Edinburgh Festival. He was also much praised for his Hylas in concert performances of *Les Troyens*, under Colin Davis, in London (1993). In recital he has become a leading exponent of lieder (in particular *Die schöne Müllerin* and *Winterreise*) and of the songs of Benjamin Britten, and is also a penetrating interpreter of the Evangelist in both Bach Passions. His recordings include Belmonte in *Die Entführung*, Sellem and Tom Rakewell in different sets of *The Rake's Progress*, *Die schöne Müllerin*, *Winterreise* (in a film made for television), *Dichterliebe*, Leoš Janáček's *Diary of One Who Disappeared* (which he has performed in London, in a production by Deborah Warner), and Britten's *Serenade*. All disclose his peculiarly attractive, silvery tenor and his innate gift for pointing every facet of a text. In 2000 Bostridge premièred and recorded *Six Songs from the Arabian*, written for him by Hans Werner Henze. (See colour plate 14.)

Alan Blyth

Bott, Catherine

(*b* Leamington Spa, 11 Sept 1952). English soprano. After studying at the GSM with Arthur Reckless she spent several years as a member of Swingle II. In 1980 she began to appear regularly in the New London Consort, and subsequently worked with other British period-instrument ensembles in Europe, Latin America and the USSR. She has established herself as a leading virtuoso in 17th-century music, from Giulio Caccini and Claudio Monteverdi to John Blow and Henry Purcell, of whose mad songs she is a noted exponent. Her recordings, which include Salome in Alessandro Stradella's *San Giovanni Battista*, Handel arias and Gabriel Fauré's *Requiem*, reveal her acute dramatic perception and distinctive sensuality. As Purcell's Dido, which she recorded with Christopher Hogwood in 1994, Bott exhibits a brooding nobility which has won many plaudits.

Jonathan Freeman-Attwood

Bouhy, Jacques (-Joseph-André)

(*b* Pepinster, 18 June 1848; *d* Paris, 29 Jan 1929). Belgian baritone and singing teacher. He studied at the Conservatoire Royal in Liège and in Paris, where he made his début at the Opéra in 1871 as Méphistophélès in *Faust*. At the Opéra-Comique, where he was first heard as W.A. Mozart's Figaro (1872), he created the title role of Jules Massenet's *Don César de Bazan*. The same year, he sang Hoël in *Le pardon de Ploërmel* (1874) and Escamillo at the première of *Carmen* (3 March 1875). At the Théâtre-Lyrique he took part in Victor Massé's *Paul et Virginie* (1876) and Gaston Salvayre's *Le bravo* (1877), both first performances. Returning to the Opéra (1878–9), he sang Alphonse (*La favorite*), Ambroise Thomas' Hamlet and Don Giovanni. In 1880 at St Petersburg he sang Méphistophélès in Charles Gounod's *Faust* and the title role in Arrigo Boito's *Mefistofele*, and in 1882 he appeared at Covent Garden in *Faust* and *Carmen*. After some years in the USA, where he founded and directed the National Conservatory of Music in New York, he returned to Paris to sing the High Priest in the first staged performance there of Camille Saint-Saëns's *Samson et Dalila* (Eden-Théâtre, 1890). From 1904 to 1907 he was again in the USA, and later he taught singing in Paris. His voice was praised by Massenet early in the singer's career, and his rendering of the Toreador's Song always evoked the warmest applause, even at the first, unsuccessful, performance of *Carmen*.

Elizabeth Forbes

Bourdin, Roger

(*b* Levallois, 14 June 1900; *d* Paris, 14 Sept 1973). French baritone. After studying at the Paris Conservatoire with ANDRÉ GRESSE and Jacques Isnardon, he made his début at the Opéra-Comique as Lescaut in *Manon* (1922) and sang there regularly until the mid-1960s in a wide range of roles, creating parts in operas by Gabriel Pierné, Jacques Ibert and Marcel Bertrand. His début at the Opéra, as Mârouf, was in 1942, and he created the title role of Darius Milhaud's *Bolivar* there in 1950. His only appearance at Covent Garden was as Pelléas to the Mélisande of MAGGIE TEYTE in 1930. He was a notable French interpreter of non-French parts, including Beckmesser, Scarpia and W.A. Mozart's Figaro. He sang Athanaël to the Thaïs of his wife, the soprano Geori Boué, at the Opéra during the 1940s. His voice was a warm, mellifluous, typically French baritone, as can be heard on his many recordings.

Alan Blyth

Bowman, James (Thomas)

(*b* Oxford, 6 Nov 1941). English countertenor. He studied at Oxford University and made his stage début in 1967 at Aldeburgh as Benjamin Britten's Oberon, a role he has sung at Covent Garden, Strasbourg, Sydney, with the WNO and at Glyndebourne, where he made his début in 1970 as Endymion in Francesco Cavalli's *Calisto*. He created the Priest-Confessor in Peter Maxwell Davies's *Taverner* (1972), his Covent Garden début; the voice of Apollo in *Death in Venice* (1973, Aldeburgh Festival); Astron (with Anne Wilkens) in Michael Tippett's *The Ice Break* (1977, Covent Garden); and sang Alan Ridout's *Phaeton* for BBC Radio. Britten dedicated his fourth Canticle, *Journey of the Magi*, to him, Peter Pears and John Shirley-Quirk. Bowman is a noted Handelian, and for the Handel Opera Society sang Otho, Scipio, Xerxes and Justinian, as well as Polinesso (*Ariodante*), which he repeated at Geneva and Buxton. His other Handel roles include Julius Caesar (Barber Institute), Ptolemy (San Francisco and the ENO), Goffredo in *Rinaldo* (Reggio nell'Emilia and Paris) and Orlando (Scottish Opera). He has also sung many other Baroque roles, including Lidio in Cavalli's *Egisto* at Santa Fe, Ruggiero in Antonio Vivaldi's *Orlando furioso* at Verona and Dallas, Claudio Monteverdi's Otho at Spitalfields and Epaphus in Niccolò Jommelli's *Fetonte* at La Scala. Bowman has been partly responsible for the present wide acceptance of the countertenor voice in modern and Baroque opera. He also sings often in oratorio and solo recitals, and is a specially fine interpreter of Elizabethan lute-songs. His voice is expressive and individual in timbre and he uses it to highly dramatic effect. His extensive recording career has included operatic roles ranging from Orlando and Julius Caesar to Britten's Oberon and voice of Apollo, lute-songs, choral works by Henry Purcell, J.S. Bach and G.F. Handel, and songs by Britten. He was created a CBE in 1997.

Alan Blyth

Braham, John

(*b* London, 20 March 1774; *d* London, 17 Feb 1856). English tenor and composer. His origins are obscure: both parents (his father is variously described as a German or Portuguese Jew) died when he was young. At the Great Synagogue in Duke's Place the boy's voice attracted the attention of the singer Leoni (Meyer Leon) and of the financier Abraham Goldsmid. Leoni, sometimes described as Braham's uncle, trained him and introduced him as a boy soprano at Covent Garden on 21 April 1787, when he sang Thomas Arne's 'The Soldier, Tir'd of War's Alarms', from *Artaxerxes*, and later at the Royalty

Theatre, Wellclose Square. When Leoni went to the West Indies and Braham's voice broke, with Goldsmid's help he became a piano teacher. After his voice had settled he spent three years at Bath studying with VENANZIO RAUZZINI. He made some appearances there, and met NANCY STORACE, a former pupil of Rauzzini. As a result he was engaged in 1796 to sing at Drury Lane in her brother Stephen's opera *Mahmoud*, left unfinished when Storace died that year, but completed by Nancy. He appeared at the Italian Opera in André-Ernest-Modeste Grétry's *Zémire et Azor*, also at the Three Choirs Festival at Gloucester, before leaving with Nancy Storace for a tour of the Continent in 1797. The couple gave concerts in Paris on the way to Italy. In 1798 they reached Florence, where Braham was heard at the Teatro della Pergola. Two years were spent at Milan, where they appeared together at La Scala in Sebastiano Nasolini's *Il trionfo di Clelia*, and where Braham emerged victorious from a contest with Mrs Billington. At Genoa he took lessons in composition with Gaetano Isola. At Livorno he was befriended by Lord Nelson. At Venice Domenico Cimarosa wrote *Artemisia* for him, but died in 1801 before completing it (the opera was performed, however, and Braham sang in it). At Trieste he appeared in Vicente Martín y Soler's *Una cosa rara*.

Braham's foreign success was noted in England. In Vienna he received offers to return to London, and did so by way of Hamburg. Towards the end of 1801 he made his adult début at Covent Garden in *The Chains of the Heart*, soon followed by *The Cabinet*; for this he wrote the music of his own part, a procedure he followed for some years, and by which he became the collaborator of various composers, including Henry R. Bishop and Thomas Attwood. His ballads, duets and patriotic songs, especially *The Death of Nelson* in *The Americans* (1811), won great popularity. Between 1804 and 1806 he appeared in Italian opera at the King's Theatre, notably in the latter year as Sesto in the first London performance of *La clemenza di Tito*. Braham was a showman who gave his various audiences what they wanted, whether singing of high quality, stirring patriotic sentiment or florid, tasteless ornament. His voice was a magnificent, durable instrument, with a range of *A* to *e''*, the scale so even that the change to falsetto was said to be imperceptible. Scott declared him 'a beast of an actor but an angel of a singer'. His diction was generally agreed to be excellent. In a letter (1816) Mary Russell Mitford wrote:

He is the only singer I have ever heard in my life who ever conveyed to my very unmusical ears any idea of the expression to which music is susceptible; no one else joins any sense to the sound. They may talk of music as married to

John Braham, drawing, 1831

immortal verse, but if it were not for Braham they would have been divorced long ago.

'Braham...can be two distinct singers', wrote Richard, Earl of Mount-Edgcumbe, who had reservations about him during the early part of his career, but on hearing him sing Handel during the 1834 Festival in Westminster Abbey was impressed not only by the undiminished brilliance of the voice but by the singer's 'most perfect taste and judgment'. He impressed Carl Maria von Weber, who wrote the part of Sir Huon in *Oberon* (1826) for him (and at Braham's insistence wrote the aria, 'O, 'tis a glorious sight to see' to replace 'From boyhood trained', and added the Preghiera 'Ruler of this awful hour'); Braham had already sung Max in the first English adaptation of *Der Freischütz* at the Lyceum in 1824.

Braham's liaison with Storace, which produced a son, lasted until 1816, when they parted on acrimonious terms and he married Frances Elizabeth Bolton. His worldly success was considerable. The Duke of Sussex was godfather to one of his sons. George IV, on a private occasion when his singing had been especially brilliant, was with difficulty restrained from knighting him on the spot. Braham made a large fortune, but his wife persuaded him to put money into two unsuccessful ventures, the purchase in 1831 of the Colosseum (an entertainment palace designed by Decimus Burton) in Regent's Park, and the building of St James's Theatre in 1835, and he was forced to resume his public career. As his voice had become lower, he appeared at Drury Lane in the baritone title roles of *William Tell* (1838) and *Don Giovanni* (1839). In 1840–42 he made a tour of North America with his son Charles that was only partly successful. In England he continued to sing at concerts in London and the provinces until his final public appearance at one of the popular Wednesday Concerts in March 1852, when he was well over 70. The Brahams had six children. Three sons, Charles, Hamilton and Augustus, became singers. The daughter, Frances, Countess Waldegrave, was a leading social and political hostess of the Victorian era. Braham's illegitimate son by Nancy Storace took holy orders and became a minor canon of Canterbury, in 1851, changing his name to Meadows.

R. Edgcumbe, 2nd Earl of Mount Edgcumbe: *Musical Reminiscences* (London, 1824, 4/1834/*R*)
J.M. Levien: *The Singing of John Braham* (London, 1945)

Ronald Crichton

Brambilla, Giuseppina

(*b* Cassano d'Adda, 1819; *d* Milan, 1903). Italian contralto, sister of MARIETTA and TERESA BRAMBILLA. She made her début in Trieste in 1841 and sang in Rome, Milan and Barcelona; then in 1846 she was engaged at Her Majesty's Theatre, London, where she appeared as Maffio Orsini, the part created by her eldest sister. In 1853 she sang Maddaleno (*Rigoletto*) at La Scala.

Elizabeth Forbes

Brambilla, Marietta

(*b* Cassano d'Adda, 6 June 1807; *d* Milan, 6 Nov 1875). Contralto, sister of GIUSEPPINA and TERESA BRAMBILLA. After studying at the Milan Conservatory with Antonio Secchi, she made her début in 1827 at the King's Theatre, London, as Arsace in Gioachino Rossini's *Semiramide*. During the season she sang two more travesty roles, Adriano (Giacomo Meyerbeer's *Il crociato*) and Romeo (Niccolò Antonio Zingarelli's *Romeo e Giulietta*), becoming a specialist in such parts. She sang Paolo at the first performance of Generali's *Francescà di Rimini* in 1828 at La Fenice. At La Scala (1838) she sang Cherubino and Arsace (*Semiramide*). Gaetano Donizetti composed two trouser roles for her, Maffio Orsini in *Lucrezia Borgia*, first given at La Scala in 1833, and Pierotto in *Linda di Chamounix*, which had its première at the Kärntnertortheater,

Vienna, in 1842. He also adapted the second tenor role of Armando di Gondi in *Maria di Rohan* for her, adding an extra number, when the opera was performed at the Théâtre Italien in Paris (1843). She also sang Pippo in *La gazza ladra* and Smeton in *Anna Bolena*. In 1848 she retired. Her voice, a true contralto, ranged from *g* to *g"*.

Brambilla, Teresa

(*b* Cassano d'Adda, 23 Oct 1813; *d* Milan, 15 July 1895). Soprano, sister of GIUSEPPINA and MARIETTA BRAMBILLA. She made her début in Milan in 1831 and sang throughout Italy with great success for 15 years. In 1846 she appeared in Paris as Abigaille in *Nabucco*. She sang Gilda at the first performance of *Rigoletto* at La Fenice (1851), while other Verdi operas in which she appeared included *Luisa Miller* and *Ernani*.

Brambilla-Ponchielli, Teresa [Teresina]

(*b* Cassano d'Adda, 15 April 1845; *d* Vercelli, 1 July 1921). Italian soprano, niece of MARIETTA BRAMBILLA. She studied with her aunts Marietta and Teresa. She made her début in 1863 as Adalgisa at Odessa, afterwards singing in Lisbon, Madrid, Paris, St Petersburg and Italy. In 1872 she sang in the revised version of Amilcare Ponchielli's *I promessi sposi* at the Teatro dal Verme, Milan, and two years later married the composer. She was a famous interpreter of the title role of *La Gioconda*, and sang Paolina in a revival of Gaetano Donizetti's *Poliuto* at the Teatro Costanzi, Rome (1883). Other roles that she sang included Leonora (*Il trovatore* and *La forza del destino*), Aida and Elsa (*Lohengrin*). She retired in 1889.

Elizabeth Forbes

Brandram, Rosina (Moult)

(*b* Southwark, London, 2 July 1845; *d* Southend, 28 Feb 1907). English contralto. She was engaged by Richard D'Oyly Carte as an understudy for Isabella Howard Paul in the original production of Gilbert and Sullivan's *The Sorcerer* (1877) and filled her place towards the end of the run. She played Kate in the New York première of *The Pirates of Penzance* (1879), and assumed the principal contralto parts in Carte's London company, beginning with Lady Blanche in *Princess Ida* (1884). Brandram was intimately connected with the Gilbert and Sullivan operas, remaining with the D'Oyly Carte company for well over 20 years. She created Katisha in *The Mikado* (1885) and the Duchess of Plaza-Toro in

The Gondoliers (1889) and took principal roles in Sullivan's later comic works, including Dancing Sunbeam in *The Rose of Persia* (1900), and in Edward German's Savoy operas.

She performed only in comic opera, nearly always in roles written for her, and seldom appeared outside London. Although typecast in matronly, sometimes unsympathetic, roles, Brandram was not unattractive. Her deep, rich voice was characterized by Gilbert (in a speech to the O.P. Club, 30 December 1906) as 'full-bodied burgundy'.

Fredric Woodbridge Wilson

Brandt, Marianne [Bischoff, Marie]

(*b* Vienna, 12 Sept 1842; *d* Vienna, 9 July 1921). Austrian mezzo-soprano. She studied in Vienna and in Baden-Baden with PAULINE VIARDOT, making her début at Olmütz in 1867 as Rachel (*La Juive*). She first appeared in Berlin in 1868 as Azucena, and was engaged there until 1882. After making her London début at Covent Garden in *Fidelio* (1872), she sang Amneris in the first Berlin performance of *Aida* (1874) and Waltraute in *Götterdämmerung* during the first Bayreuth Festival (1876). At Bayreuth she also sang Kundry at the second performance of *Parsifal* (1882). Her other Wagner roles included Brangäne, which she sang at the first Berlin (1876), London (1882) and New York (1886) performances of *Tristan und Isolde*, Ortrud, Fricka (*Die Walküre*), Magdalene, Adriano (*Rienzi*) and Erda (*Siegfried*). The extensive compass (*g* to *d'''*) of her large and well-projected voice enabled her to sing both soprano and mezzo-soprano parts; at the Metropolitan, where she appeared from 1884 to 1888, her roles included Leonore, Fidès (*Le prophète*), Siébel (*Faust*), Venus (*Tannhäuser*), the coloratura role of Astaroth, in the American première of Karl Goldmark's *Die Königin von Saba* (1885), and Eglantine, which she sang at the first American performance of Carl Maria von Weber's *Euryanthe* (1887). After her retirement in 1890 she taught in Vienna.

Elizabeth Forbes

Brandt-Forster, Ellen

(*b* Vienna, 11 Oct 1866; *d* Vienna, July 1921). Austrian soprano. She studied in Vienna with Dustmann, making her début in 1885 at Danzig as Marguerite in Charles Gounod's *Faust*. In 1886 she appeared as a flowermaiden at Bayreuth and in 1887 joined the Hofoper, Vienna, where she remained until her retirement in 1909. She sang Clarissa in *Die drei Pintos* (1889) and Lola in *Cavalleria rusticana* (1891), both first Vienna performances, and created Sophie in *Werther* (1892). A stylish singer with a pure-toned, flexible voice, she made a charming Adele in the first performance at the Hofoper of *Die Fledermaus* (1894).

Elizabeth Forbes

Brannigan, Owen

(*b* Annitsford, Northumberland, 10 March 1908; *d* Newcastle upon Tyne, 9 May 1973). English bass. He studied part-time at the GSM, London, and won its gold medal in 1942. He made his début in 1943 with the Sadler's Wells Opera as Sarastro, and sang with the company until 1948, and again from 1952 to 1958. As well as specializing in W.A. Mozart and *buffo* characters, he created Benjamin Britten's Swallow (*Peter Grimes*, 1945), Collatinus (*The Rape of Lucretia*, 1946) and Superintendent Budd (*Albert Herring*, 1947); Britten later composed Noye (*Noye's Fludde*, 1958) and Bottom (*A Midsummer Night's Dream*, 1960) for him; a comic actor of great charm, in the latter role he remains unsurpassed, as can be heard in his recording under the composer. Brannigan also created roles in operas by Malcolm Williamson and John Gardner. A member of the English Opera Group, he performed at Glyndebourne from 1947 and at Covent Garden from 1948, as well as appearing frequently in oratorio and concerts in Britain and abroad. With a voice of expressive tone and ripe verbal inflection, he gained a wide popularity in radio and television programmes of Northumbrian and other folksongs, many of which he recorded. Brannigan's other recordings include roles in Henry Purcell's *Fairy Queen* (under Britten), Francesco Cavalli's *La Calisto* (with Raymond Leppard), operas by Britten, and several by Gilbert and Sullivan (with Malcolm Sargent). He was made an OBE in 1964. In 1972 he was involved in a road accident from which he never fully recovered.

Noël Goodwin

Braun, Victor (Conrad)

(*b* Windsor, ON, 4 Aug 1935; *d* Brussels, 6 Jan 2001). Canadian baritone. He studied with LILIAN WATSON and at the Royal Conservatory of Music, Toronto. He joined the Canadian Opera Company in 1961, making his début as Escamillo. In 1963 he joined the Frankfurt Opera and in 1968 the Staatsoper in Munich. He made his Covent Garden début in 1969 as Hamlet in the first London performance of Humphrey Searle's opera and also sang there as Count Almaviva and Yevgeny Onegin and in several Verdi roles. At Santa Fe he sang Jupiter in *Die Liebe der Danae* (1982), Mandryka in *Arabella* (1983), the General in *We Come to the River*

(1984) and Holofernes in the American première of Siegfried Matthus's *Judith* (1990). His repertory also included Wolfram, which he sang at La Scala and the Metropolitan and recorded under Georg Solti. In the later part of his career he became a noted Hans Sachs, a role which he first sang in Nice (1986) and repeated at the opening of the Essen opera house, and Wozzeck, which he sang in Chicago (1988). During 1989 he sang Pizarro at Brussels, Golaud at Florence and Dr Schön in San Francisco. Braun's soft-grained voice, accomplished if not particularly individual, has developed considerable power without losing its beautiful lyric quality and was enhanced by his gifts as an actor.

Harold Rosenthal/Alan Blyth

Bréjean-Silver [Bréjean-Gravière], Georgette [née Sisout, Georgette-Amélie]

(*b* Paris, 22 Sept 1870; *d* after 1951). French soprano. She studied at the Conservatoire and made her début at Bordeaux in 1890. She joined the Opéra-Comique in 1894, making a strong impression as Manon, which remained a favourite role; Jules Massenet wrote the 'Fabliau' (as an alternative to the gavotte in Act 3) for her to sing at a performance in Brussels. She appeared in *Manon* and *Lakmé* at Monte Carlo the following season, adding *Les pêcheurs de perles* and *Guillaume Tell* a year later. At this time she sang under the name Bréjean-Gravière, changing it on her marriage to the composer Charles Silver, whose opera *La belle au bois dormant* provided her with another leading part. She also appeared as the Fairy Godmother in the première (1899) of Massenet's *Cendrillon*. On retirement she taught in Paris, having made some recordings in 1905 and 1906. Though a trifle shrill, they show exceptional accomplishments and hint at the possession of a charming manner.

J.B. Steane

Brewer, Christine

(*b* Grand Towers, IL, 26 Oct 1955). American soprano. After graduation from McKendree College in Lebanon, Illinois, she worked for several years as a schoolteacher while taking private singing lessons. She subsequently studied for a short period in Germany with BIRGIT NILSSON, whom she cites as a major influence on her vocal development. Having joined the chorus of the Opera Theatre of St Louis in 1980, she progressed, via small roles, to the part of Ellen Orford, her major operatic début (1989). Other leading roles followed at St Louis, includ-

ing Donna Anna, Ariadne, Haydn's Armida and Gloriana. Brewer made her New York City Opera début, as the Countess in *Le nozze di Figaro*, in 1993, and her Covent Garden début, in the same role, in 1994. Her sumptuous, soaring tone and gleaming top notes drew critical superlatives when she sang Ariadne at her ENO début in 1997. She has since sung the role to equal acclaim in Lyon and Santa Fe, and for her Metropolitan Opera début in 2003.

When Brewer sang her first Isolde, in concert performances at the Barbican in London in 2000, critics hailed her performance as the most affecting and beautifully sung in recent memory. She has since sung the role in the USA and at the 2005 Edinburgh Festival, and has recorded it. Another role with which she is closely associated is Leonore in *Fidelio*, which she sang at Covent Garden in 2006, having already recorded the part in English. In 2007 she scored a triumph at the Proms with her first Brünnhilde in *Götterdämmerung*. On the concert platform Brewer has been especially admired in works such as Ludwig van Beethoven's Ninth Symphony, Giuseppe Verdi's *Requiem*, and Richard Strauss's *Vier letzte Lieder*, which she has recorded with Donald Runnicles. Her other recordings include Donna Anna, Samuel Barber's *Vanessa*, W.A. Mozart's Requiem and lieder by Franz Schubert and Richard Strauss.

Richard Wigmore

Broadfoot, Eleanor.

See CISNEROS, ELEONORA DE.

Bronhill, June [Gough, June Mary]

(*b* Broken Hill, 26 Feb 1929; *d* Sydney, 25 Jan 2005). Australian soprano. She won a singing competition in Australia and in 1952 moved to England to further her career, first studying with DINO BORGIOLI, then joining the Sadler's Wells Opera company in 1954. She worked with the company through the early 1960s, singing roles that included Norina, the Queen of Night, Papagena, Zerbinetta, Leïla, Gilda and Lucy in Gian Carlo Menotti's *The Telephone*. In 1960 she appeared at Covent Garden in the title role of *Lucia di Lammermoor*. The following year she sang the title role in the first performance in the UK of Leoš Janáček's *The Cunning Little Vixen*, in which her performance was praised for its 'clear and straightforward' singing and 'telling and authentic gestures'. She followed JOAN SUTHERLAND in Gaetano Donizetti's *Lucia* on the Covent Garden tour in 1959. During the early seasons of Australian Opera at the Sydney Opera House she sang Blonde in *Die Entführung* and Adele in *Die Fledermaus*. She had special success at Sadler's Wells in operettas by Jacques Offenbach, Johann Strauss and Franz

Lehár, and especially as Hannah Glewari in *Die lustige Witwe*. She called her autobiography *The Merry Bronhill* (London, 1987) and her voice can be heard in its prime on recordings of this role, and in *The King and I* and *Lilac Time*, and especially as Sombra in *The Arcadians*. She returned to London in 1974 to sing Hanna once again at the Coliseum as well as Magda in Giacomo Puccini's *La rondine* with the English Opera Group.

She created the major role of Elizabeth Moulton-Barrett in Ronald Millar and Ron Grainer's *Robert and Elizabeth* (1964), whose vocal part, atypical for a musical, particularly suited her through its high tessitura, wide vocal range and lyricism. Other roles included Maria and later the Mother Superior in *The Sound of Music*, as well as many further appearances in *Die lustige Witwe*. On returning to Australia her versatility was demonstrated by appearances in shows ranging from *Women Behind Bars* through *A Little Night Music* to *My Fair Lady*. Her vibrant personality and her voice, clear and true with exemplary diction, easily filled the largest theatres, despite her small stature. She was awarded an OBE in 1976.

Paul Webb/R

Bronskaya, Eugenia

(*b* St Petersburg, 20 Jan/1 Feb 1882; *d* Leningrad, 12 Dec 1953). Russian soprano. She studied first with her mother in Russia and later with Teresa Arkel in Milan. After her début at Tbilisi in 1901 she sang for three years in Kiev and from 1905 to 1907 in Moscow. Returning to Italy she performed Tatyana in the Venice première of *Yevgeny Onegin*. She toured widely until 1909, when she joined the Boston Opera Company, making her début there as Micaëla in *Carmen*. Other roles included Marguerite de Valois in *Les Huguenots*, Gilda in *Rigoletto* and on one occasion the title role in *Lucia di Lammermoor*, which she undertook for an indisposed colleague as the curtain was about to rise, knowing no more than the Sextet and Mad Scene. At this period she also became well known as a recording artist, and on her return to Russia in 1911 was engaged at the Mariinsky and Bol'shoy theatres. From 1923 to 1950 she taught at the Leningrad Conservatory. Recordings show a bright voice, sometimes hardening on the high notes but used with exceptional skill, especially in staccato passages.

J.B. Steane

Broschi, Carlo.

See FARINELLI.

Brouwenstijn, Gré [Gerda Demphina]

(*b* Den Helder, 26 Aug 1915; *d* Amsterdam, 14 Dec 1999). Dutch soprano. She studied in Amsterdam and made her début there in 1940 as one of the Ladies in *Die Zauberflöte*. In 1946 she joined the newly formed Netherlands Opera, where her first successes were as Tosca and Santuzza. She made her Covent Garden début in 1951 as Aida and sang there regularly until 1964, appearing as an eloquent Elisabeth de Valois in Luchino Visconti's noted production of *Don Carlos* (1958), as Desdemona and as Leonore (with Otto Klemperer). She appeared at Bayreuth (1954–6) as Elsa, Elisabeth, Sieglinde, Gutrune and Eva; she also sang in Vienna and Stuttgart, where she took the leading role in Wieland Wagner's controversial production of *Fidelio* (1956). She sang Jenůfa at Chicago (1959) and Amelia in *Un ballo in maschera* at San Francisco (1961). She appeared at Glyndebourne as an affecting Leonore (1959, 1961, 1963) and made her farewell in that role with Netherlands Opera in 1971. Her beautiful voice was enhanced by musical intelligence and natural dignity on stage.

H. Rosenthal: 'Gré Brouwenstijn', *Opera*, vii (1959), 440–44
A. Natan: 'Brouwenstijn, Gré', *Prima donna* (Basle, 1962) [incl. discography]
D. Cairns: *Responses* (London, 1973), 140ff
A. Blyth: Obituary, *Opera*, l (2000), 291–2

Harold Rosenthal/Alan Blyth

Brownlee, John

(*b* Geelong, 7 Jan 1901; *d* New York, 10 Jan 1969). Australian baritone. He first studied in Melbourne, then with DINH GILLY in Paris, and was introduced to Covent Garden by his countrywoman Dame NELLIE MELBA, at whose farewell concert (8 June 1926) he made his London début as Marcello in the last two acts of *La bohème*. In the following February he made his first appearance at the Paris Opéra, remaining a prominent member there until 1936. At Covent Garden he sang Golaud in the 1930 revival of *Pelléas et Mélisande* and was also successful in such Verdi roles as Renato and Amonasro.

Brownlee was among the first group of artists who sang at Glyndebourne: under Fritz Busch he sang Don Alfonso in 1935, Don Giovanni in 1936, as well as the Speaker in *Die Zauberflöte* and the Count in some later performances of *Figaro*. He first appeared at the Metropolitan Opera as Rigoletto on 17 February 1937 and remained a valued member of the company until 1958, singing 348 performances of 33 roles. He also appeared widely elsewhere in North and South America, and became director (1956) and president (1966) of the Manhattan School of Music. As can be heard on the 1936 Glyndebourne recording, his Don Giovanni, if not irresistibly seductive in tone or manner, was musically very sensitive; and his singing in general, while neither so rich nor so resonant as to place him among the greatest baritones, was admirably schooled and always distinguished in style.

D. Franklin: 'John Brownlee', *Opera*, xx (1969), 209–10

Desmond Shawe-Taylor/R

Bruson, Renato

(*b* Este, nr Padua, 13 Jan 1936). Italian baritone. He studied singing at Padua and made his début in 1961 at Spoleto as Luna. After singing in many of the major Italian theatres, in 1969 he made his Metropolitian début as Enrico Ashton, returning as Luna, Germont, Don Carlo (*Forza del destino*) and Posa. In 1972 he made his début at La Scala as Antonio (*Linda di Chamounix*) and sang Ezio (*Attila*) in Edinburgh with Palermo Opera. He made his Covent Garden début in 1976 as Anckarstroem (*Ballo in maschera*), returning for Macbeth, Boccanegra, Miller, Iago and Falstaff. He has also appeared in Vienna, Berlin, Munich, Chicago, San Francisco and Los Angeles, where he sang Falstaff (1982) under Carlo Maria Giulini. A specialist in Gaetano Donizetti as well as Giuseppe Verdi, he has sung in revivals of *Belisario*, *Gemma di Vergy*, *Les martyrs*, *Le duc d'Albe*, *Torquato Tasso*, *Caterina Cornaro* and *La favorite*. Warm, well-focussed tone and eloquent phrasing have made him an ideal exponent of noble characters such as Boccanegra and Posa, but he has also been effective as Scarpia and Don Giovanni. By the time he sang Nabucco in Verona in 2000 his tone had become notably drier and sparser, though the phrasing remained as noble as ever. He has recorded many of his best roles, including Rigoletto, Boccanegra and Falstaff, producing a more serious, wise and musing reading than many.

G. Gualerzi: 'Renato Bruson', *Opera*, xxx (1979), 214–18

Alan Blyth

Bryn-Julson, Phyllis (Mae)

(*b* Bowdon, ND, 5 Feb 1945). American soprano of Norwegian parentage. Trained as a pianist at Concordia College, Moorhead, Minnesota, she was heard by Gunther Schuller, who was struck by her facility at sight-reading 12-note music. At his instigation she undertook vocal study at Tanglewood, receiving additional encouragement from Erich Leinsdorf. After further study at Syracuse University she made her official début with the Boston SO in Alban Berg's *Lulu* Suite in 1966; this led to orchestral engagements throughout the USA, including an appearance with the New York PO under Pierre Boulez. Although her repertory was broad and eclectic, she achieved her greatest successes in an extraordinary variety of testing modern works, many written specially for her. The clarity and pure timbre of her voice, her perfect pitch, three-octave range and ability to sing accurately (even in quarter-tones) made her a valued exponent of Boulez, George Crumb, György Ligeti and Lukas Foss. She has served on the faculties of Kirkland-Hamilton College (Clinton, New York) and the University of Maryland, and given masterclasses in Europe and the USA. Her first operatic role was Malinche in the American première of Roger Sessions's *Montezuma* under Sarah Caldwell (1976, Boston). The following year she made an acclaimed début at the Proms in H.W. Henze's *Das Floss der 'Medusa'*, and in 1987 sang in Igor Stravinsky's *The Nightingale* and Maurice Ravel's *L'enfant et les sortilèges* at Covent Garden. Bryn-Julson's many recordings include *The Nightingale*, *Pierrot Lunaire* (of which she was a famous exponent), Harrison Birtwistle's *Punch and Judy*, Luigi Dallapiccola's *Il prigioniero* and several works by Boulez.

Martin Bernheimer/R

Bulakhov, Pavel Petrovich

(*b* Moscow, 15/27 March 1824; *d* St Petersburg, 15/27 Oct 1875). Russian tenor. He was a member of a distinguished musical family: his father, Pyotr Alexandrovich Bulakhov (?1793–1835), and elder brother, Pyotr Petrovich Bulakhov (1822–85), were both tenors, and the younger Pyotr's daughter, YEVGENIYA ZBRUYEVA, achieved fame as the leading operatic contralto of her day. Following his operatic début in St Petersburg in 1849, Pavel Bulakhov embarked on a versatile career that embraced the spoken theatre as well as Russian and Italian opera. His principal roles included Almaviva, Lyonel (*Martha*), Sobinin (*A Life for the Tsar*) and Finn (*Ruslan and Lyudmila*). In 1856 he created the role of the Prince in Dargomïzhsky's *Rusalka* and in 1874 the Holy Fool in *Boris Godunov*. He was partnered in the former by his wife, Anis'ya Alexandrovna Bulakhova (*née* Lavrova, 1831–1920), in the role of Natasha. Like her husband, Bulakhova was particularly noted for her appearances in Mikhail Glinka's operas: apart from their creators, MARIYA STEPANOVA and Yekaterina Semyonova (1821–1906), she was the sole interpreter of the roles of Antonida and Lyudmila during the composer's lifetime.

Boris Semeonoff

Bumbry, Grace (Melzia Ann)

(*b* St Louis, 4 Jan 1937). American mezzo-soprano and soprano. She studied at Boston and with LOTTE LEHMANN in Santa Barbara. A joint winner in 1958 of the Metropolitan Opera auditions, she made her début in 1960 at the Paris Opéra as Amneris, then joined Basle Opera for four seasons. In 1961 she sang Venus at Bayreuth, the first black artist to appear there. She made her Covent Garden (1963) and Metropolitan (1965) débuts as Eboli. At Salzburg she sang Lady Macbeth (1964) and Carmen. Her roles included Azucena, Ulrica, Delilah, Fricka, C.W. Gluck's Orpheus and Santuzza, which she sang at the Vienna Staatsoper (1966). Taking on soprano roles, she sang Salome, Sélika (*L'Africaine*), Adalgisa and Norma at Covent Garden, while adding Tosca, La Gioconda, Leonora (*Trovatore* and *La forza del destino*) and George Gershwin's Bess to her Metropolitan repertory. She sang Jenůfa at La Scala (1974) and Paul Dukas's Ariane in Paris (1975), while continuing to sing mezzo roles. Her voice, particularly in the middle and lower registers, was warm and voluminous and she had a commanding presence on stage. In 1990 she sang Cassandra (*Prise de Troie*) at the opening of the Opéra Bastille in Paris, and in 1995 performed Luigi Cherubini's Medea for the first time.

A. Blyth: 'Grace Bumbry', *Opera*, xxi (1970), 506–11

Alan Blyth

Burchstein, Rose.

See RAISA, ROSA.

Burchuladze, Paata

(*b* Tbilisi, 12 Feb 1955). Georgian bass. He studied in Tbilisi, making his student début there in 1976 as Charles Gounod's Méphistophélès, then becoming a member of the Georgian State Opera, for whom he sang Leporello, Prince Gremin and King René (*Iolanta*). He studied further in Milan (1978–81), where he sang Banquo, Pagano (*I Lombardi*), Walter (*Luisa Miller*) and Zaccaria (*Nabucco*) at La Scala. He made his Covent Garden début in 1984 as Ramfis, returning as Gioachino Rossini's Don Basilio, Khan Konchak, Boris Godunov and the Inquisitor (*Fiery Angel*). Having made his US début at Philadelphia (1987) as Boris, he sang Basilio at the Metropolitan

(1989), followed by Boris and the Commendatore (1995–6). His other roles include Silva (*Ernani*), Fiesco (*Simon Boccanegra*), Philip II, Boito's Mefistofele, and Dosifey (*Khovanshchina*), of which he has made an impressive recording. His magnificent dark-toned voice and imposing stature are ideal for both the Russian repertory and Giuseppe Verdi's bass roles.

Elizabeth Forbes

Burg [Bartl], Robert

(*b* Prague, 29 March 1890; *d* Dresden, 9 Feb 1946). Czech baritone. He studied in Prague, where he made his début in 1915. After a season at Augsburg, he joined the company at Dresden and remained there from 1916 to the time of his death. He took the title role in two important premières: Ferruccio Busoni's *Doktor Faust* (1925) and Paul Hindemith's *Cardillac* (1926). He was also involved in the 'Verdi renaissance' of those years, under Fritz Busch, singing such roles as Count di Luna in *Il trovatore*, Renato in *Un ballo in maschera* and Amonasro in *Aida*. At Bayreuth he appeared first in 1933, singing Kothner in *Die Meistersinger* and Klingsor in *Parsifal* and gaining highest praise for his Alberich. A guest artist in many other German cities, he also made some appearances in Austria, Hungary and Switzerland. Whatever his best qualities, they are not well represented on records, where the voice sounds ungainly and the style often faulty: his acting ability and carrying power created a more favourable impression in the theatre.

J.B. Steane

Burgess, Sally

(*b* Durban, 9 Oct 1953). British mezzo-soprano of South African birth. She studied in London at the RCM, then joined the ENO in 1978 as a soprano, singing Zerlina, Pamina, Cherubino, Bohuslav Martinů's Julietta, Jenny (Richard Rodney Bennett's *The Mines of Sulphur*), Marzelline and Mimì. By 1981 her voice had deepened, and she took on mezzo travesty roles such as the Composer, Octavian, Orlovsky, Nicklausse and G.F. Handel's Sextus, as well as Charlotte, Pauline (*The Gambler*), Nefertiti in the British première of *Akhnaten* (1985), Sonetka (*Lady Macbeth of the Mtsensk District*), Laura in the British stage première of A.S. Dargomïzhsky's *The Stone Guest* (1987), Carmen, Judith (*Bluebeard's Castle*; see colour plate 13), the Witch (*Die Königskinder*) and Dulcinea (*Don Quichotte*). In 1983 she sang Siébel (*Faust*) at her

Covent Garden début and Smeraldina (*The Love for Three Oranges*) at Glyndebourne. For Opera North she has appeared as Hector Berlioz's Dido, Amneris, Laura (*La Gioconda*) and Azucena, all parts which, like Carmen, are particularly well suited to her vibrant voice and dramatic temperament. For Scottish Opera she has sung Fricka (1991). Having made her US début in 1994 at Portland, Oregon, as Carmen, Burgess sang the same role for her Metropolitan début the following year. In 1997 she sang in the first performance of Mark Anthony Turnage's *Twice Through the Heart* at Aldeburgh. She also enjoys a considerable career as a jazz singer, and has recorded Paul McCartney's *Liverpool Oratorio* and Julie LaVerne in *Show Boat*.

E. Forbes: 'Sally Burgess', *Opera*, xlii (1991), 16–21

Elizabeth Forbes

Burian, Karel [Burrian, Carl]

(*b* Rousinov, 12 Jan 1870; *d* Senomaty, nr Prague, 25 Sept 1924). Bohemian tenor. He made his first appearance at Brno on 28 March 1891 as Jeník in Bedřich Smetana's *The Bartered Bride*; after singing the title role in the same composer's *Dalibor* the next day, he was offered a contract. By 1899 he had reached the National Theatre in Prague, but he did not remain for long with that company, having by then become a Heldentenor much in demand in Germany. For over a decade before World War I Burian was a leading and much-admired tenor at the Dresden Opera, where he made a powerful impression in the première (1905) of Richard Strauss's *Salome* as Herod, repeating this role in the first productions of the opera in both New York and Paris in 1907. Wagner was the mainstay of his international repertory; as well as singing Tristan in the Hungarian première of *Tristan und Isolde*, he sang several of the chief Wagner roles at Covent Garden in four seasons between 1904 and 1914, and virtually all of them (*Die Meistersinger* excepted) during seven seasons at the Metropolitan. He appeared in *Parsifal* at Bayreuth in 1908. In Burian's numerous but somewhat primitive recordings, the penetrating clarity of his tone is more in evidence than the golden quality for which he was also praised. Reminiscences of Gustav Mahler and Arturo Toscanini are included in his memoirs, *Z mých pameti* (Prague, 1913).

J. Dennis: 'Karel Burian', *Record Collector*, xviii (1968–9), 149–64 [incl. discography by D. Brew and G. Sova]

Desmond Shawe-Taylor

Burnson [Burnstein], George.

See LONDON, GEORGE.

Burrowes, Norma

(*b* Bangor, Co. Down, 24 April 1944). British soprano. She studied in London at the RAM, where she sang Thérèse in Francis Poulenc's *Les mamelles de Tirésias* (1968), Claudio Monteverdi's Poppaea and Magda in *La rondine* (1969). In 1970 she won a Gulbenkian Foundation Award and made her professional début with Glyndebourne Touring Opera, as Zerlina. That year she sang Philidel in Henry Purcell's *King Arthur* with the English Opera Group and made her Covent Garden début as Fiakermilli in *Arabella*. In 1971 she appeared at Salzburg as Blonde, a part she also sang with the ENO, the Netherlands Opera, the Paris Opéra and the Metropolitan (1979), and recorded with Colin Davis. Other roles in her repertory included Fiorilla in *Il turco in Italia*, Elisa in *Il re pastore*, which she sang at Wexford in 1971, Oscar, Alison in Gustav Holst's *The Wandering Scholar* (which she recorded) and Sophie. At Glyndebourne (1970–81) she sang Papagena, Leoš Janáček's Vixen, Pamina and Susanna. Her pure, bright-toned voice, secure coloratura technique and charming appearance were much admired when she sang Zerbinetta for Scottish Opera (1975). Burrowes was also a delightful singer of Purcell and G.F. Handel, as can be heard in several recordings; she gave many recitals and appeared on television, notably as Susanna and Nannetta. She retired from performing in 1982 but has continued to teach.

Elizabeth Forbes

Burrows, (James) Stuart

(*b* Cilfynydd, nr Pontypridd, 7 Feb 1933). Welsh tenor. A schoolteacher before winning the tenor solo competition at the Royal National Eisteddfod in 1959, he studied at Carmarthen. He made his début in 1963 with the WNO as Ismaele (*Nabucco*), also singing Rodolfo (*La bohème*), Macduff, Jeník (*The Bartered Bride*), the Duke of Mantua and Ernesto (*Don Pasquale*). At Athens in 1965 he sang the title role in *Oedipus rex* under Igor Stravinsky. He made his Covent Garden début in 1967 as Beppe (*Pagliacci*), returning for 22 seasons as Fenton, Elvino (*La sonnambula*), Faust, Lensky, Jack (*The Midsummer Marriage*), and in Mozart roles. He made his San Francisco (1967) and Vienna Staatsoper (1970) débuts as Tamino and sang Don Ottavio at Salzburg (1970) and for his Metropolitan début (1971), returning there as

Belmonte, Des Grieux (*Manon*) and Alfredo. He also sang in Aix-en-Provence and Santa Fe. He was a renowned exponent of Idomeneus, Tamino and Titus. His sweet-toned voice, of great flexibility, was ideally suited to Mozart and it was used with skill. He recorded many of his best roles, notably Don Ottavio, Tamino, Lensky and Hoffmann, a part he never sang on stage, with Georg Solti and Titus with Colin Davis.

Alan Blyth

Burzio, Eugenia

(*b* Turin, 20 June 1872; *d* Milan, 18 May 1922). Italian soprano. She appeared first as a violinist, then studied singing at the Milan Conservatory, making her début in 1899 at Turin in *Cavalleria rusticana*. Specialising in the new *verismo* school, she sang throughout Italy, in South America and at St Petersburg. Among her many appearances at La Scala were admired performances in C.W. Gluck's *Armide* and Vincenzo Bellini's *Norma*. For a while she was one of the leading dramatic sopranos in Italy, but she suffered from nerves and ill-health. She made her final appearance in 1919 in Amilcare Ponchielli's *Marion Delorme*. Her recordings show a vibrant voice and a passionate style, which was imaginative and exciting at best but open to many criticisms on grounds of unevenness and over-emphasis.

M. Scott: *The Record of Singing*, i (London, 1977), 156–9

J.B. Steane

Bussani [née Sardi], Dorothea

(*b* Vienna, 1763; *d* after 1810). Austrian soprano. She was the daughter of Karl von Sardi, a professor at the military academy in Vienna. On 20 March 1786 she married the Italian bass FRANCESCO BUSSANI. She specialized in *opera buffa* and made her début creating the role of Cherubino in *Le nozze di Figaro* (1786); she also created the role of Ghita in Vicente Martín y Soler's *Una cosa rara* (1786), sang Despina in the première of *Così fan tutte* (1790) and created the role of Fidalma in Domenico Cimarosa's *Il matrimonio segreto* (1792). She always pleased the public, and a contemporary wrote that he had never heard such a beautiful and charming chest voice, nor one used with such humour and so mischievously (*Grundsätze zur Theaterkritik*, 1790). Lorenzo Da Ponte, on the other hand, wrote: 'though awkward and of little merit, by dint of grimaces and clowning and perhaps by means even more theatrical, she built up a large following among cooks, grooms, servants, lackeys

and wigmakers, and in consequence was considered a gem' (*Memorie*, 1823–7).

In 1795 she went to Florence and sang in Italy during the next decade. She appeared in Lisbon, 1807–9, and then sang at the King's Theatre, London; William Thomas Pareke later described her as having 'plenty of voice, but whose person and age were not calculated to fascinate an English audience' (*Musical Memoirs*, 1830).

D. Link: *The National Court Theatre in Mozart's Vienna: Sources and Documents 1783–1792* (Oxford, 1998)

Christopher Raeburn

Bussani, Francesco

(*b* Rome, 1743; *d* after 1807). Italian bass. He started his career as a tenor, appearing in Rome in 1763 in Guglielmi's *Le contadine bizzare*. He sang in Venice, Milan and Rome for the next 15 years, and first appeared in Vienna in 1771. In 1777 he was described in Florence as singing *primo buffo* and *mezzo carattere* roles; by this time his voice was a bass-baritone. He appeared in Venice from 1779, and in 1783 was invited to Vienna where he remained until 1794. With 20 years' experience of the theatre he was engaged not only as a singer but also as manager of scenery and costumes, and as such was paid for stage-managing W.A. Mozart's *Der Schauspieldirektor* at Schönbrunn in 1786. He also arranged pieces, and in 1784 adapted Carlo Goldoni's *Il mercato di Malmantile* as a libretto for music by Josef Bárta. He appeared regularly in the Italian repertory and sang Pippo in Bianchi's *La villanella rapita*, for which Mozart wrote the quartet 'Dite almeno' K479 (28 November 1785). Mozart intended the role of Pulchiero for him in *Lo sposo deluso* (1783–4, unfinished), and he doubled the roles of Bartolo and Antonio in the première of *Le nozze di Figaro* (1 May 1786). He was an active member of the Italian faction in Vienna during the 1780s and according to Lorenzo Da Ponte (*Memorie*, 1823–7) intrigued against him and Mozart when *Figaro* was in rehearsal. Da Ponte described Bussani as knowing something of every profession except that of a gentleman.

Bussani sang the Commendatore and Masetto in the first Vienna performance of *Don Giovanni* (1788) and created the role of Don Alfonso in *Così fan tutte* (26 January 1790). According to Da Ponte, Bussani found little favour with the new emperor, Leopold II. He achieved only moderate success as a singer as he was always in the shadow of BENUCCI, who had the stronger stage personality and was the public's favourite. In 1795 he sang in Florence, in 1799 in Rome, and in 1800–01 in Naples and Palermo. He remained active in Italy and went with his wife, the singer DOROTHEA BUSSANI (née Sardi), to Lisbon in 1807.

D. Link: *The National Court Theatre in Mozart's Vienna: Sources and Documents 1783–1792* (Oxford, 1998)

Christopher Raeburn

Butt, Dame Clara (Ellen)

(*b* Southwick, Sussex, 1 Feb 1872; *d* North Stoke, Oxon, 23 Jan 1936). English contralto. She studied with Daniel Rootham in Bristol, and in 1890 gained a scholarship at the Royal College of Music, where she was a pupil of J.H. Blower. She made her début at the Royal Albert Hall as Ursula in Arthur Sullivan's *Golden Legend* on 7 December 1892, and three days later sang the role of Orpheus in the RCM production of C.W. Gluck's opera at the Lyceum Theatre. From that date her success was assured.

It was almost entirely a success of the concert platform, and later of her own platform: that is, in her own concerts, more or less of the ballad type, given all over the British Empire. She was also much in request for other concerts, and particularly for the English festivals. Edward Elgar's *Sea Pictures* (Norwich Festival, 1899) was written for her, and she made his *Land of Hope and Glory* (1902) her own. In 1900 she married the baritone Kennerley Rumford, and thenceforward they pursued their careers together. In 1920 she made a reappearance on the operatic stage, singing Gluck's Orpheus at Covent Garden under Thomas Beecham. In the same year she was created DBE for her services during the war (she organized and sang in countless performances for war charities, including a week's run of Elgar's *Dream of Gerontius* in aid of the Red Cross).

Dame Clara was a tall woman, standing 6'2". Her voice was exceptionally powerful (someone remarked that the Albert Hall must have been built in intelligent anticipation of Butt's advent), with a trombone-like boom in the lower register; she also attained a remarkable facility. She made many records. Such majestic and powerful means, when applied to a song such as Arthur Goodhart's 'A fairy went a-marketing', may raise a smile, but the smile is tempered by admiration for the magnificent voice and the beautiful articulation of the words.

W. Ponder: *Clara Butt: her Life-Story* (London, 1928/*R*)
'Clara Butt Discography', *Record Advertiser*, ii (1971–2), no.1, pp.2–8; no.2, pp.2–9

J.A. Fuller Maitland, H.C. Colles/Andrew Porter

C

Caballé, Montserrat

(*b* Barcelona, 12 April 1933). Spanish soprano. She studied for 12 years at the Barcelona Conservatory, with (among others) Eugenia Kemmeny and Napoleone Annovazzi, winning the 1954 Liceo gold medal. She joined the Basle Opera in 1956; in three years she built up an impressive repertory, including Pamina, Tosca, Aida, Marta in Eugen d'Albert's *Tiefland*, and Richard Strauss's Arabella, Chrysothemis and Salome. In 1959 she sang her first Violetta and Tatyana, at Bremen, and the heroines of Antonín Dvořák's *Armida* and *Rusalka*. At La Scala the next year she first appeared as one of Klingsor's flowermaidens (*Parsifal*); a gradually widening international career took her to Vienna, back to Barcelona, to Lisbon and, in 1964, Mexico City (as Jules Massenet's Manon). In 1965 she replaced MARILYN HORNE at short notice in a New York concert *Lucrezia Borgia*, and achieved overnight stardom. After that many Donizetti operas were mounted for her (notably *Roberto Devereux*, *Maria Stuarda*, *Parisina* and *Gemma di Vergy*). In 1965 she also made débuts at Glyndebourne (Marschallin and W.A. Mozart's Countess) and the Metropolitan (Marguerite). At La Scala she played Lucrezia Borgia, Mary Stuart, Norma and Amelia (*Ballo in maschera*) and at Covent Garden Violetta (début, 1972), Norma, Leonora (*Il trovatore*), Amelia and Aida. In 1987 she sang Giovanni Pacini's Saffo and, in 1989, Isolde, at the Liceo, Barcelona. Other roles include Gaspare Spontini's Agnes, Gioachino Rossini's Ermione and Madama Cortese (*Il viaggio a Reims*), which she sang at Covent Garden in 1992, the year of her final operatic appearances.

Regarded by many as CALLAS's successor, Caballé was for a time the leading Verdi and Donizetti soprano of the day, able to spin effortless long legato phrases and noted for her floated *pianissimo* high notes. She was an actress of refinement and dignity, but no great dramatic intensity. Her numerous recordings include Verdi's Requiem and Johannes Brahms's *German Requiem*, Strauss and Granados songs and many operatic roles, among them some (in Puccini and Strauss operas) which she sang more frequently in earlier years, and others, such as Lucia and Fiordiligi, which she never sang on stage. In the 1980s and early 90s she became a notable recitalist, especially successful in Spanish song. She married the tenor Bernabé Marti in 1964.

Montserrat Caballé

A. Blyth: 'Montserrat Caballé Talks', *Gramophone*, li (1973–4), 174–5

J.B. Steane: *The Grand Tradition* (London, 1974/R), 537 ff

F.G. Barker: 'Montserrat Caballé', *Opera*, xxvi (1975), 342–8

R. Pullen and S. Taylor: *Montserrat Caballé: Casta Diva* (London, 1994)

Alan Blyth

Cabell, Nicole

(*b* Panorama City, CA, 17 Oct 1977). American soprano. She studied with John Malloy at the Eastman School of Music, graduating in 2001, and then joined the Lyric Opera of Chicago's Center for American Artists, where she studied with GIANNA ROLANDI. Her major professional début was in June 2005, when she sang in Michael Tippett's *A Child of our Time* with the Chicago SO. The same month she won the Cardiff Singer of the World Competition (*The Times* described her voice as 'liquid gold...the real thing'), leading to an exclusive recording contract with Decca and her first solo album, of Italian and French Romantic arias. In 2006 Cabell made débuts at Carnegie Hall, the Proms (in Benjamin Britten's *Les illuminations*), and at the Deutsche Oper, Berlin, as Gounod's Juliet (substituting at short notice for ANGELA GHEORGHIU) and Ilia in *Idomeneo*. Her London recital début followed in 2007, when she also delighted audiences as Musetta (a role she has also recorded) in Munich, Santa Fe, Washington and the Lyric Opera of Chicago.

Richard Wigmore

Cachemaille, Gilles

(*b* Orbe, 25 Nov 1951). Swiss bass-baritone. He studied at the Lausanne Conservatoire and in 1982 won three awards, including first prize in the international competition held in Paris for the performance of French song. That was also the year of his stage début in Jean-Philippe Rameau's *Les Boréades* at Aix-en-Provence, where over the following years he became a favourite. Among his roles there have been W.A. Mozart's Figaro and Leporello, which he sang on the opening night of the festival's 50th anniversary in 1998. He was a member of the Lyons Opéra from 1982 to 1985, the year of his début at Salzburg. He has subsequently sung in Vienna, Prague, Berlin and Frankfurt, as well as most of the important centres in France and Switzerland. He sang in the world première of Rolf Liebermann's *La forêt* in Geneva in 1987. In 1993 he made his début with the Glyndebourne company in Hector Berlioz's *Béatrice et Bénédict*, enjoying a more marked success as Leporello the following year. His other roles include Papageno, Don Alfonso and Golaud, all of which he has recorded. Throughout his career Cachemaille has maintained and developed an active concert repertory, ranging from J.S. Bach's Passions to Frank Martin's *Golgotha* and *Jedermann* settings. He was also the bass soloist in the first performance of Berlioz's rediscovered *Messe solennelle* under John Eliot Gardiner in 1993. A large number of recordings testify to his artistry as well as to the pleasing quality of his voice.

J.B. Steane

Caffarelli [Cafariello, Cafarellino, Gaffarello] [Majorano, Gaetano]

(*b* Bitonto, 12 April 1710; *d* Naples, 31 Jan 1783). Italian mezzo-soprano castrato. After studying under Porpora at Naples, he made his début at Rome in 1726, in a female part in Domenico Sarro's *Valdemaro*. His success was rapid: he sang in Venice, Turin, Milan and Florence before returning to Rome in 1730 as chamber virtuoso to the Grand Duke of Tuscany. He enjoyed triumphs in Johann Hasse's *Cajo Fabricio* and Nicola Porpora's *Germanico in Germania* in 1732. After singing in Pistoia, Genoa, Venice, Milan and Bologna (1730–33), he made his Naples début in Leonardo Leo's *Il castello d'Atlante* (1734), and settled there in a post in the royal chapel. Over the next 20 years he appeared at Naples in operas by Giovanni Pergolesi (including the title role in *Adriano in Siria*, 1734), Porpora, Hasse, David Perez, Leo (including Orestes in *Andromaca*, 1742), Gaetano Latilla, Sarro, Leonardo Vinci, Gioacchino Cocchi, Girolamo Abos, Giuseppe de Majo (in the serenata *Il sogno d'Olimpia*) and others, and latterly (1751–3) in Tommaso Traetta's *Farnace*, Giuseppe Conti's *Attalo rè di Bitinia*, Sextus in C.W. Gluck's *La clemenza di Tito* and Giovanni Lampugnani's *Didone*.

He appeared frequently elsewhere, in Rome again in 1735, Milan in 1736 and London in 1737–8, when he made his début at the King's Theatre in the pasticcio *Arsace* and created the title roles in G.F. Handel's *Faramondo*, *Serse* and *Alessandra Severo* (all 1738). He also appeared in Madrid by royal invitation in 1739, and in the late 1740s and early 1750s in Florence (where Horace Mann thought he sang 'most divinely well' in an anonymous *Caio Mario*), Genoa, Rome, Vienna (where his performance in Niccolò Jommelli's *Achille in Sciro* was the subject of barbed criticism from Pietro Metastasio in letters to FARINELLI), Turin, Venice, Lucca and Modena. In 1753 Louis XV invited him to Versailles, and he remained in France until 1754, singing in several works by Johann Hasse, but left under a cloud after seriously wounding a poet in a duel.

Caffarelli made his last Italian operatic appearances at Rome and Naples in 1754. In 1755 he was engaged for Lisbon, where he sang in four operas, three of them by Perez. He visited Madrid in 1756 and spent some time with Farinelli, before returning to Naples and retiring from the stage (though he continued to sing in cantatas and serenatas). In 1763 he refused an invitation to manage the S Carlo theatre. He was a favourite with royal families everywhere and amassed a substantial fortune, with which he bought himself a dukedom, an estate in Calabria and a palace in Naples. In 1770 Charles Burney recognized signs 'of his having been an amazing fine singer'.

Caffarelli's voice was a high mezzo-soprano. The compass in the two parts Handel wrote for him is *b* to *a''*. By many judges he was ranked second only to Farinelli, and by some above him. According to Burney, 'Porpora, who hated him for his insolence, used to say, that he was the greatest singer Italy had ever produced'.

Grimm reported from Paris:

It would be difficult to give any idea of the degree of perfection to which this singer has brought his art. All the charms and love that can make up the idea of an angelic voice, and which form the character of his, added to the finest execution, and to surprising facility and precision, exercise an enchantment over the senses and the heart, which even those least sensible to music would find it hard to resist.

Caffarelli's principal enemy was his own temperament; he was notorious for overbearing arrogance both to fellow artists and to the public. He had spells under house arrest and in prison, for assault, misconduct at a performance (of Latilla's *Olimpia nell'isola d'Ebuda*, 1741), when he indulged in indecent gestures and mimicry of other singers, and for humiliating a prima donna in Hasse's *Antigono* (1745). He was constantly late for concerts and rehearsals, and sometimes failed to turn up. He is said to have mellowed in old age and given large sums to charity; Burney was charmed by his politeness.

Winton Dean

Cahier, Mme Charles [née Layton Walker, Sarah (Jane); Charles-Cahier, Sarah; Black, Mrs Morris]

(*b* Nashville, TN, 8 Jan 1870; *d* Manhattan Beach, CA, 15 April 1951). American contralto. Her teachers included JEAN DE RESZKE in Paris, Gustav Walter in Vienna and Amalie Joachim in Berlin. Two years after her operatic début in Nice (1904), she was engaged by Gustav Mahler at the Vienna Hofoper, where for six seasons she sang roles that included Carmen and several in Wagner operas. She made her Metropolitan début in 1912 as Azucena and during the next two years sang Amneris and Fricka with the company; elsewhere her most famous role was Carmen. Her concert work, however, was more significant, and in 1911 Bruno Walter chose her for the première of Mahler's *Das Lied von der Erde* in Munich. The few recordings that she made document a voice that is imposing, if somewhat uncentred in tone, and a stately style.

Richard Dyer

Callas [Kalogeropoulou], (Cecilia Sophia Anna) Maria

(*b* New York, 2 Dec 1923; *d* Paris, 16 Sept 1977). Greek soprano. She was American by birth and early upbringing, and Italian by career and by marriage to

G.B. Meneghini, whose surname she incorporated with her own during the period of her marriage (1949–59). In 1937 she left the USA for Greece and in 1940 became a pupil of the well-known soprano ELVIRA DE HIDALGO at the Athens Conservatory. Two years later she sang Tosca in Athens (27 August 1942), and went on to appear, in 1944, as Santuzza, Marta (in Eugen d'Albert's *Tiefland*) and Leonore (*Fidelio*). Returning to New York with her parents in 1945, she was heard by former tenor GIOVANNI ZENATELLO, who engaged her for Amilcare Ponchielli's *La Gioconda* in Verona. This successful appearance (2 August 1947) under Tullio Serafin was the start of her real career, and she was soon in demand in Italian theatres for such heavy roles as Aida, Turandot, Isolde, Kundry and Brünnhilde. A rare versatility was shown in Venice in 1949 when, only three days after singing a *Walküre* Brünnhilde, she deputized for an indisposed colleague in the florid bel canto role of Elvira in Vincenzo Bellini's *I puritani*. Thereafter, under the guidance of Serafin, she gradually relinquished her heavier roles in order to concentrate on the earlier Italian operas. Besides adding to her repertory Bellini's Amina, Gaetano Donizetti's Lucia and Giuseppe Verdi's Leonora (*Il trovatore*), Violetta and Gilda, she was in constant demand whenever rare and vocally taxing operas of the older school were produced, such as Joseph Haydn's *L'anima del filosofo* (in its world première, 1951, Florence), C.W. Gluck's *Alceste* and *Iphigénie en Tauride*, Luigi Cherubini's *Médée*, Gaspare Spontini's *La vestale*, Gioachino Rossini's *Armida* and *Il turco in Italia*, Donizetti's *Anna Bolena* and *Poliuto*, and Bellini's *Il pirata*. She also created the role of Ariadne in Bohuslav Martinů's *Ariane* (1961, Gelsenkirchen). Her greatest triumphs were won as Norma, Medea, Anne Boleyn, Lucia, Verdi's Lady Macbeth and Violetta, and Tosca. Many of these roles she repeated in the major opera houses of the world, where her fame reached a level that recalled the careers of CARUSO and CHALIAPIN.

Callas first appeared at La Scala as Aida (12 April 1950); her débuts at Covent Garden (8 November 1952), the Lyric Theatre of Chicago (1 November 1954) and at the Metropolitan (29 October 1956) were as Norma. Her relations with the Rudolf Bing regime at the Metropolitan were uneasy, and the same could unfortunately be said, in latter days, of those with the Rome Opera and La Scala. Nevertheless, sensational publicity suggesting that she was a difficult and jealous colleague was an accusation resented by many of those who worked with her most closely. The truth was probably that an exacting, self-critical temperament coupled with recurrent vocal troubles often forced her into a difficult choice between withdrawal from contractual engagements and singing below her best form. Whether her vocal problems

Maria Callas in the title role of 'Turandot' (Puccini), La Scala, Milan

(inequality of registers, harshness in the middle voice and tremolo on sustained high notes) were mainly due to inadequate training or to some physical intractability remains uncertain.

Of Callas's artistic pre-eminence there can be no doubt. Among her contemporaries she had the deepest comprehension of the Classical Italian style, the most musical instincts and the most intelligent approach. There was authority in all that she did on the stage and in every phrase that she uttered. Her voice, especially during the early 1950s, was in itself an impressive instrument, with its penetrating individual quality, its rich variety of colour and its great agility in florid music. During the 1960s Callas's growing vocal troubles led to her gradual withdrawal from the stage; after her last operatic appearance (at Covent Garden, as Tosca, on 5 July 1965) she made only sporadic returns to the concert stage (in 1973–4) and organized some masterclasses. Fortunately, numerous recordings, notably her Tosca with Victor De Sabata, her Violetta with Franco Ghione, her Butterfly and her Lucia (both with Herbert von Karajan), remain to show that her technical defects were outweighed by her genius as an interpreter.

E. Callas: *My Daughter, Maria Callas*, ed. L.G. Blochman (New York, 1960, enlarged 2/1967/*R*)

G. Jellinek: *Callas: Portrait of a Prima Donna* (New York, 1960, 2/1986)

L. Riemens: *Maria Callas* (Utrecht, 1960)

J. Ardoin and G. Fitzgerald: *Callas* (New York, 1974)

D. Hamilton: 'The Recordings of Maria Callas', *High Fidelity and Musical America*, xxiv/3 (1974), 40–46 [with discography]

H. Wisneski: *Maria Callas: the Art behind the Music* (New York, 1975) [with performance annals 1947–74, and discography of private recordings by A. Germond]

J. Ardoin: *The Callas Legacy* (London, 1977, 2/1982) [a critical discography]

A. Stassinopoulos: *Maria Callas: the Woman behind the Legend* (New York, 1981)

J. Ardoin: 'Maria Callas: the Early Years', *OQ*, iii (1983), 6–13

J. Ardoin: *Callas at Juilliard: the Master Classes* (London, 1988)

N. Stancioff: *Callas Remembered* (London, 1988)

J. Callas: *Sisters* (London, 1989) [with appx listing early performances 1938–45]

M. Scott: *Maria Meneghini Callas* (London, 1991)

D. Brett: *Maria Callas: the Tigress and the Lamb* (London, 1998)

Desmond Shawe-Taylor

Calleja, Joseph

(*b* Attard, 22 Jan 1978). Maltese tenor. He became set on a singing career at the age of fifteen after seeing MARIO LANZA in the movie *The Great Caruso* and hearing recordings of PAVAROTTI. At sixteen he began to study with the Maltese tenor Paul Asciak, and in May 1997 he made his professional operatic début, as Macduff (*Macbeth*) in the Astra Theatre, Gozo. Later the same year he won the Belvedere International Competition in Vienna and sang Leicester in Gaetano Donizetti's *Maria Stuarda* with the Nederlandse Reisopera. In 1998 Calleja won first prize in the Caruso Competition in Milan, sang his first Nemorino (*L'elisir d'amore*), in Valletta, and made his début at the Wexford Festival in Riccardo Zandonai's *I cavalieri di Ekubù*. His US début, as Rinuccio (*Gianni Schicchi*) at the Spoleto Festival, and his German début, as Don Ottavio at the Regensburg Festival, followed in 1999, and in 2000 he made débuts in Liège (as Almaviva), Toronto (as Rodolfo in *La bohème*) and Dresden (also as Rodolfo).

At twenty-two Calleja was already attracting international attention as a lyric tenor of exceptional refinement and musicality. In 2001 he sang Ernesto (*Don Pasquale*) at La Monnaie, and during the 2002–03 season made acclaimed débuts at the Bayerische Staatsoper and the Frankfurt Opera (as Rodolfo),

Maria Callas as Tosca and Tito Gobbi as Scarpia in 'Tosca' (Puccini), Royal Opera House, London, 1964

and at Covent Garden, Welsh National Opera and the Royal Theatre, Copenhagen (as the Duke in *Rigoletto*). Other important débuts include the Liceu, Barcelona (as Nemorino, 2004), and the Vienna Staatsoper, as Elvino (*I puritani*), also in 2004. He returned to Covent Garden in 2005, as Alfredo (*La traviata*), and in 2006, as Macduff. Calleja's sensuous, high-lying tenor, with its intriguing mix of velvet and silver, and elegant sense of style, can be heard in recordings of French and Italian arias.

Richard Wigmore

Calvé [Calvet] (de Roquer), (Rosa-Noémie) Emma

(*b* Decazeville, 15 Aug 1858; *d* Millau, 6 Jan 1942). French soprano. A pupil of Jules Puget, MATHILDE MARCHESI and Rosina Laborde, she made her début as Marguerite in *Faust* at the Théâtre de la Monnaie, Brussels, on 23 September 1881, and three years later appeared in Paris, mainly at the Opéra-Comique. In 1887 she was called to La Scala, Milan, to create the heroine of Spyridon Samaras's *Flora mirabilis*; but she did not achieve lasting success until a triumphant return in 1890 as Ophelia in Ambroise Thomas' *Hamlet* (with MATTIA BATTISTINI in the title role). This was followed by appearances with FERNANDO DE LUCIA in *Cavalleria rusticana* in various Italian cities and with the same tenor in the première of Pietro Mascagni's *L'amico Fritz* (31 October 1891, Rome). Calvé soon became one of the first favourites of the international public, especially in London and New York, where her Santuzza and above all her Carmen were considered incomparable. Although these parts were to dominate her repertory, Jules Massenet wrote two roles for her, Anita in *La Navarraise* (1894, Covent Garden) and Fanny in *Sapho* (1897, Opéra-Comique), and she also created the title role of Reynaldo Hahn's *La Carmélite* (1902, Opéra-Comique). In 1904, having taken part in the 1000th performance of *Carmen* at the Opéra-Comique, she announced her intention of leaving the stage, and did not thereafter reappear at either the Metropolitan or Covent Garden; but she sang at Oscar Hammerstein's Manhattan Opera House in 1907 and 1908, and continued to give concerts in the USA (including appearances in vaudeville) until 1927. Her voice – a luscious, finely trained soprano strong in both chest and head registers (originally extending to high F), the secret of which she claimed to have learnt from Domenico Mustafà, the Italian castrato who became director of the choir at the Cappella Sistina – derived charm from its combination of absolute steadiness with rich colour. As an interpreter she was intensely dramatic and impulsive, to the point of capriciousness in later life. Her records, though disappointingly limited in repertory, are none the less extraordinary; among the best, apart from her *Carmen* excerpts, are the unaccompanied Provençal air, *O Magali*, incorporated in *Sapho*, the 'Air du mysoli' from Félicien David's *La perle du Brésil* and the folksong *Ma Lisette*, with its exquisite, sustained *pianissimo* high D♭.

E. Calvé: *My Life* (New York, 1922/R)

D. Shawe-Taylor: 'Emma Calvé', *Opera*, vi (1955), 220–23

H. Barnes and W. Moran: 'Emma Calvé: a Discography', *Recorded Sound*, no.59 (1975), 450–52

J.B. Steane: 'Singers of the Century, 2: Emma Calvé', *Opera Now* (1991), July, 65–7

Desmond Shawe-Taylor/Karen Henson

Calvesi, Vincenzo

(*b* Rome; *fl* 1777–1811). Italian tenor. His first known appearance was in Rome in 1777. He sang in comic opera in Italy until 1782, specializing in *mezzo carattere* roles. From 1782 to 1783 he sang in Dresden, and in 1785 he settled in Vienna, making his début there as Sandrino in Giovanni Paisiello's *Il re Teodoro*. Except for a year's leave of absence in 1788, which he spent mainly in Naples, he remained in Vienna until 1794. A versatile lyric tenor, he created leading roles in operas by Vicente Martín y Soler (*Una cosa rara* and *L'arbore di Diana*), Stephen Storace (*Gli sposi malcontenti* and *Gli equivoci*) and Antonio Salieri (*La grotta di Trofonio* and *Axur, re d'Ormus*), as well as Ferrando in W.A. Mozart's *Così fan tutte*. In 1785 he sang the Count in the quartet 'Dite almeno, in che mancai' κ479 and the trio 'Mandina amabile' κ480 written by Mozart for Francesco Bianchi's *La villanella rapita*. He was described in *Grundsätze zur Theaterkritik* (1790) as 'one of the best tenors from Italy…with a voice naturally sweet, pleasant and sonorous'. On his retirement from the stage in 1794 Calvesi returned to Rome, where he became one of the city's leading impresarios (*c*1796–1811).

Vincenzo's wife, Teresa, sang small roles in Vienna from 1785 to about 1789, when she left on her own to pursue her career in London and Italy. A Giuseppe Calvesi is known to have been active 1784–91; he, and not Vincenzo, sang in London in 1787 and 1788.

D. Link: *The National Court Theatre in Mozart's Vienna: Sources and Documents 1783–1792* (Oxford, 1998)

J.A. Rice: *Antonio Salieri and the Viennese Opera* (Chicago, 1998)

Dorothea Link, John A. Rice

Campanini, Italo

(*b* Parma, 30 June 1845; *d* Corcagno, nr Parma, 22 Nov 1896). Italian tenor. He studied at the Regia Scuola di Canto in Parma, making his début there in

1863 as Oloferno Vitellozzo in Gaetano Donizetti's *Lucrezia Borgia*. Engaged to sing Manrico in *Il trovatore* in Odessa, he stayed three years in Russia, returning to Italy for further study with Francesco Lamperti in Milan. In 1871, after singing Charles Gounod's Faust, Don Ottavio and Gennaro (*Lucrezia Borgia*) at La Scala, he attracted wide attention when he sang Lohengrin at Bologna under Angelo Mariani, in the first Italian performance of Richard Wagner's opera. At La Scala he also sang the title roles of Filippo Marchetti's *Ruy Blas* and *Lohengrin* (1872–3). Having made his London début in 1872 at Drury Lane as Gennaro, in 1874 he sang Kenneth in the première of Michael Balfe's *Il talismano*. In 1875 he sang Faust in *Mefistofele* in the first performance of the revised edition of Arrigo Boito's opera at Bologna, and in 1878 Don José in the London (Her Majesty's Theatre) and New York (Academy of Music) premières of *Carmen*. Having sung Gounod's Faust at the opening of the Metropolitan in 1883, he returned (1891–4) as Almaviva, Don Ottavio, Raoul (*Les Huguenots*), Lohengrin, Edgardo (*Lucia di Lammermoor*) and Boito's Faust. He sang the title role of Berlioz's *La damnation de Faust* at the Royal Albert Hall in 1894, the year he retired. His voice was reportedly neither large nor perfectly even, but was sweet, flexible, brilliant on top and used with intuitive musicality. He was the brother of the conductor Cleofonte Campanini and they made many appearances together.

Elizabeth Forbes

Campora, Giuseppe

(*b* Tortona, 30 Sept 1923; *d* Tortona, 5 Dec 2004). Italian tenor. He studied in Genoa and Milan and made his début at Bari in 1949 as Rodolfo in *La bohème*. He appeared first at La Scala in 1952 as Boris in the première of Lodovico Rocca's *L'uragano*; roles in subsequent seasons included Rodolfo, Maurizio in *Adriana Lecouvreur* and Orombello in *Beatrice di Tenda*. Abroad, he made a successful début at the Colón in 1952 and from 1955 to 1965 sang frequently at the Metropolitan in a lyric repertory ranging from Edgardo in *Lucia di Lammermoor* to the title role in *Les contes d'Hoffmann*. His active and durable career took him to most of the leading Italian houses, and he travelled widely throughout Europe and the USA. In later years he appeared also in operettas such as *Die Fledermaus* and *Das Land des Lächelns*. His recordings, which include several complete operas, show a style that is reliable rather than imaginative and a serviceable voice, not very distinctive in timbre but of pleasing quality.

J.B. Steane

Caniglia, Maria

(*b* Naples, 5 May 1905; *d* Rome, 15 April 1979). Italian soprano. She studied at the Conservatorio di Musica S Pietro a Majella, Naples, and made her début in Turin in 1930 as Chrysothemis in *Elektra*. That year she made her first appearance at La Scala as Maria in Ildebrando Pizzetti's *Lo straniero*, and sang there regularly until 1943, and again from 1948 to 1951. She appeared at Covent Garden in 1937 and 1939, and with the Scala company there in 1950; she was at the Metropolitan during the 1938–9 season. Among the roles she created were Manuela in Italo Montemezzi's *La notte di Zoraima* (1931, Milan), Roxanne in Franco Alfano's *Cyrano de Bergerac* (1936, Rome) and the title role in Ottorino Respighi's *Lucrezia* (1937, Rome), all of which she sang with her customary involvement.

Caniglia sang most of Giuseppe Verdi's lyric-dramatic soprano roles, from Leonora in his first opera, *Oberto*, produced during the Verdi year (1951) at La Scala, to Alice in Arturo Toscanini's *Falstaff* (1935, Salzburg). She was much admired as Tosca, Adriana Lecouvreur and Fedora and recorded several operas with GIGLI including *Tosca*, *Un ballo in maschera*, *Aida* and *Andrea Chénier*; but she is heard at her best as Leonora in *La forza del destino* under Gino Marinuzzi, where her gifts as a genuine *lirico spinto* soprano and her generous, outgoing personality compensate for occasional technical fallibility.

Harold Rosenthal/Alan Blyth

Cannetti, Linda

(*b* nr Verona, 8 Nov 1878; *d* Milan, 14 March 1960). Italian soprano. She studied with Melchiorre Vidal in Vienna and made her début at Fossombrone in *Faust* in 1899. Later that year she sang in *Lohengrin* with the tenor Francesco Bravi, whom she subsequently married. His early death brought her career to a temporary halt, but on its resumption in 1909 she achieved her greatest success to date as Chrysothemis in the Italian première of *Elektra*, at La Scala. In 1913 she appeared in another Richard Strauss première in Italy, that of *Feuersnot*, and at Turin sang the title role in the world première of Riccardo Zandonai's *Francesca da Rimini* (1914). Other notable events included commemorative performances of Boito's *Mefistofele* under Arturo Toscanini and a personal triumph in Buenos Aires in Italo Montemezzi's *L'amore dei tre re*. She retired in 1928. Her recordings show warmth of voice and emotion, with a quick, somewhat uneven vibrato, probably more acceptable then than it is now.

J.B. Steane

Cantelo, April (Rosemary)

(*b* Purbrook, Hants., 2 April 1928). English soprano. She studied in London and, after singing in the Glyndebourne chorus, made her début in 1950 with the company at Edinburgh as Barbarina and Echo. At Glyndebourne she also sang Blonde (1953) and Marzelline (1963). With the English Opera Group she created Helena in Benjamin Britten's *A Midsummer Night's Dream* (1960) and sang Emmeline in Henry Purcell's *King Arthur* (1970). In Malcolm Williamson's operas she created Beatrice (*Our Man in Havana*, 1963), Swallow (*The Happy Prince*, 1965), Ann (*Julius Caesar Jones*, 1966) and Berthe (*The Violins of St Jacques*, 1966). She was a very gifted singing actress, demonstrating her skill as Manon Lescaut in H.W. Henze's *Boulevard Solitude* and Jenny in Kurt Weill's *Aufstieg und Fall der Stadt Mahagonny* (both first British productions). She directed a production of Purcell's *The Fairy-Queen* in New Zealand in 1972. Her voice was a pure, clear lyrical soprano, not large, but capable of flexibility and variety of expression.

Alan Blyth

Capecchi, Renato

(*b* Cairo, 6 Nov 1923; *d* Milan, 30 June 1998). Italian baritone. Trained in Lausanne and Milan, he was first heard as a prizewinner on Italian radio. His stage début was in *Aida* at Reggio nell'Emilia (1949), and he appeared in the first of many seasons at La Scala in 1950 and at the Metropolitan Opera in *La traviata* (1951). He later became most closely associated with such comic parts as Bartolo, Gianni Schicchi, and Melitone (*La forza del destino*), in which he made his Covent Garden début (1962). In 1977 he sang a highly acclaimed Falstaff at Glyndebourne. His repertory was extensive, and his career lasted into old age. Widely appreciated as a singer of unusual intelligence, clever timing and clear enunciation, he took part in many premières, including operas by Riccardo Malipiero and Girogio Ghedini, and in the first performances in Italy of Sergey Prokofiev's *War and Peace* (1953, Florence) and Dmitry Shostakovich's *The Nose* (1964, Florence). His career continued energetically; 1986 brought his first Sharpless (Philadelphia), 1987 his début in Montreal, and 1988 the role of the Mastro di Cappella in the première of Sylvano Bussotti's *L'ispirazione* (Florence). He taught in many opera studios in Europe and the USA, where his productions included *Don Giovanni* (1987, Milwaukee), and he produced his own television shows. Many of his best roles, such as Dulcamara, Bartolo and Melitone, are recorded, but he was an artist who needed to be seen, being one of the best singing actors of his time.

J.B. Steane

Cappuccilli, Piero

(*b* Trieste, 9 Nov 1929; *d* Trieste, 12 July 2005). Italian baritone. He studied singing under Luciano Donaggio at the Teatro Giuseppe Verdi, Trieste, where he appeared in small parts. His official début was at the Teatro Nuovo, Milan, as Tonio in *Pagliacci* (1957). In 1960 he was chosen by Walter Legge to sing Enrico in a recording of *Lucia di Lammermoor* with MARIA CALLAS, and in the same year he sang Germont in *La traviata* at the Metropolitan. His début (as Enrico) at La Scala in 1964 confirmed his position, strengthened in many subsequent seasons there, as one of Italy's foremost baritones. He appeared at Covent Garden first in *La traviata* (1967) and crowned a worthy career in that house by singing in *Cavalleria rusticana* and *Pagliacci* the same evenings at the age of 60. He sang in most other leading European opera houses as well as in South Africa and South America, and in 1969 he made the first of many successful appearances at Chicago. His performances in *Don Carlos* under Herbert von Karajan (1975, Salzburg) and *Simon Boccanegra* under Claudio Abbado (La Scala and Covent Garden, 1976) showed a development of interpretative powers and technique, a remarkable feature of which was his breath control. His warm, ample voice can be heard in many important recordings.

J.B. Steane

Caradori-Allan [née de Munck], Maria (Caterina Rosalbina)

(*b* Milan, 1800; *d* Surbiton, 15 Oct 1865). Alsatian soprano of Italian birth. She was taught by her mother, whose maiden name of Caradori she took when making her début at the King's Theatre, London, in 1822, as Cherubino in *Le nozze di Figaro*. She also appeared in Italy, and was engaged at Venice in 1830 where she created the role of Giulietta in Vincenzo Bellini's *I Capuleti e i Montecchi*. Her other roles included Emilia in Gioachino Rossini's *Otello*, Rosina in *Il barbiere di Siviglia*, Zerlina, and Amina in *La sonnambula*; but it was as a concert and oratorio singer that she became best known. She took part in the London Philharmonic Society performance of Ludwig van Beethoven's Ninth Symphony given on 21 March 1825, and she sang at all the English cathedral festivals, including Westminster Abbey in 1834. She was engaged for the Manchester Festival of 1836, and at the concert on 14 September, which included Joseph Haydn's *The Creation* and W.A. Mozart's Requiem, she sang a duet from Saverio Mercadante's *Andronico* with the dying MARIA MALIBRAN, who fainted after an encore and never sang again.

Near the end of her career Caradori-Allan sang in the first performance of Felix Mendelssohn's *Elijah*, given at Birmingham in 1846, but the composer was disappointed with her performance: 'It was all so pretty, so pleasing, so elegant, at the same time so flat, so heartless, so unintelligent, so soulless', he wrote to Livia Frege. Henry Chorley, writing about her stage performances, considered her 'one of those first-class singers of the second class, with whom it would be hard to find a fault, save want of fire'.

R. Edgcumbe, 2nd Earl of Mount Edgcumbe: *Musical Reminiscences of an Old Amateur* (London, 1824, 4/1834/*R*)
H.F. Chorley: *Thirty Years' Musical Recollections* (London, 1862/*R*, abridged 2/1926/*R* by E. Newman)

Elizabeth Forbes

Carden, Joan

(*b* Richmond, Melbourne, 9 Oct 1937). Australian soprano. She studied in Melbourne then in London, making her début at Sadler's Wells (1963) as the Water-Melon Seller in Malcolm Williamson's *Our Man in Havana*. A technically capable Gilda for the Australian Opera led to her Covent Garden début in the same part in 1974. She sang Donna Anna at Glyndebourne (1977) and for the touring Metropolitan Opera (1978), and Konstanze for Scottish Opera (1978). Her Australian Opera roles include Ellen Orford, Tatyana (*Yevgeny Onegin*), the title roles in *Lakmé* and *Alcina*, two Leonoras (*Il trovatore* and *La forza del destino*), several Mozart roles and the four heroines in *Les contes d'Hoffmann*. She gradually moved away from the coloratura to the lyric-dramatic repertory, singing Tosca in concert at Adelaide in 1990 and reviving the part on stage in 1995. Her Butterfly was much admired for its well-focussed, graceful singing.

Roger Covell

Carelli, Emma

(*b* Naples, 12 May 1877; *d* nr Rome, 17 Aug 1928). Italian soprano. She was born into a musical family, and in 1895 made her début in the title role of Saverio Mercadante's *La vestale* during the centenary celebrations at Altamura. After appearances in Naples and at the Dal Verme in Milan, she went to La Scala, singing Desdemona to TAMAGNO's

Otello and, in 1900, Tatyana in the Italian première of *Yevgeny Onegin*. A spectacular tour of South America was followed by her greatest success, as the title character, Zazà, in the opera by Ruggero Leoncavallo. In 1898 she married the left-wing politician Walter Mocchi, who later became a theatrical impresario and acquired the Costanzi in Rome. Carelli took over the management in 1912, her first season including the Rome première of Richard Strauss's *Elektra*, in which she sang the title role to great acclaim, having coped with a fire in the theatre earlier that evening. She ran the theatre for 15 years, maintaining an enterprising repertory with distinguished casts and despite serious financial losses. She died in a car accident in 1928. Her few and rare recordings are not attractive as pure singing but have plenty of energy and temperament.

K. Hardwick: 'Emma Carelli', *Record Collector*, xi (1957), 173–83; xii (1958–60), 36–7 [with discography]

J.B. Steane

Carestini, Giovanni [Cusanino]

(*b* Filottrano, nr Ancona, *c*1704; *d* ?Filottrano, *c*1760). Italian soprano, later alto, castrato. He was taken to Milan at the age of 12 under the protection of the Cusani family, and first performed there in Giuseppe Vignati's *Porsena* in 1719. Several northern appearances preceded his Roman début in 1721 (Alessandro Scarlatti's *La Griselda*), where he sang alongside BERNACCHI, his teacher. He remained for two years, creating Fausta in Giovanni Bononcini's *Crispo* (1721); he then graced the Viennese court in 1723–4, appearing in Johann Fux's *Costanza e Fortezza* in Prague. He was at Venice in 1724–6, 1729 and 1731, singing in operas by Leonardo Vinci and Nicola Porpora, and in Rome in 1727–30, where he appeared in works by Vinci and Francesco Feo; he also sang in operas by Johann Hasse and others in Naples, 1728–9. He crossed the Alps in 1731 and entered the service of the Duke of Bavaria in Munich, returning to Italy before following Handel to London in 1733. There he created the principal male roles in G.F. Handel's *Arianna in Creta* (1734), *Oreste* (1734), *Parnasso in festa*, *Terpsichore*, *Ariodante* (1735) and *Alcina* (1735), also singing in revivals and pasticcios, and in Handel's oratorios (*Deborah*, *Acis and Galatea*, *Esther* and *Athalia*). Back in Naples in 1735, his salary was higher than CAFFARELLI's. During a second London engagement, for six months ending in May 1740, he enjoyed little success. In the 1740s he appeared in Italy, was in Maria Theresa's employ by 1744 and sang under Hasse in Dresden, 1747–9. Brief Italian appearances preceded a Berlin engagement, 1750–54; he then moved to

St Petersburg under Francesco Araja until 1756. His career declined rapidly; a Naples audience was hostile in 1758. Carestini was at first 'a powerful and clear soprano' (Charles Burney), with a compass of *b* to *c‴*; later he had 'the fullest, finest, and deepest counter-tenor that has perhaps ever been heard'. Handel's roles for him call for a two-octave compass, *a* to *a″*; Hasse's *Demofoonte* (1748) requires *e*♭ to *g′*. His reputation was enormous. Hasse remarked: 'He who has not heard Carestini is not acquainted with the most perfect style of singing'; Johann Quantz added: 'He had extraordinary virtuosity in brilliant passages, which he sang in chest voice, conforming to the principles of the school of Bernacchi and the manner of FARINELLI'. Others, including Burney, commented on his superb acting, and his handsome and majestic profile.

Dale E. Monson

Carey, (Francis) Clive (Savill)

(*b* Sible Hedingham, 30 May 1883; *d* London, 30 April 1968). English baritone. He studied at Cambridge and in London and with JEAN DE RESZKE in Paris and Nice. He directed *Die Zauberflöte* and sang Papageno at Cambridge University in 1911 when Edward J. Dent's English translation was first used. Engaged at the Old Vic opera company (1920–24) as singer and director, he appeared in *Le nozze di Figaro*, *Don Giovanni* and *Die Zauberflöte*. He taught in Australia at Adelaide (1924–7), where he also worked in the straight theatre, and in 1928 he toured North America in *The Beggar's Opera*, singing Captain Macheath. In the 1930s he worked at Sadler's Wells Opera, where he was director in 1945–6, after a further period of teaching in Adelaide and also Melbourne (1939–45). A stylish performer, particularly of Mozart roles, and an accomplished actor, he was an imaginative director, much concerned with the elimination of accumulated tradition and returning to composers' intentions, and a fine teacher.

Elizabeth Forbes

Carli, Antonio Francesco

(*fl* 1706–23). Italian bass. There may have been two singers of this name (? father and son). The Anton Francesco Carli who sang in six operas (five of them by C.F. Pollarolo) in Venice between 1689 and 1699 is reported as a tenor. He was probably the singer who appeared at Modena in 1690, Mantua in 1697, Piacenza in 1698 (in Giovanni Bononcini's *Camilla*), Parma in 1699 (a tenor part in A. Scarlatti's *La caduti de' Decemviri*) and Reggio nell'Emilia in 1700. The

Carli who sang in most or all of the later productions was a bass: Turin in 1703, Genoa in 1703, 1706 and 1715, Bologna in 1708, Florence in 1708 and 1719–20 (eight operas, as a virtuoso of the Tuscan court), Reggio nell'Emilia in 1712, Rome in 1717 (as Bajazet in Francesco Gasparini's *Il trace in catena*), and repeatedly in Venice (1706–18 and 1722–3) in 28 operas including works by Pollarolo, Antonio Caldara, Antonio Lotti, Tomaso Albinoni and Gasparini, and Handel's *Agrippina* (1709), in which he was the original Claudius. The tessitura and compass of this part (*C* to *e′*) point to a singer of exceptional powers, capable of sudden leaps and changes of register. Handel's very taxing bass cantata *Nell'Africane selve* may have been composed for Carli. There is a caricature of him by A.M. Zanetti in the Cini collection.

Winton Dean

Carolsfeld, Ludwig Schnorr von.

See SCHNORR VON CAROLSFELD, LUDWIG.

Carolsfeld, Malvina Schnorr von.

See SCHNORR VON CAROLSFELD, MALVINA.

Carosio, Margherita

(*b* Genoa, 7 June 1908; *d* 10 Jan 2005). Italian soprano. She studied at the Paganini Conservatory, Genoa, and made her début at nearby Novi Ligure in 1924 at the age of 16 in the title role of *Lucia di Lammermoor*. In 1928 she sang Musetta, and Fyodor in *Boris Godunov* with CHALIAPIN, at Covent Garden. The next year she made her début at La Scala as Oscar and from 1931 to 1939, and 1946 until 1952, never missed a season there. At La Scala she created Gnese in Ermanno Wolf-Ferrari's *Il campiello* (1936) and Egloge in Pietro Mascagni's *Nerone* and sang Aminta in the first Italian performance of Richard Strauss's *Die schweigsame Frau*. In 1939 she sang Rosina at the Salzburg Festival. She returned to London in 1946 with the S Carlo company as Violetta, one of her most appealing roles. Her piquant charm, exquisite phrasing and fine musicianship admirably suited her for Adina in *L'elisir d'amore*, which she sang at La Scala in 1950 and also recorded.

Harold Rosenthal/Alan Blyth

Carreras, José [Josep]

(*b* Barcelona, 5 Dec 1946). Spanish tenor. He studied with Jaime Francisco Puig. After graduating from the Barcelona Conservatory he made his operatic

José Carreras in the title role of 'Don Carlos' (Verdi), Osterfestpiele, Salzburg, 1986

début in Barcelona as Ismaele (*Nabucco*). Initially, his career was helped by support from two compatriots: Rafael Frühbeck de Burgos, who engaged him for Giuseppe Verdi's Requiem in Madrid in 1970, and MONTSERRAT CABALLÉ, with whom he sang at his sensational London début in 1971 in a concert performance of *Maria Stuarda*. After winning the Giuseppe Verdi Competition in 1972, Carreras appeared in Italy and Paris. The same year he made his American début with the New York City Opera as Pinkerton, and subsequently sang at the Hollywood Bowl (Duke of Mantua) and as Rodolfo (*La bohème*) with the San Francisco Opera in 1973. In 1974 he made his Metropolitan début as Cavaradossi and sang Alfredo at Covent Garden, where he was also greatly admired as Nemorino, Rodolfo and Stiffelio. At Salzburg he sang Don Carlos (see illustration) and Radames under Herbert von Karajan.

In 1987, at the peak of his career, he contracted leukaemia, but after extensive treatment he returned to the stage and to a demanding mixture of operatic roles and appearances for charity. The sweetness of timbre and purity of phrasing that typified his singing in the first part of his career made him one of the most popular lyric tenors of his generation. Later in his career he won acclaim beyond the opera-going public as one of the 'Three Tenors' in appearances and recordings with LUCIANO PAVAROTTI

and PLACIDO DOMINGO (see illustration at DOMINGO, PLACIDO). Carreras, though on occasion tempted to essay roles heavier than ideal for his resources, has at his best justified comparisons with JUSSI BJÖRLING and the young GIUSEPPE DI STEFANO. His recorded repertory is wide and includes many roles in works by Gaetano Donizetti, Verdi and Giacomo Puccini, where the fervent and elegaic qualities of his singing can be heard; he has also recorded *West Side Story* with Leonard Bernstein. His most recent new part is the title role in Wolf-Ferrari's *Sly*, which he sang in Zürich in 1998 and in Washington the following year, and recorded. He has published an autobiography, *Cantar con el alma* (Barcelona, 1989; Eng. trans. as *Singing from the Soul*, 1991).

N. Goodwin: 'José Carreras', *Opera*, xxxviii (1987), 507–12

Martin Bernheimer/Alan Blyth

Cartagenova, Gian [Giovanni]-Orazio [Joao Oracio]

(*b* Vicenza, 1800; *d* Vicenza, 26 Sept 1841). Italian baritone. His career began in 1823 in Milan with minor bass parts. In 1826, he joined the Italian troupe under Franciszek Mirecki, singing in the Lisbon première of Mirecki's *I due forzati*. Obligations at the S Carlos continued under Saverio Mercadante, creating roles in the 1828 premières of Mercadante's *Adriano in Siria* (Osroa), *Gabriella di Vergy* (Fayel) and the expressly revised *Ipermestra* (Danao). He then sang in Cadiz, in Ferdinando Paer's *Agnese*, and in Madrid, in operas by Mercadante, Gioachino Rossini, Vincenzo Bellini, Giovanni Pacini and Nicola Vaccai. After considerable success on the Iberian peninsula, he returned to Italy, probably in 1831.

In the 1830s Cartagenova sang regularly at La Scala, Milan, and had successes in London and Vienna. He was in demand by leading composers, and created the principal roles in Mercadante's *I Normanni a Parigi* (1832), Bellini's *Beatrice di Tenda* (1833, Filippo), Mercadante's *La gioventù di Enrico V* (1834) and many other operas. These efforts led to the pivotal role-creations in Mercadante's *Il giuramento* (1837) and Pacini's *Saffo* (1840); each role was written specifically for Cartagenova, and both show his important contribution to consolidating the vocal and psychological transition from *basso cantante* to Romantic baritone. Together with RONCONI, he helped to shape the identity of the new baritone register. He is remembered essentially as a singing actor, and he frequently moved audiences to tears.

Riccardo La Spina

Caruso, Enrico

(*b* Naples, 25 Feb 1873; *d* Naples, 2 Aug 1921). Italian tenor. Born of poor parents, he first sang as a child in churches. He studied with Guglielmo Vergine and made his début in the title role of Mario Morelli's *L'amico francesco* at the Teatro Nuovo, Naples (1895). He continued to sing, not always successfully, in small theatres in southern Italy, and to study under Vincenzo Lombardi until 1897. In May that year he achieved his first real success at Palermo in *La Gioconda*. The foundations of his career were laid at appearances in Milan (Teatro Lirico), which included the premières of Francesco Cilea's *L'arlesiana* (Federico, 1897) and *Adriana Lecouvreur* (Maurizio, 1902) and Umberto Giordano's *Fedora* (Loris, 1898); at his Buenos Aires début in 1899; his Rome début in Pietro Mascagni's

Iris, also in 1899; and finally, during the 1900–01 season, when a relatively unsuccessful appearance in *La bohème* at La Scala was followed by a triumph in *L'elisir d'amore*. Caruso sang in *L'elisir* at the S Carlo, Naples, also in 1901, but after his controversial reception he resolved never to sing again in Naples.

On 14 May 1902 Caruso made his successful début in *Rigoletto* at Covent Garden, causing a sensation with the beauty and power of his voice and the ebulliance of his personality, and where he subsequently appeared from 1904 to 1907 and in 1913 and 1914. He also sang in Spain, Germany, Austria, France and Uruguay. But the theatre where he most often sang was the Metropolitan, where he made his début in *Rigoletto* on 23 November 1903. Over the next decade he performed there periodically, creating Dick Johnson in *La fanciulla del West* in 1910; from 1912 he sang there continuously. In all he gave more than 850 performances with the company in New York or on tour, comprising no fewer than 38 roles; his most frequent appearances were as Canio, Enzo, Radames, Rodolfo and Cavaradossi. He returned to Italy only for benefit performances of *Pagliacci* in Rome (1914, at the Costanzi) and Milan (1915, at the Verme). He sang several times in Latin America (Havana, Mexico City, São Paulo) in 1917–20. His last public appearance was in Fromental Halévy's *La Juive*, at the Metropolitan on 24 December 1920. He died of a lung ailment.

Because of his incomplete and irregular training, Caruso began his career with certain technical deficiencies. In his early years he was ill at ease in the upper register, often using falsetto or transposing. He did not achieve security in his high notes, at least up to the high B, until about 1902. In his early years, too, his dark tone gave rise to ambiguities; his voice was often regarded as almost a baritone. This, however, became one of Caruso's resources, once he had mastered production. The exceptional appeal of his voice was, in fact, based on the fusion of a baritone's full, burnished timbre with a tenor's smooth, silken finish, by turns brilliant and affecting. This enabled him in the middle range to achieve melting sensuality, now in caressing and elegiac tones, now in outbursts of fiery, impetuous passion. The clarion brilliance of his high notes, his steadiness, his exceptional breath control and his impeccable intonation, formed a unique instrument, creating the legend of the twentieth century's greatest tenor.

The winning quality of the sound, the tender *mezza voce* (particularly in the early years) and his phrasing, based on a rare mastery of legato and portamento, enabled Caruso to sing the French and Italian lyric repertory (particularly *Faust*, *Les pêcheurs de perles*, *Manon*, *Manon Lescaut*, *La bohème* and *Tosca*), as well as such lighter operas as *L'elisir d'amore* and *Martha*. In addition, his noble, incisive

Enrico Caruso in 'Pagiliacci' (Leoncavallo), 1920

declamation, his broad, generous phrasing and his vigour in dramatic outbursts made Caruso a notable interpreter of Giuseppe Verdi (*Rigoletto*, *Ballo*, *Forza*, *Aida*, *La Juive*, *L'Africaine*, *Samson et Dalila*). In this repertory his performances were characterized by the irresistible erotic appeal of his timbre allied to a temperament as warm and vehement as his voice. His numerous recordings, now faithfully remastered on CD, not only made him universally famous; they also did much to encourage the acceptance of recording as a medium for opera. Beginning with the famous series recorded by Fred Gaisberg in a Milan hotel in 1902, they chronicle the whole gamut of Caruso's career. It has been aptly remarked that Caruso made the gramophone and it made him.

M.H. Flint: *Impressions of Caruso and his Art as Portrayed at the Metropolitan Opera House* (New York, 1917)

S. Fucito and B.J. Beyer: *Caruso and the Art of Singing* (New York,1922/*R*)

D. Caruso: *Enrico Caruso: his Life and Death* (New York, 1945/*R*)

F. Robinson: *Caruso: his Life in Pictures* (New York, 1957) [incl. discography by J. Secrist]

J. Freestone and H.J. Drummond: *Enrico Caruso: his Recorded Legacy* (London, 1960)

A. Favia-Artsay: *Caruso on Records* (Valhalla, NY, 1965)

'A Century of Caruso', *ON*, xxxvii/16 (1972–3) [whole issue]

J.R. Bolig: *The Recordings of Enrico Caruso* (Dover, DE, 1973)

H. Greenfield: *Caruso* (New York, 1983)

M. Scott: *The Great Caruso* (London, 1988)

E. Caruso jr and A. Farkas: *My Father and my Family* (Portland, OR, 1991)

Rodolfo Celletti/Alan Blyth

Enrico Caruso, self-portrait, 1919

Carvalho, Caroline [Miolan, Miolan-Carvalho; née Félix-Miolan, Marie]

(*b* Marseilles, 31 Dec 1827; *d* Château-Puys, nr Dieppe, 10 July 1895). French soprano. She studied first with her father, François Félix-Miolan, an oboist, and then with the tenor GILBERT DUPREZ at the Paris Conservatoire, where she won a *premier prix* in singing. After touring France with Duprez (1848–9) she made her stage début in a benefit performance for him at the Opéra on 14 December 1849, singing in the first act of *Lucia di Lammermoor* and the trio from the second act of *La Juive*. She was immediately engaged by the Opéra-Comique. In 1853 she married Léon Carvalho (after their marriage she began to use the name Caroline Carvalho rather than Marie Miolan). From 1856 until 1867 she sang at the Théâtre Lyrique, creating four Gounod heroines: Marguerite in *Faust* (1859), in which her smooth, light lyric voice and excellent coloratura were well displayed, Baucis in *Philémon et Baucis* (1860), Mireille (1864) and Juliette (1867). Her other successful roles at the Lyrique included Zerlina, Cherubino and Pamina.

She first appeared at Covent Garden in 1859, singing the title role in the first London performance of Giacomo Meyerbeer's *Dinorah*, and won greater acclaim than any new soprano since VIARDOT. She returned to London each year until 1864 and again in 1871–2, singing Gilda, Mathilde (*Guillaume Tell*), Marguerite de Valois, Marguerite and Countess Almaviva, among other roles. She also appeared in Berlin and St Petersburg, and on 9 June 1885 made her farewell appearance at the Opéra-Comique as Marguerite. After her retirement she taught singing; her most famous pupil was Maria Delna.

H. Morley: *The Journal of a London Playgoer from 1851–66* (London, 1866, 2/1891/*R*)

Harold Rosenthal/Karen Henson

Casa, Lisa Della.

See DELLA CASA, LISA.

Cassel, (John) Walter

(*b* Council Bluffs, IA, 15 May 1910; *d* Bloomington, IN, 3 July 2000). American baritone. He studied with Frank La Forge and made his début in 1942 as Brétigny in Jules Massenet's *Manon* at the Metropolitan but left the company in 1945, dissatisfied with its casting policy. He ventured into musical comedy but continued to appear in opera with various companies, including those at Philadelphia, Pittsburgh, Cincinnati, New Orleans and San Antonio. After World War II he sang at the Vienna Staatsoper and in Düsseldorf before appearing with the New York City Opera between 1948 and 1960, making his début as Escamillo. In 1955 he rejoined the Metropolitan, remaining until 1974. He created the roles of Horace Tàbor in Douglas Moore's *The Ballad of Baby Doe* (1956, Central City, Colorado) and Petruccio in Vittorio Giannini's *The Taming of the Shrew* (1958, New York City Opera). From 1970 to 1972 he sang the role of Johann Strauss sr in E.W. Korngold's *The Great Waltz* in London, then performed in Italy and Spain. His well-modulated, resonant voice was suited to the works of Richard Wagner (Telramund, the Dutchman, Kurwenal) and Richard Strauss (John the Baptist, Orestes, the Music Master).

Charles Jahant

Cassilly, Richard

(*b* Washington DC, 14 Dec 1927; *d* Boston, 30 Jan 1998). American tenor. He studied at the Peabody Conservatory, Baltimore, and made his début as a concert singer in 1954. At the end of that year he sang in Gian Carlo Menotti's *The Saint of Bleecker Street* on Broadway, and that led to his engagement with the New York City Opera as Vakula in P.I. Tchaikovsky's *Cherevichki*. In 1959 he appeared for the first time at the Chicago Lyric Opera, as Laca in *Jenůfa*, returning in 1972 as the Lord Mayor in Gottfried von Einem's *Besuch der alten Dame* (American première). His European début was in the title role of Heinrich Sutermeister's *Raskolnikoff* at Geneva in 1965, the year he joined the Hamburg Staatsoper, where he made his début as Canio. His first appearance at Covent Garden was as Laca in 1968, and he returned as Siegmund, Florestan, Othello, Peter Grimes (an imaginative portrayal), which he also sang for Scottish Opera, and a Tannhäuser particularly praised for its clear enunciation and total involvement in the character. In 1970 he made his débuts at the Vienna Staatsoper (Tannhäuser), Munich (Othello) and La Scala (Samson), in 1972 at the Paris Opéra (Siegmund) and in 1973 at the Metropolitan (Radames). In 1974

he sang Arnold Schoenberg's Aaron at Hamburg, and he recorded the part under Pierre Boulez. He returned to the Metropolitan to sing Canio, Tristan, Camille Saint-Saëns' Samson, Captain Vere (*Billy Budd*), the Drum Major (*Wozzeck*), Herod, and Jimmy Mahoney (*Aufstieg und Fall der Stadt Mahagonny*), which he also sang for Scottish Opera in 1986. He had a powerful, vibrant voice of heroic proportions and superb diction, singing his roles with intelligence and intensity, though not always with well-coordinated tone.

Alan Blyth

Castagna, Bruna

(*b* Bari, 15 Oct 1905; *d* Pinamar, Argentina, 10 July 1983). Italian mezzo-soprano. She studied in Milan and made her début in 1925 at the Teatro Sociale, Mantua, as Marina in *Boris Godunov*. In the same year she made her first appearance at La Scala and remained there till 1928. She also sang at the Teatro Colón, Buenos Aires, taking part in the South American première of Nikolay Rimsky-Korsakov's *Sadko*. In 1930 she returned on Arturo Toscanini's invitation to La Scala, where in 1933 she had a great success in *L'italiana in Algeri*. Opera and recital work took her to Australia and Egypt and then to the USA, where for a decade she was a leading mezzo at the Metropolitan Opera. She made her début there in 1936 as Amneris, after which Lawrence Gilman wrote of her 'remarkable voice, sensuously beautiful, voluptuous, richly expressive'. Her Carmen was considered the best for many years; she retired in this role in the 1949–50 season at Philadelphia. She then taught in Milan. She can be heard in a few recordings of live performances from the Metropolitan.

P. Jackson: *Saturday Afternoons at the Old Met* (Portland, OR, 1992)

J.B. Steane

Castellan, Jeanne Anaïs

(*b* Beaujeu, Rhône, 26 Oct 1819; *d* after 1858). French soprano. She studied at the Paris Conservatoire with Giulio Bordogni, ADOLPHE NOURRIT and LAURE CINTI-DAMOREAU, and in 1836 won a *premier prix* for singing. She began her stage career in Italy, appearing at Varese in 1837, and later at Turin, Bergamo, Rome, Milan and Florence, where in 1840 she married the singer Enrico Giampetro. In the winter of 1843–4 she sang in New York and Boston. She made her London début at a Philharmonic concert (13 May 1844), and appeared in Italian opera alternately in St Petersburg (1844–6) and with Benjamin Lumley's company at Her Majesty's Theatre (1845–7). Her first London role was Lucia (1 April 1845), and she chose the same role for her débuts at the Théâtre-Italien, Paris (1847), and Covent Garden (1848). At the Paris Opéra in 1849 she sang Berthe in the première of Giacomo Meyerbeer's *Le prophète*, and the following year she was particularly successful at Covent Garden in *Mosè* and *Nabucco* (which were given, respectively, as *Zora* and *Anato*). She continued to appear at Covent Garden until 1853, and for several more years at provincial music festivals and on concert tours abroad; her last appearance in England was at the 1858 Birmingham Festival. Most accounts of her agree that she possessed considerable agility and an extensive range, remarkably unified in tone quality; but several critics found fault with her intonation, and considered her cadenzas and ornamentation over-ambitious or inappropriate: Henry Chorley wrote in 1847 that 'She now attempts such feats as only one born a Garcia can accomplish; often fails signally, and never succeeds completely'.

H.F. Chorley: *Thirty Years' Musical Recollections* (London, 1862/*R*, abridged 2/1926/*R* by E. Newman)

Philip Robinson

Castris, Franceso de.

See DE CASTRIS, FRANCESCO.

Catalani, Angelica

(*b* Sinigaglia, 10 May 1780; *d* Paris, 12 June 1849). Italian soprano. She received very little formal musical instruction and made her début at La Fenice at the age of 17 in Simon Mayr's *La Lodoiska*. In 1800 she sang in Domenico Cimarosa's *Gli Orazi ed i Curiazi* in Trieste, and the following season in the same composer's *Clitennestra* at La Scala. After appearances in Florence and Rome, in 1804 she went to Lisbon, and in 1806 she made her London début at the King's Theatre in M.A. Portugal's *Semiramide*, also singing in Portugal's *Il ritorno di Serse* and *La morte di Mitridate*, Mayr's *Che originali* (*Il fanatico per la musica*) and Sebastiano Nasolini's *La morte di Cleopatra*.

Between 1808 and 1814 at the King's she appeared in Giovanni Paisiello's *La frascatana* and *Didone*, sang Sesostris in Nasolini's *La festa d'Iside*, and sang in Vincenzo Pucitta's *La vestale*, *Le tre sultane* and *La caccia di Enrico IV*, Niccolò Piccinni's *La buona figliuola* and Ferdinando Paer's *Camilla*. She also sang Vitellia (*La clemenza di Tito*) and Susanna in the first London performance of

Le nozze di Figaro (1812). Moving to Paris, she took over the direction of the Théâtre Italien in 1814, continuing to sing in operas written for her by Pucitta and Portugal. In 1817 she embarked on an extended tour of Europe, returning to London in 1824 for a few performances of *Che originali* (*Il fanatico per la musica*); then she gave up the stage. A beautiful woman with a superb, perfectly controlled voice, and a fine actress, she lacked the taste or education to make the most of her gifts.

Elizabeth Forbes

Cavalieri, Catarina [Cavalier, Catharina Magdalena Josepha]

(*b* Vienna, 18 March 1755; *d* Vienna, 30 June 1801). Austrian soprano. During a versatile career, confined almost exclusively to Vienna, she appeared with equal success in comic and serious roles in both the Italian and German repertories. Until late in her career Cavalieri possessed an impressive upper range, to *d'''*. An extraordinary stamina and flexibility are reflected in consistently large-scale bravura arias. Of her début in Vienna (19 June 1775 at the Kärntnertortheater), as Sandrina in Pasquale Anfossi's *La finta giardiniera*, Prince Khevenhüller wrote that she possessed a very strong chest voice and met with 'well-deserved approbation'. In 1776–7 she belonged to a troupe of Italian singers led by V. Fanti. In 1778 she sang Sophie in Ignaz Umlauf's *Die Bergknappen*, the inaugural production of the National Singspiel, and went on to sing 18 leading roles in the company including Nannette in Antonio Salieri's *Der Rauchfangkehrer* (1781) and Konstanze in W.A. Mozart's *Die Entführung* (1782). Of the challenging *fioriture* in 'Ach ich liebte', Mozart wrote to his father (26 September 1781): 'I have sacrificed Konstanze's aria a little to the flexible throat of Mlle Cavallieri'; this and another bravura showcase in the same act, 'Martern aller Arten', came willingly from the astute Mozart, eager to ingratiate himself with Cavalieri and her protector, the court composer Salieri. When Joseph II inaugurated *opera buffa* at the Burgtheater, Cavalieri was put to use both as a serious and comic lead, creating Enrichetta in Stephen Storace's *Gli sposi malcontenti* (1785). During 1781 Cavalieri sang in at least six different Singspiels. A notice by M.A. Schmitt (*Meine Empfindungen im Theater*, 1781) of Salieri's *Der Rauchfangkehrer* said:

> Demoiselle Cavalieri, who has the reputation among connoisseurs of being one of the first singers, and who through her beautiful singing also pleases the ordinary man, played the girl. Her acting is improving daily and it is noticeable

how much more trouble she takes if she is playing with others whose own acting contains more animation and accuracy, and a firmer assurance. In speech she is not yet natural enough: she overemphasizes final syllables and clips the last words of her speeches so much that she becomes unintelligible. Her arms are still a little too stiff, bent too far forward and not loose enough: but she has already considerable expression in her bearing, has fine deportment, and soon will delight us as an actress as much as she does with her voice.

Cavalieri is best known through Mozart's music for her. Her aria as Mme Silberklang in *Der Schauspieldirektor* (1786) has athletic tunes, with driving, vigorous two-note phrases and quaver scales. For her appearance as Donna Elvira in the first Vienna production of *Don Giovanni* (1788), Mozart composed a large-scale aria ('Mi tradì') for her in which she clearly no longer commanded her earlier high notes. For the revival of *Le nozze di Figaro* (1789), in which Cavalieri sang the Countess, Mozart rewrote 'Dove sono', eliminating the repeat of the intimate, restrained initial material and adding *fioriture* in the faster section. He also intended her to sing the role of Bettina in the unfinished *Lo sposo deluso*.

Early in her career, Cavalieri was said to want 'animation and accuracy, and a firmer assurance', and criticized for almost 'unintelligible' speech (Schmitt). The Viennese dramatist Tobias Philipp von Gebler, writing in 1780–81, said she had 'a strong and pleasant voice, in both the high and the low notes, a combination which one seldom encounters, [she] sings equally well the most difficult passages'. Karl von Zinzendorf noted that in a duet in Giuseppe Sarti's *Giulio Sabino* 'Cavalieri drowned MARCHESINI's voice with her shouts' (4 August 1785), but two days later recorded that 'she screamed less'.

Patricia Lewy Gidwitz

Cavalieri, Lina [Natalina]

(*b* Viterbo, 25 Dec 1874; *d* Florence, 7 Feb 1944). Italian soprano. Of the humblest origin, she began her career at the age of 14 singing in cafés and soon became celebrated for her exceptional beauty. Encouraged by the tenor Francesco Marconi to devote herself to opera, she studied with Maddelena Mariani-Masi and made her début in 1900 at the S Carlos, Lisbon, in *Pagliacci*, immediately afterwards singing in *La bohème* at the S Carlo, Naples. Although mostly engaged in Paris, Monte Carlo and, above all, St Petersburg, she also sang in New York (Metropolitan and Manhattan Opera House) between 1907 and 1910, and in London in 1908 (Covent Garden) and 1911 (London Opera House). With an agreeable though limited voice, she was an elegant, natural actress and preferred roles that allowed her to display her attractive figure in splendid jewels and spectacular costumes: Violetta, Manon (both Massenet and Puccini), Thaïs, Fedora, Tosca. She was married four times; one of her husbands (from 1913 to 1919) was the tenor LUCIEN MURATORE. Between 1914 and 1921 she starred in several films. Her autobiography *Le mie verità* was published in Rome in 1936.

M. Scott: *The Record of Singing*, i: *To 1914* (London, 1977), 151–2

W.R. Moran, ed.: *Herman Klein and the Gramophone* (Portland, OR, 1990)

Rodolfo Celletti/Valeria Pregliasco Gualerzi

Cebotari, Maria

(*b* Kishineu, 10/23 Feb 1910; *d* Vienna, 9 June 1949). Austrian soprano of Russian birth. She studied with Oskar Daniel in Berlin and made her début at the Dresden Staatsoper in 1931 as Mimì, remaining there until 1936; in 1935 she created Aminta in *Die schweigsame Frau* and returned in 1940 to create Juliet in Heinrich Sutermeister's *Romeo und Julia*. She sang at the Berlin Staatsoper (1936–44) and at the Vienna Staatsoper (1946–9). She first appeared at Covent Garden with the Dresden company in 1936 as Susanna, Zerlina and Sophie, soubrette roles in which she was then irresistible; she returned there in 1947 with the Vienna Staatsoper as Countess Almaviva, Donna Anna and Salome, the role that proved the apex of her career. She appeared regularly in Salzburg in Mozart roles, and there created Lucile in *Dantons Tod* (1947). Her repertory also included Butterfly and Violetta, both memorably moving, Tatyana, Arabella and Turandot. Cebotari was a sensitive artist and a fine actress, with a clear, beautiful voice and a charming stage presence. Her ecstatic account of Salome's final scene on disc explains why Strauss greatly admired her in that role.

J.B. Steane: *Singers of the Century* (London, 1996), 166–70

Harold Rosenthal/Alan Blyth

Cernay [Pointu], Germaine

(*b* Le Havre, 1900; *d* Paris, 1943). French mezzo-soprano. At the Paris Opéra in 1925 she sang Euryclea in Fauré's *Pénélope* but for most of her career was at the Opéra-Comique, where she

Fyodor Chaliapin as Ivan the Terrible in 'The Maid of Pskov' (Rimsky-Korsakov)

made her début in Franco Alfano's *Risurrezione* with MARY GARDEN in 1927. She appeared there in the French stage première of Pierre de Bréville's *Eros vainqueur* (1932) and also sang Charlotte in *Werther*, Mignon and Carmen as well as many secondary parts such as Suzuki in *Madama Butterfly* and Mallika in *Lakmé*. She enjoyed some success at the Monnaie in Brussels and had a special reputation as a singer of J.S. Bach. Her strong, bright-toned voice and forthright rather than subtle style can be heard in recordings which include the roles of Mignon and Geneviève (*Pelléas et Mélisande*).

J.B. Steane

Chaliapin [Shalyapin], Fyodor (Ivanovich)

(*b* nr Kazan', 1/13 Feb 1873; *d* Paris, 12 April 1938). Russian bass. Widely considered the greatest singing actor of his day, he was largely self-taught and sang with small provincial companies before having any formal training. After study (1892–3) in Tbilisi he successfully sang a wide variety of roles there and in St Petersburg, where he belonged to the Imperial Opera (at the Mariinsky Theatre) (1894–6) leaving to join S.I. Mamontov's private opera in Moscow. There he became renowned for his carefully thought-out performances of such roles as Boris and Varlaam, Dosifey (*Khovanshchina*), Ivan the Terrible (*The*

Maid of Pskov; see illustration), the Viking Guest (*Sadko*), the Miller (A.S. Dargomïzhsky's *Rusalka*) and Holofernes (A.K. Serov's *Judith*), while creating Nikolay Rimsky-Korsakov's Salieri in 1898. He was a member of the Bol'shoy Opera in Moscow (1899–1914) and made frequent guest appearances at the Mariinsky and in the provinces. Chaliapin's international career began in 1901 at La Scala, as Arrigo Boito's Mefistofele. He made his Metropolitan Opera début in 1907 in the same role and during the 1907–8 season sang Don Basilio (*Il barbiere*), Leporello and Méphistophélès (*Faust*; see illustration in ZENATELLO, GIOVANNI). He took part in the Sergey Diaghilev seasons in Paris (1908, 1909, 1910 and 1913), sang in Monte Carlo where he created the title role in Jules Massenet's *Don Quichotte* (1910), London (1913–14) and rejoined the Mariinsky Theatre as soloist and artistic director (1918). In 1921 he left Russia and, on 9 December, sang Boris at the Metropolitan. He continued to sing throughout the world until his final illness. He made two films and some 200 recordings, chronicling virtually all his roles and much of his recital repertory. Live performances in London of *Faust*, *Boris Godunov* and *Mozart and Salieri* demonstrate his larger-than-life portrayals late in his stage career. The recordings of songs show the extraordinary breadth of his tonal range and his masterly inflections of Russian.

Chaliapin's voice was sufficiently flexible to allow him to sing baritone roles like Yevgeny Onegin, Valentin (*Faust*) and Anton Rubinstein's Demon, as well as such bass roles as Oroveso (*Norma*) and Philip II (*Don Carlos*). In *Prince Igor* he sang Galitsky, Konchak and Igor. He was a perfectionist as far as his own make-up, costuming and musical and dramatic preparation were concerned, and untiringly attentive to the staging of the operas he appeared in. Those who worked with him or who knew him off stage testify to his almost superhuman vital force, warmth and fierce intolerance of artistic mediocrity.

H.T. Finck: 'Chaliapine, the Russian "Mephistopheles"', *The Century*, new ser., lxxxi (1910–11), 230–37

B. Semeonoff: 'Chaliapin's Repertoire and Recordings', *Record Collector*, xx (1971–2), 171–230 [with discography by A. Kelly]

V. Borovsky: *Chaliapin: a Critical Biography* (London, 1988) [with discography by A. Kelly and V. Garrick]

Harold Barnes/Alan Blyth

Chance, Michael

(*b* Penn, Bucks., 7 March 1955). English countertenor. He read English at King's College, Cambridge, where he was a choral scholar, and quickly established a reputation. He made his British operatic début as Apollo in Francesco Cavalli's *Giasone* (1983, Buxton Festival) and his European début as Andronicus in G.F. Handel's *Tamerlano* (1985, Lyons). Other roles have included Otho, in Claudio Monteverdi's *L'incoronazione di Poppea* and in Handel's *Agrippina*, and Ptolemy in Handel's *Giulio Cesare*. He sang with Kent Opera as the Military Governor in the première of Judith Weir's *A Night at the Chinese Opera* (1987, Cheltenham Festival) and in 1988 achieved a notable success in the title role of *Giasone* at the Innsbruck Early Music Week. In 1989 he appeared at Glyndebourne as Oberon in Benjamin Britten's *A Midsummer Night's Dream* (a role he subsequently sang with the Netherlands Opera and Australian Opera) and as Apollo in *Death in Venice* with the Glyndebourne Touring Opera. In 1990 he sang with the Netherlands Opera in Monteverdi's *Il ritorno d'Ulisse in patria*, and in 1997 appeared as C.W. Gluck's Orpheus at the ENO. His recordings include *Agrippina*, *Tamerlano*, *Jephtha*, *Semele*, *Orfeo* (Monteverdi and Gluck), *Giasone*, W.A. Mozart's *Ascanio in Alba* and Alexander Goehr's *The Death of Moses*, in addition to music ranging from Elizabethan lute songs through Bach Passions and cantatas to Carl Orff's *Carmina burana*. Several works have been specially composed for him by, among others, Goehr, Richard Rodney Bennett, Tan Dun, John Tavener, Anthony Powers and Elvis Costello. Chance's secure technique and natural-sounding, unstrained vocal projection have made him much in demand in both opera and oratorio.

Nicholas Anderson

Charles-Cahier, Sarah.

See CAHIER, MME CHARLES.

Charton-Demeur [de Meur], Anne [Arsène]

(*b* Saujon, Charente Maritime, 5 March 1824; *d* Paris, 30 Nov 1892). French dramatic mezzo-soprano. She studied with Bizot at Bordeaux and made her operatic début there in 1842 playing the title role in Gaetano Donizetti's *Lucia di Lammermoor*; as Mlle Charton she subsequently toured in Toulouse and Brussels. On 18 July 1846 she made a successful London début at Drury Lane, singing Madeleine in Adolphe Adam's *Le postillon de Longjumeau*; she later sang Angèle in Daniel Auber's *Le domino noir*. At Drury Lane she met the Belgian flautist Jules-Antoine Demeur (*b* Hodimont-lez-Verviers, 23 Sept 1814), whom she married on 4 September 1847. Demeur gave up this position of first flute at the Théâtre de la Monnaie to travel with his wife on her engagements.

In 1849–50 Mme Charton-Demeur was the leading female singer for Mitchell's French company at St James's Theatre, London; she also sang at a Philharmonic Society concert in 1850. She performed her first Italian role at Her Majesty's Theatre on 27 July 1852 as Amina in Bellini's *La sonnambula* and on 5 August she sang there in the Duke of Saxe-Coburg-Gotha's *Casilda*. Her performances at the Paris Opéra-Comique in 1849 and 1853 met with little success. Between 1849 and 1852 she appeared in Madrid, St Petersburg, Vienna, New York and Havana to great acclaim. She returned to Paris in 1862 to perform at the Théâtre Impérial Italien as Desdemona in Gioachino Rossini's *Otello*.

One of Charton-Demeur's most interesting and permanent associations was with Hector Berlioz. In the first performance of *Béatrice et Bénédict*, at the new theatre at Baden-Baden in 1862, she sang the title role under his direction. He wrote in his *Mémoires* that she sang 'with warmth, delicacy, great energy, and rare beauty of style'. He subsequently asked her to sing the role of Dido in the first performances of *Les Troyens à Carthage* at the Théâtre Lyrique in 1863, a role she had helped create in performances of the uncompleted work for private audiences. Although he realized that her voice was unequal to the vehemence required in certain scenes, Berlioz wrote that he 'was intensely moved by certain pieces in *Les Troyens*....above all Dido's monologue "Je vais mourir" overwhelmed me'. She had generously accepted a fee far below what she had been offered simultaneously by a Madrid theatre; when receipts for *Les Troyens* did not meet expectations her contract was cancelled and she left for Madrid, but soon returned to the Théâtre Lyrique. She maintained her friendship with Berlioz and was present when he died in 1869. At about that time she formally retired from singing, but occasionally appeared in concerts of Berlioz's music, including the Berlioz Festival at the Opéra in 1870 where she sang the duo nocturne from *Béatrice et Bénédict* with CHRISTINE NILSSON. She also sang Dido in 1879 at J.E. Pasdeloup's Concerts Populaires.

Thomasin La May

Chassé (de Chinais), Claude Louis Dominique [de]

(*b* Rennes, 1699; *d* Paris, 25 Oct 1786). French bass. Born into an untitled and impoverished branch of a family of the lesser Breton nobility, he made his début at the Paris Opéra as Léandre in the 1721 revival of André Campra's *Les fêtes vénitiennes*; this was followed by Saturn in Jean-Baptiste Lully's *Phaëton* (1721 revival). Though he was highly, even disproportionately, appreciated in minor parts, he

did not sing principal roles until the retirement of Gabriel-Vincent Thévenard in 1729. He created the title role in Michel Pignolet de Montéclair's *Jephté* in 1732, the first biblical opera staged at the Opéra. For Jean-Philippe Rameau he created Theseus (*Hippolyte et Aricie*, 1733), Huascar (*Les Indes galantes*, 1735) and Pollux (1737). He also took the leading *basse-taille* roles in revivals of works by Lully, Campra, André Destouches and Henry Desmarets. He withdrew from the stage between 1738 and 1742, to try to recover his *titres de noblesse* and re-establish his fortune. His place in the company was taken by FRANÇOIS LE PAGE, but he returned to the Opéra in 1742 as Hylas in a revival of Destouches' *Issé*. He created leading roles in Rameau's *Naïs*, *Zoroastre* and *Acante et Céphise*, and sang all the principal *basse-taille* parts in the continuing revivals of the staple 17th- and early 18th-century repertory. He retired in 1757. His intensity and intelligence in declamation and action made him arguably the greatest male singing actor of the 18th century in Paris, who could stand comparison at the highest level with the members of the Comédie-Française. Voltaire envisaged him as the ideal protagonist for his biblical tragedy *Samson*, predicting that he would be as dramatically effective as the leading actor Quinault-Dufresne. His sonorous voice was of great power and beauty, though subject to harsh attack (*saccades*) and to *chevrotement*, according to Charles Collé.

Philip Weller

Chementi, Margherita.

See CHIMENTI, MARGHERITA.

Chernov, Vladimir

(*b* Caucasus, 22 Sept 1953). Russian baritone. In 1983, after studies at the Moscow Conservatory and Accademia della Scala, he joined the Kirov Opera. A prizewinner at the Glinka (1981) and Tchaikovsky (1983) competitions, and a finalist in the Voci Verdiane Concorso in Busseto (1983), he appeared at Covent Garden with the Kirov in 1987. In 1989 and 1990 he made auspicious débuts in Boston (Marcello), Los Angeles (his first Posa), Seattle (Andrey Bolkonsky in *War and Peace*), Glasgow (Don Carlo in *La forza del destino*), Rome (Miller in *Luisa Miller*) and returned to Covent Garden as Gioachino Rossini's Figaro. In the 1990–91 season he made débuts at the Metropolitan Opera (Miller) and San Francisco (Ezio in *Attila*), and very quickly became one of the most active Russian baritones in the West. Successes in other major centres include Ford at Salzburg, Rossini's Figaro in Brussels and

Buenos Aires, Anckarstroem (*Un ballo in maschera*) in Chicago and Berlin, and Simon Boccanegra in Paris; he is a regular at the Met in Verdi, including such parts as Luna and Stankar (*Stiffelio*, 1993), and was a linchpin of Covent Garden's Verdi Festival, with appearances as Francesco Foscari (1995), Giacomo (*Giovanna d'Arco*, 1996) and Belfiore (*Un giorno di regno*, 1999, in concert). Chernov has sung in other major houses and festivals including Munich, Hamburg, Vienna, Bologna, Verona, Orange, Zürich, Barcelona and Mexico City, and further roles have included Yeletsky, Yevgeny Onegin, Germont, Enrico, Zurga, Guglielmo (*Le villi*), Alphonse (*La favorite*) and Filippo Maria Visconti (*Beatrice di Tenda*). In 2001 he sang the title role in a new production of *Simon Boccanegra* in Ferrara. His recordings include Yeletsky and many of his Verdi roles. He combines a charismatic stage presence with a beautiful, deeply expressive tone quality that has also made him much sought after as a recitalist.

John Allison

Chiara, Maria(-Rita)

(*b* Oderzo, 24 Nov 1939). Italian soprano. She studied in Venice and Turin, making her début in 1965 as Desdemona at the Doge's Palace, Venice. Engagements in the major Italian theatres led to appearances throughout Europe and in South America. She made her Covent Garden début as Liù in 1973, her US début (in Chicago) as Manon Lescaut and her Metropolitan début as Violetta in 1977. Chiara's roles included Anna Bolena, Mathilde (*Guillaume Tell*), Elsa, Jules Massenet's Manon, Vincenzo Bellini's Juliet, Micaëla, Adriana Lecouvreur and Maddalena (*Andrea Chénier*), as well as many Verdi heroines, notably Aida, which she sang in Luxor (1987) and at the 50th anniversary season at the Baths of Caracalla, Rome (1991). However, her beautiful, soft-grained voice was best displayed in Puccini, as Tosca, Mimì, Suor Angelica, Butterfly and, in particular, Liù.

Elizabeth Forbes

Chilcott, Susan

(*b* Timsbury, Somerset, 8 July 1963; *d* Blagdon, Somerset, 4 Sept 2003). English soprano. At the age of twelve she began singing lessons with Mollie Petrie, who was to remain her teacher and mentor, and from 1982 to 1986 she studied at the GSMD. After singing mainly in oratorio and recitals, she made her professional operatic début as Frasquita in Scottish Opera's 1991 production of *Carmen*,

returning to Glasgow the following year as First Lady in *Die Zauberflöte*. Her major breakthrough came in 1994, when she sang Ellen Orford in *Peter Grimes* at La Monnaie, a performance described as 'treasurable for the assurance with which she moved and for a soprano voice of great beauty and expressivity'. The same year her portrayal of Tatyana in *Yevgeny Onegin* for Glyndebourne Touring Opera was widely praised for its mingled vulnerability and dramatic urgency.

Chilcott made her ENO début in 1995 as Rusalka, but for the next few years she worked largely outside the UK, mainly at La Monnaie (where she sang Verdi's Desdemona, the Composer in *Ariadne auf Naxos*, and Hermione in Philippe Boesmans's *Wintermärchen*), at the Théâtre Musical de Paris (Fiordiligi and Tatiana), and at the Nederlandse Opera (Kát'a Kabanová and Blanche in *Dialogues des Carmélites*). In 1999 she scored a triumph as Kát'a for Scottish Opera, and in 2001 sang Lisa in *The Queen of Spades* for Welsh National Opera and a tender, poignant Desdemona for Glyndebourne. That year she was diagnosed with breast cancer. In the last two years of her life she gave three of her most memorable portrayals: Lisa (opposite DOMINGO) in her 2002 Covent Garden début; a touching and witty Helena (*A Midsummer Night's Dream*) in her Metropolitan Opera début the same year; and finally, in March 2003, a blazing, sensual Jenůfa for Welsh National Opera. Chilcott was also a delightful recitalist, notably in a programme of Shakespeare and Emily Dickinson settings she devised with the actress Fiona Shaw and the pianist Iain Burnside. Her small legacy of recordings includes Gustav Mahler's Second Symphony, *Wintermärchen* and songs by Benjamin Britten and Aaron Copland.

Richard Wigmore

Chimenti [Chementi], Margherita ['La Droghierina']

(*b* Rome; *fl* 1733–46). Italian soprano. She sang at Camerino (in Leonardo Vinci's *Artaserse*) and Viterbo in 1733, and sang male parts in operas by Giovanni Pergolesi and Leonardo Leo in Naples (1734–5), and at Venice (1736). She spent two seasons at the King's Theatre in London (1736–8), first with the Opera of the Nobility, then with John Jacob Heidegger and G.F. Handel, again generally in male roles, making her début in Johann Hasse's *Siroe* and appearing in operas by Riccardo Broschi, Giovanni Pescetti, Francesco Veracini and Egidio Duni. She created the parts of Adolfo in Handel's *Faramondo* and Atalanta in *Serse* (both 1738), and appeared in two pasticcios, one of them Handel's *Alessandro Severo* (Claudius). She sang in Handel's benefit oratorio on 28 March 1738. Mrs Pendarves called her 'a tolerable good woman with a pretty voice'. Her Handel parts indicate a limited technique and the compass (c♯' to d'') of a mezzo-soprano. After leaving London she sang at Livorno (1739–40), Florence (1741 and 1743–4, when Horace Mann considered her 'not worth hearing'), in two operas in Turin in 1741, three in Venice in 1741–2, two in Bologna in 1742, and in Duni's *Catone in Utica* in Naples in 1746.

Winton Dean

Chishko, Oles' [Aleksander] Semyonovich

(*b* Dvurechnïy Kut, nr Khar'kiv, 21 June/3 July 1895; *d* Leningrad, 4 Dec 1976). Russian-Ukrainian composer, tenor and teacher. In 1914 he entered Khar'kiv University, where he attended lectures in law and sciences. He received his early music training at the Khar'kiv Music College as a pupil of Federico Bugamelli for singing and Pietari Akimov for composition. He completed the singing course as an external student at the Khar'kiv Music and Drama Institute. He then worked in the Ukraine for some years as an opera and concert singer, teacher and conductor. In the 1920s he took part in the work of the All-Ukraine Association of Revolutionary Musicians; in 1928 he organized a composers' workshop at its Odessa branch, and later he joined the Association of Proletarian Musicians of the Ukraine.

Chishko completed his education at the Leningrad Conservatory (1931–4) under P.B. Ryazanov (composition), Y.N. Tyulin (harmony), Khristofor Kushnaryov (counterpoint) and M.O. Steinberg (orchestration), and in 1932 he joined the Composers' Union. During the 1930s he sang at the Malïy with the Leningrad PO and on radio, and he organized the song and dance ensemble of the Baltic fleet (1939–41), spending the war years in Tashkent. After his return to Leningrad in 1944 he engaged in various activities as composer, performer (he was Pierre in the first performance of Sergey Prokofiev's *War and Peace*) and teacher (in 1948 he was appointed reader at the Leningrad Conservatory and from 1957–65 was assistant professor there). His awards include the titles Honoured Art Worker of the Uzbek SSR (1944) and Honoured Art Worker of the RSFSR (1957), and the Badge of Honour. He became a member of the Communist Party in 1948.

Vocal works occupy a dominant place in Chishko's output; they include folksong arrangements for various ensembles and compositions that served as points of departure for his major stage works. *Bronenosets Potyomkin* ('Battleship Potyomkin') has been produced on almost all the opera stages of the USSR and was one of the first of the 'song operas', playing an important part in the development of Soviet opera. Chishko's other operas have also met with success, and his works for folk orchestras have helped to expand the repertories of these ensembles.

A. Klimovitsky

Chookasian, Lili

(*b* Chicago, 1 Aug 1921). American contralto. She studied with Philip Manuel and made her début in 1959, singing Adalgisa with the Arkansas Opera Theater, Little Rock. She made her European début in 1961 at Trieste as Herodias. After further study, with ROSA PONSELLE, she made her Metropolitan début as La Cieca (*La Gioconda*, 1962) and sang at Bayreuth (1965). During the next 15 years her roles included Geneviève, Mistress Quickly, Ulrica, Azucena, Amneris, Auntie (*Peter Grimes*) and La Frugola, the Princess and Zita (*Il trittico*). She has also sung with the New York City Opera (*The Medium*, 1963) and with many other leading companies, including those of Mexico City and Hamburg (both in *Aida*) and Buenos Aires, as well as at the Salzburg Festival. She created the role of the Queen in Thomas Pasatieri's *Inez de Castro* (April 1976) at Baltimore. Her dark, rich voice and strong sense of character were vividly displayed when she sang Maddalena in *Andrea Chénier* at the Metropolitan Opera in 1977.

Richard Lesueur, Elizabeth Forbes

Christofellis, Aris

(*b* Athens, 5 Feb 1960). Greek male soprano. He studied the piano and singing at the Athens Conservatory and the Ecole Normale de Musique in Paris, and continued his vocal studies with Fofi Sarandopoulo, with whom he developed a remarkable range of over three octaves. He made his recital début in Bordeaux in 1984 and his operatic début, in Antonio Vivaldi's *L'Olimpiade*, in Frankfurt in 1986. He has subsequently sung in many 18th-century operas, among them G.F. Handel's *Il pastor fido* and *Arminio*, Niccolò Jommelli's *Armida abbandonata* and Giovanni Paisiello's *L'idolo cinese*. His recordings include Vivaldi's *Ottone in villa* and *L'Olimpiade* and discs of soprano castrato arias. Christofellis has also made a detailed study of the vocal techniques and ornamentation of the 18th-century castratos and has unearthed a number of forgotten works.

He combines a bright, penetrating timbre with impressive agility and a sure command of style.

Michael Hardy

Christoff, Boris (Kirilov)

(*b* Plovdiv, 18 May 1914; *d* Rome, 28 June 1993). Bulgarian bass. He first studied law, but was heard in the famous Gusla Choir by King Boris of Bulgaria, who sent him to Rome to study singing with RICCARDO STRACCIARI; he continued in Salzburg with Muratti. Returning to Italy in 1946, he made his operatic début as Colline at Reggio di Calabria. The following season he sang Pimen at both Rome and La Scala. He first sang Boris Godunov in 1949 at Covent Garden, creating a sensation; he repeated the role in many leading houses, including La Scala and the Opéra, and in 1974 sang it at Covent Garden to celebrate the 25th anniversary of his first appearance there. He first sang his other great role, Philip II in *Don Carlos*, at Florence in 1950, and repeated it, memorably, in Luchino Visconti's Covent Garden staging in 1958. His repertory also included Khan Konchak, Rocco, King Mark, Hagen and Gurnemanz, Charles Gounod's and Arrigo Boito's Mephistopheles, Dosifey, the title role in G.F. Handel's *Giulio Cesare*, and most of Giuseppe Verdi's leading bass roles. He made his American début as Boris at San Francisco in 1956 and sang at Chicago from 1957 to 1963. He was also a fine recitalist, and made an extensive series of recordings of Russian song, most notably of Modest Musorgsky. His last major appearance was in concert in New York in 1980.

Christoff was hailed by many as CHALIAPIN's successor because of his identification with the great singing-acting parts in the Russian repertory. He was also an outstanding Verdi singer, notably as Philip II in *Don Carlos* at Covent Garden (1958). His voice, though not large, was of fine quality, smooth, round, well projected and perfectly controlled. His many operatic recordings include two of *Boris Godunov* in which he sings three roles, Boris, Pimen and Varlaam. He was able, through his personal magnetism and theatrical skill, to generate tension whenever he was on stage. His dramatic powers, and his ability to give words their fullest meaning and expressive weight, placed him among the great singing actors of his day.

A. Bozhkov: *Boris Khristov* (Sofia, 1985; Eng. trans., 1991, with discography by A. Blyth)

A. Blyth: 'Boris Christoff, 1914–1993', *Opera*, xliv (1993), 1045–8 [obituary]

Harold Rosenthal/Alan Blyth

Ciccimarra, Giuseppe

(*b* Altamura, Apulia, 22 May 1790; *d* Venice, 5 Dec 1836). Italian tenor. He was engaged for many years in Naples, where he took part in six Rossini premières: at the Teatro del Fondo he sang Iago in *Otello* (1816); at the S Carlo he sang Goffredo in *Armida* (1817); Aaron in *Mosè in Egitto* and Ernesto in *Ricciardo e Zoraide* (1818); Pylades in *Ermione* (1819) and Condulmiero in *Maometto II* (1820). He sang Nathan in Simon Mayr's oratorio *Atalia* (1822) at the S Carlo in a performance directed by Rossini and described by Gaetano Donizetti in a letter to the composer. He retired in 1826.

Elizabeth Forbes

Cigna, Gina [Sens, Genoveffa; Sens, Ginetta]

(*b* Angère, Paris, 6 March 1900; *d* Milan, 26 June 2001). Italian soprano of French birth. She studied with EMMA CALVÉ, HARICLEA DARCLÉE and ROSINA STORCHIO, and auditioned for Arturo Toscanini at La Scala in 1926 and the following year made her début there as Freia, under the name Genoveffa Sens (she married the tenor Maurice Sens in 1923). In 1929, as Gina Cigna, she returned there and sang every season until 1943, establishing herself as a leading Italian dramatic soprano. She was particularly admired as Norma, La Gioconda, Turandot and in Verdi; she also took part in important revivals of *Alceste* (1935) and *L'incoronazione di Poppea* (1937) at Florence, and was the Kostelnička in the first performance in Italy of *Jenůfa* (1941, Venice). Cigna made her Covent Garden début as Marguerite in *La damnation de Faust* in 1933, and returned there in 1936, 1937 and 1939. She sang at the Metropolitan (1937–8), and also in San Francisco and Chicago. In 1947, following a car accident, she retired, devoting much of the rest of her life to teaching. She was a highly dramatic and musical singer though her dark voice, with its attractive rapid vibrato, inclined to hardness under pressure. Her pre-war recordings of Norma and Turandot show the physical excitement of her singing and her dramatic involvement.

Harold Rosenthal/Alan Blyth

Cinti-Damoreau [née Montalant], Laure (Cinthie)

(*b* Paris, 6 Feb 1801; *d* Paris, 25 Feb 1863). French soprano. She studied the piano at the Paris Conservatoire and singing with Charles-Henri Plantade. Angelica Catalani devised her stage name of Cinti by italianizing her middle name, and she made her operatic début at the Théâtre Italien in *Una cosa rara* (8 January 1816). After the collapse of Catalani's management in 1818, Cinti was re-engaged the following year when a new company was formed at the Théâtre Louvois. There her roles included Cherubino and Rosina, and in 1822 John Ebers engaged her for a season at the King's Theatre, London. Her mastery of florid singing, acquired by emulating her colleagues at the Théâtre Italien, led in 1825 to her engagement at the Paris Opéra where she remained until 1835, apart from an interruption in the summer of 1827, when she left to sing in Brussels and married the tenor V.C. Damoreau (1793–1863). She created the principal soprano roles in Gioachino Rossini's *Le siège de Corinthe* (1826), *Moïse* (1827), *Le comte Ory* (1827) and *Guillaume Tell* (1829), and Elvire in Daniel Auber's *La muette de Portici* (1829) and Isabelle in Giacomo Meyerbeer's *Robert le diable* (1831). Although she was the Opéra's most highly paid singer, she accepted a more attractive offer from the Opéra-Comique, where from 1836 to 1841 she appeared in a succession of new operas by Auber. In 1844 she toured America with the violinist Alexandre Artôt, and continued to sing in concerts until 1848. She taught singing at the Paris Conservatoire (1833–56) and published a *Méthode de chant* (1849), other singing manuals and some songs. Her voice, outstanding for its purity of tone and intonation, was likened to a perfect piano, and her ornamentation was stylish and varied. She was a Rossini rather than a Meyerbeer singer, lacking FALCON's emotional and dramatic power; but she successfully redirected her career elsewhere when Falcon threatened to eclipse her at the Opéra.

Philip Robinson

Ciofi, Patrizia

(*b* Casole d'Elsa, nr Siena, 1967). Italian soprano. She studied at the Istituto Musicale Pietro Mascagni in Livorno, where her principal teacher and mentor was Anastasia Tomaszewska-Schepis, and subsequently took part in masterclasses with CARLO BERGONZI and SHIRLEY VERRETT at the Accademia Chigiana in Siena. She made her début in Gino Negri's *Giovanni Sebastiano* at the Teatro Comunale, Florence, in 1989, and over the next few years performed mainly bel canto roles in various Italian opera houses. In 1996 she sang her first Lucia (*Lucia di Lammermoor*), a role that became one of her calling cards, in Savona, and the following year made a sensational La Scala début as Violetta, returning to La Scala in 1998 as Adina (*L'elisir d'amore*). She later sang Violetta to equal acclaim for the reopening of La Fenice, Venice, in 2004.

Ciofi made further notable débuts at the Opéra Bastille, as Nanetta (*Falstaff*), in 1999, and at Covent Garden, as Gilda, in 2002. That year she created a sensation when she took over at short notice from NATALIE DESSAY in *Lucie de Lammermoor* (Gaetano Donizetti's French adaptation of the Italian original) at the Théâtre du Châtelet in Paris and in Lyons. Ciofi's other roles include W.A. Mozart's Susanna (which she sang on her return to the Opéra Bastille in 2001), Blonde (Florence, 2002) and Fiordiligi (Turin, 2003), G.F. Handel's Asteria (*Tamerlano*), Morgana (*Alcina*) and Polinessa (*Radamisto*), Amina (*La sonnambula*), which she first sang at the Martina Franca Festival in 1994, and all four heroines in *Les contes d'Hoffmann* (Marseilles, 2004). She has also been admired in several Rossini roles at the Rossini Opera Festival, Pesaro, including Fiorilla (*Il turco in Italia*), Desdemona and Amenaide (*Tancredi*). On disc, Ciofi's pure, bright, agile voice and delightful sense of character can be heard as Susanna in *Le nozze di Figaro* (a wonderfully spirited, resourceful portrayal), Euridice in Claudio Monteverdi's *Orfeo*, Amina, Desdemona, Polinessa, Idaspe (Antonio Vivaldi's *Bajazet*) and Teresa (*Benvenuto Cellini*), and in a disc of Handel duets with JOYCE DiDONATO.

Richard Wigmore

Cisneros, Eleonora de [Broadfoot, Eleanor]

(*b* Brooklyn, NY, 1 Nov 1878; *d* New York, 3 Feb 1934). American mezzo-soprano. She studied with Francesco Fanciulli and Adeline Murio-Celli in New York and sang for JEAN DE RESZKE, who arranged for her to sing at the Metropolitan Opera. During the 1899–1900 season she performed Rosweisse and Amneris. She went to Paris for further studies with Angelo Tabadello and at Turin in 1902 sang Brünnhilde, Ortrud, Venus, Dalila and Amneris. From 1904 to 1908 she sang regularly at Covent Garden. At La Scala she created the role of Candia in Alberto Franchetti's *La figlia di Iorio* in 1906; she also sang in the first performances there of *The Queen of Spades* (1906), *Salome* (1906) and *Elektra* (1909). She claimed to be the first American singer to perform at Bayreuth, during the 1908 season. From 1906 to 1908 she was a leading singer at Oscar Hammerstein's Manhattan Opera House and then appeared with the Chicago-Philadelphia Opera Company until 1916. In 1911 she performed in London and Australia with the Melba Opera Company. She continued to sing, mostly in Europe, into the 1920s, but after making tours on behalf of the war effort during World War I her career suffered. With a large, statuesque bearing and a voice of remarkable volume and range, she was able to sing such dramatic soprano roles as Santuzza, Gioconda and Kundry, as well as mezzo-soprano and alto roles including Carmen, Laura (*La Gioconda*), Urbain (*Les Huguenots*) and Azucena.

Susan Feder

Clark, Graham (Ronald)

(*b* Littleborough, Lancs., 10 Nov 1941). English tenor. At first a sports teacher, he studied with Bruce Boyce, then in 1973 took small roles in *The Gambler* and *A Life for the Tsar* at Wexford. In 1975 he joined Scottish Opera, singing Brighella (*Ariadne auf Naxos*), Malcolm, Jaquino, Ernesto, Pedrillo, the Italian Singer (*Der Rosenkavalier*), Zorn and David (*Die Meistersinger*). He performed the title role in the British première of Alberto Ginastera's *Bomarzo* for the ENO (1976), followed by Rinuccio, Ramiro, Almaviva, Hoffmann, Rodolfo and, for Opera North, Count Ory. Realizing that conventionally romantic parts were not for him, Clark took roles at the ENO such as the Pretender (*Boris Godunov*), Hermann (*Queen of Spades*), Aleksey (*The Gambler*), Albert Gregor (*The Makropulos Affair*), Busoni's Mephistopheles, Don Juan (A.S. Dargomïzhsky's *The Stone Guest*) and Mr Brouček. He sang for 12 consecutive seasons at Bayreuth (1981–92), as David, the Young Sailor and Melot, Loge and Mime. Having made his Metropolitan début in 1985 as Števa (*Jenůfa*), he created Bégéarss in John Corigliano's *The Ghosts of Versailles* in 1991; other Metropolitan roles include Herod, Captain Vere, which he also sang at Covent Garden (1995), and Albert Gregor. In 1991–2 he sang the Producer (Luciano Berio's *Un re in ascolto*) at Opéra-Bastille and the Painter (*Lulu*) and Captain (*Wozzeck*) at the Théâtre du Châtelet, Paris, and Basilio and Vašek in Chicago. A superb, athletic actor with a strong, penetrating voice and exceptionally clear diction, he excels particularly as Mime in *Siegfried*, which he sang at Covent Garden in 1995, and as Loge, and has made vivid recordings of both roles. His other recordings include David (*Die Meistersinger*), the Steersman (*Der fliegende Holländer*) and roles in Francis Poulenc's *Les mamelles de Tirésias* and György Ligeti's *Le Grand Macabre*.

E. Forbes: 'Graham Clark', *Opera*, xliii (1992), 1283–91

Elizabeth Forbes

Cledière, Bernard

(*fl* 1673–80). French *haute-contre*. Recruited in Languedoc together with François Beaumavielle, he sang at the Paris Opéra in Jean-Baptiste Lully's *Cadmus et Hermione* (1673, the Sun and First Prince), *Thésée* (1675 and 1677; title role), *Atys* (1676 and 1682; title role), *Alceste* (1677, Admetus), *Isis* (1677, Mercury) and *Bellérophon* (1679 and 1680, St Germain; title role). By 1682 he had left the Opéra to join the Musique du Roi. His position as principal *haute-contre* passed to the high *haute-taille* DUMESNIL, with whom he had shared the role of Alpheius (*Proserpine*) in 1680; Cledière had sung it at St Germain, while Dumesnil, making his début, had taken it over for the Paris performances.

Philip Weller

Clément, Edmond

(*b* Paris, 28 March 1867; *d* Nice, 24 Feb 1928). French tenor. He studied singing at the Paris Conservatoire and made his début at the Opéra-Comique in 1889 in Charles Gounod's *Mireille*. He took part in the premières of Camille Saint-Saëns's *Phryné* and Alfred Bruneau's *L'attaque du moulin* (both 1893) as well as the first performances in Paris of *Falstaff* and *Butterfly*. In 1896 he was in the first *Don Giovanni* ever given at the Opéra-Comique, and in 1904 sang Don José in the 1000th performance of *Carmen* at that theatre. In 1909 he made his début at the Metropolitan in *Werther* and appeared in the only performances there of *Fra Diavolo* (1910). With the Boston Opera Company in 1912 he sang his first Hoffmann, a performance reputedly ideal in its mixture of masculinity and dreaminess, with finely shaded singing. His Don José also developed into a masterly portrayal. He returned to France to fight in World War I and was wounded; later he devoted himself to teaching, but gave a memorable last recital at the age of 60 in Paris, in November 1927. His recordings are models of their kind, with slim, clearly defined tone, a polished style and unostentatious personal charm.

J.B. Steane

Coates, Edith (Mary)

(*b* Lincoln, 31 May 1908; *d* Worthing, 7 Jan 1983). English mezzo-soprano. She studied at Trinity College of Music, London. In 1924 she joined the Old Vic opera chorus and was soon singing small roles. When the company moved to Sadler's Wells in 1931 she became its leading mezzo-soprano, singing in the first English performances of *The Snow Maiden* (as Lel') and *The Tale of Tsar Saltan*, both in 1933, and appearing as Eboli in 1938. In 1945 she created Auntie in *Peter Grimes*. Having made her Covent Garden début in 1937 she became a member of the company in 1947, remaining until

1967. Though not invariably successful in dramatic parts like Azucena, Fricka, Amneris and Carmen, she had striking acting ability and stage presence. She created roles in *The Olympians* (1949) and *Gloriana* (1953) and sang the Countess in the first production in English of *The Queen of Spades* (1950). In 1966 she created Grandma in Grace Williams's *The Parlour* for the WNO (1961). She was made an OBE in 1977.

C. Hardy: 'Edith Coates', *Opera*, ii (1950–51), 69–72

Harold Rosenthal/R

Coates, John

(*b* Girlington, Yorks., 29 June 1865; *d* Northwood, Middlesex, 16 Aug 1941). English tenor. While engaged in business he sang as a baritone for the Carl Rosa Company in Manchester and Liverpool. In 1893 he took lessons in London from William Shakespeare, who pronounced his voice a tenor, but he appeared as a baritone at the Savoy Theatre in Arthur Sullivan's *Utopia Limited* and then toured the USA in it. There followed regular work in musical comedy in London and the provinces, and a second American tour.

He then retired to study the tenor repertory. He appeared at the Globe Theatre in *The Gay Pretenders* and made his Covent Garden début as Faust and sang Claudio in the first performance of Charles Villiers Stanford's *Much Ado about Nothing*. The turning-point in his career came when, at 37, he was launched as a tenor at the Three Choirs Festival (Worcester, 1902) as Edward Elgar's Gerontius. From then Coates was recognized as a master in whatever he touched – Siegfried, Tristan, Lohengrin (in Germany, and with the Beecham and Moody-Manners companies), Elgar's *The Apostles* and *The Kingdom* (first and later performances) and the traditional oratorios. He sang Mark in the British première of Ethel Smyth's *The Wreckers* at His Majesty's Theatre in 1909, when he also returned to Covent Garden singing Faust and Lohengrin. He sang Don José and Pedro in the British première of *Tiefland* (1910) for the Beecham Opera, and Tannhäuser and Tristan for Raymond Roze's English opera season (1913). His recitals covered lieder, French songs, Elizabethan and Tudor music; in addition he was a champion of contemporary English songs.

For Coates, vocal problems seemed not to exist. Perhaps the quality of voice did not flatter, and lacked opulence to some extent; but it was capable of astonishing variety of colour and was pointed directly and with intensity at the listener. His art was an ineffaceable memory by reason of his outstanding musical intelligence and subtlety, and his poetic and inventive imagination. His vision of the piano's essence in lieder has rarely been equalled by other singers and made those who accompanied him his grateful debtors. Coates was an aristocrat among singers and one of the most distinguished English tenors of the 20th century.

G. Moore: *Am I too loud? Memoirs of an Accompanist* (London, 1962)
'John Coates', *Record Advertiser*, iii/2 (1972–3), 2–3 [with discography]

Gerald Moore

Cobb, Richard Barker.
See TEMPLE, RICHARD.

Cobelli, Giuseppina

(*b* Maderno, Lake Garda, 1 Aug 1898; *d* Barbarano, nr Salò, 10 Aug 1948). Italian soprano. She studied in Bologna and Hamburg, making her début at Piacenza in 1924 as La Gioconda. After a season in the Netherlands, she was engaged by La Scala, making her début as Sieglinde (1925). Her roles included Isolde, Kundry, Fedora, Eboli, Margherita, Minnie and Adriana Lecouvreur, in which part she gave her last Scala performance in 1942. She created Silvana in Ottorino Respighi's *La fiamma* (1934, Rome) and in 1937 sang Octavia (*L'incoronazione di Poppea*) at the Maggio Musicale in Florence. A beautiful woman with a highly individual voice and dramatic temperament, she had a special affinity for *verismo* heroines. She made only two recordings, each of which explains why she was so much admired at La Scala.

Harold Rosenthal/Alan Blyth

Codecasa, Teresa.
See SAPORITI, TERESA.

Colbran, Isabella [Isabel] (Angela)

(*b* Madrid, 2 Feb 1785; *d* Castenaso, Bologna, 7 Oct 1845). Spanish soprano. After study with Francisco Pareja, Gaetano Marinelli and Girolamo Crescentini, she made her concert début in Paris (1801) and her stage début in Spain (1806), and the following year came to Italy, where she sang at Bologna; a contemporary account gave her compass then as almost three octaves, from *g* to *e'''*. In 1808–9 she sang in the premières of Giuseppe Nicolini's *Coriolano*, Vincenzo Federici's *Ifigenia* and Vincenzo Lavigna's *Orcamo* at La Scala, Milan, and in 1811 she was engaged for Naples by the impresario Domenico Barbaia, whose mistress she became; she remained there for over a decade. A highly dramatic singer who excelled in tragedy, especially in Gaspare Spontini's *La vestale* and Simon Mayr's *Medea in Corinto*, for which she created the title role (1813), she strongly influenced the operas that Rossini composed for Naples. *Elisabetta, regina d'Inghilterra* (1815), *Otello* (1816), *Armida* (1817), *Mosè in Egitto, Ricciardo e Zoraide* (1818), *Ermione, La donna del lago* (1819), *Maometto II* (1820) and *Zelmira* (1822) all contained parts written to display her special vocal and dramatic gifts. Colbran and Rossini, who had lived together for some years, were married at Castenaso on 15 March 1822, on their way to Vienna. *Semiramide*, the final opera that he composed for her, was produced at La Fenice, Venice, in 1823. The following year she accompanied Rossini to London and, after a disastrous appearance as Zelmira, retired from the stage. By then, her voice was in decline and her intonation had grown insecure; in her prime, from 1807 to about 1820, she was greatly admired in Italy for the brilliance and power of her voice and the command of her stage presence. In 1836 she was legally separated from the composer, but continued to live with Rossini's father until her death. She composed four volumes of songs.

Elizabeth Forbes

Coletti, Filippo

(*b* Anagni, 11 May 1811; *d* Anagni, 13 June 1894). Italian baritone. He studied at Real Collegio di Musica in Naples, making a successful début at the Teatro del Fondo (1834) in Rossini's *Il turco in Italia*. His talents attracted the attention of Pierre Laporte, impresario of Her Majesty's Theatre, London, who in 1840 engaged him to replace the popular favourite TAMBURINI, thereby provoking a riot vividly described by R.H. Barham in one of his *Ingoldsby Legends*. Returning defeated to Naples, Coletti created the roles of Lusignano in Gaetano Donizetti's *Caterina Cornaro* (1844) and Carlo Gusmano in Giuseppe Verdi's *Ernani* (1844) and *Alzira* (1845). When Tamburini defected to Covent Garden the following year, Coletti was re-engaged at Her Majesty's by Laporte's successor, Benjamin Lumley, where he created Francesco in Verdi's *I masnadieri* opposite JENNY LIND (1847). For the next four seasons he remained the leading Italian baritone on the London stage, being especially admired as the Doge in Verdi's *I due Foscari*. It was for him that Verdi lowered the part of Germont in the definitive version of *La traviata*, in whose first performance he took part at the Teatro Benedetto, Venice (1854). He also sang in the first Rome performance (1851) of *Rigoletto* (given under the title *Viscardello*). His last

creation of importance was the title role of Saverio Mercadante's *Pelagio* at the Teatro S Carlo, Naples (1857), given at a time when Verdi was seriously considering him for the name part of the *Re Lear* that he never wrote. Coletti retired from the stage in 1869; in 1880 he published a treatise, *La scuola di canto italiano*, in Rome. Although he undertook comic roles, it was as a 'baritono nobile' that Coletti excelled. H.F. Chorley praised him as 'an expressive, sound singer of the modern school'; to Thomas Carlyle he seemed 'a man of deep and ardent sensibility…originally an almost poetic soul'. First in bel canto roles, then in Verdi, his performances were distinguished by their dramatic integrity and eschewal of mere virtuosity.

H.F. Chorley: *Thirty Years' Musical Recollections* (London, 1862)

B. Lumley: *Reminiscences of the Opera* (London, 1864)

J.E. Cox: *Musical Recollections of the Last Half-Century* (London, 1872)

J.W. Davison: *From Mendelssohn to Wagner: the Memoirs of J.W. Davison Compiled by his Son, Henry Davison* (London, 1912)

Harold Rosenthal/Julian Budden

Colini [Collini], Filippo

(*b* Rome, 21 Oct 1811; *d* ?May 1863). Italian baritone. In both contemporary and modern sources he is sometimes confused with Virgilio Collini or FILIPPO COLETTI. He studied with Camillo Angiolini at the Collegio Romano from 1819 to 1827, where he sang in the choir. His first concert appearance was in 1831. Early in 1835 he appeared at the opera house in Fabriano, and during the autumn made his début at the Teatro Valle, Rome. Thereafter he was engaged at major Italian theatres in Palermo (1838–41, 1852–4), Naples (1841–2, 1848, 1855–7), Genoa (1842–3, 1854–5), Milan (1844–5) and Rome (1844, 1845–6, 1848–9, 1849–50), among others, and in Paris and Vienna.

During his early career his repertory consisted mainly of works by Gaetano Donizetti, especially *Torquato Tasso*; later he concentrated on Giuseppe Verdi's operas, in particular *Nabucco, Ernani, Macbeth* and *Luisa Miller*. He sang Luigi XIV in the première of Fabio Campana's *Luisa di Francia* (1844), Severo in Donizetti's *Poliuto* (1848) and Inquaro in Eugenio Terziani's *Alfredo* (1852), and he created roles in three Verdi operas: Giacomo in *Giovanna d'Arco* (1845), Rolando in *La battaglia di Legnano* (1849) and Stankar in *Stiffelio* (1850). The gracefulness, flexibility and delicacy of his high baritone voice is said to have compensated for his meagre interpretational abilities.

Roberta Montemorra Marvin

Collier, Marie

(*b* Ballarat, 16 April 1927; *d* London, 7 Dec 1971). Australian soprano. She studied in Melbourne, making her début there in 1954 as Santuzza, then touring as Magda in *The Consul*. After further study in Milan and London, she joined the Covent Garden company in 1956, making her début as Musetta. Among the roles she sang there were Tosca, Aida, Butterfly, Liù, Elisabeth de Valois, Lisa (*Queen of Spades*), Manon Lescaut, Jenůfa, Chrysothemis (which she recorded for Georg Solti) and Marie (*Wozzeck*). In 1962 she created the role of Hecuba in Michael Tippett's *King Priam*, and the following year sang Katerina Izmaylova in the first British staging of Dmitry Shostakovich's opera. In all, she sang 293 performances at the Royal Opera. At Sadler's Wells she sang Venus, Tosca and Concepcion (*L'heure espagnole*), and the leading roles in two British premières, *Kát'a Kabanová* (1951) and *The Makropulos Affair* (1964). At the Metropolitan, New York, she created the role of Christine in Marvin David Levy's *Mourning Becomes Electra* (1967). She appeared in San Francisco as Minnie in *La fanciulla del West* (1965), Emilia Marty (1965) and the Woman in *Erwartung* (1968).

Collier gained wide publicity when in 1965 she took over Maria Callas's performances of *Tosca* at Covent Garden. Her vibrant, lustrous voice, flamboyant personality and acute instinct for drama were spectacularly displayed as Emilia Marty, Katerina Izmaylova and Renata in Sergey Prokofiev's *The Fiery Angel*, which she sang for the New Opera Company of London in 1965.

A. Blyth: 'Marie Collier', *Opera*, xix (1968), 953–7

Alan Blyth

Conelly, Claire.

See CROIZA, CLAIRE.

Coni, Paolo

(*b* Perugia, 1 Aug 1957). Italian baritone. After early studies he won the Mattia Battistini Prize at Rieti, where he made his début in 1983 as Enrico in *Lucia di Lammermoor*. In the following years he sang in a wide repertory throughout Italy, coming to La Scala in 1988. This was also the year of his début at the Metropolitan, New York, as Belcore in *L'elisir d'amore*. He has sung in Chicago and San Francisco, and in the 1990s sang principal baritone roles in most of the leading European houses. With the La Scala company in Japan and with La Fenice on tour in Warsaw he extended his reputation as a successor in Verdi roles to PIERO CAPPUCCILLI, whom he somewhat resembles in tone and style. Comparisons have also been made with RENATO BRUSON, from whom he took over the role of Simon Boccanegra at Genoa in 1992, when he was commended for the carrying power of a warm and flexible voice. In 1996 signs of tiredness were observed in his upper register, although the noble quality of his voice and the assurance of his stage presence continued to command admiration. Recordings include performances of *La traviata* and *Don Carlos* under Riccardo Muti taken 'live' from La Scala: without any striking individuality of timbre or expression, he produces ample, well-rounded tone and is scrupulously attentive to details of the score.

J.B. Steane

Connell, Elizabeth

(*b* Port Elizabeth, 22 Oct 1946). Irish soprano of South African birth. She studied at the London Opera Centre, making her début in 1972 as a mezzo-soprano at Wexford as Varvara (*Kát'a Kabanová*). With Australian Opera (1973–4) she sang Venus, Kostelnička and Amneris. Engaged by the ENO (1975–80), she sang Eboli, Azucena, Mariya Bolkonskaya (*War and Peace*), Herodias, Waltraute (which she recorded under Reginald Goodall), Kabanicha, Eglantine (*Euryanthe*), Gioachino Rossini's Isabella, Béla Bartók's Judith, Sieglinde, Santuzza, Donna Elvira and Marina. She made her Covent Garden début in 1976 as Viclinda (*I Lombardi*). After Ortrud and Brangäne at Bayreuth (1980–81), she cancelled all engagements, reappearing in 1983 as a soprano. Following performances of Fiordiligi at La Scala, she sang Electra (*Idomeneo*) in Salzburg and Norma in Geneva. She made her Metropolitan début as Vitellia (1985), returned to Covent Garden as Leonora in *Trovatore* and Leonore in *Fidelio*, and sang Reiza (*Oberon*) at Edinburgh. Connell's soprano repertory includes Donna Anna, Marie (*Wozzeck*), Luigi Cherubini's *Medée*, Senta, Elsa, Elizabeth, Ariadne and Chrysothemis. Since her first Lady Macbeth in Sydney in 1977, she has made a speciality of the part throughout Europe and in the USA; her other Verdi roles include Elisabeth de Valois, Amelia (*Ballo in maschera*), Odabella and Abigaille. She sang Brünnhilde (*Die Walküre*) at Santiago in 1995 and Isolde for the ENO in 1996. A highly dramatic singer, she has a powerful, flexible voice equally suitable for Verdi and Wagner.

E. Forbes: 'Elizabeth Connell', *Opera*, xxxix (1988), 670–75

Elizabeth Forbes

Connolly, Sarah

(b Middlesborough, 13 June 1963). English mezzo-soprano. She studied at the RCM in London and then privately with David Mason and Gerald Martin Moore. After singing with the BBC Singers and the Glyndebourne Festival Chorus, she made her professional operatic début, as Anina in *Der Rosenkavalier*, with WNO in 1994. She is a company member of the ENO, where she has sung roles including the Fox in *The Cunning Little Vixen*, the Messenger in Claudio Monteverdi's *Orfeo*, Ottavia (*L'incoronazione di Poppea*), Ruggiero (*Alcina*) and Henry Purcell's Dido. In 2000 she created the role of Susie in Mark-Anthony Turnage's *The Silver Tassie*, and in 2001 her Lucretia was much admired for its dignity and contained passion. Outside Britain, in 2000 Connolly made notable débuts in the US, singing the title role of *Ariodante* with New York City Opera, and in Florence, where she sang Nero in *Poppea*. She returned to the US the following season to sing Ino and Juno (*Semele*) with San Francisco Opera and Romeo (*I Capuleti e i Montecchi*) with New York City Opera. On the concert platform she has performed with many leading orchestras and conductors, including Philippe Herreweghe, Oliver Knussen and Giuseppe Sinopoli, with whom she gave the world première of Matteo d'Amico's *Rime d'amore* in Rome. In 1997 she made her Proms début, in Arthur Honegger's *Jeanne d'Arc au bûcher*, and her Australian début, as the Angel in *The Dream of Gerontius*. Her full, warm, cleanly focussed mezzo and incisive characterization can be heard on recordings of Bach cantatas, Jean-Philippe Rameau's *Les fêtes d'Hébé*, Antonio Vivaldi's *Juditha triumphans* and Ralph Vaughan Williams's *Sir John in Love*.

Richard Wigmore

Conti, Gioacchino
['Egizziello', 'Gizziello']

(b Arpino, 28 Feb 1714; d Rome, 25 Oct 1761). Italian soprano castrato, probably the son of Nicola Conti. His nicknames derived from Domenico Gizzi, who taught him singing. His début at Rome in Leonardo Vinci's *Artaserse* (1730) was a spectacular success. He sang at Naples in operas by Vinci (1732–3), and in Vienna (1734), Genoa, Venice (1735, two operas, including Leonardo Leo's *La clemenza di Tito*) and other Italian cities. In 1736 he was engaged by G.F. Handel for London and made his Covent Garden début in a revival of *Ariodante* on 5 May; a week later he created the role of Meleager in *Atalanta*. The press reported that he 'met with an uncommon Reception'; the poet Thomas Gray admired him 'excessively' in every respect except the shape of his mouth, which 'when open, made an exact square'. According to Charles Jennens, Handel considered him 'a rising genius'. The next season, Conti appeared in Handel's new operas *Arminio* (as Sigismond), *Giustino* (Anastasius) and *Berenice* (Alessandro) and in several revivals. He also sang in Handel's oratorio *Esther* (with several new arias) and probably in *Il trionfo del tempo*, and was to have taken part in a revival of *Deborah* which was cancelled.

Conti sang in Rome in 1738, 1741–3 and later, at Padua in 1739 in G.B. Lampugnani's *Didone abbandonata*, and in 1742 in Florence, where he made a great impression but was taken seriously ill. He may have gone to Lisbon in 1743. He sang at the S Carlo, Naples, in 1746 in Egidio Duni's *Catone in Utica* and Niccolò Jommelli's *Eumene*. In 1747 the theatre engaged both Conti and his rival CAFFARELLI; the rivalry caused much excitement. He was often heard at Venice, in operas by Jommelli, J.A. Hasse and G.B. Pescetti (1746–7, 1749–50), and appeared at Lucca (1749) and Padua (1751, in Baldassare Galuppi's *Artaserse*). From 1752 to 1755 he was employed by the Lisbon court theatre and sang in many operas, most of them by David Perez; he is said to have narrowly escaped with his life from the Lisbon earthquake (1755), and 'was impressed with such a religious turn by the tremendous calamity, that he retreated to a monastery, where he ended his days' (Charles Burney), but not before he had imparted much sage and practical counsel to Gaetano Guadagni. His retirement may, however, have been due to ill-health. Conti was one of the greatest of 18th-century singers. He was an exceptionally high soprano with a compass of at least two octaves (c' to c''') and the only castrato for whom Handel wrote a top C. The four parts Handel composed for him indicate brilliance, flexibility and unusual powers of pathetic and graceful expression. In character Conti was the antithesis of Caffarelli, being as gentle as the latter was overbearing.

Winton Dean

Coote, Alice

(b Frodsham, Cheshire, 10 May 1968). English mezzo-soprano. She studied initially at the GSMD in London, but left before completing her course. After a break she continued her studies at the RNCM in Manchester, where she was encouraged by JANET BAKER and BRIGITTE FASSBAENDER and won the Fassbaender Award for Lieder. In 1992, while still at the RNCM, she won the Decca Kathleen Ferrier Prize, and in 1995–6 spent a year at the National Opera Studio, London. In her major operatic début, as Penelope (*Il ritorno d'Ulisse in patria*) at Opera North in 1997, Coote was widely praised by the critics for her rich, lustrous tone and subtly expressive phrasing. At Opera North she has since sung Cherubino, Tamiri (*Il re pastore*), Dorabella and Zenobia (*Radamisto*). She made her ENO début in 1999 as Proserpina (*Orfeo*), and in 2000 scored a triumph there as a sultry, voluptuous Poppea. The same year she was acclaimed as Ruggiero (*Alcina*) with Stuttgart Opera at the Edinburgh Festival.

Subsequent débuts have included the Wigmore Hall (2001) and the New York Lincoln Center (2004) with her regular pianist, Julius Drake, the Chicago Lyric Opera, as Hänsel (2001), the Salzburg Festival, as Dryade (*Ariadne auf Naxos*, 2001), Covent Garden, as Cherubino (2002), San Francisco (Ruggiero, 2002), Los Angeles, where she sang her first Octavian in 2005, Frankfurt, as Sesto in *La clemenza di Tito* (another role début, also 2005), and the Metropolitan, as Cherubino (2006). She returned to Covent Garden in 2003 to sing the title role of *Orlando*, but had to cancel after three performances due to illness. Her other operatic roles include C.W. Gluck's Orfeo, which she sang for the ENO in 2001, the Composer (*Ariadne auf Naxos*, Welsh National Opera, 2004) and Benjamin Britten's Lucretia.

In 2001 Coote sang at the Last Night of the Proms, and the following year performed Gustav Mahler's *Das Lied von der Erde* at the Edinburgh Festival. At the BBC Chamber Proms in 2003 she and Julius Drake gave the world première of the song cycle *The Voice of Desire* written for them by Judith Weir. She has also been admired as the Angel in *The Dream of Gerontius*, in Hector Berlioz's *Les nuits d'été*, which she sang at the Proms in 2003, and in lieder. Her début CD recital, of songs by Mahler, Robert Schumann's *Frauenliebe und -leben* and Joseph Haydn's *Arianna a Naxos*, was widely praised both for the satin beauty of her voice and her gift for penetrating without artifice to the heart of a song. Coote's other recordings include William Walton's *Gloria*, G.F. Handel's *The Choice of Hercules* and the Messaggiera in Claudio Monteverdi's *Orfeo*.

Richard Wigmore

Coralli, La.

See LAURENTI, ANTONIA MARIA.

Corbelli, Alessandro

(*b* Turin, 21 Sept 1952). Italian baritone. After studying with GIUSEPPE VALDENGO, he made his début as Marcello at Bergamo in 1974. He sang Pacuvio (Gioachino Rossini's *La pietra del paragone*) at the Piccola Scala and in Edinburgh (1982), Dandini at Philadelphia (1984) and Glyndebourne (1985). He made his Scala début in 1983 and his Covent Garden début as Taddeo (*L'italiana in*

Algeri) in 1988. His repertory includes Sharpless (his Opéra début role, 1983), W.A. Mozart's, Giovanni Paisiello's and Rossini's Figaro, Papageno, Guglielmo, Don Alfonso, which he sang at Salzburg (1991) and Florence (1994), Prosdocimo (*Il turco in Italia*), Raimbaud (*Le comte Ory*), Malatesta, Belcore, which he sang in Chicago (1991), Ford, Belfiore (*Un giorno di regno*) and Ping. At La Scala Corbelli has sung roles such as Varbel (*Lodoïska*), Lord Cockburn (*Fra Diavolo*), De Siriex (*Fedora*) and Leporello, possibly his best part. Though his light, flexible voice, superb diction and great gifts as an actor make him naturally suited to comedy, as can be heard in several Rossini recordings, he sings more serious roles such as Sharpless and Escamillo with equal conviction.

Elizabeth Forbes

Corelli, Franco [Dario]

(*b* Ancona, 8 April 1921; *d* Milan, 29 Oct 2003). Italian tenor. He studied at Pesaro and made his début in 1951 at Spoleto in *Carmen*, subsequently appearing in various Italian theatres. In 1954 he sang at La Scala, returning there until 1965. He made a sensational Covent Garden début, as Cavaradossi, in 1957, and was first heard in 1961 at the Berlin Städtische Oper and at the Vienna Staatsoper in 1963. After his Metropolitan début as Manrico (1961), he was engaged at that house every year during the following decade, in that time singing 282 performances of 18 roles. He appeared at the Paris Opéra and the Vienna Staatsoper in 1970 and at the Verona Arena in 1970 and 1972.

The possessor of a large, stentorian voice, Corelli was limited at first to *verismo* roles in the middle of the tenor range. But later he developed a strong and extended upper register and acquired the ability to inflect and vary his tone. Long the finest exponent of the Italian spinto tenor repertory (Ernani, Manrico, Radames, Don Alvaro, Andrea Chénier, Calaf, all preserved on disc), he successfully tackled some extremely difficult roles at La Scala between 1958 and 1962: Gualtiero in *Il pirata*, the title role in Gaetano Donizetti's *Poliuto* and Raoul in *Les Huguenots*. His handsome appearance and, in certain operas (especially *Carmen*), his vivid acting, made him a magnetic presence on stage. Among his recordings, those of Poliuto from La Scala and Pollione (*Norma*) in the studio (both with CALLAS), Calaf (to NILSSON's Turandot) and Don Alvaro (in a video from Naples) show why Corelli is widely regarded as one of the great tenors of the 20th century.

C.L. Osborne: 'Franco Corelli', *High Fidelity*, xvii/2 (1967), 63–7

Rodolfo Celletti/Alan Blyth

Corena, Fernando

(*b* Geneva, 22 Dec 1916; *d* Lugano, 26 Nov 1984). Swiss bass. He studied with Enrico Romani in Milan. After his début in 1937 he returned to Zürich for the war but made a postwar début in Trieste in 1947 (Varlaam). He appeared throughout Italy in roles as disparate as Escamillo, Sparafucile and Scarpia, and in 1949 sang in the première of Goffredo Petrassi's *Il cordovano* at La Scala. The *buffo* repertory soon became his abiding speciality, however; he made his Metropolitan début as Leporello in 1954, becoming the logical and worthy successor to SALVATORE BACCALONI. He sang in Edinburgh two years later (Giuseppe Verdi's *Falstaff*) and at Covent Garden as Dr Bartolo in 1960 and 1969. He also appeared in Vienna, at the Salzburg Festival, notably as Osmin in Giorgio Strehler's production of *Die Entführung aus dem Serail*, and in Berlin, Buenos Aires, Verona and Amsterdam; his other roles included Don Pasquale, Gianni Schicchi, Dulcamara, Don Alfonso, Sulpice in *La fille du régiment*, Mustafà and Lescaut in *Manon*. With the passing of time, Corena made up in comic invention for what he began to lack in vocal opulence. His wit, style and flair for improvisation remained exemplary. He is well represented in recordings of both serious and comic roles.

Martin Bernheimer

Cornelius, Peter [Petersen, Lauritz Peter Corneliys]

(*b* Labjerggaard, Jutland, 4 Jan 1865; *d* Snekkersten, nr Copenhagen, 30 Dec 1934). Danish baritone, later tenor. He studied with Jens Nyrop, and made his début in Copenhagen in 1892 as Escamillo, then continued to sing baritone roles including Kothner, Don Giovanni, Amonasro and Iago. After further study he made his tenor début in 1899 as the Steersman in *Der fliegende Holländer*. In 1902 he sang Siegmund and by 1914 he had added Siegfried, Lohengrin, Walther, Tannhäuser and Tristan to his repertory. He sang Siegfried at Bayreuth in 1906 and at Covent Garden in 1908–9 in Hans Richter's famous *Ring* in English; at Covent Garden he also sang Renaud in a revival of the first British production of C.W. Gluck's *Armide*. He made guest appearances in Paris, Budapest, Karlsruhe, Stockholm and Oslo. He retired in 1922, but in 1927 sang Tannhäuser when the tenor engaged fell ill. He made many recordings, the best of them in the period 1907–12, which show his gift for keen dramatic characterization.

Harold Rosenthal/R

Cortis [Corts], Antonio

(*b* on board ship between Oran, Algeria, and Altea, 12 Aug 1891; *d* Valencia, 2 April 1952). Spanish tenor. He studied in Madrid, where he sang in the chorus at the Teatro Real. At first he sang minor roles, then began to assume leading roles (Cavaradossi, Don José and Turiddu) in Barcelona and Valencia. In 1917 he sang in South America, where his roles included Beppe (*Pagliacci*). He was a regular guest at the Teatro Costanzi, Rome (1920–23); he also appeared in Milan, Naples and Turin, and in 1927 sang Radames at the Verona Arena. He sang in Chicago (1924–32) and San Francisco (1924–6). His roles in the USA included Edgardo, Manrico, Radames, Chénier, Canio, Cavaradossi, Des Grieux (*Manon Lescaut*), Enzo (*La Gioconda*) and Don José. His only Covent Garden season was in 1931 when he sang Calaf, and Hippolytus in Romano Romani's *Fedra* opposite PONSELLE. After 1935 he sang only in Spain, making his last stage appearance in 1951 at Zaragoza as Cavaradossi. Cortis's voice had a typically Spanish ring and power, demonstrated in his many recordings, most notably of Calaf's arias. His voice was similar to CARUSO's and he was known as the 'Caruso espagnol'.

'Antonio Cortis', *Record Collector*, xx (1971–2), 51–70 [with discography by J. León and J. Dennis]

Harold Rosenthal/Alan Blyth

Cosselli, Domenico

(*b* Parma, 27 May 1801; *d* Marano, nr Parma, 9 Nov 1855). Italian baritone. After studying in Parma he joined the chorus of the Teatro Ducale there in 1820. By 1823 he was singing leading roles in *Tancredi* and *La Cenerentola*, and he became a Rossini specialist. He appeared at all the chief Italian theatres, singing in *Le comte Ory*, *Zelmira* and *Semiramide*. He created roles in several operas by Gaetano Donizetti: Olivo in *Olivo e Pasquale* (1827, Rome), Azzo in *Parisina* (1833, Florence) and Enrico Ashton in *Lucia di Lammermoor* (1835, Naples). He also sang several Bellini roles: Valdeburgo in *La straniera* (1832, Venice); Ernesto in *Il pirata* and Filippo in *Beatrice di Tenda* (1834, Naples); and Riccardo in *I puritani* (1837, Faenza). In 1843 he retired from the stage.

Elizabeth Forbes

Cossotto, Fiorenza

(*b* Crescentino, Vercelli, 22 April 1935). Italian mezzo-soprano. A pupil of Ettore Campogalliani, she made her début in 1957 at La Scala (as Sister Mathilde in the première of *Dialogues des Carmélites*), returning there almost continuously up to the 1972–3 season and appearing in *La favorite*, *Les Huguenots*, *Il trovatore*, *Aida*, *Don Carlos*, *Barbiere*, *Cavalleria rusticana* (Santuzza), *Norma* and other operas. She began her international career in 1958, singing Jane Seymour in Gaetano Donizetti's *Anna Bolena* at the Wexford Festival. In 1959 she first appeared at Covent Garden (Neris in Luigi Cherubini's *Médée* with CALLAS) and caused a sensation as Cherubino at the Royal Festival Hall, London, with Carlo Maria Giulini. She then sang in Barcelona, Vienna, Paris, Chicago (1964) and New York (Amneris at the Metropolitan, 1968), as well as in all the leading Italian theatres. She was still singing major roles into the 21st century, including an engagement as the princess in *Suor Angelica* in Liège in 2005. Cossotto has a full, resonant voice, particularly clear and easily produced in the top register. Notable among her many recordings are her vocally opulent, dramatically exciting Amneris, Lady Macbeth, Leonora (*La favorite*) and Adalgisa (where her coloratura singing is outstanding). Her Amneris is preserved on a video made at the Verona Arena.

Rodolfo Celletti/Alan Blyth

Cossutta, Carlo

(*b* Trieste, 8 May 1932; *d* Udine, 22 Jan 2000). Italian tenor. He studied in Buenos Aires, making his début at the Teatro Colón in 1958 as Cassio and in 1964 creating the title role of Alberto Ginastera's *Don Rodrigo*. In 1964 he made his European début at Covent Garden as the Duke in *Rigoletto*. He returned as Don Carlos, Gabriele Adorno, Manrico and Turiddu and, in 1974, for his first Otello; in these roles his generous volume, ringing tone and sturdy manner won praise. He made his American début in 1963 at Chicago as Abdallo (*Nabucco*) and his Metropolitan début in 1973 as Pollione (*Norma*). He sang widely in the USA and Europe and in 1974 sang Radames with La Scala in Moscow. His recordings of *La vida breve*, Otello (under Georg Solti) and Samson demonstrate his dark, dramatic voice and eloquence.

Harold Rosenthal/Alan Blyth

Cotogni, Antonio

(*b* Rome, 1 Aug 1831; *d* Rome, 15 Oct 1918). Italian baritone. He studied in Rome, making his début there in 1852 at the Teatro Metastasio as Belcore. He sang at La Scala and in Bologna as Posa in the first Italian performance of *Don Carlos* (1867). At Covent Garden (1867–89) he made his début as Valentin and sang a great many roles, including Don Giovanni,

Papageno, W.A. Mozart's and Gioachino Rossini's Figaro, William Tell, Enrico Ashton, Belcore, Malatesta, Alphonse (*La favorite*), Hoël, Hamlet, Nevers, Nélusko, Mercutio, Germont, Amonasro, Luna, Rigoletto and Escamillo, and Barnaba in the first London performance of *La Gioconda* (1883). He gave his farewell at St Petersburg in 1898. A versatile artist, whose flexible voice was ideally suited to Italian opera, he also sang Telramund.

Elizabeth Forbes

Cotrubas, Ileana

(*b* Galati, 9 June 1939). Romanian soprano. She studied in Bucharest and made her début there in 1964 as Yniold. After further study in Vienna, she sang with the Frankfurt Opera (1968–71). She first sang at Salzburg in 1967 as the Second Boy (*Die Zauberflöte*), returning for Bastienne, Konstanze and Pamina. She made her Glyndebourne début in 1969 as Mélisande, later singing Calisto, Susanna and Titania. In Vienna she sang Zerlina, Sophie and Nedda. At Covent Garden, where she first appeared in 1971, her roles included Tatyana, Violetta, Adina, Norina, Amina and Antonia, and she sang Manon at the Paris Opéra in 1974. She sang Mimì at La Scala in 1975 as well as for her 1977 début at the Metropolitan, where she subsequently sang Gilda, Micaëla and Ilia. Taking on heavier roles, she sang Elisabeth de Valois at Florence, Marguerite at Hamburg (1985), Amelia (*Simon Boccanegra*) at Naples, Magda (*La rondine*) in Chicago (1986), Alice Ford at Monte Carlo (1987) and Desdemona at Barcelona (1988). She retired in 1989. Her sweet-toned, agile voice and gentle personality conveyed vulnerability and pathos to great dramatic effect, as can be heard in her recordings of W.A. Mozart and Violetta with Carlos Kleiber and Gilda with Carlo Maria Giulini.

A. Blyth: 'Ileana Cotrubas', *Opera*, xxvii (1976), 428–33
A. Blyth: 'Cotrubas Says Farewell', *Opera*, xl (1989), 410–12

Alan Blyth

Courtis, Jean-Philippe

(*b* Airaines, 24 May 1951). French bass. He studied the oboe and conducting before turning to singing at the Paris Conservatoire. He sang Johann in *Werther* at the 1979 Aix-en-Provence Festival and made his Paris Opéra début the following year in Jean-Philippe Rameau's *Dardanus*. He performed several other roles at the Opéra and Opéra-Comique in the early 1980s, including Mr Plunket in H.W. Henze's *The English Cat* and Frère Bernard in the world première of Olivier Messiaen's *Saint François d'Assise* in 1983. His international career dates from April 1987 when he created the role of Malfortune in the world première of Rolf Liebermann's *La forêt* in Geneva. Appearances in Bonn, Cologne, Vienna, Amsterdam and Salzburg followed. Courtis sang Don Diègue in the first staged performance of Claude Debussy's reconstructed *Rodrigue et Chimène* in Lyons, and McCreah in a revival of Gilbert Bécaud's *L'opéra d'Aran*. His repertory, which focusses principally on French roles, also includes Jules Massenet's *Don Quichotte*, George Enescu's *Oedipe* and Frank Martin's *Golgotha*. Among his recordings are *Pelléas et Mélisande* (Arkel) with Claudio Abbado, *Les Troyens* (Narbal) with Charles Dutoit and Massenet's *Esclarmonde* and *Grisélidis*, both with Patrick Fournillier.

Patrick O'Connor

Crabbé, Armand (Charles)
[Morin, Charles]

(*b* Brussels, 23 April 1883; *d* Brussels, 24 July 1947). Belgian baritone. He used the name Charles Morin when appearing in small roles. He studied in Brussels and with Cottone in Milan and made his début at La Monnaie in 1904 as the Nightwatchman in *Die Meistersinger*. From 1906 to 1914 he sang at Covent Garden, where his roles included Valentin, Alfio, Silvio and Ford; he returned in 1937 as Gianni Schicchi. At La Scala he sang Rigoletto, Marcello, Beckmesser, Lescaut and the title role of Giordano's *Il re* (1929), which he created. He joined Oscar Hammerstein's Manhattan Opera in 1907 and appeared at Chicago (1910–14), and at the Teatro Colón, Buenos Aires, in the 1920s. One of his most successful roles was Mârouf, which Henri Rabaud transposed for him from tenor to baritone. Crabbé continued to appear until the early 1940s, mainly in Antwerp. He published *Conseils sur l'art du chant* (Brussels, 1931) and *L'art d'Orphée* (Brussels, 1933). His recordings show his voice to have been typical of the French school in its forward tone and precise diction.

W.R. Moran: 'Notes from a Wandering Collector', *Record News*, iv (1959–60), 28–35 [with partial discography]

Harold Rosenthal/Alan Blyth

Craig, Charles (James)

(*b* London, 3 Dec 1919; *d* Banbury, 23 Jan 1997). English tenor. He first sang as part of an entertainment unit during war service. In 1947 he joined the chorus at Covent Garden and sang small roles with the company. Thomas Beecham, impressed with his voice, financed his further study (with DINO BORGIOLI) and engaged him as soloist for concerts in 1952. The following year Craig joined the Carl Rosa Opera Company, making his début as Rodolfo. He came to more general notice when he sang Des Grieux (*Manon Lescaut*) and a viscerally exciting Benvenuto Cellini with the company in 1957. He also sang with Sadler's Wells Opera (from 1956), appearing as Manrico, Samson, Luigi (*Il tabarro*), Cavaradossi and Andrea Chénier. In 1959 he appeared opposite JOAN HAMMOND in *Rusalka* at Sadler's Wells. That was also the year of his Covent Garden début in a major role, Pinkerton to JURINAC's Butterfly. Turiddu followed in the famous Franco Zeffirelli staging of *Cavalleria rusticana* and *Pagliacci* (later, Craig became an impassioned Canio). Other notable appearances were Arturo Talbot to SUTHERLAND's Elvira (*I puritani*, 1964), Don Alvaro (in Sam Wanamaker's controversial staging of *La forza del destino*, 1962), Calaf, Radames, a wily Golitsïn in *Khovanshchina*, and Sergey in the British première of *Katerina Izmaylova*. In Paris in 1964 he sang Pollione to the Norma of CALLAS. For Scottish Opera he sang Siegmund, Florestan and his first Otello, the role he then sang all over Italy and Germany (and at Chicago in 1966) but not in London until 1981 with the ENO, and finally at Covent Garden in 1983. Probably the best English lyric-dramatic tenor of the postwar era, Craig sang all his roles with Italianate fervour and innately musical phrasing. Though his acting was never subtle, it had rude sincerity and honest conviction. His moving Otello is preserved on a live recording under Mark Elder (1983, in English); there are also recordings of extracts from *Un ballo in maschera*, from Scottish Opera, and *Madama Butterfly* in English with MARIE COLLIER, a frequent stage partner.

C. Halbik: 'Charles Craig', *Opera*, xii (1961), 698–702

Obituaries: E. Forbes, *The Independent* (25 Jan 1997); A. Blyth, *Opera*, xlviii (1997), 534–6

Alan Blyth

Crass, Franz

(*b* Wipperfürth, 9 Feb 1928). German bass-baritone. He made his first appearance at the age of 11 as the Second Boy in *Die Zauberflöte*. He then studied singing at the Cologne Musikhochschule, and made his début at Krefeld in 1954 as the King in *Aida*. Engagements followed at Hanover (1956–62) and Cologne (1962–4); after 1964 he divided his time between Hamburg, Munich, Frankfurt and Vienna, with guest appearances in most leading European theatres. Crass first appeared at Bayreuth in 1959 as King Henry in *Lohengrin* and returned each year until 1973, singing the Dutchman, Biterolf, Fasolt, King Mark and Gurnemanz. He also appeared at Salzburg, as Rocco and Sarastro, and at La Scala from 1960, when he sang Don Fernando (*Fidelio*). In 1966 he sang Barak in the British première of *Die Frau ohne Schatten*, given by the Hamburg Staatsoper at Sadler's Wells. His repertory also included the roles of Philip II, Otto Nicolai's Falstaff and Béla Bartók's Bluebeard. He retired from the stage in 1980. Otto Klemperer chose him to sing in the *Missa solemnis* in London in 1960 and in W.A. Mozart's Requiem in 1964. His large concert repertory included works by J.S. Bach, G.F. Handel, Joseph Haydn and Leoš Janáček. Crass possessed a well-schooled bass-baritone voice of lyric rather than dramatic quality, which can be heard at its best in his recordings of Sarastro, Rocco and the Dutchman.

Harold Rosenthal/R

Crespin, Régine

(*b* Marseilles, 23 Feb 1927; *d* Paris, 5 July 2007). French soprano. She studied with Georges Jouatte and Paul Cabanel at the Paris Conservatoire, and made her operatic début at Mulhouse in 1950, as Elsa, the role of her Paris Opéra début the same year. In the next six years, despite further appearances in Paris (as Vita in Vincent d'Indy's *L'étranger*, Desdemona and Charles Gounod's Marguerite), her career was more successfully advanced in the provinces, in French opera (Salome in Jules Massenet's *Hérodiade*, Brunehild in Ernest Reyer's *Sigurd*), and also in the German and Italian roles, sung in French, with which her international reputation was later made – notably Sieglinde, the Marschallin and Tosca. In 1956 she returned to the Opéra as Carl Maria von Weber's Rezia; subsequent successes there led to engagements at Bayreuth, as Wieland Wagner's 'Mediterranean enchantress' Kundry (1958–60), and Sieglinde (1961); and at Glyndebourne (1959–60), as the Marschallin. In this role, an aristocratic, rather melancholy elegance of style and a delicate mastery of nuance, both vocal and dramatic, won her wide praise, particularly in Berlin, Vienna and New York (Metropolitan début 1962). At Covent Garden she played the Marschallin (début 1960), Tosca, Elsa and, less happily, Beethoven's Leonore. She undertook her first Ariadne in Chicago (1964), and her first *Walküre* Brünnhilde at the 1967 Salzburg Easter Festival; but, with the onset of vocal difficulties marked by unease in her highest register, she relinquished the latter role. Having retrained her voice with the German teacher Rudolf Bautz, she began to undertake mezzo roles such as Carmen,

Régine Crespin

Francis Poulenc's Madame de Croissy and (on disc) Massenet's Dulcinée. When she retired in 1989 she had already gained a considerable reputation as a singing teacher at the Paris Conservatoire.

Crespin was the first French singer after GERMAINE LUBIN to command the heroic roles of German and French opera with equal authority; in addition to the idiomatic assurance of her Wagner, she was distinguished for the classical nobility of style in such French roles as Julia in *La vestale*, Hector Berlioz's Dido, and the titular heroines of *Iphigénie en Tauride* and Gabriel Fauré's *Pénélope*. She was Madame Lidoine at the Paris première of *Dialogues des Carmélites* (1957), and Phaedra in the 1959 La Scala revival of Ildebrando Pizzetti's opera. Although her vocal timbre was not ideally suited to Italian opera, she was a moving Amelia (*Un ballo in maschera*), Desdemona and Tosca. Her singing, in opera and concert, was notable for a remarkable finesse of diction, phrase shaping and tone-colour, capable of transforming a powerful but flawed dramatic soprano into an instrument of smooth, lustrous beauty; in her prime, the eloquence of her soft high phrases was matched by few other singers. A recitalist of great accomplishment, she performed Hugo Wolf subtly, and Poulenc and Jacques Offenbach with irresistible wit. Her recorded roles include Offenbach's Métella, Grand-Duchess and Périchole, Madame Lidoine, the Marschallin, Sieglinde, the *Walküre* Brünnhilde and Carmen; and, among other works, haunting accounts of Berlioz's *Nuits d'été* and

Maurice Ravel's *Shéhérazade*. She published a frank and moving account of her life and career, *La vie et l'amour d'une femme* (Paris, 1982; Eng. trans., rev., 1997, as *On Stage, Off Stage*).

A. Tubeuf: 'Régine Crespin', *Opera*, xv (1963), 227–32
M. Loppert: 'Crespin on the Marschallin', *Opera*, xxxv (1984), 362–7

Max Loppert

Crimi, Giulio

(*b* Paterno, nr Catania, 10 May 1885; *d* Rome, 29 Oct 1939). Italian tenor. He studied in Catania and made his début in *Il trovatore* at Palermo in 1910. He then sang throughout Italy, appearing at La Scala in *Aida* and *La battaglia di Legnano* in 1916. His international career began in 1914 with highly successful performances as Giacomo Puccini's Des Grieux in Paris and London, where he also sang in the British première of Italo Montemezzi's *L'amore dei tre re*. He appeared in Buenos Aires in 1916, and then in Chicago in the American première of Pietro Mascagni's *Isabeau*. He joined the Metropolitan, where a major event in his first year was the world première of Giacomo Puccini's *Trittico* (1918): he appeared in both *Il tabarro* and *Gianni Schicchi*. Back in Italy he enjoyed a last success in *L'Africaine* at the Costanzi, Rome, in 1924, and then retired to teach, his most famous pupil being TITO GOBBI. On recordings, Crimi's full-bodied voice impresses favourably – less so the style and reliability of its usage.

J. B. Steane

Cristoforeanu, Florica

(*b* Rîmnicu Sărat, 16 May 1887; *d* Rio de Janeiro, 1 March 1960). Romanian soprano. She studied the piano, and later singing, in Bucharest and Milan (at the Giuseppe Verdi Conservatory, with Vanerí Filippi and Bodrilla), making her début as Lucia at Capodistria in 1908. After touring widely in western Europe she returned to Bucharest for performances in operetta (1910–13). Growing international fame led to her appearances at opera houses throughout Europe, notably at Barcelona, and also at the Teatro Colón, Buenos Aires. She made her début as Santuzza at La Scala, where she also appeared from 1928 to 1932 as Salome under Richard Strauss, as Mariola in the première of Ildebrando Pizzetti's *Fra Gherardo* (1928), and as Carmen and Charlotte (*Werther*). By the time she retired she had mastered a repertory of more than 90 roles, embracing mezzo, dramatic, lyric and coloratura parts in opera and operetta. In Bucharest her Cio-Cio-San, Minnie (*La fanciulla del West*), Kundry and Adriana Lecouvreur were especially admired. Her range, both vocal and dramatic, was exceptional, enhanced by a richly coloured timbre and an intense commitment to all her roles. After her death her memoirs *Amintiri din cariera mea lirică* were published (Bucharest, 1964).

Viorel Cosma

Croiza [Conelly], Claire

(*b* Paris, 14 Sept 1882; *d* Paris, 27 May 1946). French mezzo-soprano. She made her début in Nancy in 1905 (in Isidore De Lara's *Messalina*). The following year she began her long association with the Théâtre de la Monnaie, Brussels (début as Delilah, 1906), where her wide repertory included Hector Berlioz's Dido, Clytemnestra in *Iphigénie en Aulide* and Richard Strauss's *Elektra*, Erda, Carmen, Gaetano Donizetti's Léonor, Charlotte and Gabriel Fauré's Penelope. At the Paris Opéra she appeared in 1908 as Delilah. At Jacques Rouché's Théâtre des Arts in 1913 she sang in the Vincent d'Indy editions of *Poppea* and André Destouches' *Les éléments* and an act of C.W. Gluck's *Orphée*. She sang the title role in Gustave Doret's *La tisseuse d'orties* at its first performance in 1926 at the Opéra-Comique, and in the first staged performance of Claude Debussy's *La damoiselle élue* in 1919 at the Théâtre du Vaudeville.

From 1922 Croiza taught at the Ecole Normale and from 1934 at the Conservatoire. Her instinct for the French language and her intelligence, clarity of tone and passionate reserve caused her to be admired as much by poets as by musicians; Paul Valéry hailed her as possessing 'la voix la plus sensible de notre génération'. Camille Saint-Saëns, d'Indy and Fauré admired her unreservedly, as, later, did Debussy and Albert Roussel. Her silvery yet warm tone, and that 'volupté du son' based on pure, perfect utterance of the words, can be heard on her recordings.

B. Bannerman: 'Recollections of Claire Croiza', *British Institute of Recorded Sound: Bulletin*, no.1 (1956), 12–29 [with discography]

Martin Cooper

Crook, Howard

(*b* Passaic, NJ, 15 June 1947). American tenor. He studied at Illinois State University and began his career primarily as a concert singer, making his opera début as Eisenstein (*Die Fledermaus*) in Cleveland in 1970. His subsequent roles have included Belmonte and Pelléas at Amsterdam (1983 and 1984), Jean-Baptiste Lully's Atys and Jean-Philippe Rameau's Castor at Aix-en-Provence (1987 and 1991), and Admetus in Lully's *Alceste* at the Théâtre des Champs-Elysées, Paris. His agile technique and lyrical projection of high-lying roles have proved especially effective both in French Baroque repertory and in the Bach Passions, in which

Crook is an admired Evangelist. His recordings include Claudio Monteverdi's Vespers, Lully's *Alceste*, *Armide* and *Acis et Galatée*, Rameau's *Castor et Pollux* and *Les Indes galantes*, Jean-Marie Leclair's *Scylla et Glaucus*, *Messiah* and J.S. Bach's Passions.

Nicholas Anderson

Crooks, Richard (Alexander)

(*b* Trenton, NJ, 26 June 1900; *d* Portola Valley, CA, 1 Oct 1972). American tenor. He studied with Sidney H. Bourne and Frank La Forge, and first sang in opera at Hamburg as Cavaradossi in 1927. Appearances with the Berlin Staatsoper and in other European centres followed, in roles such as Walther and Lohengrin. He made his American opera début in 1930 in Philadelphia as Cavaradossi, and his Metropolitan début as Jules Massenet's Des Grieux in 1933. He sang leading lyric roles, mostly French and Italian, with the company and elsewhere in the USA for the next ten seasons, then pursued a concert career. Crooks had a beautiful voice which, though limited in the upper register, was admired for its smoothness of tone and production, as can be judged from his many recordings of opera, lieder and lighter music.

K.S. Mackiggan: 'Richard Crooks', *Record Collector*, xii (1958–60), 125–42, 147–55, 258–61; xx (1971–2), 258–70 [with discography by C.I. Morgan]

C.I. Morgan: 'Richard Crooks: a Biography', *Record Advertiser*, ii/6 (1971–2), 2–12; iii/1 (1972–3), 2–16 [with discography]

Max De Schauensee/R

Cross, Joan (Annie)

(*b* London, 7 Sept 1900; *d* Aldeburgh, 12 Dec 1993). English soprano, teacher and producer. She began her musical life as a violinist while a pupil at St Paul's Girls' School, London. Continuing her studies at Trinity College of Music, she found Emile Sauret unmoved by her playing and turned to singing, making rapid progress under the tuition of Dawson Freer. Her career started in 1923 when she accepted the offer of unpaid chorus work at the Old Vic. After taking various comprimario parts she soon found herself singing roles such as Elisabeth (*Tannhäuser*) and Aida. As principal soprano of Sadler's Wells (1931–46), she was recognized as a consummate singing-actress in an exceptionally wide range of roles, from Henry Purcell's Dido to Rosalinde (*Die Fledermaus*), Butterfly, Elsa, Sieglinde and the Marschallin. She made her Covent Garden début, as Mimi, in 1931 and sang Kupava and Militrisa in the English premières of Nikolay Rimsky-Korsakov's *Snow Maiden* and *Tale of Tzar Saltan* (both 1933).

On assuming the directorship of the Sadler's Wells Opera Company in 1943, Cross combined administration with singing. Her decision to reopen the theatre in June 1945 with the première of Benjamin Britten's *Peter Grimes*, in which she created the role of Ellen Orford, won her respect, but also enmity, leading to her departure from the company. In a new and unexpected phase of her life's work, she created a further four Britten roles over the next decade: the Female Chorus in *The Rape of Lucretia* (1946, Glyndebourne), Lady Billows in *Albert Herring* (1947, Glyndebourne), Queen Elizabeth in *Gloriana* (1953, Covent Garden), and Mrs Grose in *The Turn of the Screw* (1954, Venice). Her work as a teacher and opera producer involved her in many pioneering causes. She was a founder-member of the English Opera Group and co-founder of the Opera School (now the National Opera Studio) in 1948. Her first major production was *Der Rosenkavalier* for Covent Garden (1947), though her greatest successes were more often abroad, particularly in Norway.

Cross possessed a distinctive voice of grave beauty which she used with an unerring sense of style. A singer of sincerity, intelligence and technical skill, she was a complete operatic performer for whom words and music were of equal importance. She made a relatively small number of recordings between 1924 and 1955, including an admired Mrs Grose conducted by the composer. Never one for compromise or make-do, her outspokenness sometimes clouded her professional and personal relationships. Awarded a CBE in 1951, Cross also wrote several fine English singing translations of operas and a volume of memoirs (unpublished).

C. Hardy: 'Joan Cross', *Opera*, i/1 (1950), 22–8

H. Rosenthal: *Sopranos of Today* (London, 1956)

Obituaries: E. Forbes, *The Independent* (14 Dec 1993); F. Granville Barker, *The Guardian* (14 Dec 1993)

Bryan Crimp

Crozier, Nancy.

See EVANS, NANCY.

Cruvelli [Crüwell], (Jeanne) Sophie (Charlotte)

(*b* Bielefeld, 12 March 1826; *d* Nice or Monaco, 6 Nov 1907). German soprano. A pupil of Francesco Lamperti, she made her début at La Fenice, Venice, in 1847 as Odabella (*Attila*). She repeated the same role in Udine, followed by Lucrezia (*I due Foscari*). Giuseppe Verdi's early operas suited her voice, which was large and powerful if not always under perfect control, and in 1848 she sang Elvira (*Ernani*) and

Abigaille (*Nabucco*, given as *Nino*) at Her Majesty's Theatre in London, as well as Leonore (*Fidelio*) and Countess Almaviva. She appeared in Milan in 1849–50, singing roles including Odabella, Elvira, Abigaille, Rosina and Norma. She made her Paris début in 1851 as Elvira, and at the Théâtre Italien she also sang in *Norma*, *La sonnambula*, *Fidelio* and *Semiramide*. In 1854 she transferred to the Opéra (her performance is reported in *Dwight's Journal*, iv (1853–4), 150–51), appearing as Valentine (*Les Huguenots*), Julia (*La vestale*) and Rachel (*La Juive*). She then returned to London, where she sang in Gioachino Rossini's *Otello*, in *Fidelio* and as Donna Anna at Covent Garden. She created Hélène in *Les vêpres siciliennes* at the Paris Opéra in 1855; she had an opulent voice with a range of nearly three octaves and sang with a ferocity perfectly suited to the part. She retired the following year after her marriage to Baron Vigier and organized the French première of *Lohengrin* in her Cercle de la Méditerranée music salon (1881, Nice).

Elizabeth Forbes

Cuberli [Terrell], Lella

(*b* Austin, TX, 29 Sept 1945). American soprano. She studied at Dallas, where, as Lella Terrell, she sang Kate (*Madama Butterfly*) and Inès (*La favorite*) in 1970–71. After further study in Milan she sang Anne Trulove at Siena in 1973 and for some years pursued her career mainly in Italy. At Martina Franca (1976–82) she sang Amenaide (*Tancredi*), Adalgisa (*Norma*) and Giovanni Paisiello's Nina and Rosina. At La Scala (1978–84) she sang Konstanze (*Entführung*), Amyntas (*Il re pastore*), Ginevra (*Ariodante*), Rodelinda and Giunio (*Lucio Silla*). Her other roles at the major Italian opera houses have included Donna Elvira, Fiordiligi, the title role of *Elisabetta, regina d'Inghilterra*, Lucia, Vincenzo Bellini's Giulietta, Giuseppe Verdi's Desdemona, Mélisande and Countess Almaviva, a part she also sang at Aix-en-Provence, Salzburg and Vienna. In Brussels she sang Violetta (1987) and Gioachino Rossini's Desdemona (1994). Returning to the USA, she made her débuts in Chicago (1989) as Amenaide, and the Metropolitan (1990) as Semiramide. She made her Covent Garden début in 1990 as Mathilde (*Guillaume Tell*), then sang *Anna Bolena* in Madrid (1991) and Donna Anna in Salzburg (1994), a role she has recorded with Daniel Barenboim. Although Cuberli's beautiful voice is not large, it is firmly produced, flexible and used with impeccable style, especially in Mozart and Rossini.

Elizabeth Forbes

Cuénod [Cuenod], Hugues (Adhémar)

(*b* Corseaux-sur-Vevey, 26 June 1902). Swiss tenor. He studied in Geneva, Basle and Vienna, making his stage début at the Théâtre des Champs-Elysées in Paris in 1928. He has appeared in many character roles in the main opera houses. He created the role of Sellem in Igor Stravinsky's *The Rake's Progress* (1951, Venice) and sang the Astrologer in *The Golden Cockerel* (1954, Covent Garden). He made his Glyndebourne début in 1954 as Sellem, going on to sing over 470 performances there, his roles including Don Basilio, the travesty parts of Erice and Linfea in Cavalli's *L'Ormindo* and *La Calisto*, Triquet (*Yevgeny Onegin*) and the Cock (*The Cunning Little Vixen*). He sang Triquet in Geneva in 1986, and in 1987 (aged 85) made his Metropolitan Opera début as Emperor Altoum (*Turandot*). A cultivated musician with a wide command of languages, he made pioneering discs of Claudio Monteverdi under Nadia Boulanger (1937–9), and also made outstanding recordings of lute-songs, of François Couperin, and of the Evangelist in J.S. Bach's *St Matthew Passion*. He was a subtle, stylish singer, as effective in Monteverdi or Francesco Cavalli as in Maurice Ravel or Stravinsky; a fine interpreter of lieder, he used his high, light tenor with exquisite taste in all the music he performed. On stage his interpretations were full of humour, where that was called for, and he was also a master of the grotesque.

Alan Blyth

Cura, José

(*b* Rosario, Santa Fé, 5 Dec 1962). Argentine tenor. He began his career at the age of 15 as a choral conductor and studied composition at the National University of Rosario. After spending several years composing and conducting (1984–8), he studied singing with Horacio Amauri and, after moving to Italy, with Vittorio Terranova. His stage début came in 1992 at Verona when he sang the Father in H.W. Henze's *Pollicino*, followed by Albert Gregor in *The Makropulos Affair* at Turin in 1993, Ismaele (*Nabucco*) at Genoa and Alvaro (*La forza del destino*) at Turin, both in 1994. After winning the Operalia Competition, run by DOMINGO, Cura made his US début in Chicago as Loris (*Fedora*), also in 1994. In 1995 he was acclaimed at his Covent Garden début in the title role of *Stiffelio* and at the Opéra Bastille, Paris, as Ismaele. His other Covent Garden roles have included Loris, Camille Saint-Saëns's Samson (which he has recorded with Colin Davis), Don José and Andrea Chénier, the last in concert. He made his début at La Scala in 1997 as Enzo (*La Gioconda*), and the same year he sang his first Otello, with Claudio Abbado in Berlin. Other important roles include

Radames, Turiddu (which he recorded for television with Riccardo Muti in 1996), Canio, Giacomo Puccini's Des Grieux, Roberto (*Le villi*) and Osaka (*Iris*). In 2001 he sang Otello both at the Vienna Staatsoper and at Covent Garden, an interpretation praised for its vocal splendour but criticized by some for underplaying the character's agony. Cura has emerged as that rare phenomenon, a true *lirico spinto* tenor in the mould of Domingo, who has helped launch Cura's career and conducted his highly successful first recital, consisting of all the tenor arias from Puccini's operas. Cura's charismatic appearance and acting enhance his exciting, confidently produced voice. Like Domingo, he has recently begun to develop a parallel career as a conductor.

Alan Blyth

Curioni, Alberico

(*b* Milan, 1785; *d* Torno, Como, March 1875). Italian tenor. He sang from an early age in the major Italian cities, including Milan, Naples, where he created Alberto in Gioachino Rossini's *La gazzetta* (1816), and Pesaro, where he sang Giannetto in *La gazza ladra* (1818). He made his London début in 1821 at the King's Theatre as W.A. Mozart's Titus and sang there until 1837. His roles included Rossini's Otello, Agorante (*Ricciardo e Zoraide*) and King James (*La donna del lago*), Carolino (Simon Mayr's *Il fanatico per la musica*), Ferrando, Adriano in the London première of *Il crociato in Egitto* (1825) and Pollione with GIULIA GRISI in her first *Norma* (1835). He created Orombello in *Beatrice di Tenda* (1833, Venice). Reputed to have a 'sweet, mellifluous-toned voice', he also had a fine stage presence.

Elizabeth Forbes

Curtin [née Smith], Phyllis

(*b* Clarksburg, WV, 3 Dec 1921). American soprano. She attended Wellesley College and studied with the bass Joseph Regneas, singing in the American première of *Peter Grimes* (1946, Tanglewood) while still a student. Her first significant opera appearances were with the New England Opera Theatre in Boston as Lisa in *The Queen of Spades* and Lady Billows in Benjamin Britten's *Albert Herring*, followed in 1953 by a début with the New York City Opera in Gottfried von Einem's *Der Prozess*. Her extensive and varied roles at the City Opera over the next ten years included all the major Mozart heroines, Violetta, Salome, William Walton's Cressida, and Susannah in Carlisle Floyd's opera, a role she created (1955, Talahassee). Engagements in Vienna, Buenos Aires, Frankfurt and with the Metropolitan Opera (début 1961), La Scala and Scottish Opera

in the 1960s brought her international repute. She made numerous recital and concert appearances throughout the USA and Europe and was particularly known for her singing of contemporary works, many of which were composed for her. Curtin sang in the American premières of Britten's *War Requiem* (1963) and Dmitry Shostakovich's Symphony no.14 (1969), recording the latter under Eugene Ormandy. Although she lacked the star qualities of more celebrated operatic sopranos, her singing was always much respected for its cultivated musicality, interpretative grace and vocal purity. She has taught at the Aspen School of Music and the Berkshire Music Center, and was a member of the faculty of Yale University from 1974 until 1983, when she became dean of Boston University's School of the Arts. She retired from singing in public in 1984.

Peter G. Davis

Cuzzoni, Francesca

(*b* Parma, 2 April 1696; *d* Bologna, 19 June 1778). Italian soprano. Her parents were Angelo, a professional violinist, and Marina Castelli. She was a pupil of Francesco Lanzi; her first known appearance was in an anonymous *La virtù coronata, o Il Fernando* (1714, Parma). She sang in 1716–17 at Bologna in operas by Giovanni Bassani, Giuseppe Buini, Francesco Gasparini and Giuseppe Orlandini and by 1717–18 was 'virtuosa di camera' to the Grand Princess Violante of Tuscany, singing at Florence, Siena, Mantua, Genoa and Reggio nell'Emilia in operas by Orlandini, C.F. Pollarolo and Antonio Vivaldi (*Scanderbeg*). She made her Venice début in 1718 as Dalinda in Pollarolo's *Ariodante*, with FAUSTINA BORDONI as Ginevra; the future rivals appeared there again in two operas the following year. Cuzzoni sang at Florence and Milan in 1719, at Turin, Bologna and Florence in 1720, at Padua in 1721 and in five more operas at Venice in 1721–2; in Orlandini's *Nerone* she played Poppaea, with Faustina as Octavia and Diana Vico as Agrippina.

She went to London at the end of 1722, having married the composer and harpsichordist Pietro Giuseppe Sandoni on the way. Her reputation preceded her. Her King's Theatre début on 12 January 1723 as Teofane in G.F. Handel's *Ottone* was sensational. The part had not been composed for her and at rehearsal she refused to sing her first aria, 'Falsa immagine', until Handel threatened to pitch her out of the window; but her triumph was complete. At her benefit on 25 March 'some of the Nobility gave her 60 Guineas a Ticket' (in addition to her salary of £2000 a season). She remained a member of the company until the Royal Academy closed in June 1728 and sang in every opera: Handel's *Flavio* (Emilia,

Francesca Cuzzoni,
Farinelli and
J.J. Heidegger,
drawing by
Dorothy Boyle,
Countess of
Burlington (1734)

1723; see illustration in BERENSTADT, GAETANO), *Giulio Cesare* (Cleopatra, 1724; she and SENESINO had an outstanding success), *Tamerlano* (Asteria, 1724), *Rodelinda* (title role, 1725), *Scipione* (Berenice, 1726), *Alessandro* (Lisaura, 1726), *Admeto* (Antigona, 1727), *Riccardo Primo* (Costanza, 1727), *Radamisto* (Pilissena in the 1728 revival), *Siroe* (Laodice, 1728) and *Tolomeo* (Seleuce, 1728), Attilio Ariosti's *Coriolano*, *Vespasiano*, *Aquilio consolo*, *Artaserse*, *Dario*, *Lucio Vero* and *Teuzzone*, Giovanni Bononcini's *Erminia*, *Farnace*, *Calpurnia* and *Astianatte*, and the pasticcios *Elpidia* and *Elisa*. The exuberance of her admirers soon led to quarrels, first with the partisans of Senesino and later with those of Faustina Bordoni, who made her London début in *Alessandro* in 1726. The rivalry between the two great sopranos was notorious and became a public scandal when ovations, whistles and catcalls in turn led to a scuffle on stage during *Astianatte* (in which she created the role of Andromache) on 6 June 1727. Cuzzoni was dismissed by the Academy, but reinstated when the king threatened to withdraw his subsidy. The final Academy season seems to have been less cantankerous, despite (or because of) John

Gay's satirical portrait of the ladies as Polly and Lucy in *The Beggar's Opera*.

Cuzzoni spent winter 1728–9 in Vienna at the invitation of Count Kinsky, the imperial ambassador in London; she made a great impression but was not engaged for the opera because she demanded an exorbitant salary. She sang at Modena and Venice in 1729. John Jacob Heidegger wished to engage both prima donnas for the Second Royal Academy that autumn, but Handel, who according to Paulo Rolli had never liked Faustina and wanted to forget Cuzzoni, preferred new voices. In 1730–31 Cuzzoni sang at Piacenza, Bologna, in Johann Hasse's *Ezio* and Domenico Sarro's *Artemisia* at Naples, and in three operas, including Hasse's *Artaserse*, in Venice, in which she created Mandane (1730). During 1731–2 she appeared again in Venice and Florence in operas by Hasse and her husband, and at Genoa in the carnival seasons of 1733 and 1734, still in close association with Sandoni; she created Emirena in his *Adriano in Siria* (1734). She was one of the first singers approached by the Opera of the Nobility, in opposition to Handel, in 1733; she arrived in April 1734 and joined the cast of Nicola Porpora's *Arianna in Nasso*, singing the title role. She sang in four more operas by Porpora (*Enea nel Lazio*, *Polifemo*, *Ifigenia in Aulide* and *Mitridate*), Hasse's *Artaserse*, Handel's *Ottone* (her old part, but under Nobility management), Sandoni's *Issipile*, Francesco Veracini's *Adriano in Siria*, the pasticcio *Orfeo* and Francesco Ciampi's *Onorio*. She seems to have aroused less enthusiasm on this visit.

Cuzzoni sang in Leonardo Leo's *Olimpiade* and Antonio Caldara's *Ormisda* at Florence in 1737–8; the following carnival season she performed operas by Leo and Giuseppe Arena in Turin, receiving the huge sum of 8000 lire. Later in 1739 she was at Vienna, and in September 1740 she was a member of Angelo Mingotti's opera company at Hamburg. She sang in Amsterdam in 1742 with the Wolfenbüttel Kapellmeister Giovanni Verocai (she and Sandoni had now separated) and is said to have published there a new setting of Pietro Metastasio's *Il Palladio conservato* (no copy is known). After 1749 she was plagued with debts and an aging voice; her time was spent alternately in prison for debt or giving concerts to pay her debtors. In February 1750 she performed in Paris before the French queen; in 1750 and 1751 she revisited London and sang at concerts, but was coldly received. She spent her last years in Bologna, supporting herself, it is said, by making buttons. She died in obscurity and extreme poverty.

Cuzzoni in her prime was by universal consent a superb artist. Charles Burney expressed the views of various writers, including Pier Francesco Tosi, Johann Joachim Quantz and particularly Giovanni Battista Mancini (*Pensieri e riflessioni pratiche spora il canto figurato*, 1774):

> It was difficult for the hearer to determine whether she most excelled in slow or rapid airs. A native warble enabled her to execute divisions with such facility as to conceal every appearance of difficulty; and so grateful and touching was the natural tone of her voice, that she rendered pathetic whatever she sung, in which she had leisure to unfold its whole volume. The art of conducting, sustaining, increasing, and diminishing her tones by minute degrees, acquired her, among professors, the title of complete mistress of her art. In a cantabile air, though the notes she added were few, she never lost a favourable opportunity of enriching the cantilena with all the refinements and embellishments of the time. Her shake was perfect, she had a creative fancy, and the power of occasionally accelerating and retarding the measure in the most artificial and able manner, by what the Italians call *tempo rubato*. Her high notes were unrivalled in clearness and sweetness, and her intonations were so just and fixed, that it seemed as if it was not in her power to sing out of tune.

Tosi praised her 'delightful soothing *Cantabile*', and contrasted her pre-eminence in 'Pathetick' with Faustina's dramatic fire in 'Allegro'. Quantz, who heard her often in 1727, said that 'her style of singing was innocent and affecting', and her graces 'took possession of the soul of every auditor, by her tender and touching expression'. She could move an audience to tears in such simple arias as 'Falsa immagine' and Rodelinda's 'Hò perduto il caro sposo'. She was probably at her best on her first visit to London, and the wonderful series of parts Handel wrote for her, especially Cleopatra, Asteria, Rodelinda and Antigone, seem perfectly calculated to bring out the qualities mentioned above. They call for a fluid use of the whole compass from c' to b''' (Quantz said she sang up to c'''') and offer repeated openings for her famous trill, which was slow and sensuous. Cuzzoni was the first female high soprano to distinguish herself in prime roles. Although not inclined to extremely fast passagework, she was capable of singing coloratura arias extremely difficult for their variety of rhythm and figuration, such as 'Sprezzando il suol' in Porpora's *Enea* or 'Da tempeste' in *Giulio Cesare*; features include short florid passages, unexpectedly rising to the higher register and then abruptly truncated on a staccato note (usually a or b''). Other arias, such as 'Conservati fedele' in Hasse's *Artaserse* or the Largo 'Ombre, piante', again in *Rodelinda*, show an equally definite propensity to the noble and the pathetic. Cuzzoni was neither a great actress nor a beautiful woman. Horace Walpole, with reference to *Rodelinda*, said:

> she was short and squat, with a doughy cross face, but fine expression; was not a good actress; dressed ill; and was silly and fantastical. And yet on her appearing in this opera, in a *brown silk gown*, trimmed with silver, with the vulgarity and indecorum of which all the old ladies were much scandalized, the young adopted it as a fashion, so universally, that it seemed a national uniform for youth and beauty.

The best likeness of Cuzzoni is a print after Enoch Seeman, reproduced in Sir John Hawkins's *History*. She appears in many caricatures, including a drawing by the Countess of Burlington (see illustration), two operatic scenes engraved by John Vanderbank (1723) and Joseph Goupy (1729), and original drawings by A.M. Zanetti and Marco Ricci.

Winton Dean/Carlo Vitali

Cziak, Benedikt.

See SCHACK, BENEDIKT.

D

Dabadie, Henri-Bernard

(*b* Pau, 19 Jan 1797; *d* Paris, May 1853). French baritone. He studied at the Paris Conservatoire and made his début in 1819 at the Opéra as Cinna in Gaspare Spontini's *La vestale*. During the 16 years he sang at the Opéra, he created several roles in operas by Gioachino Rossini: Pharaoh in *Moïse et Pharaon* (1827), Raimbaud in *Le comte Ory* (1828) and William Tell (1829). He sang Pietro in the first performance of Daniel Auber's *La muette de Portici* (1828). Having created Jolicoeur in Auber's *Le philtre* (1831) in Paris, he sang Belcore (the same character as Jolicoeur) at the première of Gaetano Donizetti's *L'elisir d'amore* (Milan, 1832). Back at the Opéra he sang Count Dehorn in the first performance of Auber's *Gustave III* (1833) and created Ruggiero in Fromental Halévy's *La Juive* in 1835, the year of his retirement. His flexible, warm-toned and high-lying voice is reflected in the Rossini roles that he created. His wife, the soprano Louise Dabadie, frequently sang with him.

Elizabeth Forbes

Daddi, Francesco

(*b* Naples, 1864; *d* Chicago, 1945). Italian tenor, later bass. He trained as a singer and pianist at the Naples Conservatory and made his stage début at Milan in 1891. The following year at the Dal Verme he sang Beppe in the première of *Pagliacci*, and this was also his role in his single season at Covent Garden in 1900. He sang in the Rome première of Pietro Mascagni's *Le maschere* in 1901. Having become one of Italy's leading comprimario tenors, he emigrated to the USA in 1907, singing with the Manhattan Company usually in small parts but also as Corentin in *Dinorah* with TETRAZZINI. From 1911 to 1920 he appeared regularly in Chicago, where he enjoyed considerable success in comic bass roles such as Dr Bartolo in *Il barbiere di Siviglia*. His recordings, made as a tenor, include Beppe's Serenade in *Pagliacci* and many Neapolitan songs graced by an agreeable lyric voice and an idiomatic sense of style.

J.B. Steane

Dahl, Anne Margrethe

(*b* Oslo, 19 April 1966). Norwegian soprano. She studied at the Royal Danish Academy of Music,

Copenhagen, and made her stage début as Donna Anna with the Århus Summer Opera. From 1991 to 1999 she appeared regularly with the Danish National Opera in roles including W.A. Mozart's Countess Almaviva and Vitellia (*La clemenza di Tito*), Marguerite (*Faust*), Gilda, Rosalinde (*Die Fledermaus*), Mimì and Anne Truelove (*The Rake's Progress*). In 1999 she became a company principal with the Royal Opera, Copenhagen, where she has sung, among other roles, the Queen of Night, Violetta, Musetta, Fiordiligi, Donna Anna and Manon Lescaut. In 2000 Dahl created the role of Aunt Lydia in *The Handmaid's Tale* by Poul Ruders. She also appears frequently in concert and as a recitalist, and in 2007 was acclaimed for her performances of Bright Sheng's *The Phoenix* with the Danish National SO on their Far East tour. Among her recordings are Carl Orff's *Carmina burana* and songs by Rued Langgaard.

Richard Wigmore

Dalberg [Dalrymple], Frederick

(*b* Newcastle upon Tyne, 7 Jan 1908; *d* South Africa, May 1988). South African bass of English birth. He studied in Dresden, making his début in 1931 at Leipzig as Monterone (*Rigoletto*), later singing King Henry (*Lohengrin*), Osmin, Sarastro, Philip II and many Wagner roles. He appeared at Munich, Dresden, Vienna and Berlin, where he spent the war years. At Bayreuth (1942–4 and 1951) he sang Hagen, Fafner and Pogner. After an engagement at Munich, he joined Covent Garden in 1951. There he created John Claggart in *Billy Budd* (1951), Sir Walter Raleigh in *Gloriana* (1953) and Calkas in William Walton's *Troilus and Cressida* (1954). He sang the Doctor in the British stage première of *Wozzeck* (1952), and his repertory included King Mark, Hunding, Caspar, Pizarro, Ochs, Kečal, Sparafucile and W.A. Mozart's Bartolo. From 1957 to his retirement in 1970 he was engaged at Mannheim, where, as well as Daland, Gurnemanz and Fasolt, his roles included Don Pasquale, Boris and Dikoj (*Kát'a Kabanová*). He created Cousin Brandon in Paul Hindemith's *Long Christmas Dinner* (1961). A most versatile singer, he excelled in German roles. His daughter Evelyn (*b* Leipzig, 23 May 1939) sang in Europe and South Africa as a mezzo-soprano.

Elizabeth Forbes

Dalla Rizza, Gilda

(*b* Verona, 12 Oct 1892; *d* Milan, 4 July 1975). Italian soprano. She studied with Alerano Ricci at Bologna, making her début there in 1912 as Charlotte. She created Magda in *La Rondine* at Monte Carlo (1917) and was also the first Italian Suor Angelica and Lauretta (1919, Rome); at the first Covent Garden performances (1920) she failed to repeat her successes in these roles. After a performance of *La fanciulla del West* at Monte Carlo in 1921 Giacomo Puccini said, 'At last I've seen my Fanciulla'; although he wrote Liù with her in mind, the role was created by another singer. Having first appeared at La Scala in 1915 as Yaroslavna (*Prince Igor*), she was engaged there from 1923 to 1939; her Violetta caused a sensation. She created 13 of the 58 roles in her repertory, including Riccardo Zandonai's Giulietta and Mariella in Pietro Mascagni's *Il piccolo Marat*; she was the first Italian Arabella at Genoa in 1936. She was also a famous interpreter of Fedora. She retired from the stage in 1939, but played Angelica once more during the 1942 Puccini celebrations at Vicenza. A beautiful woman, generally considered a great singing actress, she was called the 'Duse of the Lyric Theatre'. Her early acoustic recordings give a fair indication of why her impassioned singing was so much admired by her contemporaries.

M.J. Matz: 'Gilda dalla Rizza', *ON*, xxxiv/13 (1969–70), 22–3

M. Scott: *The Record of Singing*, ii: *1914–1925* (London, 1979), 82–4

Harold Rosenthal/R

Dal Monte, Toti
[Meneghelli, Antonietta]

(*b* Mogliano Veneto, 27 June 1893; *d* Treviso, 25 Jan 1975). Italian soprano. She studied in Venice with Barbara Marchisio and made her début at La Scala in 1916 as Biancafiore in Riccardo Zandonai's *Francesca da Rimini*. In 1922 she sang Gilda at La Scala, and thereafter Rosina, Amina, Lucia, Linda di Chamounix, Norina and, notably, Violetta and Butterfly; she sang Rosalina in the première of Umberto Giordano's *Il re* in 1929. In the USA she sang Lucia and Gilda at the Metropolitan (1924) and appeared with the Chicago Civic Opera (1924–8). Her only Covent Garden appearances were in 1925 as Lucia and Rosina, after which she joined MELBA's company for the latter's farewell tour. Her recordings, including a complete *Madama Butterfly* (with GIGLI), show her highly individual timbre and subtle inflection of the text.

A.C. Renton: 'Toti dal Monte', *Record Collector*, iv (1949), 147–50 [with discography by G. Whelan]

D. Reutlinger: 'The Maestro's Singers: Toti Dal Monte, Soprano', *Il maestro*, i/3–4 (1969), 2–4 [with discography]

Harold Rosenthal/Alan Blyth

Dalmorès, Charles
[Boin, Henry Alphonse]

(*b* Nancy, 21 or 31 Dec 1871; *d* Los Angeles, 6 Dec 1939). French tenor. He began his musical career as a horn player in Paris, where he was at first refused admission to the Conservatoire because he was 'too good a musician to waste his time in being a mediocre singer'. He made his operatic début at Rouen in 1899, as Siegfried. He then went to the Brussels Opera, and in 1904 first sang at Covent Garden in *Faust*. He appeared in the British premières of Jules Massenet's *Hérodiade*, Camille Saint-Saëns's *Hélène*, M.-A. Charpentier's *Louise* and Raoul Laparra's *Habañera*, as well as in the world première of Franco Leoni's *L'oracolo* (1905). He also made a special study of Wagner, under Franz Emmerich, and in 1908 sang Lohengrin at Bayreuth. One of the most valued singers in Oscar Hammerstein's company at the Manhattan Opera House, New York (1906–10), he made his début there as Charles Gounod's Faust and later sang Don José, Manrico and Pelléas among other roles. He sang regularly with the Boston and Philadelphia-Chicago companies, and as a member of the Chicago Opera (1910–18) where his roles included Tristan and Parsifal. He later taught singing in France and the USA. A sensitive musician and a colourful personality, he was also admired for his acting. Recordings show that his powerful voice was used with much technical accomplishment and a sense of style.

J.B. Steane

Dal Prato [Del Prato], Vincenzo

(*b* Imola, 5 May 1756; *d* Munich, 1828). Italian castrato. He studied with Lorenzo Gibelli and made his début at the opera house in Fano in 1772. After touring extensively in Germany and the Netherlands, he sang at Stuttgart in 1779 for the future Russian Tsar Paul I. In 1780 Dal Prato was appointed to the court of Carl Theodor in Munich, where he spent the rest of his career. His voice was a high mezzo. His most famous role was Idamantes in W.A. Mozart's *Idomeneo* (1781), and he also sang in Antonio Salieri's *Semiramide* (1782), Ignaz Holzbauer's *Tancredi* (1783) and Georg Vogler's

Castore e Polluce (1787). Mozart complained about the inexperienced singer's poor stage presence and had to teach Dal Prato his music. But Dal Prato was apparently eager to learn, and Mozart referred to him as his 'molto amato castrato Dal Prato'. His singing was admired more for its grace and polished execution than its power or dramatic qualities.

A. Heriot: *The Castrati in Opera* (London, 1956), 121–22
J. Rushton: '"La vittima è Idamante": did Mozart have a Motive?', *COJ*, iii (1991), 1–21

Paul Corneilson

Dalrymple, Frederick.

See DALBERG, FREDERICK.

D'Alvarez [Alvarez de Rocafuerte], Marguerite [Margarita]

(*b* Liverpool, 1886; *d* Alassio, 18 Oct 1953). Mezzo-soprano of Peruvian parentage. She studied in Brussels and made her operatic début at Rouen as Delilah in 1907 or 1908. In 1909 she joined Oscar Hammerstein's Manhattan Opera Company, first appearing as Fidès in *Le prophète*. With the Boston Opera Company in 1913 she made a strong impression as the Mother in Ermanno Wolf-Ferrari's *I gioielli della Madonna*, and at Covent Garden in 1914 her Amneris in *Aida* won acclaim for the power, rich quality and ease of her singing. She appeared as Carmen at La Scala and as Léonor in *La favorite* at Marseilles. After 1918 she sang principally in concerts, specializing in French and Spanish song, and gave her last London recital in 1939. She appeared in the film *Pandora and the Flying Dutchman* (1951) and wrote a colourful autobiography, *Forsaken Altars* (London, 1954), published also as *All the Bright Dreams* (New York, 1956). Her recordings show an exceptionally rich and well-produced voice but are too few to do justice to her wide repertory.

J.B. Steane

Dam-Jensen, Inger

(*b* Fredriksberg, 13 March 1964). Danish soprano. She trained at the Royal Danish Conservatory and the Danish Opera School before winning the Cardiff Singer of the World Competition in 1993. She has sung regularly at the Royal Danish Opera in Copenhagen since 1993, where her roles have included Susanna, Rosina, Norina, Adina, a much admired Ophelia in Ambroise Thomas' *Hamlet*, Gilda, Musetta, Cleopatra, Sophie and Zdenka, the last two both notable for the effortless ease of her top notes. She made her Covent Garden début with the Royal Danish Opera as Ninetta (*The Love for Three Oranges*) in 1995. Dam-Jensen has since appeared with Covent Garden as an admired Blonde (1996) and Despina (1998), and at the Opéra Bastille (as Pamina), and in 1996 made her Glyndebourne début as Fiakermilli (*Arabella*). Her concert repertory includes G.F. Handel's *Solomon*, Gustav Mahler's Fourth Symphony (which she has recorded) and *Des Knaben Wunderhorn*, *Peer Gynt*, Richard Strauss lieder, songs by Carl Nielsen and Benjamin Britten's *Les illuminations*. She possesses a bright, attractive lyric-coloratura soprano, particularly suited to Strauss, and is a vivid actress. In 2005 she sang Bella in Michael Tippett's *The Midsummer Marriage* at Covent Garden.

Alan Blyth/Richard Wigmore

Damrau, Diana

(*b* Günzburg an der Donau, 31 May 1971). German soprano. She studied at the Staatliche Hochschule für Musik in Würzburg, and in Salzburg with Hanna Ludwig, and began her professional operatic career in Würzburg in 1999, specialising in coloratura roles. After engagements in Mannheim and Frankfurt, she made a number of important débuts in 2002, including the Vienna Staatsoper, as the Small Woman in the world premiere of Friedrch Cerha's *Der Riese von Steinfeld*, Munich, Hamburg, Dresden and the Salzburg Festival, where she scored a triumph as the Queen of Night, a role that has become something of a calling card. She returned to Salzburg as a delightful, feisty Blonde (*Die Entführung*) in 2003, the year of her Covent Garden début as the Queen of Night. Damrau's La Scala début, in Antonio Salieri's *L'Europa riconosciuta*, followed in 2004. The same year she won plaudits as a stunning Zerbinetta at Covent Garden. Her Metropolitan Opera début in 2005, also as Zerbinetta, was equally sensational.

Damrau's other operatic successes include the Gym Teacher in the world première of Lorin Maazel's *1984* at Covent Garden (2006). She has also made her mark as a recitalist, appearing regularly at the Salzburg Festival, the Vienna Musikverein and the Schubertiade in Schwarzenberg. She made her Carnegie Hall recital début in 2007. Her recordings include W.A. Mozart's *Zaide* and lieder by Gustav Mahler, Hugo Wolf, Richard Strauss and Alexander Zemlinsky.

Richard Wigmore

Danco, Suzanne

(*b* Brussels, 22 Jan 1911; *d* Fiesole, 10 Aug 2000). Belgian soprano. She received her entire musical education at the Brussels Conservatory, where she carried off many prizes and diplomas, for piano and the history of music as well as for singing. The unusual breadth of her musical culture was shown by her command of many different styles. In opera she was best known for her Mozartian interpretations, notably of Fiordiligi and Donna Elvira, which were applauded throughout Italy as well as at the festivals of Edinburgh, Glyndebourne and Aix-en-Provence. In England she sang parts as different as those of Mimì (1951, Covent Garden) and of Marie in a BBC concert performance of Alban Berg's *Wozzeck*; and she made a touching and exquisite heroine in Ernest Ansermet's first recording of *Pelléas et Mélisande*. As a concert singer she was in demand for unusual music of all periods and schools, but was most at home in the songs of Claude Debussy, Maurice Ravel and Hector Berlioz, of which she left several recordings. Her versatility was the more remarkable in that her clear, cool soprano offered no great richness or variety of colour; but it had been admirably trained, and could manage the roulades of W.A. Mozart as easily as the most difficult intervals of Berg.

Desmond Shawe-Taylor

D'Andrade [De Andrade], Francisco

(*b* Lisbon, 11 Jan 1859; *d* Berlin, 8 Feb 1921). Portuguese baritone. He studied in Milan with Sebastiano Ronconi and made his début in 1882 at San Remo as Amonasro. He sang in Spain and Portugal and in Italy, where he appeared at the Teatro Costanzi, Rome, and at La Scala, Milan. In 1886 he made his London début at Covent Garden as Rigoletto; during his five-year association with the Royal Italian Opera he also sang Renato (*Un ballo in maschera*), Don Carlo (*Ernani*), Valentin, Barnaba (*La Gioconda*), Don Giovanni, W.A. Mozart's and Gioachino Rossini's Figaro, Amonasro, Germont, Count di Luna, Alphonse (*La favorite*), Hoël (*Dinorah*), Riccardo (*I puritani*), Telramund, Escamillo, Nevers (*Les Huguenots*), Zurga, Count Almaviva and Enrico Ashton. With his brother António, a tenor, D'Andrade took part in the first performance of *Donna Bianca* (1888, Lisbon) by the Portuguese composer Alfredo Keil. D'Andrade sang regularly at Frankfurt (1891–1910) and, having first visited Berlin in 1889, became a member of the Hofoper (later Staatsoper), from 1906 to his retirement in 1919. A very elegant and cultured singer, he had a beautiful, evenly produced voice with a powerful upper register. Among his most admired characterizations was Don Giovanni, which he sang at the 1901 Salzburg Festival.

Elizabeth Forbes

D'Angeri, Anna

(*b* Vienna, 14 Nov 1853; *d* Trieste, 14 Dec 1907). Italian soprano. After study with MATHILDE MARCHESI she made her début in 1872, as Sélika in *L'Africaine* at the Teatro Sociale in Mantua. Sensational success followed at the Vienna Hofoper, where she sang until 1880. She appeared in London from 1874, notably as Ortrud and Venus in the British premières of *Lohengrin* and *Tannhäuser*. She created the title role of Carlos Gomes's *Maria Tudor* at Milan in 1879. An admired Leonora (*Il trovatore*), Elvira (*Ernani*) and Elisabeth de Valois, she was chosen by Giuseppe Verdi to appear as Amelia in the revised version of *Simon Boccanegra* (1881, La Scala). She was sought for the role of Desdemona in the première of *Otello* but by this time she had retired, having married Vittorio Dalem, the director of the Teatro Rossetti in Trieste.

David Cummings

Daniels, Barbara

(*b* Newark, OH, 7 May 1946). American soprano. After studying at Cincinnati College-Conservatory, she made her début in 1973 with West Palm Beach Opera as W.A. Mozart's Susanna. In 1974 she was engaged at Innsbruck, where her roles included Fiordiligi and Violetta; at Kassel (1976–8) she added Liù, Jules Massenet's Manon and Zdenka to her repertory and took part in the première of Walter Steffens's *Unter dem Milchwald* (1977, Hamburg). At Cologne (1978–82) she sang roles such as Elisetta (*Il matrimonio segreto*), Martha, Micaëla, Musetta and Alice Ford. She made her Covent Garden début (1978) as Rosalinde in *Die Fledermaus*, her San Francisco début (1980) as Zdenka and her Metropolitan début (1983) as Musetta. Her repertory, which had earlier included Adèle (*Le comte Ory*), G.F. Handel's Agrippina, Mimì, Butterfly, Mařenka and Charles Gounod's Marguerite, began to change as her lyric soprano became more powerful and dramatic. In 1991 she sang Minnie, which has developed into her finest role, at the Metropolitan and she has also taken on such parts as the Marschallin, Giacomo Puccini's Manon and Tosca. Her recordings include Musetta under Leonard Bernstein and Minnie under Leonard Slatkin.

Elizabeth Forbes

Daniels, David

(*b* Spartanburg, SC, 12 March 1966). American countertenor. He began studying as a tenor with GEORGE SHIRLEY at the University of Michigan before re-studying as a countertenor. He sang

Nero (*L'incoronazione di Poppea*) at Glimmerglass for his stage début in 1994, repeating the role at the Staatsoper in Munich in 1997. He returned to Glimmerglass in 1995 as Tamerlano and in 1998 as Arsace (*Partenope*). His London début was at the ENO as Benjamin Britten's Oberon in 1996, after which he appeared with the Royal Opera at the Barbican as Sextus (*Giulio Cesare*) in 1997. The same year he appeared at the New York City Opera as Arsamene (*Serse*). His first appearance at Glyndebourne was as an admirably expressive Didimus (*Theodora*) in 1996, the year of his Salzburg Festival début as Hamor (*Jephtha*). He made his Metropolitan début as Sextus in 1999, and in 2000 sang a thrilling Rinaldo at the New York City Opera and the Munich Opera Festival. In 2001 he scored a triumph as C.W. Gluck's Orpheus at Covent Garden, his début at the theatre, and in the 2004–05 season was equally acclaimed as Bertarido (*Rodelinda*) at the Metropolitan. Daniels also sings frequently in oratorio, most notably in G.F. Handel, and won plaudits for his David in *Saul* at the 1999 Edinburgh Festival. His rich yet flexible voice, used with a vivid dramatic sense, has more strength and vibrancy, and a wider tessitura, than that of most countertenors, as can be heard on a disc of Handel arias with Roger Norrington, *Rinaldo*, Antonio Vivaldi's *Il Bajazet*, a video of *Theodora* from Glyndebourne, 'Serenade', in which he sings songs by Franz Schubert, Charles Gounod, Francis Poulenc and Ralph Vaughan Williams with remarkable success, and a recital of mélodies by Hector Berlioz, Gabriel Fauré and Maurice Ravel.

R. Milnes: 'David Daniels', *Opera*, xlix (1998), 1154–61

Alan Blyth/Richard Wigmore

Darclée [Haricly, de Hartulary], Hariclea

(*b* Brăila, 10 June 1860; *d* Bucharest, 10 or 12 Jan 1939). Romanian soprano. She studied in Paris with JEAN-BAPTISTE FAURE, and in 1888 made her début at the Opéra in *Faust*. In 1890 she scored a great success at La Scala in Jules Massenet's *Le Cid*, and was immediately engaged by all the leading Italian theatres. Between 1893 and 1910 she appeared frequently in Moscow, St Petersburg, Lisbon, Barcelona, Madrid and Buenos Aires; she returned several times to La Scala, where in 1892 she created the title role in Alfredo Catalani's *La Wally* (1892), and to the Costanzi in Rome, where she likewise created the title roles of *Tosca* (1900) and Pietro Mascagni's *Iris* (1898). Her repertory ranged from the coloratura soprano roles (Gilda, Ophelia) to the dramatic *falcon* or heavier Verdi roles (Valentine,

Aida), including many others in the Franco-Italian lyric repertory: Violetta, Desdemona, Manon, Manon Lescaut, Mimì and Santuzza.

Among Darclée's exceptional qualities were power, tonal beauty, evenness, agility and an excellent technique. She was extremely handsome, with a stage presence as elegant as her vocal line. A certain coldness of temperament, however, diminished her conviction in the *verismo* repertory. She sang until 1918, when she appeared in *Roméo et Juliette* at the Teatro Lirico, Milan.

Darclée's son, the composer Ion Hartulary-Darclée (*b* Paris, 7 July 1886; *d* Bucharest, 2 April 1969), was known particularly as a writer of operettas.

Rodolfo Celletti/Valeria Pregliasco Gualerzi

Dauer, Johann [Joseph] Ernst

(*b* Hildburghausen, 1746; *d* Vienna, 12 Sept 1812). German tenor. He began his career in 1768, and in 1771 was engaged in Hamburg, where he sang in Singspiele. In 1775 he went to Gotha and in 1777 to Frankfurt and Mannheim. In 1779 he was engaged at the court theatre in Vienna, initially singing in the Singspiel company (making his début as Alexis in P.-A. Monsigny's *Le déserteur*) and, the following year, also acting in the spoken theatre company. He created Pedrillo in W.A. Mozart's *Die Entführung aus dem Serail* (1782) and Sturmwald in Carl Dittersdorf's *Der Apotheker und der Doktor* (1786). He was a useful though uninspired performer: according to the actor F.L. Schröder, 'He touched the heart in neither serious nor comic roles. His manner was a little cold and remote; his movement somewhat wooden' (O. Michtner: *Das alte Burgtheater als Opernbühne*, Vienna, 1970, pp.369, 521). He played secondary lovers, character roles and sturdy, unpolished lads.

Christopher Raeburn, Dorothea Link

David, Léon

(*b* Les Sables d'Olonne, Vendée, 18 Dec 1867; *d* Les Sables d'Olonne, 27 Oct 1962). French tenor. He studied in Nantes and in Paris, making his début in February 1892 at Monte Carlo as Euxenos in Noël Desjoyeaux's *Gyptis*. In June the same year he began a long engagement at the Opéra-Comique, Paris, by singing Iopas in *Les Troyens*. His repertory included Almaviva, George Brown (*La dame blanche*), Gerald (*Lakmé*), Des Grieux (*Manon*), Wilhelm Meister (*Mignon*), Nadir, Vincent (*Mireille*), Werther and Don José. Between 1900 and 1907 he sang at the Théâtre de la Monnaie, Brussels, where his roles included Belmonte and Dimitri in Franco Alfano's *Risurrezione*. In 1913 he created Paco in Manuel de Falla's *La vida breve* at Nice. His voice, a lyric tenor, was of beautiful quality. He retired from the Opéra-Comique in 1920 and was professor of singing at the Paris Conservatoire from 1924 to 1937. His autobiography, *La vie d'un ténor*, was published in 1950.

Elizabeth Forbes

Davide [David], Giovanni

(*b* Naples, 15 Oct 1790; *d* St Petersburg, 1864). Italian tenor. Son and pupil of the tenor Giacomo Davide, he appeared with his father at Siena in 1808 in Simon Mayr's *Adelaide di Guesclino*. Engagements in Brescia, Padua and Turin followed, and in 1814 he created Narciso in *Il turco in Italia* at La Scala, the first of many Rossini premières in which he took part. Two years later he went to Naples and sang in the first performances of *Otello* (as Roderigo, 1816), *Ricciardo e Zoraide* (Ricciardo, 1818), *Ermione* (Orestes, 1819), *La donna del lago* (James V, 1819) and *Zelmira* (Ilo, 1822). He also sang in *Tancredi*, *La gazza ladra*, *Matilde di Shabran*, *Bianca e Falliero*, *Mosè in Egitto*, *Semiramide* and *Otello* (in the title role). In 1830 he appeared in Paris, and the following season in London, but by then his voice, notable for its extreme agility and amazing compass of three octaves up to bb'', was beginning to decay. After his retirement he went to St Petersburg to direct the Italian opera.

Elizabeth Forbes

Davidoff [Levinson], Aleksandr

(*b* Poltava, 4 Sept 1872; *d* Moscow, 28 June 1944). Ukrainian tenor. He studied in Odessa and Kiev, joining the opera at Tbilisi in 1893. His Moscow début was with Savva Mamontov's Moscow Private Russian Opera Company in 1896. From 1900 to 1912 he sang at the Mariinsky in St Petersburg, appearing first as Hermann in *The Queen of Spades*, the opera with which he became most closely associated until increasing deafness brought his career to an end. His voice, which was that of a lyric tenor, was heavily taxed by roles such as Otello and Canio, yet his contemporary Sergey Levik held that his special ability lay in bringing lyric qualities to such roles. He also sang in Paris, where in 1934 he briefly became director of the Opéra Russe de Paris. Recordings show him as an unusually interesting and often stylish singer, at his best both graceful and expressive.

J.B. Steane

Davies, Arthur

(*b* Wrexham, 11 April 1941). Welsh tenor. After studying at the RNCM in Manchester with Joseph Ward, he made his début with the WNO in 1972 as Squeak (*Billy Budd*); over the next 12 years he sang some 35 roles, including Nemorino, Almaviva, Ferrando, Albert Herring, Yannakos (Bohuslav Martinů's *Greek Passion*), Jack (*The Midsummer Marriage*), Quint, Nero, the Fox, Jeník, Rodolfo and Don José. Having made his Covent Garden début in H.W. Henze's *We Come to the River* (1976), he then sang Alfredo, Števa (*Jenůfa*), Pinkerton and Foresto (*Attila*). Davies's roles for the ENO have included Essex (*Gloriana*), Don Ottavio, Faust, Gabriele Adorno, Lensky, Werther, Turiddu, Riccardo (*Ballo in maschera*) and the Duke, which he sang in Jonathan Miller's Mafia production of *Rigoletto* (1982–95). For Scottish Opera he has sung David (*Die Meistersinger*) and Cavaradossi, while for Opera North his roles have included Gaston in the British stage première of Giuseppe Verdi's *Jérusalem* (1990), William Walton's Troilus (which he repeated at Covent Garden), Nadir, and Rodolfo in *Luisa Miller*. In 1978 he sang the role of Genaro in the first concert performance of Sergey Prokofiev's *Maddalena* (Manchester). He has also performed in Europe, North and South America and Australia. His once light, lyric voice has grown heavier and more dramatic while retaining its flexibility and smoothness of tone.

Elizabeth Forbes

Davies, Ryland

(*b* Cwm, Ebbw Vale, 9 Feb 1943). Welsh tenor. He studied at the RMCM, where he made his début in 1964 with the WNO as Gioachino Rossini's Almaviva. At Glyndebourne he sang in the chorus, making his solo début in 1965 as the Marschallin's Major-Domo (*Rosenkavalier*). Over the next 25 years he sang Nemorino with the Glyndebourne touring company, Belmonte, Lensky, Ferrando, Flamand (*Capriccio*), Tamino, Lysander, the Prince (*The Love for Three Oranges*) and Tichon (*Kát'a Kabanová*). In 1967 he sang Essex (*Gloriana*) at Sadler's Wells and in Lisbon. He made his Covent Garden début in 1969 as Hylas (*Les Troyens*), then sang Don Ottavio, Ernesto, Fenton, Enéas (*Esclarmonde*) and Ferrando, the role of his San Francisco (1970), Paris Opéra (1974) and Metropolitan (1975) débuts. He sang Cassio (*Otello*) at Salzburg (1970), Pelléas at Stuttgart (1979), Berlin (1984) and Hamburg, and Carl Maria von Weber's Oberon at Montpellier (1987). He has a sweet-toned, lyrical voice and excellent diction, as demonstrated in his performance as

Armand de Clerval in Jules Massenet's *Thérèse* and in his recordings of Mozart (notably Idamantes with Colin Davis) and of Joseph Haydn's *The Seasons*. In the 1990s he sang a number of comprimario roles at Covent Garden and elsewhere, revealing a gift for deft and witty characterization.

Alan Blyth

Davies, Tudor

(*b* Cymmer, Glam., 12 Nov 1892; *d* Penault, Mon., 2 April 1958). Welsh tenor. He studied first while working in the local coal mine, and later at the RCM, London, under Gustave Garcia. After touring in the USA and Canada he joined the British National Opera Company, making his Covent Garden début on the first night of the 1921 season as Rodolfo in *La bohème*, a role he repeated, opposite MELBA, the following year. He created the part of Hugh the Drover in Ralph Vaughan Williams's opera at His Majesty's Theatre in 1924, and in 1925 sang in the first performance, at Manchester, of Gustav Holst's *At the Boar's Head*. With the Sadler's Wells Company (1931–41) and later the Carl Rosa (1941–6) he sang a wide range of roles until his retirement from opera in 1946. His voice came under strain, but in his prime, as gramophone records show, he sang with ringing, incisive tone and lively temperament. On record he played a prominent part in the Wagner-in-English series conducted by Albert Coates.

A.D. Hillier and J. Jarrett: 'Tudor Davies: a Biography and Discography', *Record Advertiser*, ii (1971–2), no.4, pp.2–21; no.5, pp.2–9

J.B. Steane

Dawson, Lynne

(*b* York, 3 June 1956). English soprano. She studied at the GSM, made her début as Countess Almaviva with Kent Opera in 1986 and sang Music in Claudio Monteverdi's *Orfeo* (a role she later recorded) at Florence the following year. Her other roles have included Zdenka in *Arabella* (1988) and Xiphares in *Mitridate* (1991), both at the Châtelet, Paris; Pamina for Scottish Opera (1988); Konstanze at La Monnaie (1990), a role she subsequently recorded with Christopher Hogwood; and Teresa (*Benvenuto Cellini*) at Amsterdam in 1991. She is a good linguist and has brought particular conviction and charm to the roles of Angelica in G.F. Handel's *Orlando*, Pamina, and Sandrina in W.A. Mozart's *La finta giardiniera*. Her warmly coloured, clear-textured voice, with its sensitively controlled vibrato, is admirably suited to the Baroque and Classical

repertory. Dawson's unaffected personality and interpretative freshness communicate themselves strongly in English Baroque operas, her recordings of which include *Venus and Adonis*, *Dido and Aeneas*, *The Fairy Queen* and *Timon of Athens*. Her other operatic recordings include C.W. Gluck's *Orfeo* and *Iphigénie en Aulide* and Mozart's *Zaide* and *Don Giovanni*. Dawson is also a stylish and sympathetic concert singer and has recorded music ranging from Handel oratorios and Bach cantatas, through Robert Schumann lieder, to works by Herbert Howells and Arvo Pärt.

Nicholas Anderson

Dawson, Peter

(*b* Adelaide, 31 Jan 1882; *d* Sydney, 26 Sept 1961). Australian bass-baritone. He studied at home with J.C. Stevens, then in England with CHARLES SANTLEY, singing to him at an audition G.F. Handel's 'O ruddier than the cherry', which became one of his calling cards over the next 50 years. Santley arranged Dawson's first concert tour of Britain, with EMMA ALBANI in 1902, the event that was to launch his career. Apart from appearances as the Nightwatchman in *Die Meistersinger* during the Covent Garden season of English opera in 1909 under Hans Richter, he favoured oratorio and concerts over opera, declaring the latter to be 'too much work for too little pay'. However, he did not exclude opera from his recitals and practically always mixed aria with classical song and ballads in his programmes. Dawson described himself as a 'singer of the people' and believed it essential to communicate directly with his public; to this end he sang all his repertory in English, employing impeccable diction. His bluff, outgoing personality, strong, well-produced voice and faultless technique are reflected in his many recordings (spanning half a century), all of which arrest the listener with their immediacy of interpretation. He published an autobiography, *Fifty Years of Song* (London, 1951/*R*).

Alan Blyth

De Amicis [De Amicis-Buonsollazzi], Anna Lucia

(*b* Naples, *c*1733; *d* Naples, 1816). Italian soprano. Taught by her father, she began performing in comic operas with her family in the 1750s in Italy, Paris and Brussels, then in 1762 made her London début at the King's Theatre. Following her début as a serious singer in J.C. Bach's *Orione* (1763, London), she left comic opera. As prima donna in Milan (1764–5), Venice (1764), Vienna and Innsbruck (1765), Naples (1766) and Florence (1767), she became involved in theatrical disputes and wished to retire. But after marriage (1768) to the Florentine physician Francesco Buonsollazzi she resumed her career, singing in Venice (1768–9, 1770–71) and Naples (1769–70, 1771–2, where she created Armida in Niccolò Jommelli's *Armida abbandonata*, 1770, and the title role in his *Ifigenia in Tauride*, 1771). W.A. Mozart praised her highly, especially her technical skill in difficult passagework and her musical singing, and in the role of Junia she ensured the success of his *Lucio Silla* in Milan (1772). Engagements in Naples (1773–6), Turin (1776–9) and the Italian première of C.W. Gluck's *Alceste* (title role, 1778, Bologna) concluded her brilliant career, though she sang for at least another ten years in private Neapolitan productions.

De Amicis amazed listeners with her vocal agility. Charles Burney described her as the first to sing staccato divisions, and the first to 'go up to E flat in altissimo, with true, clear, and powerful *real* voice'. She was equally impressive as an actress: Pietro Metastasio wrote that 'among the dramatic heroines … there was absolutely no one but the Signora De Amicis suited to portray the character … with the fire, the boldness, the frankness, and the expression necessary'.

Kathleen Kuzmick Hansell

De Andrade, Francisco.

See D'ANDRADE, FRANCISCO.

De Angelis, Nazzareno

(*b* Rome, 17 Nov 1881; *d* Rome, 14 Dec 1962). Italian bass. After singing as a boy in the Cappella Sistina and Cappella Giulia choirs in Rome, he studied with Giuseppe Fabbri and others. He made his début in 1903 at L'Aquila in *Linda di Chamounix*, and during the 1906–7 season appeared at La Scala in works such as *La Gioconda*, *Tristan und Isolde* and *Aida;* he also created the role of Aquiliante in Francesco Cilea's *Gloria* (1907). He returned to La Scala nearly every year until 1914, and then occasionally between 1918 and 1933, taking part in revivals of Gaspare Spontini's *La vestale* (1908), *Les vêpres siciliennes* (1909), *Médée* (1910) and *Nabucco* (1913); he scored great successes in *Norma* (1912), Italo Montemezzi's *L'amore dei tre re* (the first performance, 1913), *Mosè* (1918), *Mefistofele* (1918) and *Die Walküre* (1924), which were all, with *Il barbiere di Siviglia* and *Don Carlos*, strong points of his repertory. Between 1909 and 1925 he appeared at the leading South American theatres; he sang with the Chicago Opera in 1910–11 and appeared regularly at the Rome Opera from 1911 until his retirement in 1938. De Angelis's voice was large in volume and range, with a rich timbre skilfully varied by inflection and shading. A vigorous actor and a master of broad and expressive phrasing, he was the finest Italian bass between 1910 and 1930.

Rodolfo Celletti/Valeria Pregliasco Gualerzi

De Bassini, Achille [Bassi]

(*b* Milan, 5 May 1819; *d* Cava de' Tirreni, 3 Sept 1881). Italian baritone. He was the type of the 'noble' baritone for whom Giuseppe Verdi wrote parts exploiting a high tessitura, firm legato and dramatic power such as to make traditionalists complain that he shouted. He made his début in 1837 at Voghera in the title role of Gaetano Donizetti's *Belisario*. At La Scala he succeeded in other Donizetti roles, and as William Tell, Figaro (*Barbiere*) and Carlo (*Ernani*). He created three Verdi roles: the Doge in *I due Foscari* (1844, Rome), Seid in *Il corsaro* (1848, Trieste) and Miller in *Luisa Miller* (1849, Naples); he also sang in *Attila*. Verdi wanted him for Rigoletto in 1851. In 1859 he sang at Covent Garden as Germont, Rodolfo (*La sonnambula*) and Luna, and in Saverio Mercadante's *Il giuramento*. Perhaps because of losses in the 1848–9 revolutions, he spent years in St Petersburg, where Verdi wrote for him the part of Melitone in *La forza del destino* (1862), commenting that he had a 'humorous' vein perfectly suited to the character. He was still singing in Italy in 1871. His wife, the soprano Rita Gabussi (*b* Bologna, *c*1815; *d* Naples, 26 Jan 1891), sang at La Scala and at S Carlo, where she created Mercadante's Medea (1851) and was Verdi's original choice for Azucena. She also created a furore in the mad role of the seconda donna in Federico Ricci's *La prigione di Edimburgo* (1838, Trieste). Their son, Alberto De Bassini (*b* Florence, 14 July 1847; *d* after *c*1906), sang as a tenor in Italy and Russia, but in 1890 be became a baritone and later sang with touring companies in the USA; about 1906 he was teaching in New York. He made records in 1902–4.

John Rosselli

De Castris [De' Massimi], Francesco [Cecchino, Checchino]

(*b* Roman Campagna, *c*1650; *d* Rome, late Nov or early Dec 1724). Italian soprano castrato. In Rome he served Cardinal Camillo Massimi until 1677 (hence his nickname). By 1679, when he sang in two operas in Bologna, he was based in Ferrara in the service of Marquis Ippolito Bentivoglio, under whose patronage he often appeared in the Venetian theatres of S Giovanni Grisostomo and S Salvatore; he also sang at S Marco. His Venetian period is marked by a close connection, both personal and professional, with Giovanni Legrenzi. In 1687 he entered the employ of Ferdinando de' Medici in Florence, where from 1696 he sang in operas by C.F. Pollarolo, Alessandro Scarlatti, Giacomo Perti and others. His good looks and diplomatic abilities made him a powerful favourite; he was master of the revels and conducted court missions. The decline of his voice – which he admitted in his correspondence with Perti, 1700–01, when he asked for his roles in *Lucio Vero* and *Astianatte* to be adapted – and the hostility provoked by his position at court caused Ferdinando to exile him to Rome; there he lived in the Medici palace (1703–11), still carrying out diplomatic missions for his patron and receiving a good pension from Florence. In his younger years (*c*1680) De Castris's compass was limited (approximately *d♯'* to *g"*), and he apparently tended to stay within the higher register with coloratura passages. He mostly took the roles of seductive women, or rejected male lovers and political conspirators; later he turned to heroic characters. He should not be confused with Francesco Castri from Bologna, Domenico Cecchi ('il Cortona') or Francesco de Grandis from Verona ('Checchino').

Carlo Vitali

DeGaetani, Jan

(*b* Massillon, OH, 10 July 1933; *d* New York, 15 Sept 1989). American mezzo-soprano. She studied at the Juilliard School, making her formal New York début in 1958. In November 1970 she gave the first performance of George Crumb's *Ancient Voices of Children* at the Library of Congress in Washington, DC. Her first appearance with the New York PO was in January 1973, the year she became a professor at the Eastman School, Rochester. She performed regularly with the Contemporary Chamber Ensemble, with which she made her celebrated recording of *Pierrot lunaire* (which stresses its lyricism). In addition to the avant-garde repertory, in which she specialized, she performed and recorded medieval music (*The Play of Herod* with the New York Pro Musica), Baroque cantatas, Wolf lieder, and songs by Charles Ives and Stephen Foster. A singer of remarkable intelligence and expressive power, with a voice clear and true throughout its wide range, she appeared with the Boston SO, the Scottish National Orchestra (with which she gave the première of Peter Maxwell Davies's *A Stone Litany* in 1973), the BBC SO (with Pierre Boulez in Japan), the Berlin PO, Philadelphia Orchestra, Chicago SO, Concertgebouw Orchestra and the Waverly Consort.

She was appointed artist-in-residence at the Aspen Festival, Colorado, in 1973, and frequently gave masterclasses and concerts at American universities. Her most celebrated students included DAWN UPSHAW and RENÉE FLEMING.

Martin Bernheimer

Della Casa, Lisa

(*b* Burgdorf, nr Berne, 2 Feb 1919). Swiss soprano. She studied with Margarete Haeser in Zürich and made her début at Solothurn-Biel as Butterfly in 1941. At the Stadttheater, Zürich (1943–50), she sang such diverse roles as Serena (*Porgy and Bess*), Pamina and Gilda, and created the Young Woman in Willy Burkhard's *Die schwarze Spinne* (1949). She first appeared at Salzburg in 1947 as Zdenka (*Arabella*) and the following summer returned to sing the Countess (*Capriccio*). In 1951 she made her British début as Countess Almaviva at Glyndebourne; later that year in Munich she sang Arabella, the role with which she was most closely associated and which she sang at her Covent Garden début in 1953 with the Bayerische Staatsoper, and repeated in 1965. She became a member of the Vienna Staatsoper in 1947 and in 1952 sang Eva at Bayreuth. In 1953 she created the three female roles in *Der Prozess* at Salzburg. She sang at the Metropolitan (1953–68), making her début there as Countess Almaviva, and at San Francisco (1958). Best known in the Strauss repertory, Della Casa graduated from Sophie through Octavian to the Marschallin; she also sang Ariadne, Chrysothemis and Salome. She could spin out Strauss's soaring line with a smooth legato, and the limpid silvery quality of her voice made her an admirable Mozart singer. Her beauty and natural charm enhanced her vocal gifts. Her many recordings, including Arabella, Ariadne, the Marschallin and a seminal account of Strauss's *Vier letzte Lieder*, enshrine her finest qualities.

G. Fitzgerald: 'Lisa Della Casa', *Opera*, xix (1968), 185–91
E. Forbes: 'Lisa Della Casa: the Search for Perfection', *Opera*, xlvi (1995), 527–32

Harold Rosenthal/Alan Blyth

Deller, Alfred (George)

(*b* Margate, 31 May 1912; *d* Bologna, 16 July 1979). English countertenor. He sang as a treble and then, when no 'break' had occurred in the singing voice, as an alto in the choir of St John the Baptist, Margate. From Christ Church, Hastings, he was appointed to the choir of Canterbury Cathedral in 1938. Here, the exceptional quality of his powerful voice and dedicated musicianship were brought to the notice of Michael Tippett, who found in him the ideal countertenor soloist for the Henry Purcell revival in which he was active. In 1946 he sang in *Come, ye sons of art, away* in the inaugural concert of the BBC's Third Programme; he also became particularly associated with Purcell's song *Music for a while*, of which he made a notable first recording. In 1947 he left Canterbury for the choir of St Paul's Cathedral in London, which was also a base for the freelance work that was soon to bring him international fame. Deller became, as no other countertenor had done before him, a leading recitalist, giving prominence in his programmes to Elizabethan songs and English folksongs, often accompanied by the lutenist Desmond Dupré. In 1950 he founded the Deller Consort, which gave recitals, predominantly of Elizabethan and Italian madrigals, throughout Europe, the Americas, Australasia and East Asia. Benjamin Britten wrote Oberon in *A Midsummer Night's Dream* with his voice in mind, the première at Aldeburgh in 1960 bringing Deller praise for his singing, less for his acting (he later recorded the role with the composer). He also sang the role of Death, written for him by Alan Ridout in his one-act opera *The Pardoner's Tale* in 1971. He continued to sing, albeit with diminishing range and power, until his death, after which his work with the Deller Consort was continued by his son Mark. His unique achievement had been to restore the countertenor voice to a place it had not held in musical life for more than two centuries. He was a major force in the revival of interest in Elizabethan music, especially the lute-songs. Deller's voice, well preserved on recordings, had unusual beauty and richness, and his style, although often imitated, was entirely his own. He was noted for his smooth, light and lyrical voice, his command in dramatic arias and florid passages, and some tendency towards vocal mannerism. He was always intensely devoted to the music he sang but very personal in his way of bringing it to life in performance.

M. and M. Hardwick: *Alfred Deller: a Singularity of Voice* (London, 1968, 2/1980) [with discography]

J.B. Steane

Delle Sedie, Enrico

(*b* Livorno, 17 June 1822; *d* La Garenne-Colombes, nr Paris, 28 Nov 1907). Italian baritone. He studied with GALEFFI and made his début at San Casciano in 1851 as Nabucco, repeating the role shortly afterwards at Pistoia. The following year he appeared at Florence in *Rigoletto* and in 1855 at the Cannobiana, Milan, in *I puritani* and Federico Ricci's *Corrado*

d'Altamura. He sang at La Scala in 1859 and made his London début in 1861 at the Lyceum Theatre as Luna (*Il trovatore*). He also sang Renato in the first London performance of *Un ballo in maschera*, a part he repeated at the Théâtre Italien, Paris, and at Covent Garden in 1862. His other roles included Gioachino Rossini's Figaro, Malatesta (*Don Pàsquale*), Plumkett (*Martha*), Germont (*La traviata*) and Don Giovanni. From 1867 to 1871 he taught singing at the Paris Conservatoire. Although his voice was small, his style and musicianship were regarded as outstanding. He wrote two treatises on singing (1876, 1886) as well as the book *Riflessioni sulle cause della decadenza della scuola di canto in Italia* (Paris, 1881).

Elizabeth Forbes

Delmas, Jean-François

(*b* Lyons, 14 April 1861; *d* St Alban de Monthel, 29 Sept 1933). French bass-baritone. He studied at the Paris Conservatoire and in 1886 made his début as Saint-Bris in *Les Huguenots* at the Opéra. There he remained until 1927, singing in every season. He appeared in the premières of many French operas including *Thaïs*, in which he was the original Athanaël in 1894. He was also the Opéra's first Hans Sachs, Wotan, Hagen and Gurnemanz. His sonorous bass voice had an extensive upper range which enabled him to sing baritone roles such as Iago. He also appeared at Monte Carlo, but though of international calibre confined his career to France. His recordings are early and surprisingly few but show a commanding manner and a magnificent voice.

J.B. Steane

Del Monaco, Mario

(*b* Florence, 27 July 1915; *d* Mestre, nr Venice, 16 Oct 1982). Italian tenor. He studied at Pesaro and the Rome Opera School. In 1939 while still a student he sang Turiddu at Pesaro, making his official début in 1941 at the Teatro Puccini, Milan, as Pinkerton. His international career began in 1946 when he sang Radames at the Verona Arena and Cavaradossi, Canio and Pinkerton at Covent Garden with the S Carlo company. He made his American début in 1950 at San Francisco as Radames and Chénier, and his New York début in the same year as Giacomo Puccini's Des Grieux at the Metropolitan, where he sang until 1959. His most famous role was Otello, which he sang throughout Europe (including Covent Garden in 1962) and North America. His repertory also included Aeneas (*Les Troyens*), which he sang at La

Scala in 1960, and Siegmund, while Loris (*Fedora*) was a favourite role in the later years of his career. He possessed a thrilling natural voice of enormous power, though his reluctance to sing below *mezzo-forte* was sometimes criticized. His many recordings of complete operas, notably *Otello*, catch the visceral excitement of his voice and his dramatic presence. A volume of autobiography, *La mia vita e i miei successi*, including a list of his roles, was published in Milan in 1982.

F. Nuzzo: 'Mario Del Monaco', *Opera*, xiii (1962), 372–6

Harold Rosenthal/Alan Blyth

De Los Angeles, Victoria.

See LOS ANGELES, VICTORIA DE.

Del Prato, Vincenzo.

See DAL PRATO, VINCENZO

De Luca, Giuseppe

(*b* Rome, 25 Dec 1876; *d* New York, 26 Aug 1950). Italian baritone. After five years' vocal study with Venceslao Persichini, he made his operatic début at Piacenza on 6 November 1897 as Valentin in *Faust*. In 1902 he created the role of Michonnet in the first performance of Francesco Cilea's *Adriana Lecouvreur* at the Teatro Lirico, Milan, and in the two following years took part in the premières at La Scala of Umberto Giordano's *Siberia* (Gleby) and Giacomo Puccini's *Madama Butterfly* (Sharpless). He remained at La Scala for eight seasons, but the greater part of his career lay in the USA. He first appeared at the Metropolitan in Gioachino Rossini's *Il barbiere di Siviglia* in 1915, and he created Paquiro in Granados's *Goyescas* the following year. He created the title role in *Gianni Schicchi* in 1918, and he remained an invaluable member of the company for 20 consecutive seasons, gradually assuming all the leading roles of the Italian repertory. Although his well-schooled baritone was less powerful than those of his close contemporaries PASQUALE AMATO and TITTA RUFFO, his complete mastery of the art of singing enabled him to retain his powers almost unimpaired to an advanced age – as was observed when, after an absence of 25 years, he made an unheralded appearance at Covent Garden in 1935 as Rossini's Figaro. This, together with Rigoletto (in which he made his Metropolitan farewell in 1940), ranked among his favourite roles. On 7 November 1947, at the age of 70, almost exactly 50 years after his début, he gave his farewell New York recital.

De Luca's many records, made over 45 years, are of fine quality, the early Fonotipias exhibiting the brilliance of the young singer (and his delightful sense of humour as shown in the *buffo* duet from *Don Pasquale* with Ferruccio Corradetti), while the Victors made between 1917 and 1930 are models of classical style and the bel canto tradition. They have been reissued as a complete collection on CD, a worthy memorial to a noble artist.

A. Favia-Artsay: 'Giuseppe De Luca', *Record Collector*, v (1950), 56–69 [with discography]

Desmond Shawe-Taylor/R

De Lucia, Fernando

(*b* Naples, 11 Oct 1860; *d* Naples, 21 Feb 1925). Italian tenor. He studied in Naples, and made his début at the Teatro S Carlo in *Faust* on 9 March 1885. At first he was best known in the *tenore di grazia* repertory, notably as Almaviva, which remained a favourite role. But in the 1890s and the early 1900s his fame was increasingly linked with the impassioned tenor heroes of the new *verismo* school, especially Turiddu, Canio and Loris in Umberto Giordano's *Fedora*, in all of which he excelled alike as actor and singer. The title role in Pietro Mascagni's *L'amico Fritz*, in which he sang with CALVÉ in the Rome première of 1891 and in its first Covent Garden and Metropolitan Opera performances shortly thereafter, formed a bridge between the two parts of his repertory; and Pietro Mascagni gratefully chose him also for the premières of his *I Rantzau* (1892, Florence), *Silvano* (1895, Milan) and *Iris* (1898, Rome).

At the Metropolitan he sang only for a single season (1893–4), but his Covent Garden appearances were frequent and successful between 1892 and 1900, although there were recurrent complaints of his excessive vibrato. He was particularly popular in his native Naples, where he made his last stage appearance in 1917 in *L'amico Fritz*; he came out of retirement to give a memorable account of 'Pietà, Signore' (then attributed to Alessandro Stradella) on the occasion of CARUSO's funeral in 1921.

Between 1902 and 1922 he made some 400 records. This extensive legacy (much of it reissued on CD) is valuable because it represents an otherwise vanished style. De Lucia's technique and vocal control are astonishing, as are also his free, spontaneous and vivid treatment of musical text and ornament and his variety of nuance and tone-colour.

Perhaps the best of his records are his various excerpts from *Il barbiere di Siviglia*, *La sonnambula* and *L'elisir d'amore*; his account of Alfredo's aria in *La traviata* (a role he sang at Covent Garden at PATTI's farewell) is so tender and caressing as to efface the memory of other versions. The vocal tone in his records has often suffered from faulty reproduc-

DEMMER, JOSEPH ~ 117

tion and a resulting unnatural raising of the pitch; his upper range was never extensive, and even at the height of his career he often resorted to transposition. Recent CD transfers have been in the concert pitch.

M. Henstock: 'Fernando de Lucia', *Record Collector*, xxx (1985), 101–39, 149–212 [annotated discography]

M. Henstock: *Fernando de Lucia* (London, 1990) [with discography]

Desmond Shawe-Taylor/R

De Lussan, Zélie

(*b* Brooklyn, NY, 21 Dec 1861; *d* London, 18 Dec 1949). American mezzo-soprano of French descent. She was taught by her mother, herself a singer, and first appeared on stage at the age of nine. She gave public concerts when 16 and made her official stage début at Boston in 1884, as Arline in Michael Balfe's *The Bohemian Girl*. In 1888 she sang in London as Carmen, a role she is said to have sung more than 1000 times, and in which many considered her the equal of CALVÉ. She also became famous for her Zerlina in *Don Giovanni*, and in 1897 was London's first Musetta in *La bohème*. Her Metropolitan début in 1894 as Carmen was no less successful, and she appeared there for a further three seasons in roles including Nannetta, Zerlina and Nedda. In 1910 she sang Cherubino in Thomas Beecham's Mozart season at His Majesty's and Gertrude in *Hamlet* at Covent Garden; she also worked with smaller companies such as the Carl Rosa and Moody-Manners, with which she sang until 1913. She taught for many years in England, retaining the vitality and charm of her personality well into old age. Her recordings are few but show something of her rich voice and lively temperament.

J.B. Steane

De Marchi, Emilio

(*b* Voghera, nr Pavia, 6 Jan 1861; *d* Milan, 20 March 1917). Italian tenor. His voice was discovered during military service. He made his début at the Teatro Dal Verme, Milan, in 1886 as Alfredo, and sang in leading houses throughout Italy and Spain. In 1890 he was a member of the distinguished Italian company that visited Buenos Aires, and the following year made his début at La Scala. He was Giacomo Puccini's choice for the coveted role of Cavaradossi in the première of *Tosca* (1900, Rome), which he also sang at Covent Garden (1901, 1905) and the Metropolitan. In New York he was an admired Radames, and in 1902 sang the title role in the house première of *Ernani*. In his last seasons at La Scala his roles included Max in *Der Freischütz*

(1905) and Licinius in Gaspare Spontini's *La vestale* (1909). He made no commercial recordings, but a few fragments from *Tosca* recorded on cylinder at the Metropolitan carry dramatic conviction and ring out well on the high notes.

J.B. Steane

De' Massimi, Francesco.

See DE CASTRIS, FRANCESCO.

De Mey, Guy

(*b* Hamme, 4 Aug 1955). Belgian tenor. He studied at the Brussels Conservatory, and at Amsterdam with Erna Spoorenberg and Stella Dalberg. Later teachers included PETER PEARS and ERIC TAPPY. His operatic career has been varied and he has proved himself a fluent interpreter of styles ranging from the 17th century to the 20th, but it is in Baroque opera that he has gained widest recognition. He sang the title role in Jean-Baptiste Lully's *Atys* in Paris (1987), Florence and New York. Other roles include Alidoro in Antonio Cesti's *Orontea* (1986, Innsbruck), Jean-Philippe Rameau's Hippolytus (1987, Reggio nell'Emilia), Aegeus in Francesco Cavalli's *Giasone* (1988, Innsbruck) and Eurymachus in Claudio Monteverdi's *Il ritorno d'Ulisse in patria* (1989, Mézières). He is also a noted singer of Bach, particularly the Evangelist in the *St Matthew Passion*, which he has recorded to acclaim. His operatic recordings include Claudio Monteverdi's *Orfeo* and *L'incoronazione di Poppea*, *Orontea*, Cavalli's *Xerse* and *Giasone*, *Atys*, G.F. Handel's *Alessandro*, Georg Philipp Telemann's *Der geduldige Socrates* and Rameau's *Platée*.

Nicholas Anderson

Demmer, Joseph
[Friedrich Christian; Fritz]

(*b* Cologne, *c*1768; *d* Mannheim, 2 April 1811). German tenor. Demmer's principal claim to fame is that he created the role of Florestan in the first version of *Fidelio* at the Theater an der Wien on 20 November 1805. Ludwig van Beethoven was apparently dissatisfied with his performance and engaged another tenor when a revised version of the opera was staged in 1806. Demmer moved from Vienna that same year and during his final years was engaged at the Hoftheater, Mannheim. He also sang under the name Friedrich Christian (or 'Fritz') Demmer.

Richard Wigmore

Dens, Michel (Maurice Marcel)

(*b* Roubaix, 22 June 1911). French baritone. After studies in his home town, he made his début at Lille in 1938, later singing in Bordeaux, Grenoble and Toulouse. In 1947 he made his début at the Opéra-Comique, Paris, as Albert in *Werther*, later singing Scarpia, Figaro, Escamillo and Ourrias in Charles Gounod's *Mireille*, a role he recorded with great distinction. In 1951 he created the role of Rodolphe in Emmanuel Bondeville's *Madame Bovary*. During the 1950s Dens was the leading baritone at the Paris Opéra, particularly admired as Rigoletto and Iago. He had one of the most beautiful and characterful voices of his time. He was equally at home in lighter music and made many recordings of operettas, both French and Viennese. In Paris he often appeared in the operetta repertory at the Théâtre de la Gaîté. Dens had one of the longest careers of any singer in the 20th century, appearing as late as 1988 as Ménélas in *La belle Hélène*. He was for a time the director of Presence de l'Art Lyrique.

Patrick O'Connor

De Reszke, Edouard

(*b* Warsaw, 22 Dec 1853; *d* Garnek, Poland, 25 May 1917). Polish bass, brother of JEAN DE RESZKE. He studied with Francesco Steller and Filippo Coletti, and made his début as the King in the first Paris performance of *Aida* at the Opéra in 1876. He was then engaged for two seasons at the Théâtre Italien. He sang Indra in Jules Massenet's *Le roi de Lahore* at Milan (1879) and made his London début at Covent Garden in the same role (1880). He also sang Saint-Bris (*Les Huguenots*), Rodolfo (*La sonnambula*) and Don Basilio (*Il barbiere di Siviglia*). At La Scala, Milan, he sang in the premières of Carlos Gomes's *Maria Tudor* (1879) and Amilcare Ponchielli's *Il figliuol prodigo* (1880); in 1881 sang Fiesco in the first performance of the revised version of *Simon Boccanegra* and also appeared as Silva (*Ernani*). He sang Alvise in the first London performance of *La Gioconda* (1883).

With his brother Jean in the tenor roles, he sang Phanuel in the first Paris performance of *Hérodiade* (1884) and created the role of Don Diègue in *Le Cid* in Paris (1885); thereafter his career closely followed that of his brother, in London, Chicago and New York. His vast repertory included Méphistophélès, Friar Laurence, Don Pedro (*L'Africaine*), Rocco and Leporello, which he sang at a special centenary performance of *Don Giovanni* at the Opéra in 1887. His huge voice and giant stature made him a magnificent exponent of Wagner roles, and he sang Daland, King Henry (*Lohengrin*),

Hans Sachs, King Mark, the Wanderer (*Siegfried*), Pogner, Hunding and Hagen. He retired in 1903, soon after his brother.

Elizabeth Forbes

De Reszke, Jean

(*b* Warsaw, 14 Jan 1850; *d* Nice, 3 April 1925). Polish baritone, later tenor, brother of EDOUARD DE RESZKE. He studied with Francesco Ciaffei and ANTONIO COTOGNI as a baritone, making his début (under the name of Giovanni di Reschi) at La Fenice, Venice, in 1874 as Alphonse XI (*La favorite*), the role of his London début at Drury Lane the same year. He also sang Valentin and Don Giovanni. In 1876 (now as Jean de Reszke), he sang Melitone (*Forza*) and Gioachino Rossini's Figaro in Paris, then retired to restudy as a tenor with SBRIGLIA. His first appearance as a tenor, in the title role of *Robert le diable* at Madrid in 1879, was not a success and he did not sing again until 1884, when he made a triumphant reappearance as John the Baptist in the first Paris performance of Jules Massenet's *Hérodiade*, at the Théâtre Italien. The following year he created the title role in *Le Cid* at the Opéra, where he was engaged for five seasons, singing Radames, Vasco da Gama (*L'Africaine*) and the title roles of *Le prophète* and *Faust*.

In 1887 he made his tenor début in London at Drury Lane as Radames, later singing Lohengrin (his first Wagnerian role) in Italian. During the next four years he sang Vasco da Gama, Raoul (*Les Huguenots*), Faust, Lohengrin, Riccardo (*Un ballo in maschera*), Romeo, Walther, Don José and Otello at Covent Garden. He made his American début in 1891 at Chicago as Lohengrin, with his brother Edouard as King Henry, then made his Metropolitan début as Romeo, with Edouard as Friar Laurence. In 1893 Jean sang the title role in the first staged performance of Hector Berlioz's *La damnation de Faust* at Monte Carlo. In 1894 he sang Werther in Chicago, New York and London. Taking on the heavier Wagner roles, he sang Tristan (1895), young Siegfried (1896) and Siegfried in *Götterdämmerung* (1898). His last new role was Canio, of which he gave a single performance at the Opéra (1902). His beautiful voice, fine musicianship and handsome appearance made him unsurpassed in the French repertory, as well as in the Wagner roles he sang with such distinction. His pupils included CARMEN MELIS, ARTHUR ENDRÈZE, MIRIAM LICETTE, MAGGIE TEYTE, LOUISE EDVINA, LEO SLEZAK, BIDÚ SAYÃO, JOHANNES SEMBACH, KATHLEEN HOWARD, VLADIMIR ROSING and STEUART WILSON.

Elizabeth Forbes

Dérivis, (Nicholas) Prosper

(*b* Paris, 28 Oct 1808; *d* Paris, 11 Feb 1880). French bass, son of Henri-Etienne Dérivis. He studied in Paris and made his début there at the Opéra in 1831. During the next 20 years he sang an enormous repertory, including Bertram (*Robert le diable*), William Tell, Leporello, Don Giovanni and Balthazar (*La favorite*). He sang a Herald in the first performance of *La Juive* (1835) and later took the part of Cardinal Brogny in that opera. He created Nevers in *Les Huguenots* (1836), Balducci in *Benvenuto Cellini* (1838) and Félix in Gaetano Donizetti's *Les martyrs* (1840). At La Scala he sang Zaccaria in the first performance of *Nabucco* (1842) and Pagano at the première of *I Lombardi* (1843). He created the Prefect in Donizetti's *Linda di Chamounix* in Vienna (1842). In 1851 he sang Zacharie in Giacomo Meyerbeer's *Le prophèt.*

Elizabeth Forbes

Dermota, Anton

(*b* Kropa, Slovenia, 4 June 1910; *d* Vienna, 22 June 1989). Slovene tenor. He first appeared in Cluj in 1934, then was invited by Bruno Walter to Vienna, where in 1936 he made his début as the First Man in Armour (*Die Zauberflöte*) and went on to sing Alfredo; the same year he had sung Zorn (*Die Meistersinger*) at Salzburg, where in 1938 he sang Belmonte and Don Ottavio. In 1947 he appeared at Covent Garden with the Vienna Staatsoper as Don Ottavio, Ferrando and Narraboth. Although he won most renown as a Mozart tenor, Dermota also appeared in the Italian and German repertory, and in 1955 he was accorded the honour of singing Florestan at the reopening of the Vienna Staatsoper; in 1956 he took part in the première there of Frank Martin's *Der Sturm*. His large repertory included Ernesto, Rodolfo, Pinkerton, Jeník, Hoffman, Lensky, Jules Massenet's Des Grieux (one of his most successful roles), Flamand, Eisenstein and the title role in Hans Pfitzner's *Palestrina*. He was also a distinguished lieder singer and exponent of Gustav Mahler's *Das Lied von der Erde*. His plangent, slightly reedy tone and musicianly phrasing can be heard on a number of recordings, most notably as David in *Die Meistersinger* under Hans Knappertsbusch and as Tamino in performances under Herbert von Karajan and Wilhelm Furtwängler.

Harold Rosenthal/Alan Blyth

Dernesch, Helga

(*b* Vienna, 3/13 Feb 1939). Austrian soprano and mezzo-soprano. After studying at the Vienna Hochschule für Musik she was engaged by the Berne Opera, making her début in 1961 as Marina (*Boris Godunov*). Engagements followed at Wiesbaden (1963–5) and Cologne (1965–8). At Bayreuth, where she first appeared in 1965, she sang Freia, Gutrune and Eva. With Scottish Opera she sang Gutrune (1968), her first Leonore (1970), Brünnhilde, Isolde, Ariadne, the Marschallin and Cassandra (*Les Troyens*). At the Salzburg Easter festivals under Herbert von Karajan she sang Brünnhilde (*Siegfried* and *Götterdämmerung*), Leonore and Isolde on stage and in recordings. At Covent Garden, where she made her début in 1970 as Sieglinde, she sang Chrysothemis, the Dyer's Wife and, in 1987, the Nurse (*Die Frau ohne Schatten*). She made her Chicago (1971) and Vienna Staatsoper (1972) débuts as Leonore. She created the title role of Wolfgang Fortner's *Elisabeth Tudor* at Berlin in 1972 and Goneril in Aribert Reimann's *Lear* at Munich in 1978. She then began to sing mezzo roles, including Clytemnestra, Herodias, Adelaide (*Arabella*), Mistress Quickly and Fricka. In 1985 she sang Marfa (*Khovanshchina*) at the Metropolitan and in 1986 created Hecuba in Reimann's *Troades* in Munich. She sang the Electress in *Der Prinz von Homburg* at Cologne in 1992, Madame de Croissy in *Dialogues des Carmélites* at the Metropolitan in 1994 and the Princess in *Suor Angelica* at Hamburg in 1995. Her voice had great richness and power, and her strikingly handsome stage appearance and intense acting made her a compelling performer.

T. Smillie: 'Helga Dernesch', *Opera*, xxiv (1973), 407–12

Harold Rosenthal/Alan Blyth

Derzhinskaya, Kseniya Georgiyevna

(*b* Kiev, 25 Jan/6 Feb 1889; *d* Moscow, 9 June 1951). Russian soprano. She studied singing in Kiev, and from 1913 to 1915 sang at the Moscow opera house Narodniy Dom. She was a soloist at the Bol'shoy from 1915 to 1948, and was greatly influenced by Konstantin Stanislavsky and the conductor Václav Suk. Under the latter she sang Lisa (*The Queen of Spades*), Nastas'ya (P.I. Tchaikovsky's *The Enchantress*), Fevroniya (Nikolay Rimsky-Korsakov's *The Legend of the Invisible City of Kitezh*) and Ortrud. Other roles included Mariya (Tchaikovsky's *Mazepa*), the Snow Maiden and Charles Gounod's Marguerite. She was one of the outstanding Russian singers of her time, distinguished by the wide range and beautiful timbre of her strong voice, the completeness of her interpretations and her dramatic gift. Her portrayals of Russian women were particularly successful. In 1926 she sang in a concert performance of *Kitezh* at the Paris Opéra, with great success.

I.M. Yampol'sky

Deschamps-Jehin, (Marie) Blanche

(*b* Lyons, 18 Sept 1857; *d* Paris, June 1923). French contralto. She studied in Lyons and Paris, and made her début in 1879 as Mignon at the Théâtre de la Monnaie, where she also created Jules Massenet's *Herodias* (1881) and Uta in Ernest Reyer's *Sigurd* (1884). At the Opéra-Comique, Paris, she created Margared in *Le roi d'Ys* (1888), Madame de la Haltière in Massenet's *Cendrillon* (1899) and the Mother in *Louise* (1900). At Monte Carlo she sang the title role in the first performance of César Franck's *Hulda* (1894) and created the Baroness in Massenet's *Chérubin* (1905). She made her début at the Paris Opéra in 1891 as Léonor (*La favorite*), later singing Fidès, Amneris, Hedwige (*Guillaume Tell*), Delilah, Gertrude (*Hamlet*), Ortrud, Fricka, and Véronique in the first performance of Alfred Bruneau's *Messidor* (1897). Her repertory also included Carmen, Azucena, Brangäne, Erda and Hatred in C.W. Gluck's *Armide*. Her voice, a true contralto, was rich-toned and flexible.

Elizabeth Forbes

Desderi, Claudio

(*b* Alessandria, 9 April 1943). Italian bass-baritone and conductor. He studied in Florence, making his début in 1969 with the Maggio Musicale in Edinburgh as Gaudenzio (*Il Signor Bruschino*). He has sung at all the major Italian theatres, including La Scala, with whose company he came to Covent Garden in 1976 as Alidoro and Dandini. In 1977 he sang Martio in a modern version of Stefano Landi's *Sant'Alessio* at Salzburg. At Glyndebourne (1981–8) he has sung Gioachino Rossini's Bartolo, Don Magnifico, W.A. Mozart's Figaro and Don Alfonso (both of which he has recorded) and Falstaff. He made his début with the Royal Opera as Figaro (1987), returning as Don Magnifico and Leporello. His repertory includes Count Robinson (*Il matrimonio segreto*), Schicchi, Dulcamara, the Viceroy (*La Périchole*), Nick Shadow, Rossini's Macrobio (*La pietra del paragone*), Mustafà (*L'italiana in Algeri*), Signor Bruschino and Raimbaud (*Le comte Ory*), which he sang at La Scala in 1991. A fine comic actor with a flexible voice and superb diction, Desderi has also developed a secondary career as a conductor and is artistic director of the Teatro Verdi in Pisa.

Elizabeth Forbes

Desmatins, Mlle

(*fl* 1682–*c*1708). French soprano. She made her début in a minor role in Jean-Baptiste Lully's *Persée* (1682), and sang the confidante Sidonie to Le

ROCHOIS' Armide in 1686. Desmatins herself sang Armide in 1703. Roles she created include Briseis (Lully and Pascal Collasse's *Achille et Polyxène*, 1687) and Juno (Collasse's *Enée et Lavinie*, 1690). In 1697 she played the first of the Hesperides in the prologue and alternated with Le Rochois in the title role of André Destouches' *Issé*. She sang Medea in Lully's *Thésée* in 1698 (a role sung previously by SAINT-CHRISTOPHLE and Le Rochois) and the title role in the 1699 revival of Collasse's *Thétis*. In 1704 she created the title role in Henry Desmarets and André Campra's *Iphigénie en Tauride*, took the title role in the revival of Destouches' *Didon* and sang Io in the revival of Lully's *Isis*. The following year she sang Lully's Angélique (*Roland*) and Sthenobea (*Bellérophon*); in 1706 she sang his Alcestis and created the title role in Marin Marais' *Alcyone*. She disappeared from cast lists in 1707–8, whereupon most of her roles passed to Françoise Journet.

Philip Weller

Desmond, Astra

(*b* Torquay, 10 April 1893; *d* Faversham, 16 Aug 1973). English contralto. She studied singing in London (at the RAM, under BLANCHE MARCHESI) and Berlin, and gave her first recital in London in 1915. Although she made some operatic appearances with the Carl Rosa Company, at Covent Garden and at Glastonbury, where she was the first to sing the title role in Rutland Boughton's *Alkestis*, she made her career mainly as a concert and oratorio singer. From 1920 she was closely associated with Edward Elgar's choral works at the Three Choirs festivals and elsewhere; her rich and flexible voice, coupled with rare qualities of restraint and intelligence, made her an outstanding interpreter of the part of the Angel in *The Dream of Gerontius*. The same virtues distinguished her intelligently planned recitals, and British music lovers owe her a debt of gratitude for her serious studies of Scandinavian song. She was the first to introduce the songs of Yrjö Kilpinen to English audiences, and she gave numerous recitals of Edvard Grieg's songs in the original Norwegian, besides recording several of them (and much Purcell). Desmond served as president of the Society of Women Musicians. She was made a CBE in 1949.

Desmond Shawe-Taylor

Dessay, Natalie

(*b* Lyons, 19 April 1965). French soprano. She studied at the Bordeaux Conservatoire and in Paris. After winning a prize in the 1990 Mozart Competition in Vienna, she sang in Lyons as Zerbinetta, Blonde

*Mlle Desmatins
by Robert Le Vrac
Tourniers*

and Madame Herz (*Der Schauspieldirektor*), then made her début in Geneva in 1991 as Adele in *Die Fledermaus*. Her first appearance as Olympia in *Les contes d'Hoffmann* in Roman Polanski's production at the Opéra Bastille in 1992 led to engagements at the Vienna Staatsoper, La Scala and the Metropolitan Opera, on each occasion as Olympia. In Vienna she has subsequently sung Zerbinetta, Sophie and Aminta in *Die schweigsame Frau*. She sang her first Konstanze (*Die Entführung*) in Geneva in 2000. Her repertory also includes Morgana in G.F. Handel's *Alcina*, the title role in Léo Delibes' *Lakmé*, Aspasia in W.A. Mozart's *Mitridate* and the Queen of Night (the role of her Salzburg Festival début in 1997), all of which she has recorded. Among her other

recordings are *mélodies* by Gabriel Fauré and a disc of Mozart operatic arias. Dessay is the first French coloratura soprano for many years to have made an international career, and some commentators have hailed her appearance as part of a renewal of the often lamented 'lost' French vocal style.

Patrick O'Connor

Dessì [Dessy], Daniela

(*b* Genoa, 14 May 1957). Italian soprano. She studied at the Parma Conservatory with Carla Castellani and at the Accademia Chigiana, Siena. Her career began with concert singing and sacred music, and she turned increasingly to opera after her début in 1979 as Serpina in Giovanni Pergolesi's *La serva padrona* with Opera Giocosa at Genoa. She also sang Lauretta (*Gianni Schicchi*) there the same year, but then concentrated on earlier opera, including works by Domenico Cimarosa, Claudio Monteverdi (*L'incoronazione di Poppea*), G.F. Handel, Niccolò Jommelli, Antonio Salieri (*Les Danaïdes*) and Giovanni Paisiello. Her success as Desdemona at Barcelona with PLACIDO DOMINGO led to her American début in the same role with him in Los Angeles. Engagements throughout Italy and elsewhere in Europe embraced a wider and growing repertory of W.A. Mozart, Gioachino Rossini, Gaetano Donizetti, Giuseppe Verdi and Giacomo Puccini roles, in which she is admired for depth of passionate feeling combined with sensitivity to verbal inflection. She has made a number of recordings including Gilda (*Rigoletto*), Alice Ford (*Falstaff*) and Elisabeth (*Don Carlos*) the title role in Donizetti's *Alina, regina di Golconda*, all with Riccardo Muti, Mimì under Gianluigi Gelmetti and operas by Cimarosa, Pergolesi (*Adriano in Siria*), Tommaso Traetta and Antonio Vivaldi.

Noël Goodwin

Emmy Destinn as Minnie in the première of 'La fanciulla del West'(Puccini), Metropolitan Opera, New York, 1910

Destinn [Kittl], Emmy
[Destinnová, Ema]

(*b* Prague, 26 Feb 1878; *d* Cěské Budějovice, 28 Jan 1930). Czech soprano. She studied singing under Marie Loewe-Destinn, adopting the latter's name in gratitude; in later life she used exclusively the Czech form of her stage name. On 19 July 1898 she made a highly successful début as Santuzza at the Berlin Kroll Oper, where she remained for ten years and became a great favourite in a wide repertory. Her international career began after a much acclaimed Senta at Bayreuth in 1901. She made her London début in 1904 as Donna Anna at Covent Garden; she returned to London every season until 1914, and was particularly admired there for her Butterfly (of which she was the first English exponent) and Aida. From 1908 to 1916 she also sang regularly at the Metropolitan, creating the part of Minnie in the première of *La fanciulla del West* (1910), and extending her Verdi roles to include *Il trovatore*, *Un ballo in maschera* and Alice Ford in *Falstaff*. She was a famous Salome (the first to sing this role in Berlin and Paris), and a notable interpreter of Senta.

During World War I Destinn's position as a declared sympathizer with the Czech national movement led to her being interned in her own castle of Stráž nad Nežákou. After the war she found it difficult to regain her former international standing. She returned to Covent Garden, however, for the peace season of 1919, in *Aida* and *Un ballo in maschera*; and she sang again at the Metropolitan during the seasons of 1919–20 and 1920–21. Among the most emotional occasions of her career were her appearances in Prague, just before and just after World War I, as the heroine of Bedřich Smetana's patriotic opera *Libuše*. She was one of the greatest artists of her generation, equally gifted as singer and actress, with a voice of markedly individual timbre and emotional warmth, and of great flexibility; her trill, for example, was unusually distinct and even for so full a voice. She made over 200 records for several companies, many reissued on CD; not all catch the calibre of her voice, though the best give a fair idea of her considerable art.

A. Rektorys and J. Dennis: 'Emmy Destinn', *Record Collector*, xx (1971–2), 5–47, 93–4 [with discography]

Desmond Shawe-Taylor/R

D'Ettore, Guglielmo.

See ETTORE, GUGLIELMO.

Deutekom, Cristina [Engel, Stientje]

(*b* Amsterdam, 28 Aug 1932). Dutch soprano. She studied at the Amsterdam Conservatory, joined the chorus of the Nederlandse Opera and, after singing small roles with the company, scored a major success in 1963 as the Queen of Night, which quickly took her to débuts in the same role in Munich and Vienna, at the Metropolitan Opera (1967) and Covent Garden (1968), and in the 1971 recording under Georg Solti. Her virtuosity and flexibility in coloratura technique, in spite of occasional hardness in tone, brought her further success as Donna Anna, Armida (Gioachino Rossini), Konstanze, Fiordiligi, Duchess Hélène (*Les vêpres siciliennes*), Elvira (*I puritani*), Lucia and Norma as well as Odabella (*Attila*), which she recorded in 1973. The Cristina Deutekom Competition for opera singers is held at the Twentse Schouwburg, Enschede, in the eastern Netherlands.

Noël Goodwin

Devriès, Fidès

(*b* New Orleans, 22 April 1851; *d* 1941). Dutch soprano. Daughter of Rosa de Vries-van Os, and sister of JEANNE, Maurice and Hermann Devriès. She was born in New Orleans, during her mother's two-year appointment at the French Opera there. Fidès studied in Paris and made her début in 1869 at the Théâtre Lyrique in Fromental Halévy's *Le val d'Andorre*. After singing at the Théâtre de la Monnaie, in 1871 she was engaged at the Paris Opéra, making her début as Marguerite, later singing Isabelle (*Robert le diable*), Inès (*L'Africaine*) and Ophelia, which she sang in the 100th performance of *Hamlet* (1874). At the Théâtre Italien she sang Amelia (*Simon Boccanegra*) and Salome (*Hérodiade*), then in 1885 she created Chimène in Jules Massenet's *Le Cid* at the Opéra. She sang Elsa in the first Paris performance of *Lohengrin* at the Eden-Théâtre in 1887. In Monte Carlo she added Aida, Violetta and Leïla (*Les pêcheurs de perles*) to her repertory and in 1889 took her farewell to the stage as Gilda.

Elizabeth Forbes

Devriès, Jeanne

(*b* New Orleans, before July 1850; *d* 1924). Dutch soprano. She was born into a family of singers, including her sister FIDÈS DEVRIÈS. Jeanne studied with GILBERT DUPREZ in Paris, making her début there in 1867 at the Théâtre Lyrique as Amina (*La sonnambula*). The same year she created Catharine in Georges Bizet's *La jolie fille de Perth* and also sang Lady Harriet (*Martha*), Zerlina and Rosina. After an engagement at the Théâtre de la Monnaie she sang mostly in France, excelling in coloratura roles such as Amina and Marguerite.

Elizabeth Forbes/R

Diadkova, Larissa

(*b* Zelenodolsk, 1955). Russian mezzo-soprano. Following studies at the Leningrad Conservatory, she joined the Kirov Opera in 1978, and was a prizewinner at the 1984 Glinka competition. Her repertory with the Kirov has been large, including Ratmir (*Ruslan and Lyudmila*), Konchakovna (*Prince Igor*), Marfa (*Khovanshchina*), Nezhata (*Sadko*), Kashcheyevna (*Kashchey the Deathless*), Olga (*Yevgeny Onegin*), Paulina and the Countess (*Queen of Spades*), Lyubov' (*Mazepa*), the Duenna (*Betrothal in a Monastery*) and Mother Superior (*The Fiery Angel*); many of these roles are recorded. With the Kirov she has sung around the world; other notable appearances include her Metropolitan Opera début (1996) as Madelon in *Andrea Chénier*, La Cieca in *La Gioconda* at La Scala (1997), Jocasta in *Oedipus rex* in Amsterdam, Madame Arvidson in *Un ballo in maschera* at Verona and Dallas (1998), Azucena at the Metropolitan, and Amneris in Houston and Florence (1999). In 1998 she sang Yevpraxia in the Royal Opera's concert performances of P.I. Tchaikovsky's *Enchantress*, and she was acclaimed as Amneris at a concert performance of *Aida* in London in 2000. The thrilling immediacy of her burnished mezzo and her admirable verbal clarity make her a singer worthy of the great Russian tradition.

John Allison

Díaz, Justino

(*b* San Juan, Puerto Rico, 29 Jan 1940). American bass. His studies at the University of Puerto Rico and the New England Conservatory were followed by training with Friedrich Jagel. He first appeared with the New England Opera Theater in 1961, and made his Metropolitan Opera début in 1963 (Monterone) as a winner of the Auditions of the Air. Appearances for the American Opera Society, Casals Festival (Puerto Rico) and Spoleto Festival followed. In 1966 his career was firmly established by his performances at the opening night of the new Metropolitan Opera at Lincoln Center as Antony in Samuel Barber's *Antony and Cleopatra*, and under Herbert von Karajan at the Salzburg Festival as Escamillo. Subsequent appearances included La Scala, Hamburg and the Vienna Staatsoper. He sang in the performance of Alberto Ginastera's *Beatrix Cenci* that inaugurated the Kennedy Center Opera House in Washington, DC

(1971), made his Covent Garden début as Escamillo in 1976 and returned as Iago in 1990. Díaz established himself as one of the leading basses of the Metropolitan, where his evenly produced, warm *basso cantante* was heard in a wide range of Italian roles. He has also been heard at Philadelphia (Don Giovanni, 1980), San Francisco (Scarpia, 1982), Milan (Count Asdrubale in *La pietrà del paragone*, 1982) and Cincinnati (Attila, 1984) He subsequently took on baritone parts, singing Iago for Franco Zeffirelli's cinema version of *Otello* (1986) and at Covent Garden in 1990, and becoming a noted Scarpia. His recordings include roles in *Medea*, *La Wally*, *Lucia di Lammermoor* and oratorios by G.F. Handel.

Richard Bernas

DiDonato, Joyce

(*b* Prairie Village, nr Kansas City, KS, 13 Feb 1969). American mezzo-soprano. She studied first at the Academy of Vocal Arts in Philadelphia, graduating in 1995, and subsequently on the Houston Grand Opera Studio Program. In 1998, her final year as a student there, she won second prize at the Plácido Domingo Operalia Competition in Hamburg, and created the role of Meg in a workshop production of Mark Adamo's *Little Women*. She made her major professional début, as Katerina Maslova in Tod Machover's *Resurrection*, at the Houston Grand Opera in 1999, and a sensational European début in 2000, as Angelina in *La Cenerentola* at La Scala. DiDonato made similarly acclaimed débuts at the Opéra Bastille, as Rosina, in 2001, at Covent Garden, as the Fox (*The Cunning Little Vixen*) in 2003, and at the Aix Festival, as Dejanira (G.F. Handel's *Hercules*) in 2004. In the USA she sang Meg in the first full professional production of *Little Women* at the New York City Opera in 2000, and Sister Helen Prejean in Jake Heggie's *Dead Man Walking*, also at the New York City Opera, in 2002. She first appeared at the Met in 2005, as Cherubino and then as Stéphano in Charles Gounod's *Roméo et Juliette*.

DiDonato returned to Covent Garden in 2005 as a sassy, fiery Rosina of dazzling vocal accomplishment, and early in 2006 repeated her searingly intense portrayal of Dejanira at the Brooklyn Academy of Music, New York, and the Barbican, London. Her other roles include Dorabella, Isabella (*L'italiana in Algeri*), Sesto in *La clemenza di Tito* and Elisabetta in *Maria Stuarda*, which she first performed in Geneva in 2005. She is also an admired recitalist (reviewing her 2004 Wigmore Hall début, *Opera Now* praised her 'fusion of prized vocalism and open-hearted expression'), and has performed in concert, often in the music of Handel, with such conductors as John Eliot Gardiner, Marc

Minkowski, Riccardo Muti, William Christie and John Nelson. DiDonato's lustrous, easily produced mezzo and discerning musicianship can be heard on recordings including *Benvenuto Cellini* (Ascanio), *La Cenerentola*, *Radamisto*, *Little Women*, *Resurrection*, a disc of Handel duets (with PATRIZIA CIOFI) and an enterprising programme of American songs.

Richard Wigmore

Didur, Adam [Adamo]

(*b* Wola Sekowa, nr Sanok, 24 Dec 1874; *d* Katowice, 7 Jan 1946). Polish bass. He studied in Lemberg with Valery Wysocki and in Milan with Franz Emmerich. He made his début in 1894 in Rio de Janeiro, and sang at the Warsaw Opera, 1899–1903, taking such leading roles as the title part in *Mefistofele*, always a favourite of his. After appearances in Spain he sang at La Scala (1904–6) and in Russia (1909). In 1905 he made his Covent Garden début as Colline in *La bohème*, returning in 1914 to sing Baron Archibaldo in the British première of Italo Montemezzi's *L'amore dei tre re* and, among other roles, Charles Gounod's Méphistophélès. Having made his American début in 1907 at the Manhattan Opera House as Alvise (*La Gioconda*), he joined the Metropolitan Opera, where he was engaged for 25 seasons; he made his début there in 1908 as Ramfis, and created Ashby in *La fanciulla del West*, the Woodcutter in *Königskinder* (both 1910), Talpa in *Il tabarro* and Simone in *Gianni Schicchi* (both 1918). He also sang Boris Godunov (1913), Baron Archibaldo (1915), Galitsky and Konchak in *Prince Igor* (1915), all American premières. He was again praised for his portrayals of Gounod's and Arrigo Boito's devils and sang such baritone roles as Tonio and Count Almaviva. From 1945 until his death in 1946 he directed the Katowice Opera. Didur's voice had a black timbre of a certain biting quality, and he was a splendid actor. On a number of early recordings the strength and character of his singing more than compensate for some technical infelicities.

L. de Noskowski: 'Adamo Didur', *Record Collector*, xvi (1964–6), 4–23 [with discography by J. Dennis]

Leo Riemens, Alan Blyth

Di Giovanni, Edoardo.

See JOHNSON, EDWARD.

Dimitrova, Ghena

(*b* Beglej, Pleven, 6 May 1941; *d* Milan, 11 June 2005). Bulgarian soprano. After studies at the Bulgarian State Conservatory, Sofia, she joined the National

Opera and made her début as Abigaille (*Nabucco*) at Sofia in 1967. In 1970 success in an international competition in Sofia brought her engagements in Italy (including her La Scala début as Amelia in *Ballo in maschera*, 1973), France and Spain, five seasons at the Teatro Colón, Buenos Aires (from 1977), and her Vienna Staatsoper début (1978). Her American début was at Dallas in 1981 as Elvira (*Ernani*). She sang Turandot at La Scala in 1983 and made her Covent Garden début in the same role the following year. She sang Lady Macbeth on the Royal Opera tour to Greece in 1986, and Aida in the 'onsite' production at Luxor, 1987. In 1988 she made her début at the Metropolitan Opera as Turandot, which she also sang with the company of La Scala in Korea and Japan that year. Dimitrova was a powerful *lirico spinto* soprano whose often thrilling singing compensated for an intermittent lack of dramatic involvement. Among her notable recordings are Abigaille, Amneris and Turandot, as well as discs of arias by Giuseppe Verdi, Giacomo Puccini and P.I. Tchaikovsky.

H.E. Phillips: 'Crisis of Will', *ON*, lii/11 (1987–8), 27–9

Noël Goodwin

D'Intino, Luciana

(*b* San Vito al Tagliamento, nr Pordenone, 22 Aug 1959). Italian mezzo-soprano. She won attention as a prizewinner at Spoleto and the Maria Callas awards. A début as Azucena in *Il trovatore* was followed in 1984 with 'a dark-toned Rosina, rather lacking in sparkle' (*Opera*) at the Macerata Festival. Appearances in rare operatic revivals included the roles of Ernestina in Gioachino Rossini's *L'occasione fa il ladro* and Pippo in *La gazza ladra*, both at Pesaro, and Phaethon in Niccolò Jommelli's *Fetonte* at La Scala. She made her American début in 1989 as Fenena in a concert performance of *Nabucco* at Carnegie Hall in New York, appearing the following year at the Metropolitan as Federica in *Luisa Miller*. With a steadily broadening concert repertory, D'Intino gained the reputation of an exceptionally musical singer, and it was in this capacity rather than for great volume or opulence of tone that her Eboli won praise in the revival of *Don Carlos* at La Scala in 1993. Her voice was found rather too light for Dalila at Macerata and Amneris in Buenos Aires, but she has continued to impress in the bel canto repertory, such as *I Capuleti e i Montecchi*, which she sang at Genoa in 1996. Among her recordings, those of *Don Carlos* and *La gazza ladra* (as Lucia), both made 'live', testify to her fine powers of nuance as well as to the beauty of her well-mannered voice.

J.B. Steane

Di Stefano, Giuseppe

(*b* Motta Sant'Anastasia, nr Catania, 24 July 1921; *d* Santa Maria Hoe, 3 March 2008). Italian tenor. He studied in Milan with LUIGI MONTESANTO. He made his début in 1946 at the Teatro Municipale, Reggio nell'Emilia, as Jules Massenet's Des Grieux, and first sang at La Scala in 1947. He made his Metropolitan début in 1948 as the Duke in *Rigoletto* and continued to appear there until 1965. Until 1953 he sang lighter roles such as Wilhelm Meister (*Mignon*), Elvino (*La sonnambula*), Pietro Mascagni's Fritz and Nadir. His singing at that time was notable for its warm, sensual timbre and expressive, impassioned phrasing, which were enhanced by his generous, outgoing personality. As he began to take on heavier parts his singing became more rough-hewn and less elegant, and the voice larger and less pure. By 1957 he had added Don José, Canio, Turiddu, Radames, Don Alvaro (*La forza del destino*) and Osaka (*Iris*) to his repertory; thus, when he made his British début at Edinburgh in 1957, his Nemorino had less vocal charm than had been expected. He sang Cavaradossi at Covent Garden in 1961, but during the 1960s his appearances became sporadic. Di Stefano made numerous recordings, many of them with CALLAS, notably *Tosca* (1953, under Victor De Sabata) and *Lucia di Lammermoor* (1955, under Herbert von Karajan); these show his passionate, exuberant style at its most winning. He published a book on opera singing, *L'arte del canto* (Milan, 1989).

T. Semrau: 'Giuseppe di Stefano', *Record Collector*, xxxix (1994), 165–82
G. Gualerzi: 'Di Stefano and Corelli at 75', *Opera*, xlvii (1996), 1137–44

Harold Rosenthal/Alan Blyth

Dobrski, Julian

(*b* Nowe, 31 Dec 1811 or 1812; *d* Warsaw, 2 May 1886). Polish tenor. He studied in Warsaw with C.E. Soliva. After making his début in *Il barbiere di Siviglia* at the Wielki Theatre, Warsaw, on 20 September 1832, he performed there in operas by Vincenzo Bellini, Gaetano Donizetti, Giacomo Meyerbeer, Carl Maria von Weber, Ferdinand Hérold, Daniel Auber, Fromental Halévy and Giuseppe Verdi. He sang in Turin and Genoa (1846–8) and was forced to leave his native country after taking part in the spring revolution of 1848. On 1 January 1858 he created Jontek in the revised *Halka* at the Wielki; Stanisław Moniuszko transformed a melody in mazurka rhythm into the Act 4 aria 'Szumiąjodły' ('Fir trees sway') specially for him. He captivated audiences by the beauty of his tone as well as the dramatic power of his performances. On

25 February 1858, after a performance of *Ernani*, he received in tribute to his 25 years on the stage a solid gold diamond-encrusted wreath, engraved with the titles of all the operas in which he had appeared. In 1861 he again incurred the displeasure of the authorities for his patriotic attitude and was prematurely dismissed from the Wielki Theatre. However, in 1865 he returned to Warsaw to sing; he created Stefan in Moniuszko's *The Haunted Manor* and gave his last operatic performance there that year, in Halévy's *La Juive*. He had taught since 1861, and later he held important teaching posts in Warsaw. He was also editor of *Echo*, a collection of songs by foreign composers, which was begun in 1861.

Irena Poniatowska

Dobson, John

(*b* Derby, 17 Nov 1930). English tenor. He studied in London and Italy, making his début in 1956 at Bergamo as Pinkerton. In 1959 he sang Godvino (*Aroldo*) at Wexford and joined the Royal Opera, for whom he has sung over 85 roles in 30 years. For the WNO he sang Alfredo (1963) and Luigi (*Il tabarro*, 1966). His Covent Garden repertoire included David, Loge, Mime, Jaquino, Andres (*Wozzeck*), Turiddu, Rodolfo, Pang, Robert Boles (*Peter Grimes*), Snout, Shuisky, Sellem (*The Rake's Progress*) and Spalanzani. He created Paris in *King Priam* at Coventry (1962), Luke in *The Ice Break* (1977) and sang in the British première of Luciano Berio's *Un re in ascolto* (1989). A totally reliable singer, he was a splendid character actor.

Elizabeth Forbes

Dolores de Padilla.

See ARTOT DE PADILLA, LOLA.

Dolukhanova, Zara [Zarui] (Agas'yevna)

(*b* Moscow, 15 March 1918; *d* Moscow, 4 December 2007). Russian mezzo-soprano. She studied with V. Belyayeva-Tarasevich at the Gnesin music school and graduated from the Gnesin Institute in 1957. In 1939 she made her début at the Yerevan Opera but soon left the stage for the concert hall. She was, however, one of the singers who took part in re-establishing Gioachino Rossini's florid mezzo roles in the repertory: she broadcast performances of Cinderella and Rosina (also Cherubino) and recorded extracts of *Semiramide*. She was appointed a soloist with the All-Union Radio and Television in 1944, and with

the Moscow PO in 1959. Dolukhanova was outstanding among Russian singers of her day. She used the wide range and agility of her coloratura voice with controlled ease, giving polished performances of such differing composers as Modest Musorgsky, P.I. Tchaikovsky, Sergey Prokofiev, Giuseppe Verdi and Claude Debussy; she also gave the first performance (1955) of Dmitry Shostakovich's cycle *From Jewish Folk Poetry*. In all her interpretations she displayed a keen style, and she went to the heart of whatever she sang. She toured widely, in east Europe, and in Italy, France, Britain, Argentina, the USA, Japan, New Zealand and other countries.

I.M. Yampol'sky/R

Domanínská [Klobásková, Vyčichlová], Libuše

(*b* Brno, 4 July 1924). Czech soprano. She studied at Brno Conservatory, made her début as Blaženka in Bedřich Smetana's *The Secret* with the Brno Opera (1945) and soon became a leading member of the company. Her soft, warm, 'jugendliche dramatische' soprano, gifted in cantilena and capable of delicate expressive nuances, was primarily valuable in Smetana. But she won great success as Leoš Janáček's Jenůfa, Kát'a Kabanová and Vixen, in which the outstanding character of her voice was supported by sensitive dramatic feeling. In 1955 she joined the Prague National Theatre and with that company sang at the Edinburgh and Holland festivals and the Helsinki Sibelius festival. She also appeared at the Teatro Colón, Buenos Aires, and from 1958 to 1968 as a regular guest at the Vienna Staatsoper. As well as her Czech roles, she sang in Russian and Soviet operas and in Giuseppe Verdi, Giacomo Puccini and W.A. Mozart. She sang in Janáček's *Glagolitic Mass* at La Scala, and her repertory included a wide range of oratorios and cantatas by J.S. Bach, G.F. Handel, Joseph Haydn, Mozart, Ludwig van Beethoven and Antonín Dvořák, and songs.

Alena Němcová

Domgraf-Fassbänder, Willi

(*b* Aachen, 19 Feb 1897; *d* Nuremberg, 13 Feb 1978). German baritone. He studied with Jacques Stückgold and Paul Bruns in Berlin and GIUSEPPE BORGATTI in Milan. He made his début at Aachen in 1922 as Count Almaviva. Engagements followed at the Deutsche Oper, Berlin, at Düsseldorf and at Stuttgart. In 1930 he became first lyric baritone at the Berlin Staatsoper, where he remained until 1946. In addition to his German roles, his repertory there included Rigoletto, Luna, Escamillo, Silvio and Marcello.

He first appeared in England at Glyndebourne on the opening night of the first season in 1934, when he sang Figaro. His warm, pleasing baritone was enhanced by his mercurial personality and good looks. He returned to Glyndebourne in 1935 and 1937 as Figaro, Guglielmo and Papageno, which he also sang at Salzburg under Arturo Toscanini in 1937. After the war he appeared in Hanover, Vienna, Munich and Nuremberg. In the latter part of his career he scored a great personal success in the title roles of Werner Egk's *Peer Gynt* and of *Wozzeck*, in which his gifts as a singing actor were fully used. His Figaro and Guglielmo (1935, Glyndbourne) were recorded, and he also made many individual recordings. His daughter, and former pupil, is the mezzo-soprano BRIGITTE FASSBAENDER.

Harold Rosenthal/Alan Blyth

Domingo, Plácido [Placido]

(*b* Madrid, 21 Jan 1941). Spanish tenor. Taken by his family to Mexico in 1950, he studied the piano, conducting (under Igor Markevich) and finally singing. In 1957 he made his début as a baritone in the zarzuela *Gigantes y cabezudos*. His first important tenor role was Alfredo in Monterrey, Mexico, in 1961, the year he made his American début as Arturo (*Lucia di Lammermoor*) in Dallas. From 1962 to 1965 he was a member of the Israeli National Opera, singing some 300 performances of ten operas, some of them in Hebrew. In 1965 he made his New York début at the City Opera as Pinkerton and with that company in 1966 sang the title role in the first North American performance of Alberto Ginastera's *Don Rodrigo*. He first sang at the Metropolitan as Maurizio (*Adriana Lecouvreur*, 1968), at La Scala as Ernani (1969), and at Covent Garden as Cavaradossi (1971). He made notable appearances as Vasco da Gama (*L'Africaine*) at San Francisco in 1972, as Arrigo (*Les vêpres siciliennes*) in Paris and later in New York, and as Otello in Hamburg and Paris in 1975. That year he also sang Giuseppe Verdi's Don Carlos at Salzburg. In 1976 he appeared as Turiddu and Canio in a double bill in Barcelona – on one occasion singing the Prologue to *Pagliacci* when the baritone was taken ill; he repeated both roles at Covent Garden later that year. In 1982–3 at the Metropolitan he sang Paolo (Riccardo Zandonai's *Francesca da Rimini*), Aeneas (*Les Troyens*) and Lohengrin; his repertory has also included Hoffmann, Don José, Pollione, Edgardo, Riccardo, Radames, Chénier, Don Alvaro (*La forza*

Plácido Domingo, José Carreras and Luciano Pavarotti in concert as 'The Three Tenors'

del destino), Werther, Giacomo Puccini's Des Grieux, Rodolfo, Calaf, Siegmund, Parsifal, Samson and several zarzuelas. He created the title role of Moreno Torroba's *El poeta* in Madrid in 1980 and Gian Carlo Menotti's Goya in Washington, DC, in 1986.

After a career lasting more than 35 years, Domingo's voice showed little sign of decline. In his 60s he was still impressive in such roles as Hermann in *The Queen of Spades* (which he sang at the Metropolitan in 2001 and at Covent Garden in 2002), Idomeneo, Siegmund and Danilo Danilowitsch (*Die lustige Witwe*). Domingo has also conducted operas on several occasions, having made his début in this capacity in *La traviata* at the New York City Opera in 1973; his Metropolitan conducting début was in *La bohème* in the 1984–5 season. In 1998 he conducted *Aida* at the Metropolitan, 24 hours after singing Samson there. He was appointed artistic director of Washington National Opera in 1996 and of Los Angeles Opera in 2000. He became general director at the Los Angeles Opera in 2003.

Domingo is widely regarded as the leading *lirico spinto* tenor of the late 20th century, a consummate musician and an actor of exceptional passion. His singing is always marked by exemplary intelligence and taste. While he has undertaken a wide range of roles, he became particularly identified with Verdi's Otello (see colour plate 9), of which he has been a wholehearted, eloquent exponent who suggested the heroic dimension of the character through force of personality. Domingo recorded this role three times (including the Franco Zeffirelli film of 1986), and recorded almost all his other principal roles, several more than once, and appeared on many video recordings of his stage appearances (notably in the title role of the Covent Garden *Andrea Chénier*). All evince his thorough-going commitment, warm and flexible tone, command of line and fiery declamation. If he has not always been the most subtle of interpreters in terms of vocal colouring and shades of meaning, he has virtually never deviated from the high standards he sets himself in matters of technique and style. In 2000 Domingo was a recipient of the Kennedy Center Honors, the highest accolade for achievement in the arts bestowed in the USA, and was made an honorary KBE in 2002. He has received honorary doctorates from several universities. (See colour plate 9.)

H. Rosenthal: 'Placido Domingo', *Opera*, xxiii (1972), 18–23
J.B. Steane: *The Grand Tradition* (London, 1974/R), 541–2
P. Domingo: *My First Forty Years* (New York, 1983)
D. Snowman: *The World of Plácido Domingo* (New York, 1985/R)
D. Snowman: *Plácido Domingo's Tales from the Opera* (Portland, OR, 1995)

Harold Rosenthal/Alan Blyth

Dominguez, Oralia

(*b* San Luis Potosí, 15 Oct 1928). Mexican contralto. She studied at the Mexican National Conservatory and made her début with the Mexico City Opera in 1950. Three years later she first appeared in Europe, at La Scala in *Adriana Lecouvreur*. Engagements at other leading opera houses followed, including S Carlo, Naples, the Vienna Staatsoper and Paris Opéra, and she made her Covent Garden début as Sosostris in the première of Michael Tippett's *The Midsummer Marriage* (1955). She combined a well-trained and voluptuous voice of exotic timbre with agility of technique, which was heard to advantage in the title role of Gioachino Rossini's *L'italiana in Algeri* at the 1957 Glyndebourne Festival, and her engaging sense of comedy made her a much-admired Mistress Quickly in Giuseppe Verdi's *Falstaff* at Glyndebourne (1959–60) and Covent Garden (1967–8). Her recordings include roles in operas from Claudio Monteverdi to Richard Wagner, notably Erda under Herbert von Karajan (*Rheingold* 1967, *Siegfried* 1969).

Noël Goodwin

Donalda [Lightstone], Pauline

(*b* Montreal, 5 March 1882; *d* Montreal, 22 Oct 1970). Canadian soprano. She studied at the Royal Victoria College, Montreal, and went to Paris in 1902, taking her stage name from her benefactor, Donald A. Smith (Lord Strathcona). After studies with Edmond Duvernoy and PAUL LHÉRIE, she made her début as Jules Massenet's Manon in Nice in 1904. The following year she made her Covent Garden début as Micaëla with DESTINN and DALMORÈS. Later she sang several roles there, including Mimì with CARUSO, and was Ah-joe in the première of Franco Leoni's *L'oracolo* (1905). In 1919 she was London's first Concepcion in Maurice Ravel's *L'heure espagnole*. She also sang at the Théâtre de la Monnaie in Brussels, the Opéra-Comique in Paris and the Manhattan Opera in New York. Donalda won admiration for her rich timbre and vivacious style. She retired in 1922 and taught in Paris until 1937; she then returned to Montreal, where she founded the Opera Guild in 1941. That organization gave several Canadian premières and she remained president until its demise in 1969.

A.E. Knight: 'The Life of Pauline Donalda', *Record Collector*, x (1955–6), 265–74 [with discography]
R.C. Brotman: *Pauline Donalda* (Montreal, 1975)

Gilles Potvin

Donath, Helen

(*b* Corpus Christi, TX, 10 July 1940). American soprano. After studies at Del Mar College, Corpus Christi, she studied with Paola Novikova in New York. She appeared in concert and recital in New York and Texas from 1958 to 1960, then won a contract at Cologne, where her parts included Wellgunde (the role of her début in 1961), Liù, Boris Blacher's Juliet, Micaëla and Branghien in Frank Martin's *Le vin herbé*. In 1963 she moved to Hanover and received special recognition in the theatre and on television as Jeanne in Werner Egk's *Die Verlobung von San Domingo*. Donath made her débuts at Salzburg (Pamina) in 1967 and San Francisco (Sophie) in 1971, a role she also sang at her Chicago début three years later. She also appeared as Sophie with the Vienna Staatsoper at the Bol'shoy (1971). Her La Scala début, as Micaëla, followed in 1972, and her Covent Garden début, as Anne Trulove, in 1979. She has sung such roles as Susanna, Ilia (*Idomeneo*), Zerlina, Marzelline (*Fidelio*), Aennchen (*Der Freischütz*), Oscar, Mélisande, Mimì, Liù and Bohuslav Martinů's Julietta in many of the leading European houses. In 1991 she undertook the Governess in *The Turn of the Screw* in Los Angeles, and in 1993 she sang Eva in Dresden. She has been equally active in oratorio and recital and has recorded much of her repertory, including Mozart masses and the Governess under Colin Davis and, among her other opera roles, Eva and Marzelline (under Herbert von Karajan), Sophie and C.W. Gluck's Amor (under Georg Solti), and Micaëla (under Lorin Maazel). Her lyric soprano has been notable for its flexibility, purity and ease in the upper register.

Martin Bernheimer/Alan Blyth

Dönch, Karl

(*b* Hagen, 8 Jan 1915; *d* Vienna, 16 Sept 1994). German bass-baritone. He studied at the Dresden Conservatory and made his début in 1936 at Görlitz. In 1947 he joined the Vienna Staatsoper, where he was often heard as Beckmesser, a role he recorded under Hans Knappertsbusch (1950) with SCHÖFFLER as Hans Sachs; further success came in 1951 as the Doctor (*Wozzeck*), which he recorded under Pierre Boulez (1966). He sang in the premières of Gottfried von Einem's *Dantons Tod* (1947, Salzburg), Rolf Liebermann's *Penelope* (1954, Salzburg) and Frank Martin's *Der Sturm* (1956, Vienna). A versatile actor-singer who made much of comedy-character, he sang in major German theatres, at La Scala, and in New York and Buenos Aires. He was also in demand for operetta and recorded several roles in

the 1950s. He was director of the Vienna Volksoper from 1973 to 1987, where he enlarged the repertory to include such works as *Albert Herring* and *From the House of the Dead*.

Noël Goodwin

Donnelly, Malcolm

(*b* Sydney, 8 Feb 1943). Australian baritone. He studied in Sydney, where he made his début in 1966, and then in London before joining Scottish Opera (1972), with which he sang Count Almaviva, Malatesta, the Music-Master (*Ariadne auf Naxos*), James Stewart (Thea Musgrave's *Mary, Queen of Scots*), Harašta (*The Cunning Little Vixen*) and Enrico Ashton. At Wexford (1977–8) he sang Herod (*Hérodiade*) and Sebastiano (*Tiefland*). For the ENO his numerous roles include Pizarro, Germont, Napoleon (*War and Peace*), Count di Luna, Ourrias (*Mireille*), Tonio, Mazeppa, Rigoletto, Scarpia, Ford, Simon Boccanegra and Macbeth. With Opera North he has sung the Dutchman, Prince Igor, Jack Rance and Captain Balstrode; he has also appeared with Australian Opera, most notably as Macbeth, a role well suited to his powerful voice and strong personality.

Elizabeth Forbes

Donzelli, Domenico

(*b* Bergamo, 2 Feb 1790; *d* Bologna, 31 March 1873). Italian tenor. After studying with Eliodoro Bianchi he made his début at Bergamo in 1808 in Simon Mayr's *Elisa*. He then completed his studies in Naples with Viganoni and Gaetano Crivelli. For the next decade he sang florid tenor roles throughout Italy, appearing in Gioachino Rossini's *Tancredi*, the first performance of *Torvaldo e Dorliska* (1815, Rome), *L'inganno felice* and *La Cenerentola*. Then his voice began to grow heavier, and he turned to a different repertory. In 1825 he made his Paris début at the Théâtre Italien in the title role of Rossini's *Otello*. During six seasons in Paris he sang in the first performances of Rossini's *Il viaggio a Reims* (1825), Fromental Halévy's *Clari* (1829) and Louise Bertin's *Fausto* (1831). He sang from 1829 at the King's Theatre, taking part in the first London performances of Vincenzo Bellini's *Il pirata* (1830) and *La straniera* (1832). He created Pollione in *Norma* at La Scala (1831), and later sang the role in London, Venice, Bologna, Trieste and Sinigaglia (Senigallia). He appeared in many Donizetti operas, including *Fausta*, *Anna Bolena*, *Parisina*, *Belisario*, *Lucia di Lammermoor* and *Roberto Devereux*. Two of the greatest successes of his later career were as

Masaniello in Daniel Auber's *La muette de Portici* and the title role in Saverio Mercadante's *Il bravo*. He retired in 1844.

Elizabeth Forbes

Dooley, William

(*b* Modesto, CA, 9 Sept 1932). American baritone. He studied in Rochester and Munich, and made his début in 1957 at Heidelberg as Posa. He was then engaged at Bielefeld (1959) and in 1962 joined the Deutsche Oper, Berlin, with which he has remained active. In 1964 he made his début at the Metropolitan Opera as Yevgeny Onegin; he sang there for 14 seasons, and also appeared in Santa Fe, Chicago, Vienna and Florence. Among his roles are Pizarro, Telramund, Kothner, the Dutchman, Amonasro, Macbeth, the four villains (*Les contes d'Hoffmann*), Escamillo and John the Baptist (*Salome*), but he excels in modern works. He created Cortez in Roger Sessions's *Montezuma* (1964, Berlin); the Captain of the Guard in *The Bassarids* (1966, Salzburg); Mizoguchi in Toshirō Mayuzumi's *Kinkakuji* (1976, Berlin); Oberlin in Wolfgang Rihm's *Jakob Lenz* (1979, Hamburg); Tiresias in Rihm's *Oedipus* (1987, Berlin); and Eagle in Marc Neikrug's *Los Alamos* (Berlin, 1988). He has also sung Wozzeck, Dr Schön, Baron d'Houdoux (*Neues vom Tage*), Gorjančikov (*From the House of the Dead*), Nick Shadow and Major Mary (*Die Soldaten*).

Elizabeth Forbes

Dorman, Mrs.

See ELIZABETH YOUNG.

Dorus-Gras [née Van Steenkiste], Julie(-Aimée-Josephe [Joséphine])

(*b* Valenciennes, 7 Sept 1805; *d* Paris, 6 Feb 1896). Belgian soprano. She studied at the Paris Conservatoire and made her début at the Théâtre de la Monnaie, Brussels, in 1825. She sang Elvire at the first Brussels performance of Daniel Auber's *La muette de Portici* (1829), and she also took part in the historic performance of that opera on 25 August 1830 that allegedly sparked off the Belgian revolution. In 1831 she was engaged at the Paris Opéra, and during the next 15 years created many roles there, including Alice in *Robert le diable* (1831), Eudoxie in *La Juive* (1835), Marguerite de Valois in *Les Huguenots* (1836), Teresa in *Benvenuto Cellini* (1838) and other roles by Auber and Fromental Halévy. In 1839 she appeared in London on the concert platform, and in 1847 she sang the title role of *Lucia di Lammermoor*

in English at Drury Lane, with Hector Berlioz conducting. In 1849, when she sang at Covent Garden in three of her most famous roles, Elvire (*La muette de Portici*), Alice and Marguerite de Valois, she was still, according to Henry Chorley, 'an excellent artist, with a combined firmness and volubility of execution which have not been exceeded, and were especially welcome in French music'. She had a high, flexible voice, and became a noted Isabelle in *Robert le diable*, a role that probably suited her better than Alice. She was not a particularly convincing actress, but the accuracy of her singing and the brilliance of her voice ensured her success.

H.F. Chorley: *Thirty Years' Musical Recollections* (London, 1862/*R*, abridged 2/1926/*R* by E. Newman)

Elizabeth Forbes

Dotti, Anna Vincenza

(*b* Bologna; *fl* 1711–28). Italian contralto. During the period 1711–16 she sang repeatedly in Bologna and in Mantua, Genoa, Florence, Livorno (in Giovanni Bononcini's *Camilla*), Reggio nell'Emilia and Venice (three operas, two of them by Antonio Vivaldi). Between 1717 and 1720 she appeared in 12 operas in Naples, including the version of G.F. Handel's *Rinaldo* with additions by Leonardo Leo at the royal palace in 1718, in which she was Almirena. From autumn 1724 she was for three seasons a member of the Royal Academy company in London as second woman to CUZZONI, singing in G.F. Handel operas, Attilio Ariosti's *Artaserse*, *Dario* and *Lucio Vero*, Bononcini's *Astianatte* and the pasticcios *Elpidia* and *Elisa*. She created Irene in *Tamerlano* (1724) and Eduige in *Rodelinda* (1725), and appeared in revivals of *Giulio Cesare*, *Ottone* and probably *Floridante*. After FAUSTINA BORDONI's arrival in spring 1726 Dotti was allotted less important parts; Handel gave her only one aria in *Alessandro* and *Admeto*, in both of which (as on other occasions) she played male roles. On leaving London she enjoyed considerable success in Brussels (autumn 1727), and sang in an opera there in 1728. Her compass was narrow (*a* to *e'*), and her lower notes evidently weak. She is sometimes confused with Anna Maria Dotti, who sang in two operas at Venice in 1708. One of the two sang in Antonio Lotti's *Teuzzone* at Bologna in November 1711.

Winton Dean

Douglas, Nigel [Leigh Pemberton, Nigel Douglas]

(*b* Lenham, Kent, 9 May 1929). English tenor. He studied in Vienna with ALFRED PICCAVER, making his début in 1959 at the Kammeroper as Rodolfo

(*La bohème*), then singing at the Volksoper. Later he created L'Heureux in Heinrich Sutermeister's *Madame Bovary* (1967, Zürich), Philip in John Gardner's *The Visitors* (1972, Aldeburgh) and Basil in William Mathias's *The Servants* for the WNO (1980), with which he also sang Alwa (*Lulu*), the Captain (*Wozzeck*), Loge and Herod. With the ENO he sang the Devil in Rimsky-Korsakov's *Christmas Eve* (1988) and the Earl of Kent in Aribert Reimann's *Lear* (1989), both first British stage productions. A noted exponent of Benjamin Britten's operas, he has sung Peter Grimes, Vere, Aschenbach and Lechmere (*Owen Wingrave*), which he created both on BBC Television (1971) and at Covent Garden (1973), where he sang Herod in 1988. He occasionally directed the New Sadler's Wells Opera and provided the company with new English texts. He also sings, translates and directs operetta. The dryness of his voice is offset by superb diction and the excellence of his acting.

Elizabeth Forbes/R

Dow, Dorothy

(*b* Houston, 8 Oct 1920; *d* Galveston, 26 Feb 2005). American soprano. She studied at the Juilliard School, making her début in 1946 at Buffalo as Santuzza. In 1947 she created Susan B. Anthony in Virgil Thomson's *The Mother of Us All* at Columbia University. Engaged at Zürich (1948–50), she sang Elisabeth (*Tannhäuser*) at La Scala (1950), returning for Marie (*Wozzeck*), La Gioconda, Chrysothemis, Danae and William Walton's Cressida. She sang the Woman in the American première of *Erwartung* (Washington, DC, 1951). At Glyndebourne she sang Lady Macbeth (1952) and Ariadne (1953). She sang Irmengard in Gaspare Spontini's *Agnes von Hohenstaufen* at Florence (1954) and Renata in the first staged performance of Sergey Prokofiev's *The Fiery Angel* at Venice (1955). A most dramatic singer of imposing stage presence, she had an opulent voice that she used with great expressiveness.

Elizabeth Forbes

Driscoll, Loren

(*b* Midwest, WY, 14 March 1928). American tenor. He studied at Syracuse and Boston, where he made his début in 1954 as Dr Caius (*Falstaff*). In 1957 he sang Tom Rakewell at Santa Fe, returning for the American premières of Paul Hindemith's *Neues vom Tage* (1961) and H.W. Henze's *Boulevard Solitude* (1967). He sang at the New York City Opera (1957–9) and at Glyndebourne as Ferrando in 1962 before joining the Deutsche Oper, Berlin. There he remained for over 20 years, singing in the première

of Roger Sessions's *Montezuma* (1964), creating Lord Barrat in *Der junge Lord* (1965) and singing Eumaeus in *Il ritorno d'Ulisse* (1968) and First Officer in Wilhelm Dieter Siebert's *Der Untergang der Titanic* (1979). At Salzbug he created Dionysus in *The Bassarids* (1966), also singing the role at La Scala and Santa Fe (1968). He made his Metropolitan début in 1966 as David (*Die Meistersinger*), created the Architect in Aribert Reimann's *Melusine* (1971) at Schwetzingen, repeating it at Edinburgh, and took part in the première of Nicolas Nabokov's *Love's Labour's Lost* at Brussels (1973). A stylish singer, specializing in 20th-century music, he had a repertory which included Don Ottavio, Almaviva, Valzacchi (*Der Rosenkavalier*), Flamand (*Capriccio*), the Bishop of Budoja (*Palestrina*), Sándor Szokolay's Hamlet, Andres (*Wozzeck*) and the Painter (*Lulu*), which he recorded.

Alan Blyth

Dua, Octave [Haegen, Leo van der]

(*b* Ghent, 28 Feb 1882; *d* Brussels, 8 March 1952). Belgian tenor. He made his début as Jeník in the first performance in French of *The Bartered Bride* (1907, Brussels) and for a while continued to sing lyric roles. His real talent was as a comedian, character actor and comprimario tenor, in which capacity he sang with the Chicago company (1915–22) with a period at the Metropolitan (1919–21). In both cities he was particularly admired for his portrayal of Truffaldino in *The Love for Three Oranges*, which he sang at its première in Chicago in 1921. He also made a special place for himself in English operatic life, appearing in London first under Thomas Beecham in 1914, then as an 'outstanding' Torquemada in the English première of *L'heure espagnole* at Covent Garden in 1919, and in almost every season at Covent Garden and on tour from 1924 to 1939. Ernest Newman in *The Sunday Times* considered him 'without an equal today' in his field. Some early recordings show a pleasing voice, but essentially he was a stage artist and here the best testimonials are the tributes regularly paid him by the critics.

J.B. Steane

Dubosc, Catherine

(*b* Lille, 12 March 1959). French soprano. She studied piano and cello at the Strasbourg Conservatoire, then singing with Gerda Hartmann. In 1980 she entered the Ecole d'Art Lyrique of the Paris Opéra, where her teachers were Denise Dupleix and HANS HOTTER. She received further tuition from ERIC TAPPY at the Lyons Opéra before joining that company in 1985 for two seasons. She has sung many

Mozart roles, including Susanna, Despina and Pamina, as well as Marzelline, Nannetta (Giuseppe Verdi's *Falstaff*) and Blanche de la Force in Francis Poulenc's *Dialogues des Carmélites*. Other roles include Gretel (1987, Geneva) and Hypsipyle in Francesco Cavalli's *Giasone* (1988, Utrecht). She has also appeared at the Opéra-Comique and the Théâtre du Châtelet in Paris, and at Nancy, Montpellier, Avignon, Geneva, Edinburgh and Strasbourg. Her recordings include *Giasone*, *Dialogues des Carmélites*, André Campra's *Tancrède*, Jean-Marie Leclair's *Scylla et Glaucus*, C.W. Gluck's *Le rencontre imprévue* and Sergey Prokofiev's *The Love for Three Oranges*.

Nicholas Anderson

Duesing, Dale

(*b* Milwaukee, 26 Sept 1947). American baritone. After studying at Lawrence University, he sang in Bremen (1972) and Düsseldorf (1974–5), where his roles included Dandini and the King (*Die Kluge*). In 1976 he took part in the première of Andrew Imbrie's *Angle of Repose* at San Francisco and sang Olivier (*Capriccio*) at Glyndebourne; he made his Metropolitan début in 1979 as Harlequin (*Ariadne auf Naxos*). He has also appeared at Chicago, Seattle, Santa Fe, Salzburg and La Scala. His repertory includes Claudio Monteverdi's Otho, W.A. Mozart's and Gioachino Rossini's Figaro, Guglielmo, Papageno, Belcore, Pelléas, Wolfram, Yevgeny Onegin, Marcello, Demetrius and Billy Budd, the last a role particularly well suited to his vocal and dramatic gifts. He created the role of the Narrator in Nicholas Maw's *Sophie's Choice* (Covent Garden, 2002).

Elizabeth Forbes

Dufranne, Hector

(*b* Mons, 25 Oct 1871; *d* Paris, 4 May 1951). Belgian bass-baritone. He made his début in 1898 at La Monnaie in Brussels, as Valentin in *Faust*, having studied at the Brussels Conservatory with Désirée Demest. In 1900 he appeared as Thoas in *Iphigénie en Tauride* with the Opéra-Comique in Paris, where he became one of the leading and longest-serving members of the company. He sang in many premières, including those of Jules Massenet's *Grisélidis* (Marquis de Saluces, 1901) and *Thérèse* (Girondin André Thorel, 1907), and Maurice Ravel's *L'heure espagnole* (Don Inigo Gomez, 1911). He was also the Opéra-Comique's first Scarpia in *Tosca* and the Opéra's first John the Baptist in *Salome* (1910). Above all, he was associated with the role of Golaud

in *Pelléas et Mélisande*, which he sang at the première (1902) and later in New York (1910). In 1914 he sang the role in his single appearance at Covent Garden and in 1939, for the last time, at Vichy. He won high praise for both his singing and his acting in New York and later became a favourite at Chicago, where he sang Celio in the world première of *The Love for Three Oranges* (1921), conducted by the composer. At a private performance in Paris he took the part of Don Quixote in the stage première of Manuel de Falla's *El retablo de maese Pedro* (1923). His admirable voice, well placed and finely produced, served him well through a long career and is impressively heard in some historically important recordings, particularly those of *L'heure espagnole* and *Pelléas et Mélisande* (1928).

J.B. Steane

Dugazon [née Lefèbvre], Louise-Rosalie

(*b* Berlin, 18 June 1755; *d* Paris, 22 Sept 1821). French soprano. Her father, François Jacques Lefèbvre, was a dancer at the Paris Opéra, and she began her own career as a dancer. André Grétry advised her to become a singer and oversaw her studies with the soprano Marie Favart. Grétry wrote an ariette for her in *Lucile*, which was performed at the Comédie-Italienne in 1769, and she made her official début there in 1774 as Pauline in his opera *Silvain*. After a brief marriage in 1776 to actor and writer Jean-Baptiste-Henri Gourgaud, known as Dugazon, she sang under that name for the rest of her career. For political reasons she did not sing on the stage in 1792–4.

She took part in about 60 premières at the Comédie-Italienne and Opéra-Comique, including several by Grétry: *Les mariages samnites* (1778), *Aucassin et Nicolette* (1782), *Le comte d'Albert* (1788) and notably as Laurette in Grétry's *Richard coeur-de-lion* (1784). It is Laurette who sings 'Je crains de lui parler la nuit', quoted nostalgically by the countess in P.I. Tchaikovsky's *The Queen of Spades*. She created roles in several operas by Nicolas Dalayrac including *La dot* (1785), *Nina* (1786), in which she sang the title role, possibly her most successful part, and *Maison à vendre* (1800). Her dramatic talents gave her singing an expressiveness and versatility that was highly acclaimed. Later, she renounced romantic roles to play young matrons, for example in Etienne-Nicolas Méhul's *Euphrosine et Coradin* (1791). Zémaïde in Adrien Boieldieu's *Le calife de Bagdad* (1800) was another favourite role that she created; she took her farewell as Zémaïde in 1804 before an audience that included the Emperor Napoleon and Empress Joséphine. In that year the main performing troupes in Paris combined for her benefit at the Opéra. Greatly loved by audiences during her 30-year career, she gave her name to various types of role: 'jeune Dugazon' represents a light, soubrette-like but expressive Romantic role, such as she sang until the late 1780s, and 'mère Dugazon' for the more mature mezzo characters of her later career. The 'soprano dugazon', or soubrette in opéra comique, was light and agile in character, but neither virtuosic nor dramatic, and was named after Dugazon who was famous for her interpretations of such roles. A one-act opera by Charles Hess, Madame Dugazon, was performed at the Opéra-Comique in 1902. Three of her sisters sang and danced at the Opéra-Comique, and her son Gustav Dugazon was a composer.

Elizabeth Forbes/R

Duhan, Hans

(b Vienna, 27 Jan 1890; d Baden, nr Vienna, 6 March 1971). Austrian baritone. A singer with a thorough musical training (he studied the piano and the organ, as well as singing, at the Vienna Music Academy), he is remembered principally as the first artist to make complete recordings of Franz Schubert's Winterreise and Die schöne Müllerin. His career in opera, though it lasted from 1910 to 1940, was largely confined to Vienna and Salzburg, where in addition to the usual baritone roles in W.A. Mozart he sang Pedrillo in Die Entführung. He made his début at Troppau and joined the Vienna Staatsoper in 1914. At the première of Ariadne auf Naxos (1916, revised version) he doubled as the Music-Master and Harlequin. He was especially admired in Mozart and Albert Lortzing, but the overuse of his light baritone voice in operas such as Die Meistersinger led to vocal difficulties and encouraged him to concentrate on lieder and teaching (among his pupils was the baritone HERMANN UHDE). In later years he worked as stage director, conductor and composer. Recordings show a voice limited in colour as well as volume, though used with skill and intelligence.

J.B. Steane

Dumesnil [Duménil, Dumény, Du Mesny, du Mény]

(fl 1677–1700; d 1702). French tenor. His voice was discovered by Jean-Baptiste Lully, who had him trained successfully in deportment and gesture, but unsuccessfully in musical notation. He had 'une très belle représentation' and acted nobly, yet all his life learnt his roles by rote. He made his début in 1677 as Triton in Lully's Isis, and sang Alpheius (Lully's Proserpine, 1680) in Paris, taking over from CLEDIÈRE.

He created Perseus (Persée, 1682), Amadis (1684), Médor (Roland, 1685), Renaud (Armide, 1686) and Acis (Acis et Galatée, 1686) for Lully, as well as the roles of Achilles (Lully and Pascal Collasse's Achille et Polyxène, 1687), Peleus (Collasse's Thétis et Pélée, 1689), Aeneas, in both Enée et Lavinie (Collasse, 1690) and Didon (Henry Desmarets, 1693), Bacchus (Marin Marais' Ariane et Bacchus, 1696) and Amadis (André Destouches' Amadis de Grèce, 1699). Perhaps his greatest success was as Phaethon (Lully, 1683). He sang the title roles in revivals of Lully's Atys (1689 and 1699) and Thésée (1688 and 1698).

His sonorous and prodigiously high tenor voice enabled him to pass for an haute-contre: in fact he was an 'haute-taille, des plus hautes' (François Parfaict). His lack of technical musical ability apparently caused him to sing out of tune frequently, and he often appeared drunk on stage. He was obviously a gallant: the ribbons he took from the actrices de l'Opéra were many. However, he seems to have met his match in Mlle Maupin who, disguised as a man, ambushed and out-duelled him one night. She took his watch as a token with which to embarrass him the following day at the Opéra when he recounted the escapade. Dumesnil went to England to sing every Easter after the Académie season and returned each time with earnings of at least 1000 pistoles. He retired in 1700.

Philip Weller

Dun, Mlle

(b Paris; d Paris, 1713). Daughter of JEAN DUN (I) and sister of JEAN DUN (II). She made her début in the October 1708 revival of André Destouches' pastorale-héroïque Issé as the first of the Hesperides. According to the brothers Parfaict (Dictionnaire des théâtres de Paris, Paris, 1756), she was 'très applaudie' as a performer of minor roles. She appeared in Marin Marais' Sémélé (1709), Jean-Baptiste Stuck's Méléagre (1709) and Manto la fée (1711), André Campra's Hésione (1709), in Louise Bertin's Diomède (1710) and Joseph-Francois Salomon's Médée et Jason (1713). Like her father she appeared in several entrées of Les fêtes vénitiennes, creating a total of six roles between June and December 1710. She was described by the Parfaicts as possessing a figure 'peu gracieuse' but having a tender and delicate voice coupled with good taste in her singing.

James R. Anthony/R

Dun [née Catin], Mlle

(d after 1756). Wife of JEAN DUN (II). She entered the Opéra in 1721 and was employed as a member of the chorus, although on occasion she was assigned such minor roles as an Amazon in Jean-Baptiste Lully's *Bellérophon* (revival of 1728) and Terpsichore in Michel Pignolet de Montéclair's *Jephté* (1732).

James R. Anthony/R

Dun, Jean (i) [père]

(*d* Paris, 1735). French bass, father of JEAN DUN (ii) and MLLE DUN. His career at the Opéra, spanning 36 years, began in 1684 when he created the roles of Arcalaus and Florestan in Jean-Baptiste Lully's *Amadis*. He appeared in more than 37 operas, often playing more than one character in the same work: in André Campra's *opéra-ballet Les fêtes vénitiennes*, for example, he created roles in three entrées. He often reappeared in revivals over several years: he created the roles of Jupiter and the Oracle in Pascal Collasse's *Thétis et Pélée* in 1689, repeating them in 1699, and in the revivals of 1708 and 1712 he sang as a triton. He retired from the Opéra in 1720 after creating the role of Fabio in 1718 in the entrée 'La vieillesse'from Campra's *opéra-ballet Les âges*.

James R. Anthony/R

Dun, Jean (ii) [fils]

(*b* Paris; *d* 1772). Bass. Son of JEAN DUN, also a bass, and brother of MLLE DUN. He made his début at the Opéra singing in the trio of fates in a revival of Jean-Baptiste Lully's *Isis* in 1717. In 1718 he created Valère in André Campra's *Les âges*, singing opposite his father in the same entrée. Highly regarded, he sang in more than 20 operas, often appearing in more than one role in the same work. He created roles in four operas by Jean-Philippe Rameau: Jupiter and Pluto in *Hippolyte et Aricie* (1733), Osman-Bacha (*Les Indes galantes*, 1735), Jupiter in *Castor et Pollux* (1737), and Hymas and Eurilas (*Les fêtes d'Hébé*, 1739). A 1738 inventory of the Opéra described him thus: 'good musician, sings well, but he has not got a clear voice' (see G. Sadler, *EMc*). He retired from the Opéra as a singer in 1741 and soon afterwards joined the orchestra there, playing the bass viol until 1759. His wife, also known as MLLE DUN (née Catin), sang minor roles with the Opéra.

G. Sadler, *EMc*, xi, 1983, pp.453–67

James R. Anthony

Duncan, (Robert) Todd

(*b* Danville, KY, 12 Feb 1903; *d* Washington DC, 28 Feb 1998). American baritone. After attend-

ing Butler University, Indianapolis (BA 1925), and Columbia University Teachers College (MA 1930), he joined the voice faculty of Howard University in Washington, DC, where he remained until 1945. He made his début in 1934 as Alfio in *Cavalleria rusticana* with the Aeolian Opera in New York, and later became the first black member of the New York City Opera, where he first appeared as Tonio (1945). Also active in musical theatre, he created Porgy in George Gershwin's *Porgy and Bess* at the Alvin Theatre, New York (1935). He appeared in the London production of *The Sun Never Sets* (1938) and as the Lord's General in Vernon Duke's *Cabin in the Sky* (1940, New York); his performance as Stephen Kumalo in Kurt Weill's *Lost in the Stars* (1949–50) won him the Donaldson and New York Drama Critics' awards in 1950. Duncan also made two films, *Syncopation* (1942) and *Unchained* (1955).

R. Abdul: *Blacks in Classical Music* (New York, 1977)
P. Turner: *Afro-American Singers* (Minneapolis, 1977)

Dominique-René De Lerma

Duparc, Elisabeth ['Francesina']

(*d* 1773). French soprano. Trained in Italy, she sang in several operas at Florence in 1731 and 1734–5. In 1736 she was engaged by the Opera of the Nobility for London, making her King's Theatre début in Johann Hasse's *Siroe*, and singing in operas by Riccardo Broschi, Giovanni Battista Pescetti, Francesco Veracini and Egidio Duni. The following season (1737–8) she appeared in operas by Pescetti and Veracini, the G.F. Handel pasticcio *Alessandro Severo* (Sallustia) and Handel's new operas *Faramondo* (Clotilde) and *Serse* (Romilda). From then she was known almost exclusively as a Handel singer. She was his leading soprano at the King's Theatre in early 1739 and 1744–5, at Lincoln's Inn Fields in 1739–40 and 1740–41 and at Covent Garden in early 1744 and 1746. She sang in many oratorios (including the first performances of Handel's *Saul* (Michal) and *Israel in Egypt*), probably in *Giove in Argo* (1739), in the *Ode for St Cecilia's Day* and *L'Allegro* (1739–40), *Imeneo* (Rosmene) and *Deidamia* (title role) in 1740–41, *Semele* (title role) and *Joseph and his Brethren* (Asenath) in 1744, *Hercules* (Iole) and *Belshazzar* (Nitocris) in 1745 and the *Occasional Oratorio* in 1746. She also sang in both the English and bilingual versions of *Acis and Galatea*, the title roles in *Esther* and *Deborah* and in *Alexander's Feast* and *Messiah*. At the second performance of *Israel in Egypt* (11 April 1739) Handel added three Italian arias and one English aria for her. Though seldom heard at concerts, she had a part in a 'New Eclogue'

*Elisabeth Duparc
(Francesina)
with the composer
George Frideric
Handel*

by Veracini at the New Haymarket Theatre on 9 March 1741 and sang Handel arias at the annual Musicians Fund benefit at Covent Garden on 10 April 1745. In January 1752 she took part in a concert at the Great Room, Dean Street. She was also a painter.

Francesina's bright soprano improved greatly under Handel's tuition, and she became a worthy successor to STRADA and even CUZZONI. Many of her arias resemble Cuzzoni's in their demand for rapid and agile decoration, frequent trills and a melodious warbling style; Handel gave her several bird songs. His high opinion of her powers of characterization and all-round musicianship is clear from the many superb parts he wrote for her. Charles Burney ranked her as a singer of the second

class, but also wrote of 'her lark-like execution', 'a light, airy, pleasing movement, suited to [her] active throat'. Her compass was *c'* to *b''*.

Winton Dean

Duperron(-Duprez), Alexandrine.

Soprano, wife of GILBERT DUPREZ.

Duprez, Caroline

(*b* Florence, 10 April 1832; *d* Pau, 17 April 1874). French soprano. The daughter of GILBERT DUPREZ and Alexandrine Duperron, she made her début, as Ines, at Reims. She appeared with her father in Paris and other French cities, and then London (1851). In 1852 she went to the Opéra-Comique, where she appeared in a number of premières, including Giacomo Meyerbeer's *L'étoile du Nord* (1854).

Duprez, Gilbert(-Louis)

(*b* Paris, 6 Dec 1806; *d* Paris, 23 Sept 1896). French tenor and composer. He sang as a treble in François-Joseph Fétis's incidental music to Jean Racine's *Athalie* at the Comédie-Française and later studied with Alexandre Choron. His début at the Odéon (*Il barbiere di Siviglia*, 1825) and the première of his opera *La cabane du pêcheur* at Versailles the next year met with mixed success; he continued his studies in Italy after the Odéon closed in 1828. He soon distinguished himself as a *tenore di grazia*, but revealed his gifts as a dramatic tenor in Vincenzo Bellini's *Il pirata* at Turin in 1831. In the service of the impresario Alessandro Lanari, he enjoyed an almost uninterrupted run of successes in leading romantic roles, beginning with Arnold in the Italian première of *Guillaume Tell* (1831, Lucca), where he was the first tenor to sing the top high C as a chest note. Duprez scored a triumph as Percy in Gaetano Donizetti's *Anna Bolena* in Florence in 1831 (repeating his success at his first appearance in Rome in 1834), before going on to create further Donizetti roles there – Ugo in *Parisina* (1833) and Henry II in *Rosmonda d'Inghilterra* (1834). The highlight of his stay in Italy was perhaps his creation of Edgardo in *Lucia di Lammermoor* (1835, Naples); apparently he advised his close friend Donizetti on the structure and composition of the last scene. With the interpretation of these roles his voice became progressively darker.

Returning to France, he was engaged at the Opéra, where he made his début in *Guillaume Tell* (1837), achieving immediate and overwhelming success with Paris audiences. His 'chest' C, in spite of the disappointment of Gioachino Rossini, who compared it to 'the squawk of a capon with its throat cut', aroused wild enthusiasm and affected the taste of the public, who would listen to *Guillaume Tell* only when Duprez was singing. He created leading roles in Fromental Halévy's *Guido e Ginevra* (1838), *La reine de Chypre* (Gérard, 1841) and *Charles VI* (Duke of Bedford, 1843), Hector Berlioz's *Benvenuto Cellini* (title role, 1838), Daniel Auber's *Le lac des fées* (Albert, 1839), Donizetti's *Les martyrs* (Polyeucte, 1840), *La favorite* (Fernand, 1840) and *Dom Sébastien* (title role, 1843) and Giuseppe Verdi's *Jérusalem* (Gaston, 1847), and established himself as NOURRIT's successor in *Robert le diable*, *Les Huguenots*, *La Juive* and *La muette de Portici*. He also sang in London (1844–5, *Lucia*) and toured Germany (1850). He taught at the Paris Conservatoire (1842–50) and in 1853 founded

his Ecole Spéciale de Chant. Among his many students were EMMA ALBANI, CAROLINE CARVALHO, ADÈLE ISAAC and ALBERT NIEMANN.

According to the critic P. Scudo, Duprez was already outstanding as a student for the breadth and incisiveness of his phrasing, though his voice then was not large. Gradually he became the first great *tenore di forza*, despite a vocal tessitura limited in its lower range (as shown in his refusal to sing Pollione in *Norma* at Rome in 1834). In France he was praised as the first true Romantic tenor and for his excellent declamation and the smoothness of his *canto spianato*; but his acting style was said to be exaggerated. Presumably through forcing his voice, and also because of the great number of performances he gave during his years in Italy where he had to sing as many as six times a week, a decline set in early; Berlioz greatly admired him in the vigorous music of *Benvenuto Cellini* in 1838, though noting (*Mémoires*) that his voice had coarsened somewhat. The story of the famous tenor's rise and fall in Berlioz's *Les soirées de l'orchestre* is largely based on Duprez's career. He composed a number of operas throughout his career, and his writings include *L'art du chant* (1845) and *Souvenirs d'un chanteur* (1880), a valuable account of his times and distinguished contemporaries.

In 1827 he married Alexandrine Duperron (*d* 1872), a soprano who made her début at the Odéon that same year. She had a reasonably successful career, often singing with her husband during the Italian period. Her repertory included Imogene in *Il pirata* (1831, Turin) and Adalgisa (1834, Rome), a role in which she was warmly applauded. She retired from the stage about 1837. Their daughter CAROLINE DUPREZ was a *soprano leggero* who also sang with her father.

Sandro Corti

Dupuy, Martine

(*b* Marseilles, 10 Dec 1952). French mezzo-soprano. She studied in Marseilles, and after winning several international singing competitions she sang Eurydice in André Campra's *Le carnaval de Venise* at Aix-en-Provence in 1975. At Martina Franca (1976–86) she sang Isaura (*Tancredi*), Ismene (Tommaso Traetta's *Antigona*), Vincenzo Bellini's Romeo, which became one of her finest roles, Lady Pamela (*Fra Diavolo*), Arsace (*Semiramide*) and G.F. Handel's Julius Caesar. She made her Metropolitan début in 1988 as Handel's Sextus. Dupuy's other roles include Claudio Monteverdi's Nero, Octavia and Penelope, W.A. Mozart's Sextus and Cecilius (*Lucio Silla*), Antonio Vivaldi's Pharnaces, Bellini's Adalgisa,

Nancy (*Martha*), Ada (Gaetano Donizetti's *Il diluvio universale*), Armide (C.W. Gluck), Charlotte, Nicklausse and Giulietta (*Les contes d'Hoffmann*), Eboli and Mother Marie (*Dialogues des Carmélites*), which she has also recorded. However, her impeccable style, smoothly produced voice and strong coloratura technique are best displayed in her bel canto repertory, which embraces such roles as Gioachino Rossini's Arsace, Cenerentola, Rosina, Isabella, Néocles (*Le siège de Corinthe*) and Malcolm (*La donna del lago*), which she sang at La Scala (1992) and has recorded, Donizetti's Maffio Orsini and Jane Seymour, and Adalgisa in *Norma*.

Elizabeth Forbes

Durastanti, Margherita

(*fl* 1700–34). Italian soprano. Her first known appearances were in a pasticcio at Venice in 1700 and in two operas at Mantua (where she may have been in court service) in 1700–01. From 1707 she was in the service of Marquis Ruspoli at Rome, her colleagues including Antonio Caldara and G.F. Handel, who composed for her many of his finest solo cantatas and the part of Magdalene in the oratorio *La Resurrezione*. She was prima donna at the S Giovanni Grisostomo theatre in Venice, 1709–12, where she sang in nine operas by Antonio Lotti and C.F. Pollarolo and created the title part in Handel's *Agrippina* (1709). She sang at Bologna and Reggio nell'Emilia in 1710–11, Milan and Reggio nell'Emilia again in 1713, Parma in 1714, Florence in 1715, and in 1715–16 in five operas at Naples, including Alessandro Scarlatti's *Carlo rè d'Alemagna* and *La virtù trionfante*. Francesco Veracini engaged her for Dresden in 1719. Handel heard her there singing Gismonda in Lotti's *Teofane*, and he engaged her for the Royal Academy in London, where she made her début in the first production, Bernardo Porta's *Numitore*, in 1720, and played the title roles in Handel's *Radamisto* and Domenico Scarlatti's *Narciso*. The following season she sang in Giovanni Bononcini's *Astarto*, the revival of *Radamisto* (now as Zenobia; her old role was taken by SENESINO), *Arsace* (by Giuseppe Orlandini and Filippo Amadei), the composite *Muzio Scevola* and *Odio ed amore*.

In February 1721 Durastanti bore a daughter (she was married to one Casimiro Avelloni), to whom King George I and the Princess Royal stood as godparents on 2 March, and in the autumn she was singing in Munich. She missed the London season that year owing to illness, but returned in 1722–4, appearing in Handel's *Floridante* (Rossane), *Ottone*, *Flavio* and *Giulio Cesare*, and in operas by Bononcini and Attilio Ariosti. She was singing in Paris in summer 1724. She rejoined Handel's company in 1733–4, singing in *Ottone*, *Sosarme*, *Il pastor fido*, *Arianna* and several pasticcios. Durastanti had a longer personal association with Handel than any other singer. The operatic parts he wrote for her – Agrippina, Radamisto, Cloelia in *Muzio Scevola* (1721), Gismonda in *Ottone* (1723), Vitige in *Flavio* (1723), Sextus in *Giulio Cesare* (1724) and Tauride in *Arianna* (1734) – show an exceptionally wide range of character, suggesting that she was a gifted actress. Her voice was never a high soprano, and its compass gradually dropped from *d'–a"* in *Agrippina* to *b–g"* in 1733–4, when her tessitura was that of a mezzo-soprano. She frequently played male roles. Charles Burney said that her 'person was coarse and masculine', but she seems to have been a dramatic singer and a good musician.

Winton Dean

Duval, Denise

(*b* Paris, 23 Oct 1921). French soprano. She made her début at Bordeaux in 1943 as Lola (*Cavalleria rusticana*), then appeared at the Folies Bergères. In 1947 she made her début at the Opéra-Comique as Butterfly and was chosen by Francis Poulenc to create Thérèse in *Les mamelles de Tirésias*, a role written with her charm and intelligence in mind. At the Opéra-Comique she also created Francesca in Reynaldo Hahn's *Le oui des jeunes filles* (1949). At the Opéra (where she made her début in 1947 as Salome in *Hérodiade*), she sang Thaïs, Rosenn (*Le roi d'Ys*), the Princess in Henri Rabaud's *Mârouf*, Portia in Hahn's *Le marchand de Venise*, Maurice Ravel's Concepción, and sang Blanche in the Paris première of *Dialogues des Carmélites* (1957). She created Elle in *La voix humaine* (1959, Opéra-Comique), a vulnerable, subtle portrayal of a part admirably suited to her gifts, and repeated the role in the American première at Carnegie Hall and the British première with the Glyndebourne company at Edinburgh (1960). At Glyndebourne she sang an affecting and ideally waif-like Mélisande (1962). She is also a famous Ciboulette. A very beautiful woman with great dramatic intelligence, Duval was a most gifted singing actress, as the roles composed for her by Poulenc demonstrate. She recorded all three of these roles, together with a delightful Concepción in André Cluytens's set of *L'heure espagnole*. She retired in 1965 due to ill health.

André Tubeuf, Elizabeth Forbes

Dux, Claire

(*b* Witkowicz, 2 Aug 1885; *d* Chicago, 8 Oct 1967). Polish soprano. She studied in Berlin and made her début in Cologne as Pamina in 1906. From 1911 to 1918 she was a member of the Royal Opera, Berlin, where she sang the leading lyrical German and Italian roles. In 1911 she sang in Britain for the first time, with Thomas Beecham at His Majesty's Theatre, and in 1913 she was Covent Garden's first Sophie in *Der Rosenkavalier*. In 1921 she went to the USA, where she appeared frequently with the Chicago Civic Opera, also making concert tours throughout the country. After a brief return to Germany she settled in Chicago and retired from the stage, but still sang occasionally in concerts. Dux's voice was a lyric soprano of the utmost purity, controlled by a firm technique, and capable of exquisite *pianissimo*. She was admired as an actress, and her Sophie, Eva and Pamina were particularly distinguished. In later years her lieder singing was much praised, but on the evidence of her records her style in this field was not as faultless as in opera. Beecham called her 1914 Drury Lane Pamina 'the most exquisite exhibition of bel canto that London has heard for more than a generation' (*A Mingled Chime*, London, 1944).

Alan Blyth

Dvorsky, Peter

(*b* Partizánske, nr Topol'čany, 27 Sept 1951). Slovak tenor. He studied at the Bratislava Conservatory and the Scuola della Scala in Milan. After his début, with the Bratislava opera in 1972 as Lensky, he won the Moscow Tchaikovsky Competition in 1974 and the Geneva International Competition the next year. He first sang at the Vienna Staatsoper in 1977 (the Italian Singer in *Der Rosenkavalier*), and appeared as Alfredo at the Metropolitan Opera the same year. In 1978 Dvorsky sang Rodolfo at La Scala and the Duke in *Rigoletto* at Covent Garden, returning in 1988 as Lensky and as Riccardo (*Un ballo in maschera*); he has also appeared at the Bol'shoy, at the Teatro Colón, Buenos Aires, and with the Chicago Lyric Opera as well as in most major European centres, including Salzburg (Cavaradossi, 1989) and Edinburgh (Faust, 1990). He deploys his lyric tenor with strong dramatic feeling and much tonal beauty, if variable technique. He has recorded several operas by Gaetano Donizetti, Giacomo Puccini and Giuseppe Verdi, and has been particularly admired in his recordings of Czech operas, including Leoš Janáček's *Jenůfa* and *The Makropulos Affair* and Eugen Suchoň's *The Whirlpool*.

Noël Goodwin

E

Eaglen, Jane

(*b* Lincoln, 4 April 1960). English soprano. She studied with Joseph Ward at the RNCM, Manchester, making her début in 1984 with the ENO as Lady Ella (*Patience*). Other roles for the ENO have included Donna Elvira, Sinais (*Mosè*), Elizabeth I (*Maria Stuarda*), Leonora (*Il trovatore*), Eva, Micaëla, Santuzza, Tosca, Fata Morgana (*The Love for Three Oranges*) and Ariadne. She made her Covent Garden début in 1986 as Berta (*Il barbiere*), returning as First Lady (*Die Zauberflöte*). For Scottish Opera she has sung Mimì, Fiordiligi, Donna Anna, Brünnhilde (*Die Walküre*) and Norma (1993). Embarking on an international career, Eaglen sang Mathilde (*Guillaume Tell*) in Geneva, W.A. Mozart's Electra, Senta, Brünnhilde and Donna Anna at the Vienna Staatsoper, Brünnhilde at La Scala and in Chicago, and Norma at Ravenna (1994), where she returned as Abigaille (*Nabucco*) in 1995; that year she also sang Amelia (*Ballo in maschera*) at the Opéra-Bastille in Paris and Odabella (*Attila*) in Houston. In 1996 she made her Metropolitan début as Donna Anna and sang Brünnhilde in a complete *Ring* cycle in Chicago. Eaglen sang her first Isolde, to great critical acclaim, in Seattle in 1998. In 2000 she sang a majestic Turandot at the Metropolitan, repeating the role at Covent Garden the following year. She has recorded *Norma* (a notably fiery interpretation), *Tosca* and Simon Mayr's *Medea in Corinto*. Though her voice, vibrant, powerful and dramatic, has the stamina required for Wagner, it retains the legato line and flexibility for bel canto roles.

H. Finch: 'Jane Eaglen', *Opera*, xlvi (1995), 511–16
M.J. White: 'The Norma Conquest', *ON*, lx (1996), 18–21

Elizabeth Forbes

Eames, Emma

(*b* Shanghai, 13 Aug 1865; *d* New York, 13 June 1952). American soprano. After early studies in Boston and with MATHILDE MARCHESI in Paris, she made a brilliant début at the Opéra on 13 March 1889 as Charles Gounod's Juliet, with JEAN DE RESZKE. In 1890 she created Colombe in Camille Saint-Saëns's *Ascanio*. After two seasons in Paris, she made both her Covent Garden and her Metropolitan débuts in 1891. During the following decade she sang leading roles in W.A. Mozart, Richard Wagner, Gounod and Giuseppe Verdi in London and New York, continuing at the Metropolitan until her farewell to the house, as Tosca, in 1909. Eames's unexpected retirement from the operatic stage came while she was still at the height of her powers. Her lyric soprano was of singularly pure and beautiful quality, and her technique was masterly. Although sometimes considered cold in timbre and temperament, she was nevertheless admired in such emotional roles as Sieglinde and Tosca. The best of her recordings, including arias from *Roméo et Juliette*, *Faust* and *Tosca*, and Franz Schubert's 'Gretchen am Spinnrade', reveal considerable fullness and power as well as the expected technical perfection.

E. Eames: *Some Memories and Reflections* (New York, 1927/ R) [with discography]
L. Migliorini and J. Dennis: 'Emma Eames', *Record Collector*, viii (1953), 74–96 [with discography and commentary]
A.F.R. Lawrence and S. Smolian: 'Emma Eames', *American Record Guide*, xxix (1962), 210–17 [with discography and commentary]

Desmond Shawe-Taylor/Alan Blyth

Easton, Florence

(*b* Middlesbrough-on-Tees, 25 Oct 1884; *d* New York, 13 Aug 1955). English soprano. She studied in Paris and London, and made her début as the Shepherd in *Tannhäuser* (1903, Newcastle upon Tyne). She toured North America with H.W. Savage's English Grand Opera Company (1905–7); both she and her husband, the American tenor Francis MacLennan, were then engaged at the Berlin Hofoper, 1907 to 1913, and for the following three years at the Hamburg Städtische Oper. Before World War I, Easton made only a few Covent Garden appearances, notably as Butterfly in 1909. In November 1915 she sang at Chicago in *Siegfried*, and two years later began her long and fruitful association with the Metropolitan Opera, which lasted without interruption until 1929. Her pure tone, sound technique and excellent musicianship singled her out even in the brilliant assembly of singers collected by Giulio Gatti-Casazza. She was immensely versatile, with a repertory ranging from Brünnhilde to Carmen and the reputed ability to appear at a moment's notice in any one of over 100 roles. At the Metropolitan she sang some 35 roles, among them Lauretta in the première of

Emma Eames,
1895

Giacomo Puccini's *Gianni Schicchi* (14 December 1918). She made isolated reappearances at Covent Garden, as Turandot in 1927, and as Isolde and the *Siegfried* Brünnhilde with MELCHIOR in 1932. She gave her farewell performance, at the Metropolitan, on 29 February 1936 as Brünnhilde in *Die Walküre*, receiving an ovation for her still splendid singing and interpretation. Her art is adequately represented on disc, notably her final duet from *Siegfried* with Melchior.

J. Stratton: 'Florence Easton', *Record Collector*, xxi (1973–4), 195–239, 256 [with discography]

Desmond Shawe-Taylor/R

Eda-Pierre, Christiane

(*b* Fort de France, Martinique, 24 March 1932). Martinique soprano. She studied in Paris, making her début in 1958 at Nice as Leïla (*Les pêcheurs de perles*). She sang Pamina at Aix-en-Provence (1959), Lakmé at the Opéra-Comique (1961) and made her début at the Paris Opéra (1962) as Fatima (Jean-Philippe Rameau's *Les Indes galantes*). In 1964 she took part in the first public performance of Rameau's *Les boréades* at La Maison de la Radio, Paris. In Chicago (1966–76) she sang Leïla, Igor Stravinsky's Nightingale and Antonia (*Les contes d'Hoffmann*), and at Wexford Lakmé (1970) and Imogene in *Il pirata* (1976). Having sung Countess Almaviva with the Paris Opéra at the

Metropolitan (1976), she made her début with the Metropolitan company as Konstanze (1980), and in Brussels (1982–4) sang three further Mozart roles: Electra, Vitellia and Donna Elvira. She created the Angel in Olivier Messiaen's *Saint François d'Assise* at the Opéra in 1983 (a part she later recorded) and sang the title role in Robert Schumann's *Genoveva* on its French stage première at Montpellier (1985). With an attractive stage personality and a highly flexible voice, Eda-Pierre excelled above all in coloratura roles such as Konstanze (of which she made an admired recording with Colin Davis), the Queen of Night, Zerbinetta, Olympia, which she sang at Salzburg (1980), and Catharine Glover (*La jolie fille de Perth*), which she recorded for the BBC. She was also a fine interpreter of modern music and created several works specially written for her: Pierre Capdevielle's *Les amants captifs* (1960) and Gilbert Amy's *D'un espace déployé* (1973); Charles Chaynes' cantata *Pour un monde noir* (1978) and his monologue *Erzébet* (1983).

Elizabeth Forbes

Eddy, Nelson

(*b* Providence, RI, 29 June 1901; *d* Miami Beach, 6 March 1967). American baritone and actor. He moved with his family in 1915 to Philadelphia, where he studied singing with DAVID BISPHAM. He made his début in a musical play (*The Marriage Tax*) at the Philadelphia Academy of Music in 1922, and also sang roles with the Philadelphia Civic Opera and the Philadelphia Operatic Society before appearing at the Metropolitan Opera House in 1924. He spent the years 1928 to 1933 giving concert tours throughout the USA. He made his first film in 1933 and achieved fame two years later when he starred with JEANETTE MACDONALD in *Naughty Marietta*, the success of which led to their appearing together in seven further film musicals, including *Rose Marie* (1936), *Maytime* (1937), *New Moon* (1940) and *Bitter Sweet* (1940). Eddy made several recordings and continued to perform on radio, television and in concerts up to the time of his death.

'Eddy, Nelson', *CBY 1943*
E. Knowles: *The Films of Jeanette MacDonald and Nelson Eddy* (South Brunswick, NJ, 1975)

Robert Skinner

Edelmann, Otto

(*b* Brunn am Gebirge, nr Vienna, 5 Feb 1917; *d* Vienna, 14 May 2003). Austrian bass-baritone. He studied in Vienna with Theodore Lierhammer and

Grüner Graarud, making his début in 1937 at Gera as W.A. Mozart's Figaro. From 1938 to 1940 he was engaged at Nuremberg. In 1947 he joined the Vienna Staatsoper, where he made his début as the Hermit (*Der Freischütz*). At the first two postwar Bayreuth festivals (1951, 1952) he sang Hans Sachs, recording the role in 1951 with Herbert von Karajan; he again sang Sachs at the Edinburgh Festival (1952, with the Hamburg Opera) and at his Metropolitan début (1954). He sang Ochs in the first opera performance in the new Grosses Festspielhaus, Salzburg, in 1960. His repertory also included Leporello, Rocco, Amfortas, King Henry (*Lohengrin*), Gurnemanz, Plunkett (*Martha*) and Dulcamara. Apart from his genial Hans Sachs, his recordings include an exuberant Ochs in Karajan's famous 1956 *Rosenkavalier* and Pizarro in Wilhelm Furtwängler's 1953 *Fidelio*.

Harold Rosenthal/Alan Blyth

Edvina [Martin], (Marie) Louise (Lucienne Juliette)

(*b* Montreal, 1880; *d* London, 13 Nov 1948). Canadian soprano. She studied with JEAN DE RESZKE in Paris. She made her début as Marguerite (*Faust*) in 1908 at Covent Garden, where she sang every season until 1914, and again in 1919, 1920 and 1924. She was the first London Louise, Thaïs, Maliella (*I gioielli della Madonna*), Francesca da Rimini (Riccardo Zandonai) and Fiora in *L'amore dei tre re* (Italo Montemezzi). Her repertory also included Tosca, Desdemona and Mélisande. She sang with the Boston Opera (1911–13), appearing also in its Paris season in 1914; in Chicago (1915–17); and once at the Metropolitan (1915) as Tosca. Her last operatic performance was in that role at Covent Garden in 1924. Her pure, refined singing was enhanced by her attractive stage personality. Among her recordings, her 'Depuis le jour' from *Louise* stands out for its delicacy and imagination.

H.H. Harvey: 'Maria Louise Edvina', *Gramophone*, xxx (1952–3), 7 [with discography]

Harold Rosenthal/Alan Blyth

Egizziello.

See CONTI, GIOACCHINO.

Egmond, Max (Rudolf) van

(*b* Semarang, Java, 1 Feb 1936). Dutch bass-baritone. He studied at the Hilversum Muzieklyceum with Tine van Willigen, and won prizes in competitions at 's-Hertogenbosch, Brussels and Munich. He began his career in 1954 in the *St Matthew Passion* at Naarden and subsequently appeared as a concert singer and recitalist throughout Europe and North and South America. His operatic performances, mostly with Netherlands Opera, included the world première of Jurriaan Andriessen's *Het zwarte blondje* (1962), Antony Hopkins's *Three's Company* (1963), Quinault in *Adriana Lecouvreur* (1966), Pluto in Agostino Agazzari's *Eumelio* (1974) and Meraspes in G.F. Handel's *Admeto* (1977). He was professor of singing at the Amsterdam Muzieklyceum (1972–80) and at the Sweelinck Conservatorium Amsterdam (1980–95), where Peter Kooy was his pupil. In 1978 he became a professor at the Baroque Performance Institute, Oberlin, Ohio. He has also given master-classes in Baroque performance practice and the art of the lied. Egmond retired from public performance in 1995. His affinity with Baroque music, particularly that of J.S. Bach, and his thorough knowledge of authentic performance practice are reflected in his many recordings, notably of Bach cantatas (under Nikolaus Harnoncourt and Gustav Leonhardt) and the Passions, Claudio Monteverdi's *Orfeo* and *Il ritorno d'Ulisse*, Jean-Baptiste Lully's *Alceste* and Handel's *Admeto*. His warm, gentle timbre and superb diction are also well displayed in his recordings of Franz Schubert, including *Winterreise* with Jos van Immerseel, and Robert Schumann lieder.

Elizabeth Forbes/R

Ehrenbergů [Ehrenbergová], Eleanora

(*b* nr Prague, 1 Nov 1832; *d* Prague, 30 Aug 1912). Czech soprano. She made her debut at the Estates Theatre, Prague, as Lucia di Lammermoor, in 1854 and then appeared in coloratura roles in Stettin, Hamburg and Leipzig. In 1862 she returned to Prague as a member of the Czech company at the Provisional Theatre. Here she sang the role of Mařenka in the première of Bedřich Smetana's *The Bartered Bride*, conducted by the composer, in 1866. Two years later she created another Smetana role, Jitka in *Dalibor*. In the earlier part of her career, Ehrenbergů was admired in W.A. Mozart (as Konstanze, Donna Anna and Queen of the Night), Gioachino Rossini, Gaetano Donizetti and Giacomo Meyerbeer. During the 1870s and early 1880s, she undertook several roles by Giuseppe Verdi, and the part of Venus in Richard Wagner's *Tannhäuser*. She was also a distinguished concert singer.

Richard Wigmore

Elias, Rosalind

(*b* Lowell, MA, 13 March 1929). American mezzo-soprano. She studied at the New England Conservatory and while still a student appeared as Claudio Monteverdi's Poppaea. Further study at the Berkshire Music Center, Tanglewood, was followed by four years with the New England Opera Company, 1948–52. She then studied in Italy with Luigi Ricci and Nazareno de Angelis, sang at La Scala, and the S Carlo, Naples, and joined the Metropolitan in 1954. There she sang over 45 roles in more than 450 performances, and created roles in two operas by Samuel Barber: Erika in *Vanessa* (1958) and Charmian in *Antony and Cleopatra* (1966). She was much admired for her rich tone and clarity of vocal character as Cherubino, Octavian, Olga and Carmen. Her British stage début was with Scottish Opera as Gioachino Rossini's Cenerentola in 1970, and in 1975 she sang Baba the Turk at Glyndebourne. In the 1980s she directed several operas in the USA, including *Carmen*.

Noël Goodwin

Elizza, Elise [Letztergroschen, Elisabeth]

(*b* Vienna, 6 Jan 1870; *d* Vienna, 3 June 1926). Austrian soprano. Her teacher in Vienna was Adolf Limley, who became her husband. She sang first in operetta, then joined the opera company at Olomouc in 1894. The following year she made her début, as Inès in *L'Africaine*, at the Vienna Staatsoper, where she remained as a valued and versatile member of the company until 1919. Her roles there ranged from the Queen of Night to Brünnhilde, though she was probably happiest in the lyric-coloratura repertory, such as Violetta and Marguerite de Valois in *Les Huguenots*. She later taught in Vienna, where LOTTE LEHMANN was among her pupils. A prolific early recording artist, she reveals on records a voice of exceptional beauty with a highly accomplished technique and a sensitive style.

J.B. Steane

Elkins, Margreta [Geater, Margaret]

(*b* Brisbane, 16 Oct 1932). Australian mezzo-soprano. Her teachers included Pauline Bindley in Melbourne and Harold Williams in Sydney. She made her début as Carmen (1953, Brisbane) with the Sydney-based National Opera of Australia, followed by Azucena (1954), Suzuki and Siebel. In 1958 she became a resident principal at Covent Garden. She regularly partnered SUTHERLAND in *Norma*, as

Adalgisa, and in *Alcina*, as Ruggiero. She returned to Australia with the Sutherland-Williamson company (1965) and eventually became a member of the Australian Opera in 1976. Tall, with a commanding stage presence and a creamy, rounded voice with a soprano extension, she has excelled as Amneris, Octavian, Herodias, Maffio Orsini, Brangäne and Delilah. She was Helen in the first performances of *King Priam* (1962, Coventry and London).

Roger Covell

Ellis [Elsas], Mary

(*b* New York, 15 June 1900; *d* London, 30 Jan 2002). American soprano. After an operatic training she appeared in New York at the Metropolitan Opera House during the last days of World War I, where she created the role of the Novice in *Suor Angelica*, and later also sang Lauretta (*Gianni Schicchi*) during the first run of performances of *Il trittico*. She sang Giannetta to CARUSO's Nemorino and Fyodor to CHALIAPIN's Boris before turning to lighter music in 1924, when she created the title role in Oscar Hammerstein and Rudolf Friml's *Rose Marie*, and then began acting in plays and films. She was admired by Ivor Novello, who brought her to London to take the leading female role, that of opera singer Militza Hajos, in the first of his Drury Lane musicals, *Glamorous Night* (1935), whose success was partly due to Ellis's varied talents. Her operatic training showed in the strength and quality of her higher notes, and made her ideal as opera singer Maria Ziegler in Novello's *The Dancing Years* (1939). It was in this role that she introduced one of Novello's most poignant songs, 'My Dearest Dear', which was written to show the purity of her voice to its most dramatic effect. Her third role for Novello, as the opera singer Marie Foretin in *Arc de Triomphe* (1943), was less successful. She spent the rest of the war doing charitable work and afterwards moved into straight theatre, appearing as Mrs Crocker Harris in Terrence Rattigan's *The Browning Version* (1949). By the time she returned to musical theatre for Noël Coward's *After the Ball* (1954), her voice, though still attractive, had lost its original range and she accepted no further musical roles.

Ellis's continued popularity, despite the failure of *After the Ball*, rested on recordings of the Novello shows and the public's memory of her performances. During the 1930s she enjoyed the rare combination of a voice that was as comfortable in opera as in operetta, a glamorous appearance and an acting ability that allowed her to dominate such vast auditoriums as that of Drury Lane. Her autobiography was published as *Those Dancing Years* (London, 1982).

Paul Webb

Elming, Poul

(*b* Ålborg, 21 July 1949). Danish baritone, later tenor. He studied at the conservatories at Ålborg and Århus, and with Paul Lohmann at Wiesbaden, before making his début, as a member of the Jutland Opera, in Århus in 1979. He sang many leading baritone roles with the company, including Malatesta, Giorgio Germont and Posa, before retraining as a tenor at the Juilliard School in New York. Elming made his début as a tenor at the Royal Opera in Copenhagen in 1989 in the title role of *Parsifal*, adding Erik the same season. In 1990 he made his successful first appearance at the Bayreuth Festival as Siegmund. He has returned to Bayreuth in succeeding years either as Siegmund or as Parsifal, and also performed these roles at Covent Garden, the Berlin Staatsoper, the Vienna Staatsoper, Chicago, San Francisco and elsewhere. In 1994 he made his Covent Garden début, as Siegmund, and added Max (*Der Freischütz*) to his repertory in Madrid and Copenhagen. In 2000 he created the role of Luke in Poul Ruders's *The Handmaid's Tale* (*Tjenerindens Fortaelling*), at the Royal Danish Opera, Copenhagen. He has also appeared widely as a concert artist, particularly in works by Scandinavian composers. Elming's heroic, typically Scandinavian timbre and notable gifts as an interpreter can be heard and seen in Daniel Barenboim's recording of *Die Walküre* from Bayreuth (1992).

Alan Blyth

Elmo, Cloe

(*b* Lecca, 9 April 1910; *d* Ankara, 24 May 1962). Italian mezzo-soprano. She studied in Rome, making her début as Santuzza at Cagliari in 1934. She then sang Orpheus in Rome, and from 1936 to 1945 she was leading mezzo-soprano at La Scala, where her roles included Mistress Quickly, Ulrica, Azucena and the Princess (*Adriana Lecouvreur*). In 1947 she was engaged at the Metropolitan, and while in America was chosen by Arturo Toscanini to sing Mistress Quickly in his broadcast performance and recording of *Falstaff*. She returned to La Scala in 1951 and created roles in Lodovico Rocca's *L'uragano* and Juan José Castro's *Proserpina y el extranjero* (1952); she also created Moraima in Giorgio Ghedini's *Re Hassan* (1939, Venice) and Goneril in Vito Frazzi's *Re Lear* (1939, Florence), and sang Signora Susanna in the first staged performance of Gian Francesco Malipiero's *Il festino* (1954, Bergamo). She also sang works by J.S. Bach under Otto Klemperer and Bernardino Molinari. She had a richly coloured voice and a dynamic stage personality.

Harold Rosenthal/R

Elvira, Pablo

(*b* San Juan, 24 Sept 1938; *d* Bozeman, MT, 5 Feb 2000). Puerto Rican baritone. He enrolled in the Puerto Rico Conservatory (1960) to study the trumpet and singing; from 1966 when he was a finalist in the Metropolitan Opera auditions he devoted himself exclusively to singing. He taught at the Indiana University School of Music (1966–74), but left to perform in South America, Europe, Israel, Puerto Rico and the USA. He appeared with the New York City Opera and the Metropolitan, where he made his début as Tonio in 1979. Although he performed a wide repertory he had particular success as Figaro (Gioachino Rossini), Rigoletto, Tonio and Germont. Elvira's work was grounded in solid musicianship and artistic consistency; his voice was characterized by clarity, expressive phrasing and broad dramatic qualities.

Donald Thompson

Elwes, Gervase (Cary)

(*b* Billing Hall, Northampton, 15 Nov 1866; *d* nr Boston, MA, 12 Jan 1921). English tenor. He was educated at the Oratory School, Birmingham, and Christ Church, Oxford. He served in the diplomatic service from 1891 to 1895. After singing as an amateur, he studied in London and Paris. From 1903 he made professional appearances, singing at the leading provincial festivals besides giving solo recitals. He performed many new songs by Rebecca Clarke, Teresa del Riego and Lady Irène de Poldowski. In 1904, under Felix Weingartner in London, he first sang Edward Elgar's Gerontius, with which he became closely identified; in 1905 he gave the first performance of Roger Quilter's song cycle *To Julia* , and in 1909 of Ralph Vaughan Williams's, *On Wenlock Edge*. He also appeared in Germany, Belgium and the USA. He was on his way to an engagement at Harvard University when he was killed in a train accident. The high place that Elwes held among British singers owed more to a temperament sensitive to every implication of the music, as his few recordings reveal, than to his natural vocal gifts. The Musicians Benevolent Fund was founded in 1921 as the Gervase Elwes Memorial Fund.

W. and R. Elwes: *Gervase Elwes: the Story of his Life* (London, 1935)

J.N. Hyde: 'Gervase Elwes', *Record Collector*, xvii (1966–8), 182–9 [with discography]

J.A. Fuller Maitland, H.C. Colles/R

Elwes [Hahessy], John Joseph

(*b* London, 20 Oct 1946). English tenor. He studied in London with George Malcolm at Westminster Cathedral, where he was a chorister, and at the RCM. From the age of 14 he lived with the family of the tenor GERVASE ELWES (1866–1921) and later took their name. He made his début in 1968 at the Proms in Ralph Vaughan Williams's *Serenade to Music*. He has appeared in operas by Claudio Monteverdi, Jean-Philippe Rameau, G.F. Handel, C.W. Gluck and W.A. Mozart and in many others in concert performances. He sang the title roles in Monteverdi's *Orfeo* and *Il ritorno d'Ulisse in patria*, and Nerone in *L'incoronazione di Poppea*. His recordings of operas by Rameau have been widely acclaimed and include *Les Indes galantes* (1974), *Zaïs* (1977), *Pygmalion* (1981), *Le temple de la gloire* (1982) and *Zoroastre* (1983). Other recordings include Vaughan Williams's *The Pilgrim's Progress* (1972), Monteverdi's *Orfeo* (1974), Francesco Cavalli's *Serse* (1985), Antonio Vivaldi's *L'incoronazione di Dario* (1986) and Tomaso Albinoni's *Cleomene* (1988). Since the late 1970s he has lived in France and worked mainly on the Continent. His wide tessitura has made him much sought after in French Baroque opera, where an ability to sustain clarity and lyricism in exceptionally high registers is required.

Nicholas Anderson

Endrèze [Kraeckmann], Arthur

(*b* Chicago, 28 Nov 1893; *d* Chicago, 15 April 1975). American baritone. He studied in Paris with JEAN DE RESZKE and made his début in 1925 at Nice as Don Giovanni. In 1928 he sang Karnac in *Le roi d'Ys* at the Opéra-Comique, then in 1929 he was engaged at the Paris Opéra, making his début as Valentin (*Faust*). He also sang Nevers (*Les Huguenots*), Athanaël (*Thaïs*), Herod (*Hérodiade*), Hamlet, Mercutio, Telramund, Kurwenal, Iago, Amonasro, Germont and Rigoletto. He created Mosca in Henri Sauguet's *La chartreuse de Parme* (1939) and sang Creon in the first Paris performance of Darius Milhaud's *Médée* (1940). At Monte Carlo he sang Nilakantha (*Lakmé*), Scarpia and the Duke of Kilmarnock in Franco Alfano's *L'ultimo lord* (1932), and created Metternich in Arthur Honegger and Jacques Ibert's *L'aiglon* (1937). In 1946 he made his farewell at the Opéra as Jacob in Etienne-Nicolas Méhul's *Joseph*. He had a warm, lyrical voice especially well suited to the French repertory.

Elizabeth Forbes

Engel, Stientje.

See Deutekom, cristina.

Equiluz, Kurt

(*b* Vienna, 13 June 1929). Austrian tenor. He became alto soloist with the Vienna Boys' Choir, and studied music at the Music Academy. In 1950 he joined the State Opera Chorus and soon became a valued comprimario with Scaramuccio in *Ariadne auf Naxos*, a part he made his own, singing it also at Florence and Salzburg. He was admired for his cameos in *Die Meistersinger* (Balthasar Zorn) and as Pedrillo in *Die Entführung*. His distinctive, well-focussed voice can be heard in several small roles on records (including Scaramuccio in the famous recording with Herbert von Karajan), but the most memorable part of his legacy is probably his singing of the Evangelist in J.S. Bach's Passions and his contributions to the complete cycle of Bach cantatas directed by Nikolaus Harnoncourt and Gustav Leonhardt. Equiluz was professor of oratorio at Graz from 1964 to 1981, when he joined the Vienna Music Academy to teach oratorio and lieder. He continued to give recitals well into his 60s.

J.B. Steane

Karl Erb in the title role of 'Parsifal' (Wagner)

Erb, Karl

(*b* Ravensburg, 13 July 1877; *d* Ravensburg, 13 July 1958). German tenor. Entirely self-taught (he was a civil servant until his voice was discovered), he made his début in Wilhelm Kienzl's *Der Evangelimann* at Stuttgart on 14 June 1907. From 1908 to 1910 he gained valuable experience at Lübeck before returning to Stuttgart for the seasons 1910–12. In 1913 he joined the Hofoper in Munich, after a successful guest appearance as Lohengrin. His reputation grew rapidly as he matured and increased his repertory, which eventually numbered some 70 parts (including the principal Mozart roles and *Parsifal, Euryanthe, Der Corregidor,* and *Iphigénie en Aulide*). A highpoint in his career was the first performance of Hans Pfitzner's *Palestrina* in 1917, in which he took the title role with great distinction. He left Munich in 1925 but continued to give guest performances in opera until 1930 (his last role was Florestan under Wilhelm Furtwängler in Berlin). From that time he devoted himself entirely to lieder and concert singing, though he had long been admired for his renditions of the songs of Franz Schubert and Hugo Wolf in particular; he was also famous for his interpretation of the Evangelist in the Bach Passions. In 1927 he and his wife, maria Ivogün, sang the princi-pal roles in *Die Entführung aus dem Serail* at Covent Garden.

Erb continued to sing and record at an advanced age. To fine natural musicianship he added incomparable diction. His voice was soft-grained yet powerful and from an early age it seems to have had the distinctive nasal quality evident in the recordings of his middle and later years. Though he made all too few recordings in his prime, some notable treasures have been preserved. These include his Evangelist in Günther Ramin's abridged recording of the *St Matthew Passion* (1941) and the title role of Wolf's *Der Corregidor* (made in 1944), as well as sensitive and moving accounts of lieder by Schubert, Robert Schumann, Johannes Brahms and Wolf (for the Hugo Wolf Society). Among writers who paid tribute to Karl Erb were Romain Rolland and Thomas Mann – in the latter's novel *Dr Faustus* Erb may be recognized as the model for Erbe, the 'tenor of almost castrato heights', who in masterly fashion sang the role of the narrator in Adrian Leverkühn's oratorio *Apocalipsis cum figuris* under Otto Klemperer in a fictitious ISCM concert at Frankfurt in 1926.

Peter Branscombe

Eremans [Erremans, Heremance], Mlle

(*fl* 1721–43). French soprano. She made her début in the 1721 revival of André Destouches' *Issé* as First Hesperides in the prologue and was immediately praised for her light, beautiful and flexible voice. In the 1721 revival of Jean-Baptiste Lully's *Phaëton* she sang Astraea in the prologue to the Saturn of the young Claude Chassé. She sang the title role in three performances of *Armide* (1724), for which she was praised by Mlle Le rochois, but did not generally take such dramatic roles: her Phaedra in the 1742 revival of Jean-Philippe Rameau's *Hippolyte et Aricie* was an exception. She created Venus in both François Francoeur's and François Rebel's *Pirame et Thisbé* (1726) and Rameau's *Dardanus* (1739), and Hébé in Rameau's *Les Indes galantes* (1735). She also sang in the opéra-ballet *Les fêtes nouvelles* at the Paris Opéra in 1734. A frequent understudy and replacement for Mlle Antier, she retired in 1743. Eremans was married to FRANÇOIS LE PAGE.

Philip Weller

Ericson, Barbro

(*b* Halmstad, 2 April 1930). Swedish mezzo-soprano. She studied in Stockholm, making her début there in 1956 as Eboli with the Royal Opera, of which she was a member for over 20 years. She appeared with the Stockholm company at Covent Garden (1960) as Mary (*Der fliegende Holländer*) and at Expo Montreal (1967) as Ulrica and Baba the Turk. At Bayreuth she sang Venus and Kundry (1964). She made her début at the Metropolitan Opera in 1968 as Fricka. Her repertory included Amneris, Nicklausse, Carmen, Brangäne, Ortrud, Suzuki, Herodias and Leda, which she sang in the Swedish première of Richard Rodney Bennett's *The Mines of Sulphur* (1967, Stockholm). Among her later roles were Mistress Quickly, Magdelone (*Maskarade*), Madame de Croissy (*Dialogues des Carmélites*) and Clytemnestra, which she sang at Madrid (1981). A singer of great intensity with an opulent, rich-toned voice, she was an excellent comic actress, as she demonstrated in the première of György Ligeti's *Le Grand Macabre* (1978), when she created Mescalina.

Elizabeth Forbes

Ershov (Ershoff), Ivan Vasil'yevich.

See YERSHOV, IVAN VASIL'YEVICH.

Escalaïs, Léon [Léonce-Antoine]

(*b* Cuxac d'Aude, nr Toulouse, 8 Aug 1859; *d* Paris, Nov 1941). French tenor. He studied at the Paris Conservatoire and made his début in 1882 at the Théâtre du Château d'Eau in Frédéric Duvernoy's *Sardanapale*. The following year he was engaged by the Opéra, where one of his most successful roles was that of Arnold in *Guillaume Tell*. He had a big, heroic voice and was in great demand for such operas as *Il trovatore* and *L'Africaine*, and also *La Juive*, in which he appeared at La Scala. In 1892 he left Paris for Lyons, where he became director, returning to the capital to great acclaim in 1908. He also enjoyed a spectacular success at the French Opera in New Orleans. His powerful voice and ringing high notes are well demonstrated in recordings made in 1905 and 1906, which show a skilled technician, somewhat unimaginative in style and interpretation.

J.B. Steane

Esswood, Paul (Lawrence Vincent)

(*b* West Bridgford, Notts., 6 June 1942). English countertenor. He studied at the RCM, London, under Gordon Clinton, 1961–4. From 1964 to 1971 he was a lay vicar at Westminster Abbey. His début was in a broadcast performance of *Messiah* under Charles Mackerras in 1965; from that time he quickly established a reputation as a leading countertenor, in Britain and elsewhere, particularly Germany and the Netherlands, in both sacred and secular repertories. In 1968 he first appeared in opera, in Francesco Cavalli's *Erismena* at Berkeley, California, singing soon thereafter in operas by Alessandro Scarlatti (including *Tigrane*, 1969, Basle), G.F. Handel and others, including Claudio Monteverdi, in whose *Il ritorno d'Ulisse in patria* (Vienna), *Orfeo* (Salzburg) and *L'incoronazione di Poppea* (Amsterdam) he appeared in 1971. Esswood took part in recordings of several works by Monteverdi (notably the Vespers), Handel, Henry Purcell and J.S. Bach (notably the complete cantatas with Nikolaus Harnoncourt and Gustav Leonhardt). In 1978 he created the role of Death in Krzysztof Penderecki's *Paradise Lost* in Chicago, repeating it the next year at La Scala and becoming the first countertenor to appear there. He sang Oberon in Benjamin Britten's *A Midsummer Night's Dream* (1988, Cologne) and created the title role in Philip Glass's *Akhnaten* at Stuttgart (1984). He sang the title role of *Admeto* at Karlsruhe (1990) and that of *Riccardo Primo* for the English Bach Festival at Covent Garden (1991). He sang with various specialist early music ensembles and was a founder of the *a cappella* male group Pro Cantione Antiqua. Esswood's singing was distinguished by his cool and pure tone, unusually even across his entire compass, his clear articulation and his keen sense of line.

Stanley Sadie

Estes, Simon (Lamont)

(*b* Centerville, IA, 2 Feb 1938). American bass-baritone. He studied with Charles Kellis at the University of Iowa, and after further training at the Juilliard School sang at the Deutsche Oper, Berlin (début as Ramfis in *Aida*), at Lübeck and at Hamburg. His success at the first Tchaikovsky Vocal Competition in Moscow (1966) led to engagements in both North America and Europe, including the role of Carter Jones in Gunther Schuller's *The Visitation* for San Francisco (1967). In 1978 he became the first black male artist to take a major role at Bayreuth when he sang the title role in *Der fliegende Holländer*, a performance of astonishing presence, preserved on video. Estes made his Metropolitan début in 1982 as the Landgrave in *Tannhäuser*. Among his other roles were Philip II, Wotan (at Berlin and the Metropolitan), Oroveso, Boris, John the Baptist, Porgy (including the first Metropolitan performances of Gershwin's work, 1985), the title role in Giuseppe Verdi's *Attila*, the four villains in *Les contes d'Hoffmann* and Charles Gounod's Méphisthophélès. He was a regular soloist in major choral works, notably Verdi's Requiem, which he recorded impressively under Carlo Maria Giulini.

Martin Bernheimer/Alan Blyth

Etcheverry, (Henri-)Bertrand

(*b* Bordeaux, 29 March 1900; *d* Paris, 14 Nov 1960). French bass-baritone. He studied in Paris and made his début in 1932 as Ceprano (*Rigoletto*) at the Opéra, where he sang until the mid-1950s. Among the roles he created there were Tiresias in George Enescu's *Oedipe* (1936) and the Prince of Morocco in Reynaldo Hahn's *Le marchand de Venise* (1935); he also sang Bluebeard in the first performance at the Opéra of Paul Dukas' *Ariane et Barbe-bleue*, as well as roles in Werner Egk's *Peer Gynt* and Hans Pfitzner's *Palestrina* in their first productions in France. His repertory at the Opéra included Don Giovanni, Wotan, Boris and Méphisthophélès. He first appeared at the Opéra-Comique in 1937 as Golaud, a role he also sang at Covent Garden and La Scala. His roles at the Opéra-Comique included Seneca (*L'incoronazione di Poppea*), Ourrias (*Mireille*) and Nourabad (*Les pêcheurs de perles*). His Golaud is preserved in the 1942 recording of *Pelléas et Mélisande*, conducted by Roger Désormière.

Harold Rosenthal/R

Ettore [d'Ettore], Guglielmo

(*b* Sicily, *c*1740; *d* Ludwigsburg, wint. 1771–2). Italian tenor. He sang in Naples in Niccolò Jomelli's *Temistocle* in 1757 and Johann Hasse's *Achille in Sciro* in 1759. He later moved to Bologna where Padre Martini heard him and recommended him to Andrea Bernasconi in Munich. In 1761 he was engaged there, remaining in service until 1771. He appeared in several Italian centres in the 1760s, among them Venice and Verona in 1765, in operas by Giuseppe Sarti, and Turin, where in 1767 he sang in Ferdinando Bertoni's *Tancredi* and Quirino Gasparini's *Mitridate, rè di Ponto*. By then he was a Cavaliere ('d'Ettore'). He sang the title role in Bernasconi's *La clemenza di Tito* at Munich in 1768 and Admetus in Pietro Guglielmi's *Alceste* the next year in Milan. Charles Burney reported that he was the most applauded of the singers in Antonio Sacchini's *Scipio in Cartagena* in Padua in 1770; elsewhere he referred to him as reckoned 'the best singer of his kind on the serious opera stage'. C.F.D. Schubart wrote that he had 'never heard anyone sing with the feeling of a d'Ettore' (*Schubart's Leben und Gesinnungen*, Stuttgart, 1791–3, i, p. 94). Ettore's range extended from *A* to *d"* and his vocal abilities included a capacity for wide leaps. In 1770–71 he sang the title role in W.A. Mozart's *Mitridate* in Milan; the young composer had to write five versions of his entrance aria to satisfy the tenor, and Ettore ultimately included an aria by Gasparini (displaying his splendid top *c"*) in place of another of Mozart's. Relations were so strained that eight years later the mention of Ettore's name evoked unpleasant memories for Mozart. Ettore was engaged at the Württemberg court on 28 January 1771 but died the next winter. His compositions, which are unpublished, include arias and many 'Duetti Notturni' written in a fluent melodic style.

H.J. Wignall: *Mozart, Guglielmo d'Ettore and the Composition of Mitridate* (Ann Arbor, 1995)

Harrison James Wignall

Evans, Anne [Lucas, Anne Elizabeth Jane]

(*b* London, 20 Aug 1941). English soprano. She studied at the RCM, London, and then in Geneva, where she made her début in 1967 as Annina (*La traviata*) and sang Countess Ceprano (*Rigoletto*) and Wellgunde. In 1968 she joined Sadler's Wells Opera (later the ENO), making her début as Mimì and singing Countess Almaviva, the Marschallin and Penelope Rich (*Gloriana*). With the WNO (1974–89) she sang Senta, Chrysothemis, the Empress and the Dyer's Wife (*Die Frau ohne Schatten*), Leonore in *Fidelio*, Donna Anna and Brünnhilde in a complete *Ring* cycle, also given at Covent Garden (1986). Having sung Ortlinde and Third Norn at

Bayreuth (1983), Evans returned as Brünnhilde (1989–92), a role she has also sung in Berlin, Paris and with the Royal Opera (1995–6), and recorded under Daniel Barenboim. Her Wagner repertory, to which her strong, clear voice is particularly suited, also includes Elsa, Eva, Kundry, Elisabeth (the role of her Metropolitan début in 1992), Isolde, which she first sang with the WNO (1993), and Sieglinde, which she sang in San Francisco in 1995.

R. Milnes: 'Anne Evans', *Opera*, xxxvii (1986), 256–63

Elizabeth Forbes

Evans, Sir Geraint (Llewellyn)

(*b* Cilfynydd, 16 Feb 1922; *d* Aberystwyth, 19 Sept 1992). Welsh baritone. He studied with Theo Hermann in Hamburg and later with Fernando Carpi in Geneva and at the GSM, London. He joined the Covent Garden company in 1948, making his début as the Nightwatchman (*Die Meistersinger*). In his second season he sang W.A. Mozart's Figaro (his début role at La Scala in 1960 and at the Vienna Staatsoper a year later). His repertory widened to include Escamillo, Lescaut, Marcello, Papageno, Balstrode, Sharpless, Dulcamara and Bottom (Benjamin Britten). At Covent Garden he created Mr Flint (*Billy Budd*, 1951), Mountjoy (*Gloriana*, 1953) and Antenor (*Troilus and Cressida*, 1954). He sang at Glyndebourne, 1950–61, in Mozart roles and as Abbate Cospicuo (*Arlecchino*), the Music-Master (*Ariadne auf Naxos*) and Falstaff, the role of his Metropolitan début in 1964. Evans sang regularly at Salzburg from 1962 as Figaro, Leporello and Wozzeck and with the leading American companies, having made his début at San Francisco in 1959 as Beckmesser. He first appeared at the Paris Opéra in 1975 as Leporello. He was knighted in 1969 and in 1973 celebrated the 25th anniversary of his Covent Garden début, as Don Pasquale. In 1984 he made his farewell appearance at Covent Garden, as Dulcamara, and in the same year his autobiography, *A Knight at the Opera*, was published in London. His voice, while lacking an italianate richness (his Rigoletto and Scarpia were unsuccessful), was resonant and carefully trained, but it was above all for his resourceful and genial wit that he was admired, notably as Don Pasquale, Beckmesser and Falstaff and as W.A. Mozart's Figaro, Leporello and Alfonso. He recorded all these roles, along with Balstrode and Mr Flint, and made inimitable contributions to several Gilbert and Sullivan recordings.

L. Dunlop: 'Geraint Evans', *Opera*, xii (1961), 231–6

Harold Rosenthal/R

Evans [Crozier], Nancy

(*b* Liverpool, 19 March 1915; *d* Suffolk, 20 Aug 2000). English mezzo-soprano. She studied in Liverpool with John Tobin, then with MAGGIE TEYTE and Eva de Reusz. She made her début in recital in Liverpool (1933), singing for the first time in London a year later, accompanied by Gerald Moore. Her stage début was in Arthur Sullivan's *The Rose of Persia* (1938, London); in 1939 she sang small roles at Covent Garden. During the war she sang widely for the Entertainments National Services Association. Joining what was to become the English Opera Group in 1946, she alternated with FERRIER in the title role of Benjamin Britten's *The Rape of Lucretia* at Glyndebourne; in 1947 she created Nancy in *Albert Herring*, and later sang Polly in Britten's version of *The Beggar's Opera*, Henry Purcell's Dido, and Lucinda Woodcock in Thomas Arne's *Love in a Village*. She travelled with the English Opera Group to the Netherlands, Belgium, Switzerland and Scandinavia. On stage her lively presence enhanced her warm-toned singing. In 1968 she created the Poet and seven other characters in Malcolm Williamson's *The Growing Castle* (Dynevor Castle, Wales). A noted concert singer, she was the dedicatee and first performer (at the 1948 Holland Festival) of Britten's *A Charm of Lullabies*; in recital she specialized in the French and 20th-century British song repertory. She married first Walter Legge, then Eric Crozier. Evans's recordings, all showing her innate sense of style, included Purcell's Dido, Britten's Lucretia and English songs.

Harold Rosenthal/R

Ewing, Maria (Louise)

(*b* Detroit, 27 March 1950). American mezzo-soprano and soprano. She studied at the Cleveland Institute (1968–70) with ELEANOR STEBER and in later years with JENNIE TOUREL and O.G. Marzolla. But the decisive encounter of her student days was with James Levine; under his direction she made her début in 1973 at the Ravinia Festival. After appearances at Miami, Boston, Cologne, Chicago and Santa Fe, in 1976 she sang Cherubino at Salzburg, then made her Metropolitan début in the same role. She then sang there Rosina, Mélisande and Blanche (Poulenc's *Dialogues des Carmélites*), Zerlina, Dorabella, the Composer, Carmen and Marie (*Wozzeck*). In Europe her roles included Cenerentola, Dorabella, Jacques Offenbach's La Périchole and Katerina Izmaylova (*Lady Macbeth of the Mtsensk District*), which she sang to acclaim at the Opéra-Bastille, Paris, in 1993. She appeared in Peter Hall's productions at Glyndebourne as Carmen, Dorabella and Poppaea. She made her Covent Garden début as Salome (1988), returning as Carmen (1991). In Los Angeles she sang Tosca (1989) and Butterfly (1991). From 1997 her career was confined to occasional concert appearances. Her bewitching stage presence and magnetic acting were seconded by a vibrant, wide-ranging voice which was not always under perfect control. Her Carmen (at Glyndebourne and at Covent Garden) and her Salome (Covent Garden), preserved on video, reveal her artistry at its most compelling.

Elizabeth Forbes/Alan Blyth

F

Falcon, (Marie) Cornélie

(*b* Paris, 28 Jan 1814; *d* Paris, 25 Feb 1897). French soprano. She studied with Felice Pellegrini and ADOLPHE NOURRIT at the Paris Conservatoire, and in 1831 won *premiers prix* for singing and lyric declamation. She made her début at the Opéra as Alice in Giacomo Meyerbeer's *Robert le diable* (1832). Her acting ability and dramatic voice greatly excited Meyerbeer, who wrote for her the part of Valentine in *Les Huguenots* (29 February 1836). Other notable creations were Rachel in Fromental Halévy's *La Juive* (25 February 1835) and the title role in Louise Bertin's *Esmeralda* (14 November 1836); her repertory also included Donna Anna, Julie in Gaspare Spontini's *La vestale* and Gioachino Rossini's French heroines. Her success at the Opéra led to overwork followed by loss of voice. In March 1837 she broke down during a performance of Louis Niedermeyer's *Stradella*. She resumed a busy schedule of performances shortly afterwards, but continued to experience vocal difficulties. She stopped singing in October and after a last appearance in *Les Huguenots* (15 January 1838), she twice visited Italy in the hope of recovering her voice. She returned to the Opéra on 14 March 1840 to sing parts of *La Juive* and *Les Huguenots* at a benefit performance, but her voice had been permanently damaged. Successful concerts with CINTI-DAMOREAU in Russia in the winter of 1841–2 were followed by some private performances in Paris and rumours of miraculous medical cures, but Falcon never appeared on stage again.

In later years the designation 'Falcon soprano' was given to the type of roles in which she excelled, and those written expressly for her give some indication of her vocal strengths. Using little ornamentation, she specialized in long lyrical lines, large upward leaps and sustained high notes. Her voice was noted for its crystalline clarity and the ease with which it could rise above an orchestra, aided by a fast, narrow vibrato. Despite the strength of her top and bottom registers, GILBERT DUPREZ (who sang with her several times) suggested that her inability to create a smooth link between the two contributed to her vocal demise. (See colour plate 6.)

Philip Robinson/Benjamin Walton

Farinelli [Broschi, Carlo; Farinello]

(*b* Andria, Apulia, 24 Jan 1705; *d* Bologna, 16/17 Sept 1782). Italian soprano castrato, the most admired of all the castrato singers. He was also a talented composer and instrumentalist.

In 1740, Farinelli wrote of his birth to Count Pepoli, 'I do not claim I was born from the third rib of Venus, nor that my father was Neptune. I am Neapolitan and the Duke of Andria held me at the baptismal font, which is enough to say that I am a son of a good citizen and of a gentleman'. Farinelli's father, Salvatore Broschi, was a petty official in Andria and later in Barletta. There is evidence that the family moved from Barletta to Naples in 1711, but none for the often-repeated assertion that Farinelli's father was a musician. He may have received some musical training from his brother, the composer Riccardo Broschi, who was seven years his elder. In 1717, the year of his father's death, he began private study in Naples with Nicola Porpora, the teacher of many fine singers. As Giovenale Sacchi, his first biographer, and Padre Martini, who often met him during the years of his retirement, attest, the stage name of Farinelli came from a Neapolitan magistrate, Farina, whose three sons had sung with the Broschi brothers and who later patronized the young singer.

Farinelli made his public début in 1720 in Porpora's serenata *Angelica*, based on the first printed libretto of Pietro Metastasio. This marked the beginning of a lifelong friendship between singer and librettist, who always referred to each other as 'dear twin' ('caro gemello') in reference to their operatic 'twin birth' in this work, in which Farinelli, aged only 15, sang the small role of the shepherd Tirsi. Two years later his performing career began in earnest. In 1722–4 he sang in Rome and Naples in operas by Porpora, Carlo Francesco Pollarolo and Leonardo Vinci, among others, and was quickly promoted into leading roles; at this time he often sang the part of the prima donna, such as the title role in Porpora's *Adelaide* (1723, Rome). His earliest surviving image, a caricature by Pierleone Ghezzi (1724), 'Farinello Napolitano famoso cantore di Soprano', shows him costumed as a woman.

From 1724 to 1734 Farinelli achieved extraordinary success in many northern Italian cities, including Venice, Milan and Florence. His appearance at Parma in 1726 at the celebrations on the marriage of the duke, Antonio Farnese, marks his first association with the Farnese family, who played a critical role in his later life through Elisabetta Farnese, niece of the duke and wife of Philip V of Spain. From 1727 to 1734 he lived in Bologna, where both he and his brother were enlisted in the Accademia Filarmonica in 1730. In 1732 he was granted rights of citizenship and purchased a country estate outside the city, where he would retire in 1761. In Bologna he met Count Sicinio Pepoli, with whom he began to correspond in 1731; his 67 letters to Pepoli provide rich detail of the singer and the period. In Turin, he met the English ambassador, Lord Essex, who in 1734 played a critical role in negotiating for his performances in London, and may have been responsible for commissioning the formal portrait of 1734 by Bartolomeo Nazari, the first of many imposing depictions that serve to transform Farinelli's image from the caricatures of Ghezzi, Marco Ricci, Antonio Maria Zanetti (all before 1730; for a slightly later caricature, based on Ricci's, see Cuzzoni, francesca).

Attempts had been made to lure Farinelli to London since 1729. G.F. Handel failed to secure him for his company, but Farinelli signed a contract in 1734 with the competing company, where Porpora was the leading composer. From 1734 to 1737 he performed in operas by Porpora, J.A. Hasse and by his own brother, Riccardo, and his singing took the city by storm. The extensive commentary, public and private, is rarely less than ecstatic. When, in 1737, he decided to break his contract and go to Madrid at the command of 'Their Catholic Majesties' (as described by Benjamin Keene, British ambassador to Spain), the resentment was equally strong. *The Daily Post* reported on 7 July 1737 (Lindgren, 1991):

> Farinello, what with his Salary, his Benefit Night, and the Presents made him by some of the wise People of this Nation, gets at least 5000 l. a Year in England, and yet he is not asham'd to run about like a Stroller from Kingdom to Kingdom, as if we did not give him sufficient Encouragement, which we hope the Noble Lords of the Haymarket will look upon as a great Affront done to them and their Country.

Farinelli had been called to Madrid by the queen in the hope that his singing would help cure the debilitating depression of Philip V. It became his responsibility to serenade the king every night (the exact number of arias differs in reports between three and nine), an obligation he apparently maintained until the king's death in 1746. That Farinelli's activities encompassed more than singing the same arias every night to the ailing king is especially well documented in the period after Philip V's death and the accession of Ferdinand VI (1746–59). In 1747 he was appointed artistic director of the theatres at Buen Retiro (Madrid) and Aranjuez, marking the begin-

ning of a decade of extraordinary productions and extravaganzas in which he collaborated extensively with Metastasio. Only Metastasio's side of this correspondence survives: the 166 letters, beginning on 26 August 1747, detail many of Farinelli's projects, from the importation of Hungarian horses (with which Metastasio was engaged from Vienna for a year and a half) to the redirection of the River Tagus in Aranjuez to enable elaborate 'water music' or *embarcadero* for the royal family. 17 of the 23 operas and serenatas produced under Farinelli's direction between 1747 and 1756 had texts by Metastasio, many of them revised for the Spanish performances. Metastasio's letters preserve one side of an engaging conversation about all aspects of performance. His new serenata, *L'isola disabitata*, was set by Giuseppe Bonno and performed in 1754, the year the Aranjuez theatre was inaugurated; Metastasio wrote to Farinelli after hearing about the production: 'I have been present at Aranjuez all the time I was reading your letter…I have seen the theatre, the ships, the embarkation, the enchanted palace; I have heard the trills of my incomparable Gemello; and have venerated the royal aspect of your divinities'. Farinelli's 'royal aspect' was also captured by the painter and set designer Jacopo Amigoni in two large canvases of 1750–52. The most imposing portrait, however, is the last, painted about 1755 by Corrado Giaquinto, showing him full length in his chivalric robes with Ferdinand VI and Queen María Barbara revealed in an oval behind him by flying putti (see colour plate 1 for a detail from this portrait).

The Giaquinto portrait marks the apogee of Farinelli's career. Metastasio's *Nitteti*, set by Nicola Conforto, had its première in 1756. After Ferdinand VI's death in 1759, Farinelli was asked to leave Spain, and retired to his villa in Bologna where he installed his extensive collections of art, music and musical instruments. He nurtured hopes of returning to Spain or of attaining a position of similar authority elsewhere, but they proved to be vain. He lived out his years corresponding with Metastasio (who died in April 1782) and receiving the homage of musicians and nobility, including G.B. Martini, Charles Burney, C.W. Gluck, W.A. Mozart, the Electress of Saxony and Emperor Joseph II, and died shortly after his 'twin'.

Farinelli's voice was by all accounts remarkable. J.J. Quantz, who first heard him in Naples in 1725 and then again at Parma and Milan in 1726, published a description:

> Farinelli had a penetrating, full, rich, bright and well-modulated soprano voice, whose range extended at that time from *a* to *d'''*. A few years afterwards it had extended lower by a few notes,

but without the loss of any high notes, so that in many operas one aria (usually an adagio) was written for him in the normal tessitura of a contralto, while his others were of soprano range [Farinelli's later repertory indicates that his lower range ultimately extended to *c*]. His intonation was pure, his trill beautiful, his breath control extraordinary and his throat very agile, so that he performed even the widest intervals quickly and with the greatest ease and certainty. Passage-work and all varieties of melismas were of no difficulty whatever for him. In the invention of free ornamentation in adagio he was very fertile (Marpurg, 1754).

The *messa di voce* was the cornerstone of 18th-century vocal pedagogy and Farinelli's was legendary. In a letter to Count Sicinio Pepoli from Vienna in March 1732, the singer described his audience before the Habsburg emperor Charles VI: 'I presented him with three *messe di voce* and other artful effects, which his generosity allowed him to admire'. The emperor also advised Farinelli, as the singer reported to Burney: 'Those gigantic strides [leaps], those never-ending notes and passages…only surprise, and it is now time for you to please;…if you wish to reach the heart, you must take a more plain and simple road'. Earlier, Quantz had criticized his acting. Burney states how much Farinelli learnt from these early critiques, so that he 'delighted as well as astonished every hearer', but both criticisms followed Farinelli throughout his career. In London, after the initial wild enthusiasm, some dissatisfaction began to be voiced, and in May and June 1737 Farinelli cancelled several performances, excusing himself on grounds of 'indisposition'. On 11 June, he sang a farewell aria of his own, expressing his gratitude to Britain.

Farinelli's prodigious vocal abilities, about which there can be no doubt, were coupled with deep musicianship. He composed and he played the keyboard and the viola d'amore. In addition to his London farewell, for which he wrote both text and music, he composed an aria for Ferdinand VI (1756), and he sent 'flotillas' of manuscripts to Metastasio. One packet, received after Metastasio's death in 1782 by the composer Marianne von Martínez, elicited an enthusiastic response; she wrote: 'I have received much applause from many musical experts for the great naturalness and fancy that exists generally [in your keyboard works] and particularly in the first sonata in F and in the second in D, with the graceful rondo well constructed and then ornamented with pleasing variations'. Farinelli and Metastasio earlier exchanged settings of the aria 'Son pastorello amante'; on receipt of Farinelli's version, Metastasio wrote (13 June 1750): 'Your

music to my canzonet is expressive, graceful, and the legitimate offspring of one arrived at supremacy in the art' (Heartz, 1984).

Farinelli was a legend even during his life. Fictionalized accounts began to appear in the 1740s in England (including in 1744 a comic opera by J.F. Lampe), flourished in the 19th century (Eugène Scribe wrote three fictionalized accounts in 1816, 1839 and 1843, the last set to music by Daniel Auber) and continue to this day, (as in the novels by L. Goldman: *The Castrato*, New York, 1973; M. David: *Farinelli: mémoires d'un castrat*, Paris, 1994; and F. Messmer: *Der Venusmann*, Berne, 1997). These fictions are often rich in imagined political and sexual intrigue (as in the 1994 film *Farinelli*). Despite the mythologizing, all contemporary evidence points to Farinelli as a person of noble sentiment and character. As Burney wrote:

> Of almost all other great singers, we hear of their intoxication by praise and prosperity, and of their caprice, insolence, and absurdities, at some time or other; but of *Farinelli*, superior to them all in talents, fame, and fortune, the records of folly among the *spoilt children* of Apollo, furnish not one disgraceful anecdote.

D. Heartz: 'Farinelli and Metastasio: Rival Twins of Public Favour', *EMc*, xii (1984), 358–66

J. Rosselli: 'The Castrati as a Professional Group and a Social Phenomenon, 1550–1850', *AcM*, lx (1988), 143–79

D. Heartz: 'Farinelli revisited', *EMc*, xviii (1990), 430–43

L. Lindgren: 'Musicians and Librettists in the Correspondence of Gio. Giacomo Zamboni (Oxford, Bodleian Library, MSS Rawlinson Letters 116–138)', *RMARC*, no.24 (1991), 1–194

K. Bergeron: 'The Castrato as History', *COJ*, viii (1996), 167–84 [on the film *Farinelli*]

E.T. Harris: 'Twentieth-Century Farinelli', *MQ*, lxxxi (1997), 180–89 [on the film *Farinelli*]

T. McGeary: 'Farinelli in Madrid: Opera, Politics, and the War of Jenkins' Ear', *MQ*, lxxxii (1998), 383–421

Ellen T. Harris/R

Farrar, Geraldine

(*b* Melrose, MA, 28 Feb 1882; *d* Ridgefield, CT, 11 March 1967). American soprano. She studied in Boston, New York and Paris; soon after her début at the Königliches Opernhaus, Berlin (*Faust*, 15 October 1901), she became a pupil of LILLI LEHMANN, to whose Donna Anna she was later to sing Zerlina at Salzburg. After five years in Berlin, Farrar joined the Metropolitan Opera in New York, where she first appeared as Charles Gounod's Juliet in 1906, and quickly became one of the leading stars of the company. She remained at the Metropolitan

Geraldine Farrar by Frances Benjamin Johnston, c. 1910

until 1922, when she made her farewell as Ruggero Leoncavallo's Zazà on 22 April. With her personal beauty, clear tone and shapely phrasing she excelled in such lyrical parts as Zerlina and Cherubino, Manon and Mignon, as well as in several Puccini roles, among them the heroine in the 1918 première of *Suor Angelica*. She was also the first Goose Girl in Englebert Humperdinck's *Königskinder* (1910), the first Caterina in Umberto Giordano's *Madame Sans-Gêne* (1915) and the first American Louise in Gustave Charpentier's unsuccessful sequel, *Julien* (1914). Farrar's seductive and strongly personal timbre is well captured on a long series of Victor records, which have been successfully transferred to CD. They offer, among other worthwhile performances, a substantial souvenir of her Butterfly and her Carmen, two of her most popular roles.

G. Farrar: *The Story of an American Singer* (New York, 1916, 2/1938 as *Such Sweet Compulsion*, 3/1970 with discography)
W.R. Moran: 'Geraldine Farrar', *Record Collector*, xiii (1960–61), 194–240 [with discography], 279–80; xiv (1961–2), 172–4; xx (1971–2), 163–4
E. Nash: *Always First Class: the Career of Geraldine Farrar* (Washington DC, 1982)

Desmond Shawe-Taylor/R

Farrell, Eileen

(*b* Willimantic, CT, 13 Feb 1920; *d* Park Ridge, NJ, 23 March 2002). American soprano. She studied with Merle Alcock and Eleanor McLellan, and concentrated on concert singing until her belated operatic début in 1956 as Santuzza in Tampa, Florida. That year she sang Leonora (*Il trovatore*) in San Francisco, returning in 1958 as Luigi Cherubini's Medea; Chicago appearances followed, and, in 1960, her much delayed Metropolitan début as Gluck's Alcestis. Her relationship with the Metropolitan management was not easy and she sang there sporadically for only five seasons. Although her voice, temperament and histrionic gifts would have suited the great Wagnerian roles admirably, she sang Brünnhilde and Isolde only in concert performances, notably with the New York PO under Leonard Bernstein. She was equally celebrated for her singing of J.S. Bach (with the Bach Aria Group) and the blues (at the 1959 Spoleto Festival and on subsequent recordings). She was an intelligent actress; her voice was huge, warm, vibrant and, apart from difficulties at the extreme top in later years, remarkably well controlled. Her recordings, especially of Giuseppe Verdi and Richard Wagner, demonstrate the imposing strength and vitality of her singing. Her memoir, *Can't Help Singing: the Life of Eileen Farrell* was published in 1999.

Martin Bernheimer/R

Fassbaender, Brigitte

(*b* Berlin, 3 July 1939). German mezzo-soprano. She studied with her father, WILLI DOMGRAF-FASS-BÄNDER, at the Nuremberg Conservatory, and made her début at the Staatsoper, Munich, in 1961 as Nicklausse. After playing Hänsel, Carlotta (*Die schweigsame Frau*), and the various pages and maids of the repertory, she scored a great success in 1964 as Clarice (Gioachino Rossini's *La pietra del paragone*). Later her roles included C.W. Gluck's Orpheus, Sextus (*La clemenza di Tito*), Cherubino, Dorabella, Carmen, Azucena, Eboli, Brangäne and Marina. Her débuts at Covent Garden (1971) and the Metropolitan Opera (1974) were as Octavian, a part in which her dashing looks and her warm, darkly attractive tone won her particular praise, as they did for her wicked Orlofsky. In 1973 she sang Fricka (*Das Rheingold*) at the Salzburg Festival and in 1976 created Lady Milford in Gottfried von Einem's *Kabale und Liebe* in Vienna; she has also appeared in San Francisco, Paris and Japan. Charlotte (*Werther*), Mistress Quickly, Countess Geschwitz, Clytemnestra, the Nurse (*Die Frau ohne Schatten*) and Clairon (*Capriccio*) were among the successful roles of her later career. To every one she brought an intensity of acting and utterance all her own, as can be heard in her recordings of Dorabella, Sextus, Hänsel, Charlotte (live from Munich),

Geschwitz (twice) and Orlofsky. Fassbaender was also one of the most perceptive and original interpreters of lieder, her recordings of *Winterreise* and *Schwanengesang* are psychologically searing in her own unique, idiosyncratic manner. She retired from public performance in 1995. From the early 1990s she has been increasingly active as an opera director and made her British directing début with *Der ferne Klang* for Opera North (1992).

S. Gould: 'Brigitte Fassbaender', *Opera*, xxxii (1981), 789–95

T. Castle: 'In Praise of Brigitte Fassbaender: Reflections on Diva-Worship', *En travesti: Women, Gender Subversion, Opera*, ed. C.E. Blackmer and P.J. Smith (New York, 1995), 20–58

Alan Blyth

Faull, Ellen

(*b* Pittsburgh, 14 Oct 1918). American soprano. After studying at the Curtis Institute and Columbia University, she became a leading singer of the New York City Opera, making her début there in 1947 as Donna Anna. She created Abigail Borden in Jack Beeson's *Lizzie Borden* (1965), and appeared in the New York première of Douglas Moore's *Carry Nation* (1968) and the American première of Ermanno Wolf-Ferrari's *I quatro rusteghi* (1951); among her traditional roles were Countess Almaviva, Leonora (*Il trovatore*) and Butterfly. She performed with most of the important American opera companies. Her attractive *lirico spinto* was able to spin out long, limpid phrases in Giuseppe Verdi, yet also to deliver the vehement coloratura of Donna Anna's music with fire and meaning.

Thor Eckert Jr

Faure, Jean-Baptiste

(*b* Moulins, 15 Jan 1830; *d* Paris, 9 Nov 1914). French baritone. He studied at the Paris Conservatoire, making his début in 1852 as Pygmalion (Victor Massé's *Galathée*) at the Opéra-Comique, where he also created Hoël in Giacomo Meyerbeer's *Le pardon de Ploërmel* (1859) and sang at the 1853 première of Ambroise Thomas' *La Tonelli*. He made his London début at Covent Garden in 1860 as Hoël, and during the next decade sang Alphonse (*La favorite*), Fernando (*La gazza ladra*), Nevers (*Les Huguenots*), Don Giovanni, William Tell, Méphistophélès in the first Covent Garden performance of *Faust* (1863), Belcore, Peter the Great (*L'étoile du Nord*), Count Rodolfo (*La sonnambula*) and W.A. Mozart's Figaro. His début at the Paris Opéra was in 1861 as Julien (Józef Poniatowski's *Pierre de Médicis*); there he created Pedro in Massé's *La mule de Pedro* (1863), Nélusko

in *L'Africaine* (1865), Posa in *Don Carlos* (1867) and the title role in Thomas' *Hamlet* (1868; see colour plate 10), also singing Méphistophélès in the first performance at the Opéra of *Faust* (1869). In 1870 he sang Lothario in the first London performance of *Mignon* at Her Majesty's Theatre. Returning to Covent Garden (1871–5), he sang Hamlet, Caspar (*Der Freischütz*). Cacico (*Il Guarany*), Lothario and Assur (*Semiramide*). He sang Don Giovanni at the first performance of Mozart's opera given at the new Palais Garnier (1875), and then created Charles VII in Auguste Mermet's *Jeanne d'Arc* (1876). He retired from the stage in 1886. Although he possessed a fine, resonant, even and extensive voice, Faure was chiefly notable for the innate musicality and stylishness of his singing and for his great gifts as an actor. He taught singing at the Paris Conservatoire from 1857 to 1860 and published two books on the art of singing. His voice can be heard on a private cylinder recorded in Milan (*c*1897–9), singing 'Jardins d'Alcazar' from *La favorite*.

Elizabeth Forbes

Favero, Mafalda

(*b* Portomaggiore, nr Ferrara, 6 Jan 1903; *d* Milan, 3 Sept 1981). Italian soprano. She studied with VEZZANI in Bologna and in 1926 made her début at Cremona, under the name of Maria Bianchi, as Lola (*Cavalleria rusticana*); her 'official' début was at Parma in 1927 as Liù. After singing Elsa and Margherita she was engaged at La Scala, where she made her début as Eva in 1928. She continued to sing there until 1950. A leading singer throughout Italy, she sang Norina, Liù and Zerlina at Covent Garden (1937, 1939) and in 1938 made her only American appearances, at San Francisco and the Metropolitan (where she made her début as Mimì). Her repertory included Carolina (*Il matrimonio segreto*), Susanna, Violetta, Martha, Suzel (*L'amico Fritz*), Zazà and – her most famous role – Giacomo Puccini's Manon Lescaut. In addition, she created several roles, including the title role in Pietro Mascagni's *Pinotta* (1932), Laura in Riccardo Zandonai's *La farsa amorosa* (1933) and, at La Scala, Gasparina in Ermanno Wolf-Ferrari's *Il campiello* (1936) and Finea in his *La dama boba* (1939). Her voice and vibrant, appealing style can be heard in a number of recordings that also catch the immediate eloquence of her interpretations. She was considered one of the finest Italian sopranos between the wars.

Harold Rosenthal/Alan Blyth

Feinhals, Fritz

(*b* Cologne, 4 Dec 1869; *d* Munich, 30 Aug 1940). German baritone. After studies in Italy he made his début in 1895 as Silvio in *Pagliacci* at Essen, where he remained for two seasons. After a year in Mainz, in 1898 he joined the Munich Opera, where he was last heard in 1927. His Covent Garden début as Telramund won high praise in 1898, but he did not sing there again until Ernest Van Dyck's German season of 1907 when in addition to Telramund his roles were Hans Sachs, Kurwenal, Wolfram and Wotan (*Die Walküre*). He also appeared in Paris, Vienna, and Rostock, and in 1908–9 at the Metropolitan. There, in addition to the Wagnerian repertory, he sang Amonasro, and Sebastiano in the American première of Eugen d'Albert's *Tiefland*. In 1917 he sang Borromeo in the world première of *Palestrina* at Munich, where he later taught. Though W.J. Henderson of the New York *Sun* wrote of his 'glorious voice', recordings made at about this time (1908) make painful listening. The volume is ample but the tone unsteady, the method providing scant evidence of his Italian training.

J.B. Steane

Fel, Marie

(*b* Bordeaux, 24 Oct 1713; *d* Chaillot, 2 Feb 1794). French singer. One of the most famous singers of the Académie Royale de Musique, Marie Fel had a long and brilliant career on the operatic stage. She learnt the Italian style of singing from Mme Van Loo, a celebrated Italian singer who married the painter Carle Vanloo and came to Paris in 1733. She made her début on 29 October 1734 as Venus in the prologue of *Philomèle* by Louis Lacoste and at the Concert Spirituel des Tuileries on 1 November in a motet by Joseph de Mondonville. Her appeal increased rapidly. She performed regularly at the Concerts chez la Reine, small court gatherings where operas being given in Paris were previewed or repeated. As she continued to sing major roles, she also frequently performed *cantatilles*, airs in French or Italian inserted between the acts of an opera. From 1739 she began to assume leading roles and, with the famous *haute-contre* PIERRE DE JÉLYOTTE, gave performances which charmed every opera audience. Her flexibility and clear articulation particularly suited the technically demanding *ariettes*. F.M. Grimm, in a letter to the abbé Raynal (*Mercure de France*, May 1752, p.187), praised her mastery of the Italian style.

In 1757 she appeared with her pupil SOPHIE ARNOULD, who replaced her at the Opéra the following year. She continued to sing at the Tuileries, and was applauded for her interpretation of Latin and French motets, especially those of Mondonville. In 1752 she performed the *Salve regina* which

J.-J. Rousseau had written for her (*Confessions* (Geneva, 1782), ix: 1756).

Her sensitivity and intelligence brought her many admirers, among them Grimm and the librettist Louis de Cahusac. The painter Quentin La Tour called her his 'Céleste'; his pastel of her, displayed at the Salon du Louvre in 1757, has become famous. During her long career she performed in over a hundred premières and revivals, including major roles in most of Jean-Philippe Rameau's works: *Castor et Pollux* (Amour in 1737, Télaïre in 1754), *Fêtes d'Hébé* (Hébé, 1739, 1747, 1756), *Dardanus* (1739, 1744), *Hippolyte et Aricie* (1742 revival), *Les Indes galantes* (1743), *Fêtes de Polymnie* (1745), *Le temple de la gloire* (1745), *Zaïs* (Zélidie, 1748), *Naïs* (Naïs, 1749), *Platée* (Folly, 1745, 1749), *Zoroastre* (Amélite, 1749 and 1756), *La guirlande* (Zélide, 1751), *Acante et Céphise* (Céphise, 1751), *La naissance d'Osiris* (Pamilie, 1754).

Some of her other roles were in works by Jean-Baptiste Lully, André Campra and J.-J. Mouret (they are listed by Pitou), as well as Altisidore in Joseph Bodin de Boismotier's *Don Quichote chez la duchesse* (1743), the title role in Jean-Marie Leclair's *Scylla et Glaucus* (1746), Chloé in Boismortier's *Daphnis et Chloé* (1747), Hero in René de Béarn Brassac's *Léandre et Héro* (1750), Aurore in Mondonville's *Titon et l'Aurore* (1753), Colette in Rousseau's *Le devin du village* (1753) and Alcimadure in *Daphnis et Alcimadure* (1754), Mondonville's pastorale in Languedoc dialect.

M. Cyr: 'Eighteenth-Century French and Italian Singing: Rameau's Writing for the Voice', *ML*, lxi (1980), 318–37
S. Pitou: *The Paris Opéra: an Encyclopedia of Opera, Ballets, Composers and Performers* (London, 1983)
G. Sadler: 'Rameau's Singers and Players at the Paris Opéra: a Little-known Inventory of 1738', *EMc*, xi (1983), 453–67

Mary Cyr

Feldman, Jill

(*b* Los Angeles, 21 April 1952). American soprano. She studied singing privately in San Francisco, and later in Basle, and took a degree in musicology from the University of California at Santa Barbara. She made her American operatic début in 1979 as Music in Claudio Monteverdi's *Orfeo*, and the next year made her European début at the Spoleto Festival as Clerio in Francesco Cavalli's *Erismena*. In 1984 she sang the title role in a notable revival (concert performance) of Marc-Antoine Charpentier's *Médée*, directed by William Christie, at the Salle Pleyel, Paris. She has sung throughout Europe, specializing in Baroque roles and touring as a soloist and with ensembles. Her recordings include Jean-Philippe

Rameau's *Anacréon*, Antonio Cesti's *Orontea*, Cavalli's *Xerse*, Charpentier's *Médée*, *Actéon*, *Les arts florissants* and *Le malade imaginaire*, and W.A. Mozart's *Ascanio in Alba*. Feldman's accomplished technique, her fine sense of drama and a vocal range capable of subtle nuances of colour assist her in projecting an authoritative stage presence. Among her operatic roles that of Medea in Charpentier's opera is outstanding for its vivid characterization and subtle interpretation of the text. Feldman also has a flourishing concert career, and has recorded works ranging from early Italian songs to songs by Luigi Cherubini and Giacomo Meyerbeer.

Nicholas Anderson

Félix-Miolan, Marie.

See CARVALHO, CAROLINE.

Feller, Carlos

(*b* Buenos Aires, 30 July 1925). Argentine bass. He studied in Buenos Aires, making his début in 1946 at the Colón, where he sang for a decade. He made his London début in Domenico Cimarosa's *Il maestro di cappella* at Sadler's Wells (1958). For Glyndebourne he sang Don Alfonso and W.A. Mozart's Figaro in 1959 and the following year sang Dr Bombasto (*Arlecchino*) at Edinburgh. After appearing in Frankfurt and Brussels, he was engaged at Cologne, where he sang until he was over 70. He made his Metropolitan Opera début as Don Alfonso in 1988. His repertory included Leporello, Mozart's and Gioachino Rossini's Dr Bartolo, Don Magnifico, Geronimo (*Il matrimonio segreto*), Don Pasquale, Dulcamara, Baculus (*Der Wildschütz*), Otto Nicolai's Falstaff, Lord Tristan (*Martha*) and Varlaam. A superb *basso buffo*, he also sang heavier roles such as Polonius (Sándor Szokolay's *Hamlet*), the Doctor (*We Come to the River* and *Wozzeck*), Schigolch (*Lulu*) and Claggart.

Elizabeth Forbes

Fenton [Besswick], Lavinia

(*b* Westminster, London, 7 Oct 1710; *d* Greenwich, 24 Jan 1760). English actress and singer. She made her acting début in 1726 at the Haymarket Theatre, London, and sprang to fame in 1728 when she created Polly Peachum in *The Beggar's Opera* at Lincoln's Inn Fields Theatre. After she had sung the part more than 60 times, she retired, becoming mistress of the third Duke of Bolton (Charles Powlett, or Paulet), who married her immediately after the death of his wife in 1751 – 23 years after

taking her off the stage. William Hogarth's painting of *The Beggar's Opera* (1731; Tate collection) shows the duke, in a box on stage, staring lovingly at her. The toast of the town by the age of 17, she combined ingenuous sweetness and youthful charm.

Oxford DNB (O. Baldwin and T. Wilson)

Elizabeth Forbes, Olive Baldwin,
Thelma Wilson

Fernandi, Eugenio

(*b* nr Turin, 1922; *d* New Jersey, 15 Aug 1991). Italian tenor. He studied in Turin with AURELIANO PERTILE, then at the opera school of La Scala, where he began his career in small parts. He then progressed to major roles in the Italian regions before achieving success at the Metropolitan in his début there as Pinkerton in 1958; thereafter, until 1962, he was admired as Edgardo (to CALLAS's Lucia), Don Carlos, Faust, Rodolfo (*La bohème*), Radames, Enzo Grimaldi (*La Gioconda*) and the Italian Singer (*Der Rosenkavalier*). He sang to acclaim at the Vienna Staatsoper from 1958 and took the title role in *Don Carlos* at the Salzburg Festival (1958, 1960) under Herbert von Karajan. Walter Legge asked him to sing Calaf in Callas's 1957 recording of *Turandot*, and he also recorded, in 1959, the Giuseppe Verdi Requiem under Tullio Serafin. His singing on disc reveals a ringing yet plangent tenor and a fine sense of phrasing.

Alan Blyth

Ferrani [Zanazzio], Cesira

(*b* Turin, 8 May 1863; *d* Pollone, nr Biella, 4 May 1943). Italian soprano. She studied with Antonietta Fricci in Turin, where she made her début in 1887 as Micaëla and later sang Gilda. After singing in Venice and Genoa, where she took part in the first performance of Pietro Mascagni's *Le maschere* (1891), she created the title role in Giacomo Puccini's *Manon Lescaut* at Turin (1893), repeating the role in Buenos Aires, Rome and other cities. She sang Suzel (*L'amico Fritz*) at Monte Carlo (1895), then created Mimì in *La bohème* at Turin (1896). At La Scala she sang Mélisande in the first Milan performance of *Pelléas et Mélisande* with Arturo Toscanini (1908). Her repertory included Juliet, Jules Massenet's Sapho and Charlotte, Amelia (*Simon Boccanegra*), Elisabeth (*Tannhäuser*), Elsa and Eva (*Die Meistersinger*). She retired from the stage after a final appearance as Mélisande (Rome, 1909), a role in which she was much admired, and devoted herself to teaching in her native city, opening her salon to the intellectuals of Turin.

Adriana Ferrarese

Albanesi Sc.

Sig.ra Andriana Ferrarese, Principal Singer at the King's Theater.

Tho' sweeter notes than Philomela's Lay;
Melt on her Lips, and snatch the sense away;
Yet 'midst these sounds, new Pleasures are in store,
We now the Singer th'Actress now adore. LR

At the same time as GEMMA BELLINCIONI, the first Santuzza, established a model of the dramatic soprano entirely in the grip of passion, Ferrari succeeded in asserting her aristocratic style, emphasizing polished singing over sheer volume. While this made her the Puccini soprano *par excellence*, it inevitably precluded her from singing Tosca.

Her voice is preserved on a series of discs recorded by the Gramophone and Typewriter Company in Milan in 1903.

Elizabeth Forbes/Marco Beghelli

Ferrarese [Ferraresi, Ferrarese del Bene], **Adriana** [Andreanna, Andriana]

(*b* Valvasano [now Friuli], 19 Sept 1759; *d* after 1803). Italian soprano. As a student at the Ospedale dei Mendicanti in Venice from 1778 to 1782 she sang in oratorio. She has long been identified with a Francesca Gabrielli, '*detta* la Ferrarese', whom Charles Burney heard at the Ospedaletto in Venice in 1770; E.L. Gerber (in his *Historisch-biographisches Lexikon der Tonkünstler*, 1790–92) may have been the first to assume that Burney's Gabrielli and Adriana Ferrarese were one and the same, but no solid evidence links them. She eloped with Luigi del Bene in December 1782 and appeared in a serious opera in Livorno during autumn 1784, before going to London in 1785. During her two years there she sang initially in serious opera, including Luigi Cherubini's *Demetrio* (1785), and then, because she was overshadowed in that genre by Gertrud Mara, in comic, where she was assigned the serious roles. By autumn 1786 she was back in Italy, where she sang exclusively in *opera seria*, including Angelo Tarchi's Iphigenia and C.W. Gluck's Alcestis.

Ferrarese made her Vienna début on 13 October 1788 as Diana in Vicente Martín y Soler's *L'arbore di Diana*, in which she sang two substitute arias;

the *Rapport von Wien* remarked: 'connoisseurs of music claim that in living memory no such voice has sounded within Vienna's walls. One pities only that the acting of this artist did not come up to her singing'. She went on to create Eurilla in Antonio Salieri's *La cifra* (1789), Eugenia in the Vienna première of Giovanni Paisiello's *La molinara*, and her most famous role, W.A. Mozart's Fiordiligi (26 January 1790). Her tenure of 30 months coincided with the peak of the librettist Lorenzo Da Ponte's influence in Vienna; she was dismissed with Da Ponte, with whom she was romantically involved, in early 1791, and continued her career, in serious opera, throughout Italy until the turn of the century.

Music written for Ferrarese tends to emphasize *fioriture*, *cantar di sbalzo* (large leaps) and the low end of her range. Adaptations of existing music for revivals and new music written for her tend to enhance the serious style at the expense of the comic, but her success with the Viennese suggests that she could also interact effectively with comic characters in recitative and ensembles. Nonetheless, her strength lay in her purely vocal abilities, which Joseph Weigl (*Il pazzo per forza*) and Salieri (*La cifra*) in particular exploited in the music they wrote for her. Her singing won much praise, notably from Count Karl Zinzendorf, who wrote that 'La Ferrarese chanta à merveille' (27 February 1789). The casting of Ferrarese as Susanna for the 1789 revival of *Le nozze di Figaro* met with only qualified enthusiasm from Mozart, who wrote that 'the little aria [K577] I have made for Ferrarese I believe will please, if she is capable of singing it in an artless manner, which I very much doubt' (19 August 1789); he also composed a large-scale rondò, K579, to replace 'Deh, vieni, non tardar'. As Fiordiligi in *Così fan tutte* her vain temperament and formidable vocal resources were exploited to perfection by Da Ponte and Mozart, creating a rigid *seria* character who is the object of comic intrigue.

P. Lewy Gidwitz: 'Mozart's Fiordiligi: Adriana Ferrarese del Bene', *COJ*, viii (1996), 199–214

Patricia Lewy Gidwitz, John A. Rice

Ferrari-Fontana, Edoardo

(*b* Rome, 8 July 1878; *d* Toronto, 4 July 1936). Italian tenor. He turned to singing after starting a career in medicine and then working in the Italian Embassy at Montevideo. After touring South America in operetta he was encouraged by Tullio Serafin to study for opera; his début was as Tristan (Turin, 1910), and he soon established himself as the leading Italian Wagnerian tenor of his day. At La Scala

he sang Pollione in *Norma* (1912), and the following year he appeared as Avito in the première of *L'amore dei tre re*. This he repeated, with Arturo Toscanini, at the Metropolitan in 1914, singing with 'a magnificent robust voice with pealing upper tones'. He also appeared in Buenos Aires and was a member of the Boston Company, where he sang Tristan in 1912 (with his wife, MARGARETE MATZENAUER, as Isolde in some performances). From 1926 he taught in Toronto. His few recordings show a voice of fine quality, compact in production, and used with taste and imagination.

J.B. Steane

Ferraris, Ina Maria

(*b* Turin, 6 May 1882; *d* Milan, 11 Dec 1971). Italian soprano. She studied with Vittorio Vanzo in Milan, gave her first concert in London in 1906 and two years later made her operatic début at Bologna as Philine in *Mignon*. In 1911, at La Scala, she sang Sophie in the first Italian production of *Der Rosenkavalier*. She remained at La Scala for some 20 years, singing light roles, until her retirement in 1934, after which she taught; she was also popular in South America. In 1917, at Monte Carlo, she created the role of Lisette in the première of *La rondine*. On recordings she is best known for her part in some enchanting duets from *Der Rosenkavalier* and *Hänsel und Gretel* with CONCHITA SUPERVIA, mementos of their association in both operas at La Scala.

J.B. Steane

Ferrier, Kathleen (Mary)

(*b* Higher Walton, Lancs., 22 April 1912; *d* London, 8 Oct 1953). English contralto. She studied with J.E. Hutchinson and then ROY HENDERSON. Established as one of England's leading concert artists, she made her stage début as Lucretia in the première of Benjamin Britten's *The Rape of Lucretia* at Glyndebourne in 1946. The following year she sang C.W. Gluck's Orpheus there. These remained her only operatic roles. Her recordings of *Orfeo ed Euridice* (one, abridged, deriving from the Glyndebourne production, the other from a broadcast from the 1951 Holland Festival) give some idea of the strength and beauty of her interpretation. Covent Garden staged *Orfeo ed Euridice* for her in 1953 with John Barbirolli as conductor. She could sing only two of the four scheduled performances before illness forced her to cancel; these were her last public appearances.

Kathleen Ferrier

Ferrier's warm, ample and beautiful voice was firm through all its range. She used it with increasing expressiveness, overcoming an initial inflexibility.

N. Cardus, ed.: *Kathleen Ferrier: a Memoir* (London, 1954, 2/1969) [with discography]
W. Ferrier: *The Life of Kathleen Ferrier* (London, 1955)
C. Rigby: *Kathleen Ferrier: a Biography* (London, 1955)
N. Cardus: 'Kathleen Ferrier', *Gramophone Record Review* (1957), 974–5, 1027–8 [with discography by F. F. Clough and G. J. Cuming]
M. Leonard: *Kathleen* (London, 1988)
P. Campion: *Ferrier: a Career Recorded* (London, 1992) [discography]

Alan Blyth

Festa (Maffei), Francesca

(*b* Naples, 1778; *d* St Petersburg, 9/21 Nov 1835). Italian soprano. She studied in Naples with GIUSEPPE APRILE and in Rome with GASPARO PACCHIEROTTI, making her début in 1799 at the Teatro Nuovo, Naples. She sang at La Scala between 1805 and 1824, creating Fiorilla in Gioachino Rossini's *Il turco in Italia* (1814). Her roles included Donna Anna, Cenerentola and Desdemona in Rossini's *Otello*, which she sang at the Teatro S Benedetto, Venice (1818). She also appeared in Paris, Munich and St Petersburg.

Elizabeth Forbes

Figner, Nikolay Nikolayevich

(*b* Nikiforovka, nr Kazan', 9/21 Feb 1857; *d* Kiev, 13 Dec 1918). Russian tenor. He studied in St Petersburg and Naples, where he made his début in Charles Gounod's *Philémon et Baucis* in 1882. After further appearances in Italy he sang in Latin America in 1884 and 1886, and in 1887 sang Raoul (*Les Huguenots*) at the Imperial Opera, St Petersburg. After his Covent Garden début in the same year, as the Duke in *Rigoletto*, he returned to the Imperial Opera, where he appeared regularly with his second wife, MEDEA MEI-FIGNER until their divorce in 1904. He took part in the premières of P.I. Tchaikovsky's *The Queen of Spades* (1890) and *Iolanta* (1892), and Eduard Nápravník's *Dubrovsky* (1895) and *Francesca da Rimini* (1902). From 1910 to 1915 he directed and sang at the Narodnïy Dom opera house. His repertory included Tchaikovsky's Lensky and Andrey Morozov (*Oprichnik*), the Prince in Alexander Dargomïzhsky's *Rusalka*, Nero (Anton Rubinstein), Kuratov in Nápravník's *Nizhniy-Nougoroders*, Grigory (*Boris Godunov*), Don José, Faust, Werther, Arturo (*I puritani*), Fernand (*La favorite*), Enzo (*La Gioconda*), Radames, Vasco da Gama (*L'Africaine*), Lohengrin, Canio and Turiddu. Figner's voice, although dry, was extremely expressive; he took enormous pains with diction, acting and costuming, cutting a figure of romantic elegance which held audiences enthralled.

A. Favia-Artsay: 'The Fabulous Figners', *Hobbies*, lxi/Dec (1954), 22–35

Harold Barnes/R

Fink, Bernarda

(*b* Buenos Aires, 29 Aug 1955). Argentine mezzo-soprano of Slovenian parentage. She studied at the Arts Institute of the Teatro Colón, and in 1985 won Argentina's New Lyric Voices prize. Moving to Europe, she sang with leading orchestras and conductors, specializing in the music of the Baroque and earlier periods. As well as returning to the Colón, she appeared with immediate success in opera in Geneva and Prague, followed by a début at Salzburg as Dorabella in *Così fan tutte*. She has been widely admired as C.W. Gluck's Orpheus, singing the role under René Jacobs's direction in Paris, London, Montreux and Valencia. She has also become a noted recitalist, with concerts at Carnegie Hall in New York, the Wigmore Hall, London, the Sydney Opera House, Tokyo, Paris and Vienna. Fink's voice, rich and pure in quality, has character in it and takes well to recording. Fine examples of her art can be heard in recordings of several Claudio Monteverdi and G.F. Handel operas and C.W. Gluck's *Orfeo*, all conducted by René Jacobs, while a bold but tasteful performance of Hugo Wolf's *Die Zigeunerin* shows her aptitude in a quite different repertory.

J.B. Steane

Finley, Gerald

(*b* Montreal, 30 Jan 1960). Canadian baritone. He studied at the RCM and the National Opera Studio in London before making his professional stage début as Sid (*Albert Herring*) at Glyndebourne in 1986. He has returned to Glyndebourne on several occasions, most notably as Figaro in *Le nozze di Figaro* for the inaugural performances in the new house in 1994 (an occasion preserved on video), a portrayal near-ideal in both vocal and dramatic terms. He was equally admirable as Papageno both in Roger Norrington's 'Mozart Experience' on the South Bank in London, then in John Eliot Gardiner's semi-staged, touring performances of *Die Zauberflöte* in 1995, also recorded on video and CD. His other Mozart recordings include Masetto and Guglielmo. He sang Demetrius in *A Midsummer Night's Dream* at Aix (1991), and appeared in Mozart's *Der Schauspieldirektor* the same year at the Salzburg Festival. Finley created the title role in Tobias Picker's *Fantastic Mr Fox* in Los Angeles in 1998 and scored a notable success in the principal role of Harry Heegan in the première of Mark-Anthony Turnage's *The Silver Tassie* at his ENO début in 2000. He has also made a considerable name for himself in concert and recital (making his Wigmore Hall début in 1989), and has recorded works including Henry Purcell's *Indian Queen*, Joseph Haydn's *The Creation*, Hector Berlioz's *L'enfance du Christ*, Johannes Brahms's *A German Requiem*, songs by Frank Bridge and works by Benjamin Britten and Anton Webern. His interpretations of a wide repertory of song disclose his firm, warm, easily produced baritone and his natural gift for unaffected, discerning interpretation.

Alan Blyth

Finnilä, Birgit

(*b* Falkenberg, 24 Jan 1931). Swedish contralto. She studied at Göteborg and in London at the RAM. After some years as a concert singer, she made her stage début in 1967 as C.W. Gluck's Orpheus at Göteborg. She appeared at La Scala, the Opéra, in Munich and Geneva and at Salzburg, where she sang Erda in the Easter Festival (1973–4); her repertory included Brangäne and Hedwige (*Guillaume Tell*). She sang the Seashell (*Die ägyptische Helena*) at Carnegie Hall, New York (1979) and made her Metropolitan début in 1981 as Erda, the role that best displayed her deep, resonant voice.

Elizabeth Forbes

Fischer, Hanne

(*b* Copenhagen, 3 March 1966). Danish mezzo-soprano. She studied at the Royal Danish Conservatory, and made her professional opera début, as Cherubino, at the Royal Opera, Copenhagen, in 1993. The same year she was engaged at the Kiel Opera, where her roles included Cherubino, Siebel (*Faust*), Idamante (*Idomeneo*), Dorabella (*Così fan tutte*), Hänsel and Flosshilde (*Das Rheingold*). She made her Glyndebourne début as Annio (*La clemenza di Tito*) in 1995, returning there as a charming Isolier (*Le comte Ory*) in 1997 and 1998. Since 1997 Fischer has been a company principal at the Royal Opera, singing a repertory that includes Rosina in *Il barbiere di Siviglia*, Dorabella, Suzuki (*Madama Butterfly*), Idamante, the Composer (*Ariadne auf Naxos*), Sextus (*La clemenza di Tito*), C.W. Gluck's Orpheus and Fricka in *Rheingold*. She has also appeared in opera in Bonn, Berlin, Hamburg and at the Théâtre des Champs-Elysées in Paris, and has appeared frequently in concert in Denmark and elsewhere.

In 2000 Fischer was widely praised for her moving performance in the Copenhagen world première of *The Handmaid's Tale* by Poul Ruders, as Offred's double (in the 'time before' flashbacks). Five years later she sang in the première, also in Copenhagen, of *Kafka's Trial* by the same composer. In 2007 she won plaudits as Fricka in David McVicar's production of *Rheingold* at Strasbourg. Fischer's recordings include *The Handmaid's Tale*, *Kafka's Trial* and Robert Schumann's dramatic ballads *Des Sängers Fluch* and *Vom Pagen und der Königstochter*.

Richard Wigmore

Fischer, (Johann Ignaz [Karl]) Ludwig

(*b* Mainz, 18 Aug 1745; *d* Berlin, 10 July 1825). German bass. He studied the violin and cello, but first attracted attention at the age of 18 with his singing in a church choir and in student operetta in Mainz. He soon received a position at court as a supernumerary, and was noticed by the tenor ANTON RAAFF with whom he studied after 1770 in Mannheim, and where he created the role of Kaled in Vogler's *Der Kaufmann von Smyrna* (1771). In 1772 he became *virtuoso da camera* at the court there (according to the libretto of Antonio Salieri's *La fiera di Venezia*, 1772) and was given a grant by Elector Carl Theodor to continue his education with Raaff. In February 1775 he took over instruction in singing at the Mannheim Seminarium Musicum. He created the role of Rudolf in Ignaz Holzbauer's serious German opera, *Günther von Schwarzburg* (1777), and by 1778 he received the highest salary among Mannheim court singers. In that year he moved with the court to Munich, where in 1779 he married Barbara Strasser (*b* Mannheim, 1758; *d* after 1825). From 1780 to 1783 the couple worked for the court theatre in Vienna, where Fischer sang Osmin in the first performance of *Die Entführung*, much to the satisfaction of W.A. Mozart, who frequently wrote about him in his letters and arranged the aria *Non so d'onde viene* (κ512) and may have written the recitative and aria *Aspri rimorsi atroci* (κ432/421*a*) for him. He also created the role of Herr von Bär in Salieri's *Der Rauchfaugkehrer* (1781). When the Singspiel company was replaced by an Italian *opera buffa* company in 1783 Fischer went to Paris, where he performed at the Concert Spirituel with much success. He then secured his reputation with a tour of Italy and in 1785 visited Vienna, Prague and Dresden. The couple served the Prince of Thurn and Taxis in Regensburg from 1785 until Fischer received a lifelong appointment in Berlin, with J.F. Reichardt's intervention, in 1789. The title role of Reichardt's *Brenno* (1789) was the first of many collaborations between Fischer and the composer. From this time on Fischer ceased appearing in comic roles. Guest appearances in London (at Johann Salomon's invitation in 1794 and 1798), Leipzig (1798), Hamburg (1801–2) and elsewhere added to his fame until he gave up public performance in 1812, and retired on a pension in 1815.

In his day Fischer was regarded as Germany's leading serious bass singer. His voice, which was said to range from *D* to *a'*, was praised by Reichardt as having 'the depth of a cello and the natural height of a tenor'. Others, too, repeatedly compared his voice to a tenor's in its flexibility, lightness and precision. He also composed, but his only extant work is the virtuoso song pair *Der Kritikaster und der Trinker* (Berlin, 1802), containing the popular drinking song 'Im kühlen Keller sitz' ich hier'. His handwritten autobiography, which goes up to 1790, is located in the Staatsbibliothek zu Berlin. His son Joseph Fischer (*b* Berlin, 1780; *d* Mannheim, 1862) was a bass singer and lied composer of some success, and his daughters Josepha Fischer-Vernier (*b* 1782) and Wilhelmine (*b* 1785) were also distinguished singers.

Roland Würtz/Paul Corneilson, Thomas Bauman

Fischer-Dieskau, Dietrich

(*b* Berlin, 28 May 1925). German baritone. He was one of the leading singers of his time, an artist dis-

Dietrich Fischer-Dieskau as Barak in 'Die Frau ohne Schatten'(Strauss), Bavarian State Opera, 1963

tinguished by his full, resonant voice, cultivated taste and powerful intellect. He studied in Berlin with Georg Walter before being drafted into the German army and taken prisoner by the British in Italy in 1945. After the war he resumed his studies, now with Hermann Weissenborn. He made his concert début in Johannes Brahms's *German Requiem* at Freiburg in 1947 and his stage début the next year as Posa in *Don Carlos*, under Heinz Tietjen at the Städtische Oper, Berlin, where he then became a leading baritone. Also in 1948 he broadcast *Winterreise* on Berlin radio, and at Leipzig gave his first solo recital. In 1949 he began regular appearances at the Vienna Staatsoper and at the Bavarian Staatsoper, Munich, and in 1952 at the Salzburg Festival. He sang at the Bayreuth Festival, 1954–6, as the Herald (*Lohengrin*), Wolfram (a performance of outstanding nobility), Kothner and Amfortas. In 1961 he created the role of Mittenhofer in H.W. Henze's *Elegy for Young Lovers* at the Schwetzingen Festival. His first London appearance was in Frederick Delius's *A Mass of Life* under Thomas Beecham in 1951. That, and his performances at Kingsway Hall of *Die schöne Müllerin* (which he then recorded for the first time with Gerald Moore) and his *Winterreise* the following year, established his fame in Britain. Among his frequent return visits, two were particularly notable: the first performances of Benjamin Britten's *War*

Requiem in 1962 in the rebuilt Coventry Cathedral, and his *Songs and Proverbs of William Blake* (composed for Fischer-Dieskau) at the 1965 Aldeburgh Festival. That year he made his highly successful Covent Garden début as Mandryka in *Arabella*.

Some of Fischer-Dieskau's most vivid roles, with the dates when he first sang them, were: Wolfram (1949), John the Baptist (*Salome*, 1952), Don Giovanni (1953), Ferruccio Busoni's Faust (1955), Amfortas (1955), Count Almaviva (1956), Renato (1957), Falstaff (1959), Paul Hindemith's Mathis (1959), Wozzeck (1960), Yevgeny Onegin (1961), Barak (*Die Frau ohne Schatten*, 1963), Macbeth (1963), Don Alfonso (1972) and the title role in the première of Aribert Reimann's *Lear* (1978). He recorded many of these parts and in addition, most notably, both Olivier and the Count in different sets of *Capriccio*, Papageno (with Karl Böhm), Gunther in Georg Solti's *Götterdämmerung*, Kurwenal in the famous Furtwängler *Tristan und Isolde*, the Dutchman, and Wotan (in Herbert von Karajan's *Das Rheingold*). After much hesitation as to its suitability for his voice, he undertook the role of Hans Sachs at the Deutsche Oper, Berlin, under Eugen Jochum in the 1975–6 season, and recorded it at the same time.

In spite of all this operatic activity, and a brief spell as a conductor in the early 1970s, Fischer-Dieskau's greatest achievement was in lieder. His repertoire consisted of more than 1000 songs, a feat unequalled by any other singer. He recorded all of Franz Schubert's, Robert Schumann's and Hugo Wolf's songs appropriate for a male singer, most of Ludwig van Beethoven's, Johannes Brahms's and Richard Strauss's songs, and many by Felix Mendelssohn, Franz Liszt and Carl Loewe. He has also written books on Schubert and Schumann, compiled *The Fischer-Dieskau Book of Lieder* (London, 1976) and published a book of memoirs, *Nachklang* (Stuttgart, 1988; Eng. trans., as *Echoes of a Lifetime*, 1989). His interpretations set standards by which other performances were judged. They were based on command of rhythm, a perfect marriage of tone and words, an almost flawless technique and an unerring ability to impart the right colour and nuance to a phrase. He was sometimes criticized for giving undue emphasis to certain words and overloading climaxes. Though his Italian was excellent and his Count Almaviva, Don Giovanni, Posa, Iago and Falstaff were substantial achievements, he was probably at his happiest in German roles such as Busoni's Faust, the Speaker, Wolfram, Kurwenal, Barak, Mandryka, Mathis and Wozzeck. Since his retirement from singing Fischer-Dieskau has taken up conducting again and has made a number of recordings with his wife, the soprano JULIA VARADY.

J. Demus and others: *Dietrich Fischer-Dieskau* (Berlin, 1966)

K. Whitton: *Dietrich Fischer-Dieskau: Mastersinger* (London, 1981)

H.A. Neunzig: *Dietrich Fischer-Dieskau: eine Biographie* (Stuttgart, 1995; Eng. trans., 1998)

Alan Blyth

Fisher, Sylvia (Gwendoline Victoria)

(*b* Melbourne, 18 April 1910; *d* Melbourne, 25 Aug 1996). Australian soprano. She studied at the Melba Memorial Conservatorium in Melbourne with Mary Campbell, then privately with Adolf Spivakovsky. While a student she made her operatic début (1932) as Hermione in Jean-Baptiste Lully's *Cadmus et Hermione*, her only stage performance before she moved to Europe in 1947. She joined the Covent Garden company in 1948, making her début that December as Leonore, and remained a member of the ensemble until 1958. Her many London roles included the Marschallin, Ellen Orford, a moving Mother Marie in the British première of *Dialogues des Carmélites*, Elsa, Agathe and Sieglinde, and she was compared with Lotte Lehmann for warmth of stage presence and vocal radiance. She scored a notable success as Kostelnička Buryjova in the first British production of *Jenůfa* (1956); she also sang Turandot, Brünnhilde (*Die Walküre*) and Isolde, but they were vocally too demanding so she later wisely abandoned them. After some years of retrenchment, she had a second career with the English Opera Group from 1963 as Lady Billows (*Albert Herring*), the Female Chorus (*The Rape of Lucretia*) and Mrs Grose (*The Turn of the Screw*); she created the role of Miss Wingrave in 1971 and repeated it at Covent Garden in 1973. When *Gloriana* was revived at Sadler's Wells in 1966, she triumphed as a commanding and dignified Elizabeth I. Her final appearances were in 1973 as a powerful Marfa Kabanicha (*Kát'a Kabanová*) for the ENO. She always managed to convey the essence of a role through her sympathetic identification with it, most notably as the Marschallin, Lady Billows, Elizabeth I and Miss Wingrave.

Harold Rosenthal/Roger Covell

Flagstad, Kirsten (Malfrid)

(*b* Hamar, 12 July 1895; *d* Oslo, 7 Dec 1962). Norwegian soprano. She came of a musical family: her father was a conductor, her mother a pianist and coach. While still a student, she made her début on 12 December 1913 at the National Theatre, Oslo, as Nuri in Eugen d'Albert's *Tiefland*. For the next 18 years she sang only in Scandinavia, where

Kirsten Flagstad as Brünnhilde in 'Siegfried' (Wagner), Metropolitan Opera, New York, 1937

she appeared in a wide variety of parts, including operetta, musical comedy and even revue. On 29 June 1932 she sang her first Isolde, at Oslo; this was also her first public performance in the German language. ELLEN GULBRANSON, the regular Bayreuth Brünnhilde of the previous generation, chanced to hear her, and recommended her to Bayreuth, where she sang small parts in 1933, and Sieglinde and Gutrune in 1934. An engagement at the Metropolitan ensued, and her first appearance there, on 2 February 1935 as Sieglinde, followed four days later by Isolde, was the beginning of her world fame. Her first Brünnhilde performances, later in 1935, set the seal on her success (see illustration). In 1936 and 1937 she sang Isolde, Brünnhilde and Senta at Covent Garden, arousing as much enthusiasm in London as in New York.

In 1941 Flagstad returned to Norway to join her second husband, who was arrested as a Nazi collaborator after World War II and died in 1946 while awaiting trial. Although she herself was acquitted of political offence by a Norwegian tribunal, her return to Nazi-occupied Norway during the war and a certain political naivety in her nature caused her afterwards to be looked at askance in America.

Flagstad's return to English musical life, on the other hand, was quite uncontroversial. She returned to Covent Garden in 1948 as Isolde, and thereafter sang for three more seasons in her other Wagnerian roles, including Kundry and Sieglinde as well as all three Brünnhildes; her farewell came in *Tristan* on 30 June 1951. At the age of 55 she could still sing these heavy roles with majestic effect. In 1950, at the Albert Hall, she gave the first performance of Richard Strauss's *Vier letzte Lieder* with Wilhelm Furtwängler as conductor. In 1951 and 1952 she sang Henry Purcell's Dido in the little Mermaid Theatre (then located in Bernard Miles's garden in St John's Wood, London), and when the permanent Mermaid Theatre opened its doors in the City of London, she reappeared in the same role, bidding farewell to the operatic stage there on 5 July 1953.

Meanwhile, she sang Leonore in *Fidelio*, under Furtwängler, at the Salzburg Festival (1948–50) and her Wagner roles in many major houses. In 1957, in honour of the 50th anniversary of Edvard Grieg's death, she sang some of his songs, in Norwegian national costume, at a Promenade Concert. During her retirement she continued to be active, as director for a few years of the newly formed Norwegian

State Opera, and in the recording studio, for which she even learnt music that was new to her, such as the part of Fricka in *Das Rheingold*. Over a period of more than 30 years she made many superb recordings. The complete *Tristan und Isolde* and her Brünnhilde in the complete *Ring*, live from La Scala (1950), both under Furtwängler, undoubtedly offer the finest memorial to her art; especially valuable, too, are her later sets of songs by Grieg and Jean Sibelius. The majority of her discs were reissued on CD to mark her centenary in 1995.

Although Flagstad was not a singer of naturally ardent temperament, she was always a superlative musician, with a rock-like sense of rhythm and flawless intonation. The lasting purity and beauty of her tone, unsurpassed in the Wagner repertory, probably owed much not only to natural gifts and sound training, but to the enforced repose of the war years and the fact that she undertook no heavy roles until middle life. At 40 she sang with a voice of radiant quality in the upper range, and with heroic power which responded with an effect of ease to Wagner's utmost demands; but as Leonore, Senta, Elisabeth and Elsa she then revealed flaws in her legato. Later, her scale was perfectly consolidated. Her Isolde was a stately Nordic princess, more proud than passionate. No other Brünnhilde in her time seemed so much a Valkyrie born.

J. Dennis: 'Kirsten Flagstad', *Record Collector*, vii (1952), 172–90 [with discography]

L. Biancoli: *The Flagstad Manuscript* (New York and London, 1953)

E. McArthur: *Flagstad: a Personal Memoir* (New York, 1965/R)

H. Vogt: *Flagstad: Singer of the Century* (London, 1987)

Desmond Shawe-Taylor/Alan Blyth

Fleming, Renée

(*b* Rochester, NY, 14 Feb 1959). American soprano. She studied at SUNY and made some early appearances singing George Gershwin with the New Harlem SO. After further study at the Juilliard School, and under JAN DEGAETANI, and early appearances at the Houston Opera Studio, she won a Fulbright Scholarship to work in Europe with ARLEEN AUGÉR and ELISABETH SCHWARZKOPF. In 1986 she sang her first major operatic role, Konstanze in *Die Entführung aus dem Serail*, at the Salzburg Landestheater. Some of the most coveted awards, such as the Richard Tucker and George London prizes, fell to her, and in 1988 she gained a Metropolitan Opera Audition Award, with a house début in 1991 as Countess Almaviva in *Le nozze di Figaro* (a role she repeated there in 2000). This was also the role which introduced her to Vienna, Paris, San Francisco and Buenos Aires. At Glyndebourne

she sang Fiordiligi in *Così fan tutte* (1992), and Covent Garden heard her first as Dirce in Luigi Cherubini's *Médée* (1989). She returned to Covent Garden as the Marschallin in 2000. The same year her Donna Anna at the Metropolitan Opera was widely praised for its virtuosity and dramatic urgency. On recordings she came to notice with a brilliant performance in the title role of Gioachino Rossini's *Armide* at the Pesaro Festival of 1993. Fleming also confirmed her growing reputation as a concert artist in a recital at Lincoln Center that same year. On the opening night of the Metropolitan season 1995–6, her Desdemona to DOMINGO's Otello placed her among the leading singers of the day. The beauty of her voice and the charm of her acting were equally acclaimed on her Bayreuth début as Eva in *Die Meistersinger* in 1996. She has also been in demand for world premières, including John Corigliano's *The Ghosts of Versailles* (Metropolitan Opera, 1991), Conrad Susa's *The Dangerous Liaisons* (San Francisco, 1994) and André Previn's *A Streetcar Named Desire* (San Francisco, 1998), which brought perhaps the greatest personal triumph of her career. Her voice combines the moderate power of a lyric soprano with the fullness and intensity of a more dramatic type. From the first, her recordings revealed an extensive range, considerable accomplishment in florid singing, and a distinctive, vibrant timbre. Later years have brought a deepening of her expressive powers in a steadily growing recorded repertory which includes such roles as Gaetano Donizetti's Rosmonde, Jules Massenet's Thaïs and Antonín Dvořák's Rusalka, Schubert lieder and Richard Strauss's *Vier letzte Lieder*.

J.B. Steane

Fleta, Miguel

(*b* Albalate de Cinca, 28 Dec 1893; *d* La Coruña, 30 May 1938). Spanish tenor. He studied at the Barcelona Conservatory and then in Milan with Luisa Pierrich, whom he later married. He made his début in 1919 at Trieste in Riccardo Zandonai's *Francesca da Rimini*, then sang in Vienna (1920), Rome (1920–22, including the première of Zandonai's *Giulietta e Romeo*), Monte Carlo (1921), Madrid (1921–2) and Buenos Aires (1922), in *Rigoletto*, *Aida*, *Tosca* and, above all, in *Carmen*. He appeared at the Metropolitan (1923–5), at La Scala (1924), where he returned to sing Calaf in the first *Turandot* in 1926, and at the Teatro Colón from 1922 to 1927; his Paris début, singing Cavaradossi, followed in 1928. His repertory included *Lucia*, *Pagliacci*, *Andrea Chénier* and *Manon*. He had a beautiful voice remarkable for its colour, range, evenness, sensual warmth and ease of inflection and expression, and was considered by Giacomo Puccini to be the ideal performer of his works. He had also an exuberant and passionate temperament, but lacked taste and style, and failed to care for his voice, so that by 1928 he was already in decline. His virtues and failings are vividly exemplified in many recordings.

J.A. León: 'Miguel Fleta', *Record Collector*, xv (1963–4), 99–108 [with discography]

Rodolfo Celletti/R

Flórez, Juan Diego

(*b* Lima, 13 Jan 1973). Peruvian tenor. He initially intended to pursue a career in popular music (his father, Rubén Flórez, was a noted folk guitarist and singer), only deciding on a classical career after he entered the Conservatorio Nacional de Música in Lima in 1990. In 1993 he gained a scholarship to the Curtis Institute of Music in Philadelphia, where he sang several Rossini, Bellini and Donizetti roles. His professional operatic début came at the Rossini Opera Festival in Pesaro in 1996, when he stepped out of the chorus at short notice to take the tenor lead in *Matilde di Shabran*. His mellifluous, easily produced voice and astonishing agility won critical accolades, and the same year he made a triumphant La Scala début in C.W. Gluck's *Armide* under Riccardo Muti. His 1997 Covent Garden début, in a concert performance of Donizetti's *Elisabetta al castello di Kenilworth*, likewise provoked critical superlatives. As Tim Ashley noted in the *Guardian*, 'everyone was convinced that a great tenor had arrived' (2 Feb 2000).

Flórez has subsequently appeared in most of the world's leading opera houses, where he has confirmed his reputation as the finest *tenore di grazia* of his generation. He made his Vienna Staatsoper début as Rossini's Figaro, one of his favourite roles, in 1999 and his Metropolitan Opera début, also as Figaro, in 2002. At Covent Garden he has sung Rodrigo in Rossini's *Otello*, Don Ramiro in *La cenerentola* (both 2000), Elvino in *La sonnambula* (2002) and Ernesto in *Don Pasquale* (2004). He has been equally admired in such roles as Fenton, Lindoro (*L'italiana in Algeri*) and Rinuccio (*Gianni Schicchi*). Flórez's recordings include W.A. Mozart's *Mitridate*, Rossini's cantata *Le nozze di Teti, e di Peleo* and three award-winning discs of bel canto arias.

Richard Wigmore

Focile, Nuccia

(*b* Militello, Sicily, 25 Nov 1961). Italian soprano. She studied with Elio Battaglia in Turin, where she made her début in 1986 as Oscar in *Un ballo in maschera*. In that year she also won the Pavarotti

Competition in Philadelphia. The clarity of her voice and the charm of her youthful appearance helped to fit her ideally for the lighter Mozart roles and others such as Norina in *Don Pasquale* and Nannetta in *Falstaff*, which she sang at Covent Garden in 1988. In the first five years of her career Focile sang in many of the major Italian houses, including La Scala, and was a frequent visitor to the USA and Britain, where she was particularly popular with the WNO. In Paris her roles have included Tatyana in *Yevgeny Onegin* (1992) and Charles Gounod's Juliet (1994). She made her Metropolitan Opera début as Mimi in 1995, returning there in the same role in 2000. The voice gaining weight, she has added roles such as Amelia Boccanegra and Butterfly, and also developed her concert repertory. She has made some solo recordings (including songs by Gaetano Donizetti, Giuseppe Verdi and Giacomo Puccini) but is probably heard best as Susanna in *Le nozze di Figaro* with Charles Mackerras and as a delightful Eleonora in Donizetti's *L'assedio di Calais*.

J.B. Steane

Foli, Giovanni.

Early stage name of JOHN McCORMACK.

Ford, Bruce (Edwin)

(*b* Lubbock, TX, 15 Aug 1956). American tenor. His steady rise to a leading position among Mozart and Rossini tenors of his generation has been grounded in gifts of musicianship as well as technique, which have also equipped him to master many other musical styles, ranging from Jean-Philippe Rameau through Giuseppe Verdi to contemporary US composers such as Carlisle Floyd and Philip Glass. After study at the universities of West Texas State and Texas Tech, and a period with Houston Opera Studio, he made his début at Houston and spent periods in Germany (Wuppertal, 1983–5, Mannheim, 1985–7). A remarkable facility in both the highest and lowest registers and in intricate *fioriture* has given Ford unusual authority over Gioachino Rossini's vocal writing, both in comic and serious tenor roles: he has sung Agorante (*Ricciardo e Zoraide*) at Pesaro, Almaviva at Covent Garden, James (*La donna del lago*) at La Scala, and Orestes (*Ermione*) at Glyndebourne. His wide vocal compass has also afforded him an impressive command of W.A. Mozart's Mithridates (notably at Covent Garden in 1992 and 1994). And in other Mozart roles, such as Belmonte, Ferrando (which he has sung at Salzburg) and Tamino, his graceful, long-breathed control of line and dynamics makes ample amends for an occasional rawness of timbre. Ford's recordings include Almaviva, Giacomo Meyerbeer's *Il crociato in Egitto* and Simon Mayr's *Medea in Corinto*.

Max Loppert

Formes, Karl Johann

(*b* Mülheim, 7 Aug 1815; *d* San Francisco, 15 Dec 1889). German bass. He made his début at Cologne in 1842 as Sarastro. Engaged at the Kärntnertortheater, Vienna, he created Plumkett in Flotow's *Martha* (1847). Forced to leave Vienna for political reasons, in 1849 he sang in London for the first time at Drury Lane. He made his Covent Garden début in 1850 as Caspar (*Der Freischütz*) and sang there regularly until 1868. His roles included Bertram (*Robert le diable*), Marcel (*Les Huguenots*), Leporello, Rocco and Peter the Great (*L'étoile du nord*). He also took part in the première of the three-act revision of Louis Spohr's *Faust* (1852) and the first London performance of Hector Berlioz's *Benvenuto Cellini* (1853), in which he sang the Cardinal. In 1857 he appeared at the New York Academy of Music, returning there for the next 20 years. In 1872 he took part in the première in the USA of Heinrich Marschner's *Der Templer und die Jüdin*. After his retirement from the stage in 1878, he taught singing in San Francisco. His voice combined a solid, resonant lower register with considerable flexibility, and he was particularly admired as Caspar.

His brother Theodor (*b* Mülheim, 24 June 1826; *d* Endenich, 15 Oct 1875), a tenor, made his début in 1846 at Budapest as Edgardo (*Lucia di Lammermoor*). After singing in Olmütz, Vienna and Mannheim, he was engaged at the Berlin Hofoper (1851–64), where he sang the title roles in the first local performances of *Tannhäuser* (1856) and *Lohengrin* (1859). Two other brothers, Wilhelm (1831–1884) and Hubert, were also singers.

H. Rosenthal: *Two Centuries of Opera at Covent Garden* (London, 1958)

Elizabeth Forbes

Forrester, Maureen (Kathleen Stuart)

(*b* Montreal, 25 July 1930). Canadian contralto. After studies with Sally Martin, Frank Rowe and Bernard Diamant, she concentrated on a concert career. Her New York début (Town Hall, 1956) attracted extraordinary critical attention and engagements soon followed with leading American orchestras. In Europe she appeared at festivals in Berlin, Montreux and Edinburgh, and the Holland festival, earning particular praise for her Mahler singing; she sang in Giuseppe Verdi's Requiem under Malcolm Sargent at a Promenade Concert in 1957. Her first major

operatic engagement was as C.W. Gluck's Orpheus, in Toronto in 1962. Subsequently she sang, among other roles, Cornelia in *Giulio Cesare* (1966, New York City Opera), La Cieca in *La Gioconda* (1967, San Francisco), Erda (1975, Metropolitan), Madame Flora in Gian Carlo Menotti's *The Medium*, Mistress Quickly, Brangäne, Arnalta (*L'incoronazione di Poppea*), Ulrica, Clytemnestra, Mme de Croissy (*Dialogues des Carmélites*) and the Countess (*The Queen of Spades*), which she sang at La Scala in 1990. A character actress of considerable wit, she was a singer of rare tonal opulence with a high standard of musicianship and interpretative imagination. She has made many recordings, including C.W. Gluck's Orpheus, G.F. Handel operas and works by Gustav Mahler.

M. Forrester and M. McDonald: *Out of Character* (Toronto, 1986) [autobiography]
J.T. Hughes: 'The Art of Maureen Forrester', *International Classical Record Collector*, ii/2 (1995), 50–54

Martin Bernheimer/R

Forsell, (Carl) John [Johan] (Jacob)

(*b* Stockholm, 6 Nov 1868; *d* Stockholm, 30 May 1941). Swedish baritone. He made his début as Gioachino Rossini's Figaro at the Stockholm Opera in 1896 and sang there regularly until 1911, and as a guest until 1938. In 1909–10 he appeared with success at Covent Garden as Don Giovanni, and at the Metropolitan in numerous roles including Telramund, Amfortas, Germont, Tonio and Prince Yeletsky. He was notable, especially as Don Giovanni, not only for the beauty and skill of his singing, but for the vivacity and zest of his whole dramatic performance – qualities which were still evident as late as 1930, when his fiery and elegant Don Giovanni, in Italian at Salzburg, provided a marked contrast to the sedateness of an otherwise German-speaking cast. From 1924 to 1939 Forsell was director of the Stockholm Opera; from 1924 to 1931 he taught at the Stockholm Conservatory, where his pupils included JUSSI BJÖRLING and SET SVANHOLM. He made numerous recordings, all in Swedish, between 1903 and 1925.

C.L. Bruun: 'John Forsell', *Record News* [Toronto], iv (1959–60), 256–63, 292–6 [discography]
K. Liliedahl: *John Forsell: a Discography* (Trelleborg, 1972, 2/1977)

Desmond Shawe-Taylor

Forti, Anton

(*b* Vienna, 8 June 1790; *d* Vienna, 16 June 1859). Austrian baritone. He began his career playing the viola in the orchestra of the Theater an der Wien. In 1808 he was engaged as a singer by Prince Esterházy for his theatre at Eisenstadt. During his three seasons there he sang Dandini in the German-language première of Nicolo Isouard's *Cendrillon*. From 1813 to 1834 he appeared at the Kärntnertortheater in Vienna. A very stylish singer and actor, he excelled in Mozart roles, especially Don Giovanni, the Count in *Le nozze di Figaro* and Sarastro. In 1823 he created Lysiart in *Euryanthe*. He also sang a number of tenor roles, including Gioachino Rossini's Othello, Mozart's Titus and Max (*Der Freischütz*). His wife Henriette (1796–1818) sang Cherubino, and Zerlina to her husband's Don Giovanni.

Elizabeth Forbes

Fouchécourt, Jean-Paul

(*b* Blanzy, 30 Aug 1958). French tenor. He trained as a conductor and saxophonist before turning to singing. He quickly acquired a reputation in French Baroque music, singing principal *haute-contre* roles in Jean-Baptiste Lully, André Campra and Jean-Philippe Rameau, most notably with Les Arts Florissants under William Christie. He subsequently toured the world in opera from Claudio Monteverdi to W.A. Mozart, and more recently has undertaken light tenor roles in 19th- and 20th-century repertory such as Jacques Offenbach's *Les contes d'Hoffmann* at the Metropolitan, New York, and Maurice Ravel's one-act operas throughout Europe. Despite his versatility, he remains best known as an exponent of early French dramatic music, and his fluent, sensual delivery, acute theatrical sense and command of refined nuance have adorned many performances and recordings of works by Lully (*Phaëton* and *Atys*), Joseph de Mondonville, Campra, Marc-Antoine Charpentier and Rameau (*Les indes galantes* and *Hippolyte et Aricie*). Fouchécourt's comic virtuosity and mimicry in Rameau's *Platée*, which he sang with the Covent Garden Company in 1997–8, have been exceptionally well received. He is also an admired concert singer and a sensitive exponent of *mélodies*.

Jonathan Freeman-Attwood

Francesina.

See DUPARC, ELISABETH.

Franci, Benvenuto

(*b* Pienza, Siena, 1 July 1891; *d* Rome, 27 Feb 1985). Italian baritone. He studied in Rome at the S Cecilia Conservatory with COTOGNI and Enrico Rosati, and made his début there in 1918 at the Teatro Costanzi in Pietro Mascagni's *Lodoletta*. In 1919 he appeared at the S Carlo, as Renato, then at leading Italian theatres, including La Scala (1923–36) and the Rome Opera (1928–49). He created roles in operas by Umberto Giordano, including Neri in *La cena delle beffe* (1924, Milan), Riccardo Zandonai and Arrigo Boito, including Fanuèl in *Nerone* (1924, Milan); his German roles included Hans Sachs and Barak. He also sang in Madrid, Barcelona, Buenos Aires and at Covent Garden (1925, 1931 and 1946). He retired in 1953. He had a large and penetrating voice, especially in the middle register, and was remarkable for his vehement singing in many dramatic Verdi roles, particularly Count di Luna, Rigoletto, Don Carlo (*La forza del destino*) and Amonasro, as well as Barnaba in *La Gioconda*, Gérard in *Andrea Chénier* and Scarpia, as can be heard in his recordings of arias from most of his roles.

Rodolfo Celletti

Frantz, Ferdinand

(*b* Kassel, 8 Feb 1906; *d* Munich, 26 May 1959). German bass-baritone. He studied privately and made his début in 1927 at Kassel as Ortel (*Die Meistersinger*); after engagements in Halle, Chemnitz and Hamburg, in 1943 he was engaged by the Staatsoper in Munich, of which he remained a member until his death. He established himself as a leading Heldenbariton, singing Wotan, Hans Sachs, Kurwenal and the Dutchman; such was the range of his voice that he also sang King Mark, Daland, the Landgrave, King Henry (*Lohengrin*), Méphistophélès and Galitsky (*Prince Igor*). He made guest appearances in Vienna, Milan, Paris and London where he sang Jupiter in the first performance in England of *Die Liebe der Danae* in 1953 (with the Bayerische Staatsoper), and Wotan in 1954. He made his Metropolitan début in 1949 as Wotan, and also appeared there as Pizarro. Frantz's beautifully schooled voice, significant use of the text and sympathetic personality are well represented in his recording of Wotan in Wilhelm Furtwängler's *Ring* with the Rome RAI SO (1953) and as Hans Sachs in Rudolf Kempe's notable recording of *Die Meistersinger* (1956). He was married to the soprano Helena Braun.

Harold Rosenthal/Alan Blyth

Franz, Paul [Gautier, François]

(*b* Paris, 30 Nov 1876; *d* Paris, 20 April 1950). French tenor. He studied with Louis Delaquerrière in Paris and joined the Opéra in 1909, making his début as Lohengrin, and singing there until his retirement in 1938. He was the first Paris Parsifal in 1914, and his many roles included Aeneas (*Les Troyens*), John the Baptist (*Hérodiade*), Rodrigue (*Le Cid*), Raoul (*Les Huguenots*), Ernest Reyer's Sigurd and Richard Wagner's Siegmund, Siegfried and Tristan. Franz made his Covent Garden début in 1910 as Samson, returning regularly until 1914. His London roles included Julien (*Louise*), Radames and Otello. In 1937 he joined the teaching staff of the Paris Conservatoire. Franz had a large, rich voice with an especially fine middle register and a particularly aristocratic style of declamation. He made distinguished recordings of French repertory, most notably as Sigurd and Samson, and of Wagner.

Harold Rosenthal/Alan Blyth

Fraschini, Gaetano

(*b* Pavia, 16 Feb 1816; *d* Naples, 23 May 1887). Italian tenor. He studied in Pavia and made his début there in 1837 as Tamas in Gaetano Donizetti's *Gemma di Vergy*. In 1839 he sang in *Torquato Tasso* at Bergamo and in 1840 in *Marino Faliero* at La Scala. Engaged at the S Carlo, Naples, from 1840 to 1853 he sang in the first performances of Giovanni Pacini's *Saffo* (Faone), *La fidanzata corsa*, *La stella di Napoli*, *La regina di Cipro*, *Merope* and *Romilda di Provenza*. He created Gerardo in *Caterina Cornaro* (1844); other Donizetti operas in which he sang included *Linda di Chamounix*, *Maria di Rohan*, *La favorite*, *Poliuto* and *Lucia di Lammermoor*. He was dubbed the 'tenore della maledizione' because of the force with which he delivered Edgardo's curse in *Lucia*, and was noted above all as an early *tenore di forza*.

He was chosen by Giuseppe Verdi to create Zamoro in *Alzira* (1845, Naples), Corrado in *Il corsaro* (1848, Trieste), Arrigo in *La battaglia di Legnano* (1849, Rome) and the title role of *Stiffelio* (1850, Trieste). He also appeared in *Oberto*, *Ernani*, *I Lombardi*, *I masnadieri*, *Luisa Miller* and *Il trovatore*. In 1856 he sang Henri in *Les vêpres siciliennes* at Rome, in 1858 Gabriele Adorno in *Simon Boccanegra* at Naples, and he created Riccardo in *Un ballo in maschera* (1859, Rome). It is a commentary on his technique and taste that, after so many forceful roles, he could still be expected to sing with the refinement and elegance necessary for Riccardo's music. He sang in the first London performance of *I due Foscari* at Her Majesty's Theatre (1847), in *La forza del destino* at Madrid (1863), and *La traviata* and *Rigoletto* at the Théâtre Italien, Paris (1864). He made his last appearance, as Gennaro in *Lucrezia Borgia* at Rome in 1873, when, though in his late fifties, he still retained the firmness and security of his voice.

Elizabeth Forbes

Fremstad, Olive [Rundquist, Olivia]

(*b* Stockholm, 14 March 1871; *d* Irvington-on-Hudson, NY, 21 April 1951). American mezzo-soprano and soprano of Swedish birth. Of illegitimate birth, she was adopted by an American couple of Scandinavian origin who took her to Minnesota. She studied in New York, and later in Berlin with LILLI LEHMANN. After a notable stage début as Azucena with the Cologne Opera (21 May 1895) she sang there as a mezzo for three years, during which she also appeared in minor roles in the Bayreuth *Ring* of 1896 and made a mark at the Vienna Opera as Brangäne. After a further period of study in Italy she joined the Munich Opera for three years, from 1900, singing a great variety of parts, among which her Carmen was specially popular. During the Covent Garden seasons of 1902 and 1903 she made a very favourable impression in various Wagner roles. On 25 November 1903 she made her Metropolitan début as Sieglinde, and remained at the house with increasing success for 11 consecutive seasons, singing under both Gustav Mahler and Arturo Toscanini in her Wagner repertory, which soon included Isolde, Brünnhilde and Kundry. She also appeared as Giacomo Meyerbeer's Selika, Carmen, Tosca, Santuzza, Salome and C.W. Gluck's Armide; the

Olive Fremstad, 1911

last two roles she introduced to America. She was still at the height of her powers when disagreements with the manager, Giulio Gatti-Casazza, caused her to leave the Metropolitan after singing Elsa on 23 April 1914. This final performance provoked one of the most remarkable demonstrations of affection and admiration in the history of the house.

Her vocal qualities were transcendent; it is clear from the fascinating account given by her secretary, Mary Watkins Cushing, that her vivid temperament made her often a difficult colleague as well as an interpreter of genius. Her few recordings, made in 1911–12, are constrained and unworthy of her reputation; the best of them is 'O don fatale' from *Don Carlos*. Thea Kronberg, the heroine of Willa Cather's *The Song of the Lark*, is a fictional portrait of Fremstad.

L. Migliorini and J. Dennis: 'Olive Fremstad', *Record Collector*, vii (1952), pp. 51–65 [with discography]
M.W. Cushing: *The Rainbow Bridge* (New York, 1954/R1977 with discography by W.R. Moran)

Desmond Shawe-Taylor/R

Freni [Fregni], Mirella

(*b* Modena, 27 Feb 1935). Italian soprano. She studied with Ettore Campogalliani at Bologna and in 1955 made her début at Modena as Micaëla. After a season with the Netherlands Opera, she sang Zerlina at Glyndebourne (1960–61), returning in 1962 as Susanna and Adina. She made her Covent Garden début as Nannetta, and later appeared there as Zerlina, Susanna, Violetta, Mimì, Micaëla, Charles Gounod's Marguerite, and Tatyana (1988). In 1962 she sang Elvira (*I puritani*) at Wexford and first appeared at La Scala as Mimì; subsequent roles included Marie (*La fille du régiment*), Jules Massenet's Manon and Amelia (*Simon Boccanegra*), which she also sang at Covent Garden during the 1976 Scala visit and Elvira (*Ernani*). She made her Metropolitan début in 1965 as Mimì, and her repertory there included Suzel, Charles Gounod's Juliet, Liù and Tatyana (1989). At Salzburg, where she made her début in 1966 as Micaëla, she took on heavier roles, singing Desdemona (1970), Elisabeth de Valois (1975) and Aida (1979). She later added Giacomo Puccini's Manon Lescaut and Butterfly to her repertory, and sang Adriana Lecouvreur at San Francisco (1985), Bologna (1988) and Munich (1990). She sang Lisa (*Queen of Spades*) at La Scala in 1990. In the last years of her career she sang Fedora in several theatres. The purity, fullness and even focus of her voice are evident in her many recordings, most notably in her Mimì, Aida, Micaëla and Tatyana.

Harold Rosenthal/Alan Blyth

Frezzolini [Frezzolini-Poggi], Erminia

(*b* Orvieto, 27 March 1818; *d* Paris, 5 Nov 1884). Italian soprano. She is identified with Romantic opera and especially with Giuseppe Verdi, two of whose heroines she created: Giselda in *I Lombardi* and *Giovanna d'Arco*, at La Scala, Milan (in 1843 and 1845 respectively). Trained mainly by her father, GIUSEPPE FREZZOLINI, a noted bass, and Domenico Ronconi, she had bel canto skills but sang in the new manner called for by Verdi's works, uniting smooth legato and dramatic power. Her sensational début, at Florence in 1837, was in the title role of Vincenzo Bellini's *Beatrice di Tenda*; this remained one of her most effective parts, along with Gaetano Donizetti's Lucrezia Borgia (in which she caused another sensation, at La Scala in 1840), Bellini's Elvira (*I puritani*), and Verdi's Giselda, Gilda (*Rigoletto*) and Leonora (*Il trovatore*). She also created the title role in Carlo Coccia's *Giovanna II, regina di Napoli* (1840, Milan). She was compared to MARIA MALIBRAN for boldness, intensity and pathos, with an added sweetness of timbre; F.-J. Fétis wrote of her beauty and nobility on stage. After an early London season (1841) and many Italian engagements, she spent the years between 1847 and 1857 in St Petersburg, Madrid, London and Paris. Vocal decline and financial extravagance led her during the years 1857–60 to tour, at times hazardously, in the USA and Cuba and, as late as 1874, to appear in minor Italian theatres; Mark Twain records a concert in Naples in 1867 greeted with both applause and hisses. Her brief marriage in 1841 to the tenor ANTONIO POGGI ended in legal separation; her letters show her aware of the difficult position of women in a male-dominated world. After Poggi died (1875) she married a French doctor.

M. Twain: *The Innocents Abroad* (New York, 1869), ii, chap. 2
J. Rosselli: *Singers of Italian Opera* (Cambridge, 1992)

John Rosselli

Frezzolini, Giuseppe

(*b* Orvieto, 9 Nov 1789; *d* Orvieto, 16 March 1861). Italian bass. He studied in Orvieto, making his début in 1819 at Terni in Stefano Pavesi's *Ser Marcantonio*. He appeared in Florence, Siena, Modena, Turin, Venice and at La Scala, where in 1827 he sang in the first performance of Saverio Mercadante's *Il montamaro*. The same year he created Pasquale in Gaetano Donizetti's *Olivo e Pasquale* at Rome; he sang in the premières of Donizetti's *Alina, regina di Golconda* (1828, Genoa) and Giovanni Pacini's *Il talismano* (1829, Milan). In 1832 he created Dulcamara in *L'elisir d'amore* (Teatro della Cannobiana, Milan), and sang the part again in Berlin in 1834, when the work was performed in German under the title *Der Liebestrank*, and in 1835, in Italian, in Vienna. In 1840 he sang in the first performance of Alberto Mazzucato's *I corsari* at La Scala and, as Mamm' Agata, in the first Viennese performance of Donizetti's *Convenienze ed inconvenienze teatrali*. His repertory included the bass *buffo* parts in operas by Gioachino Rossini and Luigi Ricci. The soprano, ERMINIA FREZZOLINI, was his daughter.

Elizabeth Forbes

Friant, Charles

(*b* Paris, 1890; *d* Paris, 22 April 1947). French tenor. His father was a principal dancer at the Opéra, Paris, and he himself sang in the chorus and appeared in the première of Vincent d'Indy's *L'étranger* as a boy. He later trained with Sarah Bernhardt and joined her company as an actor, then going to the Conservatoire to study singing in 1910. His operatic début was in the Paris première of Jules Massenet's *Cléopâtre*. From 1920 to 1939 he was a member of the Opéra-Comique, appearing in a wide repertory but enjoying special success in Massenet operas such as *Manon*, *Werther* and *Le jongleur de Notre Dame*. Premières included *Le roi Candaule* by Alfred Bruneau and *Le Hulla* by Marcel Samuel-Rousseau. He also sang at Monte Carlo and La Monnaie, Brussels. His recordings, especially those from *Werther*, are distinctively stylish and expressive.

J.B. Steane

Friberth [Frieberth, Friebert, Friedberg], Carl [Karl]

(*b* Wullersdorf, Lower Austria, 7 June 1736; *d* Vienna, 6 Aug 1816). Austrian tenor, librettist and composer, brother of the composer Joseph Frieberth, with whom he is often confused. He was a musician in the Esterházy retinue from 1 January 1759, numbering among the highest-paid singers; also in 1759, Prince Paul Esterházy sent him to Italy to study singing. Joseph Haydn wrote a number of roles and arias for him and for his wife of 1769, the former Maria Magdalena Spangler, and seems to have aided their careers at Eisenstadt out of friendship. The couple took the roles of Tobias and Sarah in the première of *Il ritorno di Tobia* (Vienna, 1775), and Friberth wrote the libretto (in Italian) to Haydn's opera *L'incontro improvviso* of the same year (based on L.H. Dancourt's *La rencontre imprévue*, set by C.W. Gluck in 1764), in which he created the role of Ali. He may also have adapted *Lo speziale* (Sempronio, 1768), *Le pescatrici* (Fresellino,

1770) and *L'infedeltà delusa* (Filippo, 1773). He also created Don Pelagio in *La canterina* (1767). He had an immense range (Frisellino's 'Tra tuoni e lampi' in *Le pescatrici* reaches *c'''*), and he was an accomplished actor. After leaving Esterházy's service in 1776, Friberth became Kapellmeister at Vienna's two Jesuit churches (the Kirche Am Hof and the Universitätskirche) and at the Minoritenkirche. He retained these posts until his death and devoted himself primarily to the composition of church music, including nine masses. He also sang in Katharina Schindler's troupe (1776), published 24 lieder in Joseph von Kurzböck's *Sammlung deutscher Lieder für das Klavier* (iii, 1780), and from 1771 was a member of the Vienna Tonkünstler-Societät, which he later served in various important administrative capacities. An Italian journey of 1796, underwritten by Prince Esterházy, is said to have brought him the pope's Order of the Golden Spur. Some Italian and Latin vocal pieces by him are extant, and there are editions of nine of his lieder (DTÖ, liv, Jg.xxvii/2, 1920/R).

Mary Hunter/R

Frick, Gottlob

(*b* Ölbronn, nr Pforzheim, 28 July 1906; *d* Mühlacker, 18 Aug 1994). German bass. He studied at the Musikhochscule in Stuttgart and was a chorus member at the Stuttgart Opera (1927–31). He was engaged at Coburg in 1934, making his début as Daland. After periods at Freiburg and Königsberg he was engaged at the Dresden Staatsoper, where he created Caliban in Heinrich Sutermeister's *Die Zauberinsel* (1942) and the Carpenter in Joseph Haas's *Die Hochzeit des Jobs* (1944), and sang Rocco, Otto Nicolai's Falstaff, Prince Gremin, the Peasant in Carl Orff's *Die Kluge*, and, especially, the Wagnerian bass roles. He joined the Berlin Städtische Oper in 1950 and the Bavarian and Vienna Staatsopern in 1953. He first sang at Covent Garden in 1951, as Hunding and Hagen, and appeared there regularly from 1957 to 1967 in the Wagner repertory and as Rocco. He also appeared at Bayreuth, Salzburg (where he took part in the première of Werner Egk's *Irische Legende*), the Metropolitan, La Scala and other leading theatres. Although he officially retired in 1970 he continued to make occasional appearances in Munich and Vienna, and in 1971 sang Gurnemanz at Covent Garden. In 1976 the Stuttgart Opera staged *Die lustigen Weiber von Windsor* to honour his 70th birthday. Frick had a strong, firmly centred yet flexible bass voice which was immediately recognizable; he sang with the utmost intelligence and with incisive diction. He recorded all his major roles, notably his Rocco (three times), Hagen and Gurnemanz.

W. Schwinger: 'Gottlob Frick', *Opera*, xvii (1966), pp. 188–93

Harold Rosenthal/Alan Blyth

Frijsh, Povla

(*b* Aerø, 3 Aug 1881; *d* Blue Hill, ME, 10 July 1960). Danish soprano. After studying with Ove Christensen she went to Paris at the age of 17 to work with JEAN PÉRIER and made her recital début there three years later. She toured with the Cortot-Thibaud-Casals trio, from whom she acknowledged learning much about phrasing and timing. She appeared in Paris in recital with Raoul Pugno and was chosen by Gustav Mahler to sing in his Second Symphony in Cologne (1910). She made her American début in New York in 1915 and gave annual recitals there until 1947. Frijsh's voice was distinctive in timbre and expressively used. Although she sang in opera only twice – in Paris (*L'incoronazione di Poppea*) and in Copenhagen (Peter Heise's *Drot og marsk*) – her sense of drama was extraordinary: she made a hair-raising experience of Franz Schubert's *Gruppe aus dem Tartarus*, yet could sing César Cui's *La fontaine de Csarskoë-Zelo* in the purest bel canto. She was always interested in new songs, encouraging composers such as Virgil Thomson, Randall Thompson, Samuel Barber and Rebecca Clarke by including their works in her programmes. She was the first to sing many of Francis Poulenc's songs in New York, and she gave the New York premières of Ernest Bloch's *Poèmes d'automne* and Charles Loeffler's *Canticum fratris solis* (1925). In her later years she was active as a teacher. Her complete recordings have been issued on CD.

P.L. Miller: 'Povla Frijsh', *American Record Guide*, xiii (1946–7), 7–10

Philip l. Miller

Frittoli, Barbara

(*b* Milan, 1969). Italian soprano. She studied at the Conservatorio di Musica G. Verdi in Milan and made her professional operatic début in Valentino Bucchi's *Il giuoco del barone* at the Teatro Comunale, Florence, in 1989. During the next few years she established a reputation as one of the leading Italian sopranos of her generation, specialising in W.A. Mozart (Countess Almaviva, Donna Anna, Donna Elvira, Fiordiligi) and lyric Italian and French roles. She made several important débuts in 1992: as Mimì at the San Carlo, Naples; in the title

role of *Beatrice di Tenda* at La Scala; and as Micaëla (*Carmen*) in Philadelphia. Micaëla was also the role of her débuts at the Vienna Staatsoper (1993) and the Metropolitan Opera (1995). In 1997 she sang her first Liù, at the Opéra-Bastille. Her other Italian roles include Amelia (*Un ballo in maschera*) and Desdemona, with which she made her début at the Salzburg Easter Festival in 1996.

Among her Mozart roles, her powerful yet touching Fiordiligi has been admired in Vienna (1994), Naples, and on her débuts at Covent Garden and Glyndebourne (both 1998). Frittoli returned to Covent Garden to sing Alice Ford (1999), and to Glyndebourne as Donna Anna (2000). She has sung Donna Elvira at the Vienna Staatsoper, the Opéra-Bastille, the San Carlo, Naples, and the Salzburg Festival (1999), and in 2001 added a notably fiery Elettra (*Idomeneo*) to her Mozart roster, singing the role at the Edinburgh Festival and in the recording with Charles Mackerras. In concert she has been acclaimed in such works as Giuseppe Verdi's Requiem, Johannes Brahms's *German Requiem*, Gioachino Rossini's *Stabat mater* and Richard Strauss's *Vier letzte Lieder*, which she sang at the Proms in 2003. Frittoli's other recordings include an eloquent Leonora in *Il trovatore* – a triumphant first foray into *lirico-spinto* territory – Mimì, Liù, Nedda (*Pagliacci*), and discs of Mozart and Verdi arias.

Richard Wigmore

Fuchs, Marta

(*b* Stuttgart, 1 Jan 1898; *d* Stuttgart, 22 Sept 1974). German soprano. She studied in Stuttgart, Munich and Milan. She made her début as a mezzo in Aachen in 1928, where she stayed until 1930, and was then engaged by Fritz Busch for the Dresden Staatsoper; among her roles were Octavian, Amneris, Azucena, Eboli and Ortrud. Gradually she assumed dramatic soprano roles, the first being Kundry (1933, Amsterdam; 1933–7, Bayreuth). She became the most important soprano at Bayreuth from 1938, when she succeeded LEIDER as Brünnhilde (1938–42), sharing Isolde with her in 1938. She sang at Covent Garden with the Dresden company in 1936 (Donna Anna, the Marschallin and Ariadne), and in Paris (1938) with the Berlin Staatsoper, of which she was also a member. She retired in 1945. Fuchs had a warm and expressive voice, and was among the most impressive interpreters of Brünnhilde of her day, as her recording of Act 2 of *Die Walküre* confirms. She was also an accomplished singer of lieder, and made notable recordings of Franz Schubert's *Erlkönig* and Hugo Wolf's *Geh, Geliebter*.

Leo Riemens/Alan Blyth

Fugère, Lucien

(*b* Paris, 22 July 1848; *d* Paris, 15 Jan 1935). French baritone. After failing as a sculptor, he began his singing career in Parisian cabarets, making his début at the *café-concert* Ba-ta-clan on 3 March 1870. On that occasion he introduced to the public Robert Planquette's celebrated march *Le régiment de Sambre-et-Meuse*. At the end of 1873 he was engaged by the Bouffes-Parisiens, and in 1877 by the Opéra-Comique where, until 1910, he sang more than 100 roles, over 30 of them in first performances, including Fritelli in Emmanuel Chabrier's *Le roi malgré* (1887), Chevalier des Grieux in Jules Massenet's *Le portrait de Manon* (1894), Pandolfe in *Cendrillon* (1899), the Father in *Louise* (1900) and the Devil in *Grisélidis* (1901). He was also famous as Papageno and Figaro, and as Leporello, which he sang at Covent Garden in 1897. In 1910 he was Sancho Panza in the Paris première of Massenet's *Don Quichotte* (the score of which the composer dedicated to Fugère) at the Gaîté-Lyrique, and appeared there regularly from 1910 to 1913, including the première of Henry Février's *Carmosine* (1913). He returned to the Opéra-Comique in 1919 in André Messager's *La basoche*, celebrating his artistic jubilee there in 1920. He appeared only once at the Opéra, in a gala performance on 1 April 1919. Henri de Curzon described him as 'a basse-chantante of easy baritone range, with a ringing clarity in the lower register and a skilful refinement in the upper', and praised his 'comic verve filled with originality, the subtlety of which never allows it to fall into caricature or vulgarity'. The recordings he made in 1902 are much in demand with collectors. In 1929 he wrote, with Raoul Duhamel, a *Nouvelle méthode pratique du chant français par l'articulation*. It was sharply criticized by H. Malherbe for being a hazardous and complicated system for 'gymnasts, pugilists, painters and mimes', but at least it served Fugère, who at the age of 85 sang Gioachino Rossini's Bartolo to triumphant acclaim at the Théâtre de la Porte-St-Martin.

V. Girard: 'Lucien Fugère', *Record Collector*, v (1953), 101 [with discography]

HAROLD ROSENTHAL

Furlanetto, Ferruccio

(*b* Pordenone, Sicily, 16 May 1949). Italian bass. He made his début in 1974 at Lonigo (Vicenza) as Sparafucile, then sang at various Italian opera houses. At Aix-en-Provence (1976–7) he sang Dr Grenvil and Cecil (*Roberto Devereux*). Having made his US début in 1978 at New Orleans as Zaccaria (*Nabucco*), he sang Alvise (*La Gioconda*) at San Francisco the following year. At Glyndebourne (1980–81) his roles were Melibeo (Joseph Haydn's *La fedeltà premiata*) and Gioachino Rossini's Don Basilio. He has sung Phanuel (*Hérodiade*) and Ernesto (*Parisina*) at Rome; Oberto, Charles Gounod's Méphistophélès and Don Giovanni at San Diego (1985–93); Mahomet II at the Paris Opéra (1985); Philip II, W.A. Mozart's Figaro, Leporello, Don Alfonso and Don Giovanni at Salzburg (1986–95); Fernando (*La gazza ladra*) at Pesaro (1989); and Don Pasquale at La Scala (1994). He made his Covent Garden début as Leporello in 1988, and between 1990 and 1992 sang Leporello, Don Giovanni and Figaro at the Metropolitan. Furlanetto's other roles include Rossini's Assur, Mustafà and Don Magnifico, and Giuseppe Verdi's Ramfis and Fiesco. A lively actor with an incisive, dark-toned voice, he has recorded several of his Mozart roles, including Leporello with Herbert von Karajan and Figaro and Don Alfonso with James Levine.

ELIZABETH FORBES

G

Gadski, Johanna

(*b* Anklam, Prussia, 15 June 1872; *d* Berlin, 22 Feb 1932). German soprano. She studied in Stettin and made an early début (1889) at the Kroll Opera, Berlin, singing there and elsewhere in Germany for the next five years. In 1895 she began a successful three-year association with the Damrosch Opera Company in the USA, and from 1899 to 1901 was active at Covent Garden and at Bayreuth, where she sang Eva (1899). Between 1900 and 1917, however, her main centre was the Metropolitan, where (after a previous appearance as Elisabeth in *Tannhäuser* on tour in Philadelphia) she made her house début on 6 January 1900 as Senta; she became one of the Metropolitan's most valuable Brünnhildes and Isoldes, excelling also in many Verdi roles such as Aida, Leonora (*Il trovatore*) and Amelia. After the USA's declaration of war on Germany, her reputation suffered during the war hysteria of that time. From 1929 until her death (in a car accident) she was active and successful in a Wagnerian touring company in the USA organized at first by Sol Hurok and then by herself. She sang even the heaviest Wagner roles with unfailing beauty of voice and purity of style, and showed the same qualities in her Italian parts. Her powers are well documented in the large number of records which she made between 1903 and 1917, notably in her Wagner excerpts and in scenes from *Aida* and *Il trovatore* with CARUSO, HOMER and AMATO.

L. Migliorini and N. Ridley: 'Johanna Gadski', *Record Collector*, xi (1957), pp. 196–231 [with discography], 257–85; xii (1958–60), 36

Desmond Shawe-Taylor

Gaffarello.

See CAFFARELLI.

Gailhard, Pierre [Pedro]

(*b* Toulouse, 1 Aug 1848; *d* Paris, 12 Oct 1918). French bass and opera director. He studied singing in Toulouse and with Révial at the Paris Conservatoire. On 4 December 1867 he made his début at the Opéra-Comique as Falstaff in Ambroise Thomas' *Le songe d'une nuit d'été*, and was engaged at the Opéra in 1870. There he created the roles of Richard in Auguste Mermet's *Jeanne d'Arc* (1876), Simon in Victorin Joncières' *La reine Berthe* (1878) and Pedro in Thomas' *Françoise de Rimini* (1882). He appeared regularly at Covent Garden from 1879 to 1883, his roles there including Osmin, Girot in Ferdinand Hérold's *Le pré aux clercs*, and Méphistophélès, of which he was generally considered to be the finest interpreter since FAURE. His voice was warm and vibrant, but also powerful, and he was said to be unequalled in vehemence in the scene of the Benediction of the Swords (*Les Huguenots*). Yet he also had the necessary light touch for comic operas. In 1884 he was appointed manager of the Opéra, a position he held jointly with Jean Eugene Ritt (1884–91) and then with Eugène Bertrand (1893–9); on Bertrand's death in 1899 he became sole manager (until 1906). His regime was perhaps most distinguished for its excellent Wagner productions. Gailhard also wrote the scenarios for two works by Paul Vidal, *Maladetta* (1893) and *Guernica* (1895). On 6 July 1886 he was appointed a Chevalier of the Légion d'Honneur.

Harold Rosenthal

Galeffi, Carlo

(*b* Malamocco, Venice, 4 June 1882; *d* Rome, 22 Sept 1961). Italian baritone. After studies with Giovanni Di Como, Enrico Sbriscia and Teofilo De Angelis, he made his début at the Teatro Quirino, Rome, in 1903 in *Lucia di Lammermoor*. His first great successes were in Palermo (1908) and at the S Carlo, Naples, in *Aida* and *Rigoletto* (1909) and during 1910 and 1911 he appeared in Lisbon, Buenos Aires, Boston and at the Metropolitan. His first appearance at La Scala was in 1912 in *Don Carlos*, and he sang there for 18 seasons (the last time in 1940). He was also engaged at Chicago (1919–21) and returned to Buenos Aires, where he stayed until 1952. Galeffi had a full, smooth voice with an extensive range; it was remarkable for its affecting warmth. His passionate phrasing and dramatically eloquent enunciation made him a first-rate Rigoletto and a fine Verdi interpreter generally (*Nabucco*, *La traviata*, *Un ballo in maschera*, *Il trovatore*, *Don Carlos*). His other important roles included Tonio and Gioachino Rossini's Figaro. He took part in the first performances of Pietro Mascagni's *Isabeau* (1911) and *Parisina* (1913), Italo Montemezzi's *L'amore di tre re*

(1913) and Arrigo Boito's *Nerone* (1924), and sang at the Italian premières of *Gianni Schicchi* (title role, 1919, Milan) and *Il tabarro* (Michele, 1919, Rome).

G. Lauri-Volpi: 'Carlo Galeffi (1884–1961): a Tribute', *Opera*, xii (1961), pp. 802–3

Rodolfo Celletti/Valeria Pregliasco Gualerzi

Gall, Yvonne

(*b* Paris, 6 March 1885; *d* Paris, 21 Aug 1972). French soprano. She studied at the Paris Conservatoire and in 1908 was engaged by André Messager at the Opéra as Woglinde in the first production there of *Götterdämmerung*. Keeping the French lyric roles such as Marguerite, Manon and Thaïs at the centre of her career, she developed a powerful voice and added more dramatic parts such as Elsa and, in 1923, Isolde to her repertory. At Monte Carlo she sang in the premières of operas by Raoul Gunsbourg, the impresario of the house: *Le vieil aigle* (1909), *Le cantique des cantiques* (1922) and *Lysistrata* (1923). Abroad, she appeared with success in Buenos Aires and in Chicago, where she sang in the first American performance of *L'heure espagnole*. Tosca was the part in which she appeared at La Scala and in her only performances at Covent Garden (1924); Ernest Newman remarked that she presented 'three capable Toscas, a different one in each act'. One of her last appearances was as Phoebe in Jean-Philippe Rameau's *Castor et Pollux* at the Maggio Musicale, Florence, in 1936. Her bright, very French soprano is heard in many recordings, notably in one of the first complete operas on record, Charles Gounod's *Roméo et Juliette* (1912).

J.B. Steane

Galli, Filippo

(*b* Rome, 1783; *d* Paris, 3 June 1853). Italian bass. He made his début in 1801 at Naples as a tenor. On the advice of Giovanni Paisiello and of Luigi Marchesi, he became a bass, making his second début in Gioachino Rossini's *La cambiale di matrimonio* at Padua in 1811. The next year he sang Tarabotto in *L'inganno felice* at the Teatro S Moisè, Venice, the first of nine Rossini premières in which he took part, and made his début at La Scala as Polidoro in Pietro Generali's *La vedova stravagante*. During the next 13 years he appeared in over 60 different operas at La Scala, including 26 first performances. In one season (1814) he appeared in three operas by Ferdinando Paer and sang Guglielmo (*Così fan tutte*), the title role of *Don Giovanni*, Dandini in the first performance of Stefano Pavesi's *Agatina* and Selim at the première of *Il turco in Italia*. Other

Rossini premières at La Scala included *La pietra del paragone* (Count Asdrubale, 1812) and *La gazza ladra* (Fernando, 1817).

Elsewhere, Galli sang Mustafà at the première of *L'italiana in Algeri* at the Teatro S Benedetto, Venice (1813), the Duke of Ordow at the première of *Torvaldo e Dorliska* (1815, Teatro Valle, Rome), and created the title role of *Maometto II* at the S Carlo, Naples (1820); he made his Paris début in 1821 at the Théâtre Italien in *La gazza ladra*. His last Rossini creation was Assur in *Semiramide* at La Fenice (1823). He appeared in London at the King's Theatre between 1827 and 1833, and at the Teatro Carcano, Milan, he sang Henry VIII at the first performance of *Anna Bolena* (1830). He continued to sing, in Mexico and Spain, for another decade, returning to La Scala in 1840 to take the title role in Gaetano Donizetti's *Marino Faliero*. He was a chorus master in Madrid and Lisbon, and then taught at the Paris Conservatoire for some years.

The wide range of Galli's magnificent voice and its extreme flexibility are fully demonstrated by the roles that Rossini wrote for him, while his power as an actor can be imagined from Donizetti's Henry VIII.

H. Weinstock: *Donizetti and the World of Opera in Italy, Paris and Vienna in the First Half of the Nineteenth Century* (New York, 1963/R)

Elizabeth Forbes

Galli-Curci [née Galli], Amelita

(*b* Milan, 18 Nov 1882; *d* La Jolla, CA, 26 Nov 1963). Italian soprano of Italian-Spanish parentage. She graduated from the Milan Conservatory in 1903 with a first prize as a pianist; on the advice of Pietro Mascagni she also had some vocal lessons there with Carignani and Sara Dufes, but she was mainly self-taught. She made her début at Trani on 26 December 1906 as Gilda, a role that remained a favourite throughout her career. In 1908 she appeared in Rome with De Luca in the Italian première of Georges Bizet's posthumous *Don Procopio*. During the next eight years she became increasingly successful in the coloratura repertory not only in Italy but in Spain, Egypt and Russia, and in South and Central America.

Galli-Curci made a spectacular début at Chicago as Gilda on 18 November 1916. She remained with the Chicago company for eight consecutive seasons, singing Rosina, Amina, Lucia, Linda di Chamounix, Violetta, Dinorah, Juliette, Manon and Lakmé, and an occasional Mimì and Madama Butterfly. She made her début at the Metropolitan in *La traviata* on 14 November 1921, appearing as a regular member of the company in these and other similar parts until

Amelita Galli-Curci in the title role of 'Dinorah' (Meyerbeer)

her farewell in *Il barbiere di Siviglia* on 24 January 1930. By that time she had begun to show signs of vocal distress; and, after an operation in 1935 for the removal of a throat tumour, her attempted return to the stage, for a single performance of *La bohème* in Chicago in 1936, was unsuccessful. She was never heard in opera in London; and her English concert tours, in 1924, 1930 and 1934, though at first very popular, did not show her at the height of her powers. She was married twice: to the artist Luigi Curci (1910, divorced 1920); then, in 1921, to Homer Samuels, her accompanist.

Galli-Curci possessed a limpid timbre of exceptional beauty and an ease in florid singing that sounded natural rather than acquired; her highest register, up to *e'''*, remained pure and free from shrillness. Her style, though devoid of dramatic intensity, had a languorous grace and charm of line capable of conveying both gaiety and pathos. Her numerous Victor records, especially those made before 1925 by the acoustic process, deserved their enormous vogue, being among the best of their kind ever made; during the post-1925 electric period she successfully repeated some of her excellent duet recordings with TITO SCHIPA and GIUSEPPE DE LUCA, but by then her work had begun to be affected by false intonation and other flaws. Most of her recordings have been successfully remastered on CD.

C.E. Le Massena: *Galli-Curci's Life of Song* (New York, 1945/R)

A. Favia-Artsay: 'Amelita Galli-Curci', *Record Collector*, iv (1949), pp. 162–79 [with discography by G. Whelan]

Desmond Shawe-Taylor

Galli-Marié [née Marié de l'Isle, Marié], Célestine(-Laurence)

(b Paris, Nov 1840; d Vence, nr Nice, 22 Sept 1905). French mezzo-soprano. She was taught by her father, Félix Mécène Marié de l'Isle, a double bass player who became a tenor at the Opéra and eventually a conductor. She made her début in Strasbourg in 1859 as Célestine Marié, but shortly after married a sculptor named Galli (who died in 1861) and took the professional name Galli-Marié. Emile Perrin, director of the Opéra-Comique, engaged her after hearing her in a performance of Michael Balfe's *The Bohemian Girl* in Rouen. She first appeared at the Opéra-Comique to considerable acclaim as Serpina in Giovanni Pergolesi's *La serva padrona* (1862) and sang there regularly until 1885, creating the title roles of *Mignon* (1866) and *Carmen* (1875), as well as creating important roles in works by François-Auguste Gevaert, Ernest Guiraud, Aimé Maillart, Victor Massé, Jules Massenet and Emile Paladilhe (who was her lover). Though principally associated with the Opéra-Comique, she toured in France and Europe, singing in the Italian première of *Carmen* at Naples and performing in London with a French company at Her Majesty's Theatre in 1886, as well as in Spain. With her return to the Opéra-Comique as Carmen in 1883 the work finally achieved the success in Paris it had enjoyed elsewhere in Europe. Her last appearance in the capital was in this, her most famous role, in a performance with MELBA (Micaëla), JEAN DE RESZKE (Don José) and Jean Lassalle (Escamillo) in December 1890 at the Opéra-Comique, to raise funds for a monument to Bizet. She was praised for her intelligence, natural acting ability (as both comedian and tragedian) and musicianship; her voice was not distinguished for its range or volume, but for the warmth of its timbre.

Harold Rosenthal/Karen Henson

Galusin, Vladimir

(b Rubtsovsk, 1957). Russian tenor. A graduate of the Novosibirsk Conservatory, he began his career at Novosibirsk Opera in 1981. In 1990 he joined the Kirov Opera, where his roles at home and on tour have ranged from Grigory (*Boris Godunov*), Mikhail (*The Maid of Pskov*), Grishka Kuter'ma (*The Legend of the Invisible City of Kitezh*) and Hermann (*The Queen of Spades*) to Aleksey (*The Gambler*) and Sergey (*Lady Macbeth of the Mtsensk District*); many of these are recorded. From the mid-1990s he also appeared with opera companies and festivals around the world, notably at Bregenz (*Kitezh*, 1995), Amsterdam (*Luisa Miller*), Florence (*Turandot*), New York (*Boris Godunov*) and Buenos Aires (*Yevgeny Onegin*), all in

1997, Vienna (*Don Carlos*, 1998), and Verona (*Aida*), Macerata (*Otello*) and Paris (*Queen of Spades*) in 1999; he returned to Madrid in 2000 for Don Alvaro in *La forza del destino*. Other roles include Giacomo Puccini's Des Grieux and Pinkerton. Galusin's virile, ringing tone is more italianate than Russian, but his vivid, almost expressionistic acting makes him an exciting interpreter of both repertories.

John Allison

Garbin, Edoardo

(b Pauda, 12 March 1865; d Brescia, 12 April 1943). Italian tenor. His teachers in Milan were Alberto Selva and Vittorio Orefice. In 1891 he made his début at Vicenza in *La forza del destino*, appearing at La Scala two years later as Fenton in the world première of *Falstaff*. He subsequently married his Nannetta, ADELINA STEHLE, with whom he then appeared for many years, principally in the Puccini operas. His other important première was that of Ruggero Leoncavallo's *Zazà* in 1900 (Dufresne), also at La Scala, where he remained until 1918. His European successes were not repeated in London where he met with a critical press in 1908. His records show a voice that often bewilders the ear, sometimes ringing, sometimes white in tone, and mixing some rather forced singing with passages of considerable delicacy.

J.B. Steane

García, Manuel (del Pópulo Vicente Rodríguez)

(b Seville, 21 Jan 1775; d Paris, 10 June 1832). Spanish composer, tenor, director and singing teacher, father of PAULINE VIARDOT, MARIA MALIBRAN, and the baritone and noted teacher Manuel Garcia. He was baptized Manuel del Pópulo Vicente Rodríguez in the church of S María Magdalena on 23 January 1775, the son of Gerónimo Rodríguez Torrentera (1743–1817) and Mariana Aguilar (1747–1821).

Contrary to rumours of being orphaned or illegitimate which have persisted to the present in biographical studies, García seems to have lived a stable family life with his parents, maternal grandmother and sisters Maria and Rita until he was at least 14, when his name disappears from the parish censuses of S María Magdalena. After musical studies in Seville with Antonio Ripa and Juan Almarcha, García made his début in Cádiz, where he married the singer Manuela Morales in 1797. The next year the couple joined Francisco Ramos's company in Madrid. García's début with the company, in a *tonadilla*, took place on 16 May

1798 in the Teatro de los Caños del Peral. The premières of his own *tonadillas*, *El majo y la maja* and *La declaración*, followed in December 1798 and July 1799. In 1800–01 García was in Málaga, where he achieved considerable success as a composer and singer. In a letter to the Marquis of Astorga dated 29 November 1800 he expressed an interest in returning to Madrid to promote the cause of Spanish opera. The king's permission was solicited by Astorga in March 1801. Back in Madrid, as well as singing in the capacity of first tenor, García shared directing responsibilities at the Caños del Peral with an actor from Cartagena, Isidoro Maiquez. Opera alternated with theatrical performances, and Maiquez was famous for his interpretation of Shakespeare's Othello, a role with which García later became identified in the guise of Gioachino Rossini's Otello.

In August and September 1804 García, together with Manuela Morales and the singer Joaquina Briones (who later became his second wife), gave performances in Cádiz. In October he returned to the Caños del Peral to sing in the opera *La esclava persiana*. On 28 April 1805 he sang in his monologue opera *El poeta calculista* for the first time. It was a tremendous success: the aria 'Yo que soy contrabandista' gained enduring popularity throughout Europe (both of his daughters later interpolated it in the lesson scene of *Il barbiere di Siviglia*, and in 1836 Franz Liszt composed a *Rondeau fantastique* based on it).

On 2 October 1806 García submitted a request to be named composer to the Teatro del Príncipe in Madrid. His qualifications were substantiated by the composer Blas de Laserna and the violinist Josef Barbieri (*apoderado* of the theatre and grandfather of the composer Francisco Asenjo Barbieri), and his request was granted. However, political problems in the administration prevented him from taking up the post, and he left Spain. The last opera he composed in Spain, *Los ripios de maestro Adán*, was performed on 18 January 1807. After brief stays in Valladolid, Burgos, Vitoria, Bayonne and Bordeaux, García and Joaquina Briones settled in Paris. He made his début at the Théâtre de l'Impératrice in Paer's *Griselda* on 11 February 1808.

In 1811 García travelled to Italy; he sang at Turin before making his début at the Teatro S Carlo in Naples on 6 January 1812 in Marcos Portugal's *Oro non compra amore*. At this time he began formal vocal training (for the first time in his life) with the tenor Giovanni Ansani. García's *Il califfo di Bagdad* and *Tella e Dallaton, o sia La donzella di Raab* were performed in Naples in 1813 and 1814 respectively, and it was there that in 1815 he created the role of Norfolk in Rossini's *Elisabetta, regina d'Inghilterra*. In 1816 in Rome he sang Almaviva in the pre-

Manuel García in the title role of 'Otello' (Rossini)

mière of *Il barbiere di Siviglia* under its original title *Almaviva, ossia L'inutile precauzione*.

Towards the end of 1816 García and his wife returned to Paris to sing at the Théâtre Italien. Paolino in *Il matrimonio segreto* was the role of García's *rentrée* on 16 October. *Il califfo di Bagdad* had its Paris première on 22 May 1817 at the Théâtre Italien. It was performed regularly until García and his wife left the company after a contretemps with the director, ANGELICA CATALANI, purportedly resulting from García's receiving more applause than she in a single performance of M.A. Portugal's *La morte di Semiramide* on 20 September 1817. He turned to the Opéra-Comique, where his first French opera, *Le prince d'occasion*, was performed on 13 December 1817. In 1818 he travelled to London, appearing at the King's Theatre with great success in *Otello* and *Il barbiere di Siviglia*.

Now in his vocal prime, García returned to Paris the next year and became a sensation in roles such as Almaviva, Otello and Don Giovanni. In 1824 García returned to London for one more season; he opened a singing academy in Dover Street, and published *Exercises and Method for Singing* (1824). The following October he embarked for New York with his wife and children, Manuel, Maria (later Maria Malibran) and Pauline (Pauline Viardot). There he directed the first performances of opera in Italian in the USA. As well as Rossini's operas (*Otello, Barbiere, Cenerentola, Tancredi, Il turco in Italia*) and his own (*L'amante astuto, La figlia dell'aria*), García, at the urging of Lorenzo da Ponte, presented W.A. Mozart's *Don Giovanni*. From New York he went in 1827 to Mexico City, where he was received with great enthusiasm. After a debate on language which raged for months in the Mexican press, García obligingly translated Rossini's and his own operas into Spanish. *El amante astuto* was chosen for the anniversary celebration on 5 October 1828 of the nation's constitution of 1824.

García had planned to remain in Mexico, but political events forced him to leave and in 1829 he returned to Paris. He won tumultuous applause on his reappearance, as Almaviva, but his voice was in decline and he was not even able to finish his final performance of *Don Giovanni* on 23 December 1829. Undaunted, he dedicated himself to teaching, for which he seems to have been specially gifted. Among his most successful students, apart from his children, were the tenor ADOLPHE NOURRIT, the Countess (María de las Mercedes Santa Cruz y Montsalvo) Merlin and HENRIETTE MÉRIC-LALANDE. He continued to perform, and his tremendous energy 'in spite of his white hair' was noted in the *Revue musicale* of March 1831. His last appearance, in August 1831, was in a *buffo* role in a student performance of Count Beramendi's *Le vendemie di Xeres*. His death certificate shows that he died on 10 June the following year. He was buried in Père Lachaise cemetery.

Throughout García's career critics commented above all on the remarkable flexibility of his voice. He was also praised for his musicianship, skilful acting and gift of invention. This last led to reproofs for his tendency towards crowd-pleasing ornamentation. The voice was, according to F.-J. Fétis, a deep tenor. Indeed, it is possible that it was a baritone with a highly developed falsetto which allowed García to tackle the demands of Rossini's *Otello* as well as the fireworks of his own arias. The depth of his voice enabled him to take the title role of *Don Giovanni* which, according to Fétis, he sang with a 'Herculean force'. His expert delivery of recitative, as well as the Andalusian fire of his stage presence, made him ideally suited to dramatic roles such as Otello and Don Giovanni. García's dynamic perfectionism left its impact on three continents and his legacy, in the hands of his children, was carried into the 20th century.

James Radomski/R

García, Pauline.

See VIARDOT, PAULINE.

Garden, Mary

(*b* Aberdeen, 20 Feb 1874; *d* Inverurie, Scotland, 3 Jan 1967). American soprano of Scottish birth. Taken to the USA in 1883, she studied singing in Chicago with Sarah Robinson-Duff, supported financially by wealthy patrons David and Florence Mayer. In 1896 the Mayers financed her further studies in Paris, chiefly with Trabadelo and LUCIEN FUGÈRE. When her patrons withdrew their support in 1899, Garden was coached by the American soprano SIBYL SANDERSON, through whom she met Albert Carré, director of the Opéra-Comique, and Jules Massenet. After much preparation she was engaged for the Opéra-Comique, making an acclaimed unscheduled début as Gustave Charpentier's Louise on 10 April 1900 when, after the first act, Marthe Rioton succumbed to illness. Other leading roles soon followed: she created Marie in Lucien Lambert's *La Marseillaise* and Diane in Gabriel Pierné's *La fille de Tabarin*. She was coached by Sanderson for *Thaïs* at Aix-les-Bains, then sang Manon and André Messager's *Madame Chrysanthème* at Monte Carlo (conducted by the composer). Her success was sealed when Claude Debussy chose her (against the wishes of Maurice Maeterlinck) to sing Mélisande in the première of *Pelléas et Mélisande* (1902; see illustration). The devoted efforts of Garden, Carré and the conductor Messager pulled *Pelléas* from the near-disaster of the *repetition générale* to full triumph by the end of the season. At Covent Garden, where she appeared in the 1902 and 1903 seasons, she sang Manon, Juliet and Charles Gounod's Marguerite, as well as the title role in the première of Herbert Bunning's *The Princess Osra* (1902), but London did not please her and she was never to return to the house. Meanwhile, at the Opéra-Comique she sang in Massenet's *Grisélidis* (1902), then created the title role in Xavier Leroux's *La reine Fiammette* (1903). She carried off superbly the coloratura writing in the role of Violetta (1903), triumphed in Camille Saint-Säens's *Hélène* in 1905 and the same year created Massenet's Chérubin, a role specially written for her, at Monte Carlo.

By now Garden was recognized as a supreme singing-actress, with uncommonly vivid powers of characterization (her dramatic style influenced by both Sarah Bernhardt and Coquelin Ainé) and a rare subtlety of colour and phrasing. Two years after creating Chrysis in Camille Erlanger's *Aphrodite* (1906), the Paris opera sensation of 1906–7, she left the Opéra-Comique for the Opéra, where she sang Ophelia in Ambroise Thomas' *Hamlet* and, in 1909, the title part in Henry Février's *Monna Vanna*. Enticed by Oscar Hammerstein for his battle against the Metropolitan, Garden's début at the Manhattan Opera House was in the American première of *Thaïs* (25 November 1907). She was hailed as the supreme singing-actress – some critics had reservations about her voice, but none questioned her remarkable gift for tone colouring, subtle phrasing and 'forward'

*Mary Garden
as Mélisande
in 'Pelléas et
Mélisande'
(Debussy)*

style. With an imported Parisian supporting cast, *Pelléas* (1908) achieved popular success, and the same year she astonished America with her impersonation of a young boy in Massenet's *Le jongleur de Notre Dame*. As Salome (1909), her lascivious kissing of the severed head of the Baptist outraged the guardians of morality even more than her Dance of the Seven Veils (which she executed chastely in a body-stocking). By now a household name in America, in 1910 she began a long association with the Chicago Grand Opera, where she was admired in such roles as Fanny in Massenet's *Sapho*, the Prince in *Cendrillon*, Carmen, Tosca and Dulcinée in *Don Quichotte*. After two disastrous forays into film with Samuel Goldwyn (including a silent version of *Thaïs*), other powerful stage interpretations followed, including the title roles in Massenet's

Cléopâtre and the première of Février's *Gismonda* (both 1919), Fiora in Italo Montemezzi's *L'amore dei tre re* (1920), Charlotte in *Werther* (1924), Katiusha in Franco Alfano's *Risurrezione* (1925, in French) and the heroine of Arthur Honegger's *Judith* (1927), the last two both American premières.

Garden was a controversial director of the Chicago Opera Association in the 1921–2 season (uniquely, for a director, continuing to sing leading roles), and was responsible for innovative works, including the première of Sergey Prokofiev's *The Love for Three Oranges* (1921). Prokofiev wrote *The Fiery Angel* for her but she declined to sing it. After retiring from the opera stage in 1934, she worked as a talent scout for MGM and gave lecture-recitals and talks, mainly on Debussy. She was decorated by the French and Serbian governments during

World War I and made a Chevalier of the Légion d'Honneur in 1921. For much of her life she openly encouraged young singers and even secretly paid for them to receive training. She herself died in penury, almost forgotten.

O. Thompson: 'Mary Garden', *The American Singer* (New York, 1937), pp. 265–77

M. Garden and L. Biancolli: *Mary Garden's Story* (New York, 1951/*R*)

G. Whelan: 'The Recorded Art of Mary Garden', *Gramophone*, xxix (1951–2), pp. 367–72 [with discography]

H. Cuénod: 'Remembrances of an Enchantress', *High Fidelity*, xiv/7 (1964), pp. 36–8

R.D. Fletcher: '"Our Own" Mary Garden', *Chicago History*, ii/1 (1972), pp. 34–46

D. Shawe-Taylor: 'Mary Garden (1874–1967)', *Opera*, xxxv (1984), pp. 1079–84

M.T.R.B. Turnbull: *Mary Garden* (Aldershot, 1996) [incl. discography]

Michael T.R.B. Turnbull/R

Gardoni, Italo

(*b* Parma, 12 March 1821; *d* Paris, 26 March 1882). Italian tenor. He made his début in 1840 at Viadana in the title role of Gaetano Donizetti's *Roberto Devereux* and then sang in Turin, Berlin, Milan, Brescia and Paris, first at the Opéra, later at the Théâtre Italien. He made his London début in 1847 at Her Majesty's Theatre, creating Carlo in Giuseppe Verdi's *I masnadieri*. He also sang Pylades (*Iphigénie en Tauride*), Don Ottavio, Tamino, Faust and Florestan. At Covent Garden he made his début in 1855 as Count Ory, then sang Nemorino, Danilowitz in Giacomo Meyerbeer's *L'étoile du nord* and Corentin in *Dinorah* (1859), both first British performances. He sang regularly in London and Paris until 1874, when he retired. His repertory included Rodrigo (Rossini's *Otello*), Giannetto (*La gazza ladra*), Elvino, Arturo, Fra Diavolo and Alfredo. Versatile both as singer and actor, he had a light but well-focussed voice.

Elizabeth Forbes

Garrett, Lesley

(*b* Doncaster, 10 April 1955). English soprano. She studied at the RAM from 1977 to 1979 and while there made her mark as a spirited Lazuli in Emmanuel Chabrier's *L'étoile* (1979); the same year she won the Kathleen Ferrier Prize and entered the National Opera Studio. After appearances in small roles at Batignano, she made her official stage début as Dorinda (G.F. Handel's *Orlando*) in 1980 at the Wexford Festival, singing W.A. Mozart's

Zaide there the following year. In 1981 she sang Carolina (*Il matrimonio segreto*) at the Buxton Festival and in 1982 Susanna at Opera North. After singing Despina for Glyndebourne Touring Opera, she joined the ENO in 1984 where, among other roles, she has sung Bella (*The Midsummer Marriage*, 1985), Atalanta (*Serse*, 1985), Zerlina (1985), Yum-Yum (1986), Jacques Offenbach's Eurydice (1988), Oscar (*Un ballo in maschera*, 1989), Susanna (1990), Adèle (1991), Rose (*Street Scene*, 1992), Dalinda (*Ariodante*, 1993), the title role in *The Cunning Little Vixen* (1995) and Rosina (1998), in all of which she sang and acted with a natural command of the stage. With her outgoing personality and powers of communication, thanks not least to her perfect diction, she has been an enthusiastic proselytizer of opera on television, notably in her own programmes 'Viva la Diva' and 'Lesley Garrett – Tonight', and on her mixed recitals on CD. In all this, however, she has never compromised her musicianship, excellent technique or keen sense of style.

R. Milnes: 'Lesley Garrett', *Opera*, xlvii (1996), pp. 499–506

Alan Blyth

Garrigues, Malvina.

See Schnorr von Carolsfeld, Malvina.

Garrison [Siemonn], Mabel

(*b* Baltimore, 24 April 1886; *d* New York, 20 Aug 1963). American soprano. She studied singing at the Peabody Conservatory with W.E. Heinendahl and Pietro Minetti, and later in New York with Oscar Saenger and Herbert Witherspoon. Using her married name of Siemonn, she made her stage début with the Aborn Opera Company in Boston as Philine in Ambroise Thomas' *Mignon* in 1912. She joined the Metropolitan Opera two years later, making her official début as Frasquita in *Carmen* in November 1914. She only attracted real attention, however, when she substituted at short notice for Raymonde Delaunois as Urbain in *Les Huguenots* the following month. Similarly, she made a fine impression two years later when she replaced Frieda Hempel as the Queen of Night, and she scored her greatest success as the Queen of Shemakha in Nikolay Rimsky-Korsakov's *The Golden Cockerel*, covering for Maria Barrientos, in 1918. Among her other roles were Olympia, Gilda, Martha, Rosina, Adina (*L'elisir d'amore*) and Lucia di Lammermoor, Oscar and Mme Herz (*Der Schauspieldirektor*).

After her final Lucia at the Metropolitan in 1921, Garrison performed extensively in Europe for several years. She sang Rosina with the Chicago Civic Opera in 1926 and later took part in a series of Baroque operas under Werner Josten in Northampton, Massachusetts, which included the American premières (in English) of G.F. Handel's *Serse* (1928) and *Rodelinda* (1931). Also a recitalist, she was admired for the clarity of her voice and her smooth and elegant style.

A. Favia-Artsay: 'Historical Records: Mabel Garrison', *Hobbies*, lix/8 (1954), pp. 22–3

G.M. Eby: 'The Two Careers of Mabel Garrison', *ON*, xxiii/4 (1958–9), pp. 24–7

Philip L. Miller

Gasdia, Cecilia

(*b* Verona, 14 Aug 1960). Italian soprano. After winning the RAI Maria Callas competition in 1981, she sang Giulietta (*I Capuleti e i Montecchi*) in Florence. The following year she took over at short notice the title role of *Anna Bolena* at La Scala, and sang Amina (*La sonnambula*) at S Carlo. She has appeared throughout Europe and the USA, making her Metropolitan début in 1986 as Charles Gounod's Juliet. Her repertory includes Giuseppe Verdi's Violetta, Gilda, Hélène (*Jérusalem*) and Desdemona; Giacomo Puccini's Lauretta, Mimì, Musetta and Liù, as well as Alice (Antonio Salieri's *Falstaff*), Nedda, Teresa (*Benvenuto Cellini*) and Salome (*Hérodiade*). A specialist in bel canto, Gasdia excels particularly in such roles as Gioachino Rossini's Zelmira, Armida, Hermione and Corinna (*Il viaggio a Reims*), all of which she has recorded, and Vincenzo Bellini's Beatrice di Tenda. She has a well-schooled voice, with a brilliant coloratura technique, and phrases stylishly.

Elizabeth Forbes

Gasteen, Lisa

(*b* Brisbane, 13 Nov 1957). Australian soprano. When she began to study at the Brisbane Conservatory, as a mezzo, her interest was primarily in jazz singing. Her real classical training began when her teacher began to train her as a soprano. In 1982 she won the Australian regional finals of the Metropolitan Opera Auditions, and in 1984 she was awarded the Covent Garden Scholarship. Gasteen made her operatic début in 1985 with the Lyric Opera of Queensland (now Opera Queensland) as the High Priestess (*Aida*) followed by Desdemona (*Otello*). She became a regular guest artist with the Australian Opera (now Opera Australia), in roles including Leonore (*Fidelio*), Elsa (*Lohengrin*), Donna Elvira

and Donna Anna (*Don Giovanni*), Aida, Elisabetta (*Don Carlo*) and Elisabeth (*Tannhäuser*). For Victoria State Opera she has sung Elisabetta, Elisabeth, Desdemona, Aida and Leonora (*Il trovatore*).

In 1991 Gasteen won the Cardiff Singer of the World Competition, and the following year she sang Donna Anna in Prague (with Charles Mackerras) and made her début with Scottish Opera, as Leonora (*Il trovatore*). Over the next few years the demands of her young family meant that she remained based in Australia, where she sang mainly Italian roles. In 1996 she sang an acclaimed Kaiserin (*Die Frau ohne Schatten*) at the Melbourne International Festival, and the following year made her Metropolitan Opera début, as Aida.

Gasteen's voluminous yet supple soprano, with its bright, athletic top and sumptuous lower register, has been admired throughout Europe and the United States, above all in Richard Strauss and Richard Wagner. She made a triumphant Covent Garden début as Isolde in 2002, returning as Elektra in 2003, as Isolde, again, in 2004 and as Brünnhilde in the 2005–6 *Ring* cycle. In 2004 she sang her first Senta, for Opera Australia, and the following year made her Vienna Staatsoper début, as Brünnhilde. In concert Gasteen has performed in works such as Gioachino Rossini's *Stabat mater*, *Elijah*, Leoš Janáček's *Glagolitic Mass*, Ludwig van Beethoven's Ninth Symphony and Giuseppe Verdi's *Requiem*. Her discs include a recital of Italian arias, Marta in Eugen D'Albert's *Tiefland* and Brünnhilde in *Die Walküre*, recorded during the State Opera of South Australia's *Ring* cycle in Adelaide in November 2004.

Richard Wigmore

Gatti [Pesci], Gabriella

(*b* Rome, 5 July 1908; *d* Rome, 22 Oct 2003). Italian soprano. She studied singing after gaining a diploma for the piano, made her professional début at the Maggio Musicale Fiorentino in 1933 as Anna (*Nabucco*) and the following year sang an acclaimed Desdemona at the Rome Opera. She sang up to 1953 in all the leading Italian theatres, most often in Rome and Florence, but also at La Scala between 1938 and 1947 where she sang in *La damnation de Faust* in the 1946–7 season. Her voice was lyrical in character, graceful in timbre and expression, and she stood as an example of the refined, classical style at a time when the opposite manner prevailed among Italian sopranos. She was a notable Mathilde in *Guillaume Tell* (the role of her farewell in Rome) and Desdemona in Giuseppe Verdi's *Otello*, though her wide repertory included Claudio Monteverdi's

Orfeo, Elisabeth (*Tannhäuser*), W.A. Mozart's Countess Almaviva, Abigaille (*Nabucco*), Helen of Troy (in Arrigo Boito's *Mefistofele*) and Marie in *Wozzeck*, of which she gave the Italian première (1942, Rome).

L. Morris Hall: 'Gabriella Gatti', *Record Collector*, xxxi (1986), pp. 171–229 [with discography]

Rodolfo Celletti/Valeria Pregliasco Gualerzi

Gauci, Miriam

(*b* Malta, 3 April 1957). Maltese soprano. She studied in Malta and Milan, winning international prizes at La Scala, Treviso and Bologna, where she made her début in Francis Poulenc's *La voix humaine* in 1984. Her well-managed voice, of moderate volume and fine quality, fitted her well for the lyric Italian repertory and she was soon in demand throughout Europe and the USA. At Santa Fe in 1987 she made her US début as Butterfly, the role with which she has become most closely associated. Later that year she appeared as Mimì in *La bohème* with PLACIDO DOMINGO on the opening night of the season at Los Angeles. In 1992 her recording of *Madama Butterfly* and a solo recital aroused wide interest and speculation that here might be a successor to MIRELLA FRENI. Her career has continued successfully, and though her stage presence was sometimes felt to lack colour she can be deeply touching in roles such as Giuseppe Verdi's Desdemona and Giacomo Puccini's Sister Angelica. In 1997 she appeared at the Vienna Staatsoper singing both Margherita and Elena in Arrigo Boito's *Mefistofele* and was re-engaged for performances of *Don Carlos*, *Pagliacci* and Verdi's *Requiem* under Riccardo Muti.

J.B. Steane

Gautier, François.

See FRANZ, PAUL.

Gaveaux [Gavaux, Gaveau], Pierre

(*b* Béziers, 9 Oct 1760; *d* Charenton, nr Paris, 5 Feb 1825). French singer and composer. At the age of seven he became a choirboy at Béziers Cathedral, where he was a soloist for nearly ten years. Intended for the clergy, he studied Latin and began philosophical studies while working at composition with the cathedral organist, Abbé Combès. On the death of the Bishop of Béziers he accepted a post as first tenor at St Séverin, Bordeaux. He continued his musical studies under the direction of Franz Beck and his early success as a composer of motets

decided his vocation. He abandoned his clerical plans and was engaged as a conductor and tenor at the Grand Théâtre de Bordeaux. In 1788 he was active in Montpellier and toured in the south of France, and the following year was called to Paris to sing in the Théâtre de Monsieur, which at that time was in the Tuileries. His light and agreeable voice had a fine timbre so that he could sing such major roles as Floreski in Luigi Cherubini's *Lodoïska* in 1791 and Romeo in Daniel Steibelt's *Roméo et Juliette* in 1793. He was, moreover, an excellent musician and an intelligent actor, and was highly valued as a member of the company because of his competence and dynamism. He remained with the company when it moved to the Théâtre Feydeau, where he created the role of Jason in Cherubini's *Médée* (1979) and began his career as a composer of dramatic works with minor *opéras comiques*; these remained fashionable from his *Le paria, ou La chaumière indienne* (1792) to *Le traité nul* (1797).

When the companies of the Théâtres Favart and Feydeau merged in 1801, Gaveaux remained a member, but he took only secondary roles as his voice was losing its grace and it was becoming difficult for him to keep up with such rivals as Jean Elleviou or JEAN-BLAISE MARTIN. In 1804 he was appointed a singer in the imperial chapel. He was affected by mental illness and left the stage in 1812.

Apparently cured, he resumed his publishing activities, directing the shop in the Passage Feydeau himself from 1813 to 1816. He wrote one more *opéra comique*, *Une nuit au bois, ou Le muet de circonstance* (1818). In 1819 he retired to a mental asylum.

Paulette Letailleur/R

Gay [née Pichot Gironés], María

(*b* Barcelona, 13 June 1879; *d* New York, 29 July 1943). Spanish mezzo-soprano. She studied with Juan Gay Planella, her first husband, and then in Paris with Ada Adini. She sang in concerts at Brussels, and soon afterwards (in 1902) appeared there at the Théâtre de la Monnaie as Carmen. Until the late 1920s she performed at the world's leading opera houses, including Madrid, Covent Garden (1906), La Scala (1906–7), the Metropolitan (1908–9) and Chicago, where she sang regularly between 1910 and 1927. She was a mainstay of the Boston Opera Company and its short-lived successor (1909–14, 1915–17), singing such roles as Delilah, Amneris and Santuzza. With her second husband, the tenor GIOVANNI ZENATELLO, she featured prominently in the first open-air seasons in the Verona Arena (from 1913) and, after her retirement, directed a school of singing in New York. If her merits as a singer were debatable (though her middle and lower registers were rich and resonant) she owed her fame above all to her realistic Carmen.

Q. Eaton: 'Shameless Siren', *ON* (8 Jan 1972), pp. 6–7
M. Scott: *The Record of Singing*, i: *To 1914* (London, 1977), pp. 166–7

Rodolfo Celletti/Valeria Pregliasco Gualerzi

Gayarre, Julián (Sebastián)

(*b* Valle de Roncal, Pamplona, 9 Jan 1844; *d* Madrid, 2 Jan 1890). Spanish tenor. After studying in Madrid with Melchiorre Vidal, and Milan, he made his début in 1867 as Danieli (*Les vêpres siciliennes*) at Varese. He sang in Bilbao, Parma, Vienna, St Petersburg, Milan, where he created Enzo in *La Gioconda* (1876), Rome, where he sang in the première of Giuseppe Libani's *Il conte verde* (1873), and Henri in Gaetano Donizetti's posthumous *Le duc d'Albe* (1882). He made his Covent Garden début in 1877 as Fernand (*La favorite*) and over the next decade sang Don Ottavio, Elvino, Arturo, Edgardo, Gennaro (*Lucrezia Borgia*), Ernani, the Duke, Riccardo (*Un ballo in maschera*), Faust, Raoul, John of Leyden (*Le prophète*), Vasco da Gama, Alim (*Le roi de Lahore*) and Sobinin in the first performance in Britain of *A Life for the Tsar* (1887). He also sang Max, Lohengrin and Tannhäuser, roles much heavier than his usual repertory. The *Miserere grande*, sung in Seville during Holy Week, was written for Gayarre by the Spanish composer Hilarión Eslava. In 1889 he collapsed while singing Nadir (*Les pêcheurs des perles*) in Madrid and died a month later. His friend Manuel Giró composed a Requiem for Gayarre. His voice, beautiful in timbre and even in quality throughout its range, was used with great skill and admirable taste.

Elizabeth Forbes

Gaye [first name unknown]

(*fl* 1676–81). French baritone. He created and revived principal *basse-taille* roles in Jean-Baptiste Lully's early *tragédies*: Aegeus (*Thésée*, 1675, revived 1677), Celaenus (*Atys*, 1676), Hierax (*Isis*, 1677) and Jupiter (*Le triomphe de l'amour*, 1681). Durey de Noinville attributes the creation of the title role in *Cadmus et Hermione* (1673) and that of Alcides in *Alceste* (1674) to Gaye, although François Parfaict names François Beaumavielle in both instances: the casting may have been different for performances at court and in Paris. In *Proserpine* (1680) the role of Pluto was apparently sung at St Germain by Gaye and in Paris by Beaumavielle.

Philip Weller

Gazzaniga, Marietta

(*b* Voghera, nr Milan, 1824; *d* Milan, 2 Jan 1884). Italian soprano. After her début at Voghera in 1840 as Jane Seymour in *Anna Bolena* and Romeo in *I Capuleti e i Montecchi*, she sang in Italian cities, notably in Verdi roles. She created the title role in *Luisa Miller* (1849, Naples) and Lina in *Stiffelio* (1850, Trieste). Verdi claimed in 1852 that he had disliked her in both; he was irritated just then at the failure of *Rigoletto* in Bergamo, which was blamed on her performance as Gilda. She went on nonetheless with such lyric coloratura parts as well as with heroic ones (Norma and Paolina in *Poliuto* at Bologna in 1852). She undertook several North and Central American tours, during the first of which (1857–8) her husband, Count Malaspina, died of smallpox on the voyage to Havana. In New York in 1866–7 an admiring critic reported 'greater purity and less vehement forcing of tone'. She went on singing in the Americas each year until 1870; by then she had exchanged her old part of Leonora in *Il trovatore* for the lower-lying part of Azucena.

G.C.D. Odell: *Annals of the New York Stage* (New York, 1927–49)
M. Conati: *La bottega della musica: Verdi e la Fenice* (Milan, 1983)

John Rosselli

Gedda [Ustinoff], Nicolai (Harry Gustaf)

(*b* Stockholm, 11 July 1925). Swedish tenor. His Russian father was a member of the Kuban Don Cossack Choir and subsequently choirmaster at the Russian Orthodox church in Leipzig; his mother, whose maiden name he adopted professionally, was Swedish. He studied with CARL-MARTIN OEHMAN and at the Swedish Royal Academy of Music in Stockholm. In 1951 he made his début at the Swedish Royal Opera in the première of Heinrich Sutermeister's *Der rote Stiefel*; in the following year he sang there as Chapelou in *Le postillon de Lonjumeau*, to immediate acclaim. He made his début at La Scala as Don Ottavio in 1953 and at the same theatre created the Groom in Carl Orff's *Il trionfo di Afrodite*. In 1954 he sang Huon in *Oberon* at the Paris Opéra, and the next year made his Covent Garden début as the Duke of Mantua in *Rigoletto*. He sang regularly for 22 seasons at the Metropolitan from 1957, the year of his American début (at Pittsburgh as Faust), creating Anatol in Samuel Barber's *Vanessa* (1958) and singing Kodana in the first American performance of Gian Carlo Menotti's *Le dernier sauvage* (1964). At the 1961 Holland Festival he sang Hector Berlioz's

Nicolai Gedda as the Duke of Mantua in 'Rigoletto'
(Verdi), Bavarian State Opera, 1966

Cellini, a role he repeated at Covent Garden in 1966, 1969 and 1976.

A fine linguist, speaking and singing in seven languages, Gedda commanded the range of vocal and idiomatic style for Cellini, Hans Pfitzner's Palestrina, P.I. Tchaikovsky's Hermann, Lohengrin, Faust, Riccardo, Pelléas, Pinkerton and Nemorino (which he sang at Covent Garden in 1981). He continued to sing fluently into his 70s. He was also an accomplished recitalist, his repertory encompassing songs in German, French, Russian and Swedish. His many recordings include his concert repertory and his major roles in both opera and operetta, most notably Dmitry, Lensky, Cellini and Charles Gounod's Faust, which indicate the plaintive yet virile quality of his tone and his sure, instinctive understanding of the style needed for different genres. He published a volume of memoirs, *Gåvan är inte gratis* [The present is not free] (Stockholm, 1978).

G. Storjohann: 'Nicolai Gedda', *Opera*, xvii (1966), pp. 939–44

J.B. Steane: *The Grand Tradition* (London, 1974/R), pp. 471–3

Harold Rosenthal/Alan Blyth

Geistinger, Marie

(*b* Graz, 26 July 1836; *d* Klagenfurt, 28 or 29 Sept 1903). Austrian soprano. Some sources suggest 1833

or 1828 as her year of birth. She performed in Graz as a child and appeared in Munich (1850), Vienna (1852), Berlin (1854–6), Hamburg (1856–7), Riga (1859) and Berlin again (1863–5). She then made her name at the Theater an der Wien in Vienna in the leading roles in Jacques Offenbach's *La belle Hélène*, *La Grande-Duchesse de Gérolstein* and *Barbe-bleue*. She became joint manager and created the role of Rosalinde in *Die Fledermaus* (1874) as well as leading roles in Johann Strauss the younger's *Indigo* (1871), *Carneval in Rom* (1873) and *Cagliostro in Wien* (1875). She subsequently sang in Leipzig (1877–80), made major reappearances in Vienna and Berlin and toured America with the Grand Opera Company four times (1881, 1891, 1896, 1899), appearing on both coasts. She possessed a full, well-schooled soprano, with an imposing coloratura.

Andrew Lamb

Gélin, Nicolas

(*b* Prangey, nr Langres, 15 Nov 1726; *d* after 1779). French bass. He joined the Paris Opéra about 1750, singing Neptune and Polyphemus in the 1752 revival of Jean-Baptiste Lully's *Acis et Galatée*. He then created Borée and Eole in Joseph de Mondonville's *Titon et l'Aurore* (1753). He took principal roles after the retirement of CLAUDE CHASSÉ in 1757, but faced stiff competition from HENRI LARRIVÉE, who rose swiftly to prominence after his début in 1755. Though subordinate, Gélin stood his ground, singing Thoas in the last revival of Henry Desmarets and André Campra's *Iphigénie en Tauride* in 1762, and creating important roles in Antoine Dauvergne's *tragédies lyriques* of the early 1760s. For C.W. Gluck he sang Calchas to Larrivée's Agamemnon in the première of *Iphigénie en Aulide* (1774) the High Priest in *Alceste* (1776), and Hidraot in *Armide* (1777); he also created roles for Gossec. He retired in 1779.

Philip Weller

Genast, Eduard

(*b* Weimar, 15 July 1797; *d* Wiesbaden, 3 Aug 1866). German bass-baritone. Son of the singer and actor Anton Genast, a friend and colleague of J.W. von Goethe, he made his début in 1814, aged just 17, as W.A. Mozart's Osmin. Shortly afterwards he was engaged at the Hofoper in Dresden. Here he created the role of Jacob in E.-N. Méhul's *Joseph*, in performances conducted by Carl Maria von Weber. He continued his career at the Leipzig Opera, where in 1828 he sang Lord Ruthven in the première of Heinrich Marschner's *Der Vampyr*. The following year he returned to the Weimar Hoftheater. Genast also composed two operas, lieder, and other vocal works. He was married to the singer and actress Caroline Christine Genast-Böhler.

Richard Wigmore

Gencer [Ceyrekgil], (Ayshe) Leyla

(*b* Istanbul, 10 Oct 1928; *d* Milan, 9 May 2008). Turkish soprano. A pupil of Giannina Arangi-Lombardi, she made her début at Ankara in 1950 as Santuzza, the role of her Italian début at the Arena Flegrea, Naples, in 1953. She sang at La Scala in 1957 as Madame Lidoine in the world première of Francis Poulenc's *Dialogues des Carmélites*. Subsequently she appeared throughout Europe and America, but until her retirement in 1983 was most often heard in Italy. Although her voice was limited in volume and not very even, she was able, thanks to her technique, strong temperament and theatrical intelligence, to tackle with success such dramatic roles as Gioconda and Aida. Lighter roles such as Gilda and Amina made the best use of her vocal flexibility and impressive soft singing; but her interpretative powers found most scope in the dramatic coloratura repertory, particularly in Gaetano Donizetti and early Giuseppe Verdi: *Elisabetta, regina d'Inghilterra, Anna Bolena, Maria Stuarda, Lucrezia Borgia, Attila, I due Foscari* and *La battaglia di Legnano*.

R. Celletti: 'Leyla Gencer', *Opera*, xxiii (1972), pp. 692–6
F. Cella: *Leyla Gencer* (Venice, 1986) [with discography]

Rodolfo Celletti/Valeria Pregliasco Gualerzi

Gens, Véronique

(*b* Orléans, 19 April 1966). French soprano. Having won prizes in her native city, and in early music at the Paris Conservatoire, Gens made her début with Les Arts Florissants in 1986. Under William Christie's guidance she quickly became a proficient and appealing interpreter of, among others, Henry Purcell, Jean-Baptiste Lully and Jean-Philippe Rameau, including appearances at the Aix-en-Provence Festival in *The Fairy-Queen* (1989) and *Castor et Pollux* (1991), both recorded. She sang in Lully's *Phaëton* at the reopening of the Lyons Opera in 1993, followed at the same theatre with Countess Almaviva (1994). The same season she took part in a production, jointly staged by the Théâtre du Châtelet and Covent Garden, of Purcell's *King Arthur*. She has since added Idamante, Donna Elvira and Lully's Galatea to her stage repertory. In addition to Christie, Gens has worked with such conductors as Marc Minkowski, Jean-Claude Malgoire, Philippe Herreweghe, René Jacobs and Christophe Rousset in the Baroque repertory, and in 1998 recorded an admired Fiordiligi in Jacobs's

set of *Così fan tutte*. She sang the same role to acclaim in the 2000 Aix-en-Provence Festival. With Herreweghe, in concert and on disc, she has undertaken Mary in Hector Berlioz's *L'enfance du Christ*. She is also a sympathetic, involving interpreter of French *mélodies* as can be heard on a disc of Gabriel Fauré, Claude Debussy and Francis Poulenc and a Berlioz recording. Her flexible, soft-grained voice, deployed with an innate sense of style, is used with eloquence and a strong sense of dramatic purpose.

Alan Blyth

Gentili, Serafino

(*b* Venice, 1775; *d* Milan, 13 May 1835). Italian tenor. He made his début in 1796 at Ascoli Piceno. From 1800 to 1803 he sang in Naples, and between 1812 and 1828 he appeared frequently at La Scala. He created Lindoro in Gioachino Rossini's *L'italiana in Algeri* (1813) at the Teatro S Benedetto, Venice. He also sang in Paris and Dresden.

Elizabeth Forbes

Genz, Stephan

(*b* Erfurt, 1973). German baritone. As a boy treble he was a member of the Thomanerchor in Leipzig, and at fifteen he began to study singing with Hans-Joachim Beyer at the Hochschule für Musik in Leipzig. He continued his studies with MITSUKO SHIRAI and Hartmut Höll at the Staatliche Hochschule für Musik in Karlsruhe, and also took lessons with DIETRICH FISCHER-DIESKAU and ELISABETH SCHWARZKOPF. His recital career began to develop after he won the Johannes Brahms Competition in Hamburg in 1994. He made a highly praised Wigmore Hall début in 1997 and has given lieder recitals in many of Europe's most prestigious venues, including the Théâtre du Châtelet and the Théâtre des Champs-Elysées in Paris, the Concertgebouw, the Schubertiade at Feldkirch and Hohenems, and the Aix, Edinburgh, Verbier and Florence Maggio Musicale festivals. He has also made recital tours in the USA, making an acclaimed US début at the Frith Collection, New York, in 2000, and in Japan.

After a season at the Deutsche Oper Berlin (1996–7), Genz appeared at the Lausanne Opera, making his début as Harlekin (*Ariadne auf Naxos*) in 1999, at La Scala, also as Harlekin (2000), at the Aix Festival (début as Guglielmo, 2000), at the Opéra Bastille, where he made his début as Pierrot/Fritz in *Die tote Stadt* in 2001, at the Hamburg Staatsoper (Guglielmo, 2002) and at the Teatro Regio, Parma (Papageno, 2005). He is also much in demand as a concert singer, working with such conductors as

John Eliot Gardiner, Philippe Herreweghe, René Jacobs and Sigiswald Kuijken. On disc his mellifluous, subtly coloured baritone and refined beauty of line have been admired as Harlekin and Olivier (*Capriccio*), in Gabriel Fauré's Requiem and a Mozart aria recital with his brother, tenor Christoph Genz, and in several recordings of lieder. His first solo album, of lieder by Ludwig van Beethoven (including *An die ferne Geliebte*), won the 1999 *Gramophone* magazine vocal award.

Richard Wigmore

Gergalov, Aleksandr

(*b* 5 July 1955). Russian baritone. A principal with the Kirov Opera, he made his début with the company as Gioachino Rossini's Figaro in 1982, the year he graduated from the Leningrad Conservatory. He was a prizewinner at Geneva (1985) and in the Chaliapin All-Russian Vocalists Contest (1989). His important roles include Onegin, Di Luna and the Marquis of Posa. He was much admired as Andrey Bolkonsky in *War and Peace* at the Mariinsky Theatre in 1991, televised in Europe and recorded on disc and video. Other parts recorded with the Kirov include Yeletsky (*Queen of Spades*), the Venetian (*Sadko*), Prince Ivan (*Kashchey the Immortal*) and Ferdinand (Prokofiev's *Betrothal in a Monastery*). His focussed voice is distinctive for its dark, eloquent tone.

John Allison

Gerhaher, Christian

(*b* Straubing, 24 July 1969). German baritone. He took singing lessons with PAUL KUEN and Raimund Grumbach and attended the Opera School at the Musikhochschule in Munich while also studying philosophy and medicine, graduating with a medical doctorate. Here he met his regular piano partner, Gerold Huber, and took part in masterclasses with FISCHER-DIESKAU, SCHWARZKOPF and BORKH. In 1998 he won the Prix International Pro Musicis and was engaged for two years at the Würzburg Stadttheater, where his roles included Papageno, Guglielmo and Albert (*Werther*). At the same time he developed an admired lieder partnership with Huber, making débuts at Carnegie Hall's chamber music hall in New York and the Schubertiade in Feldkirch in 1999, and at the Wigmore Hall in 2000. As a concert singer Gerhaher has performed with many leading orchestras and conductors, including Helmuth Rilling, Nikolaus Harnoncourt, Philippe Herreweghe and Trevor Pinnock. In 2003 he made his début with the Berlin PO under Simon Rattle,

in Benjamin Britten's *War Requiem*, returning the following year for Carl Orff's *Carmina burana*. His operatic roles since leaving Würzburg in 2000 have included Kilian in *Der Freischütz* (which he recorded with Bruno Weil in 2001), Count Almaviva (which he sang at the Opéra du Rhin, Strasbourg, in 2004) and Claudio Monteverdi's Orfeo, with which he made a notable début at the Alte Oper, Frankfurt, in 2005. Gerhaher's rounded, evenly produced high baritone and direct, expressive style are heard to particular advantage in his recordings of Franz Schubert's song cycles (of which *Die schöne Müllerin* and *Winterreise* won awards), *Dichterliebe*, Johannes Brahms's *Vier ernste Gesänge*, Gustav Mahler's *Kindertotenlieder* and Joseph Haydn's *Creation*.

Richard Wigmore

Gerhardt, Elena

(*b* Leipzig, 11 Nov 1883; *d* London, 11 Jan 1961). German soprano and mezzo-soprano, active in England. She studied at the Leipzig Conservatory (1900–04), whose director, Arthur Nikisch, having heard her sing as a student, took the unprecedented step of accompanying her himself at her first public recital on her 20th birthday. At that time she made several pioneering records of lieder with Nikisch, with whom she was romatically involved. After a few stage appearances at the Leipzig Opera in 1905–6 (as Mignon and Charlotte), she devoted herself wholly to concert work, and soon became a notable interpreter of German song. She sang for the first time in England in 1906, and in the USA in 1912. After World War I she soon resumed her international career, but continued to live in Leipzig. In 1932 she married Fritz Kohl, the director of the Leipzig radio, who was arrested in the following year under the Nazi regime. When he was eventually released, he and his wife left Germany in 1934 and settled in England, where Gerhardt had always been very popular. Her fame increased during World War II when she took part in several of the National Gallery Concerts organized by Myra Hess. She continued to sing for some years after the war, both in public and for the BBC, but devoted herself increasingly to teaching.

Gerhardt's voice deepened to mezzo-soprano during her maturity, and became an ideal instrument for the lieder repertory, enabling her to sing many nominally masculine songs without any sense of strain or incongruity. For instance, her numerous performances of *Winterreise* had a memorably exalted and tragic character. Her recitals and records contributed notably to the then growing fame of Hugo Wolf. In her best vocal period, the sensuous beauty of her floating tones in Johannes

Brahms's *Feldeinsamkeit* or in the *da lontano* final verse of Schubert's *Der Lindenbaum* could hold an audience enthralled. In later years minor technical faults intruded, but seemed unimportant beside her penetrating interpretations, her mastery of light and shade, her humour, rhythmic energy and wide variety of tone-colour. Although her style was very much of its period (especially in her liberal use of portamento), she made every song she sang a part of her own warm and rich personality.

E. Gerhardt: *Recital* (London, 1953/R) [with appx: 'Elena Gerhardt and the Gramophone', and discography by D. Shawe-Taylor]

W. Radford: 'Elena Gerhardt', *Recorded Sound*, no.40 (1970), 671–7

Desmond Shawe-Taylor/Alan Blyth

Gerl [née Reisinger], **Barbara**

(*b* Vienna or ?Pressburg [now Bratislava], 1770; *d* Mannheim, 25 May 1806). Singer and actress, wife of FRANZ XAVER GERL. By 1780 she was a member of Georg Wilhelm's troupe, playing in Moravia and Silesia; she is listed in the Gotha *Theater-Kalender* for 1781: 'children's roles, and sings in operettas'. Later numbers of the *Theater-Kalender* trace her rise from soubrette roles to 'first dancer' and player of queens etc. During these years Wilhelm's company performed at Olmütz (Olomouc), Troppau (Opava), Brünn (Brno) and Vienna (the 'Fasantheater auf dem Neustift', and in 1783 also in the Kärntnertortheater), and in many provincial Austrian towns. Early in 1789 she joined EMANUEL SCHIKANEDER's company at Regensburg, making her début as Kalliste in a German version of Pietro Guglielmi's *La sposa fedele* (*Robert und Kalliste*). That summer she, Franz Gerl and BENEDIKT SCHACK joined Schikaneder in Vienna when he began his directorship at the Freihaus-Theater auf der Wieden. Barbara Gerl took the principal female roles in Schikaneder's sequel to Vicente Martín y Soler's *Una cosa rara*, called *Der Fall ist noch weit seltner*, in May 1790, and in *Robert und Kalliste* and Schikaneder's *Der Stein der Weisen* (in which she and Schikaneder sang the duet 'Nun, liebes Weibchen' K625/592a, written or orchestrated by W.A. Mozart), both in September. She also performed in a number of spoken plays. On 30 September 1791 she achieved her one link with immortality by creating the part of Papagena in *Die Zauberflöte*. She and her husband appear to have left Schikaneder's company in 1793; they were at Brünn from 1794 until 1801 and from 1802 in Mannheim, where she died shortly after the birth of her second child.

Peter Branscombe

Gerl [Görl], **Franz Xaver**

(*b* Andorf, Upper Austria, 30 Nov 1764; *d* Mannheim, 9 March 1827). Austrian bass and composer. The son of a village schoolmaster and organist, by 1777 he was an alto chorister at Salzburg, where he must have been a pupil of Leopold Mozart. He was at the Salzburg Gymnasium, 1778–82, and then studied logic and physics at the university. In autumn 1785 he went to Erlangen as a bass, joining the theatrical company of Ludwig Schmidt, who had earlier been at Salzburg. In 1786 he joined G. F. W. Grossmann's company, performing in the Rhineland, and specialized in 'comic roles in comedies and Singspiels'. By 1787 he was a member of EMANUEL SCHIKANEDER's company at Regensburg, making his début in Giuseppe Sarti's *Wenn zwei sich streiten* (*Fra i due litiganti*) and appearing as Osmin in *Die Entführung*. From summer 1789 he was a member of Emmanuel Schikaneder's company at the Freihaus-Theater auf der Wieden, Vienna. On 2 September 1789 he married the soprano Barbara Reisinger (*see* GERL, BARBARA). His name first appears as one of the composers of *Der dumme Gärtner aus dem Gebirge* (*Der dumme Anton*), Schikaneder's first new production at his new theatre, on 12 July 1789; it is unlikely that this was Gerl's first theatre score since Schikaneder would hardly have entrusted such an important task to a novice. *Der dumme Anton* proved so successful that it had no fewer than six sequels; Gerl certainly performed in two of these, though he and BENEDICT SCHACK may not have written all the scores. Between 1789 and 1793 Gerl wrote music for several more plays and Singspiels.

Gerl played a wide variety of parts in plays and operas (including Don Giovanni and Figaro in German) during his Vienna years, though he is most often associated with the role of Sarastro in *Die Zauberflöte*, which he created on 30 September 1791 and continued to sing at least until November 1792 (the 83rd performance, announced by Schikaneder as the 100th). The Gerls appear to have left the Freihaus-Theater in 1793; they were at Brünn (Brno), 1794–1801, and from 1802 Gerl was a member of the Mannheim Hoftheater. Apart from operatic roles he also appeared frequently in plays; he retired in 1826. That year he married Magdalena Dengler (née Reisinger – his first wife's elder sister), the widow of Georg Dengler, director of the Mainz theatre.

Although the paucity of the surviving material and the difficulty of identifying Gerl's contribution to joint scores make it impossible to evaluate him as a composer, the works he wrote were popular in their day. His career as a singer is better documented. When Friedrich Ludwig Schröder, the greatest actor-manager of his age, went to Vienna in 1791 he was told not to miss hearing Schack and Gerl at Schikaneder's theatre. At the end of May he heard Paul Wranitzky's *Oberon*, in which both were singing, and thought Gerl's singing of the Oracle 'very good'. Mozart's high regard for his qualities is evident in the aria 'Per questa bella mano' (к612), written for Gerl in March 1791, and above all in Sarastro's music. Mozart's friendly relationship with Gerl is attested by the fact that Gerl was one of the singers who is said, on Mozart's last afternoon, to have joined the dying composer in an impromptu sing-through of the Requiem (the others were Schack and Mozart's brother-in-law Franz Hofer).

Peter Branscombe/R

Gerville-Réache, Jeanne

(*b* Orthez, 26 March 1882; *d* New York, 5 Jan 1915). French mezzo-soprano. Her studies with Rosine Laborde attracted the attention of both EMMA CALVÉ, a former pupil of Laborde, and the 78-year-old PAULINE VIARDOT who coached her for her début as C.W. Gluck's Orpheus at the Opéra-Comique in 1899. She took part in the world première of Camille Erlanger's *Le Juif polonais* (Paris, 1900), and in 1902, as Geneviève, in that of *Pelléas et Mélisande*. She appeared in Brussels and London, and in 1907 was engaged by Oscar Hammerstein I for the new Manhattan Opera Company, where she repeated her original role in the American première of *Pelléas* and scored a special success as Delilah, a role she had studied with Camille Saint-Saëns. In 1910 in the first American production of *Elektra* she sang Clytemnestra, a role she promptly renounced. In Chicago she entered the Wagnerian repertory as Fricka and Brangäne. Everything pointed to a brilliant continuation of her career but at the age of 32 she contracted fatal blood-poisoning. By most accounts she had one of the most beautiful voices of the century, with temperament to match – a view borne out by her few recordings, which also show some stylistic faults such as broken phrasing.

J. McPherson and W.R. Moran: 'Jeanne Gerville-Réache', *Record Collector*, xxi (1973–4), 53–79

J. B. Steane

Geszty, Sylvia

(*b* Budapest, 28 Feb 1934). Hungarian soprano. She studied in Budapest, making her début at the State Opera in 1959. Engaged at the Berlin Staatsoper (1961–70), she sang C.W. Gluck's Cupid, Oscar, Susanna, Gilda, Queen of Shemakha and the Queen of Night, which was her début role at Covent Garden (1966) and Salzburg (1967). At Hamburg she sang Olympia, the Fiakermilli and Musetta. Engaged at Stuttgart (1971), she sang Norina and Manon (H.W. Henze's *Boulevard Solitude*), which she repeated in Edinburgh (1977). She made her Glyndebourne début (1971) as Zerbinetta, returning for Konstanze (1972), which she sang at Salzburg. In 1973 she made her American début with the New York City Opera, in Los Angeles, as Sophie. Her roles included Donna Anna, Fiordiligi, Giovanni Paisiello's Rosina and G.F. Handel's Alcina. She sang Gismonda in Domenico Cimarosa's *Il marito disperato* at Schwetzingen (1976). Her light, silvery voice, effortless coloratura and spirited acting were perfectly suited to Zerbinetta, which she sang in East and West Berlin, Munich, Vienna and Düsseldorf, and also recorded for Rudolf Kempe.

Alan Blyth

Gheorghiu, Angela

(*b* Adjud, 7 Sept 1965). Romanian soprano. She studied with Arta Florescu at the Enescu Academy in Bucharest and made her professional début at 18 as Solveig in Edvard Grieg's *Peer Gynt* and her opera début at the Cluj Opera as Mimì in 1990, the year she won the Belvedere International Competition in Vienna. She first appeared at Covent Garden as Zerlina in 1992 and the same year sang an acclaimed Mimì there. Further Covent Garden appearances have been as Nina in Jules Massenet's *Chérubin*, Liù, Micaëla and Adina. However, her most admired appearance was as a vocally and dramatically near-ideal Violetta in Richard Eyre's staging of *La traviata* (1994), conducted by Georg Solti and preserved on CD and video, in which her deeply eloquent singing is supported by her dark looks and a naturally affecting interpretation. Gheorghiu first sang at the Vienna Staatsoper in 1992 as Adina, returning as Mimì and Nannetta, and made her Metropolitan début, as Mimì, in 1993. In 1999 she sang Suzel in *L'amcio Fritz* in Monte Carlo, partnered by her husband ROBERTO ALAGNA. Her voice is one of the most natural and individual of her generation, capable both of notable flexibility and of expressing intense feeling. Among recordings that catch the essence of her art are Tosca, Magda in *La rondine*, Juliette in Charles Gounod's opera, the title role in *Manon*, and Charlotte in *Werther*, in all of which she is partnered by Alagna. On video, from the Lyons Opéra, a delightfully insouciant Adina to Alagna's Nemorino reveals her gifts in comedy. She is also an accomplished recitalist, as revealed in a CD recital embracing songs in many idioms and languages.

A. Blyth: 'Angela Gheorghiu', *Opera*, l/3 (1999), pp. 254–60

Alan Blyth

Ghiaurov, Nicolai

(*b* Velingrad, 13 Sept 1929; *d* Modena, 2 June 2004). Bulgarian bass. He was a pupil of Christo Brambarov at the Bulgarian State Conservatory and then continued his studies in Leningrad and Moscow. He made his début at Sofia in 1955 as Don Basilio in *Il barbiere*, winning the Concours International de Chant de Paris the same year, and in 1958 made the first of many appearances in Italy at the Teatro Comunale, Bologna, in *Faust*; from 1959 he also sang, to great acclaim, at La Scala, where his roles included Boris and Philip II. He made his début at Covent Garden in 1962 (as Padre Guardiano) and at the Metropolitan in 1965 (as Méphistophélès), as well as touring Germany with the Sofia Opera. He first appeared at the Vienna Staatsoper in 1957, as Ramfis, singing regularly there from 1962; his roles included Ivan Khovansky (1989). At the Opéra he sang Jules Massenet's Don Quichotte (1974), and he appeared at the Salzburg Festival, notably as Boris in 1965 and Philip II in 1975. These were among his most notable roles; he also sang Boris at the Metropolitan in 1990. He possessed a voice of unusually rich and varied colour allied to an excellent vocal technique and remarkable musicality. A vigorous and painstaking actor, as an interpreter he tended to express the strong and violent emotions rather than the finer and more intimate shades of meaning. He left notable souvenirs of his appreciable art on disc, among them his Philip II under Georg Solti, Boris under Herbert von Karajan and his Don Quichotte. He was a sonorous bass soloist in Carlo Maria Giulini's recording of the Verdi Requiem and the video of the same work conducted by Karajan.

A. Blyth: 'Nicolai Ghiaurov', *Opera*, xxviii (1977), pp. 941–7

Rodolfo Celletti/Alan Blyth

Ghiuselev, Nikola.

See GYUZELEV, NIKOLA.

Giacomini, Giuseppe

(*b* Veggiano, nr Padua, 7 Sept 1940). Italian tenor. He studied at Padua and Milan, making his début in 1967 at Vercelli as Pinkerton. Having sung in Vienna and Berlin (1972), at La Scala (1974) and the Paris Opéra (1975), he made his Metropolitan début in 1976 as Don Alvaro, returning as Don Carlos, Macduff, Pinkerton, Canio and Manrico. He made an impressive Covent Garden début in 1980 as Dick Johnson, returning in other lyric and spinto roles: Turiddu (which he has recorded), Manrico, Cavaradossi, Radames, Pollione and Calaf. Giacomini's other parts range from Edgardo and Don José through Giacomo Puccini's Des Grieux and Luigi (*Il tabarro*), both of which he has recorded, to Lohengrin (in Italian) and Giuseppe Verdi's Otello, which he first sang in 1986 at San Diego and has repeated in Vienna, Naples and Monte Carlo. In 1990 he created Nanni in Marco Tutino's *La lupa* at Livorno. His powerful, firmly focussed voice is well suited to the heavier Italian repertory, while his dramatic involvement has greatly increased over the years.

Elizabeth Forbes

Giaiotti, Bonaldo

(*b* Ziracco, nr Udine, 25 Dec 1932). Italian bass. He studied with Alfredo Starno in Milan where he made his début at the Teatro Nuovo in 1957. Within the next three years he established himself as one of the leading Italian basses of his time, and was engaged in 1960 by the Metropolitan, New York, remaining a valued member of the company for the next 25 years. The priestly roles in *La forza del destino* and *Aida* were his speciality, though the part he sang most frequently in the house was that of Timur in *Turandot*. At La Scala he was introduced as Rodolfo in *La sonnambula* (1986), and at the Verona Festival of 1992 he appeared as King Philip in *Don Carlos*. He also made a concert tour of South America in 1970. His sonorous, evenly produced voice served him well over a long career, and can be heard in many recordings. Among these is *Luisa Miller* (1975, with Peter Maag), where Count Walter's aria in Act 1 is a fine example of his art.

J.B. Steane

Giannini, Dusolina

(*b* Philadelphia, 19 Dec 1902; *d* Zürich, 29 June 1986). American soprano. She studied first with her father, the Italian tenor Ferruccio Giannini, then with MARCELLA SEMBRICH, and made her operatic début at Hamburg as Aida in 1925. Subsequent engagements took her to Berlin, Vienna and Covent Garden, as well as to Salzburg (1934–6), where she sang Donna Anna under Bruno Walter and Alice Ford under Arturo Toscanini. In 1938 she created the part of Hester Prynne in *The Scarlet Letter*, an opera by her brother, Vittorio Giannini. Her career at the Metropolitan began with Aida in 1936 and lasted until 1941, during which period she also played Donna Anna, Santuzza and Tosca. After appearing in Chicago (1938–42) and San Francisco (1939–43) she took part in the first season of New York City Opera (1943), as Tosca at the opening, and then Carmen and Santuzza. She retired some 20 years later and devoted herself to teaching. Giannini's voice was a true dramatic soprano, backed by strong temperament and impeccable musicianship, as revealed by her recordings, notably her Aida. She must be rated a 'freelance' prima donna, who never belonged to any company but made numerous 'star' and guest appearances. She was also a noted concert singer.

W.R. Moran: 'Dusolina Giannini and her Recordings', *Record Collector*, ix (1954), pp. 26–51 [with discography]

Max De Schauensee/R

Gietz, Gordon

(*b* Calgary, 5 Aug 1963). Canadian tenor. He joined the Calgary Boys' Choir at the age of eleven, and the Calgary Opera Chorus in 1983, while studying for a maths degree at Calgary University. When he began to be offered small roles he decided on a career in singing, and spent two years as a member of the Atelier Lyrique, the training school of the Opéra de Montréal, for whom he sang Rodolfo in *La bohème* in 1989. In 1991 he joined the Opéra as house lyric tenor, singing roles such as Beppe in *I Pagliacci*, Tybalt (*Roméo et Juliette*), Tebaldo (*I Capuleti e I Montecchi*), Ferrando (*Così fan tutte*), Paris (*La belle Hélène*) and Hoffmann. His major European début was as Cassio (*Otello*) in Monte Carlo in 1993. He sang Tamino for Netherlands Opera in 1999, and in 2001 made débuts at the Opéra Bastille, as Don Ottavio, and at Glyndebourne, as Lysander in *A Midsummer Night's Dream*. His La Scala début, in *Dialogues des Carmélites*, followed in 2004. He returned to Covent Garden, in Michael Tippett's *Midsummer Marriage*, in the 2005–06 season. Gietz has also been much admired for his compelling performances in contemporary opera. His world premières include the role of Stingo in Nicholas Maw's *Sophie's Choice* at Covent Garden in 2002, Yonas in Kaija Saariaho's *Adriana Mater* at the Opéra Bastille in 2006 and Jonathan Harvey's *Wagner Dream* at Netherlands Opera in 2007.

Richard Wigmore

Gigli, Beniamino

(*b* Recanati, 20 March 1890; *d* Rome, 30 Nov 1957). Italian tenor. In Rome, after lessons from Agnese Bonucci, he won a scholarship to the Liceo Musicale; his teachers were COTOGNI and Enrico Rosati. In 1914 he won an international competition at Parma, and on 14 October that year made a successful début in *La Gioconda* at Rovigo. In 1915 his Faust in Arrigo Boito's *Mefistofele* was highly appreciated at Bologna under Tullio Serafin and at Naples under Pietro Mascagni. Spain was the scene of his first successes abroad, in 1917. The climax of his early career was his appearance in the memorial performance of *Mefistofele* at La Scala on 19 November 1918. On 26 November 1920 he made a brilliant début (again in *Mefistofele*) at the Metropolitan Opera, where he remained as principal tenor for 12 consecutive seasons, singing no fewer than 28 of his total of 60 roles.

In the lyrical and romantic repertory, Gigli was regarded as the legitimate heir of CARUSO (MARTINELLI excelled in the more dramatic and heroic parts). The operas in which he was most often heard were *La bohème*, *La Gioconda*, *L'Africaine*, *Andrea Chénier* and *Mefistofele*. His Covent Garden début was in *Andrea Chénier* on 27 May 1930, with subsequent appearances in 1931, 1938 and 1946. In 1932 he left the Metropolitan, declining to accept a substantial reduction of the salary paid him before the Depression. Thereafter he pursued his career more actively in Italy, elsewhere in Europe, and in South America, returning to the Metropolitan, for five performances only, in 1939. A favourite of Mussolini, Gigli was at first under a cloud after the dictator's fall, but returned to sing in *Tosca* at the Rome Opera in March 1945, and in November 1946 reappeared at Covent Garden with the S Carlo company in *La bohème*, with his daughter, Rina Gigli, as Mimì. He continued to appear in opera at Naples and at Rome as late as 1953, and in concerts almost until his death.

Smoothness, sweetness and fluency were the outstanding marks of Gigli's singing. His style was essentially popular, both in its virtues and its limitations: natural, vital and spontaneous on the one hand, but always liable to faults of taste – to a sentimental style of portamento, for instance, or the breaking of the line by sobs, or ostentatious bids for stage applause 'like a picturesque beggar appealing for alms' (Ernest Newman). He missed refinement in W.A. Mozart, and was unequal to the technical demands of 'Il mio tesoro'; in Giuseppe Verdi he was more at home, although notably happier when, as in the second scene of *Un ballo in maschera* or the last act of *Rigoletto*, his grandees had adopted popular disguise; best of all in Giacomo Puccini and the melodramatic lyricism of *Andrea Chénier* and *La Gioconda*. His mellifluous cantilena in such pieces as Nadir's romance in *Les pêcheurs de perles* was consummately beautiful. Gigli was something less than a great artist; but as a singer pure and simple he was among the greatest.

His many recordings offer a complete portrait of his long career; outstandingly successful are the arias from *Mefistofele*, *Martha*, *L'elisir d'amore*, *La Gioconda* and *Faust*, duets with GIUSEPPE DE LUCA from *La forza del destino* and *Les pêcheurs de perles*, and the complete recordings of *Andrea Chénier* and *La Bohème*. Gigli was also a seductively charming interpreter of Neapolitan and popular songs, and delighted 1930s cinema audiences with his portrayals of ingenuous and lovestruck tenors.

A.-M. and G. Cronstrom: 'Beniamino Gigli', *Record Collector*, ix (1954–5), pp. 199–269; xiii (1960–61), 184–8 [with discography]

T. Peel and J. Holohan: 'Beniamino Gigli Discography', *Record Collector*, xxxv (1990), pp. 110–18

Desmond Shawe-Taylor/Alan Blyth

Gilfry, Rodney

(*b* Covina, CA, 11 March 1959). American baritone. He made his European début in 1986 at Hamburg as W.A. Mozart's Figaro. After singing Demetrius (*A Midsummer Night's Dream*) at Los Angeles in 1988, he returned in roles that included the four villains (*Les contes d'Hoffmann*), Mozart's and Gioachino Rossini's Figaro, Orestes (*Elektra*), Ford, Papageno, Guglielmo, Don Giovanni (of which he has made a vivid recording under Gardiner) and Malatesta. In 1988 he also sang Petya in Rolf Liebermann's *La forêt* at Schwetzingen and, in 1989, Lescaut (*Manon*) and Otho (*L'incoronazione di Poppea*) at Geneva. From 1990 he has appeared regularly at Zürich, where he has undertaken such roles as Mercutio (*Roméo et Juliette*), Ernesto (*Il pirata*), Jules Massenet's Herod, and Ford. Gilfry's other parts have included the title role in the US première of Wolfgang Rihm's *Oedipus* at Santa Fe (1991), Olivier (*Capriccio*) at Chicago (1994) and Valentin (*Faust*) in San Francisco (1995). He made his Metropolitan début as Demetrius in 1996, returning as Guglielmo in 2000. His strong lyric baritone and fine stage presence make him an ideal Billy Budd, a role he sang at Geneva (1994), for his débuts at Covent Garden (1995) and the Opéra Bastille (1996) and in Dallas and Los Angeles. In 1998 he created the role of Stanley Kowalski in André Previn's *A Streetcar Named Desire* in San Francisco, and in 2002 sang Nathan in the premiere of Nicholas Maw's *Sophie's Choice* at Covent Garden.

Elizabeth Forbes

Gilly, Dinh

(*b* Algiers, 19 July 1877; *d* London, 19 May 1940). French baritone. After studies in Toulouse and Rome he won a *premier prix* at the Paris Conservatoire in 1902 and made his début on 14 December of that year as Silvio in *Pagliacci* at the Opéra, where he remained until 1908. He sang in Latin America, Spain, Germany and Monte Carlo. From 1909 to 1914 he was a member of the Metropolitan Opera, with which he sang Sonora in the world première of *La fanciulla del West*, Rigoletto, Count di Luna, Amonasro, Lescaut (*Manon*), Albert (*Werther*) and other leading roles. In 1911 he made his Covent Garden début as Amonasro and also sang Jack Rance (in the first London *Fanciulla*), Sharpless, Rigoletto and Athanaël in *Thaïs*. He appeared in several later seasons and was last heard in 1924 as Germont. He was admired as a highly musical and expressive singer, an excellent linguist and a fine actor. He taught in London, where his pupils included JOHN BROWNLEE. Between 1908 and 1928 he made approximately 40 recordings displaying a rounded tone, a sophisticated style and a dramatic presence.

H. Harvey: 'Dinh Gilly', *Record Collector*, v (1950), pp. 147–54 [with discography by J. Dennis]

M. Scott: *The Record of Singing*, ii (London, 1979), pp. 40–41

Harold Barnes/R

Giménez, Raúl (Alberto)

(*b* Santa Fé, 14 Sept 1950). Argentine tenor. He studied in Buenos Aires, making his début there in 1981 as Ernesto (*Don Pasquale*). In 1984 he sang Filandro (Domenico Cimarosa's *Le astuzie femminili*) at Wexford, returning as Lurcanio (*Ariodante*). He made his US début at Dallas (1989) and his Covent Garden début (1990) as Ernesto, returning as Almaviva and Don Ramiro (*La Cenerentola*). His repertory also includes Ferrando, Fenton, Elvino (*La sonnambula*), Tonio (*La fille du régiment*) and Lynceus (Antonio Salieri's *Les Danaïdes*), which he sang at Ravenna (1990) and has recorded; but his high-lying, keenly focussed voice and virtuoso coloratura technique are heard to best advantage in Gioachino Rossini, in whose operas he is a specialist: as Gernando/Carlo (*Armida*), Giocondo (*La pietra del paragone*), Florville (*Signor Bruschino*), Roderick Dhu and James V (*La donna del lago*), Count Alberto (*L'occasione fa il ladro*), Lindoro (*L'italiana in Algeri*) and Argirio (*Tancredi*), which he sang at La Scala (1993). Giménez's Rossini recordings include Don Ramiro, Narciso (*Il turco in Italia*) and Almaviva, the role of his Metropolitan début in 1996.

Elizabeth Forbes

Giorgi, Geltrude.

See RIGHETTI, GELTRUDE.

Giorgi-Belloc, Teresa.

See BELLOC-GIORGI, TERESA.

Giraldoni, Eugenio

(*b* Marseilles, 20 May 1871; *d* Helsinki, 23/24 June 1924). Italian baritone, son of the baritone LEONE GIRALDONI and the soprano and violinist Carolina Ferni (1839–1926). Eugenio was taught by his mother and made his début in 1891 as Escamillo at Barcelona. He became well known throughout Italy and in South America and in 1900 was given the role of Scarpia in the world première of *Tosca* at the Costanzi in Rome. He repeated the part later that year at La Scala and in other houses including Covent Garden (1906), but was generally considered to exaggerate the sadism and underplay the refinement of the part. In his single season at the Metropolitan, in 1904, he was also found somewhat coarse in his performances. He nevertheless continued to be in great demand in Europe and South America. He was a widely admired Boris, a part he first sang at Buenos Aires in 1909. He was also Italy's first Yevgeny Onegin in 1900 and Golaud in the Rome première of *Pelléas et Mélisande*. Other roles outside the standard Italian repertory were Hans Sachs, Telramund, Ochs and Anton Rubinstein's Demon. He was considered the best singer of Gérard in *Andrea Chénier* and in 1906 took part in the première of Alberto Franchetti's *La figlia di Iorio*. He retired from the stage in 1921 and thereafter taught in Helsinki. His recordings, magnificent in quality of voice, often show him as a colourful stylist too; strangely, they do not include any excerpts from *Tosca*.

J.B. Steane

Giraldoni, Leone

(*b* Paris, 1824; *d* Moscow, 19 Sept/1 Oct 1897). Italian baritone, father of EUGENIO GIRALDONI. He studied in Florence, making his début in 1847 at Lodi. After singing in Florence and, from 1855, at La Scala, he created the title role of *Simon Boccanegra* at La Fenice in 1857 and Renato in *Un ballo in maschera* at the Teatro Apollo, Rome, in 1859. He also sang other Verdi roles, notably Count di Luna (*Il trovatore*). In 1877 he sang Gioachino Rossini's Figaro at La Scala, and in 1878 at Cagli he took part in the first performance of Agostino Mercuri's *Il violino del diavolo*, written for his wife, Carolina Ferni, a virtuoso violinist as well as a singer. He created the title role of Gaetano Donizetti's posthumously produced *Il duca d'Alba* at the Teatro Apollo, Rome (1882), and after his retirement in 1885 taught singing in Moscow. A sensitive artist, he had a rich, high-lying voice.

Elizabeth Forbes

Girardeau, Isabella

(*fl* 1709–12). Italian soprano. Very little is known of her: Charles Burney thought she was an Italian married to a Frenchman and tentatively identified her with one Isabella Calliari. She was a member of the Queen's Theatre company in London from January 1710 (perhaps October 1709) until spring or summer 1712 and sang in six pasticcios, John Jacob Heidegger's *Almahide* (1710), Francesco Mancini's *Idaspe fedele* (1710, 1712), Alessandro Scarlatti's *Pirro e Demetrio*, Giovanni Bononcini's *Etearco* (1711), Francesco Gasparini's *Antioco* (1712) and *Ambleto* (1712), and in G.F. Handel's *Rinaldo* (1711), in which she was the original Almirena. This is an exceptionally modest part for an *opera seria* heroine, and neither elaborate nor taxing (the compass is *d'* to *a''*); moreover much of the material was not new. Girardeau was evidently no great virtuoso; but she could not have lacked power, for in *Ambleto* she had 'a noisy song for trumpets and hautbois obligati' (Burney). She is said to have been a bitter rival of ELISABETTA PILOTTI-SCHIAVONETTI, Handel's first Armida.

Winton Dean

Giraud, Fiorello

(*b* Parma, 22 Oct 1868; *d* Parma, 28 March 1928). Italian tenor. The son of the tenor Lodovico Giraud (1846–82), he studied in Parma and made his début as Lohengrin at Vercelli in 1891. His success was rapid and the following year he created Canio (*Pagliacci*) at the Teatro Dal Verme, Milan. Unlike Fernando Valero, who created Turiddu in *Cavalleria rusticana*, Giraud was not invited to sing the part throughout the world, and when engaged at Monte Carlo in 1897 it was only to sing Cassio to Tamagno's Otello. Otherwise, appearances abroad were limited to Spain, Portugal and South America. In Italy his reputation as a Wagnerian tenor grew steadily, and in 1907 he sang Siegfried in the première at La Scala of *Götterdämmerung*, under Arturo Toscanini. Later in the same season he was also Italy's first Pelléas. Other premières included Vincenzo Tommasini's *Medea* (1906, Trieste) and Stefano Donaudy's *Sperduti nel buio* (1907, Palermo). His few recordings, which include some Wagner but nothing of *Pagliacci*, show a strong, vibrant voice used with imagination and skill, though with a limited upper range.

J.B. Steane

Gismondi [Resse; Hempson], Celeste

(*d* London, 11 March 1735). Italian soprano. Acclaimed for her interpretation of intermezzo soubrette roles in Naples between 1725 and 1732, she succeeded Santa Marchesini as partner to the bass Gioacchino Corrado. During that period she created the female roles in all of Johann Hasse's intermezzos and in others by Leonardo Vinci and Domenico Sarro. In 1732 she married an Englishman named Hempson who took her to London, where she sang under various names from November 1732 to 1734 in works by G.F. Handel and others. She created the role of Dorinda in Handel's *Orlando* (1733) and took part in performances of his *Alessandro*, the pasticcio *Catone*, *Tolomeo* and *Deborah* as well as works by Nicola Porpora (*Arianna in Nasso*, *Davide e Bersabea* and *Enea nel Lazio*) and Giovanni Bononcini (*Astarto*).

She had a voice of brilliant quality particularly suited to syllabic declamation but also capable of virtuoso passages; arias written for her often parody the emotional heights of serious roles. Dorinda's music calls for a compass from *b♭* to *b♭"*.

Franco Piperno

Gizziello.

See CONTI, GIOACCHINO.

Gjevang, Anne

(*b* Oslo, 24 Oct 1948). Norwegian mezzo-soprano. She studied in Oslo, Rome and Vienna, and made her début at Klagenfurt in 1972 as Baba the Turk. She was successively a member of the companies in Ulm (1973–7), Bremerhaven (1977–9) and Karlsruhe (1979–80). Her Bayreuth début in 1983 as Erda led to engagements at Covent Garden and the Metropolitan Opera in the same role. In Zürich (1985–90) her repertory included Carmen, Ulrica, Maddalena (*Rigoletto*) and Isabella (*L'italiana in Algeri*). She created the role of Lady Macbeth in Antonio Bibalo's *Macbeth* at Oslo in 1990. A versatile singer-actress, Gjevang is also an impressive concert singer. Her distinctive voice, with its northern contralto colouring, can be heard in recordings ranging from *Messiah* and W.A. Mozart's *Mitridate* to Gustav Mahler's symphonies nos. 3 and 8 and Carl Nielsen's *Saul og David*.

Andrew Clark

Glossop, Peter

(*b* Sheffield, 6 July 1928). English baritone. He studied in Sheffield, making his début in 1949 as Coppélius/Dr Miracle. In 1952 he joined Sadler's Wells chorus and was soon singing principal roles: Gérard, Scarpia, Gioachino Rossini's Figaro, Zurga, Ramiro (*L'heure espagnole*), Yevgeny Onegin, Rigoletto and Luna. He made his Covent Garden début in 1961 as Demetrius (*A Midsummer Night's Dream*), after singing the part in Edinburgh; later roles at Covent

Garden included Renato, Amonasro, Germont, Posa, Iago, Boccanegra, Rigoletto, Nabucco, Marcello, Billy Budd, Escamillo, Choroebus (*Les Troyens*) and John the Baptist. He sang Lescaut in the British première of H.W. Henze's *Boulevard Solitude* (1962, Sadler's Wells) and Tarquinius in *The Rape of Lucretia* (English Opera Group, 1963). He made his La Scala début in 1965 as Rigoletto, his Paris and San Francisco débuts in 1966 as Posa. He sang Rigoletto in concert at Newport, Rhode Island, for the Metropolitan in 1967, then made his house début in 1971 as Scarpia, returning as Don Carlo (*Forza*), Falstaff, Mr Redburn (*Billy Budd*), Balstrode (*Peter Grimes*) and Wozzeck. He appeared in Vienna and Salzburg (1970), where he sang Iago for Herbert von Karajan, later recording the role. His repertory also included Macbeth, Don Carlo (*Ernani*), Tonio and Mandryka, which he sang for the ENO (1980). Although he was not the subtlest of actors, his portrayals were always sung and projected with eager conviction.

Alan Blyth

Gluck, Alma [Fiersohn, Reba]

(*b* Bucharest, 11 May 1884; *d* New York, 27 Oct 1938). American soprano of Romanian birth. She was taken to the USA in infancy and studied singing in New York, making a highly successful début

Alma Gluck

with the Metropolitan Opera at the New Theatre on 16 November 1909 as Sophie in Jules Massenet's *Werther*. She sang for seven seasons between 1909 and 1918 at the Metropolitan, where her roles included the Happy Spirit in C.W. Gluck's *Orfeo ed Euridice* (under Arturo Toscanini), Marguerite, Venus, Gilda and Mimì. After a period of further study with MARCELLA SEMBRICH, she devoted herself almost wholly to concert singing. In the popular ballad repertory she achieved a success similar to that of JOHN MCCORMACK, rivalling him in purity of tone and line and clarity of enunciation; she was also a distinguished interpreter of more serious music, especially G.F. Handel. By her first husband Gluck had a daughter who, as Marcia Davenport, became well known as a novelist and writer on music; her second husband, the violinist Efrem Zimbalist, often played obbligato accompaniments to her recordings.

M. Davenport: *Of Lena Geyer* (New York, 1936) [*roman à clef* based on Gluck's career]

B.T. Eke: 'Alma Gluck', *Record Collector*, i/8 (1946), pp. 5–10; vi (1951), 33–45, 53 [with discography by H. Chitty]

Desmond Shawe-Taylor

Gobbato, Angelo (Mario Giulio)

(*b* Milan, 5 July 1943). Italian bass-baritone and director resident in South Africa. He studied the

Tito Gobbi as Iago in 'Otello' (Verdi)

piano and singing privately while reading science at the University of Cape Town. His singing teachers were Albina Bini, Adelheid Armhold and FREDERICK DALBERG in Cape Town and, in 1965–6, CARLO TAGLIABUE and Anna Pistolesi in Milan. He made his début as Kecal (*The Bartered Bride*) in Cape Town in 1965. Gobbato is best known for *buffo* roles such as Dr Bartolo (*Il barbiere*), Don Pasquale and Figaro (*Il barbiere* and *Figaro*); he was awarded the first Nederburg Prize for opera in 1971 for his portrayal of Papageno. He was resident producer at the Nico Malan Opera House in Cape Town, 1976–81, and head of the opera school of the University of Cape Town, 1982–8. In 1989 he was appointed director of opera for the Cape Performing Arts Board. He has directed – mainly from the Italian repertory – for all the arts councils in South Africa.

James May

Gobbi, Tito

(*b* Bassano del Grappa, 24 Oct 1913; *d* Rome, 5 March 1984). Italian baritone. He studied in Rome with GIULIO CRIMI and made his début in 1935 at Gubbio as Rodolfo (*La sonnambula*). In 1937 he appeared at the Teatro Adriano, Rome, as Germont. He sang regularly at the Teatro Reale dell'Opera, Rome, from 1938; his first great success there was as Wozzeck in the Italian première of Alban Berg's opera (1942). He first appeared at La Scala in 1942 as Belcore, the role in which he made his Covent Garden début with the Scala company in 1951. He appeared regularly in London, especially in Verdi roles, including Posa (1958), Boccanegra, Iago, Rigoletto and Falstaff. He also sang Don Giovanni, Almaviva, Gianni Schicchi and Scarpia (see illustration in CALLAS, MARIA).

Gobbi made his American début as Gioachino Rossini's Figaro in San Francisco in 1948; from 1954 to 1973 he sang regularly in Chicago in a repertory that included Gérard, Michonnet, Jack Rance and Tonio, and he made his Metropolitan Opera début in 1956 as Scarpia. At Rome he created roles in Lodovico Rocca's *Monte Ivnor* (1939), G.F. Malipiero's *Ecuba* (1941), Mario Persico's *La locandiera* (1941), Adriano Lualdi's *Le nozze di Haura* (1943) and Jacopo Napoli's *Il tesoro* (1958) and at Milan in G.F. Ghedini's *L'ipocrita felice* (Lord Inferno,1956). His repertory consisted of almost a hundred roles. Intelligence, musicianship and acting ability, allied to a fine though not large voice, made Gobbi one of the dominant singing actors of his generation. He directed several operas, notably *Simon Boccanegra* in Chicago and London, and wrote *Tito Gobbi: My Life* (London, 1979) and *Tito Gobbi on his World of Italian Opera* (London, 1984). Gobbi's highly individual timbre and diction and his ability to colour his tone made him an ideal recording artist, as can be heard in his Rigoletto, Boccanegra, Iago, Falstaff and Gianni Schicchi.

D. De Paoli: 'Tito Gobbi', *Opera*, vi (1955), pp. 619–22
J.W. Freeman: 'Tito Gobbi Talks', *ON*, xxxvi/17 (1971–2), pp. 14–16
A. Blyth: 'Gobbi: the Singer and the Man', *British Music Yearbook 1975*, pp. 3–21 [with discography by J.B. Steane]
H. Rosenthal: 'Tito Gobbi 1913–84', *Opera*, xxxv (1984), pp. 476–84

Harold Rosenthal/Alan Blyth

Goerne, Matthias

(*b* Karl-Marx-Stadt [now Chemnitz], 31 March 1967). German baritone. A pupil of Hans Beyer, he later studied with ELISABETH SCHWARZKOPF and DIETRICH FISCHER-DIESKAU, winning international prizes such as the Hugo Wolf Competition of 1990. In that year he sang in the *St Matthew Passion* under Kurt Masur with a distinction that brought him to the notice of other leading conductors in Germany. He launched an operatic career in 1992, singing the title role of H.W. Henze's *Der Prinz von Homburg* at Cologne. In the following years he sang regularly with the Dresden Staatsoper and in 1997 made his début at Salzburg as Papageno, the role which also introduced him to the Metropolitan Opera (1998). In 1999 he sang his first Wozzeck, in Zürich. Nevertheless, it is as a concert artist, and particularly a lieder recitalist, that he has gained his most conspicuous successes. In Britain he gave a highly acclaimed recital at the Wigmore Hall in 1994, and at the 1998 Edinburgh Festival he gave a performance of *Winterreise*, with Alfred Brendel, which was widely considered one of the finest in memory. He has met with similar triumphs in New York and made an especially strong impression with his advocacy of Hanns Eisler's *Hollywood Songbook*. Goerne's platform manner induces a sense of deep absorption, fully borne out in the quality of his singing. The voice is rich and well rounded rather than penetrative, although capable of taking on a harder edge in the expression of anger or irony. He has made a number of admired recordings, including Bach cantatas and the *St Matthew Passion*, *Winterreise*, *Dichterliebe*, Robert Schumann's Heinrich Heine and Joseph Eichendorff *Liederkreise* and Justinus Kerner songs op.35, a disc of German operatic arias and a notable contribution to the Hyperion Schubert Song Edition.

J.B. Steane

Gogorza, Emilio [Edoardo] de

(*b* Brooklyn, NY, 29 May 1874; *d* New York, 10 May 1949). American baritone of Spanish descent. He spent his youth in Spain and France and in England, where he sang as a boy soprano. He returned to New York and studied with Cleito Moderati and Emilio Agramonte. He made his début as assistant to MARCELLA SEMBRICH in 1897. Because he was extremely short-sighted he never sang in opera, but he soon found a place as a leading recitalist and festival soloist, often appearing jointly in recitals with EMMA EAMES, whom he married in 1911. From about 1898 he was very active in various recording studios, using a variety of pseudonyms (Carlos Francisco, M. Fernand, Herbert Goddard etc.); eventually under his own name he became one of the most successful and prolific Victor Red Seal artists. Because of his own success and his association with many of the leading singers of his day, he became artistic director for Victor and supervised many recording sessions. In 1925 he joined the faculty of the Curtis Institute. His voice was a vibrant and virile baritone of wide range and ample power, as can be heard on recordings with Eames reissued on CD. He was master of many styles, especially admired in music of the French and Spanish schools, but he had a gift of lending distinction to simple home songs and popular selections. He contributed some memoirs to *Opera News* (Nov 1937).

Philip Lieson Miller

Goldberg, Reiner

(*b* Crostau, nr Bautzen, 17 Oct 1939). German tenor. He studied in Dresden, making his début in 1966 at the Landestheater as Luigi (*Il tabarro*). In 1973 he joined the Staatsopern of Dresden and Berlin and took part in the première of Ernst Meyer's *Reiter der Nacht* in Berlin, where in 1976 he sang Huon in a performance of *Oberon* to mark the 150th anniversary of Weber's death. In 1982 he sang Walther at Covent Garden, Erik at the Salzburg Easter Festival and Florestan at the Salzburg Summer Festival. He sang Tannhäuser at La Scala (1984) and Walther, Siegfried (*Götterdämmerung*) and Erik at Bayreuth (1987–92). His repertory also included Parsifal, which he sang under Armin Jordan on the soundtrack of H.J. Syberberg's film of the opera, Max, Bacchus, Faust, Hermann (*The Queen of Spades*), Sergey (*Lady Macbeth of the Mtsensk District*), the Drum Major (*Wozzeck*) and the title role of Paul Dessau's *Verurteilung des Lukullus*. In 1991 Goldberg sang young Siegfried in concert at Amsterdam, and both Siegfrieds at Covent Garden, where he returned for Florestan (1993), the role of his Metropolitan début in 1992. He had an incisive, well-focussed voice with a notably powerful upper register, as can be heard on several recordings, including Florestan and Siegmund (under Bernard Haitink), Siegfried in both *Siegfried* and *Götterdämmerung* (with James Levine), the Drum Major, and Emperor Pao in Alexander Zemlinsky's *Der Kreidekreis*.

Elizabeth Forbes

Goltz, Christel

(*b* Dortmund, 8 July 1912). German soprano. She studied with Ornelli-Leeb in Munich and before she was 20 was singing in operetta at the Deutsches Theater. In 1935 she sang Agathe in *Der Freischütz* at Fürth. After a season at Plauen, where she added Santuzza, Eva and Octavian to her repertory, in 1936 she was engaged at Dresden; she remained a member of the company until 1950, creating Juliet in Heinrich Sutermeister's *Romeo und Julia* (1940) and singing Carl Orff's Antigone. In 1947 Goltz sang in Berlin at both the Staatsoper and the Städtische Oper; she then began to appear in Vienna and Munich, as Electra, Salome, Alcestis, the Countess (*Capriccio*), Leonore and Tosca. In 1951 she made her Covent Garden début as Salome and the following year sang Marie in *Wozzeck*, a role she also sang at Salzburg, Vienna and Buenos Aires. At Salzburg she created the title role in Rolf Liebermann's *Penelope* in 1954; later that year she made her Metropolitan début as Salome. During the 1957–8 season she sang her first Isolde; at that time her repertory included nearly 120 operas. Goltz had a clear, brilliant voice, three octaves in range, and her acting was intense. She recorded Salome (under Joseph Keilberth and Clemens Krauss) and the Dyer's Wife (under Karl Böhm).

Harold Rosenthal/R

Gomez, Jill

(*b* New Amsterdam, British Guiana, 21 Sept 1942). British soprano. She studied in London, making her début with Glyndebourne Touring Opera in 1968 as Adina. At Glyndebourne (1969–84) she was affecting as Mélisande, Callisto, Anne Trulove and Helena (*A Midsummer Night's Dream*). She made a memorable impression when she created Flora in Michael Tippett's *The Knot Garden* at Covent Garden (1970). Her subsequent roles there included Titania and Lauretta. For Scottish Opera she sang Elizabeth Zimmer (*Elegy for Young Lovers*), Anne Trulove, Fiordiligi, Countess Almaviva, Pamina and Leïla (*Les pêcheurs de perles*). With the English Opera Group she again made her mark in a new role, the

Countess in Thea Musgrave's *The Voice of Ariadne* (1974), and also sang a subtle Governess (*The Turn of the Screw*). At Wexford she sang Thaïs (1974) and Rosaura in *La vedova scaltra* (1983). She has sung at Frankfurt, Zürich, Vienna, Lyons and Florence, where she took part in *The Fairy-Queen* (1987). For Kent Opera (1977–88) she sang Tatyana, Violetta, Amyntas (*Il rè pastore*) and Donna Anna. She sang Helena at Sadler's Wells in 1990 and also recorded the role. Her other roles included G.F. Handel's Cleopatra, Cinna (*Lucio Silla*) and Teresa (*Benvenuto Cellini*). Her voice, bright and expressive, is limited in tonal colour; a gifted singing-actress, she is heard at her most vivid in recordings of stage works by Manuel de Falla and of Spanish songs.

Alan Blyth

Gorchakova, Galina

(*b* Novosibirsk, 1 March 1962). Russian soprano. After studies at the Novosibirsk Conservatory, she joined the Opera House in Sverdlovsk (now Yekaterinburg) in 1988, her early roles including Tatyana, Santuzza, Cio-Cio-San, Liù, Tamara (Anton Rubinstein's *Demon*) and Katerina (*Lady Macbeth of the Mtsensk District*). Winning auditions in St Petersburg, she moved on to the Kirov Opera in 1991, and with that company was quickly recognized as an artist of rare individuality. Her international career began with an appearance as Renata in Sergey Prokofiev's *Fiery Angel* at the 1991 Proms in London, and she made her Covent Garden and Metropolitan Opera débuts the following year in the same role, taking it to La Scala in 1994. She returned to Covent Garden in 1993 as Tatyana, which, together with P.I. Tchaikovsky's Lisa, became a calling card around the world. Other Tchaikovsky roles include Maria (*Mazepa*) and Iolanta, and in concert Natal'ya (*The Oprichnik*) and Kuma (*The Enchantress*). With the Kirov she has also sung Gorislava (*Ruslan and Lyudmila*), Yaroslavna (*Prince Igor*), Princess Olga (*The Maid of Pskov*), Volokhova (*Sadko*), Fevroniya (*Legend of the Invisible City of Kitezh*) and Clara (*Betrothal in a Monastery*), many of which have been recorded on disc and video. Tosca introduced her to Houston in 1996, and in 1998 in Rotterdam she added Manon Lescaut to her repertory. Her Verdi roles have included Leonora (including the original version of *La forza del destino*) and Elisabeth de Valois. She made her Australian début in recital at the 1999 Sydney Festival, and has a large repertory of Russian song. Although her gleaming voice can lack flexibility, it has thrilling amplitude throughout its considerable range.

John Allison

Görl, Franz Xaver.

See GERL, FRANZ XAVER.

Gorr, Rita [Geirnaert, Marguerite]

(*b* Zelzaete, 18 Feb 1926). Belgian mezzo-soprano. She studied in Ghent, then at the Brussels Conservatory. In 1949 she made her début in Antwerp as Fricka in *Die Walküre*. Thereafter she sang at the Strasbourg Opera until 1952, the year in which she made her Paris débuts (at the Opéra-Comique as Charlotte and at the Opéra as Magdalene). Her large voice, of rich, metallic timbre, ranging freely over two octaves, was joined to a powerfully dramatic temperament. In Richard Wagner (notably as Fricka and Ortrud) and Giuseppe Verdi (Eboli, Azucena, Ulrica and Amneris) she gave grandly exciting performances; a noble breadth of expression won her special praise in the French repertory – Delilah, Iphigenia (*Iphigénie en Tauride*), Margared (*Le roi d'Ys*), Jules Massenet's Herodias and Charlotte, Luigi Cherubini's Medea and Hector Berlioz's Dido. She first sang at Bayreuth in 1958, at La Scala in 1960 and at the Metropolitan in 1962. She made her London début at Covent Garden in 1959 and sang there until 1971. Later roles included Madame de Croissy (*Dialogues des Carmélites*), which she sang at Seattle and Lyons in 1990. Recordings of her Amneris, Ortrud, Margared and Delilah give a sense of the excitement she created on stage.

J. Bourgeois: 'Rita Gorr', *Opera*, xii (1961), pp. 637–40

Harold Rosenthal/Alan Blyth

Gottlieb, (Maria) Anna [Nanette]

(*b* Vienna, 29 April 1774; *d* Vienna, 4 Feb 1856). Austrian singer and actress. She came from a theatrical family; both her parents were in the German theatre company of the Nationaltheater, and, as one of four sisters who all acted in the theatre as children, she first appeared in the Burgtheater at the age of five. She was just 12 when she created the role of Barbarina in W.A. Mozart's *Le nozze di Figaro* (1 May 1786); she also created Pamina in *Die Zauberflöte* (30 September 1791). That role represented the artistic peak of her career (although she was not yet 18). She had been engaged by EMANUEL SCHIKANEDER in 1789 for his Freihaus-Theater and stayed there three years, singing mainly in Singspiel.

In 1792 she began her long and popular career in the Theater in der Leopoldstadt. The repertory was principally Singspiel and, later, musical parodies; thus Anna Gottlieb was not an opera singer in the accepted sense. She had not only to sing and act but also to dance. In 1796 she surprised the public by playing in a piano duet in Thaddäus Weigl's *Idoly*. Her greatest successes were in the roles she created in Singspiels and travesties to words by Joachim Perinet and C.F. Hensler, director of the Leopoldstädter Theater, set by Wenzel Müller and Ferdinand Kauer: in *Das Neusonntagskind* (1793, Perinet and Müller), as Hulda in *Das Donauweibchen* (1798, Hensler and Kauer), a role she performed over a thousand times, as Evakathel in *Evakathel und Schnudi, oder Die Belagerung von Ypsilon* (1804, Perinet and Müller) and in the title role of *Die neue Alceste* (1806, Perinet and Müller). Under Hensler's direction (1803–17) she was the mainstay of the company and in the 1790s she received favourable criticisms for her acting and singing in works such as C.W. Gluck's *Die Pilgrim von Mekka* (*La rencontre imprévue*). By 1808 the notices were lukewarm, and from that year until 1811 she was absent from the stage. She reappeared with diminishing success, finally singing mainly secondary roles.

Gottlieb was praised in a review (*Wiener Zeitung für Theater, Musik und Poesie*) of *Die travestierte Palmyra* (1813), a take-off of Antonio Salieri's *Palmira*, by Perinet with music by Gebel:

If ever an artist in this theatre has the feeling and predisposition for parody, it is she. Her acting and singing are calculated to be precisely the opposite of the original character. Thus are her pathos, carriage and behaviour humorous throughout, and she parodies all the prima donnas superbly and with especial felicity sings bravura arias and difficult passages with an indistinctness exactly like the Italian florid singing no-one ever understands anyway.

In *Maria Stuttgartin* (1815), a parody of Friedrich von Schiller's *Maria Stuart*, she did not know her part; and in 1828 her contract was summarily terminated by Rudolf Steinkeller, the new director at the Leopoldstadt. She received no pension and in the course of the next eight years she periodically petitioned the emperor for a pension, explaining that her only means of livelihood was working with her hands and that, with the approach of old age (she said at 58), this was no longer possible.

Describing the first Mozart Festival in Salzburg in 1842 Wilhelm Kuhe wrote (*My Musical Recollections*, 1896): 'there entered a very tall, thin and eccentric-looking woman who at once exclaimed as though addressing an audience, "I am the first Pamina"... she seemed to think that she had at least an equal claim with Mozart to be an object of universal veneration'. She was the last surviving singer in Vienna who had known Mozart, and she died during the celebrations of his centenary in 1856.

Christopher Raeburn/R

Graham, Susan

(*b* Roswell, NM, 23 July 1960). American mezzo-soprano. She studied at the Manhattan School of Music and then won the Metropolitan Opera National Council Auditions in 1988. After engagements with the St Louis Opera (Erika in *Vanessa*) and in Seattle, Chicago and Washington, she made her first Metropolitan appearances in the 1991–2 season as Octavian and Cherubino. She sang Cecilius (*Lucio Silla*) at Salzburg in 1993 and made her Covent Garden début the following year in the title part of Jules Massenet's *Chérubin*. She has also appeared at the Vienna Staatsoper, La Scala, Glyndebourne and the Paris Opéra, variously as Cherubino, Octavian, the Composer, Hector Berlioz's Beatrice, Charlotte (*Werther*) and Marguerite (*La damnation de Faust*). In 1995 she sang the title role in the première of Alexander Goehr's *Arianna* at Covent Garden. Other premières include John Harbison's *The Great Gatsby* (1999, Metropolitan Opera) and Jake Heggie's *Dead Man Walking* (2000, Chicago). In 2000 she scored a triumph in the leading role of C.W. Gluck's *Iphigénie en Tauride* at the Salzburg Festival. In all these roles she has disclosed a firm, expressive voice, fresh in timbre, free at the top, together with an innate feeling for the stage and a commanding presence. Graham has also proved herself an accomplished recitalist, with a particular gift for American song and *mélodies*. Her recordings of Béatrice, French operatic arias, *La damnation de Faust* and *Les nuits d'été* confirm her affinity with French music and her keen, personal inflection of all that she sings.

Alan Blyth

Gramm, Donald

(*b* Milwaukee, 26 Feb 1927; *d* New York, 2 June 1983). American bass-baritone. He studied at the Wisconsin College-Conservatory of Music (1935–44) and at 15 took singing lessons with George Graham. His opera début was in *Lucia di Lammermoor* at the 8th Street Theater of Chicago when he was 17. Formal study followed at the Chicago Musical College (1944) and later with Martial Singher at the Music Academy of the West, Santa Barbara. His New York début was with the Little Orchestra Society (*L'enfance du Christ*, 1951). He became a member of the New York City Opera the following year (Colline in *La bohème*),

and began a long, mutually beneficial relationship with Sarah Caldwell's Boston Opera in 1958. A singer of extraordinary versatility and intelligence, Gramm sang with every leading company in the USA and at Spoleto, Aix-en-Province and Glyndebourne (Nick Shadow, 1975; Falstaff, 1976). He participated in the American premières of Carl Orff's *Der Mond*, Bohuslav Martinů's *The Marriage*, Darius Milhaud's *Medée*, Frank Martin's *Der Sturm*, Benjamin Britten's *Gloriana* and *Owen Wingrave*, Alban Berg's *Lulu*, Arnold Schoenberg's *Moses und Aron* and *Jakobsleiter*, Giuseppe Verdi's *Don Carlos* in the original French version, and Vittorio Giannini's *The Taming of the Shrew*, among others. More traditional roles included Méphistophélès, Figaro and Ochs. He was also active in the concert hall and particularly adept in the music of J.S. Bach and Berg. Gramm's voice was not particularly large, but he used it with uncommon sensitivity to nuance, and fidelity to the composer's instructions. He was an elegant stylist, and a remarkably convincing actor. In 1981 he ventured into stage direction with *Figaro* at Wolf Trap.

Martin Bernheimer/R

Grandi, Margherita [Garde, Marguerite]

(*b* Hobart, 4 Oct 1894; *d* Milan, 29 Jan 1972). Australian mezzo-soprano, later soprano. She studied in London (1912–17) at the RCM and in Paris, from 1919, with EMMA CALVÉ. Engaged (under the name of Djemma Vécla, an anagram of Calvé) as a mezzo-soprano in 1922 at Monte Carlo, she sang Carmen, Charlotte and Arrigo Boito's Margherita, and created the title role of Jules Massenet's *Amadis*. After further study in Italy with Giannina Russ, she made her soprano début in 1932 under her married name of Grandi at the Teatro Carcano, Milan, as Aida, a role she repeated at Verona (1946). She sang Arrigo Boito's Helen of Troy at La Scala in 1934. She made her British début in 1939 at Glyndebourne as Lady Macbeth, then spent the war in Italy, singing Maria in the Italian première of *Friedenstag* at Venice (1940) and Octavia (*L'incoronazione di Poppea*) at Rome (1943). In 1947 she made her London début singing Tosca and Donna Anna at the Cambridge Theatre, then sang Lady Macbeth with the Glyndebourne company at Edinburgh. She returned to Edinburgh in 1949 as Amelia (*Un ballo in maschera*) and created Diana in Arthur Bliss's *The Olympians* at Covent Garden (1949), where she also sang Leonora (*Il trovatore*) and, in 1951, made her stage farewell as Tosca. She had a generous, vibrant voice which was allied to a style of rare sweep and conviction. Grandi is heard singing Brian Easdale's operatic aria in the film *The Red Shoes* (1948), and she is represented on disc by extracts from *Macbeth* and *Don Carlos*.

Harold Rosenthal/R

Granforte, Apollo

(*b* Legnano, nr Verona, 20 July 1886; *d* Gorgonzola, nr Milan, 11 June 1975). Italian baritone. As a young man he emigrated to South America where he studied with Guido Capocci and made his début as Germont in *La traviata* at Rosario, Argentina, in 1913. He returned to Italy during World War I, singing in Rome and Milan. He extended his international reputation through Australian tours with MELBA in 1924 and then with an eminent company of Italian singers in 1928 and 1932. In 1935 he sang in the world première of Pietro Mascagni's *Nerone* at La Scala. Other world premières included Ernst Krenek's *Cefalo e Procri* (1934, Venice) and G.F. Malipiero's *Giulio Cesare* (1936, Genoa). His wide repertory included John the Baptist, the Wanderer, Telramund and Amfortas. After the war he taught at the Ankara Conservatory, then in Prague and finally in Milan where RAFFAELE ARIÈ was among his pupils. His recordings include the leading baritone roles in *Otello*, *Pagliacci*, *Tosca* and *Trovatore*.

A.A. Delicata: 'Apollo Granforte', *Record Collector*, xii (1958–60), pp. 173–94, 258

J.B. Steane

Graziani, Francesco

(*b* Fermo, 26 April 1828; *d* Fermo, 30 June 1901). Italian baritone, brother of LODOVICO GRAZIANI. He made his début in 1851 at Ascoli Piceno in Gaetano Donizetti's *Gemma di Vergy* and the following season sang at Macerata in Giuseppe Verdi's *I masnadieri*. He appeared at the Théâtre Italien, Paris, from 1853 to 1861 and made his London début at Covent Garden in 1855 as Don Carlo in *Ernani*, continuing to sing there regularly for the next 25 years. Though his repertory was enormous, ranging from W.A. Mozart (*Don Giovanni* and *Le nozze di Figaro*), Gioachino Rossini (*Otello*, *La donna del lago* and *Guillaume Tell*), Gaetano Donizetti (*Lucia di Lammermoor*, *Linda di Chamounix* and *La favorite*), and Vincenzo Bellini (*La sonnambula* and *I puritani*) to Friedrich Flotow's *Martha*, Charles Gounod's *Faust*, Giacomo Meyerbeer's *L'Africaine* and Ambroise Thomas' *Hamlet*, it was in Verdi roles that he excelled. He was the first Luna in Paris (1854) and in London (1855), and he also sang Germont, Rigoletto and Renato in both capitals. At Dublin in 1859 he sang the title role in the first per-formance of *Macbeth* in the British Isles. He sang Don Carlo in the première of *La forza del destino* at St Petersburg (1862), Posa in the first London *Don Carlos* (1867) and Amonasro in the first London *Aida* (1876). His final appearance at Covent Garden was in *La traviata* in 1880. He was said to possess one of the finest baritone voices heard in the second half of the 19th century.

Elizabeth Forbes

Graziani, Lodovico

(*b* Fermo, 14 Nov 1820; *d* Fermo, 15 May 1885). Italian tenor. He was the brother of Giuseppe, FRANCESCO and Vincenzo Graziani. He made his début at Bologna in 1845 and appeared at the Théâtre Italien, Paris, in 1851 as Gennaro (*Lucrezia Borgia*). He sang Alfredo at the first performance of *La traviata* at La Fenice, Venice (1853), and made his début at La Scala in 1855 in Giuseppe Apolloni's *L'ebreo*; he also appeared there as the Duke in *Rigoletto* and as Henri in *Les vêpres siciliennes* (given as *Giovanna di Guzman*). He sang the title role in Gaetano Donizetti's *Dom Sébastien* at the S Carlo, Naples, in 1856 and returned to La Scala in 1862 to sing Riccardo in *Un ballo in maschera*. In 1865 he sang Vasco de Gama in the first Italian performance of Giacomo Meyerbeer's *L'Africaine* at Bologna.

Elizabeth Forbes

Grécy, Mlle.

See SCIO, JULIE-ANGÉLIQUE.

Greene, (Harry) Plunket

(*b* Old Connaught House, Co. Wicklow, 24 June 1865; *d* London, 19 Aug 1936). Irish bass-baritone. He studied in Stuttgart (under Anton Hromada from 1883), Florence (under Luigi Vannuccini) and London (under J.B. Welsh and Alfred Blume). His first public appearance was in *Messiah* at the People's Palace, Stepney, on 21 January 1888, and he was soon a regular oratorio soloist. But he made his mark most decisively in the recitals he gave with the pianist Leonard Borwick from 1893, in which his interpretations of Robert Schumann and Johannes Brahms were widely admired.

Greene appeared at Covent Garden as the Commendatore (*Don Giovanni*) in 1890, but his operatic career was short-lived, and he became best known as a festival and oratorio singer, especially for his part in many first performances of Hubert Parry's works and in that of Edward Elgar's *Dream of Gerontius* (1900). In 1899 he married Parry's daughter Gwendolen. Charles Villiers Stanford wrote many of his finest songs for Greene, whose remarkable powers of interpretation, particularly the beauty of his enunciation, made him one of the leading exponents of English song. He believed passionately that songs should be sung in the language of the audience. His voice declined prematurely, but his intimate way of singing retained all its old fascination, as can be clearly heard in the most valuable of his records, the four 78 r.p.m. sides issued in 1934 when he was nearly 70, of which, 'The Hurdy-Gurdy Man' (*Der Leiermann*) creates an unforgettable impression. His writings include *Interpretation in Song* (London, 1912/R), *From Blue Danube to Shannon* (London, 1934) and *Charles Villiers Stanford* (London, 1935).

S. Wilson: 'Harry Plunket Greene', *Recorded Sound*, no.32 (1968), 327–8
M. Ritchie: 'Plunket Greene as a Teacher', *Recorded Sound*, no.32 (1968), 328–9 [with discography]
Record Advertiser, vol. i (1970–71), no.6, 2–4 [with discography]

Desmond Shawe-Taylor/Alan Blyth

Gregor, József

(*b* Rákosliget, 8 Aug 1940; *d* Budapest, 27 Oct 2006). Hungarian bass. He studied with György M. Kerényi and Endre Rösler at the Bartók Conservatory in Budapest (1957–9). After singing in a choir, he joined the Szeged Opera, making his début as Sarastro in 1964. In 1990 he was appointed Intendant of the company. He was a regular guest at the Budapest Opera, and also appeared in Belgium, France, Germany, the Netherlands and the USA. With a resonant voice and ebullient personality well suited to *buffo* roles (his speciality), he received acclaim as Mozart's Osmin and Leporello, and as Don Pasquale and Falstaff; he also sang in recordings of neglected operas such as Giovanni Paisiello's *Il barbiere di Siviglia*, Antonio Salieri's *Falstaff* and Domenico Cimarosa's *Il pittore parigino* (he sang in a performance of the last at Monte Carlo in 1988). Gregor's other roles included Gioachino Rossini's Moses and Giuseppe Verdi's Attila.

Péter P. Várnai

Greindl, Josef

(*b* Munich, 23 Dec 1912; *d* Vienna, 16 April 1993). German bass. He studied in Munich with PAUL BENDER and ANNA BAHR-MILDENBURG, made his début in 1936 at Krefeld as Hunding, sang at Düsseldorf (1938–42), was then engaged by the

Berlin Staatsoper, and moved to the Städtische (later Deutsche) Oper in 1949. He first appeared at Bayreuth as Pogner in 1943 and from 1951 to 1970 he sang there regularly in the Wagnerian bass repertory; he also sang Hans Sachs at Covent Garden (1963). In 1952 he made his Metropolitan début as King Henry. He appeared as Moses in the first complete German stage performance of *Moses und Aron* (1959, Berlin). His repertory included Don Alfonso, Boris, Rocco, Osmin, Philip II, Otto Nicolai's Falstaff and David Orth in *Die Bürgschaft*. At Salzburg he sang the Commendatore, Rocco and Lodovico, and was a magnificent Sarastro; he also sang in the première of Carl Orff's *Antigonae* (1949). Greindl had a rich and voluminous voice which was warm in timbre, although not always ideally steady. He used it expressively in Wagner, both in the saturnine roles of Fafner and Hunding and in his sympathetic portrayals of King Mark and Pogner, all of which he recorded.

Harold Rosenthal/Alan Blyth

Gresse, André

(*b* Lyons, 23 March 1868; *d* Paris, 1937). French bass. The son of LÉON GRESSE, he studied in Paris, making his début in 1896 at the Opéra-Comique as the Commendatore. During five years there he created Césaire in Jules Massenet's *Sapho* (1897) and the President in Camille Erlanger's *Le Juif polonais* (1900); he also sang Gaveston (*La dame blanche*), Nilakantha (*Lakmé*), Count des Grieux (*Manon*), Nourabad (*Les pêcheurs de perles*) and Colline. In 1901 he was engaged by the Opéra, where he remained for 25 years, singing 60 roles. These included Le Révérend, which he sang at the première of Massenet's *Bacchus* (1909), Ramfis, Méphistophélès, Gesler (*Guillaume Tell*), Leporello, Sparafucile, Friar Laurence (*Roméo et Juliette*), Alphonse (*La favorite*), Varlaam, Osmin, King Mark, Fasolt, Hunding, Wotan, Hagen (*Götterdämmerung* and Ernest Reyer's *Sigurd*), Pogner, Don Diègue (*Le Cid*) and Sancho Panza (*Don Quichotte*), which he had created at Monte Carlo in 1910. The very wide range of his powerful voice allowed him to sing many baritone as well as bass roles. His pupils included ANDRÉ PERNET, ROGER BOURDIN and TEFTA TASHKO-KOÇO.

Elizabeth Forbes

Gresse, Léon(-Pierre-Napoléon)

(*b* Charolles, 22 July 1845; *d* Marly-le-Roi, 13 April 1900). French bass. He sang first as an amateur, then obtained engagements at Le Havre and Toulouse. He made his Paris début at the Opéra in 1875 as a Gravedigger (*Hamlet*), then sang Saint-Bris (*Les Huguenots*) and Gesler (*Guillaume Tell*). Engaged in 1878 at the Théâtre de la Monnaie, Brussels, he created Phanuel in *Hérodiade* (1881) and Hagen in Ernest Reyer's *Sigurd* (1884), which role he also sang at the Paris première (1885). He remained at the Opéra until his death, singing a wide repertory that included Balthazar (*La favorite*), Brogni (*La Juive*), Sparafucile, Bertram (*Robert le diable*), Don Pedro (*L'Africaine*), Don Diègue (*Le Cid*), the King (*Hamlet*), Friar Laurence (*Roméo et Juliette*) and Lodovico (*Otello*). The first Hunding (1893) and Pogner (1897) in Paris, he created Père Saval in Augusta Holmès's *La montagne noire* (1895). He was succeeded as a principal bass at the Opéra by his son, ANDRÉ GRESSE.

Elizabeth Forbes

Grigorian, Gegam

(*b* Erevan, 29 Jan 1951). Armenian tenor. Studies at the Erevan Conservatory and La Scala's Scuola di Perfizionamento Artistico laid the foundation for a career that has embraced the Russian and Italian repertory of the 19th century. Following his début in 1971 at the Erevan National Theatre as Edgardo in *Lucia di Lammermoor*, and a short apprenticeship with the Lithuanian Opera in Vilnius, he appeared regularly at the Bol'shoy and in other Soviet theatres, singing such roles as the Pretender (*Boris Godunov*), Radames, Cavaradossi and Pollione (which he recorded with the Bol'shoy). He became a Kirov Opera principal in 1989, and with the company at home, on tour and on record has sung many roles, including Lensky, Hermann, Andrey (*Mazepa*), Vaudémont (*Iolanta*), Vladimir (*Prince Igor*), Princeling Vsevolod (*Legend of the Invisible City of Kitezh*), Pierre Bezukhov (*War and Peace*) and Alvaro (*La forza del destino*, in the original version). Significant débuts included Covent Garden (1993, as Lensky) and the Metropolitan (1995, as Hermann), and he has also appeared in Washington, Buenos Aires, Monte Carlo, Paris, Rome and Genoa. Grigorian's other roles include Riccardo, Ernani, Canio and Turiddu, all notable for their idiomatic style. A stocky presence on the stage, Grigorian is capable of vocal refinement, although he is admired most of all for the exciting thrust of his singing.

John Allison

Grimaldi, Nicolo.

See NICOLINI.

Grisi, Giuditta

(*b* Milan, 28 July 1805; *d* Robecco d'Oglio, nr Cremona, 1 May 1840). Italian mezzo-soprano, elder sister of GIULIA GRISI. The niece of Josephina Grassini, she studied with her aunt and at the Milan Conservatory. She made her début in Vienna in 1826 in Gioachino Rossini's *Bianca e Falliero*. After engagements in Florence, Parma and Turin, she sang in Venice for several seasons. It was in Vincenzo Bellini's music above all that she excelled; in 1830 she appeared in *Il pirata* and sang Romeo in the première of *I Capuleti e i Montecchi*, which she also sang at La Scala. Other roles at La Scala included Elisabetta in Gaetano Donizetti's *Otto mesi in due ore*, given under its alternative title of *Gli esiliati in Siberia* (1831), and the title role in Luigi Ricci's *Chiara di Rosembergh*, which she created the same year. During 1832 she appeared in *La straniera* in Venice, London and Paris. In 1833 she sang the title role of *Norma* at Bologna, and the following season sang Romeo and Norma in Madrid. She retired in 1838, after an engagement at the Teatro Valle in Rome.

Elizabeth Forbes

Grisi, Giulia

(*b* Milan, 22 May 1811; *d* Berlin, 29 Nov 1869). Italian soprano, sister of GIUDITTA GRISI. She studied with the composer M.A. Marliani and with Giacomelli in Bologna, where she made her début in the 1828–9 season in Gioachino Rossini's *Zelmira* (Emma) and also sang in his *Torvaldo e Dorliska* and *Il barbiere di Siviglia*, and in Giacomo Cordella's *Lo sposo di provincia*. After singing at the Pergola, Florence, she made her début at La Scala in the first performance of Feliciano Strepponi's *Ullà di Bassora*, also creating Adalgisa in *Norma* (1831) and Adelia in Gaetano Donizetti's *Ugo, conte di Parigi* (1832). She then broke her contract and left Italy, never to sing there professionally again. Grisi made her Paris début at the Théâtre Italien in the title role of *Semiramide* (1832) and in the next two years sang Desdemona (Gioachino Rossini's *Otello*), Giulietta (*I Capuleti e i Montecchi*), Anne Boleyn, Ninetta (*La gazza ladra*) and Ellen (*La donna del lago*). In 1834 she made her London début at the King's Theatre as Ninetta, and sang Donna Anna, Pamyre (*Le siège de Corinthe*) and Amina (*La sonnambula*).

From 1835 until 1847 (except for 1842) Grisi alternated between the two capitals. In Paris she created Elvira in *I puritani*, Elena in *Marino Faliero* (both 1835) and Norina in *Don Pasquale* (1843), also singing in Donizetti's *Parisina*, *Roberto Devereux*, *Belisario*, *Maria di Rohan* and *Gemma di Vergy*,

Giulia Grisi with her sister, Giuditta Grisi, drawing by Deveria, 1833

in Bellini's *Il pirata* and in Giuseppe Verdi's *I due Foscari*. In London she sang the title roles in *Norma* and *Beatrice di Tenda*, Donizetti's *Lucrezia Borgia* and *Fausta* and Rossini's *La Cenerentola*, as well as Carolina and Elisetta (*Il matrimonio segreto*), Giselda (*I Lombardi*), W.A. Mozart's Susanna, and Mistress Ford in Michael Balfe's *Falstaff*. Transferring to Covent Garden, she sang Semiramis at the opening of the Royal Italian Opera (1847). Later roles included Léonore (*La favorite*), Valentine (*Les Huguenots*), Fidès (*Le prophète*), Alice (*Robert le diable*) and Leonora (*Il trovatore*). Her professional partner in many of these operas, and her lifelong companion, was the tenor GIOVANNI MARIO (she was separated, though not divorced, from the man she had married in 1836). Accompanied by Mario, she visited St Petersburg (1849), New York (1854) and Madrid (1859), before retiring in 1861. On the day of Rossini's funeral in Paris (21 November 1868), she sang in the *Stabat mater* at S Croce in Florence. Grisi's voice, perfectly placed and even over a range of two octaves, c' to c''', easily made the transition from the florid writing of Rossini and Donizetti to the more forceful style of Verdi and Giacomo Meyerbeer. If she lacked the interpretative genius of PASTA or MALIBRAN, she was an impressive singing actress, magnificent in such roles as Donna Anna, Semiramis and Norma, where her passionate involvement was allowed full scope.

T.G. Kaufman: 'Giulia Grisi: a Re-Evaluation', *Donizetti Society Journal*, iv (1980), 180–96 [see also 'A Chronology of Grisi's Operatic Performances', ibid., 197–223; 'Grisi's Repertory', ibid., 224–5]

E. Forbes: *Mario and Grisi* (London, 1985)

Elizabeth Forbes

Grist, Reri

(*b* New York, 29 Feb 1932). American soprano. She studied in New York while working in the theatre (she was in the first cast of *West Side Story*, 1957) and made her operatic début in 1959 at Santa Fe as Blonde. She sang the Queen of Night at Cologne (1960) and Zerbinetta at Zürich, where she was engaged from 1961 to 1964. She made her Covent Garden début in 1962 as the Queen of Shemakha (*The Golden Cockerel*), later singing Olympia, Gilda, Susanna and Oscar (*Un ballo in maschera*). At San Francisco (1963–9) she sang Rosina, Despina, Sophie, Burgundian Lady (*Carmina burana*), Adèle and Zerbinetta. She made her Salzburg début as Blonde (1965), returning there as Susanna and Despina. Having made her Metropolitan début in 1966 as Rosina, she returned as Sophie, Norina and Adina, which she also sang in Vienna (1973). With a light, silvery voice of wide compass and great agility, and an ebullient personality, Grist excelled as Zerbinetta and Oscar, both of which she recorded, and in the Mozart soubrette roles. She also sang frequently in concert and recital, with a repertory that included Alban Berg and Anton Webern.

Alan Blyth

Gritton, Susan

(*b* Reigate, 31 Aug 1965). English soprano. She studied with David Mason (1984–7) and at the National Opera Studio (1992–3), and won the Kathleen Ferrier Prize in 1994. Her concert début was in W.A. Mozart's Requiem with John Eliot Gardiner in 1991, her stage début at Glyndebourne as Barbarina in the opening performances of the new house in 1994. She has subsequently sung Susanna and Zerlina at Glyndebourne, roles in *Platée*, *Paul Bunyan* and *The Pilgrim's Progress* with Covent Garden on tour, Belinda at the Berlin Staatsoper and Marzelline at the Rome Opera. She was a notable Sister Constance in *Dialogues des carmélites* at the ENO in 1999, and returned to the ENO as a vivid Sharpears (*The Cunning Little Vixen*) in 2001. She appears regularly in concert in Baroque music, to which her pure yet characterful soprano and fine-grained phrasing are ideally suited. Among the most notable of her many recordings are Antonio Vivaldi's *Ottone in villa*, G.F. Handel's *Deborah*, a delightful Miss Wordsworth in Benjamin Britten's *Albert Herring* and numerous Henry Purcell discs. (See colour plate 4.)

Alan Blyth

Grobe, Donald (Roth)

(*b* Ottawa, IL, 16 Dec 1929; *d* Berlin, 1 April 1986). American tenor. He studied at the Mannes College of Music, New York, and with Martial Singer. He made his début as Borsa (*Rigoletto*) in Chicago in 1952. After engagements at Krefeld-Mönchengladbach and Hanover, in 1960 he joined the Deutsche Oper, Berlin. There he created Wilhelm in H.W. Henze's *Der junge Lord* (1965) and Arundel in Wolfgang Fortner's *Elisabeth Tudor* (1972); he was Aschenbach in the German première of Benjamin Britten's *Death in Venice* (1974) and took part in the première of Aribert Reimann's *Die Gespenstersonate* (1984). He first appeared at the Edinburgh Festival in 1965 with the Munich company, as Ferrando in *Così fan tutte*; he returned, with the Deutsche Oper, in 1971 as Oleander in Reimann's *Melusine*, and in 1975 as Alwa in *Lulu*. He made his Covent Garden début with the Munich company in 1972, as Flamand in *Capriccio* and Henry Morosus in *Die schweigsame Frau*, and his Metropolitan Opera début during the 1968–9 season as Froh. He also created Claude Vallée in Ján Cikker's *The Play of Love and Death* (1969, Munich). His repertory also included Hoffmann, Eisenstein and Tom Rakewell. Although his voice was not outstandingly beautiful, he was a highly intelligent singer and a gifted actor.

Harold Rosenthal/R

Groop, Monica

(*b* Helsinki, 14 April 1958). Finnish mezzo-soprano. She studied in Helsinki at the Sibelius Academy and made her début in 1986 at Savonlinna, then joined the Finnish National Opera, where her roles have included Olga (*Yevgeny Onegin*), Charlotte (*Werther*), Sextus (*La clemenza di Tito*), Dorabella and Octavian. In 1989 she was a finalist in the Cardiff Singer of the World Competition. Groop sang Cherubino at Aix-en-Provence in 1991, and the same year made her Covent Garden début as Wellgunde and Waltraute, returning in 1994 as Varvara (*Kát'a Kabanová*). In 1995 she added two further roles to her repertory: the Composer (*Ariadne auf Naxos*) at Frankfurt and Mélisande at Los Angeles. In 1996 she sang Zerlina in *Don Giovanni* (with Georg Solti) in the inaugural production of the re-opened Opéra Palais Garnier in Paris, and in 1999 made a widely praised Glyndebourne début as Sextus. The same year she gave a Salzburg Festival recital accompanied by András Schiff, a frequent partner in recital. Groop's rich, even, firmly focussed voice and elegant sense of phrase are no less admirably displayed on the concert platform. Her recordings include J.S. Bach's *Christmas Oratorio*, Bach cantatas and arias, Antonio Vivaldi's *Ottone in Villa*, Zerlina, *Elijah*, Grieg and Sibelius songs, the complete songs of Allan Pettersson and the chamber version of *Das Lied von der Erde*.

Elizabeth Forbes

Grossi, Eleonora

(*fl* 1868–71). Italian mezzo-soprano. She sang in London at Covent Garden (1868–9) as Nancy (*Martha*), Urbain (*Les Huguenots*) and Pippo (*La gazza ladra*). She created Amneris in *Aida* at Cairo on 24 December 1871. To judge from these roles, she had a flexible voice of considerable dramatic weight.

Elizabeth Forbes

Groves, Paul

(*b* Lake Charles, LA, 25 Nov 1964). American tenor. After studying at Louisiana State University and the Juilliard School, he entered the Metropolitan Opera's Young Artists Development Program, winning the Met's National Council Auditions in 1991. The following year he made his Met début as the Steersman in *Der fliegende Holländer*. His success in the role has led to regular appearances in the house, in roles such as W.A. Mozart's Belmonte, Idamante, Ferrando and Don Ottavio, Almaviva (*Il barbiere di Siviglia*), the Duke (*Rigoletto*), Camille de Rosillon (*Die lustige Witwe*), Des Grieux (Jules Massenet's *Manon*), Tom Rakewell and Lysander (*A Midsummer Night's Dream*).

Having honed a reputation above all as a stylish and mellifluous Mozart tenor, Groves made his Salzburg Festival début, as Don Ottavio, in 1995, and his La Scala début, as Tamino, in 1996. Tamino was also the role of his Covent Garden début in 2003. Groves's other roles include Nadir (*Les pêcheurs de perles*), which he sang for his Lyric Opera of Chicago début in 1998, Hector Berlioz's Faust, Fenton, the role of his San Francisco début in 2001, Nemorino (Washington début, 2006), Renaud (*Armide*) and Pylade (*Iphigénie en Tauride*), which he performed at Covent Garden in 2007. In 2006 he created the role of Jianli in Tan Dun's *The First Emperor* at the Metropolitan Opera, and the following year made his New Orleans Opera début in the title role of *Les contes d'Hoffmann*. Groves also has a flourishing concert career in the USA and Europe, in such works as Berlioz's Requiem and *L'enfance du Christ*, *A Child of our Time*, Benjamin Britten's *War Requiem* and *Serenade*, and Gustav Mahler's *Das Lied von der Erde*. He made an admired Alice Tully

Hall recital début in 1996. His recordings include Admète (*Alceste*), and Pylade, Tebaldo (*I Capuleti e i Montecchi*), Roger Water's opera *Ça Ira*, Maurice Ravel cantatas and *mélodies* by Henri Duparc.

Richard Wigmore

Gruberová, Edita

(*b* Bratislava, 23 Dec 1946). Slovak soprano. She studied at the Bratislava Conservatory, as well as in Prague and Vienna. Her début was in 1968 in Bratislava as Rosina (*Il barbiere*), and two years later she was engaged for the Queen of Night at the Vienna Staatsoper. There she became a regular member of the company in 1972 and within a few years had established herself as one of the world's leading coloratura sopranos. As the Queen of Night she made débuts at Glyndebourne in 1974 and at the Metropolitan in 1977, the year in which she first appeared at the Salzburg Festival, as Thibault (*Don Carlos*) under Herbert von Karajan. Her other major successes have included appearances as Zerbinetta, Gilda, Violetta, Lucia, Konstanze, Manon, Oscar and Donna Anna (at La Scala in 1987). Gruberová has featured prominently in the revival of Gioachino Rossini and in other bel canto operas, and made her Covent Garden début as Giulietta in Vincenzo Bellini's *I Capuleti e i Montecchi* in 1984. She also sang Marie (*La fille du régiment*, 1987) and Semiramis (1992) at Zürich; and Queen Elizabeth I (*Roberto Devereux*) in Vienna in 1990. She combines a voice of exceptional range, agility and tonal clarity with an engaging stage personality and a natural gift for comedy. Her numerous recordings include W.A. Mozart's most brilliant concert arias (in which her virtuosity is unsurpassed), many of her Mozart and bel canto roles, notably Queen of Night, Giulietta, and Lucia, and Zerbinetta with both Kurt Masur and Georg Solti.

Noël Goodwin

Grümmer, Elisabeth

(*b* Niederjeutz, nr Diedenhofen [now Thionville, Lorraine], 31 March 1911; *d* Warendorf, Westphalia, 6 Nov 1986). German soprano. She studied in Aachen and made her début there as the First Flowermaiden in *Parsifal* in 1940, following it with Octavian. From 1942 to 1944 she was first lyric soprano in Duisburg and in 1946 joined the Städtische (later Deutsche) Oper, Berlin, where she sang until 1972. She sang Ellen Orford in the first Berlin performance of *Peter Grimes* and appeared as Agathe, Desdemona, Pamina and Eva. She sang this last role in Dresden and London and at Bayreuth, where her roles also included Elsa, Freia and Gutrune. In 1952 she appeared with the Hamburg Staatsoper in Edinburgh as Agathe, Pamina and Octavian and in 1953 made her first appearances in Vienna and Salzburg. She also sang at Glyndebourne (Ilia and Countess Almaviva), the Metropolitan (Elsa, 1967) and New York City Opera (Marschallin, 1967), and was an accomplished interpreter of lieder. Grümmer's beautiful voice, clarity of diction and innate musicianship are evident in her recordings, which include the roles of Donna Anna, Agathe, Elsa, Elisabeth, Eva and Hänsel.

A. Blyth: 'Remembering Elisabeth Grümmer', *Opera*, xxxviii (1987), 150

Harold Rosenthal/Alan Blyth

Grün, Friederike (Sadler-)

(*b* Mannheim, 14 June 1836; *d* Mannheim, Jan 1917). German soprano. She studied in Mannheim, joining the Hofoper chorus there in 1857. She was engaged at Frankfurt (1862), Cologne, Kassel, the Berlin Hofoper (1866) and, after further study in Milan, at Stuttgart (1870); she also made appearances in Vienna. Her repertory included Agathe, Norma, Valentine and Elisabeth, which she sang in the Italian première of *Tannhäuser* at Bologna in 1872. Her last engagement was at Coburg (1875–7). Although her voice was a dramatic soprano, she created Fricka, a mezzo role, in the first complete *Ring* at Bayreuth (1876).

Elizabeth Forbes/R

Grünbaum, Therese [née Müller]

(*b* Vienna, 24 Aug 1791; *d* Berlin, 30 Jan 1876). Austrian soprano. She studied with her father, the composer Wenzel Müller, appearing on the stage while still a child (including the part of Lilli in Ferdinand Kauer's *Das Donauweibchen*). While engaged in Prague, she sang Zerlina in 1807 and later became a famous Donna Anna. For her benefit performance of the title role of E.-N. Méhul's *Héléna* in 1815, Carl Maria von Weber composed a special scena and aria (J178). In 1816 she moved to the Kärntnertortheater, Vienna, where in 1819 she sang Desdemona in the first Viennese performance of Gioachino Rossini's *Otello* and in 1823 created Eglantine in Weber's *Euryanthe*. Later she sang in Munich (1827) and Berlin (1828–30). She had a brilliant, flexible voice with secure technique. After retiring from the stage she became a noted teacher. Her husband was the tenor Johann Christoff Grünbaum (1785–1870), who sang in Prague,

Vienna and Berlin. Their daughter, Caroline Grünbaum (*b* Prague, 18 March 1814; *d* Brunswick, 26 May 1868), had a successful career as a soprano and created Anna in Heinrich Marschner's *Hans Heiling* in Berlin (1833).

Elizabeth Forbes

Grundheber, Franz

(*b* Trier, 27 Sept 1937). German baritone. He studied in Hamburg, at Indiana University and the Music Academy of the West in San Diego. He made his début in 1966 at the Hamburg Staatsoper, and has continued to sing there regularly, while developing an extensive international career. He made his Vienna Staatsoper début, as Mandryka, in 1983, and his Salzburg Festival début, as Olivier (*Capriccio*), in 1985. Grundheber is an outstanding Wozzeck and Barak (*Die Frau ohne Schatten*), roles which display his gift for portraying tragic figures in a heroic light. Grundheber has also enjoyed successes as Cardillac, the Dutchman, Ruprecht (*The Fiery Angel*), Rigoletto (which he sang at Covent Garden in 1997) and Macbeth. Notable among his recordings are Wozzeck (with Claudio Abbado) and Tiresias (*Oedipus rex*).

Andrew Clark

Guadagni, Gaetano

(*b* Lodi or Vicenza, 16 Feb 1728; *d* Padua, 11 Oct 1792). Italian alto castrato, later soprano. In 1746 he travelled from Cremona, by way of Mantua, to Padua, where in the summer he took up employment as an alto at the *cappella* of S Antonio; in autumn of that year he sang at the Teatro S Moisè, Venice. In the 1748–9 season he was engaged by the Haymarket Theatre, London, as a member of G.F. Crosa's company of comic singers. G.F. Handel, whose attention he had caught, transferred to him the parts in *Messiah* and *Samson* originally written for Susanna Cibber and wrote for him the part of Didymus in *Theodora* (1750). Charles Burney claimed to have been of assistance to him in studying his roles; he later depicted Guadagni's voice as a 'full and well-toned countertenor', adding that during his first stay in England Guadagni 'was more noticed in singing English than Italian'. As an actor Guadagni was greatly influenced by David Garrick, who 'took great pleasure in forming him'. Micah's aria 'Return, oh God of hosts' (*Samson*) became a showpiece of Guadagni's in a number of London concerts (the last of which took place on 30 April 1753). Shortly afterwards he is said to have been a pupil of the soprano castrato Gioacchino Conti in

Lisbon. In 1754 he sang at the Concert Spirituel, Paris, and at Versailles and in 1755 he was again in London (as Lysander in *The Fairies* by J.C. Smith at Drury Lane). From 1756 to 1761 he played various roles in Italian theatres, including Sammete in Tommaso Traetta's *Nitteti* (1757, Reggio Emilia), Arbaces in J.C. Bach's *Artaserse* and the title role in Niccolò Piccinni's *Il Tigrane* (both 1761, Turin). In addition to his 'most beautiful voice' he was admired for his restrained style and the appropriate manner of acting which he adapted to the characters he played; but there was also trouble with impresarios because 'he rarely does his duty.' At Parma, nevertheless, he was increasingly in demand, singing two important pre-reform operas by Traetta, *Le feste d'Imeneo* in 1760 and *Enea e Lavinia* in 1761.

Early in 1762 he went to Vienna, where he made his début as Horatius in Johann Hasse's *Il trionfo di Clelia* and a month later sang Bacchus in C.W. Gluck's *Arianna*. On 5 October 1762 he created the title role in C.W. Gluck's *Orfeo ed Euridice*, probably his most famous role. A year later he created Orestes in Traetta's *Ifigenia in Tauride*, in 1764 he sang the title role in a revised version of Gluck's *Ezio* and in 1765 and created the title role in Gluck's *Telemaco*. In addition to these, his most important Viennese roles, he also sang in numerous concerts there from 1762. Early in 1764 he went to Frankfurt with Gluck for the emperor's coronation, and in summer 1765 he went to Innsbruck for the wedding of Archduke Leopold, where he created the role of Romulus in Hasse's *Romolo ed Ersilia*. In October 1765 Guadagni was in Padua, from where he tried to contact the impressario Count Giacomo Durazzo. He returned to Venice and was appointed to sing for the doge at an annual salary of 2000 ducats, though he had permission to take up other engagements during the carnival. In spring 1767 he offered his assistance to Prince Kaunitz for the intended opera performance at the wedding ceremonies in Vienna of the Archduchess Josepha and King Ferdinand IV of Naples (letter of 18 March 1767). In 1767–8 he sang in Venice in operas by Josef Mysliveček, Baldassare Galuppi, G.B. Borghi and P.A. Guglielmi. For Ferdinando Bertoni he returned to Metastasian roles in *Ezio* (1767) and *Il trionfo de Clelia* (1769, Padua). In 1768 he was appointed for the second time at the *capella* of S Antonio in Padua and in summer 1769 he went to London. In 1770 he sang Orpheus at the Haymarket Theatre, in a pasticcio which, in addition to Gluck's music, contained pieces by J.C. Bach and P.A. Guglielmi and an aria by Guadagni himself, 'Men tiranne', a minuet-like Larghetto in F major (in place of Gluck's F minor); this piece was published in *The Favourite Songs in the Opera Orfeo* (London, 1770). Guadagni's 'attitudes, action

and impassioned and exquisite manner of singing the simple and ballad-like air: Che farò, acquired his very great and just applause' (Burney; the air appeared in Domenico Corri's *A Select Collection of the most Admired Songs*, Edinburgh, c1779). Soon, however, Guadagni found himself rejected by the public, because – according to Burney – in order not to interrupt the progress of the stage action he did not bow to acknowledge applause and refused to repeat arias.

After staying in a number of towns in northern Italy, including Verona and Venice (where in 1772 he was awarded the title Cavaliere di S Marco), he went to Munich, where he sang the title roles in a new pasticcio of *Orfeo* in 1773 and in Antonio Tozzi's version in 1775. In 1776, after creating the title role in Bertoni's *Orfeo ed Euridice* in Venice, he went to Potsdam, where he sang before Frederick the Great, who presented him with a golden snuff-box set with diamonds. In 1781 Antonio Calegari wrote the last original part for him, that of Deucalion in *Deucalione e Pirra*. Guadagni settled in Padua and continued to sing sacred music in the Basilica del Santo and to take the part of Orpheus, as a soprano role, in domestic marionette theatre performances. That in later years Guadagni was a soprano is also confirmed by an Italian aria by him with a range from c' to g'' ('Pensa a serbarmi, o cara', from Metastasio's *Ezio*). Burney provided a comprehensive judgment of Guadagni as both actor and singer:

As an actor he had no equal on any stage in Europe: his figure was uncommonly elegant and noble; his countenance replete with beauty, intelligence, and dignity; and his attitudes and gestures were so full of grace and propriety, that they would have been excellent studies for a statuary. But though his manner of singing was perfectly delicate, polished, and refind, his voice seemed, at first, to disappoint every hearer… The music he sang was of the most simple imaginable; a few notes, with frequent pauses, and opportunities of being liberated from the composer and the band were all he wanted. And in these extemporaneous effusions he proved the inherent power of melody divorced from harmony, and unassisted even by unisonous accompaniment.

Guadagni favoured a syllabic style (to which he readily applied his stupendous *messa di voce*, or simple extempory solo passages interspersed with suggestive pauses); but he was not averse to energetic displays of agility. His technical and stylistic abiliites were, however, generally used according to their dramatic relevance.

In contrast with several anecdotes concerning Guadagni's generosity and unselfishness (in C.F. Cramer's *Magazin der Musik* and in J.N. Forkel's *Almanach*, 1783) there is a rather hostile one in C.D. von Dittersdorf's autobiography. Durazzo mentions Guadagni's grand airs when he was singing at Venice. A portrait of Guadagni (together with Giovanni Manzuoli) is in Antonio Fedi's *Parnaso* (*c*1790).

Two sisters of Guadagni, Lavinia Alessandra and (presumably) Angiola, sang in a performance of Piccinni's *La buona figliuola* on 19 May 1764 at the Laxenburg Castle theatre before the imperial court. In the same year the former also sang Livietta in Galuppi's *Le nozze* in Vienna; the latter had performed earlier in Venice (1760) and later sang there with her brother (1767).

Gerhard Croll/Irene Brandenburgr

Guasco, Carlo

(*b* Solero, Alessandria, 13 March 1813; *d* Solero, 13 Dec 1876). Italian tenor. He qualified as a surveyor, trained with an unknown teacher and, briefly, with Giacomo Panizza, and made his début at La Scala in 1837 as the Fisherman in Gioachino Rossini's *Guillaume Tell*, which was billed as 'Vallace' for reasons of censorship. In 1841 he took part in the first performance of Federico Ricci's *Corrado d'Altamura* at La Scala. He went on to sing the lyric tenor parts of Vincenzo Bellini and Gaetano Donizetti, creating Riccardo, Count de Chalais in the latter's *Maria di Rohan* (1843, Vienna) and – in the same poetic vein – Oronte in Giuseppe Verdi's *I Lombardi* (1843, Milan). Only under protest did he undertake, in Venice (1844), the more forceful title role in *Ernani*, which Verdi till then could not cast satisfactorily; though hoarse several nights running, he succeeded well enough to go on to create Foresto in *Attila* (1846, Venice). His voice was said to be penetrating and incisive. Between 1844 and 1848 he sang several times in Madrid and St Petersburg, once in London, and at Nice and Marseilles. At Bergamo he sang Donizetti's Crispus (*Fausta*) and Percy (*Anna Bolena*). He retired in 1849 but sang again in Paris and Vienna in 1852–3; by then he was in vocal decline.

John Rosselli/R

Gudehus, Heinrich

(*b* Altenhagen, nr Celle, 30 March 1845; *d* Dresden, 9 Oct 1909). German tenor. He studied with MALVINA SCHNORR VON CAROLSFELD at Brunswick and with Gustav Engel in Berlin, where he made his début in 1871 as Nadori in Louis Spohr's *Jessonda*. After further study, he reappeared at Rīga (1875) as Raoul in *Les Huguenots*. From 1880 to 1890 he was engaged at Dresden, making his début there as Lohengrin. He sang Parsifal at the second performance of Richard Wagner's opera at Bayreuth (1882), returning there as Tristan (1886) and Walther (1888). In 1884 he appeared at Covent Garden, singing Walther, Max (*Der Freischütz*), Tannhäuser and Tristan, and sang at the Royal Albert Hall in the first concert performance in England of Parsifal. He made his New York début at the Metropolitan in 1890 as Tannhäuser, also singing Raoul, Lohengrin, John of Leyden (*Le prophète*), Florestan, Walther, Siegfried, Siegmund and Tristan. On his return to Europe he was engaged at the Berlin Royal Opera House, remaining there until his retirement in 1896. One of the second generation of Wagnerian heroic tenors, he was also much admired in the dramatic French repertory.

Elizabeth Forbes

Gueden, Hilde

(*b* Vienna, 15 Sept 1917; *d* Klosterneuburg, 17 Sept 1988). Austrian soprano. She studied at the Vienna Conservatory and first appeared at the Volksoper in 1935 in Robert Stolz's operetta *Servus! Servus!*. She then went to Zürich, making her operatic début there in 1939 as Cherubino. In 1941 she was engaged at the Staatsoper in Munich. At Richard Strauss's suggestion she sang Sophie in *Der Rosenkavalier*, first in German and then in Italian (1942, Rome). She sang Zerlina at Salzburg in 1946 and was then engaged at the Vienna Staatsoper, where she sang until 1973. She made her London début at Covent Garden with the Vienna company in 1947, returning in 1956 as Gilda, the role of her Metropolitan début in 1951. In 1948 she appeared at the Edinburgh Festival with the Glyndebourne company as Despina and Zerlina. In nine seasons at the Metropolitan she sang Susanna, Zdenka, Mimì, Micaëla and Anne Trulove in the American première of *The Rake's Progress* (1953). In 1954 at Salzburg she sang Zerbinetta, displaying a newly acquired coloratura technique. She scored further successes as Aminta in Strauss's *Die schweigsame Frau* (1959, Salzburg) and in the title role of his *Daphne* (1964, Vienna). Gueden's vocal and dramatic abilities made her a much sought-after artist in modern works including Benjamin Britten's *The Rape of Lucretia* and Boris Blacher's *Romeo und Julia*, in both of which she sang at Salzburg. Her recordings, including Sophie in Erich Kleiber's *Der Rosenkavalier*, Rosalinde in Herbert von Karajan's second recording of *Die Fledermaus*, Hanna Glawari in Stolz's *Die lustige Witwe* and Eva in Hans Knappertsbusch's *Die Meistersinger*, adumbrate her winning ways as regards tone and phrasing.

H. Liversidge: 'Hilde Gueden', *Gramophone Record Review*, no.58 (1958), 809–13 [with discography by F.F. Clough and G.G. Cuming]

Harold Rosenthal/Alan Blyth

Guéymard, Louis

(*b* Chapponay, 17 Aug 1822; *d* Corbeil, nr Paris, July 1880). French tenor. He made his début at the Paris Opéra in 1848 in the title role of *Robert le diable*, which he also sang at the 500th performance of Giacomo Meyerbeer's opera (1867). In 1849 he created Jonas in *Le prophète* and the following year sang John of Leyden, the title role. He sang in the première of Charles Gounod's *Sapho* (1851), created Rodolphe in Gounod's *La nonne sanglante* (1854), Henri in Giuseppe Verdi's *Les vêpres siciliennes* (1855) and Adoniram in Gounod's *La reine de Saba* (1862). His repertory included Raoul (*Les Huguenots*), Arnold (*Guillaume Tell*), Edgardo, Manrico and Eléazar (*La Juive*), which he also sang at Covent Garden in 1852, Robert le diable and Masaniello. After leaving the Opéra he sang with the French Opera Company in New Orleans (1873–4). He was married to the soprano PAULINE GUÉYMARD-LAUTERS.

Elizabeth Forbes

Louis Guéymard in the title role of 'Robert le Diable' (Meyerbeer), painting by Gustave Courbet, 1857

Guéymard-Lauters [née Lauters], Pauline

(*b* Brussels, 1 Dec 1834; *d* 1876 or later). Belgian soprano. She made her début in 1854 at the Théâtre Lyrique, Paris. From 1861 to 1876 she was engaged at the Paris Opéra, making her début there as Valentine (*Les Huguenots*). She created Balkis in Charles Gounod's *La reine de Saba* (1862); Alda in Auguste Mermet's *Roland à Roncevaux* (1864); Eboli in Giuseppe Verdi's *Don Carlos* (1867) and the Queen in Ambroise Thomas' *Hamlet* (1868). Her roles also included Leonora (*Il trovatore*), Donna Anna, C.W. Gluck's Alcestis, Fidès (*Le prophète*) and Léonor (*La favorite*). She was married to the tenor LOUIS GUÉYMARD.

Elizabeth Forbes

Guglielmi, Giacomo

(*b* Massa, 16 Aug 1782; *d* ? Naples, after 1830). Tenor, son of the composer Pietro Alessandro Guglielmi. According to F. Piovano he studied solfège with Ferdinando Mazzanti, voice with Niccolò Piccinni's nephew and the violin with Capanna. After his début in 1805 at the Teatro Argentina, Rome, he sang, mostly in comic opera, at Parma, Naples, Florence, Bologna and Venice. He then went to Amsterdam and in 1809 to Paris for two years. By 1812 he had returned to Naples, to sing leading roles; he sang there again in 1819–20 and 1825. In 1820–21 he sang in Malta. His last stage appearance was probably in Parma in 1827 in an opera by Saverio Mercadante. After retiring from the stage he was held in considerable esteem as a teacher; among his pupils were GIULIA GRISI and ENRICO TAMBERLIK. Reports about his teaching ability circulated into the early 1830s, and his singing method was published in Toulouse in 1842. He created the role of Don Ramiro in *La Cenerentola* (1817, Rome). F.J. Fétis judged his voice to be 'pleasant, but of weak power; he sang with more taste than spirit'.

James L. Jackman, Kay Lipton and Mary Hunter/ Kay Lipton

Gulak-Artemovsky, Semyon Stepanovich

(*b* Gulakovshchina, nr Gorodishche [now in Ukraine], 4/16 Feb 1813; *d* Moscow, 5/17 April 1873). Ukrainian baritone, playwright and composer. The son of a priest, he was educated in a local church school. On the recommendation of the Metropolitan of Kiev, who commended his vocal abilities, he was later enrolled in the episcopal choir at the cathedral of St Sophia, transferring in 1830 to the choir of St Michael's monastery, the seat of the Kiev vicariate. In 1838 M.I. Glinka, who was touring Ukraine to recruit singers for the court chapel choir, heard him sing and offered to take him to St Petersburg. There he gave him singing lessons, and in 1839 sent him to France and Italy for professional training and to gain operatic experience. He returned to Russia in January 1842 and spent the next 22 years singing leading roles in the St Petersburg opera theatres. Possessing a fine, wide-ranging baritone voice, his repertory included the roles of Enrico Ashton in *Lucia di Lammermoor*, Sir Riccardo Forth in *I puritani* and the Unknown in Verstovsky's *Askold's Grave*. One of the few singers of his generation with the ability to sing in languages beside his native Russian, Gulak-Artemovsky frequently performed with the Italian troupe in St Petersburg. Perhaps his most important achievement was in the creation (alternately with Osip Petrov) of the hero Ruslan in Glinka's original production of *Ruslan and Lyudmila* (1842); he received high praise from A.N. Serov for this role as well as for his interpretation of the Hermit in *Der Freischütz*.

As a composer Gulak-Artemovsky is known principally for his popular opera *Zaporozhets za Dunayem* ('A Cossack beyond the Danube'), for which he wrote both music and text between 1861 and 1862. The opera, which uses Ukrainian folk melodies, received its première at the Mariinsky Theatre in April 1863, with Gulak-Artemovsky taking the title role of Ivan Karas. His interest in folk music is illustrated further by his arrangement of the tune *Stoit yavir nad vodoyu* ('The Sycamore Stands by the Water'), which he dedicated to the Ukrainian poet Taras Shevchenko, and by his collection of Ukrainian folktunes, *Narodni ukraïns'ki pisni z golosom* (Kiev, 1868, 2/1883). Two other stage works, *Ukrainskaya svad'ba* ('The Ukrainian Wedding') and *Noch' nakanune Ivanova dnya* ('The Night before St John's Day'), appeared in 1851 and 1852 respectively. Gulak-Artemovsky retired from the stage in 1864 and spent the rest of his life in Moscow.

Geoffrey Norris/Nigel Yandell

Gulbranson, Ellen

(*b* Stockholm, 4 March 1863; *d* Oslo, 2 Jan 1947). Swedish soprano. She studied with Mathilde Marchesi in Paris, and also with Marchesi's daughter Blanche, who successfully transformed her from a mezzo-soprano into a dramatic soprano. She made her début in Stockholm in 1889 as Amneris and sang Brünnhilde and Ortrud there in 1898. She was a leading figure among the second generation of Bayreuth singers, whose fame was largely due to the Wagner festivals there. In 1896, 20 years after the opening of Bayreuth, she shared the role of Brünnhilde with LILLI LEHMANN, but thenceforward remained its sole exponent until 1914, appearing also as Kundry during five seasons. Her Covent Garden Brünnhilde in 1900 made no great mark in the proximity of Milka Ternina and NORDICA; but when she returned in 1907 to sing in two *Ring* cycles under Hans Richter, she was found to have greatly improved. Gulbranson made a few recordings by the unreliable Edison and Pathé 'hill and dale' system.

Desmond Shawe-Taylor

Guleghina, Maria

(*b* Odessa, 9 Aug 1959). Ukrainian soprano of Armenian-Ukrainian ancestry. As a student at the Odessa Conservatory she won first prize in the Glinka Competition and third prize in the Tchaikovsky Competition, and in 1985 began singing at the State Academic Opera, Minsk. Her major roles there included Yolanta and Elisabeth de Valois. Soon after her international début, as Amelia in *Un ballo in maschera* at La Scala in 1987, she left the Soviet Union and established herself in non-Russian parts: with the exception of Lisa in *The Queen of Spades*, which she has also recorded with the Kirov Opera, she has concentrated on the Italian repertory. Other early La Scala performances included Lucrezia in *I due Foscari* (1988) and Tosca (1989), the role in which she made débuts in Hamburg (1990), Berlin, Vienna, San Francisco and Chicago; her interpretation of Tosca is preserved on a recording with Riccardo Muti, taken from performances at La Scala in 2000. In 1995 she made her Rome début as Lady Macbeth and her Paris début as Abigaille, both parts she has repeated widely. Her Abigaille at the Metropolitan in 2001 was widely praised for its reckless abandon. She first appeared in London at a Barbican concert as Elvira in *Ernani* (a role she tackled on stage in Vienna in 1999), and made her Covent Garden début in 1996 as Fedora. She has sung Maddalena de Coigny at the Metropolitan Opera and Odabella in Houston, and undertook her first Manon Lescaut at La Scala in 1998. She sang her first Norma at Orange in 1999. Further roles include Aida and Santuzza, and she has also recorded Leonora (*Oberto*) and Giorgetta (*Il tabarro*). Guleghina's glamorous stage presence is allied to bright and powerful tone that never turns hard, making her one of the outstanding dramatic sopranos of her generation.

John Allison

Gura, Hermann

(*b* Breslau [now Wrocław, Poland], 5 April 1870; *d* Bad Wiessee, 13 Sept 1944). German baritone and producer, son of the bass-baritone Eugen Gura. He studied in Munich with Hasselbeck and Zenger and made his début in Weimar in 1890 in the title role of *Der fliegende Holländer*. After engagements in Riga (1890–91), at the Kroll Theatre, Berlin (1891–2), Aachen (1892–3), Zürich (1893–4), Basle (1894–5) and Munich (1895–6), he joined the Schwerin Hoftheater as singer and producer, remaining there until 1908. In 1911 he was appointed director of the Berlin Komische Oper, and in 1913 was responsible for the staging of *Der Rosenkavalier* at its first London performance, and other operas during Thomas Beecham's 1913 Covent Garden season; he also sang Beckmesser. During the 1920s he was a director at the Helsinki Opera, then taught singing in Berlin and founded the Deutsche Gastspieloper. He was married three times, his last wife being the soprano Annie Gura-Hummel, who sang the Goose Girl in the first London performance of Engelbert Humperdinck's *Königskinder*.

Harold Rosenthal/R

Gutheil-Schoder, Marie

(*b* Weimar, 16 Feb 1874; *b* Bad Ilmenau, Thuringia, 4 Oct 1935). German soprano. She studied in Weimar, where she made her début in 1891. After an apprenticeship in secondary roles, she had a notable success in 1895 as Carmen. She was then engaged by Gustav Mahler for the Vienna Staatsoper where, in spite of being dubbed 'the singer without a voice', she remained as one of the most admired artists from 1900 to 1926. During this time she became most closely associated with the operas of W.A. Mozart, and of Richard Strauss who coached her in Electra and Octavian for the Viennese premières of *Elektra* and *Der Rosenkavalier*; she also appeared as Salome. At Salzburg she sang Susanna in *Le nozze di Figaro*, and at Covent Garden, in a single appearance under Thomas Beecham in 1913, Octavian. She gained additional respect among musicians for her support of some avant-garde composers, especially Arnold Schoenberg, whose *Erwartung* she sang at its première in Prague in 1924. On retirement as a singer she taught and directed at Vienna and Salzburg. Her few recordings, made in 1902, reveal very little about her. The admiration of other artists, such as Bruno Walter and LOTTE LEHMAN, tells far more, as does the faith reposed in her by Mahler and Strauss. Her singing was famous for its subtlety and refinement; and about the voice, Erwin Stein wrote that it was 'the perfect instrument of a great artist'.

J.B. Steane

Gyuzelev [Ghiuselev], Nikola

(*b* Pavlikeni, 17 Aug 1936). Bulgarian bass. He studied at Sofia and joined the Bulgarian National Opera in 1960, making his début as Timur. In 1965 he toured France, Germany and Italy with the company and made his Metropolitan début as Ramfis. He sang in most major European theatres, including La Scala, the Paris Opéra, the Vienna Staatsoper and Covent Garden, where he made his début in 1976 as Pagano (*I Lombardi*). His repertory included Boris, Dosifey (*Khovanshchina*), Alexander Borodin's Galitsky (which he sang at Covent Garden in 1990), Don Giovanni, Gioachino Rossini's Don Basilio, Oroveso (*Norma*), Henry VIII (*Anna Bolena*), Charles Gounod's and Arrigo Boito's Mephistopheles and the four villains in *Les contes d'Hoffmann*. His rich, dark-toned voice was most effective in Giuseppe Verdi, notably as Philip II, Attila, Silva (*Ernani*) and Fiesco (*Simon Boccanegra*).

Elizabeth Forbes

Hackett, Charles

(*b* Worcester, MA, 4 Nov 1889; *d* New York, 1 Jan 1942). American tenor. On the recommendation of LILLIAN NORDICA he studied at the New England Conservatory with Arthur J. Hubbard, and later with Vincenzo Lombardi in Florence. In 1914 he made his début in Genoa as Wilhelm Meister, which also served for his La Scala début (1916). He appeared at the Paris Opéra as a servant in *Maria di Rohan* in 1917, returning as the Duke and Romeo in 1922. After a season in Buenos Aires (1917–18) he made his Metropolitan début in 1919 as Almaviva; there he later sang Lindoro (*L'italiana in Algeri*), Rodolfo, Pinkerton, Romeo and Alfredo. At Monte Carlo (1922–3) he sang Cavaradossi and Des Grieux (*Manon*). He was closely identified with the Chicago Opera (1922–35) and took part in the première of Charles Cadman's *A Witch of Salem* (1926) and Hamilton Forrest's *Camille* (1930). In the same year, he appeared at Covent Garden as Almaviva, Fenton, and Romeo in MELBA's farewell performance. He continued to sing until 1939. Hackett made a number of records, including duets with Maria Barrientos and PONSELLE; they document a secure technique and a certain elegance, though there is also a sense of routine about them. That sense is completely dispelled by the sweep and finesse of his style in a recording of a Metropolitan Opera broadcast of Charles Gounod's *Roméo et Juliette* from 1935.

L.F. Holdridge: 'Charles Hackett', *Record Collector*, xxii (1974–5), 173–214

Richard Dyer, Elizabeth Forbes

Hadley, Jerry

(*b* Princeton, IL, 16 June 1952; *d* Poughkeepsie, NY, 18 July 2007). American tenor. After vocal studies at the University of Illinois and with Thomas Lo Monaco in New York, he made his début as Lyonel in *Martha* (1978, Sarasota). Several seasons at the New York City Opera, beginning in 1979 (as Arturo in *Lucia di Lammermoor*), established him as a leading lyric tenor: his roles included Des Grieux (*Manon*), Pinkerton, Tom Rakewell, Werther and Charles Gounod's Faust. His European début in Vienna as Nemorino in 1982 was followed by appearances in Berlin, Geneva, Glyndebourne, Hamburg, London

and Munich. He made his Metropolitan Opera début as Des Grieux in 1987. His lyrical, italianate voice and dramatic immediacy made him a fine interpreter of the Mozart, French lyric and Italian repertories. In 1999 he created the lead role in John Harbison's *The Great Gatsby*. He was an equally accomplished artist in the concert hall in works such as *Messiah*, *Elijah* and Benjamin Britten's *War Requiem*, all of which he recorded. Among his many operatic recordings are *Faust*, *Werther*, *La bohème* and *The Rake's Progress*, in all of which his firm line and ardent manner are in evidence.

Cori Ellison/Alan Blyth/R

Haefliger, Ernst

(*b* Davos, 6 July 1919; *d* Davos 17 March 2007). Swiss tenor. He studied at Zürich and Geneva, and in Vienna with JULIUS PATZAK. He made his début in 1949 at Salzburg, creating Tiresias in Carl Orff's *Antigonae*. While engaged at the Städtische (later Deutsche) Oper, Berlin (1952–74), he sang Belmonte at Glyndebourne (1956), Idamantes at Salzburg (1961) and Tamino in Chicago (1966). He created roles in Boris Blacher's *Zwischenfälle bei einer Notlandung* (1966, Hamburg) and *Zweihunderttausend Taler* (1969, Berlin), and in several operas by Frank Martin. His repertory included Ferrando, Don Ottavio, Pelléas, Jeník, Busoni's Calaf, Froh and Palestrina, his most striking characterization. He was an admired interpreter of the Evangelist in both Bach Passions, and of Franz Schubert's *Die schöne Müllerin* and *Winterreise*. Haefliger's voice was notable for its clarity and focus rather than its tonal quality, which tended towards the monochrome. His scrupulous attention to verbal articulation and his understanding of the niceties of phrasing were always evident in Bach and in song recitals, as can be heard on many recordings. He also recorded several of his Mozart roles and an eloquent Florestan in *Fidelio*, all with Ferenc Fricsay conducting.

Alan Blyth

Hafgren [Hafgren-Waag, Hafgren-Dinkela], Lilly

(*b* Stockholm, 7 Oct 1884; *d* Berlin, 27 Feb 1965). Swedish soprano. She was trained first as a pianist and was advised by Siegfried Wagner to take up

1. Farinelli in the court of Philip V of Spain, detail of a painting by Corrado Giaquinto

Above: 2. Anastasia Robinson by John Vanderbank, 1723
Right: 3. Marie Pélissier by François Drouais

4. Susan Gritton as Sophie and Diana Montague as Octavian in 'Der Rosenkavalier' (Strauss), English National Opera, London, 2003

5. Christopher Maltman and Toby Spence in 'Così fan tutte' (Mozart), English National Opera, London, 2002

6. Nicholas Levasseur as Bertram [left] with Adolph Nourrit as Robert [centre] and Cornelie Falcon as Isabelle [right], in 'Robert le diable' (Meyerbeer), Opera Garnier, Paris

7. *John Tomlinson as Dosifey in 'Khovanshchina' (Musorgsky), English National Opera, London, 2003*

singing. Her studies in Frankfurt and Milan being completed, she was invited to Bayreuth, where in 1908 she made her début as Freia in *Das Rheingold*. Further roles there were Elsa in *Lohengrin* and Eva in *Die Meistersinger*, in which role she reappeared in 1924. From 1908 to 1912 she was with the opera at Mannheim, after which there followed six years at the Hofoper in Berlin. Her large repertory now ranged from Brünnhilde and Isolde to Pamina and Countess Almaviva, Tosca, Carmen and Charlotte in *Werther*. She sang the Empress in the Berlin première of *Die Frau ohne Schatten* and the title role in that of *Ariadne auf Naxos*. She travelled widely in Europe, appearing at La Scala as Brünnhilde in the seasons of 1925, 1926 and 1930. Her operatic career continued in Dresden until 1934, and she was also a noted recitalist. For a time she appeared under the name of Hafgren-Waag after her first marriage and Hafgren-Dinkela after her second. Her voice on records is bright in tone, conveying a strong sense of dramatic commitment.

J.B. Steane

Hagegård, Håkon

(*b* Karlstad, 25 Nov 1945). Swedish baritone. He studied in Stockholm, making his début at the Royal Opera in 1968 as Papageno, the role he later sang in Ingmar Bergman's film of *The Magic Flute* (*Trollflöjten*, 1975). He first appeared at Glyndebourne as the Count in *Capriccio* (1973), returning as Count Almaviva and Guglielmo. After his Metropolitan début as Malatesta (1978) he sang Gioachino Rossini's Figaro, Eisenstein and Wolfram, the role of his Covent Garden début in 1987. He has also appeared with Scottish Opera, La Scala and Drottningholm, and in Paris, Copenhagen, Hamburg, Geneva, Zürich, Santa Fe, San Francisco and Chicago. Among his other roles are Don Giovanni (which he has recorded), Pacuvio (*La pietra del paragone*), Yevgeny Onegin, Posa, Rigoletto, Ford and Pelléas. In 1991 he sang Beaumarchais in the première at the Metropolitan of John Corigliano's *The Ghosts of Versailles*, and the following year created the Officer in Ingvar Lidholm's *Ett drömspel* ('A Dream Play') at the Royal Opera, Stockholm, a role he subsequently recorded. With the years his light, lyrical voice has grown more powerful, without losing its beauty of tone or flexibility. Hagegård is also an admired concert singer, and has made notable recordings of Johannes Brahms's *German Requiem*, lieder by Franz Schubert, Hugo Wolf and Gustav Mahler and songs by Edvard Grieg, Wilhelm Stenhammar and Ture Rangström.

Elizabeth Forbes

Hagley, Alison

(*b* London, 9 May 1961). English soprano. She studied at the GSM, then at the National Opera Studio. After appearances in G.F. Handel at the Batignano Festival in 1985 and in *La finta giardiniera* at the Camden Festival the following year, she made her Glyndebourne début in 1988 as the Little Owl in *L'enfant et les sortilèges*, returning as Papagena, Zerlina, Nannetta and, most notably, as a delightful and quick-witted Susanna at the reopening of the new house in 1994, a performance preserved on video. Her ENO début in 1991 was as Lauretta in *Gianni Schicchi*, and she has subsequently returned there to sing Gretel and Nannetta. In 1992 she was a subtle and affecting Mélisande in Peter Stein's staging of *Pelléas et Mélisande* with the WNO, with Pierre Boulez conducting. For Scottish Opera she has undertaken Musetta and Adèle (*Die Fledermaus*) and for the Staatsoper in Munich Susanna, Zerlina and Bella (*The Midsummer Marriage*). After smaller roles at Covent Garden, Hagley sang Susanna there in 1997. She was Dorabella in Simon Rattle's recording of *Così fan tutte*, based on live performances, in 1995. She is also a noted concert singer, and took part in Paul McCreesh's admired recording of Handel's *Solomon*, where her warm, finely phrased singing epitomizes her work in all fields.

Alan Blyth

Haizinger [Haitzinger], Anton

(*b* Wilfersdorf, Lower Austria, 14 March 1796; *d* Karlsruhe, 31 Dec 1869). Austrian tenor. After teaching in Vienna he studied harmony with Wölkert and singing with Mozzati; he later continued his studies with Antonio Salieri. He was engaged at the Theater an der Wien as *primo tenore* in 1821 and made a successful début as Gianetto (*La gazza ladra*); he then sang Don Ottavio, Lindoro (*L'italiana in Algeri*) and Florestan to WILHELMINE SCHRÖDER-DEVRIENT's Leonore (1822). He created Adolar in *Euryanthe* at the Kärntnertortheater in 1823; Julius Benedict described his performance in the première. The following year he sang the tenor solos in Beethoven's Ninth Symphony and *Missa solemnis* in the presence of the composer. He made successful visits to Prague, Pressburg, Frankfurt, Mannheim, Stuttgart and Karlsruhe, where he settled in 1826. In 1827 he married the actress and singer Amalie Neumann (1800–84), widow of the actor Karl Neumann. Together with Schröder-Devrient he gave a short season at the Opéra-Comique in Paris in 1831, singing Florestan, Max (*Der Freischütz*), and Huon in the Paris première of *Oberon*. In 1833 he sang Max, Tamino, Florestan and Adolar (in the London première of *Euryanthe*) with the German opera company at Covent Garden. Richard Mount Edgcumbe described his voice as 'very beautiful', although Henry Chorley found it 'throaty and disagreeable'. He returned to England in 1841, and visited St Petersburg in 1835. He established a school of dramatic singing in Karlsruhe with his wife, and also published some music, including a song, *Vergiss mein nicht*, and a *Lehrgang bei dem Gesangunterricht in Musikschulen* (1843).

One of the finest German tenors of his generation, Haizinger contributed much to the success of *Fidelio* and of Weber's operas, especially as a partner to Schröder-Devrient. The dramatist P.A. Wolff wrote that, 'To hear Haitzinger is something extraordinary. It is a pity that he has not made much progress as an actor; but one forgives him everything when one considers his moving voice, his expressive delivery, his admirable technique' (letter to F.W. Gubitz, 31 January 1826).

John Warrack/Elizabeth Forbes

Hale, Robert

(*b* San Antonio, TX, 22 Aug 1943). American bass-baritone. He studied in Boston, making his début in 1966 with the Goldovsky Opera. In 1967 he joined New York City Opera, where he sang W.A. Mozart's Figaro, Count Almaviva, Don Giovanni, Raimondo, Henry VIII (*Anna Bolena*), Oroveso, Giorgio (*I puritani*) and the Father (*Louise*). At San Diego (1978) he sang Claudius (*Hamlet*), and at Buenos Aires (1980) the four *Hoffmann* villains. Meanwhile, after singing the Dutchman in Stuttgart (1978), he began to take on heavier roles: Pizarro, Iago, Mephistopheles (Charles Gounod and Arrigo Boito), Scarpia and Escamillo, which he sang in Germany and at Zürich, Lisbon and San Francisco. Having made his Covent Garden début as John the Baptist (1988), he returned as Orestes (*Elektra*, 1994). His débuts at La Scala (1989) and the Metropolitan (1990) were both as the Dutchman. At Salzburg he has sung Pizarro and Barak (*Die Frau ohne Schatten*). An imposing presence, great dramatic intensity and a strong, expressive voice make him a superb Wotan, a role he has sung throughout Europe and in North and South America, and also recorded.

Elizabeth Forbes

Hallstein, Ingeborg

(*b* Munich, 23 May 1937). German soprano. She made her début in 1956 at Passau as Musetta and in 1959 became a member of the Staatsoper in Munich. In 1960 she sang Rosina in *La finta semplice* at Salzburg; in 1962 she sang the Queen of Night at the Theater an der Wien, Vienna, and at Covent Garden. She sang in all the major cities of Europe, sang Scolatella in the Kassel premiere of H.W. Henze's *Il re cervo* (1963); in the premiere of *Being Beauteous* (Berlin, 1964), and created Autonoe in *The Bassarids* (1966, Salzburg). Her repertory included Konstanze, Fiordiligi, Susanna, Norina, Marie (*Zar und Zimmermann*), Aennchen (*Der Freischütz*), Violetta, Gilda, Nedda, Sophie and Zerbinetta, the role which best displayed her brilliant coloratura technique. She was professor of singing at the Musikhochschule in Würzburg from 1979 until 2006.

Elizabeth Forbes

Hamari, Julia

(*b* Budapest, 21 Nov 1942). Hungarian mezzo-soprano. She studied in Budapest at the Liszt Academy of Music and in 1964 won a prize that enabled her to continue her studies in Stuttgart. Although her career developed mainly in the concert hall – she became renowned as a contralto soloist, notably in J.S. Bach, and a lieder singer – she also sang a successful Carmen at Stuttgart, and was a member of the Deutsche Oper am Rhein in the 1970s; among her other roles have been Fatima (*Oberon*), Cornelia (*Giulio Cesare*) and C.W. Gluck's Orpheus, all of which she recorded. Her British operatic début was at Glyndebourne in 1979 as Celia in Joseph Haydn's *La fedeltà premiata*, and she first appeared at the Metropolitan Opera as Rosina (*Il barbiere*) in 1984. Hamari's singing was distinguished by a confident technique and smooth, full tone. Her other recordings included Lola (*Cavalleria rusticana*), Olga (*Yevgeny Onegin*), Giovanna (*Ernani*), Magdalene (*Die Meistersinger*) and the Mother (*Hänsel und Gretel*), in addition to Bach cantatas and other choral works.

Noël Goodwin

Hammond, Dame Joan (Hood)

(*b* Christchurch, 24 May 1912; *d* Bowral, NSW, 26 Nov 1996). Australian soprano of New Zealand birth. She studied in Sydney, where in 1928 she made her début as Giovanna (*Rigoletto*), then sang Venus and Helmwige (1935). After further study in Vienna, London and Florence, she was engaged at the Vienna Volksoper in 1938 to sing Nedda, Martha and Konstanze; in 1939 she sang Mimì and Violetta at the Staatsoper. Engaged by the Carl Rosa company (1942–5), she sang Butterfly, Tosca, Violetta, Marguerite (*Faust*) and the Marschallin. In 1947 she returned to Vienna, then made her Covent Garden début in 1948 as Leonora (*Il trovatore*), returning as Mimì, Beethoven's Leonore and Aida. She made her American début with the New York City Center Opera in 1949, and sang Elisabeth de Valois (1951) and Rusalka (1959) at Sadler's Wells, Tatyana and Fevroniya (*The Invisible City of Kitezh*) in Russian in Barcelona, Aida and Tatyana in Leningrad and Moscow (1957), and Desdemona and Tosca (1957) and Salome (1960) in Australia for the Elizabethan Theatre Trust. Hammond's other roles included Pamina, Donna Anna and Elvira, Agathe, Elisabeth, Elsa, Norma and Turandot. Her record of 'O my beloved father' from *Gianni Schicchi* sold over a million copies and won a golden disc in 1969. She had a strong, vibrant voice, which she used intelligently to project the meaning of what she sang. Her warm personality allied to her expressive manner made her an instantly communicative, if not specially subtle, artist. An operation in 1964 left her partially deaf, and she announced her retirement the following year. *A Voice, a Life*, her autobiography, was published in 1970. She was made a DBE in 1974.

A. Blyth: 'Joan Hammond at 80', *Opera*, xliv (1993), 158–62
Obituary, *The Times* (28 Nov 1996)

Alan Blyth

Hammons, Thomas

(*b* Shawnee, OK, 24 Dec 1951). American bass-baritone. He studied at Cincinnati College-Conservatory and made his professional operatic début with Santa Fe Opera, as the Doctor in Stephen Oliver's *The Duchess of Malfi*, in 1978. He has subsequently been acclaimed for his roles in two important world premières: as Henry Kissinger in John Adams's *Nixon in China* (1987, Houston), and as both the first officer and the terrorist 'Rambo' in the same composer's *The Death of Klinghoffer* (La Monnaie, 1991). Since his Metropolitan debut in 1996, as the Sacristan in *Tosca*, he has sung for the house each season in buffo roles including Bartolo (*Il barbiere di Siviglia*). Hammons has also appeared at many of the other major US and Canadian opera houses, in roles including Peter Quince, Don Alfonso, the Bosun (*Billy Budd*), and Dulcamara (*L'elisir d'amore*), which he sang at the Opéra de Montréal in 2002.

Richard Wigmore

Hampson, (Walter) Thomas

(*b* Elkhart, IN, 28 June 1955). American baritone. He studied in Spokane and Los Angeles, making his début in 1978 at Spokane in *Hänsel und Gretel*. In 1981 he won first prize at the Metropolitan Opera

Auditions. Engaged at Düsseldorf (1981–4), he sang the Herald (*Lohengrin*), Harlequin (*Ariadne auf Naxos*), Belcore, and Nanni (Joseph Haydn's *L'infedeltà delusa*). He sang H.W. Henze's Prince of Homburg at Darmstadt, Guglielmo at St Louis (1982), Malatesta at Santa Fe (1983) and Count Almaviva at Aix-en-Provence (1985). In 1984 he was engaged at Zürich, where over the next decade his roles included Jules Massenet's Lescaut, G.F. Handel's Julius Caesar, Marcello, Don Giovanni, Gioachino Rossini's Figaro (also the role of his Covent Garden début in 1993), Posa (*Don Carlos*) and the Prince of Homburg. In 1986 he made his Vienna Staatsoper début as Guglielmo, and his Metropolitan début as Count Almaviva, which he also sang at his Salzburg début (1988). Other roles at the Metropolitan have included Billy Budd and Coroebus (*Les Troyens*). At San Francisco he has sung Claudio Monteverdi's Ulysses (1990) and created Valmont in Conrad Susa's *Dangerous Liaisons* (1994). In 1998 he sang the title tole in *Guillaume Tell* at the Vienna Staatsoper, and the following year performed the title role in *Werther*, in the composer's downward transposition, at the Metropolitan. His movement towards heavier repertory is exemplified by two recent roles: the title role in Ferruccio Busoni's *Doktor Faust*, which he sang at the Metropolitan in the 2000–01 season, and Amfortas, which he performed at the Opéra National, Paris, in 2001. A charismatic actor, Hampson has a grainy, flexible voice perfectly suited to W.A. Mozart's three Da Ponte operas, all of which he has recorded to acclaim. His other operatic recordings include Gioachino Rossini's Figaro, Yevgeny Onegin, Marcello, Ambroise Thomas' Hamlet and a disc of Verdi arias. He is also an outstanding recitalist with an enterprisingly wide repertory: in addition to his many recordings of lieder, he has performed and recorded little-known songs by American composers, including Charles Ives, Charles Griffes and Edward MacDowell, and created *Night Speech*, a song cycle by Stephen Paulus, at Spokane (1989). He has been particularly closely associated with the songs of Gustav Mahler, and has co-edited the *Knaben Wunderhorn* songs for the critical edition of the Gustav Mahler Gesellschaft (Universal Edition, Vienna).

R.V. Lucano: 'A Conversation and then Some with Thomas Hampson', *Fanfare*, xv/2 (1991–2), 225–33
E. Seckerson: 'Hit and Myth', *Gramophone*, lxix/April (1992), 38–41

Elizabeth Forbes

Hann, Georg

(*b* Vienna, 30 Jan 1897; *d* Munich, 9 Dec 1950). Austrian bass. After study with Theodor Lierhammer in Vienna, he joined the Staatsoper in Munich in 1927. There he sang a wide variety of roles ranging from the deep bass of Sarastro to dramatic baritone parts such as Scarpia and Tonio. In 1942 he created La Roche in *Capriccio*. He also appeared at the Salzburg festivals of 1931, 1946 and 1947, and was a guest artist in Vienna and Berlin. At Covent Garden he sang in *Salome* in 1924 and reappeared there, with the Vienna Staatsoper, in 1947 as Leporello and Pizarro. His strong personality, vivid characterization and tendency to roughness and exaggeration are evident in many recordings of opera and lieder, some of them taken from wartime broadcasts; among the best is his Daland in *Der fliegende Holländer*.

J.B. Steane

Hansen-Eidé, Kaja Andrea Karoline.

See NORENA, EIDÉ.

Harper, Heather (Mary)

(*b* Belfast, 8 May 1930). Northern Ireland soprano. She studied in London and made her début in 1954 as Lady Macbeth with the Oxford University Opera Club. She sang First Lady (*Die Zauberflöte*) in 1957 at Glyndebourne, returning as Anne Trulove in 1963. With the New Opera Company she created Lucie Manette in Arthur Benjamin's *A Tale of Two Cities* (1957) and sang the Woman in the British stage première of *Erwartung* (1960). Her Covent Garden début was as Helena (*A Midsummer Night's Dream*) in 1962, and she returned as Ellen Orford, Micaëla, Blanche (*Dialogues des Carmélites*), Gutrune, Eva, Antonia, Mrs Coyle (*Owen Wingrave*), which she had created on television (1971), Arabella and Nadia in the première of Michael Tippett's *The Ice Break* (1977). At Bayreuth (1967–8) she sang Elsa and in Buenos Aires (1969–72) Arabella, Donna Elvira, Marguerite and Vitellia (*La clemenza di Tito*). She was highly praised as the Governess (*The Turn of the Screw*) with the English Opera Group (1972), although Ellen Orford was her most sympathetic role, admirably suited to her firm, expressive, well-projected voice and eloquent enunciation. She retired from opera in 1984, but sang Nadia in a concert performance of *The Ice Break* at the 1990 Proms in London.

On the concert platform Harper was at home in music ranging from Monteverdi madrigals, J.S. Bach and G.F. Handel (of whom she was a specially admired interpreter) through Gustav Mahler, Frederick Delius and Ralph Vaughan Williams to Anton Webern and Luigi Dallapiccola. She had the technical assurance and confidence in her own abilities to encompass the demands of Richard Strauss's

Vier letzte Lieder and Tippett's Third Symphony, in which she was the soloist in the première (1972). She recorded both these works and much else in her extensive repertory, notably the Female Chorus (*The Rape of Lucretia*), Helena and Mrs Coyle with the composer and Ellen Orford with Colin Davis.

A. Blyth: 'Heather Harper', *Opera*, xxii (1971), 594–600

Alan Blyth

Harrell, Mack

(*b* Celeste, TX, 8 Oct 1909; *d* Dallas, 29 Jan 1960). American baritone, father of the cellist Lynn Harrell. He studied at the Juilliard School and in 1939 won the Metropolitan Opera Auditions of the Air and made his début with the company as Biterolf in *Tannhäuser*. He created Samson in Bernard Rogers's *The Warrior* (1947) and continued to appear at the Metropolitan until 1958, singing a wide repertory that included Masetto, Papageno, Kothner, Amfortas, John the Baptist, Captain Balstrode (*Peter Grimes*) and Nick Shadow, his best-known role, which he sang in the American première of *The Rake's Progress* in 1953. He appeared with New York City Opera, making his début in 1944 as Germont, and in Chicago and San Francisco. His repertory also included Escamillo, Marcello, Valentin, Luna, Golaud and Wozzeck, which he recorded, and he took part in the US premières of Darius Milhaud's *Christophe Colomb* (1952, Carnegie Hall) and his *David* (1956, Hollywood Bowl). He taught at the Juilliard School from 1945 to 1956. Harrell possessed a sturdy lyric baritone of remarkable beauty and was a considerable musician and artist, but perhaps the most notable aspect of his singing was the directness of its human appeal.

Richard Dyer, Elizabeth Forbes

Harshaw, Margaret

(*b* Philadelphia, 12 May 1909; *d* Libertyville, IL, 7 Nov 1997). American mezzo-soprano, later soprano. She studied at the Juilliard School with Anna Schoen-René. After winning the Metropolitan Opera Auditions of the Air in 1942, she made her Metropolitan début as the Second Norn in *Götterdämmerung* and in subsequent seasons sang such roles as Azucena, Amneris and Mistress Quickly. At San Francisco (1944–7) her roles included Ulrica, Brangäne and Claude Debussy's Geneviève. During the 1950–51 season she changed to soprano parts, succeeding Helen Traubel in the heroic Wagnerian repertory (Isolde, Senta, Kundry and Brünnhilde), and remaining with the Metropolitan until the close of the 1963–4 season. During this period she also fulfilled engagements at Covent Garden (1953–6), where she excelled as Brünnhilde in Rudolf Kempe's *Ring* cycles, Glyndebourne (appearing as Donna Anna in 1954) and elsewhere. She was a convincing actress and possessed a good, though by no means great, Wagnerian voice; her tone was evenly produced over a wide range. She later taught at Indiana University, Bloomington, and became one of the finest singing teachers in the USA.

Max De Schauensee/R

Harwood, Elizabeth (Jean)

(*b* Kettering, 27 May 1938; *d* Fryerning, Essex, 21 June 1990). English soprano. After studying in Manchester, in 1960 she won the Kathleen Ferrier Memorial Prize, and made her début as Second Boy (*Die Zauberflöte*) at Glyndebourne, where she later sang Fiordiligi, Countess Almaviva and the Marschallin. In 1961 she joined Sadler's Wells, where her roles included Susanna, Konstanze, Adèle (*Le comte Ory*), Zerbinetta and Jules Massenet's Manon. In 1963 she toured Australia, singing Lucia, Adina and Amina. She made her Covent Garden début in 1967 as the Fiakermilli, returning for Marzelline, Gilda, Bella (*The Midsummer Marriage*), Norina, Donna Elvira and Teresa (*Benvenuto Cellini*). For Scottish Opera (1967–74) she sang Fiordiligi, Sophie and Lucia. After Herbert von Karajan heard her at Aix-en-Provence, in 1970 she was invited to Salzburg, where she sang Konstanze, Fiordiligi, Countess Almaviva and Donna Elvira. She also appeared at La Scala (1972) and the Metropolitan (1975). Her voice, capable of both brilliant coloratura and lyrical warmth, was used with elegance, complemented by a charming stage presence. Her recorded legacy includes Hanna Glawari (*Die lustige Witwe*) and Musetta under Karajan, Benjamin Britten's Titania under the composer, Bella, Robert Schumann's *Szenen aus Goethes Faust* and *Messiah*, and an important video of her Violetta in *La Traviata* (BBC production).

M. Kennedy: 'Elizabeth Harwood: an Appreciation', *Opera*, xli (1990), 932–3

Alan Blyth

Hasse, Faustina.

See BORDONI, FAUSTINA.

Haugland, Aage

(*b* Copenhagen, 1 Feb 1944; *d* Copenhagen, 23 Dec 2000). Danish bass. He was a soloist with the Copenhagen Boys' Choir and later studied music and medicine at the university there; he made his début with the Norwegian Opera in 1968 in Bohuslav Martinů's *Comedy on the Bridge*. In 1973 he became a member of the Danish Royal Opera, with which he had a permanent contract as First Bass. His British début was in 1975 as Hunding at Covent Garden, and he sang a formidable Hagen with the ENO the same year, later recording the role with Reginald Goodall. In 1979 he made his American début at St Louis as Boris, then sang Ochs at the Metropolitan, where he subsequently took several other roles. He sang King Henry in *Lohengrin* for his début at La Scala in 1981 and Hagen at Bayreuth in 1983. Haugland's big, warm and evenly produced voice was also heard to advantage as Rocco, Fafner, Gremin, Prince Ivan Khovansky and Klingsor, the last two of which he recorded. Notable among his other recordings are operas by Danish composers, including Peter Heise's *Drot og Marsk* ('King and Marshal'), Carl Nielsen's *Maskarade* and *Saul og David*, and Per Nørgård's *Siddhartha*. In March 2000 he sang the role of the Commander in the world première of Poul Ruders's *The Handmaid's Tale*.

Noël Goodwin/John Shea

Hawlata, Franz

(*b* Eichstätt, 26 Dec 1963). German bass. He studied at the Musikhochschule in Munich with ERNST HAEFLIGER, HANS HOTTER and Erik Werba. His stage début was in 1986 at the Theater am Gärtnerplatz in Munich, where he was under contract and built his repertory. He has since appeared in many major houses in a wide variety of roles, among them Baron Ochs at the WNO, Covent Garden and the Metropolitan (début 1995), Rocco in *Leonore* on tour and on disc with John Eliot Gardiner, and Osmin in *Die Entführung aus dem Serail* (Salzburg Festival, 1996). At the Vienna Staatsoper he was admired as Otto Nicolai's Falstaff (1994) and with Covent Garden (at Sadler's Wells Theatre) as Kecal (*The Bartered Bride*) in 1998. In the Italian repertory Hawlata's roles include Sparafucile and Colline. Among his recordings his Mephisto in Louis Spohr's *Faust* and Water Goblin in *Rusalka* are outstanding. His strong, flexible bass and gifts as an actor make his Osmin, Caspar (*Der Freischütz*) and Ochs among the most admirable of the day.

Alan Blyth

Heilbronn, Marie

(*b* Antwerp, 1851; *d* Nice, 31 March 1886). Belgian soprano. She studied in Paris and made her début in 1867 at the Opéra-Comique, as Alice in the first performance of Jules Massenet's *La grand'tante*. In 1870 she appeared at La Monnaie as Violetta, the role of her début at Covent Garden in 1874, and in 1878 at the Théâtre Ventadour as Juliet in Victor Capoul's *Les amants*. She returned in 1879 as Ophelia (*Hamlet*). The same year she appeared at the Paris Opéra as Marguerite and in 1880 she sang Zerlina and Ophelia there. At Monte Carlo in 1883 she sang Susanna, Philine (*Mignon*), Marguerite, Victor Massé's Galatea and Rose in Aimé Maillart's *Dragons de Villars*. In 1884 she created the title role of Massenet's *Manon* at the Opéra-Comique. She was immensely gifted and very attractive in appearance.

Elizabeth Forbes

Heilmann, Uwe

(*b* Darmstadt, 7 Sept 1960). German tenor. He studied in Detmold, made his début there as Tamino in 1981 and joined the Stuttgart Staatsoper in 1985. There he rapidly established himself as the house's leading Mozartian tenor with admired performances as Tamino, Don Ottavio and Belmonte. He made his début at the Metropolitan in 1990 as Belmonte, the role with which he also made his La Scala début in 1994. Heilmann also developed a flourishing career as a concert singer, especially in J.S. Bach and the major choral works, and was an acclaimed interpreter of lieder, notably at the Hohenems and Salzburg festivals. Among his many recordings, those of his four most celebrated Mozart roles (Tamino, Belmonte, Titus and Don Ottavio), Flamand (*Capriccio*) and *Die schöne Müllerin* stand out, all displaying his incisive tenor, his fine line and his gift for characterization through the text. In 1999 he retired from singing to devote himself to academic study.

Alan Blyth

Heinefetter, Sabine

(*b* Mainz, 19 Aug 1809; *d* Illenau, 18 Nov 1872). Soprano. She made her début in 1824 in Peter Ritter's *Der Mandarin* at Frankfurt. She was advised by Louis Spohr to sign a contract for life with the Kassel Opera; but in 1829 she fled to Paris, where she studied with Davidde Banderali and Giovanni Tadolini and sang at the Théâtre Italien until 1842. She created Adina in *L'elisir d'amore* at the Teatro Cannobiana, Milan (1832), and sang Alaide in *La straniera* at Danzig (1833). In 1846 she appeared in Marseilles, where she married shortly afterwards. She continued to sing occasionally until 1856.

Heink, Ernestine.

See SCHUMANN-HEINK, ERNESTINE.

Heldy, Fanny [Deceuninck, Marguerite Virginia Emma Clémentine]

(*b* Ath, nr Liège, 29 Feb 1888; *d* Paris, 13 Dec 1973). French soprano of Belgian birth. After studies at the Liège Conservatoire she made her début as Elena in Raoul Gunsbourg's *Ivan le Terrible* in 1910 at La Monnaie, Brussels, in October 1910, remaining there until 1912. She appeared at Monte Carlo (1914–18), Warsaw and St Petersburg and made her Paris début in February 1917 as Violetta at the Opéra-Comique, which became her artistic home for more than two decades; her roles there included Rosina, Butterfly, Manon, Olympia, Antonietta and Giulietta, and Tosca. She made her début at the Opéra as Charles Gounod's Juliet in December 1920. In addition to the conventional repertory, to which she invariably brought particular distinction, she created many roles, among them Portia in Reynaldo Hahn's *Le marchand de Venise* (1935, Opéra). Maurice Ravel's Concepción she made her own; Arturo Toscanini chose her for Mélisande and Louise at La Scala; her Violetta was unforgettable for both brilliance and pathos. She first appeared at Covent Garden in 1926 as Manon. Returning to Monte Carlo she sang Nelly Harfield in Gunsbourg's *Venise* (1928), Freddie in Franco Alfano's *L'ultimo Lord* (1932), the Duc de Reichstadt in the première of *L'aiglon* (1937) and Carmen and Octavian (1939). Despite the metallic quality of her voice, she was the leading singing actress of her day in the French repertory. Her discs include a dimly recorded but important *Manon* (1923) and souvenirs of her Violetta, Marguerite, Thaïs, Louise and Concepción, which catch the individual, Gallic tang of her voice.

André Tubeuf/R

Hempel, Frieda

(*b* Leipzig, 26 June 1885; *d* Berlin, 7 Oct 1955). German soprano, later naturalized American. She studied in Leipzig and Berlin, after which her early career was centred at the Berlin Königliche Oper (début on 22 August 1905 as Mrs Ford in *Die lustigen Weiber von Windsor*). She was first heard at Covent Garden in 1907 in a double bill as W.A. Mozart's Bastienne and Engelbert Humperdinck's Gretel, then as Eva and Mrs Ford. Her fine schooling and purity of tone immediately marked her out, but her big London success came during Thomas Beecham's Drury Lane season of 1914, when she sang the Queen of Night (perhaps her most famous part) and the Marschallin, a role she had introduced to Berlin in 1911 and to New York in 1913. Her Metropolitan début in 1912, as Marguerite de Valois in a brilliantly cast *Les Huguenots*, began a period of seven years with that company, during which she settled in New York where she became a naturalized American. She sang Eva and Euryanthe there under Arturo Toscanini, besides many of the lighter Verdi, Rossini and Donizetti parts, in which she was regarded as the natural successor of SEMBRICH. After a farewell Metropolitan appearance, in *Crispino e la comare*, on 10 February 1919, she devoted herself mainly to a concert career. Her refined, exhilarating style is worthily represented on her many recordings.

'Frieda Hempel', *Record Collector*, x (1955–6), 53–71 [with discography]

Desmond Shawe-Taylor/R

Hempson, Celeste.

See GISMONDI, CELESTE.

Hemsley, Thomas

(*b* Coalville, Leics., 12 April 1927). English baritone. He studied privately and made his début in 1951 as Henry Purcell's Aeneas at the Mermaid Theatre, London, playing opposite FLAGSTAD. In 1953 he sang Hercules (C.W. Gluck's *Alceste*) at Glyndebourne, returning as Masetto, the Music-Master (*Ariadne auf Naxos*), Don Fernando and Dr Reischmann in the British première of H.W. Henze's *Elegy for Young Lovers* (1961). Engaged at Aachen (1953–6), the Deutsche Oper am Rhein (1957–63) and Zürich (1963–7), he sang more than 100 roles, including Guglielmo, the Speaker, Germont and Marcello. He created Demetrius (*A Midsummer Night's Dream*) with the English Opera Group at Aldeburgh (1960), subsequently recording the role under the composer. He sang Beckmesser at Bayreuth (1968–70) and made his Covent Garden début in 1970 creating Mangus in *The Knot Garden*. For Scottish Opera he sang Dr Malatesta and Balstrode and created Caesar in Iain Hamilton's *The Catiline Conspiracy* (1974). His roles for the WNO (1977–85) included Gioachino Rossini's Dr Bartolo, Dr Kolenatý (*The Makropulos Affair*) and Don Alfonso, while for Kent Opera he sang Falstaff (1980). After retirement he became increasingly active as a teacher, adjudicator and director.

Hemsley was also an intelligent lieder singer; his *Winterreise* (which he recorded) was greatly admired, and he several times performed the complete *Italienisches Liederbuch* and *Spanisches Liederbuch* of Hugo Wolf with IRMGARD SEEFRIED. He was a noted interpreter of Jesus in J.S. Bach's Passions and of the baritone solos in *Belshazzar's Feast* and the *War Requiem*, parts which well displayed his flexible, if slightly dry, baritone, incisive enunciation and keen dramatic sense.

Alan Blyth

Henderson, Roy (Galbraith)

(*b* Edinbugh, 4 July 1899; *d* Bromley, Kent, 16 March 2000). Scottish baritone. He studied at the RAM (1920–25). He made his début at the Queen's Hall in 1925 in Frederick Delius's *A Mass of Life*, and made such a favourable impression that he sang in all further performances until 1946. He made his Covent Garden début in 1928 as Donner, later singing Kothner and the Herald (*Lohengrin*). In 1934 he sang Count Almaviva in the Glyndebourne Festival's opening performance, *Le nozze di Figaro*, returning there until 1939 as Papageno, Masetto and Guglielmo. He also appeared with the company in London and on tour as Peachum in *The Beggar's Opera* (1939–40). He was an eloquent interpreter of Elijah, Jesus in J.S. Bach's *St Matthew Passion*, and the baritone solos in Ralph Vaughan Williams's *Sea Symphony* and Delius's *Sea Drift* (which he recorded). He sang in the first performances of Vaughan Williams's *Dona nobis pacem* and *Five Tudor Portraits*, Delius's *Idyll* and George Dyson's *The Canterbury Pilgrims*. Although Henderson's voice was not intrinsically beautiful, he used it with intelligence and charm. A gifted teacher, he numbered KATHLEEN FERRIER among his pupils. He took part in the Glyndebourne Mozart recordings as Count Almaviva and Masetto, and made many discerning recordings of English songs.

Alan Blyth

Hendricks, Barbara

(*b* Stephens, AR, 20 Nov 1948). American-Swedish soprano. She studied at the Juilliard School and with JENNIE TOUREL and first established herself as an accomplished concert singer. In 1973 she recorded the role of Clara in *Porgy and Bess* with Lorin Maazel, and the following year made her début in San Francisco as Erisbe in Francesco Cavalli's *Ormindo*, subsequently singing the title role of *Calisto* at Glyndebourne and Jeanne in Werner Egk's *Die Verlobung in San Domingo* at the St Paul Opera Summer Festival. In 1975 she sang the title role in *The Cunning Little Vixen* at Santa Fe and Nannetta (*Falstaff*) at Boston, and in 1976 took part in the world première of David Del Tredici's *Final Alice* under Georg Solti. That year she also made her Salzburg Festival début, in Gustav Mahler's Second Symphony, returning to Salzburg as Pamina in 1981. Hendricks made her Paris Opéra début as Charles Gounod's Juliet in 1982 and the same year sang Nannetta in Los Angeles and at Covent Garden. In 1985 she sang Liù at Bonn, and in 1987 she made her Metropolitan début as Richard Strauss's Sophie. Her light, bright-toned voice is well suited to both soubrette and lyric roles, and her repertory includes Susanna, her début role at La Scala in 1987, Ilia, Antonia, Norina and Mimì, all of which she has recorded. Hendricks is also a charming recitalist, at her best in *mélodies* and the lighter songs of Franz Schubert and Richard Strauss. She became a Swedish citizen after her marriage.

Elizabeth Forbes

Henry, Didier

(*b* Paris, 24 May 1953). French baritone. He studied at the Paris Conservatoire and the School of the Grand Opéra, and won competitions in Paris in 1978 and Athens in 1981. He subsequently joined the company at Lyons, where he sang Marcello in *La bohème*. At the Massenet festivals in St Etienne he has sung in revivals of *Amadis* (1988), *Cléopâtre* and *Grisélidis*. In 1990 he sang the title role in Ambroise Thomas' *Hamlet* at Metz, then sang Pelléas in the first performance in Russia of Claude Debussy's *Pelléas et Mélisande* in Moscow, conducted by Manuel Rosenthal. Henry's repertory also includes Orestes in *Yevgeny Onegin*, *Iphigénie en Tauride* (which he sang at La Scala in 1991), Blondel in A.-E.-M. Grétry's *Richard Coeur-de-lion*, Albert in *Werther*, Lescaut in *Manon Lescaut*, Valentin in *Faust* and three roles in *The Love for Three Oranges*, which he has recorded under Kent Nagano. Among his other operatic recordings are *Pelléas et Mélisande* and *L'enfant et les sortilèges*, both with Charles Dutoit, *Amadis* and Pietro Mascagni's *Il piccolo Marat*. He is also an admired recitalist, and has recorded *mélodies* by Francis Poulenc.

Patrick O'Connor

Henschel, Dietrich

(*b* Berlin, 22 May 1967). German baritone. He studied with Hanno Blanschke in Munich and in DIETRICH FISCHER-DIESKAU's class in Berlin. While a student he won prizes in several German competitions and at the International Hugo Wolf Competition. He made his professional stage début in Michèle Reverdy's *Le précepteur* in Munich in

1990. From 1993 to 1995 he was a member of Kiel Opera, where his warm, incisive, evenly produced baritone, frequently likened to that of his erstwhile teacher Fischer-Dieskau, was heard in roles including Claudio Monteverdi's Orfeo, Papageno, Count Almaviva, Valentin (*Faust*) and Pelléas. He has since sung in other major opera houses, notably Stuttgart, Lyons (where he scored a notable triumph as Ferruccio Busoni's Doktor Faust in 1997), the Deutsche Oper Berlin (where he made his début, also in 1997, in H.W. Henze's *Der Prinz von Homburg*), Zurich, Geneva, the Théâtre du Châtelet and the Opéra Bastille. His other roles include Don Giovanni and Wozzeck. Henschel is equally admired as a lieder and oratorio singer. He has performed with many leading conductors and orchestras in Europe and made frequent recital tours in Europe, the USA and Japan, including staged performances of *Winterreise* directed by Peter Stosser. Among his many recordings are J.S. Bach's *St Matthew Passion*, Joseph Haydn's *The Seasons*, Johannes Brahms's *German Requiem*, Engelbert Humperdinck's *Königskinder*, *Doktor Faust* (which won a 2000 Grammy award), Arnold Schoenberg's *Die Jakobsleiter*, and lieder by Franz Schubert (including notably robust, stoical interpretations of *Die schöne Müllerin* and *Winterreise*), Gustav Mahler, Hugo Wolf, E.W. Korngold and Othmar Schoeck.

Richard Wigmore

Henschel, Jane

(*b* Wisconsin, 2 March 1952). American mezzo-soprano. She studied with Ruth Michaelis and Nina Hinson at the University of Southern California, and started her career in concert and oratorio. In 1978 she joined the opera company at Aachen, moving to Wuppertal in 1981 and Dortmund in 1983. In these years she built up a large repertory, including the major mezzo roles in Giuseppe Verdi and Richard Wagner. Her international career gained momentum in 1992 when she made an impressive début at Covent Garden as the Nurse in *Die Frau ohne Schatten*: the review in *Opera* reported that she was 'the controlling presence whenever she was on stage'. In the following years she reappeared as Waltraute and as Fricka, a role she sang also in the *Ring* at La Scala. Henschel has been closely associated with 20th-century operas such as *Erwartung* (which she has sung in New Zealand), *The Rake's Progress* (Glyndebourne and Boston) and *Punch and Judy* (Amsterdam). One of the most adaptable of singers, with an extensive repertory outside opera, she has been in steady demand throughout Europe and the USA and more recently in Japan. Her recordings include Gustav Mahler's Eighth

Symphony and a vibrant, richly characterized portrayal of Baba the Turk in *The Rake's Progress* conducted by Seiji Ozawa.

J.B. Steane

Hensel, Heinrich

(*b* Neustadt, 29 Oct 1874; *d* Hamburg, 23 Feb 1935). German tenor. He studied in Vienna and Frankfurt and made his début at Freiburg in 1897, remaining a member of the ensemble there until 1900. After engagements at Frankfurt, where he created the Prince in Engelbert Humperdinck's *Dornröschen* (1902), and Wiesbaden, he became the leading Heldentenor at the Hamburg Opera (1912–29). He was chosen by Siegfried Wagner to create the tenor lead in *Banadietrich* (1910, Karlsruhe) and to sing Parsifal at Bayreuth, where he also sang Loge (1911–12). During the 1911–12 season he visited the USA, singing Siegmund, Siegfried and Lohengrin at the Metropolitan and Siegmund in Chicago. He appeared at Covent Garden from 1911 to 1914 in

the Wagner repertory and sang Parsifal in the first staged London production in 1914. His lyrical style is preserved in a number of acoustic recordings of Wagner.

Harold Rosenthal/Alan Blyth

Heppner, Ben

(*b* Murrayville, BC, 14 Jan 1956). Canadian tenor. He studied at the University of British Columbia and during the mid-1980s sang lyrical roles with the Toronto-based Canadian Opera Company Ensemble. In 1986 he sang Sandy in Peter Maxwell Davies's *The Lighthouse* at the Guelph Spring Festival, then decided to re-study as a dramatic tenor with William Neill. He won the Birgit Nilsson prize (1988) in New York, then sang Bacchus (*Ariadne auf Naxos*) in Melbourne and the Prince (*Rusalka*) in Philadelphia. He went on to sing Lohengrin in Stockholm and San Francisco (1989), Walther von Stolzing at Seattle, La Scala and Covent Garden (1990), Bacchus at Santa Fe and Frankfurt, and Florestan at Cologne and Vienna.

Ben Heppner, 2000

In 1991 Heppner performed as Laca (*Jenůfa*) in Brussels, Erik (*Der fliegende Holländer*) in Geneva and Idomeneo in Amsterdam; the following year he sang Dvořák's Dimitrij in Munich and W.A. Mozart's Titus at Salzburg, created the title role of William Bolcom's *McTeague* at Chicago (1992) and made his Metropolitan début as Laca. He returned to Covent Garden as a memorable Peter Grimes (1995) and to Toronto as Canio (1996). He sang an enormously successful Tristan, with Jane Eaglen as Isolde, at the Metropolitan in 1999. In 2000 Heppner returned to the Vienna Staatsoper after an absence of several years to sing the Emperor in *Die Frau ohne Schatten*, and the same year sang Florestan in a new production of *Fidelio* at the Metropolitan. In 2001 he made his Paris Opéra début, as Peter Grimes, and sang Hector Berlioz's Aeneas in concert, under Colin Davis, at the Barbican in London. Serious vocal problems resulted in a performance hiatus in 2002, but he returned with a triumphant *Les Troyens* at the Metropolitan in 2003, and all fears for his voice were quelled when he followed that performance with a reprisal of his 1999 Tristan. He has made notable recordings of Walther von Stolzing, Lohengrin, Grimes, Erik, Florestan, Huon (*Oberon*), Jean (*Hérodiade*), Chénier and Calaf, all of which display his powerfully dramatic voice, with its solid middle register and ringing top notes, and his vivid sense of character. Heppner is also a noted interpreter of such non-operatic works as Gustav Mahler's Eighth Symphony and *Das Lied von der Erde*.

P. Dyson: 'Ben Heppner', *Opera*, xlvi (1995), 1146–53

Elizabeth Forbes/R

Herincx, Raimund [Raymond] (Frederick)

(*b* London, 23 Aug 1927). English bass-baritone. He studied in Belgium and Milan, making his début in 1957 as Arrigo Boito's Mefistofele for the WNO, with whom he later sang Germont, Scarpia, Pizarro and Nabucco. For Sadler's Wells (1957–67) he sang Count Almaviva, Jack Rance, Nick Shadow, Rigoletto, Messenger/Creon (*Oedipus rex*), Baron Prus (*The Makropulos Affair*) and Agénor (Malcolm Williamson's *The Violins of St Jacques*). He created Segura in Williamson's *Our Man in Havana* (1963). He made his Covent Garden début in 1968 as King Fisher (*The Midsummer Marriage*), which he also sang with the WNO in Lisbon, Adelaide and San Francisco (American première, 1983); later he sang Donner, Rangoni, Escamillo and Alfio and created Faber in *The Knot Garden* (1970), White Abbot in *Taverner* (1972), which he also sang in Boston (American première, 1986), and the Governor in *We Come to the*

River (1976). He sang Wotan for the ENO (1974–7) and in Seattle (1977–81) and made his Metropolitan début in 1977 as Mathisen (*Le prophète*). He sang Mr Redburn (*Billy Budd*) at San Francisco (1978), Telramund at Barcelona (1979) and the *Hoffmann* villains for Opera North (1983). He was particularly successful at portraying villainy and anger.

Alan Blyth

Herold, Vilhelm Kristoffer

(*b* Hasle, Bornholm, 19 March 1865; *d* Copenhagen, 15 Dec 1937). Danish tenor. He studied in Denmark and Paris and made his début at the Royal Theatre, Copenhagen, as Charles Gounod's Faust in February 1893; later that year he appeared at the World's Columbian Exposition in Chicago. He sang at the Swedish Royal Opera (1901–3, 1907–9) and made his Covent Garden début in 1904 as Lohengrin, his most famous role; his voice was said to resemble that of JEAN DE RESZKE in sweetness and beauty of timbre. In Denmark his Canio (*Pagliacci*) was equally esteemed. He also sang Walther, and in 1905 Roméo and Faust, admired for control, musicianship and presence. He returned to Covent Garden in 1907 as Walther and also sang in Berlin, Dresden and other German cities, but continued to sing in Copenhagen until he retired in 1915. He was director of the Kongelige Opera, Copenhagen, 1922–4, after which he taught (LAURITZ MELCHIOR was among his pupils). He recorded excerpts from his roles, showing his restrained, thoughtful style. He was made a *Kammersänger* in 1901.

Leo Riemens/Alan Blyth

Hidalgo, Elvira de

(*b* Aragon, 27 Dec 1892; *d* Milan, 21 Jan 1980). Spanish soprano. She studied in Barcelona and Milan, making her début in 1908 at the San Carlo as Rosina, the role of her Metropolitan début in 1910, when she also sang Amina. She appeared at La Scala, Rome, Buenos Aires and Covent Garden, where she sang Gilda in 1924 with the British National Opera Company. Returning to the Metropolitan (1924–6), she sang Gilda and Lucia. At San Francisco (1925) she sang Rosina, Violetta and Martha, then toured the USA in *Il barbiere* with CHALIAPIN. Her repertory included Elvira (*I puritani*), Linda di Chamounix and Marguerite de Valois (*Les Huguenots*). She retired in 1932, then taught in Athens (where her pupils included MARIA CALLAS), Ankara and Milan. Her recordings show her bright, agile soprano voice to advantage.

Alan Blyth

Hill, Karl

(*b* Idstein im Taunus, 9 May 1831; *d* Sachsenberg bei Schwerin, 12 Jan 1893). German baritone. He studied in Frankfurt, making his début in 1868 as Jacob (E.-N. Méhul's *Joseph*) at Schwerin, where he was engaged until 1890. He sang Alberich in the first *Ring* cycle, at Bayreuth in 1876, and Klingsor in the first performance of *Parsifal* (1882). His repertory included the Dutchman and Hans Sachs as well as W.A. Mozart's Count Almaviva, Don Giovanni and Leporello. Signs of insanity forced him to retire from the opera house.

Elizabeth Forbes

Hill, Martyn

(*b* Rochester, 14 Sept 1944). English tenor. After being a choral scholar at King's College, Cambridge, he studied at the RCM (keyboard and voice) and with Audrey Langford. The first ten years of his career were mostly concerned with medieval and Renaissance music, often with David Munrow's consorts, and with the Consort of Musicke, founded by Anthony Rooley and James Tyler. After Munrow's death he moved on to the Baroque era and then eventually to the Romantic period, concentrating from the early 1980s on lieder (he contributed admirably to Graham Johnson's complete edition of Franz Schubert song on CD) and 20th-century works while retaining his interest in Baroque repertory. This versatility has allowed him to deploy his well-groomed tenor and innate musicality through a wide range of music. In opera, he has sung Arbace in *Idomeneo* with Nikolaus Harnoncourt at Zürich and the title part in the same work at Glyndebourne (1985), where he also sang Belmonte (1988). For Scottish Opera he was Peter Quint (*The Turn of the Screw*, 1988). Other roles included Ferrando, Flamand (*Capriccio*) and Tom Rakewell. His lengthy discography encompasses, among others, John Dowland, Henry Purcell, G.F. Handel, W.A. Mozart, Ludwig van Beethoven, Luigi Cherubini, Gustav Holst, Gerald Finzi (*Dies natalis*, particularly suited to his voice and style), Benjamin Britten and Robin Holloway.

Alan Blyth

Hillebrecht, Hildegard

(*b* Hanover, 26 Nov 1927). German soprano. She studied in Düsseldorf and made her début in 1951 at Freiburg as Leonora (*Il trovatore*). After engagements at Zürich (where she sang the Daughter in the première of the revised version of *Cardillac*, 1952), Düsseldorf and Cologne, she joined the Bayerische Staatsoper in 1961. At Salzburg (1956–64) she sang Ilia, Ariadne and Chrysothemis, and at San Francisco (1965) Elsa and Ariadne. She also sang at the Deutsche Oper, Berlin, where she created Anticlea in Luigi Dallapiccola's *Ulisse* (1968). Her roles included Tosca, Amelia (*Ballo*), Hélène (*Les Vêpres siciliennes*), Elisabeth de Valois and Desdemona, as well as Leonore, Senta, Elisabeth, Sieglinde, Jenůfa and Ursula (*Mathis der Maler*). A dignified actress, she had a vibrant, creamy-toned voice, especially well suited to Richard Strauss. Her best roles were the Empress, which she sang at Covent Garden in 1967, the Marschallin, which she sang in Copenhagen (1970), and Ariadne, which she recorded for Karl Böhm. She made her farewell in Munich in 1977 as the Second Norn.

Alan Blyth

Hill Smith, Marilyn

(*b* Carshalton, 9 Feb 1952). English soprano. She studied at the GSM under Arthur Reckless and Vilem Tausky, then gained widespread recognition touring the USA, Canada, Australasia and the UK in Gilbert and Sullivan operas, also performing principal roles in early French opera with the English Bach Festival. She made her operatic début with the ENO (1978) as Adèle (*Die Fledermaus*), for which her roles have included Despina, Blonde, Susanna, Olympia, Zerbinetta, Fiakermilli, Thérèse (*Les mamelles de Tirésias*), and Venus and Chief of Secret Police in the British première of *Le Grand Macabre* (1982). She made her Covent Garden début in 1981 as First Niece in *Peter Grimes*, followed by principal roles with the Royal Opera, Scottish Opera (Cunegonde in *Candide*), Welsh Opera (Musetta and Konstanze) and Canadian Opera, Lyric Opera of Singapore, New Sadler's Wells (Angèle in *Der Graf von Luxemburg* and Countess Maritza), D'Oyly Carte and the new Carl Rosa company. She has performed in opera, oratorio and in concert at many of the major European festivals including the BBC Proms, Aldeburgh, Paris, Athens and Cologne, and has made regular appearances on television and radio.

Hill Smith is adept at a wide variety of musical styles, and her award-winning recordings range from Jean-Philippe Rameau to Franz Lehár. She is most acclaimed for her interpretation of operetta and has made a noted contribution to the recording of rare works by Johann Strauss II. Her voice is warm yet silver-toned with an innate intelligence of phrasing and clarity of diction. Max Schönherr was an enthusiastic admirer, while Mary Ellis deemed her ability to sing in true Viennese style 'a technique that is all but lost these days'.

Peter Kemp

Hislop, Joseph

(*b* Edinburgh, 5 April 1884; *d* Upper Largo, Fife, 6 May 1977). Scottish tenor. He studied with Gillis Bratt in Stockholm, making his début there as Faust at the Swedish Royal Opera (12 September 1914). After five years in Scandinavia he spent a season in Italy at the S Carlo, Naples, before making his Covent Garden début on 14 May 1920 in *La bohème*, eliciting the commendation 'my ideal Rodolfo' from Giacomo Puccini. He appeared in Chicago (1920–21) and at the Manhattan Opera House in New York (1921) and then joined Antonio Scotti's US tour. In 1923 he sang at La Fenice in Venice and the Regio in Turin, and became the first British tenor to take a leading role at La Scala (Edgardo in *Lucia di Lammermoor*). At the Colón (1925) and the Opéra-Comique he impressed by his convincing acting and vocal style. He appeared in a film, *The Loves of Robert Burns* (directed by Herbert Wilcox), and made over 120 records for HMV and Pathé, which cover most of his repertory and include notable accounts of his Edgardo and Faust. He retired in 1937. In a new career in teaching at Stockholm, his pupils included BIRGIT NILSSON and JUSSI BJÖRLING. From 1947 he was artistic adviser at Covent Garden and then Sadler's Wells, and he later taught at the GSM.

M.F. Bott: 'Joseph Hislop', *Record Collector*, xxiii (1976–7), 198–237; xxv (1979–80), 36–42

M.T.R.B. Turnbull: *Joseph Hislop, Gran Tenore* (Aldershot, 1992) [incl. complete discography]

Michael T.R.B. Turnbull

Hnatyuk, Dmytro

(*b* Starosiliya, Chernivets'ka region, 28 March 1925). Ukrainian baritone. After graduating from the Kiev Conservatory he became a member of the company of the Kiev Theatre of Opera and Ballet. His roles include Rigoletto, Gioachino Rossini's Figaro, Ostap in M.V. Lysenko's *Taras Bulba* and the title roles in *Yevgeny Onegin* and *Mazepa*, which give scope to his strong and penetrating voice. He has toured in the USA, Japan and Australia. He served as principal stage director of the Kiev Shevchenko Opera and Ballet Theatre.

Virko Baley

Hofer [née Weber; Mayer], (Maria) Josepha

(*b* Zell, 1758; *d* Vienna, 29 Dec 1819). German soprano, sister of ALOYSIA LANGE. She was the eldest daughter of the singer and violinist Fridolin Weber (1733–79). After her father's death she moved to Vienna, and was then engaged as a soprano at Graz, 1785–7. On 21 July 1788 she married the court musician Franz de Paula Hofer (1755–96), and began performing at the suburban Theater auf der Wieden the next January. According to contemporary reports, she commanded a very high tessitura but had a rough edge to her voice and lacked stage presence. In September 1789 W.A. Mozart, her brother-in-law, wrote for her the bravura insertion aria 'Schon lacht der holde Frühling' (κ580, for a German version of Giovanni Paisiello's *Il barbiere di Siviglia*). Two years later he composed the role of the Queen of Night in *Die Zauberflöte* for her; she finally ceded the part to Antonia Campi in 1801. Josepha's second husband, from 1797, was (Friedrich) Sebastian Mayer (1773–1835), who created Pizarro in Beethoven's *Fidelio* (*Leonore*) in 1805. In that year Josepha retired from the stage, to be replaced by her daughter Josefa Hofer.

Thomas Bauman

Höffgen, Marga

(*b* Mülheim an der Ruhr, 26 April 1921; *d* Baden, 7 July 1995). German contralto. After study at the Berlin Hochschule für Musik and with Weissenborn she gave her first public concert in Berlin in 1952. The following year she sang in J.S. Bach's *St Matthew Passion* under Herbert von Karajan in Vienna. Her first and for some years her only operatic roles were Erda in the *Ring*, which she sang for the first time on the stage at Covent Garden in 1959, and the First Norn. She sang Erda for the first time at Bayreuth in 1960, and also sang the part in Vienna, Buenos Aires and elsewhere. She recorded roles in *Siegfried*, *Parsifal*, *Die Meistersinger* and *Die Zauberflöte*. Her first love, however, was the concert platform. Her expressive, beautifully focussed contralto, perhaps heard to best advantage in Herbert von Karajan's 1954 recording of the B minor Mass, was particularly associated with the music of Bach and Richard Wagner.

Peter Branscombe

Holl, Robert

(*b* Rotterdam, 10 March 1947). Dutch bass-baritone. After studying in the Netherlands he won first prize at the 1971 's-Hertogenbosch competition and went to study further with HANS HOTTER in Munich, where he won first prize in the ARD Competition the following year. Engaged at the Staatsoper there from 1973 to 1975, he sang roles such as the Commendatore, the Doctor (*Pelléas et Mélisande*) and Padre Guardiano (*La forza del des-*

tino). Since 1975 he has devoted much of his time to concert and recital work, appearing at the Vienna, Salzburg, Holland and Seville festivals and taking part in the Schubertiade at Hohenems. Holl is a sympathetic Bach singer, as can be heard in his recordings of the Passions, the B minor Mass and several cantatas, and brings authority and nobility of line to such works as Joseph Haydn's *The Creation* and *The Seasons*, Ludwig van Beethoven's *Missa solemnis* and Dmitry Shostakovich's Symphony no.13. His soft-grained yet sonorous voice and expressive diction are also heard to advantage in lieder, and he has made impressive recordings of songs by Franz Schubert, Johannes Brahms, Hugo Wolf and Hans Pfitzner. In recent years Holl has been acclaimed for his noble, lyrical singing of two Wagnerian roles: Amfortas, which he first sang in Zürich in 1996, and Hans Sachs, which he performed at Bayreuth in 1996, 1998 and 1999.

Elizabeth Forbes/R

Hollweg, Werner

(*b* Solingen, 13 Sept 1936; *d* Freiburg im Breisgau, 1 Jan 2007). German tenor. He prepared for a commercial career but took up singing in 1958 and studied in Detmold, Lugano and Munich, making his début with the Vienna Kammeroper in 1962. He joined the Bonn Opera for four seasons from 1963, and from 1968, when he sang Belmonte, appeared more widely in Germany, at the Vienna Staatsoper and regularly at the Salzburg Festival. He developed a close working relationship with Nikolaus Harnoncourt, with whom he recorded the title role in *Idomeneo* and Eisenstein in *Die Fledermaus*. A stylish lyric tenor, particularly in W.A. Mozart, he made his Covent Garden début in 1976 as Titus; in 1989 he sang in the première of York Höller's *Der Meister und Margarita* in Paris. Hollweg's other operatic recordings include the title role in Mozart's *Mitridate*, both Soliman and Gomatz in *Zaide*, Hugo Wolf's *Der Corregidor* and Desmoulins in Gottfried von Einem's *Dantons Tod*. He was also a much-admired concert soloist, and recorded such works as *Messiah*, Joseph Haydn's *The Creation* and *The Seasons*, Franz Schubert's *Lazarus* and Gustav Mahler's *Das klagende Lied*.

Noël Goodwin

Holm, Richard

(*b* Stuttgart, 3 Aug 1912; *d* Munich, 20 July 1988). German tenor. He studied in Stuttgart with Rudolf Ritter and made his début at Kiel in 1937. After engagements at Nuremberg and Hamburg, in

1948 he joined the Staatsoper in Munich. In 1950 he sang Belmonte at Glyndebourne. He made his Metropolitan début in 1952 as David. At Covent Garden in 1953 he sang David and Flamand in the British première of *Capriccio*, given by the Munich company. He returned to London as Loge, 1958–60 and 1964–6; he also appeared at Bayreuth, Salzburg and Vienna. His extensive repertory included Tamino, which he sang in Felsenstein's 1954 production of *Die Zauberflöte* at the Komische Oper, Berlin, and Robespierre in Gottfried von Einem's *Dantons Tod*. At Munich he created Wallenstein in Paul Hindemith's *Die Harmonie der Welt* (1957) and Black in Werner Egk's *Die Verlobung in San Domingo* (1963), and in 1975 he sang Aschenbach in *Death in Venice*. He also sang in oratorio. His voice, though not large, was well schooled and pleasing, and he was a sensitive performer; his recordings include the tenor solo part of *The Creation* and the role of Max in *Der Freischütz*.

Harold Rosenthal/R

Hölzel, Gustav

(*b* Budapest, 2 Sept 1813; *d* Vienna, 3 Dec 1883). Austrian bass-baritone. The son of an actor-singer, he made his stage début at the age of 16 in Sopron, then sang in Graz, Berlin and Zürich. Engaged at the Vienna Hofoper in 1840, he remained there for more than 20 years. In 1843 at the Kärntnertortheater he created Di Fiesco in Gaetano Donizetti's *Maria di Rohan*. Dismissed from the Hofoper in 1863 for altering the words of Friar Tuck's song in Heinrich Marschner's *Der Templer und die Jüdin*, he appeared at Darmstadt, Nuremberg, the Theater an der Wien and the Munich Hofoper, where he created Beckmesser in *Die Meistersinger* in 1868. In New York he took part in the American première of *Der Schauspieldirektor* (1870). An excellent comic actor, he sang Baculus (*Der Wildschütz*) at his farewell performance in 1877. Other roles included Leporello, Don Basilio and Van Bett (*Zar und Zimmermann*).

Elizabeth Forbes

Holzmair, Wolfgang

(*b* Vöcklabruch, 24 April 1952). Austrian baritone. He studied with HILDE RÖSSL-MAJDAN and Erik Werba at the Vienna Music Academy. In 1981 he won the singing competition at 's-Hertogenbosch and in 1982 first prize at the second international Lied competition in Vienna, organized by the Musikverein. From 1983 to 1986 he was engaged at the Berne Opera and then from 1986 to 1989 at Gelsenkirchen. His roles included Guglielmo,

Papageno, Gioachino Rossini's Figaro, Valentin, Harlequin, (*Ariadne auf Naxos*), Eisenstein (*Die Fledermaus*) and Danilo (*Die lustige Witwe*). At the same time he was developing his career on the concert platform. He gained international attention when he sang the role of Hans Scholl in Udo Zimmermann's *Die weisse Rose* at the Zürich Opera (1987). He has won praise for his Papageno in London, Paris and Los Angeles, and for his Pelléas in Vienna and Paris, both roles suiting his high, light baritone. But he has been most admired for his skills as a lieder interpreter, where his warm, appealing, typically Viennese tone, forthright manner and attention to word-painting enhance his readings of a wide variety of songs by Franz Schubert, Robert Schumann and Hugo Wolf. Holzmair has been particularly praised as the protagonist of *Die schöne Müllerin*, which he has recorded twice, in 1983 with Jörg Demus and in 1997 with Imogen Cooper. He and Cooper, who have formed a close artistic rapport, have also recorded the other Schubert cycles and Schumann's Heinrich Heine *Liederkreis* and *Dichterliebe*. In 1992 he gave the first performance of Luciano Berio's orchestrations of early songs by Gustav Mahler. Holzmair is also an intelligent interpreter of *mélodies*.

Alan Blyth

Louise Homer as Marina in 'Boris Godunov'
(Musorgsky)

Homer [née Beatty], Louise (Dilworth)

(*b* Shadyside, Pittsburgh, 30 April 1871; *d* Winter Park, FL, 6 May 1947). American contralto. She studied music at Philadelphia and Boston, then married the composer Sidney Homer in 1895 and went to Paris, where she studied singing and acting with Fidèle Koenig and PAUL LHÉRIE, the first Don José. She made her operatic début at Vichy in 1898, as Léonor in *La favorite*. At Covent Garden in 1899 she sang Lola and Amneris, returning in 1900 for Ortrud and Maddalena after a winter season at La Monnaie in Brussels. Her American début (1900) was with the Metropolitan Opera on tour in San Francisco as Amneris, in which role she also made her first New York appearance. Homer began a long and successful Metropolitan career, singing chiefly in Italian and French opera, but she soon assumed leading Wagnerian roles; she was also a notable Orpheus in Arturo Toscanini's 1909 revival of C.W. Gluck's opera, created the Witch in Engelbert Humperdinck's *Königskinder* (1910) and was the first to sing the title role in Horatio Parker's *Mona* (1912). After resigning from the Metropolitan in 1919, she sang with other major American companies including the Chicago Grand Opera (1920–25) and the San Francisco and Los Angeles operas (1926). She returned to the Metropolitan in 1927 and made her last appearance there in 1929, as Azucena. A performer of great artistic integrity, she had a beautiful voice and a majestic stage presence. Among her many recordings the ensembles with CARUSO, MARTINELLI, GIGLI and others are particularly successful. Samuel Barber was her nephew.

S. Homer: *My Wife and I* (New York, 1939/*R*)

D. Reutlinger: 'Louise Homer: a Discography', *The Maestro*, iv–v (1972–3), 62–5

A. Homer: *Louise Homer and the Golden Age of Opera* (New York, 1974)

Herman Klein, Desmond Shawe-Taylor,
Katherine K. Preston

Höngen, Elisabeth

(*b* Gevelsberg, Westphalia, 7 Dec 1906; *d* Vienna, 7 Aug 1997). German mezzo-soprano. She studied in Berlin with Ludwig Horth and made her début at Wuppertal in 1933, singing Lady Macbeth during her first season; after engagements at Düsseldorf and Dresden, in 1943 she became a member of the Vienna Staatsoper. She appeared at Salzburg (1948–50) as Orpheus, Benjamin Britten's Lucretia and Clairon (*Capriccio*) and in 1959 as Bebett in the première of Heimo Erbse's *Julietta*. She sang at Covent Garden in 1947 with the Vienna company as Dorabella, Herodias and Marcellina, returning in 1960 as Clytemnestra. In 1951 she sang Fricka and Waltraute at Bayreuth, in 1952 she appeared at the Metropolitan Opera, making her début as Herodias. Her repertory also included Eboli, Amneris, Carmen, Venus, Baba the Turk, the Nurse and Barak's Wife, and Adriano (*Rienzi*). She retired in 1971. Her expressive voice was always used most musically, and her dramatic gifts were remarkable. Her recordings include the Nurse in Karl Böhm's first version of *Die Frau ohne Schatten* and Waltraute in Wilhelm Furtwängler's *Ring* from La Scala.

Harold Rosenthal/R

Hopf, Hans

(*b* Nuremberg, 2 Aug 1916; *d* Munich, 25 June 1993). German tenor. He studied in Munich with PAUL BENDER and in Oslo with Ragnvald Bjärne. In 1936 he made his début as Pinkerton with the Bayerische Landesbühnen, a touring ensemble; engagements followed in Augsburg (1939–42), Dresden (1942–3) and Oslo (1943–4). He joined the Berlin Staatsoper in 1946 and in 1949 was engaged by the Staatsoper in Munich. Hopf sang the tenor part in the performance of Ludwig van Beethoven's Ninth Symphony under Wilhelm Furtwängler that reopened Bayreuth in 1951, and also sang Walther; between 1961 and 1966 he returned as Siegfried, Tannhäuser and Parsifal. At the 1954 Salzburg Festival he sang Max (*Der Freischütz*). He appeared at Covent Garden (1951–3) as Radames and Walther and at the Metropolitan, where he made his début in 1952 as Walther and sang mostly in the Wagner repertory. He made his La Scala début in 1963 as Siegfried and first appeared at the Teatro Colón in 1958 as Walther. His repertory also included Otello and the Emperor (*Die Frau ohne Schatten*), which he recorded under Karl Böhm. His strong, reliable voice can also be heard as Walther on Herbert von Karajan's recording of *Die Meistersinger* from Bayreuth.

Harold Rosenthal/R

Horne, Marilyn (Bernice)

(*b* Bradford, PA, 16 Jan 1929). American mezzo-soprano. She studied at the University of Southern California, taking part in LOTTE LEHMANN's master-classes. She dubbed the voice of Dorothy Dandridge in the film *Carmen Jones* in 1954, the year of her début at Los Angeles (as Háta in *The Bartered Bride*), then spent three seasons at Gelsenkirchen (1956–9), singing soprano and mezzo roles. In 1960 she first appeared at San Francisco, as Marie in *Wozzeck* (the role of her Covent Garden début in 1964). An

association with JOAN SUTHERLAND, which began in New York in 1961 with a concert performance of *Beatrice di Tenda* in which she sang Agnese, brought many notable performances – as Arsace to Sutherland's Semiramide (1965, Boston), and as Adalgisa to her Norma (1967, Covent Garden; her Metropolitan début, 1970). She sang Néocles in *Le siège de Corinthe* at La Scala (1969), Carmen at the Metropolitan (1972), and G.F. Handel's Rinaldo in Houston (1975). Among her other Rossini roles were Malcolm in *La donna del lago* (1981, Houston; 1985, Covent Garden), Falliero in *Bianca e Falliero* (1986, Pesaro), Andromache in *Ermione* (1987, Pesaro), Calbo in *Maometto II* (1988, San Francisco) and Isabella in *L'italiana in Algeri* (1989, Covent Garden). In the latter part of her career she sang Mistress Quickly (1988, San Francisco) and Delilah (1988, Théâtre des Champs-Elysées). In 1991 she did a comic turn as the 'exotic' Samira in the première of John Corigliano's *The Ghosts of Versailles*. Horne had a voice of extraordinary range, rich and tangy in timbre, with a stentorian chest register and an exciting top. Her recordings include several Rossini roles, Laura in *La Gioconda*, Juno in *Semele*, C.W. Gluck's Orpheus, Anita in Jules Massenet's *La Navarraise* and Zerlina. In concert she once achieved the feat of singing in a single programme Rossini arias and Brünnhilde's Immolation Scene, proof of her exceptional versatility. Throughout her lengthy career she was an admired recitalist, singing lieder, *mélodies*, Spanish and American songs with equal aplomb. She has written an autobiography, *My Life* (New York, 1984). She announced her retirement from performing in 1998.

M.R. Scott: 'Marilyn Horne', *Opera*, xviii (1967), 963–7

Alan Blyth

Hotter, Hans

(*b* Offenbach am Main, 19 Jan 1909; *d* Munich, 6 Dec 2003). German bass-baritone. He studied philosophy and music in Munich then worked as a church singer and later as an organist and choir-master. He learnt singing with Matthäus Roemer, made his operatic début at Troppau (1930) and after a brief engagement at Breslau spent the seasons 1932–4 in Prague. He then moved to Hamburg and in 1937 was offered a guest contract at Munich; he finally settled in Munich in 1940 but continued to appear regularly with other leading German companies, and in Vienna (where he made his début as Jochanaan in 1939). Hotter's international fame was delayed by the war, but from his first appearances at Covent Garden (as the Count and Don Giovanni with the Vienna Staatsoper

Hans Hotter
as Wotan in
'Der Ring des
Nibelungen'
(Wagner),
Bavarian State
Opera

during the September 1947 season) he became a favourite with British audiences, especially in Richard Wagner; he sang his first Hans Sachs at Covent Garden in 1948, in English. In 1950 he was invited to the Metropolitan Opera, and in 1952 his association with Bayreuth began. During the 1950s and 1960s he was generally recognized as the world's leading Wagnerian bass-baritone, renowned especially as Hans Sachs and as Wotan (see illustration), embodying the grandeur of Wagner's conception in a style at once rhetorical and noble. Though his voice could be unsteady and lack focus, its unmistakable quality, matched by his intense declamation and his commanding physical presence, made him one of the greatest operatic artists of the mid-20th century. Although he made

many recordings, it is to be deplored that he did not in his prime record Wotan, or such other of his finest parts as Borromeo in *Palestrina*, Sachs and the Dutchman. However, originally pirated recordings of live performances have gradually become commercially available, including his Dutchman, in a German broadcast under Clemens Krauss in 1944, King Mark, in Herbert von Karajan's 1952 Bayreuth performance, and Gurnemanz, live from Bayreuth under Hans Knappertsbusch in 1962; although technically disappointing, they reveal the full glory of his voice. His La Roche was captured in Wolfgang Sawallisch's studio recording of *Capriccio*. Among the roles he created are the Kommandant in Richard Strauss's *Friedenstag* (1938, Munich), Olivier in *Capriccio* (1942, Munich) and Jupiter in *Die Liebe der Danae* at the unofficial première (1944, Salzburg).

Hotter produced the *Ring* at Covent Garden (1961–4) and appeared elsewhere as a producer. He was also a distinguished concert and recital artist; his retirement from the operatic stage in 1972 was not accompanied by a reduction in his other activities. An artist of intelligence and dedication, he was able without loss of quality to reduce his warm, ample voice to convey the intimacy and subtlety of lieder and of roles requiring a lightness and flexibility generally unattainable by singers best known in heavier roles. He recorded *Winterreise* with Michael Raucheisen in 1942 (and then with Gerald Moore in 1955 and in two further versions) and made superb recordings of lieder by Franz Schubert, Robert Schumann, Carl Loewe, Johannes Brahms, Hugo Wolf and Gustav Mahler. Hotter published his memoirs, in German, in 1996. A translation appeared in 2006 (Han Hotter: *Memoir*, trans. and ed. by Donald Arthur).

D. Cairns: 'Hotter's Farewell', *Responses* (London, 1973), 155–7

P. Turing: *Hans Hotter: Man and Artist* (London, 1983)

A. Blyth: 'Hans Hotter at 90', *Opera*, i (1999), 36–42 [Survey of his recordings]

Peter Branscombe

Howard, Kathleen

(*b* Clifton, Ont., 17 July 1880; *d* Hollywood, CA, 15 Aug 1956). Canadian mezzo-soprano. Her vocal studies were in Buffalo, New York, Berlin and (with JEAN DE RESZKE) in Paris. After making her début as Azucena in Metz in 1907, she sang in Darmstadt (1909–12), as well as appearing in London and St Petersburg (1911). She sang with the New York Century Opera Company, 1914–15. Her Metropolitan Opera début was in 1916 as the Third Lady in *Die Zauberflöte*, and she remained a company comprimaria until 1928, singing 39 roles, including Zita in the première of *Gianni Schicchi* (1918). She recorded for Edison and Pathé. After retiring from singing, she appeared in several films opposite W.C. Fields and was fashion editor of *Harper's Bazaar*. She published an autobiography, *Confessions of an Opera Singer* (New York, 1918).

Cori Ellison

Howell, Gwynne (Richard)

(*b* Gorseinon, 13 June 1938). Welsh bass. He studied at the RMCM, where he sang on stage the roles of Hunding, Fasolt and Pogner. In August 1968 he joined Sadler's Wells, making his début as Monterone (*Rigoletto*), and playing, among other parts, the Commendatore, Colline, and the Cook (*The Love for Three Oranges*). His Covent Garden début was as First Nazarene in *Salome* (1970); his many parts there have included Richard Taverner in the première of Peter Maxwell Davies's *Taverner*, Timur, the Landgrave, Sarastro, Pimen and Padre Guardiano. With the ENO he has sung leading roles including Hans Sachs (1984), Gurnemanz (1986) and Philip II (1992). A voice of mellow, well-rounded timbre (slightly less imposing at the bottom of its compass) and a tall, dignified figure aid his natural aptitude for *basso cantante* roles. (See colour plate 13.)

A. Blyth: 'Gwynne Howell', *Opera*, xlii (1991), 1018–25

Max Loppert

Huberdeau, Gustave

(*b* Paris, 1874; *d* Paris, 1945). French bass-baritone. He studied at the Paris Conservatoire and made his début at the Opéra-Comique, gaining experience in a wide variety of secondary roles and taking part in premières such as that of Jules Massenet's *Grisélidis* (1901), in which he sang Gondebaud. His career prospered further when he joined the Manhattan Company in 1909; for the American première of *Grisélidis* he played the Devil, and he also sang Orestes in the American première of *Elektra* (1910). From 1913 to 1920 he appeared with the Chicago Opera Company and was a visitor to Covent Garden, where he sang Méphistophélès, Arkel, and the Father in the British première of Pietro Mascagni's *Iris* (1919). He also sang Rambaldo in the première of *La rondine* at Monte Carlo in 1917. He continued to sing throughout France in the 1920s, appearing at Monte Carlo in 1927, still in a wide repertory, including Hunding in *Die Walküre*. His recordings are rare and show a sturdy voice, somewhat dry in quality.

J.B. Steane

Hüni-Mihacsek, Felice

(*b* Pécs, 3 April 1891; *d* Munich, 26 March 1976). Hungarian soprano. She studied in Vienna with Rosa Papier, making her début there at the Staatsoper in 1919 as the First Lady (*Die Zauberflöte*). She remained a member of the Vienna company until 1926, when she joined the Staatsoper in Munich, singing there regularly until 1944 with occasional postwar appearances until 1953. Originally a lyric soprano, taking such roles as the Queen of Night, Fiordiligi and Mařenka, she gradually assumed more dramatic roles, including Donna Anna, Elisabeth,

Antonia, the Marschallin, Eva and Elsa. Hüni-Mihacsek, who was also an accomplished concert artist, was generally considered one of the outstanding Mozart sopranos of the inter-war period.

Harold Rosenthal/R

Hunter, Rita (Nellie)

(*b* Wallasey, 15 Aug 1933; *d* Sydney, 29 April 2001). English soprano. She studied with Edwin Francis in Liverpool and Redvers Llewellyn in London. After a two-year period in the Sadler's Wells chorus, and a tour with the Carl Rosa Company, a scholarship enabled her to study in 1959 with EVA TURNER. In 1960 she became a principal at Sadler's Wells, making her début as Marcellina; other roles included Senta, Santuzza and Odabella (*Attila*). However, it was not until Reginald Goodall's first vernacular performance of the *Ring* at the London Coliseum (beginning with *Die Walküre*, 1970), in which she was Brünnhilde, that the potential of her well-defined, vibrant dramatic soprano began to be realized: her tone, style and inflections, at once powerful and delicate, seemed to revive the spaciously noble manner of Richard Wagner singing of an earlier era. In 1972 she made a dramatic Covent Garden début, as Senta, stepping in at the last min-

ute for an indisposed ANJA SILJA. Flexibility, of both style and timbre, allowed her to encompass Verdi roles with marked success – in particular Amelia (*Un ballo in maschera*) and Leonora (*Il trovatore*); she proved herself a touching actress. Her first original-language Brünnhilde was at the Metropolitan, in December 1972; she returned there as Santuzza and Norma, and also sang in San Francisco, Munich and Nice. Hunter recorded Brünnhilde, in German and English, and Eglantine in the first complete *Euryanthe*. In 1981 she moved to Australia, where she added the roles of Abigaille (*Nabucco*), Isolde and Elektra to her repertory. In 1983 she returned to London to sing Leonora in *Il Trovatore* with the ENO. She was made CBE in 1980 and published an autobiography, *Wait till the Sun Shines, Nellie* (London, 1986), in which she discussed her fraught working relationship with Goodall.

E. Forbes: 'Rita Hunter', *Opera*, xxvii (1976), 14–20

Max Loppert

Hunt-Lieberson [Hunt], Lorraine

(*b* San Francisco, 1 March 1954; *d* Santa Fe, NM, 3 July 2006). American mezzo-soprano. She first studied the violin and viola, changing to singing in

Lorraine Hunt-Lieberson in Peter Sellars's staging of Bach's cantatas, nos. 82 and 199, Barbican, London, 2001

1981 when she won competitions sponsored by the Metropolitan and the Boston Opera. After that her stage career was mainly, although not exclusively, concentrated on Baroque repertory. One of her earliest successes was as Sextus in Peter Sellars's controversial staging of *Giulio Cesare*. She also appeared in his productions of *Oedipus rex* as Jocasta, *Don Giovanni* as Donna Elvira, *L'incoronazione di Poppea* as Octavia, and *Serse*, in which she took the title part. Hunt later scored major successes as Irene in Sellars's 1996 staging of G.F. Handel's *Theodora* at Glyndebourne, and in the title parts of Marc-Antoine Charpentier's *Médée* with William Christie's Les Arts Florissants and of *Ariodante* at Göttingen, and as Myrtle Wilson in the world première of John Harbison's *The Great Gatsby* at the Metropolitan. In 1996–7 she sang Charlotte (*Werther*) at the Lyons Opéra, Sextus at the Paris Opéra and Phèdre (*Hippolyte et Aricie*) with Christie at the Palais Garnier, Paris. She also undertook Carmen at the Opéra Bastille in 1998 and the title role in a concert performance of *The Rape of Lucretia* at the 1999 Edinburgh Festival. In 2001 she returned to the Edinburgh Festival, singing a magnetic, sensual Dido in Part 2 of *Les Troyens*. On the concert platform Hunt-Lieberson's repertory included *Les nuits d'été*, Alban Berg's *Sieben frühe Lieder*, Benjamin Britten's *Phaedra* (which she successfully recorded) and Gustav Mahler's *Lieder eines fahrenden Gesellen*, with which she made her Proms début in 1998. In December 2000 she sang in the première of John Adams's nativity oratorio *El Niño* at the Théâtre du Châtelet in Paris. In 2001 she was widely acclaimed for her singing of two J.S. Bach cantatas (nos. 82 and 199) in stagings by Peter Sellars, first in Boston and subsequently in New York, Paris, London and Lucerne. Her other recordings include the title roles in *Médée* and *Theodora*, and a disc of Robert Schumann lieder. Her deeply eloquent Irene at Glyndebourne is preserved on video and discloses her warm, vibrantly expressive tone at its best, while the flexibility and dramatic involvement of her singing are vividly revealed in her recording of *Ariodante*. She married the composer Peter Lieberson in 1999.

Alan Blyth

Hüsch, Gerhard (Heinrich Wilhelm Fritz)

(*b* Hanover, 2 Feb 1901; *d* Munich, 21 Nov 1984). German baritone. He studied with Hans Emge and made his début at Osnabrück in Albert Lortzing's *Der Waffenschmied* in 1923. Engagements followed at Bremen, Cologne (1927–30) and Berlin (1930–42), first at the Städtische Oper and then

at the Staatsoper. He sang at Covent Garden in 1930 as Falke in Bruno Walter's production of *Die Fledermaus*, then as Papageno the following year, and again in 1938 under Thomas Beecham, with whom he also recorded the role. At Bayreuth in 1930 and 1931 he sang an outstanding Wolfram in *Tannhäuser*. His repertory included Count Almaviva, Germont, Sharpless and Storch (*Intermezzo*). Hüsch possessed a lyric baritone that could be soft and sweet in Italian opera, sonorously warm and resonant in German. He had a notable feeling for words, and his performances of Schubert's song cycles, which he also recorded, remain models of style. His other recordings include Hugo Wolf lieder and excerpts from his operatic roles.

D. Hammond-Stroud: 'Gerhard Hüsch – an Appreciation', *Opera*, xxxvi (1985), 164–6

Harold Rosenthal/Alan Blyth

Hutt, Robert

(*b* Karlsruhe, 8 Aug 1878; *d* Berlin, 5 Feb 1942). German tenor. He studied in Karlsruhe, where he made his début in 1903. Düsseldorf and Frankfurt claimed him from 1910 to 1917, and he then began a ten-year engagement with the Berlin Staatsoper. Though he sang a wide range of heroic parts, such as Manrico in *Il trovatore*, he became principally associated with Richard Wagner and Richard Strauss. At Covent Garden in 1913 and 1914 he sang Walther in *Die Meistersinger* and Parsifal (at the British stage première), and at Drury Lane appeared as Bacchus in the last four of the performances in which Thomas Beecham introduced *Ariadne auf Naxos* to English audiences. In 1920 he sang the Emperor in the Berlin première of *Die Frau ohne Schatten*. He was also a member of the German opera company led by Leo Blech which played at the Manhattan Opera House, New York, in 1923, and the following year he sang there in the New York première of Eugen d'Albert's *Die toten Augen*. His recordings include songs by Strauss in which he is accompanied by the composer and excerpts from a performance of *Die Meistersinger* showing his style assured and his voice still sturdy at the age of 50.

J.B. Steane

Huttenlocher, Philippe

(*b* Neuchâtel, 29 Nov 1942). Swiss baritone. He studied at Fribourg with Juliette Bise and became a professor of singing at the Musikhochschule in Saarbrücken. He began his career as a member of the Ensemble Vocal de Lausanne under Michel

Corboz, and in 1975 sang the title role in the famous Jean-Pierre Ponnelle production of *Orfeo* (Claudio Monteverdi) conducted by Nikolaus Harnoncourt at the Zürich Opera, which toured throughout Europe and was recorded both in sound and video. Although known especially for his performances of Baroque music (Bach cantatas, operas by Monteverdi and Jean-Philippe Rameau), his repertory ranges from Monteverdi and Heinrich Schütz to contemporary Swiss composers. Huttenlocher has participated in numerous recordings, singing mainly under Michael Corboz, Harnoncourt and Helmuth Rilling. He is admired for his warm, light baritone, his clear articulation and his keen sense of style.

Martin Elste

Hvorostovsky, Dmitry

(*b* Krasnoyarsk, Siberia, 16 Oct 1962). Russian baritone. He studied in Krasnoyarsk, making his début there in 1986. After appearing at the Kirov the following year he made a concert tour of the USA with a group of Russian singers, then, in 1989, won the Singer of the World Competition at Cardiff and made his west European début at Nice as Yeletsky (*The Queen of Spades*). Subsequently he sang Yevgeny Onegin in Venice, Yeletsky in Amsterdam and Silvio (*Pagliacci*) in Barcelona, then in 1992 made his Covent Garden début as Riccardo (*I puritani*), returning as Onegin and Yeletsky (2001). He made his stage début in the USA as Germont in Chicago (1993) and his Metropolitan début as Yeletsky (1995). His other roles include Gioachino Rossini's Figaro, Alphonse XI (*La favorite*), Don Giovanni and Count Almaviva, both of which he has sung at Salzburg, and the Marquis of Posa, the role in which he made his La Scala début (1992). Hvorostovsky has made notable recordings of Onegin, Yeletsky and Germont, and is also a distinguished recitalist, as can be heard in several recordings of Russian songs and a disc of Neapolitan songs. His beautiful, cultivated voice is of moderate size but strongly projected, while his dramatic involvement has grown steadily with experience.

Elizabeth Forbes

Hyde, Walter

(*b* Birmingham, 6 Feb 1875; *d* London, 11 Nov 1951). English tenor. He studied at the RCM under Gustave Garcia and as a student appeared in *Euryanthe* and Charles Villiers Stanford's *Much Ado about Nothing*. He made his début at Terry's

Theatre, London, in *My Lady Molly* (1903), and in 1906 sang in the première of Liza Lehmann's *Vicar of Wakefield*. In 1908 he sang Pinkerton, and Siegmund in the English *Ring* under Hans Richter, at Covent Garden, where he appeared regularly until 1923–4; he also sang Siegmund in his Metropolitan début in 1910. A distinguished Mozartian, he was a member of the Thomas Beecham and the British National Opera companies. He sang Sali in the first London performance of Frederick Delius's *A Village Romeo and Juliet* (1910) and took part in the première of Gustav Holst's *The Perfect Fool* (14 May 1923). His repertory also included Walther and Parsifal. He made a number of acoustic recordings, on which his clear articulation of the text and firm tone are evident.

Harold Rosenthal/R

Hynninen, Jorma

(*b* Leppävirta, 3 April 1941). Finnish baritone. While teaching at a Kuopio primary school he studied at the conservatory there, and continued his studies at the Sibelius Academy in Helsinki. Having made his Helsinki début in 1969 (Silvio, *Pagliacci*), he undertook many lyric baritone roles there before making his international début as Pelléas at La Scala in 1977. But Hynninen's intense, fiery eloquence as a singing actor first drew widespread attention when he created the role of Topi in Aulis Sallinen's *The Red Line* (1978, Helsinki; repeated in London, 1979, Moscow, 1982, and New York, 1983); to the leading roles of the two successive Sallinen operas, *The King Goes Forth to France* (1984, Savonlinna) and *Kullervo* (1992, Los Angeles), he brought similar magnetism of personality and lean, fine-grained beauty of voice. Hynninen has inspired other Finnish composers, notably Einojuhani Rautavaara (title roles in *Thomas*, 1985 and *Vincent*, 1990), to write operas for him. More recently he has broadened his Verdi and Wagner repertory to include Macbeth, Telramund and Amfortas. A passionate exponent of the Finnish song repertory (much of which he has committed to disc), he is no less vivid in lieder, as his recordings of Franz Schubert, Robert Schumann and Johannes Brahms confirm. He has made many international appearances in, and several recordings of, the baritone part in Jean Sibelius's *Kullervo* Symphony. In 1984 Hynninen became artistic director of the Finnish National Opera, and in 1993 artistic director of the Savonlinna Festival.

H. Finch: 'Jorma Hynninen', *Opera*, xlvi (1995), 768–73

Max Loppert/R

I

Incledon, Charles [Benjamin]

(*b* St Keverne, Cornwall, bap. 5 Feb 1763; *d* Worcester, 11 Feb 1826). English tenor. The son of a medical practitioner, he disliked his baptismal name and took the name Charles instead. He was a chorister at Exeter Cathedral under William Jackson and was locally renowned as a boy soloist before he joined the navy, where he attracted attention as a singer. In 1784 he made his stage début in Southampton as Alphonso in Samuel Arnold's *Castle of Andalusia* and the next year moved to Bath, where he sang with the Bath-Bristol theatre company and studied with VENANZIO RAUZZINI, who helped him get an engagement in London at Vauxhall Gardens. He sang at Covent Garden (1790–1815), quickly establishing himself as the leading English stage tenor. He appeared in many operas and afterpieces by William Shield and others. Incledon was popular in Dublin, particularly as Young Meadow in *Love in a Village* and Orpheus in an adaptation of C.W. Gluck's *Ofeo ed Euridice* and from 1802 toured widely with a series of solo entertainments. Incledon made a successful visit to North America in 1817–18, although his voice was then past its prime. His acting was not generally admired, but his dramatic rendering of the ballad *The Storm* (with painted backdrop of a ship in distress) held audiences spellbound. His West Country accent and somewhat flashy personality limited his success as a concert artist, but he sang in several Covent Garden oratorio seasons and was a soloist in the first London performance of Joseph Haydn's *The Creation* (1800). Haydn had heard him in Shield's *The Woodman* (1791) and noted: '[Incledon] has a good voice and quite a good style, but he uses the falsetto to excess. He sang a trill on high C and ran up to G'. For many of his contemporaries his impassioned performances of nautical and sentimental ballads exemplified true English singing. William Robson (1846) remembered that 'never was so sound, so rich, so powerful, so sweet an English voice as Incledon's'.

His eldest son, Charles Venanzio Incledon (1791–1865), sang at Drury Lane in 1829–30 and later lived in Vienna as a teacher of English.

'Mr. Incledon': *Quarterly Musical Magazine and Review*, i (1818), 78–80

'Mr Incledon', *The Musical World*, xiii (1838), 63–5

W. Robson: *The Old Play-Goer* (London, 1846)

T.J. Walsh: *Opera in Dublin 1705–1797* (Dublin, 1973)

T.J. Walsh: *Opera in Dublin 1798–1820* (Oxford, 1993)

Olive Baldwin, Thelma Wilson

Inghilleri, Giovanni

(*b* Porto Empedocle, Sicily, 9 March 1894; *d* Milan, 10 Dec 1959). Italian baritone. He was trained first as a pianist and discovered his voice while working as a répétiteur. In 1919 he made his début as Valentin in *Faust* at the Carcano, Milan, and then went on to sing with considerable success throughout Italy, at the Costanzi in Rome, the S Carlo in Naples (the first of many seasons in 1922, the last being 1948) and La Scala. He was enthusiastically received at his début in *Pagliacci* at Covent Garden in 1928, and returned there for the next two seasons and again in 1935. A highlight of his career in London was the 1930 *Traviata* with PONSELLE and GIGLI where his 'steadiness of tone, flawless phrasing and ease of manner' were commended as a model. He sang at Chicago in 1929, and later in France and Spain. In 1936 he appeared in the première of G.F. Malipiero's *Giulio Cesare* in Genoa. He continued to prove his worth as a musicianly singer (he was also a composer of opera, ballet and songs) until his retirement in 1953, after which he taught singing in Milan. Recordings show the fine voice and authoritative style that distinguished him in the 1920s; when he returned to the studios after the war, his style had deteriorated, though his tone remained impressive.

J.B. Steane

Isaac [Lelong], Adèle

(*b* Calais, 8 Jan 1854; *d* Paris, 22 Oct 1915). French soprano. She studied with GILBERT DUPREZ in Paris, making her début in 1870 at the Théâtre Montmartre in Victor Massé's *Les noces de Jeannette*. In 1873 she first sang at the Opéra-Comique, as Marie (*La fille du régiment*). She also sang Charles Gounod's Juliet and W.A. Mozart's Susanna, and in 1881 created the four female lover roles (Olympia/Antonia/Giulietta/Stella) in *Les contes d'Hoffmann*. From 1883 to 1885 she was engaged at the Opéra, where her roles included Ophelia (*Hamlet*), Marguerite (*Faust*), Adèle (*Le comte Ory*), Zerlina, Marguerite de Valois (*Les Huguenots*), Isabelle (*Robert le diable*), Ambroise

Thomas's Francesca da Rimini and Mathilde (*Guillaume Tell*). In 1887 she created Minka in Emmanuel Chabrier's *Le roi malgré lui* at the Opéra-Comique. She retired in 1894. Her brilliant, flexible voice was especially suited to Mozart.

Elizabeth Forbes

Isokoski, Soile

(*b* Posio, 14 Feb 1957). Finnish soprano. She studied at the Sibelius Academy in Helsinki and made her recital début there in 1986. In 1987 she won the Lappeenranta Competition and was engaged as a soloist at the Finnish National Opera, making her début the same year as Mimì. Other early competition successes included second prize in the 1987 BBC Singer of the World Competition and first prize in the Elly Ameling Competition (1988) and the Tokyo International Competition (1990). At the Finnish National Opera she established a reputation above all in the lyric Mozart roles, to which her warm, gleaming, seamlessly integrated voice and refined legato are ideally suited. Isokoski made her Vienna Staatsoper début, as Pamina, and her Salzburg Festival début, as First Lady, in 1993, and her débuts at Covent Garden, as Fiordiligi, and at the Opéra Bastille, Paris, as Countess Almaviva, in 1997. She has returned to Covent Garden as Eva (*Die Meistersinger*, 2000) and Mozart's Countess (2005). Other important débuts include La Fenice, Venice, as Donna Elvira (1996), the Berlin Staatsoper (1994), the Metropolitan Opera, as the Countess (2002), and the Proms, where she scored a triumph with Richard Strauss's *Vier letzte Lieder* in 1999. Among her other roles are the Marschallin (which she has sung in Vienna, Cologne and Paris), Liù, Elsa (*Lohengrin*), which she first sang in Athens in 1999, Agathe, Alice Ford (her first Verdi role, which she sang at the Berlin Staatsoper in 1997) and Antonia in *Les contes d'Hoffmann*.

Isokoski's recordings include Fiordiligi, Donna Elvira, a disc of Mozart arias, lieder by Franz Schubert and Robert Schumann, and a gloriously sung Strauss recital (including the *Vier letzte Lieder*) that won the 2002 *Gramophone* award and drew favourable comparisons with classic recordings of the past.

Richard Wigmore

Ivogün, Maria [Kempner, Ilse]

(*b* Budapest, 18 Nov 1891; *d* Beatenberg, Switzerland, 2 Oct 1987). Hungarian soprano. She was the daughter of the singer Ida von Günther, from whom she derived her own stage name. Heard by Bruno Walter at an unsuccessful audition for the Vienna Hofoper, she was instantly engaged for Munich, where she appeared in 1913, first as Mimì and then as the Queen of Night. She remained at Munich until 1925, singing such roles as Konstanze, Zerbinetta (in which Richard Strauss described her as 'simply unique and without rival', and made a point of having her engaged for *Ariadne* productions whenever possible), Zerlina, Marzelline, Norina, Gilda, Oscar (*Un ballo in maschera*) and Nannetta, often performing opposite her first husband, the tenor KARL ERB, with whom she also recorded duets at that period. In 1917 she sang the part of Ighino at the première of Hans Pfitzner's *Palestrina* (with Erb in the title role), and also created the title part in the same composer's *Das Christelflein*. In 1924 she created a sensation when she sang Zerbinetta at Covent Garden under Walter; a memento of the occasion exists in her exhilarating account of Zerbinetta's aria. The same season she also performed Gilda, and returned for Konstanze in 1927. She made her début at the Salzburg Festival as Zerlina in 1925, the year she moved to Berlin, where she appeared at both the Städtische Oper and the Staatsoper. There she added to her repertory heavier roles such as Manon, Mignon and Tatyana. She never sang at the Metropolitan but appeared as Rosina in Chicago (1921–2). Ivogün's operatic career faded somewhat prematurely in the early 1930s but she continued to give frequent recitals with the pianist Michael Raucheisen, whom she married in 1933. All who saw and heard her remarked on her personal charm, light and airy to match her vocal qualities. Her numerous recordings bear out the evidence of her contemporaries. After retirement she taught in Berlin, where her pupils included ELISABETH SCHWARZKOPF and RITA STREICH.

A. Frankenstein: 'Maria Ivogün', *Record Collector*, xx (1971–2), 98–119 [with discography by J. Dennis], 283–4
A. Blyth: 'Maria Ivogün: an Appreciation', *Opera*, xxxviii (1987), 1372–3

Alan Blyth

J

Jachmann-Wagner, Johanna.

See WAGNER, JOHANNA.

Jacobs, René

(*b* Ghent, 30 Oct 1946). Belgian countertenor and conductor. He studied classical philology at the University of Ghent, later taking singing lessons from Louis Devos in Brussels and Lucie Frateur in The Hague and attending Alfred Deller's masterclasses. He has performed with many of the leading early and Baroque ensembles including those directed by Alan Curtis (with which he made his début in 1974 as Clerio in Francesco Cavalli's *Erismena*, in Amsterdam), Nikolaus Harnoncourt, Gustav Leonhardt and Sigiswald Kuijken. During the 1970s he founded his own group, Concerto Vocale, which he has successfully directed in operas by Cavalli and G.F. Handel. He conducted *L'incoronazione di Poppea* in his own performing edition at Montpellier in 1989, and at the Festwochen der Alten Musik in Innsbruck the following year. In recent years he has won acclaim as a Mozart conductor, both through his performances (including *Così fan tutte* at the Aix Festival) and through his stylish and thought-provoking recording of *Così fan tutte*. Jacobs also teaches performing practice in Baroque singing at the Schola Cantorum, Basle. His recordings as a singer include Antonio Cesti's *Orontea*, Jean-Baptiste Lully's *Le bourgeois gentilhomme*, Marc-Antoine Charpentier's *David et Jonathas*, Handel's *Admeto, Alessandro, Partenope* and *Tamerlano*, and many Bach cantatas with Leonhardt and Harnoncourt. Recordings under his direction include *L'incoronazione di Poppea*, Cavalli's *Giasone* and *Calisto*, Handel's *Flavio* and *Giulio Cesare* and G.P. Telemann's *Orpheus*. He both directed and sang the title role in Cavalli's *Xerse*. As an opera director he is imaginative, with a lively dramatic sense and a strong rapport with singers.

Nicholas Anderson

Jadlowker, Hermann

(*b* Riga, 17 July 1877; *d* Tel-Aviv, 13 May 1953). Latvian tenor. After training as a cantor (which permanently influenced his style), he studied at the Vienna Conservatory with Joseph Gänsbacher and made his début at Cologne in 1899 as Gomez in Conradin Kreutzer's *Nachtlager in Granada*. In 1900 he went to Stettin, then to Riga, and in 1906 to the court theatre in Karlsruhe, where he began to attract international attention, particularly through his singing of Georges Brown in *La dame blanche* and of Raoul. The German emperor heard him during a Wiesbaden festival and arranged for his engagement at the Royal Opera House, Berlin, in 1909. From 1910 to 1912 he sang at the Metropolitan, where he made his début as Faust, created the King's Son in Engelbert Humperdinck's *Königskinder* opposite FARRAR (1910) and sang Rodolfo (*La bohème*), Turiddu, Canio, Lohengrin, Max and Pinkerton. In 1912 Richard Strauss chose him for Bacchus in the première of *Ariadne auf Naxos*.

Although intrinsically a lyric tenor with amazing coloratura agility, Jadlowker sang such roles as Florestan, Tannhäuser, Parsifal and Otello, which gradually took their toll. He left the Berlin company in 1921 and thereafter seldom appeared in opera, though he sang Armand Mirabeau in the first performance of Franz Lehár's *Frasquita*. He left a wide range of recordings, which show the skill of his coloratura and the peculiarly doleful timbre of his voice.

A. Frankenstein: 'Hermann Jadlowker', *Record Collector*, xix (1970–71), 5–31 [with discography by T. Kaufmann, D. Brew and J. Dennis]

Leo Riemens/Alan Blyth

Jäger, Ferdinand

(*b* Hanau, 25 Dec 1839; *d* Vienna, 13 June 1902). German tenor. He studied in Dresden, where he made his début in 1865. Engagements in Cologne, Hamburg, Stuttgart and Kassel followed. Recommended to Richard Wagner as a possible Siegfried, Jäger did not sing in the first *Ring* cycle at Bayreuth (1876) although coached in the role by the composer. But he sang Siegfried in both *Siegfried* and *Götterdämmerung* in the Vienna premières (1878–9), at the Munich Hofoper in private performances before King Ludwig II and at the Viktoria Theater, Berlin (1881). He sang Parsifal at Bayreuth (1882), after Winkelmann and Gudehus. Despite his fine voice and a physique perfect for the role, he never quite obtained real success as Siegfried.

Elizabeth Forbes

Janowitz, Gundula

(*b* Berlin, 2 Aug 1937). German soprano. She studied in Graz and made her début in 1960 as Barbarina at the Vienna Staatsoper, where she was engaged for 30 years. Early roles there included Pamina (which she recorded with Otto Klemperer), Henry Purcell's Dido, Mimì, Marzelline and, in 1964, the Empress (*Die Frau ohne Schatten*). At Bayreuth (1960–62) she sang a flowermaiden and Woglinde; at Aix-en-Provence (1963) Pamina; and at Glyndebourne (1964) Ilia. She made her Metropolitan début in 1967 as Sieglinde, which she also sang at the Salzburg Easter Festival (1967–8) and recorded for Herbert von Karajan. At Salzburg she sang Donna Anna, Countess Almaviva, Fiordiligi (1968–72), the Marschallin and Ariadne (1978–81). In 1972 she sang a memorable Agathe with Karl Böhm in a new production of *Der Freischütz* in Vienna, and in 1973 was W.A. Mozart's Countess at the reopening of the Paris Opéra. She appeared at Frankfurt, Hamburg, Munich, Berlin and La Scala, and made her Covent Garden début in 1976 as Donna Anna, returning as Ariadne (1987). Her other roles included Leonore (which she recorded under Leonard Bernstein), Elisabeth, Eva, Freia, Arabella, the Countess (*Capriccio*), Aida, Odabella and Amelia (*Boccanegra*).

Janowitz was also an accomplished lieder singer, outstanding in Franz Schubert and Richard Strauss, and a noted oratorio soloist. Her acting, once merely dignified, later became more committed. Her singing was sometimes criticized for being a little cool; but her voice, a full-toned lyric soprano of uncommon purity, was one of the most beautiful to be heard in the 1960s and 1970s. Among her most admired recordings are Countess Almaviva, Ariadne and the Countess in *Capriccio*, Strauss's *Vier letzte Lieder* with Karajan and various choral works. She was appointed opera director at Graz, in 1990, but she resigned the following year.

J.B. Steane: *Singers of the Century*, ii (London, 1998), 241–5

Alan Blyth

Jansen [Toupin], Jacques

(*b* Paris, 22 Nov 1913; *d* Paris, 13 March 2002). French baritone. He studied in Paris and made his début at the Opéra-Comique in 1941 as Pelléas, which became his most famous role. He recorded it with Roger Désormière in 1942 and sang it frequently in Europe and America, including the Theater an der Wien, Vienna (1946), the Holland Festival, Amsterdam (1948), Covent Garden and the Metropolitan (1949). At the Opéra-Comique he also sang much operetta, to which his small but keenly projected voice was well suited; his roles there included Valérien in Reynaldo Hahn's *Malvina* (1945) and the title role in Gabriel Pierné's *Fragonard* (1946). At the Opéra he appeared as Ali in Jean-Philippe Rameau's *Les Indes galantes* (1952), and at Aix-en-Provence he sang Cithaeron in Rameau's *Platée* (1956). He was also a notable Danilo in *Die lustige Witwe*, a role he sang over 1500 times. Jansen appeared in a number of films, and provided the singing voice for several others.

Elizabeth Forbes/R

Janssen, Herbert

(*b* Cologne, 22 Sept 1892; *d* New York, 3 June 1965). German baritone. Having served as an officer in World War I, he studied with Oskar Daniel in Berlin and made his début there at the Staatsoper on 5 May 1922 as Herod in Franz Schreker's *Der Schatzgräber*; he remained with the company until 1938, singing a wide variety of lyrical roles, especially in the works of Giuseppe Verdi and Richard Wagner, parts that soon brought him world fame. At Covent Garden (1926–39) and at Bayreuth (1930–37) he was regarded as a notable exponent of the Dutchman, Wolfram, Kurwenal, Kothner, Gunther and Amfortas, all of which he performed with a warm and sympathetic timbre, fine legato, clear enunciation and vivid acting. He was also a remarkable Prince Igor and Orestes (*Elektra*). Distaste for the Nazi regime having caused him to leave Germany in 1938, he sang that year in Buenos Aires and thereafter regularly at the Metropolitan, where he was a mainstay of the German wing from 1939 to 1952. After the retirement of FRIEDRICH SCHORR in 1943, he was persuaded to take over the heavier roles of Wotan and Hans Sachs, to which his voice was not so happily suited. His gifts as a lieder singer were mainly shown in his recordings, notably those made for the Hugo Wolf Society. Reissued on CD, these reveal the interior nature of his interpretations. His Wagner singing is preserved in several off-the-air recordings from the Metropolitan and in the virtually complete Bayreuth *Tannhäuser* of 1930.

T. Hart: 'Herbert Janssen', *Record Collector*, xvi (1964–6), 242–63 [with discography]; xxi (1973–4), 84

Desmond Shawe-Taylor/Alan Blyth

Jélyotte, Pierre de

(*b* Lasseube, 13 April 1713; *d* 12 Oct 1797). French singer and composer. He received his early musical training at Toulouse, where he studied singing, the harpsichord, the guitar, the cello and composition. In 1733 he went to Paris and made his début at the opera in a revival of Collin de Blamont's *Les fêtes grecques et romaines*. In the next years at the opera he continued to sing minor roles, and his popularity quickly grew. In 1738, when the *haute-contre* Tribou retired, Jélyotte took the main part in a revival of Jean-Baptiste Lully's *Atys*. Subsequently he created many of Jean-Philippe Rameau's leading roles, usually with the soprano MARIE FEL. These include the title roles in *Dardanus* (1739), *Platée* (1745) and *Zoroastre* (1749). With Fel he also performed in J.-J. Cassanéa de Mondonville's *Daphnis et Alcimadure* in 1754, a tragedy written in their native Languedoc dialect.

Jélyotte often took part in performances at court. *Zeliska*, his *comédie-ballet* (one vaudeville in *Mercure de France*, March 1746), had its première at Versailles in 1746. In 1745 he had been appointed *maître de guitare* to the king and he later became first cellist for the Théâtre des Petits Appartements of Madame de Pompadour. In the *concerts spirituels* that she organized he performed his own motets (now lost) or those of Mondonville. *Ecoutez l'histoire*, a *romance* by him, survives. At the Paris Concert Spirituel, however, he made only infrequent, unannounced appearances (see, for example, *Mercure de France*, May 1752, p. 185). He retired from the opera in 1765 but continued to perform occasionally in soirées at the Prince of Conti's home. An oil painting by M.B. Ollivier records one of these performances, in which Jélyotte is playing the guitar beside the young W.A. Mozart (aged seven) seated at a harpsichord during his first visit to Paris. Several other portraits of Jélyotte are known (they are listed by J.G. Prod'homme); to those should be added an anonymous miniature (Musée des Beaux-Arts, Dijon) on ivory formerly presumed, on unknown authority, to be a portrait of Claude Balbastre – he is accompanying himself on the guitar, and a score of *Atys* stands open before him on the harpsichord.

One of the extraordinary features of Jélyotte's voice was the ease with which he traversed the upper register of the *haute-contre* range (*f♯'* to *d''*). Some of Rameau's roles originally written for TRIBOU (such as Castor in *Castor et Pollux*, 1737) and later revised for Jélyotte (1754) demand a high tessitura and agility in rapid runs. One of the most difficult ariettes in all of Rameau's works, 'Règne, Amour' from *Zaïs* (1748), was also written for him. Rameau's librettist, Louis de Cahusac, pointed to the talents of Fel and Jélyotte as an important factor in the success of Rameau's works:

> We enjoy nowadays two singers who have carried taste, precision, expression and lightness of singing to a point of perfection that one would never before have thought possible. The art owes its greatest progress to them, for without doubt it is to the possibilities that M Rameau saw in their brilliant, flexible voices that opera owes its remarkable pieces with which this illustrious composer has enriched French singing.

Mary Cyr

Jerger, Alfred

(*b* Brno, 9 June 1889; *d* Vienna, 18 Nov 1976). Austrian bass-baritone. After studying musicology and conducting at the Vienna Music Academy under Albert Fuchs, Hermann Grädener and Gutheil, he joined the staff of the Zürich Opera in 1913; he conducted operetta performances, worked as an actor, and in 1917 sang Lothario in *Mignon*. That year he so impressed Richard Strauss with his performance as Baron Ochs that he was invited to join the Munich Hofoper (1919), and after two seasons moved to Vienna. In all, he sang some 150 roles with the Vienna Staatsoper from 1920 until he retired in 1964, and in addition he was active as a producer (Vienna, Oslo, Spain and Covent Garden – *Der Rosenkavalier*, 1960) and as a reviser of librettos. For two decades Jerger was a remarkably versatile singer at Vienna (Don Giovanni and Leporello, Sachs and Beckmesser, Méphistophélès, Scarpia, the Grand Inquisitor and King Philip II; he was also very successful in the title role of Ernst Krenek's *Jonny spielt auf*, and for many years his Pizarro and his Mozart roles were familiar at the Salzburg Festival). In 1924 he created the Man in Arnold Schoenberg's *Die glückliche Hand*. He was a renowned Strauss singer – Storch, Barak, John the Baptist, Orestes, Ochs and other parts; at Dresden in 1933 he created the role of Mandryka in *Arabella*, a part he sang at Covent Garden in 1934. At the end of World War II Jerger was appointed temporary director of the Vienna Staatsoper and was largely responsible for its being able to perform *Le nozze di Figaro* as early as May 1945. In 1947 he became a professor at the Vienna Music Academy (among his pupils was LEONIE RYSANEK), and at 80 he sang the Notary in Georg Solti's *Der Rosenkavalier* recording. Between the wars Jerger made a series of fine recordings.

Peter Branscombe

Maria Jeritza as Ariadne in the première of 'Ariadne auf Naxos' (Strauss), Stuttgart, 1912

Jeritza, Maria [Mizzi] [Jedlitzka, Marie]

(*b* Brno, 6 Oct 1887; *d* Orange, NJ, 10 July 1982). Moravian soprano, active in Austria and the USA. After studies in Brno and Prague, she made her début at Olmütz in 1910 as Elsa; she then joined the Vienna Volksoper and in 1912 appeared at the Hofoper. She quickly became an immense favourite in Vienna, where she sang regularly for over two decades; she was especially admired as Tosca, Minnie and Turandot, and in many Strauss roles. She was the first Ariadne in both versions of *Ariadne auf Naxos* (1912, Stuttgart, see illustration; 1916, Vienna), and the first Empress in *Die Frau ohne Schatten* (1919, Vienna). Her Salome was a remarkably vivid assumption. Having sung Marietta in the first Vienna performance of E.W. Korngold's *Die tote Stadt*, she repeated this role for her Metropolitan début later in the same year (19 November 1921). Of greater musical significance was her Jenůfa in both the first Viennese (1918) and first New York (1924) performances of Leoš Janáček's opera. During the next 12 years she became recognized as the Metropolitan's most glamorous star since the days of GERALDINE FARRAR and appropriately introduced to New York both Giacomo Puccini's *Turandot* and Richard Strauss's *Die ägyptische Helena*. Her Covent Garden perfor-

mances were confined to seven roles during 1925 and 1926, whereas at the Metropolitan she sang 290 performances in 20 roles. After World War II she made isolated appearances in Vienna and New York (having become a naturalized American). Though endowed with an ample and lustrous voice, Jeritza belonged to the category of artist known as a 'singing actress', freely yielding both dramatically and vocally to impulses that were sometimes more flamboyant than refined. In her numerous recordings, faults of taste and technique co-exist with genuine vocal achievements. Archival material from the Vienna Staatsoper in the 1930s testifies to the magnetic effect she had on audiences.

M. Jeritza: *Sunlight and Song: a Singer's Life* (New York, 1924/R)

Desmond Shawe-Taylor/R

Jerusalem, Siegfried

(*b* Oberhausen, 17 April 1940). German tenor. After 17 years as an orchestral bassoonist he studied singing at Stuttgart, making his début there in 1975 as First Prisoner in *Fidelio*. He sang his first major Wagner role, Lohengrin, in several leading German houses, including Berlin, where he became a member of the Deutsche Oper in 1978. At Bayreuth he has sung Froh, the Young Sailor (*Tristan*; 1977), Parsifal, Walther and Lohengrin (1979–81), Siegmund (1983–6), Siegfried (1988–92), Tristan (1993–5) and Loge (1994–5). Having made his Metropolitan début in 1980 as Lohengrin, he returned as Loge (1987), Siegfried (1990–91) and Parsifal (1992). His Met Siegfried and Parsifal, both under James Levine, are recorded on video. He first sang at Covent Garden, as Erik, in 1986. Although his repertory includes Tamino, Florestan (both of which he has recorded), Idomeneus, C.W. Gluck's Orestes (a high baritone part), Max (*Freischütz*), Don Alvaro (*Forza del destino*), Lensky, Boris (*Kát'a Kabanová*) and Assad (*Königin von Saba*), his powerful, expressive voice and dramatic involvement are shown to best advantage in his Wagner roles, above all Siegfried, which he has sung with notable success in Berlin, Vienna and at Covent Garden (1995–6), and has recorded with both Bernard Haitink and Daniel Barenboim. Jerusalem is also an admired concert singer, and he has made impressive recordings of such works as Ludwig van Beethoven's Ninth Symphony, *Das Lied von der Erde* and *Gurrelieder*.

A. Blyth: 'Siegfried Jerusalem', *Opera*, xliii (1992), 904–9

Elizabeth Forbes

Jessner, Irene

(*b* Vienna, 28 Aug 1901; *d* Toronto, 10 Jan 1994). Canadian soprano. She studied at the Neues Konservatorium in Vienna with Victor Fuchs. Her début was in Teplice in 1930 as Elsa in *Lohengrin*, after which she appeared in Brno, Buenos Aires, Chicago, Munich, Philadelphia, Prague and San Francisco. In 1936 she made her Metropolitan début as Ortlinde in *Die Walküre* and remained with the company until 1952, singing a broad repertory including Hänsel, Tosca and many Mozart, Strauss and the lighter Wagner roles. She recorded for Columbia and Victor. In 1952 Jessner joined the voice faculty at the University of Toronto, where her pupils included TERESA STRATAS.

Cori Ellison

Jo, Sumi

(*b* Seoul, 22 Nov 1962). Korean soprano. She studied in Italy, making her début in 1986 at Trieste as Gilda. In 1988 she sang Thetis/Fortune in Niccolò Jommelli's *Fetonte* at La Scala, and Barbarina at Salzburg, where she returned as Oscar (1989) and the Queen of Night (1993). In 1990 she made her US début in Chicago as the Queen of Night, a role she has subsequently sung to acclaim at Los Angeles, Florence and Covent Garden (1993), where her previous roles included Olympia (1991), Adina (*L'elisir d'amore*) and Elvira in *I puritani* (1992). Jo's repertory also embraces Zerbinetta (Lyons, 1989), Oscar at Salzburg, Sister Constance (*Dialogues des Carmélites*), Matilde (*Elisabetta, regina d'Inghilterra*), Richard Strauss's Sophie, Amina (*La sonnambula*) and Countess Adèle (*Le comte Ory*), which she sang at Aix-en-Provence in 1995. Her pure-toned and extremely flexible coloratura soprano is used with great musicality, as she demonstrates in several Rossini recordings and in her three recordings of the Queen of Night under Armin Jordan, Georg Solti and Arnold Östman.

Elizabeth Forbes

Jobin, Raoul

(*b* Quebec, 8 April 1906; *d* Quebec, 13 Jan 1974). Canadian tenor. He studied first in Quebec, then in Paris. There Henri Büsser engaged him for the Opéra, where he made his début as Charles Gounod's Tybalt in 1930 and sang minor roles for two years. After two seasons in Bordeaux, he returned to the Opéra in 1935; there he sang Romeo, Faust, Raoul and Lohengrin, and created Fabrice in Henri Sauguet's *Chartreuse de Parme* (1939). At the Opéra-Comique he sang Don José, Julien, Werther, Hoffmann, Jules Massenet's Des Grieux and Cavaradossi. He left France in 1939 and made his Metropolitan début in 1940 as Des Grieux, later singing Tonio (*La fille du régiment*), Faust, Don José, Romeo, Pelléas and Canio. He also sang Gérald (*Lakmé*) in San Francisco (1940) and Don José in Chicago (1941). He returned to the Opéra, where his roles (1949–52) included Mârouf, Walther, Radames and Arrigo Boito's Faust. On retirement he opened a singing school in Montreal. His firm, bright-toned voice and enthusiastic style can be heard to advantage in a number of recordings, notably as Don José, Romeo, Hoffmann and Tonio, and as Admetus (opposite FLAGSTAD) in C.W. Gluck's *Alceste*.

André Tubeuf/Alan Blyth

Johnson, Edward
[Di Giovanni, Edoardo]

(*b* Guelph, ON, 22 Aug 1878; *d* Guelph, 20 April 1959). Canadian tenor and impresario. His father hoped he would become a lawyer, but in 1899 he took his savings and went to New York to study music. In 1902 he was the hero in Reginald De Koven's *Maid Marian* in Boston, and he starred on Broadway (1908) in Oscar Straus's *A Waltz Dream*. On CARUSO's advice he went to Florence (1909) to work with Vincenzo Lombardi. As Edoardo di Giovanni he made his operatic début in Padua (1912) in *Andrea Chénier*, and sang in many Italian premières, including *Parsifal* in Italian (his La Scala début, 1914), Giacomo Puccini's *Il tabarro* and *Gianni Schicchi* (1919, Rome), and works by Ildebrando Pizzetti and Franco Alfano.

Johnson left Italy to become the leading lyric tenor of the Chicago Opera (1919–22) and the Metropolitan Opera (1922–35) where he was a favourite as Pelléas, Romeo and Peter Ibbetson, a role he created in the Deems Taylor opera. Also in his repertory were Siegfried and Faust (1923, Covent Garden). His musicianship, romantic appearance and ability to project a character were coupled with a lyric voice of good quality and range, a sound technique and a seldom-used but easy high E. He followed Herbert Witherspoon, Giulio Gatti-Casazza's successor, as general manager of the Metropolitan (1935–50), instituted the Auditions of the Air and successfully guided the Metropolitan through the war period. On retirement (1950) Johnson moved to Guelph, but remained chairman of the board of Toronto's Royal Conservatory of Music. He held honours from many countries, but was especially proud that a Guelph school and a music foundation bore his name.

R.A. Simon: 'Profile: General Director', *New Yorker* (14 Dec 1935), 30–33

R. Mercer: *The Tenor of his Time: Edward Johnson of the Met* (Toronto, 1976)

Ruby Mercer

Johnston, James

(*b* Belfast, 13 Aug 1903; *d* Belfast, 17 Oct 1991). Irish tenor. He studied privately and made his début in 1940 in Dublin as the Duke of Mantua in *Rigoletto*. In 1945 he was engaged by Sadler's Wells; while their leading tenor (1946–50) he sang Gabriele Adorno in the English première of *Simon Boccanegra* (1948), as well as Don Carlos, Pinkerton, Jeník and Hugh the Drover. He made his début at Covent Garden in 1949 as Alfredo, and the same year created Hector in Arthur Bliss's *The Olympians* there; he went on to become a principal tenor at Covent Garden (1951–8), singing Manrico (to CALLAS's Leonora), Radames, Don José, Cavaradossi and Calaf. He sang Macduff at Glyndebourne in 1952. Johnston had a ringing tone and unaffected delivery, and sang with rare fervour.

Alan Blyth

Jones, Della

(*b* Neath, 13 April 1946). Welsh mezzo-soprano. She studied in London and Geneva, where she made her début in 1970 as Fyodor (*Boris Godunov*), later singing Olga (*Yevgeny Onegin*) and the Schoolboy (*Lulu*). She sang Clytemnestra (*Iphigénie en Aulide*) at Oxford in 1972, and in 1977 she joined the ENO, where her roles have included Cherubino, Dorabella, G.F. Handel's Sextus, Rosina, Cenerentola, Isolier (*Le comte Ory*), Ninetta (*La gazza ladra*), Isabella (*L'italiana in Algeri*), Suzuki and Dolly, which she created in Iain Hamilton's *Anna Karenina* (1981). With Scottish Opera she has sung Hänsel, Clori (*Egisto*) and Donna Elvira, and with the WNO, Hector Berlioz's Dido, Herodias (*Salome*), Brangäne and Handel's Ariodante. Jones made her Covent Garden début in 1983 as the Female Cat (*L'enfant et les sortilèges*), then sang Rosina, Melibea (*Il viaggio a Reims*) and Marcellina. In 1990 she sang Ruggiero (*Alcina*) in Geneva and Paris. She has also sung in Venice, Bordeaux, Los Angeles, Antwerp and San Diego. Her repertory also includes Henry Purcell's Dido, Baba the Turk, Ruggiero (Alcina), Donna Elvira, Adalgisa, Magdalene, Claudio Monteverdi's Nero, Zerlina, Agrippina and C.W. Gluck's Armide, which she sang in Versailles in 1992. She sang Lucrezia in Berthold Goldschmidt's *Beatrice Cenci* in concert at Berlin (1994), and Samira in John Corigliano's *The Ghosts of Versailles* at Chicago (1995). Her numerous recordings include several Handel operas and ora-

torios, Vitellia (*Clemenza di Tito*), Rosina and Peter Maxwell Davies's *Resurrection*. She brings to all her roles a wide vocal range, a superb coloratura technique and uncommon dramatic flair.

H. Canning: 'Della Jones', *Opera*, xli (1990), 1159–64

Elizabeth Forbes

Jones, Dame Gwyneth

(*b* Pontnewynydd, 7 Nov 1936). Welsh soprano. She studied at the RCM and in Siena, Zürich and the International Opera Studio, Geneva. Engaged as a mezzo at Zürich in 1962, she made her début as Annina (*Der Rosenkavalier*). After singing Lady Macbeth for the WNO, she joined the Royal Opera in 1963, singing Lady Macbeth and Octavian on tour. Established as a soprano, she made her Covent Garden début in 1964 as Leonore, then sang Leonora (*Il trovatore*), Elisabeth de Valois, Santuzza, Desdemona, Donna Anna, Aida, Tosca, Salome, Chrysothemis, the Marschallin and Sieglinde. The last of these was her début role at Bayreuth (1966), where she also sang Eva, Kundry, Elisabeth/Venus, Senta, and Brünnhilde in the 1976 Centenary *Ring*, which appeared on videotape and disc. Jones sang regularly at the Vienna Staatsoper, in Munich, Paris, Milan, San Francisco, Chicago and the Metropolitan, making her début in 1972 as Sieglinde. Her later repertory included Isolde, Ortrud, the Empress and the Dyer's Wife, Helen (*Die ägyptische Helena*), Richard Strauss's Electra, Turandot (Royal Opera at Los Angeles, 1984), Minnie, and Woman in *Erwartung*. She sang Brünnhilde in the *Ring* at Covent Garden in 1991. Alun Hoddinot's Ninth Symphony (*A Vision of Eternity*) set three poems by William Blake and Percy Bysshe Shelley for Jones (1992). Her strong, vibrant *lirico spinto* soprano and handsome stage presence, together with total emotional and dramatic involvement in her roles, gave tremendous excitement to her performances. Her voice could, though, develop an uncomfortable beat under pressure, especially in later years, and this often detracts from the value of her recordings. She was created DBE in 1986.

K. Loveland: 'Gwyneth Jones', *Opera*, xxi (1970), 100–06

A. Blyth: 'Gwyneth Jones', *Gramophone*, l (1972–3), 26–7

J. Rockwell: 'Gwyneth Jones', *ON*, xxxvii/7 (1972–3), 18–19

T. Haberfeld: *Gwyneth Jones* (Zürich, 1991)

Alan Blyth

Jörn, Karl

(*b* Riga, 5 Jan 1873; *d* Denver, 19 Dec 1947). Latvian tenor. He studied with Jacobs Ress in Berlin and in 1896 made his début in *Martha* at Freiburg. Appearances at Zürich and Hamburg led to his engagement at the Berlin royal opera in 1902, where he remained until 1908. Covent Garden first heard him in a British double première, in 1906, of Ede Poldini's one-act *Vagabund und Prinzessin* and Peter Cornelius's *Der Barbier von Bagdad*. In the two following seasons he sang Walther in *Die Meistersinger*; his Loge in *Das Rheingold* was considered one of the best ever heard. He joined the Metropolitan in 1908, proving his adaptability in W.A. Mozart and Richard Wagner, Jules Massenet (*Manon*) and Pietro Mascagni (*Cavalleria rusticana*) and in a special performance of Ludwig van Beethoven's Ninth Symphony under Arturo Toscanini. He also sang Jeník in the American première of *The Bartered Bride* (1909). Taking American citizenship in 1916, he retired from singing to develop an invention for mineral-divining; then, losing his fortune, he returned in 1928, joining JOHANNA GADSKI's touring company and singing (with great success) his first Tristan and Siegfried. He taught in New York and Denver and gave a final performance as Lohengrin shortly before his death. His sturdy voice and lyric style can be heard in many recordings; they cover a wide repertory and include two of the earliest made of complete operas, *Faust* and *Carmen*, both recorded in 1908 with EMMY DESTINN.

J.B. Steane

Rosemary Joshua

Joshua, Rosemary

(*b* Cardiff, 16 Oct 1964). Welsh soprano. After studying at the RCM, she made her professional operatic début, as Pamina, with Opera Northern Ireland in 1989. The same year she first appeared at the ENO, singing one of the Graduates in Kurt Weill's *Street Scene*. In 1992 she enhanced her growing reputation with her début as Zerlina for Scottish Opera, and as Princess Ida for the ENO. Her major international début came in 1993 when she enchanted audiences as Angelica (*Orlando*) at the Aix Festival, repeating the role at Montpellier in 1996 and Lyons in 1997. At the ENO she has subsequently sung Susanna, Sophie (*Der Rosenkavalier*) and Semele (1999), a memorably sexy portrayal nominated for a Laurence Olivier Award. Joshua made her Glyndebourne début, as Anne Trulove, in 2000, her début at the Théâtre des Champs-Elysées, as Sharpears in *The Cunning Little Vixen*, in 2002, and her Covent Garden début, as a sparkling Zerlina, in 2003. Three other important débuts in the 2002-03 season were at the Metropolitan Opera, as Adèle in *Die Fledermaus* (a portrayal described by Martin Bernheimer in the *Financial Times* as 'compellingly zany and virtuosic'); at La Scala, in *The Cunning Little Vixen*; and at the Staatsoper in Munich, as Susanna. On the concert platform she has sung with many leading orchestras and conductors, including Simon Rattle, Roger Norrington, Mark Elder, Charles Mackerras, René Jacobs and Nikolaus Harnoncourt.

Joshua's silvery, finely focussed soprano, graceful phrasing and pearly coloratura have given her a reputation as something of a Handel specialist. In addition to Angelica (which she has recorded) and Semele, her other Handel opera roles include Ginevra in *Ariodante*, which she sang in San Diego in 2002, Cleopatra (Florida Grand Opera, 2000) and Poppea (*Agrippina*), which she has sung in Cologne, Brussels and Paris. She has also recorded the title role in *Partenope* with Alan Curtis, catching all the Neapolitan queen's wayward, caressing sensuality. Among her other recordings are Belinda (*Dido and Aeneas*), Venus (John Blow's *Venus and Adonis*), Gretel (*Hänsel und Gretel*), Michal (*Saul*) and Sophie in a disc of excerpts from *Der Rosenkavalier*.

Richard Wigmore

Journet, Françoise

(*b* Lyons; *d* Paris, 1720). French soprano. She sang at the Lyons opera for three or four years, moving to Paris shortly before 1700. She sang Mélisse in the première of André Destouches' *Amadis de Grèce* (1699), a role she repeated in 1711. At first she was not well received by the public, but was encouraged to persevere by MLLE DESMATINS, with whom she seems to have alternated in the title role of Henry Desmarets and André Campra's *Iphigénie en Tauride*. She subsequently alternated with Mlle Armand as Clorinde in the first revival of Campra's *Tancrède* (1707), having previously appeared as Iole to Desmatins' Dejanira in Marin Marais' *Alcide* (1705).

Journet created the title role in Marais' *Sémélé* (1709) and Ilione in Campra's *Idoménée* (1712) and sang in Jean-Baptiste Lully revivals: as Hermione (*Cadmus*, 1711), Angélique (*Roland*, 1716), Io (*Isis*, 1717) and Stheneboea (*Bellérophon*, 1718). She took Polyxena in the only revival of Lully and Pascal Collasse's *Achille et Polyxène* (1712) and twice sang the title role in Destouches' *Issé* (1708 and 1719) and in Collasse's *Thétis et Pélée* (1708 and 1712). She repeated the title role of *Iphigénie en Tauride* in the 1711 revival and surpassed herself in the famous 1719 revival. The same year, she was the heroine in the revival of Marais' *Alcyone*. When she died, her roles were taken over by MARIE ANTIER.

She was said to have beauty of voice, nobility of presence and a particular personal fascination. Her tender, moving eloquence of gesture, combined with a majestic deportment, were recorded in a famous full-length portrait by Jean Raoux. Her duets with THÉVENARD were apparently much admired.

Philip Weller

Journet, Marcel

(*b* Grasse, 25 July 1867; *d* Vittel, 25 Sept 1933). French bass. He reportedly studied singing in Paris and made his operatic début at Béziers in 1891 in *La favorite*. He sang at La Monnaie, 1894–1900, and then was based in Paris, appearing both at the Opéra and at the Opéra-Comique, where he sang in the French première of Giacomo Puccini's *La bohème* (1898). He made his Covent Garden début in 1897 as the Duke of Mendoza in Frédéric d'Erlanger's *Inès Mendo*. That season he sang the Landgrave in a French version of *Tannhäuser*; he returned regularly until 1907 and again in 1927 and 1928. He was engaged at the Metropolitan Opera, 1900–08, and then sang at the Opéra until 1931. He appeared frequently in other centres, including Monte Carlo (where he sang in the première of Reynaldo Hahn's *Nausicaa*, 1919), Buenos Aires, Chicago, Madrid and Barcelona, and was heard regularly at La Scala, 1917–27, where in 1924 he created Simon Magus in Arrigo Boito's posthumous *Nerone*. Endowed with a powerful, resonant voice with a range which allowed him to sing such baritone parts as Tonio and Scarpia, he had a large repertory of French and Italian roles and many Wagnerian ones including Klingsor, Hans

Sachs, Wotan, Titurel and Gurnemanz. His art is preserved on a number of recordings, most notably his Méphistophélès in Charles Gounod's *Faust*.

M. Scott: *The Record of Singing*, ii (London, 1979), 42–4

Harold Barnes

Jungwirth, Manfred

(*b* St Pölten, 4 June 1919). Austrian bass. He studied in St Pölten and Vienna, making his début in 1942 at Bucharest as Méphistophélès and King Henry (*Lohengrin*). Engaged at Innsbruck (1945), Zürich (1948) and Frankfurt (1960), he also sang at the Komische Oper, Berlin, and Deutsche Oper am Rhein. He made his British début in 1965 at Glyndebourne as Ochs, which was also his début role at the Vienna Staatsoper (1967), San Francisco (1971), the Metropolitan (1974) and Dallas (1982); he also sang it at Munich, Nice, Rome and Trieste. He created the Vicar in Gottfried von Einem's *Besuch der alten Dame* (1971, Vienna). His repertory included Osmin, Rocco, which he sang at La Scala (1978), the King (*Aida*), Pietro (*Boccanegra*), Cuno (*Der Freischütz*), Sacristan (*Tosca*), Severolus (*Palestrina*), Truffaldino (*Ariadne auf Naxos*), Count Waldner (*Arabella*), the role of his Covent Garden début (1981), and La Roche (*Capriccio*), which he sang at Salzburg (1985) and Florence (1987). His ripe, dark-coloured voice and comic talents were displayed to best advantage as Ochs, which he recorded with Georg Solti.

Alan Blyth

Jurinac, Sena [Srebrenka]

(*b* Travnik, 24 Oct 1921). Austrian soprano of Yugoslav birth. She studied at the music academy at Zagreb and was a singing pupil of Milka Kostrenčić. She made her début at the Zagreb Opera just after her 21st birthday, as Mimì, and in 1945 she joined the Vienna Staatsoper (Cherubino, 1 May), remaining with the company. She appeared at the Salzburg Festival in 1947, soon after sang Dorabella in two of the Vienna company's performances at Covent Garden, and the following year made a deep impression in the same role with the Glyndebourne Opera Company at the Edinburgh Festival. At Glyndebourne, where she first appeared in 1949 and at once became a great favourite, she impressed with an assumption of Fiordiligi (1950) as accomplished as her Dorabella had been the year before. Although best known early in her career for W.A. Mozart, she built up an extensive repertory covering a wide range of parts. She appeared at most of the world's leading opera houses, maturing from roles such as Octavian, Marzelline and Ilia (*Idomeneo*) to the Countess Almaviva, the Marschallin, Leonore and Electra. Among her other notable roles were the Composer (*Ariadne auf Naxos*), the two ladies in *Don Giovanni*, Elisabeth (*Tannhäuser* and *Don Carlos*, the latter commemmorated in a series of Austrian stamps issued to celebrate the centenary of the Vienna Staatsoper in 1969), Jenůfa, Cio-Cio-San and Tosca, Desdemona, and later Marie (*Wozzeck*), Poppaea and Iphigenia (*Iphigénie en Tauride*).

Jurinac's voice was beautifully pure, rich and even throughout its range, and although she did not always sound to best advantage in her numerous recordings, the finest of them faithfully convey the integrity, eloquence and commitment that made an unforgettable impression on two generations of opera-lovers. The ardent, youthful singer of the 1940s and 50s grew into the sensitive, reflective artist of the 60s and 70s. Although she appeared frequently as a concert and lieder singer, she will be remembered as one of the outstanding operatic sopranos of her time, generous of voice and radiant of personality. This is reflected in her recordings of Ilia, Marzelline, Leonore and Octavian, and the second version of *Ariadne auf Naxos* with Erich Leinsdorf in 1959.

Earl of Harewood: 'Sena Jurinac', *Opera*, i/5/(1950), 26–9

U. Tamussino: *Sena Jurinac* (Augsburg, 1971) [with discography]

A. Blyth: 'Great Voices: Sena Jurinac', *Gramophone*, lxvii (1989–90), 1953–4

J. Hunt: *Three Italian Conductors, Seven Viennese Sopranos* (London, 1991) [incl. discography]

Peter Branscombe

K

Kabaivanska, Raina

(*b* Burgas, 15 Dec 1934). Bulgarian soprano. She studied at the Bulgarian State Conservatory and made her début in Sofia in 1957 as Tatyana. In 1961, after further study in Italy, she appeared at La Scala in Vincenzo Bellini's *Beatrice di Tenda*; her American début was at San Francisco in 1962 as Desdemona. She returned regularly to La Scala and has since sung in all the major Italian opera houses and often in the opera festivals at Martina Franca; she also appeared at the Metropolitan (début in 1962 as Nedda), Covent Garden (where her Desdemona, opposite MARIO DEL MONACO in 1964, received great critical acclaim), Moscow, Salzburg and Vienna. In 1973 she sang Hélène in CALLAS's production of *Les vêpres siciliennes* at the rebuilt Teatro Regio, Turin. In 1971 she became a permanent guest artist at Hamburg. She made her Paris début in 1975 at the Opéra as Leonora (*La forza del destino*). Butterfly and Tosca were considered her greatest roles, and her repertory also included the Countess (*Capriccio*), Elizabeth (*Roberto Devereux*), Adriana Lecouvreur and Francesca da Rimini. At Rome in 1981 she sang the title role in the first 20th-century production of Gaetano Donizetti's *Fausta*, and in 1984 sang the title role in Gaspare Spontini's *La vestale* at Genoa. Late in her career she added roles in *The Makropulos Affair*, *The Turn of the Screw* and *La voix humaine*. Her voice was a strong and agreeable lyric soprano, secure in the top register and capable of warm, expressive shading; she was a natural and highly individual actress with a fine stage presence, particularly suited to the *verismo* repertory, as can be amply confirmed in her video recordings of *Tosca*, recorded on location in Rome, and of *Butterfly* caught at the Arena di Verona.

Rodolfo Celletti/R

Kalter [Aufrichtig] Sabine

(*b* Jarosław, 28 March 1890; *d* London, 1 Sept 1957). Polish mezzo-soprano. She studied in Vienna and made her début at the Volksoper in 1911. From 1915 to 1935 she was engaged at Hamburg, and was especially successful in Giuseppe Verdi and Richard Wagner, and as Delilah, C.W. Gluck's Orpheus, Fidès (*Le prophète*) and Marina (*Boris Godunov*). Being Jewish, she had to leave Germany in 1935; she settled in London, where she sang with much success at Covent Garden, 1935–9, as Ortrud (the role of her début there), Fricka, Waltraute, Brangäne, Herodias (*Salome*) and Háta (*The Bartered Bride*). From 1939 she sang in concert and recital and taught in London. She had a warm, beautiful voice and strong dramatic ability. She made few recordings, among them Brangäne in a complete 1936 *Tristan* with MELCHIOR and FLAGSTAD.

Harold Rosenthal/R

Kanawa, Kiri Te.

See TE KANAWA, KIRI.

Kappel, Gertrude

(*b* Halle, 1 Sept 1884; *d* Pullach, 3 April 1971). German soprano. She studied in Leipzig, making her début in 1903 as Leonore at Hanover, where she was engaged until 1924. At Covent Garden she sang Brünnhilde (1912–14) and also Isolde, Sieglinde, Senta, the Marschallin and Electra (1924–6). She appeared at the Vienna Staatsoper (1921–7), at Salzburg, where she sang Donna Anna (1922), and at the Staatsoper in Munich (1927–31). She made her Metropolitan début in 1928 as Isolde, later singing Ortrud, Fricka, Brünnhilde, the Marschallin and Electra (the first Metropolitan performance, 1932). She sang Isolde at San Francisco in 1933 and retired in 1937. Her 1924 recordings of 'Pace, pace, mio Dio' (*La forza del destino*) and the closing scene of *Götterdämmerung* reveal the wide range of her voice and the richness and security of her singing.

Alan Blyth

Karnéus, Katarina

(*b* Stockholm, 26 Nov 1965). Swedish mezzo-soprano. She studied with Ulla Blom at Trinity College of Music in London and at the National Opera Studio, sponsored by WNO and Glyndebourne Festival Opera. She made her professional operatic début as Cherubino with WNO, and her international début as Carmen with the Opéra-Comique in Paris. After winning the Cardiff Singer of the World Competition in 1995 she was invited to appear at the Proms in London, the Salzburg Festival, the Edinburgh Festival and other leading venues, and to work with such conductors as Rafael Frühbeck de Burgos, Charles Mackerras and Roger Norrington. Karnéus has remained closely associated with WNO, for whom she has sung roles including Sextus, Rosina, Angelina (*La Cenerentola*), C.W. Gluck's Orpheus and Octavian (her début in the role, 2000). Her Metropolitan Opera début, as Varvara (*Kát'a Kabanová*), was in 1999, and the same year she made her début with the Staatsoper in Munich, as Annius (*La clemenza di Tito*), returning to Munich in 2000 as Sextus and in 2001 as Sextus and as Dorabella. Karnéus has also appeared with the Glyndebourne Festival Opera (as Dorabella), the Paris Opéra (as Dorabella and Meg Page) and the Netherlands Opera. She is much in demand as a concert singer and recitalist, and has made two acclaimed solo discs for EMI, one of songs by Gustav Mahler, Richard Strauss and Joseph Marx, the other of Maurice Ravel's *Chansons madécasses*. Her glowing, richly coloured mezzo is allied to a formidable technique (her dazzling coloratura in such roles as Angelina and Rosina has provoked critical superlatives) and a compelling stage presence.

Richard Wigmore

Kasarova, Vesselina

(*b* Stara Zagora, 18 July 1965). Bulgarian mezzo-soprano. She studied with Ressa Koleva at the conservatory in Sofia, where she made her first appearances with the Sofia National Opera in such roles as Rosina (her stage début), Dorabella, Preziosilla and Fenena (*Nabucco*). She joined the Zürich Opera in 1989, making her début as Second Norn, followed by Olga and Anna (*Les Troyens*). In 1998 she returned to the house, scoring a particular success in the title part of Jacques Offenbach's *La Périchole* with Nikolaus Harnoncourt. She was briefly engaged at the Vienna Staatsoper in 1991, the year she made her début at the Salzburg Festival as Annius (*La clemenza di Tito*). But it was a concert performance of *Tancredi* at Salzburg the following year which really established her credentials as a dedicated artist with a strong, vibrant mezzo and great fluency in her runs. Kasarova made her Covent Garden début as Rosina in 1993 and returned as Sextus in *La clemenza di Tito* in 2000. In 1998 she appeared at the Munich Festival as Jane Seymour (*Anna Bolena*) and made her début at the Rossini Festival at Pesaro in the title part of *La Cenerentola*. In 1999 she sang the role of Ruggero (*Alcina*) at Barcelona and Sextus and Isabella (*L'italiana in Algeri*) at the Staatsoper in Munich. Among other roles in Kasarova's repertory are Zerlina,

Charlotte and Vincenzo Bellini's Romeo, which she has recorded to considerable acclaim. A recital of Mozart arias with Colin Davis likewise testifies to her vivid powers of communication and consummate technique. She is also an accomplished exponent of French and Russian song, and of lieder, as revealed in a recording of songs by Franz Schubert, Johannes Brahms and Robert Schumann.

A. Blyth: 'Vesselina Kasarova: The Voice of Romeo', *Gramophone*, lxxvi/Sept (1998), 10–12

Alan Blyth

Kastorsky, Vladimir

(*b* Bol'shiye Saly, 2/14 March 1871; *d* Leningrad [now St Petersburg], 2 July 1948). Russian bass. He studied with Stanislaus Gabel in St Petersburg and made his début in the provinces, going to the Mariinsky, St Petersburg [later Leningrad], in 1895. There he remained until 1930, singing in a wide repertory which included Wagnerian roles such as Wotan and King Mark. In 1908 he sang Pimen at Paris in the first performances of *Boris Godunov* outside Russia. For many years he taught singing in Leningrad, and at an advanced age appeared at the Bol'shoy in a supporting role in *The Queen of Spades*. He also became a famous singer of folksongs, especially with a male-voice quartet which toured extensively. A voice of fine quality, almost baritonal in timbre, is heard in recordings, impressive also in the low register, evenly produced, tastefully directed and well preserved in later years.

J.B. Steane

Katul'skaya, Yelena Kliment'yevna

(*b* Odessa, 21 May/2 June 1888; *d* Moscow, 19 or 20 Nov 1966). Russian soprano. She studied privately in Odessa (1904) and St Petersburg (1905–7), then entered the St Petersburg Conservatory and graduated from Natal'ya Iretskaya's class in 1909. She made her début as Lakmé at the Mariinsky Theatre, St Petersburg, where she sang until 1911, then went to the Bol'shoy, Moscow (1913–45). Her roles included Nikolay Rimsky-Korsakov's Volkhova, Swan Princess (*Tale of Tsar Saltan*) and Snow Maiden; Marguerite and Juliet; Cio-Cio-San and Jules Massenet's Manon. A sensitive, cultured musician, she had a lyrical voice of beautiful timbre and wide range. She was also well known as a recitalist, with an extensive repertory ranging from Russian folksong and works by Soviet composers to early Italian and modern French music. From 1948 she taught at the Moscow Conservatory, as a professor from 1950.

I.M. Yampol'sky

Keenlyside, Simon

(*b* London, 3 Aug 1959). English baritone. He studied with John Cameron at the RNCM, where he sang Lescaut in *Manon* (1987). His professional stage début was as Count Almaviva (*Le nozze di Figaro*) in 1988 at Hamburg. He then moved to Scottish Opera (1988–94), where he sang Billy Budd, Gioachino Rossini's Figaro, Marcello, Danilo (*Die lustige Witwe*), Belcore and Papageno, the last-named hailed as a virtuoso performance. He made his Covent Garden début, as Silvio, in 1989, followed by Guglielmo, which was also the role of his admired Glyndebourne début in 1995. His début at La Scala in 1995 was Papageno (with Riccardo Muti), and he returned to the house for Count Almaviva and Ubalde (C.W. Gluck's *Armide*) in 1999. He made his first Metropolitan appearance, as Belcore, in 1996, the year in which he scored a notable success as Ambroise Thomas' Hamlet at Geneva, catching all the role's inwardness. This was followed in 1997 by an ardent Pelléas at San Francisco and a mercurial Don Giovanni at Ferrara with Claudio Abbado. Keenlyside's interpretation of the title part in Claudio Monteverdi's *Orfeo*, in which he toured with René Jacobs in 1998–9, was notable for its single-minded intensity; and he revealed his comic gifts as Gioachino Rossini's Figaro at the Berlin Staatsoper, and as Dandini at the Paris Opéra (both 1998), where he also sang Yeletsky in 1999. In 2000 he was a compelling, athletic Billy Budd at Covent Garden, conveying the character's goodness with no hint of insipidity (see colour plate 8). His operatic recordings include Don Giovanni (with Abbado) and Ned Keene (*Peter Grimes*). He is also an accomplished interpreter of lieder (as revealed on recordings of Franz Schubert and Robert Schumann) and *mélodies*, and he has regularly performed the song cycles of Gustav Mahler in concert. All his performances are distinguished by his mellow yet incisive tone and high intelligence as an interpreter.

R. Milnes: 'Simon Keenlyside', *Opera*, xlviii (1997), 1284–90

Alan Blyth

Kelemen, Zoltán

(*b* Budapest, 12 March 1926; *d* Zürich, 9 May 1979). Hungarian bass-baritone. He studied in Budapest and Rome, making his début in 1959 at Augsburg as Kecal. After an engagement at Wuppertal, in 1961 he joined the Cologne Opera, remaining there until his death; he took part in the première of Bernd Alois Zimmermann's *Die Soldaten* (1965) and made his London début with the company at Sadler's Wells (1969) as the Mayor in *Der junge Lord*. He first appeared at Bayreuth in 1962 as Ortel and a Nobleman (*Lohengrin*); in 1964 he sang Alberich, the role of his Salzburg (1965), Metropolitan (1968) and Covent Garden (1970) débuts, and which he recorded for Herbert von Karajan. A fine Mozartian, he was an earthy Leporello, a suave Alfonso and an amusing, menacing Osmin. His other roles included Pizarro, Don Magnifico, Falstaff (Otto Nicolai and Giuseppe Verdi), Dulcamara, the Grand Inquisitor, Ochs, Gianni Schicchi, Rangoni and Klingsor, which he also recorded. Kelemen was a powerful actor and coloured his rich, agile voice cleverly to suggest humour or malevolence as a character required.

Alan Blyth

Kelly, Michael (William)

(*b* Dublin, 25 Dec 1762; *d* Margate, 9 Oct 1826). Irish tenor, composer, theatre manager and music publisher. The eldest of the 14 children of Thomas Kelly (Deputy Master of Ceremonies at Dublin Castle, and a wine merchant), Michael Kelly grew up amid the rich musical life of Dublin, and received singing lessons from various immigrant Italians, notably Francesco Passarini and VENANZIO RAUZZINI. His piano teachers included Michael Arne. He made an impromptu début as the Count in Niccolò Piccinni's *La buona figliuola* on 17 May 1777, and went on to sing in Charles Dibdin's *Lionel and Clarissa* and Michael Arne's *Cymon*, before leaving Dublin in 1779, on Rauzzini's advice, to study in Naples.

His most influential teachers were Fedele Fenaroli and GIUSEPPE APRILE, and he enjoyed the patronage of Sir William Hamilton. He made his Italian début in Florence in May 1781, and then sang in various Italian cities including Venice where in 1783 his fortunes took a decisive turn. Count Durazzo, Joseph II's ambassador in Venice, recruited him for the newly created Italian opera company in Vienna. Over the four years Kelly spent there, taking secondary or comic tenor roles, he sang with the best singers of the day, including NANCY STORACE, FRANCESCO BENUCCI and STEFANO MANDINI. Kelly worked with Stephen Storace, Vicente Martín y Soler and Giovanni Paisiello, but his most memorable association was with W.A. Mozart, who wrote the roles of Don Basilio and Don Curzio in *Le nozze di Figaro* for him. He also created the role of Valente in Storace's *Gli sposi malcontenti* (1785), Corrado in Martín y Soler's *Una cosa rara* and Eufemio of Ephesus in Storace's *Gli equivoci* (both 1786).

In his *Reminiscences* he left a vivid picture of his acquaintance with Mozart, both socially and in the opera house. Although Kelly's comments on musical life in Vienna are often superficial, he saw humanity in the round with keen observation and humorous detachment. It is these qualities which make the book so attractive: its first volume, particularly, is a valuable source of information about the music and manners of the time. Even if written with the aid of a rough diary or notes, the *Reminiscences*, which run to some 170,000 words, are a remarkable testimony to Kelly's memory. They were ghosted, not long before Kelly's death, by Theodore Hook, who was described by his great-great-nephew, the English music critic Martin Cooper (1910–86), as 'a man of the theatre, professional writer, almost a professional wag and something of a crook'. Perhaps some of Hook's character colours Kelly's narrative.

In February 1787, with the Storaces and Attwood, Kelly left Vienna for London, visiting Mozart's father in Salzburg en route. Kelly quickly established himself as the principal tenor at Drury Lane, making his début on 20 April. He continued to sing there until 1808, creating the lead roles in several of Stephen Storace's English operas, including Lord William in *The Haunted Tower* (1789), the Seraskier in *The Siege of Belgrade* (1791) and the robber captain in *The Iron Chest* (1796), as well as the Prisoner in the Iron Mask in Thomas Shaw's *The Island of St Marguerite* (1789). But he was unable to sustain a singing career at the King's Theatre in the Haymarket, where he made his first appearance in June 1789 and where he created Iarbas in Storace's *Dido, Queen of Carthage* (1792). In 1793 he became its stage manager, and continued with few interruptions in that capacity for nearly 31 years. Kelly won greater approval for his technique than for the quality of his voice. In his *Memoirs of the Life of John Philip Kemble* (1825), James Boaden wrote:

> His voice had amazing power and steadiness, his compass was extraordinary. In vigorous passages he never cheated the ear with the feeble wailings of falsetto, but sprung upon the ascending fifth with a sustaining energy that often electrified an audience.

Lord Mount Edgcumbe, however, no mean judge, expressed a less favourable view in his *Musical Reminiscences* (1825):

> Though he was a good musician and not a bad singer, having been long in Italy, yet he had retained, or regained, so much of the English

Michael Kelly

vulgarity of manner that he was never greatly liked at this theatre [Drury Lane].

Kelly claimed to have written over 60 theatre pieces between 1797 and 1821. For many of these, however, he contributed just a few songs; at other times he wrote in collaboration. He commanded a limited but prolific vein of melodic invention and seems to have relied on others for harmony and orchestration.

Kelly never married, though he lived with Anna Maria Crouch for some years in what seems to have been a platonic relationship. Kelly was buried in the churchyard of St Paul's, Covent Garden. His niece, Frances Maria Kelly (1790–1882), was an actress and singer of considerable distinction.

M. Kelly: *Reminiscences* (London, 1826, 2/1826/*R* with introduction by A.H. King); ed. R. Fiske (London, 1975)
S.M. Ellis: *The Life of Michael Kelly, Musician, Actor and Bon Viveur* (London, 1930)
T. Walsh: *Opera in Dublin, 1798–1820: Frederick Jones and the Crow Street Theatre* (Oxford, 1993)

Alec Hyatt King/R

Kenny, Yvonne (Denise)

(*b* Sydney, 25 Nov 1950). Australian soprano. She studied in Sydney and Milan, making her début in 1975 at the Queen Elizabeth Hall, London, in the title role of Gaetano Donizetti's *Rosmonda d'Inghilterra*.

The following year she made her Covent Garden début in the première of H.W. Henze's *We Come to the River*, then sang roles ranging from G.F. Handel (Semele and Alcina) and W.A. Mozart (Ilia, Pamina, Servilia and Susanna) to Aennchen, Micaëla, Sophie (*Der Rosenkavalier* and *Werther*), Adina and Benjamin Britten's Helena (*A Midsummer Night's Dream*). In 1984 she created the title role in Gavin Bryars's *Medea* in Lyons. Her roles with Australian Opera have included Mélisande, Jules Massenet's Manon, Leïla, Countess Adèle, Fiordiligi and Handel's Alcina and Cleopatra. At Zürich she added two further Mozart roles to her repertory: Giunia (*Lucio Silla*) and in 1991 Aspasia (*Mitridate, rè di Ponto*), a part she also sang to acclaim at Aix-en-Provence and Covent Garden. Kenny's other Mozart roles include Konstanze, Donna Elvira, Donna Anna, which she sang at Glyndebourne in 1991, and the Countess, which she performed in Washington, DC, and in Munich. She sang Romilda (*Xerxes*) for ENO, and made a notable impression as the Countess (*Capriccio*) in Berlin (1993) and Vienna (1995). She is also admired as an oratorio singer, particularly in Handel, and as a recitalist. Her opera recordings include Adelia (*Ugo conte di Parigi*), the title roles in *Emilia di Liverpool* and Johann Mayr's *Medea in Corinto*, Penelope Rich in *Gloriana* and several of her Mozart roles. In these and in her recordings of such works as *Messiah*, *Elijah* and Gustav Mahler's Fourth Symphony, Kenny reveals a full-toned, flexible voice, a stylish sense of phrase and an excellent coloratura technique.

H. Canning: 'Yvonne Kenny', *Opera*, xliii, 1992, 1385–93

Elizabeth Forbes

Kern, Adele

(*b* Munich, 25 Nov 1901; *d* Munich, 6 May 1980). German soprano. She studied in Munich, making her début there in 1924 as Olympia in *Les contes d'Hoffmann*. She was a member of the famous Clemens Krauss ensembles, first in Frankfurt, later in Vienna and finally in Munich from 1937 to 1943, and again briefly after World War II. In 1938 she sang the part of Mi in Franz Lehár's *Das Land des Lächelns*. She appeared frequently at Salzburg between 1927 and 1935, as Susanna, Despina, Marzelline and Sophie; she also sang at the Teatro Colón (1928) and Covent Garden (1931, 1934). She possessed a light, high, silvery voice of great charm which can be heard in recordings of excerpts from her main roles. Her Zerbinetta was a highlight of the Munich summer festivals in the late 1930s. She retired in 1947.

Harold Rosenthal/R

Khokhlov, Pavel (Akinfiyevich)

(*b* Spassky, Tambov, 21 July/2 Aug 1854; *d* Moscow, 20 Sept 1919). Russian baritone. He studied law in Moscow, also taking lessons in violin and piano, and in singing first with Yury Arnol'd (who upset Khokhlov's voice by making him study bass parts) and later with Aleksandra Aleksandrova-Kochetova. He made his début at the Moscow Bol'shoy as Valentin (19 Feb/3 March 1879), remaining with the company until his retirement in 1900; he also appeared at the Mariinsky in St Petersburg (1881, 1887–8), and sang in concerts in the provinces. His rich, warm voice and generous artistry quickly made an impression, and he was particularly successful as Yevgeny Onegin (singing the role at the first Bol'shoy performance, 11/23 January 1881, and thereafter 138 times in Moscow alone) and as Anton Rubinstein's Demon; he also appeared in Prague (1889) in these two roles, which he virtually made his own. A scrupulous stylist, conscientious in his constantly refreshed study of a role, he was a master both of bel canto and of a more flexible declamatory style, and moreover had a fine stage presence. Various factors, including overwork and drink, led to an early vocal decline, as noted by P.I. Tchaikovsky, who liked and admired Khokhlov, in a letter to Yuuliya Shpazhinskaya of 23 September/5 October 1886. His other roles included Don Giovanni, Giuseppe Verdi's Renato, Di Luna and Giorgio Germont, Richard Wagner's Wolfram and Telramund, Giacomo Meyerbeer's Nélusko and Nevers, Carl Maria von Weber's Ottokar, and many Russian roles including Boris Godunov and Prince Igor.

John Warrack

Kibkalo, Yevgeny (Gavrilovich)

(*b* Kiev, 12 Feb 1932). Russian baritone. He graduated from Vladimir Politkovsky's class at the Moscow Conservatory in 1956, was engaged that year as a soloist by the Bol'shoy, then studied at the La Scala opera school in 1963. His distinctive qualities were his beautiful, even voice and warm tone, his musicality and his excellent sense of ensemble. He sang in the first Bol'shoy performances of Sergey Prokofiev's *War and Peace* (Andrey) and *The Story of a Real Man* (Aleksey); his other roles included P.I. Tchaikovsky's Yeletsky, Mazepa and Yevgeny Onegin; Gioachino Rossini's and W.A. Mozart's Figaro; and Demetrius in Benjamin Britten's *A Midsummer Night's Dream*. He performed in many countries, and was made People's Artist of the RSFSR in 1959. In that year he appeared as Shaklovity in a film version of *Khovanshchina*.

I.M. Yampol'sky/R

Kiepura, Jan

(*b* Sosnowiec, 16 May 1902; *d* Harrison, NY, 15 Aug 1966). Polish tenor. He studied in Warsaw with Tadeusz Leliva, making his début in Lwów as Faust in 1924. He sang at the Vienna Staatsoper (1926–37) as Cavaradossi, Calaf, Rodolfo (*La bohème*), Manrico, Don José and created the Stranger in E.W. Korngold's *Das Wunder der Heliane* (1927, Hamburg). In 1928 Kiepura sang Cavaradossi at the Paris Opéra and Calaf to acclaim at La Scala, where he created Marchese Marcarille in Felice Lattuada's *Le preziose ridicole* (1929). He made his American début at Chicago in 1931 as Cavaradossi and his Metropolitan début in 1938 as Rodolfo, singing there until 1942 as Don José, the Duke, Jules Massenet's Des Grieux and Cavaradossi. He also sang in Chicago (1939–42). Between the wars he took part in symphonic and choral concerts in Kraków. With his wife, the soprano Marta Eggerth, he appeared on Broadway, on tour and in London at the Palace Theatre (1955) in *The Merry Widow*. He made a number of romantic films in the 1930s, which show his ebullient personality, handsome appearance and velvet-toned lyric voice with superb top notes. Other recordings, including popular hit songs by Walter Jurmann, reveal his easy, forward production and lyrical charm.

Leo Riemens/Alan Blyth/R

Kindermann, August

(*b* Potsdam, 6 Feb 1817; *d* Munich, 6 March 1891). German bass-baritone. In 1836 he joined the chorus of the Berlin Hofoper, and in 1839 he was engaged at Leipzig, where he took part in the first performance of Albert Lortzing's *Caramo*. He also created the title role of Lortzing's *Hans Sachs* (1840) and Eberbach in *Der Wildschütz* (1842). In 1846 he went to Munich, where he was engaged at the Hofoper until his retirement in 1889. His very large repertory included W.A. Mozart's Figaro and Sarastro, Hidraot in C.W. Gluck's *Armide*, Indra (*Le roi de Lahore*) and many of Richard Wagner's baritone and bass roles. He sang Wotan in the first performances of *Das Rheingold* (1869) and *Die Walküre* (1870); his repertory also included King Henry (*Lohengrin*), Fafner, Hunding, Hagen, King Mark and Titurel, which he sang at the first performance of *Parsifal* at Bayreuth (1882). For the 40th anniversary of his engagement at Munich he sang Stadinger in Lortzing's *Der Waffenschmied* (1886). His son and three daughters all became singers, the best known of them being Hedwig Reicher-Kindermann.

Elizabeth Forbes

King, James (Ambros)

(*b* Dodge City, KS, 22 May 1925; *d* Naples, FL, 20 Nov 2005). American tenor. After study with Martial Singher and Max Lorenz he began his career as a baritone. As a winner of the American Opera Auditions in Cincinnati, he was sent to Europe in 1961 where he made his professional début in Florence, singing Cavaradossi. His first resident appointment took him to the Deutsche Oper, Berlin (1962), and engagements followed at Salzburg (1962), Vienna (1963), Bayreuth (1965) and La Scala (1968). In the USA he sang at San Francisco, making his début in 1961 as Don José, and at the Metropolitan, where he first appeared in 1966 as Florestan. He sang the Emperor in both the Metropolitan and Covent Garden premières of *Die Frau ohne Schatten*. In 1983 at La Scala he sang the title role in the revival of Luigi Cherubini's *Anacreon*. King's bright, incisive tone, easy top voice and remarkable stamina made him particularly successful in the more lyrical Wagner roles such as Walther von Stolzing, Parsifal (recorded under Pierre Boulez at Bayreuth) and Lohengrin, and as Bacchus in *Ariadne auf Naxos*, which he recorded with Rudolf Kempe; his repertory also included Otello, Siegmund (which can be heard in Karl Böhm's Bayreuth recording of the *Ring* as well as Georg Solti's studio version), the title role in Hans Pfitzner's *Palestrina*, Aegisthus, which he sang at Salzburg in 1989, and the Drum-Major at the Metropolitan in 1990. King was also a sterling soloist in works such as Ludwig van Beethoven's Ninth Symphony, Giuseppe Verdi's Requiem and Gustav Mahler's *Das Lied von der Erde*, all of which he recorded.

Martin Bernheimer/Alan Blyth

Kipnis, Alexander

(*b* Zhitomir, Ukraine, 1/13 Feb 1891; *d* Westport, CT, 14 May 1978). American bass of Ukrainian birth. He studied conducting at the Warsaw Conservatory and singing in Berlin with Ernst Grenzebach. Interned as a Russian alien on the outbreak of World War I, he was soon released and began his career at Hamburg and Wiesbaden, where he spent five years with the Wiesbaden Opera. In 1919 he joined the Berlin Charlottenburg opera (later the Städtische Oper), where he became leading bass (1922–30). Thereafter he was a member of the Berlin Staatsoper (1930–35) and the Vienna Staatsoper (1935–8). In 1934, however, he became an American citizen.

By then he had established himself everywhere as an outstanding Wagner and Mozart bass and a highly distinguished interpreter of Italian and Russian roles. He was much in demand at Bayreuth, singing there between 1927 and 1933, and appeared at the 1937 Salzburg Festival as Sarastro under Arturo Toscanini. In England he sang often at Covent Garden (first as Marcel in *Les Huguenots*, 1927) and for one season at Glyndebourne (Sarastro, 1936); he repeated the latter role at Salzburg in 1937. But his career took him increasingly to America, both North and South. He was particularly appreciated in Chicago, where he was a regular member of the company from 1923 to 1932, and where his 30 roles included as many in Italian and French operas as in German. Between 1926 and 1936 he took part in six seasons at the Colón, Buenos Aires. After a surprisingly late début at the Metropolitan (in 1940 as Gurnemanz) he remained in New York until his retirement in 1946, singing his first Boris Godunov there in 1943. Pogner, King Mark, Ochs and Philip II were among his other most successful roles. With a voice of wide range and variety of colour, as well as of unusual refinement and flexibility for a bass, he also made his mark as a lieder singer, contributing extensively and valuably to the albums of the Hugo Wolf and Johannes Brahms Song Societies. The best of his many operatic recordings are those made in Berlin in the early 1930s, especially Osmin's first song from *Die Entführung* and 'Il lacerato spirito' from *Simon Boccanegra*. Kipnis's papers are in the Mugar Memorial Library, Boston University. His son, Igor Kipnis, was a noted harpsichordist and critic.

A. Frankenstein, E. Arnosi and J. Dennis: 'Alexander Kipnis', *Record Collector*, xxii (1974–5), 51–79 [with discography]; xxiii (1976–7), 166–71 [addenda by C. Dillon]

Desmond Shawe-Taylor/R

Kirchschlager, Angelika

(*b* Salzburg, 1966). Austrian mezzo-soprano. After studying piano at the Mozarteum, she entered the Vienna Music Academy in 1984 to study singing (with Gerhard Kahry and WALTER BERRY) and percussion. Early operatic experiences with the Wiener Kammeroper led to major débuts at Graz, as Octavian, in 1992, and with the Vienna Staatsoper, as Cherubino, in 1993. Her US début, in Seattle, followed in 1997. As a member of the Vienna Staatsoper, Kirchschlager quickly won renown for her bittersweet, sensuous voice, musical refinement and dramatic intensity in roles such as Sesto (*La clemenza di Tito*), Dorabella, Idamante, Rosina (*Il barbiere di Siviglia*), Valencienne (*Die lustige Witwe*) and the Composer (*Ariadne auf Naxos*). She made her La Scala début, as Zerlina, in 1999, and a triumphant Covent Garden début in 2002 as Sophie in the world première of Nicholas Maw's *Sophie's*

Choice. She has returned to Covent Garden to sing Nicklausse (*Les contes d'Hoffmann*, 2003) and Mélisande (2007). In her first Handel role, she was a charismatic Sesto in David McVicker's award-winning production of *Giulio Cesare* at Glyndebourne in 2005. The following year she gave the world première of Julian Anderson's *Heaven is Shy of Earth* at the Proms.

Kirchschlager is a naturally communicative lieder singer with a special affinity for Johannes Brahms and Gustav Mahler. She has appeared frequently at such venues as the Vienna Musikverein, the Wigmore Hall, the Salzburg Festival, Carnegie Hall (debut 2002) and the annual Schubertiade at Schwarzenberg. Among her recordings are discs of arias by J.S. Bach and G.F. Handel, lieder by Gustav and Alma Mahler and E.W. Korngold, Cherubino in René Jacobs' *Le nozze di Figaro*, a duet recital, *Women's Lives and Loves*, with FELICITY LOTT, and a disc of lullabies entitled *When Night Falls*.

Richard Wigmore

Kirkby, Dame (Carolyn) Emma

(*b* Camberley, Surrey, 26 Feb 1949). English soprano. She studied classics at Oxford and singing with Jessica Cash. Her uncommonly pure, crystalline voice, deployed with minimal vibrato, her natural declamation, agile coloratura and her sensitivity to words have been widely admired by interpreters of early, Renaissance and Baroque music and have served as a model for many specialists in this repertory. She made her operatic début as Mother Nature in Matthew Locke and Christopher Gibbons's *Cupid and Death* at Bruges in 1983 and her first American appearances as Dorinda in G.F. Handel's *Orlando* in a 1989 tour. Kirkby has sung frequently under the direction of Andrew Parrott, Anthony Rooley and Christopher Hogwood in a repertory ranging from 14th-century Italian songs to arias by Joseph Haydn and W.A. Mozart, and has been a regular member of Gothic Voices, Chiaroscuro and Rooley's Consort of Musicke. In 1989 she sang Venus in Daniel Purcell's, John Weldon's and John Eccles's settings of *The Judgment of Paris* at the BBC Promenade Concerts. Her many recordings include *Dido and Aeneas*, *Venus and Adonis*, *Orlando*, Claudio Monteverdi's *Orfeo*, Johann Hasse's *Cleofide*, discs of G.F. Handel cantatas and arias, and a wide range of Italian cantatas and madrigals, English songs and Baroque and Classical choral works. In 2001 Kirkby made the world première recording of the newly identified Handel *Gloria*. She was made a Dame Commander of the British Empire in 2007.

Nicholas Anderson

Kirkby-Lunn, Louise.

See LUNN, KIRKBY.

Kirsten, Dorothy

(*b* Montclair, NJ, 7 July 1910; *d* Los Angeles, 18 Nov 1992). American soprano. She studied at the Juilliard School of Music, then with Astolfo Pescia in Rome. She made her début in 1940 as Pousette in *Manon* with the Chicago Opera Company, where she also sang Musetta to GRACE MOORE's Mimì. She made her début at the New York City Opera, as Violetta, in 1944, and at the Metropolitan, as Mimì, the following year; she sang at the Metropolitan intermittently for 30 years, making her farewell as Tosca in 1975. Her roles in the house included Violetta, Louise (which she had studied with Gustave Charpentier), Marguerite, Charles Gounod's Juliet, Manon Lescaut (her favourite part), Minnie and Fiora (*L'amore dei tre re*). She also appeared regularly at the San Francisco Opera, where she undertook Cressida in the American première of William Walton's opera in 1955 and sang Blanche in Francis Poulenc's *Dialogues des Carmélites*. She made guest appearances in Sacramento, France, England, the Soviet Union and South America, and also appeared in the film *The Great Caruso* (1951). Kirsten recorded extracts from several of her roles (most notably her feisty Minnie), which reveal her gleaming, if not particularly beguiling, *lirico spinto* soprano and her unfailingly secure technique. She published an autobiography, *A Time to Sing* (1982).

L. Rasponi: *The Last Prima Donnas* (New York, 1982), 284
A. Blyth: Obituary, *Opera*, xliv (1993), 163–4

Max De Schauensee

Klimentova, Maria Nikolayevna

(*b* Moscow, 1857; *d* Moscow, 1946). Russian soprano. She studied at the Moscow Conservatory and while still a student there, in 1879, she created Tatyana in *Yevgeny Onegin* at the Malïy Theatre. She joined the Bol'shoy in 1880 and sang there for a decade. She took part in another Tchaikovsky première, as Oxana in *Cherevichki* (1887), and continued to sing Tatyana throughout her career, as well as Tamara (*The Demon*) and other Russian and French roles. Later she taught in Paris, and remained there until near her death.

Elizabeth Forbes

Klobásková, Vyčichlová.

See DOMANÍNSKÁ, LIBUŠE.

Klose, Margarete

(*b* Berlin, 6 Aug 1902; *d* Berlin, 14 Dec 1968). German mezzo-soprano. After study in Berlin with Marschalk and Bültemann she made her début at Ulm in 1927. From 1928 to 1931 she was a member of the Mannheim Opera, first coming to the notice of a wider public during the Paris Wagner season of 1929 when the first *Ring* in German was given at the Champs-Elysées by the Bayreuth ensemble. From 1931 she was a member of the Berlin Staatsoper. In 1935 she sang Ortrud under Thomas Beecham at Covent Garden and in 1936 she began to appear at Bayreuth. She was heard in London again in 1937 as Fricka, Waltraute and Brangäne, and in 1939 she appeared in Rome for the first time. In December 1945 she sang C.W. Gluck's *Orfeo ed Euridice* with the re-formed Berlin Staatsoper in its opening opera at the Admiralspalast. She went on to sing in North and South America, at the Salzburg Festival and in Italy, Spain, London, Vienna and Coburg. In 1949 she moved from the Berlin Staatsoper to the Städtische Oper, returning to her old company in 1958 and retiring in 1961. Klose's clear, rich voice and dignified stage bearing fitted her admirably for the Wagnerian mezzo roles in which she was best known (as can be heard in many recordings); she was a distinguished Clytemnestra in *Elektra* and *Iphigénie en Aulide*, and she also appeared with success as Gluck's Orpheus, Carmen, the Kostelnička (*Jenůfa*), Delilah and Albert's mother (*Albert Herring*), and in many of the Verdi mezzo roles.

Peter Branscombe

Kmentt, Waldemar

(*b* Vienna, 2 Feb 1929). Austrian tenor. He studied singing at the Vienna Music Academy under Adolf Vogel, Elisabeth Rado and Hans Duhan. While a student he toured the Netherlands and Belgium with an ensemble from the academy that included WALTER BERRY and Fritz Uhl, singing in *Die Fledermaus* and *Le nozze di Figaro*. In 1950 he sang the tenor part in Ludwig van Beethoven's Ninth Symphony under Karl Böhm in Vienna, and the following year sang the Prince in Prokofiev's *The Love for Three Oranges* at the Vienna Volksoper. He was soon singing Mozart roles at the Theater an der Wien (the home of the Staatsoper until 1955) and sang Jaquino in *Fidelio* at the opening performance of the rebuilt Staatsoper. Kmentt sang regularly at the Salzburg Festival, where his roles included Idamantes, Ferrando, Gabriel in Frank Martin's *Le mystère de la Nativité*, and Tamino. In 1968 he sang Idomeneus at La Scala. He sang Walther von Stolzing at Bayreuth (1968–70) and was an engaging Eisenstein (*Die Fledermaus*), as his recording with Herbert von Karajan confirms. He continued to sing comprimario roles at the Vienna Staatsoper until well into his 60s. His repertory included Erik, Bacchus and the Emperor (*Die Frau ohne Schatten*). Kmentt also appeared regularly in concerts and as a recitalist, and recorded Ludwig van Beethoven's *Missa solemnis* with Otto Klemperer. His sappy, flexible tenor was seconded by a typically Viennese charm of manner.

Harold Rosenthal/Alan Blyth

Kniplová [née Pokorná], Naděžda

(*b* Ostrava, 18 April 1932). Czech soprano. Raised in a musical family, she studied singing at the Prague Conservatory with Jarmila Vavrdová (1947–53) and at the Academy of Musical Arts with Ungrová and Zdeněk Otava (1954–8). After engagements at Ústí nad Labem (1957–9) and the Janáček Opera, Brno (1959–64), she became a principal of the Prague National Theatre, having won prizes at the Geneva (1958), Vienna and Toulouse (1959) competitions. From her Brno days she was noted for the dramatic force of her performances; the sonorous, metallic, dark timbre of her voice was particularly well suited to the dramatic soprano roles of Czech opera – notably Bedřich Smetana's Libuše, Milada (*Dalibor*) and Anežka (*Two Widows*), and Leoš Janáček's Kostelnička, Kabanicha and Emilia Marty. She also sang Tosca, Aida, Senta, Ortrud, Brünnhilde and Isolde. In Brno she created splendid characterizations of Sergey Prokofiev's Renata (*The Fiery Angel*), Katerina in Bohuslav Martinů's *The Greek Passion*, Dmitry Shostakovich's Katerina Izmaylova and Béla Bartók's Judith (*Bluebeard's Castle*). Her many international appearances, notably those at Vienna, Munich, Hamburg, San Francisco and New York, were praised for their dramatic intensity, though some critics commented on a certain lack of vocal purity or steadiness.

Alena Němcova

Knote, Heinrich

(*b* Munich, 26 Nov 1870; *d* Garmisch, 12 Jan 1953). German tenor. His long career was almost entirely centred on Munich, where he remained for nearly 40 years, concentrating on the heroic Wagner repertory, until his farewell in *Siegfried* on 15 December 1931. Between 1901 and 1913 he made many successful appearances at Covent Garden, and was even more appreciated at the Metropolitan (1904–8), where his performance fees were, at one time, twice those earned by VAN ROOY. Knote was a superior, if typical, Wagnerian Heldentenor, who made many pre-1914 recordings and a further Wagner series as

late as 1930, demonstrating the amazing endurance of his vocal powers.

Desmond Shawe-Taylor

Knüpfer, Paul

(*b* Halle, 21 June 1866; *d* Berlin, 4 Nov 1920). German bass. He studied at Sondershausen, where he made his début in 1885. He sang in Leipzig (1887–98), then from 1898 he was engaged at the Berlin Hofoper (later Staatsoper) until his retirement in 1920. He took part in the disastrous première of Ruggero Leoncavallo's *Der Roland von Berlin* (1904) and sang Ochs in the Berlin première of *Der Rosenkavalier* (1911). He made his Bayreuth début in 1901, alternating as Gurnemanz and Titurel, then sang there regularly till 1906 as the Landgrave, Hunding and King Mark, and returned in 1912 as Pogner. At Covent Garden (1904–8 and 1913–14) he made his début as King Mark, then sang his other Wagner roles, including King Henry and Hagen, as well as Otto Nicolai's Falstaff, Abul Hassan in the first Covent Garden *Barbier von Bagdad* (1906), Ochs in the British première of *Der Rosenkavalier* (1913) and Gurnemanz in the British stage première of *Parsifal* (1914). He was equally gifted in serious or comic roles. His voice was mellow and flexible, though it deteriorated in later years. His many recordings give some idea of his expressive range. He was married to the soprano Marie Egli.

Alan Blyth

Kochańska, Prakseda Marcelina.

See SEMBRICH, MARCELLA.

Kocherga, Anatoly

(*b* Vinnitsa district, 1946). Ukrainian bass. Studies at the Kiev Conservatory and prizes in the Glinka (1971) and Tchaikovsky (1974) competitions led to a period with the Kiev Opera. His international career was launched in 1989, when he sang Shaklovity in the Vienna Staatsoper's *Khovanshchina* under Claudio Abbado. Engagements at Bregenz, Amsterdam (both as Kochubey in *Mazepa*), the Opéra Bastille and La Scala (respectively as Boris Godunov and the Sergeant in *Lady Macbeth of the Mtsensk District*) followed, and he has repeated these roles with success elsewhere and recorded them. Since his Boris at the 1994 Salzburg Easter and Summer festivals he has been particularly associated with the part, singing it in Venice, Turin, Montpellier and with the Vienna Staatsoper in Japan; he has also sung Dosifey (*Khovanshchina*) in

Brussels. He has sung Gremin in Amsterdam (1997) and Field Marshal Kutuzov (*War and Peace*) in Paris (2000). Non-Russian roles earlier in his career included the Commendatore, but subsequently have been mainly in Giuseppe Verdi, including Sparafucile (1997, San Francisco), Pistol, Banquo and the Grand Inquisitor. Non-operatic assignments such as Modest Musorgsky's *Songs and Dances of Death*, Dmitry Shostakovich's 13th Symphony and Leoš Janáček's *Glagolitic Mass* are equally well suited to his imposing voice and presence.

John Allison

Kollo, René

(*b* Berlin, 20 Nov 1937). German tenor. The grandson of Walter Kollo and son of Willi Kollo, both operetta composers, he began his career in light music. After studying with Elsa Varena in Berlin, he made his operatic début at Brunswick in 1965, and was then engaged at Düsseldorf (1967–71). At first he sang lyrical roles: Froh, Lensky, Eisenstein, Vladimir (*Prince Igor*), the Steersman for his Bayreuth début in 1969, Matteo (*Arabella*) at La Scala (1970) and W.A. Mozart's Titus and Tamino at Salzburg (1974). Appearing in Munich, Vienna, Hamburg, Berlin, Venice and Milan he took on heavier Wagnerian roles, notably Parsifal, Erik, Lohengrin and Walther, a part he sang at Bayreuth (1973) and the Salzburg Easter Festival (1974). In 1976 he made débuts at the Metropolitan as Lohengrin and Covent Garden as Siegmund and sang the title role in *Siegfried* in the Bayreuth centenary *Ring*. His other roles included Florestan, Hermann (*Queen of Spades*), Laca (*Jenůfa*), Matteo (*Arabella*), Max (*Der Freischütz*), Bacchus, Tristan, which he sang at Bayreuth in 1981, Tannhäuser, Siegfried (*Götterdämmerung*), Otello, which he sang at Frankfurt in 1988, Canio and Peter Grimes. Kollo's many recordings include Florestan, most of his Wagner and Strauss roles and *Das Lied von der Erde*. He was an intelligent singer, and though his voice inevitably lost the lyrical quality so notable in his 1975 recording of Paul in E.W. Korngold's *Die tote Stadt*, it always kept its firmness and characteristic brightness of timbre.

B. Kayser: 'René Kollo', *Opera*, xl (1989), 1415–21

Elizabeth Forbes

Komissarzhevsky, Fyodor Petrovich

(*b* Kiev province, 1838; *d* Sanremo, 1/14 March 1905). Russian tenor. After studying in St Petersburg and with E. Repetto in Milan, he made his début in 1863 at the Mariinsky Theatre, where he quickly

attained the rank of leading tenor, a position he held until 1880. Among the many roles he created were Don Juan (*The Stone Guest*, 1872), Grigory/Pretender/Dmitry (*Boris Godunov*, 1874), Sinodal (*The Demon*, 1875) and the title role in *Vakula the Smith* (1876). He had a small voice of velvety timbre, heard to advantage in parts such as Gennaro (*Lucrezia Borgia*), Faust, Fra Diavolo and Jontek (*Halka*). He was noted for his impeccable diction and for his refined phrasing and characterization. From 1883 to 1888 he was a professor at the Moscow Conservatory, teaching drama as well as singing; Konstantin Stanislavsky was one of his pupils.

Boris Semeonoff

Konetzni(-Wiedmann) [Konerczny], Anny

(*b* Ungarisch-Weisskirchen, 12 Feb 1902; *d* Vienna, 6 Sept 1968). Austrian soprano, sister of HILDE KONETZNI. After a short period in the Volksoper chorus, she studied at the Vienna Conservatory with Erik Schmedes and made her stage début at Chemnitz in 1927 as a contralto. She sang Brünnhilde to her sister's Siegelinde. After guest appearances in the *Ring* at Paris in 1929 she joined the Berlin Staatsoper in 1931, singing Helena (*Les vêpres siciliennes*), Ariadne and the Marschallin in her first season. In 1933 she appeared at Buenos Aires, then became a member of the Vienna Staatsoper. In 1935 she sang Brünnhilde under Thomas Beecham at Covent Garden, returning in three of the next four seasons, and was invited back for *Die Walküre* in 1951. This was her début role at the Metropolitan, where she appeared in the 1934–5 season as Brünnhilde, Venus, Ortrud and Isolde. She also sang several roles at Salzburg, including Reiza (*Oberon*) under Bruno Walter in 1934 and Isolde for Arturo Toscanini in 1936, and appeared in Rome, Paris and other leading centres. Her voice, in its prime a strong, pure dramatic soprano, was not supported by a particularly impressive stage presence. She retired in 1955, and illness obliged her to give up teaching at the Vienna Music Academy in 1957. Her singing is preserved in various compilations of recordings originally made between the 1930s and 50s; of these the most impressive are excerpts from *Tristan* and *Parsifal*.

Peter Branscombe

Konetzni, Hilde

(*b* Vienna, 21 March 1905; *d* Vienna, 20 April 1980). Austrian soprano, sister of ANNY KONETZNI. She studied at the Vienna Conservatory and made her début at Chemnitz in 1929 (Sieglinde to her sister's Brünnhilde). In 1932 she joined the German Theatre in Prague, and after a successful guest appearance as Elisabeth in *Tannhäuser* in Vienna she joined the Staatsoper in 1936. That year she first sang at Salzburg (Donna Elvira). Her Covent Garden début was in 1938 (First Lady in *Zauberflöte* and Chrysothemis in *Elektra*); she is remembered especially for stepping into the Marschallin's clothes at a moment's notice to save a *Rosenkavalier* performance when LOTTE LEHMANN fell ill. She appeared in *The Bartered Bride*, *Tannhäuser*, the *Ring* and *Don Giovanni* the following season at Covent Garden, and was heard as Leonore (*Fidelio*) during the 1947 Vienna Staatsoper season. She also sang at Glyndebourne (Donna Elvira in 1938) and in the USA, and in 1955 returned to sing Sieglinde and Gutrune in the Covent Garden *Ring*. Although she and her sister both sang the Marschallin, Hilde Konetzni tended to prefer the more lyrical roles. Towards the end of her career she added to an extensive repertory a number of small character parts of the kind beloved of Viennese audiences. Her Leonore survives in an incandescent Vienna concert performance under Karl Böhm from 1944. She also created the title role in Heinrich Sutermeister's monodrama *Niobe* in Zurich in 1946. Towards the end of her career she added to an extensive repertory, principally of lyrical roles, a number of small character parts, including one in the Salzburg première in 1961 of Rudolf Wagner-Régeny's *Das Bergwerk zu Falun*. She recorded Richard Strauss songs with the composer as accompanist, while her Sieglinde and Gutrune in Wilhelm Furtwängler's La Scala *Ring* (1950) and Sieglinde in the RAI broadcast relays of 1953 are worthy mementos of her Wagner.

Peter Branscombe

Kónya, Sándor

(*b* Sarkad, 23 Sept 1923; *d* Ibiza, 20 May 2002). Hungarian tenor. He studied in Budapest, Detmold and Milan, making his début in 1951 at Detmold as Turiddu. He sang at Darmstadt in 1954, and the following year joined the Städtische (later Deutsche) Oper, Berlin. He was also a member of the Frankfurt Opera Company. In 1956 he created Leandro in H.W. Henze's *König Hirsch*, and sang Nureddin (*Der Barbier von Bagdad*) at Edinburgh. He made his Bayreuth (1958), Paris (1959), Florence, Metropolitan (1961) and Covent Garden (1963) débuts as Lohengrin, his best-known role. At La Scala (1960) he sang Parsifal; at San Francisco (1960–65) he appeared as Dick Johnson, Lohengrin, Pinkerton, Radames, Don Alvaro and Riccardo

(*Ballo*). At the Metropolitan, where he sang until 1975, his roles included Walther, Parsifal, Erik, Max, Edgardo (*Lucia*), Don Carlos, Cavaradossi and Calaf. His strong, clear voice, equally suitable for German or Italian roles, lay between the lyrical and the heroic.

Alan Blyth

Korjus, Miliza

(*b* Warsaw, 17 Aug 1913; *d* Culver City, CA, 27 Aug 1980). Polish soprano. Daughter of a Swedish diplomat, she travelled widely in her youth, studying, it is said, in as many as 16 conservatories; she also learnt from recordings of famous coloratura sopranos such as TETRAZZINI and GALLI-CURCI. In 1929 she gave her first public recital and toured eastern Europe. She was engaged by the Berlin Staatsoper in 1933, making her début as Gilda in *Rigoletto*. Other lyric and coloratura roles followed, but she became most widely known through some best-selling records and her appearance in *The Great Waltz* (1938), a film about the life of Johann Strauss. In the same year Korjus toured the United States where she reappeared with considerable success at Carnegie Hall, New York, in 1944, having meanwhile lived in Mexico. She continued to give concerts but never returned to opera or films. The best of her recordings, such as the Prayer from *Lakmé*, show a distinctive tone and style. Her range and flexibility were exceptional and, with her attractive appearance, might have ensured a career comparable to that of her contemporary, LILY PONS: perhaps there was not room in the USA for both.

J.B. Steane

Környei [von Konvey], Béla

(*b* Krumau [now Český Krumlov, Czech Republic], 18 May 1875; *d* Budapest, 22 April 1925). Hungarian tenor. He sang bass in the Folk Theatre chorus, later taking solo parts at Temesvár (now Timişoara, Romania) as a baritone and returning to the Folk Theatre in 1907 as Don José. The heroic power and beauty of his voice, which compensated for dramatic deficiencies, assured his success, principally in Giuseppe Verdi and Giacomo Puccini. From 1915 to 1918 he was a member of the Vienna Staatsoper, where he created Bacchus in the second version of *Ariadne auf Naxos* (1916). In 1918 he returned to Budapest, where he died while still at the height of his career. Numerous recordings preserve his art.

Péter P. Várnai

Korsov, Bogomir Bogomirovich
[Gering, Gottfried]

(*b* St Petersburg, 19 Feb/3 March 1843; *d* Tbilisi, 1920). Russian baritone. After studies in St Petersburg with Luigi Piccioli and in Milan with Giovanni Corsi, he made his début in Turin in 1868. He returned to Russia the following year, singing at the Mariinsky, until 1882, and thereafter at the Bol'shoy until 1904. In Moscow he created the roles of Mazeppa (1884), the Fiend (P.I. Tchaikovsky's *The Slippers*, 1887) and Aleko (1893). Other important roles included the title roles in *Boris Godunov*, Anton Rubinstein's *The Demon* and Judas in *Die Maccabäer* (1877), and Camille Saint-Saëns's *Henry VIII* (Russian première, 1897, Moscow). His German antecedents were said to be reflected in the care he applied to all aspects of his characterizations.

Boris Semeonoff

Koryakin, Mikhail Mikhaylovich

(*b* Kochetka, Kharkiv province, 19/31 March 1850; *d* St Petersburg, 18/30 Jan 1897). Russian bass. After completing his studies with Alexandra Alexandrova-Kochetova at the Moscow Conservatory in 1878, he made successful débuts that year in both Moscow and St Petersburg, remaining at the Mariinsky Theatre until his untimely death at the height of his career. He took part in the premières of important Russian operas, notably as Thibaut in *The Maid of Orléans* (1881), Bermyata in *The Snow Maiden* (1882), Gremin in the premiere of the revised version of *Yevgeny Onegin* (1885); Kichiga in *The Enchantress* (1887) and Konchak in *Prince Igor* (1890). A true *basso profondo*, he excelled in comic and fantastic parts, but his extensive repertory also embraced more conventional roles, such as Ivan Susanin and the Village Head (*May Night*).

Boris Semeonoff

Koshetz [Koshits], Nina (Pavlovna)

(*b* Kiev, 18/30 Dec 1894; *d* Santa Ana, CA, 14 or 15 May 1965). Ukrainian soprano. The daughter of Pavel Koshitz, a leading tenor at the Bol'shoy, she was trained in Moscow, first as a pianist, and then as a singer under Sergey Taneyev. She made her début as Tatyana in *Yevgeny Onegin* with the Zimin Private Opera company in 1913, and remained with the company until 1919. During this period she also toured Russia and in 1917 appeared as Tatyana at the Mariinsky, Petrograd. Other roles included Lisa in *The Queen of Spades*, Marina in *Boris Godunov*, Tosca, and Electra in Taneyev's *Oresteya*. In 1920 she left Russia and joined the Chicago Opera Association,

singing Fata Morgana in the première of *The Love for Three Oranges* in 1921. She sang as a guest artist with the Russian Opera Company in New York and on tour in 1922, and in 1924 was at the Colón, Buenos Aires. The later 1920s were spent largely in France, where she sang at the Paris Opéra in 1925, and at the Trocadéro in 1927 in the first Paris production of Nikolay Rimsky-Korsakov's *Sadko*. There were further concert seasons and occasional operatic appearances in Europe and the USA; in 1940 she retired to Hollywood, where she managed a restaurant and appeared in several films. Her few recordings, prized by collectors, show a clear, steady voice excitingly combined with an imaginative, emotionally charged style.

J. Dennis: 'Nina Pavlovna Koshetz', *Record Collector*, xvii (1966–8), 53–61 [with discography by V. Liff]
M. Scott: *The Record of Singing*, ii (London, 1979), 23–5

J.B. Steane

Köth, Erika

(*b* Darmstadt, 15 Sept 1927; *d* Speyer, 21 Feb 1989). German soprano. She began her musical studies in Darmstadt in 1942 with Elsa Blank and after an interruption resumed them in 1945. She made her début in 1948 at Kaiserslautern as Philine in *Mignon*; engagements followed at Karlsruhe (1950–53), Munich (from 1953) and Berlin (from 1961). She sang at Covent Garden in 1953 with the Munich company as the Fiakermilli (*Arabella*) and the Italian Soprano in the English première of *Capriccio*. She appeared regularly at Salzburg (1955–64) as the Queen of Night and Konstanze, and at Bayreuth (1965–8) as the Woodbird. It was as a coloratura singer that she established herself in Germany. Her repertory included Lucia, Donna Elvira, Susanna, Violetta, Gilda, Sophie and Zerbinetta. She also sang Igor Stravinsky's Nightingale and Anne Trulove.

Harold Rosenthal/R

Kowalski, Jochen

(*b* Wachow, Brandenburg, 30 Jan 1954). German countertenor. He studied in Berlin, making his début while still a student as David in *Die Meistersinger* at the Komische Oper and then joining the company. In 1985 he sang the title role of G.F. Handel's *Giustino*, and repeated the part in Vienna (1986) and Schwetzingen (1989). His unusually wide repertory includes the title role and Ptolemy in Handel's *Giulio Cesare*, Daniel (*Belshazzar*), Annius (*La clemenza di Tito*), Fyodor (*Boris Godunov*), Benjamin Britten's Oberon and C.W. Gluck's Orpheus, which he sang during the Komische Oper's visit to Covent

Garden (1989) and with the Royal Opera in 1991. With that house he also sang Prince Orlovsky (*Die Fledermaus*), Orpheus and Pharnaces (*Mitridate, re di Ponto*), which he repeated in Amsterdam (1992). He sang Otto (*L'incoronazione di Poppea*) in Salzburg in 1993, and the following year appeared as Gioachino Rossini's Tancredi in Berlin. In 1995 he created Creon in Rolf Liebermann's *Freispruch für Medea* in Hamburg. He also appeared in Munich, Houston, Paris and Düsseldorf. Kowalski's recordings include Didimus (*Theodora*), Orpheus and discs of Baroque arias. His voice, sweet-toned, flexible and unusually resonant for a countertenor, is equally well suited to Baroque, Classical and contemporary music, while he is a powerful and expressive actor.

Elizabeth Forbes

Kožená, Magdalena

(*b* Brno, 26 May 1973). Czech mezzo-soprano. She studied at the Brno Conservatory and with Eva Blahová at the college of Peforming Arts in Bratislava. In 1995 she won the International Mozart Competition in Salzburg and the following year was engaged at the Vienna Volksoper. In Brno she has sung roles including Dorabella and Isabella (*L'italiana in Algeri*). Further afield, she made her Drottningholm Festival début, as Paris in C.W. Gluck's *Paride ed Elena*, in 1998, and her débuts at the Châtelet in Paris, as Gluck's Orpheus, and the Vienna Festival, as Nero in *L'incoronazione di Poppea*, in 2000. In 2001 she appeared as Cherubino in the Aix-en-Provence Festival. Kožená devotes much of her time to concert and recital work, and has performed throughout Europe with Marc Minkowski and Les Musiciens du Louvre. Her recordings include an acclaimed solo début recital of Czech songs for DG, Bach cantatas and a disc of Handel Italian cantatas, in which her agility, dramatic flair and subtlety of colouring have been widely admired.

Richard Wigmore

Kozlovsky, Ivan Semyonovich

(*b* Mar'yanovka, Kiev province, 11/24 March 1900; *d* Moscow, 21 Dec 1993). Ukrainian tenor. He graduated from the Kiev Institute of Music and Drama in 1920, having made his début in 1918 at Poltava. He joined the Bol'shoy Theatre in 1926 and was made People's Artist of the USSR in 1940. Kozlovsky was the most popular Soviet singer of his time. The distinctive features of his singing were his clear, silvery tone and flexible upper register extending to *e‴*, his remarkable technique, expressive use of words and

finished phrasing. A versatile artist and a fine actor, he sang such contrasting roles as Lensky, Berendey (*The Snow Maiden*), Lohengrin and the Holy Fool (*Boris Godunov*). From 1938 to 1941 Kozlovsky directed his own opera company and took part in C.W. Gluck's *Orfeo ed Euridice* and Jules Massenet's *Werther*.

I.M. Yampol'sky

Kraeckmann, Arthur.

See ENDRÈZE, ARTHUR.

Krásová, Marta

(*b* Protivín, 16 March 1901; *d* Vráž u Berouna, 20 Feb 1970). Czech mezzo-soprano. She took up singing on the advice of the violinist Otakar Ševčík and studied with Olga Borová-Valoušková, Růžena Maturová and, in Vienna, M. Ullanovský. In 1922 she joined the Slovak National Theatre in Bratislava, where under the conductor Oskar Nedbal she changed from soprano to mezzo roles. She made her début at the Prague National Theatre as Azucena (1926) and was a member of the company from 1928 to 1966.

To her musicality, excellent technique, breath control and wide range was allied a great talent as an actress with graceful movement and a rich imagination. She was an outstanding Isabella in Zdeněk Fibich's *Bride of Messina*, Róza in *The Secret*, Ježibaba in *Rusalka* and Death in Rudolf Karel's *Death the Neighbour*; her non-Czech roles included Amneris, Eboli, Carmen, C.W. Gluck's Orpheus and the Countess in *The Queen of Spades*. Her finest performance was as the Kostelnička in Leoš Janáček's *Jenůfa*. She regularly sang lieder, achieving her greatest success in Antonín Dvořák's Biblical Songs and in Gustav Mahler. Josef Bohuslav Foerster, Vítězslav Novák and K.B. Jirák dedicated songs to her. She appeared as a guest in many opera houses in Europe and in the USA (1937) including Hamburg, Dresden, Madrid, Paris, Moscow and Warsaw, and made many recordings, including Dvořák's *Stabat mater* with the Czech PO under Václav Talich. She was made National Artist in 1958.

Alena Němcová

Kraus, Alfredo

(*b* Las Palmas, Canary Islands, 24 Sept 1927; *d* Madrid, 10 Sept 1999). Spanish tenor. A pupil of Mercedes Llopart, he made his début in 1956 at Cairo in *Rigoletto* and *Tosca* and was soon appearing in various Italian theatres, making his La Scala début in 1958. He then sang in Spain, at Covent Garden (1959, Edgardo opposite SUTHERLAND's Lucia) and again at La Scala (1960, Elvino), where he frequently returned. He also sang frequently in the USA, particularly at the Metropolitan where he made his début in 1966 in *Rigoletto* and subsequently sang Nemorino, Ernesto, Tonio (*La fille du régiment*), Charles Gounod's Romeo and other roles. Kraus's voice was smooth, bright and well schooled, with an extensive top register up to *d''*. He was considered the best light lyric tenor of his generation, and the elegance and stylishness of his singing, combined with warmth of expression and a handsome stage presence, made him the ideal interpreter of such aristocratic roles as Don Ottavio, Almaviva, Alfredo, Faust and Jules Massenet's Des Grieux, Werther and Hoffmann, which he sang at Covent Garden in 1991. He continued singing into his 70s with little deterioration in his tone quality. He recorded extensively; among his early sets, his Ferrando in Karl Böhm's *Così fan tutte* and Fenton in Georg Solti's *Falstaff* reveal his plangent tone and elegant style at their best, as does his Alfredo to CALLAS's Violetta in a live recording of *La traviata* from Lisbon (1958). His later recording of Werther is a valuable souvenir of his work in French opera.

R. Celletti: 'Alfredo Kraus', *Opera*, xxvi (1975), 17–21
E. Forbes: 'Alfredo Kraus and Werther', *Opera*, xlii (1991), 1131–6

Rodolfo Celletti/Alan Blyth

Kraus, Ernst

(*b* Erlangen, 8 June 1863; *d* Wörthsee, 6 Sept 1941). German tenor. He studied in Munich with Anna Schimon-Regan, and later in Milan with Cesare Galliera. He made his début at Mannheim in 1893 as Tamino; after two seasons with the Damrosch Opera Company in the USA he was engaged as leading Heldentenor at the Royal Opera House, Berlin (later Staatsoper), from 1898 to 1924. He sang regularly at Bayreuth from 1899 to 1909 as Walther, Erik, Siegmund and Siegfried, and created Heinrich in Ethel Smyth's *Der Wald* (1902). He sang the title role in the German première of *Dalibor* (1904) and Herod in the first London *Salome* at Covent Garden in 1910, having already appeared there between 1900 and 1907 in the Wagnerian repertory. He sang at the Metropolitan during the 1903–4 season, making his début as Siegmund. Kraus was one of the earliest Wagner singers to record extensively, the early process catching some hardness in his forceful tenor. His son Richard Kraus was a conductor.

Harold Rosenthal/Alan Blyth

Kraus, Otakar

(*b* Prague, 10 Dec 1909; *d* London, 28 July 1980). British baritone of Czech birth. He studied in Prague and with Fernando Carpi in Milan, made his début at Brno in 1935 as Amonasro, then sang with the Bratislava Opera (1936–9). He settled in England in 1940 and appeared at the Savoy Theatre in that year in Modest Musorgsky's *The Fair at Sorochintsï*. From 1943 to 1946 he sang with the Carl Rosa Opera Company, created Tarquinius in *The Rape of Lucretia* (1946) and joined the English Opera Group. After a season with the Netherlands Opera (1950–51), he joined the Covent Garden company and sang there until 1973, creating Diomede in *Troilus and Cressida* (1954) and King Fisher in *The Midsummer Marriage* (1955). He was also a notable Amonasro, Iago, Scarpia and Orestes. His formidable Alberich was much admired at Covent Garden, where he sang under Rudolf Kempe; Kempe then took him to Bayreuth, where he repeated the role (1960–62), later preserved on CD. In 1951 he created Nick Shadow in *The Rake's Progress* at Venice (which was recorded) and repeated the part at La Scala and Glyndebourne. After leaving Covent Garden he taught in London; his pupils included GWYNNE HOWELL, ROBERT LLOYD and JOHN TOMLINSON. Kraus established himself as a first-rate singing actor, always a vital and striking stage figure and a master of make-up.

H. Rosenthal: 'Otakar Kraus', *Opera*, xxiv (1973), 1067–72

Harold Rosenthal/Alan Blyth

Krause, Tom

(*b* Helsinki, 5 July 1934). Finnish baritone. Studying medicine at Helsinki he became interested in jazz and dance music, developing a talent for singing that took him to the Vienna Akademie für Musik in 1956. He made his operatic début in Berlin (1959) as Escamillo and quickly gained a reputation in opera and concert throughout Germany and Scandinavia. His career was based in Hamburg, where, with the basic repertory of W.A. Mozart, Giuseppe Verdi and Richard Wagner, he also appeared in such rarities as Gioachino Rossini's *La pietra del paragone* (1963) and G.F. Handel's *Jephtha* (1964); he was awarded the rank of Kammersänger there in 1967. The Herald in *Lohengrin* was his first role at Bayreuth (1962) and the Count in *Capriccio* his first in England (1963, Glyndebourne). He sang in the American première of Benjamin Britten's *War Requiem* and made his début at the Metropolitan Opera as Mozart's Count Almaviva in 1967, reappearing there every season until 1973. From 1968, when he performed Don Giovanni, he has appeared regularly at the

Salzburg Festival, singing in Olivier Messiaen's *Saint François d'Assise* there in 1998. His Paris Opéra début occurred in 1973 and he has also sung at La Scala and Covent Garden. Krause's other major roles include Don Alfonso, Guglielmo, Pizarro, Amonasro, Amfortas, Titurel (which he sang at the Opéra Bastille, Paris, in 1999) and Golaud. He took part in the premières of Ernst Krenek's *Der goldene Bock* (1964) and Humphrey Searle's *Hamlet* (1968), both in Hamburg. In 1990 *Opera* magazine described his Don Alfonso (*Così fan tutte*) as 'unforgettable' and sung 'in wonderful voice'. His recordings include recitals of German lieder and songs by Modest Musorgsky and Jean Sibelius as well as a wide range of religious and operatic music; all show a firm, resonant voice, a sound technique and a power of vivid characterization.

J.B. Steane/R

Krauss, Fritz

(*b* Lehenhammer, 16 June 1883; *d* Überlingen, 28 Feb 1976). German tenor. After studying in Munich, Berlin and Milan, he made his début in Bremen in 1911. Engagements followed in Danzig and Kassel, and he was a house tenor at Cologne from 1915 to 1921, when he was called to the Staatsoper in Munich. There he enjoyed his greatest successes until his retirement in 1943. In 1931 he created the role of Asmus Modiger in Hans Pfitzner's *Das Herz*. He was also a regular guest at the Vienna Staatsoper, took the role of Ferrando in the first performances of *Così fan tutte* ever given at the Salzburg Festival, and was much admired at Covent Garden in 1926–7 as Walther von Stolzing, Don Ottavio, Belmonte and Florestan. However, to judge from recordings, Krauss's most impressive role was Lohengrin, which showed his strong, shining tenor at its best. He was also a notable Huon (*Oberon*), Radames, Tannhäuser, Siegmund, Parsifal and Hoffmann.

Alan Blyth

Krebs, Helmut

(*b* Dortmund, 8 Oct 1913; *d* Dahlem, 30 Aug 2007). German tenor. After studies at the Dortmund conservatory and the Berlin Hochschule für Musik, he made his stage début in 1938 at the Berlin Grosse Volksoper. Following a spell at Düsseldorf from 1945, he joined the Deutsche Oper (Berlin) in 1947, remaining there until his retirement over 40 years later. In 1953 he made his British début as Belmonte (*Entführung*) and Idamantes (*Idomeneo*) at Glyndebourne. The following year he sang Aaron in the first performance (unstaged), in Hamburg,

of *Moses und Aron*, and later appeared in the premières of H.W. Henze's *König Hirsch* (1956) and *Der junge Lord* (1965). He also sang at Covent Garden, La Scala and the Vienna Staatsoper. He was made Kammersänger in 1963. Outside opera, Krebs's evenly controlled technique, wide vocal range, expressive declamation and highly individual timbre were well suited to Baroque music and lieder. He sang the title role in a recording of Claudio Monteverdi's *Orfeo* under August Wenzinger, and made many recordings of J.S. Bach's cantatas and Henze's *Der junge Lord*. His interpretations of the Evangelist in Bach's Passions have been especially admired. Late in his career he recorded music by Bach, W.A. Mozart and Hugo Wolf for the BBC. He began teaching at the Berlin Hochschule für Musik in 1957, and at the Frankfurt Hochschule für Musik in 1966. In 1988 he returned to the Deutsche Oper to sing in Leoš Janáček's *From the House of the Dead*.

Nicholas Anderson

Krull, Annie [Maria Anna]

(*b* nr Rostock, 12 Jan 1876; *d* Schwerin, 14 June 1947). German soprano. She studied in Berlin and made her début at Plauen in 1898. In 1901 she created Diemut in Richard Strauss's *Feuersnot* and sang in the première of Ignacy Jan Paderewski's *Manru*, both in Dresden, where she established herself as principal dramatic soprano until 1912. She created the title role in Strauss's *Elektra* in 1909, repeating the role in 1910 under Thomas Beecham at Covent Garden, where she was compared to her disadvantage with London's first Electra, EDYTH WALKER. Salome was another role in which she was much admired. She spent her last seasons at Mannheim, Weimar and Schwerin, where in 1916 she retired to teach. Her recordings include Act 2 of *Tannhäuser* (1909), in which her Elisabeth is strongly characterized and finely sung.

J.B. Steane

Krusceniski [Riccioni, née Kruszelnicka], Salomea [Krushel'nytska, Solomiya]

(*b* Bilyavyntsi, Halychyna [now Tarnopol'] province, 11/23 Sept 1872; *d* L'viv, 16 Nov 1952). Ukrainian soprano, later naturalized Italian. She studied with Valery Wysocki in Lemberg (now L'viv) and made her début there in 1893, then appeared at Kraków. In 1895 she continued her studies at Milan with Fausta Crespi and during the 1895–6 season at Cremona she appeared in Giacomo Puccini's *Manon Lescaut* and in *Les*

Huguenots. Until 1902 she sang mostly in Odessa, Warsaw and St Petersburg, but a brilliant début at the S Carlo, Naples, in 1903 inaugurated her career in the leading theatres of Italy (La Scala in 1906–7, 1909 and 1915), Spain, Buenos Aires and Uruguay (1906–1913). At La Scala in 1907 she created the title role in Francesco Cilea's *Gloria* in a performance conducted by Arturo Toscanini. She became Italian by marriage in 1910 and retired from the stage in the early 1920s, continuing her concert career until 1929.

A woman of singular beauty and complex personality, she had a flexible, warm and well-focussed voice. At first a fine interpreter of Giacomo Meyerbeer and Giuseppe Verdi, she later appeared in Alfredo Catalani's *Loreley*, *Madama Butterfly* (in the revised version at Brescia in 1904), *Adriana Lecouvreur* and, during the same period, in the works of Richard Wagner (particularly as Brünnhilde) and of Richard Strauss (Salome, Elektra). Though passionate in temperament, Krusceniski avoided the vulgar over-exuberance of many singing actresses of the *verismo* period. She was in fact guided by original and subtle ideas about the theatre, which in some roles, such as Aida and Salome, led her to a highly stylized characterization, marked by hieratic attitudes or an enigmatic oriental languor.

E. Arnosi and J. Dennis: 'Salomea Kruszelnicka', *Record Collector*, xviii (1968–9), 77–88 [with discography by R.L. Autrey]

Rodolfo Celletti/Valeria Pregliasco Gualerzi/R

Kruszelnicka, Salomea.

See KRUSCENISKI, SALOMEA.

Kuen, Paul

(*b* Sulzberg bei Kempten, 8 April 1910; *d* Allgau, April 1997). German tenor. He studied in Munich and made his début in 1933 at Konstanz. After singing in Bamberg, Freiburg, Nuremberg and Dresden, in 1947 he was engaged at the Munich Staatsoper. A fine singer and a superb actor, he had a wide repertory that included Monostatos (*Die Zauberflöte*), Don Basilio (*Le nozze di Figaro*), David (*Die Meistersinger*), Kilian (*Der Freischütz*), Valzacchi (*Der Rosenkavalier*), Baba Mustapha (*Der Barbier von Bagdad*) and the Captain (*Wozzeck*). His most successful part was Mime (*Das Rheingold* and *Siegfried*), which he sang at Bayreuth (1951–7), Covent Garden (1953–4), the Metropolitan (1961–2) and at many other opera houses. He also sang the Witch in *Hänsel und Gretel*.

Elizabeth Forbes

Kuhlmann, Kathleen

(*b* San Francisco, 7 Dec 1950). American mezzo-soprano. After attending the Lyric Opera Center for American Artists, Chicago, she made her début in 1979 as Maddalena (*Rigoletto*) with the Lyric Opera, with which she also sang Bersi (*Andrea Chénier*) and Princess Clarice (*The Love for Three Oranges*). She made her European début in 1980 at Cologne as Preziosilla (*La forza del destino*), followed by Rosina and Nancy (*Martha*). In 1982 she made her débuts at La Scala as Meg Page, San Francisco, and at Covent Garden as Ino/Juno (*Semele*), returning to Covent Garden as Carmen and, in 1992, as Bradamante (*Alcina*). Kuhlmann's other roles include Rosina, Pauline (*The Queen of Spades*), Claudio Monteverdi's Octavia and Penelope, C.W. Gluck's Orpheus, Cenerentola (the role of her Glyndebourne début in 1983), Dorabella, Nicklausse and Charlotte (*Werther*), which she sang for her Metropolitan début in 1989, Arsace, and Isabella (*L'italiana in Algeri*). She has a rich, vibrant tone, an agile florid technique and an exciting dramatic temperament, as can be heard in her recording of Bradamante.

Elizabeth Forbes

Kullman, Charles

(*b* New Haven, CT, 13 Jan 1903; *d* New Haven, 8 Feb 1983). American tenor. He studied at Yale University and the Juilliard School of Music, and also sang at the Indiana University Arts Center. After making his début with the American Opera Company as Pinkerton in 1929 he went to Europe and sang the same role with the Kroll Oper in Berlin in 1931. He later appeared at the Berlin Staatsoper and Covent Garden, and in Vienna and Salzburg. He made his Metropolitan début in 1935 in Charles Gounod's *Faust*. For 25 seasons he sang with the company while still making guest appearances elsewhere. Kullman was one of the most versatile tenors ever to sing with the Metropolitan. He was able to adapt his lyric voice to heavy roles, and his repertory ranged from Tamino and Rinuccio to Tannhäuser and Parsifal. He had an appealing vocal quality and a pleasing stage personality. He was also an admired concert singer and sang in the famous 25th anniversary performance in Vienna of *Das Lied von der Erde* under Bruno Walter in 1936. The recording of the occasion offers a fine souvenir of Kullman's voice and artistry.

C.I. Morgan: 'Charles Kullman', *Record Collector*, xx (1972), 243–58

P. Jackson: *Saturday Afternoons at the Old Met* (New York, 1992)

Alan Blyth

Kunc, Zinka.

See MILANOV, ZINKA.

Kunz, Erich

(*b* Vienna, 20 May 1909; *d* Vienna, 8 Sept 1995). Austrian bass-baritone. A pupil of Theo Lierhammer and Hans Duhan at the Vienna Akademie für Musik, he made his début at Troppau in 1933. After various provincial engagements he became a member of the Vienna Staatsoper in 1940. In 1943 he first sang Beckmesser at Bayreuth, and he soon became a regular singer at Salzburg and other festivals. Covent Garden heard him as Leporello, Guglielmo and Figaro during the 1947 Vienna Staatsoper season; in 1948 he sang Guglielmo with the Glyndebourne company at the Edinburgh Festival, and in 1950 he sang the same role at Glyndebourne, where he had been a member of the chorus in 1936. In 1953 he sang at the Metropolitan Opera for the first time.

An accomplished singing actor with a fine sense of humour and a gift for timing, he excelled in such roles as Papageno, Beckmesser and Figaro. For British tastes his Leporello was found too Austrian, not Italian enough, but with his endearing stage manner he was a firm favourite with Viennese audiences from the beginning, often playing small parts in operetta or Volksoper performances with consummate gusto and vocal skill. He was also an accomplished singer of popular Viennese songs, and recorded a considerable number. His many recordings of opera include Beckmesser, Papageno, Figaro, Leporello and Guglielmo.

A. Blyth: 'Erich Kunz', *Opera*, xliv (1995), 1285–7 [obituary tribute]

Peter Branscombe

Kurt(-Deri), Melanie

(*b* Vienna, 8 Jan 1880; *d* New York, 11 March 1941). Austrian soprano. She studied in Vienna with Fannie Müller and in 1902 made her début at Lübeck as Elisabeth. After a season in Leipzig she withdrew for further study with LILLI LEHMANN and her sister Marie in Berlin. She joined the Hoftheater, Brunswick, in 1905 and was engaged at Berlin (1908–15). She sang at Covent Garden in 1910 as Sieglinde and Brünnhilde (*Die Walküre*) and in 1914 as Kundry. From 1915 to 1917 she sang at the Metropolitan Opera, making her début as Isolde and singing, as well as the Wagner repertory, the title role in *Iphigénie en Tauride*, Leonore (*Fidelio*), Pamina, Santuzza and the Marschallin. In 1920 she joined the Berlin Volksoper, where she sang

until 1925. She possessed a rich, powerful dramatic soprano voice, evinced in her recordings of Wagner, and had outstanding dramatic presence.

Harold Rosenthal/R

Kurz, Selma

(*b* Biala, Silesia, 15 Oct 1874; *d* Vienna, 10 May 1933). Austrian soprano. Although she made her début in Hamburg as Mignon in 1895, her first appearance at Vienna in the same role in 1899 established that city as the centre of her artistic and private life. She was highly successful in many and varied roles, including Tosca and even Sieglinde, but became particularly famous in the coloratura repertory, notably as Giuseppe Verdi's Gilda and Oscar. In 1900 she created the role of the Princess in Alexander von Zemlinksy's *Es war einmal*. Gifted with a voice of remarkable purity, sweetness and ease, she also possessed a shake of amazing perfection and duration, which she was accustomed to display – not inappropriately – in an inserted cadenza to Oscar's teasing 'Saper vorreste'. Between 1904 and 1907, and again in 1924, she dazzled Covent Garden audiences in these and other parts. In 1916 she became the first Zerbinetta in the revised version of Richard Strauss's *Ariadne auf Naxos* in Vienna, where she continued to sing until 1926. Among her many successful recordings are the unaccompanied 'Lockruf' from Karl Goldmark's *Königin von Saba* and numerous versions of her *cheval de bataille*, 'Saper vorreste'.

D. Halban: 'Selma Kurz', *Record Collector*, xiii (1960–61), 51–6 [with discography by A.E. Knight]; xvii (1966–8), 46

D. Halban: 'My Mother Selma Kurz', *Recorded Sound*, no.49 (1973), 128–40 [with discography by A. Kelly, J.F. Perkins and J. Ward]

Desmond Shawe-Taylor

Kusche, Benno

(*b* Freiburg, 30 Jan 1916). German bass-baritone. He studied at Karlsruhe and made his début at Koblenz in 1938 as Melitone (*La forza del destino*). The next year he was engaged at Augsburg. In 1946 he was engaged by the Staatsoper in Munich, where he sang for over 30 years. At Salzburg in 1949 he took part in the first performance of Carl Orff's *Antigonae*. He made his Covent Garden début in 1951 as Beckmesser; in 1953 he appeared there with the Munich company, as La Roche in the British première of *Capriccio*. At Glyndebourne he sang Leporello (1954), Don Fernando in *Fidelio* (1963) and La Roche (1963 and 1964). In 1971 he made his Metropolitan début as Beckmesser. Kusche's repertory included Papageno (which he sang in Walter Felsenstein's 1954 production of *Die Zauberflöte* at the Komische Oper, Berlin), Alberich, Faninal, Figaro, Don Alfonso and Gianni Schicchi. His gifts as a character baritone were deployed most tellingly as Beckmesser and Alberich, both of which he recorded under Rudolf Kempe, and as Faninal, which he sang in the 1979 video recording of Otto Schenk's Munich staging.

Harold Rosenthal/Alan Blyth

Kuznetsova, Mariya Nikolayevna

(*b* Odessa, 1880; *d* Paris, 26 April 1966). Russian soprano. She first went into ballet at St Petersburg, then trained as a singer with Joakim Tartakov. Her operatic début at the Mariinsky Theatre as Marguerite in *Faust* was a triumph, and she remained with the company until 1913. Among the premières in which she took part was Nikolay Rimsky-Korsakov's *The Legend of the Invisible City of Kitezh* (Fevroniya, 1907). From 1908 she developed a reputation abroad, and Paris became her second artistic home. At the Opéra she appeared in Emmanuel Chabrier's *Gwendoline* (1910), Jules Massenet's *Roma* (1912; she had sung in the first performance earlier that year at Monte Carlo), as Aida and Norma, and created roles in Raoul Gunsbourg's *Venise* (1913) and Massenet's *Cléopâtre* (1914). She made her Covent Garden début in 1909 and took part in the famous Thomas Beecham Russian season at Drury Lane in 1914; there she sang Yaroslavna in the first performances of *Prince Igor* in England. As a dancer she also had a great success with her appearances in 1914, first in Paris then at Drury Lane, as Potiphar's wife, in Richard Strauss's ballet *Josephs-Legende*, a role which she created. In the USA she sang with the Manhattan Company and at Chicago, where in 1916 she created a sensation in the first production in America of *Cléopâtre*. She returned to Russia but fled from the Revolution to Sweden, disguised as a cabin-boy and hidden in a trunk. Her operatic career continued and she also sang operetta for a while (at Paris in 1934 she replaced SUPERVIA in Franz Lehár's *Frasquita*). She was still singing in 1936, when a company of Russian émigrés she had formed in 1929 visited Japan. Kuznetsova's repertory ranged from Salome, Aida and Norma to the lighter lyric roles such as Mimì and Charles Gounod's Juliet. With an expressive voice and excellent technique she was the first Russian singer after CHALIAPIN to attach as much importance to acting as to singing. Her vibrant tone and expressive style are well caught on recordings, which include a number of Russian and Spanish songs.

D.C. Kinrade: 'Marija Nikolaevna Kuznecova', *Record Collector*, xii (1958–60), 156–9 [with partial discography by H. Barnes]

J.B. Steane, Harold Barnes

L

Labbette, Dora [Perli, Lisa]

(*b* Purley, 4 March 1898; *d* Purley, 3 Sept 1984). English soprano. She studied at the GSM, winning the gold medal, and with Lisa Lehmann on a Melba Scholarship. Boosey's Ballad Concerts and her Wigmore Hall début in 1917 led to a long recital and oratorio career with Thomas Beecham, the Hallé, the Promenade Concerts, and the Three Choirs and Delius festivals. She specialized in English songs, especially those of Frederick Delius. Her involvement with opera, inspired by Dinh Gilly, began with Mimì at Covent Garden (1935); for her operatic career she assumed the name of Lisa Perli. Her voice was true, pure and youthful, and she was an outstanding actress, ideal for Charles Gounod's heroines, Mélisande, Delius's Vreli (*A Village Romeo and Juliet*) and Giuseppe Verdi's Desdemona. Her many records include the first complete *Messiah* and Act 4 of *La bohème*, both under Beecham. The war cut short her London career in 1939.

Alan Jefferson

Labia, Fausta.

Italian soprano, sister of MARIA LABIA.

Labia, Maria

(*b* Verona, 14 Feb 1880; *d* Malcesine, Lake Garda, 10 Feb 1953). Italian soprano. She studied with her mother, Cecilia Labia, making her début in 1905 as Mimì in Stockholm. In 1907 she appeared at the Komische Oper, Berlin, as Tosca, returning subsequently as Carmen, Marta (*Tiefland*) and Salome, among other roles. She sang at the Manhattan Opera House, New York (1908–9), La Scala (1912) and the Paris Opéra (1913). In 1916 she was imprisoned for a year in Ancona as a suspected German agent. Resuming her career after the war, she sang Giorgetta in the first European performance of *Il tabarro* (1919, Rome), repeating the role in that year in Buenos Aires. In the first Scala production of Wolf-Ferrari's *I quattro rusteghi* (1922) she played Felice, a role that became her favourite and in which she continued to appear until 1936. Her performances in *verismo* operas were said to be impulsive and, for their day, 'shamelessly sensual'. She used her warm, not especially large, voice with particular

reliance on the chest register. Some early recordings remain of her Tosca and Carmen.

Her elder sister, Fausta (*b* Verona, 3 April 1870; *d* Rome, 6 Oct 1935), had a relatively short career (1892–1912), which included performances as Sieglinde under Arturo Toscanini at La Scala. She retired shortly after her marriage to the tenor Emilio Perea.

R. Celletti: 'Maria Labia', *Record News*, iii (Toronto, 1958–9), 32–4 [with discography]

Harold Rosenthal/R

Labinsky, Andrey

(*b* Kharkiv, 14/26 July 1871; *d* Moscow, 8 Aug 1941). Russian tenor. He studied with Stanislaus Gabel at the St Petersburg Academy and sang in the chorus of the Mariinsky Opera. There he made his début as a soloist in 1897, remaining until 1911 and singing in a wide repertory which included Lohengrin and Don José as well as the Russian operatic roles. In 1902 he created Afer in Nikolay Rimsky-Korsakov's *Servilia*; in 1907 he created Vsevolod in *The Invisible City of Kitezh* and undertook a recital tour through eastern Russia to Japan. From 1912 to 1924 he was a leading tenor at the Bol'shoy in Moscow, where he appeared in such diverse roles as Radames and Almaviva. In 1920 he was appointed professor at the Moscow Conservatory, and at the time of his death was principal vocal coach at the Bol'shoy. His recordings include some brilliant performances and also show him to have been a creative stylist.

J.B. Steane

Lablache, Luigi

(*b* Naples, 6 Dec 1794; *d* Naples, 23 Jan 1858). Italian bass. The son of an expatriate French merchant and an Irishwoman, he became the most famous bass of his generation. He entered the Conservatorio della Pietà dei Turchini, Naples, at the age of 12, and began his operatic career as a *buffo napoletano* at the Teatro S Carlino in 1812. After further study and an engagement as *buffo* at Messina, in 1813 he became first *basso cantante* at Palermo, where he remained for several years. His reputation grew, and in 1821 he made a triumphant début at La Scala as Dandini in Gioachino Rossini's *La Cenerentola*. He sang at La Scala until 1828, creating Arnoldo in Saverio Mercadante's *Elisa e Claudio* (1821) and Sulemano in Giacomo Meyerbeer's *L'esule di Granata* (1822). He also appeared at Rome, Turin, Venice and, in 1824, Vienna, where he was a leading member of Domenico Barbaia's company. Ferdinando I of Naples, then in Vienna, appointed Lablache a singer in his royal chapel and had him engaged for the Teatro S Carlo, where for several years he appeared in new operas by Vincenzo Bellini and Gaetano Donizetti, as well as distinguishing himself in such roles as Assur in Rossini's *Semiramide*.

On 30 March 1830, Lablache made a brilliant London début as Geronimo in Domenico Cimarosa's *Il matrimonio segreto* at the King's (from 1837 Her Majesty's) Theatre, where he subsequently appeared every season until 1852, except for 1833 and 1834. Lord Mount-Edgcumbe described him on his London début as 'a bass of uncommon force and power. His voice was not only of deeper compass than almost any ever heard, but when he chose, absolutely *stentorian*, and he was also gigantic in his person; yet when he moderated its extraordinary strength, he sang pleasingly and well.'

While his reputation rested chiefly on his interpretation of comic roles, in which he excelled, he was equally impressive in serious roles such as Elmiro in Rossini's *Otello*, Assur in *Semiramide*, Henry VIII in *Anna Bolena* and Oroveso in *Norma*. In 1839 Richard Wagner wrote an additional aria for this role for him, but Lablache declined to sing it. His Paris début took place on 4 November 1830 at the Théâtre Royal Italien, where he continued to appear regularly until 1851 and created his most important roles, including Sir George Walton in Bellini's *I puritani* (25 January 1835) and the title role in Donizetti's *Marino Faliero* (12 March 1835). *I puritani* enjoyed such success that for the next six years this opera opened and closed each season with its original cast of GIULIA GRISI, GIOVANNI BATTISTA RUBINI, TAMBURINI and Lablache. In England, Lablache appeared in opera and sang at provincial music festivals and, in 1836 and 1837, was Princess Victoria's singing teacher. He was the first Don Pasquale in Donizetti's opera (Théâtre Royal Italien, 3 January 1843), and his interpretation of this role, in which he displayed 'real comic genius' (H.F. Chorley), became definitive.

After the opening in 1847 of the Royal Italian Opera, Covent Garden, Lablache was one of the few artists to remain faithful to Benjamin Lumley's management at Her Majesty's (where he created Massimiliano in Giuseppe Verdi's *I masnadieri* in

Luigi Lablache in 'Il Barbiere di Siviglia' (Rossini)

1847). With his readiness to take small roles without condescension he acquired a larger and more varied repertory than any other singer of comparable standing; Lumley described him as 'the greatest dramatic singer of his time'. On the closure of Her Majesty's in 1852 Lablache visited St Petersburg, and in 1854, after his return, he became a leading member of Frederick Gye's company at Covent Garden. In 1855, when he was over 60, he was still singing some of his most famous roles, including Leporello, Don Pasquale, Bartolo in *Il barbiere* (see illustration) and Balthazar in Donizetti's *La favorite*. His health began to deteriorate in 1856, and he retired from the stage.

Lablache wrote a *Méthode de chant* which was published in Paris but it added little to his reputation. His eldest son, Federico Lablache, was an operatic bass, and his daughter-in-law, Mme Demeric Lablache, sang for many years as a mezzo-soprano with J.H. Mapleson's company. One of his daughters, Cecchina, married the pianist Sigismond Thalberg.

Philip E.J. Robinson/Elizabeth Forbes

La Droghierina.

See CHIMENTI, MARGHERITA.

Lafont, Jean-Philippe

(*b* Toulouse, 4 Feb 1951). French baritone. He studied in Toulouse and then at the Opéra-Studio in Paris, where he made his début as Papageno in 1974, and in 1977 sang Nick Shadow in *The Rake's Progress*. In the same year he sang Guglielmo at Albi. In 1978 he created roles in Antoine Duhamel's *Gambara* at Lyons. He subsequently sang regularly in Toulouse (where he took part in the première of Marcel Landowski's *Montségur* in 1985) and in 1987 in the title role of *Falstaff*. At the Opéra-Comique in Paris he has taken part in the revivals of Charles Gounod's *Le médecin malgré lui*, F.-A. Philidor's *Tom Jones* and the Jacques Offenbach triple bill, *Vive Offenbach!*, and in 1982 sang all four sinister roles in *Les contes d'Hoffmann*. In 1983 he made his American début at Carnegie Hall in a concert performance of *Benvenuto Cellini*; his Metropolitan début was as Escamillo in 1988, and in 1991 he sang Jack Rance in *La fanciulla del West* at La Scala. One of the most versatile French baritones of his generation, Lafont also includes in his repertory roles such as the High Priest (*Alceste*), Rigoletto, Amonasro, Barak (*Die Frau ohne Schatten*), Leporello, Sancho Panza, William Tell, Golaud, Nabucco, Thoas (*Iphigénie en Tauride*), Count Almaviva, Creon (*Medée*), Astor (Luigi Cherubini's *Démophon*), Assur (*Semiramide*), Ourrias, Ramiro (*L'heure espagnole*), Michele (*Il tabarro*), and the title role in Ferruccio Busoni's *Doktor Faust*. In 1996 he created the role of the villain, Scarpiof, in Landowski's *Galina* in Lyons. He appeared in Geneva, Nîmes, Brussels, Perugia, Rome, Naples, Bonn, and Aix-en-Provence, where in 1982 he sang Boreas (Jean-Philippe Rameau's *Les boréades*). His many recordings include Claude Debussy's *La chute de la maison Usher* with Georges Prêtre, *Les mamelles de Tirésias* with Seiji Ozawa, *Falstaff* with John Eliot Gardiner and *La belle Hélène* with Michel Plasson. He has also appeared as an actor in the films *Parole de Flic* and *Babette's Feast*.

Patrick O'Connor/R

Laguerre [Lagarde, Legar, Legard, Le Garde, Legare, Leguar, Leguerre etc.], John

(*b* c1700; *d* London, 28 March 1748). English baritone and painter. The various spellings of his name in playbills, advertisements and cast-lists have caused much confusion, with some writers asserting that more than one person is involved. Laguerre first appeared in Italian opera, having a minor role in G.F. Handel's *Radamisto* (1720). He then joined John Rich's company at Lincoln Inn Fields and Covent Garden, where between 1721 and 1740 he sang in pantomimes, afterpieces, ballad operas and burlesques. He sang again for Handel, creating Curio in *Giulio Cesare* (1724), his English theatre roles being taken by other singers on Italian opera nights. His most popular roles were Hob in *Flora* and Gaffer Gubbins in *The Dragon of Wantley*. He sang Corydon in the first public performance of Handel's *Acis and Galatea* in March 1731. In 1724 he married the dancer and actress Mary Rogeir; they always worked together and after her death in 1739 his career declined. In 1741 he was imprisoned for debt, but was allowed to sing in his benefit performance on 23 April. In 1746 he was taken on by Rich as a scene painter. He had published engravings of theatrical subjects, having been trained by his father, the French-born mural painter Louis Laguerre, who died at the theatre on John's first benefit night in 1721. 'Honest Jack Laguerre' had a reputation as a wit, a mimic and an amusing companion.

Olive Baldwin, Thelma Wilson

Lajeunesse, Emma.

See ALBANI, EMMA.

Lakes, Gary

(*b* Dallas, TX, 26 Sept 1950). American tenor. He studied at Seattle, where he made his début in 1981 as Froh. After winning the Melchior Auditions at the Juilliard School, New York, he sang Florestan in Mexico City (1983), Achilles (*Iphigénie en Aulide*) at Waterloo, New Jersey (1984), and Camille Saint-Saëns's Samson in Charlotte, North Carolina (1985). He made his Metropolitan début in 1986 as the High Priest (*Idomeneo*) and has subsequently sung many roles there, notably Walther von der Vogelweide, Bacchus (which he recorded with James Levine), Siegmund, Grigory, Florestan, Parsifal and Aeneas (*Les Troyens*). He also appeared in San Francisco, Buenos Aires and many of the leading European opera houses, sang Aeneas at Lyons (1989), and made an acclaimed début at the Châtelet, Paris, as Samson in 1991. Lakes's other recordings include Heurtal in Albéric Magnard's *Guercoeur*, Aeneas and the title role in Carl Maria von Weber's *Oberon*. He has an imposing stage presence and a powerful, brilliant-toned voice, heard to particular advantage in the French heroic tenor repertory.

Elizabeth Forbes

Lamiraux-Lalande, Henriette.

See MÉRIC-LALANDE, HENRIETTE.

Lampe, Mrs.

See YOUNG, ISABELLA (i).

Lane, Gloria

(*b* Trenton, NJ, 6 June 1930). American mezzo-soprano, later soprano. She studied in Philadelphia and made her début there as the Secretary in the première of Gian Carlo Menotti's *The Consul* (1950), the opera of her London début (Cambridge Theatre) the next year. She sang Desideria in another Menotti première, *The Saint of Bleecker Street*, on Broadway (1954), and was Baba the Turk in the Glyndebourne revival of *The Rake's Progress* (1958) and Carmen at Covent Garden (1960). Other engagements took her to La Scala, the Vienna Staatsoper, the Deutsche Oper, Berlin, and to France, Denmark and Italy as well as Boston, Chicago and San Francisco. Changing to dramatic soprano, she first sang Santuzza with the New York City Opera in 1971, and Ariadne and Lady Macbeth at Glyndebourne the next year. She combines a forceful stage personality with a strong voice in both registers, and a keen sense of rhythm, if not very subtle shading.

Noël Goodwin

Langan, Kevin

(*b* New York, 1 April 1955). American bass. While studying with MARGARET HARSHAW at Indiana University Music School, he was heard by ELISABETH SCHWARZKOPF and Walter Legge, who sponsored his Wigmore Hall début recital in 1979. The same year he joined the San Francisco Opera, making his début there as the Old Hebrew in *Samson et Dalila* in 1980. He has subsequently sung a very large range of roles for the company and other leading US opera houses, including W.A. Mozart's Osmin, Figaro, Bartolo (which he has recorded), Leporello, Commendatore and Sarastro, Giuseppe Verdi's Sparafucile, Ramfis, Padre Guardiano (*La forza del destino*) and Phillip II, Henry VIII (*Anna Bolena*) and Méphistophélès (Charles Gounod's *Faust*). He made his European opera début, as Osmin at the Opéra de Lyon, in 1982, his Carnegie Hall recital début in 1983 and his Metropolitan Opera début, as Colline (*La bohème*), in 1990. In 1996 he created the role of Henry Mosher in the world première of Tobias Picker's *Emmeline* at Santa Fe. Langan is admired for both his sonorous depth of tone and

his imposing stage presence. In recent years he has added several Wagner roles to his repertory, including Titurel and Daland, which he sang for Portland Opera in 2007.

Richard Wigmore

Langdon, Michael [Birtles, Frank]

(*b* Wolverhampton, 12 Nov 1920; *d* Hove, E. Sussex, 12 March 1991). English bass. He joined the Covent Garden chorus in 1948, making his solo début in 1950 as the Nightwatchman (*The Olympians*) in Manchester. Graduating to principal roles, he created Lieutenant Ratcliffe in *Billy Budd* (1951), the Recorder of Norwich in *Gloriana* (1953), the He-Ancient in *The Midsummer Marriage* (1955) and the Doctor in *We Come to the River* (1976). His other roles included Osmin, Sarastro, Fafner, Hunding, Hagen, Daland, Don Basilio, Rocco, Kecal, Varlaam, the Grand Inquisitor (*Don Carlos*), Bottom, Waldner (*Arabella*) and Ochs, his best-known part, which he studied in Vienna with ALFRED JERGER and sang more than 100 times. His repertory also included Méphistophélès, Osmin, Sarastro, the Commendatore, Gioachino Rossini's Moses, Otto Nicolai's Falstaff, Carl Nielsen's Saul and Don Pasquale; for Scottish Opera he created the title role of Orr's *Hermiston* at Edinburgh (1975). His final appearances were as Frank in *Die Fledermaus* at Covent Garden in 1985. Langdon was a notable Claggart (*Billy Budd*) in a production for television and on Benjamin Britten's recording. He had a large, rather dry-toned voice, equally suitable to comic or tragic parts. On retiring from the stage he became director of the National Opera Studio (1978–86). His autobiography, *Notes from a Low Singer*, was published in 1982.

H. Rosenthal: 'Michael Langdon', *Opera*, xxvi (1975), 1111–16

E. Downes and E. Forbes: 'Michael Langdon (1920–1991)', *Opera*, xlii (1991), 511–15

Alan Blyth

Lange [née Weber], (Maria) Aloysia [Aloisia, Aloysia Louise] (Antonia)

(*b* Zell or Mannheim, *c*1761; *d* Salzburg, 8 June 1839). German soprano. She was the sister of JOSEPHA HOFER, and sister-in-law of W.A. Mozart, who married her sister Constanze in 1782. She studied in Mannheim with G.J. Vogler and with Mozart, her association with whom produced seven concert arias and the role of Mme Herz in *Der Schauspieldirektor* (as well as a series of letters by Mozart notable

Aloysia Lange as Zémire in 'Zémire et Azor' (Grétry), lithograph by Johann Esaias Nilson, 1784

for their elucidation of his views on vocal performance and training). Their first encounter, during Mozart's stay in Mannheim in 1777–8 (when he fell in love with her), resulted in the concert arias K294, 316/300 *b* and probably 538. In 1778 she moved from Mannheim to Munich, where she made her début as Parthenia in Anton Schweitzer's *Alceste* (Carnival 1779); she was then engaged for the new National Singspiel in Vienna, where she made her début on 9 September 1779 as Hännchen in a German adaptation of F.-A. Philidor's *Le rosière de Salency*. She married the court actor and painter Joseph Lange on 31 October 1780.

When in 1782 Joseph II removed German opera to the neighbouring Kärntnertortheater and reinstated Italian comic opera at the Burgtheater, she was retained as a leading singer of the Italian troupe.

For her début, as Clorinda in Pasquale Anfossi's *Il curioso indiscreto* (1783), Mozart composed two substitute arias, K418 and 419. Lange participated regularly in Italian opera for only eight months; probably she fell out of favour because of disagreements over salary and roles as well as missed performances. In 1785 she was among the German singers transferred to the less prestigious Kärntnertortheater, where she revived many roles of her early career with the important addition of Konstanze in Mozart's *Die Entführung* (1785–8). Lange continued to appear occasionally at the Burgtheater, notably for a German revival in 1785 of C.W. Gluck's *La rencontre imprévue*, for the Vienna première of Mozart's *Don Giovanni* (as Donna Anna) and for Domenico Cimarosa's *Il fanatico burlato*, both in 1788. She was retained by Leopold II for his *opera seria* venture in

Vienna in 1790, as a seconda donna. In 1795 Aloysia undertook a concert tour with her sister Constanze, continuing her successes as Mozart's Sextus, a role she had performed in Vienna.

A report in the *Deutsches Museum* (1781) states that she 'has a very pleasing voice, though it is too weak for the theatre', and Gerber pronounced her voice 'more suited for an ordinary room than the theatre'. Leopold Mozart corroborates this view in a letter to his daughter of 25 March 1785:

> It can scarcely be denied that she sings with the greatest expression: only now I understand why some persons I frequently asked would say that she has a very weak voice, while others said she has a very loud voice. Both are true. The held notes and all expressive notes are astonishingly loud; the tender moments, the passage work and embellishments, and high notes are very delicate, so that for my taste the one contrasts too strongly with the other. In an ordinary room the loud notes assault the ear, while in the theatre the delicate passages demand a great attentiveness and stillness on the part of the audience.

Mozart's compositions give the clearest picture of her voice. His sensitivity to Lange's small instrument may be seen in the light orchestration and relatively high tessitura. Her music exploits expressive, cantabile delivery and gives ample opportunity for portamento and the addition of ornaments. Her *fioriture* consist primarily of scale work and *abbellimenti* spun out in varied, flexible rhythmic configurations, and there is an almost casual assaying of her remarkable upper range, extending to g''' (as Blanka in Ignaz Umlauf's *Das Irrlicht*, 1782, she sang to a'''). Gebler regarded her as 'a splendid singer, [with] a tone and an expression that goes to the heart [and] an extraordinary upper range; she correctly performs the most difficult passages and blends them with the song as it should be done'.

Patricia Lewy Gidwitz

Langridge, Philip (Gordon)

(*b* Hawkhurst, Kent, 16 Dec 1939). English tenor. From 1958 he studied the violin at the RAM, playing professionally for a short period until 1964; in 1962 he began singing lessons with Bruce Boyce, continuing later with Celia Bizony. One of the most versatile British singers of the day, he has a large concert repertory that extends from Claudio Monteverdi and the 18th- and 19th-century oratorios to first performances of works by Richard Rodney Bennett, Alexander Goehr, Heinz Holliger, Elisabeth Lutyens and Anthony Milner. But it is as

a singing-actor of extraordinarily wide range that he has become internationally celebrated. Whether in operas by contemporary composers (he co-created the title role of Harrison Birtwistle's *The Mask of Orpheus* in 1986 and sang at the British première of Michael Tippett's *New Year* in 1990, among many others), those of the postwar period (he has given memorable accounts of Benjamin Britten's Grimes, Vere, Quint and, finest of all, Aschenbach) or others stretching back to the beginnings of the medium, Langridge has consistently revealed an acuity of stylistic understanding and a rare directness of dramatic delivery. His voice, individual rather than beautiful and tending to lack power and ring at the top of its compass, has nevertheless served him in the dramatic tenor roles of Leoš Janáček (Zivný in *Osud*, Laca in *Jenůfa*, Gregor in *The Makropulos Affair*) as impressively as it has in Jean-Philippe Rameau, G.F. Handel, W.A. Mozart (notably Don Ottavio and Idomeneus, both of which he has sung at Glyndebourne), Hector Berlioz, Modest Musorgsky, Arnold Schoenberg and Igor Stravinsky. The same intelligence, natural musicianship and finely focussed diction have shed light on the song repertory. Langridge's many recordings include *Peter Grimes*, *The Rake's Progress*, Aron in *Moses und Aron* (the role of his Salzburg début in 1987), *Osud*, lieder by Franz Schubert and several outstanding discs of English song. He was made a CBE in 1994. He is married to the mezzo-soprano ANN MURRAY.

C. Pitt: 'Philip Langridge', *Opera*, xxxvii (1986), 499–507

Max Loppert

Lanigan, John

(*b* Seddon, Victoria, 7 Jan 1921; *d* Victoria, Canada, 1 Aug 1996). Australian tenor. He studied in Melbourne and London, making his début at the Stoll Theatre in 1949 as Fenton and Rodolfo. In 1951 he sang Thaddeus (*The Bohemian Girl*) at Covent Garden and began a 25-year engagement with the Royal Opera, first appearing as the Duke (*Rigoletto*). For a decade he sang lyric roles, Tamino, Alfredo, Pinkerton, Des Grieux (*Manon*), Jeník, Essex (*Gloriana*), Almaviva and Laca (*Jenůfa*). He created Jack in *The Midsummer Marriage* (1955) and Hermes in *King Priam* (1962, Coventry). Later he displayed rare vocal and dramatic versatility in character parts: as Mime, Spalanzani (*Les contes d'Hoffmann*), Pandarus (*Troilus and Cressida*), Il 'Tinca' (*Il tabarro*), Dr Caius, the Drunken Guest (*Katerina Ismaylova*), the Rector (*Peter Grimes*), Flute, Sir Philip (*Owen Wingrave*) and Shuysky, his most effective role. He created Jones in Richard Rodney Bennett's *Victory* (1970), the Cardinal/Archbishop in Peter Maxwell Davies's *Taverner* (1972) and the Soldier/Madman in H.W. Henze's *We Come to the River* (1976).

Elizabeth Forbes

Lanza, Mario [Cocozza, Alfred Arnold]

(*b* Philadelphia, 31 Jan 1921; *d* Rome, Italy, 7 Oct 1959). American tenor. He first studied singing while working as a piano mover in Philadelphia and in 1942 was awarded a summer scholarship at the Berkshire Music Center. Shortly afterwards he entered the Special Services of the armed forces and sang regularly for military radio shows during World War II. After his discharge he made a series of concert appearances, including a performance at the Hollywood Bowl in 1946. In 1947 he embarked on a world tour with the Bel Canto Trio which also included Frances Yeend and GEORGE LONDON. His first film role, in *That Midnight Kiss* (1949), brought him immediate national recognition and fame. He subsequently made six further films, including *The Great Caruso* (1951) and *The Toast of New Orleans* (1950), in which he sang his greatest hit, *Be my love* (Nicholas Brodszky and Sammy Cahn). Although he possessed a voice of great power and range, Lanza sang in only one opera, Giacomo Puccini's *Madama Butterfly*, with the New Orleans Opera (1948). He was idolized as a romantic figure with a marvellous voice who chose films over opera. In the early 1950s he presented his own radio show. At this time his problems with obesity became increasingly severe, and they may have contributed to his early death at the age of 38.

Jean W. Thomas

Larin, Sergey

(*b* Daugavpils, Latvia, 9 March 1953; *d* Bratislava, 13 Jan 2008). Russian tenor. After linguistic studies in Gor'kiy (now Nizhniy Novgorod) and singing lessons in Vilnius, he made his début at the Lithuanian Opera and Ballet Theatre, as Alfredo, in 1981. His Western début did not take place until 1990, when he appeared as Lensky at the Vienna Staatsoper; but unlike some compatriots he has not concentrated primarily on Russian roles: his calling cards at major houses in Western Europe have included Don José, Calaf, Cavaradossi (the role of his Metropolitan Opera and Paris Opéra débuts) and Don Carlos (which he sang at the 1998 Salzburg Festival), and his non-Russian repertory also includes the Prince (*Rusalka*) and Florestan. It was in *Carmen* that he made his Covent Garden début in 1991. He has sung three roles in *Boris*

Godunov, beginning as the Simpleton, moving on to Shuysky and finally assuming the Pretender with the Kirov Opera at the Metropolitan in 1992 and at the 1994 Salzburg Festival. That Salzburg production has been preserved on disc, and his other important recordings include Calaf (on disc and video), Andrey in P.I. Tchaikovsky's *Mazepa*, Sergei in *Lady Macbeth of the Mtsensk District*, and a disc of Russian songs. Larin is a highly expressive performer, possessed of a heroically charged tenor tone which he is capable of scaling down as the situation demands. His portrayals of complex characters and the internalized drama he finds in the song repertory suggest that he belongs to the old, psychological tradition of Russian theatre.

John Allison

Larmore, Jennifer

(*b* Atlanta, GA, 21 June 1958). American mezzo-soprano. She studied at Westminster Choir College at Princeton with R.H. McIvor, and privately with John Bullock and REGINA RESNIK. She sang in the European première of Gian Carlo Menotti's *The Egg* at Spoleto in 1977 and made her official début as W.A. Mozart's Sextus at Nice in 1986. Since then she has built an impressive reputation in the operas of G.F. Handel, Mozart and Gioachino Rossini. Larmore made her Covent Garden début as Rosina in 1992 and her first appearance at La Scala, as Isolier (*Le comte Ory*), in the same year, returning to La Scala for *L'enfant et les sortilèges*. Her Metropolitan début, as Rosina, followed in 1995. In 1998 she sang her first Carmen, opposite DOMINGO, at the Los Angeles Opera, and in 2001 scored a notable success at the Metropolitan Opera in *L'italiana in Algeri*. Her full, flexible mezzo and forthright characterization can be heard on her recordings of the title roles of *Giulio Cesare* and *La Cenerentola*, as Rosina in *Il barbiere di Siviglia* and as Arsace in *Semiramide*. She is a lively and persuasive actress.

Alan Blyth

La Rochois.

See LE ROCHOIS, MARIE.

Larrivée, Henri

(*b* Lyons, 9 Jan 1737; *d* Paris, 7 Aug 1802). French baritone. At first a singer in the Opéra chorus, he began his career as a soloist in 1755 when he played a High Priest in Jean-Philippe Rameau's *Castor et Pollux*; later he sang Jupiter and finally Pollux. Apart from other roles in operas of Rameau and Jean-Baptiste Lully, he created Ricimer in F.-A. Philidor's *Ernelinde* (1767) and the title role in F.-J. Gossec's *Sabinus* (1773). For C.W. Gluck he created Agamemnon (in *Iphigénie en Aulide*, 1774), Hercules (in *Alceste*, 1776), Ubalde (in *Armide*, 1777) and Orestes (in *Iphigénie en Tauride*, 1779); he also played Orestes in Niccolò Piccinni's *Iphigénie* (1781), A.-E.-M. Grétry's *Andromaque* (1780) and J.-B Lemoyne's *Electre* (1782). He venerated Gluck (although the composer criticized his acting) and overcame a lack of sympathy with Piccinni to sing Roland with such success as to give rise to Nicolas Framery's 'Epître à M. Larrivée' (*Journal de Paris*, 4 February 1778). Subsequently he created Danaus in Antonio Salieri's *Les Danaïdes* (1784). He last appeared as Agamemnon in 1797. He had a wide range and a flexible voice which, according to F.-J. Fétis and others, became nasal on high notes.

Larrivée's wife, Marie Jeanne Larrivée (née Le Mière) (*b* Sedan, 29 Nov 1733; *d* Paris, Oct 1786), was a soprano who appeared at the Opéra from 1750, mostly in minor roles; but she created the title role of Philidor's *Ernelinde* (1767) and Eponine in Gossec's *Sabinus* (1773).

Julian Rushton

Larsén-Todsen, Nanny

(*b* Hagby, 2 Aug 1884; *d* Stockholm, 26 May 1982). Swedish soprano. She studied in Stockholm, Berlin and Milan and made her début in 1906 with the Royal Opera, Stockholm, where she continued to sing until 1923, first in lyric roles, including Donna Anna, Reiza, Aida, Tosca and the Marschallin, before taking on the heavier Wagner repertory. At La Scala (1923–4) she sang Isolde under Arturo Toscanini; at the Metropolitan (1925–7) she made her début as Brünnhilde (*Götterdämmerung*) and, in addition to Wagner, sang Fidelio, Leonore, Rachel (*La Juive*) and Gioconda. At Covent Garden (1927 and 1930) she sang Brünnhilde, while at Bayreuth (1927–31) her roles were Isolde, Kundry and Brünnhilde. She also appeared at the Paris Opéra and with the state operas of Berlin and Vienna. Most notable of her recordings are her Isolde, based on Bayreuth performances of 1928, and Brünnhilde's Immolation Scene from the same year, which show her strong, evenly produced tone and appreciable sensitivity.

Leo Riemens/Alan Blyth/R

Laschi, Filippo

(*b* Florence, *fl* 1739–89). Italian tenor. He was a singer and actor of unusual ability and a champion of Italian comic opera in the mid-18th century, mentioned in admiring terms by W.A. Mozart and Charles Burney. Initially he sang serious roles but from 1741 (Giovanni Chinzer's *La serva favorita*) he preferred comedy parts. He was a leading figure in the success of Neapolitan, Roman and Florentine comic opera in Venice between 1743 and 1745, singing with Pietro Pertici, FRANCESCO BAGLIONI, Grazia Mellini, Pellegrino Gaggiotti and other specialists in the genre. With a company directed by G.F. Crosa, and initially including Pertici and the soprano ANNA MARIA QUERZOLI (whom he married; LUISA LASCHI was their daughter), he introduced this repertory to London (1748–50), Brussels (1749) and Amsterdam (1750), and from 1753 he was involved in first performances of many of Carlo Goldoni's *commedie per musica*. The Goldoni repertory remained a constant element in his activity until the mid-1760s, after which he worked in Vienna (1765–8) where, among other works, he sang Apollo in the premiere of C.W. Gluck's *Alceste* (1767). Laschi sang in various Italian centres in the 1770s and was a teacher of the Mozart bass LUIGI BASSI and the tenor MICHAEL KELLY; he was also the composer of arias sung in pasticcios (such as *The Maid of the Mill*, 1765) and in 1780 played the cembalo at the Pergola Theatre in Florence. He held posts as a *virtuoso di camera* of the Grand Duke of Tuscany and Charles of Lorraine.

Richard G. King, Franco Piperno, Saskia Willaert

Laschi [Mombelli], Luisa

(*b* Florence, 1760s; *d c*1790). Italian soprano. Her first known appearances were in 1782 in Vicenza and Bologna. She made her Viennese début on 24 September 1784 in Domenico Cimarosa's *Giannina e Bernardone*. The *Wiener Kronik* said: 'she has a beautiful clear voice, which in time will become rounder and fuller; she is very musical, sings with more expression than the usual opera singers and has a beautiful figure! Madam Fischer (Storazi [i.e. NANCY STORACE]) has only more experience, and is otherwise in no way superior to Dem Laschi'. On 21 January 1785 Laschi replaced Storace, who was about to give birth, as Rosina in Giovanni Paisiello's *Il barbiere di Siviglia* 'very well, and was much applauded' (Karl von Zinzendorf). She left at Easter for an engagement in Naples – where she met her future husband, the tenor DOMENICO MOMBELLI – but returned to Vienna at Easter 1786. There, on 1 May 1786, she created the role of the Countess in *Le nozze di Figaro*. She had a further success on 15 May in Pasquale Anfossi's *Il trionfo delle donne*. On 1 August she appeared, probably for the first time in Vienna with Mombelli, in Giuseppe Sarti's

I finti eredi. On 29 September the emperor wrote to his chamberlain, Count Rosenberg, with a jocular reference to *Figaro*: 'The marriage between Laschi and Mombelli may take place without waiting for my return, and I cede to you *le droit de Seigneur*'. In November 1786 she created the role of Queen Isabella in Vicente Martín y Soler's *Una cosa rara*, and in 1787 created Cupid in his *L'arbore di Diana*, a role that required her to appear alternately as a shepherdess and as Cupid. A contemporary reviewer described her portrayal: 'Grace personified …; ah, who is not enchanted by it, what painter could better depict the arch smile, what sculptor the grace in all her gestures, what singer could match the singing, so melting and sighing, with the same naturalness and true, warm expression?'

In January 1788 she appeared in the première of Antonio Salieri's *Axur re d'Ormus* and in May sang Zerlina in the first Vienna performance of W.A. Mozart's *Don Giovanni*; Mozart composed a new duet to be sung by her and Francesco Benucci. She was already seven months pregnant but continued singing until the day before her confinement and reappeared four weeks later. But there were difficulties between the Italian company and the management, and the emperor gave the Mombellis notice. In September Luisa created the role of Carolina in Salieri's *Il talismano* and in February 1789 she made her farewell appearance as Donna Farinella in *L'ape musicale*; nothing further seems to be known about her, but in 1791 Domenico, apparently a widower, married the ballerina Vincenza Viganò, by whom he had 12 children.

D. Link: *The National Court Theatre in Mozart's Vienna: Sources and Documents 1783–1792* (Oxford, 1998)

Christopher Raeburn

Lassalle, Jean

(*b* Lyons, 14 Dec 1847; *d* Paris, 7 Sept 1909). French baritone. He studied at the Paris Conservatoire and made his début as St Bris in *Les Huguenots* at Liège in 1868. There followed four years in the Netherlands and the French provinces; then, in 1872, he was engaged for the reopening of the Paris Opéra, where for a while he was the highest-paid male singer and where he remained as the leading baritone until his retirement in 1901. Premières in the house included Jules Massenet's *Le roi de Lahore* and Camille Saint-Saëns's *Henry VIII*, and in Brussels he sang in the première of Ernest Reyer's *Sigurd*. In 1879 he appeared at La Scala and in Madrid. At Covent Garden, where he was closely associated with the DE RESZKE brothers, he was heard from 1879 to 1881 and again from 1888 to 1893. Lassalle had a great success, as both singer and actor, as

Nélusko in *L'Africaine* and another in the London première of Anton Rubinstein's *Demon*. Other roles in London included Don Giovanni, William Tell, Hamlet and Rigoletto, with the later addition of Hans Sachs, the Dutchman, and Telramund in *Lohengrin*. Of these Wagnerian roles, the last two, along with Wolfram in *Tannhäuser*, were in his repertory at the Metropolitan, where he made his début in 1892 and sang for the last time in 1897. His few and rare recordings were made after his retirement, but they still show a well-preserved voice and, in the aria from *Le roi de Lahore*, a fine example of the elegant style for which his period is known.

J. B. Steane

Laubenthal, Rudolf

(*b* Düsseldorf, 18 March 1886; *d* Pöcking, nr Starnberg, 2 Oct 1971). German tenor. He studied with LILLI LEHMANN in Berlin and made his début in 1913 at the Charlottenburg opera, where he remained until 1923, the year of his Metropolitan début as Walther. He sang in the first American performances of *Jenůfa*, *Die ägyptische Helena* and *Švanda the Bagpiper*. At Covent Garden (1926–30) he sang Erik, Siegfried, Tristan and Walther. He continued to appear in Munich, Vienna and other European theatres until 1937. His repertory included Arnold (*Guillaume Tell*), Hoffmann and John of Leyden (*Le prophète*). A handsome man and an intelligent actor, he was renowned as Tristan and Siegfried, and recorded excerpts from both roles.

Harold Rosenthal/R

Laurence, Elizabeth [Scott, Elizabeth Jane]

(*b* Harrogate, 22 Nov 1949). English mezzo-soprano. She studied at Trinity College, London. In 1986 she sang Mallika (*Lakmé*) at Monte Carlo, Jocasta (*Oedipus rex*) in Madrid and Nancy (*Albert Herring*) with Glyndebourne Touring Opera, for whom she created Anna Arild (Nigel Osborne's *Electrification of the Soviet Union*) in 1987. She also created Behemoth in York Höller's *Der Meister und Margarita* at the Paris Opéra (1989). Her Covent Garden début was as Second Audition in the British première of *Un re in ascolto* (1989), which she also sang at Opéra Bastille (1991). Her roles include Cherubino, Erda, Béla Bartók's Judith and Maurice Ravel's *Concepcion*. With her warm-toned, flexible voice and handsome appearance, she excels in parts such as Lady de Hautdesert in Harrison Birtwistle's *Gawain*, which she created at Covent Garden (1991).

Elizabeth Forbes

Laurenti [Novelli], **Antonia Maria**
['La Coralli', 'Corallina']

(*fl* 1714–41). Italian contralto. She belonged to the famous musical Laurenti family of Bologna and may have been the daughter of Bartolomeo Girolamo Laurenti (1644–1726). Her first recorded appearance in opera was in 1714, in Padua. Until 1719 she was active on the stage in several Italian cities, taking leading roles. Francesco Veracini recruited her (at the high salary of 2375 thalers) for the company that performed at Dresden in 1719. In 1720 she resumed her career in Italy. Under her nickname 'La Coralli' she is referred to obliquely in Benedetto Marcello's satire *Il teatro alla moda* (1720). Antonio Denzio invited her to Prague in 1726. There she married the tenor Felice Novelli (*fl* 1717–62) on 8 March 1727. The pair returned to Italy and thereafter often performed in the same productions. Of especial note is the appearance of Novelli and Laurenti as a comic pair in Francesco Mancini's intermezzo *La serva favorita* (1730, Turin). Laurenti's last known appearance was in the pasticcio *Sirbace* (1741, Ferrara).

Michael Talbot

Lauri-Volpi [Volpi], [Rubini], **Giacomo**

(*b* Rome, 11 Dec 1892; *d* Valencia, 17 March 1979). Italian tenor and writer on opera singers. He studied at the Rome Conservatory with COTOGNI and later with Enrico Rosati. He made his début (under the name Giacomo Rubini) at Viterbo in 1919 as Arturo (*I puritani*) and in 1920 sang Des Grieux (*Manon*) under his own name in Rome. Engaged at La Scala as the Duke of Mantua in 1922, he sang there regularly in the 1930s and 40s. He was a member of the Metropolitan Opera from 1923 to 1933, singing in 232 performances of 26 operas; his roles included Calaf in the American première of *Turandot* (1926) and Rodolfo in the first Metropolitan *Luisa Miller* (1929). His only Covent Garden appearances were in 1925 as Chénier and 1936 as the Duke, Cavaradossi and Radames, perhaps his most striking role. He sang Arrigo Boito's Nero to open the Teatro Reale dell'Opera, Rome, in 1928 and Arnold in the centenary production of *Guillaume Tell* at La Scala in 1929. His repertory also included Raoul (*Les Huguenots*), Otello and Manrico. His bright, ringing tone and beautiful legato made him one of the finest lyric-dramatic tenors of his day; his many recordings capture the virile brio of his exemplary style. He wrote a number of books, including *Voci parallele* (Milan, 1955) and *Misteri della voce umana* (Milan, 1957).

C. Williams and T. Hutchinson: 'Giacomo Lauri-Volpi', *Record Collector*, xi (1957), 245–72; xii (1958–60), 34–5, 66–7, 108; xx (1971–2), 239 [with discography]

Harold Rosenthal/Alan Blyth

Lavrovskaya [Lawrowska], **Yelizaveta Andreyevna**

(*b* Kashin, Tver' province, 1/13 Oct 1845; *d* Petrograd [now St Petersburg] 4 Feb 1919). Russian mezzo-soprano. She studied at the St Petersburg Conservatory. In 1867 her performance in a student presentation of C.W. Gluck's *Orfeo* greatly impressed the Grand Duchess Yelena Pavlovna, who sent her to Paris to take lessons from PAULINE VIARDOT. In 1868 she made her professional début in the contralto role of Vanya in M.I. Glinka's *A Life for the Tsar*, and later sang Ratmir in *Ruslan and Lyudmila*. This testifies to her considerable range of voice, for she was to sing Carmen, Mignon and many other mezzo-soprano roles (although she refused to sing the role of Laura in Alexander Dargomïzhsky's *The Stone Guest* for being 'not sufficiently singable'). She was also well known as a sensitive recitalist and concert singer, not only in Russia but also in western Europe; she sang at the Monday Popular Concerts at the Crystal Palace, London, in 1873 and at the Paris Exhibition in 1878. She was much admired by M.A. Balakirev, at whose Russian Musical Society and Free School concerts she regularly appeared, and she sang at the first concert given by P.I. Tchaikovsky in 1871. He dedicated to her his Six Romances op.27 (1875), and it was she who in 1877 suggested to him Alexander Pushkin's *Yevgeny Onegin* as a suitable subject for an opera. She made further appearances at the Mariinsky, St Petersburg (1889–90 season), as well as at the Bol'shoy, Moscow (1890–91 season). In 1888 she was appointed professor of singing at the Moscow Conservatory; Tchaikovsky considered her to be an 'excellent' teacher. In 1871 she married Prince Tsertelev.

Edward Garden

Lawrence, **Marjorie (Florence)**

(*b* Dean's Marsh, nr Melbourne, 17 Feb 1909; *d* Little Rock, AR, 13 Jan 1979). Australian soprano, later naturalized American. She studied in Paris and made her opera début at Monte Carlo in 1932 as Elisabeth in *Tannhäuser*. In 1933 she first appeared, as Ortrud, at the Paris Opéra, where, during the next three years, she sang Brünnhilde, Salome (*Hérodiade*), Rachel (*La Juive*), Aida, Donna Anna, Brunehild (*Sigurd*), Brangäne and Valentine. She made her Metropolitan début in New York as the

Walküre Brünnhilde on 18 December 1935, continuing to appear there for six seasons, mostly in the Wagnerian repertory but also as the heroines of *Alceste, Salome* and *Thaïs*. Although she had polio in 1941, she resumed her career in 1943 in specially staged performances during which she was always seated. In 1946 she returned to Paris as Amneris. Lawrence possessed a large, vibrant and expressive voice. Her singing, though not always secure, gave pleasure because of its physical impact and distinctive sound. She left vivid examples of her art on disc, notably her Brünnhilde, Senta and Salome.

M. Lawrence: *Interrupted Melody: the Story of my Life* (New York, 1949)
J. Rockwell: Obituary, *New York Times* (15 Jan 1979)
W. Hogarth: 'Majorie Lawrence', *Record Collector*, xxxii (1987), 2–18

Max De Schauensee/Alan Blyth/R

Layton-Walker, Sarah (Jane).

See CAHIER, MME CHARLES.

Lázaro, Hipólito

(*b* Barcelona, 13 Dec 1887; *d* Barcelona, 14 May 1974). Spanish tenor. Success in amateur zarzuela performances, and a period with Adolfo Bracale's opera company in Eygpt led to his operatic début at Barcelona in *La favorita*. He then studied with Enrico Colli in Milan. In 1913 he sang in Pietro Mascagni's *Isabeau* at Genoa under the composer, who subsequently engaged him as Ugo for the première of his *Parisina* at La Scala. In 1914 he made his first tour of South America, where he enjoyed some of his greatest successes. He appeared at the Metropolitan in 1918, making a strong impression there with the high tessitura of *I puritani*. Back in Italy he received acclaim for his part (the Prince of Fleury) in the première of Mascagni's *Il piccolo Marat* at the Costanzi, Rome, in 1921, and he repeated his success, also under Mascagni, in Paris in 1928. He was Gianetto in the première of *La cena delle beffe* in 1924, but withdrew from further performances after disagreements with the composer, Umberto Giordano. He was engaged for the 1925–26 season by Bracale in Egypt when Mascagni was principal conductor. His contentious disposition probably hindered the development of his career in the 1930s, when he appeared in Santa Cruz de Tenerife although he continued to sing to the end of his life, giving a farewell concert in New York in 1944 and making his final operatic appearances in Havana in 1950. A bright, penetrating voice with magnificent high notes is heard on recordings

that also show him to have been capable of some delightful as well as some deplorable stylistic effects. He also wrote an egotistical autobiography, *El libro de mi vida* (Havana, 1949, 2/1968).

J.B. Richards: 'Hipolito Lazaro', *Record Collector*, xvi (1964–6), 53–94

J.B. Steane

Lazzari, Virgilio

(*b* Assisi, 20 April 1887; *d* Castel Gandolfo, 4 Oct 1953). Italian bass, later naturalized American. He sang with the Vitale Operetta Company, 1908–11, then studied in Rome with COTOGNI. He made his operatic début at the Teatro Costanzi, Rome, in 1914. After singing in South America, in 1917 he made his North American début at Boston. He sang with the Chicago Opera (1918–33), then made his Metropolitan début as Don Pédro (*L'Africaine*), remaining with the company until 1951 and singing 20 roles. From 1934 to 1939 he appeared at the Salzburg Festival, where he sang Pistol (*Falstaff*), Bartolo and Leporello, the role of his only Covent Garden appearance (1939). His most famous role was that of Archibaldo (Italo Montemezzi's *L'amore dei tre re*), which he sang first in 1916 in Mexico City and as late as 1953 in Genoa. Although not blessed with a great voice, Lazzari was considered one of the best singing actors in his particular repertory.

Harold Rosenthal/R

Lear [née Shulman; married name Stewart], Evelyn

(*b* Brooklyn, NY, 8 Jan 1926). American soprano. In addition to performing the standard repertory, she has participated in the premières of several contemporary operas. She studied at the Juilliard School and later in Berlin. Engaged by the Berlin Städtische (later Deutsche) Oper, she made her début in 1959 as the Composer. In 1961 she created the title role in Giselher Klebe's *Alkmene* in Berlin and in 1963 Jeanne in Werner Egk's *Die Verlobung in San Domingo* at the opening celebrations of the rebuilt Nationaltheater, Munich. She made her Metropolitan début as Lavinia in the first performance of Marvin David Levy's *Mourning Becomes Electra* (1967). With her first performance in Vienna of Alban Berg's *Lulu* in 1962 she became closely associated with the role, singing it in London with the Hamburg company that year and recording it under Karl Böhm. She made her Covent Garden début in 1965 as Donna Elvira. Her repertory included both Cherubino and Countess Almaviva,

Fiordiligi, Pamina, Claudio Monteverdi's Poppaea, G.F. Handel's Cleopatra, Mimì, Desdemona, Tatyana, Marie (*Wozzeck*), Emilia Marty and Octavian. From 1972 she began to undertake heavier roles, including Tosca and the Marschallin. She created Arkadina in Thomas Pasatieri's *The Seagull* (1974), Magda in Robert Ward's *Minutes to Midnight* (1982) and Ranyevskaya in Rudolf Kelterborn's *Kirschgarten* (1984, Zürich). Her voice, though not large, was of distinctively warm and affecting quality, well produced and projected. In 1985 she made her farewell at the Metropolitan as the Marschallin and sang Countess Geschwitz at Florence, repeating the role in Chicago (1987) and San Francisco (1989). Lear was also a distinguished recitalist, singing in seven languages. She married the baritone THOMAS STEWART.

Harold Rosenthal/R

Leblanc, Georgette

(*b* Tancarville, 8 Feb 1875; *d* Le Cannet, nr Cannes, 27 Oct 1941). French soprano. She studied in Paris, making her début in 1893 at the Opéra-Comique as Françoise in the first performance of Alfred Bruneau's *L'attaque au Moulin*. She also sang Fanny in Jules Massenet's *Sapho*. Engaged at the Théâtre de la Monnaie (1894–6), she sang Anita (*La Navarraise*), Thaïs and Carmen. In Brussels, she began a 20-year personal association with Maurice Maeterlinck, who wanted her to create the heroine of *Pelléas et Mélisande*; Claude Debussy, however, insisted that MARY GARDEN should sing the role. Instead, Leblanc sang Ariane at the first performance of Paul Dukas' *Ariane et Barbe-bleue* at the Opéra-Comique (1907). She also created Ygraine in Jean Nouguès' *La mort de Tintagiles* (1905). She first sang Mélisande in 1912 at Boston, where she also acted in the play. In 1930 she published *Souvenirs (1895–1918)*, an account of her liaison with Maeterlinck.

Elizabeth Forbes

Lefèbvre, Louise-Rosalie.

See DUGAZON, LOUISE-ROSALIE.

Leggate, Robin

(*b* West Kirby, Cheshire, 18 April 1946). English tenor. He studied at Oxford and Manchester and made his début in 1975 as Richard II in Alan Bush's *Wat Tyler* at Sadler's Wells Theatre. He first sang at Covent Garden in 1977 as Cassio; his subsequent roles there have included Joe (*La fanciulla del West*), Gaston, Elemer, Tamino, Narraboth, the Novice

(*Billy Budd*), Malcolm, Jaquino, the Painter and the Negro (*Lulu*), Andrey Khovansky (*Khovanshchina*), Paris (*King Priam*), Edmondo (*Manon Lescaut*), Lysander, Ovlur (*Prince Igor*), and the Holy Fool (*Boris Godunov*). He has sung with Opera North, the WNO and Scottish Opera, in Hamburg, Paris and at Glyndebourne. A versatile character actor with a smooth, well-focussed voice, he also sings lyric roles such as Don Ottavio, Ferrando, Lensky, Oberon, Gonzalve (*L'heure espagnole*) and Bob Cratchit (Thea Musgrave's *A Christmas Carol*).

Elizabeth Forbes

Legros [Le Gros], Joseph

(*b* Monampteuil, Laon, 7 or 8 Sept 1739; *d* La Rochelle, 20 Dec 1793). French tenor and composer. Having been a choirboy at Laon Cathedral, Legros developed a powerful, sweet-toned *haute-contre* suited to the high tessitura of French opera. Recruited by François Rebel and François Francoeur, he made his début at the Paris Opéra in 1764, shortly before the retirement of JÉLYOTTE, in J.-J. Cassanéa de Mondonville's *Titon et l'Aurore*. Although a stiff actor he became the Opéra's leading *haute-contre* until his retirement (accelerated by obesity) in 1783.

Legros played the title roles in Jean-Philippe Rameau's principal *tragédies lyriques*, and created over 30 other roles. He adapted without apparent difficulty to the new italianate style, singing Sandomir in F.-A. Philidor's *Ernelinde* in 1767 and at subsequent revivals. He was the first Achilles in C.W. Gluck's *Iphigénie en Aulide* (1774) and on its revival the following year led a patriotic demonstration with the aria 'Chantez, célébrez votre reine'. His popularity influenced the adaptation of the castrato role of Orpheus in the French version of Gluck's opera to suit his range (exceptionally, the compass is extended to *e b* ''). Legros subsequently created the principal tenor roles in Gluck's *Alceste*, *Armide*, *Iphigénie en Tauride* and Cynire (rather than Narcissus) in *Echo et Narcisse*. For Niccolò Piccinni he created Médor (*Roland*), the title role in *Atys* and Pylades (*Iphigénie en Tauride*); his last role was the eponymous hero in Antonio Sacchini's *Renaud*.

Legros was director of the Concert Spirituel from 1777, and promoted music by Joseph Haydn and W.A. Mozart; but he too often he allowed commercial considerations to outweigh his artistic judgment. With L.-B. Desormery he rewrote the second entrée of François Grenet's *opéra-ballet*, *Le triomphe de l'harmonie* (performed at the Opéra as *Hylas et Eglé* in 1775). He composed another opera, *Anacréon*, which was not performed, and some songs.

Julian Rushton

Lehane, Maureen

(*b* London, 18 Sept 1932). English mezzo-soprano. She studied at the GSM and in Berlin. She made a speciality of G.F. Handel, and sang leading roles – often castrato roles, which she sang with much spirit – in some 20 of his stage works for the Handel Opera Society in London and elsewhere, mostly during the 1960s and 70s. Her Glyndebourne début was in 1967 as Melide in Francesco Cavalli's *L'Ormindo*, and her repertory includes operas by Antonio Vivaldi, J.C. Bach, Henry Purcell (*Dido and Aeneas*) and Gioachino Rossini (*La Cenerentola*) as well as works by Hugo Cole, Alan Ridout and her husband, Peter Wishart. With a voice admired for range, flexibility and fullness of tone, she toured Europe, the Middle and Far East and the USA; she has also given masterclasses in Handel interpretation and, with her husband, edited three volumes of Purcell songs.

Noël Goodwin

Lehmann, Lilli

(*b* Würzburg, 24 Nov 1848; *d* Berlin, 17 May 1929). German soprano. Sister of MARIE LEHMANN, she studied with her mother, the singer Marie Loewe, in Prague, and made her début there in 1865 as the First Boy in *Die Zauberflöte*, later taking over the part of Pamina. In 1868 she was engaged at Danzig, and in 1869 she sang for the first time at the Berlin Hofoper, as Marguerite de Valois in *Les Huguenots*. The following year, after appearances in Leipzig, she was engaged permanently in Berlin. She took part in the first complete *Ring* cycle at Bayreuth (1876), delighting Richard Wagner with her singing as Woglinde, Helmwige and the Woodbird. She also created Christine in Ignaz Brüll's *Das goldene Kreuz* (1875). She made her London début at Her Majesty's Theatre in June 1880 as Violetta in *La traviata*, and also sang Philine in Ambroise Thomas' *Mignon*. In 1882 she was heard in Vienna for the first time, and in 1884 she returned to London, appearing at Covent Garden as Isolde and as Elisabeth in *Tannhäuser*.

In 1885 Lehmann broke her contract with the Berlin Hofoper and went to New York, where she made her début at the Metropolitan as Carmen. During her first season she also sang Brünnhilde in *Die Walküre*, Sulamith in the first American performance of Karl Goldmark's *Die Königin von Saba*, Berthe in *Le prophète*, Marguerite in *Faust*, Irene in *Rienzi* and Venus in *Tannhäuser*. She took part in the first New York performances of *Tristan und Isolde* (1886), Goldmark's *Merlin* (1887), *Siegfried*

Lilli Lehmann [centre] with Minna Lammert [left] and Marie Lehmann [right], as Rhinemaidens in the première of 'Der Ring des Nibelungen' (Wagner), Bayreuth, 1876

(1887) and *Götterdämmerung* (1888), as well as the first complete *Ring* cycle given in the USA (March 1889). In 1891 she returned to Berlin and in 1896 she sang Brünnhilde at Bayreuth. During her final season at the Metropolitan (1898–9) she sang Fricka in *Das Rheingold*, and at Covent Garden, where she returned in 1899, her last appearances were as Isolde, Sieglinde, Ortrud, Leonore, Donna Anna and Norma. Between 1901 and 1910 she sang at the Salzburg Festival (Donna Anna and the First Lady in *Die Zauberflöte*) and also became the festival's artistic director. She continued to appear on the concert platform until 1920. She had started to teach in Berlin as early as 1891, and among her many famous pupils were OLIVE FREMSTAD and GERALDINE FARRAR.

Lehmann's enormous repertory ranged from the light, coloratura parts of her youth to the dramatic roles which she sang with superb authority and technical skill during the middle and later years of her career. As it grew more powerful, her voice retained all its flexibility, and she could turn from Wagner or Giuseppe Verdi to W.A. Mozart or Vincenzo Bellini with astonishing ease; W.J. Henderson wrote that dramatically 'she was possessed of that rare combination of traits and equipment which made it possible for her to delineate the divinity in womanhood and womanhood in divinity, the mingling of the unapproachable goddess and the melting pitying human being' (*The Art of Singing*, New York, 1938). However, not all of Lehmann's critics were unstinting in their praise. Hugo Wolf, writing in the *Wiener Salonblatt* of 25 January 1885, objected to her making a virago of Isolde, and he felt that her interpretation of the part was neither rounded nor fully worked out, though it contained many beautiful, even gripping details.

L. Lehmann: *Meine Gesangskunst* (Berlin, 1902, 3/1922; Eng. trans., 1902, as *How to Sing*, enlarged 3/1924/*R*)
L. Lehmann: *Mein Weg* (Leipzig, 1914, 2/1920; Eng. trans., 1914/*R*)

Elizabeth Forbes

Lehmann, Lotte

(*b* Perleberg, 27 Feb 1888; *d* Santa Barbara, CA, 26 Aug 1976). German soprano, active in England and the USA. She studied in Berlin, and began her career in 1910 with the Hamburg Opera. In 1916 she moved to Vienna, scoring an instant success as the Composer in the newly revised version of Richard Strauss's *Ariadne auf Naxos*; she was later to be his first Dyer's Wife in *Die Frau ohne Schatten* (1919, Vienna) and Christine in *Intermezzo* (1924, Dresden). She remained in Vienna until 1938,

when political events drove her from Austria. During her long Viennese career she sang a wide range of French and Italian roles (Giacomo Puccini specially esteemed her Suor Angelica), as well as the German repertory with which she became most closely associated. From 1924 she was a great favourite at Covent Garden, returning almost every year until 1938, by which time she had also established herself in the USA, where she became a naturalized citizen.

Internationally, Lehmann's most famous roles were Ludwig van Beethoven's Leonore, and Richard Wagner's Elisabeth, Elsa, Eva and above all Sieglinde. But the part with which she became increasingly identified was that of Strauss's Marschallin – a portrayal of which Richard Capell wrote: 'The lyric stage of the time knew no performance more admirably accomplished; it seemed to embody a civilization, the pride and elegance of old Vienna, its voluptuousness, chastened by good manners, its doomed beauty'. Over her long and fruitful career Lehmann developed and refined her lieder style, and her recitals, which continued until 1951, won her a following no less devoted than her operatic public. Her many recordings, most of which have been transferred successfully to CD, convey a vivid impression of her warm, generous voice and urgent, impulsive style. She wrote a volume of autobiography, *Anfang und Aufstieg*, published in Vienna in 1937 (as *Wings of Song*, London, 1938), and several studies in interpretation. After retirement she taught at the Music Academy of the West, Santa Barbara, and gave masterclasses.

B. Glass: *Lotte Lehmann: a Life in Opera and Song* (Santa Barbara, CA, 1988) [with discography by G. Hickling]
A. Jefferson: *Lotte Lehmann 1888–1976* (London, 1988) [with discography by F. Juynboll]

Desmond Shawe-Taylor/R

Lehmann, Marie

(*b* Hamburg, 15 May 1851; *d* Berlin, 9 Dec 1931). German soprano. Sister of LILLI LEHMANN. Like her sister, she was taught by her mother, Marie Loewe. She made her début in 1871 at Leipzig as Aennchen in *Der Freischütz* and then sang at Breslau, Cologne, Hamburg and Prague. In 1872 she sang in the performance of Ludwig van Beethoven's Ninth Symphony at the laying of the foundation stone of the Bayreuth Festspielhaus, and in 1876 took part in the first complete *Ring* cycle at Bayreuth, singing Wellgunde and Ortlinde (see illustration at LEHMANN, LILLI). From 1882 to 1896 she was engaged at the Vienna Hofoper. Her repertory included Marguerite de Valois (*Les Huguenots*),

Donna Elvira (*Don Giovanni*), Adalgisa (*Norma*) and Antonina in Gaetano Donizetti's *Belisario*. She returned to Bayreuth in 1896 to sing the Second Norn in *Götterdämmerung*.

Elizabeth Forbes/R

Leider, Frida

(*b* Berlin, 18 April 1888; *d* Berlin, 4 June 1975). German soprano. She made her début at Halle in 1915, and filled other engagements at Rostock, Königsberg and Hamburg until her move in 1923 to the Berlin Staatsoper, where she was principal dramatic soprano for some 15 years. She appeared there in numerous Mozart, Verdi and Strauss operas as well as in *Fidelio* and in the big Wagner roles that brought her international fame. In 1924 she made her Covent Garden début as Isolde and Brünnhilde, at once becoming the favourite Wagnerian soprano of the house, to which she returned every year until 1938; her other roles there included Donna Anna, Leonora (*Il trovatore*) and C.W. Gluck's Armide. Between 1928 and 1938 she was a regular Brünnhilde, Isolde and Kundry at Bayreuth. Her American career was centred on Chicago, where she was heard in *Fidelio*, *Der Rosenkavalier*, *La Juive* and *Un ballo in maschera*, in addition to her Wagnerian parts.

Leider was a splendid artist with a dark-coloured, ample and well-trained voice of lovely quality, and a fine-spun legato and purity of phrase that enabled her to excel in Mozart and Italian opera as well as in Wagner. During her best years she made many valuable recordings, often in company with MELCHIOR, SCHORR and her other regular Wagnerian associates. These have all appeared in CD transfers, worthy mementos of her treasurable art.

F. Leider: *Das war mein Teil* (Berlin, 1959; Eng. trans., 1966/R, as *Playing my Part*) [with discography by H. Burros]
D. Shawe-Taylor: 'Frida Leider (1888–1975)', *Opera*, xxxix (1988), 905–8

Desmond Shawe-Taylor/R

Leiferkus, Sergey (Petrovich)

(*b* Leningrad [now St Petersburg], 4 April 1946). Russian baritone. He studied in Leningrad, where he was engaged at the Malïy Opernïy Teatr from 1972 to 1978. He first sang at the Kirov (now the Mariinsky) Theatre in 1977 as Prince Andrey (*War and Peace*) and went on to sing Gioachino Rossini's Figaro, Robert (*Iolanta*), Don Giovanni and other roles. In 1982 he sang the Marquis in Jules Massenet's *Grisélidis* at Wexford, returning

for Hans Heiling, Boniface (*Le jongleur de Notre-Dame*) and the Fiddler (*Königskinder*). He has sung Don Giovanni and Yevgeny Onegin for Scottish Opera, Zurga (*Les pêcheurs de perles*) and Escamillo for the ENO and Scarpia and Zurga for Opera North. In 1987 Leiferkus toured Britain with the Kirov Opera as Yevgeny Onegin and Tomsky (*The Queen of Spades*). He made his Royal Opera début as Luna in 1989, returning as Prince Igor, Ruprecht (*The Fiery Angel*), Iago, Onegin, Scarpia and Telramund. In 1992 he sang Tomsky at Glyndebourne and made his Metropolitan début as Onegin, returning as Iago in 1994. He sang at the Wexford festival while this was under the directorship of Elaine Padmore. Among his other roles are Nabucco, Amonasro, Anckarstroem in *Un ballo in maschera* (which he sang to acclaim in San Francisco in 2000) and Rangoni (*Boris Godunov*). Leiferkus's operatic recordings, all displaying his rich, intense timbre and incisive diction, include Don Pizarro, Iago and Telramund as well as four of his finest Russian roles: Tomsky, Mazeppa, Rangoni and Ruprecht. He is also a fine recitalist, and has made outstanding recordings of Russian songs that reveal his brilliant gifts of characterization and, as in Modest Musorgsky's *The Peepshow* and *Song of the Flea*, an ebullient sense of humour.

E. Forbes: 'Sergey Leiferkus', *Opera*, xli (1990), 175–80

Elizabeth Forbes

Leigh, Adele

(*b* London, 15 June 1928; *d* London, 23 May 2004). English soprano. After studying drama she went to the Juilliard School and was a pupil of MAGGIE TEYTE. From 1948 to 1956 she was a resident soprano at Covent Garden, making her début as Xenia (*Boris Godunov*) and having particular success as Cherubino, Pamina and Manon as well as creating Bella in Michael Tippett's *The Midsummer Marriage* (1955). She returned in 1961 as Octavian, and in 1963 joined the Vienna Volksoper as principal operetta soprano, until 1972. Her American début was as Musetta at Boston in 1966. She later came out of retirement to sing Gabrielle (*La vie parisienne*) at the Brighton Festival in 1984 with Phoenix Opera, and Heidi Schiller in Stephen Sondheim's *Follies* in London in 1987. Her bright-toned lyric soprano and musical sensibility were widely admired, as were her personal charm and glamorous appearance.

H. Rosenthal: *Sopranos of Today* (London, 1956)

Noël Goodwin

Lemaure, Catherine-Nicole

(*b* Paris, 3 Aug 1704; *d* Paris, 1786). French soprano. Entering the Paris Opéra chorus in about 1719, she sang Astraea in the 1721–2 revival of Lully's *Phaëton* in December, and was promoted to sing Libya in January. She quickly came to sing such principal parts as Hippodamie in the première of Mouret's *Pirithoüs* and the title role in Lacoste's *Philomèle* (both 1723). Her temperament was capricious and volatile, however, and she left the Opéra without warning in 1725 after a performance of Destouches and Lalande's *Les élémens*. She returned in 1726, only to cause an uproar when her rivalry with MARIE PÉLISSIER caused acrimonious disputes among 'les politiques de l'Opéra' during the opening run of Francoeur and Rebel's *Pirame et Thisbé*. Lemaure disappeared again in 1727–30, returning to sing in Campra's *Hésione*. She sang Oriane (Lully's *Amadis*, 1731) with triumphant success, created Iphise (Montéclair's *Jephté*, 1732) and sang the title role in Destouches' *Issé* (1733 revival), in which she was considered 'miraculeuse' by J.-B. Formont. She sang Iphigenia in the 1734 revival of Desmarets' *Iphigénie en Tauride*. Threatened with imprisonment if she did not appear in the 1735 revival of *Jephté*, Lemaure deliberately sang poorly and was hissed by the parterre. When she refused to continue, she was escorted (still in costume) to Fort l'Evêque, where she was detained overnight before returning the following day to take up her role with better grace. Her 1740 performances of Iphise and Oriane were greeted with enthusiastic ovations, and in 1744 she supplanted Pélissier as Iphise in Rameau's *Dardanus*, a role Pélissier had created.

Her personal fascination in performance, the 'transcendent beauty' of her voice, and the prodigious transformation which came over her as soon as she began to sing on stage, were vividly described by J.-B. de La Borde (in his *Essai sur la musique*). Voltaire contrasted the rapturous physiological emotion of her voice with the supreme technical art of Pélissier. Lemaure retired in 1744, more by caprice than because of any vocal incapacity, but was still cited with admiration (by Voltaire and the *Mercure*) well into the 1760s and 70s.

Philip Weller

Lemeshyov [Lemeshev], Sergey (Yakovlevich)

(*b* Knyazevo, Tver' province, 27 June/10 July 1902; *d* Moscow, 26 June 1977). Russian tenor. He studied at the Moscow Conservatory and with Konstantin Stanislavsky at the Bol'shoy Opera Studio. He made his début in 1926 in Sverdlovsk (now Yekaterinburg). In 1931 he joined the Bol'shoy Theatre. Lemeshyov's lyrical voice, with its individual tone, and the integrity of his characterizations imbued his performances with special charm, and they were noted for their intelligence, fastidious detail and fine acting. His repertory included Lensky, Bayan (*Ruslan and Lyudmila*), Vladimir (*Prince Igor*), Berendey and Levko (*The Snow Maiden* and *May Night*), Vladimir Dubrovsky in Eduard Nápravník's *Dubrovsky*, Charles Gounod's Faust and Romeo, the Duke of Mantua and Almaviva. His recordings include the romance 'O, day mne zabven'ye' ('O grant me oblivion') from *Dubrovsky*. As a director he produced *La traviata* at the Malïy Theatre, Leningrad, and *Werther* at the Bol'shoy, both in 1951. He published *Put' k iskusstvu* ('The Path to Art', Moscow, 1968). He was made People's Artist of the USSR in 1950.

I.M. Yampol'sky

Lemnitz, Tiana (Luise)

(*b* Metz, 26 Oct 1897; *d* Berlin, 26 Jan 1994). German soprano. She studied with Anton Kohmann in Frankfurt and made her début at Heilbronn in 1920 in Albert Lortzing's *Undine*; from 1922 to 1928 she sang at Aachen. She became leading lyric soprano at Hanover (1928–33) and then, after a year in Dresden, joined the Berlin Staatsoper in 1934, remaining there until she retired in 1957. In Berlin her roles ranged from Mimì and Micaëla to Aida and Desdemona, from Pamina and Mařenka to Sieglinde. Later she sang the Marschallin, Milada (Bedřich Smetana's *Dalibor*), Jenůfa, and Nastas'ya (P.I. Tchaikovsky's *The Enchantress*).

Lemnitz made her Covent Garden début in 1936 as Eva and returned for Octavian, Elsa, Pamina and Sieglinde; her career was otherwise mostly confined to central Europe. She was also a distinguished singer of lieder. Her warm, appealing voice and presence made her an ideal interpreter of the lyric roles of W.A. Mozart, Carl Maria von Weber, Richard Wagner and Richard Strauss. In 1935 she sang in the first performance of the operetta *Die grosse Sünderin* composed for the Berlin Staatsoper by Eduard Künneke. Among the best of her many recordings are the arias from *Der Freischütz* and *Lohengrin*, her exquisite Pamina in Thomas Beecham's classic recording of *Die Zauberflöte* and her Octavian in Rudolf Kempe's *Der Rosenkavalier*.

R. Seeliger: 'Tiana Lemnitz', *Record Collector*, xv (1963–4), 29–43 [with discography by R. Seeliger and B. Park]
A. Blyth: Obituary, *Opera*, xlv (1994), 427–8

Harold Rosenthal/Alan Blyth

Lotte Lenya as Jenny in Georg Wilhelm Pabst's 1931 film of 'Die Dreigroschenoper' (Weill)

Lenya [Lenja], Lotte [Blamauer, Karoline Wilhelmine]

(*b* Vienna, 18 Oct 1898; *d* New York, 27 Nov 1981). American singing actress of Austrian birth. After studying dance in Zürich (1914–20) she moved to Berlin to embark on a dancing career. Two years later she turned to the spoken theatre, where by the end of the decade she had established a brilliant reputation in plays by, among others, Frank Wedekind, Marieluise Fleisser and, above all, Bertolt Brecht

and his outstanding musical collaborator, Kurt Weill. Her marriage to Weill in 1926 was followed by a striking appearance at the 1927 Baden-Baden Festival in his and Brecht's one-act 'Songspiel' *Mahagonny*. With her creation of Jenny in *Die Dreigroschenoper* (1928, Berlin) and her subsequent recordings and film version of that role, her international reputation was assured. While continuing a noteworthy career as an actress, she sang the part of Jenny in the Berlin version of Weill's *Aufstieg und Fall der Stadt Mahagonny* (with new material specially composed for her, 1930) and created three further roles in works by Weill: Anna I in the *ballet chanté Die sieben Todsünden* (1933, Paris), Miriam in *The Eternal Road* (1937) and the Duchess in *The Firebrand of Florence* (1945), the latter two receiving their premières in New York where the couple had emigrated in 1935.

Soon after Weill's death in 1950 Lenya began to devote much of her time to the revival of some of his important works from the German years, most notably through her re-creation, in Marc Blitzstein's English translation, of Jenny in the long-running New York production of *The Threepenny Opera* (from 1954). Her live and recorded performances won for her and for Weill a new or renewed reputation in many lands, and established a 'classical' and much imitated Weill singing style whose abrasive timbre and low tessitura (generally requiring transposition down a 4th) were markedly different from those of Lenya's Berlin years, when she sang with an almost boyish soprano. What had survived from those years, and most remarkably matured, was a combination of dramatic insight and musical instinct, of intelligence, wit, coolness and passion, which arose from a strictly inimitable empathy with Weill's music. Although her tastes in both popular and classical music were broad and she enjoyed a critical *succès d'estime* in the Broadway production of *Cabaret* (1966), as a musical performer she confined herself almost entirely to the songs of her husband and to the one extended work he composed especially for her, *Die sieben Todsünden*; this was enough to establish her as one of the outstanding *diseuses* of her time.

No less important to Weill's later reception was Lenya's role in creating the Kurt Weill Foundation for Music (1962), a non-profit organization richly endowed by Weill's posthumous royalties (the couple was childless) and dedicated to the study and propagation of his music. Much information on Lenya's career and personality can be found in the holdings of its Weill-Lenya Research Center in New York and the pages of its biannual newsletter. Her papers are now housed in the Weill-Lenya Archive at the Beinecke Rare Book and Manuscript Library of Yale University.

D. Spoto: *Lenya: a Life* (New York, 1989)

L. Symonette and K. Kowalke, eds.: *Speak Low (when you Speak Love): the Letters of Kurt Weill and Lotte Lenya* (Berkeley, 1996)

D. Farneth, ed.: *Lenya the Legend: a Pictorial Autobiography* (New York, 1998)

David Drew/J. Bradford Robinson

Leonov, Leon Ivanovich [Charpentier]

(*b* St Petersburg, *c*1813; *d* Oct 1872). Russian tenor. The illegitimate son of John Field, the Irish composer and pianist, and a French mother, he appeared with his father as a child prodigy in Moscow. Having begun his career as a tenor in 1833, he was engaged in St Petersburg at the Bol'shoy Theatre, where he created Sobinin in *A Life for the Tsar* (1836) and Finn in *Ruslan and Lyudmila* (1842). Later he sang at the Mariinsky Theatre (1860–64). His repertory included the title role of *Robert le diable* and Gioachino Rossini's Count Almaviva as well as many parts in Russian operas.

Elizabeth Forbes

Le Page, François

(*b* Joinville, 27 Feb 1709; *d* after 1780). French baritone (*basse-taille*). His first roles at the Paris Opéra were Don Carlos and Silvandre (*L'Europe galante*, 1736 revival), Mars (*Castor et Pollux*, 1737) and Pan (*Cadmus*, 1737 revival). His position as third *basse-taille*, after CLAUDE CHASSÉ and JEAN DUN, improved during the former's absence, 1738–42. He created Ismenor and Teucer in Jean-Philippe Rameau's *Dardanus* (1739), roles that reverted to Chassé in the 1744 revival, when Le Page was relegated to Antenor. In 1740 he sang the title role in Michel Montéclair's *Jephté* for the triumphant return of Mlle Lemaure as Iphise, and the following year appeared as André Destouches' Hylas to Lemaure's Issé. Le Page sang in the first performances of Rameau's *Zaïs* (1748, Cindor) and *Naïs* (1749, Jupiter and Tiresias) and took smaller roles in *Zoroastre*, *Platée* and *Acante et Céphise*. He was married to MLLE EREMANS, and retired in 1752.

Philip Weller

Le Rochois, Marie ['La Rochois']

(*b* Caen, *c*1658; *d* Paris, 8 Oct 1728). French soprano and singing teacher, commonly but incorrectly known as Marthe le Rochois. She may have studied with Michel Lambert, who presumably brought her to the attention of his son-in-law, Jean-Baptiste Lully. In 1678 she entered the Paris Opéra, where Lully chose her to create the roles of Arethusa in *Proserpine* (1680), Merope in *Persée* (1682), Arcabonne in *Amadis* (1684), Angélique in *Roland* (1685), Armide in *Armide* (1686) and Galatea in *Acis et Galatée* (1686). She also sang in Lully revivals, as Medea in *Thésée* (1688), Cybele in *Atys* (1689) and Hermione in *Cadmus et Hermione* (1690). In the post-Lully period she created Polyxena in the Lully—Pascal Collasse *Achille et Polyxène* (1687), Thetis in Collasse's *Thétis et Pélée* (1689), Lavinia in Collasse's *Enée et Lavinie* (1690), Dido in Henry Desmarets' *Didon* (1693) and Medea in Marc-Antoine Charpentier's *Médée* (1693). Fearing the loss of her voice, Le Rochois was absent from the Opéra from 1694 to 1696, when she returned as Ariadne in Marin Marais' *Ariane et Bacchus*. In 1697 she created the roles of Venus in Desmarets' *Vénus et Adonis* and Roxane in André Campra's *L'Europe galante*. Her final role (shared with MLLE DESMATINS) was Isis in André Destouches' *pastorale-héroïque*, performed in December 1697. She retired in 1698.

Le Rochois was best known for her performance of Armide, the memory of which caused Le Cerf de la Viéville (*Comparaison de la musique*, 1704–6) to 'shiver' with delight. Titon du Tillet (*Le Parnasse françois*, 1732) called her the 'greatest actress and the best model for declamation to have appeared on the stage':

> Although she was of mediocre height, dark complexioned and possessed a rather ordinary figure as seen off-stage,…On stage she made one forget all the most beautiful Actresses; she had the air of a Queen or Goddess, her head nobly placed, with an admirable sense of Gesture; all her actions were correct and natural. She knew what to do during the *Ritournelle* which played while an Actress came on-stage, and she was a master of pantomime.

Although most French observers seem to have been in general agreement with Titon's appraisal, J.E. Galliard, in his English translation (1709) of François Raguenet's *Paralèle des italiens et des françois*, added: 'I saw that woman at Paris: she was a good figure enough and had a tolerable voice, but then she was a wretched actress and sang insufferably out of tune'.

Upon retirement from the Opéra, Le Rochois purchased a small country house outside Paris where she received important musicians, actors and actresses, who profited from her 'pleasant conversation, her knowledge and her good taste' (Titon du Tillet). Of strong moral character and untouched by professional jealousy, she gave singing lessons in her retirement to a new generation of opera singers, chief among whom were Mlles Françoise Journet and Marie Antier. After a long illness, she died in an apartment on the rue St Honoré and was buried at St Eustache.

James R. Anthony/R

Le Roux, François

(*b* Rennes, 30 Oct 1955). French baritone. He studied with François Loup, then at the Opéra-Studio in Paris with Vera Rozsa and ELISABETH GRÜMMER. In 1980 he joined the Lyons Opéra, remaining with the company for the following five years. His repertory there included the major Mozart baritone roles – Don Giovanni, Papageno, Guglielmo, Count Almaviva and Figaro – but perhaps his most significant role there was Pelléas, which he first sang in 1985 and repeated to acclaim at La Scala, Covent Garden (where he made his début in 1989 as Papageno) and the Vienna Staatsoper. He appeared as Ramiro in *L'heure espagnole* at Glyndebourne in 1987, and in 1991 created the title role in Harrison Birtwistle's *Gawain* at Covent Garden. He has sung many new works in concert, including John Casken's *My Way of Life* (1990) and *Still Mine* (1994). Le Roux is also a notable interpreter of *mélodies*, showing an exact understanding of music and text, as his recording of Reynaldo Hahn songs confirms. Among his other notable recordings are Gawain and his vulnerable, ardent Pelléas with Claudio Abbado. Although Le Roux's voice is not voluminous, he uses it with consistent subtlety and imagination.

Alan Blyth

Lesne, Gérard

(*b* Montmorency, 15 July 1956). French countertenor. Mainly self-taught, he joined the Clemencic Consort in Vienna in 1979 and since then has appeared with many of the leading European early music ensembles, including the Ensemble Clément Janequin, La Grande Ecurie et la Chambre du Roy, the Chapelle Royale, Hesperion XX and Les Arts Florissants. In 1985 he founded his own vocal and instrumental ensemble, Il Seminario Musicale, with which he has appeared in concerts and festivals throughout Europe. Although he has sung a number of operatic roles, he shows closer affinity with sacred music of the 17th and 18th centuries, for which his lightly textured, pure-toned voice is particularly well suited. His recordings include Alessandro Stradella's *S Giovanni Battista*, Marc-Antoine Charpentier's *David et Jonathas*, G.F. Handel's *Poro*, Antonio Vivaldi's *L'incoronazione di Dario*, *Leçons de ténèbres* by Charpentier and François Couperin, cantatas by Alessandro Scarlatti, Antonio Caldara,

J.S. Bach, Handel and Bononcini, and sacred music by Claudio Monteverdi, Vivaldi, Giovanni Pergolesi and Niccolò Jommelli.

Nicholas Anderson

Levasseur, Nicholas (Prosper)

(*b* Bresles, nr Beauvais, 9 March 1791; *d* Paris, 7 Dec 1871). French bass. He entered the Paris Conservatoire in 1807 and made his début at the Opéra as the Pacha in A.-E.-M. Grétry's *La caravane du Caire* (1813). However, the Opéra's repertory lacked deep bass roles, and for two seasons he sang in Italian opera at London, making his début at the King's Theatre in Johann Mayr's *Adelasia e Aleramo* (1815). He returned to the Opéra as an understudy but in 1819 joined the Théâtre Italien, first appearing as Almaviva in *Le nozze di Figaro*. The following year he appeared at La Scala, Milan, in the première of Giacomo Meyerbeer's *Margherita d'Anjou*. At the Théâtre Italien, Levasseur sang in many Rossini operas new to Paris, notably in the title role of *Mosè* (1822), a role he repeated with considerable success when Rossini revised the work for the Opéra (1827) (though Rossini himself reportedly forgot to attend the first performance as he was playing dominoes in the Opéra café). In 1828 he rejoined the Opéra as one of its leading singers, and was one of the celebrated trio that included NOURRIT and CINTI-DAMOREAU. Over the next 12 years he created virtually every important new bass role in the Opéra's repertory, including Bertram in *Robert le diable* (1831 see colour plate 6), whose 'ironie moqueuse' in the *duo bouffe* was particularly praised, Brogni in *La Juive* (1835), Marcel in *Les Huguenots* (1836) and Balthazar in *La favorite* (1840). Other roles he created included the Tutor (*Le comte Ory*, 1828), Walter Furst (*Guillaume Tell*, 1829), Moses (*Mosè in Egitto*, 1819, *Moïse et Pharon*, 1827), and Zacharie (*Le prophète*, 1849). His pure, expressive voice was, like that of Louis Ponchard, inspired by C.W. Gluck, W.A. Mozart and the Italian school; he also had a talent for comic effects as well as for serious roles. He left the Opéra in 1845, but at Meyerbeer's request returned to sing in the première of *Le prophète* (16 April 1849), and finally retired in 1853. His ease with intimate scenes meant that he was also suited to salon performances, and he was one of the singers involved in Charles Lebouc's soirées of *musique classique et historique* organized for audiences of amateurs. Levasseur taught at the Conservatoire from 1841 to 1869, and on his retirement he was made a Chevalier of the Légion d'Honneur. He became blind shortly before his death.

Philip Robinson/Sarah Hibberd

Levasseur [Le Vasseur], **Rosalie** [Marie-Rose-**(Claude-)**Josephe]

(*b* Valenciennes, 8 Oct 1749; *d* Neuwied am Rhein, 6 May 1826). French soprano. She made her début at the Paris Opéra in 1766 as Zäide in André Campra's *L'Europe galante* and appeared there regularly until 1785. Known as Mlle Rosalie during her first ten years at the Opéra, she was well received in minor roles or as a substitute for Mme Larrivée until, in 1776, she was entrusted with Eurydice and Iphigenia in revivals of C.W. Gluck's operas. She was then preferred over her rival, SOPHIE ARNOULD, to create the title role in the French *Alceste*. The mistress from 1770 of the Austrian ambassador Mercy-Argenteau, by whom she had a son, she became Gluck's close friend and favourite interpreter, creating the title roles in *Armide* (1777) and *Iphigénie en Tauride* (1779). She was successful in the title role of F.-A. Philidor's *Ernelinde* (1777 revival), but less so in Niccolò Piccinni's works, relinquishing his Angélique (*Roland*) and Sangaride (*Atys*) to other singers. Her reputation lay not in vocal beauty but in intelligent use of the voice as an adjunct to accomplished acting.

J.G. Prod'homme: 'Rosalie Levasseur, Ambassadress of Opera', *MQ*, ii (1916), 210–43

Julian Rushton

Levinson, Aleksandr.

See DAVIDOFF, ALEKSANDR.

Lévy, Paul.

See LHERIE, PAUL.

Lewis, Keith (Neville)

(*b* Methven, 6 Oct 1950). New Zealand tenor. He studied in New Zealand, then at the London Opera Centre (1974–6) and with RICHARD LEWIS and others. His début was as Ferrando at the St Céré Festival in France in 1977, followed that year by Don Ottavio for Glyndebourne Touring Opera and the next summer at Glyndebourne, where he returned in later seasons. He created the roles of Christ/Father in John Tavener's *Thérèse* for his Covent Garden début in 1979; other débuts include the Paris Opéra in 1983 as Aménophis in *Moïse* (Gioachino Rossini), San Francisco Opera in 1984 as Don Ottavio, and the Deutsche Oper, Berlin, in 1985 as Ferrando. In 1988 he added Hector Berlioz's Faust to his repertory at Hamburg and in 1989 Charles Gounod's at Berlin. He has sung frequently in Australian opera productions, and in 1992 sang Pyrrhus in the British première of Rossini's *Ermione* at the Queen Elizabeth Hall. The mellifluous style of his lyric tenor is combined with smooth projection and ardently expressive character. His recordings include Don Ottavio under Bernard Haitink with the Glyndebourne company (1984).

A. Simpson and P. Downes: *Southern Voices: International Opera Singers of New Zealand* (Auckland, 1992), pp. 260–75

Noël Goodwin

Lewis, Richard [Thomas, Thomas]

(*b* Manchester, 10 May 1914; *d* Eastbourne, 13 Nov 1990). English tenor. He studied in Manchester with Norman Allin and made his début in 1941 with the Carl Rosa Company, singing Almaviva and Pinkerton. After World War II he resumed his studies in London. In 1947 he sang the Male Chorus (*Rape of Lucretia*) at Glyndebourne and at Covent Garden, adding Peter Grimes with the resident company the same season and later singing Tamino and Alfredo. For Glyndebourne (1948–74) he sang Don Ottavio, Ferrando, Admetus (*Alceste*), Idomeneus, Tom Rakewell (British première of *The Rake's Progress*, at Edinburgh, 1953), Bacchus, Florestan and Claudio Monteverdi's Nero and Eumaeus. He created Gwyn in Arwell Hughes's *Menna* (WNO, 1953). For Covent Garden Lewis created Troilus in William Walton's *Troilus and Cressida* (1954), Mark in *The Midsummer Marriage* (1955) and Achilles in *King Priam* (1962, Coventry) and sang Don José, Hoffmann, Hermann, Captain Vere, and Aron in the first British staging of *Moses und Aron* (1965), which he also sang at Boston in its American stage première (1966). He made his San Francisco début in 1955 as Don José, then sang Troilus, Jeník, Grigory, Jules Massenet's Des Grieux, the Captain (*Wozzeck*), Alwa (*Lulu*), Jason, Pinkerton, Eisenstein and Herod. At the Deutsche Oper, Berlin, he created Amphitryon in Giselher Klebe's *Alkmene* (1961). His mellifluous, flexible voice was used with great intelligence, as can be heard on his two recordings of *Idomeneo* and in recorded extracts from *Così fan tutte* and *Troilus and Cressida*. Lewis also had a notable career on the concert platform. He took part in the première of Igor Stravinsky's *Canticum sacrum* (1956, Venice), and was a leading exponent of the tenor parts in all the main oratorios. He was particularly renowned for his Gerontius, which he twice recorded.

H.D. Rosenthal: 'Richard Lewis', *Opera*, vi (1955), 144–8
A. Blyth: 'Richard Lewis 1914–1990', *Opera*, xlii (1991), 33–6
N. Ross-Russell: *There will I Sing: the Making of a Tenor* (London, 1996)

Alan Blyth

Lhérie [Lévy], Paul

(*b* Paris, 8 Oct 1844; *d* Paris, 17 Oct 1937). French tenor, later baritone. He studied in Paris, making his début at the Opéra-Comique in 1866 as Ruben in E.-N. Méhul's *Joseph*. At the Théâtre de la Monnaie he sang Fabrice in Friedrich Flotow's *L'ombre* (1871) and Reinhild in F.-A. Gevaert's *Le billet de Marguerite*. Back at the Opéra-Comique, he created Charles II in Jules Massenet's *Don César de Bazan* (1872), Benoît in Léo Delibes' *Le Roi l'a dit* (1873) and Don José in *Carmen* (1875). In 1882 he became a baritone and in 1884 sang Posa in the revised version of Giuseppe Verdi's *Don Carlos* at La Scala. At Covent Garden in 1887 he sang Zurga, Rigoletto, Germont, Luna and Alphonse (*La favorite*). In 1891 he created the Rabbi David in Pietro Mascagni's *L'amico Fritz* at the Teatro Costanzi, Rome; in 1894 he sang Gudleik in the first performance of César Franck's *Hulda* at Monte Carlo and then retired.

Elizabeth Forbes

Licette, Miriam

(*b* Chester, 9 Sept 1892; *d* Twyford, 11 Aug 1969). English soprano. She studied under BLANCHE MARCHESI, JEAN DE RESZKE, GIUSEPPE SABBATINI, and Helen M. Hardelot, making her début in Rome as Butterfly (1911). After further successful European appearances, she returned to England, where she became one of the leading lyric sopranos of her day, singing with the Thomas Beecham Opera Company (1916), the British National Opera Company (1922), and at Covent Garden (1919–1929). In 1938–39 she sang in *Un ballo in maschera* and *Der Zigeunerbaron* with the Carl Rosa Opera Company. Her roles included Mimì, Desdemona, Eva and Louise, and she was specially admired in W.A. Mozart. Her voice was pure and steady, with firmly placed tone and a remarkably even scale, well represented in Beecham's complete recording in English of *Faust* (1930). Her name is commemorated in the Miriam Licette Scholarship administered by the Musicians Benevolent Fund.

J.B. Steane

Lichtenegger, Mathilde.

See MALLINGER, MATHILDE.

Liebling, Estelle

(*b* New York, 21 April 1880; *d* New York, 25 Sept 1970). American soprano and teacher. Trained in Paris by Mathilde Marchesi and in Berlin by Selma Nicklass-Kempner, she made her début at the Dresden Hofoper in the title role of Gaetano Donizetti's *Lucia di Lammermoor* at the age of 18. She then sang with the Stuttgart Opera and at the Opéra-Comique, and appeared three times at the Metropolitan Opera (1902–4), where her début role was Marguerite in *Les Huguenots*. After her 50th birthday she turned her energies to teaching and was on the faculty of the Curtis Institute from 1936 to 1938. Thereafter she settled in New York, where her pupils included BEVERLY SILLS. She wrote an influential book on singing technique, *The Estelle Liebling Coloratura Digest* (New York, 1943).

Karen Monson/R

Ligabue, Ilva

(*b* Reggio nell'Emilia, 23 May 1932; *d* Palermo, 22 Aug 1998). Italian soprano. Trained at the Scuola della Scala, Milan, she made her début there in 1953 as Marina in *I quattro rusteghi*. Engagements followed elsewhere in Italy and in Germany; she achieved a major success at Glyndebourne in 1958 as Alice (*Falstaff*) and returned as Fiordiligi and Donna Elvira. In 1961 she sang Vincenzo Bellini's Beatrice at La Scala and made her American début with the Chicago Lyric Opera as Margherita (*Mefistofele*). She also sang Alice at Covent Garden (1963) and appeared at the Vienna Staatsoper, in Buenos Aires and elsewhere. A lyric soprano of great tonal beauty and musical sensibility, she had a captivating stage presence. Her recordings include Alice with Georg Solti and Leonard Bernstein, and Asteria in Arrigo Boito's *Nerone*.

Noël Goodwin

Lightstone, Pauline.

See DONALDA, PAULINE.

Lima, Luis

(*b* Córdoba, Argentina, 12 Sept 1948). Argentine tenor. After studying in Buenos Aires and Madrid, he made his début in 1974 at Lisbon as Turiddu. He was then engaged at Mainz and also sang in Stuttgart, Hamburg, Munich and Berlin; in 1977 he sang Edgardo (*Lucia di Lammermoor*) at La Scala. He made his début at the Metropolitan in 1978 as Alfredo, at the Teatro Colón in 1982 as Cavaradossi and at Covent Garden in 1984 as Nemorino. He has also appeared at Verona, Rome, Paris, Geneva, Salzburg and Savonlinna, where in 1986 he sang Don Carlos. His repertory includes Don José, Hoffmann, Charles Gounod's Romeo, Faust and

Vincent, Hector Berlioz's and Arrigo Boito's *Faust*, Riccardo (*Ballo*) and Rodolfo (*Bohème*). A lyric tenor with an elegant style, he has sometimes taken roles that are too heavy for his voice.

Elizabeth Forbes

Lind [Lind-Goldschmidt], Jenny [Johanna Maria]

Jenny Lind

(*b* Stockholm, 6 Oct 1820; *d* Wynds Point, Herefordshire, 2 Nov 1887). Swedish soprano. She was nicknamed 'the Swedish nightingale'. In 1830 she was enrolled at the Royal Opera School, Stockholm. She made her début in 1838 as Agathe in *Der Freischütz*; later that year she sang Pamina and Euryanthe. She appeared in *La vestale*, *Robert le diable* (1839), *Don Giovanni* (as Donna Anna), *Lucia di Lammermoor* (1840) and *La straniera*, and as Norma, which she sang for the first time in 1841. Her voice began to show signs of fatigue, the middle register being particularly worn, and she went to Paris to consult the younger Manuel Garcia, who imposed a period of rest before taking her as a pupil. When she returned to Stockholm, appearing in *Norma* in October 1842, an improvement in her voice and technique was immediately apparent. The middle register remained veiled in tone and relatively weak for the rest of her career, but the notes from *c"* to *a"* had become marvellously strong and flexible, and her range extended to *g'''*.

Lind's new roles included Valentine (*Les Huguenots*), Ninetta (*La gazza ladra*), Countess Almaviva, and Amina (*La sonnambula*), which she sang for the first time in 1843. During the next season she added *Il turco in Italia*, C.W. Gluck's *Armide* and *Anna Bolena* to her repertory. In 1844 she went to Germany, making her début in Berlin in *Norma* and in 1845 singing Vielka in Giacomo Meyerbeer's *Ein Feldlager in Schlesien*, written for her but created by LEOPOLDINE TUCZEK-EHRENBURG. Returning to Stockholm, she sang Marie (*La fille du régiment*) for the first time.

Lind made her Viennese début at the Theater an der Wien in April 1846 as Norma. She then toured extensively in Germany, taking part, with Felix Mendelssohn, in the Lower Rhine Festival at Aachen during May and June, when she sang in Joseph Haydn's *Creation* and G.F. Handel's *Alexander's Feast*. She also appeared at Munich, Stuttgart, Karlsruhe, Mannheim and Nuremberg. Returning in January 1847 to Vienna, she scored an immense success as Marie. Her triumphant London début was at Her Majesty's in May of the same year, when she sang (in Italian) Alice in *Robert le diable* before Queen Victoria and Prince Albert, followed by *La*

sonnambula and *La fille du régiment* with even greater success. She also created Amalia in *I masnadieri* (22 July) and sang Susanna. Having decided to give up the theatre, she sang in Sweden during the winter, making her last Stockholm appearance as Norma in April 1848. She then sang for a second season at Her Majesty's followed by an extensive tour of Great Britain. In December she sang Mendelssohn's *Elijah* at the Exeter Hall, London. Persuaded to give six extra farewell performances at Her Majesty's, she made her final stage appearance there as Alice on 10 May 1849. In 1850 she embarked on an eight-month concert tour throughout the USA, visiting 93 cities. She continued to sing in concerts and oratorios, both in Germany and in England, where she lived from 1858 until her death. In 1883, the year of her last public performance, she became professor of singing at the RCM. Lind's stage reputation was based largely on four operas, *La sonnambula*, *Robert le diable*, *La fille du régiment* and *Norma*. Her interpretation of Norma failed because of her temperamental inability to realize the character fully; thus Amina, Alice and Marie were probably her most satisfying operatic achievements (though her own preference was for Julia in *La vestale*).

B. Lumley: *Reminiscences of the Opera* (London, 1864/*R*)

H.S. Holland and W.S. Rockstro: *Memoir of Madame Jenny Lind-Goldschmidt: her Early Art-Life and Dramatic Career, 1820–1851* (London, 1891/*R*)

J.M.C. Maude: *The Life of Jenny Lind* (London, 1926/*R*)

J. Bulman: *Jenny Lind: a Biography* (London, 1956)

G. Denny: *Jenny Lind, the Swedish Nightingale* (New York, 1962)

W.P. Ware and T.C. Lockard, eds.: *The Lost Letters of Jenny Lind* (London, 1966)

A.F. Block: 'Two Virtuoso Performers in Boston: Jenny Lind and Camilla Urso', *New Perspectives on Music: Essays in Honor of Eileen Southern*, ed. J. Wright and S.A. Floyd (Warren, MI, 1992), 355–72

Elizabeth Forbes

Lipkowska [née Marschner], Lydia (Yakovlevna) [Lipkovskaya, Lidiya]

(*b* Babino, 25 May/6 June 1882; *d* Beirut, 22 March 1958). Russian soprano. She studied at the St Petersburg Conservatory, and sang in St Petersburg at the Imperial Opera (1906–8 and 1911–13) and in private opera companies (1913–15). In 1909 she sang at the Théâtre du Châtelet, Paris and then in the USA, appearing with the companies of Boston (1909) and Chicago (1910), and singing with the Metropolitan Opera (1909–11). She made her Covent Garden début as Mimì in 1911, later appearing as Ermanno Wolf-Ferrari's Susanna, Gilda and Violetta. At Monte Carlo in 1914 she took part in the first performances of Amilcare Ponchielli's *I Mori di Valenza* with GEORGY BAKLANOV and GIOVANNI MARTINELLI. After emigrating to France in 1919, she appeared with different émigré opera troupes in western Europe, toured the USSR (1928–9) and later lived and taught in Romania; among her students was the soprano VIRGINIA ZEANI. Lipkowska returned to Paris in 1945 before settling in Lebanon. Her repertory included Lakmé, Lucia, Nikolay Rimsky-Korsakov's Marfa (*The Tsar's Bride*), the Snow Maiden and Ol'ga (*Ivan the Terrible*), and P.I. Tchaikovsky's Tatyana and Iolanta. According to contemporary critics she was a good actress with an attractive presence and a pure voice capable of expressing uncomplicated emotions. She made 29 recordings between 1911 and 1914 which reveal her refinement of tone.

M. Scott: *The Record of Singing*, i (London, 1977), 25–7

Harold Barnes/Alan Blyth

Lipovšek, Marjana

(*b* Ljubljana, 3 Dec 1946). Slovenian mezzo-soprano. She studied at Graz and in Vienna, joining the Staatsoper in 1979 and then singing at Berlin, Hamburg, Frankfurt and Madrid. In 1986 she created Rosa Sacchi in Krzysztof Penderecki's *Die schwarze Maske* at Salzburg, where she has subsequently sung the Nurse (*Die Frau ohne Schatten*), Octavia (*L'incoronazione di Poppea*), Mistress Quickly,

Marina (*Boris Godunov*), Clytemnestra and Countess Geschwitz (*Lulu*). Her repertory also includes Dorabella, Carmen, Ulrica (*Un ballo in maschera*), Azucena, Amneris, Magdalene, Marina (*Boris Godunov*), Brangäne, Marfa (*Khovanshchina*), the Composer, Octavian and Delilah. In 1990 Lipovšek made her Covent Garden début as Clytemnestra and her Metropolitan début as Fricka, a role she has also sung in Munich, Barcelona, Chicago and at La Scala. In 1994 she sang Judith (*Bluebeard's Castle*) in Florence and in 1995 her first Kundry in Munich. Her operatic recordings include Marfa, Brangäne, Waltraute, Marina, Mistress Quickly and the Sphinx in Georges Enescu's *Oedipe*; all display her rich, vibrant, warm-toned voice, with its notably strong middle and lower registers, and her vivid gifts of characterization. Lipovšek also has a flourishing career as a concert singer, and has made admired recordings of works ranging from J.S. Bach's Passions to *Das Lied von der Erde* and *Oedipus rex*.

Elizabeth Forbes

Lipp, Wilma

(*b* Vienna, 26 April 1925). Austrian soprano. She studied in Vienna with ANNA BAHR-MILDENBURG and ALFRED JERGER, and made her début there as Rosina in 1943, joining the Staatsoper two years later. As the Queen of Night in 1948, she won wider fame; this was also the role of her débuts at La Scala (1950, under Otto Klemperer) and Paris (during the 1953 Staatsoper visit). In 1951 she sang the Woodbird at Bayreuth and made her début at Covent Garden as Gilda, returning in 1955 for Violetta. At Glyndebourne in 1957 she sang Konstanze and Nanetta, the role in which she made her début at San Francisco in 1962. Her career, which began in soubrette and coloratura roles, including Blonde, Servilia (*La clemenza di Tito*), Adèle, Sophie and the Italian singer (*Capriccio*) later progressed to more lyrical ones, including Ilia (*Idomeneo*), a notable Pamina, Donna Elvira, Countess Almaviva, Alice Ford and Eva. Lipp's pure, sweet tone and accurate coloratura are displayed in her recordings of the Queen of Night under Herbert von Karajan and Karl Böhm.

Alan Blyth

Lisitsian [Lisitsyan], Pavel [Pogos] Gerasim

(*b* Vladikavkaz, 24 Oct/6 Nov 1911; *d* Moscow, 6 July 2004). Armenian baritone. He studied in Leningrad, and made his début there in 1935. He first sang with the Bol'shoy Opera in 1940 and was for many years the company's leading baritone. He appeared at the Metropolitan as Amonasro in 1960, when he undertook a concert tour of the USA. He was a notable Yevgeny Onegin, Yeletsky, Escamillo, Napoleon (*War and Peace*) and Janusz (*Halka*), and also sang in the standard Italian and Russian repertories. He was, in addition, acknowledged as an authoritative interpreter of Russian song. Lisitsian had one of the century's most beautiful baritone voices allied to considerable artistry, as can be heard on his many recordings; he was also a fine actor.

Alan Blyth

List [Fleissig], Emanuel

(*b* Vienna, 22 March 1888; *d* Vienna, 21 June 1967). Austrian bass, later naturalized American. He was a chorister at the Theater an der Wien, then emigrated to the USA, where he sang in vaudeville and then studied with Josiah Zuro. Returning to Vienna in 1920, he made his début at the Volksoper in 1922 as Méphistophélès. The next year he went to the Charlottenburg Opera, Berlin, and from 1925 to 1933 was a member of the Staatsoper. He made his Covent Garden début in 1925 as Pogner and returned (1934–6) as Hunding, Hagen, King Mark, Ramfis and Ochs, his most famous role. He sang at the Metropolitan (where he made his début as the Landgrave in *Tannhäuser*) from 1933 to 1950 and at San Francisco, Chicago and Buenos Aires. At Salzburg between 1931 and 1935 he sang Osmin, the Commendatore, Rocco and King Mark, and at the 1933 Bayreuth Festival, Fafner, Hunding and Hagen. Forced to leave Germany, he became a naturalized American and did not return to Berlin until 1950. List had a deep, rich bass which, with his imposing presence, admirably fitted him for the Wagner villains he so tellingly portrayed. He recorded several of his Wagner roles, including Hunding on Bruno Walter's famous 1935 recording of *Die Walküre*, Act 1.

Harold Rosenthal/R

Little(-Augustithis), Vera (Pearl)

(*b* Memphis, 10 Dec 1928). American mezzo-soprano. Trained in Alabama and in Europe, she made her début in 1958 as Carmen at the Städtische (later the Deutsche) Oper, Berlin, where she continued to sing for 30 years. She created Begonia in H.W. Henze's *Der junge Lord* in Berlin (1965) and Beroe in his *The Bassarids* at Salzburg (1966). Her repertory included Claudio Monteverdi's Octavia, Erda, Delilah, Clytemnestra, Gaea (*Daphne*) and many Verdi roles, to which her vibrant, rich-toned

voice was well suited. She also sang modern parts, such as Baba the Turk, Jocasta, Circe and Melanto (Luigi Dallapiccola's *Ulisse*), with great proficiency.

Elizabeth Forbes

Litvinne, Félia (Vasil'yevna)
[Schütz, Françoise Jeanne]

(*b* St Petersburg, ? 11 Oct 1860; *d* Paris, 12 Oct 1936). Russian soprano of German and Canadian descent. She studied with PAULINE VIARDOT and VICTOR MAUREL in Paris, making her début with the Théâtre Italien troupe as Amelia (*Simon Boccanegra*) in 1883. She then sang throughout Europe, in New York, at La Monnaie as Brünnhilde in the first *Die Walküre* in French (1887), the Opéra, La Scala, and in Rome and Venice. From 1890 she appeared in the imperial theatres in Moscow and St Petersburg. Litvinne made her Metropolitan début in 1896 as Valentine (*Les Huguenots*) and sang, among other roles, Aida, Donna Anna, Brünnhilde (*Siegfried*) and Sélika (*L'Africaine*). In 1899 she appeared at Covent Garden, as Isolde, returning periodically until 1910; in her last season she sang Brünnhilde in *Götterdämmerung*. She sang in several Russian *Ring* cycles, 1899–1914, and, with CHARLES DALMORÈS, in the French premières of *Götterdämmerung* and *Tristan* under Alfred Cortot in 1902. An excellent musician and linguist, she had a large, flexible voice and great stage presence. Her recordings (1902–8, several with Cortot as her pianist) vividly convey her vibrant, impassioned singing.

H.M. Barnes and V. Girard: 'Félia Litvinne', *Record Collector*, viii (1953), 124–32, 143, 235; xx (1971–2), 147–56 [discography by L.C. Witten], 283

M. Scott: *The Record of Singing*, i (London, 1977), 91–2

Harold Barnes/Alan Blyth

Ljungberg, Göta

(*b* Sundsvall, 4 Oct 1893; *d* Lidingö, nr Stockholm, 30 June 1955). Swedish soprano. She studied in Stockholm with Gillis Brand, then in Milan and Berlin, making her début in 1917 as Gutrune with the Swedish Royal Opera, where she was engaged until 1926 and was admired for her intelligence, appearance and acting ability. The sensational success of her Covent Garden début in 1924 as Sieglinde led to her engagement at the Berlin Staatsoper. Her later London roles were Salome, Kundry, Tosca, Elisabeth (*Tannhäuser*) and the title role of Eugene Goossens's *Judith*, which she created (1929). At the Metropolitan (1932–5), she sang Salome and Richard Wagner heroines, and created Lady Marigold Sandys in Howard Hanson's *Merry*

Mount (1934). Ljungberg was visually and vocally ideal as Salome, and her recording of the final scene of Richard Strauss's opera shows the vibrant, clear and sensuous quality of her voice. Her recordings of Sieglinde and Kundry reveal similar vocal and dramatic excitement. She retired in 1935.

Leo Riemens/Alan Blyth

Lloyd, Robert

(*b* Southend-on-Sea, 2 March 1940). English bass. He studied with OTAKAR KRAUS in London, and made an auspicious début in 1969 at the Collegiate Theatre as Don Fernando in *Leonore*. He sang with Sadler's Wells Opera, then in 1972 joined the Royal Opera, Covent Garden, where he has sung more than 60 roles, including Sarastro, the Commendatore, Don Basilio, Philip II, the Landgrave, Heinrich der Vogler, Gurnemanz, Daland, Fasolt, Arkel, Fiesco, Banquo, Ashby (*La fanciulla del West*), Walter Furst (*Guillaume Tell*), Rocco, Sir Giorgio (*I puritani*), Frère Laurent, Philosophe (*Chérubin*) and Ramfis, all of which have displayed his considerable gifts as a singing actor. He also sang with Scottish Opera and has appeared at Glyndebourne, Aix-en-Provence, Amsterdam, Munich, Madrid, San Francisco and Chicago. In 1991 he sang Gurnemanz at La Scala and the Metropolitan, where he returned (1995/6) as Arkel, Fiesco and Sarastro. His acting ability, fine presence and resonant voice are superbly displayed in the title role of *Boris Godunov*, which he sang in the Andrey Tarkovsky production at Covent Garden (1983) and at the Kirov Opera (1990), preserved on video. In 1999 he gave a charismatic portrayal of the colliery leader Tyrone O'Sullivan in the world première of Alun Hoddinott's *Tower* in Swansea. His many operatic recordings include Osmin, Sarastro, Rossini's Don Basilio, The Grand Inquisitor, Banquo, Bottom and Gurnemanz in Hans-Jürgen Syberberg's film version of *Parsifal*. Lloyd is also a distinguished soloist in choral works, his firm tone and authoritative phrasing making him particularly effective in Giuseppe Verdi's Requiem and in *The Dream of Gerontius*. He was made a CBE in 1991.

R. Milnes: 'Robert Lloyd', *Opera*, xxxiv (1983), 368–74

Elizabeth Forbes

Loewe, Sophie (Johanna Christina)

(*b* Oldenburg, 24 May 1812; *d* Budapest, 29 Nov 1866). German soprano. She studied in Vienna and with Francesco Lamperti in Milan. In 1831 she was in Naples, where she sang Adelaide in Gioachino Rossini's *Tancredi*. The following year she sang Elisabetta in Gaetano Donizetti's *Otto mesi in due ore*

at the Kärntnertortheater, Vienna. After an engagement at Berlin, where she sang Isabelle (*Robert le diable*) and Amina (*La sonnambula*), in 1841 she sang at Her Majesty's Theatre, London, as Alaide (*La straniera*), Donna Elvira and Elena (*Marino Faliero*). The same year she created the title role of Donizetti's *Maria Padilla* at La Scala. In 1844 she sang Elvira in the first performance of *Ernani* and in 1846 she created Odabella in *Attila*, both at La Fenice. She also sang Abigaille (*Nabucco*) and Giselda (*I Lombardi*) at Parma. In 1848 she retired. A forceful singer, she excelled in dramatic parts such as Norma and the soprano roles in Giuseppe Verdi's early operas.

Elizabeth Forbes

London [Burnstein, Burnson], George

(*b* Montreal, 30 May 1920; *d* Armonk, NY, 24 March 1985). American bass-baritone of Canadian birth. In 1941 he made his opera début, as George Burnson, singing Dr Grenvil (*La traviata*) at the Hollywood Bowl. His international career began in 1949 when he sang Amonasro in Vienna. Engagements followed at Glyndebourne, La Scala, the Metropolitan Opera, where he appeared from 1951 to 1964, Bayreuth and the Bol'shoy, where he was the first non-Russian to sing Boris (1960), a role he later recorded in Moscow. A long collaboration with Wieland Wagner culminated in London's singing Wotan in the complete *Ring* in Cologne (1962–4). His repertory also included Don Giovanni and Count Almaviva (both of which he recorded), Charles Gounod's Méphistophélès, Escamillo, the multiple villains in *Les contes d'Hoffmann*, the Dutchman, Scarpia, Mandryka (which he recorded impressively under Georg Solti) and the title role in Gian Carlo Menotti's *Le dernier sauvage*. At the height of his career London's performances were distinguished by a rare dramatic individuality and vocal power, as the best of his recordings confirm. Perhaps his finest achievement was his commanding, anguished Amfortas, which he twice recorded under Hans Knappertsbusch at Bayreuth. From 1968 he concentrated on arts administration, serving successively at the Kennedy Center, Washington, DC (1975–9), the National Opera Institute and the Opera Society of Washington. He was also active as a producer and staged the first complete English-language *Ring* in the USA (1975, Seattle), a production that forswore Wieland Wagner's modernism in favour of storybook realism.

J. Wechsberg: 'The Vocal Mission', *New Yorker* (26 Oct, 2 Nov 1957)
T. Page: Obituary, *New York Times* (26 March 1985)
T. Stewart: 'George London', *ON*, l/1 (1985–6), 32–3

Martin Bernheimer/Alan Blyth

Lopardo, Frank

(*b* New York, 23 Dec 1957). American tenor. He studied at the Juilliard School with Robert White (1980–81) and made his stage début as Tamino at the Opera Theatre of St Louis in 1984. He first appeared in Europe as Fenton in Amsterdam in 1986, followed by Almaviva in 1987, the year in which he made his débuts at the Vienna Staatsoper (as Lindoro in *L'italiana in Algeri*) and Glyndebourne (as Ferrando). He made his début at Chicago, as Elvino (*La sonnambula*), in 1988, his Salzburg Festival début as Don Ottavio in 1990 and his San Francisco début, in the same role, in 1991. His Metropolitan début in 1990 was as Gioachino Rossini's Almaviva and he has returned for, among other roles, Ferrando, Don Ottavio, Tamino, Fenton, Rodolfo and Idreno (*Semiramide*). He made a much-admired Covent Garden début, as Lindoro, in 1989, and in 1994 appeared there as Alfredo to ANGELA GHEORGHIU's Violetta, a performance that was recorded live. Lopardo also sings regularly in concert in a wide-ranging repertory. His dark-grained, mellifluous tenor is deployed with agility and intelligence in all his roles, most notably on disc as Ottavio, Ferrando, Lindoro, Ernesto (*Don Pasquale*) and Alfredo.

Alan Blyth

Lorengar, Pilar [García, Pilar Lorenza]

(*b* Zaragoza, 16 Jan 1928; *d* Berlin, 2 June 1996). Spanish soprano. She studied in Madrid, and with Angeles Ottein, making her début in zarzuelas in 1949. In 1955 she sang Cherubino at Aix-en-Provence, Rosario in a New York concert performance of *Goyescas* (her American début) and Violetta at Covent Garden, where she returned as Donna Anna, Countess Almaviva, Fiordiligi and Alice Ford. She sang Pamina at Glyndebourne (1956) and Buenos Aires (1958), and Ilia (*Idomeneo*) at Salzburg (1961). In 1964 she sang the title role in Pablo Sorozábal's revised version of *Pepita Jiménez* in Madrid. She sang at San Francisco (1964–5) as Desdemona, Liù, Mélisande and Eva. In 1966 she made her Metropolitan début as Donna Elvira, later singing Elsa, Eva, Agathe and Butterfly. She appeared in most major European opera houses, but it was at the Deutsche Oper, Berlin, where she was engaged from 1958 for over 30 years, that she chiefly made her career, broadening her repertory to include Regina (*Mathis der Maler*), Elisabeth de Valois, Mařenka, Tatyana, Jenůfa, Mimì, Tosca, Manon Lescaut, Valentine (*Les Huguenots*), Maddalena (*Andrea Chénier*), which she sang at Lyons in 1989, and Queen Isabella in the German première of Manuel de Falla's *Atlántida* in 1961. She retired from the Deutsche Oper in 1991. Though

not the deepest of interpreters, Lorengar achieved great success through her attractive stage presence, pearly tone and refined phrasing. Notable among her many recordings are her Fiordiligi, Violetta and Giuseppe Mazza's *El maestro campanone*.

A. Blyth: Obituary, *Opera*, xlvii (1996), 903–4

Harold Rosenthal/Alan Blyth

Lorenz, Max

(*b* Düsseldorf, 10 May 1901; *d* Vienna, 12 Jan 1975). German tenor. After studying with Ernst Granzebach in Berlin he made his début at the Dresden Staatsoper as Walther (*Tannhäuser*), becoming a principal tenor in 1928 and in 1932 appearing as Menelaus in *Die Ägyptische Helena*. From 1933 he was at the Berlin Staatsoper, and he also appeared at the Metropolitan, making his début as Walther (*Die Meistersinger*) in 1931 and singing there until 1934 and again in 1947–50; he also sang at Bayreuth (from 1933 and in 1952) and Covent Garden (1934, 1937). He joined the Vienna Staatsoper in 1937 and appeared at many Salzburg festivals, creating roles in such new works as Gottfried von Einem's *Der Prozess* (Josef K., 1953), Rolf Liebermann's *Penelope* (1954) and Rudolf Wagner-Régeny's *Das Bergwerk zu Falun* (1961). Lorenz was a prominent Wagnerian tenor, celebrated as Tristan, Siegfried and Walther in particular; he was also a notable Florestan, Otello, Bacchus (Richard Strauss's *Ariadne*) and Herod.

Peter Branscombe

Los Angeles, Victoria de

(*b* Barcelona, 1 Nov 1923; *d* Barcelona, 15 Jan 2005). Spanish soprano. She came from a musical family and studied the piano, the guitar and singing at home as well as at the Barcelona Conservatory. After her operatic début at Barcelona (1941, Mimì), she soon became a leading opera and concert singer, internationally as well as in Spain. Having been invited by the BBC to sing Salud in a 1948 studio broadcast of Manuel de Falla's *La vida breve*, she made her début at Covent Garden in 1950, and at the Metropolitan in the following year, and sang regularly in both houses until 1961. Although she successfully tackled the lighter Wagnerian roles, such as Eva and Elsa, she excelled as the more lyrical heroines of *La bohème*, *Madama Butterfly* and *Manon*. At the Metropolitan she was especially admired in her début role of Marguerite, and as Mélisande and Desdemona; and in two successive years (1961 and 1962) she appeared at Bayreuth as Elisabeth. During the later 1960s she took part in several productions at the Teatro Colón, Buenos Aires, and she sang in

Victoria de Los Angeles, 1965

Otello at Dallas in 1969. In 1978 she sang the title role of *Carmen* with the New Jersey State Opera at Newark. By that time, however, she had mostly confined her appearances to the concert platform, where her personal and vocal charms made her a great and continuing favourite.

Victoria de Los Angeles possessed a warm, vibrant instrument of unusual clarity and flexibility, somewhat dark and southern in quality but capable of much tonal variety. In her best years the timbre of her voice was exceptionally sweet, and she was a most communicative artist in both song and opera. Among the best of her operatic recordings are *La bohème* and *Carmen*, conducted by Thomas Beecham, *Il barbiere di Siviglia*, two sets of *Madama Butterfly*, *Manon* (with Pierre Monteux) and *La vida breve*. From early in her career she made a speciality of recording Spanish songs, from the Middle Ages to the 20th century. Los Angeles studied lieder with GERHARDT, and was a particularly accomplished interpreter of Johannes Brahms, both in recital and on disc. She was also a delightful exponent of *mélodies*.

C. Hardy: 'Victoria de los Angeles', *Opera*, viii (1957), 210–16

B. James 'Victoria de los Angeles', *Audio & Record Review*, ii/6 (1963), 12–15 [with discography by F.F. Clough and G.J. Cuming]

A. Porter: 'A Heavenly Creature', *International Opera Collector* (wint. 1998), 8–10

Desmond Shawe-Taylor

Lott, Dame Felicity

(*b* Cheltenham, 8 May 1947). English soprano. She studied at the RAM, and made her stage début in 1973 with Unicorn Opera, Abingdon, as Seleuce (*Tolomeo*). She first appeared at the ENO in 1975 as a touchingly artless Pamina. An impressive Fiordiligi and an impassioned Natasha in *War and Peace* followed. In 1976 her Covent Garden début was in H.W. Henze's *We Come to the River*, and she later appeared there as Anne Trulove, Blanche (*Dialogues des Carmélites*), Ellen Orford, Eva and the Marschallin, all roles that exhibited her gifts for clear tone, alert musicianship and interior feeling. At Glyndebourne she has been admired as a Straussian. Her Octavian, Arabella, Madeleine and particularly her Christine Storch (preserved on video) all brought out a touch of insouciant charm in her singing and acting. Munich, Dresden and Vienna all acknowledged her gift by casting her as, variously, the Marschallin, Arabella and Madeleine. The Marschallin was also the role of her Metropolitan début in 1990. Her Louise in Brussels and her Jenifer (*The Midsummer Marriage*) for WNO were notable successes in other genres. Lott has also been admired as a soloist in all the major oratorios and as a recitalist, and is a founder-member of the Songmakers' Almanac. She has gained a justified reputation in lieder and *mélodies*, her interpretations marked by the subtle nuances she brings to the text. Her gift for sensuousness is notably preserved on her recordings of Claude Debussy and Francis Poulenc, her sense of humour in Jacques Offenbach. Her gifts as a Mozartian are shown in her recordings of Countess Almaviva (with Bernard Haitink) as well as Fiordiligi and Donna Elvira (with Charles Mackerras). She was made a CBE in 1990 and a DBE in 1996.

E. Forbes: 'Felicity Lott', *Opera*, xl (1989), 1174–80

Alan Blyth

Luart [Lawaert], Emma

(*b* Brussels, 14 Aug 1892; *d* Brussels, 26 Aug 1968). Belgian soprano. She trained at the Brussels Conservatory and after singing in the summer season at Ostend in 1913 made her official début at The Hague the following year. From 1918 to 1922 she sang at La Monnaie in Brussels, appearing mostly in lyric roles such as Louise, Mélisande and Manon, which became her most famous part. She then transferred to the Opéra-Comique in Paris, where she remained till World War II. Her début role there was Lakmé, and premières in which she took a leading part included Marcel Samuel-Rousseau's *Le bon roi Dagobert* and Gabriel Pierné's one-act *Sophie Arnould*. At Monte Carlo in 1923 she sang in the first performances outside Russia of Modest Musorgsky's *The Fair at Sorochintsï* with JOHN MCCORMACK. On her retirement she taught singing in Brussels. A characteristically bright 'French' voice is heard in her recordings along with a touching expressiveness, especially in the excerpts from *Manon*.

J.B. Steane

Lubin, Germaine (Léontine Angélique)

(*b* Paris, 1 Feb 1890; *d* Paris, 20–27 Oct 1979). French soprano. She studied at the Paris Conservatoire (1909–12) and with FÉLIA LITVINNE and LILLI LEHMANN. She made her début as Antonia in *Les contes d'Hoffmann* at the Opéra-Comique, where she also sang Richard Strauss's Ariadne, Gabriel Fauré's Penelope, Charlotte, Louise and Camille (*Zampa*). At the Opéra (1916–44) she sang a very varied repertory, at first lyric roles such as Marguerite (Charles Gounod and Arrigo Boito), Juliet, Thaïs, Aida and Ernest Reyer's Salammbô; later she took on heavier roles, including Agathe, Fidelio, Cassandra, Elsa, Eva, Elisabeth, Sieglinde, Electra, Octavian and the Marschallin. She created Nicéa in Vincent d'Indy's *La légende de Saint Christophe* (1920), Empress Charlotte in Darius Milhaud's *Maximilien* (1932) and Gina, Duchess Sanseverina in Henri Sauguet's *La chartreuse de Parme* (1939). She was admired for her classical dignity and repose in C.W. Gluck's *Alceste* and *Iphigénie en Aulide*, and as Telaira in Jean-Philippe Rameau's *Castor et Pollux* (Maggio Musicale, 1935). She was also acclaimed for her singing of the title role in Paul Dukas' *Ariane et Barbe-bleue* in the London première at Covent Garden in 1937. Lubin's friendship with the Wagners and her sympathy with Germany (though she described herself as 'a quarter Polish, a quarter Arab and half Alsatian') brought her career to an abrupt close in 1944 after the liberation of Paris. She was imprisoned for three years and thereafter sang only in recitals (1952 and 1954). Her rounded, expressive voice can be heard on a number of recordings, of which several Wagner extracts are especially noteworthy.

H. Barnes: 'Germaine Lubin Discography', *Recorded Sound*, xix (1965), 367

M. de Schauensee: 'Lubin Revisited', *ON*, xxx/12 (1965–6), 27–8

Martin Cooper/Elizabeth Forbes/R

Luca, Giuseppe de.

See DE LUCA, GIUSEPPE.

Lucchesina, La.

See MARCHESINI, MARIA ANTONIA.

Lucchesino, Il.

See PACINI, ANDREA.

Luccioni, José

(*b* Bastia, 14 Oct 1903; *d* Marseilles, 5 Oct 1978). Corsican tenor. He abandoned his formal education to work for Citroën motors, but while doing his military service he was encouraged to seek proper voice teachers. He studied in Paris with LÉON DAVID and LÉON ESCALAÏS, and won second prize in a singing competition, whereupon he was engaged to sing at the Paris Opéra, making his début in 1931 in Alfred Bruneau's *Virginie*. Success came to him the following year in Rouen, as Cavaradossi. He was re-engaged at the Opéra, where for the next 15 years he became the leading heroic tenor. His international career began in Monte Carlo, where he sang Dmitry opposite CHALIAPIN as Boris. He also appeared in Chicago, Barcelona, Rome (where, in 1936, he created Franco Alfano's *Cyrano de Bergerac*) and at Covent Garden, where he sang Don José to SUPERVIA's Carmen and Calaf opposite TURNER as Turandot. Among his other roles were Matho in Ernest Reyer's *Salammbô*, Otello, which he sang 120 times at the Opéra, and Samson, which he recorded complete in 1947. Luccioni's true tenor voice was matched by a compelling dramatic skill. He also made two films, *Colomba* (1933) and *Le bout de la route* (1949).

Patrick O'Connor

Lucia, Fernando de.

See DE LUCIA, FERNANDO

Ludwig, Christa

(*b* Berlin, 16 March 1928). German mezzo-soprano. The daughter of the singers Anton Ludwig and Eugenia Besalle, she studied with her mother and FELICE HÜNI-MIHACZEK, making her début in 1946 as Orlofsky at Frankfurt, where she sang until 1952. After engagements at Darmstadt and Hanover, she joined the Vienna Staatsoper in 1955 and remained there for more than 30 years, creating Miranda in Frank Martin's *Der Sturm* (1956) and Claire Zachanassian in Gottfried von Einem's *Der Besuch der alten Dame* (1971). Having first sung at Salzburg in 1954 as Cherubino, she took part in Rolf Liebermann's *Die Schule der Frauen* (1957),

Christa Ludwig as Leonore in 'Fidelio' (Beethoven), Bavarian State Opera

sang the title role of *Iphigénie en Aulide* in 1962, and returned there until 1981, when she sang Mistress Quickly. Ludwig made her American début in Chicago in 1959 as Dorabella. At the Metropolitan (1959–90) her roles included Cherubino, the Dyer's Wife, Dido in the first American production of *Les Troyens* (1973), Fricka, Waltraute, Ortrud, Kundry, the Marschallin, Charlotte and Clytemnestra. At Bayreuth she sang Brangäne (1966) and Kundry (1967). She made her Covent Garden début in 1968 as Amneris, returning as Carmen (1976). She also appeared at Hamburg, Munich, Rome, San Francisco, La Scala and the Paris Opéra. Her repertory included Leonore (*Fidelio*) and Lady Macbeth, as well as Claudio Monteverdi's Octavia, Eboli and Marie (*Wozzeck*). She was also a renowned interpreter of lieder, especially those of Johannes Brahms and Gustav Mahler. Her voice was rich, even-toned and expressive, and she was a compelling actress. Ludwig's many operatic recordings include Dorabella under Karl Böhm, Leonore with Otto Klemperer, Venus and Kundry for Georg Solti, Ortrud for Rudolf Kempe and Octavian under Herbert von Karajan. She also recorded much of her large concert and lieder repertory, notably J.S. Bach's *St Matthew Passion*, Brahms's Alto Rhapsody, and *Das Lied von der Erde* (all with

Klemperer). From 1957 to 1971 she was married to the bass-baritone WALTER BERRY. At the time of her retirement in 1994 she gave an outspoken television interview with Thomas Voigt (now available on video), in which she discussed her career and her working relationships with Klemperer, Karajan and others.

C. Osborne: 'Christa Ludwig', *Opera*, xxiv (1973), 216–22

Alan Blyth

Lunn, (Louise) Kirkby [Kirkby-Lunn]

(*b* Manchester, 8 Nov 1873; *d* London, 17 Feb 1930). English mezzo-soprano. She studied in Manchester and then at the RCM with Albert Visetti. While still a student she sang Margaretha in the English première of Robert Schumann's *Genoveva* (1893) and the Marquise de Montcontour in Léo Delibes's *Le roi l'a dit*. She sang Nora in Charles Villiers Stanford's *Shamus O'Brien* at the Opéra-Comique in 1896, then joined the Carl Rosa company, where her roles included Julia in Arthur Sullivan's sacred music drama *The Martyr of Antioch* and Ella in the première of Hamish MacCunn's *Diarmid*, both at Covent Garden (1897). In 1901 she reappeared there as the Sandman in *Hänsel und Gretel* and Siébel in *Faust*; she continued to sing at Covent Garden until 1914, appearing in several London first performances, notably as Pallas in Camille Saint-Saëns's *Hélène* and in the title role in *Hérodiade* (both 1904), Hate in C.W. Gluck's *Armide* (1906) and Delilah (1909), as well as Orpheus, Ortrud, Brangäne, Fricka, Carmen, Olga (*Yevgeny Onegin*) and Amneris. She appeared at the Metropolitan (1902–3 and 1906–8). She sang Kundry in English in Boston (1904), and later with the British National Opera Company at Covent Garden (1922). She possessed a large, rich voice, which ranged from *g* to *b♭″*; recordings confirm its size and its steady, somewhat severe quality. Her stage performances were sometimes considered rather cool; Saint-Saëns said he thought her Delilah was a clever embodiment 'même avec son peu de chaleur'.

J.B. Richards: 'Louise Kirkby Lunn', *Record Collector*, xix (1970–71), 101–43; 'The Kirkby Lunn Recordings', xix (1970–71), 172–88 [discography]

Harold Rosenthal/R

Lussan, Zélie de.

See DE LUSSAN, ZÉLIE.

Luxon, Benjamin

(*b* Redruth, Cornwall, 24 March 1937). English baritone. He studied at the GSM and in 1963 joined the English Opera Group, for which his roles included Benjamin Britten's Sid, Tarquinius and Demetrius, and Henry Purcell's King Arthur (1970). He created the title role in Benjamin Britten's television opera *Owen Wingrave* (1971), subsequently recording the part with the composer, and took the roles of the Jester, Death and Joking Jesus in the première of Peter Maxwell Davies's *Taverner* at Covent Garden (1972). Other roles he sang there included Owen Wingrave, Yevgeny Onegin, Wolfram, Marcello, Falke (*Fledermaus*) and Diomede (*Troilus and Cressida*). At Glyndebourne (1972–80) he sang Claudio Monteverdi's Ulysses, Count Almaviva, Don Giovanni, Papageno, the Forester (*The Cunning Little Vixen*) and Ford. With the ENO (1974–90) he sang Posa, Papageno, Falstaff and Gianni Schicchi. He sang Wozzeck in Glasgow (1983), Sherasmin (*Oberon*) in Edinburgh (1986), Captain Balstrode in Philadelphia (1987) and Wozzeck again in Los Angeles (1988), where he returned as Falstaff (1990). His strong personality and warm, expressive voice were as effective in contemporary works as in his most famous role, Yevgeny Onegin, which he sang at the Metropolitan (1980), Frankfurt (1984), La Scala, Geneva (1986), Amsterdam, Paris and Prague. Luxon was also a sympathetic interpreter of lieder and of Russian and, especially, English songs, as can be heard on several recordings. He was made a CBE in 1986.

Alan Blyth

Lytton [Jones], Sir H(enry) A(lbert) [Henri, H.A.]

(*b* London, 3 Jan 1865; *d* London, 15 Aug 1936). English baritone. In 1884, with his wife, 'Louie Henri', he joined the chorus of the D'Oyly Carte company touring Arthur Sullivan's *Princess Ida*. In 1887 he deputized at the Savoy Theatre as Robin Oakapple in *Ruddigore*, and during the 1890s appeared at the Savoy in Gilbert and Sullivan revivals, playing mostly heavier baritone roles. He created roles for Sullivan and Edward German in *The Rose of Persia* (1899), *The Emerald Isle* (1901), *Merrie England* (1902) and *A Princess of Kensington* (1903) before appearing in musical comedy. In 1906–7 and 1908–9 he again appeared at the Savoy under W.S. Gilbert, and then from 1909 until 1934 toured with the D'Oyly Carte company in the principal comedy roles. He was a versatile performer, with a sound baritone and winning stage presence. He was knighted in 1930.

H. A. Lytton: *The Secrets of a Savoyard* (London, 1922)
H. A. Lytton: *A Wandering Minstrel* (London, 1933)

Andrew Lamb

Maas, Joseph

(*b* Dartford, Kent, 30 Jan 1847; *d* London, 16 Jan 1886). English tenor. He started his career as a chorister at Rochester Cathedral, studying singing with the organist, J.L. Hopkins, and later with Susannah (or possibly Louisa) Pyne in London and Antonio Sangiovanni in Milan. He made his début in February 1871, replacing Sims Reeves at a concert given by the Henry Leslie Choir. His first stage appearance was as Babil in Dion Boucicault's spectacle *Babil and Bijou* at Covent Garden in August 1872, after which he went to the USA as a member of Clara Kellogg's English Opera Company. In 1878 he sang Gontran in the first performance in England of Ignaz Brüll's *Das goldene Kreuz* at the Adelphi Theatre under Carl Rosa, who then engaged him as principal tenor. He sang the title role in the English première of *Rienzi* (1879), Wilhelm Meister and Radames in the first English-language performances of *Mignon* and *Aida* (1880), and Des Grieux in the first London performance of *Manon* (1885). In 1883 he sang Lohengrin at Covent Garden, and his repertory also included Faust and Gaetano Donizetti's Edgar. Maas appeared regularly in concerts and oratorio, especially in the Handel festivals. He was heard in Paris and Brussels in 1884 and 1885; in August 1885 he sang at the Birmingham Festival in the first performances in England of Antonín Dvořák's *The Spectre's Bride* and Charles Villiers Stanford's *Three Holy Children*. He was an indifferent actor, but his voice was said to be of a pure and beautiful quality, and his cantabile style was greatly admired.

Obituary, *The Athenaeum* (23 Jan 1886), 145

Obituary, *MT*, xxvii (1886), 93–4

G. Hauger: 'Joseph Maas: a Centenary Memoir', *Opera*, xxxvii (1986), 136–41

Harold Rosenthal/George Biddlecombe

McCormack, John [Foli, Giovanni]

(*b* Athlone, 14 June 1884; *d* Dublin, 16 Sept 1945). Irish tenor, later naturalized American. He began his studies in Dublin, and in 1905 went to Milan to study with Vincenzo Sabatini. The following year he made his stage début under the assumed name of Giovanni Foli in Pietro Mascagni's *L'amico Fritz* at the Teatro Chiabrera in Savona, near Genoa. After further engagements in small Italian theatres

he made his Covent Garden début as Turiddu (*Cavalleria rusticana*) in the autumn season of 1907, confirming his success the same season in *Rigoletto* and *Don Giovanni*. From 1908 to 1914 he took part in every summer season at Covent Garden, adding to his repertory (often with TETRAZZINI or MELBA in the cast) *Il barbiere di Siviglia*, *La sonnambula*, *Lucia di Lammermoor*, *Faust*, *Roméo et Juliette*, *Lakmé*, *La bohème* and *Madama Butterfly*. He made his New York début at the Manhattan Opera House as Alfredo in *La traviata* (1909) and took the same role in his Metropolitan début the following year, becoming a favourite with the public in Boston and Chicago as well as New York. In 1911 he created the part of Paul Merrill in Victor Herbert's *Natoma*. McCormack was already laying the foundations of his future career as a concert singer and soon, being by his own admission a poor actor, he decided to abandon the stage. Thereafter, partly because of his Irish nationalism (which for a time made him unpopular in England), he spent his time mainly in the USA, and in 1917 became an American citizen. His concert work revealed him as a remarkable interpreter, not only of G.F. Handel, W.A. Mozart and the Italian classics, but also of German lieder. The preponderance in his programmes of sentimental and popular ballads alienated many musical people as much as it pleased the wider public; but, whatever the song, he never debased his style. Meanwhile his repertory of serious music grew continually.

In 1928 McCormack was made a papal count by Pope Pius XI. By then he had returned to live in Ireland, and for another decade he continued to give concerts in many parts of the world, especially in the British Isles. In autumn 1938 he made a farewell tour, but during the war he emerged from retirement for some broadcasts, and to tour in aid of the Red Cross.

McCormack's numerous recordings show the singular sweetness of his tone and perfection of his style and technique in his prime – for example, in his famous version of Mozart's 'Il mio tesoro' and in Handel's 'O sleep' (*Semele*) and 'Come, my beloved' (i.e. 'Care selve' from *Atalanta*) – while later records of lieder and of Irish folksongs illustrate other aspects of his versatile art. He was always, according to Ernest Newman, 'a patrician artist...with a respect for art that is rarely met with among tenors'. McCormack bequeathed his papers to University College, Dublin.

*John McCormack,
signed portrait*

P.V.R. Key and J. Scarry, eds.: *John McCormack: his Own Life Story* (Boston, 1918/*R*)

L.A.G. Strong: *John McCormack: the Story of a Singer* (London, 1941/*R*)

P.C. Hume, *The King of Song* (New York, 1964)

P.W. Worth and J. Cartwright: *John McCormack: a Comprehensive Discography* (New York and London, 1986)

Desmond Shawe-Taylor/R

McCracken, James (Eugene)

(*b* Gary, IN, 16 Dec 1926; *d* New York, 29 April 1988). American tenor. His début was as Rodolfo in *La bohème* at Central City, Colorado, in 1952. He made his Metropolitan Opera début in 1953 as Parpignol in the same opera and took many other comprimario roles before leaving for Europe in 1957. He was engaged at Bonn as Max, Radames and Canio. The turning-point in his career was an engagement as Otello with the Washington Opera in 1960; it became, and remained, his most celebrated role, and he recorded it under John Barbirolli. He sang in most of the world's leading houses, including Boston and Zürich, and his repertory included Florestan, Don José, Calaf, Manrico and Don Alvaro, Tannhäuser, Bacchus (*Ariadne auf Naxos*),

Hermann, Samson and John of Leyden (*Le prophète*). A powerful and convincing actor, McCracken had an emotional intensity and a dark-timbred tenor of exceptional fervour. His other recordings include Florestan, Don José and John of Leyden. He married the mezzo-soprano Sandra Warfield.

A. Williamson: 'James McCracken', *Opera*, xviii (1967), 7–14

J. McCracken and S. Warfield: *A Star in the Family* (New York, 1971)

S. Wadsworth: 'Finding Tannhäuser', *ON*, xlii/11 (1977–8), 14–15, 32

J. Hines: 'James McCracken', *Great Singers on Great Singing* (Garden City, NY, 1982), 156–63

B. Paolucci: 'America's Heroic Tenor: James McCracken', *Ovation*, vi/8 (1985), 15–17, 30

Martin Bernheimer

MacDonald, Jeanette

(*b* Philadelphia, 18 June ?1901; *d* Houston, 14 Jan 1965). American soprano. She is best known for her performances in film musicals in operetta style; she first appeared opposite Maurice Chevalier in *The Love Parade* (1929), and then with NELSON EDDY in such films as *Naughty Marietta* (1935), *Rose Marie* (1936), *Sweethearts* (1938) and *New Moon* (1940). Although her voice lacked flexibility and warmth, MacDonald projected an image of charm and beauty appropriate to the romantic heroines she portrayed. She left film work in 1942 in order to make concert tours, radio appearances and recordings. She also began a brief career in opera in 1943, when she appeared with EZIO PINZA in Charles Gounod's *Roméo et Juliette* in Montreal; her only other role was as Marguerite in *Faust* with the Chicago Civic Opera and Cincinnati Summer Opera the following year. MacDonald was married to the actor and composer Gene Raymond, whose songs she performed in her concert programmes.

Jean W. Thomas

McDonnell, Tom [Thomas] (Anthony)

(*b* Melbourne, 27 April 1940). Australian baritone. After studying in Melbourne, he sang Belcore (*L'elisir d'amore*) in Brisbane. He joined Sadler's Wells Opera (later the ENO) in 1967. His first major role was W.A. Mozart's Figaro and in 1968 he sang Marcel Sciocca in Malcolm Williamson's *The Violins of St Jacques*. In 1969 he sang Yevgeny Onegin with Glyndebourne Touring Opera. His roles with the ENO include Germont, Schaunard, Escamillo, Papageno and Andrey, which he sang at the first London performance of Sergey Prokofiev's

War and Peace (1972) and at the opening of the Sydney Opera House (1973). He also sang Wolfram (*Tannhäuser*) with the Australian Opera. In 1974 he created Lieutenant September in Gordon Crosse's *The Story of Vasco* and sang the Captain (Adonis) in the first London stage performance of H.W. Henze's *The Bassarids*. He made his Covent Garden début in the première of Henze's *We Come to the River* (1976) and created Yuri in Michael Tippett's *The Ice Break* (1977); for the ENO he created Atahuallpa in Iain Hamilton's *The Royal Hunt of the Sun*, and at the Collegiate Theatre he sang in the première of Nicola LeFanu's *Dawnpath* (1977). For Opera Factory he sang Faber (*The Knot Garden*), Don Alfonso and Seneca, took part in the first performance of Nigel Osborne's *Hell's Angels* (1986), and created the role of Aristaeus in Harrison Birtwistle's *The Mask of Orpheus* at the London Coliseum. A powerful actor, he excels in dramatic roles.

Elizabeth Forbes

McEathron, Margaret Nixon.

See NIXON, MARNI.

McIntyre, Sir Donald (Conroy)

(*b* Auckland, 22 Oct 1934). British bass-baritone of New Zealand birth. He studied in London and made his début in 1959 with the WNO as Zaccaria (*Nabucco*). At Sadler's Wells (1960–67) he sang over 30 roles, including W.A. Mozart's Figaro, Attila, the Dutchman, Caspar and Pennybank Bill in the first British staging of *Mahagonny* (1963). He made his Covent Garden début in 1967 as Pizarro, later singing Barak (*Die Frau ohne Schatten*), Golaud, Shaklovity (*Khovanshchina*), Balstrode, Escamillo, Nick Shadow, Scarpia, John the Baptist, Orestes, Axel Heyst in the première of Richard Rodney Bennett's *Victory* (1970), Sarastro, Count des Grieux, Kurwenal and Wotan, the role of his Metropolitan début in 1975. At Bayreuth (1967–80) he sang Telramund, Amfortas, the Dutchman, and Wotan in the 1976 centenary *Ring* cycle under Pierre Boulez, which was recorded. McIntyre first sang Gurnemanz with the WNO (1981), later recording the role with Reginald Goodall, and Hans Sachs at Zürich (1984), and sang Prospero in the British première of Luciano Berio's *Un re in ascolto* (1989, Covent Garden) and Baron Prus in *The Makropulos Affair* at the Metropolitan in 1996. He has appeared at Vienna, Munich, Berlin, Chicago, La Scala and Paris. With his strongly projected, full-toned voice and fine stage presence, he is a compelling singing actor. He was appointed OBE in 1977 and knighted in 1992.

A. Blyth: 'Donald McIntyre', *Opera*, xxvi (1975), 529–36

A. Simpson and P. Downes: *Southern Voices: International Opera Singers of New Zealand* (Auckland, 1992), 132–47

Alan Blyth

McLaughlin, Marie

(*b* Hamilton, Lanarks., 2 Nov 1954). Scottish soprano. She studied in Glasgow and London, making her début in 1978 as Anna Gomez (*The Consul*) with the ENO. She made her Covent Garden début in 1981 as Barbarina and has subsequently sung there roles including Zerlina, Iris (*Semele*), Susanna, Marzelline, Adina, Norina, Titania, Zdenka, Musetta and Nannetta. At Glyndebourne she has sung Micaëla (1985), Violetta (1987) and Donna Elvira. She made her Metropolitan début (1986) as Marzelline, returning as Susanna and Zdenka. She has also sung in Chicago and throughout Europe, making her Salzburg début in 1990 as Marzelline. McLaughlin's later roles with the ENO have included Gilda, Tatyana (1989) and Karolina (Bedřich Smetana's *The Two Widows*), while at Geneva she has added to her repertory Jenny (*Mahagonny*) and Blanche (*Dialogues des Carmélites*). She has a charming stage presence and a full-toned yet flexible lyric voice, heard to advantage in recordings of Susanna, Zerlina, Despina and Marzelline, and of Schubert and Strauss lieder.

A. Clark: 'Marie McLaughlin', *Opera*, xliv (1993), 1391–9

Elizabeth Forbes

McNair, Sylvia

(*b* Mansfield, OH, 23 June 1956). American soprano. She studied opera with Virginia McWatters and VIRGINIA ZEANI and song with John Wustman at Indiana University, made her concert début in *Messiah* at Indianapolis (1980) and her stage début as Sandrina in Joseph Haydn's *L'infedeltà delusa* at the Mostly Mozart Festival, New York (1982). In 1984 she made her European début, creating the title role of Rudolf Kelterborn's *Ophelia* at Schwetzingen. She subsequently appeared in the USA as Pamina at Santa Fe and Hero (*Béatrice et Bénédict*) and Morgana (*Alcina*) at St Louis, and in Europe as Susanna at Amsterdam, Pamina in Berlin, and Pamina and Susanna at the Vienna Staatsoper. In 1989 she gave a ravishing interpretation of Anne Trulove at Glyndebourne, where her Ilia was equally admired. Ilia also introduced her to Covent Garden (1989), the Salzburg Festival (1990), where she returned for a seductive Poppaea in *L'incoronazione di Poppea*, and the Opéra-Bastille in Paris (1991).

Her début at the Metropolitan was in 1991 as Marzelline. She sang Pamina at Salzburg (1997) and G.F. Handel's Cleopatra at the Metropolitan (1999). McNair is also a distinguished concert artist – her London début in W.A. Mozart's C minor Mass with John Eliot Gardiner was a personal triumph – and a pleasing recitalist. In 1994 André Previn composed his Four Songs for her. McNair's pure, silvery tones and refined phrasing have adorned all her performances, even when her style has seemed a shade bland. Of her many recordings, those of Poppaea and Ilia, both with Gardiner, represent her at her most beguiling.

Alan Blyth

MacNeil, Cornell

(*b* Minneapolis, 24 Sept 1922). American baritone. He trained as a machinist before winning a scholarship to the Hartt School of Music, Hartford, Connecticut, where he studied with FRIEDRICH SCHORR. From 1946 he took small parts in Broadway musicals. In 1950 Gian Carlo Menotti chose him to sing the role of Sorel in the première at Philadelphia of *The Consul*. This led to performances with a number of small American opera companies, and an engagement with the New York City Opera (1952–5), where he developed his gifts in the Italian repertory. Guest appearances included his débuts in San Francisco as Escamillo (1955) and Chicago as Giacomo Puccini's Lescaut (1957). His reputation was firmly, and internationally, established in 1959, when he made his débuts at La Scala (as Carlo in *Ernani*) and the Metropolitan Opera (as Rigoletto), in both cases substituting for indisposed singers. In 1960 he opened the Metropolitan season in the company's first production of *Nabucco*, and he continued to sing with the company until 1987; his roles included Nabucco, Amonasro, Luna, Gérard, Barnaba (*La Gioconda*), the Dutchman, Boccanegra, Guy de Montfort (*Les vêpres siciliennes*), Carlo (*La forza del destino*), Iago and Trinity Moses (*Mahagonny*). MacNeil's Covent Garden début (as Macbeth in 1964) was praised for his pure and even legato, less for his dramatic involvement. This was the main objection to his performances, and it might be said that his many recordings, which include Rigoletto and Amonasro, present a better view of his art than did his stage appearances. His voice was a true Verdian baritone, crowned by a magnificent top register, though not always well knit to the middle. The high tessitura of Di Luna (*Il trovatore*), for example, was delivered with a technical control that few contemporary singers could rival. He appeared in Franco Zeffirelli's film version of *La traviata*, and in his later career developed into a powerful interpreter of *verismo* roles, notably Scarpia. In 1988 he sang Giorgio Germont to his son Walter's Alfredo at Glyndebourne.

Richard Bernas

Maddalena, James

(*b* Lynn, MA, 1954). American baritone. He studied at the New England Conservatory and made his professional debut with the Boston Pops Orchestra in 1974. Since 1981 he has collaborated regularly with director Peter Sellars, beginning with roles in typically provocative productions of operas by G.F. Handel, Joseph Haydn and W.A. Mozart (Count Almaviva in *Figaro*, Guglielmo in *Così fan tutte*). Maddalena first achieved international success with his powerful portrayal of Richard Nixon in the 1987 première of John Adams's *Nixon in China* at the Houston Grand Opera. He subsequently repeated the role at the Netherlands Opera, the Edinburgh Festival, the Washington Opera, the Frankfurt Opera, at the Adelaide Festival, in Paris and elsewhere, and also recorded it. His other premières include the Captain in Adams's *The Death of Klinghoffer* at La Monnaie (1991), Hobson in David Carlson's *The Midnight Angel* in St Louis (1993), Elliot Goldenthal's Vietnam oratorio *Fire Water Paper* (1995) and Stewart Wallace's *Harvey Milk* at the Houston Grand Opera (also 1995). In 2001 he performed the role of Gideon March in Mark Adamo's *Little Women* at the Houston Grand Opera. While Maddalena has specialised in contemporary American opera, he also has a large concert repertory ranging from J.S. Bach to Paul Hindemith.

Richard Wigmore

Madeira [née Browning], Jean

(*b* Centralia, IL, 14 Nov 1918; *d* Providence, RI, 10 July 1972). American contralto. She studied at the Juilliard School of Music and under the name Jean Browning made her début in 1943 at the Chautauqua Summer Opera as Nancy (*Martha*). In 1947 she was chosen by Gian Carlo Menotti to alternate with Marie Powers in the European tour of *The Medium*. She joined the Metropolitan in 1948, making her début as the First Norn. From 1955 she sang mostly in Europe: she appeared as Clytemnestra, one of her greatest roles, at Salzburg (1956), as Carmen at Vienna and Aix-en-Provence and as Erda at Covent Garden, Bayreuth and Munich. She created Circe in Luigi Dallapiccola's *Ulisse* (1968, Berlin) and continued to sing until 1971. She had a rich, dark voice and was a compelling figure on the stage. Her arresting Erda can be heard on Georg Solti's recording of *Das Rheingold*,

and her vividly characterized Clytemnestra on Karl Böhm's *Elektra*.

Harold Rosenthal/Alan Blyth

Magli, Giovanni Gualberto

(*bur.* Florence, 8 Jan 1625). Italian castrato. A Florentine, he was a pupil of Giulio Caccini and entered Medici service on 23 August 1604. In 1607 he was lent to Prince Francesco Gonzaga of Mantua for the first performances of Claudio Monteverdi's *Orfeo*: he played Music and at least one other role, acquitting himself well despite the difficulty of learning the music. Magli then performed in the wedding festivities for Prince Cosimo de' Medici and Maria Magdalena of Austria in 1608. He came under the protection of Don Antonio de' Medici, who arranged two years' paid leave (from 18 October 1611) to study vocal and instrumental technique in Naples. Magli again left Florence in October 1615 to serve the elector of Brandenburg, but his salary payments had resumed by September 1622.

T. Carter: 'A Florentine Wedding of 1608', *AcM*, lv (1983), 89–107

J. Whenham, ed.: *Claudio Monteverdi: 'Orfeo'* (Cambridge, 1986)

W. Kirkendale: *The Court Musicians in Florence during the Principate of the Medici, with a Reconstruction of the Artistic Establishment* (Florence, 1993)

Tim Carter

Maison, René

(*b* Frameries, 24 Nov 1895; *d* Mont d'Or, Haut Doubs, 11 July 1962). Belgian tenor. He studied in Brussels and Paris, and made his début in 1920 at Geneva, as Rodolfo (*La bohème*). His reputation grew with three successive seasons, beginning in 1925, at Monte Carlo, where his roles included Faust, Hoffmann and Huon in *Oberon*. From 1928 to 1931 he was a member of the company at Chicago, undertaking heavier roles such as Lohengrin, Florestan and Parsifal. In Paris he sang at the Opéra-Comique and at the Opéra, where in 1934 he created the role of Eumolpus in Igor Stravinsky's *Perséphone*. From 1934 to 1937 he was principal dramatic tenor at the Colón; he also had a career at the Metropolitan from 1935 to 1943. One of his greatest successes there was as Julien in *Louise*, which he also sang at Covent Garden in 1935. His only other London role was Lohengrin in 1931, when his acting and physical presence (he was 6 feet 4 inches in height) impressed, though his singing was criticized for roughness in the loud passages and 'a rather falsetto character of voice' in the soft (Ernest Newman in the *Sunday Times*). On retirement he taught in

New York and Boston, his pupils including RAMÓN VINAY. Recordings show an expressive style and a strong voice, well heard in 'live' performances from the Metropolitan.

J.B. Steane

Malanotte, Adelaide

(*b* Verona, 1785; *d* Salò, 31 Dec 1832). Italian contralto. She made her début in 1806 at Verona, then sang in Turin and at the Teatro Valle, Rome, in the first performance of Nicola Manfroce's *Alzira* (1810). She repeated *Alzira* in Monza (1811), sang in Florence (1812), then created the title role of Gioachino Rossini's *Tancredi* (1813) at La Fenice, scoring a great success. She later sang Tancredi in Ferrara and Bologna and, in 1818, at the S Carlo, where she was heard by Ferdinand Hérold. He did not like the timbre of her voice but thought her style, taste and intonation perfect.

Elizabeth Forbes

Malfitano, Catherine

(*b* New York, 18 April 1948). American soprano. After making her début at the Central City Opera in 1972 as Nannetta, she sang Rosina with the Minnesota Opera Company (1972–3). From 1973 to 1979 she sang regularly with the New York City Opera, and at the Houston Opera Studio. She made her European début as Susanna at the 1974 Holland Festival, her Metropolitan Opera début as Gretel (1979) and her Vienna Staatsoper début as Violetta (1982). She has performed with most of the principal American companies and sung the leading roles in the premières of several works. In 1980 she appeared as Servilia in Jean-Pierre Ponnelle's film of *La clemenza di Tito*. She sang Konstanze at the Paris Opéra (1984), the title roles in *Lulu* (1985) and *Daphne* (1988) at the Munich Festival and Butterfly at Covent Garden (1988). Her first Salome was with the Deutsche Oper, Berlin, under Giuseppe Sinopoli in 1990; she sang the role later at the WNO and Covent Garden, where she was also a notable Lina in Giuseppe Verdi's *Stiffelio* (1993) and a powerful Tosca (2000). Her later roles have included Kát'a Kabanová, Emilia Marty (*The Makropoulos Affair*), which she sang at the Metropolitan in the 2000–2001 season, the title role in *Lady Macbeth of the Mtsensk District*, Kundry, and Senta, which she first performed at the Lyric Opera of Chicago in 2001. In October 1999 she sang Beatrice in the world première of William Bolcom's *A View from the Bridge* in Chicago. Malfitano is a singing-actress of exceptional talent, bringing an originality and depth of interpretation to all her roles, as can be gauged from

her videos of *Stiffelio* and *Salome*, both recorded at Covent Garden, and *Tosca*, recorded on location in Rome (1992).

Michael Walsh/Alan Blyth

Malibran [née García], Maria(-Felicia)

(*b* Paris, 24 March 1808; *d* Manchester, 23 Sept 1836). Spanish mezzo-soprano. She was the daughter of the tenor MANUEL GARCÍA and sister of the mezzo-soprano PAULINE VIARDOT. She studied with her father, a rigorous teacher whose harshness towards her was notorious, and made her London début at the King's Theatre in June 1825 as Rosina (*Il barbiere*); subsequently she sang Felicia in the first British performance of Giacomo Meyerbeer's *Il crociato in Egitto*. *Il barbiere* opened the García family's season at the Park Theatre, New York, in November 1825. (*Tancredi*, Gioachino Rossini's *Otello*, *Il turco in Italia* and *La Cenerentola*, *Don Giovanni* and two pieces by Manuel García were also in the repertory.) After the failure of her marriage to Eugène Malibran, Maria Malibran returned to Europe in 1827. She made her Paris début at the Théâtre Italien in *Semiramide* in 1828, where she also created the title role in Fromental Halévy's *Clari* (1828). She reappeared at the King's Theatre in 1829 in *Otello*, and then sang alternately in Paris and London until 1832, when she went to Italy.

She made her Italian début at the Teatro Valle, Rome, on 30 June 1832 as Desdemona; moving to Naples she sang the same role at the Teatro del Fondo on 6 August and Rosina in *Il barbiere di Siviglia* at the S Carlo on 7 September, followed by *La Cenerentola*, *La gazza ladra*, *Semiramide* and *Otello*, scoring a tremendous success at every performance. In Bologna she sang Romeo in *I Capuleti e i Montecchi* on 13 October, substituting the final scene of Nicola Vaccai's *Giulietta e Romeo* for that of Vincenzo Bellini. In May 1833 at Drury Lane she sang *La sonnambula* in English; it was so successful that it later transferred to Covent Garden. She returned to the S Carlo, Naples, in November 1833, singing her usual Rossini and Bellini roles, as well as operas by Giovanni Pacini, Lauro Rossi and Carlo Coccia: she sang *Norma* on 23 February 1834 in Naples, and repeated it at La Scala on 15 May. She visited Venice early in 1835, singing Desdemona and Norma at La Fenice. On 8 April she gave one performance of *La sonnambula* at the Teatro Emeronitio, which was in dire financial straits, raising enough money to guarantee the future of the theatre, renamed Teatro Malibran. In May she sang Amina and Leonore in *Fidelio* in English at Covent Garden, then in September returned to La Scala. New roles included Vaccai's Romeo and the title role of his *Giovanna Grey*, which she created on 23 February 1836. She also created the title role in Gaetano Donizetti's *Maria Stuarda* on 30 December 1835, causing a famous scandal by ignoring some changes that the Milanese censors had insisted upon. Bellini adapted the role of Elvira in *I puritani* (1835, Paris) for her to sing in Naples, but the opera was turned down by the management and she never sang it.

Her first marriage having eventually been annulled, she married the violinist Charles de Bériot in March 1836, and at Drury Lane in May of that year created the title role in Michael Balfe's *The Maid of Artois*, which he had written for her. A riding accident when she was pregnant resulted in her death during the Manchester Festival. To judge from the parts adapted for her by both Donizetti and Bellini, the compass (*g* to *e'''*), power and flexibility of Malibran's voice were extraordinary. Her early death turned her into something of a legendary figure with writers and poets during the later 19th century. A portrait by Henri Decaisne shows her in the role of Desdemona (see colour plate 11).

Memoirs of the Public and Private Life of the Celebrated Madame Malibran (London, 1836)
A. Fitzlyon: *Maria Malibran* (London, 1987)

Elizabeth Forbes

Mallinger [née Lichtenegger], Mathilde

(*b* Zagreb, 17 Feb 1847; *d* Berlin, 19 April 1920). Croatian soprano. After studying at the Prague Conservatory with G.B. Gordigiani and in Vienna with Richard Loewy, she was engaged at the Hofoper, Munich, where she made her début in 1866 as Norma. While at Munich she sang Elsa in *Lohengrin*, Elisabeth in *Tannhäuser* and Eva at the first performance of *Die Meistersinger* (21 June 1868). She was then engaged at Berlin, making her début as Elsa in 1869, and remained there until her retirement in 1882. She took part in the first Berlin performances of *Die Meistersinger* (1870) and of *Aida* (1874), and her repertory also included Leonore in *Fidelio*, Agathe in *Der Freischütz*, Sieglinde in *Die Walküre*, Valentine in *Les Huguenots* and the Mozart roles of Pamina, Donna Anna and Countess Almaviva. Her voice, essentially a lyric soprano, was not large but so well schooled that she could sing heavier, dramatic roles without strain. After her retirement she taught singing in Prague and later in Berlin, where LOTTE LEHMANN was among her pupils.

Elizabeth Forbes

Malten [Müller], Therese

(*b* Insterburg [now Chernyakhovsk], East Prussia, 21 June 1855; *d* Neuzschieren, nr Dresden, 2 Jan 1930). German soprano. After studying with Gustav Engel in Berlin, she made her début in 1873 as Pamina in *Die Zauberflöte* at Dresden, where she was engaged for the next 30 years. Richard Wagner heard her as Senta in a performance of *Der fliegende Holländer* at Dresden in September 1881 and invited her to Bayreuth the following summer to share the role of Kundry in *Parsifal* with MATERNA and BRANDT. She also sang Kundry at Munich in the private performance of *Parsifal* given for King Ludwig (3 May 1884) and at the Royal Albert Hall, in the first concert performance in London (10 November 1884). She had previously made her London début at Drury Lane as Leonore in *Fidelio* (24 May 1882), a role she repeated in Munich (15 August 1884). At Dresden she sang Isolde (1884), Brünnhilde in *Die Walküre* and *Siegfried* (1885) and many other roles in French, Italian and German operas, ranging from C.W. Gluck's *Armide* to Pietro Mascagni's *Cavalleria rusticana* (1891). Returning to Bayreuth she sang Isolde (1886), Eva in *Die Meistersinger* (1888) and Kundry for the last time in 1894. She also took part in the *Ring* cycles presented by Angelo Neumann in St Petersburg and Moscow (1889). Her voice was notable for its extensive compass; its middle register was described as rich and powerful and the higher and lower notes as equally strong and pleasing.

Elizabeth Forbes

Maltman, Christopher

(*b* Cleethorpes, 7 Feb 1970). English baritone. After reading biochemistry at Warwick University he studied singing at the RAM in London and in 1997 won the Lieder Prize in the Cardiff Singer of the World competition. The following year he became a company member of the ENO, where he has appeared as Gioachino Rossini's Figaro (a role he has also sung at the Deutsche Oper, Berlin), Mozart's Count Almaviva and Tarquinius, which he has also performed at the Montpellier Festival. His resonant, high-lying baritone, muscular yet subtly inflected, has also been admired as Ned Keene (the role of his Glyndebourne début), Billy Budd, which he has sung for WNO and at the Seattle Opera (2000), and Dandini (*La Cenerentola*). Maltman is a noted recitalist, and has appeared at the Wigmore Hall, the Konzerthaus in Vienna, the Edinburgh and Hohenems Festivals and elsewhere. In 2000 he made recital débuts at the Salzburg Mozarteum and Carnegie Hall, New York. His recordings include discs of English songs and a thoughtful, finely sung version of Robert Schumann's *Dichterliebe*. (See colour plate 5.)

Richard Wigmore

Mandini, Maria

(*fl* 1782–91). French soprano, wife of STEFANO MANDINI. The daughter of a Versailles court official, she was engaged with her husband in the Italian opera company in Vienna; she made her début there in 1783 as Madama Brillante in Domenico Cimarosa's *L'italiana in Londra* and then sang Countess Belfiore in Giuseppe Sarti's *Fra i due litiganti*. She is known to have created three roles, all small parts: Marina in Vicente Martín y Soler's *Il burbero di buon cuore* (1786), Marcellina in *Le nozze di Figaro* (1786) and Britomarte in Martín y Soler's *L'arbore di Diana* (1787). The high tessitura of her aria 'Il capro e la capretta', which Mozart wrote for her as Marcellina, belies any claim that she was a mezzo-soprano. She was apparently an attractive but poor singer. Karl von Zinzendorf wrote of her performance as Marina: 'La Mandini let us see her beautiful hair'. As Britomarte she was said to sound 'like an enraged cat', and the performing score contains a pencilled comment at the head of her only aria: 'canta male'. All that is known of her later career is that she sang with her husband in Naples and Paris.

Christopher Raeburn/Dorothea Link

Mandini (Alberto) Paolo

(*b* Arezzo, 1757; *d* Bologna, 25 Jan 1842). Italian tenor and baritone, brother of STEFANO MANDINI. He is sometimes confused with Stefano because, like him, Paolo had a wide range and sang both tenor and baritone roles. A pupil of Saverio Valente, he made a successful début at Brescia in 1777 and sang widely in Italy before joining Joseph Haydn's company at Eszterháza in 1783–4. He appeared as Don Fabio in Domenico Cimarosa's *Il falegname*, Gianetto in Pasquale Anfossi's *I viaggiatori felici*, Armidoro in Cimarosa's *L'amor costante*, the Marquis in Giuseppe Sarti's *Le gelosie villane* and the Count in Francesco Bianchi's *La villanella rapita*. Haydn wrote Idreno for him in *Armida*. For the 1785–6 season he joined his brother in Vienna, where he made his début in Anfossi's *I viaggiatori felici* as Gianetto and sang Paulino in Bianchi's *La villanella rapita*. He achieved greater success in Venice in 1787, in Cimarosa's *L'amor costante* among other operas. In 1788–9 he sang the title role in Giovanni Paisiello's *Il rè Teodoro* in Venezia in Parma, Milan and Bologna, and appeared in Vicente Martín y Soler's *L'arbore di Diana* as Silvio (Milan) and *Una cosa rara* (Parma). He then returned to Vienna, where he created Sandrino in Antonio Salieri's *La cifra* (1789), and returned briefly to Eszterháza (March–September 1790). He later joined his brother in St Petersburg.

Christopher Raeburn/Dorothea Link

Mandini, Stefano

(*b* 1750; *d* ?c1810). Italian baritone. His first known appearance, in Ferrara in 1774, was followed by a string of engagements throughout Italy. At Parma in 1776 he was described as 'primo buffo mezzo carattere'. In 1783 he and his wife, the soprano MARIA MANDINI, were engaged by Joseph II for his new Italian opera company in Vienna, Stefano making his début on 5 May 1783 as Milord Arespingh in Domenico Cimarosa's *L'italiana in Londra*. That season he distinguished himself as Mingone in Giuseppe Sarti's *Fra i due litiganti*, Don Fabio in Cimarosa's *Il falegname* and as Count Almaviva in Giovanni Paisiello's *Il barbiere di Siviglia*; in the last, Zinzendorf noted, he excelled in all four disguises in Almaviva's role. In 1784 he sang in *Le vicende d'amore* (P.A. Guglielmi), *La finta amante*, *La vendemmia* (Giuseppe Gazzaniga) and created the title role in Paisiello's *Il re Teodoro in Venezia*. The following season he created Artidoro in Stephen Storace's *Gli sposi malcontenti* and Plistene in Antonio Salieri's *La grotta di Trofonio*. He also sang in Francesco Bianchi's *La villanella rapita*, for which W.A. Mozart wrote a quartet (к479) and a trio (к480). Mandini as Pippo sang in both these numbers.

Mandini created three roles in 1786: the Poet in Salieri's *Prima la musica e poi le parole*, Count Almaviva in Mozart's *Le nozze di Figaro* and Lubino in Vicente Martín y Soler's *Una cosa rara*. He also sang in Giuseppe Sarti's *I finti eredi* and Giovanni Paisiello's *Le gare generose*. In 1787–8 he appeared as Leandro in Paisiello's *Le due contesse* and created Doristo in Martín y Soler's *L'arbore di Diana* and Biscroma in Salieri's *Axur re d'Ormus*. He was then released to go to Naples. In 1789–91 he and his wife sang at the Théâtre de Monsieur in Paris, having considerable success in *Il barbiere di Siviglia*, *Una cosa rara* and *La villanella rapita*, and in Venice (1794–5). The *Annalen des Theaters*, in a report from Paris, described Mandini as an outstandingly good actor and singer. In the summer of 1795 while on his way to St Petersburg, he stopped in Vienna to give six guest performances of Niccolò Piccinni's *La Griselda* and Paisiello's *La molinara*. He stayed several years in St Petersburg, where the painter Elisabeth-Louise Vigée Le Brun remarked that he was an excellent performer and sang wonderfully. It is uncertain whether he or his younger brother PAOLO MANDINI appeared in Berlin in 1804. An extremely versatile singer, he acquitted himself well both as the comic servant (e.g. Doristo) and as the serious lover (e.g. Lubino). His wide range permitted him to portray Count Almaviva as a tenor for Paisiello and as a baritone for Mozart. Three canzonette, for which he composed both the text and the music, were published in London.

Christopher Raeburn/Dorothea Link

Manfredini-Guarmani, Elisabetta

(*b* Bologna, 1790; *d* after 1817). Italian soprano. After making her début in 1809 at Bologna, she created roles in four operas by Gioachino Rossini: Amira in *Ciro in Babilonia* (1812) at Ferrara; Amenaide in *Tancredi* (1813) and Aldimira in *Sigismondo* (1814) at La Fenice, Venice; and the title role of *Adelaide di Borgogna* (1817) at the Teatro Argentina, Rome. At La Scala she created Mandane in Ferdinando Paer's *L'eroismo in amore* (1815) and sang the title role of Johann Mayr's *Ginevra di Scozia* (1816). She also sang in Turin. To judge from the music composed for her by Gioachino Rossini, she had a voice of exceptional flexibility.

Elizabeth Forbes

Mangin, Noel

(*b* Wellington, 31 Dec 1931; *d* Auckland, 4 March 1995). New Zealand bass. After training initially as a tenor, he made his début as a bass-baritone in Auckland in 1957 as Giorgio Germont. Three years later he made his Australian début as Sarastro, by which time his voice had developed a true bass depth and resonance. After further study in Paris with Dominique Modesti (1961–2), he sang with Sadler's Wells Opera (1963–7) and at the Hamburg Staatsoper from 1967 until he began a freelance career in 1977. In Hamburg he sang Black Will in the première of Alexander Goehr's *Arden Must Die* in 1967. From 1979 he regularly sang Fafner, Hunding and Hagen in Seattle Opera's annual bilingual *Ring* productions, and from 1977 he made frequent appearances with Victoria State Opera. Mangin claimed to have 189 roles in his repertory, of which the most notable were Don Pasquale, Ochs and, especially, Osmin, which he recorded twice. He was made a Kammersänger at Hamburg in 1976 and created an OBE in 1981.

A. Simpson and P. Downes: *Southern Voices: International Opera Singers of New Zealand* (Auckland, 1992), 91–103

Peter Downes

Manners, Fanny.

See MOODY, FANNY.

Manning [Payne], Jane (Marian)

(*b* Norwich, 20 Sept 1938). English soprano. She studied with GREENE at the RAM (1956–60), with Frederik Husler at the Scuola di Canto, Cureglia, Switzerland (1964), and in London with Frederick Jackson and Yvonne Rodd-Marling. She made her professional début in London in 1964 singing Anton Webern, Luigi Dallapiccola and Olivier Messiaen, and has continued to specialize in 20th-century music, to which her gifts – clear tone, precise pitching and an enthusiastic aptitude for new 'effects' – are well suited. Some of the problems, and joys, of performing modern works are discussed in her essay 'Contemporary Vocal Technique', *Composer*, no. 38 (1971), 13–15. She has also published *New Vocal Repertory* (London, 1986–98), and contributed a chapter on the interpretation of Messiaen vocal music to *The Messiaen Companion* (London, 1995). Particularly associated with new British music, she has given the first performances of works by Richard Rodney Bennett, Harrison Birtwistle, Peter Maxwell Davies, Antony Hopkins, Nicola Le Fanu, David Lumsdaine, Elizabeth Maconchy, Anthony Payne (whom she married in 1966) and others; in 1973 she received a special award from the Composers' Guild of Great Britain and in 1988 she founded the group Jane's Minstrels. Her recordings, with them and as a soloist, include works by Arnold Schoenberg, Elisabeth Lutyens and Payne, the complete song cycles of Messiaen and the complete vocal works of Erik Satie. Extensive work for the BBC has taken her from light music to *Pierrot lunaire*, David Lumsdaine's *Aria for Edward John Eyre* and Milton Babbitt's *Philomel*. As a member of The Matrix she has performed Perotinus and John Cage, and she has also appeared in oratorio and Classical opera. She teaches in the USA (since 1982) and in England, where she became a visiting professor at the RCM in 1995. She was appointed OBE in 1990.

Paul Griffiths

Manowarda, Josef von

(*b* Kraków, 3 July 1890; *d* Vienna, 24 Dec 1942). Austrian bass of Polish birth. He studied in Graz, where he sang from 1911 to 1915. After three years at the Vienna Volksoper and a further period of study, he made his début at the Staatsoper as the Spirit Messenger in the première of *Die Frau ohne Schatten* (1919). He continued to sing regularly in Vienna even after 1934, when he moved to Berlin. He was heard first at Salzburg in 1922 and at Bayreuth in 1931; he became closely associated with both festivals, his Mozart roles including Osmin in *Die Entführung*, while at Bayreuth he sang most of the Wagnerian bass parts. Elsewhere he also took the bass-baritone roles of Wotan and Hans Sachs. Recordings, some of actual performances, capture the authority and power of his stage performances but also expose unevenness in his vocal production.

J.B. Steane

Mantius, Eduard

(*b* Schwerin, 18 Jan 1806; *d* Ilmenau, Thuringia, 4 July 1874). German tenor. He studied in Leipzig and made his début in 1830 as Tamino at the Berlin Hofoper, where he was engaged until 1857. In 1849 he created Slender in Otto Nicolai's *Die lustigen Weiber von Windsor*. His repertory of over 150 roles included Adolar (*Euryanthe*), Raoul (*Les Huguenots*), Arnold (*Guillaume Tell*), Pylades (*Iphigénie en Tauride*) and Florestan, which he sang at his farewell performance in Berlin. He had a powerful, brilliant voice as effective in W.A. Mozart as in heavier German or French roles.

Elizabeth Forbes

Manuguerra, Matteo

(*b* Tunis, 5 Oct 1924; *d* Mt Pellier, 20 July 1998). French baritone. He settled in Argentina after World War II and at 35 entered the Buenos Aires Conservatory. In 1963 he returned to France to accept a three-year contract as first baritone in Lyons. He moved to the Paris Opéra in 1966, singing in *Faust*, *Rigoletto*, *La traviata*, *Carmen* and *Lucia di Lammermoor*. Engagements throughout Europe followed. His American début was in Seattle in 1968 (*Andrea Chénier*), and he joined the Metropolitan Opera as Enrico Ashton in *Lucia* in 1971. He attracted special attention the next year in a concert performance of *L'Africaine* in New York, and became known for Verdi roles such as Renato, Don Carlo (*La forza del destino*) and Macbeth. He sang Rigoletto at Chicago (1977), Houston (1983) and Buenos Aires (1986), and Renato (*Un ballo in maschera*) at Naples in 1989. A baritone of uncommon fervour, taste and versatility, Manuguerra brought equal authority to the French and Italian repertories, as several recordings, particularly of Verdi operas, confirm.

Martin Bernheimer

Mařák, Otakar

(*b* Esztergom, Hungary, 5 Jan 1872; *d* Prague, 2 July 1939). Czech tenor. He studied at the Prague Conservatory with Paršova-Zikešová. In 1899 he made his début at Brno as Faust and from 1900 he appeared at the New German Theatre, Prague. He sang under Gustav Mahler at the Vienna Hofoper, created Gennaro in Ermanno Wolf-Ferrari's *I gioielli della Madonna* (1911, Berlin) and sang in the première of Ferruccio Busoni's *Die Brautwahl* (1912, Hamburg). In 1913 he was the first London Bacchus (*Ariadne auf Naxos*), and the following year he sang in Chicago as Parsifal in the local première of Richard Wagner's

opera. He was principal tenor at the Prague National Theatre from 1914 and retired from the stage in 1934. His recordings, including a complete *Pagliacci*, give a fair indication of his vocal and dramatic strengths.

David Cummings/R

Marc, Alessandra

(*b* Berlin, 29 July 1957). American soprano. She trained with Marilyn Cotlow in the USA and in 1983 made her début as Mariana in a concert performance of Richard Wagner's *Das Liebesverbot* at the Waterloo Festival. The quality and power of her voice attracted immediate attention, and she was soon singing major roles such as Tosca, Ariadne and Aida. Particularly admired were her Maria in Richard Strauss's *Friedenstag*, which she later recorded, at Santa Fe and Lisabetta in Umberto Giordano's *La cena delle beffe* at the Wexford Festival of 1987. Aida was the role of her début in Chicago, San Francisco and at the Metropolitan; it also introduced her to Vienna in 1992. Marc made her Covent Garden début in 1994 as Turandot, a role she has since sung widely in Italy, France, Israel and the Metropolitan Opera (2000). In song recitals her voice has been found almost overpowering, as it was by some when she made her concert début at the Wigmore Hall, London, in 1990. Large-scale choral works such as Ludwig van Beethoven's *Missa solemnis* and Giuseppe Verdi's Requiem (which she has recorded with Daniel Barenboim) have suited her well. Although she has been somewhat neglected by the major recording companies, her magnificent voice, with its mezzo-tinted timbre, is impressively heard as Strauss's Elektra and Chrysothemis and in an operatic recital on the Delos label.

J.B. Steane

Marchesi, Blanche

(*b* Paris, 4 April 1863; *d* London, 15 Dec 1940). French soprano, daughter of SALVATORE MARCHESI and MATHILDE MARCHESI. She studied with her mother in Paris, singing at many private and charity concerts there, and made her professional concert début in London in 1896. Her first operatic appearance was in 1900 at Prague, as Brünnhilde in *Die Walküre*. She sang with the Moody-Manners Opera Company for several seasons, appearing at Covent Garden in 1902 as Elisabeth in *Tannhäuser*, Elsa in *Lohengrin*, Isolde, Leonora in *Il trovatore* and Santuzza in *Cavalleria rusticana*. She taught singing for many years in London and wrote her memoir, *A Singer's Pilgrimage* (London, 1923/R), and a book on singing.

Elizabeth Forbes

Marchesi [née Graumann], Mathilde (de Castrone)

(*b* Frankfurt, 24 March 1821; *d* London, 17 Nov 1913). German mezzo-soprano and singing teacher, wife of SALVATORE MARCHESI and mother of BLANCHE MARCHESI. Although she appeared on the opera stage only once, her influence on opera as a teacher was enormous. She studied with Felice Ronconi in Frankfurt and with Otto Nicolai in Vienna, making her concert début in 1844 at Frankfurt and taking part in the Lower Rhine Festival at Düsseldorf in May 1845. In October of that year she went to Paris for two years of study with Manuel Garcia. When he moved to London, she followed and sang very successfully in concerts there during 1849, and then sang in Germany and the Netherlands. In 1852 she married Salvatore Marchesi, with whom she had often appeared on the concert platform. She made her only stage appearance, as Rosina in *Il barbiere di Siviglia* in Bremen in 1853.

In 1854 Marchesi became professor of singing at the Vienna Conservatory, a post she held for seven years; during this period her pupils included Caroline Dory, Antoinetta Fricci, Gabrielle Krauss and Ilma di Murska. In 1861 she moved to Paris and gave lessons privately while continuing her concert and recital appearances. In 1864 she and her husband made a long tour of the British Isles; the following year she went to Cologne and remained there for three years. In 1868 she returned to the Vienna Conservatory and taught there for a decade; she resigned in 1878 but continued to teach privately in Vienna. Her pupils came from all over Europe and the USA, and included ANNA D'ANGERI, Katherina Klafsky and EMMA NEVADA.

In 1881 she opened her own school of singing in Paris, which continued to attract pupils from many parts of the world for over 25 years. She taught, among others, SUZANNE ADAMS, EMMA CALVÉ, EMMA EAMES, MARY GARDEN, NELLIE MELBA, SYBIL SANDERSON and Blanche Marchesi, her daughter. Her vocal method, based on that of her teacher Garcia, was published in Paris in 1886, and she also wrote a practical guide for students and a volume of autobiography.

Elizabeth Forbes/R

Marchesi, Salvatore, Cavaliere de Castrone, Marchese della Rajata

(*b* Palermo, 15 Jan 1822; *d* Paris, 20 Feb 1908). Italian baritone and singing teacher, husband of MATHILDE MARCHESI and father of BLANCHE MARCHESI. He studied in Palermo and in Milan with Francesco Lamperti. Forced to leave Italy because of his lib-

eral political ideas, he made his début in New York in 1848 as Carlo in *Ernani*. On returning to Europe he studied further with Manuel Garcia in London and sang there in concert in 1850, when he met the German mezzo-soprano Mathilde Graumann. After their marriage in 1852 he appeared at the Berlin Opera in *Ernani*, *Il barbiere di Siviglia* and Gaetano Donizetti's *Lucrezia Borgia*. Further engagements in Germany followed, and in December 1853 he sang at Ferrara, again in *Ernani*. After a period spent teaching at the Vienna Conservatory, in 1863 he returned briefly to the stage. He sang Leporello and Charles Gounod's Mephistopheles (in Italian) at Her Majesty's Theatre, where in 1864 he again sang Mephistopheles, this time in the first performance of *Faust* in English. He translated several French and German opera librettos into Italian, including those for Richard Wagner's *Der fliegende Holländer*, *Tannhäuser* and *Lohengrin*. The composer of a number of songs, he also wrote a book on singing and vocal exercises.

Elizabeth Forbes

Marchesini, Maria Antonia ['La Lucchesina']

(*fl* 1736–9). Italian mezzo-soprano. She sang in three operas at the Teatro Nuovo, Naples, in 1736 and was engaged for London by the Opera of the Nobility, making her début at the King's Theatre in the pasticcio *Sabrina* in 1737. She next appeared in Egidio Duni's *Demofoonte*, and the impressario John Jacob Heidegger re-engaged her for the 1738 autumn season when she sang in the pasticcios *Arsace* and *Alessandro Severo* (Albina), G.F. Handel's *Faramondo* (Rosimonda) and *Serse* (Arsamene), Giovanni Pescetti's *La conquista del vello d'oro* and Antonio Veracini's *Partenio*. Still in London in 1739, she sang in Pescetti's *Angelica e Medoro* at Covent Garden and may have appeared in Handel's *Il trionfo del tempo* and *Jupiter in Argo*. She probably created the Witch of Endor in Handel's oratorio *Saul*. In May 1738 she married the portrait and scene painter Jacopo Amiconi in London. Her parts in *Faramondo* and *Serse* suggest a singer of limited accomplishments; the compass is *a* to *g"*, with a low tessitura. She took male roles in *Demofoonte*, *Serse* and several other operas.

Winton Dean

Marchetti Fantozzi [née Marchetti], Maria (?Vincenza)

(*b* ?1760; *d* ? after 1800). Italian soprano. She was one of the leading singers of *opera seria* during the

1780s and 90s. Around 1783 she married the tenor Angelo Fantozzi and thereafter usually identified herself as Maria Marchetti Fantozzi. She was praised throughout Italy for her acting as well as her singing, particularly in Naples, where she performed in at least nine different operas in 1785–6. Marchetti was a specialist in the portrayal of passionate, tragic heroines like Semiramide and Cleopatra; she was thus ideally suited to create the role of Vitellia in W.A. Mozart's *La clemenza di Tito*. Music written for her by Luigi Cherubini, Giacomo Tritto and Niccolò Zingarelli, as well as Mozart, shows her to have been an extraordinary virtuoso, with a large range and a capacity for difficult coloratura.

J.A. Rice: 'Mozart and his Singers: the Case of Maria Marchetti Fantozzi, the First Vitellia', *OQ*, xi/4 (1994–5), 31–52

John A. Rice

Marchi, Emilio de.

See DE MARCHI, EMILIO.

Marcolini, Marietta

(*b* Florence, *c*1780; *d* 1814 or later). Italian contralto. In 1800 she was singing at the Teatro S Benedetto, Venice; in 1803 she took part in the first performance of P.C. Guglielmi's *La serva bizzarra* at the Teatro Nuovo, Naples. In 1806 she sang at Livorno and Pisa, then at the Teatro Argentina, Rome, in the premières of Giacomo Tritto's *Andromaca e Pirro* and Giuseppe Nicolini's *Traiano in Cacia* (1807). In 1810 she sang at the première of Domenico Puccini's *Il trionfo di Quinto Fabio* at Livorno. Marcolini made her début at La Scala in the first performances of Carlo Bigatti's *L'amante prigioniero* and of Ercole Paganini's *Le rivali generose* (1809). She created roles in five operas by Gioachino Rossini: Ernestina in *L'equivoco stravagante* (1811) at Bologna; the title role of *Ciro in Babilonia* (1812) at Ferrara; Clarice in *La pietra del paragone* (1812) at La Scala; Isabella in *L'italiana in Algeri* (1813) at the Teatro S Benedetto; and the title role of *Sigismondo* (1814) at La Fenice, Venice. She was also a renowned exponent of Rossini's Tancredi.

Elizabeth Forbes

Mardones, José

(*b* Fontecha, nr León, 14 Aug 1868; *d* Madrid, 4 May 1932). Spanish bass. He studied in Madrid, where he made his début in zarzuelas. In 1908 he joined the Lisbon S Carlos Opera and in 1909 made his North American début in *Aida* with the new Boston Opera. His best role in the most flourishing years of his career was Arrigo Boito's Mefistofele, which he repeated at the Metropolitan in 1920. He had become leading bass there in 1917, remaining until 1926 and singing in the first performances there of *La forza del destino, Luisa Miller, Le roi de Lahore* and Gaspare Spontini's *La vestale*. Returning to Spain, he resumed singing after an illness and made some fine recordings when nearly 60. His reputation was that of an indifferent actor with one of the most magnificent voices of the age. The voice is mightily impressive on recordings, which are also by no means wooden or characterless as interpretations.

J.B. Steane

Maréchal, Adolphe (Alphonse)

(*b* Liège, 26 Sept 1867; *d* Brussels, 1 Feb 1935). Belgian tenor. He studied at the Liège Conservatory and made his début at Dijon in 1891. After singing for some years in provincial French houses he was engaged by the Opéra-Comique in 1895, where he sang in several premières, most notably those of *Louise* in 1900 (Julien) and *Grisélidis* in 1901. This led to another important Massenet première, at Monte Carlo, where in 1902 he created the title role in *Le jongleur de Notre Dame*, playing 'his difficult role with infinite address and virtuosity', according to the *Journal de Monaco*. He made his Covent Garden début in 1902 as Don José, acting with 'marked and picturesque power' (*Musical Times*). He also appeared in *Faust, Manon* and the première, under Messager, of Herbert Bunning's *The Princess Osra*, with MARY GARDEN in the title role and the English libretto translated into French. He retired after a crisis of voice and health in 1907. Among his few and rare recordings is a solo from *Le jongleur* which shows a finely tutored voice and an eloquent style.

J.B. Steane

Margiono, Charlotte

(*b* Amsterdam, 24 March 1955). Dutch soprano. After studying with Aafje Heynis at the Arnhem Conservatory, she sang a delightful Mařenka in Harry Kupfer's staging of *The Bartered Bride* at the Komische Oper in 1985, then was admired as Susanna in Berne in 1988, Vitellia (*La clemenza di Tito*) at the Aix Festival the same year and Amelia (*Simon Boccanegra*) with the Netherlands Opera in 1989. She gained international recognition when she undertook Fiordiligi in Jürgen Flimm's arresting production of *Così fan tutte* at Amsterdam in

1990 with Nikolaus Harnoncourt conducting (also recorded), and the same year won plaudits for her Agathe at Amsterdam and her Vitellia with John Eliot Gardiner at the Holland Festival; she was also praised in the latter role at the Salzburg Festival in 1991 with Colin Davis. Her other Mozart parts include Countess Almaviva (sung at Aix, 1991, and recorded with Harnoncourt), Donna Elvira (recorded with Gardiner) and Pamina. In 1995 she sang Agathe at the Maggio Musicale in Florence, conducted by Wolfgang Sawallisch, and the following year appeared as Desdemona in Amsterdam. In 1999 she added to her repertory Marguerite in a concert performance of *La damnation de Faust* with Bernard Haitink in Amsterdam. Margiono is a noted concert singer, especially in the *Missa solemnis*; her recording of the work with Gardiner discloses the lyrical warmth and refined style of her approach. She also gives recitals, often with the mezzo-soprano Birgit Remmert.

Alan Blyth

Mariani, Luciano

(*b* Cremona, 1801; *d* Castell'Arquato, Piacenza, 10 June 1859). Italian bass. In 1823 he was singing at La Fenice, where he created Oroe in *Semiramide*. He sang Olivo (Gaetano Donizetti's *Olivo e Pasquale*) at the Teatro della Cannobiana, Milan (1830). He created Rodolfo in *La sonnambula* at the Teatro Carcano, Milan (1831), and Alfonso in *Lucrezia Borgia* at La Scala (1833). At the Teatro Comunale, Bologna, he sang Oroveso (*Norma*) and Rodolfo (1834). His sister was ROSA MARIANI.

Elizabeth Forbes

Mariani, Rosa

(*b* Cremona, 1799; *d* after 1832). Italian coloratura contralto. She was the sister of the bass LUCIANO MARIANI. She made her début in Cremona, in 1818, and sang Arsace in the première of *Semiramide* at La Fenice in 1823. She toured Italy with her brother, and appeared at the King's Theatre, London, in 1832.

Elizabeth Forbes/R

Marié de l'Isle, Célestine.

See GALLI-MARIE, CELESTINE.

Marié de l'Isle, (Claude Marie) Mécène

(*b* Château-Chinon, 1811; *d* Paris, 1882). French tenor, later baritone. He sang in the chorus of the Opéra-Comique, Paris, then in 1838 made his début as a soloist at Metz. Returning to the Opéra-Comique, he sang Albert in the first performance of Antoine Clapisson's *La symphonie* (1839) and created Tonio in Gaetano Donizetti's *La fille du régiment* (1840). Engaged at the Opéra in 1841, he sang Eléazar (*La Juive*), Max (*Der Freischütz*), Arnold (*Guillaume Tell*), Raoul (*Les Huguenots*), Fernand (*La favorite*) and Robert le diable. He then became a baritone and, after singing in Italy, in 1848 he returned to the Opéra, where he sang the title role of *Guillaume Tell*, Nevers (*Les Huguenots*), Alphonse (*La favorite*) and Raimbaud (*Le comte Ory*). After retiring from the stage he taught in Paris, his best-known pupil being his daughter, CÉLESTINE GALLI-MARIÉ, who created Carmen.

Elizabeth Forbes

Marini, Ignazio

(*b* Tagliuno, Bergamo, 28 Nov 1811; *d* Milan, 29 April 1873). Italian bass. He made his début in 1832 at Brescia and was then engaged at La Scala, where he created Guido in Gaetano Donizetti's *Gemma di Vergy* (1834), sang Talbot in *Maria Stuarda* (1835), created the title role of Giuseppe Verdi's *Oberto* and sang Gran Sinisalco in the first performance of Donizetti's *Gianni di Parigi* (1839). In 1840 he sang Murena in *L'esule* in a performance given at Bergamo in honour of Donizetti, who was then further revising the opera. At the Teatro Apollo, Rome, he sang the title role of *Marino Faliero* (1840) and created Arnoldo in Donizetti's *Adelia* (1841). In 1846 he created the title role of *Attila* at La Fenice. Engaged at Covent Garden, 1847–9, he sang Silva (*Ernani*), Marcel (*Les Huguenots*), Bertram (*Robert le diable*), W.A. Mozart's Figaro and Leporello. His vast repertory included Gioachino Rossini's Moses, Elmiro (*Otello*) and Mustafà; Vincenzo Bellini's Oroveso, Rodolfo (*La sonnambula*), Filippo (*Beatrice di Tenda*) and Giorgio (*I puritani*); and Donizetti's Belisarius, Nottingham (*Roberto Devereux*) and Félix (*Poliuto*). He sang in New York, Havana and St Petersburg, where in 1862 he appeared as the Alcalde in the first performance of *La forza del destino*. His wife, the soprano Antonietta Marini-Rainieri, created Leonora in *Oberto* (1839) and the Marchesa del Poggio in *Un giorno di regno* (1840) at La Scala.

Elizabeth Forbes

Mario, Giovanni Matteo, Cavaliere de Candia

(*b* Cagliari, 17 Oct 1810; *d* Rome, 11 Dec 1883). Italian tenor. He was an army officer but was forced to desert and go into exile because of his association with Giuseppe Mazzini's 'Young Italy' party. He studied in Paris with Louis Ponchard and Giulio Bordogni and was coached by Giacomo Meyerbeer himself for his Opéra début as Robert le diable (1838); he also sang the title role of *Le comte Ory*. His London début, as Gennaro in *Lucrezia Borgia*, was at Her Majesty's (1839); Lucrezia was sung by GIULIA GRISI, his stage partner for the next 22 years and his lifelong companion. He also appeared as Nemorino and Pollione. He returned to Paris to make his début at the Théâtre Italien as Nemorino and sang in the first performance of Fromental Halévy's *Le drapier* at the Opéra.

Thereafter, Mario and Grisi divided their time between Paris and London. In winter 1840–41 Mario transferred to the Théâtre Italien. He sang Orombello in *Beatrice di Tenda*, the first of ten new roles, including Almaviva, that year. He began to take over parts written for RUBINI or habitually sung by him, among them Arturo (*I puritani*) and Elvino (*La sonnambula*). He took on four Donizetti roles during the next two years, Edgardo, Percy (*Anna Bolena*), Carlo (*Linda di Chamounix*) and Ernesto in the première of *Don Pasquale*. In 1843 he sang four Rossini roles, Otello, Gianetto (*La gazza ladra*), Lindoro (*L'italiana in Algeri*) and Don Ramiro (*La Cenerentola*). During the next three seasons in London he created the title role of Michael Costa's *Don Carlos* (1844) and sang Paolino in *Il matrimonio segreto*, Ferrando, and Oronte in *I Lombardi*. In Paris he took over Gualtiero, a favourite Rubini role, in *Il pirata* (1844) and sang Jacopo in *I due Foscari* (Giuseppe Verdi wrote a cabaletta especially for him).

In 1847 Mario and Grisi transferred from Her Majesty's Theatre to Covent Garden, where he sang with the Royal Italian Opera every season (except 1869) until his retirement in 1871. During the winters he appeared at St Petersburg (1849–53, 1868–70), Paris (1853–64), New York (1854) and Madrid (1859, 1864). He was able to return to Italy but never sang there professionally. At Covent Garden his roles included James (*La donna del lago*), Fernand (*La favorite*), Raoul (*Les Huguenots*), Masaniello (*La muette de Portici*), John of Leyden (*Le prophète*), Raimbaut (*Robert le diable*), Eléazar (*La Juive*) and Tamino; he also sang the Duke in the London première of *Rigoletto* (1853).

In St Petersburg he sang in Jules Alary's *Sardanapale* (1852) and in New York took the role of Idreno (*Semiramide*). At the Théâtre Italien he appeared as Manrico, Alfredo and Lyonel (*Martha*). On 15 May 1858 he sang in *Les Huguenots* at the reopening of Covent Garden after the 1856 fire. He attempted the title role of *Don Giovanni* but soon reverted to the part of Ottavio. He appeared in the Paris première of *Un ballo in maschera* (1861); his last new roles at Covent Garden were in Charles Gounod's *Faust* (1864) and *Roméo et Juliette* (1867).

Mario's voice was a lyric tenor of great sweetness and beauty, with a range from *c* to *c''*; for the roles he inherited from Rubini he added a falsetto extension up to *f''*. Nemorino, Ernesto and Gennaro were the successes of his earlier years, while the Duke of Mantua, Raoul and Faust were the most admired roles of his maturity. Almaviva, which he sang more than a hundred times in London alone, personified for 30 years his vocal charm and dramatic grace.

G. Pearse and F. Hird: *The Romance of a Great Singer: a Memoir of Mario* (London, 1910/R)
E. Forbes: 'The Purloined Cabaletta', *About the House*, iv/3 (1972–6), 51–3
E. Forbes: *Mario and Grisi* (London, 1985)

Elizabeth Forbes

Marschner, Lydia.

See LIPKOWSKA, LYDIA.

Martin, (Nicolas-)Jean-Blaise [Blès]

(*b* Paris, 24 Feb 1768; *d* Ronzières, nr Lyons, 28 Oct 1837). French baritone. He studied music at an early age and auditioned unsuccessfully for the Opéra as both a violinist and a singer. He made his début at the Théâtre de Monsieur in 1789 in *Le marquis de Tulipano*, a French version of Giovanni Paisiello's opera *Il matrimonio inaspettato*. Lessons with LOUISE-ROSALIE DUGAZON and François Joseph Talma helped him to overcome his deficiencies as an actor and in 1794 he moved to the Théâtre Favart, remaining there until it merged with the Feydeau to form the Opéra-Comique in 1801. Martin specialized in comic servant roles in new operas by N.-M. Dalayrac, Adrien Boieldieu, E.-N. Méhul, Nicolo Isouard and others. He retired from the Opéra-Comique in 1823 but returned briefly in 1826 and 1833, when he appeared in Léon Halévy's *Les souvenirs de Lafleur*, a pasticcio incorporating songs from his most successful roles. He was also a member of the imperial chapel (later the royal chapel) from its foundation until July 1830, and taught singing at the Paris Conservatoire from 1816 to 1818 and 1832 to 1837.

Martin's voice combined the range and quality of a tenor and a baritone, spanning two and a half octaves from *E♭* to *a'*, with an additional octave in falsetto. His exceptional range influenced vocal characterization in *opéras comiques* for over a century, and high-lying 'baryton Martin' roles can be found in operas by Ferdinand Hérold (*Zampa*), Charles Gounod (Valentin in *Faust*), Georges Bizet (Escamillo in *Carmen*, Ernesto in *Don Procopio*, the Duke of Rothsay in *La jolie fille de Perth* and Splendiano in *Djamileh*), Claude Debussy (Pelléas) and Maurice Ravel (Ramiro in *L'heure espagnole*). Martin was also noted for his facility in rapid vocalization, sometimes inappropriately applied. He composed a one-act *opéra comique*, *Les oiseaux de mer*, produced at the Théâtre Feydeau in 1796.

Philip Robinson

Martin, Riccardo [Whitefield, Hugh]

(*b* Hopkinsville, KY, 18 Nov 1874; *d* New York, 11 Aug 1952). American tenor. He studied in Paris, making his début in 1904 at Nantes as Faust; after further study in Italy, he sang Andrea Chénier at

Riccardo Martin as Dick Johnson in 'La fanciulla del West' (Puccini), c. 1911

Verona, then made his American début in 1906 at New Orleans as Canio. He toured with the San Carlo Opera Company and in 1907 made his Metropolitan début as Arrigo Boito's Faust; he remained with the company until 1915, creating Quintus in Horatio Parker's *Mona* (1912) and Christian in Walter Damrosch's *Cyrano* (1913), and singing Pinkerton, Cavaradossi and Rodolfo. He made his Covent Garden début in 1910 as Pinkerton, also singing Giacomo Puccini's Des Grieux, Radames, Faust, Cavaradossi, Angel Clare (Frédéric d'Erlanger's *Tess*) and, in 1911, Canio and Dick Johnson. He appeared at Boston and in Chicago (1920–23) as Radames, Nicias (*Thaïs*) and Don José. He had a voice of great beauty, though lacking in individuality, and a fine presence, but he suffered comparison with CARUSO throughout his career.

M. de Schauensee: 'A Tribute to Riccardo Martin', *ON*, xvii/6 (1952–3), 12–13

Richard LeSueur/Elizabeth Forbes

Martinelli, Giovanni

(*b* Montagnana, 22 Oct 1885; *d* New York, 2 Feb 1969). Italian tenor. After study in Milan, he made his stage début there at the Teatro Dal Verme in Giuseppe Verdi's *Ernani* in 1910. In the following year he sang Dick Johnson in *La fanciulla del West* at Rome under Arturo Toscanini, later his 'passport role' to many theatres. He appeared at Covent Garden during five seasons between 1912 and 1937, singing over 90 performances in 15 operas, among which the *Otello* and *Turandot* of his last season were particularly memorable. The Metropolitan Opera, however, became the centre of his career for 31 consecutive seasons from 1913, with a few still later appearances in 1945. He sang with the company in 926 performances in a total of 38 operas, and in 1915 created Lefèbvre in the première of Umberto Giordano's *Madame Sans-Gêne*. In 1923 he sang with the San Francisco Opera Company during their first season.

Over the years Martinelli developed an unimpeachable technique and scrupulous style, and after the death of CARUSO became the leading exponent of such dramatic and heroic roles as Verdi's Manrico, Radames, Don Alvaro and, eventually, Otello. He displayed his skills as a singing actor in the roles of Samson and Eléazar (*La Juive*). The clarion ring of his upper register, the distinctness and purity of his declamation and the sustained legato phrasing made possible by remarkable breath control were the outstanding features of his mature style; he retained his vocal powers to an advanced age, making his final appearances as Emperor Altoum (*Turandot*) as late as 1967. His many recordings, especially those made by the Victor company between 1914 and 1939, well display his splendid tone and style. Even more compelling are his off-the-air recordings from the Metropolitan, of which *Otello* is the most important.

J.B. Richards and J.A. Gibson: 'Giovanni Martinelli', *Record Collector*, v (1950), 171–93 [incl. discography]
R. Bebb: 'The Art of Giovanni Martinelli', *Recorded Sound*, no.53 (1974), 247–57
W.J. Collins: 'Giovanni Martinelli', *Record Collector*, xxv (1979–80), 149–215, 221–55 [incl. discography]

Desmond Shawe-Taylor/Alan Blyth

Marton [née Heinrich], Eva

(*b* Budapest, 18 June 1943). Hungarian soprano. She studied in Budapest, making her début there in 1967 as Kate Pinkerton at the Margaret Island Festival. With the Hungarian State Opera (1968–72), she sang the Queen of Shemakha (*The Golden Cockerel*), Rodelinda, Countess Almaviva and Tatyana. From 1972 to 1977 she was engaged at Frankfurt; she made her Metropolitan début in 1976 as Eva, returning as Chrysothemis, La Gioconda, the Empress (*Die Frau ohne Schatten*), Elsa, Ortrud, Tosca, Salome and Turandot, and at Bayreuth sang Elisabeth and Venus (1977–8). Marton's repertory also includes Donna Anna, Aida, Elisabeth de Valois, Leonora (in both *Il trovatore* and *La forza del destino*), Maddalena (*Andrea Chénier*), Mathilde, Fedora, Brünnhilde, Ariadne and Ludwig van Beethoven's Leonore, which she sang at Salzburg in 1982; she returned to Salzburg in 1992 as the Dyer's Wife (*Die Frau ohne Schatten*). Having made a notable Covent Garden début as Turandot in 1987, she sang Richard Strauss's Electra there in 1994. She has appeared in Vienna, Florence, Berlin, Paris, Brussels, Zürich, Hamburg, Chicago, Manila, Verona and La Scala. She has recorded many of her most successful roles, including Turandot, Electra, Salome, Minnie (*La fanciulla del West*), Leonora (*Il trovatore*), Ortrud, Brünnhilde, Maddalena and Fedora. Although at times prone to stridency, her powerful, incisive voice, with its gleaming top register, is equally impressive in the Italian spinto repertory and the heavier Wagner and Strauss roles.

A. Blyth: 'Eva Marton', *Opera*, xli (1990), 276–82

Elizabeth Forbes

Marusin, Yury

(*b* Perm', 8 Dec 1947). Russian tenor. He studied in Leningrad (now St Petersburg), where he made his début at the Malïy Theatre in 1972. After further study in Milan (1977–8) he joined the Kirov Opera, making his British début in 1987 with that company at Covent Garden as Lensky, also singing Hermann and Grigory. He has sung the Tsarevich (*The Tale of Tsar Saltan*) at La Scala and Reggio nell'Emilia (1988), Golitsïn (*Khovanshchina*) at the Vienna Staatsoper (1989), Anatol' Kuragin (*War and Peace*) at the Kirov and in San Francisco, and Prince Andrey Khovansky at Edinburgh (1991). His roles also include Faust, Rodolfo, Pinkerton, the Duke, Alfredo, Don Carlos, Don Alvaro, Vaudémont (*Iolanta*) and Bayan (*Ruslan and Lyudmila*), which he has sung in San Francisco and in Palermo (1995). Although the strong beat in his voice is not to all tastes, he is a powerful singing actor, specially effective as Hermann, a role he has sung in St Petersburg, Paris, Toronto, Madrid and at Glyndebourne (1992 and 1995).

Elizabeth Forbes

Marzia, Maria Anna.

See ALBONI, MARIETTA.

Mason, Edith (Barnes)

(*b* St Louis, 22 March 1893; *d* San Diego, 26 Nov 1973). American soprano. She studied in Cincinnati, and in Paris with Enrico Bertran and EDMOND CLÉMENT, making her début in Marseilles in 1911. She sang with the Boston Opera Company, with which she first appeared as Nedda (*Pagliacci*) in 1912, in Montreal (1912) and Nice (1914), and with the Century Company, New York (1914–15), before making her Metropolitan Opera début in 1915 as Richard Strauss's Sophie; she performed at the Metropolitan until 1917, singing Micaëla, Gretel and Musetta, took part in the première of Reginald De Koven's *The Canterbury Pilgrims* (1917), and performed again in the 1935–6 season. She was heard in Paris at the Théâtre du Vaudeville (1919–20) and later at the Opéra, where she sang Juliet, Charles Gounod's Marguerite and Gilda, and Opéra-Comique. At Monte Carlo (1920–21) she sang Thaïs, Salome (*Hérodiade*), Antonia, Marguerite de Valois and Butterfly. She appeared at La Scala as Mimì under Arturo Toscanini (1923), at Covent Garden (1930) as Martha, Juliet and Gilda; at Florence in 1933 and at Salzburg in 1935 as Nannetta (*Falstaff*). A long, important career at Chicago, where she was first engaged by MARY GARDEN, began in 1921; she was the first Chicago Sophie (1925) and Snow Maiden in Nikolay Rimsky-Korsakov's opera, and also the principal interpreter there of Gilda, Gounod's Marguerite and Arrigo Boito's Margherita. She also played

Jules Massenet's Thaïs, Elsa (*Lohengrin*), Fiora (in Italo Montemezzi's *L'amore dei tre re*), and, notably, Butterfly. Her stage appearances were marked by the natural beauty and easy production of her voice (amply confirmed in her recordings), her meticulous attention to the musical text, and the graceful restraint of her acting. She retired in 1939, after playing Desdemona to MARTINELLI and TIBBETT, but in 1941 made a single reappearance in Chicago as Mimì. She was twice married to the conductor Giorgio Polacco.

O. Thompson: *The American Singer* (New York, 1937/R), 283, 351
A.E. Knight: 'Edith Mason,' *Record Collector*, x (1955–6), 75–87 [incl. discography]

Richard D. Fletcher/R

Massard, Robert

(*b* Pau, 15 Aug 1925). French baritone. After studying in Pau and Bayonne, he made his début on 8 June 1952 as the High Priest in *Samson et Dalila* at the Paris Opéra, remaining with the company until 1976. In 1952 he also scored a success as Thoas (*Iphigénie en Tauride*) at the Aix-en-Provence Festival, an interpretation preserved on disc. His big, easy baritone established him from the outset as a favourite for repertory parts throughout France. He sang in many leading houses, his roles including Thoas, Enrico Ashton, Ramiro (*L'heure espagnole*), Valentin and Escamillo. But it was in the important revivals of C.W. Gluck and Hector Berlioz that he proved indispensable: his Orestes with the Covent Garden Opera at the 1961 Edinburgh Festival was praised as stylish, vigorous and impassioned; by contrast, his slow-witted Fieramosca (*Benvenuto Cellini*), which he sang in Paris and London, was a clever character study. Massard created the Harpist in Henry Barraud's *Numance* in 1955 and sang the Count in the first Opéra-Comique production of *Capriccio* (1957), as well as Orpheus in Milhaud's *Les malheurs d'Orphée* and Nero in *L'incoronazione di Poppea* at Aix. Successes outside France included Rigoletto (1962, Bol'shoy) and Valentin (1967, La Scala). Among his recordings, his Orestes, Escamillo (to CALLAS's Carmen), Fieramosca and Athanaël (*Thaïs*) stand out for the compact vigour of his singing.

André Tubeuf/Alan Blyth

Massol, Jean-Etienne August
[Eugène Etienne Auguste]

(*b* Lodève, 23 Aug 1802; *d* Paris, 30 Oct 1887). French baritone. He made his Opéra début as a

tenor, singing Licinius in *La vestale* (17 November 1825), but Nourrit's pre-eminence restricted him to secondary roles until the mid-1830s, when he began to appear, with increasing success, in baritone roles such as William Tell. In 1840 he created Sévère in Gaetano Donizetti's *Les martyrs*. In 1845 he left the Opéra for Brussels, where he returned in 1848–9 as director of La Monnaie. He made his London début in 1846 as Nevers (*Les Huguenots*) at Drury Lane, and appeared with the Royal Italian Opera at Covent Garden, 1848–50, most impressively as Alphonse (*La favorite*), Pietro (*La muette de Portici*) and Nevers. In 1850 he returned to the Opéra as principal baritone and created Reuben in Daniel Auber's *L'enfant prodigue*, repeating the role at Her Majesty's Theatre in the following season. Massol's imposing physique and voice made him a most effective 'heavy' baritone. His last notable creation at the Opéra was Ahasuerus in Fromental Halévy's *Le Juif errant* (1852).

Philip Robinson

Masterson, (Margaret) Valerie

(*b* Birkenhead, 3 June 1937). English soprano. She studied in Liverpool, at the RCM and with Adelaide Saraceni in Milan. In 1963–4 she made her début at the Landestheater, Salzburg, singing Frasquita, Nannetta, Fiorilla (*Il turco in Italia*) and in *Der Schauspieldirektor*. She then joined the D'Oyly Carte company, taking most principal Gilbert and Sullivan soprano roles (1966–70). After singing Konstanze at the Coliseum in 1971, she joined the Sadler's Wells Opera, later ENO; her roles have included Adèle (*Le comte Ory*), the Countess, Cleopatra (*Giulio Cesare*), Romilda (*Xerxes*), Violetta, Oscar, Manon, Sophie, the Marschallin, Louise, Mireille, Juliet, Pamina and Adele (*Die Fledermaus*). At Aix-en-Provence (1975–9) she sang Matilde (*Elisabetta, regina d'Inghilterra*), Fiordiligi, Morgana (*Alcina*) and Countess Almaviva. At Covent Garden she sang Marguerite, Semele, Micaëla, The Anne Who Steals in the British première of Aulis Sallinen's *The King Goes Forth to France* (1987), the New Prioress (*Dialogues des Carmélites*, 1987) and she created the Wife of the Second Soldier in H.W. Henze's *We Come to the River* (1976). She made her début at the Opéra in 1978 as Marguerite, followed by Drusilla (*L'incoronazione di Poppea*) and Cleopatra (1987). In 1980 she made her American début, in San Francisco, as Violetta and first appeared at Glyndebourne, as Konstanze. In 1991 she returned to Aix as Mercy in W.A. Mozart's *Die Schuldigkeit des ersten Gebots*. To her clean, forward, smooth vocal production with its ease and lustre in high phrases are added excellent diction and an attractive stage presence. Her clear voice, fluent technique and vital use of the text can be heard in her recordings of Gilbert and Sullivan, and in her Violetta from the ENO.

H. Rosenthal: 'Valerie Masterson', *Opera*, xxx (1979), 1128–34

Harold Rosenthal/R

Materna(-Friedrich), Amalie

(*b* St Georgen, 10 July 1844; *d* Vienna, 18 Jan 1918). Austrian soprano. She made her début in 1865 at Graz and then appeared in operetta at the Karlstheater, Vienna. In 1869 she first sang at the Vienna Court Opera, as Selika in *L'Africaine*, and was engaged there for 25 years. She sang Amneris in the first Vienna performance of *Aida* (29 April 1874), the title role at the première of Karl Goldmark's *Die Königin von Saba* (10 March 1875) and Viviane at the première of his *Merlin* (1886). Her voice grew to be immensely powerful, but it never lost its youthful bright timbre and was ideal for the role of Brünnhilde, which she sang in the first complete *Ring* cycle at Bayreuth (1876), in the first Vienna performances of *Die Walküre* (1877) and *Siegfried* (1878), and in the first Berlin *Ring* at the Victoria Theatre (1881). In 1882 she sang Kundry at Bayreuth in the first performance of *Parsifal*, repeating the role there at every festival until 1891. After a concert tour of the USA with WINKELMANN and SCARIA, she made her début at the Metropolitan, New York, on 5 January 1885 as Elisabeth in *Tannhäuser*, and also sang Valentine in *Les Huguenots*, Rachel in *La Juive* and Brünnhilde in *Die Walküre*. Her final performance in Vienna was as Elisabeth on 31 December 1894. After her retirement she taught in Vienna, where she made one last public appearance in 1913, singing Kundry at a concert commemorating the centenary of Richard Wagner's birth.

Elizabeth Forbes

Mathis, Edith

(*b* Lucerne, 11 Feb 1938). Swiss soprano. She studied at the International Opera Studio, Zürich, and in Lucerne where she made her début in 1956 as the Second Boy (*Die Zauberflöte*). She appeared in 1959 at the Cologne Opera, then, in 1963, at the Deutsche Oper, Berlin. She first sang at Salzburg in 1960 as Ninetta (*La finta semplice*), returning regularly. She took part in the première of Gottfried von Einem's *Der Zerrissene* (1964, Hamburg) and created Luise in H.W. Henze's *Der junge Lord* (1965, Berlin), later recording the part. At Glyndebourne she sang Cherubino (1962–3) and Sophie (1965).

She made her Covent Garden début in 1970 as Susanna, a role she recorded for Karl Böhm, later singing Sophie and Despina. At the Metropolitan (1970–76) her roles included Pamina (which she recorded with Herbert von Karajan), Marzelline, Aennchen and Zerlina. She sang in Vienna and Munich, where she created Queen Mary in Heinrich Sutermeister's *Le roi Bérenger* (1985). Mathis's repertory also included Nannetta, Zdenka, Mélisande, Agathe which she sang at Barcelona (1986), and the Marschallin, which she sang for the first time in 1990 at Berne. She sang the title role of Othmar Shoeck's *Massimilla Doni* in a recording issued to coincide with a concert performance at the Lucerne Festival in 1986. Her fresh, pure-toned voice, instinctive sense of style and attractive stage manner made her one of the outstanding Mozart sopranos of her day. She has also been a distinguished concert singer and recitalist, as can be heard in her recordings of J.S. Bach cantatas, Joseph Haydn's *The Creation* and *The Seasons* and lieder by Franz Schubert and Johannes Brahms. She married the conductor Bernhard Klee.

Alan Blyth

Mattei, Peter

(*b* Pitéa, 3 June 1965). Swedish baritone. He studied in Stockholm, first at the Swedish Royal Academy of Music and then at the Operahögskolan, and made his professional début in the 1990 Drottningholm Festival, as Nardo in W.A. Mozart's *La finta giardiniera*. He returned to Drottningholm for Antonio Salieri's *Falstaff* in 1992. Mattei made his Scottish Opera début, as a dangerous, charismatic Don Giovanni, in 1995, and the following year made his Salzburg Festival début, as Don Ferrando (*Fidelio*). Other major débuts include Glyndebourne, as Mozart's Count Almaviva (2000), the Metropolitan Opera, in the same role (2002), Aix, as Don Giovanni (also 2002), and La Scala, as Wolfram in *Tannhäuser* (2005).

Mattei's warm, incisive lyric baritone and histrionic gifts have also been admired as Guglielmo, Papageno, Onegin (which he has sung at La Monnaie and at the 2007 Salzburg Festival), Belcore (*L'elisir d'amore*), Marcello (*La bohème*) and Posa (*Don Carlos*). His concert repertory includes Christus in the St *Matthew Passion*, Johannes Brahms's *German Requiem*, Alexander Zemlinsky's *Lyrische Symphonie* and the Gustav Mahler song cycles. On disc he can be heard as Don Giovanni and Coroebus (*Les Troyens*), and in works including Mahler's Eighth Symphony and Jean Sibelius's *Kullervo* Symphony.

Richard Wigmore

Matters, Arnold

(*b* Adelaide, 11 April 1904; *d* Adelaide, 21 Sept 1990). Australian bass-baritone. After winning the Sun Aria Competition at Ballarat, he was invited by NELLIE MELBA to sing with her in Melbourne and encouraged by her to seek training and a career abroad. He studied in Adelaide with Frederick Bevan and Clive Carey and in London with W. Johnstone Douglas. From 1932 he sang with Sadler's Wells Opera, making his début as Valentin in Charles Gounod's *Faust*, combining a fine voice with admirable theatrical gifts; his Falstaff, in particular, was a ripe and humorous study. His repertory included Don Giovanni, Hans Sachs and Wotan. He also sang small roles during international seasons at Covent Garden and produced opera for Sadler's Wells and elsewhere. Matters returned to Australia in 1941 for war service with an entertainment unit. He again joined Sadler's Wells in 1944 and sang the title role in the first performance in England (1948) of *Simon Boccanegra*. He was the original Pilgrim in Ralph Vaughan Williams's *The Pilgrim's Progress* (1951) at Covent Garden, and created Cecil in Benjamin Britten's *Gloriana* (1953). In 1954 he returned to Adelaide to teach at the Elder Conservatorium (1954–66), producing *Tosca* and *Otello* for the Elizabethan Trust Opera (now Opera Australia) 1957 touring season. His recordings include the role of Mícha in *The Bartered Bride*, conducted by Thomas Beecham.

Harold Rosenthal/Roger Covell

Mattila, Karita (Marjatta)

(*b* Somero, 5 Sept 1960). Finnish soprano. In 1981, while still a student at the Sibelius Academy in Helsinki, she won the Lappeenranta Competition and made her professional début, as Donna Anna at Savonlinna, returning the following year as Lady Billows. In 1983 she became the first Cardiff Singer of the World. She made her international début in 1984 as W.A. Mozart's Countess Almaviva with the Finnish National Opera in Brussels, and Mozart dominated the early part of her career. Donna Elvira was the role of her British (Scottish Opera) and American (Washington) débuts, both in 1985, and over the next few years she added Fiordiligi (Covent Garden and Paris débuts, 1986), Pamina and Ilia. By the early 1990s she had broadened her repertory; Agathe, Eva and Chrysothemis (which she sang with Claudio Abbado in Salzburg in 1995) reflected an increasing weight and richness in her voice, and Elsa followed in San Francisco in 1996. She was Hanna Glawari at the Opéra Bastille in 1997 and sang her first Leonore in Helsinki in 2000. She appeared as Emma in Franz Schubert's *Fierrabras* at the 1988 Vienna Festival. Her Italian roles have included Musetta, Manon Lescaut, Amelia Boccanegra and, above all, Elisabeth in *Don Carlos*, which she has recorded both on disc and video. Mattila's voice is also well suited to Slavonic music, and in addition to Tatyana she has been an outstanding Lisa (*Queen of Spades*), notably at the Metropolitan Opera (1995) and Covent Garden (2000), and Jenůfa, first at Hamburg in 1998 and then at Covent Garden in 2001 – an interpretation of burning emotional immediacy. She is a communicative interpreter of lieder and Finnish song. Her radiant voice has a grandeur that is indivisible from her strikingly tall and blonde stage presence, making Mattila the leading lyric soprano of her generation.

J. Allison: 'Karita Mattila', *Opera*, xlvii (1996), 1260–68

John Allison

Matzenauer, Margaret(e)

(*b* Temesvár [now Timişoara, Romania], 1 June 1881; *d* Van Nuys, CA, 19 May 1963). American contralto. Born of German parents who were musicians, she learnt to play the piano as a child and had already appeared in opera before studying in Graz with Georgine von Januschowsky-Neuendorff and in Berlin with Antonia Mielke and Franz Emerich. She made her début in Strasbourg as Puck in *Oberon* in 1901 and sang more than 15 roles in her first season there. She made guest appearances with many companies including those of Bayreuth in 1911 (Waltraute, Flosshilde and the First Norn). Later that year she made her American début at the Metropolitan Opera as Amneris under Arturo Toscanini. During her 19 seasons at the Metropolitan she took part in a great number of new productions and revivals, notably *Fidelio*, *Samson et Dalila* and *Le prophète* (both with CARUSO), and *Jenůfa*. She appeared at Covent Garden in 1914, as both Kundry and Ortud. Enthusiastically praised for her acting, Matzenauer had a photographic memory (she performed Kundry at 24 hours' notice having never sung the part before), and her musicianship was exceptional. Although her voice was a sumptuous contralto, she was often listed as a soprano and her repertory was vast. In a single season in the 1920s she sang Isolde, Brünnhilde, Delilah, Azucena and Amneris, and although her ventures into the soprano repertory took their toll on her voice, it retained its contralto richness. As a concert artist she is especially remembered for her performances of *Das Lied von der Erde* under Wilhelm Mengelberg, the American première of *Oedipus rex* under Sergey

Koussevitzky and many Bach works under Artur Bodanzky. After leaving the Metropolitan she continued to give concerts and recitals, appeared occasionally in opera, and was active as a teacher. She is known to have made 85 recordings. With her second husband, the tenor EDOARDO FERRARI-FONTANA, she performed *Tristan and Isolde* in 1912 with the Boston Opera Company.

P.L. Miller: 'Margaret Matzenauer', *Record Collector*, xxiii (1976–7), 5–47 [incl. discography]

Philip Lieson Miller

Maurel, Victor

(*b* Marseilles, 17 June 1848; *d* New York, 22 Oct 1923). French baritone. He studied in Marseilles, then at the Paris Conservatoire with François-Eugène Vauthrot and Duvernoy. He made his début in Marseilles (1867) in *Guillaume Tell*, and the following year appeared at the Paris Opéra as the Count di Luna and in *Les Huguenots*, *L'Africaine* and *La favorite*, but overshadowed by JEAN-BAPTISTE FAURE, he decided to continue his career abroad. After appearances in St Petersburg, Cairo and Venice, he made his début at La Scala, as Cacico in the première of Carlos Gomes's *Il Guarany* (19 March 1870), where he also created Cambro in Gomes's *Fosca* (1873); he sang Posa in the Italian première of *Don Carlos* at Naples (1872). He returned to the Paris Opéra in 1879 and sang there regularly until 1894. At La Scala he sang the title role in the revised version of *Simon Boccanegra* (24 March 1881); his performance led Giuseppe Verdi to choose him as the first Iago (5 February 1887) and the first Falstaff (9 February 1893). He sang at Covent Garden (1873–9, 1891–5 and 1904), where he was the first London Telramund and Wolfram and the first Covent Garden Dutchman. He sang Amonasro in the first American production of *Aida* (26 November 1873, Academy of Music, New York) and later appeared at the Metropolitan Opera (1894–6, 1898–9). He sang Herod (in Italian) at the Paris première of *Hérodiade* (1884) and created the role of Tonio in *Pagliacci* at the Teatro Dal Verme, Milan (21 May 1892). At the Opéra-Comique he created the role of Mathis in Camille Erlanger's *Le Juif polonais* (1900). Maurel was outstanding not so much for the timbre or resonance of his voice as for his perfect breath control and skill as an actor. (He appeared on the dramatic stage for a brief period in the early 1900s.) In addition to his career as a performer, he was co-director of the Théâtre Italien, Paris (1883–5), and drew upon his training as a painter in designing the production of Charles Gounod's *Mireille* at the Metropolitan (1919). For a time he had an opera

studio in London, and from 1909 until his death he taught in New York. He wrote a number of books on singing and opera staging: *A propos de la mise-en-scène du drame lyrique Otello: étude précédée d'aperçus sur le théâtre chanté en 1887* (Rome, 1888); *Le chant renové par la science* (Paris, 1892); *Un problème d'art* (Paris, 1893); *A propos de la mise-en-scène de Don Juan: réflexions et souvenirs* (Paris, 1896); *Appréciation de la presse parisienne sur Victor Maurel dans Don Juan, à l'Opéra-Comique* (Paris, 1896) [pubd by Maurel]; *L'art du chant* (Paris, 1897); *Dix ans de carrière* (Paris, 1897/*R*) [memoirs] and 'Conférence sur l'enseignement de l'art du chant', *Voix d'opéra: écrits de chanteurs du XIXe siècle: Duprez, Faure, Maurel, Roger* (Paris, 1988) [talk given in Milan in 1890].

F. Rogers: 'Victor Maurel: his Career and his Art', *MQ*, xii (1926), 580–601
D. Shawe-Taylor: 'Victor Maurel', *Opera*, vi (1955), 293–7

Harold Rosenthal/Karen Henson

Mayer, Josepha.

See HOFER, JOSEPHA.

Mayr, Richard

(*b* Salzburg, 18 Nov 1877; *d* Vienna, 1 Dec 1935). Austrian bass. Having first studied medicine in Vienna, he was persuaded by Gustav Mahler to take up a career as a singer. After several years' work at the Vienna Music Academy, he made his début in 1902 at Bayreuth, as Hagen, and was at once engaged by Mahler for the Vienna Hofoper. Making his début there as Silva (*Ernani*), he sang at Vienna for more than 30 successive years; he displayed amazing versatility in a round of leading parts of various schools, serious and comic, extending from Wotan, Gurnemanz and Sarastro to Figaro, Leporello and Ochs. The Richard Strauss—Hugo von Hofmannsthal correspondence shows that both men would have preferred Mayr for the original Dresden production of *Der Rosenkavalier*; he played Ochs a few months later in the Vienna première, and was soon recognized everywhere as the ideal exponent of a part which he sang to perfection and played with inimitable gusto and virtuosity. It was as Ochs that he made his first Covent Garden appearance, in 1924, in the famous cast that included LOTTE LEHMANN, DELIA REINHARDT and ELISABETH SCHUMANN with Bruno Walter as conductor; he often returned to London in this and other roles. He made his Metropolitan début as Pogner in 1927, soon adding *Der Rosenkavalier* to his New York repertory, and remaining for three seasons with the company. In Vienna he sang Barak in the première of *Die Frau ohne Schatten* in 1919 and Count Waldner in the Viennese première of *Arabella*. He was naturally a mainstay of the Salzburg festivals, taking part in every one between 1921 and 1934. The most important of his recordings is the abridged *Rosenkavalier* of 1933, which gives a capital impression of the ripeness and spontaneity of his style and the richness of his voice.

Desmond Shawe-Taylor

Mazurok, Yury (Antonovich)

(*b* Kraśnik, 18 July 1931). Polish baritone. He studied in Moscow, and in 1963 joined the Bol'shoy Theatre, where he later became a soloist. He won prizes in competitions at Prague (1960), Bucharest (1961) and Montreal (1967). His performances were noted for his firm, beautiful tone, vivid temperament and imposing stage presence, although he was criticized for a lack of wholehearted commitment in his acting and for his limited range of gesture and expression. His roles included Yevgeny Onegin and Yeletsky, Andrey and Tsaryov (*War and Peace* and *Semyon Kotko*), and Gioachino Rossini's Figaro. In 1975 he made his Covent Garden début as Renato, and in 1978 his Metropolitan début as Germont. He frequently sang at the Vienna Staatsoper, including Escamillo in Franco Zeffirelli's 1979 production of *Carmen*. In 1987 he sang Scarpia at Wiesbaden. He was also a noted interpreter of Russian songs.

I.M. Yampol'sky/R

Mazzoleni, Ester

(*b* Sebenico (now Šibenik), Dalmatia, 12 March 1883; *d* Palermo, 17 May 1982). Italian soprano. She studied with the soprano Amelia Pinto and made her début in 1906 in *Il trovatore* at the Teatro Costanzi, Rome. She became well known throughout Italy, appearing at La Scala first in 1908. Her roles there included Medea in the first Italian performances of Luigi Cherubini's opera (1909) and the heroines of Gaspare Spontini's *La vestale* and *Fernando Cortez*. She also sang Isolde, Norma and a wide range of dramatic roles, travelling occasionally to Spain, France and Hungary. In 1913 she sang Aida at the opening of the Verona Arena, to which she returned for the commemorative ceremonies 50 years later. She retired in 1926 and then taught in Palermo. She sang and acted in a highly charged, emotional style, her voice vibrant and her treatment of the vocal line emphatic, so that her many recordings offer some excitement as well as instructive demonstration of the methods of another age.

M. Scott: *The Record of Singing, ii: 1914 to 1925* (London, 1979)

G. Feliciotti and others: 'Ester Mazzoleni', *Record Collector*, xxxix (1994), 84–105, 314 only

J.B. Steane

Mei, Eva

(*b* Fabriano, Ancona, 3 March 1967). Italian soprano. She studied at the Florence Conservatory and sang Aspasia in Antonio Salieri's *Axur, re d'Ormus* at Siena in 1989. She made her début at the Vienna Staatsoper as Konstanze in 1990, going on to sing Donna Anna in Zürich and Amsterdam and the Queen of Night in Budapest. She appeared in Genoa as Musetta, then sang Violetta at the Berlin Staatsoper and Norina (*Don Pasquale*) at the Staatsoper in Munich. She sang Ludwig van Beethoven's *Missa solemnis* at the 1992 Salzburg Festival, and the following year made notable débuts at La Scala as Amenaide (*Tancredi*) and at Covent Garden as the Queen of Night. She has returned to Covent Garden as Konstanze. Her other roles include Alcina, Violetta, Adalgisa, Zerbinetta, Aspasia (*Mitridate*) and Fanny (Gioachino Rossini's *La cambiale di matrimonio*). Mei uses her light, flexible, clearly focussed lyric-coloratura soprano with taste and a keen sense of character, as revealed in her recordings of Adalgisa, Amenaide, Norina, Antonio Salieri's Aspasia and works such as Ludwig van Beethoven's *Missa solemnis*, Joseph Haydn's *Harmoniemesse* and Giovanni Pergolesi's *Stabat mater*. In 1999 she scored a notable success in *Il viaggio a Reims* at the Rossini Opera Festival in Pesaro.

Elizabeth Forbes

Meier, Waltraud

(*b* Würzburg, 9 Jan 1956). German mezzo-soprano. While studying languages at Würzburg University she took private singing lessons, making her début at Würzburg in 1976 as Lola (*Cavalleria rusticana*). Over the next few years, first at Mannheim (1976–8) and then at Dortmund (1980–83), she sang more than 35 roles, including Cherubino, Nicklausse and Concepcion, Fricka, Octavian, Carmen, Santuzza and Azucena. Her triumphant Bayreuth début as Kundry in 1983 established her as one of the world's leading Wagner singers, subsequently confirmed in Bayreuth appearances as Brangäne and Waltraute and recordings of Wagnerian mezzo roles. She made her Metropolitan Opera début as Fricka in 1987, and her Vienna Staatsoper début as Venus (*Tannhäuser*) – her first major Wagner soprano role – in 1988. She has also enjoyed notable successes as Eboli (the role of her Covent Garden début in 1984), P.I. Tchaikovsky's Joan of Arc, Hector Berlioz's Marguerite, Camille

Saint-Saëns's Dalila and Marie in *Wozzeck*, Venus, Ortrud and the Composer, and as an interpreter of lieder and *mélodies*. Meier's début as Isolde in 1993 at Bayreuth, and her recording of the role with Daniel Barenboim, signalled a decisive move into dramatic soprano repertory. She has also sung in Cologne, Hamburg, Hannover, Stuttgart, Munich, Vienna, Paris and Dallas. She is also an admired concert singer in works such as Johannes Brahms's Alto Rhapsody, and Wagner's *Wesendonck-Lieder*. Meier has a highly distinctive voice of laser-like intensity and is a vibrant and intelligent actress. On discs, her Kundry has been recorded no fewer than six times – with Barenboim (audio and video), Reginald Goodall, James Levine (Bayreuth audio, Met video), Christian Thielemann, and Kent Nagano (video).

A. Clark: 'Waltraud Meier', *Opera*, xlii (1991), 886–91

Andrew Clark/R

Mei-Figner [Figner, née Mei], Medea (Ivanovna)

(*b* Florence, 4 April 1859; *d* Paris, 8 July 1952). Russian soprano of Italian birth. She married the tenor NIKOLAY FIGNER in 1889. She studied (as a mezzo) in Florence and made her début (Sinalunga, 1874) as Azucena, appearing subsequently in Turin (the Queen in *Hamlet* with MAUREL), Florence, Odessa, Barcelona and Madrid. She sang in South America with Tamagno and Figner, and by 1886 she was singing soprano roles. In April 1887 she sang Valentine (*Les Huguenots*) with Figner at the Imperial Theatre, St Petersburg. After opening the summer season at Covent Garden with GAYARRE and D'ANDRADE in *La favorite*, she and Figner returned to the St Petersburg Opera where they reigned until their divorce (1904) and where she remained until 1912. P.I. Tchaikovsky chose her as the first Lisa in *The Queen of Spades* (1890) and she was the first Iolanta (1892). She appeared in the premières of Eduard Nápravnik's *Dubrovsky* (Masha, 1895) and *Francesca da Rimini* (1906). Her repertory included Tat'yana, Natal'ya (*Oprichnik*), Marguerite (*Faust*), Carmen, Violetta, Desdemona, Gioconda, Mimì, Tosca, Elsa, Elisabeth and the three Brünnhildes. Admired for her handsome presence, she combined a high degree of musicianship with a rich flexible voice. She remained in Russia until 1930, singing (until 1923) and teaching. Between 1901 and the late 1920s she made at least 23 recordings.

J. Dennis: 'Medea Mei-Figner', *Record Collector*, iv (1949), 42, 51–3 [with discography]

Harold Barnes

Melba, Dame Nellie [Mitchell, Helen Porter]

(*b* Richmond, Melbourne, 19 May 1861; *d* Sydney, 23 Feb 1931). Australian soprano of Scottish descent. She had already had some training and concert experience before 1886, the year she left Australia for further study in Europe. She studied in Paris with MATHILDE MARCHESI, and made her operatic début on 13 October 1887 at the Théâtre de la Monnaie, Brussels, as Gilda; in the following year she appeared at Covent Garden as Lucia and at the Paris Opéra as Ophelia. Her rare beauty of tone and finish of technique created an instant stir, and these virtues soon began to be matched by equivalent qualities of taste and musicianship, notably as the Gounod heroines Juliette and Marguerite. She had studied both parts with the composer, and often sang them with JEAN DE RESZKE, who became a decisive influence on her musical development.

Melba's Lucia in 1893 began an association with the Metropolitan Opera that lasted irregularly until 1910; she also sang for Oscar Hammerstein's Manhattan Opera Company and in Chicago, and organized occasional operatic seasons in Australia in partnership with the J.C Williamson company in 1911, 1924 and 1928. In 1904 she created Camille Saint-Saëns's Hélène at Monte Carlo. But Covent Garden always remained, as she said, her 'artistic home'; she sang there almost every year until World War I, and occasionally thereafter, making her farewell appearance in a mixed programme on 8 June 1926 – when direct recordings were made of the occasion, including the diva's emotional speech. After the brilliant French and Italian roles of her early career, Melba had come to concentrate increasingly on the role of Giacomo Puccini's Mimì; from 1899 (with the Royal Italian Opera) until her retirement it became the most famous of all her parts. Although her timbre was often called silvery, it also possessed in her prime what the American critic W.J. Henderson described as 'a clarion quality', adding that 'from B flat below the clef to the high F ... the scale was beautifully equalized throughout and there was not the smallest change in the quality from bottom to top'. These virtues are well exemplified in the best of the 150 recordings she made between 1904 and 1926 (most transferred to LP and CD). Her name became commercially valuable, and both peach melba and melba toast were named after her. She was created DBE in 1918 and after her retirement from the stage became president of the Melba Memorial Conservatorium in Melbourne.

N. Melba: *Melodies and Memories* (London, 1925/*R*)
J.A. Hetherington: *Melba* (London, 1967)

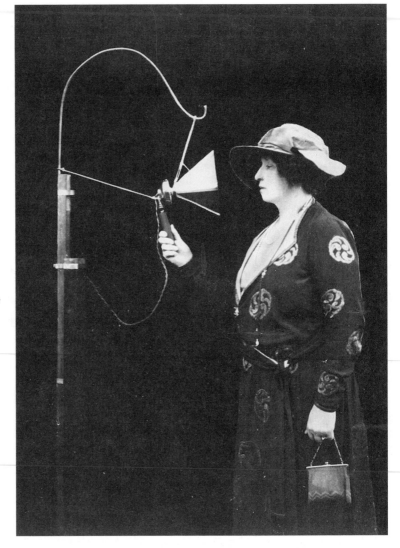

Nellie Melba
broadcasting a
song recital at the
Marconi works
on 15 June 1920,
the first advertised
British programme
broadcast

W. Hogarth: Discography, *Record Collector*, xxvii (1981–3), 72–87

W.R. Moran, ed.: *Nellie Melba: a Contemporary Review* (Westport, CT, 1984) [with and discography]

T. Radic: *Melba: the Voice of Australia* (Melbourne, 1986)

Desmond Shawe-Taylor/R

Melchert, Helmut

(*b* Kiel, 24 Sept 1910). German tenor. He studied in Hamburg, making his début in 1939 at Wuppertal. In 1943 he was engaged at the Hamburg Staatsoper, remaining there for over 30 years. In 1957 he sang Aron in the first stage performance of Arnold Schoenberg's *Moses und Aron* at Zürich. He repeated the role many times, in Berlin, Paris, Milan, Rome and Buenos Aires. Though a fine Florestan, Loge and Shuysky, he specialized in 20th-century works. In 1960 he created the role of the Elector in H.W. Henze's *Der Prinz von Homburg* In 1966 he created Tiresias in Henze's *The Bassarids* at Salzburg and sang in the premières of Boris Blacher's *Zwischenfälle bei einer Notlandung* and Gunther Schuller's *The Visitation* at Hamburg. In 1968, he appeared in the première of created Luigi Dallapiccola's *Ulisse*, again in the role of Tiresias. In 1969 he created roles in Lars Johan Werle's *Resan* and Krzystof Penderecki's *The Devils of Loudun* at Hamburg. His vast repertory included Aegisthus (*Elektra*), Herod (*Salome*), the Captain and the Drum Major (*Wozzeck*), Novagerio (*Palestrina*), Robespierre (Gottfried von Einem's *Dantons Tod*) and Igor Stravinsky's Oedipus.

Elizabeth Forbes

Melchior, Lauritz [Hommel, Lebrecht]

(*b* Copenhagen, 20 March 1890; *d* Santa Monica, CA, 18 March 1973). Danish tenor, later naturalized American. He studied at the Royal Opera School, Copenhagen, and made his début at the Royal Opera on 2 April 1913 as Silvio in *Pagliacci*, going on to sing various other baritone roles. The advice of Mme Charles Cahier and subsequent studies with Vilhelm Herold revealed the true nature of Melchior's voice, and he made a second début at the same theatre on 8 October 1918 in the title role of *Tannhäuser*. With the help of Hugh Walpole, who heard him sing in London in 1919, Melchior was enabled to study the Richard Wagner repertory intensively with ANNA BAHR-MILDENBURG and others and made a third, or 'international', début at Covent

Lauritz Melchior in the title role of 'Tannhäuser' (Wagner)

Garden on 14 May 1924 as Siegmund. Later that year he sang Siegmund and Parsifal at Bayreuth, where he returned regularly until 1931. From 1926 to 1939 he appeared every year at Covent Garden, where he quickly became a mainstay of the Wagner repertory; Otello was his only non-Wagnerian London role. He was a regular singer in Berlin, 1925–39, and in Hamburg, 1927–30, and also appeared in Bremerhaven. Melchior's Metropolitan début on 17 February 1926, as Tannhäuser, and subsequent appearances in 1926–7, were not outstandingly successful; his great New York period began only with his return, after a year's absence and further study (mainly with Egon Pollak in Hamburg), to sing Siegfried and Tristan in 1929. Thenceforward his activities centred on this house, until disagreements with the Rudolf Bing regime caused him to take his leave, as Lohengrin, on 2 February 1950. During those years he made frequent guest appearances in Europe and in Buenos Aires. Latterly he scored some success in Broadway shows and films, but made occasional concert and radio appearances in his old repertory, even singing Siegmund with the Danish Radio Orchestra to celebrate his 70th birthday.

In his later years Melchior sang little but Wagner, and concentrated on the heaviest roles, in each of which he appeared over 100 times (as Tristan, over 200). These figures suggest something of the stamina and endurance that made him the only Wagner tenor of recent times who could still sound fresh in the last acts of *Tristan* and *Götterdämmerung*. A certain baritonal warmth remained a welcome characteristic, but there was no corresponding constriction in his top notes; Siegfried's lusty high C always rang thrillingly. These virtues, coupled with vivid and expressive enunciation, induced his admirers to overlook his dramatic limitations and even some musical defects – vagueness in rhythm and note values – which caused him to avoid the more lyrical and musically complex role of Walther. The heroic scale of his singing, even as experienced through recordings, marks him as the outstanding Heldentenor of the twentieth century.

From 1913 Melchior recorded extensively. His best pre-war years are documented by his Siegmund (with LOTTE LEHMANN and Bruno Walter) and by a composite but almost complete account of the young Siegfried's music, supplemented by extracts from *Götterdämmerung*, *Tristan*, *Lohengrin* and *Parsifal*, with FRIDA LEIDER or KIRSTEN FLAGSTAD (1939–40). There are also many privately issued Wagner recordings, mainly from Metropolitan broadcasts. He set up the Lauritz Melchior Heldentenor Foundation to provide scholarships to gifted young singers.

H. Hansen: *Lauritz Melchior: a Discography* (Copenhagen, 1965, 2/1972)

S. Emmons: *Tristanissimo* (New York, 1990) [with discography by H. Hansen]

Desmond Shawe-Taylor

Melis, Carmen

(*b* Cagliari, 16 Aug 1885; *d* Longone al Segino, nr Como, 19 Dec 1967). Italian soprano. Her teachers included ANTONIO COTOGNI and JEAN DE RESZKE. She made her début as Thaïs at Novara in 1905 and had a great success at Naples the following year in Pietro Mascagni's *Iris*; she also sang in Rome and toured Russia and Poland in 1907. From 1909 to 1913 she was with Oscar Hammerstein's company at the Manhattan Opera House, New York, where she was admired for her Latin temperament as well as for her voice. In Boston her roles included Desdemona and Helen of Troy, with the Giacomo Puccini heroines at the centre of her repertory. She sang at Covent Garden in 1913, appearing in *Pagliacci* and *La bohème* with CARUSO, and giving her part in *I gioielli della Madonna* 'all its romance and savagery' (*The Times*). On her return in 1929 the voice had faded, and she contributed an overplayed Musetta and an undersung Tosca. She remained a favourite for many years at La Scala, where in 1924 she sang Ginevra in the première of Umberto Giordano's *La cena delle beffe*, and in Buenos Aires, where she undertook more unexpected roles such as the Marschallin and Sieglinde. She later taught, numbering RENATA TEBALDI among her pupils. Her recordings, which include a complete *Tosca* (1929), show a voice of beautiful quality in the middle register, used with warmth and imagination.

J.B. Steane

Mellon, Agnès

(*b* Epinay-sur-Seine, 17 Jan 1958). French soprano. She studied with Nicole Fallien and Jacqueline Bonnardot in Paris, and with Lilian Loran in San Francisco. Later she became a member of the Paris Opéra; she has also appeared at the Opéra-Comique. She has established an international reputation in Renaissance and Baroque music, her roles including Tibrino and Love in Antonio Cesti's *Orontea* (1986, Innsbruck), Eryxene in Johann Hasse's *Cleofide* (1987) and Telaira in Jean-Philippe Rameau's *Castor et Pollux* (1991, Aix-en-Provence). Mellon's natural-sounding declamation, carefully controlled vibrato and purity of tone make for a rewarding partnership with period instruments. Her recordings include Baroque choral works and many Baroque operas, among them Francesco Cavalli's *Xerse* and *Giasone*, Jean-Baptiste Lully's *Atys*, Marc-Antoine Charpentier's *Actéon*, *Les arts florissants*, *Medée* and *David et Jonathas*, Rameau's *Anacréon*, *Zoroastre*, *Castor et Pollux* and *Pigmalion*, Jean-Marie Leclair's *Scylla et Glaucus*, Henry Purcell's *Dido and Aeneas*, Hasse's *Cleofide* and Luigi Rossi's *Orfeo*. She married the French countertenor, DOMINIQUE VISSE.

Nicholas Anderson

Mel'nikov, Ivan Aleksandrovich

(*b* St Petersburg, 21 Feb/4 March 1832; *d* St Petersburg, 25 June/8 July 1906). Russian baritone. He received his early musical training as a choirboy. After working for some years in trade, he began to study singing with Gavriil Lomakin in 1861 and in 1862–6 participated, either as chorister or soloist, in the Free Music School concerts conducted by Lomakin. After further study in Milan with E. Repetto, a master of bel canto, Mel'nikov made his St Petersburg début in 1867, as Riccardo in Vincenzo Bellini's *I puritani*, and was immediately acclaimed as an artist of the highest order. He appeared regularly at the Mariinsky Theatre in 1890, in both foreign and Russian roles, and he was the first interpreter of more than a dozen characters from 19th-century Russian opera. Among his best-known roles were Ruslan in M.I. Glinka's *Ruslan and Lyudmila* (in 1871 V.V. Stasov described him as the greatest of the Ruslans), the Miller in Dargomïzhsky's *Rusalka*, the title role in Modest Musorgsky's *Boris Godunov* (which he created in 1874), Amonasro in *Aida*, Wolfram in *Tannhäuser*, and the title role in Alexander Borodin's *Prince Igor* (which he created in the year of his retirement). He also created Don Carlos in *The Stone Guest* (1872), Tokmakov in *The Maid of Pskov* (1873), the title role in Anton Rubinstein's *The Demon* (1875) and the Charcoal Burner in *May Night* (1880). With the exception of *Iolanta*, he sang in every opera by P.I. Tchaikovsky, who greatly admired his gifts. He created Prince Vyazminsky in *The Oprichnik* (1874), Prince Kurlyatev in *The Enchantress* (1887), the Devil in *Cherevichki* (1886) and Tomsky in *The Queen of Spades* (1890), but he was unsuccessful as Onegin, a part he sang when his voice was past its best. He remained, however, a great favourite with St Petersburg audiences until he retired after a farewell performance in *Prince Igor* in 1890. Although Mel'nikov came to the Russian stage at a time when standards were generally low, his voice was said to be exact in all registers, with a mild timbre capable of projecting both lyric tenderness and dramatic force. Modest Tchaikovsky remarked that he excelled in both declamatory passages and

Ivan Aleksandrovich
Mel'nikov as
Kochubey in
'Mazepa'
(Tchaikovsky),
St Petersburg,
1884

cantilena. After his retirement Mel'nikov became a director at the Mariinsky Theatre (1890–92) and also founded an amateur choir, which was noted for its fine performances. He published three collections of choral pieces, the first in 1890, for women's voices, and two others in 1894, for men's and mixed voices.

M. Montagu-Nathan: 'Shaliapin's Precursors', *ML*, xxxiii (1952), 232–8

M. Montagu-Nathan/Jennifer Spencer

Meneghelli, Antonietta.

See DAL MONTE, TOTI.

Mentzer, Susanne

(*b* Philadelphia, 21 Jan 1957). American mezzo-soprano. She studied at the Juilliard School and with Norma Newton, and made her stage début in Houston in 1981 as Albina in Gioachino Rossini's *La donna del lago*. After her European début at Cologne

and Rodolfo. Merritt has subsequently developed an international reputation as a Rossini specialist, his unusually wide vocal range, extending to *d″*, allowing him to sing the composer's high-lying roles without strain. He has performed Erisso (*Maometto II*), Contareno (*Bianca e Falliero*), Pyrrhus (*Ermione*) and Otello at Pesaro; James (*La donna del lago*) and Idreno (*Semiramide*) at Covent Garden, the former for his début there in 1985; Count Libenskof (*Il viaggio a Reims*) for his La Scala début (1988) and subsequently in Vienna; Aménophis (*Moïse et Pharaon*) at the Paris Opéra; Antenore (*Zelmira*) in Venice and Rome; and Argirio (*Tancredi*) in Los Angeles and Chicago. He has also appeared at Madrid, Florence, Naples and Parma. Merritt's repertory also includes such roles as C.W. Gluck's Pylades, Arturo (*I puritani*), Percy (*Anna Bolena*), Nemorino, Léopold (*La Juive*), Cellini, Aeneas (*Les Troyens*), Arrigo (*Vespri siciliani*), Admetus (*Alceste*), Leukippos (*Daphne*) and Arnold Schoenberg's Aaron, which he sang to acclaim in Amsterdam in 1995. In recent years he has moved increasingly into character roles such as the Captain in *Wozzeck*, which he performed in Hamburg in 1998, and Lilaque in H.W. Henze's *Boulevard Solitude*, which he sang at Covent Garden in 2001. Merritt has recorded several of his Rossini parts and other roles ranging from Faust, Arrigo and several Donizetti parts to Sobinin (*A Life for the Tsar*).

R. Milnes: 'Chris Merritt', *Opera* (1992), festival issue, 6–12

Elizabeth Forbes/R

Mesplé, Mady

(*b* Toulouse, 7 March 1931). French soprano. She studied at the Toulouse Conservatory and in 1953 joined the Liège Opera, making her début as Lakmé. After three seasons she was engaged at La Monnaie, singing Lucia and the Queen of Night. In 1956 she joined the Opéra-Comique, where she created the title role in Henri Tomasi's *Princesse Pauline* (1962) and Kitty in Gian Carlo Menotti's *Le dernier sauvage* (1963). At Aix-en-Provence she sang Zémire (*Zémire et Azor*; 1956) and Zerbinetta (1966). She made her début at the Opéra as Sister Constance of St Denis in the French première of *Dialogues des Carmélites* (1958). Her repertory included Mireille, Philine (*Mignon*), Ophelia, Norina, Oscar, Charles Gounod's Juliet, Sophie (*Werther*), and The Fire, The Princess and The Shepherdess (*L'enfant et les sortilèges*) and Ciboulette. She sang throughout Europe and the USA, making her Metropolitan début as Gilda (1973). A high soprano of rare distinction, she had an individuality of timbre and a refinement of phrase beyond the usual coloratura singer, she was also a noted concert performer and recitalist, including in her adventurous 20th-century repertory Anton Webern's cantatas. Mesplé has made delightful recordings of many French operettas; her other recordings include Erik Satie's *Socrate*, Madame Herz in W.A. Mozart's *Der Schauspieldirektor*, Lakmé and Daniel Auber's *Manon*, in addition to several discs of *mélodies*.

Max Loppert, Elizabeth Forbes

Metternich, Josef

(*b* Hermühlheim, nr Cologne, 2 June 1915; *d* Feldafing, 21 Feb 2005). German baritone. He studied in Cologne and Berlin and sang with the Cologne and Bonn choruses. His solo début was in 1941 in *Lohengrin* with the Berlin Städtische Oper, to which he returned in 1945 as Tonio (*Pagliacci*), winning esteem in the Italian as well as the German repertory. He made his Covent Garden début in 1951 as the Dutchman and also sang at La Scala and the Vienna Staatsoper; his first appearance at the Metropolitan Opera was in 1953 as Don Carlo (*La forza del destino*), and he returned in both Italian and German roles. In 1954 he became a member of the Staatsoper in Munich, where he created Johannes Kepler in Paul Hindemith's *Die Harmonie der Welt* (1957) and later sang Kothner (*Die Meistersinger*) under Joseph Keilberth at the reopening of the rebuilt Nationaltheater (1963). He was a powerful and reliable, if not always very imaginative, singer. His recordings include John the Baptist under Rudolf Moralt (1952) and Mandryka under Lovro von Matačić with SCHWARZKOPF (1955).

Noël Goodwin

Metzger(-Lattermann), Ottilie

(*b* Frankfurt, 15 July 1878; *d* Auschwitz, ?Feb 1943). German contralto. She was a pupil of Selma Nicklass-Kempner in Berlin, and made her début at Halle in 1898. After three years at Cologne she became the leading contralto at the Hamburg Opera, and when CARUSO appeared as guest artist she sang with him in *Carmen* and *Aida*. In 1901 she appeared for the first time at Bayreuth, where she was heard last in 1912, her great roles being Erda and Waltraute in *Götterdämmerung*. She also sang at Hamburg in the premières of Siegfried Wagner's *Bruder Lustig* (1905), Leo Blech's *Versiegelt* (1908) and Eugen d'Albert's *Izegl* (1909). From 1916 to 1921 she sang with the Dresden Staatsoper. Although her career centred on Germany, she was also heard in Vienna, St Petersburg and New York, where she sang under Blech with the German

Opera Company which toured the USA in 1922 and 1923. At Covent Garden she made her début in 1902, singing in *Die Meistersinger*, *Siegfried* and *Tristan*. In 1910 she appeared as Clytemnestra in *Elektra* and later that year as the first London Herodias in *Salome*; she also made a strong impression as Carmen. Following her second marriage, to the bass-baritone Theodor Lattermann, she used the composite name of Metzger-Lattermann and developed a distinguished career as a concert singer, her accompanists including Richard Strauss and Hans Pfitzner. She later taught in Berlin until the Nazis came to power when, as she was Jewish, she took refuge in Brussels, only to be deported to Auschwitz in 1942. Her recordings, made between 1904 and 1910, show a strong, deep tone, ideally suited to Erda's scene in *Siegfried*.

J.B. Steane

Meur, Arsène de.

See CHARTON-DEMEUR, ANNE.

Mey, Guy de.

See DE MEY, GUY.

Meyer, Kerstin (Margareta)

(*b* Stockholm, 3 April 1928). Swedish mezzo-soprano. She studied in Stockholm, at the Salzburg Mozarteum, and in Siena, Rome and Vienna. She made her début in 1952 as Azucena with the Swedish Royal Opera and became permanently associated with that company. She sang Carmen in Wieland Wagner's controversial 1959 production in Hamburg, where she also created Mrs Claiborne in Gunther Schuller's *The Visitation* (1966), Alice Arden in *Arden Must Die* (1967) and Gertrude in Humphrey Searle's *Hamlet* (1968). In 1960 she sang Dido (*Les Troyens*) at Covent Garden, later appearing as Octavian and Clytemnestra. After her début as Carolina in the first English-language performances of H.W. Henze's *Elegy for Young Lovers* (1961), she became a favourite at Glyndebourne; her roles there included Claude Debussy's Geneviève, Claudio Monteverdi's Octavia, Clairon (*Capriccio*), Elisabeth in the première of Nicholas Maw's *The Rising of the Moon* (1970) and Claire in the first British performance of Gottfried von Einem's *Der Besuch der alten Dame* (1973), a role she also sang in Stockholm (1976) in her own Swedish translation of the opera. At Salzburg she created Agave in *The Bassarids* (1966); she also appeared at the Metropolitan (1960–63) and Bayreuth (1962–5). She created Spermando (Amando) in György Ligeti's *Le Grand Macabre*

(1978, Stockholm). In recitals she often sang in duo with ELISABETH SÖDERSTRÖM. Her voice, though not large, was used with skill and dramatic flair. Among her recordings are excerpts from her Orpheus and Octavian, as well as duets with Söderström.

Harold Rosenthal/R

Michaels-Moore, Anthony
[Moore, Anthony Michael Frederick]

(*b* Grays, Essex, 8 April 1957). English baritone. He grew up in a musical household (his father, John, is a noted amateur choral conductor) and studied at Newcastle University (1975–8) and at the Royal Scottish Academy of Music and Drama (1984–5). In 1985 he was joint winner of the Pavarotti Competition in Philadelphia, which led to his US opera début there (Guglielmo, 1988). After roles with Scottish Opera-Go-Round and Opera North (including the Messenger in *Oedipus rex* and Escamillo), in 1987 he joined Covent Garden, where he sang a wide range of lyric baritone roles. As his warm-toned voice gained in size, dramatic intensity and focus he made impressive figures of such Verdi parts as Stankar (*Stiffelio*) and Egberto (*Aroldo*), and Macbeth and Simon Boccanegra in the first versions of both operas. In 2000 he was acclaimed for his Scarpia at Covent Garden. Playing romantically charged characters such as Enrico Ashton (*Lucia di Lammermoor*), Posa, Onegin (which he performed memorably at the ENO in 2000), Ambroise Thomas' Hamlet and Umberto Giordano's Gérard (in which he made his 1996 Colón début), he invests both notes and words with unforced eloquence which, combined with his natural stage command, lends his performances rare distinction. Among many international appearances Michaels-Moore has sung at La Scala (Licinius in *La vestale*, 1993, a role he has also recorded), in Madrid (Don Fernando in the first Spanish stage performances of Roberto Gerhard's *The Duenna*, 1992) and at the Metropolitan and San Francisco, where he appeared as Rodrigo in *Don Carlos* in 1998. He is also a noted concert singer in works such as *The Dream of Gerontius*, *The Kingdom* and *Elijah*.

R Milnes: 'Anthony Michaels-Moore', *Opera*, xlvi (1995), 1029–35

Max Loppert

Micheau, Janine

(*b* Toulouse, 17 April 1914; *d* Paris, 18 Oct 1976). French soprano. She studied in Toulouse and at the Paris Conservatoire, and made her début in 1933 at the Opéra-Comique as the Newspaper Girl in

Louise. In 1935 in Amsterdam she sang Mélisande, which she later repeated elsewhere in Europe and in San Francisco. Her French roles at the Paris Opéra-Comique (1933–56) included Mireille, Olympia and Georges Bizet's Leïla; she was also an acclaimed Zerbinetta and was the first French Anne Trulove in 1953. At the Opéra (1940–56) she sang Juliet, Gilda, Violetta, Pamina, Sophie (*Der Rosenkavalier*) and Creusa in Darius Milhaud's *Médée*, and created the role of Manuela in his *Bolivar* (1950). She made her Covent Garden début as Micaëla in 1937 and sang Violetta and Micaëla in Chicago in 1946. She retired in 1968. In all her roles Micheau was admired for the care, skill and taste with which she used a characteristically French voice, light and flexible with a wide range and conspicuously even production. Her voice and style are best displayed in her recordings of Juliet, Leïla and Micaëla.

Martin Cooper/R

Micheletti, Gaston

(*b* Tavaco, 5 Jan 1892; *d* Ajaccio, 21 May 1959). Corsican tenor. He studied at the Paris Conservatoire, made his début at Reims as Faust (1922) and three years later joined the Opéra-Comique, where he remained until his retirement in 1946. During this period he sang a large repertory of lyric-dramatic roles, appearing on such occasions in the company's history as the 500th performance of *Les contes d'Hoffmann* (1927) and the 1000th of *Carmen* (1930). Among world premières in which he took a leading part were those of Raoul Laparra's *Le joueur de viole* (1925) and Camille Fournier's *Le chevalier de Mauleon* (1927). He also appeared in Brussels, Nice and Monte Carlo. On records he is most widely remembered in excerpts from *Carmen* with CONCHITA SUPERVIA, whom he partnered on stage in 1930; but his worth as a fine singer on his own account is well attested by solo recordings, many of which are as pleasing for their stylistic qualities as for the resonance of his full-bodied, securely placed voice.

J.B. Steane

Migenes [Migenes-Johnson], Julia

(*b* New York, 13 March 1945). American soprano. As a child she appeared as Dolore in a Metropolitan Opera production of *Madama Butterfly*. After graduating from the High School of Music and Art in New York, she appeared on Broadway (*West Side Story* and *Fiddler on the Roof*) and then made her New York City Opera début as Annina in Gian Carlo Menotti's *The Saint of Bleecker Street* (1965). In the early 1970s she pursued her career in Europe

and studied in Cologne with Gisela Ultmann, a formative influence on her vocal technique and dramatic style. She became a popular performer with the Vienna Volksoper (1973–8), where her roles included Despina, Susanna, Blonde and Toinette, which she created in Franz Wolpert's *Der eingebildete Kranke* (1975). She returned to the USA to sing Musetta in *La bohème* with the San Francisco Opera in 1978, and a year later first appeared with the Metropolitan Opera as Jenny in *Aufstieg und Fall der Stadt Mahagonny*. Other roles at the Metropolitan included Nedda, Musetta and the title role in *Lulu*, where her acting and singing in the 1985 production were highly praised. She also sang Lulu at the Vienna Staatsoper in 1983. She sang Salome in Geneva, Jacques Offenbach's Eurydice at the Deutsche Oper, Berlin (1983), and Jules Massenet's Manon in her Covent Garden début (1987). At Los Angeles the following year she sang Olympia, Antonia and Giulietta (*Les contes d'Hoffmann*).

As a classical crossover artist, Migenes has more recently made successful ventures into television (she has hosted her own television variety shows in Germany and Britain), popular music and Broadway; in 1998–9 she toured with a one-woman entertainment, 'Diva on the Verge'. In 1984 she gained wide attention for her title role performance in Francesco Rosi's cinematic version of *Carmen*, starring opposite PLÁCIDO DOMINGO. Her video recording of Francis Poulenc's *La voix humaine* (1991) is also highly regarded, as is her performance as the lovelorn prostitute, Jenny, in a video of Kurt Weill's *Dreigroschenoper* (1991). Migenes's other recordings include recreations of the Broadway hits *Man of La Mancha*, *Kismet* and Charles Strouse's *Rags*, excerpts from Viennese operettas and recitals of traditional ballads.

F. Gannon: 'Carmen Chameleon: a Profile of Julia Migenes-Johnson', *Saturday Review*, xii/4 (1985), 26–30, 59
J. Kaufman: 'Diva on the Verge', *Wall Street Journal* (24 July 1998)

Kathleen Haefliger

Mikhaylova [Michailova], Mariya [Maria] (Aleksandrovna) [Alexandrovna]

(*b* Khar'kiv, 22 May/3 June 1866; *d* Molotov [now Perm'], 18 Jan 1943). Russian soprano. She studied in St Petersburg, Paris and Milan, and made her début in 1892 as Marguerite de Valois (*Les Huguenots*) at the Imperial Opera, St Petersburg; she remained there until 1912, making frequent tours in Russia and one each to Prague (1903) and Tokyo (1907). She created the role of Electra in Aleksandr Taneyev's *Oresteya* (1895); her repertory also included W.A. Mozart's and Daniel Auber's Zerlina, Aennchen (*Der Freischütz*), Carolina (*Il matrimonio segreto*), Berthe (*Le prophète*), Juliet, Nannetta (*Falstaff*), Gilda, Lakmé, Micaëla, Tamara (*The Demon*) and M.I. Glinka's Lyudmila and Antonida (*A Life for the Tsar*). With a pure, musical voice, she was the first singer to achieve world fame through the gramophone alone. She also undertook many salon engagements.

A. Favia-Artsay: 'Marie Michailowa', *Hobbies* (June 1954), 22–5

H. Barnes: 'Maria Michailova', *Record Collector*, xxxvii (1992), 3–25

Harold Barnes/Alan Blyth

Milanov [née Kunc; Ilić], Zinka

(*b* Zagreb, 17 May 1906; *d* New York, 30 May 1989). Croatian soprano. She studied at the Zagreb Academy of Music, and with Milka Ternina, Maria Kostrenčić and Fernando Carpi, making her début as Leonora (*Il trovatore*) at Ljubljana in 1927; she was the leading soprano at the Zagreb Opera from 1928 to 1935, singing such roles as Sieglinde, the Marschallin, Rachel and Minnie. After appearances at the Deutsches Theater, Prague, in 1937 and at the Salzburg Festival the same year (where she sang an acclaimed Verdi Requiem with Arturo Toscanini), she began a long association with the Metropolitan Opera, making her début as Leonora (*Il trovatore*) and appearing every season (except for 1941–2 and 1947–50) until her farewell performance as Maddalena de Coigny (*Andrea Chénier*) in 1966; with the company she gave 424 performances in 14 works – notably as the principal Verdi and Puccini heroines, but also as Norma, Donna Anna, Santuzza, Maddalena de Coigny and La Gioconda. In 1951 her brother, the pianist and composer, Božidar Kunc, moved to New York to assist her in her career. She appeared at the Teatro Colón (1940–42), San Francisco and Chicago, but her European performances after 1939 were few: as Tosca at La Scala (1950), and as Tosca and Leonora at Covent Garden (1956–7).

Milanov's *lirico spinto* voice was one of translucent beauty as well as great power, and she was able to spin out the most exquisite *pianissimo* phrases, although she was not always wholly reliable in pitch or steadiness. While she rarely delved deeply into a character, she dominated her roles by virtue of her majestic deportment. Her voice can be heard in pristine form in relays from the Metropolitan in the 1940s, notably as Amelia (*Un ballo in maschera*) and La Gioconda. Among her studio recordings, her Leonora (*Il trovatore*) and Aida reveal her lustrous tone and finely moulded phrasing, as do a 1939

broadcast of the *Missa solemnis* and a 1940 broadcast of the Verdi Requiem, both under Toscanini.

E.K. Einstein jr: 'Zinka Milanov: a Discography', *Grand Baton*, v/2 (1968), 7–16, 21

R. Jacobson: 'The Most Beautiful Voice in the World', *ON*, xli/22 (1976–7), 11–15

A. Blyth: 'Zinka Milanov: an Appreciation', *Opera*, xl (1989), 929–32

Harold Rosenthal/Alan Blyth/R

Milde, Hans (Feodor) von

(*b* Petronell, nr Vienna, 13 April 1821; *d* Weimar, 10 Dec 1899). Austrian baritone. He studied in Vienna and with the younger Manuel Garcia in Paris. From 1845 to 1884 he was engaged at the Hofoper, Weimar, where in 1850 he sang Telramund in the first performance of *Lohengrin*, conducted by Franz Liszt. He also sang the Dutchman and, later, Hans Sachs and Kurwenal. He took part in the revival of Hector Berlioz's *Benvenuto Cellini* (1852), created the title role of Peter Cornelius's *Der Barbier von Bagdad* (1858) and Ruy Diaz in the same composer's *Der Cid* (1865). He sang the High Priest in the first stage performance of *Samson et Dalila*, at Weimar (1877). He married the soprano ROSA VON MILDE-AGTHE.

Elizabeth Forbes

Milde-Agthe, Rosa von [née Agthe, Rosa]

(*b* Weimar, 25 April 1825; *d* Weimar, 25 Jan 1906). German soprano. She studied in Weimar, where she was engaged at the Hofoper from 1845 to 1867. Under the name of Rosa Agthe, in 1850 she sang Elsa in the first performance of *Lohengrin*, conducted by Franz Liszt. The following year she married the baritone HANS VON MILDE. She created Margiana in Peter Cornelius's *Der Barbier von Bagdad* (1858) and Chimène in the same composer's *Der Cid* (1865). Her repertory also included Lucia, Pamina, both of C.W. Gluck's Iphigenias, Leonore (*Fidelio*) and Lady Harriet (*Martha*).

Elizabeth Forbes

Mildenburg von Bellschau, Anna.

See BAHR-MILDENBURG, ANNA.

Milder-Hauptmann, (Pauline) Anna

(*b* Constantinople, 13 Dec 1785; *d* Berlin, 29 May 1838). Austrian soprano. She was brought up in Constantinople and Bucharest, before moving to

Vienna, where she studied with Giuseppe Tomaselli and Antonio Salieri (on EMANUEL SCHIKANEDER's recommendation) and also had instruction from Sigismund Neukomm (on Joseph Haydn's advice). She made her début as Juno in F.X. Süssmayr's *Der Spiegel von Arkadien* (1803), and sang Leonore in all three versions of Ludwig van Beethoven's *Fidelio* (1805, 1806 and 1814). Her voice was described by Haydn as 'like a house' and by G.A. Griesinger as 'like pure metal'.

In 1808 she made a successful tour, and was admired by Napoleon, among others; in 1816 she was appointed court *prima donna assoluta* in Berlin. In 1810 she married a jeweller, Peter Hauptmann, whose difficult personality seems to have lain behind a later faltering in her career. She achieved her greatest triumph in 1812 in C.W. Gluck's *Iphigénie en Tauride*, and was largely responsible for the Gluck revival in Vienna and Berlin. Gluck's heroines suited her imposing presence and her magnificent full, rich and flawless voice; she made Joseph Weigl's *Das Waisenhaus* and *Die Schweizerfamilie* famous. Luigi Cherubini wrote *Faniska* for her (1806) and she sang in the first Vienna performance of his *Médée* (1814). In addition, Franz Schubert wrote *Der Hirt auf dem Felsen* and the second *Suleika* song for her, and she also created the title role in Conradin Kreutzer's *Adel von Budoy* (1821, Königsberg). In 1829 she created the role of Irmengard in Gaspare Spontini's unsuccessful *Agnes von Hohenstaufe*. Leaving Berlin over a quarrel with Spontini, she visited Russia, Sweden and Denmark; in the same year she sang in Felix Mendelssohn's historic revival of J.S. Bach's *St Matthew Passion*. Her last public appearance was in Vienna in 1836.

F.A. Marshall/Christopher H. Gibbs

Miles, Alastair

(*b* Harrow, Middx, 11 July 1961). English bass. He studied with Rudolf Piernay, Richard Standen and Bruce Boyce at the GSM, and then at the National Opera Studio (1986–7). He made his operatic début with Opera 80 as Trulove (1985), and the following year made an outstanding impression in a concert performance of Gioachino Rossini's *Otello* in London. In 1988 Miles made his débuts in minor roles at the ENO, WNO and Covent Garden, and the same year appeared as Dikoj (*Kát'a Kabanová*) with Glyndebourne Touring Opera. In 1989 he sang Colline at the ENO, the Spirit Messenger (*Die Frau ohne Schatten*) and Raimondo (*Lucia di Lammermoor*) with the WNO, and Lamoral (*Arabella*) at Glyndebourne. He has subsequently undertaken major roles with the same companies and appeared in Amsterdam, Vienna and San Francisco,

most notably as W.A. Mozart's Figaro (a role he has recorded with Charles Mackerras), Gioachino Rossini's Don Basilo and Alidoro, Rodolfo (*La sonnambula*), Raimondo, Zaccaria, Fiesco, and Charles Gounod's and Hector Berlioz's Méphistophélès. He made a much-praised Metropolitan début in 1997 as Sir George (*I puritani*). In 1999 he scored a triumph in the title role of Arrigo Boito's *Mefistofele* at the ENO, and in the following year sang Elmiro in Rossini's *Otello* at Covent Garden. On the concert platform and on disc he has been much admired in G.F. Handel, especially as Saul, as Elijah and in the Verdi *Requiem*. Miles's true, firm bass is deployed with ease and flexibility through a wide range, and he has become an impressive actor. He is also an accomplished recitalist, at home in several idioms.

Alan Blyth

Millo, Aprile [April]

(*b* New York, 14 April 1958). American soprano. Brought up in Los Angeles, she received her musical education primarily from her parents, who were both opera singers; she later studied with Rita Patanè in New York. While a student at the San Diego Opera Center (1977–80), she sang the High Priestess in *Aida*, but then resolved to accept only leading roles. She won prizes in Busseto (1978) and Barcelona (1979). Her first major role was Aida, in Salt Lake City in 1980, followed by Elvira (*Ernani*) at La Scala in 1982. She made her Metropolitan Opera début in 1984 as Amelia in *Simon Boccanegra*, replacing an ill colleague. She has since made the company her artistic home, singing the Verdi heroines in which she specializes: Aida, Desdemona, Elisabeth de Valois, Elvira and Leonora (*Il trovatore*), as well as Liù. She also worked with Eve Queler's Opera Orchestra of New York, and has sung in concert performances of *Andrea Chénier*, *La battaglia di Legnano*, *I Lombardi*, *Il pirata* and *La Wally* at Carnegie Hall. In 1985 she appeared as Aida in Hong Kong with the American group Ambassadors for Opera. In Europe, she has sung in Bologna, Bonn, Rome (where she sang Luisa Miller), Verona and Vienna. She possesses a spinto voice of power, warmth and temperament which has made her one of the finest singers of her generation.

Cori Ellison

Milnes, Sherrill (Eustace)

(*b* Hinsdale, IL, 10 Jan 1935). American baritone. After studies at Drake and Northwestern universities, and with ROSA PONSELLE, he became an apprentice at Santa Fe, then made his début with the touring Opera Company of Boston as Masetto (1960). In 1961 he sang Gérard (*Andrea Chénier*) with the Baltimore Civic Opera, and in 1964 Gioachino Rossini's Figaro at the Teatro Nuovo, Milan. With New York City Opera (1964–6) he sang Valentin, Ruprecht in the American première of *The Fiery Angel*, John Sorel (*The Consul*) and, in 1982, Ambroise Thomas' Hamlet, a role he recorded with flair. He made his Metropolitan début in 1965 as Valentin, remaining with the company for more than 25 years; in 1967 he created Adam Brant in Marvin Levy's *Mourning Becomes Electra*. His repertory included Escamillo, Tonio, Don Giovanni, Barnaba, Jack Rance, Scarpia, Athanaël (*Thaïs*), Alphonse (*La favorite*), Sir Riccardo Forth (*I puritani*) and the leading Verdi baritone roles, in particular Amonasro, Carlo (*Ernani* and *La forza del destino*), Boccanegra, Rigoletto, Iago and Montfort. In 1971 he made his Chicago début as Posa and first sang at Covent Garden as Renato, returning in 1983 as Macbeth. He sang Falstaff for the first time in 1991. He has appeared at Central City, Colorado, Macerata, Cincinnati, San Diego, Tanglewood and Hanover. Milnes's brilliant top voice, general fervour and command of legato was in the line of succession to LAWRENCE TIBBETT, LEONARD WARREN and ROBERT MERRILL. Among his many recordings his Macbeth (Riccardo Muti) and Carlo in *La forza del destino* (James Levine) catch most tellingly the dramatic thrust of his style.

S. Milnes: 'A Role in Hand', *ON*, xxxvi/2 (1971–2), 12–14

W. Sargeant: 'Sherrill Milnes', *New Yorker* (29 March 1976)

J. Spong: *The First Forty-Five* (West Des Moines, IA, 1978)

T. Lanier: 'Sherrill Milnes', *Opera*, xxxi (1980), 538–44

J. Hines: 'Sherrill Milnes', *Great Singers on Great Singing* (Garden City, NY, 1982), 173–81

Martin Bernheimer, Elizabeth Forbes

Mingardo, Sara

(*b* Mestre, nr Venice, 2 March 1961). Italian contralto. She studied at the Benedetto Marcello Conservatory in Venice and won a scholarship to the Accademia Chigiana in Siena. In 1987 she made her professional opera début as Fidalma in Domenico Cimarosa's *Il matrimonio segreto* in L'Aquila and Sulmona, and the following year sang the title role in *La Cenerentola* in Treviso and Rovigo. From 1989 she appeared in many of the leading opera houses in Italy, including La Fenice, La Scala, Milan and San Carlo in Naples. Her major international début was in 1995, when she sang the title role of G.F. Handel's *Riccardo Primo* with Christophe Rousset at Fontevraud. The following year she made her Salzburg Festival début, as

Emilia in *Otello* with Claudio Abbado. Mingardo has also sung at La Monnaie in Brussels and the Châtelet in Paris and at festivals including Bregenz and Aix-en-Provence. She has worked with conductors such as John Eliot Gardiner (with whom she performed and recorded a vivid, witty Mistress Quickly), Roger Norrington, Colin Davis (*Béatrice et Bénédict* and *Les Troyens*) and Myung-Wha Chung. In 2000 she made an acclaimed US opera début as Andromaca in Gioachino Rossini's *Ermione* at the Santa Fe Opera Festival. Besides her Rossini roles and such parts as C.W. Gluck's Orpheus and Ottone in *L'incoronazione di Poppea*, Mingardo is particularly renowned for her singing of Handel, and has performed the role of Julius Caesar in Montpellier and Paris with Christophe Rousset, Rinaldo at the Beaune International Baroque Festival and in Paris, and Andronico (*Tamerlano*) with Trevor Pinnock at the Maggio Musicale Fiorentino. Her extensive concert repertory includes Gustav Mahler's Second Symphony, Johannes Brahms's *Alto Rhapsody*, Edward Elgar's *The Dream of Gerontius* and Rossini's *Stabat mater* and *Petite messe solennelle*, in addition to works by J.S. Bach, Handel and Antonio Vivaldi. Mingardo's rich, velvety timbre, agility and dramatic intensity can be heard on recordings of *Riccardo Primo* (with Rousset), vocal works by Vivaldi, Bach cantatas (with John Eliot Gardiner) and Giovanni Pergolesi's *Stabat mater*.

Richard Wigmore

Minter, Drew

(*b* Washington DC, 11 Nov 1955). American countertenor. He attended Indiana University and studied privately with Marcy Lindheimer, Myron McPherson, RITA STREICH and Erik Werba. Early in his career he was a member of early music ensembles, including the Waverly Consort in New York. He is a founder-member of the Newberry Consort, with whom he has performed and recorded extensively. His stage début was in the title role of G.F.Handel's *Orlando* at the St Louis Baroque Festival in 1983. He has since appeared in Boston, Brussels, Los Angeles, Milwaukee and Omaha, where his clear, ringing voice has won praise, particularly in operas by Handel, Stefano Landi and Claudio Monteverdi. In 1989 he made his Santa Fe Opera début as the Military Governor in the American première of Judith Weir's *A Night at the Chinese Opera* and also sang Endymion (*Calisto*). He sang the title role in Handel's *Ottone* at Göttingen in 1992 and subsequently recorded the part. Among his other Handel recordings are *Agrippina, Berenice, Esther, Floridante, Giustino, Messiah, Sosarme, Susanna* and *Theodora*.

Cori Ellison/R

Minton, Yvonne (Fay)

(*b* Sydney, 4 Dec 1938). Australian mezzo-soprano. She studied at the Conservatorium in Sydney and in 1960 moved to London, where she began a concert career before making her operatic début in 1964 as Benjamin Britten's Lucretia in a City Literary Institute production; the same year she created Maggie Dempster in Nicholas Maw's *One Man Show*. She then joined the Covent Garden company and over the next 12 years sang more than 30 major roles, including Marina (*Boris Godunov*) and Marfa (*Khovanshchina*), and Helen in Michael Tippett's *King Priam*. She created (and later recorded) Thea in *The Knot Garden* (1970) and had notable success as Octavian, the role of her débuts at Chicago (1970), the Metropolitan Opera (1973) and the Paris Opéra (1976); she also recorded the part under Georg Solti. Her appearance as Brangäne at Bayreuth in 1974 was followed by Fricka and Waltraute in the centenary *Ring*, and she sang Kundry at Covent Garden in 1979. Also in 1979 she sang Countess Geschwitz in the first three-act *Lulu* in Paris, which she also filmed and recorded. Minton's other recordings include Dorabella under Otto Klemperer (1971), W.A. Mozart's Sextus (1976) under Colin Davis, Geneviève (*Pelléas*) under Pierre Boulez (1970) and Fricka under Marek Janowski (1981–4). Among Minton's finest roles was the castrato role of Sextus in *La clemenza di Tito*. Her warm fullness of tone and striking stage personality were combined with interpretative skill and imagination. She was made a CBE in 1980. After a short period of retirement she sang Leokadja Begbick (*Mahagonny*) at Florence in 1990 and Clytemnestra at Adelaide in 1991 and returned to Covent Garden as Countess Helfensteen in *Mathis der Maler* (1995).

H. Rosenthal: 'Yvonne Minton', *Opera*, xxviii (1977), 834–41
J. Burnie: 'Singing a Different Song', *Sunday Times Magazine* (27 Oct 1985)

Noël Goodwin

Miolan [Miolan-Carvalho], Caroline.

See CARVALHO, CAROLINE.

Mirate, Raffaele

(*b* Naples, 3 Sept 1815; *d* Sorrento, Nov 1895). Italian tenor. He studied with Crescentini and made his début in 1837 at the Teatro Nuovo, Naples, in Gaetano Donizetti's *Torquato Tasso*. He went on singing the Rossini-Bellini-Donizetti repertory – at the Théâtre Italien, Paris, La Scala (Amenophis in Rossini's *Mosè in Egitto*, 1840), and elsewhere – but in 1845 appeared in Rome in Verdi roles (Jacopo in *I due Foscari* and Charles VII in *Giovanna d'Arco*). Verdi's librettist F.M. Piave compared him to the previously supreme lyric tenor, MORIANI. As the highest paid singer at La Fenice, Venice, in 1850 and 1851 he created, in the latter year, the Duke in Giuseppe Verdi's *Rigoletto*. A more forceful Duke than some later tenors, he was said to have a brilliant and intense timbre and incisive phrasing; Verdi approved of his singing the heavier part of Manrico in *Il trovatore* (1853–4, Venice; 1855, Milan). He sang in Boston and New York in 1855, in Buenos Aires in 1857 and 1860, retired in 1861, but appeared again in 1863–6 at the S Carlo, Naples, where he sang Leicester in *Maria Stuarda* (1865) and took part in the first performance of Saverio Mercadante's *Virginia* (1866); by then he was in serious decline.

J. Rosselli: *Singers of Italian Opera* (Cambridge, 1992)

John Rosselli

Miricioiu, Nelly

(*b* Adjud, 31 March 1952). Romanian soprano, naturalized British. She studied in Iaşi and Milan, making her début in Iaşi as the Queen of Night, and was then engaged at Braşov Opera (1975–8). With Scottish Opera (1981–3) she sang Violetta, Tosca and Manon Lescaut. In 1982 she sang the three heroines in *Les contes d'Hoffmann* at the Opéra-Comique and made her Covent Garden début as Nedda, returning as Musetta, Marguerite, Antonia and Valentine (*Les Huguenots*). She sang Violetta with great success for the ENO (1984), and has subsequently performed the role throughout Europe and in the USA. Her repertory also includes Lucia, Gilda, Mimì (which she sang for her Metropolitan début in 1989), Butterfly, Magda (*La Rondine*), Lucia, Olympia, Juliet and Yaroslavna (*Prince Igor*). As Miricioiu's beautiful, vibrant voice has become more flexible she has taken on a number of bel canto roles, singing Gioachino Rossini's Armida, Gaetano Donizetti's Maria Stuarda and Anna Bolena in Amsterdam (1989–92), Amenaide (*Tancredi*) in Salzburg (1992), Norma in Washington and Rossini's Ermione in Brussels (1995), and Semiramide in Geneva (1998). Her recordings include a much admired Tosca, Mercadante's *Orazi e Curiazi*, Rossini's *Ricciardo e Zoraide* and *mélodies* by Henri Duparc.

Elizabeth Forbes

Mitchell, Leona

(*b* Enid, OK, 13 Oct 1949). American soprano. She began her career with the Michigan Opera

Theatre in Detroit and in 1971 won first place in a study programme sponsored by the San Francisco Opera. In 1972 she made her professional début as Micaëla at the San Francisco Spring Opera Theater. Her Metropolitan Opera début, also as Micaëla, took place in December 1975; that year she also sang Bess in Lorin Maazel's recording of George Gershwin's opera. At the Metropolitan she has sung Pamina, the Prioress (*Dialogues des Carmélites*), Butterfly, Musetta, Leonora (*La forza del destino*) and Elvira (*Ernani*). She made her European début at the Geneva Opera (1976) as Liù, a role she repeated in 1980 at Covent Garden and the Paris Opéra. Her voice has been described as a cross between LEONTYNE PRICE's husky chest tones and MIRELLA FRENI's radiant upper register. Although Mitchell's early career was as a lyric soprano, in the early 1980s she started to move into the spinto repertory.

S. Wadsworth: 'Here to Sing: Soprano on the Rise: Leona Mitchell', *ON*, xliii/14 (1979), 10–13

H. Waleson: 'A Lyric Soprano Ventures into Heavier Fare', *New York Times* (20 March 1983)

Michael Walsh

Mitterwurzer, Anton

(*b* Sterzing, Tyrol, 12 April 1818; *d* Döbling, Vienna, 2 April 1876). Austrian baritone. He studied in Vienna, making his début in 1838 at Innsbruck. From 1839 until his retirement in 1870 he was a member of the Dresden Hofoper, where he made his début as the Hunter in Conradin Kreutzer's *Das Nachtlager in Granada*, took part in the première of Heinrich Marschner's *Kaiser Adolf von Nassau* (1845) and created Wolfram in *Tannhäuser* (1845). He also sang Kurwenal in the first performance of *Tristan und Isolde* (1865, Munich). His repertory included Aubry in *Der Vampyr*, Bois-Guilbert in *Der Templer und die Jüdin* and the title role of *Hans Heiling*. An intelligent singer with a powerful voice, he was also an excellent actor. The Austrian composer and conductor Johann Gänsbacher was his uncle.

Elizabeth Forbes

Mödl, Martha

(*b* Nuremberg, 22 March 1912; *d* Stuttgart, 16 Dec 2001). German soprano and mezzo-soprano. She studied at the Nuremberg Conservatory, made her début as Hänsel at Remscheid in 1942 and was then engaged at Düsseldorf (1945–9), singing Dorabella, Octavian, the Composer (*Ariadne auf Naxos*), Clytemnestra, Eboli, Carmen and Alban Berg's Marie. In 1949 she joined the Hamburg Staatsoper and became a dramatic soprano. In 1950–51 she

appeared as Lady Macbeth in Berlin and subsequently sang Kundry, Venus, Isolde and Brünnhilde (*Die Walküre*). In 1951 she sang Kundry at the first postwar Bayreuth Festival, a performance which was recorded live. She sang there regularly until 1967, notably as Brünnhilde and Isolde, and later adding the mezzo role of Waltraute to her repertory.

Mödl first appeared in England in the 1949–50 Covent Garden season, as Carmen. She sang at Edinburgh in 1952 with the Hamburg company and in 1958 with the Stuttgart Opera, which she had joined in 1953. In 1955 she sang Leonore at the reopening of the Vienna Staatsoper. She appeared at the Metropolitan (1956–60) and sang the Nurse (*Die Frau ohne Schatten*) at the reopening of the Munich Nationaltheater (1963). In the 1960s she sang at Monte Carlo and Toulouse. She sang in the premières of Aribert Reimann's *Melusine* (1971, Schwetzingen), Wolfgang Fortner's *Elisabeth Tudor* (1972, Berlin), Gottfried von Einem's *Kabale und Liebe* (1976, Vienna) and Reimann's *Die Gespenstersonate* (1984, Berlin). Returning to the mezzo repertory, she continued to sing into her 80s roles such as the Housekeeper (*Die schweigsame Frau*), the Countess (*The Queen of Spades*) and the Mother (Fortner's *Die Bluthochzeit*). Mödl was a highly individual singer and a performer of great dramatic intensity. Her recordings include Brünnhilde in Wilhelm Furtwängler's *Ring* (1953) and Isolde (1952, Bayreuth). Her voice can also be heard in a 1953 German film of Otto Nicolai's *Die lustigen Weiber con Windsor*. UTE VINZING was her pupil.

Harold Rosenthal/Alan Blyth

Moffo, Anna

(*b* Wayne, PA, 27 June 1932; *d* New York, 10 March 2006). American soprano. She studied at the Curtis Institute, Philadelphia, and in Rome with LUIGI RICCI and Mercedes Llopart, making her début in 1955 at Spoleto as Norina. In 1956 she sang Zerlina at Aix-en-Provence and appeared throughout Italy, making her American début the following year as Mimì in Chicago. She joined the Metropolitan Opera in 1959, making her début as Violetta; she appeared regularly in New York during the 1960s and early 1970s in such roles as Pamina, Norina, Gilda, Luisa Miller, the four heroines of *Les contes d'Hoffmann*, Juliet, Charles Gounod's Marguerite, Manon, Mélisande and the title role in *La Périchole*. She sang Gilda at Covent Garden (1964), and appeared in Vienna, Salzburg, Berlin and elsewhere. A lyric soprano of warm, full, radiant tone, she also undertook coloratura parts. As Violetta she was internationally acclaimed, notably as a guest artist in Walter Felsenstein's production at the Komische Oper, Berlin, the range and versatility of her voice, and her charming stage presence, being put to particularly good use. After a vocal breakdown in 1974–5 she made a fresh start in 1976, singing the title roles in *Thaïs* (1976, Seattle), *Adriana Lecouvreur* (1978, Parma), and Kate in Vittorio Giannini's *The Taming of the Shrew* (1979, Vienna, VA). Among her many recordings are Nannetta (in Herbert von Karajan's first *Falstaff*), Richard Wagner's version of *Iphigénie en Aulide* (with DIETRICH FISCHER-DIESKAU, *L'amore dei tre re* (Italo Montemezzi), *Carmen* and *Hänsel und Gretel*, Lucia, Luisa Miller and, on film, Violetta in *La traviata*.

J. Hines: 'Anna Moffo', *Great Singers on Great Singing* (Garden City, NY, 1982), 182–8

Harold Rosenthal/Alan Blyth

Mojica, José

(*b* Mexico City, 14 Sept 1896; *d* Lima, 21 Sept 1974). Mexican tenor. Born in poverty, but gifted with a fine voice and good looks, he joined the Chicago Opera Company in 1919 and remained until 1930, when he went into films, returning once more to sing Fenton in *Falstaff* in 1940. In 1928 he popularized the love song *Júrame* (Promise me) by the Mexican composer María Grever. His parts ranged from Pelléas, which he sang opposite MARY GARDEN, to Don Basilio in *Le nozze di Figaro*. In 1921 he sang the Prince in the première of *The Love for Three Oranges*, in which he scored a further success the following year in New York. On his mother's death in 1943 he gave up his career and became Father José Francisco de Guadaloupe, a Franciscan priest, working as a missionary in Peru. He undertook a concert tour of Central America to raise funds in 1954, and later wrote his autobiography, *Yo pecador* (I, a sinner) (Mexico City, 1956). His recordings show an attractive lyric voice often used with skill and imagination.

J.B. Steane

Moll, Kurt

(*b* Buir, nr Cologne, 11 April 1938). German bass. He studied at the Hochschule für Musik, Cologne, then privately with Emmy Mueller. He made his début as Lodovico (*Otello*) at Aachen, where he was engaged from 1961 to 1963, and then sang at Mainz and Wuppertal before joining the Hamburg Staatsoper in 1970. From 1972 he has been a regular guest at Munich, Vienna and Paris, and has also appeared at Salzburg and Bayreuth. His roles

include most of the leading bass parts in Richard Wagner's operas, his King Mark and Pogner being particularly vivid portrayals, and he uses his true, strong and flexible bass equally well in less serious roles such as Osmin, which he recorded with considerable success under Karl Böhm. He is a noble Sarastro, with the low notes resonant and firm. He is also an appreciable interpreter of such Verdi roles as Fiesco and Padre Guardiano. He first appeared in the USA as Gurnemanz (1974, San Francisco). In 1975 he created the King in Günter Bialas's *Der gestiefelte Kater* at the Schwetzingen Festival in the Hamburg Staatsoper production and added the title role in Jules Massenet's *Don Quichotte* (given with the same company) to his repertory. He made his Covent Garden début as Caspar in Götz Friedrich's production of *Der Freischütz* in 1977, returning as Osmin in 1987 and Daland in 2000; his Metropolitan début was in 1978 as the Landgrave, and he has subsequently appeared there in several Wagner operas. In 1984 he sang the title role in *Der barbier von Bagdad* at the Munich opera festival. Moll is also a distinguished concert and oratorio singer, and made his American début as a recitalist in Carnegie Hall in 1984. His extensive discography includes all his Wagnerian roles, lieder and oratorio.

Alan Blyth

Mombelli, Anna and Ester.

Italian singers, daughters of DOMENICO MOMBELLI.

Mombelli, Domenico

(*b* Villanova Monferrato, nr Alessandria, 17 Feb 1751; *d* Bologna, 15 March 1835). Italian tenor and composer. He began his career as organist at Crescentino, where in 1776 he staged his own three-act opera, *Didone*, to a libretto by Pietro Metastasio. He came to prominence as a singer in 1780, when he first appeared in Venice in Pasquale Anfossi's *Nitteti*; he returned there frequently until 1800. Although he sang in Rome, Turin, Reggio nell'Emilia, Padua and Bologna during this period, his main centre of activity other than Venice was Naples, especially the Teatro S Carlo, where he first appeared in 1783 in Giuseppe Sarti's *Medonte* and Domenico Cimarosa's *Oreste*, and returned periodically until 1803.

Mombelli's first wife was LUISA LASCHI, Mozart's first Countess Almaviva, with whom he sang in Vienna in 1786. Laschi died, probably in 1790, and in 1791 he married the dancer Vincenza Viganò, a niece of Luigi Boccherini and sister of the choreographer Salvatore Viganò. They had 12 children, of whom two, Ester (*b* Bologna, 1794) and Anna (*b* Milan, 1795), became singers; with them and a bass, Mombelli formed a travelling company which appeared in Lisbon, Padua and Milan (1806–11).

In 1805 Mombelli became friendly with the 13-year-old Gioachino Rossini, who composed for him the principal role in *Demetrio e Polibio* to a text by Vincenza Mombelli. The work was performed in 1812 at the Teatro Valle, Rome, with Domenico as Demetrius, Ester as Lisinga and Anna as Siveno. For some years Mombelli held the copyright of *Demetrio e Polibio* and performed in it at the Teatro Carcano, Milan (1813) and in other cities. Castil-Blaze reports that he sang in Florence at over 70 years of age. He was one of the best 'serious' tenors of the Classical period in Italy: in 1816 he was described by Duke Cesarini Sforza as incomparable 'nelle parti forti e vibrate'. By then his voice was in decline and he turned increasingly to teaching, first in Florence and then in Bologna. His published works include two sets of ariettas for voice and keyboard, six duets for two sopranos and the rondò *Tu mi sprezzi*.

Elizabeth Forbes, Colin Timms

Mombelli, Luisa.

See LASCHI, LUISA.

Monaco, Mario del.

See DEL MONACO, MARIO.

Moncrieff, Gladys (Lillian)

(*b* Bundaberg, Queensland, 13 April 1892; *d* Gold Coast, Queensland, 9 Feb 1976). Australian soprano. After showing promise as a child performer in Queensland she successfully auditioned with the J.C. Williamson management for professional training and from 1914, sang principal roles in Gilbert and Sullivan and musical comedy. After a South African tour with the company she achieved lasting success as Teresa in Harold Fraser-Simson's *The Maid of the Mountains* (1921, Melbourne), eventually playing the role some 2800 times. Contemporary critics wrote of the purity, richness, power and wide range of her voice, her conviction of style and her clear enunciation. She had a considerable success in London in Franz Lehár's *Die blaue Mazur* (1927). Her subsequent Australian appearances included the leading roles in two Australian musicals by Varney Monk, *Collit's Inn* (1933) and *The Cedar Tree* (1934), many revivals of operettas and musical comedies, and concert tours up to her retirement in 1959. Moncrieff became one of the most consistently admired and affectionately regarded performers (often referred to as 'Our Glad') in Australia. Her autobiography, *My Life of*

Song, written with Lillian Palmer (and including a discography), was published in Adelaide in 1971.

Roger Covell

Monelli, Raffaele

(*b* Fermo, 5 March 1782; *d* S Benedetto del Tronto, Adria, 14 Sept 1859). Italian tenor, brother of SAVINO MONELLI. He studied in Fermo, making his début in 1808. He took part in two Gioachino Rossini premières: as Duke Bertrando in *L'inganno felice* and as Dorvil in *La scala di seta*, both in 1812 at the Teatro S Moisè, Venice.

Elizabeth Forbes/R

Monelli, Savino

(*b* Fermo, 9 May 1784; *d* Fermo, 5 June 1836). Italian tenor. His brother was the tenor RAFFAELE MONELLI. Savino studied in Fermo. In 1817 he created roles in Gioachino Rossini's *La gazza ladra* (Giannetto) at La Scala and *Adelaide di Borgogna* (Adelberto) at the Teatro Argentina, Rome. He sang Don Ramiro in the first performance of Gaetano Donizetti's *Chiara e Serafina* (1822) at La Scala and Enrico at the première of Donizetti's *L'ajo nell'imbarazzo* (1824) at the Teatro Valle, Rome.

Elizabeth Forbes/R

Mongini, Pietro

(*b* Rome, 1830; *d* Milan, 27 April 1874). Italian tenor. He started his career as a bass, but by 1853 was singing tenor roles at Genoa. In 1855 he made his Paris début at the Théâtre Italien as Edgardo in *Lucia di Lammermoor*, and in 1857 sang at Reggio nell'Emilia in the first performance of Achille Peri's *Vittor Pisani* and in Gaetano Donizetti's *Anna Bolena*. He first appeared at La Scala in 1858 as Arnold in *Guillaume Tell*, and made his London début in 1859 as Elvino in *La sonnambula* at Drury Lane, where he also sang Arrigo in the first London performance of Giuseppe Verdi's *Les vêpres siciliennes* (in Italian). In 1860 he sang Manrico (*Il trovatore*) at La Scala and Huon in Carl Maria von Weber's *Oberon* at Her Majesty's Theatre. He returned to London every year from 1862 to 1873, appearing either at Her Majesty's, where his many roles included Don Alvaro in the first London performance of *La forza del destino* (1867), or at Covent Garden, where he made his début as Gennaro in *Lucrezia Borgia* (1868). On 24 December 1871 he created the role of Radamès in the first performance of *Aida*, at the Cairo Opera House. According to contemporary reports, his genuinely heroic tenor voice was not used with much subtlety or intelligence, but in such roles as Arnold, Manrico and Alvaro the sheer brilliance of sound and the excitement of his performances compensated for any lack of artistry.

Elizabeth Forbes

Montagnana, Antonio

(*b* Venice; *fl* 1730–50). Italian bass. In 1730 he sang at Rome and in 1731 at Turin in operas by Nicola Porpora, who is said to have been his teacher. He was a member of G.F. Handel's company at the King's Theatre, 1731–3, and may have made his début as Leo in *Tamerlano*. During the 1731–2 season he sang in revivals of *Poro*, *Admeto*, *Flavio* and *Giulio Cesare*, in first productions of *Ezio* (Varus) and *Sosarme* (Altomaro), and in Attilio Ariosti's *Coriolano* and the pasticcio *Lucio Papirio dittatore*. The following season he was in Leonardo Leo's *Catone*, revivals of G.F. Handel's *Alessandro*, *Tolomeo* and probably *Floridante*, and the first production of *Orlando* (Zoroastro). He sang Haman in *Esther* and Polyphemus in *Acis and Galatea* during Handel's first London oratorio season (May and June 1732), and Abinoam and the Chief Priest of Israel in the first performance of *Deborah* (17 March 1733). Handel composed the part of Abner in *Athalia* for him and cast him as Emireno in a planned revival of *Ottone*, but in the early summer he left the company with SENESINO and BERTOLLI to join the Opera of the Nobility. The anonymous pamphlet *Harmony in an Uproar*, published in February 1734, implies that he broke a formal contract to do so. He sang with the Opera of the Nobility throughout its four London seasons (1733–7) in at least 15 operas at Lincoln's Inn Fields and the King's Theatre, including Porpora's *Arianna in Nasso* (Piritous, 1733 première), *Enea nel Lazio*, *Polifemo*, *Ifigenia in Aulide* and *Mitridate*, Johann Hasse's *Artaserse* and *Siroe*, Francesco Veracini's *Adriano* and *La clemenza di Tito*, Giovanni Bononcini's *Astarto* and Handel's *Ottone*. In 1737–8 he was a member of John Jacob Heidegger's company at the King's, appearing in two pasticcios, G.B. Pescetti's *La conquista del vello d'oro*, Veracini's *Partenio* and two new Handel operas, *Faramondo* and *Serse*, as Gustavo and Ariodate. For ten years from 1740 he was attached to the royal chapel at Madrid, where he sang in many operas and cantatas.

When he arrived in London, Montagnana was a remarkable singer, a genuine bass with powerful low notes, considerable agility and a compass of more than two octaves (E to f'), as seen in the music composed for him by Handel, who regularly expanded the parts he sang in revivals. But by 1738 his powers were on the wane and in his last two Handel parts his compass had shrunk to G to $e\,b'$. Charles Burney,

refering to the earlier period, singled out his voice's 'depth, power, mellowness and peculiar accuracy of intonation in hitting distant intervals'. In *Orlando* a listener reported that he sang 'with a voice like a Canon' – presumably ballistic rather than clerical.

Winton Dean

Montague, Diana

(*b* Winchester, 8 April 1953). English mezzo-soprano. She studied in Manchester, then sang in the Glyndebourne chorus, making her solo début in 1977 as Zerlina with the Glyndebourne Touring Opera. While engaged at Covent Garden (1978–83) she sang Kate Pinkerton, Laura (*Luisa Miller*), the Lady Artist (*Lulu*), Annius, Parséis (*Esclarmonde*), Nicklausse and Cherubino, the last a role she has also sung with the ENO and Scottish Opera and at the Salzburg and Aix-en-Provence festivals. She sang Wellgunde and Siegrune at Bayreuth (1983) and has appeared in Lyons, Nancy, Brussels, Lausanne, Frankfurt, Edinburgh and at the Metropolitan, where she made her début in 1987 as Annius. Her repertory includes Proserpine (Claudio Monteverdi's *Orfeo*), Henry Purcell's Dido, Idamantes, Dorabella, Isolier (*Le comte Ory*), the Fox (*The Cunning Little Vixen*) and Mélisande. She has a creamy voice, a handsome presence and, adept in the Classical style, excels as Gluck's Orpheus, which she sang at Glyndebourne in 1989, and in the title role of *Iphigénie en Tauride*, which she sang for WNO in 1992. (See colour plate 4.)

Elizabeth Forbes

Montalant, Laure.

See CINTI-DAMOREAU, LAURE.

Montesanto, Luigi

(*b* Palermo, 23 Nov 1887; *d* Milan, 14 June 1954). Italian baritone. He studied in Palermo and made his début there in 1909 as Escamillo. He sang at Buenos Aires from 1910, appearing as John the Baptist in the local première of *Salome*, and sang Gioachino Rossini's Figaro in the opening season of the Théâtre des Champs-Elysées in Paris (1913). At the Metropolitan he created Michele in *Il tabarro* (1918), thereafter appearing in Chicago during the 1920s. Until 1940 he was successful at the leading Italian houses as Scarpia, Rigoletto, Wolfram and Germont. He appeared in Britain in joint recitals with TOTI DAL MONTE. After his retirement he taught in Milan; GIUSEPPE DI STEFANO was among his pupils.

David Cummings

Moody [Manners], Fanny

(*b* Redruth, Cornwall, 23 Nov 1866; *d* Dundrum, Co. Dublin, 21 July 1945). English soprano. She studied with CHARLOTTE SAINTON-DOLBY, making her stage début as Arline in *The Bohemian Girl* at Liverpool in 1887 with the Carl Rosa Opera Company, of which she remained the leading soprano until 1898. In 1896–7 she made an opera tour of South Africa with her husband, the bass Charles Manners. The following year they founded the Moody-Manners Company (1898–1916). In 1892 she sang Tatyana in the first English performance of *Yevgeny Onegin* at the Olympic Theatre, London. She created the title role in Emilio Pizzi's *La Rosalba*, and Militza in C. McAlpin's *The Cross and the Crescent*, in the Covent Garden seasons that she organized with Manners (1902–3). Her repertory also included Elsa, Charles Gounod's Marguerite and Juliet, Leonora (*Il trovatore*) and Santuzza. Her pleasant light soprano voice and charming stage personality were widely admired.

P. Graves: 'The Moody-Manners Partnership', *Opera*, ix (1958), 558–64

Harold Rosenthal/R

Moore, Grace

(*b* Nough, TN, 5 Dec 1898; *d* nr Copenhagen, 26 Jan 1947). American soprano. She studied singing with Marafioti in New York and then appeared in revue and operetta. In 1926 she sailed for Europe and after working with Richard Berthélemy at Antibes made her Opéra-Comique début as Mimì in 1928. That year she made her Metropolitan début in the same role, remaining there until the 1931–2 season and returning in several seasons up to 1946, singing such roles as Lauretta, Tosca, Manon, Fiora (*L'amore dei tre re*) and Louise. She appeared at Covent Garden in 1935 as Mimì and continued to give concerts internationally until her death in an air accident. She also appeared in numerous Broadway shows and made several films, the most important of which were Abel Gance's *Louise* and *One Night of Love* (1934). Moore had a glamorous personality, earning the American accolade 'star of stage, screen and radio', and a sensuous, substantial voice, though it lacked technical finish.

G. Moore: *You're Only Human Once* (Garden City, NY, 1944/R)

Max De Schauensee/R

Moreau, Fanchon [Françoise]

(*b* 1668; *d* after 1743). French soprano. Although Titon du Tillet (*Le Parnasse françois*, 1732) stated that she left the stage about 1708, her name disappears from cast lists in 1702; he added that she was still living in 1743. According to J.-B. Durey de Noinville (*Histoire du théâtre de l'Opéra de l'Académie royale de musique en France*, 1753, 2/1757), she made her début in 1683 in the prologue of Jean-Baptiste Lully's *Phaëton* (probably as Astraea). From 1683 to 1692 (when her older sister Louison left the Opéra) both sisters were entered as 'Mlle Moreau' in cast lists. It is known, however, that it was Fanchon who created the role of Oriane in Lully's *Amadis* (1684) and Sidonie in his *Armide* (1686).

Between 1692 and 1702 she appeared in several Lully revivals: as Oriane in *Amadis* (1701), Sangaride in *Atys* (1699), Aegle in *Thésée* (1698), Libya in *Phaëton* (1702) and as Proserpina (1699). She also sang major roles in the first performances at the Paris Opéra of many *préramiste* stage works, among them M.-A. Charpentier's *Médée* (Creusa), André Campra's *L'Europe galante* and A.C. Destouches' *Issé*. She was a mistress of the dauphin (as was her sister, Louison), and later of Philippe de Vendôme for 20 years. François Couperin's bawdy canon *La femme entre deux draps* names Fanchon as one of the women 'between two sheets'; she was the inspiration for his harpsichord piece 'La tendre Fanchon'.

James R. Anthony

Morena [Meyer], Berta

(*b* Mannheim, 27 Jan 1878; *d* Rottach-Egern, Tegernsee, 7 Oct 1952). German soprano. She studied in Munich with Sophie Röhr-Brajnin and AGLAJA ORGÉNI, and made her début in 1898 at the Munich Hofoper as Agathe (*Der Freischütz*). She remained with the company until her farewell in 1927, being especially admired in Wagner roles. She made her Metropolitan début in 1908 as Sieglinde and later sang Elisabeth, Leonore, Brünnhilde and Santuzza there. When she appeared at Covent Garden in 1914, as Isolde, Sieglinde and Kundry, she was praised more as an actress (she was a woman of great beauty and distinctive stage presence) than as a singer.

Harold Rosenthal/R

Moriani, Napoleone

(*b* Florence, 10 March 1806/1808; *d* Florence, 4 March 1878). Italian tenor. He made his début at Pavia in 1833 in Giovanni Pacini's *Gli arabi nelle Gallie*. Between 1840 and 1844 he frequently sang in Vienna and Germany; in 1841 he was made a *Kammersänger* to the Austrian emperor. From 1844 to 1846 he appeared alternately in London and Madrid (where he was awarded the Order of Isabella), and made his Paris début in 1845 at the Théâtre Italien; he also sang at Lisbon and Barcelona, then for two years in Italy. His last important engagements were at the Théâtre Italien (1849–50) and Madrid (1850).

Moriani combined sweetness of tone with great dramatic intensity. With his gaunt good looks he excelled in death scenes: impressed by his performance in revivals of Gaetano Donizetti's *Lucia di Lammermoor* and *Pia de' Tolomei*, composers wrote for him parts portraying the hero in a prolonged death agony, as in Nicola Vaccai's *La sposa di Messina* (1839, Venice) and Federico Ricci's *Luigi Rolla* (1841, Florence). He also sang in the premières of Saverio Mercadante's *Le due illustri rivali* (1838, Venice) and Donizetti's *Maria de Rudenz* (Enrico, 1838, Venice) and *Linda di Chamounix* (Carlo, 1842, Vienna). For a revival of *Attila* at La Scala in 1847 Giuseppe Verdi wrote an alternative romanza for him, to be inserted in the last act.

Julian Budden

Morin, Charles.

See CRABBÉ, ARMAND.

Morison, Elsie (Jean)

(*b* Ballarat, Victoria, 15 Aug 1924). Australian soprano. She studied with CLIVE CAREY both at the Melbourne Conservatory and at the RCM. She made her English concert début at the Royal Albert Hall in *Acis and Galatea* in 1948 and that autumn joined Sadler's Wells Opera, appearing regularly there until 1954. She was ideally cast when she sang Anne Trulove in the first British staging of *The Rake's Progress* (1953, Edinburgh) and at her Glyndebourne début the following year. After a notable Covent Garden début (1953) as Mimì, she sang there regularly until 1962. In such roles as Susanna, Pamina, Marzelline, Micaëla, Antonia (*Les contes d'Hoffmann*), Mařenka, and Blanche in the British première of Francis Poulenc's *Dialogues des Carmélites* (1958), she was admired for the touching sincerity of her acting and the lyrical warmth of her voice. In 1955 she created the title role of Arwel Hughes's *Menna* for the WNO and, to mark the Frederick Delius centenary, sang in a touring production of *A Village Romeo and Juliet*. Among her recordings, those of Henry Purcell, G.F. Handel and Michael Tippett's *A Child of our Time* capture well the grace and conviction of her singing. She was married to the conductor Rafael Kubelík.

Harold Rosenthal/Alan Blyth

Morris, James

(*b* Baltimore, 10 Jan 1947). American bass-baritone. He studied with PONSELLE in Baltimore and MOSCONA in Philadelphia, making his début with the Baltimore Civic Opera in 1967 as Crespel (*Les contes d'Hoffmann*). In 1970 he joined the Metropolitan Opera, beginning with the King (*Aida*) and similar parts, graduating to Don Giovanni and other principal roles from 1975. He was heard mainly in lyric Italian roles, including Banquo at his British début (1972, Glyndebourne) and Guglielmo at the Salzburg Festival (from 1982; he recorded the part under Riccardo Muti). A suggestion that he should sing Wotan led him to study with HANS HOTTER, and he first sang the role in *Walküre* at Baltimore in 1984. He added the *Rheingold* Wotan at San Francisco the next year (when he also first sang the Dutchman at Houston), and sang the three *Ring* Wotans first in Munich in 1987 under Wolfgang Sawallisch. The role brought him conspicuous success also at the Deutsche Oper, Berlin (1987), the Metropolitan Opera (1989) and Covent Garden (*Rheingold*, 1988; *Walküre*, 1989; *Siegfried*, 1990; and the complete cycle, 1991), while he recorded it concurrently under both Bernard Haitink and James Levine. Morris resists typecasting as Wotan, and has sung to acclaim roles such as Hans Sachs, Scarpia, Macbeth, Philip II (which he sang in San Francisco in 1998) and Claggart. He also sang in premières of operas by Thomas Pasatieri. His other recordings range from Macheath in *The Beggar's Opera* and Cecil in Gaetano Donizetti's *Maria Stuarda* to Amonasro, Amfortas, the Dutchman, Timour in Jules Massenet's *Le roi de Lahore* and Dr Miracle (*Les contes d'Hoffmann*). At the Metropolitan Opera alone he has sung over 50 roles. His imposing presence is matched by his firm, weighty tone and command of line. His dramatic interpretations, if not always markedly individual, are supported by clear musical insight.

H. Canning: 'James Morris', *Opera*, xxxix (1988), 1177–83
P. Thomason: 'Basso continuo', *ON*, lix (1994–5), 20–23

Noël Goodwin

Moscona, Nicola [Mosconas, Nicolai]

(*b* Athens, 23 Sept 1907; *d* Philadelphia, 17 Sept 1975). Greek bass. He studied with Elena Theodorini at the Athens Conservatory and began singing professionally in 1929. After performing throughout Greece and in Egypt and Italy, he made his Metropolitan Opera début in 1937 as Ramfis in *Aida*. He spent the next 25 seasons as a principal bass there, singing over 30 different roles, including Pimen, Colline, Raimondo (*Lucia di Lammermoor*), Sparafucile and

Ferrando (*Il trovatore*). He was a favourite singer of Arturo Toscanini, who chose him to participate in his recordings of *La bohème*, *Mefistofele*, *Rigoletto* and the Verdi Requiem, which reveal his firm tone and feel for shaping a phrase.

Cori Ellison/Alan Blyth

Moser, Edda (Elisabeth)

(*b* Berlin, 27 Oct 1938). Austrian soprano of German birth. She studied at the Berlin Conservatory and made her début at the Städtische Oper in 1962 as Kate Pinkerton, after which she sang for a year in the Würzburg Opera chorus; engagements followed at Hagen and Bielefeld. She has appeared regularly at Vienna, Salzburg (from 1970) and Hamburg; since her Metropolitan début in 1968 as Wellgunde (*Das Rheingold*) her roles there have included Donna Anna, the Queen of Night, Armida in *Rinaldo* and Liù. Equally at home in contemporary music, she sang the title role of Siegried Matthus's *Omphale* at Cologne (1979). Her repertory ranges from Konstanze and Aspasia (W.A. Mozart's *Mitridate*) to the three heroines of *Les contes d'Hoffmann*, Ariadne, and Marie (*Wozzeck*). Moser's voice is a powerful dramatic coloratura soprano, used with remarkable accuracy and musicianship.

Harold Rosenthal/R

Moser, Thomas

(*b* Richmond, VA, 27 May 1945). American tenor. He studied in Richmond, Philadelphia and in California, making his début in 1975 at Graz. In 1979 he sang W.A. Mozart's Titus at the New York City Opera, and over the following decade performed in many of Europe's leading opera houses in a repertory that included Don Ottavio, Tamino, Idomeneus, C.W. Gluck's Pylades and Achilles, the title role of Franz Schubert's *Fierrabras*, Paul (*Die tote Stadt*) and Franz I (Ernst Krenek's *Karl V*). At the 1984 Salzburg Festival he created the role of the Tenor in Luciano Berio's *Un re in ascolto*. In the 1990s he began to take on heavier roles: Florestan (which he sang at La Scala in 1990 and repeated there in 1999), Fritz (*Der ferne Klang*), the Emperor (*Die Frau ohne Schatten*), Max (*Der Freischütz*), Don José and Hector Berlioz's Faust. In 1993 Moser made his Metropolitan début as Bacchus and sang Adolar (*Euryanthe*) at Aix-en-Provence; he sang his first Lohengrin in Geneva in 1994 and his first Peter Grimes at the Théâtre du Châtelet, Paris, in 1995, and made an impressive Covent Garden début in 1997 as Palestrina. His strong, sinewy, even-toned voice has retained its flexibility as it has

grown weightier and more baritonal, while he sings Classical, Romantic and modern works with equal conviction. His many recordings include operatic roles ranging from Gluck and Mozart to Don José, the Young Sailor (*Tristan und Isolde*) and Fritz, and works such as *The Creation*, *La damnation de Faust*, Berlioz's *Roméo et Juliette*, *Das Lied von der Erde* and *Gurrelieder*.

Elizabeth Forbes/R

Mravina [Mravinskaya], Yevgeniya Konstantinovna

(*b* St Petersburg, 4/16 Feb 1864; *d* Yalta, 12/25 Oct 1914). Russian soprano. She studied with IPPOLIT PETROVICH PRYANISHNIKOV, then with DESIRÉE ARTÔT in Berlin and MATHILDE MARCHESI in Paris, making her début at Vittorio Veneto in August 1885. From 1886 to 1897 she was a principal soloist at the Mariinsky Theatre. In 1895 she created the coquettish Oxana in Nikolay Rimsky-Korsakov's *Christmas Eve*, a role particularly suited to her consummate acting ability, lyric purity of tone and supreme musical intelligence. Other roles she sang to perfection were Antonida in *A Life for the Tsar*, Lyudmila in M.I. Glinka's second opera and Tatyana in P.I. Tchaikovsky's *Yevgeny Onegin*. She also sang in operas by Charles Gounod, Giacomo Meyerbeer and Richard Wagner. She made three European tours, in 1891–2, 1902–3 and finally in 1906, but by that time her voice and health were already deteriorating.

Edward Garden

Müller, Maria

(*b* Theresienstadt [now Terezín, nr Litoměřice], 29 Jan 1898; *d* Bayreuth, 13 March 1958). Czech soprano. She studied in Vienna with ERIK SCHMEDES and made her début as Elsa at Linz in 1919. Engagements followed at the Neues Deutsches Theater in Prague and in Munich, and in 1925 she made her début as Sieglinde (a role which was to become one of her best) at the Metropolitan. She remained there until the 1934–5 season, singing in a number of American premières including Franco Alfano's *Madonna imperia* (1928), Ildebrando Pizzetti's *Fra Gherardo* (1929), *Švanda the Bagpiper* (1931) and *Simon Boccanegra* (1932). She first sang in Berlin at the Städtische Oper as Euryanthe in 1926 and later sang at the Staatsoper until 1943. After World War II she retired to live at Bayreuth, where she had sung regularly from 1930 to 1944 as Senta, Eva, Elisabeth, Elsa and Sieglinde, all of which are recorded. At Salzburg she appeared as Eurydice

Muzio, Claudia [Muzzio, Claudine]

(*b* Pavia, 7 Feb 1889; *d* Rome, 24 May 1936). Italian soprano. Her father was a stage director at Covent Garden and the Metropolitan, her mother a chorus singer. Among her teachers was Annetta Casaloni, Giuseppe Verdi's first Maddalena (*Rigoletto*), who probably helped her to obtain engagements at Turin in 1911 and 1914–15. She had made her début at Arezzo on 15 January 1910 in Jules Massenet's *Manon*; her first appearance at La Scala, as Desdemona, was during the 1913–14 season. In the Covent Garden summer season of 1914 she attracted considerable attention in some of her best roles, including Desdemona, Margherita (*Mefistofele*), Tosca and Mimì (the two last with Caruso in the cast), but was never to return to that theatre. In the USA, however, she quickly became a much valued member first of the Metropolitan company (début as Tosca, 1916), where she remained for seven consecutive seasons and reappeared briefly in 1934, and where she sang Giorgetta (*Il tabarro*) in the première of Giacomo Puccini's *Trittico* (1918); and subsequently of the Chicago Civic Opera (début as Aida, 1922), to which she returned for nine seasons with only a single break. During this period she was also much in demand in the principal South American houses; in Italy she made some notable appearances under Arturo Toscanini at La Scala in 1926–7 (*La traviata*, *Il trovatore*, *Tosca*), but thereafter sang mostly in Rome where she created the title role in Licinio Refice's *Cecilia* (1934).

Muzio's extensive repertory embraced all the leading Verdi and Puccini roles, as well as those of the *verismo* school – which last, however, she interpreted in a more subtle and refined manner than was usual. Nobility and sweetness of voice and aspect, together with intense drama and pathos, were marked features of her style; good judges thought her one of the finest artists of her time. Although she made many recordings, few of them do her full justice. The early groups (1911, 1917–18, 1920–25) are marred by low technical standards, although in subsequent reissues on CD the compelling quality of her voice can be clearly heard. In many of the technically excellent recordings made in 1934–5, however, her tone has lost much of its pristine freshness and steadiness. Among this last group, however, there are some unforgettable achievements, notably her infinitely pathetic reading of Germont's letter in the last act of *La traviata*.

J.B. Richards: 'Claudia Muzio', *Record Collector*, xvii (1966–8), 197–237, 256–63 [incl. discography by H.M. Barnes]

G. Gualerzi: 'The Divine Claudia', *Opera*, xxxvii (1986), 643–51

Desmond Shawe-Taylor

Claudia Muzio in 'La fiamma' (Respighi)

Mysz-Gmeiner [née Gmeiner], Lula

(*b* Kronstadt [now Braşov, Romania], 16 Aug 1876; *d* Schwerin, 7 Aug 1948). German contralto. She came of a musical family: her sister Ella, likewise a contralto, appeared at Covent Garden in 1911 in Engelbert Humperdinck's *Königskinder*, her brother Rudolf was also a successful singer, and her sister Luise was a pianist. Lula Gmeiner first studied the violin under Olga Grigorovich at Kronstadt, 1882–92, and then singing under Rudolf Lasse there, 1892–6, afterwards with Gustav Walter in Vienna (where she is said to have impressed Johannes Brahms), with Emilie Herzog, Etelka Gerster and LILLI LEHMANN in Berlin, and with Raimund von Zur Mühlen in London. She began her concert career at the turn of the century, and in 1900 married Ernst Mysz, an Austrian naval officer. She was regarded as an outstanding interpreter of lieder, comparable with JULIA CULP and ELENA GERHARDT, although less famous internationally than those singers. She was appointed *Kammersängerin*, and was a professor at the Hochschule für Musik in Berlin, 1920–45. Among her pupils were PETER ANDERS (who later became her son-in-law) and, briefly, ELISABETH SCHWARZKOPF. In the 1920s Mysz-Gmeiner made several lieder recordings, notably a Franz Schubert series to commemorate the centenary of the composer's death; although by that time she had trouble in maintaining pitch, the best of those recordings, especially *Die junge Nonne*, well capture the intimacy and purity of her style.

Eric Blom/Desmond Shawe-Taylor

Myszuga, Aleksander [Mishuga, Ołeksandr; Myshuga, Olexander]

(*b* Nowy Witków, nr Lwów, 7 June 1853; *d* nr Freiburg, 9 March 1922). Polish tenor of Ukrainian descent. After making his début in Stanisław Moniuszko's *The Haunted Manor* (1880, Lwów), he studied with Bruni in Milan and with GIOVANNI SBRIGLIA in Paris. In Italy he used the stage name 'Filippi'; he also sang in Lwów, at the Wielki Theatre in Warsaw (1884–92), five times in Vienna, and in Prague (1887, 1900), Paris (1892), St Petersburg (1903) and many times in Kiev. His voice, with a register extending to c'', was well suited to lyrical parts, but he also sang dramatic roles, notably in *Les Huguenots* and *Aida*, and was highly successful in Moniuszko's *Halka*. Myszuga had been a disciple of Walery Wysocki in Lwów and upheld Wysocki's pedagogical methods as a teacher in Kiev (1905–11) and Warsaw (1911–14); in 1918 he founded a music school in Stockholm.

Irena Poniatowska

N

Nachbaur, Franz (Ignaz)

(*b* Giessen, nr Friedrichshafen, 25 March 1835; *d* Munich, 21 March 1902). German tenor. After studying in Milan with Francesco Lamperti and at Stuttgart with Jan Pišek, he made his début in 1857 at Pessau, then appeared at Meiningen, Cologne, Hanover and Prague (1860–63), where he sang Lionel in Friedrich Flotow's *Martha* and Charles Gounod's Faust, and Darmstadt (1863–8), where his roles included Gounod's Romeo. He began a 23-year association with the Hofoper, Munich, on 24 June 1867 as Flotow's Alessandro Stradella and sang Walther at the first performance of *Die Meistersinger* (1868), Froh at the première of *Das Rheingold* (1869), the title role in *Rienzi* (1871) and Radames in *Aida* (1877). In 1878 he sang Lohengrin in Rome and in 1882 made his London début as Adolar in Carl Maria von Weber's *Euryanthe* at Drury Lane. He also sang in Berlin, Hamburg and Moscow. His farewell appearance in Munich on 13 October 1890, when he sang Chapelou in Adolphe Adam's *Le postillon de Lonjumeau*, was his 1001st performance at the Hofoper. Although he sang many heavy dramatic roles including Siegmund (*Die Walküre*), a superb technique preserved the suppleness and lyricism of his voice throughout a long career.

Elizabeth Forbes

Nantier-Didiée, Constance (Betzy Rosabella)

(*b* St Denis, Ile de Bourbon [now Ile de la Réunion], 16 Nov 1831; *d* Madrid, 4 Dec 1867). French mezzo-soprano. She studied with GILBERT DUPREZ at the Paris Conservatoire and in 1849 won the *premier prix* for opera. In 1850 she made her début at the Teatro Carignano, Turin, as Emilia in Saverio Mercadante's *La vestale*. She appeared in *Luisa Miller* at the Théâtre Italien in 1852, and the next year began a three-year engagement at Covent Garden, where she made her début as Gondì in *Maria di Rohan* and sang in the English premières of *Rigoletto* and *Benvenuto Cellini*. In 1854–6 she sang in Spain and North America, then for two years at the Théâtre Italien. On 15 May 1858 she returned to Covent Garden to sing Urbain (*Les Huguenots*) at the gala opening of the present theatre, where she continued to appear until 1864. Giacomo Meyerbeer

and Gounod wrote her additional music for productions there of *Dinorah* (1859) and *Faust* (1863). She was the first Preziosilla in *La forza del destino* (1862, St Petersburg), and had a wide repertory of comic, dramatic and travesty roles.

H.F. Chorley: *Thirty Years' Musical Recollections*, London, 1862/*R*, abridged 2/1926/*R* by E. Newman

Philip Robinson

Nash, (William) Heddle

(*b* London, 14 June 1894; *d* London, 14 Aug 1961). English tenor. He studied with GIUSEPPE BORGATTI in Milan, where he made his début as Almaviva in *Il barbiere di Siviglia* in 1924. He sang in Genoa, Bologna and Turin before returning to London in 1925, when he was engaged by the Old Vic company and at once made his name as the Duke in *Rigoletto*, also singing Tamino, Faust and Tonio (*La fille du régiment*). Tours with the British National Opera Company followed, during which he sang a wide variety of roles, among them Almaviva, Fenton, Turiddu, Romeo, Jules Massenet's Des Grieux and David (*Meistersinger*). In 1929 he made his début at Covent Garden, when his Don Ottavio was compared with that of McCORMACK; he sang there regularly until the war, as Almaviva, Rodolfo, Pinkerton, Eisenstein, Faust, Rinuccio (*Gianni Schicchi*), Pedrillo, Roméo (on tour) and David. In 1947–8, the first postwar season, he returned as Des Grieux and David. He was a mainstay of the early Glyndebourne seasons, singing every Ferrando, Don Basilio and Pedrillo from 1934 to 1938, and Don Ottavio in 1937. In 1940 he sang in New Zealand as part of the centennial celebrations for European settlement. During World War II he appeared with the Carl Rosa Opera Company in London. He created Dr Manette in Arthur Benjamin's *A Tale of Two Cities* at Sadler's Wells in 1957, his final stage appearance.

Nash was also a markedly popular concert and oratorio singer. He was particularly admired in G.F. Handel and as Gerontius, which he first performed in 1932, at Edward Elgar's insistence, and which he sang in the work's first complete recording in 1945. In recital he attempted a wide repertory, and was well known for his advocacy of Franz Liszt's songs. Charm, grace, romantic ardour and what Richard Capell in *Grove5* termed 'a minstrel-like effect of spontaneity' represented a rare natural gift enhanced by technical assurance; these qualities were epitomized in his noted account of the Serenade from Georges Bizet's *La jolie fille du Perth*. Among the best of his early recordings are solos from *Don Giovanni* and G.F. Handel's *Jephtha*, the pioneering sets of *Faust* (under Thomas Beecham) and the first complete *Così fan tutte*, made at Glyndebourne in 1935. He later made many worthwhile recordings for HMV, including Handel arias and Nadir's Romance from *Les pêcheurs de perles*.

J. Jarrett: 'Heddle Nash', *Record Advertiser*, iii/5 (1972–3), 2–11
A. Blyth: 'Heddle Nash: a Centenary Note', *Opera*, xlv (1994), 670–73

Alan Blyth

Nast, Minnie

(*b* Karlsruhe, 10 Oct 1874; *d* Füssen, 20 June 1956). German soprano. She studied at the Karlsruhe Conservatory and made her début at Aachen in 1897. She sang in Dresden from 1898 to 1919 and then taught there until the bombing of the city in 1945. She toured the USA and Canada in 1905 and was also heard in Russia, the Netherlands and England, where, at Covent Garden, her principal roles were Aennchen, Marzelline and Eva. This was in the 1907 winter season; its tragic sequel, the shipwreck in which many of the company lost their lives, made her determined never to go overseas again. She sang mostly light and soubrette roles, specializing in W.A. Mozart and, in 1911, creating the part of Sophie in *Der Rosenkavalier*. Her technical accomplishment and clear tone are well preserved in some early solo recordings; she also recorded her original part in the trio from *Der Rosenkavalier* and sang Micaëla in the first recording of *Carmen*.

J.B. Steane

Natzka, Oscar

(*b* Matapara, 15 June 1912; *d* New York, 5 Nov 1951). New Zealand bass. He was at first a blacksmith, but in 1935 won a scholarship to study at Trinity College of Music in London with Albert Garcia. In 1938 he was engaged to sing at Covent Garden, where he made his début as Wagner in *Faust* and later created the leading role of De Fulke in George Lloyd's *The Serf*. He also sang in *Rigoletto* and *Die Meistersinger*. After war service with the Royal Canadian Navy, he returned to sing leading bass roles at Covent Garden in 1947, notably Sarastro; the next year he made his début at the New York City Opera as Sparafucile in *Rigoletto*. Thereafter he sang widely in North America in opera and concerts, but in 1951 he was taken ill during a performance of *Die Meistersinger* in New York, and 13 days later he died. Possessor of an outstandingly powerful and resonant bass voice, he made a number of recordings of ballads and operatic arias in the late 1930s and the 1940s.

A. Simpson and P. Downes: 'Oscar Natzka', *Southern Voices: International Opera Singers of New Zealand* (Auckland, 1992), 52–63

Peter Downes

Naudin, Emilio

(*b* Parma, 23 Oct 1823; *d* Bologna, 5 May 1890). Italian tenor. He studied in Milan, making his début in 1843 at Cremona in Giovanni Pacini's *Saffo*. After singing in all the major Italian theatres, in 1858 he made his London début at Drury Lane. From 1863 to 1875 he sang regularly at Covent Garden. His roles there included Ernesto, Nemorino, Edgardo, Pollione, Elvino, Fra Diavolo, Masaniello, Don Ottavio, Robert le diable, Danilowitz (*L'étoile du nord*) and Vasco da Gama, which he had created in *L'Africaine* at the Paris Opéra in 1865. His repertory also included Alfredo, Manrico, the Duke (*Rigoletto*) and the title role of *Don Carlos*, which he sang at the first London performance of Giuseppe Verdi's opera, in 1867. He sang Lohengrin in the English provinces (1875) and Tannhäuser in Moscow (1877).

Elizabeth Forbes

Navarrini [Navarini], Francesco

(*b* Cittadella, nr Padua, 26 Dec 1853; *d* Milan, 21 or 23 Feb 1923). Italian bass. He studied in Milan and made his début at Treviso (1878) in *Lucrezia Borgia*. After a season at Malta, he sang in various Italian cities, acquiring a large repertory and making his first appearance at La Scala in 1883 as Alvise in *La Gioconda*. His portrayal there of the Grand Inquisitor in the first Italian presentation of *Don Carlos* was highly praised, and he soon took his place as the theatre's principal lyric bass. He sang Lodovico in the première of *Otello* (1887) and was the Pogner of the production under Arturo Toscanini of *Die Meistersinger* (1898). Abroad he appeared in London, Paris and Madrid, and from 1894 to 1912 was a favourite in Russia. At Monte Carlo his singing of the Slander Song in *Il barbiere di Siviglia* was a highlight of the 1900 season, and in 1902 he visited the USA as a member of Pietro Mascagni's touring company. His virtues as a singer are demonstrated in his 16 recordings of 1907: a fine, sonorous voice, evenly produced, and exemplifying the traditional graces of the best Italian school.

P. Padoan: 'Francesco Navarrini', *Record Collector*, xl, 1995, 53–69

J.B. Steane

Negri, Anna [Antonia]

Possibly a sister of MARIA ROSA NEGRI.

Negri, Maria Caterina

(*b* Bologna; *fl* 1719–45). Italian contralto, sister of MARIA ROSA NEGRI. She studied under Antonio Pasi and made her first known stage appearance at Bologna in Giovanni Bononcini's *Trionfo di Camilla*, after which she sang in Modena (1720), Florence (1721), Livorno (1722), Milan (1722 and 1723), Faenza (1723) and Ferrara (1724). During the period 1724–7 she was attached to the company of Antonio Denzio at the theatre of Count Sporck in Prague, where she sang Alcina in Antonio Bioni's *Orlando furioso*. She appeared in three operas by Antonio Vivaldi in Venice in 1727–8, then found engagements at Forlì and Livorno (1729), Genoa (1730) and Naples (1733), where she appeared in Giovanni Pergolesi's *Lo frate 'nnamorato*. From November 1733 until summer 1737 she was a member of G.F. Handel's company in London, singing in 11 of his operas, the serenata *Parnasso in festa* and a number of pasticcios and oratorio revivals, including *Deborah* (Sisera), *Esther* (Mordecai) and probably *Il trionfo del tempo*. In 1735 she appeared in *Aminta, a Pastoral Opera* in Dublin. After leaving London she sang in Florence (1737–8), Lisbon (1740–1), Parma (1743), Rimini (1744) and Gorizia (1745). The parts Handel composed for her – Carilda in *Arianna in Creta*, Polinesso in *Ariodante*, Bradamante in *Alcina*, Irene in *Atalanta*, Tullius in *Arminio*, Arsace in *Berenice*, Philoctetes in *Oreste* and Cloride in *Parnasso in festa* – suggest a singer of moderate competence, though an occasional aria demands an agile technique. The compass is *a* to *e"*. She often played male roles.

She should not be confused with the singer Caterina Bassi Negri (*fl* 1734–46), known as Caterina Bassi before her marriage to the singer Giovanni Domenico Negri in 1739 or 1740.

Winton Dean, Daniel E. Freeman

Negri, Maria Rosa [Risack, Rosa Negri]

(*b* Bologna, *c*1715; *d* Dresden, 4 Aug 1760). Italian mezzo-soprano, sister of MARIA CATERINA NEGRI. She was engaged for Dresden in 1730 and accompanied her sister Caterina Negri to London in 1733. She sang in four Handel operas, all revivals, during the period 1733–6, and probably in the 1734 revival of *Deborah*. Handel wrote the part of Euterpe in *Parnasso in festa* for her, and probably the original role of Dalinda in *Ariodante*, although this was altered for soprano before performance. She was in Dublin with her sister in 1735–6 and in London in 1737 when she created Amantius in Handel's *Giustino*. In Dresden she sang in a series of operas by Johann Hasse, including *Cajo Fabricio* (1734), *La clemenza di Tito* (1738), *Arminio* (1745) and *La spartana generosa* (1747). In 1743 she appeared with her sister at Parma as Rosa Negri Risack. Handel appears to have thought little of her; the parts of Melo in *Sosarme* (1734), Eurilla in *Il pastor fido* (1734) and Morgana in *Alcina* (1736) were much shortened and simplified for her. Their compass is *a* to *f"*; her Hasse parts are more rewarding and call for expressiveness, fluent if limited coloratura and a compass *b* to *g"*.

An Anna or Antonia Negri, known as La Mestrina, she sang frequently at Venice (1728–42), as well as at Parma, Modena and elsewhere, and married the tenor Pellegrino Tomj. According to Moritz Fürstenau she was a sister of Maria Rosa and was engaged for Dresden at the same time, but no parts sung by her at Dresden have been discovered, and there may be confusion with another singer.

Winton Dean

Negrini (Villa), Carlo

(*b* Piacenza, 24 June 1826; *d* Naples, 14 March 1865). Italian tenor. He studied in Milan, then sang in the La Scala chorus, making his début as a soloist in 1847 as Jacopo (*I due Foscari*). After singing in Como and Constantinople, in 1850 he returned to La Scala as Oronte (*I Lombardi*). In 1852 he sang Pollione and Ernani at Covent Garden. He created Gabriele Adorno in *Simon Boccanegra* (1857) and Glauco in Errico Petrella's *Jone* (1858), both at La Scala, and sang throughout Italy. His roles included Gioachino Rossini's Otello, Poliuto, John of Leyden, Rodolfo (*Luisa Miller*), Manrico and Riccardo (*Ballo*). FRANCESCO MERLI was his pupil.

Elizabeth Forbes

Neidlinger, Gustav

(*b* Mainz, 21 March 1910; *d* Bad Ems, 26 Dec 1991). German bass-baritone. He studied in Frankfurt with Otto Rottsieper and made his début in 1931 at Mainz, where he remained until 1934, taking supporting *buffo* bass roles. After an engagement in Plauen (1934–6) he joined the Hamburg Staatsoper, where his roles included Kecal, Bartolo and van Bett in *Zar und Zimmermann*. In 1950 he moved to the Württembergisches Staatsoper, Stuttgart, where his roles included Leporello, Iago, Falstaff, Ochs, Faninal, Barak and Kaspar in Werner Egk's *Der Zaubergeige*. He appeared at Bayreuth from 1952 to 1975 as Alberich, Kurwenal, Klingsor, the Nightwatchman, Hans Sachs and Telramund. He sang with the Stuttgart company at the Royal Festival Hall, London, in 1955 as Pizarro and Kurwenal, and at the 1958 Edinburgh Festival as Lysiart (*Euryanthe*) and Kurwenal. In 1963 he made his Covent Garden début as Telramund. He did not sing in New York until 1972, when he appeared at the Metropolitan as Alberich. He was a guest at most European opera houses during the 1950s and 60s, appearing regularly at the Vienna Staatsoper from 1956. His Alberich, which is preserved in many Bayreuth recordings as well as Georg Solti's studio *Ring*, was sung with a smoothness and even beauty of tone quite unusual in the part.

Harold Rosenthal/R

Nelepp, Georgy

(*b* Bobruika, Ukraine, 20 April 1904; *d* Moscow, 18 June 1957). Russian tenor. He studied at the Leningrad Conservatory and made his début, as Lensky, with the Kirov in 1930, remaining with the company until 1944. In that year he moved to the Bol'shoy, where he had his most significant success. Nelepp possessed a lyric-dramatic tenor capable of an amazing range and intensity of expression, making him an ideal exponent of such roles as Florestan, Gustavus III, Manrico, Radames, Don José, Sobinin (*A Life for the Tsar*), Dmitry (*Boris Godunov*), Golitsïn (*Khovanshchina*), Yury (*The Enchantress*), Hermann, Andrey (*Mazepa*) and Sadko, several of which he recorded. He sang in approximately 20 complete opera sets, among which his agonized portrayal of the obsessive Hermann in the Melodiya recording of *The Queen of Spades* is an unrivalled achievement.

Alan Blyth

Nelli, Herva

(*b* Florence, 1909; *d* Sharon, CT, 31 May 1994). American soprano of Italian birth. She was taken by her parents to the USA when she was 12 and trained at Pittsburgh. Her earliest appearances were with the Salmaggi Company at the Brooklyn Academy

in 1946, where she sang Norma, Leonora (*Il trovatore*) and Aida. Then she sang with La Scala company of Philadelphia (1946–7), adding Santuzza and Gioconda to her repertory. She was introduced to Arturo Toscanini by LICIA ALBANESE and he immediately cast her as Desdemona for a concert performance of *Otello*. This was recorded, as were her subsequent performances with Toscanini in *Aida*, *Falstaff* (Alice Ford), *Un ballo in maschera* and Verdi's *Requiem*. Nelli made her Metropolitan début, as Aida, in 1953 and appeared there until 1961. She also appeared in Verdi roles at San Francisco, New Orleans and Chicago. In 1948 she sang Gioconda in Genoa and Aida at La Scala, following her appearance there with Toscanini in a concert to mark the reopening of the house. She possessed a firm, technically secure, if not strikingly individual, spinto voice; under Toscanini's tutelage, her interpretations were often shapely and eloquent.

Alan Blyth

Németh, Maria

(*b* Körmend, 13 March 1897; *d* Vienna, 28 Dec 1967). Hungarian soprano. She studied in Budapest and Naples, with Giannina Russ in Milan and with Felice Kaschovska. She made her début in Budapest in 1923 as Sulamith (*Die Königin von Saba*). From 1924 to 1946 she was a member of the Vienna Staatsoper, where her voice and temperament enabled her to sing Giacomo Puccini, Giuseppe Verdi, W.A. Mozart and Richard Wagner with equal success. She was considered a superb Turandot, a role she sang at Covent Garden in 1931. She also appeared in Italy, and as Donna Anna at the Salzburg Festival. Her last appearance was as Santuzza in 1946. Her recordings show the inherent beauty of her voice and the security of her technique, most notably in the roles of Sulamith, Turandot and Leonora in *La forza del destino*.

Harold Rosenthal/Alan Blyth

Nes, Jard van

(*b* Zwolle, 15 June 1948). Dutch mezzo-soprano. She studied at the conservatory in The Hague with Herman Woltman and made her concert début in 1975 at the Holland Festival, where she later created the title role in Theo Loevendie's *Naima* (1985). She made her opera début at the Netherlands Opera as Bertarido (*Rodelinda*) in 1983, and her other operatic roles included Magdalene (*Die Meistersinger*) and Brangäne (*Tristan und Isolde*). At her Salzburg Festival début in 1990 she sang the Third Lady in *Die Zauberflöte*, conducted by Georg Solti, but her

Corrado, console di Milano and *La sonnambula* (1860). From 1862 to 1869 he appeared at the Théâtre Italien, Paris, and he made his Covent Garden début (under the pseudonym Nicolini) in 1866, singing opposite Patti in *Lucia di Lammermoor*, but without great success. In 1871 he returned to London to sing in *Faust* and *Robert le diable* at Drury Lane, and from 1872 to 1884 he was engaged every season at Covent Garden. He appeared in many roles, including Pery in Carlos Gomes's *Il guarany* (1872), Lohengrin (1875), Radamès in *Aida* (1876) and Fabio in Jules Cohen's *Estella* (1880), all first London performances, and he sang Celio at the première of Charles Ferdinand Lenepveu's *Velléda* (1882). His voice had a wide vibrato that some of his contemporaries found distressing, but his fine stage presence and intense acting were particularly appreciated in such roles as Charles Gounod's Faust and Romeo. He accompanied Patti on tours of Europe (to Vienna, Milan, Brussels, Berlin, Hamburg and other cities), and of the USA and South America. In 1886 he became her second husband, and that year made his final stage appearance, as Almaviva in *Il barbiere di Siviglia* at Drury Lane, though he continued to sing in concerts for some time.

H. Klein: *The Reign of Patti* (London, 1920)

Elizabeth Forbes

Nielsen, Alice

(*b* Nashville, TN, 7 June 1868 or 1876; *d* New York, 8 March 1943). American soprano. Her year of birth is ordinarily given as 1876, but according to her death record, she died at the age of 74. She began as a singer in church choirs, and made her professional début in 1893 with the Pike Opera Company in Oakland, California. She was then engaged to sing at the Tivoli Theatre in San Francisco, where she soon became a favourite. Henry Clay Barnabee heard her sing, and offered her a position with what was then America's leading light opera company, the Bostonians. She spent two years with the ensemble, singing such roles as Maid Marian in Reginald De Koven and H.B. Smith's *Robin Hood* and Yvonne in Victor Herbert's *The Serenade*. After she left the troupe (taking with her several of its leading players and precipitating its demise), she starred in two operettas which Herbert composed especially for her, *The Fortune Teller* (1898; also in London, 1901) and *The Singing Girl* (1899). In 1902 she abandoned the popular musical stage to study opera in Rome. The following year she made her European début in Naples as Marguerite in Charles Gounod's *Faust*. Success in London with *The Fortune Teller* had brought her to the notice of the impresario Henry Russell, who

introduced her to Covent Garden audiences in 1904. She was a 'fresh and charming' Zerlina at her début there in *Don Giovanni*; she also sang Mimì to Caruso's Rodolfo and Gilda to Victor Maurel's Rigoletto, as well as Susanna and Micaëla. She sang at the S Carlo, Naples, before returning in 1905 to New York, where her appearances in *Don Pasquale* at the Casino Theatre failed to impress. With Henry Russell's San Carlo Opera Company she sang in *Don Pasquale* in a gruelling tour of the USA. In 1909 she joined the newly formed Boston Opera Company, under the direction of Russell, and remained with them as principal lyric soprano until 1914. By World War I her popularity had waned, and she attempted a return to Broadway in Rudolf Friml's *Kitty Darlin'* (1917). The critical consensus was that her small, pure voice and youthful appeal had faded; she later played small parts in a few non-musicals, then quietly retired.

Gerald Bordman/R

Nielsen, Inga

(*b* Holbaek, 2 June 1946; *d* Copenhagen, 10 Feb 2008). Danish soprano. After studying in Vienna and Stuttgart, she made her début in 1971 at Gelsenkirchen; engagements followed at Münster, Berne and Frankfurt. She sang a flowermaiden at Bayreuth (1979); her roles at this period included Zerlina, Blonde, Ilia, Norina, Nannetta and Aennchen. She sang Donna Clara in Alexander Zemlinsky's *Der Zwerg* with the Hamburg Staatsoper at Edinburgh in 1983, later recording the role, and created Minette in H.W. Henze's *The English Cat* at Schwetzingen, repeating the role in the French and American premières of the opera in Paris and Santa Fe (1985). Nielsen sang Amenaide (*Tancredi*) at Wexford (1986), Konstanze at Salzburg and for her Covent Garden début (1987), Fiordiligi at Strasbourg (1989) and Christine (*Intermezzo*) at Geneva (1991). As her pure-toned, agile soprano grew in volume, she took on such roles as Agathe, Salome, the Marschallin, Ursula (*Mathis der Maler*), which she sang at Covent Garden in 1995, Elsa, which she first sang at Hamburg in 1998 and the Empress (*Die Frau ohne Schatten*), which she performed at La Scala in 1999. Nielsen was equally active as a concert singer, and recorded works including Bach cantatas and his *St John Passion*, Robert Schumann's *Der Rose Pilgerfahrt* and Gustav Mahler's Eighth Symphony. Her operatic recordings include Leonore and Salome, both widely acclaimed for their combination of vocal finesse and dramatic conviction, in addition to roles in W.A. Mozart's *Il re pastore* and Peter Heise's *King and Marshall*.

Elizabeth Forbes

Niemann, Albert

(*b* Erxleben, nr Magdeburg, 15 Jan 1831; *d* Berlin, 13 Jan 1917). German tenor. He made his début in 1849 at Dessau, singing small roles and chorus parts. After studying with Friedrich Schneider and Albert Nusch, in 1852 he was engaged at Halle. Two years later he moved to Hanover, where the king paid for him to study further with GILBERT DUPREZ in Paris. Having first sung Tannhäuser (at Insterburg) in 1854, Lohengrin in 1855 and Rienzi in 1859, he was chosen by Richard Wagner to sing in the first Paris performance of *Tannhäuser*. He was granted a year's leave of absence from Hanover, his contract with the Paris Opéra running from 1 September 1860 to 31 May 1861 at a salary of 6000 francs a month. After the fiasco of the first (13 March 1861) and two subsequent performances, Wagner withdrew his score and Niemann returned to Hanover.

In 1864 Niemann made a very successful guest appearance in Munich, singing Tannhäuser, Lohengrin, Faust and Manrico (*Il trovatore*). From 1866 until his retirement in 1889, he was engaged in Berlin, where he sang in the first local performances of *Die Meistersinger* (1870), *Aida* (1874) and *Tristan und Isolde* (1876), also taking part in a gala performance of Gaspare Spontini's *Olympie* (1879). He created the role of Siegmund in the 1870 première of *Die Walküre* at Munich and also sang it during the first complete *Ring* cycle at Bayreuth (1876) and in the first cycle given in London, at Her Majesty's Theatre (1882). It was also as Siegmund that he made his New York début at the Metropolitan (1886). During his two seasons there he sang in the first New York performances of *Tristan und Isolde* (1886), Gaspare Spontini's *Fernand Cortez* (1888), and *Götterdämmerung* (1888). His last appearance in Berlin was as Florestan (*Fidelio*) in 1888.

Of immense physical stature, Niemann was unrivalled as Siegmund and Tristan during his lifetime. His powerful, heroic tenor voice could express, according to a contemporary, not only 'love and hate, sorrow and joy, pain and delight, but also anger, despair, scorn, derision and contempt'.

Elizabeth Forbes

Nilsson [Svennsson], (Märta) Birgit

(*b* Västra Karup, 17 May 1918; *d* Västra Karup, 25 Dec 2005). Swedish soprano. She studied at the Swedish Royal Academy of Music, Stockholm, where her teachers included JOSEPH HISLOP. In 1946 she made her début at the Swedish Royal Opera, Stockholm, as Agathe (*Der Freischütz*), later singing Leonore, Lady Macbeth, the Marschallin, Sieglinde, Donna Anna, Venus, Senta, Aida, Tosca

Birgit Nilsson as Isolde in 'Tristan und Isolde' (Wagner)

and Lisa (*The Queen of Spades*). In 1951 she sang Electra (*Idomeneo*) at Glyndebourne, creating a stir with her keen-edged, forthright singing. During the 1954–5 season she sang her first *Götterdämmerung* Brünnhilde and Salome at Stockholm and made her Munich début as Brünnhilde in the complete *Ring*. Also in 1954 she first appeared in Vienna and, as Elsa, began her long association with Bayreuth, returning (1957–70) as Isolde, Sieglinde and Brünnhilde. In particular, her interpretation of Isolde in Wieland Wagner's 1966 production was of searing vocal and dramatic power. She first sang at Covent Garden in the 1957 *Ring*, returning as Isolde, Amelia (*Un ballo in maschera*), with the Swedish Royal Opera in 1960), Richard Strauss's Electra, Turandot and Leonore. She made her American début at San Francisco in 1956, and she first sang at the Metropolitan in 1959 as Isolde. Her only new role in the 1970s was the Dyer's Wife (*Die Frau ohne Schatten*), which she sang at Stockholm in 1975.

Nilsson was generally considered the finest Wagnerian soprano of her day. Her voice was even throughout its range, pure in sound and perfect in intonation with a free ringing top; its size was phenomenal. Her dramatic abilities were considerable. Electra was possibly her finest achievement, although the sheer power and opulence of her voice, coupled with a certain coolness, made her an ideal Turandot. In both of these, as well as in Wagnerian roles, her phenomenal stamina was perfectly suited to the rigorous demands of the music. Her many recordings include Brünnhilde and Isolde, in both of which she was unrivalled, as well as the title roles in *Turandot* and *Elektra*; moreover, even her readings of the roles for which she was less renowned, such as Leonore, Aida and Tosca, have had few if any equals since. Her second recording of Isolde (1966, Bayreuth) and her Electra remain perhaps her most thrilling achievements.

W. Jefferies: 'Birgit Nilsson', *Opera*, xi (1960), 607–12

W. Weaver: 'The Prima Donna at Work: Die Nilsson and La Nilsson', *HiFi/MusAm*, xv/2 (1965), 48–51, 119

A. Blyth: 'Birgit Nilsson', *Gramophone*, xlvii (1969–70), 1123

J. Young: 'Skanska: Birgit Nilsson on Home Ground', *ON*, xxxix/15 (1974–5), 48–51

B. Nilsson: *Mina minnesbilder* (Stockholm, 1977; Eng. trans., 1981, as *My Memoirs in Pictures*)

S. Wadsworth: 'And Still Champ…Birgit Nilsson Revisited', *ON*, xliv/13 (1979–80), 8–12, 35

Harold Rosenthal/Alan Blyth

Nilsson, Christine [Kristina Törnerhjelm]

(*b* Sjöabol, nr Växjö, 20 Aug 1843; *d* Stockholm, 22 Nov 1921). Swedish soprano. She studied with Franz Berwald in Stockholm, where she sang publicly from an early age, and then with P.F. Wartel, N.-J.-J. Masset and Enrico Delle Sedie in Paris. Her stage début was in 1864 as Violetta in *La traviata* at the Théâtre Lyrique, where she sang until 1867. She made her London début in 1864 at Her Majesty's Theatre as Violetta, also appearing as Marguerite in *Faust*. Although contracted to sing in the first performance of Georges Bizet's *La jolie fille de Perth* at the Théâtre Lyrique, she transferred instead to the Opéra and sang Ophelia at the première of Ambroise Thomas' *Hamlet* (1868) and Marguerite in the Opéra's first performance of *Faust* (1869).

She made her Covent Garden début in 1869 in the title role of *Lucia di Lammermoor*, and during the season also sang in the first London performance of *Hamlet*. In 1870 she sang in Julius Benedict's oratorio *The Legend of St Cecilia* for her benefit at the Paris Opéra, was London's first Mignon at Drury Lane and embarked on a tour of the USA managed by Maurice Strakosch. She sang in the first New York performance of *Mignon* at the Academy of Music (1871).

At Drury Lane Nilsson appeared in Mozart, Meyerbeer, Wagner and Verdi roles and took part in the first performance (sung in Italian) of Michael Balfe's posthumous opera *The Talisman* (1874). At Her Majesty's Theatre she sang in the first London performance of Arrigo Boito's *Mefistofele* (1880). She travelled extensively, visiting St Petersburg and Moscow several times between 1872 and 1875, and her Brussels début was on 3 April 1875, when she

sang Ophelia at the Théâtre de la Monnaie. In 1877 she was heard in Vienna and in 1878 at the Court Theatre, Munich.

Returning to New York in 1883 for the opening season of the Metropolitan Opera House, she sang Marguerite in the inaugural performance of *Faust* (22 October) and the title role in the first local performance of Amilcare Ponchielli's *La Gioconda* (20 December), and shortly afterwards she retired from the stage. Her voice, though not large, was pure and brilliant in timbre, immensely flexible and perfectly even in scale for two and a half octaves up to top *E*. Ophelia, Marguerite and Mignon were probably her finest roles, while an attractive appearance and a graceful stage personality were great assets in such parts as Violetta. Berwald wrote his opera *Drottningen av Golconda* ('The Queen of Golconda') for her, but it was not performed until many years after her death.

H. Headland: *Christine Nilsson: the Songbird of the North* (Rock Island, IL, 1943)

Elizabeth Forbes

Nimsgern, Siegmund

(*b* St Wendel, Saarland, 14 Jan 1940). German bass-baritone. He studied with Sibylle Fuchs in Saarbrücken, where he made his début in 1967 as Lionel in P.I. Tchaikovsky's *The Maid of Orléans* and sang in George Enescu's *Oedipe* (1971). In 1972 he was engaged at the Deutsche Oper am Rhein, and the following year made his début at Covent Garden as Amfortas. He sang Telramund at the 1976 Salzburg Easter Festival and made his Metropolitan début in 1978 as Pizarro, returning in 1981 as John the Baptist (*Salome*). His repertory also included Don Giovanni, William Tell, Caspar, Macbeth, Boccanegra, Amonasro, Iago, Escamillo and Scarpia, which he first sang in Chicago (1982). His malign Pizarro was a particularly vivid interpretation, as can be heard on his recording with Kurt Masur. He excelled in Richard Strauss (Barak, Kunrad in *Feuersnot*, Mandryka and Altair in *Die ägyptische Helena*), while his Wagner roles included Gunther, Alberich, Klingsor (both of which he recorded), Kurwenal, the Dutchman and Wotan, which he sang at Bayreuth (1983–5). His voice was keenly focussed and finely projected, while his scrupulous musicianship made him a noted interpreter of such 20th-century roles as Béla Bartók's Bluebeard (of which he made a commanding recording with Pierre Boulez) and Sergey Prokofiev's Ruprecht (*The Fiery Angel*). Nimsgern's evenness of production and firm legato were also admired in the concert repertory, especially in J.S. Bach, and he made recordings of the *Christmas Oratorio*, the *St Matthew Passion* and several cantatas.

Elizabeth Forbes

Nissen, Hans Hermann

(*b* Zippnow, nr Marienwerder [now Kwidzyn], 20 May 1893; *d* Munich, 28 March 1980). German bass-baritone. He studied in Berlin and later in England with Manuel Garcia, and made his début in 1924 at the Grosse Volksoper, Berlin. The next year he was engaged by the Staatsoper in Munich, where he remained until 1967. He sang Wotan and Hans Sachs at Covent Garden in 1928 and 1934, and appeared in the Wagnerian repertory at Chicago (1930–32) and the Metropolitan (1938–9). He sang Hans Sachs at Salzburg in 1936–7 and at Bayreuth in 1943, and made guest appearances in Paris, Milan, Vienna, Berlin and elsewhere. In addition to Wagner roles, his repertory included Renato, Amonasro, Barak, Borromeo (*Palestrina*) and Orestes. Although his voice was not large, it was firm and evenly produced, and was used with great artistry and refinement. Among his recordings is a warm account of Hans Sachs in Karl Böhm's 1938 recording of Act 3 of *Die Meistersinger*.

Harold Rosenthal/Alan Blyth

Nixon, Marni [McEathron, Margaret Nixon]

(*b* Altadena, CA, 22 Feb 1930). American soprano. After studying singing and opera with Carl Ebert, Jan Popper, Boris Goldovsky and Sarah Caldwell, She embarked on a varied career, involving film and musical comedy as well as opera and concerts. She has appeared extensively on American television, dubbed the singing voices of film actresses in *The King and I*, *West Side Story* and *My Fair Lady*, and acted in several commercial stage ventures. Her light, flexible, wide-ranging soprano and uncanny accuracy and musicianship have made her valuable in more classical ventures, and have contributed to her success in works by Anton Webern, Igor Stravinsky, Charles Ives, Paul Hindemith and Alexander Goehr, many of which she has recorded. Her opera repertory includes Zerbinetta (*Ariadne auf Naxos*), W.A. Mozart's Susanna, Blonde and Constanze, Violetta, La Périchole and Philine (*Mignon*), performed at Los Angeles, Seattle, San Francisco and Tanglewood. In addition to giving recitals, she has appeared with orchestras in New York (under Leonard Bernstein), Los Angeles, Cleveland, Toronto, London and Israel. She has taught at the California Institute of Arts (1969–71)

and joined the faculty of the Music Academy of the West, Santa Barbara, in 1980.

Martin Bernheimer/R

Noble, Dennis (William)

(*b* Bristol, 25 Sept 1899; *d* Jávea, Alicante, Spain, 14 March 1966). English baritone. He studied in London with DINH GILLY before making his début with the British National Opera Company in 1924 as Silvio. He was soon elevated to the international seasons at Covent Garden, where he appeared regularly until 1939. His roles included both Figaros, Rigoletto, Germont (to PONSELLE's Violetta), Tonio, Valentin and a much-praised Amonasro. He also sang leading parts in the premières of four operas by British composers: Eugene Goossens's *Judith* and *Don Juan de Mañara*, Albert Coates's *Pickwick* (Sam Weller) and George Lloyd's *The Serf*. In the 1947–8 season he reappeared at Covent Garden as Jules Massenet's Lescaut and Escamillo. He also appeared in New York, Cleveland, Brussels, Rome and elsewhere in Italy. He was the first, and markedly effective, soloist in William Walton's *Belshazzar's Feast*, and was an alternately fiery and dejected exponent of Elijah. His firm, easily produced tone, emphasis on a consistently true line and gift for placing words naturally on it were enhanced by his excellent stage presence. He was equally adept at projecting comedy, heroism, pathos and tragedy as his many recordings, made for Columbia and HMV, amply confirm. Most notable among them are the extracts from *Rigoletto* and *La traviata*, arias from *Faust* and *Pagliacci* and solos from *Elijah*, all of which show Noble's exemplary articulation and definition of tone and text.

Alan Blyth

Noël, Victoire.

See STOLZ, ROSINE.

Noni, Alda

(*b* Trieste, 30 April 1916). Italian soprano. She studied in Trieste and Vienna, making her operatic début as Rosina at Ljubljana in 1937. After performances at Zagreb, Belgrade and Trieste, she joined the Vienna Staatsoper in 1942 and sang such roles as Despina, Norina, Gilda, Oscar and Zerbinetta, which she recorded in 1944 in a performance of *Ariadne auf Naxos* in honour of Richard Strauss's 80th birthday. In 1946 she made her London début at the Cambridge Theatre as Norina. She appeared at La Scala from 1949 to 1953, making her début as Carolina (*Il matrimonio segreto*) and also singing Armidoro (Niccolò Piccinni's *La buona figliuola*), Papagena, Zerlina and Nannetta during the 1950 visit of La Scala to Covent Garden. With Glyndebourne Opera at the 1949 Edinburgh Festival she sang Oscar, and at Glyndebourne itself (1950–54) Blonde, Despina and Clorinda (*La Cenerentola*), which she recorded. Her other recordings include Adina and an irresistibly vital Norina. She excelled in comic roles and her repertory, which included operas by Luigi Cherubini, Daniel Auber and Ermanno Wolf-Ferrari, displayed to advantage her limpid and attractive coloratura soprano.

Harold Rosenthal/Alan Blyth

Nordica [Norton], Lillian [Lilian]

(*b* Farmington, ME, 12 May 1857; *d* Batavia, Java [now Jakarta, Indonesia], 10 May 1914). American soprano. She studied with John O'Neill at the New England Conservatory, graduating in 1876. Engaged by Patrick Gilmore, she made her concert début with his band (September 1876), then toured America – and, in 1878, Europe – with the ensemble; her London début was at the Crystal Palace (21 May 1878). She left Gilmore to study with Antonio Sangiovanni in Milan; he coined her stage name and arranged for her operatic débuts – as Donna Elvira in *Don Giovanni* (Teatro Manzoni, Milan, March 1879) and as Violetta (Teatro Guillaume, Brescia, April 1879). She sang in St Petersburg (1880–82) and continued summertime studies in Paris with GIOVANNI SBRIGLIA; she also studied Marguerite (*Faust*) and Ophelia (*Hamlet*) with Charles Gounod and Ambroise Thomas, making her Paris Opéra début in the former role (22 July 1882). In 1882 she married Frederick Gower, who disappeared three years later in the midst of their divorce proceedings. Nordica's American operatic début, as Lillian Norton-Gower, was at the New York Academy of Music as Marguerite (26 November 1883). It marked the beginning of a long association with James Mapleson, with whose company she also made her Covent Garden début (12 March 1887).

Nordica subsequently sang at Drury Lane (1887), Covent Garden (1888–93) and the Metropolitan Opera, where she made her début as Leonora in *Il trovatore* (27 March 1890). In the 1890s she turned her attention to the music of Richard Wagner. After extensive coaching by Cosima Wagner, she sang Elsa in the first production of *Lohengrin* at Bayreuth in 1894. At the height of her Metropolitan Opera career (1893–1907) she was known primarily as a Wagnerian. In 1896 she married a Hungarian tenor, Zoltan Dome, whom she divorced in 1904. Between 1897 and 1908 she sang at the Metropolitan and with the Damrosch-Ellis Company (1897–8), at Covent Garden (1898, 1899, 1902), and with Oscar Hammerstein's Manhattan Opera Company (1907–8). From 1908 Nordica devoted herself to concert performances; her final appearance with the Metropolitan was in December 1909. That year she married George Washington Young; they lived in Ardsley-on-the-Hudson, New York. Nordica's final operatic appearance was in Boston (March 1913); shortly afterwards she embarked on a world concert tour. In December the steamer on which she was travelling struck a reef off New Guinea; Nordica contracted pneumonia, from which she later died.

Although not a strong actress, Nordica had a rich voice and a remarkable coloratura range. She knew 40 operatic roles in English, Italian, German, French and Russian. A resolute and shrewd – but also generally good-natured – individual, she owed her stature as a great Wagnerian soprano to hard work, constant study and determination. Late in her career she became a strong proponent of opera in English; she was also an ardent suffragist and had an unfulfilled dream of establishing a Bayreuth-like American Institute for Music.

L. Nordica: *Lilian Nordica's Hints to Singers* (New York, 1923)

I. Glackens: *Yankee Diva: Lillian Nordica* (New York, 1963)

Katherine K. Preston

Norena, Eidé [Hansen-Eidé (neé Hansen), Kaja Andrea Karoline]

(*b* Horton, nr Oslo, 26 April 1884; *d* Lausanne, 19 Nov 1968). Norwegian soprano. She studied with ELLEN GULBRANSON in Oslo, where she made her début as Cupid (C.W. Gluck's *Orfeo*) in 1907. She sang at the Nationale Theater in Oslo (1908–18) and then at the Swedish Royal Opera, Stockholm; in 1924 she was engaged to sing Gilda at La Scala. She first appeared at Covent Garden in 1924 and was a regular visitor to London where her Desdemona (1937) was especially distinguished. At the Paris Opéra (1925–37), her roles included the Queen of Shemakha (*The Golden Cockerel*), Marguerite de Valois (*Les Huguenots*), Mathilde (*Guillaume Tell*) and Ophelia (*Hamlet*). Norena sang at the Metropolitan (1933–8), making her début as Mimì, and also in Vichy and Monte Carlo, where her Marguerite de Valois and Juliette were much admired. In Amsterdam she sang the three heroines of *Les contes d'Hoffmann*. Her lovely voice, sincere feeling and restrained, impeccable style are preserved on recordings of her Violetta, Desdemona, Marguerite de Valois and Juliette.

Harold Rosenthal/Alan Blyth

Norman, Jessye

(*b* Augusta, GA, 15 Sept 1945). American soprano. She studied at Howard University, the Peabody Conservatory and the University of Michigan (with, among others, Pierre Bernac and Elizabeth Mannion). She won the Munich International Music Competition in 1968 and made her operatic début in 1969 at the Deutsche Oper, Berlin, as Elisabeth (*Tannhäuser*), later appearing there as Countess Almaviva. Further engagements in Europe included Aida at La Scala and Cassandra (*Les Troyens*) at Covent Garden, both in 1972. The following year she returned to Covent Garden as Elisabeth. For her American stage début she sang Jocasta in Igor Stravinsky's *Oedipus rex* and Henry Purcell's Dido with the Opera Company of Philadelphia (1982); she appeared first at the Metropolitan Opera in 1983, once again as Cassandra and later as Dido in *Les Troyens*. Other roles she has sung include C.W. Gluck's Alcestis, Strauss's Ariadne, Madame Lidoine (*Dialogues des Carmélites*), the Woman (*Erwartung*), Emilia Marty (*The Makropulos Affair*), Béla Bartók's Judith, and Richard Wagner's Kundry and Sieglinde.

Norman has a commanding stage presence; her particular distinction lies in her ability to project drama through her voice. Her opulent and dark-hued soprano is richly vibrant in the lower and middle registers, if less free at the top; although her extraordinary vocal resources are not always perfectly controlled, her best singing reveals uncommon refinement of nuance and dynamic variety. Her operatic recordings include Countess Almaviva, Joseph Haydn's Rosina (*La vera costanza*) and Armida, Leonore, Euryanthe, Giuseppe Verdi's Giulietta (*Un giorno di regno*) and Medora (*Il corsaro*), Carmen, Ariadne, Salome and Jacques Offenbach's Giulietta and Helen. Norman also appeared in jazz concerts including, in 1982 her own show *A Great Day in the Morning*. As her many discs reveal, she is also a penetrating interpreter of lieder and *mélodies*, at her finest in the broader canvases of Gustav Mahler, Richard Strauss (whose *Vier letzte Lieder* she has recorded with distinction) and Claude Debussy.

'Jessye Norman Talks to John Greenhalgh', *Music and Musicians*, xxvii/12 (1979), 14–15

E. Southern: *Biographical Dictionary of Afro-American and African Musicians* (Westport, CT, 1982)

M. Mayer: 'Double Header: Jessye Norman in her Met Debut Season', *ON*, xlviii/11 (1983–4), 8–11

Martin Bernheimer/Alan Blyth

Norton, Lilian.

See NORDICA, LILLIAN.

Nourrit, Adolphe

(*b* Montpellier, 3 March 1802; *d* Naples, 8 March 1839). French tenor, son of Louis Nourrit. He studied with the elder MANUEL GARCÍA for 18 months, initially against his father's wishes, then made his début at the Opéra in 1821 as Pylades in *Iphigénie en Tauride*. He was coached intensively by Gioachino Rossini and created the roles of Néocles in *Le siège de Corinthe*, Count Ory, Aménophis in *Moïse et Pharaon* and Arnold in *Guillaume Tell*. Among the other roles he created were Masaniello (*La muette de Portici*), Robert (*Robert le diable*, see colour plate 6), Eléazar (*La Juive*) and Raoul (*Les Huguenots*). From December 1826, when he succeeded his father as first tenor at the Opéra, until his resignation in October 1836, he created the principal tenor roles in all major new productions, generating an entire repertory for the acting tenor. His success in *Moïse* and *Le siège de Corinthe* was so great that in 1827 he was appointed *professeur de déclamation pour la tragédie lyrique* at the Conservatoire, where his most famous student was the dramatic soprano CORNÉLIE FALCON.

Moïse marked a turning-point in singing at the Opéra, as the singers turned to the more open-voiced, italianate production favoured by Rossini. Here, as in all the scores written for Nourrit, the dynamics and the thickness of the orchestration below his voice part indicate that he could not have been singing in falsetto in his upper register (as has often been stated). He had a mellow, powerful voice that extended to e''. The highest he ever sang in public was d''. As Nourrit's status at the Opéra increased, so did his influence upon new productions. His advice and collaboration was sought by composers; he wrote the words of Eléazar's aria 'Rachel, quand du Seigneur' and insisted that Giacomo Meyerbeer rework the love-duet climax of Act 4 of *Les Huguenots* until it met with his approval. He also wrote four ballet scenarios including *La Sylphide* (1832), whose combination of magic and Scottian realism was inspired by *Robert le diable*. In addition, he was concerned more broadly with the social aspects of singing, particularly with the missionary role of the performer. In the early 1830s he was involved with the ideas of the Saint-Simonians, and after his retirement dreamed of founding a grand *opéra populaire* which would introduce opera to the masses.

About 1 October 1836, Charles Duponchel engaged Gilbert Duprez as joint first tenor at the Opéra. Nourrit accepted this arrangement in case he should fall ill (among other reasons). He sang *Guillaume Tell* superbly with Duprez in the audience on 5 October. On 10 October, during *La muette de Portici*, with Duprez again in the house, Nourrit suddenly went hoarse. After the performance Hector Berlioz and George Osborne walked the tenor up and down the boulevards as he despaired and talked of suicide; on 14 October he resigned from the Opéra. During this time he continued to enjoy success as a salon performer; he was the first to introduce Franz Schubert's lieder to Parisian audiences at the celebrated soirées organized by Franz Liszt, Chrétien Urhan and Alexandre Batta at the Salons d'Erard in 1837. The intimacy of the salon apparently suited him particularly well; criticized for a weak voice, he showed great nuance of feeling and dramatic range. His farewell performance from the Opéra was on 1 April 1837. He immediately set out to perform in the provinces, but a liver condition (possibly the result of alcoholism) and its effects on his singing forced him to cut short his tours. While listening to Duprez at the Opéra, on 22 November 1837, he decided to go to Italy in the hope of succeeding GIOVANNI RUBINI on his retirement, and left Paris in December 1837.

The following March he began to study in Naples with Gaetano Donizetti. He worked to eradicate nasal resonance, but as a result lost his head voice. He wanted Donizetti to write the opera for his Naples début, *Poliuto*; when it was forbidden because of its Christian subject matter, Nourrit felt betrayed. His wife, arriving in July 1838, was shocked at the sound of his voice and his thinness; he was being leeched regularly and was constantly hoarse. But his Naples début in Saverio Mercadante's *Il giuramento* (14 November 1838) was a success. As his liver disease advanced, his mental health deteriorated and his memory began to fail. On 7 March 1839 he sang at a benefit concert, was disappointed in his performance and upset by the favourable reaction of the audience. The following morning, he jumped to his death from the Hotel Barbaia.

Nourrit's brother, the tenor Auguste Nourrit (1808–53), was for some time theatre director at The Hague, Amsterdam and Brussels, and took over Adolphe's post at the Conservatoire after his death.

Evan Walker/Sarah Hibberd

Novacek, Stephanie

(*b* Iowa City, 31 Aug 1970). American mezzo-soprano. After studies at Cornell College (Iowa) and the University of Illinois, she became a member of the Houston Grand Opera Studio (1996–9). At Houston she created the role of Maria Callas in Michael Daugherty's *Jackie O* (1997) and the following year won acclaim as Jo in the world première of Mark Adamo's *Little Women*. Novacek had made her Houston Grand Opera début as the Page in

Salome in 1997, and has since sung roles for the company including Carmen, Maddalena (*Rigoletto*), Siebel (*Faust*) and Olga (*Yevgeny Onegin*). She is also a noted interpreter of Baroque opera. She sang Dido and the Sorceress in Mark Morris's production of *Dido and Aeneas* at the Brooklyn Academy of Music (1998) and has appeared in the title roles of M.-A. Charpentier's *Médée* and Jean-Baptiste Lully's *Armide*, and as Claudio Monteverdi's Ottavia (*L'incoronazione di Poppea*) and Messaggiera (*Orfeo*), the last two with Canada's Opera Atelier. In 2004 Novacek made her Covent Garden début, as Suzuki (*Madama Butterfly*), and her Geneva début, as Aljeja in Janáček's *From the House of the Dead*. The following year she made her Chicago Lyric Opera début, as Annina in *Der Rosenkavalier*.

Richard Wigmore

Novotná, Jarmila

(*b* Prague, 23 Sept 1907; *d* New York, 9 Feb 1994). Czech soprano. She studied in Prague with EMMY DESTINN, and later in Milan. She made her début in Prague as Mařenka in *The Bartered Bride* in June 1925. In 1928 she sang Gilda at the Verona Arena, and in 1931 the title role in Jacques Offenbach's *La Belle Hélène* at Berlin. From 1933 to 1938 sang at the Vienna Staatsoper, making regular appearances at Salzburg as Octavian, Eurydice, Countess Almaviva, Pamina, and Frasquita in Hugo Wolf's *Der Corregidor*. In Vienna she created the title role in Franz Lehár's *Giuditta* (1934) opposite RICHARD TAUBER; the performance was broadcast by 120 radio stations. Her American début was as Butterfly at San Francisco in 1939, and she was a valued member of the Metropolitan Opera from 1940 to 1956 where her repertory included Donna Elvira, Pamina, Octavian, Violetta, Freia and Mélisande. She returned to Europe after World War II and was heard again at Salzburg, in Paris and in Vienna. She appeared in *The Merry Widow* in San Francisco and on Broadway in the title role of E.W. Korngold's adaptation of *La belle Hélène*. Her recordings, which range from her early years in Prague to her postwar Salzburg *Rosenkavalier*, evince her charm and interpretative depth as well as occasional flaws in technique. She also appeared in films, including *The Bartered Bride*, directed by Max Ophüls in 1932, which continues to be regarded as one of the most successful translations of opera to the screen, and a dramatic role in *The Search* (1948). She made an evocative wartime recording of Czech and Slovak folksongs accompanied by the exiled Czech premier Jan Masaryk.

Harold Rosenthal/Alan Blyth

Nozzari, Andrea

(*b* Vertova, Bergamo, 1775; *d* Naples, 12 Dec 1832). Italian tenor. He studied in Bergamo and made his début in 1794 at Pavia. After singing in Rome, Milan, Parma and Bergamo, in 1803 he was engaged at the Théâtre Italien in Paris, appearing in Ferdinando Paer's *Principe di Taranto* and *Griselda*, Giovanni Paisiello's *Nina* and Domenico Cimarosa's *Il matrimonio segreto*. From 1812 he was engaged in Naples, where he sang in Gaspare Spontini's *La vestale*, Simon Mayr's *Medea in Corinto* (creating Jason in 1813) and C.W. Gluck's *Iphigénie en Aulide*. At the S Carlo he created roles in eight operas by Gioachino Rossini: Leicester in *Elisabetta, regina d'Inghilterra* (1815); Rinaldo in *Armida* (1817); Osiride in *Mosè in Egitto* and Agorante in *Ricciardo e Zoraide* (1818); Pyrrhus in *Ermione* and Roderick Dhu in *La donna del lago* (1819); Erisso in *Maometto II* (1820) and Antenore in *Zelmira*, as well as the title role of Gaetano Donizetti's *Alfredo il grande* (1823). At the Teatro del Fondo he created the title role of Rossini's *Otello* (1816), amazing the public with the force and agility of his singing and the nobility of his bearing. He retired in 1825.

Elizabeth Forbes

Nucci, Leo

(*b* Castiglione dei Pepoli, Bologna, 16 April 1942). Italian baritone. A pupil of Giuseppe Marchese, he sang Gioachino Rossini's Figaro at Spoleto in 1967, then sang in the chorus at La Scala during further study and made his fully professional début in 1975 at Venice as Schaunard. He appeared at La Scala in 1976 as Figaro, at Covent Garden in 1978 as Miller (*Luisa Miller*), and as Anckarstroem (*Un ballo in maschera*) at the Metropolitan in 1980, the Paris Opéra in 1981 and Salzburg in 1989. Nucci's repertory also includes Marcello, Lescaut, Sharpless, Mamm' Agata (*Le convenienze ed inconvenienze teatrali*), Barnaba (*La Gioconda*), Yevgeny Onegin and Charles Gounod's Mercutio, but his sonorous voice, strong technique and histrionic ability are best displayed in Giuseppe Verdi, in such roles as Giorgio Germont, Luna, Macbeth, Posa, Amonasro, Rigoletto, Iago and Falstaff, and in Gaetano Donizetti. Nucci's many Verdi recordings sometimes lack subtlety of characterization, though he is heard to advantage on disc as Anckarstroem (with Herbert von Karajan), as Donizetti's Malatesta and Belcore, and on the aria 'Eri tu' from *Un ballo in maschera* as recorded in 1989.

Elizabeth Forbes

O

Oberlin, Russell (Keys)

(*b* Akron, OH, 11 Oct 1928). American countertenor and teacher. He was educated at the Juilliard School of Music (diploma 1951). Oberlin was a founding member in 1952 of the New York Pro Musica Antiqua with Noah Greenberg, and also appeared as a countertenor with numerous opera companies, orchestras and ensembles, and in theatrical productions. Admired for his virile, sweet tone and subtle phrasing, he was a leading exponent of early music, and through his many recordings and appearances helped to popularize not only music at that time unknown but also the repertory of the countertenor voice. In 1961 he sang Oberon in the first Covent Garden production, and the US première in San Francisco, of Benjamin Britten's *A Midsummer Night's Dream*. In the mid-1960s he turned to teaching, and appeared as lecturer and lecture-recitalist at colleges and universities throughout the USA and abroad. In 1971 he was appointed professor of music at Hunter College, CUNY, and director of the Hunter College Vocal Collegium.

Patrick J. Smith

Obin, Louis-Henri

(*b* Asq, nr Lille, 4 Aug 1820; *d* Paris, 1895). French bass. He studied in Lille and Paris, making his début in 1844 as Elmiro in Gioachino Rossini's *Otello* at the Opéra, where he was engaged for nearly 25 years. In 1850 he sang in the première of Daniel Auber's *L'enfant prodigue*. He created Procida in Giuseppe Verdi's *Les vêpres siciliennes* (1855), the High Priest of Brahma in *L'Africaine* (1865) and Philip II in Verdi's *Don Carlos* (1867). His repertory included Don Basilio (*Il barbiere di Siviglia*), Leporello, the title role of *Mosè in Egitto*, Balthazar (*La favorite*), Elmiro, Brogni (*La juive*), and Bertram (*Robert le diable*), which he sang at Covent Garden in 1863. ALBERT SALÉZA was his pupil.

Elizabeth Forbes

Obraztsova, Yelena (Vasil'yevna)

(*b* Leningrad [now St Petersburg], 7 July 1937). Russian mezzo-soprano. While still a student at the Leningrad Conservatory, she appeared with success at the Bol'shoy as Marina; in 1964 she became a soloist there. Her voice, of beautiful, full timbre, was controlled with unusual flexibility and lightness; she was an effective and spontaneous actress, notably in such roles as Marfa (*Khovanshchina*), Konchakovna (*Prince Igor*), Amneris, Eboli, Carmen, Lyubasha (*The Tsar's Bride*) and Delilah. She was also successful in contemporary opera, particularly as Hélène (*War and Peace*) and Oberon (Benjamin Britten's *A Midsummer Night's Dream*). Her international appearances included those at San Francisco, the Metropolitan (during the Bol'shoy company's visit in 1975) and La Scala (as Jules Massenet's Charlotte in 1976). She sang Azucena at Covent Garden in 1985, and made her début as a producer in the Bol'shoy's 1986–7 season with *Werther*. In 1973 she was made a National Artist of the RSFSR, and in 1976 was awarded the Lenin Prize.

I.M. Yampol'sky

Ochman, Wiesław

(*b* Warsaw, 6 Feb 1937). Polish tenor. After studying in Warsaw he made his début in 1959 as Edgardo (*Lucia di Lammermoor*) in Bytom, where he was engaged until 1963, then sang at Kraków, Warsaw and Berlin. In 1967 he was engaged at the Hamburg Staatsoper and the following year made his British début at Glyndebourne as Lensky, returning as Don Ottavio and Tamino. In 1972 he sang Alfredo (*La traviata*) at Chicago and Cavaradossi at San Francisco, in 1973 Idomeneus at Salzburg and in 1974 Henri in *Les vêpres siciliennes* at the Paris Opéra. Henri was also the role of his Metropolitan début in 1975, when he also sang Alfred in the centenary performance of *Die Fledermaus* at the Theater an der Wien, Vienna. His plangent tone was particularly suited to Slavonic music, and his repertory included Grigory/Dmitry (*Boris Godunov*) which he sang at the Metropolitan in 1982, Andrey Khovansky and Vasily Golitsïn (*Khovanshchina*), Lensky, Hermann (*The Queen of Spades*), the Prince (*Rusalka*) and both Laca and Števa in *Jenůfa*. He sang the Shepherd in the first performance of Karol Szymanowski's *King Roger* on the American continent (1981, Buenos Aires), and also recorded the opera. Gradually abandoning the Mozart and lighter Italian roles he once sang so stylishly, Ochman acquired a new, heavier repertory with such roles as Erik, Florestan, Herod and Fritz in Franz Schreker's *Der ferne Klang*. His other recordings include Hermann, the Prince, Narraboth (*Salome*), Laca, Idomeneus, Jontek (*Halka*) and Stefan (*The Haunted Manor*).

Elizabeth Forbes

Oehman, Carl-Martin

(*b* Floda, nr Göteborg, 4 Sept 1887; *d* Stockholm, 26 Dec 1967). Swedish tenor. He studied the piano and the organ at the Stockholm Conservatory, and then, privately, singing in Stockholm and Milan. He appeared first in concerts in 1914, making his operatic début in *Fra Diavolo* at Göteborg three years later. The Swedish Royal Opera, which became the centre of his career, heard him first in 1919 and last in 1941. He became well known for his singing of the more lyrical Wagnerian roles, yet in his single season at the Metropolitan in 1924 he appeared only as Laca in the American première of *Jenůfa* and as Camille Saint-Saëns's Samson. At Covent Garden in 1928 he sang Tannhäuser and Walther in *Die Meistersinger*: the power of his full voice and the charm of his *mezza voce* were admired. Some of his best work was done in Berlin, where he sang in the local première of *Simon Boccanegra* (1930). As a teacher he numbered among his pupils JUSSI BJÖRLING, MARTTI TALVELA and NICOLAI GEDDA, all of whom paid warm tribute to his musicianship and clarity. On recordings he is somewhat variable, but at best the voice has fine quality and the style remarkable sensitivity.

J.B. Steane

Oelze, Christiane

(*b* Cologne, 9 Oct 1963). German soprano. She studied with Klesie Kelly-Moog and Erna Westberger, working for the first years of her career in concert and oratorio. In 1990 she made her operatic début as Despina in *Così fan tutte* at Ottawa, with a first appearance at Salzburg the following year as Konstanze in *Die Entführung*. Her performance as Anne Trulove in *The Rake's Progress* at Glyndebourne in 1994 was widely praised, and the same year audiences at Covent Garden enjoyed her delightful Zdenka in *Arabella*. She returned to Glyndebourne as an affecting, understated Mélisande in 1999 and to Covent Garden as Servilia (*La clemenza di Tito*) in 2000. In 1995 she sang Pamina in a series of performances of *Die Zauberflöte* conducted by John Eliot Gardiner that were also filmed and recorded; and in 1996 she was the Marzelline in Gardiner's revival of Ludwig van Beethoven's *Leonore*.

Her pure, delicate timbre is matched by a graceful style which can lend itself more readily to expressions of happiness than of grief and deep thoughtfulness. This was sometimes remarked upon with regard to her Pamina, and it has somewhat limited the effectiveness of her lieder singing. However, recordings such as that of songs by Anton Webern show a not inappropriate coolness as well as a charming voice and resourceful musicianship.

J.B. Steane

Oestvig, Karl Aagaard

(*b* Christiania, 17 May 1889; *d* Oslo, 21 July 1968). Norwegian tenor. He studied at Cologne and made his début in 1914 at Stuttgart, where he sang the Lay Brother/Giovanni in the first performance of Max von Schillings's *Mona Lisa* (1915). Engaged at the Vienna Staatsoper from 1919 to 1927, he created the role of the Emperor in Richard Strauss's *Die Frau ohne Schatten* (1919); from 1927 to 1930 he sang at the Berlin Städtische Oper. His repertory included Tamino, Lohengrin, Walther, Parsifal, Don José, Hoffmann, Paul in E.W. Korngold's *Die tote Stadt*, Bacchus in *Ariadne auf Naxos* and Max in Ernst Krenek's *Jonny spielt auf*, which he sang at Munich on 16 June 1928, when the performance was interrupted by a Nazi demonstration. A very stylish singer, he brought a lyrical approach even to his heavier, more dramatic roles. In 1932 he retired to Oslo, where he taught singing and produced opera.

Elizabeth Forbes

Offers, Maartje

(*b* Koudekerke, 27 Feb 1892; *d* Island of Tholen, 28 Jan 1944). Dutch contralto. She studied at The Hague and in Rotterdam, making her début in concert at Leiden. Her career in opera began in 1917 when she sang Delilah in Camille Saint-Saëns's *Samson et Dalila* at The Hague. Appearances in Paris and Milan established her for a while as one of the leading contraltos of the day; she made a special impression as Erda and as Fricka, and, in 1925, repeated her Delilah at La Scala under Arturo Toscanini. Other operatic roles included Orpheus, Azucena and Amneris. Her recordings of J.S. Bach suggest that shortness of breath must have been a limitation. During the latter part of her career she sang mostly in concerts.

J. B. Steane

Ognivtsev, Aleksandr Pavlovich

(*b* Petrovskoye, Lugansk region, 27 Aug 1920). Russian bass. In 1949 he graduated from the Kishinyov conservatory and was engaged as a soloist by the Bol'shoy. His début as Dosifey (*Khovanshchina*) and his performances as Boris soon afterwards brought him immediate recognition as a singer of unusual dramatic accomplishment and authority, with a strong, beautiful voice of velvety timbre, and an imposing stage presence. A versatile actor, he took with equal success roles in high tragedy, complex psychological drama and comedy: his repertory included Ivan the Terrible (*The Maid of Pskov*), Prince Gremin (*Yevgeny Onegin*) and René (*Iolanta*), Charles Gounod's Méphistophélès, Gioachino Rossini's Don Basilio, Philip II, and the General (Sergey Prokofiev's *Gambler*), which he sang on the Bol'shoy visit to the Metropolitan in 1975. He created Nicholas I in Y.A. Shaporin's *The Decembrists* (1953) and the Leader in A.N. Kholminov's *Optimisticheskaya tragediya* ('An Optimistic Tragedy', 1964), and sang Theseus in the first performances in the USSR of Benjamin Britten's *A Midsummer Night's Dream* (1965). His film appearances included Aleko (in Serge Rachmaninoff's opera, 1954). In 1965 he was made People's Artist of the USSR.

I.M. Yampol'sky

Ohms, Elisabeth

(*b* Arnhem, 17 May 1888; *d* Marquartstein, 16 Oct 1974). Dutch soprano. After study in Amsterdam and Frankfurt, she made her début at Mainz in 1921, and in 1923 joined the Staatsoper in Munich, where she spent the greater part of her career; she was appointed *Kammersängerin*, and married the Munich stage designer Leo Pasetti. Her many notable performances as Brünnhilde and Isolde during the Munich summer festivals made her name familiar to a wider public, and she began to make guest appearances elsewhere, notably at La Scala, in 1927 and 1928, under Arturo Toscanini in *Fidelio* and *Parsifal*, at Bayreuth in 1931 in *Parsifal* (again with Toscanini), and at Covent Garden during three seasons in Wagnerian roles and as Richard Strauss's Marschallin. At the Metropolitan during three consecutive seasons (from January 1930) she appeared in all the heavier Wagner roles. In Munich her non-Wagnerian parts, besides those mentioned, included Turandot and Strauss's Helen of Troy. Her dark-coloured, heroic soprano is well represented, among her few recordings, by a majestic 'Ozean, du Ungeheuer' from Carl Maria von Weber's *Oberon*.

Desmond Shawe-Taylor

Olczewska, Maria.

See OLSZEWSKA, MARIA.

Olenina d'Alheim [d'Al'geym; née Olenina], Mariya Alekseyevna

(*b* Istomino, Ryazan province, 20 Sept/1 Oct 1869; *d* Moscow, 27 Aug 1970). Russian mezzo-soprano. Although she had lessons in 1887 with YULIYA PLATONOVA and Aleksandra Molas, and later studied in Paris, she was never systematically trained. She made her début in Paris in 1896, singing music by Modest Musorgsky, and in Russia (St Petersburg) in 1901. From then on she led a busy concert life in St Petersburg and Moscow. She and her husband, Pierre d'Alheim (1862–1922), a French writer, author of a book on Musorgsky and translator into French of his texts, were energetic advocates of Russian music in the West. In 1908 she founded in Moscow a so-called 'Maison du Lied' with the aim of spreading classical and contemporary vocal chamber music. The Maison, which existed until 1915, organized concerts, international competitions for song arrangements and for Russian translations of texts, and published a bulletin. In 1910 Olenina d'Alheim gave recitals in London, and in 1918 she moved to Paris. She last sang in Moscow and Leningrad in 1926, though she returned to live in Moscow in 1959.

An outstanding recitalist, Olenina d'Alheim belonged, according to V.V. Stasov, to a group of artists with peculiarly Russian characteristics. Although her voice was neither particularly powerful nor particularly beautiful, she exerted a strong artistic influence. Her lofty inspiration and her grasp of the style and essence of a song made her performances totally compelling; her enunciation and declamation were beyond reproach, her phrasing noted for its expressiveness. In works such as Musorgsky's 'The Field-Marshal' (*Songs and Dances of Death*) and *Nursery* cycle, or Franz Schubert's *Der Erlkönig*, she reached heights of tragic pathos. Her repertory included music by trouvères and Minnesinger, French and Italian Renaissance composers, Russian and west European classical and contemporary composers (often rare or new works), and folksongs. The composer Mily Alekseyevich Balakirev was her brother. She published *Le legs de Moussorgski* (Paris, 1908), and the last interview with her, 'Tsel' moyey zhizni bïla znakomit' lyudey s russkoy muzïkoy' ('My life's aim was to acquaint people with Russian music'), was printed in *Literaturnaya rossiya* (12 September 1969).

I.M. Yampol'sky

Olivero, Magda [Maria Maddalena]

(*b* Saluzzo, nr Turin, 25 March 1910). Italian soprano. She studied in Turin and made her début there in 1933 as Lauretta in *Gianni Schicchi*. Her early roles included Manon Lescaut, Mimì, Elsa, Liù, Violetta (Reggio nell' Emilia and Parma) and Butterfly (Modena and Naples). During the 1939–40 season she sang Adriana Lecouvreur in Rome, Naples, Venice and Florence, becoming Francesco Cilea's preferred interpreter of the role. She added the title roles in *Francesca da Rimini* and *Suor Angelica*, Riccardo Zandonai's Giulietta and Umberto Giordano's *Fedora* to her repertory. In 1941 she married and retired, but at Cilea's urging she made her reappearance in 1951 as Adriana Lecouvreur at Brescia.

During the next 20 years Olivero became specially identified with Fedora, Tosca, Minnie and Pietro Mascagni's Iris. She made her London début in 1952 at the Stoll Theatre as Mimì and in 1963 sang Adriana Lecouvreur at the Edinburgh Festival. She sang in the USA at Dallas in 1967 as Medea, in New York in 1970 in *La voix humaine* and at the Metropolitan in 1975, when she was over 60, as Tosca. Her singular dramatic gifts and her finely articulated, sincere singing are captured on a film of her Tosca. She also made highly individual and compelling recordings of her Adriana, Liù and Fedora.

M. Olivero: 'Cilea and "Adriana Lecouvreur"', *Opera*, xiv (1963), 523–8

Harold Rosenthal/Alan Blyth

Olszewska [Olczewska], Maria [Berchtenbreitner, Marie]

(*b* Ludwigsschwaige, nr Donauwörth, 12 Aug 1892; *d* Klagenfurt, 17 May 1969). German mezzo-contralto. She studied in Munich and made her début as a Page in *Tannhäuser* at Krefeld in 1915. After an engagement at Leipzig she sang at the Hamburg Opera, where she took part in the joint première (with Cologne) of E.W. Korngold's *Die tote Stadt* (1920). She sang regularly in Vienna (1921–30). She also appeared frequently at the Staatsoper in Munich, and at Covent Garden (1924–32), where her performances in such roles as Fricka, Ortrud, Brangäne, Octavian, Orlofsky (*Die Fledermaus*) and Herodias (*Salome*) drew the highest critical acclaim. Her Carmen and Amneris were less successful. She sang in Chicago (1928–32) and at the Metropolitan (1933–5). Olszewska possessed a rich, beautiful voice and great dramatic temperament; Ernest Newman wrote that 'she makes us feel for the moment that the whole drama centres in her'. She made a number of recordings, including the role of Octavian in the renowned 1933 abridged version of *Der Rosenkavalier*. She married the baritone EMIL SCHIPPER.

H.M. Barnes: 'Maria Olczewska Discography', *British Institute of Recorded Sound Bulletin*, no.6 (1957), 17–20

Harold Rosenthal/Alan Blyth

Onegin [Onégin; née Hoffmann], (Elisabeth Elfriede Emilie) Sigrid [Lilly]

(*b* Stockholm, 1 June 1889; *d* Magliaso, Switzerland, 16 June 1943). Franco-German contralto and mezzo-soprano. Though often described as Swedish, she was in fact the daughter of a French father and a German mother. She sang first as Lilly Hoffmann; after her marriage to Baron Eugene Borisovitch Lvov Onégin (1883–1919) – a Russian émigré, pianist and composer who had adopted the surname of Pushkin's celebrated hero – she used the name Lilly Hoffmann-Onégin, but soon adopted the professional name by which she was to become famous. She studied in Munich and Milan, and later had lessons or advice from LILLI LEHMANN and MARGARETE SIEMS. She was first engaged by the Stuttgart Opera in 1912; but from 1919 to 1922, after her husband's early death, she was a member of the Hofoper in Munich, and in 1920 married Dr Fritz Penzoldt. She had two Metropolitan Opera seasons (1922–4) and one at Covent Garden (1927), in both houses singing only Amneris and Wagner roles; she also sang at Salzburg (C.W. Gluck's Orpheus, 1931–2) and at Bayreuth (1933–4). Onegin's greatest successes were in concerts, in which she would often sing Rossini arias; she was also a notable interpreter of Johannes Brahms's Alto Rhapsody. She had the finest and most highly trained voice of its kind since SCHUMANN-HEINK, whose repertory and manner of singing she emulated without approaching the older singer's fire and communicative power. Notwithstanding her rich tone and astonishing technique, her recordings suggest also something marmoreal in their smoothness and coldness of style.

J. Dennis: 'Sigrid Onegin', *Record Collector*, v (1950), 223–31 (incl. discography], 280–81; xii (1959), 200

Desmond Shawe-Taylor

O'Neill, Dennis

(*b* Pontardulais, 25 Feb 1948). Welsh tenor. He studied at Sheffield University and with Frederick Cox, and after solo appearances with Scottish Opera's

'Opera for All' (1971) he joined the Glyndebourne chorus (1974) and sang at the Wexford Festival. During two seasons as principal tenor with South Australian Opera, he created a role in Larry Sitsky's *Fiery Tales* (1976). Thereafter he sang lyric roles with Scottish Opera and the WNO, then studied further in Italy with Ettore Campogalliani and Luigi Ricci. His débuts at Covent Garden in 1979 as Flavio (*Norma*) and at Glyndebourne in 1980 as the Italian Tenor (*Der Rosenkavalier*) were followed by leading roles in both theatres and with the ENO. In 1983 he made débuts in the USA at Dallas as Edgardo (*Lucia*) and at the Vienna Staatsoper as Alfredo, a role he also sang with the Metropolitan Opera on tour in 1986 before singing Rodolfo with them in New York the next year. In 1990 he sang Gabriele Adorno in Cologne and Foresto (*Attila*) at Covent Garden, and has subsequently expanded his Verdi repertory to include such roles as Radames, Don Alvaro (*La forza del destino*), Macduff and Otello. O'Neill combines a fine-spun italianate tone with an intelligent perception of style and character. His recordings include Cavaradossi, Dick Johnson (*La fanciulla del West*) and Giuseppe Verdi's Requiem. A governor of the Welsh College of Music and Drama, he has set up a bursary in his own name to help young WNO singers to study abroad.

Noël Goodwin

Opie, Alan (John)

(*b* Redruth, Cornwall, 22 March 1945). English baritone. He studied at the GSM and the London Opera Centre, where he sang Gianni Schicchi. He made his début in 1969 as Papageno with Sadler's Wells Opera in Liverpool, then sang Rochefort (*Anna Bolena*) in Santa Fe (1970), Sid (*Albert Herring*) at Wexford (1971) and Demetrius for the English Opera Group (1972). He also appeared with the Phoenix Opera. Since joining the ENO in 1973, he has sung a wide variety of roles, ranging from Gioachino Rossini's Figaro and Dandini, Guglielmo and Valentin, to Balstrode, Junius (*Rape of Lucretia*), Cecil (*Gloriana*) and Oblonsky in the première of Hamilton's *Anna Karenina* (1981). He made his Covent Garden début in 1971 as an Officer (*Barbiere*), returning for Ping, Hector (*King Priam*), Mangus (*The Knot Garden*), Dr Falke, Paolo (*Simon Boccanegra*) and Faninal. Opie has sung Sid, W.A. Mozart's Figaro, Balstrode, the Traveller (*Death in Venice*) and Don Alfonso at Glyndebourne, Baron de Gondremarck (*La vie parisienne*) and Robert Storch (*Intermezzo*) for Scottish Opera, and Diomede (*Troilus and Cressida*) and Miller (*Luisa Miller*) for Opera North. He has also appeared in

Paris, Chicago, Cologne, Amsterdam and Munich, and made his Metropolitan début as Balstrode in 1994. A charismatic actor with a strong, vibrant voice and vivid diction, he scored a major success as Beckmesser with the ENO (1984) and at Bayreuth (1987), and has recorded the role with Georg Solti. Notable among his other recordings are Rossini's Figaro, Diomede, Smirnov (*The Bear*) and several of his Britten roles.

A. Blyth: 'Alan Opie', *Opera*, xlii (1991), 150–56

Elizabeth Forbes

Orgéni, Aglaja [Görger St Jörgen, Anna Maria von]

(*b* Rimászombat, Galicia [now Rimavská Sobota, Slovakia], 17 Dec 1841; *d* Vienna, 15 March 1926). Hungarian soprano. She studied with PAULINE VIARDOT at Baden-Baden, and made her début in 1865 at the Royal Opera House, Berlin, as Amina in *La sonnambula*. In 1866 she sang at Covent Garden in *La traviata*, *Lucia di Lammermoor* and Friedrich Flotow's *Martha*. Leaving Berlin, she sang in Leipzig, Dresden, Hanover and other cities. In 1872 she appeared in Vienna and the following year in Munich, where she sang Leonora (*Il trovatore*), Amina, and Valentine (*Les Huguenots*). Her repertory also included Agathe (*Der Freischütz*) and Marguerite (*Faust*). In 1879 she retired from the stage, but continued to sing in concert until 1886, after which she taught at the Leipzig Conservatory, becoming the first female professor at that establishment. In 1914 she moved to Vienna. She had style and great technical proficiency, especially in coloratura.

Elizabeth Forbes

Orgonasova, Luba

(*b* Bratislava, 22 Jan 1961). Slovak soprano. After studies at the Bratislava Conservatory and a period (from 1979) as soloist at the Slovak National Theatre in Bratislava, she moved to Germany in 1983 and became a member of the Pfalztheater in Kaiserslautern and, later, the Stadttheater in Hagen. Mozart roles featured in her wide repertory here, and even more so after she appeared at the Vienna Volksoper in 1988 as Donna Anna and Pamina. She repeated Pamina at both Aix-en-Provence and the Vienna Staatsoper in 1989, made her Salzburg début in 1990 as Marzelline (*Fidelio*), and sang Konstanze (the role of her Paris début) around Europe, recording the part to acclaim with John Eliot Gardiner.

Orgonasova first appeared at Covent Garden in 1993 as Aspasia (*Mitridate*), and her other Mozart parts include Ilia, Fiordiligi, Giunia (*Lucio Silla*) and Elecktra, which she sang to acclaim at the Salzburg Festival in 2000. Her operatic repertory has also embraced Agathe (which she performed and recorded with Nikolaus Harnoncourt in Berlin in 1995), Jacques Offenbach's Giulietta, Amina (*La sonnambula*), Lucia, Gilda, Violetta, Luisa Miller, Mimì and Liù, Charles Gounod's Marguerite, Micaëla, Antonia and Sophie, and Igor Stravinsky's Nightingale. Her first Handel role (Alcina in Barcelona, 1999) and subsequent performances in concert as Armida in *Rinaldo* (a role she has also recorded) showed off the pearly sheen and focussed brilliance of her coloratura. Outstanding among her non-operatic recordings are Joseph Haydn's 'Nelson' Mass, Ludwig van Beethoven's Ninth Symphony and *Missa solemnis*, Gioachino Rossini's *Stabat mater*, Giuseppe Verdi's Requiem and Benjamin Britten's *War Requiem*.

John Allison

Orlandi, Elisa

(*b* Macerata, 1811; *d* Rovigo, 1834). Italian mezzo-soprano. She made her début in 1829 and the following year sang in Gaetano Donizetti's *Olivo e Pasquale* at the Teatro della Canobiana, Milan. She created Jane Seymour in *Anna Bolena* (1830) at the Teatro Carcano, Milan, and also sang in Donizetti's *Gianni di Calais* there. In 1833 she created Eleonora in *Il furioso nell'isola di San Domingo* at the Teatro Valle, Rome. She collapsed and died during a performance of *Norma* at Rovigo, in which she was to sing Adalgisa.

Elizabeth Forbes

Osten, Eva von der

(*b* Heligoland, 19 Aug 1881; *d* Dresden, 5 May 1936). German soprano. She studied in Dresden, where she made her début at the Hofoper in 1902 as Urbain (*Les Huguenots*). She remained a member of the company until her farewell performance in 1927 as Brünnhilde (*Die Walküre*). Her most notable creation was Octavian (1911), which she also recorded, and she was in addition the first Dresden Ariadne, Dyer's Wife (*Die Frau ohne Schatten*), Kundry, Tatyana and Maliella (*I gioielli della Madonna*). She was the first Covent Garden Octavian (1913) and Kundry (1914); she also appeared as Ariadne at His Majesty's Theatre in 1913. She toured the USA with the German Opera Company (1922–4),

as Isolde and Sieglinde. Her large repertory also included Senta, Carmen, Louise, Tosca and Zazà. Osten's acting and beauty were much admired, as was her fine dramatic soprano voice. Her recordings, most notably of Elsa's solos from *Lohengrin*, show the purity of her tone. She was married to the bass-baritone FRIEDRICH PLASCHKE.

M. Scott: *The Record of Singing*, ii (London, 1979), 184–5

Harold Rosenthal/R

Otava, Zdeněk

(*b* Vítějeves, nr Polička, Bohemia, 11 March 1902; *d* Prague, 4 Dec 1980). Czech baritone. As a choirboy he impressed Leoš Janáček; subsequently he studied the piano and violin with Bohuslav Martinů. After singing lessons in Prague, he studied in Rome (with RICCARDO STRACCIARI), Milan and Vienna. He made his début in Bratislava as Iago (1925), and a year later was engaged by the Brno Opera, with which he sang Baron Prus in the première of Janáček's *The Makropulos Affair* and the title role in Ernst Krenek's *Jonny spielt auf*. From 1929 to 1972 he worked at the National Theatre in Prague, singing more than 160 roles; he also toured widely abroad. Otava's voice had a very wide range and a marked intensity, and while light, was extremely varied in colour, with an even tone, free of vibrato; his diction was absolutely clear. With his striking stage presence, he gave characteristic portrayals of Figaro, Germont, Yevgeny Onegin and Telramund, and masterly projections of such villains and conspirators as Pizarro, Scarpia and Iago. He was no less versatile and successful in the Czech repertory, and learnt a large number of contemporary roles. He was also a successful recitalist, favouring the contemporary Czech repertory. He taught at the Prague Conservatory (1941–2, 1953) and at the Academy of Musical Arts (1952–73).

Alena Němcová

Otter, Anne Sofie von

(*b* Stockholm, 9 May 1955). Swedish mezzo-soprano. She studied in Stockholm and at the GSMD in London before being engaged by the Basle Opera (1983–5), where she first appeared as Alcina in Joseph Haydn's *Orlando paladino*. She made admired débuts at Covent Garden (1985) and the Metropolitan (1988) as Cherubino, and has since delighted European and American audiences in such roles as Henry Purcell's Dido, C.W. Gluck's Orpheus, Idamantes, Dorabella,

Sextus (*La clemenza di Tito*), Tancredi, Vincenzo Bellini's Romeo, Octavian, Hänsel and Charlotte (*Werther*). In 1999 she was an affecting, intimate Alcestis in Gluck's opera at the Théâtre du Châtelet, Paris. Her recorded repertory of operas extends even further, encompassing Claudio Monteverdi's Octavia, several Handel roles (notably Ariodante), Clytemnestra (*Iphigénie en Aulide*), Olga, Judith (*Bluebeard's Castle*) and Jocasta. Von Otter is also an eloquent oratorio soloist and has made a deserved reputation as an interpreter of lieder, Scandinavian songs and, most recently, *mélodies*. In 2000 she collaborated on a crossover album with Elvis Costello. Her voice, basically firm and flexible, has an individual tang to it; she employs it intelligently to project the meaning of all she sings, and on stage she commands the personality to perform comedy and tragedy with equal aplomb. Among her many discs those of Octavia, Ariodante, Sextus, Hänsel, Octavian, Singoalla (Gunnar de Frumerie), cantatas by G.F. Handel and of songs by Ludwig van Beethoven, Giacomo Meyerbeer, Louis Spohr, Hector Berlioz, Franz Schubert, Robert Schumann and Edvard Grieg (usually with her imaginative accompanist, Bengt Forsberg), disclose her art at its considerable best.

A. Clark: 'Anne Sofie von Otter', *Opera*, xlii (1991), 627–34

Alan Blyth

Owens, Anne-Marie

(*b* South Shields, 1955). English mezzo-soprano. She studied at the GSMD with Laura Sarti and at the National Opera Studio, and made her professional début as Mistress Quickly for Glyndebourne Touring Opera. In 1985 she joined ENO, with whom she has sung many roles, including Anežka (Bedřich Smetana's *The Two Widows*), Marfa (*Khovanshchina*), Jezibaba (*Rusalka*) and Berthe in Judith Weir's *Blond Eckbert*. Among her many other roles are Brangäne (which she has sung for WNO and La Monnaie), Giuseppe Verdi's Mistress Quickly (at WNO and the Komische Oper, Berlin), Amneris and Azucena, Venus (*Tannhäuser*), Mrs Grose in *The Turn of the Screw* (Glyndebourne), and Santuzza in *Cavalleria rusticana*. Her rich, dark-toned mezzo has also been admired as Morozova in P.I. Tchaikovsky's *Oprichnik* in Cagliari, Madelon in *Andrea Chénier* for Scottish Opera, Ragonde (*Le Comte Ory*) for Garsington Opera, the Witch (*Hänsel und Gretel*) for Opera Australia, and Herodias in *Salome* for both Santa Fe Opera and Opera North. In 1996 Owens created the role of Aunt Hannah Watkins in the world première of Tobias Picker's *Emmeline* at Santa Fe, repeating the part for New York City Opera the following season. Her recordings include Harrison Birtwistle's *Mask of Orpheus*, Maurice Ravel's *Les enfants et les sortilèges* and Ralph Vaughan Williams's *Pilgrim's Progress* and *Sir John in Love*.

Richard Wigmore

P ✏

Pacchierotti [Pacchiarotti], Gasparo [Gaspare]

(*b* Fabriano, nr Ancona, bap. 21 May 1740; *d* Padua, 28 Oct 1821). Italian soprano castrato. Trained at either Forlì Cathedral or with Ferdinando Bertoni at S Marco, Venice (where he was principal soloist for three years from 28 February 1765), he remained in Venice until 1770, taking a minor operatic role at the Teatro S Giovanni Grisostomo (1766) and singing in Baldassare Galuppi's *Il re pastore* in 1769. After an appointment as primo uomo at Palermo he sang in Naples as the partner of ANNA DE AMICIS, beginning in 1771 with the première of Niccolò Jommelli's *Ifigenia in Tauride* (Orestes) and performing frequently at S Carlo up to Carnival 1776. He also sang in Bologna in Carnival 1773 (Ferdinando Bertoni's *Olimpiade*) and at the Naples court theatre in Carnival 1774 (C.W. Gluck's *Orfeo*), and for Carnival 1775 he was engaged at the Regio Ducal Teatro, Milan.

In spring 1776 he left Naples permanently, passing through Rome, Florence and Forlì (where his singing in Bertoni's *Artaserse* provoked the famous incident reported by Stendhal – the orchestra were unable to continue for the tears in their eyes). He was engaged by the theatres of Milan, Genoa, Lucca, Turin and Padua, at each singing in an opera by Bertoni. For two years (1778–80) he sang regularly at the King's Theatre in London, where Bertoni was resident composer. In July 1780 he left for Italy, singing at Lucca in the title role of Bertoni's *Quinto Fabio* (1780); at the Teatro S Benedetto, Venice, in the première of Bertoni's *Armida abbandonata* (Carnival 1780–81); and at Mantua, in Luigi Gatti's *Olimpiade* (1781). Persuaded by William Beckford, an English admirer and patron, he returned to the King's Theatre, where Bertoni was again composer, singing there with consistent success (1781–4); the London *Public Advertiser* called him 'superior to any Singer heard in this country since Farinelli'. In September 1781 Pacchierotti performed a RAUZZINI cantata with TENDUCCI and the composer for Beckford's coming-of-age party at his Fonthill estate.

Pacchierotti then appeared as primo uomo nearly every season at the Teatro S Benedetto, Venice, and sang at Trieste (1785), Genoa and Crema (1788), Padua, Milan and Bergamo (1789), faithfully promoting Bertoni's operas each season and remaining in Italy until his last London visit, in 1791, where he sang at many concerts as well as in opera. Joseph Haydn first heard him on 7 February at a Professional Concert, and little more than a week later had him perform his cantata *Arianna a Naxos*, himself accompanying at the harpsichord. At Venice in 1792 Pacchierotti sang Bertoni's Requiem for Angelo Emo, the *Dies irae* of which he made famous. The inauguration and first Carnival season of the Teatro La Fenice, Venice (1792–3), were his last operatic appearances. Pacchierotti retired to Padua a wealthy man, living in the house of Cardinal Bembo surrounded by furniture from London, an English garden and many famous visitors including Carlo Goldoni, Stendhal and Gioachino Rossini. He spent the last 28 years of his life studying Italian and English literature, and concentrating his musical interests particularly on Benedetto Marcello's psalms. He sang in public at least twice: in 1796 in Padua before Napoleon (unwillingly), and on 28 June 1814 at S Marco for Bertoni's funeral.

By all accounts the greatest of the late-18th-century castratos, Pacchierotti was last in the line of the finest male sopranos. Both Mount Edgcumbe ('the most perfect singer it ever fell to my lot to hear') and Charles Burney devoted more space to describing his genius than they accorded any other performer of the era. He was able to sing with facility from Bb to c''', had a command of many different styles, was a considerable actor and moved even casual listeners by his rendition of pathetic airs. He was the principal author of the anachronistic vocal treatise *Modi generali del canto premessi alle maniere parziali onde adornare o rifiorire le nude o semplici melodie o cantilene giusta il metodo di Gasparo Pacchiarotti* (Milan, 1836), published under the name of his friend Antonio Calegari.

L. Melville: *The Life and Letters of William Beckford of Fonthill* (London, 1910)

G. Chapman, ed.: *The Travel Diaries of William Beckford of Fonthill* (Cambridge, 1928)

S. Willier: 'A Celebrated Eighteenth-Century Castrato: Gasparo Pacchiarotti's Life and Career', *OQ*, xi/3 (1995), pp. 95–121

Kathleen Kuzmick Hansell

Pacetti, Iva

(*b* Prato, 13 Dec 1898; *d* Rome, 19 Jan 1981). Italian soprano. After study in Florence she made her début at Prato as Aida. She arrived at La Scala in 1922, and sang Helen of Troy in *Mefistofele* under Arturo Toscanini, with whom she also worked in Paul Dukas' *Ariane et Barbe-bleue*. She was the first Rome Turandot (1926) and gave her farewell performance there in the same role 21 years later. Abroad her greatest success was in South America, though she also sang at Chicago and throughout Europe. At Covent Garden she appeared in 1930, 1931 and 1938, as Desdemona, Leonora in *La forza del destino* and, most frequently, Tosca. Her pianissimo singing was admired, but *The Times* observed in 1930 that she lacked the ringing quality required, and the *Liverpool Post* nominated her 'wobbler of the season'. Her large repertory included such varied parts as the Dyer's Wife in *Die Frau ohne Schatten*, Norma and Leonore in *Fidelio*. Her best-known recording is of *Pagliacci* made in 1934 with BENIAMINO GIGLI, though the role of Nedda is one she never sang on stage.

J.B. Steane

Pacini, Andrea ['Il Lucchesino']

(*b* Lucca, *c*1690; *d* Lucca, March 1764). Italian alto castrato and composer. He sang in Venice (12 operas: 1708, début in Tomaso Albinoni's *Astarto*, 1714–16, 1726), Florence (1709–10, 1720, 1725–6, 1731–2), Genoa (1710–11, 1720, 1728), Rome (1711, 1721–2), Lucca (1711, 1714–15, 1724, 1730), Ferrara (1713, 1731), Naples (ten operas at the S Bartolomeo and the royal palace, 1713–14, 1722–3), Livorno (1717–18), Bologna (1719–20, 1722), Turin (1719), Milan (1719–20) and Parma (1724, 1729). He appeared in operas by all leading composers from Alessandro Scarlatti, Albinoni and Antonio Vivaldi to Nicola Porpora, Johann Hasse and Leonardo Vinci. He was elected a member of the Accademia Filarmonica at Bologna in 1721. From 1720 to 1730 he had the title of virtuoso to Prince Antonio of Parma. He was engaged by the Royal Academy in London as second man to SENESINO for 1724–5, making his début in the title role of G.F. Handel's *Tamerlano* and scoring a success: Lady Bristol told her husband that 'the new man takes extremely'. He sang Ptolemy in Handel's *Giulio Cesare* (Handel composed a new aria for him) and Unulfo in *Rodelinda*, and in Attilo Ariosti's *Artaserse* and *Dario* and the Vinci—Giuseppe Orlandini *Elpidia*. The parts Handel wrote for him demand a good technique but limited range (compass *a* to *e"*). In later life Pacini became a priest, and often took part in the annual celebration of S Croce at his native town. He composed a mass for its St Cecilia Festival in 1744. There are two caricatures of him by A.M. Zanetti in the Cini collection. He appears with other singers in a J.-A. Watteau drawing in the Louvre, executed on a visit to Paris in 1721.

Winton Dean

Pacini, Regina

(*b* Lisbon, 6 Jan 1871; *d* Buenos Aires, 18 Sept 1965). Portuguese soprano. She came from a family of musicians, her father, José Pacini (who was also her first teacher), being a well-known baritone and director of the S Carlos at Lisbon, where Regina made her début in 1888 as the heroine of *La sonnambula*. The following year she appeared in Milan and Palermo and in James Mapleson's last season at Her Majesty's in London. She quickly became a favourite in Spain, singing also in the 1890s in Russia, Poland and South America. In 1902 she reappeared in London, singing at Covent Garden with CARUSO in *L'elisir d'amore* and *Lucia*, and was praised by the *Musical Times* for 'vocal agility such as this generation seldom hears'. She was again Caruso's partner at Monte Carlo in 1904, and in 1905 sang there in *I puritani* and *Il barbiere* with BONCI. At the height of her career in 1907 she retired and married Marcelo de Alvear (later president of Argentina), which enabled her to exercise an influence on the musical life of the country. Her recordings are rarely without some flaw of voice or style but she is impressively fluent; the upper part of her voice was particularly lovely.

J.B. Steane

Padilla y Ramos, Mariano.

Spanish baritone, husband of DÉSIRÉE ARTÔT.

Padmore, Mark

(*b* London, 8 March 1961). English tenor. He learnt the clarinet as a child, and took up singing seriously when he gained a choral scholarship to King's College, Cambridge. After graduating in 1982 he worked as a freelance singer with such groups as the Tallis scholars, the Sixteen, Chiaroscuro, and the King's Consort. In 1987 Padmore joined the Hilliard Ensemble, with whom he toured extensively and made several recordings; then, in 1991, he became a member of William Christie's Les Arts Florissants, taking solo roles in a number of performances and recordings of French Baroque operas. These included the *Gramophone* award-winning recording of Jean-Philippe Rameau's *Hippolyte et Aricie*, in which his graceful, sweet-toned singing of the *haute-contre* role of Hippolyte was much admired. Working with Philippe Herreweghe's Collegium Vocale Ghent in the mid-1990s, he established an international reputation as a superb Bach singer; in particular, his thoughtful and dramatically immediate performances of the Evangelist in the *St John* and *St Matthew* Passions have been widely acclaimed. He has recorded both roles, and also sang the Evangelist in the staged production of the *St John Passion* by Deborah Warner at the ENO.

Though Padmore has made his name primarily as a Baroque singer, his wide repertory ranges from medieval polyphony to contemporary works, and includes the roles of Don Ottavio, Iopas in *Les Troyens* (at the Théâtre Musical de Paris), the Novice in *Billy Budd* and the tenor solos in Benjamin Britten's *War Requiem*. Among his many Baroque operatic roles are Jason in M.-A. Charpentier's *Médée*, Alphée in Jean-Baptiste Lully's *Proserpine*, the title role in Rameau's *Zoroastre* (which he has recorded with Christie), Arnalta in *L'incoronazione di Poppea*, and Handel's Jephtha, a portrayal of searing intensity which he gave with WNO in 2003 and the ENO in 2005. Padmore is also a perceptive interpreter of German and English song, as can be heard on recordings of lieder by Franz Schubert's contemporaries and songs by Benjamin Britten, Michael Tippett and Gerald Finzi.

Richard Wigmore

Pagliughi, Lina

(*b* New York, 27 May 1907; *d* Savignano sul Rubicone, nr Rimini, 2 Oct 1980). Italian soprano. Born in New York of Italian parents, she appeared in public for the first time when she was 12. She studied in San Francisco with Silvia Puerara Maracci and Domenico Brescia, and then in Milan with Manlio Bavagnoli. She made her début at the Teatro Nazionale, Milan (1927), as Gilda. Subsequently she appeared at Monte Carlo (1931), at the S Carlo, Naples (1936), as Lucia, at La Scala (1937) as Sinaïde in Gioachino Rossini's *Mosè in Egitto* and (1947) as Lucia, at Covent Garden (1938) as Gilda, at the Maggio Musicale, Florence (1940), as the Queen of Night and at the Rome Opera (1949) as Elvira (*I puritani*). Pagliughi's other roles included Rosina, Violetta and Amina, and she appeared in the title role in Umberto Giordano's *Il re*. She retired from the stage in 1954 and taught in Milan. Her vocal and stylistic gifts – sweet, pure tone, smooth, flexible technique, perfect legato and delicacy of expression – made her the leading Italian light soprano after TOTI DAL MONTE. Her unimpressive stage presence was a hindrance to her theatrical career, but she sang a great deal on the radio and made many successful recordings.

L. Di Cave: 'Lina Pagliughi', *Record Collector*, xxi (1973–4), 101–25 [with discography]

Rodolfo Celletti/Valeria Pregliasco Gualerzi

Palló, Imre

(*b* Matisfalva, 23 Oct 1891; *d* Budapest, 25 Jan 1978). Hungarian baritone. After studying at the Budapest Academy of Music under Georg Anthes, and later in Italy with MARIO SAMMARCO, he made his Royal Hungarian Opera début in 1917, as Alfio, and was soon its leading interpreter of lyric baritone roles. He sang with refined diction and velvety tone, his voice showing good balance in all registers, and he also possessed an imposing stage presence; all these qualities were notably displayed in his Verdi roles, especially Posa, Luna, Falstaff (the first in Hungary) and Simon Boccanegra. His peasant origins were advantageous in Kodály – he created the title role in *Háry János* (1926) and the Suitor in *Székely fonó* ('The Spinning Room', 1932). In 1935 he took part in Lodovico Rocca's *Il dibuk* in Rome. From 1957 to 1959 he was Intendant of the Hungarian State Opera.

Péter P. Várnai

Palmer, Felicity (Joan)

(*b* Cheltenham, 6 April 1944). English mezzo-soprano. The daughter of a music master, she studied at the GSM in London (1962–7) and then for a year with MARIANNE SCHECH at the Musikhochschule, Munich. In 1970 she won a Kathleen Ferrier Scholarship, and made her Queen Elizabeth Hall début, in Henry Purcell's *Dioclesian*; subsequent appearances in oratorio confirmed her reputation as a singer of quick musicianship and confident projection. After a decade as a soprano (début role, Purcell's Dido with Kent Opera, 1971) and wide experience as Countess Almaviva, Donna Elvira and Pamina (for the ENO), she retrained as a mezzo-soprano. She has won international renown for her magnetic presence and powerful musical command in shaping phrases and projecting words, amply compensating for occasionally edgy tone. Palmer's mezzo-soprano repertory includes the title roles in G.F. Handel's *Tamerlano* and C.W. Gluck's Orpheus (for Opera North), Juno in *Semele*, Fricka (*Das Rheingold*, 1989, for Scottish Opera), Kabanicha (*Kát'a Kabanová*) and Mistress Quickly (1988, Glyndebourne), the Countess (*Queen of Spades*), Herodias, Clytemnestra,

Gertrude in Ambroise Thomas' *Hamlet* (1990, Chicago), and the title role in the stage première of Roberto Gerhard's *The Duenna* (1992, Madrid). In 1997 she sang Richard Strauss's Clytemnestra at Covent Garden. Her many recordings reflect her two vocal 'identities' and her versatility, and include Gluck's *Armide* (which she sang at the Spitalfields Festival in 1982), Electra (*Idomeneo*), Marcellina (*Le nozze di Figaro*), many works by Handel and Edward Elgar's *The Dream of Gerontius*. She was made a CBE in 1993.

E. Forbes: 'Felicity Palmer', *Opera*, xlv (1994), 1033–8

Max Loppert

Pålson-Wettergren, Gertrud.

See WETTERGREN, GERTRUD.

Pampanini, Rosetta

(*b* Milan, 2 Sept 1896; *d* Corbola, nr Rovigo, 2 Aug 1973). Italian soprano. A pupil of Emma Molajoli, she made her début in 1920 at the Teatro Nazionale, Rome, as Micaëla in *Carmen*. She was then heard at the S Carlo, Naples (1923), at the Comunale, Bologna (1923–4) and at La Scala (1925) in *Madama Butterfly*, conducted by Arturo Toscanini; she returned there until 1930 and again between 1934 and 1937. She sang in the leading Italian theatres and appeared at the Colón, Buenos Aires (1926), at Covent Garden (1928) in *Madama Butterfly* and *Pagliacci* and as Liù in *Turandot*, returning there in 1929 and 1933, at the Berlin Städtische Oper (1929), at the Chicago Civic Opera (1931–2) and at the Paris Opéra (1935). Pampanini's pure, natural voice was full of warmth and brilliance, with a strong, resonant top register; she was considered one of the world's leading Puccini sopranos between 1925 and 1940, partly because of the variety of colour and inflection she brought to the utterances of Mimì, Cio-Cio-San and Manon, and partly because of the grace and simplicity of her bearing. She was also admired in *Andrea Chénier*, *Iris* and *Tosca*. After she retired in 1946 she taught singing in Milan; AMY SHUARD and Victoria Elliott were among her pupils.

Rodolfo Celletti/R

Pandolfini, Angelica

(*b* Spoleto, 21 Aug 1871; *d* Lenno, Como, 15 July 1959). Italian soprano. As the daughter of Francesco Pandolfini, she was brought up with a singing career in view, though she first studied the piano in Paris. She trained as a singer under Jules Massart and made her début in *Faust* at Modena in 1894. Later that year in Malta she became associated with the new *verismo* operas, and was soon known throughout Italy as an outstanding Mimì. 1897 brought her début at La Scala where, in 1902, she created the title role in Francesco Cilea's *Adriana Lecouvreur*. Her repertory also included Eva in *Die Meistersinger* (sung in Italian), Desdemona and the heroines of *La traviata* and *Aida*, both of which revealed weaknesses and presaged her early retirement in 1909. She made only five records, all extremely rare in their original form. Among them is Adriana's first aria, sung with tenderness and some endearing personal touches.

J.B. Steane

Panerai, Rolando

(*b* Campi Bisenzio, nr Florence, 17 Oct 1924). Italian baritone. He studied in Florence and Milan, making his début in 1946 in Florence as Enrico Ashton (*Lucia di Lammermoor*). At Naples (1947–8) he sang Pharaoh (*Mosè in Egitto*), Luna, Germont and Gioachino Rossini's Figaro. In 1951 he made his La Scala début as the High Priest (*Samson et Dalila*), returning as Enrico Ashton, Apollo (*Alceste*), the Husband (*Amelia al ballo*) and in the title role of *Mathis der Maler* (Italian première, 1957). In 1955 he created Ruprecht in the stage première of *The Fiery Angel* in Venice and sang W.A. Mozart's Figaro in Aix-en-Provence. He made his Salzburg début in 1957 as Ford, then sang Masetto, Paolo (*Boccanegra*) and Guglielmo, returning as Ford in 1980. At San Francisco (1958) he sang both Figaros and Marcello. In 1962 he created the title role of Guido Turchi's *Il buon soldato Svejk* (Milan). He sang all over Italy, in Vienna, Munich, Paris and at the Metropolitan. Having made his Covent Garden début in 1960 as Gioachino Rossini's Figaro, he returned in the 1980s as Don Alfonso, Don Pasquale, Falstaff and Dulcamara. He had a dark-toned, vibrant voice and incisive diction, heard to advantage on his recordings of such roles as Guglielmo, Luna, Ford, Silvio and Marcello.

Alan Blyth

Pantaleoni, Romilda

(*b* Udine, 1847; *d* Milan, 20 May 1917). Italian soprano. She studied in Milan, making her début there in 1868 at the Teatro Carcano in Jacopo Foroni's *Margherita*. She appeared at the Apollo on the Greek Island of Syros in the 1869–70 season. In 1882 she sang in the première of Tomás Giribaldi's *Manfredi di Svevia* at the Teatro Solis, Montevideo.

After singing in Rome, Genoa, Modena, Naples, Turin, Vienna and Brescia, in 1883 she made her début at La Scala as La Gioconda. She sang Anna in the first Milan performance of Giacomo Puccini's *Le villi* (1884) and created the title role, written for her, in Amilcare Ponchielli's *Marion Delorme* (1885). She sang Desdemona in the first performance of Giuseppe Verdi's *Otello* (1887), a role for which she was coached by Verdi himself, and created Tigrana in Puccini's *Edgar* (1889). Her repertory included Mathilde (*Guillaume Tell*), Paolina (*Poliuto*), Valentine (*Les Huguenots*), Sélika (*L'Africaine*), Marguerite (*Faust*) and Margherita (*Mefistofele*), as well as many Verdi roles: Leonora (*Il trovatore* and *La forza del destino*), Amelia (*Un ballo in maschera*), Elisabeth de Valois (*Don Carlos*) and Aida. She also sang Santuzza and Elsa. A magnificent singing actress, she retired in 1891 after the death of the conductor Franco Faccio with whom she had a liaison. Her brother, Adriano Pantaleoni (1837–1908), was a baritone who sang regularly at La Scala.

Elizabeth Forbes

Panzacchi [Pansacchi], Domenico

(*b* Bologna, *c*1730; *d* Bologna, 1805). Italian tenor. He is said to have been a pupil of BERNACCHI and sang in *opera seria* from 1746. In Vienna in 1748–9 he first worked with ANTON RAAFF, who was to overshadow him in parts of his later career. In 1751–7 he was at Madrid (Raaff arriving at a higher salary in 1755), and from 1760 until his pensioning in 1782 he was in the service of the Munich court (which Raaff joined after 1778), with occasional operatic engagements in Italy. He sang the title roles in Andrea Bernasconi's *Agelmondo* (1760), *Temistocle* (1762) and *Demofoonte* (1766), but he is best remembered for creating Arbaces in *Idomeneo* (1781); he was a great favourite with the Munich audiences, and Mozart found his singing and acting worthy of respect.

Dennis Libby/Paul Corneilson

Panzéra, Charles (Auguste Louis)

(*b* Geneva, 16 Feb 1896; *d* Paris, 6 June 1976). Swiss baritone. He volunteered for the French Army during World War I, then made France his home. A student at the Paris Conservatoire, he made his début as Albert in *Werther* in 1919 at the Opéra-Comique. There he sang a range of secondary roles, his only significant stage appearance being Pelléas, which he also performed in Amsterdam and Florence; his interpretation was highly praised by Claude Debussy's widow. A born recitalist, Panzéra was one of the foremost interpreters of *mélodies* of his time. In 1922 he gave the first performance of Gabriel Fauré's last song cycle *L'horizon chimérique*, dedicated to him and suiting to perfection his keen but reserved style, as his recording confirms. Through Europe and the USA, with triumphant success, he championed the art of French song, together with his wife and accompanist, the talented pianist Madeleine Baillot. Panzéra's voice was a perfect example of the baryton Martin, the timbre tenor-like with no heavy overtones. A prolific recording artist, he left superb interpretations of Henri Duparc's songs showing words and tone finely wedded, the expression restrained, never exaggerated. He retired in the early 1950s and taught at the Conservatoire. His writings include *L'art de chanter* (Paris, 1945); *L'amour de chanter* (Paris, 1957); *L'art vocal: 30 leçons de chant* (Paris, 1959); *50 mélodies françaises: leçons de style et d'interprétation/50 French Songs*, (Brussels and New York, 1964) and *Votre voix: directives générales* (Paris, 1967).

André Tubeuf/Alan Blyth

Paoli, Antonio [Marcano, Antonio Emilio Paoli; Bascarán, Ermogene Imleghi]

(*b* Ponce, 14 April 1871; *d* San Juan, 24 Aug 1946). Puerto Rican tenor. Encouraged by his elder sister Amalia, a singer active in Spain, he studied in Madrid and Milan. During his early career (and while studying singing in Milan), he adopted the name Ermogene Imleghi Bascarán. He made his début in Paris as Arnold in *Guillaume Tell* (1899) and developed a career as a dramatic tenor in the tradition of TAMAGNO. Paoli toured with a company headed by Pietro Mascagni in 1902, singing in Chicago and New York. Following his début as Otello in Madrid (1905), he sang that role some 570 times; he had also given, by the end of his career, 425 performances of Manrico. Other important appearances were at the new Teatro Colón, Buenos Aires, in 1908, and at La Scala as Samson in 1909–10. His many recordings include excerpts from *Pagliacci*, under the direction of Ruggero Leoncavallo (1907). He occasionally performed in Puerto Rico during his tours of North and South America, and retired there in the early 1920s; his last public appearances were in San Juan in 1928 as Manrico and Otello with a visiting New York company. Folllowing his retirement, in 1935 he organized in San Juan a production of *Cavalleria rusticana*. In such roles as Samson, Canio and Otello he contributed to the development of a true dramatic tenor style of characterization as distinct from that of the 'elevated baritone'.

J. López, E. Arnosi and L. Alvarado: 'Antonio Paoli', *Record Collector*, xxii (1974–5), 5 [with discography by J. Dennis]

Donald Thompson

Pape, René

(*b* Dresden, 4 Sept 1964). German bass. He was a member of the Dresden Kreuzchor (1974–81) and made his stage début in 1988 at the Berlin Staatsoper, where he has since been a member of the regular ensemble, singing Sarastro, Rocco, Ramfis, Fasolt, Hunding, King Mark and Pogner, among others. His first appearance at the Salzburg Festival was as Don Fernando (*Fidelio*) and in J.S. Bach's *St Matthew Passion* in 1990, returning the following year to undertake Sarastro in the Schaaf–Solti staging. He sang Fasolt at Bayreuth each year from 1994 to 1998. His début at La Scala was in 1991 as Sarastro, and he first appeared at the Vienna Staatsoper as Hunding (1996), at Covent Garden as Heinrich der Vogler (1997) and at the Metropolitan as Fasolt (1997). In 2000 he returned to the Metropolitan as an athletic Escamillo. His King Mark is widely acclaimed and is captured on DVD in a 2007 performance at Glyndebourne. His other roles include a saturnine, beautifully sung Leporello, heard at the 1999 Salzburg Festival. He is also a notable concert artist. His well-formed, compact bass and refined, shapely phrasing can be heard on disc as Pogner and in *The Creation*, *The Seasons* and W.A. Mozart's *Requiem*, all with Georg Solti.

Alan Blyth

Pareto, Graziella [Graciela]

(*b* Barcelona, 15 May 1889; *d* Rome, 1 Sept 1973). Spanish soprano. She studied in Milan, and made her début as Amina at Madrid in 1908, taking the role in Parma shortly afterwards. For two seasons from 1909 she appeared at the Teatro Colón, Buenos Aires, as Gilda, Adina, Rosina and Ophelia (Ambroise Thomas' *Hamlet*), parts she sang there later on her return in 1926. In Italy she sang at Rome, Naples, as Giacomo Meyerbeer's Marguerite de Valois at Turin, 1912, and reached La Scala in 1914, as Gilda. At Covent Garden in 1920 she played Norina, Violetta, and Leïla (*Les pêcheurs de perles*) under Thomas Beecham, who considered her the best *soprano leggero* of her day (in *A Mingled Chime* he described her voice as being 'of exquisite beauty, haunting pathos and flawless purity'). She appeared at Chicago (1923–5), and as Carolina (*Il matrimonio segreto*) at the 1931 Salzburg Festival. Her records, which include extracts from her leading roles, offer proof of a pure, limpid soprano, capable, as in 'Dite alla giovine' from *La traviata*, of considerable pathos.

G. Fraser: 'Graziella Pareto', *Record Collector*, xvii (1966–8), 75–89

Alan Blyth

Parly, Ticho [Christiansen, Frederick]

(*b* Copenhagen, 16 July 1928; *d* Seattle, 21 June 1993). American tenor of Danish birth. He studied in Paris, at Bloomington, Indiana, where he took part in the première of Norman Dello Joio's *The Ruby* (1955), and New York, making his début in 1958 at New Orleans as Pong (*Turandot*). Engaged at Aachen in 1959 he sang Radames. At San Francisco (1960) he sang the Emperor (*Die Frau ohne Schatten*), the Drum Major and Rinuccio. At Wuppertal (1961) his roles included Ferruccio Busoni's Mephistopheles and Peter Grimes. In 1963 he sang Leandro (H.W. Henze's *Il re cervo*, the revised version of *König Hirsch*) at Kassel and made his Bayreuth début as Vogelgesang (*Die Meistersinger*), returning as Siegmund (1966) and Siegfried (1968). In 1966 he made his débuts at Covent Garden as Siegfried, at the Paris Opéra as Tannhäuser, and at the Metropolitan and the Colón as Tristan. He sang Herod at La Scala (1967), returning as the Drum Major. For Scottish Opera he sang Siegfried (1971) and Peter Grimes (1973). He sang Loge at San Diego (1974) and at Seattle (1975–7). He appeared frequently at Copenhagen in Wagner roles and also as Florestan, Shuysky and Otello, which he sang in 1988 as a last-minute replacement. He created a sense of youthful exuberance on stage to second a strong, rather baritonal voice.

Alan Blyth

Pasero, (Giacinto Tommaso) Tancredi

(*b* Turin, 11 Jan 1893; *d* Milan, 17 Feb 1983). Italian bass. He studied with Arturo Pessina and made his début at the Politeama Chiarella, Turin, as the King of Egypt (*Aida*) in 1917. In 1924 he appeared at the Teatro Costanzi, Rome, and at the Colón, Buenos Aires, where he returned until 1930. In 1926 he made his début at La Scala in *Don Carlos*, and sang there, almost continuously, until 1951. He was engaged at the Metropolitan (1929–33), at Covent Garden (as Padre Guardiano in *La forza del destino*, 1931) and at the Paris Opéra (1935). He retired in 1955. His voice was full, mellow and even across a wide range, and he sang with a fine sense of style in a repertory extending from Sarastro to Escamillo. He was outstanding in such Italian *basso cantante* roles as Oroveso (*Norma*), Zaccaria, Ramfis, Fiesco, Mephistofele and Philip II; and in the latter part of his career he became a renowned Boris Godunov.

S. Winstanley: 'Tancredi Pasero', *Record Advertiser*, iii/4 (1972–3), 2 [with discography]

N. Linnell: 'Tancredi Pasero, 1893–1983: a Tribute', *Record Collector*, xxviii (1983–4), 141–3

Rodolfo Celletti/Valeria Pregliasco Gualerzi

Pasini [Muzii], Camilla

(*b* Rome, 6 Nov 1875; *d* Rome, 29 Nov 1935). Italian soprano. She was the sister of LINA PASINI-VITALE. Camilla made her début in Rome as Inès and went on to create Musetta in *La bohème*. She sang at La Scala in 1897 and again in 1904 after touring in South America.

David Cummings/R

Pasini-Vitale [née Pasini], Lina [Carolina]

(*b* Rome, 8 Nov 1872; *d* Rome, 23 Nov 1959). Italian soprano. After study in Rome she made her début at the Teatro Dal Verme, Milan, as Cecilia in *La tilda* by Francesco Cilea (1892). Early in her career she was successful at La Scala and in Rome and Turin as Pietro Mascagni's Iris and Suzel (*L'amico Fritz*), Micaëla, Mimì and Gretel. In 1897 she married the conductor Edoardo Vitale. From 1914 she was widely known in operas by Richard Wagner, singing Kundry in the South American première of *Parsifal* at Buenos Aires, and appearing as Brünnhilde at Rome in 1926. She retired in 1928, after singing Kundry at Naples. Her sister CAMILLA PASINI was also a singer.

David Cummings/R

Paskalis, Kostas

(*b* Levadia, Boeotia, 1 Sept 1929; *d* Athens, 9 Feb 2007). Greek baritone. He studied in Athens, making his début there in 1951 as Rigoletto. In 1958 he sang Renato in Vienna, where he was a member of the Staatsoper for 20 years. He made his British début in 1964 as Macbeth at Glyndebourne, where he also sang Don Giovanni (1967), and his Metropolitan début in 1965 as Don Carlo (*La forza*), returning as Ford. At Salzburg he created Pentheus in H.W. Henze's *The Bassarids* in 1966 and at La Scala sang Valentin (1967). He made his Covent Garden début in 1969 as Macbeth, returning for Iago, Scarpia and Rigoletto. His repertory included William Tell, Escamillo (which he recorded), Barnaba (*La Gioconda*), Yevgeny Onegin and Harlequin (*Ariadne auf Naxos*), but it was in Giuseppe Verdi that he excelled, as Posa, Rigoletto, Amonasro, Boccanegra, Luna, Germont, Nabucco and, his finest roles, Iago and Macbeth (the latter preserved on video). He was an arresting actor and had a warm, resonant voice with a wide range, although his concern for powerful characterization sometimes caused him to distort his vocal line.

Alan Blyth

Pasqua, Giuseppina

(*b* Perugia, 19 March 1855; *d* Pieve di Budrio, Bologna, 24 Feb 1930). Italian soprano and mezzo-soprano. Trained first in Perugia, she made her soprano début in Bologna as Oscar in *Un ballo in maschera* and continued training with MARIETTA PICCOLOMINI in Palermo, where she sang Marguerite de Valois in *Les Huguenots*. She then studied as a mezzo-soprano with LUIGIA ABBADIA; she sang Amneris at La Scala in 1878, and created Princess Eboli in the revised version of *Don Carlos* (1884). Her fame in Europe was such that Giuseppe Verdi engaged her as Mistress Quickly for the première of *Falstaff* at La Scala (1893). Her repertory was very wide, but she was particularly successful in *Mignon*, *La favorite*, *La Gioconda*, *Il trovatore*, *Lohengrin* and *Saffo*.

A. Lupattelli: *Giuseppina Pasqua* (Perugia, 1880)

Galliano Ciliberti

Pasta [née Negri], Giuditta (Angiola Maria Costanza)

(*b* Saronno, nr Milan, 26 Oct 1797; *d* Como, 1 April 1865). Italian soprano. She studied in Milan with Giuseppe Scappa and Davide Banderali and later with Girolamo Crescentini and Ferdinando Paer among others. In 1816 she made her début at the Teatro degli Accademici Filodrammatici, Milan, in the première of Scappa's *Le tre Eleonore*; soon after, she appeared in Paris at the Théâtre Italien as Donna Elvira, Giulietta in Niccolò Zingarelli's *Giulietta e Romeo* and in two operas by Paer. Her London début at the King's Theatre in 1817 was as Telemachus in Domenico Cimarosa's *Penelope*. She also sang Cherubino and Despina.

After singing in all the main Italian centres from 1818 (her roles included Gioachino Rossini's Cenerentola and Cimarosa's Curiazio), she achieved her first great triumph singing Rossini's Desdemona at the Théâtre Italien, Paris, in 1821, subsequently appearing there as Tancredi and Queen Elizabeth. In the following decade she established herself as Europe's greatest soprano, exerting a major influence on the styles of Vincenzo Bellini and Gaetano Donizetti and becoming one of Rossini's favourite singers. Her great roles included Zingarelli's Romeo, Simon Mayr's Medea and Giovanni Paisiello's Nina. She made a triumphant return to London in 1824 as Desdemona and also sang Zerlina and Semiramide (one of her greatest interpretations). For the next few years she alternated between London and Paris, adding roles by Giacomo Meyerbeer and Rossini (she created Corinna in *Il viaggio a Reims* in 1825) to her repertory. In 1826–7 she sang in Naples, creating the title role of Giovanni Pacini's *Niobe* at the S Carlo.

Her first Bellini role was Imogene in *Il pirata* (1830, Vienna). Subsequently she created Amina in *La sonnambula* (1831, Teatro Carcano, Milan) and the title roles in *Norma* (her début at La Scala in 1831) and *Beatrice di Tenda* (1833, La Fenice). For Donizetti she created the title role in *Anna Bolena* (1830, Teatro Carcano) and Bianca in *Ugo, conte di Parigi* (1832). After 1835, when she retired from the stage, Pasta's appearances were infrequent, though she performed in London in 1837 and Berlin and Russia in 1840–41. Her voice had begun to show signs of wear, and she lost the desire to compete with the legend she had created.

Pasta's greatness lay in her naturalness, truth of expression and individual timbre, which enabled her, within a phrase, to achieve soul-stirring emotion. She could execute intricate *fioriture* but channelled her bravura to illuminate the drama, though she was often criticized for faulty intonation. An accomplished actress, her deportment and portrayal of dignity were without peer.

K. Stern: 'Giuditta Pasta', *ON*, xlvi/12 (1981–2), 8–11

Kenneth Stern

Pataky, Kálmán [Koloman von]

(*b* Alsólendva, 14 Nov 1896; *d* Los Angeles, 3 March 1964). Hungarian tenor. After little serious study, he made his début at the Budapest Opera in 1922, as the Duke of Mantua, which led to an invitation to sing under Franz Schalk at the Vienna Staatsoper in 1926. Until the Nazi invasion of Austria, Vienna remained his base, although he often sang in Budapest and abroad (usually as Koloman von Pataky), notably at the Paris Opéra (1928), Glyndebourne (1936), La Scala (1940), Stockholm and, frequently, at the Colón, Buenos Aires. He sang Florestan under Arturo Toscanini at Salzburg in 1936. He spent the war in Hungary, returning to the Colón for a few performances in 1946. Pataky was not an accomplished actor, but his classically beautiful voice and thorough understanding of style (developed largely during his years in Vienna), his wide cultural background and gift for musical characterization made him one of the leading W.A. Mozart tenors; he was an outstanding Don Ottavio, Belmonte and Tamino. Other roles included Giacomo Puccini's Rodolfo and Des Grieux, and (though he was perhaps less well suited to these heroic roles) Radames, Cavaradossi and Turiddu. Pataky's sweet tone and refined technique are well displayed in his record-

ing of Don Ottavio in Fritz Busch's Glyndebourne *Don Giovanni*.

A. Blyth: 'Koloman von Pataky and Walter Widdop', *Opera*, xl (1989), 288–95

Péter P. Várnai/Alan Blyth

Paton, Mary Anne.

See WOOD, MARY ANNE.

Patti, Adelina [Adela] (Juana Maria)

(*b* Madrid, 19 Feb 1843; *d* Craig-y-Nos Castle, nr Brecon, Wales, 27 Sept 1919). Italian soprano, daughter of the singers Salvatore Patti and Caterina Chiesa Barilli-Patti. She received her first singing lessons from her half-brother, Ettore Barilli, and when she was seven sang in a charity concert at Tripler Hall, New York. Accompanied by her brother-in-law, Maurice Strakosch, and the violinist Ole Bull, she toured the USA as a child prodigy for three years, and in 1857 she went on another long tour, with the pianist Louis Moreau Gottschalk. She made her stage début in 1859 at the New York Academy of Music, in the title role of *Lucia di Lammermoor*, which she had studied with the conductor Emmanuele Muzio. After a tour of Philadelphia, Boston, Baltimore and other cities, during the winter of 1860–61 she sang in New Orleans and in Cuba.

Under Maurice Strakosch's management, she made her European début at Covent Garden on 14 May 1861, as Amina in *La sonnambula*; by the final curtain, the audience had succumbed completely to the spell of the 18-year-old prima donna, and Patti's quarter-century reign at Covent Garden had begun. After a tour of the British Isles, she sang in Berlin, Brussels, Amsterdam and The Hague.

She made her Paris début at the Théâtre Italien in 1862 and her first appearance in Vienna at the Carltheater in 1863, on both occasions as Amina. In October that year she sang Marguerite in Charles Gounod's *Faust* for the first time, at Hamburg. In the winter of 1865–6 she made her first visit to Italy, singing at Florence, Bologna, Rome and Turin. In November 1868 she sang a duet from Gioachino Rossini's *Stabat mater*, with MARIETTA ALBONI, at the composer's funeral in Paris and she spent the following winter in St Petersburg and Moscow.

Patti was London's first Aida in 1876 at Covent Garden, and she made her début at La Scala in *La traviata* in 1877. Her partner on those and many other occasions was the tenor ERNEST NICOLINI, whom she married in 1886, after obtaining a

Adelina Patti

divorce from her first husband, the Marquis de Caux. Returning to New York after an absence of over 20 years in 1881, she embarked on a concert tour, and for the following three winters she was engaged by James Henry Mapleson for his operatic tours of the USA, during which her fee rose to £1000 a performance. In 1885, her 25th consecutive season at Covent Garden, she sang the title role of *Carmen*, one of the very few misjudgments of her career. After another tour of the USA, she gave six farewell performances at the Metropolitan in April 1887. In 1888, after singing in Madrid and Lisbon, she appeared in Buenos Aires and Montevideo, then sang *Roméo et Juliette* at the Paris Opéra, with Gounod conducting, and JEAN and EDOUARD DE RESZKE in the cast.

In 1895 Patti gave six farewell performances at Covent Garden, two each of Violetta, Zerlina and Rosina, her last operatic appearances in London, though in 1897 she sang at Monte Carlo and at Nice, where she created her final operatic role, *Dolores* by André Pollonnais. Her final American tour opened at Carnegie Hall, New York, on 4 November 1903, and her official London farewell took place at the Albert Hall on 1 December 1906, but she continued to take part in charity concerts until 1914.

During the later stages of Patti's career, the legends that surrounded her tended to obscure the fact that at the zenith of her vocal powers, between 1863 and 1880, she was also a remarkable actress, especially in comedy. In the early years, when the compass of her perfectly placed and produced voice extended easily to *f'''*, Amina, Lucia, Violetta, Norina and Rosina were the roles in which she excelled, and her interpretations were marred only by an over-use of ornamentation. Later, her secure technique enabled her to continue to sing many of these parts, but she also became pre-eminent in a slightly heavier lyric repertory, in such roles as Semiramide, Marguerite (which at first she had found uncomfortably low), Leonora (*Il trovatore*) and Aida. Although she rarely chose to sing in works lying outside her vocal, histrionic or emotional range, *L'Africaine* and *Les Huguenots* both exceeded these limits; the other two Meyerbeer operas in which she appeared, *Dinorah* and *L'étoile du nord*, suited her talents much better. Her amazing purity of tone and vocal flexibility after singing for more than half a century are amply illustrated by the recordings she made when in her 60s and testify to her exemplary care for her phenomenal gifts. Louisiana State University library holds a collection of her letters.

H. Klein: *The Reign of Patti* (London, 1920/R)
J.F. Cone: *Adelina Patti: Queen of Hearts* (Portland, OR, 1993)

Elizabeth Forbes

Pattiera, Tino

(*b* Cavtat, nr Dubrovnik, 27 June 1890; *d* Cavtat, 24 April 1966). Croatian tenor. He studied in Vienna and after gaining experience in operetta made his début at the Dresden Hofoper in 1914 as Manrico in *Il trovatore*. His fine voice was matched by good looks, and he became the most popular tenor in Dresden, especially when paired in the 1920s with the soprano META SEINEMEYER. With her, and under Fritz Busch, he sang in some notable productions, including *La forza del destino*, *Don Carlos*, *The Queen of Spades* and *Andrea Chénier*. Although he specialized in the Italian repertory, he also sang Tannhäuser, and Bacchus in *Ariadne auf Naxos*. He

joined the Chicago Opera Company in the 1921–2 season, and was a guest artist in Berlin, Vienna, Budapest and Belgrade. He gave his last concert at Dresden in 1953 and taught for some years in Vienna. Although a highly gifted singer, he lacked the secure technique and stylistic discipline to make the best use of his voice. Recordings preserve its distinctive timbre, and his duets with Seinemeyer make it understandable that their performances together in Dresden created an enthusiasm comparable to the MELBA-and-CARUSO evenings in London.

A. Vincenti and J. Dennis: 'Tino Pattiera', *Record Collector*, xvii (1966–8), 268–85

J.B. Steane

Patzak, Julius

(*b* Vienna, 9 April 1898; *d* Rottach-Egern, Bavaria, 26 Jan 1974). Austrian tenor. After studying music and conducting under Guido Adler, Franz Schmidt and others, he took up singing in earnest, being entirely self-taught. Provincial engagements led to an invitation to join the Staatsoper in Munich in 1928, where he stayed until he joined the Vienna company in 1945. He participated during this period in the premières of Hans Pfitzner's *Das Herz* (1931), Richard Strauss's *Friedenstag* (1938, in which he created the role of the Rifleman) and Carl Orff's *Der Mond* (1939). For more than three decades he was much in demand, particularly for Mozart tenor roles, and as his voice grew larger he became an incomparable Florestan and Palestrina, the only two of his grandest roles to have been recorded completely (and these only semi-officially). His extensive repertory ranged from Singspiel and operetta through the lighter Wagner roles and Richard Strauss to Giuseppe Verdi, Giacomo Puccini and Modest Musorgsky. Late in his career he was still a marvellously subtle and stylish performer of lieder, old Viennese theatre songs and the *Heurigen* songs of his native city, and he also took up conducting again. He was much sought after as a soloist in oratorios (the Evangelist in J.S. Bach's Passions and in Franz Schmidt's *Das Buch mit sieben Siegeln*). Among his many lieder and oratorio recordings, the version of *Das Lied von der Erde* with Bruno Walter and KATHLEEN FERRIER is one of his finest. He was the first Austrian artist to be engaged by the BBC after the war, and he appeared at Covent Garden (where he had sung Tamino in 1938) as Florestan and Herod during the 1947 Vienna Staatsoper season; he returned to sing Florestan and Hoffmann with the resident company. He also made notable appearances at the Salzburg Festival, where he created Desmoulins in Gottfried von Einem's *Dantons Tod* (1947). His advocacy for new music, both opera and song, deserves mention, and he taught both at the Vienna Music Academy and at the Mozarteum, Salzburg.

Although Patzak's voice was generally considered small, it was so finely projected and allied to such intelligent phrasing, meticulous enunciation and effective stage deportment that it seldom failed to make its mark. His slightly nasal timbre was immediately recognizable. When well into his 50s, he was able to stand in as Lohengrin or continue to sing in the Beethoven, Mozart and Pfitzner operas with no loss of impact. He recorded several smaller roles, notably Mime in Wilhelm Furtwängler's RAI *Ring* of 1953, and made memorable recordings of operatic excerpts.

P. Branscombe: 'Julius Patzak', *Opera*, v (1954), 403–7
J. Dennis: 'Julius Patzak', *Record Collector*, xix (1970–71), 195–222 [with discography by D. Brew]

Peter Branscombe

Pauly [Pauly-Dresden; née Pollak], Rose

(*b* Eperjeske, 15 March 1894; *d* Kfar Shmaryahn, nr Tel-Aviv, 14 Dec 1975). Hungarian soprano. She studied in Vienna with Rosa Papier-Paumgartner, making her début during the 1917–18 season at Hamburg in a minor role in *Martha*. After singing at Gera and Karlsruhe, she went to Cologne, where she sang the title role in the German première of *Kát'a Kabanová* in 1922. She made her first appearance at the Vienna Staatsoper in 1923, singing Sieglinde, the Empress (*Die Frau ohne Schatten*) and Rachel (*La Juive*); in 1931 she created Agave in Egon Wellesz's *Die Bakchantinnen*. Engaged at the Kroll Oper, Berlin (1927–31), she sang Leonore, Donna Anna, Senta, Carmen and Maria in Ernst Krenek's *Der Diktator*. At the Berlin Staatsoper she was acclaimed as Marie (*Wozzeck*), Jenůfa and Electra. She appeared at Salzburg as the Dyer's Wife (1933) and as Electra (1934–7), the role of her débuts in 1938 at Covent Garden (where Ernest Newman praised her dramatic intensity), and at the Metropolitan. Pauly was a most versatile singer, with a rich, powerful voice, and excelled as Richard Strauss's Electra, Salome and the Dyer's Wife. She made few recordings, but extracts from *Elektra* give an idea of her compelling interpretation of the title role.

Leo Riemens/Elizabeth Forbes

Pavarotti, Luciano

(*b* Modena, 12 Oct 1935; *d* Modena, 6 Sept 2007). Italian tenor. He studied in Modena with Arrigo Pola and in Mantua with Ettore Campogalliani, making his début in 1961 at Reggio nell'Emilia as Rodolfo (*La bohème*) and quickly making an impression for his eloquent lyrical singing. In 1963 he sang Edgardo (*Lucia*) in Amsterdam and made his Covent Garden début as Rodolfo, returning as Alfredo, Elvino, Tonio (*Fille du régiment*), Gustavus III, Cavaradossi, Rodolfo (*Luisa Miller*), Radames and Nemorino (1990). In 1964 he sang Idamantes at Glyndebourne; in 1965 he made his American début at Miami as Egardo in *Lucia di Lammermoor* with JOAN SUTHERLAND, toured Australia with the Sutherland-Williams company, as Edgardo, and made his La Scala début as Rodolfo, returning for the Duke, Vincenzo Bellini's Tebaldo and Jules Massenet's Des Grieux. At La Scala he also sang in a remarkable performance of Giuseppe Verdi's Requiem to mark the centenary of Arturo Toscanini's birth. He first sang at San Francisco in 1967 as Rodolfo, and the following year made his Metropolitan début, again as Rodolfo, later singing Manrico, Fernand (*La favorite*), Ernani, Cavaradossi, Idomeneus, Arturo (*I puritani*), Radames, Rodolfo (*Luisa Miller*, 1991) and the Italian Singer (*Der Rosenkavalier*).

Pavarotti had a bright, incisive tenor with a typically free, open, italianate production and penetrating high notes. He made it a practice never to sing beyond his own means; and even when he tackled more dramatic roles such as Otello late in his career he never forced his fundamentally lyric tenor. Above all he had a directness of manner that went straight to his listeners' hearts. His voice and style were ideally suited to Gaetano Donizetti, the early and middle-period works of Verdi (he was particularly admired as Alfredo and Gustavus III) and to Giacomo Puccini's Rodolfo and Cavaradossi. His impassioned singing of Calaf's 'Nessun dorma' (*Turandot*) turned the aria into a bestseller, though in this role and some of the other heavier parts he essayed he arguably lacked the true spinto power.

Pavarotti's art is liberally preserved on disc and video, which give a true reflection of his voice and personality: no opera singer has understood better than he the new power of the media. He recorded most of his major roles, some of them twice, and was one of the 'Three Tenors' combination (with DOMINGO and CARRERAS) of the 1990s that brought opera to an unprecedentedly wide public. His genial looks and generous, outgoing personality were ideally suited to that kind of phenomenon; indeed, it might well not have existed without his enthusiastic participation. Despite his enormous popular acclaim, Pavarotti was anxious to preserve his reputation as a serious artist, and his voice retained much of its colour and vibrancy into his 60s. But in later years he was sometimes critisized for sloppy performances and carelessness. In 1999 he sang Cavaradossi at the Metropolitan, followed in 2001 by Radames, although by then the tone production had become noticeably more effortful.

Luciano Pavarotti and Mirella Freni in 'La bohème' (Puccini), Salzburg, 1976

G. Gualerzi: 'Luciano Pavarotti', *Opera*, xxxii (1981), 118–24
L. Pavarotti: *My Own Story* (London, 1981)
M. Mayer: *Grandissimo Pavarotti* (Garden City, NY, 1986)

Alan Blyth, Stanley Sadie

Pavlovskaya [née Berman], Emiliya Karlovna

(*b* St Petersburg, 28 July/9 Aug 1853; *d* Moscow, 23 March 1935). Russian soprano. She studied at the St Petersburg Conservatory, graduating in 1873. In 1873–4 she sang in western Europe, principally in Italy, and from 1876 in theatres in Kiev, Odessa, Tbilisi and Kharkiv. From 1876 until her retirement she alternated between the Bol'shoy in Moscow and the Mariinsky, creating a Tchaikovsky role at each: Mariya (*Mazepa*, 1884) and the title role in *The Enchantress* (1887), respectively. In 1885 she also sang Tatyana in the première of the revised version of *Yevgeny Onegin*. From 1895 she taught at the Bol'shoy; DMITRY SMIRNOV was one of her pupils.

Boris Semeonoff

Pears, Sir Peter (Neville Luard)

(*b* Farnham, 22 June 1910; *d* Aldeburgh, 3 April 1986). English tenor. He won a scholarship to the

RCM, London, where he spent two terms in 1933–4. At the same time he joined the BBC Chorus and then the BBC Singers (1934–8), and took lessons with ELENA GERHARDT and Dawson Freer. His life-long personal and professional relationship with Benjamin Britten began when the two met in 1936; a year later they gave their first recital together (which included Britten's *On this Island*). In 1939 they went to the USA, and while there Pears studied with Therese Behr (Artur Schnabel's wife) and Clytie Hine Mundy.

Returning with Britten to London in 1942, Pears made his stage début in the title role of *Les contes d'Hoffmann* at the Strand Theatre. The next year he joined the Sadler's Wells company, singing Gioachino Rossini's Almaviva, Rodolfo, the Duke of Mantua, Tamino, Ferrando and Vašek, and, memorably, creating the title role in *Peter Grimes* (1945). These years also saw the notable first performances, given by Pears and the composer, of Britten's *Michelangelo Sonnets* and the *Serenade* for tenor, horn and strings.

In 1946 Pears was one of the founders of the English Opera Group, with which he sang the Male Chorus in the première of *The Rape of Lucretia* (1946) and the title role in *Albert Herring* (1947), both at Glyndebourne. His other creations in Britten's dramatic works included Captain Vere in *Billy Budd* (1951, Covent Garden), Essex in *Gloriana* (1953, Covent Garden), Quint in *The Turn of the Screw* (1954, Venice), Flute in *A Midsummer Night's Dream* (1960, Aldeburgh), the Madwoman in *Curlew River* (1964, Aldeburgh), Nebuchadnezzar in *The Burning Fiery Furnace* (1966, Aldeburgh), the Tempter in *The Prodigal Son* (1968, Aldeburgh), Sir Philip Wingrave in *Owen Wingrave* (1971, BBC television) and Aschenbach in *Death in Venice* (1973, Aldeburgh). For the English Opera Group he also sang Macheath in Britten's realization of *The Beggar's Opera*, Satyavān in Gustav Holst's *Sāvitri*, and W.A. Mozart's Idomeneus; and he created Boaz in Lennox Berkeley's *Ruth* (1956). At Covent Garden he created Pandarus in William Walton's *Troilus and Cressida* (1954), and will be remembered for his acute portrayals of Tamino, Vašek and David (*Die Meistersinger*) during the 1950s. He later took part in the premières of H.W. Henze's *Novae de infinito laudes* (1963) and Witold Lutosławski's *Paroles tissées* (1965). He was made a CBE in 1957, and was knighted in 1977.

Pears was one of the founders of the Aldeburgh Festival, inaugurated in 1948, and remained a director until his death. He was an eloquent interpreter of Franz Schubert, probably the leading Evangelist of his day in J.S. Bach's Passions, an impassioned Gerontius and a noted exponent of British song. He collaborated with Britten on the libretto of *A Midsummer Night's Dream* and on realizations of several works by Henry Purcell, including *The Fairy Queen* (1967).

Britten wrote all his major tenor roles, and many of his solo vocal works, with the particular characteristics of Pears's voice in mind. Clear, reedy and almost instrumental in quality, it was capable of great expressive variety and flexibility, if no wide range of colour. Its inward, reflective timbre, tinged with poetry, was artfully exploited by Britten, from the role of Peter Grimes to that of Aschenbach, but the voice could also be commanding, almost heroic, as was shown in the more vehement sections of Captain Vere's role or in the part of the Madwoman in *Curlew River*; Pears's cheeky vein of humour was given full range as Albert Herring and as Flute. His recital partnership with Britten produced evenings of extraordinary interpretative insights, when line and tone were perfectly matched to the texts of Franz Schubert's and Robert Schumann's song cycles.

Pears continued singing until he was well into his sixties, and after his retirement was active in teaching and promoting young singers at the Britten-Pears School in Aldeburgh. His recordings include virtually all the roles Britten created for him, and his eloquent accounts of the Evangelist in J.S. Bach's Passions and Gerontius.

H. Keller: 'Peter Pears', *Opera*, ii (1950–51), 287–92

M. Thorpe, ed.: *Peter Pears: a Tribute on his 75th Birthday* (London, 1985) [incl. discography]

Sir Peter Pears

'Sir Peter Pears 1910–1986: Three Tributes', *Opera*, xxxvii (1986), 624–30

C. Headington: *Peter Pears: a Biography* (London, 1992)

P. Reed: *The Travel Diaries of Peter Pears* (London, 1995)

Alan Blyth

A. Levy: *The Bluebird of Happiness: the Memoirs of Jan Peerce* (New York, 1976)

J. Hines: 'Jan Peerce', *Great Singers on Great Singing* (Garden City, NY, 1982), 224–30

Obituary, *New York Times* (17 Dec 1984)

Martin Bernheimer/R

Peckover, Alfred.

See PICCAVER, ALFRED.

Pedrazzi, Francesco

(*b* Bologna, *c*1802; *d* after 1850). Italian tenor. He studied with Giovanni Tadolini and made his début in 1828 at Pisa. After singing in Parma, in 1832 he sang Tebaldo in Vincenzo Bellini's *I Capuleti e i Montecchi* at Bologna. He was then engaged at La Scala, where he created Gennaro in *Lucrezia Borgia* (1833) and Viscardo in Saverio Mercadante's *Il giuramento* (1837). He also sang Justinian in *Belisario* (1836). At S Carlo he sang Leicester in the first performance of Gaetano Donizetti's *Maria Stuarda* (1834), given under the title of *Buondelmonte* because of censorship problems. He retired in 1850.

Elizabeth Forbes

Peerce, Jan [Perelmuth, Jacob Pincus]

(*b* New York, 3 June 1904; *d* New York, 15 Dec 1984). American tenor. He studied with GIUSEPPE BORGATTI and from the mid-1940s was chosen by Arturo Toscanini to sing in his broadcasts and recordings of *La bohème*, *La traviata*, *Fidelio*, *Un ballo in maschera* and the last act of *Rigoletto*. He made his stage début in Philadelphia in 1938 as the Duke of Mantua and joined the Metropolitan in 1941, making his first appearance as Alfredo; he stayed with that company until 1968. He toured abroad with many ensembles, specializing in the Italian and French spinto repertories, and in 1956 he became the first American to sing with the Bol'shoy since the war. In 1971 he made his Broadway début as Tevye in *Fiddler on the Roof*. He also appeared in films such as *Tonight We Sing* and *Goodbye, Columbus* (directed by his son, Larry Peerce), and recorded popular songs in addition to Jewish liturgical music. In his prime Peerce was most admired for a remarkably even scale, a strong technique, and a voice with a dark vibrancy in the middle register and a metallic ring at the top, points confirmed by his recordings under Toscanini. Though his diminutive size precluded an ideal romantic illusion, he was an actor of restraint and dignity. The American tenor RICHARD TUCKER, was his brother-in-law.

Pélissier [Pellissier], Marie

(*b* 1706/7; *d* Paris, 21 March 1749). French soprano. She married the impresario Victor Pélissier soon after her début at the Paris Opéra in 1722, and sang at his theatre in Rouen. After her husband's bankruptcy, she returned to Paris and appeared at the Opéra in a revival of Pascal Collasse's *Thétis et Pélée* on 16 May 1726 to considerable acclaim. Later that year she attracted even greater applause for her creation of Thisbe in François Rebel and François Francoeur's *Pyrame et Thisbé*. Sensing a challenge, CATHÉRINE-NICOLE LEMAURE returned in December from one of her 'retirements', and a fierce rivalry developed between the two singers and between their respective supporters, the 'mauriens' and 'pélissiens'. On 15 February 1734 Pélissier was dismissed after a scandal involving her lover François Lopez Dulis. She fled to London, but returned to sing at the Opéra on 19 April 1735, remaining there until her retirement in October 1741. Among the many roles she created were five in operas of Jean-Philippe Rameau: Aricia in *Hippolyte et Aricie*, Emilie in *Les Indes galantes*, Telaira in *Castor et Pollux*, and Iphise in both *Les fêtes d'Hébé* and *Dardanus*.

Pélissier's voice was small and, initially at least, somewhat forced. She was nevertheless regarded as an heir to the famous MARIE LE ROCHOIS in the emotional power of her declamation and the eloquence of her gestures and facial expressions, though she never equalled Le Rochois' stature. Her portrait was painted by François Drouias (see colour plate 3).

Graham Sadler/R

Pellegrini, Valeriano

(*b* Verona, ?*c*1663; *d* Rome, 18 Jan 1746). Italian soprano castrato and composer. He sang in the Chiesa Nuova and the Cappella Sistina choir in Rome, at Cardinal Ottoboni's private concerts and in Giovanni Bononcini's *La fede publica* in Vienna (1699). From 1705 to 1716 he was in the service of the Elector Palatine at Düsseldorf, where he created the difficult role of Gheroldo (requiring a range of *c'* to *b''*) in Agostino Steffani's *Tassilone* (1709) and was knighted. During this period he also appeared at Venice (as Nero in G.F. Handel's *Agrippina*, 26 December 1709) and London. Pellegrini served the elector in other capacities; he acquired for him a large collection of medals at Verona in 1708, but in 1715 the painter Sebastiano Ricci shamelessly fobbed him off with a bogus Correggio. Pellegrini made his London début on 9 April 1712 at a concert in the Old Spring Garden, but did not appear on the stage until the following November. G.F. Handel composed for him Mirtillo in *Il pastor fido*, the title role in *Teseo* and probably Lepidus in *Silla*. He seems to have been a technically proficient rather than a glamorous singer. By 1728 he had lost his voice and become a priest. In his last years in Rome he was dependent on charity.

Winton Dean, John Rosselli

Penco, Rosina

(*b* Naples, April 1823; *d* Porretta, nr Bologna, 2 Nov 1894). Italian soprano. After an unrecorded début she sang in Dresden and Berlin in 1850, and Constantinople in 1850–51, chiefly the lyric coloratura parts of Gioachino Rossini, Vincenzo Bellini and Gaetano Donizetti, and was renowned for her trill. Before Giuseppe Verdi wrote Leonora in *Il trovatore* for her (1853, Rome) he heard that she had 'many virtues' though 'imperfect'; she was also described as 'very pretty' and 'a devil' to her fellow singers. Verdi prized her combination of agility with passionate dramatic temperament; he later suggested her for *La traviata* and for the heavier part of Amelia in *Un ballo in maschera* (which she eventually sang in 1861 at Covent Garden and the Théâtre Italien, Paris). He complained in 1858 that she had retreated into the bel canto style 'of thirty years ago' – her range included Norma, Elvira in *I puritani* and Paolina in Donizetti's *Poliuto* – instead of moving forward into 'the style of thirty years hence'. She sang frequently in Madrid (to 1857), London (1859–62), Paris (most years from 1855 to 1872) and St Petersburg (to 1874).

John Rosselli

Pennarini [Federler], Aloys

(*b* Neudorf, nr Vienna, 21 June 1870; *d* Ustí nad Labem, 23 May 1927). Austrian tenor. He studied in Vienna, making his début in 1893 at Bratislava as Turiddu, and his Bayreuth début in 1899, in *Parsifal* and *Die Meistersinger*. After engagements at Olomouc, Elberfeld, Graz and Hamburg (1900–13), he became director of the Nuremberg Opera, where he continued to sing until 1920. He made his Covent Garden début in 1902 as Lohengrin, also singing Walther, Siegmund and Siegfried, and Heinrich in the British première of Ethel Smyth's *Der Wald*. In 1904 he toured the USA with the Savage Opera Company as Parsifal. Renowned as an excellent interpreter of Richard Wagner, he had a powerful, well-managed but hard-toned voice.

Elizabeth Forbes

Perelmuth, Jacob Pincus.

See PEERCE, JAN.

Pergamenter, Karl.

See PERRON, KARL.

Peri, Jacopo ['Zazzerino']

(*b* Rome or Florence, 20 Aug 1561; *d* Florence, 12 Aug 1633). Italian composer, singer and instrumentalist. His most significant contribution was his development of the dramatic recitative for musical theatre. A performer of his own vocal compositions, Peri's contribution to the early history of opera is arguably as much vocal as compositional.

Although Peri may have been born in Rome, he claimed descent from Florentine nobles with a long record of public service. He settled in Florence at an early age, and on 1 September 1573 he was taken into the convent of SS Annunziata 'to sing laude to the organ'. His musical education continued under Cristofano Malvezzi, who included a four-part ricercare by him in his print of 1577 and the madrigal *Caro dolce ben mio* in his first book of five-part madrigals (1583). On 1 February 1579 Peri began service as organist at the Badia at a yearly salary of 15 scudi. He held the post until April 1605, and by 1586 he was also employed as a singer at S Giovanni Battista. The young Peri was praised by A.F. Grazzini for his instrumental and vocal performances, knowledge and grace, but Grazzini was annoyed that Peri's talents as a musician appeared to be insufficiently recognized. In 1584 the Duke and Duchess of Mantua spoke of Peri's endearing qualities. Pietro de' Bardi praised Peri's performances on the organ and other keyboard instruments, his compositions and his singing, in which, he said, he intelligently imitated speech in sound.

In 1588, shortly after the accession of Grand Duke Ferdinando I, Peri's name first appeared as an official employee of the Medici court with a monthly salary of six scudi, which was increased to nine scudi in September 1590. In 1589 he took part in the festivities celebrating Ferdinando's marriage to Christine of Lorraine. He performed the role of Arion in the fifth *intermedio* for Girolamo Bargagli's comedy *La pellegrina*, singing his own aria *Dunque fra torbid'onde*, in which he illustrated the miraculous powers of music. According to the descriptive

Jacopo Peri as Arion in fifth intermedio for 'La pellegrina', 1587

commentary published with the music in 1591, he captivated the audience, accompanying himself with amazing skill on the chitarrone. Peri's costume for this role is depicted in a sketch by Bernardo Buontalenti (see illustration).

With the encouragement and collaboration of Jacopo Corsi and Ottavio Rinuccini, he wrote music for the latter's short pastoral *Dafne*. Although *Dafne* was reportedly planned as early as 1594, the earliest recorded performance was during Carnival 1597–8. Details of the casting are unknown, but Peri sang the role of Apollo in some of them.

Peri's next and most significant collaboration with Rinuccini was in their opera *Euridice*, first produced for the Florentine celebrations of the wedding of Maria de' Medici and Henri IV, King of France. The première took place before a small audience

in the Palazzo Pitti on 6 October 1600 where, according to handwritten annotations on a copy of the original libretto, Peri himself took the role of Orpheus. *Euridice* received high praise, particularly from Marco da Gagliano, who was impressed not only by the work but also by Peri's own expressive singing

After 1600 Peri continued to serve the Medici court. His later professional activities were primarily in composition, although he sang the role of Neptune in an unnamed ballo on 14 February 1611, and again in a new version of the ballo, now named *Mascherate di ninfe di Senna*, on 5 May 1613.

In 1630 Peri suffered a serious illness and on 15 March 1630 prepared his will. He died three years later and was buried in the church of S Maria Novella.

C.V. Palisca: 'The First Performance of "Euridice"', *The Department of Music, Queens College of the City University of New York: Twenty-Fifth Anniversary Festschrift*, ed. A. Mell (Flushing, NY, 1964), 1–23; repr. in C.V. Palisca: *Studies in the History of Italian Music and Music Theory* (Oxford, 1994), 432–51

H.M. Brown: 'How Opera Began: an Introduction to Jacopo Peri's *Euridice* (1600)', *The Late Italian Renaissance, 1525–1630*, ed. E. Cochrane (New York and London, 1970), 401–43

T. Carter: 'Jacopo Peri (1561–1633): Aspects of his Life and Works', *PRMA*, cvi (1978–9), 50–62

T. Carter: *Jacopi Peri (1561–1633): his Life and Works* (New York and London, 1989)

William V. Porter (with Tim Carter)/R

Périer, Jean (Alexis)

(*b* Paris, 2 Feb 1869; *d* Paris, ?3 Nov 1954). French baritone. He studied with ALEXANDRE TASKIN and Romain Bussine at the Paris Conservatoire and made his début in 1892 as Monostatos (*Die Zauberflöte*) at the Opéra-Comique, where he remained (except from 1894 to 1900) until 1920. His repertory lay chiefly in operetta (he sang leading roles in the first performances of André Messager's *Véronique* in 1898 and *Fortunio* in 1907, and created Duparquet in Reynaldo Hahn's *Ciboulette*, 1923) but he also sang Don Giovanni, Lescaut, Sharpless and was the first Pelléas (Opéra-Comique, 30 April 1902) and the first Ramiro (*L'heure espagnole*). He also created the title role in Henri Rabaud's *Mârouf* (1914) and Abbé Coignard in Charles Levadé's *La rôtisserie de la Reine Pédauque* (1920). He sang Pelléas at the Manhattan Opera in 1908 and appeared at Monte Carlo, but remained firmly a part of the Parisian musical and theatrical scene. He acted in several films between 1900 and 1938. His was essentially a declamatory art, and even with limited gifts as a singer he created convincing characters with the help of his clear diction and his ability as an actor. Seven published recordings of his voice (on cylinders, later issued as discs) were made about 1905.

Harold Barnes

Perini, Flora

(*b* Rome, 20 Nov 1887; *d* Rome, Sept 1975). Italian mezzo-soprano. She studied at the Accademia di S Cecilia in Rome and made her début at La Scala in 1908 as Anacoana in Alberto Franchetti's *Cristoforo Colombo*. She made her début at the Metropolitan Opera as Lola in *Cavalleria rusticana* in 1915; there she also sang roles including Amneris and Maddalena, as well as creating Pepa in *Goyescas* (1916) and the Princess in *Suor Angelica* (1918). She remained at the Metropolitan until 1924, after

which she sang for one season in Chicago. While in the USA she made some recordings for Victor, including the classic *Rigoletto* Quartet with GALLI-CURCI, CARUSO and DE LUCA in 1917. She returned to Italy in 1925, where she sang principally at the Teatro Costanzi in Rome.

Cori Ellison

Perli, Lisa.

See LABBETTE, DORA.

Pernet, André

(*b* Rambervillers, Vosges, 6 Jan 1894; *d* Paris, 23 June 1966). French bass. He studied at the Paris Conservatoire with ANDRÉ GRESSE and made his début at Nice in 1921. After seven years in the French provinces he was engaged in 1928 by the Paris Opéra and became their leading bass; from 1931 he also appeared at the Opéra-Comique. At the Opéra he was much admired as Boris Godunov, Don Quichotte, Méphistophélès and Don Giovanni. He created, among other parts, the title roles in Darius Milhaud's *Maximilien* (1932) and George Enescu's *Oedipe* (1936) and Shylock in Reynaldo Hahn's *Le marchand de Venise* (1935). In that year he also appeared at the Orange opera festival in *La damnation de Faust*. He made guest appearances throughout Europe and appeared in the film version of Gustave Charpentier's *Louise* (1939). His many recordings reveal a firm, supple voice of ample range and a notable feeling for words.

Harold Rosenthal/R

Perra [Perras], Margarita [Margherita]

(*b* Monastir [now Bitola, Macedonia] or Salonica, 15 Jan 1908; *d* Zürich, 2 Feb 1984). Greek soprano. She studied at the Salonica State Conservatory and then at the Berlin Hochschule für Musik; there, in 1927 as Norina, she caught the attention of Bruno Walter, who engaged her for the Städtische Oper. She appeared as Nuri in Eugen d'Albert's *Tiefland* and as Cupid in C.W. Gluck's *Orfeo ed Euridice* (1927) and sang the title role in the Berlin première of Paul Graener's *Hanneles Himmelfahrt* (1928). She later moved to the Berlin Staatsoper, having toured in Spain, Argentina and Brazil. In 1935 she was engaged by the Vienna Staatsoper and was highly praised as W.A. Mozart's Konstanze under Felix Weingartner. She repeated the role in Salzburg (1935) and at Glyndebourne (1937), and had further successes as the Queen of Night, Susanna, Pamina and other Mozart roles. In 1936 she sang

Gilda at Covent Garden. Having married in 1937, she settled in Zürich and until 1944 appeared only in recitals, but returned to the operatic stage for a season in Vienna (1946–7). Her firm, well-schooled voice possessed a gently glowing tone colour.

Obituary, *Opera*, xxxv (1984), 376–7

George Leotsakos

Perron [Pergamenter], Karl

(*b* Frankenthal, Pfalz, 3 June 1858; *d* Dresden, 15 July 1928). German bass-baritone. He studied with Julius Hey in Berlin and Julius von Stockhausen in Frankfurt, making his début in 1884 at Leipzig as Wolfram. In 1892 he moved to Dresden, where he was engaged at the Hofoper until 1913. There he created John the Baptist in *Salome* (1905), Orestes in *Elektra* (1909) and Ochs in *Der Rosenkavalier* (1911). In addition to his Richard Strauss roles he sang Don Giovanni, Count Almaviva (*Le nozze di Figaro*), Hans Heiling, Nélusko (*L'Africaine*), Ambroise Thomas' Hamlet, Escamillo and Yevgeny Onegin. At Bayreuth between 1889 and 1904 he sang Amfortas, Wotan, King Mark and Daland. A powerful actor, he sang with great authority.

Elizabeth Forbes

Persson, Miah

(*b* Örnsköldsvik, 27 May 1971). Swedish soprano. She sang in choirs as a child in the provincial town of Hudiksval, and after spending a year in Paris studied singing, musicology, piano and conducting at the Kulturama conservatory in Stockholm (1991–4). She joined Opera Studio 67 in 1994, and subsequently continued her studies at the University College of Opera. Persson was engaged at the Royal Swedish Opera in 1999, singing roles such as Susanna, Pamina, Gretel, Sophie (*Der Rosenkavalier*), Frasquita (*Carmen*) and Dorinda (G.F. Handel's *Orlando*). She made her French début as Héro (*Béatrice et Bénédict*) at the Théâtre des Champs-Elysées in 1998, and has subsequently sung Nannetta (*Falstaff*) at the Aix Festival and the Champs-Elysées. After her acclaimed Salzburg Festival opera début in 2004, as Sophie, she returned in 2005 and 2006 as Sifare in *Mitridate*. In 2005 Persson sang a delightful, spirited Susanna at Covent Garden (her house début), and in 2006 she was widely praised for her elegantly sung, subtly acted Fiordiligi at Glyndebourne. Other roles include the Governess in *The Turn of the Screw* (which she has sung at Frankfurt Opera), and Almirena in *Rinaldo* (Montpellier and Innsbruck). Her clear, sweet tone,

shapely phrasing and nimble coloratura, heard on her début recital of Mozart arias, have also made her an admired singer in the Baroque and Classical concert repertory.

Richard Wigmore

Pertile, Aureliano

(*b* Montagnana, nr Padua, 9 Nov 1885; *d* Milan, 11 Jan 1952). Italian tenor. He studied with GIACOMO OREFICE in Padua and made his début at Vicenza in *Martha* in 1911. After further studies in Milan with Manlio Bavagnoli he began to attract notice in 1913–14 at the S Carlo, Naples, singing in *Madama Butterfly* and *Carmen*, and then at the Costanzi, Rome (1915–16), La Scala (1916) and at the Colón, Buenos Aires (1918). He achieved fame in 1922 for his performance in *Mefistofele* at La Scala under Arturo Toscanini, whose favourite tenor he then became. Still at La Scala, where he appeared every year until 1937, he scored notable successes as Lohengrin, Giacomo Puccini's Des Grieux, Edgardo, Andrea Chénier, Canio, Radames, Riccardo, Don Alvaro, Manrico and Fedora, and took the title roles in the premières of Arrigo Boito's *Nerone* (1924), Ermanno Wolf-Ferrari's *Sly* (1927), and Pietro Mascagni's *Nerone* (1935). He sang until 1946, in the later years appearing frequently as Otello. From 1945 he taught at the Milan Conservatory. His voice was not particularly powerful, and the tone, rather thick in the middle register, took on nasal and guttural inflections. It became smooth and mellifluous, however, in lyrical moments as well as vibrant and incisive in dramatic ones. Pertile stood out because of his fine enunciation, variety of expression and unusual interpretative gifts, as can be heard in recordings from his best years (1922–32), including solos from *Andrea Chénier* and *Adriana Lecouvreur*, and Radames in a complete *Aida* from La Scala. At his peak Pertile was widely held, in Italy and Argentina, the equal of the most famous tenors of the period. Less fortunate in the USA (he sang at the Metropolitan only during the 1921–2 season), he was very popular at Covent Garden (1927–31), especially as Manrico, Radames and Canio.

P. Morby: 'Aureliano Pertile', *Record Collector*, vii (1952), 244–60, 267–83 [with discography by H.M. Barnes and V. Girard]

Rodolfo Celletti/Valeria Pregliasco Gualerzi

Peters, Roberta

(*b* New York, 4 May 1930). American soprano. She studied with William Hermann and was engaged by the Metropolitan at 19, without previous stage experience. She made her début in 1950 as Zerlina, a last-minute replacement for Nadine Conner; her official début was to have been as the Queen of Night, two months later. By her 25th anniversary with the company she had given 303 performances of 20 roles in 19 operas, notably Gilda, Despina, Norma, Rosina, Oscar, Zerbinetta and Lucia. Later she attempted to broaden her repertory in lyric soprano roles, playing Violetta, Mimì and Jules Massenet's Manon outside New York and performing in musical comedy. She performed at Covent Garden (*The Bohemian Girl* under Thomas Beecham, 1951), in Salzburg (*Die Zauberflöte*, 1963), Vienna (1963), Munich (1964) and Berlin (1971), and with the Kirov and Bol'shoy companies (1972). A singer of considerable charm and flute-like accuracy, Peters maintained the PONS and GALLI-CURCI tradition of coloratura singing at a time when the more dramatic attitudes of CALLAS and, later, SUTHERLAND were in vogue. She recorded several of her most successful roles, including Zerbinetta and Rosina with Erich Leinsdorf and the Queen of Night with Karl Böhm.

R. Peters and L. Biancolli: *A Debut at the Met* (New York, 1967)

J. Hines: 'Roberta Peters', *Great Singers on Great Singing* (Garden City, NY, 1982), 231–9

Martin Bernheimer/R

Petersen, Lauritz Peter Corneliys.

See CORNELIUS, PETER.

Petersen, Marlis

(*b* Sindelfingen, 1968). German soprano. She took piano and flute lessons as a child, and later became a pupil of SYLVIA GÉSZTY at the Staatliche Hochschule für Musik in Stuttgart, where she won several competitions. She also studied jazz and tap dancing in at the New York City Dance School in Stuttgart. In 1993 she joined the Nuremberg Opera as a coloratura soprano, singing roles including Ännchen, Blonde, Oscar (*Un ballo in maschera*), Rosina, Lulu and the Queen of Night. She also appeared as a guest in other leading German houses, and at La Scala. In 1998 Petersen joined the company of the Deutsche Oper am Rhein in Düsseldorf, where her successes included W.A. Mozart's Susanna and Viola in Manfred Trojahn's *Was ihr wollt*. In 2002 she made sensational débuts at the Vienna Staatsoper, as Lulu, and at Covent Garden, as a dazzling Zerbinetta. Her other roles include Adèle in *Die Fledermaus* (which she sang for her Chicago Lyric Opera début in 2006), Sophie, Norina (*Don*

Pasquale) and Konstanze, the role of her Aix Festival début in 2007. The same year Petersen created the role of Aphrodite in H.W. Henze's *Phaedra* at the Berlin Staatsoper and La Monnaie, Brussels. She also has a flourishing career as a concert singer, notably in J.S. Bach, many of whose cantatas she has performed and recorded with Ton Koopman. On disc she can also be heard as Elisa in Mozart's *Il re pastore*, on a recording made at performances at the 2006 Salzburg Festival, and Joseph Haydn's *The Seasons*.

Richard Wigmore

Peterson, Curt

(*b* Colorado, 1967). American tenor. He studied at the Juilliard School's Opera Center after taking a degree in vocal performance at the University of Colorado at Boulder, and made his professional debut, as David in *Die Meistersinger*, with Opera Colorado in 1992. Since then he has made his name in North America as a fluent lyric tenor, equally adept in the bel canto repertory (with Gioachino Rossini's Count Almaviva a favourite role) and in contemporary opera. He is also a noted interpreter of the Classical oratorio repertory, and of later works such as *Carmina burana*. His other operatic roles include Nadir (*Les pêcheurs de perles*), Tonio in *La fille du régiment* (which he sang for his Opera Lyra Ottawa début in 2001), Ajax I in *La belle Hélène*, Lindoro (*L'Italiana in Algeri*), Ramiro (*Cenerentola*) and Ernesto (*Don Pasquale*). In 1996 Peterson created the role of Matthew Gurney in Santa Fe Opera's 1996 world première production of Tobias Picker's *Emmeline*, repeating the part for his New York City Opera début the following season and also for the recording. In 2001 he made his French debut, at the Nantes Opera, in a production of Manfred Gurlitt's *Soldaten*.

Richard Wigmore

Petitpas, Mlle

(*d* Paris, 24 Oct 1739). French soprano. She made her début with the Paris Opéra in January 1727 in the last three performances of the opening run of François Francoeur and François Rebel's *Pirame et Thisbé* and was well received. She created Ismene to PÉLISSIER's Polyxena in J.-N.-P. Royer's *Pyrrhus* (1730). In the première of Jean-Philippe Rameau's *Hippolyte et Aricie* (1733) she sang four parts, and was the only singer named and praised by the *Mercure* for her 'nightingale's cantilena' (*ramage de rossignol*). Her light, supple voice had a coloratura quality and great flexibility: according to J.-B. de La Borde, 'Elle avait autant de talent pour chanter les ariettes que la Pélissier pour déclamer le récitatif', though he considered Marie-Jeanne Lemière even greater in florid singing. Immediately after these performances she disappeared surreptitiously to England for an assignation, returning in April 1734. She sang Electra in the 1734 revival of Henry Desmarets and André Campra's *Iphigénie en Tauride*, and created roles in Rameau's *Les Indes galantes* (1735) and *Castor et Pollux* (1737). Her career was short and she died young.

Philip Weller

Petrenko, Yelizaveta Fyodorovna

(*b* Akhtirka, 23 Nov/5 Dec 1880; *d* Moscow, 28 Oct 1951). Ukrainian mezzo-soprano. She entered the St Petersburg (later Petrograd) Conservatory in 1902 and studied singing with Natal'ya Iretskaya and ballet with Mikhail Fokine. She made her début at the Mariinsky as Delilah in 1905 while still a student; at her graduation recital the following year her rendering of Arsace's aria from *Semiramide* created a sensation. In 1909 she sang with CHALIAPIN in *Ivan the Terrible* (*The Maid of Pskov*) during the first Sergey Diaghilev season in Paris. In 1913 she sang Marfa in a variant version by Maurice Ravel and Igor Stravinksy of *Khovanshchina*, also directed by Diaghilev in Paris. She continued at the Mariinsky until 1915 and thereafter sang elsewhere in Petrograd and in Moscow, retiring in 1922 to take up teaching. Between 1907 and 1915 she made frequent appearances in the West: in 1913 and 1914 she participated in the Russian seasons in Paris and London with Diaghilev and Thomas Beecham, creating the role of Death in Stravinsky's *The Nightingale*. She was equally at home in mezzo-soprano and contralto parts, her enormous repertory including Amneris, Carmen, Fricka, Stéphano (Charles Gounod's *Roméo et Juliette*), Ratmir (*Ruslan and Lyudmila*), Bonny Spring (*Snow Maiden*) and Paulina and the Countess (*Queen of Spades*). She sang with nearly all the great Russian singers of her day, including Chaliapin, YERSHOV and SMIRNOV. Her recordings show a voice with a warm, caressing quality, equally effective in opera and in the P.I. Tchaikovsky songs for which she became famous.

Boris Semeonoff

Petrov, Osip (Afanas'yevich)

(*b* Yelizavetgrad [now Kirovograd], 3/15 Nov 1806; *d* St Petersburg, 28 Feb/12 March 1878). Russian bass. His date of death is often given incorrectly as 27 February/11 March or 2/14 March, the latter being the date of his burial. He first sang in a church choir, at the same time teaching himself the guitar; he was also taught the clarinet by a friend. In 1826 he was taken into Zhurakhovsky's travelling company, making his début in Yelizavetgrad in C.A. Cavos's *The Cossack Poet*, and shortly after joining the troupe of Ivan Fyodorovich Stein: here he was much influenced by working with the great actor Mikhail Shchepkin. Continuing his self-education, with help from Cavos in singing and Osip Hunke for piano and theory, he made rapid progress, singing in various different operatic genres and acting in plays. In 1830 Petrov made his St Petersburg début, soon winning wide recognition for his talents. At the première of *A Life for the Tsar* (1836) he set a tradition for the interpretation of Ivan Susanin with a performance of overwhelming dramatic power: Glinka himself recounted how the chorus of Poles set upon Petrov so violently that he had genuinely to defend himself. Other roles written for Petrov and created by him include M.I. Glinka's Ruslan (1842), the Miller in Alexander Dargomïzhsky's *Rusalka* (1856), Oziya in A.N. Serov's *Judith* (1863), Vladimir in Serov's *Rogneda* (1865), Leporello in Dargomïzhsky's *The Stone Guest* (1872), Ivan the Terrible in Nikolay Rimsky-Korsakov's *The Maid of Pskov* (1873), Varlaam in Modest Musorgsky's *Boris Godunov* (1874), Prince Gudal in Anton Rubinstein's *The Demon* (1875) and the Mayor in P.I. Tchaikovsky's *Vakula the Smith* (1876). In April 1876 the Mariinsky Theatre held a celebration to mark his 50th anniversary on the stage: he was presented with a gold medal by the tsar and a diamond-studded gold wreath, on each leaf of which was engraved the name of one of the 100 operas in which he had sung. For Petrov's jubilee Tchaikovsky wrote his Nicolay Nekrasov cantata, *To Touch the Hearts of Men*.

Petrov's voice, which ranged from *B'* to *f'*, from a rich, profound bass to a flexible baritone in the high register, was greatly admired for its warmth, depth and evenness of delivery; and his vivid personality and generous perception made him especially successful as a character actor. His non-Russian roles included Gioachino Rossini's Figaro, Vincenzo Bellini's Oroveso, Giacomo Meyerbeer's Bertram, Ferdinand Hérold's Zampa and Carl Maria von Weber's Kaspar. But his embodiment of essential Russian types in a bass voice of peculiarly Russian character provided many different composers with an example and an inspiration: V.V. Stasov was not exaggerating when at the jubilee he declared that 'Petrov may be considered one of the founders of Russian opera as we know it'. Petrov married the contralto Anna Yakovlevna Vorob'yova, who sang thereafter under her married name.

John Warrack/R

Petrova, Anna Yakovlevna (Vorob'yova)

(*b* St Petersburg, 2/14 Feb 1817; *d* St Petersburg, 13/26 April 1901). Russian contralto. Her mother, Avdot'ya Vorob'yova (*d* 1836), and her mother's former husband, Yakov Stepanovich Vorob'yov (1766–1809), were leading singers of their day. Trained originally for ballet, she studied singing with M.I. Glinka, among others, and identified closely with that composer's musical outlook. After her début as Pippo in Gioachino Rossini's *La gazza ladra* in 1833, she created the part of Vanya in *A Life for the Tsar* (1836) and later Ratmir in *Ruslan and Lyudmila* (1842). She and her husband OSIP PETROV were recognized as pioneers of the Russian nationalist school of music, notably by the critic and musicologist V.V. Stasov, who described her voice as 'one of the most exceptional and astonishing in all Europe: size, beauty, strength, gentleness'. Petrova also excelled in the bel canto operas of Rossini and Vincenzo Bellini, in which her singing was compared to that of ALBONI and VIARDOT. Her reminiscences were published in *Russkaya starina*, xxvii (1880), 611–17.

Boris Semeonoff

Piccaver [Peckover], Alfred

(*b* Long Sutton, Lincs., 24 Feb 1884; *d* Vienna, 23 Sept 1958). English tenor. He was brought up in New York, where he studied at the American Institute of Applied Music. In 1907 he went to Europe and was engaged for the Neues Deutsches Theater, Prague, where he made his début as Romeo. He continued his studies with Rosario in Milan and Ludmilla Prohaska-Neumann in Prague. In 1910 he joined the Vienna Hofoper, remaining a favourite there until his retirement in 1937. He sang in the first Austrian performances of *La fanciulla del West* and *Il tabarro*. His repertory included Andrea Chénier, Radames, Lohengrin, Walther, Faust, Des Grieux, Don José, Canio, Werther, Florestan and Lensky. He sang with the Chicago Opera from 1923 to 1925 and at Covent Garden in 1924. Piccaver made many recordings, both acoustic and electric, which well convey the velvety yet voluminous character of his voice.

Harold Rosenthal/Alan Blyth

Picchi, Mirto

(*b* San Mauro a Signa, nr Florence, 15 March 1915; *d* Florence, 25 Sept 1980). Italian tenor. He studied in Florence with Giuseppe Armani and GIULIA TESS. He made his début as Radames in the season organized by La Scala at the Milan Palazzo del Sport in 1946. At first he sang Verdi and Puccini roles in Italy and abroad, appearing at the Cambridge Theatre, London (1947–8), as the Duke of Mantua, Rodolfo and Cavaradossi, and at the 1949 Edinburgh Festival as Riccardo in *Un ballo in maschera*. In 1952 he sang Pollione at Covent Garden at CALLAS's London début as Norma. From the early 1950s he specialized in contemporary music, creating roles in Juan José Castro's *Proserpina y el extranjero* (1952, La Scala), Ildebrando Pizzetti's *Cagliostro* (1953, La Scala) and *La figlia di Iorio* (1954, Naples), and Flavio Testi's *La celestina* (1963, Florence), and took part in the Italian première of *War and Peace* (1953, Florence). He scored notable successes as Peter Grimes and as Captain Vere (*Billy Budd*), and his large repertory included the Drum Major (*Wozzeck*), Tom Rakewell, Tiresias (*The Bassarids*) and Igor Stravinsky's Oedipus. His last appearance was as W.A. Mozart's Don Basilio at La Scala in 1974. Picchi's recordings of Riccardo (Edinburgh), Don Carlos (1951), Pollione (1952) and Jason to Callas's Medea at La Scala (1957) disclose his virtues as a singer of style and subtle artistry seldom found among Italian tenors, compensating for a voice somewhat lacking in native warmth.

Alan Blyth

Piccolomini, Marietta

(*b* Siena, 15 March 1834; *d* Poggio Imperiale, Florence, 23 Dec 1899). Italian soprano. She made her début in February 1852 at the Teatro della Pergola, Florence, in *Lucrezia Borgia* and later that year sang at the Teatro Apollo, Rome, in *Poliuto* and *Don Pasquale*. In 1853 she sang Gilda in *Rigoletto* at Pisa, and at Turin in 1855 she sang Violetta in *La traviata*, a role for which she became famous; she was the first Violetta in London (1856, Her Majesty's Theatre) and Paris (1856, Théâtre Italien). At Her Majesty's in 1858 she sang Arline in *La zingara*, the Italian version of Michael William Balfe's *The Bohemian Girl*, and the title role of *Luisa Miller*. She was also heard as Serpina in *La serva padrona*, Zerlina in *Don Giovanni*, Lucia, Adina in *L'elisir d'amore*, Marie in *La fille du régiment*, Amina in *La sonnambula*, Elvira in *I puritani* and Leonora in *Il trovatore*. In 1863 she married the Marchese Gaetani della Fargia and retired from the stage. Her popularity, especially as Violetta, rested more in her youthful, attractive appearance and her acting ability than in her vocal accomplishment. According to Henry Chorley, 'her voice was weak and limited… hardly one octave and a half in compass. She was not sure in her intonation: she had no execution'.

H.F. Chorley: *Thirty Years' Musical Recollections* (London, 1862/*R*, abridged 2/1926/*R* by E. Newman)

Elizabeth Forbes

As a contralto Pistocchi was active in the principal theatres. At Ferrara in 1675 a sonnet, *Ai numi dell'Adria*, was published in his honour; in the years that followed he was in Turin (1688), Parma (1688–9, 1690–92, 1699, 1701), Piacenza (1687, 1690), Rome (1693, 1694), Bologna (1694–5), Modena (1686, 1691), Genoa (1693), Pesaro (1692) and Venice (1690–92, 1699, 1704–5). On his last visit to Venice adverse comment was made on the condition of his voice, but he continued to sing for many years in religious services and private entertainments. Great though his fame was as a singer, it was even greater as a teacher of singing; his most celebrated pupils included Luigi Albarelli, VALENTINO URBANI, Antonio Pasi, Annibale Pio Fabri, ANTONIO MARIA BERNACCHI, GAETANO BERENSTADT and Giuseppe Cassani. These pupils helped to spread a fame that became almost legendary and contributed to the persistence of various anecdotes, such as Charles Burney's about the loss of his voice. P.F. Tosi's panegyric in his *Opinioni* and the fact that Pistocchi was a man of superior literary culture helped to spread an idea of Pistocchi as the defender of a 'pure' style, far removed from the preoccupation with technique of the following generation. According to Vincenzio Martinelli, however, the corruption of taste originated in his school. In fact he had among his pupils singers who showed a variety of stylistic tendencies, from the emotionalism of Antonio Pasi to the many-styled virtuosity of BERNACCHI. The trend towards vocal agility around the 1720s and 30s was, moreover, a general phenomenon and not traceable to a single school. The summit of Pistocchi's art must have consisted in the ability to ornament, which according to Tosi involved both melodic and rhythmic variation.

Sergio Duranti/R

Plançon, Pol [Paul-Henri]

(*b* Fumay, Ardennes, 12 June 1851; *d* Paris, 11 Aug 1914). French bass. A pupil of GILBERT DUPREZ and GIOVANNI SBRIGLIA, he made his début at Lyons in 1877. He first sang at the Paris Opéra in 1883 as Charles Gounod's Méphistophélès, and remained there for ten seasons, taking part in the premières of Jules Massenet's *Le Cid* (Count of Gormas) and Camille Saint-Saëns's *Ascanio* (François I) for 14 consecutive seasons (1891–1904), singing, besides his French and Italian roles, occasionally in German and even in English (as Friar Francis in the première of Charles Villiers Stanford's *Much Ado About Nothing*). In 1893 he appeared for the first time at the Metropolitan Opera, returning as leading bass for 12 of the subsequent seasons there until his

farewell to the house in 1908. In 1894 he created Garrido in *La Navarraise* at Covent Garden. Judging by the recordings that survive, Plançon was the most polished singer of his time. His beautiful *basse chantante* had been admirably schooled, and his style was extremely elegant; his many recordings (1902–8) embody standards otherwise outside the experience of a present-day listener. Not only his flawless trills and rapid scales but his cantabile and pure legato, as in 'Voici des roses' (*Faust*) and 'Vi ravviso' (*La sonnambula*), are exemplary.

J. Dennis: 'Paul Henri Plançon', *Record Collector*, viii (1953), 149–91 [incl. discography and commentary by L. Hevingham-Root]

Desmond Shawe-Taylor/R

Plaschke, Friedrich [Plaške, Bedřich]

(*b* Jaroměř, 7 Jan 1875; *d* Prague, 4 Feb 1952). Czech bass-baritone. He studied in Prague, and in Dresden with KARL SCHEIDEMANTEL. He made his début at the Dresden Hofoper in 1900 as the Herald in *Lohengrin* and remained a member of that company until 1937, creating Pöschel (*Feuersnot*), the First Nazarene (*Salome*), Arcesius (d'Albert's *Die toten Augen*), Altair (*Die ägyptische Helena*), Count Waldner (*Arabella*) and Morosus (*Die schweigsame Frau*); he was also the first Dresden Barak, Gérard (*Andrea Chénier*), Boris Godunov and Amfortas. He sang Pogner at Bayreuth in 1911 and Kurwenal, Hans Sachs and Amfortas at Covent Garden in 1914. Plaschke toured the USA with the German Opera Company, 1922–4. In Germany he was considered one of the best singing actors of his day. He left a few acoustic recordings, most notably extracts from his Hans Sachs. He was married to the soprano EVA VON DER OSTEN.

Harold Rosenthal/Alan Blyth

Platonova [Garder], Yuliya [Julia] Fyodorovna

(*b* Mitava, Latvia, 1841; *d* St Petersburg, 4/16 Nov 1892). Russian soprano. After studying in Riga and St Petersburg she made her début in 1862 at the Mariinsky Theatre as Antonida. She possessed a small but cultured voice of pleasing timbre and was noted for the clarity of her diction and her outstanding dramatic talent. She was admired and respected by many of the leading Russian composers of her time, in whose operas she created important roles, among them Mary in César Cui's *William Ratcliff* (1869), Dasha in Aleksandr Nikolayevich Serov's posthumous *Vrazh'ya sila* ('The Power of the Fiend', 1871), Donna Anna in Alexander Sergeyevich Dargomïzhsky's *The Stone Guest* (1872), and Olga in Nikolay Rimsky-Korsakov's *The Maid of Pskov* (1873). Her initiative and energy were largely responsible for a revival of *Rusalka* in St Petersburg in 1865, and for the first full production there of *Boris Godunov* in 1874, following a presentation of three scenes the previous year; Platonova sang Marina on both occasions. OLENINA D'ALHEIM was one of her pupils.

Boris Semeonoff/R

Plishka, Paul

(*b* Old Forge, PA, 28 Aug 1941). American bass. He studied at Montclair State College, and received his initial stage experience with Paterson Lyric Opera, New Jersey. In 1965 he joined the Metropolitan Opera National Company, singing W.A. Mozart's Bartolo and Giacomo Puccini's Colline. When the touring company was disbanded, he was invited to join the Metropolitan Opera at Lincoln Center, where he made his début as the Monk in *La Gioconda* (1967). He remained a member of the company throughout his career, singing leading roles in both the serious and *buffo* repertories, among them Leporello, Oroveso (*Norma*), King Mark, Varlaam, Pimen and Boris Godunov; but it is as an interpreter of Giuseppe Verdi that he is particularly admired: as Falstaff, Zaccaria, the Miller, Banquo, Philip II, Procida, Silva and Fiesco (*Simon Boccanegra*). He made his La Scala début in *La damnation de Faust* in 1974, and in 1991 sang Kutuzov (*War and Peace*) at San Francisco. His mellow, voluminous bass can be heard in recordings of *Anna Bolena*, *I puritani*, *Norma*, *Faust*, *Le Cid* and *Falstaff*.

Martin Bernheimer/R

Plowright, Rosalind (Anne)

(*b* Worksop, 21 May 1949). English soprano, later mezzo-soprano. She studied in Manchester and at the London Opera Centre, making her début in 1975 as the Page in *Salome* with the ENO. In 1976–7 she sang Countess Almaviva and Donna Elvira with Glyndebourne Touring Opera. Her later roles with the ENO have included Miss Jessel, Elizabeth I (*Maria Stuarda*), Hélène (*Les vêpres siciliennes*), Elisabeth de Valois and Tosca. Plowright made her Covent Garden début in 1980 as Ortlinde, returning as Donna Anna, Maddalena (*Andrea Chénier*), Leonora (*Il trovatore*), Ariadne, Senta and Desdemona. In 1982 she made her US début at San Diego as Medora (*Il corsaro*), followed by Violetta and Emmanuel Chabrier's

Gwendoline. She first sang at La Scala in 1983 as Suor Angelica, returning as C.W. Gluck's Alcestis (1987). After singing Luigi Cherubini's Medea (in French) at Buxton in 1984, she repeated the role at Covent Garden and (in Italian) at Lausanne. Her repertory has also included Norma, Butterfly, Lady Macbeth, Tatyana and Gioconda. Among Plowright's recordings are Gaspare Spontini's *La vestale* and impassioned interpretations of Leonora in both *Il trovatore* and *La forza del destino*. A versatile, highly dramatic artist, she has a full-toned, dark-coloured voice particularly rich in the middle register. She experienced vocal problems at the height of her career, but returned to sing Santuzza at the Berlin Staatsoper in 1996, and Giorgetta (*Il tabarro*) at the ENO in 1997. In 2000 she turned to mezzo-soprano, first appearing as Amneris for Scottish Opera.

H. Matheopoulos: *Diva* (London, 1991), 133–44

Elizabeth Forbes

Podles, Ewa

(*b* Warsaw, 26 April 1952). Polish contralto. She studied at Warsaw State Music High School and won prizes at competitions in Moscow, Toulouse, Barcelona and Rio de Janeiro. Engaged at the Wielki Theatre, Warsaw, she sang roles ranging from Cenerentola to Konchakovna (*Prince Igor*). In 1984 she sang Rosina at Aix-en-Provence and made her Metropolitan début as G.F. Handel's Rinaldo. Between 1985 and 1989 she sang Cornelia in *Giulio Cesare* in Rome, Malcolm (*La donna del lago*) in Trieste and Adalgisa in Vancouver. She made her Covent Garden début in 1990 as Hedwige (*Guillaume Tell*) and her début at La Scala as Ragonde (*Le comte Ory*) in 1991, the year she also sang Delilah at the Opéra Bastille and Arsace (*Semiramide*) at La Fenice. In 1997 she performed and recorded the role of Polinesso in Handel's *Ariodante* with Les Musiciens du Louvre. Her flexible, rich-toned voice, very individual in timbre, is ideal for the Rossini coloratura contralto roles, notably Tancredi, which she has sung at La Scala (1993) and recorded to acclaim. Podles is also admired as a concert singer, in works such as Giuseppe Verdi's Requiem and *Das Lied von der Erde*, and she is an accomplished recitalist, as can be heard on a vivid recording of Russian songs.

Elizabeth Forbes/R

Poell, Alfred

(*b* Linz, 18 March 1900; *d* Vienna, 30 Jan 1968). Austrian baritone. After qualifying as a doctor, he took singing lessons at the Vienna Academy of Music, and made his operatic début in Düsseldorf in 1929. He remained a member of the Düsseldorf company until 1940, when he was engaged as a principal baritone at the Vienna Staatsoper. During the next two decades Poell also appeared frequently as a guest at La Scala, Covent Garden, the Paris Opéra, Glyndebourne and the Salzburg Festival. While he was admired above all in W.A. Mozart (as Count Almaviva, Don Giovanni, Guglielmo and Masetto), his repertory included several Strauss roles (notably Mandryka and Faninal), Gunther (*Götterdämmerung*) and Benjamin Britten's Tarquinius. Poell sang in the world premières of Strauss's *Die Liebe der Danae* (Salzburg, 1952) and Gottfried von Einem's *Der Prozess* (Salzburg, 1953). His extensive discography includes Almaviva, Masetto, Pizarro (*Fidelio*), Faninal, Gunther, Homonay (*Der Zigeunerbaron*), and Mahler Lieder.

Richard Wigmore

Poggi, Antonio

(*b* Castel S Pietro, Bologna, 1806; *d* Bologna, 15 April 1875). Italian tenor. He studied with ANDREA NOZZARI and, after an unsuccessful appearance in Paris as James (*La donna del lago*), made his début in 1827 at Bologna as Peter the Great (Giovanni Pacini's *Il falegname di Livronia*). He sang in the first performance of Giuseppe Persiani's *Saraceni in Catania* (1832, Padua) and created Roberto in *Torquato Tasso* at the Teatro Valle, Rome (1833). He made his début at La Scala as Elvino (*La sonnambula*) in 1834, then sang in the first performance of Gaetano Donizetti's *Pia de' Tolomei* (1837, Venice). He appeared at Her Majesty's Theatre, London, in 1842. His repertory included Gioachino Rossini's Almaviva and Idreno; Vincenzo Bellini's Arturo (*La straniera* and *I puritani*), Pollione and Orombello (*Beatrice di Tenda*); Donizetti's Nemorino, Edgardo, Gennaro and Fernando (*Marin Faliero*). He sang Oronte in Giuseppe Verdi's *I Lombardi* at Venice and Florence (1843), Rome and Milan (1844). For a revival in Senigallia in July 1843, Verdi composed a new cabaletta in Act 2 for Poggi (as Oronte). He went on to create Charles VII in Verdi's *Giovanna d'Arco* at La Scala (1845). He was married to the soprano ERMINIA FREZZOLINI, but they separated in 1846 and he retired from the stage.

Elizabeth Forbes

Pointu, Germaine.

See CERNAY, GERMAINE.

Polaski, Deborah

(*b* Richland Center, WI, 26 Sept 1949). American soprano. She studied at Marion College, Indiana, and with Irmgard Hartmann in Berlin, making her début in 1976 at Gelsenkirchen. After appearing at Munich, Hamburg, Karlsruhe and Ulm, she sang Death/Judas in Gottfried von Einem's *Jesu Hochzeit* at Hanover (1980); Marie (*Wozzeck*), Isolde and Kundry at Freiburg (1983–5); Katerina Izmaylova at Mannheim (1985–6); Amelia (*Un ballo in maschera*) at Essen and Chrysothemis at Geneva (1986); Senta at La Scala and in Prague (1988); Richard Strauss's Electra (a role she has recorded) at Zürich (1991) and Salzburg (1994); and Kundry for her Metropolitan début (1992) and at Bayreuth (1993). With a powerful, vibrant voice of true dramatic proportions, she is well equipped to tackle the heavier Strauss and Wagner repertory. After singing Brünnhilde at Bayreuth in 1988, with limited success, Polaski scored a triumph when she sang the same role there in 1991 and in several subsequent seasons; she has also sung the part at Cologne (1990), the Berlin Staatsoper (1993–4) and Covent Garden (1994–5). Her other roles include the Marschallin, the Dyer's Wife, which she first sang in Amsterdam and Geneva in 1992, and Dido and Cassandra in *Les Troyens*, for which she was acclaimed at the 2000 Salzburg Festival. In addition to Electra, Polaski has recorded Ortrud in *Lohengrin* (with Daniel Barenboim) and Ermanno Wolf-Ferrari's *Sly*.

Elizabeth Forbes

Polgár, László

(*b* Budapest, 1 Jan 1947). Hungarian bass. He studied with Eva Kutrucz at the Liszt Academy of Music, Budapest, 1967–72, and later privately with HANS HOTTER and YEVGENY NESTERENKO. He made his début at the Hungarian State Opera in 1971 as Count Ceprano (*Rigoletto*). His career proper started in the early 1980s: he sang Rodolfo in *La sonnambula* at Covent Garden in 1981, Leporello in Yuri Lyubimov's famous Budapest production of *Don Giovanni* in 1982 and Gurnemanz in János Ferencsik's *Parsifal* revival the next year. He returned to Covent Garden in 1989, with the Hungarian State Opera, as Bluebeard in Béla Bartók's opera.

Polgár has made regular appearances at the Vienna Staatsoper since 1983, and in Munich and Paris from 1985, and has appeared in Zürich and Salzburg as Sarastro and Publius (*La clemenza di Tito*). But he is perhaps best known for his magnetic interpretation of Bluebeard, which he recorded with Pierre Boulez and sang again with distinction at the Aix Festival in 1998. He was a member of the Zürich

Opera from 1991. He owes his international fame to his beautifully silky, well-balanced voice and his remarkable declamation and musicality, also noted features of his concert appearances.

Péter Várnai/Alan Blyth

Poli-Randaccio, Tina [Ernestina]

(*b* nr Ferrara, 13 April 1879; *d* Milan, 1 Feb 1956). Italian soprano. She studied in Pesaro and made her début in 1902 at Bergamo in *Un ballo in maschera*. She travelled widely in Italy, Spain, Hungary and South America, mostly in lyric-dramatic and *verismo* roles. Admiring her Santuzza in *Cavalleria rusticana*, Pietro Mascagni engaged her in 1908 to sing the heroine of his *Amica* in an Italian tour. In 1910, as Brünnhilde in *Siegfried*, she made her début at La Scala, where she also appeared in the theatre's first presentation of *La fanciulla del West*. Other notable roles were Aida, La Gioconda and the heroine of Pietro Mascagni's *Parisina*. In her only season at Covent Garden (1920) she sang Tosca, a performance praised for emotional force but criticized for unevenness. Her career lasted until 1934 with an appearance as Turandót at Bologna. Recordings show a powerful voice, capable of delicacy but inclined to shrillness at the top and having the fast vibrato characteristic of Italian sopranos of the period. She was clearly an imaginative artist, sensitive to nuance and warm in feeling.

J.B. Steane

Pollack, Rose.

See PAULY, ROSE.

Pollet, Françoise

(*b* Boulogne-Billancourt, nr Paris, 10 Sept 1949). French soprano. She studied the violin and later singing at the Versailles Conservatoire and in Munich. A three-year engagement at Lübeck (1983–6, début role the Marschallin) gained her experience in W.A. Mozart, Giuseppe Verdi, Richard Wagner and Richard Strauss. Since then she has sung widely in France and abroad, and became the first French soprano since CRESPIN to gain an international reputation. Her forays into the French repertory include Valentine (*Les Huguenots*), both Cassandra and Dido in *Les Troyens*, Catherine of Aragon (Camille Saint-Saëns's *Henry VIII*) and Paul Dukas' Ariane (in the 1991 Ruth Berghaus production at the Théâtre du Châtelet, Paris).

Pollet's soft-grained, lustrous instrument is not always heard to advantage in the dramatic soprano repertory that she sometimes essays, but rather in gentler styles and moods, in which her voice attains a rare beauty of tone and style. She is a distinguished singer of lieder and *mélodies* and a lambent interpreter of the orchestral version of Olivier Messiaen's *Poèmes pour Mi*. Her recordings include *Les Troyens* (Dido) and *La damnation de Faust* (both under Charles Dutoit), *Les Huguenots*, Brahms songs and a highly praised disc of French arias.

Max Loppert

Pons, Juan

(*b* Ciutadella, Menorca, 8 Aug 1946). Catalan baritone. He studied in Barcelona and joined the Liceu chorus, singing bass roles such as Banquo, Tom (*Ballo in maschera*) and the King (*Aida*). As a baritone, he sang Ernesto (Gaetano Donizetti's *Parisina*) and Giorgio Germont in 1978, followed by Gérard (*Andrea Chénier*) in 1979. That year he made his Covent Garden début as Alfio (*Cavalleria rusticana*) and sang Egberto (*Aroldo*) in concert at Carnegie Hall, New York. His decisive breakthrough came in 1980, when he stood in at short notice as Giuseppe Verdi's Falstaff at La Scala. During the next 15 years he appeared in most of the leading European opera houses; he made his Metropolitan début in 1985 as Amonasro, and has also sung in San Francisco and Chicago. Pons's repertory includes Henry Ashton, Belcore, Scarpia, Sharpless, Jack Rance, Jules Massenet's Herod, and many of the great Verdi baritone roles, several of which he has recorded. On the opening night of the 1994–5 Met season, he sang Michele (*Il tabarro*) and Tonio (*Pagliacci*). A fine actor, with a large, evenly produced voice, he is equally assured in tragic parts such as Boccanegra and comic roles like Melitone, Gianni Schicchi and, especially, Falstaff.

Elizabeth Forbes

Pons, Lily (Alice Joséphine)

(*b* Draguignan, nr Cannes, 12 April 1898; *d* Dallas, 13 Feb 1976). American soprano of French birth. A piano student at the Paris Conservatoire, she received her first vocal instruction from Alberti de Gorostiaga, and then studied with ZENATELLO in New York. She made her operatic début in 1928 at Mulhouse as Lakmé, with Reynaldo Hahn conducting. She then sang in French provincial houses as Gretel, Cherubino, Blonde, the Queen of Night and Mimì. On the recommendation of Zenatello, she went to the Metropolitan, making her début in 1931 as Lucia. She caused a sensation and thereafter remained with the company for 28 seasons.

She had success as Gilda, Amina, Marie (*La fille du régiment*), Philine (*Mignon*), Olympia and, above all, Lakmé. In 1935 she sang Rosina at Covent Garden and Gilda and Lucia at the Paris Opéra. She sang in South America, San Francisco (where her roles included the Queen of Shemakha and Violetta), Monte Carlo and Chicago, and made several films. Married to André Kostelanetz from 1938 to 1958, she made her stage farewell at the Metropolitan in 1958 as Lucia. Pons possessed a pure, agile high coloratura voice, as can be heard on her many recordings.

B. Park: 'Lily Pons', *Record Collector*, xiii (1960–61), 245–71 [with discography]

Dennis K. McIintire/Alan Blyth

Ponselle [Ponzillo], Rosa (Melba)

(*b* Meriden, CT, 22 Jan 1897; *d* Green Spring Valley, MD, 25 May 1981). American soprano. She studied singing with her mother and then with Anna Ryan. She began to appear in film theatres and vaudeville, often with her elder sister Carmela (a mezzo-soprano who was to sing at the Metropolitan from 1925 to 1935). In 1918 her coach, William Thorner, brought her to the attention of CARUSO and Gatti-Casazza. In the first Metropolitan *La forza del destino* she made an unprecedented début – the first operatic performance of her life – as Leonora (1918), opposite Caruso and DE LUCA. She had prepared the role with Romano Romani, who remained her principal operatic and vocal tutor. She sang at the Metropolitan for 19 seasons, undertaking 22 roles.

Rosa Ponselle in the title role of 'La Gioconda' (Ponchielli)

Perhaps most celebrated as Norma, she also enjoyed extraordinary successes in *Oberon, Ernani, Don Carlos, La Gioconda, Andrea Chénier, Guillaume Tell, L'amore dei tre re, Don Giovanni* (Donna Anna), *Cavalleria rusticana, La traviata, La vestale* and *L'Africaine*. She also participated in Joseph Carl Breil's *The Legend*, Italo Montemezzi's *La notte di Zoraïma* and Romano Romani's *Fedra*. In 1935 she attempted Carmen, and experienced her only notable failure. Two years later she retired from opera, reportedly after her request for a revival of *Adriana Lecouvreur* was rejected, and vowed never again to set foot in the Metropolitan after her final performance (Carmen, 1937). She made her Covent Garden début as Norma in 1929, returning as Violetta, Leonora (*Forza*) and the heroine of Romani's *Fedra*; at the Florence Maggio Musicale in 1933 she sang Julia (*La vestale*). Although her repertory was broad, she never sang Giacomo Puccini or Richard Wagner, about which she later confessed regret.

Ponselle's voice is generally regarded as one of the most beautiful of the century. She was universally lauded for opulence of tone, evenness of scale, breadth of range, perfection of technique and communicative warmth. Many of these attributes are convincingly documented on recordings, among them a nervously vital portrayal of Violetta from a complete Metropolitan recording of *La traviata* (1935). In 1939 and 1954 she made a few private song recordings, later released commercially, the later set revealing a still opulent voice of darkened timbre and more limited range.

I. Cook: 'Rosa Ponselle', *Opera*, iii (1952), 75–81
T. Villella and B. Park: 'Rosa Ponselle Discography', *Grand Baton*, vii/1–2 (1970), 5–14
'Ponselle at 80', *Opera*, xxviii (1977), 13–25
J. Hines: 'Rosa Ponselle', *Great Singers on Great Singing* (Garden City, NY, 1982), 250–57
J.A. Drake: 'Rosa Ponselle Recalls Roles and Colleagues, 1918–1924', *OQ*, x/1 (1993–4), 85–108
M. Bernheimer: 'The Golden Soprano', *Opera*, xlviii (1997), 138–45

Martin Bernheimer/R

Popp, Lucia

(*b* Uhorská Ves, 12 Nov 1939; *d* Vienna, 16 Nov 1993). Austrian soprano of Slovak birth. After studying at Bratislava, she made her début there as the Queen of Night in 1963, then sang Barbarina in Vienna, where she was engaged at the Staatsoper, and First Boy (*Die Zauberflöte*) at Salzburg. She made her Covent Garden début in 1966, as Oscar, returning as Despina, Sophie, Aennchen, Gilda and Eva. She first appeared at the Metropolitan in 1967 as the Queen of Night (a role she recorded with

Otto Klemperer), and later sang Sophie and Pamina there. Engaged at Cologne, she sang throughout Europe in a repertory including Zerlina, Susanna, Ilia, Blonde, Konstanze, Marzelline, Rosina and Zerbinetta. In the 1980s she took on heavier roles such as Elsa, Arabella and the Marschallin in Munich; subsequently she sang the two Strauss heroines at Covent Garden. Her voice, which was initially light and perfectly suited to the soubrette and coloratura repertory, matured to encompass the more intense emotions of the roles undertaken in her later career. Popp was also a delightful concert singer and a noted interpreter of a wide range of lieder, which she sang with charm and perspicacity. Among her many cherished recordings are Susanna, Pamina, Vitellia, Sophie, Gretal, Bystrouška (*Cunning Little Vixen*) and lieder by Franz Schubert and Richard Strauss.

A. Blyth: 'Lucia Popp', *Opera*, xxxiii (1982), 132–8

Alan Blyth

Porto, Carlo (Ottolini)

(*b* *c*1800; *d* 1836 or later). Italian bass. During the 1830s he sang in Milan, Florence, Turin and Naples. He created roles in four Donizetti operas: Ernesto in *Parisina* (1833) and Clifford in *Rosmonda d'Inghilterra* (1834) at the Teatro della Pergola, Florence; Talbot in *Maria Stuarda* (1834), given as *Buondelmonte* owing to censorship, and Raimondo in *Lucia di Lammermoor* (1835) at S Carlo. He was a famous exponent of Henry VIII (*Anna Bolena*) and also sang many Bellini roles: Capellio (*I Capuleti e i Montecchi*), Rodolfo (*La sonnambula*), Oroveso (*Norma*) and Giorgio (*I puritani*), which he sang in Bologna (1836).

Elizabeth Forbes

Poulenard, Isabelle

(*b* Paris, 5 July 1961). French soprano. She studied at the Ecole Nationale d'Art Lyrique of the Paris Opéra. Her début came in 1981 at Tourcoing, as Lisette in Giovanni Paisiello's *Il Re Teodoro in Venezia* – a performance which, like many of her early appearances, was conducted by Jean-Claude Malgoire. Since then she has taken a wide variety of roles, including Despina, the Queen of Night, C.W. Gluck's Iphigenia (*Iphigénie en Aulide*) and the title role in Jean-Philippe Rameau's *Zéphyre*. Her recordings include Antonio Cesti's *Orontea*, Jean-Baptiste Lully's *Armide*, Francesco Cavalli's *Serse*, Antonio Vivaldi's *L'incoronazione di Dario*, Rameau's *Le temple de la gloire, Platée* and *Les indes galantes*, G.F. Handel's *Alessandro* and *Tamerlano* and G.P. Telemann's *Orpheus*. Her performances are not confined to the Baroque and Classical periods; she has sung in Francis Poulenc's *Dialogues des Carmélites* and in French sacred choral repertory of the 19th and 20th centuries. Poulenard's agile technique, tonal purity and light-textured voice, however, are especially well suited to 17th- and 18th-century music, in which she reveals an informed sense of style.

Nicholas Anderson

Powers, Marie

(*b* Mount Carmel, PA, 1910; *d* New York, 28 Dec 1973). American contralto. She studied in New York and in the mid-1940s toured the USA with the San Carlo Opera; her roles for the company included Azucena, Amneris and both Laura and La Cieca in *La Gioconda*. She sang Madame Flora in the New York (1947) and London (1948) premières of Gian Carlo Menotti's *The Medium*, and in 1948 made her début with the New York City Opera in his *The Old Maid and the Thief*. She also created Azelia in William Grant Still's *Troubled Island* in 1949, and the Mother in Menotti's *The Consul* (Philadelphia, 1950). At the Paris Opéra she sang Fricka (1951) and Mistress Quickly (1952). A very effective actress with a strong, deep-toned voice, she will always be associated with *The Medium* in which she played the role of Baba, both on Broadway and in the film version (1951).

Elizabeth Forbes

Pozzoni(-Anastasi), Antonietta

(*b* Venice, 1846; *d* Genoa, April 1914). Italian soprano, later mezzo-soprano. She studied in St Petersburg and Milan, making her début at La Scala in 1865 as Marguerite (*Faust*). After singing in Rome, Padua, Turin and Naples, in 1871 she sang *La traviata* in Florence, which led to her engagement to sing Aida at the première of Giuseppe Verdi's opera in Cairo. Her soprano repertory included Lady Macbeth, Hélène (*Les vêpres siciliennes*), Anna Bolena, Lucrezia Borgia, Emilia (Saverio Mercadante's *La vestale*) and Norma. In 1874 she took part in the first performance of Carlos Gomes's *Salvator Rosa* at Genoa and sang Amneris at Brescia, repeating the role in Rome, Madrid, Milan, Barcelona and Florence. Her mezzo parts included Fidès, Azucena, Ortrud, Léonor (*La favorite*) and Jules Massenet's Herodias. She retired in 1887.

Elizabeth Forbes

Prégardien, Christoph

(*b* Limburg 18 Jan 1956). German tenor. He studied at the Frankfurt Hochschule für Musik and later in Milan, Frankfurt and Stuttgart. From 1983 to 1987 he sang with the Frankfurt Opera, making his début there in 1984 as Vašek (*The Bartered Bride*) and later appearing as Hylas (*Les Troyens*), Fenton and the Steersman. His wide repertory ranges from the Baroque to the 19th century and includes the roles of Don Ottavio, Tamino and Almaviva. His operatic commitments have taken him to many German opera houses, and in 1989–90 he sang in Haydn operas at Cairo and Antwerp. He has acquired an outstanding reputation in cantata and oratorio; his dramatic sense, articulate delivery and lyrical, light-textured voice are well suited to J.S. Bach's Evangelist and to the interpretation of lieder. In this repertory his fresh and penetrating performances of Franz Schubert (usually with fortepianist Andreas Staier) have been especially acclaimed.

Prégardien's recordings include Claudio Monteverdi's *Il ritorno d'Ulisse in patria*, G.F. Handel's *Rodelinda*, W.A. Mozart's *Don Giovanni*, Joseph Haydn's *Armida* and *Creation*, J.S. Bach's *St John Passion* and *St Matthew Passion*, *Christmas Oratorio* and a number of cantatas, and lieder by Schubert, Robert Schumann, Johannes Brahms and Felix Mendelssohn. In the autumn of 2000 he began to teach at the Hochschule für Musik und Theater in Zürich.

Nicholas Anderson

Prévôt [Prevot, Prévost], Ferdinand

(*b c*1800; *d* ?Paris, in or after 1857). French baritone. His father was also a singer, and in the early years of his career he was designated Prévot *fils* or by his full name. He sang in the Opéra chorus as early as 1818 and made his solo début in 1824 in A.-E.-M. Grétry's *Anacréon chez Polycrate*. His career continued into the 1850s; though he never achieved star status among his peers, his longevity and consistency were remarkable, and he took many minor roles, notably in the premières at the Paris Opéra of Daniel Auber's *Gustave III* (1833), Fromental Halévy's *La Juive* (1835) and *Les Huguenots* (1836). Charles Hervey (*The Theatres of Paris*, 1846) called him 'a most useful member of the company, who, without being ever positively good, is never positively bad'.

Laurie C. Shulman

Prey, Hermann

(*b* Berlin, 11 July 1929; *d* Krailling vor München, 23 July 1998). German baritone. He studied in

Berlin and made his début in 1952 at Wiesbaden as Moruccio (*Tiefland*). Engaged at Hamburg (1953–60), he created Meton in Ernst Krenek's *Pallas Athene weint* (1955). A regular guest in Vienna, Berlin and Munich, he first appeared at Salzburg in 1959 as the Barber in *Die schweigsame Frau*. In 1960 he made his Metropolitan début as Wolfram, returning as Count Almaviva, Papageno and Gioachino Rossini's Figaro, the role of his San Francisco début in 1963, when he also sang Olivier (*Capriccio*). In 1962 he sang Don Giovanni at Aix-en-Provence; in 1965 he made his Bayreuth début as Wolfram and sang Storch (*Intermezzo*) with the Munich company in Edinburgh. Having made his Covent Garden début in 1973 as Rossini's Figaro, he returned as Guglielmo, Papageno, Eisenstein and Beckmesser, which he first sang at Bayreuth in 1981. Prey was also a well-schooled interpreter of lieder, of which he made many recordings, and a noted concert singer, especially in J.S. Bach. His mellifluous tone and keen phrasing, allied with a genial, relaxed manner on stage, were particularly apt in W.A. Mozart, as his recordings of Figaro, Guglielmo and Papageno reveal. He published an autobiography, *First Night Fever* (London, 1986).

Leontyne Price in 'Il trovatore' (Verdi), Salzburg, 1972

Alan Blyth

Price, (Mary Violet) Leontyne

(*b* Laurel, MS, 10 Feb 1927). American soprano. While training as a teacher at Wilberforce, Ohio, she sang with her college glee club. In 1949 she won a scholarship to the Juilliard School, New York, where she sang Alice Ford. In 1952 Virgil Thomson chose her to sing St Cecilia in a Broadway revival of his opera *Four Saints in Three Acts*; thereafter she was immediately engaged as Bess in a new production of Gershwin's opera at the Ziegfeld Theatre (1953) and on a two-year world tour. Porgy was sung by WILLIAM WARFIELD to whom she was then married. At Rome in 1954 she sang in a première concert the title role in Lou Harrison's opera *Rapunzel*. A concert career (including first performances of works by Samuel Barber and Henri Sauguet) was interrupted by a highly successful television appearance as Tosca (1955). This, and appearances at San Francisco in 1957 (as Madame Lidoine in Francis Poulenc's *Dialogues des Carmélites* and as Aida, Leonora in *Il trovatore*, Donna Elvira and in Carl Orff's *Die Kluge*), decided the course of her career. At her débuts at the Verona Arena, Vienna and Covent Garden (all 1958) and La Scala (1960), she had further triumphs as Aida. In 1959 she sang Liù and Thaïs at Chicago. In 1960 she first appeared at the Salzburg Festival, as Donna Anna, returning there in 1962–3 as Leonora in *Il trovatore*; in the latter role she had made an acclaimed Metropolitan début in 1961. Further roles there included Leonora (*La forza del destino*), Elvira (*Ernani*), Amelia (*Un ballo in maschera*), Butterfly, Minnie, Tosca, Pamina and Fiordigli. A notable appearance among many in New York was as Cleopatra in Barber's *Antony and Cleopatra*, commissioned for the opening of the new Metropolitan (1966), in which some of the lyrical passages were composed especially for her; in 1975 she played Giacomo Puccini's Manon there, and she made her farewell appearance as Aida in 1985. Though her repertory embraced Poppaea, Handel's Cleopatra, Tatyana, and Mozart and Puccini roles, it was principally in Giuseppe Verdi that she achieved fame as one of the world's foremost sopranos. Her voice was a true *lirico spinto*, able to fill Verdi's long phrases with clean, full, dusky tone. Musically she was a subtle interpreter, though her acting did not always evince dramatic involvement. Many recordings, of Mozart, Puccini and, especially, Verdi operas, as well as African-American spirituals, faithfully document her career.

A. Blyth: 'Leontyne Price Talks to Alan Blyth', *Gramophone*, xlix (1971–2), 303 only

W. Sargeant: ' Leontyne Price', *Divas* (New York, 1973), 135–67

R. Jacobson: '"Collard Greens and Caviar"', *ON*, l/1 (1985–6), 18–23, 28–31, 46–7

M. Loppert: 'Price, Rysanek, Los Angeles', *Opera*, xlvii (1996), 1277–85

Alan Blyth

Price, Dame Margaret (Berenice)

(*b* Blackwood, Mon. [now Gwent], 13 April 1941). Welsh soprano. She studied in London, making her début in 1962 with the WNO as Cherubino, then singing Nannetta, Amelia (*Boccanegra*) and Mimì. She first sang at Covent Garden in 1963 as Cherubino; later roles there included Pamina, Marzelline, Donna Anna, Fiordiligi, Countess Almaviva, Desdemona, Norma and Amelia (*Ballo in maschera*). At Glyndebourne she sang the Angel (*Jephtha*) in 1966, then Konstanze and Fiordiligi. In 1967 she appeared as Titania at Aldeburgh. She made her American début in 1969 at San Francisco as Pamina, followed by Nannetta, Fiordiligi and Aida. In 1971 Price made a sensational German début when she sang Donna Anna in Cologne; the same year she first appeared at Munich as Amelia (*Boccanegra*), returning there in Mozart roles and as Ariadne, Adriana Lecouvreur and the Marschallin. She sang in Chicago, at La Scala and at the Paris Opéra, with which she visited New York in 1976, as Countess Almaviva and Desdemona, the role of her Metropolitan début in 1985. Her repertory also embraced Giuseppe Verdi's Joan of Arc and Elisabeth de Valois. Her operatic recordings include several of her Mozart roles, Amelia (*Ballo in maschera*) and Desdemona (both with Georg Solti) and Isolde with Carlos Kleiber. Price was a thoughtful, full-throated interpreter of a wide range of lieder, continuing to give recitals and make recordings after she gave up the stage in 1994. She retired in October 1999. In her earlier years her voice was sweet and brilliant in tone, highly flexible and capable of great dramatic power. Latterly the tone lost something of its bell-like purity, but acquired a new warmth and expressiveness. She was made a CBE in 1982 and a DBE in 1993.

A. Blyth: 'Margaret Price', *Opera*, xxxvi (1985), 607–14

Alan Blyth

Printemps [Wigniolle], Yvonne

(*b* Ermont, Seine-et-Oise, 25 July 1894; *d* Neuilly, nr Paris, 18 Jan 1977). French soprano. She made her début in revue at the Théâtre Cigale in Paris at the age of 12. A career at the Opéra-Comique seemed possible, for she had a voice of delightful quality with prodigious breath control; in 1916, however, she joined the company of actors run by Sacha Guitry, whom she married three years later. Together they enjoyed a great international success in the theatre in plays and *opérettes*, including André Messager's *L'amour masqué* and Reynaldo Hahn's *Mozart*, until their divorce in 1932, after which Printemps appeared in films and two musicals – Noël Coward's *Conversation Piece* (1934) and Oscar Straus's *Les trois valses* (1937). In 1949 she appeared as Hortense Schneider, with her second husband (Pierre Fresnay) as Jacques Offenbach, in Marcel Achard's film *La valse de Paris*. Several composers wrote specially for her, including Francis Poulenc and Hahn. Her recordings of song and operetta reveal a light voice managed with skill, charm and imagination.

J.B. Steane

Prohaska, Jaro(slav)

(*b* Vienna, 24 Jan 1891; *d* Munich, 28 Sept 1965). Austrian bass-baritone. After an early career as a church organist, he studied singing at the Vienna Music Academy (1919–23) and made his début in 1922 at Lübeck. After an engagement at Nuremberg (1925–31) he joined the Berlin Staatsoper, of which he remained a member until 1952, taking part in the première of Paul Graener's *Der Prinz von Homburg* (1935). He sang regularly at Bayreuth (1933–44) as Hans Sachs, Wotan, Gunther, Telramund, Amfortas and the Dutchman. He appeared at the Teatro Colón, Buenos Aires (1935 and 1937), and at the Paris Opéra (1936 and 1940). In addition to Wagner roles his repertory included Ochs, which he sang at the 1949 Salzburg Festival. He was appointed head of the Hochschule für Musik in Berlin in 1947 and director of its opera school in 1952; among his pupils was HERMANN PREY. His recordings include his Hans Sachs (1943, Bayreuth) and Ochs (1949, Salzburg).

Harold Rosenthal/Alan Blyth

Prokina, Yelena

(*b* Odessa, 16 Jan 1965). Russian soprano. Her early tuition at the School of Arts in Odessa and the Leningrad Institute for the Theatre, Music and Cinematography was followed by vocal studies at the Leningrad Conservatory, moulding Prokina as an outstanding singer-actress. She made her début as Marguerite in Charles Gounod's *Faust* with the Kirov Opera in 1988, remaining with the company for several years to sing such parts as Desdemona, Tatyana, Emma in *Khovanshchina* and a passionately fresh Natasha in *War and Peace* (the last two preserved on disc). She appeared with the Kirov Opera at the Edinburgh Festival and in Birmingham in 1991, but it was not until 1994 that she consolidated her international reputation with widely praised portrayals of Kát'a Kabanová at Covent Garden and Tatyana at Glyndebourne. She also sang in the first Portuguese performances of *Yevgeny Onegin* (1993, Lisbon).

Although Prokina has sung as far afield as Los Angeles (Donna Anna and Lina in *Stiffelio*), Buenos Aires (Lisa in *The Queen of Spades*) and Sydney (Tatyana), her most significant performances have been in western Europe: she has established close links with the opera house in Zürich, where in 1995 she sang her first Amelia in *Simon Boccanegra* (a role she repeated at Glyndebourne in 1998), and she was Fevroniya in Harry Kupfer's Bregenz production of *The Legend of the Invisible City of Kitezh* in 1995. The latter performance, recorded on CD and video, summed up Prokina's art, with her vivid stage presence, both innocent and womanly, complementing a radiant soprano. Her other recordings include a notable disc of songs by R.M. Glière and Carl Maria von Weber's *Euryanthe*.

John Allison/R

Protschka, Josef

(*b* Prague, 5 Feb 1944). German tenor of Czech birth. He studied in Cologne and made his début in 1977 at Giessen; after singing in Saarbrücken, in 1980 he was engaged at Cologne. He has also appeared in Düsseldorf, Mannheim, Munich and Hanover and has sung Peisander (*Il ritorno d'Ulisse*) in Salzburg (1985), Idomeneus at Drottningholm (1986), Flamand (*Capriccio*) in Florence and Hoffmann at Bregenz (1987) and the title role of *Fierrabras* in Vienna (1988). His repertory includes Tamino, Don Ottavio, Max, Lionel, Faust, Werther, Jeník, Loge and Tom Rakewell. He has a strong, warm-toned and lyrical voice which has become larger and more dramatic through tackling heavier roles such as Florestan, which he sang at Hamburg (1988), Brussels (1989) and Covent Garden (1990), and Lohengrin, which he sang in Zürich (1991).

Elizabeth Forbes

Pryanishnikov, Ippolit Petrovich

(*b* Kerch', 14/26 Aug 1847; *d* Moscow, 11 Nov 1921). Russian baritone and director. He studied in St Petersburg and Milan and sang in Italy until 1877. He made his début at the Mariinsky Theatre, St Petersburg, as Anton Rubinstein's Demon (1878) and sang there until 1886, notably

as Lionel in the première of P.I. Tchaikovsky's *Maid of Orleans* and Mizgir' in the première of Nikolay Rimsky-Korsakov's *Snow Maiden*. Highly valued by Tchaikovsky, he was the first St Petersburg Yevgeny Onegin (1885) and Mazeppa (1884). He directed operas by Borodin, Rimsky-Korsakov and Leoncavallo in both Tbilisi and Moscow. GEORGY ANDREYEVICH BAKLANOV, Nikolay Bol'shakov, and Yevgeniya Konstantinova Mravina were his pupils.

David Cummings

Pushee, Graham

(*b* Sydney, 25 April 1954). Australian countertenor. While studying with David Parker in Sydney in 1973 he made his opera début, with the University of New South Wales Opera, as Oberon in the first Australian performances of *A Midsummer Night's Dream*, revealing marked theatrical gifts, an even and charactertul tone and technical agility. In 1976 he sang the title role in G.F. Handel's *Orlando* with the same company. On the basis of these opera roles and appearances in early music performances with the Sydney Renaissance Players, he received a Churchill Fellowship, enabling him to study with PAUL ESSWOOD in London and at the Schola Cantorum Basiliensis. Settling in Switzerland, he appeared in the title roles of *Poro*, *Orlando*, *Admeto*, *Giulio Cesare*, *Scipione* and *Il pastor fido* at the Karlsruhe Handel Festival. He returned to Australia in 1994 to take the title role in *Giulio Cesare* in a highly praised new production for the Australian Opera, and also sang the role in his Paris Opéra début and for Houston Grand Opera. He made his British début in 1994 with Opera North as Andronicus in Handel's *Tamerlano*, returned to the role of Oberon for Karlsruhe, Wiesbaden, Leipzig and Turin and sang Endimione in Francesco Cavalli's *La Calisto* under René Jacobs at La Monnaie in Brussels (which he recorded) and at the Deutsche Staatsoper, Berlin. Pushee's repertory also includes Ruggiero in *Alcina*, the title role in *Rinaldo* and roles in Claudio Monteverdi and Henry Purcell. Among his recordings are a disc of Handel arias, excerpts from *Giulio Cesare* and a video of the complete opera.

Roger Covell

Putnam, Ashley (Elizabeth)

(*b* New York, 10 Aug 1952). American soprano. She studied at the University of Michigan, then became an apprentice at Santa Fe. She made her début in 1976 as Lucia at Norfolk, Virginia, where she later sang the title role in the American première of Thea Musgrave's *Mary, Queen of Scots* (1978). She sang Angel More (*The Mother of Us All*) and Gilda at Santa Fe, Donna Elvira and Ophelia (*Hamlet*) at San Diego, Zdenka at Houston and Konstanze at Miami. At the New York City Opera (1978–83) her roles included Violetta, Elvira (*I puritani*), Giselda (*I Lombardi*), Adèle (*Le comte Ory*), Marie (*La fille du régiment*) and Gaetano Donizetti's Mary Stuart. She made her European début in 1978 as Musetta at Glyndebourne, where she later sang Arabella (1984) and Vitellia (1991). Returning to Santa Fe she sang Richard Strauss's Danae (1985), Fiordiligi (1988) and the Marschallin (1989), a role she also sang at Los Angeles (1994) and the Berlin Staatsoper (1995). In 1983 she sang Xiphares (*Mitridate*) at Schwetzingen and Aix-en-Provence. She made her Covent Garden début in 1986 as Jenůfa and her Metropolitan début in 1990 as Donna Elvira. The following year she also sang Fusako in the US première of H.W. Henze's *Das verratene Meer* in San Francisco. During the 1970s and 80s Putnam's flexible, silver-toned voice was well suited to the bel canto repertory. More recently she has increasingly taken on heavier, more dramatic roles such as Donna Anna, Kát'a Kabanová, Ellen Orford and Eva, which she first sang at Cleveland in 1995.

Elizabeth Forbes

Quilico, Gino

(*b* New York, 29 April 1955). Canadian baritone, son of LOUIS QUILICO. He studied music at the University of Toronto and continued vocal studies with his parents, making his début in 1978 as Mr Gobineau in a television performance of *The Medium*. After engagements in Canada and the USA, in 1980 he made his European début in Paris as Charles Gounod's Mercutio, which brought him a three-year contract at the Opéra. He made his British début as Giacomo Puccini's Lescaut with Scottish Opera at the 1982 Edinburgh Festival, followed by Valentin at Covent Garden the next year and Escamillo in 1991. Besides many roles in the French, Italian and Russian repertory and in W.A. Mozart, he has sung in the premières of *L'héritière* (J.-M. Damase) and *Montségur* (Marcel Landowski). He made his Metropolitan début in 1987 as Jules Massenet's Lescaut, returning as Valentin (1990), Figaro in the première of John Corigliano's *The Ghosts of Versailles* (1991), Escamillo, Schaunard, Belcore and Enrico (*Lucia di Lammermoor*). He has sung on several occasions with his father in the same opera, notably at the Metropolitan in *Il barbiere* and *Manon*. His high baritone voice, full-toned and pungent in character, is combined with an elegant presence. He has made several video recordings, and his CD recordings include Lescaut, Marcello, Mercutio, Orpheus (Claudio Monteverdi), Raimbaud (*Le comte Ory*), Coroebus (*Les Troyens*) and the title role in Ernest Chausson's *Le roi Arthus*. He was awarded the Order of Canada in 1992.

J.B. Steane: 'Louis and Gino Quilico', *Opera Now* (1996), Jan, 32–4

Noël Goodwin

Quilico, Louis

(*b* Montreal, 14 Jan 1925; *d* Toronto, 15 July 2000). Canadian baritone. He studied at the Conservatoire de Musique, Montréal, with MARTIAL SINGHER, the Accademia di S Cecilia, Rome, and the Mannes College, New York. His principal teacher was the pianist Lina Pizzolongo, whom he married in 1949. She died in 1991. After winning several major Canadian competitions he made his professional début with the Opera Guild of Montreal in 1954. In 1955 he won the Metropolitan Opera Auditions of the Air and the same year made his New York début with the New York City Opera. He joined the Metropolitan in 1973 and became one of its leading baritones. He performed such roles as Rigoletto (this became his calling card, and was a role he played over 500 times in his career, the last in Ottawa in 1994), Giorgio Germont, Rodrigo (*Don Carlos*), Iago, Amonasro, Scarpia, Tonio, Golaud and Falstaff at leading houses throughout the world, including Covent Garden, the Vienna Staatsoper, the Teatro Colón, the Rome Opera, the Bol'shoy, San Francisco and the Opéra de Montréal. He was also principal baritone of the Canadian Opera Company. Quilico sang in the premières of Darius Milhaud's *Pacem in terris* (1963), a work he recorded, and *La mère coupable* (1966) and André Jolivet's *Les coeurs de la matière* (1965); in 1991 he played the title role of Tony in Frank Loesser's *The Most Happy Fella* at the New York City Opera. His many recordings include operas ranging from Claudio Monteverdi to Giuseppe Verdi, Giacomo Puccini and Jules Massenet. Quilico had a clear and ringing dramatic voice, particularly well suited to Verdi. He taught at the University of Toronto (1970–87) and at McGill University (1987–90), and gave masterclasses with young professional singers. He was awarded the Companion of the Order of Canada in 1974. In 1993 he married the Canadian pianist Christina Petrowska. Following his retirement from the Metropolitan in 1998 Quilico continued to give concerts, appearing frequently with his wife. After his sudden death his widow set up the Christina and Louis Quilico Fund to help young singers, pianists and composers for the voice. His son is the baritone GINO QUILICO.

C. Petrowska: *Mr. Rigoletto: in Conversation with Louis Quilico* (Toronto, 1996)

Ezra Schabas

R

Raaff [Raff], Anton

(*b* Gelsdorf, nr Bonn, bap. 6 May 1714; *d* Munich, 28 May 1797). German tenor. Originally educated for the priesthood, he sang in several dramas at the Jesuit college in Bonn while still a boy. After being appointed to the service of Clement Augustus, Elector of Cologne, Raaff was sent in 1736 to Munich, where he studied with G.B. Ferrandini and sang in his *Adriano in Siria* (1737). The following year he studied with BERNACCHI in Bologna, remaining in Italy until 1741–2, when he returned to electoral service in Bonn. In 1749 he left for Vienna where he sang in several operas composed and directed by Niccolò Jommelli. He was in Italy in 1751–2, when he was called to the court of Lisbon; from there he went in 1755 to Madrid and, in 1759, he travelled with FARINELLI to Naples.

For the next decade Raaff was the principal tenor on the Neapolitan and Florentine stages, appearing in operas by Johann Hasse and J.C. Bach, as well as Antonio Sacchini, Niccolò Piccinni and Josef Mysliveček. In August 1770 he arrived at Mannheim, Carl Theodor's seat, where he created the title roles in Piccinni's *Catone in Utica* (1770) and Bach's *Temistocle* (1772) and *Lucio Silla* (1775). W.A. Mozart was severely critical of his singing and acting in the title role of Ignaz Holzbauer's *Günther von Schwarzburg* (1777; also a première), but was more sympathetic after hearing him sing Bach's 'Non so d'onde viene' from *Alessandro nell'Indie* at the Concert Spirituel in Paris during June 1778; Mozart tried to win his favour by composing a setting of one of the tenor's favourite texts, 'Se al labbro mio' (K295). Raaff's last role was the title part in *Idomeneo* (1781), composed for Munich where Carl Theodor had transferred his court. Though Raaff's voice was praised by C.F.D. Schubart as having an unusually large range from bass to alto, with flexible coloratura throughout, Mozart found it small in range and limited in technique. Yet Raaff sang well enough in 1787 to impress MICHAEL KELLY, who wrote that 'he still retained his fine *voce di petto* and sostenuto notes, and pure style of singing'. He was one of the last and greatest representatives of the legato technique and portamento, brought to perfection by Bernacchi and his school.

M. Kelly: *Reminiscences* (London, 1826, 2/1826), i, 282; ed. R. Fiske (London, 1975)

P. Petrobelli: 'The Italian Years of Anton Raaff', *MJb 1973–4*, 233–73

D. Heartz: 'Raaff's Last Aria: a Mozartian Idyll in the Spirit of Hasse', *MQ*, lx (1974), 517–43

Daniel Heartz (with Paul Corneilson)

Racette, Patricia

(*b* Manchester, NH, 1965). American soprano. She studied jazz and music education at North Texas State University, and then joined the Merola Opera Program of San Francisco Opera, winning the Richard Tucker Award in 1988. The following year she made her major début at San Francisco, as Alice Ford, and subsequently sang roles with the company including Liù, Desdemona, Mimì, Musetta, Micaëla, Violetta, Elisabetta (*Don Carlos*) and Luisa Miller. Her breakthrough came with the title role in the world première of Tobias Picker's *Emmeline* (Santa Fe, 1996). She followed this two years later with a triumphant Metropolitan Opera début, as Antonia in *Les contes d'Hoffmann*, in 1998, returning later the same year as Violetta. With her strong, shining lyric soprano and dramatic intensity, Racette has also been admired as Cio-Cio-San (*Madama Butterfly*) at Houston Grand Opera, Los Angeles (on her 2005 début there) and San Francisco, as Jenůfa, which she sang for her Chicago debut in 2000, and in the world premières of Carlisle Floyd's *Cold Sassy Tree* (Houston, 2000) and Picker's *An American Tragedy* (Metropolitan, 2005). Her recordings include Alexander Zemlinsky's *Der Traumgorge*.

Richard Wigmore

Radford, Robert

(*b* Nottingham, 13 May 1874; *d* London, 1 March 1933). English bass. He studied in London, making his début in 1904 at Covent Garden as the Commendatore. He sang Hunding and Hagen in 1908 in the first *Ring* cycle in English, conducted by Hans Richter; Pogner (*Die Meistersinger*) and Abbot Tunstall in the première of Edward Naylor's *The Angelus*, 1909; and, in 1910, Claudius (*Hamlet*) and Tommaso in the British première of *Tiefland*. During the war years he sang with the Beecham Opera Company on tour and in London, when his roles included Boris. Returning to Covent Garden as a founder-member of the British National Opera Company in 1922–3, he appeared as Méphistophélès, the Father (*Louise*), King Mark and Osmin. His firm, resonant voice and superb diction were particularly admired in Richard Wagner, as his recordings of Wotan in Act 2 of *Die Walküre* and of Hagen's Watch and Call of the Vassals demonstrate.

W.G. Kloet: 'Robert Radford', *Record Collector*, xiv (1961–2), 200–30 [incl. discography by J.P. Kenyon]
W. Radford: 'Robert Radford', *Recorded Sound*, no.39 (1970), 632–8

Elizabeth Forbes

Raff, Anton.

See RAAFF, ANTON.

Ragin, Derek Lee

(*b* West Point, NY, 17 June 1958). American countertenor. He studied at the Oberlin College Conservatory of Music, Ohio, and at the age of 26 won the ITT International Fellowship, which enabled him to study in Amsterdam. He has won several major prizes, including first prize in the 1986 Munich International Music Competition of the ARD. In 1983 he made his operatic début in Antonio Cesti's *Il Tito* at the Festwoche der Alten Musik, Innsbruck. His American début was as Nirenus in G.F. Handel's *Giulio Cesare* at the Metropolitan in 1988, when he was one of the first countertenors to appear there. He has appeared at the Aldeburgh, Maryland and Aix-en-Provence festivals, and in 1990 made his Salzburg Festival début as Orpheus in C.W. Gluck's *Orfeo ed Euridice*. He sings in concerts in Germany and elsewhere, but is particularly renowned for his dramatically forceful interpretations of operatic roles, recordings of which include Handel's *Giulio Cesare*, *Tamerlano* and *Flavio*, Johann Hasse's *Cleofide* and Gluck's *Orfeo*.

Nicholas Anderson

Raimondi, Gianni

(*b* Bologna, 17 April 1923). Italian tenor. He studied in Bologna with Albertina Cassani and Antonio Melandri, and in Milan with MARIO BASIOLA and Gennaro Barra Caracciolo. He made his début in 1947 at Budrio, near Bologna, in *Rigoletto*. He sang frequently at the S Carlo, Naples, from 1952 to 1979 and at La Scala from 1956 to 1972, also

appearing at the Vienna Staatsoper between 1957 and 1974 and at the Metropolitan Opera (1965–9). Endowed with an ample voice of pure, warm timbre, he had clear enunciation and an exact sense of phrasing. The facility, range and brilliance of his top register enabled him to excel in such arduous parts as Arturo (*I puritani*), Arnold (*Guillaume Tell*) and Arrigo (*Les vêpres siciliennes*). Raimondi's other notable roles included Edgardo (*Lucia di Lammermoor*), Alfredo Germont (which he recorded), Cavaradossi, Rodolfo and Pinkerton.

Rodolfo Celletti/Valeria Pregliasco Gualerzi

Raimondi, Ruggero

(*b* Bologna, 3 Oct 1941). Italian bass. A pupil of Teresa Pediconi and of Piervenanzi, he made his début at Spoleto in 1964 as Colline, followed immediately by Procida (*Les vêpres siciliennes*) at the Rome Opera; he continued to appear in Italy, notably at La Fenice and La Scala (as Timur in *Turandot*, 1967–8, returning in 1969–70). In 1969 he sang an acclaimed Don Giovanni at Glyndebourne, and in 1970 he made his Metropolitan début as Silva (*Ernani*). At Covent Garden he sang Giuseppe Verdi's Fiesco in 1972, and he appeared as Boris at La Fenice later that year. His repertory has included Jules Massenet's Don Quichotte (1982, Vienna), Charles Gounod's Méphistophélès (1985, Hamburg) and Selim in *Il turco in Italia* (1986, Pesaro). He returned to Covent Garden, as Gioachino Rossini's Moses, in 1994, and sang Iago at Salzburg in 1996 and Falstaff at the Berlin Staatsoper in 1998. He possesses the full, smooth and resonant voice of a *basso cantante* (with a certain baritonal quality and colour in the upper register) and an imposing stage presence. His career is extensively chronicled on disc, his Fiesco, Philip II and Selim particularly notable, as are his video performances as Don Giovanni in Joseph Losey's film (1979) and his Scarpia recorded live on location in Rome in 1992.

A. Blyth: 'Ruggero Raimondi Talks to Alan Blyth', *Gramophone*, l (1972–3), 2030

Rodolfo Celletti/Alan Blyth

Raisa, Rosa [Burchstein, Rose]

(*b* Białystok, 23 May 1893; *d* Los Angeles, 28 Sept 1963). American soprano of Polish birth. When she was 14 she fled to escape a pogrom and settled in Naples, where she studied with Barbara Marchisio. She made her début as Leonora in *Oberto* during the 1913 Verdi celebrations at Parma. Later that year she sang Queen Isabella (*Cristoforo Colombo*) at Philadelphia; she then sang in Chicago (1913–14) and at Covent Garden in 1914. She sang regularly in Chicago, 1916–32 and 1933–6, appearing in the first American performances of Pietro Mascagni's *Isabeau*, Italo Montemezzi's *La nave* and Ottorino Respighi's *La fiamma*. In 1936 she sang Leah in the American première of Lodovico Rocca's *Il dibuk* at Detroit.

Engaged at La Scala, she created Asteria in Arrigo Boito's *Nerone* in 1924 and Turandot in 1926. She returned to Covent Garden in 1933 as Tosca, with her husband, Giacomo Rimini, as Scarpia. She was a thrilling singer and actress, and a great dramatic soprano.

M. Scott: *The Record of Singing*, ii (London, 1979), 71–3

Harold Rosenthal/R

Ralf, Torsten (Ivar)

(*b* Malmö, 2 Jan 1901; *d* Stockholm, 27 April 1954). Swedish tenor. He studied in Stockholm and in Berlin with Hertha Dehmlow and made his début at Stettin (now Szczecin) in 1930 as Cavaradossi. After engagements at Chemnitz (1932–3) and Frankfurt (1933–5) he joined the Dresden Staatsoper, of which he remained a member until 1944. At Dresden he created Apollo in Richard Strauss's *Daphne* (1938) and sang in the recording of the work; he also appeared in the première of Heinrich Sutermeister's *Die Zauberinsel* (1942). During the 1930s and 40s he appeared regularly at the Vienna Staatsoper. He sang at Covent Garden (1935–9) as Lohengrin, Walther, Parsifal, Erik and Tannhäuser, and in 1936 was heard as Bacchus in a single performance of *Ariadne auf Naxos* given in London by the Dresden company with Strauss conducting. He returned to Covent Garden in 1948 as Radames. He sang at the Metropolitan (1945–8) in the Wagnerian repertory and as Radames and Otello, and appeared at the Teatro Colón, Buenos Aires, in 1946. Ralf had a *lirico spinto* tenor voice with a reedy but resonant timbre. His recordings include a complete *Fidelio* under Karl Böhm (1944), in which his careful musicianship and the heroic ring of his voice make his interpretation of Florestan ideal, and excerpts from the roles of Otello, Lohengrin and Walther. Ralf's two brothers, Oscar (1881–1964) and Einar (1888–1971), were also musicians. Oscar, a tenor, was a member of the Swedish Royal Opera from 1918 to 1940, and was the first Swedish tenor to sing at Bayreuth, as Siegmund in 1927; he translated many operas into Swedish and wrote an autobiography, *Tenoren han går i Ringen* ('The tenor goes into the

Ring', Stockholm, 1953). Einar, a choral conductor, was from 1940 director of the Swedish Royal Academy of Music.

Harold Rosenthal/Alan Blyth

Ramey, Samuel (Edward)

(*b* Colby, KS, 28 March 1942). American bass. He studied in Wichita and New York, making his début in 1973 as Zuniga at New York City Opera, with whom he sang until 1986; later roles with the company included Charles Gounod's Méphistophélès and Arrigo Boito's Mefistofele, Don Giovanni, Leporello, the *Hoffmann* villains, Henry VIII (*Anna Bolena*), Archibaldo, Olin Blitch (Carlisle Floyd's *Susannah*), Attila and Don Quichotte (1986). At Glyndebourne (1976–7) he sang W.A. Mozart's Figaro and Nick Shadow. He made his Chicago and San Francisco débuts (1979) as Colline. At Aix-en-Provence (1980) he sang Assur (*Semiramide*), returning as Nick Shadow (1992). He first appeared at La Scala and the Vienna Staatsoper (1981) as Figaro, the role of his début at Covent Garden (1982), where he later sang Don Basilio, Charles Gounod's and Hector Berlioz's Méphistophélès, the *Hoffmann* villains, Philip II and Attila. He sang several Gioachino Rossini roles at Pesaro between 1981 and 1989. He made his Paris Opéra début as Rossini's Moses (1983), and then sang Bertram in *Robert le diable* (1985); in 1984 he made his Metropolitan début as Argante (*Rinaldo*), returning as Sir Giorgio (*I puritani*), Escamillo, Béla Bartók's Bluebeard, Don Giovanni, Philip II and Pagano (*I lombardi*). He sang Don Giovanni at Salzburg in 1987. Ramey's other roles include Arkel, Rodolfo (*La sonnambula*) and Boris Godunov, which he first sang in Geneva in 1993. A compelling actor with a magnificent stage presence, he has a resonant, flexible, evenly produced voice particularly well suited to Rossini and the Verdi bass roles such as Philip or Attila, but no less effective as Gounod's Méphistophélès and Nick Shadow. He has recorded many of his operatic roles (including a richly comic Gaudenzio in *Il Signor Bruschino* and a subtle, dangerous Nick Shadow), in addition to such choral works as J.S. Bach's Mass in B minor, Joseph Haydn's *The Creation* and Verdi's Requiem.

M. Mayer: 'Samuel Ramey', *Opera*, xxxvii (1986), 399–405

Charles Jahant/Elizabeth Forbes

Randle, Thomas

(*b* Hollywood, CA, 21 Dec 1958). American tenor. He studied at Los Angeles and in Germany, then began his career as a concert singer. A performance in Los Angeles of Michael Tippett's *Songs for Dov*, conducted by the composer, led to his engagement at the ENO, where he made his operatic début in 1988 as Tamino. With the Los Angeles PO he has also given the US and world premières of works by Heinz Holliger and William Kraft. In 1989 he sang in Henry Purcell's *The Fairy-Queen* at Aix-en-Provence and appeared as Claudio Monteverdi's Orfeo at Valencia. He has sung Ferrando in Brussels and for Scottish Opera, Pelléas (1990) at the ENO, Olympion in *The Ice Break* at the Royal Albert Hall (1990) and Tamino at Glyndebourne (1991). He created Dionysus at the ENO in John Buller's *Bakxai* ('The Bacchae', 1992) and in 1994 sang in the première of Peter Schat's opera *Symposion* (based on the life of P.I. Tchaikovsky) with the Netherlands Opera, in *King Priam* with the ENO and *Gloriana* with Opera North at Covent Garden. The following year he sang in the première of John Tavener's *The Apocalypse* at the Proms. An excellent actor and a musical singer, he has a strong, lyrical voice with a highly distinctive timbre. His recorded repertory is mainly Baroque (*The Fairy-Queen* with Les Arts Florissants, 1989, and G.F. Handel's *Esther* under Harry Christophers, 1995) and 20th century (Tippett's *The Ice Break* with the London Sinfonietta, 1991, Benjamin Britten's *War Requiem* with the BBC Scottish SO, 1995, and Luigi Nono's *Canti di vita e d'amore* with the Bamberg SO, 1997).

Elizabeth Forbes

Randová, Eva

(*b* Kolín, 31 Dec 1936). Czech mezzo-soprano. After teaching mathematics and sport she took singing lessons, making her début as Eboli at Ostrava in 1962; she learnt the main mezzo roles before joining the Prague National Theatre in 1968. She became a member of the Stuttgart Opera in 1971, made her Bayreuth début as Waltraute in 1973, and later had conspicuous success there as Ortrud, Kundry, and Fricka in the 1976 *Ring* directed by Patrice Chéreau. At Salzburg in 1975 she sang Eboli under Herbert von Karajan, and in 1977 made her Covent Garden début as Ortrud. Her American début was at San Francisco, followed by the Metropolitan in 1981 as Fricka. She is renowned as the Kostelnička in *Jenůfa*, which she sang in Yury Lyubimov's production at Covent Garden (1986) and in a recording under Charles Mackerras (1982). Other recordings include the Fox in *The Cunning Little Vixen* (1981), Ortrud under Georg Solti (1987), Vlasta in Zdeněk Fibich's *Šárka* (1988) and Lola in Franz Schreker's *Irrelohe* (1989), which evince her dark-toned, firmly

sustained voice, incisive diction and characterization.

J. Higgins: 'The Competitive Spirit', *The Times* (17 Nov 1986) [interview]

Noël Goodwin

Rankin, Nell

(*b* Montgomery, AL, 3 Jan 1926; *d* New York, 13 Jan 2005). American mezzo-soprano. She studied at the Birmingham (Alabama) Conservatory and in New York. Her opera début was in 1949 as Ortrud at Zürich, and in her first season she sang 126 performances in a variety of roles. Engagements followed at La Scala, and at the Vienna Staatsoper in 1951 as Amneris, which she also sang for her Metropolitan début in the same year. She appeared regularly in New York for some 20 seasons and in almost as many roles, notably Ortrud, Gutrune, Ulrica and Azucena. For her débuts at Covent Garden (1953) and San Francisco (1955) she sang Carmen. Her recordings include Suzuki with TEBALDI, conducted by Alberto Erede (1951). She impressed with fullness of tone and generous phrasing more than with vitality of character.

Noël Goodwin

Rappé, Jadwiga

(*b* Toruń, 24 Feb 1952). Polish contralto. After studying at Warsaw University and the Academy of Music in Wrocław, she won first prize at the International Bach Competition in Leipzig in 1980, followed the next year by the gold medal at the International Festival of Young Soloists in Bordeaux. In 1983 she made her stage début in Warsaw. While her repertory ranges from the Baroque to contemporary music, she specializes in large-scale concert works of the 19th and 20th centuries, for which her ample, noble and steady voice is ideally suited. Although she appears less frequently in opera, she has scored notable successes as Gaea in *Daphne* (in Amsterdam) and as a grave Erda in *Das Rheingold* and *Siegfried*, a role that she has sung at the Deutsche Oper in Berlin, the Warsaw Opera and Covent Garden. In addition to Erda (with Bernard Haitink), Rappé's recordings include J.S. Bach's B minor Mass and solo alto cantatas, Ludwig van Beethoven's *Missa solemnis*, Gustav Mahler's symphonies nos. 2, 3 and 8, Arthur Honegger's *Le roi David*, Karol Szymanowski's *Stabat mater* and *Demeter* and Krzysztof Penderecki's *Polish Requiem*.

Andrew Clark

Rasi, Francesco

(*b* Arezzo, 14 May 1574; *d* Mantua, 30 Nov 1621). Italian composer, tenor, chitarrone player and poet. Like his contemporaries JACOPO PERI and GIULIO CACCINI his role as singer/composer contributed to the development of solo song and opera in the early seventeenth century.

Rasi was born into a prominent family, which later served the Medici and Gonzaga courts. In October 1592 he enrolled at the University of Pisa and in the summer of 1594 he was a pupil of Caccini. During the early 1590s he performed in Rome under the patronage of Grand Duke Ferdinando I of Tuscany. Emilio de' Cavalieri, in a letter from Rome dated 16 December 1593, reported Rasi's great success as a singer and chitarrone player and urged the grand duke to increase his salary, since he was being considered for other positions. In 1594 he may have entered the service of Carlo Gesualdo and subsequently travelled to Ferrara, Venice and Naples. He made a trip to Poland, returning to Italy by November 1597. In a letter of 17 November 1598 Cavalieri reported that Rasi had accepted an offer from the Duke of Mantua. He probably served the Gonzagas for the rest of his life.

Rasi was in Florence in 1600, when he sang in the first performances of Peri's *Euridice* (in the role of Aminta) and Caccini's *Il rapimento di Cefalo*. Both composers highly praised his artistry. At Mantua in 1607 he almost certainly created the title role in Claudio Monteverdi's *Orfeo*. Later in 1607 his singing received great praise at a seaside resort near Genoa, where he had accompanied Ferdinando Gonzaga. In 1608 in Mantua he sang in the first performances of Marco da Gagliano's *Dafne* (in the role of Apollo) and Monteverdi's *Arianna*. Later in 1608 he was in France and the Low Countries. In early 1610 Rasi, along with accomplices, was sentenced in Tuscany to be hanged, drawn and quartered for the murder of his stepmother's servant and the near murder of his stepmother; he escaped Tuscany through the protection of the Gonzagas, who arranged for him to flee to Turin. The sentence was eventually annulled in 1620, with the condition that he never return to Arezzo. In 1617 he wrote an opera, *Cibele, ed Ati*, for the wedding of Ferdinando Gonzaga and Caterina de' Medici; however, it was not performed then, and the music is lost, although the text survives in his seven-volume collection of secular and spiritual poetry, *La cetra di sette corde* (Venice, 1619), along with another libretto, *Elvidia rapita*. In 1621 he revisited Florence, Rome and Savona, and on 4 September of that year he married Alessandra Bocchineri in Pistoia, but died less than three months later. His death was mourned in an undated poem by Gabriello Chiabrera.

C. MacClintock: 'The Monodies of Francesco Rasi', *JAMS*, xiv (1961), 31–6
T. Carter and D. Butchart: 'The Original Orpheus' *MT*, cxviii (1977), 393, only [letter to ed.])

William V. Porter/R

Ratti, Eugenia

(*b* Genoa, 5 April 1933). Italian soprano. She made her début in 1954 at Sestri Levante. In 1955 she sang in the stage première of Darius Milhaud's *David* at La Scala and made her Glyndebourne début as Nannetta. In 1957 she created Sister Constance (*Dialogues des Carmélites*) at La Scala and sang Fiorilla (*Il turco in Italia*) and Elisetta (*Il matrimonio segreto*) with the Piccola Scala in Edinburgh. She made her American début in 1958 at San Francisco, singing Rosina, Musetta and Susanna. Returning to Glyndebourne, she sang Adina (1961) and the Italian Soprano in *Capriccio* (1973). She also appeared in Vienna, Munich and Paris. A spirited comic actress with a keen, expressive voice, she excelled in such roles as Vespina (*L'infedeltà delusa*), which she sang at Wexford (1969) and the Holland Festival (1970).

Elizabeth Forbes

Rautio, Nina

(*b* Bryansk, 21 Sept 1957). Russian soprano. She studied at the Leningrad Conservatory before being engaged by the Kirov from 1981 to 1987. She then joined the Bol'shoy Opera, with whom she appeared at the Metropolitan and the Edinburgh Festival in 1991, as Tatyana and Oxana (*Christmas Eve*). In 1992 she made her début at La Scala as Manon Lescaut and appeared as Aida at both the Savonlinna Festival and the Opéra Bastille. Since 1994 her roles at Covent Garden have included Amelia in *Un ballo in maschera* (her début role), Aida, Lisa and Desdemona. In 1994 she made her Vienna Staatsoper début, also as Manon Lescaut, and appeared at the Metropolitan as Aida. Rautio's other roles include Abigaille, Lady Macbeth, Leonora (*La forza del destino*) and Maddalena (*Andrea Chénier*). On the concert stage she makes a speciality of the Verdi Requiem, which she has recorded along with Manon Lescaut, arias by Giacomo Puccini and songs by P.I. Tchaikovsky. All reveal her firm, piquant, typically Russian timbre, secure technique and emotional commitment.

Alan Blyth

Rauzzini, Venanzio

(*b* Camerino, nr Rome, bap. 19 Dec 1746; *d* Bath, 8 April 1810). Italian soprano castrato and composer. After early studies in Rome and possibly also in Naples with Nicola Porpora, he made his début at the Teatro della Valle in Rome in Niccolò Piccinni's *Il finto astrologo* (7 February 1765). His first major role was in Pietro Alessandro Guglielmi's *Sesostri* at Venice during Ascension Fair 1766. In the same year he entered the service of the Elector Maximilian III Joseph at Munich, where he remained until 1772. He first appeared there in Tommaso Traetta's *Siroe* (Carnival 1767) and later that year was given leave to perform in Venice and in Vienna, where W.A. Mozart and his father heard him in Johann Hasse's *Partenope*. Charles Burney, visiting Rauzzini in August 1772, praised his virtuosity and the quality of his voice, but was most impressed by his abilities as a composer and harpsichordist. His last known operatic performance in Munich was in Andrea Bernasconi's *Demetrio* (Carnival 1772). According to Michael Kelly he was forced to leave because of difficulties with noblewomen engendered by his good looks.

Venanzio Rauzzini

Rauzzini performed for two more years in Italy before moving permanently to England. Engaged for Carnival 1773 at Milan, he was primo uomo in Mozart's *Lucio Silla* (26 December 1772) and in Giovanni Paisiello's *Sismano nel Mogol* (30 January 1773). In January Mozart wrote for him the brilliant motet *Exultate, jubilate* K165/158a. Later that year he sang at Venice and Padua, and in 1774 at Turin (Carnival) and Venice (Ascension Fair).

From November 1774 to July 1777 Rauzzini sang regularly at the King's Theatre in London, making his simultaneous début as singer and composer in the pasticcio *Armida*. William Bingley reported that his acting in Antonio Sacchini's *Motezuma* (7 February 1775) greatly impressed David Garrick. Both Burney and Lord Mount Edgcumbe, however, deemed his voice sweet but too feeble, a defect Burney ascribed to Rauzzini's devoting too much time to composition. Indeed, Rauzzini contributed arias to four other pasticcios in the season 1775–6 and wrote a comic opera, *L'ali d'amore. Piramo e Tisbe*, his best-loved opera, was first staged in London on 16 March 1775 (and probably not in Munich, 1769, as claimed in many biographical sketches); it was revived there in three other seasons and performed at many continental theatres. In the following years many of his works, both vocal and instrumental, were published in London. Rauzzini's singing also gradually won over London audiences. For his last London appearance in 1777 he composed an *Address of Thanks*, presumably the cantata *La partenza* 'sung by him and Miss Storace'. In the autumn of 1777 Rauzzini took up residence in Bath, where he managed concerts by many renowned performers, among them his pupils JOHN BRAHAM, NANCY STORACE, CHARLES INCLEDON, Mrs Billington and Mme Mara. At Dublin in 1778 he met and taught MICHAEL KELLY and promoted his career with advice to study in Naples. In the spring of 1781, again in London, Rauzzini sang in concerts with TENDUCCI and others and wrote the second act of the opera *L'omaggio di paesani al signore del contado*. He was intermittently in London during the next three seasons to stage his operas *L'eroe cinese*, *Creusa in Delfo* and *Alina, o sia La regina di Golconda*, which was heavily criticized by the *Public Advertiser* (10 May 1784). Ballets with music by him were performed at the King's Theatre in the season 1783–4, and he also directed the production of Giuseppe Sarti's *Le gelosie villane* (15 April 1784). During this period a scandal arose over his claim that certain arias in Sacchini's operas were his own. He was not in London when his incidental music for Frederick Reynolds's *Werter* (originally performed at Bath) was used at Covent Garden on 14 March 1786, and after the London première of his unsuccessful opera *La vestale* (1 May 1787) he remained permanently at Bath in his handsome town house and sumptuous country villa in Perrymead. Among his many guests was Joseph Haydn, who wrote the canon *Turk was a faithful dog and not a man* during a visit from 2 to 5 August 1794. Near the end of his life Rauzzini published a set of 12 vocal exercises with an introduction summing up his ideas on the art of singing and reflecting his own tasteful execution.

M. Kelly: *Reminiscences* (London, 1826, 2/1826/*R*1968 with introduction by A.H. King); ed. R. Fiske (London, 1975)
M. Sands: 'Venanzio Rauzzini: Singer, Composer, Traveller', *MT*, xciv (1953), 15–19, 108–11
S. Hodges: 'Venanzio Rauzzini: "The First Master for Teaching in the Universe"', *MR*, lii (1991), 12–30

Kathleen Kuzmick Hansell/R

Raveau, Alice

(*b* 1884; *d* Paris, 1951). French contralto. She studied at the Paris Conservatoire and made her début at the Opéra-Comique in 1908, singing the role that was to remain most closely associated with her: C.W. Gluck's Orpheus. She was still singing it at the company's revival in 1924, and in 1936 she took part in the first complete recording, a performance that continues to impress, as much by its intensity of feeling and care for words as by the beauty and noble power of the voice. She sang the title role in the world première of Gaston Salvayre's *Solange* (1909) and the leading female role of Diana in Samuel-Alexandre Rousseau's *Léone* (1910). At Monte Carlo in 1913 she sang Eurycleia in the world première of Gabriel Fauré's *Pénélope* and created the title role in *Yato* by Marguerite Labori. She was also a noted Charlotte in *Werther* and in 1929 sang Delilah at the Opéra. In later years she became well known as a recitalist, particularly in association with the composer and conductor Henri Tomasi. Though her fine art and rich voice can be heard in many recordings, the *Orphée* remains her most memorable achievement for the gramophone.

J.B. Steane

Reardon, John

(*b* New York, 8 April 1930; *d* Santa Fe, 16 April 1988). American baritone. After studying with MARTIAL SINGHER and MARGARET HARSHAW, he made his début in 1954 at the New York City Opera and subsequently sang with numerous companies in the USA – his Metropolitan début was in 1965 as Tomsky in *The Queen of Spades* – and Europe. His recordings include Nick Shadow. The possessor of a well-controlled lyric voice and notable acting ability, Reardon was best known for his large repertory of over a hundred roles (Scarpia, Pelléas,

Benjamin Britten's Tarquinius and roles in works by W.A. Mozart and Richard Strauss) and for the number of premières he gave, mostly with the Santa Fe Opera. These included works by Douglas Moore, Lee Hoiby (*Natalia Petrovna*, 1964; *Summer and Smoke*, 1971), Marvin David Levy and Thomas Pasatieri, as well as American premières of *The Nose*, *Cardillac*, *Dantons Tod*, *The Devils of Loudun*, *The Bassarids* and *Help, Help, the Globolinks!* He directed the opera workshop at the Wolf Trap Summer Theatre in Virginia.

J. Reardon: 'The Challenges of Modern Opera', *Music Journal*, xxix/4 (1971), pp. 28 ff

Patrick J. Smith

Rehfuss, Heinz (Julius)

(*b* Frankfurt, 25 May 1917; *d* Buffalo, NY, 27 June 1988). Swiss-Jewish bass-baritone of German birth, later active in the USA and Canada. He was brought up in Neuchâtel, and studied singing with his father, Carl Rehfuss, and operatic production with Otto Erhardt. In 1937–8 he made his début as a choral singer and stage designer at the Städtebundtheater in Biel-Solothurn; he sang in 1938–9 in Lucerne and from 1940 to 1952 at the Zürich Opera House, where he undertook more than 80 roles. With his smooth, mellifluous tone he was also an outstanding lieder and oratorio singer, particularly admired as a sensitive interpreter of Christ in J.S. Bach's Passions. From 1952 he sang at many European opera houses, notably as Don Giovanni, Boris Godunov and Golaud, and went on concert tours to America (where he later became a naturalized citizen), Asia and Africa. He also made a point of singing 20th-century music, in such roles as Dr Schön in *Lulu*, and gave the first performances of works by composers including Igor Stravinsky, Darius Milhaud, Benjamin Britten and Luigi Nono. Rehfuss taught singing during courses at Dartington Hall and Darmstadt (1947–64); he became professor of music (head of the singing and opera departments) at the State University of New York at Buffalo in 1965, and visiting professor at the Montreal Conservatory in 1961 and at the Eastman School, Rochester, New York, in 1970. In 1962 the city of Zürich awarded him the Hans Georg Nägeli Medal. Rehfuss made many recordings, including Golaud in *Pelléas et Mélisande* with Ernest Ansermet, Frank Martin's *Sechs Monologe aus 'Jedermann'* and *Le vin herbé*, and Creon and the Messenger in *Oedipus rex*, conducted by the composer.

Jürg Stenzl

Rehkemper, Heinrich

(*b* Schwerte, 23 May 1894; *d* Munich, 30 Dec 1949). German baritone. He studied in Hagen, Düsseldorf and Munich, making his début in Emmerich Kálmán's *Die Faschingsfee* at Coburg in 1919. At Stuttgart (1921–4) he sang over 40 roles and in 1925 he joined the Staatsoper in Munich, where he remained until 1943. He was a popular Papageno but also sang dramatic roles such as Macbeth, Rigoletto, Amfortas and Telramund. In 1931 he appeared in the première of Hans Pfitzner's *Das Herz*. He was also much in demand throughout Germany as a recitalist, admired by Richard Strauss, who was his accompanist on a concert tour of Norway. His recordings reveal a somewhat dry voice with limited appeal, though his singing can be tender and intense in feeling.

J. Dennis, D. Brew and R. Jones: 'Heinrich Rehkemper', *Record Collector*, xxii, (1974–5), 267–86

J.B. Steane

Reichmann, Theodor

(*b* Rostock, 15 March 1849; *d* Marbach, 22 May 1903). German baritone. He studied in Berlin, Prague and with Francesco Lamperti in Milan, making his début in 1869 at Magdeburg as Ottokar in *Der Freischütz*. After singing at Rotterdam, Strasbourg and Hamburg, he appeared for the first time in Munich in May 1874 in *Guillaume Tell*, and the following year began a permanent engagement there with Heinrich Marschner's *Hans Heiling* (1875). He sang Amonasro in *Aida* (1877), the Wanderer in *Siegfried* (1878) and the title role of Viktor Nessler's *Der Rattenfänger von Hameln* (1881), all first Munich performances. He sang Amfortas at all 16 performances of *Parsifal* at Bayreuth in 1882, returning to the festival in that role regularly until 1902, as Hans Sachs in 1888–9 and as Wolfram in *Tannhäuser* in 1891. He made his London début in 1882, when he substituted for EMIL SCARIA as Wotan in the second and third complete *Ring* cycles presented by Angelo Neumann at Her Majesty's Theatre. He first sang at Covent Garden in 1884, appearing as Telramund in *Lohengrin*, as the Dutchman and as Hans Sachs and returned in 1892 to sing Wotan (*Die Walküre* and *Siegfried*) in the *Ring* cycles conducted by Gustav Mahler. From 1883 to 1889, and again from 1893 until his death, he was engaged at the Vienna Hofoper, where he sang Iago in the first Vienna performance of Giuseppe Verdi's *Otello* (1888). He made his New York début at the Metropolitan in 1889 as the Dutchman, and during his two seasons there he sang 16 parts, which included Don Giovanni,

Count di Luna in *Il trovatore*, Renato in *Un ballo in maschera*, Solomon in *Die Königin von Saba*, Amonasro, Werner in *Der Trompeter von Säckingen*, Nélusko in *L'Africaine* and Escamillo in *Carmen*, as well as his Wagner roles. His final appearance in Munich was at the Prinzregententheater as Hans Sachs on 11 August 1902, when the resonance of his magnificently warm and even voice was said to have been as powerful as at the beginning of his career, 30 years earlier.

Elizabeth Forbes

Reina, Domenico

(*b* Lugano, 1797; *d* Lugano, 29 July 1843). Italian tenor. He studied in Milan, making his début in 1820. At the King's Theatre in 1823 he sang in the first London performances of Gioachino Rossini's *Ricciardo e Zoraide*, *La donna del lago* and *Matilde di Shabran*. Engaged at La Scala, he created Arturo in Vincenzo Bellini's *La straniera* (1829), Tamas in Gaetano Donizetti's *Gemma di Vergy* (1834) and Leicester in *Maria Stuarda* (1835). He also sang in Rome, Venice, Bergamo and Naples. His repertory included Rossini's Ilo (*Zelmira*); Donizetti's Fernando (*Marino Faliero*) and Alamiro (*Belisario*); and Bellini's Tebaldo (*I Capuleti e i Montecchi*), Orombello (*Beatrice di Tenda*), Elvino (*La sonnambula*) and Pollione.

Elizabeth Forbes

Reinhardt, Delia

(*b* Elberfeld, 27 April 1892; *d* Arlesheim, 3 Oct 1974). German soprano. She studied in Frankfurt with Maurice Strakosch and Hedwig Schako and made her début at Breslau in 1913. Three years later she was engaged by the Munich Hofoper, where she remained until 1923, being especially admired in the Mozart repertory. From Munich she went to the Berlin Staatsoper, where she appeared regularly until 1938, singing more than 60 roles including Octavian, the Empress (*Die Frau ohne Schatten*), the Composer, Christine (*Intermezzo*), Elsa, Elisabeth (*Tannhäuser*) and Eva, as well as roles in works by Darius Milhaud, Franz Schreker and Kurt Weill. She appeared at Covent Garden between 1924 and 1929 and sang Octavian in the famous performances of *Der Rosenkavalier* under Bruno Walter, with LOTTE LEHMANN, ELISABETH SCHUMANN and RICHARD MAYR. In London she also sang Cherubino, Freia, Gutrune, Micaëla, Mimì and Butterfly. She appeared at the Metropolitan Opera for two seasons, 1922–4. Recordings of her best roles show her to have been an ardent interpreter with a warm, lyrical tone. Her first husband was the baritone GUSTAV SCHÜTZENDORF, her second the conductor Georges Sébastian.

Harold Rosenthal/Alan Blyth

Reinhold, Henry Theodore

(d London, 14 May 1751). English bass of German descent. His origins are obscure; he named his second son Theodore Chriestlieb and may well have been related to the Dresden organist and composer Theodor Christlieb Reinhold. He was second bass (Mercury) in G.F. Handel's *Atalanta* in May 1736 and the sole bass the following season, when he sang in the premières of *Arminio*, *Giustino* and *Berenice*. Later in 1737 he created the comic role of the Dragon in John Frederick Lampe's *The Dragon of Wantley*, which received 68 performances in its first season. His other English stage roles included Sir Trusty in Thomas Arne's *Rosamond* and the Lion in Lampe's *Pyramus and Thisbe*. In Handel's two seasons at Lincoln's Inn Fields Theatre (1739–41) he sang Polyphemus in *Acis and Galatea* ('O ruddier than the cherry' became a song he performed at theatre benefits) and created the bass parts in *L'Allegro* and Handel's last two operas, *Imeneo* (1740) and *Deidamia* (1741). While continuing to sing English stage music, he became the composer's principal oratorio bass from 1743, when he created the role of Harapha in *Samson* and sang in the first London performance of *Messiah*. Between 1744 and Reinhold's death Handel wrote parts for him in a number of oratorios, including *Joseph and his Brethren*, *Hercules*, *Belshazzar*, the *Occasional Oratorio*, *Judas Maccabaeus*, *Joshua*, *Alexander Balus*, *Susanna*, *Solomon* and *Theodora*. He was one of the 'good Set of Singers' Handel wrote of having for *Belshazzar*, and the composer entrusted him with substantial roles and a wide range of characterizations. The compass of most of his oratorio parts is from G to e'.

Reinhold died between the two Foundling Hospital performances of *Messiah* in 1751, and Drury Lane put on a benefit for his 'Wife and four small Children in great Distress'. On his death the *General Advertiser* described him as 'not less admired for his private Character than his publick Performance'. His first name has sometimes been given as Thomas, but he is Theodore Reinhold in the records of the Royal Society of Musicians, of which he was a founder member, and his name appears in his children's baptismal records as Henry or Henry Theodore.

Olive Baldwin, Thelma Wilson

Reining, Maria

(b Vienna, 7 Aug 1903; d Vienna, 11 March 1991). Austrian soprano. She studied in Vienna, making her début in 1931 at the Staatsoper as a soubrette and remaining for two seasons. After appearances in Darmstadt (1933–5) she joined the Staatsoper in Munich. She returned to Vienna in 1937, singing there with distinction until 1958. She appeared at Salzburg from 1937 to 1941, as Eva, Euryanthe, Elisabeth (*Tannhäuser*), Countess Almaviva and Pamina, and returned as Arabella (1947) and the Marschallin (1949 and 1953). In 1938 she sang Elsa to acclaim at Covent Garden and Eva and Butterfly at Chicago; in 1949, the Marschallin at the Paris Opéra and the Marschallin and Ariadne at the New York City Opera. She had a radiant, well-schooled voice and an elegant and aristocratic stage presence. There remain complete recordings of her Marschallin in Erich Kleiber's notable account of 1954, Ariadne (1944, Vienna) and Arabella (1947, Salzburg), as well as extracts from other roles and operetta. All evince her lovely tone and careful characterization.

A. Blyth: 'Maria Reining', *Opera*, xxxix (1988), 545–50

Harold Rosenthal/Alan Blyth

Reinmar [Wochinz], Hans

(b Vienna, 11 April 1895; d Berlin, 7 Feb 1961). Austrian baritone. He studied in Vienna and Milan, making his début at Olomouc in 1919. Nuremberg, Zürich, Dresden and Hamburg claimed him in turn, until in 1928 he sang at the Staatsoper in Berlin where, apart from a break in the 1940s, he remained until 1944, joining the Komische Oper in 1952 and singing there for the last time in Robert Kurka's *The Good Soldier Schweik* two days before his death. At Bayreuth his roles included Gunther and Amfortas, and at Salzburg in 1942 he sang an admired Mandryka. He was also a guest artist at La Scala and in Vienna, Paris and Rome. His Italian training helped him to play a leading part in the Verdi revivals, such as those of *Simon Boccanegra* and *Don Carlos* in Berlin. The crowning achievement of his career was his Boris Godunov, sung in the original version at Berlin and Munich. His many recordings cover both the Italian and the German parts of his repertory, showing a voice of considerable power and beauty, used expressively and with care for evenness of production.

J.B. Steane

Reisinger, Barbara.

See GERL, BARBARA.

Remedios, Alberto (Telisforo)

(*b* Liverpool, 27 Feb 1935). English tenor. He studied at the RCM and made his début at Sadler's Wells in 1957 as Tinca (*Tabarro*). Other roles for Sadler's Wells were Don Ottavio, Tamino, Alfredo, Jake (*Aufsteig und Fall der Stadt Mahagonny*), Bacchus, Erik, Max, Florestan and Samson. In 1965 he toured Australia with the Sutherland-Williamson company, as Faust and Lensky, then made his Covent Garden début as Dmitry, followed by Erik and Mark (*The Midsummer Marriage*). In 1968 he sang a memorable Walther at Sadler's Wells and was then engaged for two seasons at Frankfurt. His roles for the ENO included Hector Berlioz's Faust, Don Alvaro, Siegmund, Siegfried, Lohengrin, Jules Massenet's Des Grieux and Tristan (1981). In 1973 he made his American début at San Francisco as Dmitry, then sang Don Carlos. In 1975 he sang Otello for the WNO and in 1976 made his Metropolitan début as Bacchus. For Scottish Opera he has sung Aeneas (*Les Troyens*), Igor Stravinsky's Oedipus and Laca. His repertory included Peter Grimes and Radames. With a strong yet lyrical voice, capable of singing W.A. Mozart and Richard Wagner, he excelled as Bacchus, Walther and the young Siegfried, and may be heard on live recordings of the famous Reginald Goodall English-language *Ring* cycle at the ENO. He was made a CBE in 1981.

E. Forbes: 'Alberto Remedios', *Opera*, xxiv (1973), 15–21

Alan Blyth

Renaud [Croneau], Maurice (Arnold)

(*b* Bordeaux, 24 July 1860; *d* Paris, 16 Oct 1933). French baritone. He made his début in autumn 1883 at La Monnaie, where he later sang in the premières of Ernest Reyer's *Sigurd* (1884) and *Salammbô* (1890) in addition to singing a wide variety of French, Italian and Wagnerian roles. From 1890 (début 19 September as Karnac in *Le roi d'Ys*) to 1891 he appeared with the Opéra-Comique and from 1891 (début 17 July as Nélusko in *L'Africaine*) to 1902 he was a member of the Opéra, returning frequently until 1914. He sang at Monte Carlo, 1891–1907, and at New Orleans in 1893. His Covent Garden début was in 1897; he returned for the next two seasons and again (1902–4) as, among others, Don Giovanni, Wolfram, Nevers (*Les Huguenots*), Escamillo, Rigoletto and Lescaut (*Manon*). He appeared with the Manhattan Opera (1906–7, 1909–10), at the Metropolitan (1910–12), in Boston and in Chicago, where he sang Rigoletto, Athanaël, Rance (*La fanciulla del West*) and Coppélius, Dapertutto and Dr Miracle (*Les contes d'Hoffmann*). Renaud had a warm, expressive voice and was considered one of the most versatile singing actors of his day.

A. de Cock and P.G. Hurst: 'Maurice Renaud', *Record Collector*, xi (1957), 75–119, 166–7; xii (1958), 37 [with discography by L. Hevingham-Root]

Harold Barnes

Rendall, David

(*b* London, 11 Oct 1948). English tenor. He studied at the RAM and the Salzburg Mozarteum and in 1973 won a Young Musician of the Year Award from the Greater London Arts Association, followed by a Gulbenkian Fellowship in 1975. He made his début with Glyndebourne Touring Opera in 1975 as Ferrando, and then sang the Italian Singer in *Der Rosenkavalier* at Covent Garden, where his roles have included Almaviva, Jules Massenet's Des Grieux, Matteo (*Arabella*), Rodrigo (*La donna del lago*), Flamand (*Capriccio*) and the Duke. In 1976 he first sang at Glyndebourne as Ferrando, returning as Tom Rakewell and Belmonte. At the ENO (1976–92) he has sung Leicester (*Maria Stuarda*), the Duke, Rodolfo and Pinkerton. His North American début was at Ottawa as Tamino in 1977, followed the next year by Rodolfo and Alfredo with New York City Opera and Don Ottavio at San Francisco. His Metropolitan début (1980) was as Don Ottavio, and he returned for Lensky, Matteo, David and Idomeneus. He has sung in Paris, Vienna, Berlin, Hamburg, Buenos Aires, San Francisco, Chicago, Santa Fe and Aix-en-Provence, where he sang W.A. Mozart's Titus in 1988. A lyric tenor of accomplished style and versatility, he is an ardent and convincing actor. His recordings include *Maria Stuarda* under Charles Mackerras (1982) and *La rondine* under Lorin Maazel (1985).

Elizabeth Forbes, Noël Goodwin

Resnik, Regina

(*b* New York, 30 Aug 1922). American mezzo-soprano (formerly soprano) and director. She studied at Hunter College, New York, and sang Lady Macbeth with the New Opera Company, New York, in 1942. She sang with the Metropolitan (1944–74), making her début as Leonora (*Il trovatore*); her roles there included Ellen Orford in the New York première of *Peter Grimes*, Alice Ford, Leonore, Donna Anna and Donna Elvira, and Sieglinde. At Bayreuth she sang Sieglinde in 1953 and Fricka in 1961. In 1955 she began to concentrate on the mezzo-soprano repertory, singing Azucena, Eboli and Herodias (*Salome*). She created the Baroness in Samuel Barber's *Vanessa* (1958) and also sang Lucretia in *The Rape of Lucretia* at Stratford, Ontario (she had sung the Female Chorus in the American première at Chicago in 1947). In 1972 she sang Claire in the American première of Gottfried von Einem's *Der Besuch der alten Dame* at San Francisco.

Resnik made her Covent Garden début in 1957 as Carmen; her roles there included Marina (*Boris Godunov*), a brilliant Mistress Quickly and a decadent Clytemnestra. She also appeared in Vienna, Salzburg and in the leading American and German opera houses. In 1971 she directed *Carmen* at Hamburg and *Elektra* in Venice. She had a vibrant voice with a strong upper register. Her acting was full of subtle detail, and her fine musicianship and keen intelligence were apparent in all her work. Among her recordings are notable accounts of her Sieglinde (1953, Bayreuth), Carmen, Clytemnestra and Mistress Quickly.

I. Cook: 'Regina Resnik', *Opera*, xiv (1963), 13–18
H. Rosenthal: *Great Singers of Today* (London, 1966)

Harold Rosenthal/Alan Blyth

Resse, Celeste.

See GISMONDI, CELESTE.

Rethberg, Elisabeth [Sättler, Lisbeth]

(*b* Schwarzenberg, nr Zwickau, 22 Sept 1894; *d* Yorktown Heights, NY, 6 June 1976). German soprano. She studied at Dresden, made her début in 1915 with the Dresden Opera, and remained with the company for seven years, singing a wide variety of roles. She made her Metropolitan début in 1922 as Aida, remaining as leading soprano for 21 consecutive seasons. During those years she returned regularly to Dresden, sang at Covent Garden in five seasons, and frequently appeared at the Salzburg Festivals. On one return trip to Europe she sang the title role in the Dresden première of Richard Strauss's *Die ägyptische Helena* in 1928. Her other Verdi roles were Desdemona, Amelia (*Un ballo in maschera* and *Simon Boccanegra*), and the Leonoras of both *Il trovatore* and *La forza del destino*. In Wagner she excelled in the 'youthful-dramatic' parts of Elisabeth, Elsa, Eva and Sieglinde; she was also an accomplished Mozart singer. Rethberg's beautiful *lirico spinto* soprano was perfectly equalized between the registers, and a combination of natural musicianship and sound training enabled her to maintain an unusually even legato in the most difficult passages. Rethberg made a large number of recordings, many of which reveal her rare beauty of tone and purity of style.

J.B. Richards: 'Elisabeth Rethberg: the Discography', *Record Collector*, iii (1948), 51–6
J.B. Richards: 'Elisabeth Rethberg's Recordings', *Record Collector*, viii (1953), 4–19
J.B. Steane: *Singers of the Century* (London, 1996), 216–20

Desmond Shawe-Taylor/R

Reuss-Belce [Baumann], Luise

(*b* Vienna, 24 Oct 1860; *d* Aibach, Augsburg, 5 March 1945). Austrian soprano. She studied in Vienna, making her début in 1881 as Elsa at Karlsruhe, where she sang Cassandra in the first complete performance of *Les Troyens* (1890). In 1897 she moved to Wiesbaden and in 1901 to Dresden, where she remained until 1911. Having made her Bayreuth début in 1882 as a flowermaiden in the première of *Parsifal*, she returned (1889–1901) as Eva, Gutrune, Fricka and Second Norn. She made her Covent Garden début in 1893 as Sieglinde and then sang Fricka (1900). Engaged at the Metropolitan (1901–3), she sang Elisabeth, Fricka and Gutrune; she also sang Iolanthe in the American première of Ethel Smyth's *Der Wald* (1903). One of the longest-living singers to have participated in a performance under Richard Wagner's aegis, she had a fine, substantial voice, particularly strong in the middle register.

Elizabeth Forbes

Reynolds, Anna [Ann]

(*b* Canterbury, 4 Oct 1931). English mezzo-soprano. She studied in Rome and made her operatic début in Parma (Suzuki, 1960). In Italy she subsequently sang a wide range of roles, including Henry Purcell's Dido, Gioachino Rossini's Tancredi, Elizabeth I (*Maria Stuarda*) and Charlotte (*Werther*), indicating the versatility of her style and stage presence. Her first opera appearance in England was at Glyndebourne in 1962, as Geneviève in *Pelléas et Mélisande*; her other Glyndebourne roles included Ortensia in Rossini's *La pietra del paragone*. At Covent Garden she played Adelaide (*Arabella*, 1967) and Andromache (Michael Tippett's *King Priam*, 1975). As a Wagnerian mezzo-soprano she took part in the von Karajan *Ring* cycles, at Salzburg and the Metropolitan; from 1970 to 1975 she regularly appeared at Bayreuth. A concert singer of great distinction, she was a notable interpreter of the Angel in *The Dream of Gerontius* and the alto solos in *Das Lied von der Erde*. Her many recordings include a collection of Gustav Mahler's songs, Robert Schumann's Eichendorff *Liederkreis*, and Bach cantatas, in which her exemplary line and expressive tone were at their most admirable.

Alan Blyth

Reyzen [Reisen; Reizen], Mark (Osipovich)

(*b* Zaytsevo, Dnepropetrovsk province, 21 June/ 3 July 1895; *d* Moscow, 25 Nov 1992). Ukrainian bass. He studied at the Khar'kiv Conservatory and made his début with the Khar'kiv Opera as Pimen in *Boris Godunov* in 1921. In the following seasons he appeared in a wide variety of roles, including Méphistophélès in *Faust*, Saint-Bris in *Les Huguenots*, Ruslan and Farlaf in *Ruslan and Lyudmila* and Dosifey in *Khovanshchina*. From 1925 to 1930 he was a member of the Leningrad Opera, where in 1928 he sang his first Boris. He then became principal bass at the Bol'shoy, Moscow, remaining there for the rest of his long career. He also sang in Germany, Hungary and France, with appearances at the Paris Opéra and at Monte Carlo in *Mefistofele* and *Il barbiere di Siviglia*. One of the greatest of Russian singers, he had a voice of exceptional beauty, scrupulously used and so well preserved that he could sing at the Bol'shoy to celebrate his 90th birthday. He was also an imposing figure and an accomplished actor. His recordings, dating from 1929 to 1980, include complete performances of *Boris Godunov*, *Khovanshchina* and *Mozart and Salieri*, together with an impressively wide repertory of songs, mainly Russian.

M. Reyzen: *Avtobiograficheskiye zapiski* [Autobiographical notes] (Moscow, 1980)
N. Linnell: 'Mark Reizen', *Record Collector*, xxviii (1983), 5–31

J.B. Steane

Rhodes, Jane (Marie Andrée)

(*b* Paris, 13 March 1929). French mezzo-soprano. She made her stage début in *La damnation de Faust* at Nancy in 1953, and took part in the première of Marcel Landowski's *Le fou* (1956). Her Opéra début was in 1958 as Hector Berlioz's Marguerite; her incursions into the dramatic soprano repertory, notably as Richard Strauss's Salome (Opéra, 1958) – perhaps invited by her lissom figure and attractively piquant stage presence – were not invariably successful; as an internationally admired Carmen, she developed an impressively 'French' portrayal, aided by a voice not large or intrinsically beautiful, but capable of exquisitely seductive inflections. In addition to an operatic repertory that included *Bluebeard's Castle*, *L'incoronazione di Poppea*, Maurice Ravel's *L'heure espagnole* and Francis Poulenc's *La voix humaine* (the last two played in a 1968 Opéra-Comique double bill), she appeared in much Jacques Offenbach. Rhodes took the role of Renata in the first recording of Sergey Prokofiev's *The Fiery Angel*

(in French). She married the conductor Roberto Benzi in 1966.

Max Loppert

Ricciarelli, Katia

(*b* Rovigo, 18 Jan 1946). Italian soprano. She studied in Venice, making her début in 1969 at Mantua as Mimì. After winning the 1970 Verdi Award at Parma, she sang Leonora (*Il trovatore*) there and Verdi's Joan of Arc in Rome, both in 1971. She made her American début at Chicago in 1972 as Lucrezia (*I due Foscari*) and first sang at La Scala in 1973 as Angelica. Having made her Covent Garden début in 1974 as Mimì, she sang Amelia (*Ballo in maschera*), Elisabeth de Valois, Luisa Miller, Lucia, Aida, Alice Ford (*Falstaff*), Desdemona and Vincenzo Bellini's Giulietta. She made her Metropolitan début in 1975 as Mimì, then sang Micaëla and her Verdi roles. At Pesaro (1981–9) she sang Ellen (*La donna del lago*), Amenaide (*Tancredi*), Madama Cortese (*Il viaggio a Reims*), Bianca (*Bianca e Falliero*) and Ninetta (*La gazza ladra*). Her repertory also included Luigi Cherubini's Medea, Mathilde (*Guillaume Tell*), Norma, Imogene (*Il pirata*), Paolina (*Poliuto*) and the title roles of *Maria Stuarda*, *Caterina Cornaro*, *Lucrezia Borgia* and *Maria di Rohan*. In 1989 she sang Maddalena (*Andrea Chénier*) at Versailles. Ricciarelli recorded many of her bel canto roles and, less successfully, Aida, Tosca and Turandot. Her vibrant, warm-toned voice was enhanced by her truthful, appealing acting.

A. Blyth: 'Katia Ricciarelli', *Opera*, xli (1990), 28–33

Alan Blyth

Ridderbusch, Karl

(*b* Recklinghausen, 29 May 1932; *d* Wels, nr Linz, 21 June 1997). German bass. He made his début at the Städtisches Theater, Münster, in 1961. He was a member of the Essen Opera before moving to Düsseldorf in 1965, where he made the Deutsche Oper am Rhein his artistic base. In 1967 he made his débuts at Bayreuth and the Metropolitan in Richard Wagner, and at Covent Garden in 1971 where he sang Fasolt, Hunding and Hagen. He sang regularly at the Vienna Staatsoper, his first appearance there in 1968, and was a notable Hans Sachs in Herbert von Karajan's production of *Die Meistersinger* at the 1974 and 1975 Salzburg Easter festivals. Ridderbusch's voice was firm, clear, sonorous and rich in timbre; his style was direct, his stage presence imposing. He appeared successfully in Giuseppe Verdi, and in *buffo* roles including Ochs and W.A. Mozart's Bartolo, but he was at his best in the serious, dramatically demanding repertory, for example the Commendatore, Rocco, Hunding, Hagen, Hans Sachs and Caspar (*Der Freischütz*). His recordings, which include Hans Sachs, his *Ring* roles and Rocco, demonstrate the warmth and conviction of his interpretations.

Gerhard Brunner/R

Riegel, Kenneth

(*b* Womelsdorf, PA, 19 April 1938). American tenor. He studied in New York, making his début in 1965 at Santa Fe as an Alchemist in *König Hirsch*. Engaged at the New York City Opera (1969–74), he made his Metropolitan début in 1973 as Iopas (*Les Troyens*), later singing Tamino, Titus, David and Hoffmann. He has also sung at many other major houses in Europe and the USA. At the Paris Opéra he sang Alwa in the first performance of the three-act version of *Lulu* (1979) and created the Leper in Olivier Messiaen's *Saint François d'Assise* (1983). His repertory initially included Don Ottavio (which he sang in Joseph Losey's filmed version), Ferrando, Belmonte and Idomeneus, but in the 1980s his voice grew heavier, and he sang such roles as Hector Berlioz's Faust, Erik, Loge, Shuysky, Albert Gregor (*The Makropulos Affair*), Oedipus, Ferruccio Busoni's Mephistopheles, and Gustav von Aschenbach. A powerful and subtle actor, Riegel scored a huge success at Hamburg in 1981 as the Dwarf in Alexander Zemlinsky's *Der Zwerg*, which he later repeated at Edinburgh, Amsterdam and Covent Garden (1985) and recorded. He returned to Covent Garden as Loge (1991) and Herod (1992), which he repeated at Salzburg. In 1994 he sang his first Peter Grimes, in Munich. Riegel's other recordings include Hector Berlioz's Faust, Shuysky, Herod and Alwa.

Elizabeth Forbes

Rigby, Jean

(*b* Fleetwood, 22 Dec 1954). English mezzo-soprano. She studied at the Birmingham School of Music, the RAM and the National Opera Studio. After winning the ENO Young Artists competition in 1981 she joined the company the next year and made her début as Mercédès (*Carmen*). A wide range of roles followed, including Benjamin Britten's Lucretia in 1984; she created Eurydice in Harrison Birtwistle's *The Mask of Orpheus* (1986) and won special distinction as Penelope in *Il ritorno d'Ulisse* (1989). Her Covent Garden début was as Thibault (*Don Carlos*) in 1983, and she appeared at Glyndebourne in 1985 as Mercédès; at Zürich in 1986 she sang Cornelia

in *Giulio Cesare* under Nikolaus Harnoncourt. Her video recordings include Dorabella, directed by Jonathan Miller, for whose *Rigoletto* production in English she sang and recorded Maddalena, and Britten's Lucretia. Her rich, velvety tone, ease of production and musical sensitivity are also heard frequently in concerts.

Noël Goodwin

Righetti [Giorgi, Giorgi-Righetti, Righetti-Giorgi], Geltrude

(*b* Bologna, 1793; *d* Bologna, 1862). Italian contralto. She studied in Bologna and gave her first public performance there in 1814. She was invited by Duke Sforza Cesarini to sing, at the express wish of Gioachino Rossini, in the première of *Il barbiere di Siviglia* (1816, Teatro Argentina, Rome), though only very late and after another singer had declined. In 1817 she created the title role in *La Cenerentola* at the Teatro Valle in Rome. During her brief career, she was appreciated for her coloratura singing, her range extending from *f* to *b b''*. She retired from the stage, probably for health reasons, in 1822. Her *Cenni d'una donna già cantante sopra il Maestro Rossini* (Bologna, 1823), a reply to an article by Stendhal published under a pseudonym in the *Revue mensuelle de Paris* (1822), gives an interesting account of the première of *Il barbiere di Siviglia*.

Bruno Cagli/R

Risack, Rosa Negri.

See NEGRI, MARIA ROSA.

Ritchie, Margaret [Ritchie, Mabel Willard]

(*b* Grimsby, 7 June 1903; *d* Ewelme, Oxon., 7 Feb 1969). English soprano. She studied at the RCM and with Plunket Greene, Agnes Nicholls and Henry Wood, and became known as a concert singer and as a leading soprano of the Intimate Opera Company. In 1944 she joined Sadler's Wells, distinguishing herself especially as Dorabella in *Così fan tutte*. In 1946 she sang Lucia in the first production, at Glyndebourne, of Benjamin Britten's *Rape of Lucretia*, and in the following year joined the English Opera Group. The part of Miss Wordsworth, the prim and innocent schoolmistress in Britten's *Albert Herring* (Aldburgh Festival, 1948), displayed to perfection her musical qualities and delightful sense of comedy, and might be called an affectionate portrait of her personality. Her voice, though small, was of pure quality and beautifully produced; she used it with an unfailing sense of style and showed unusual flexibility in the execution of florid passages.

Desmond Shawe-Taylor

Ritter-Ciampi, Gabrielle

(*b* Paris, 2 Nov 1886; *d* Paimpol, 18 July 1974). French soprano. Her mother (Cécile Ritter-Ciampi) was a principal soprano at the Opéra, her father (Ezio Ciampi) an Italian tenor and later her teacher, while her uncle was the pianist Theodore Ritter. She herself trained first as a pianist and gave some public performances at the age of 16. She then turned to singing and made her début in 1917 as Violetta. She joined the Opéra-Comique two years later, appearing there first as W.A. Mozart's Countess Almaviva and as Philine in *Mignon*. She remained with the company for many years, singing Konstanze in their first production of *Die Entführung aus dem Serail* (1937) and creating the leading role of Irène in Reynaldo Hahn's *Le oui des jeunes filles* (1949). She also appeared at the Opéra, at La Scala, in Berlin and at Salzburg in 1932. She was Monte Carlo's first Marschallin in *Der Rosenkavalier* (1926), admired for 'the perfection of her vocal art and a nobility of bearing'; she also sang there all three main soprano roles in *Les contes d'Hoffmann*. Her impressive versatility, technique and intelligence are evident in many recordings, which also preserve her brightly defined voice and responsive style.

J.B. Steane

Rivoli [Riwoli], Paulina

(*b* Vilnius, 22 July 1823 or 1817; *d* Warsaw, 12 Oct 1881). Polish soprano. Born into a family of itinerant actors, she studied at the opera school of the Wielki Theatre in Warsaw; she made her début there on 17 June 1837 in *L'italiana in Algeri*. She performed with much success in *Les Huguenots*, *La Juive* and in operas by Carl Maria von Weber, Daniel Auber, Domenico Cimarosa and Stanisław Moniuszko. She was in Italy in 1851, and in 1858 sang the title role in the Warsaw première of Moniuszko's *Halka*. Her lyrical voice was noted for its beauty of timbre. She retired in 1860.

Irena Poniatowska

Riwoli, Paulina.

See RIVOLI, PAULINA.

Rizza, Gilda dalla.

See DALLA RIZZA, GILDA.

Robbin, Catherine

(*b* Toronto, 28 Sept 1950). Canadian mezzo-soprano. She studied at the Royal Conservatory in Toronto and then privately in Paris and London. Her career has from the start centred on the Baroque and period-instrument performance. She has often performed and recorded with John Eliot Gardiner's Monteverdi Choir, most notably in *Messiah*, Ludwig van Beethoven's *Missa solemnis* and as Annius in *La clemenza di Tito* (semi-staged, 1990). With Christopher Hogwood and his Academy of Ancient Music she has sung Henry Purcell's Dido and G.F. Handel's Julius Caesar in concert. She sang Medoro in Handel's *Orlando* with Hogwood at the 1989 Proms, and also recorded the role under his baton. In 1990 she sang the title role in the North American première, in Toronto, of Handel's *Floridante*. Her other Handel opera recordings include Eduige in *Rodelinda*. Robbin's concert repertory has concentrated on Brahms (Alto Rhapsody), Hector Berlioz (she has contributed to a mixed-voice version of *Les nuits d'été* with Gardiner), the Gustav Mahler cycles and Edward Elgar's *Sea Pictures*. She has also appeared frequently with Graham Johnson's Songmakers' Almanac. Her voice is a slim, attractive mezzo, which she uses with expressive nuance and a keen feeling for style.

Alan Blyth

Robin, Mado

(*b* Yseures-sur-Creuse, nr Tours, 29 Dec 1918; *d* Paris, 10 Dec 1960). French soprano. She studied in Paris, where she made her début at the Opéra in 1945 as Gilda (*Rigoletto*) and also sang the Queen of Night. The following year she sang Lakmé at the Opéra-Comique, followed by Rosina (*Il barbiere di Siviglia*) and Olympia (*Les contes d'Hoffmann*). She appeared at many French regional theatres, in Brussels and in Monte Carlo. In 1953 she returned to the Opéra to sing Konstanze (*Die Entführung*), and in 1954 she sang in San Francisco, as Gilda and Lucia. Her extreme facility for coloratura and very high range were best displayed in roles such as Igor Stravinsky's Nightingale.

Elizabeth Forbes

Robinson, Anastasia

(*b* ?Italy, *c*1692; *d* Bath, April 1755). English soprano, later contralto. She was the eldest daughter of Thomas Robinson, a portrait painter from Leicestershire who travelled and studied in Italy. She studied music with William Croft and singing with Pietro Sandoni and the Baroness (Johanna

Maria Lindelheim). At first she exercised her talent in private, singing to her own accompaniment at weekly *conversazioni*, much patronized by society, in her father's house in Golden Square. When her father's sight failed, she turned professional to support the family and began to give concerts at York Buildings and elsewhere. The solo soprano part in G.F. Handel's *Ode for Queen Anne's Birthday* was written for her, and she presumably sang it in February 1714. On 9 June 1713 she had a benefit at the Queen's Theatre; on 20 June she introduced a new cantata there. She joined the opera company at the beginning of 1714, making her début in the pasticcio *Creso* on 27 January. She sang that spring in *Arminio* and *Ernelinda*, on several occasions with new songs, and met with immediate favour. The following season, in addition to her old parts, she played Almirena in the revival of Handel's *Rinaldo* and sang in the new pasticcio *Lucio Vero*. She created the part of Oriana in Handel's *Amadigi*, but retired after one performance owing to illness. In the 1715–17 seasons she was in Alessandro Scarlatti's *Pirro e Demetrio*, the pasticcios *Clearte* and *Vinceslao*, and revivals of *Rinaldo* and *Amadigi*. She had benefits in *Arminio* (1714), *Ernelinda* (1715) and twice in *Amadigi* (1716 and 1717); on the last occasion (21 March) Handel composed a new scene for her and NICOLINI.

Although the opera closed in summer 1717, Robinson had benefits at the King's Theatre on 15 March 1718 and 21 February 1719. It must have been during this period that her voice dropped from soprano to contralto as the result of an illness. She sang at Drury Lane from October 1719 to March 1720. On the foundation of the Royal Academy of Music she rejoined the opera company and sang in its first three productions in spring 1720: Bernardo Porta's *Numitore*, Handel's *Radamisto* (creating the part of Zenobia) and Thomas Roseingrave's arrangement of Domenico Scarlatti's *Narciso*. A Hanoverian diplomat, de Fabrice, paid tribute to her performance in *Numitore*, ranking her in beauty of voice with the brilliant DURASTANTI. Robinson missed the opening of the autumn season, but returned in spring 1721 and sang in all the premières between then and summer 1724: the composite *Muzio Scevola* (Irene), Handel's *Floridante* (Elmira), *Ottone* (Matilda), *Flavio* (Teodata) and *Giulio Cesare* (Cornelia), Giovanni Bononcini's *Ciro*, *Crispo* (Fausta), *Griselda*, *Erminia*, *Farnace* and *Calfurnia*, Attilio Ariosti's *Coriolano* and *Vespasiano*, and the pasticcios *Odio ed amore* and *Aquilio consolo*. She appeared with the rest of the company in concerts and ridottos at the theatre in March and June 1721 and February and March 1722; on the first occasion she took part in a serenata by Alessandro Scarlatti. In June 1724 she retired from the stage, having secretly married

the elderly Earl of Peterborough two years earlier; he did not acknowledge her publicly until shortly before his death in 1735.

Robinson's salary at the Royal Academy was reputed to be £1000, almost doubled by benefits and presents. In retirement she lived at Parson's Green (where she held a kind of musical academy at which Bononcini, P.F. Tosi, Maurice Greene and others performed) and, after Peterborough's death, at his seat near Southampton. She was on friendly terms with Bononcini, who had helped to advance her career (Peterborough had paid him £250 for teaching her), and obtained him a pension of £500 from the Duchess of Marlborough; Bononcini dedicated his *Farnace* to Peterborough. On 11 January 1723 she took part with Jane Barbier, the opera orchestra and the Chapel Royal choir in a private performance at Buckingham House of Bononcini's choruses to the late Duke of Buckingham's play *Julius Caesar*, conducted by the composer. She was buried in Bath Abbey.

Robinson enjoyed great personal and artistic popularity. As a singer she was remarkable for charm and expressiveness rather than virtuosity; the care with which Handel supported and sometimes doubled her part in the orchestra suggests technical limitations. His richest part for her, Oriana, which offers many openings for pathos, belongs to her soprano period (compass d' to a''). From 1720 her range diminished (b to e''), and Handel seldom taxed her with coloratura; but he gave her a highly emotional part in *Giulio Cesare* and an ironically humorous one in *Flavio*. She disliked playing termagants and found the role of Matilda in *Ottone* as first composed impossible to sing: 'a Patient Grisell by Nature' (an allusion to her success in Bononcini's *Griselda*), she was asked to play 'an abominable Scold'. Afraid to face Handel, she enlisted the help of the diplomat Giuseppe Riva (and suggested approaching Lady Darlington, the king's half-sister) to have it altered – apparently with success, for the aria to which she chiefly objected, 'Pensa, spietata madre', was replaced before performance. Robinson's letters to Riva in the Campori collection at Modena show an attractive and generous character, though Lady Mary Wortley Montagu referred to her as 'at the same time a prude and a kept mistress'. Giuseppe Riva described her as 'of moderate beauty but of the highest spirit'. She was a woman of culture and social gifts, rare in an 18th-century singer, a friend of Alexander Pope and a Roman Catholic. The one blot on her memory is her destruction of Peterborough's memoirs after his death. There is a portrait by John Vanderbank (1723; see colour plate 2).

Winton Dean

Robinson, Ann Turner [née Turner]

(*d* London, 5 Jan 1741). English soprano, the youngest daughter of the countertenor and composer William Turner. She first sang in public at the King's Theatre on 5 April 1718, when she introduced a cantata by Attilo Ariosti composed 'purposely on this Occasion'. She repeated it on 21 March at a concert with the castrato BALDASSARI. In spring 1719 she was engaged by John Hughes to replace Jane Barbier at a private concert, apparently accompanied by G.F. Handel, when according to Hughes 'her late Improvement has I think plac'd her in the first Rank of our English Performers'. Between October 1719 and March 1720 she appeared several times at Drury Lane in Ariosti's cantata *Diana on Mount Latmos*, but Ariosti mentioned her in uncomplimentary terms in letters to Giuseppe Riva in February and March. She had a benefit there on 17 May 1720. She was generally announced as 'Mrs Robinson, late Mrs Turner' or 'Mrs Turner Robinson', to distinguish her from Anastasia Robinson, who was singing at the same period and sometimes at the same theatre; but it is not always easy to tell which is meant. In the spring of 1720 both appeared together in the short first season of the Royal Academy of Music, in Bernardo Porta's *Numitore* (2 April), Handel's *Radamisto* (27 April) and Domenico Scarlatti's *Narciso* (30 May). Ann Turner Robinson was the original Polissena in *Radamisto*, but missed the final performances of all three operas. She sang a Handel cantata at her Drury Lane benefit on 20 March 1723.

She was probably the Mrs Robinson who sang regularly between the acts at Drury Lane from December 1725 to December 1726, played in Henry Carey's pantomime *Apollo and Daphne* from February 1726, and included seven Handel opera arias in her benefit programme on 28 April. She certainly had a benefit at Drury Lane on 26 March 1729, when she sang 14 Handel pieces; most of them had been composed for CUZZONI or FAUSTINA. She was in Handel's first London oratorio performances at the King's Theatre in May and June 1732, as an Israelite Woman in *Esther* and Clori in the bilingual *Acis and Galatea*. Her part in *Radamisto* shows that she was a capable singer with some brilliance at the top of her compass (*e'* to *a"*).

Winton Dean

Robinson, (Peter) Forbes

(*b* Macclesfield, 21 May 1926; *d* London, 13 May 1987). English bass. He studied at Loughborough College and at the training school of La Scala, joined the Covent Garden Opera in 1954 and made his début that year as Monterone. He took more than 60 roles with the company, the most important being the speaking part of Moses in the British première of Arnold Schoenberg's *Moses und Aron* (1965), the title role, which he created, in Michael Tippett's *King Priam* (1962) and Claggart in *Billy Budd*. In 1965 he sang in the BBC broadcast of *Der barbier von Bagdad*. He also sang frequently with the WNO, notably as Don Giovanni, Boris, Fiesco and Philip II. In 1966 he appeared at the Teatro Colón, Buenos Aires. Robinson had a dark, expressive voice, evenly produced and capable of subtle characterization, especially in such roles as Claggart and Boris.

Alan Blyth

Robson, Christopher

(*b* Falkirk, 9 Dec 1953). Scottish countertenor. He studied with PAUL ESSWOOD and Helga Mott, making his concert début in 1976 and his operatic début in 1979 at the Barber Institute, Birmingham, as Argones (*Sosarme*). He has subsequently sung with Kent Opera, Opera Factory and Scottish Opera, and at Frankfurt, Karlsruhe and Berlin. He made his ENO début at Nottingham in Claudio Monteverdi's *Orfeo* (1981) and his Covent Garden début (1988) as Athamas (*Semele*). A specialist in Baroque opera, Robson has sung Endymion (*Calisto*), Corindo (Antonio Cesti's *Orontea*) and many G.F. Handel roles, notably Julius Caesar, Ptolemy, Arsamene (*Serse*), Ezio, Andronicus and the title role in *Tamerlano*, and Polinesso (*Ariodante*). His keenly focussed, flexible voice is also heard to advantage in modern works, and he scored a huge success in the title role of Philip Glass's *Akhnaten* at Houston and with New York City Opera (both 1984), and for the ENO (1985). In 1989 he sang Edgar in the UK première of Aribert Reimann's *Lear* for the ENO, and created Ometh in John Casken's *Golem* at the Almeida Festival. In 1994 he made his début, as Julius Caesar, at the Staatsoper in Munich, returning as Arsamene the following year. A fine recitalist and concert singer, Robson has recorded works including *Messiah*, Henry Purcell odes and J.S. Bach's *Magnificat*, as well as *Golem*, Monteverdi's *Orfeo*, Michael Tippett's *The Ice Break* and Peter Maxwell Davies's *Resurrection*.

Elizabeth Forbes

Rochois, Marie le.

See LE ROCHOIS, MARIE.

Röckel, Joseph [Josef] (August)

(*b* Neunburg, Upper Palatinate, 28 Aug 1783; *d* Cöthen, 19 Sept 1870). Tenor. He was originally intended for the church, but in 1803 entered the diplomatic service. In 1804 he was engaged to sing in Vienna at the Theater an der Wien, where on 29 March 1806 he appeared as Florestan in the première of the second version of Ludwig van Beethoven's *Fidelio*. Beethoven esteemed him as artist and person, and asked his advice about cuts in the opera. Röckel subsequently taught singing at the Hofoper, where HENRIETTE SONTAG was among his pupils. After travelling to Mannheim, Trier, Bremen, Prague, Zagreb and Aachen, he went in 1830 to Paris, where he produced German operas with a German company. Encouraged by the success of this venture he remained in Paris until 1832, when he took his company to London and produced *Fidelio*, *Der Freischütz* and other German operas at the King's Theatre with such distinguished singers as SCHRÖDER-DEVRIENT and HAIZINGER. The company was conducted by J.N. Hummel, Röckel's brother-in-law. In 1835 he retired from operatic life, and in 1846 went to York as a music teacher, returning to Germany in 1853. He appears to have had an active interest in Richard Wagner.

William Barclay Squire/James Deaville

Rode, Wilhelm

(*b* Hanover, 17 Feb 1887; *d* Icking, nr Munich, 2 Sept 1959). German bass-baritone. He studied in Hanover and made his début in 1908 as the Herald in *Lohengrin* at Erfurt. After engagements at Bremerhaven, Breslau and Stuttgart, he joined the Bayerische Staatsoper, Munich (1922–32), and from 1926 sang with the Deutsches Opernhaus, Berlin, where he took part in the premières of Kurt Weill's *Die Bürgschaft* and Franz Schreker's *Der Schmied von Gent* (both 1932). He sang Wotan at Covent Garden (1928), and Count Almaviva and Don Pizarro at Salzburg (1929–32). At the Vienna Staatsoper (1930–33) he sang Scarpia, the four villains in *Les contes d'Hoffmann* and Simon Boccanegra, as well as the Wagner roles for which he was best known. In 1933 he took over as director of the Deutsches Opernhaus following Max von Schillings's death, until 1944. Forced to retire in 1945 owing to his political sympathies, he later sang at Regensburg (1949–51). He had a magnificently resonant and warm-toned voice that was heard to best advantage as Hans Sachs, Wotan, Amfortas and the Dutchman, but he never sang at Bayreuth as he was usually engaged during the summer months at the Munich Festival.

Leo Riemens/Elizabeth Forbes

Rodgers, Joan

(*b* Whitehaven, Cumbria, 4 Nov 1956). English soprano. After reading Russian at the University of Liverpool and studying at the RNCM, she made a remarkable début as Pamina at the 1982 Aix-en-Provence Festival. Engagements followed at both London opera houses and across Europe in the lyric Mozart roles – Susanna, Zerlina, Despina – and she enjoyed close working relationships with the producer Jean-Pierre Ponnelle and the conductor Daniel Barenboim, with whom she made several Mozart opera recordings. More recently, along with several highly effective appearances in G.F. Handel operas, she has enlarged both her range and her repertory by undertaking Mozart's Countess and Elvira; much praised accounts of P.I. Tchaikovsky's Iolanta, Mimì, and Mélisande with Opera North; Emmanuel Chabrier's Briséïs (a rare concert revival at the 1995 Edinburgh Festival, also recorded); a touching Blanche in Francis Poulenc's *Dialogue des Carmélites* at the ENO in 1999; and her first Marschallin, for Scottish Opera, also in 1999. In 1996 she made her Metropolitan début as Pamina. Her voice has grown in size without sacrificing its gentle, palpitating freshness of timbre and precision of delivery. In recital Rodgers has become internationally known for her expert delivery of Russian, which affords eloquent interpretations of Modest Musorgsky, Tchaikovsky and Serge Rachmaninoff; alike in *mélodies* and lieder she communicates through graceful, unforced delivery of words as well as notes. Married to the conductor Paul Daniel, she was created a CBE in 2001.

H. Canning: 'Joan Rodgers', *Opera*, xlvi (1995), 1390–98

Max Loppert/R

Roger, Gustave-Hippolyte

(*b* Paris, 17 Dec 1815; *d* Paris, 12 Sept 1879). French tenor. He entered the Paris Conservatoire in 1836 as a pupil of Blès Martin and won *premiers prix* in singing and in *opéra comique* the following year. In 1838 he made his début as Georges in Fromental Halévy's *L'éclair* at the Opéra-Comique, where he subsequently created a number of roles written for him by Halévy, Daniel Auber and Ambroise Thomas. His success rested on his considerable intelligence, fine bearing and pure tone. In 1846 he sang Faust in the first performance of Hector Berlioz's *La damnation de Faust*, and in 1848 he moved from the Opéra-Comique to the Opéra, where, in 1849, he created the role of Jean de Leyde in Giacomo Meyerbeer's *Le prophète*. Although his voice was too light for such parts, he had enormous success and continued to sing a number of leading tenor roles at the Opéra. He successfully toured Germany on several occasions. His most celebrated partners were JENNY LIND and PAULINE VIARDOT, and he enjoyed the friendship of Berlioz, Meyerbeer and many literary figures. In 1859 he sang in Félicien David's *Herculanum* at the Opéra, but shortly afterwards he lost his right arm in a shooting accident. For some years he continued to appear on stage with a mechanical arm, at the Opéra-Comique and in the provinces, and from 1868 until his death he was a professor of singing at the Conservatoire. His book *Le carnet d'un ténor* (1880) contains lively memories of his career, including an account of his visits to England in 1847 and 1848. In 1861 Berlioz orchestrated Franz Schubert's *Erlkönig* for him.

Hugh Macdonald

Rogers, Nigel (David)

(*b* Wellington, Shropshire, 21 March 1935). English tenor. He studied at King's College, Cambridge, under Boris Ord (1953–6), then privately in Rome (1957), Milan (1958–9) and at the Musikhochschule in Munich (1959–64), where he was taught by GERHARD HÜSCH. There in 1960 he helped to found the Studio der Frühen Musik, a quartet specializing in early music, with whom he made his professional début in 1961. Since 1964 he has also pursued a career as a soloist, particularly in music of the Baroque period, on the Continent, especially in Germany and the Netherlands; he has also sung in Britain and in North America. He teaches at the Schola Cantorum Basiliensis. Rogers has specialized in Claudio Monteverdi's operas, singing principal roles in *Il ritorno d'Ulisse in patria*, *L'incoronazione di Poppea*, *Il combattimento di Tancredi e Clorinda* and *Orfeo*. He has been associated with several early music groups, including Chiaroscuro, with whom he has recorded frequently and performed in many European countries, but has not confined himself to music of the 17th century and earlier; he has sung in several 20th-century works (including *Billy Budd* and Alexander Goehr's *Arden must Die*), and his recordings include J.S. Bach's *St Matthew Passion* and Franz Schubert's *Die schöne Müllerin* (with fortepiano accompaniment) as well as music by Monteverdi (notably *Orfeo*, whose title role he has recorded twice), Thomas Morley, the lute-song repertory and 16th- and 17th-century music. His keen sense of style and natural feeling for the expressive character of Baroque music, coupled with an exceptional control in florid music, made him a leading figure in the early-music revival of the 1960s and 70s. His voice, apt in scale to Baroque music, has a certain incisive quality; he has a ready command of the *trillo* and of fast-moving, elaborate lines such as those of Orpheus's 'Possente spirto' from *Orfeo*, an interpretation that has won him special praise. He has also contributed to periodicals and written a chapter on the voice in J.A. Sadie, ed.: *Companion to Baroque Music* (London, 1990).

Stanley Sadie

Rolfe Johnson, Anthony

(*b* Tackley, Northants., 5 Nov 1940). English tenor. Originally a farmer, he studied at the GSMD with Ellis Keeler and later with Vera Rozsa, RICHARD LEWIS and PETER PEARS. He made his début with the English Opera Group in 1973 as Count Vaudémont in *Iolanta* (P.I. Tchaikovsky), followed by Stroh (*Intermezzo*) and Lensky at Glyndebourne in 1974. His début with the ENO was in 1978 as Don Ottavio, and in 1983 he was highly successful both in Geneva and with Scottish Opera as Aschenbach (*Death in Venice*); during these years he toured widely in Europe and the USA in concerts and making recordings. In 1988 he made his Covent Garden début as Jupiter (*Semele*) and in 1989 sang an outstanding Ulysses (Claudio Monteverdi) with the ENO. He made his Metropolitan début as Idomeneus in 1991, repeating the role in Vienna and Salzburg the same year. In 1994 he sang Peter Grimes for Scottish Opera, Glyndebourne and the Metropolitan Opera. One of the most stylish and versatile tenors of his day, Rolfe Johnson was a founder member of the Songmakers' Almanac (1976), and has since pursued a flourishing concert career in parallel with opera; he is a renowned singer of lieder and English song, and an outstanding interpreter of Handel oratorios and of the Evangelist in the Bach Passions. His extensive discography ranges from J.S. Bach and G.F. Handel through Mozart operas (his recordings of Idomeneus and Titus have been described as models of Mozartian singing) to *Oedipus rex*, *The Rake's Progress* and many works by Benjamin Britten, notably *Peter Grimes* and the *War Requiem*. He was appointed Director of Singing Studies at the Britten–Pears School in 1990, and was made a CBE in 1992.

D.P. Stearns: 'Quick Study', *ON*, lii/10 (1987–8), 20–21, 46

A. Blyth: 'Anthony Rolfe Johnson', *Opera*, xliv (1993), 647–53

Noël Goodwin

Roman, Stella [Blasu, Florica Vierica Alma Stela]

(*b* Cluj, 23 Aug 1904; *d* New York, 12 Feb 1992). Romanian soprano. She studied in Rome with Giuseppina Baldassare-Tedeschi and subsequently made her Italian début at Piacenza in 1932. After appearing successfully at the Rome Opera, she sang the role of the Empress in the La Scala première of *Die Frau ohne Schatten* in 1940. She made her Metropolitan début as Aida in 1941. For ten years (1941–50) she alternated with ZINKA MILANOV in such operas as *Il trovatore*, *Otello*, *Ballo*, *Cavalleria rusticana*, *La Gioconda* and *Tosca*. She appeared at San Francisco during the same period, where her roles included Donna Anna, Mimì and the Marschallin; she repeated the last at the S Carlo in Naples in 1951. An unorthodox and sometimes hectic technique prevented the singer and her warm, beautiful lirico-dramatic voice from achieving greatness, but she was a fascinating artist capable of effortless, high *pianissimos* and vibrant climaxes, as can be heard in off-the-air performances from the Metropolitan, notably her Amelia (*Ballo in maschera*) and Desdemona.

P. Jackson: *Saturday Afternoons at the Old Met* (New York, 1992)

Max de Schauensee/R

Ronconi, Giorgio

(*b* Milan, 6 Aug 1810; *d* Madrid, 8 Jan 1890). Italian baritone. He studied with his father, Domenico Ronconi, a well-known singing teacher, and made his début in 1831 at Pavia as Valdeburgo (*La straniera*). The following year he sang in Gaetano Donizetti's *L'esule di Roma* at the Teatro Valle, Rome, where in 1833 he sang Cardenio in *Il furioso all'isola di San Domingo* and the title role of *Torquato Tasso*, both first performances. He also sang in five other Donizetti premières, *Il campanello di notte* (Naples, 1836), *Pia de' Tolomei* (Venice, 1837), *Maria de Rudenz* (Venice, 1838), *Maria Padilla* (Milan, 1841) and *Maria di Rohan* (Vienna, 1843), which he repeated at the Théâtre Italien, Paris. Having first sung at La Scala in 1839 as Enrico Ashton (*Lucia di Lammermoor*), he created the title role of Giuseppe Verdi's *Nabucco* there in 1842. The same year he made his London début at Her Majesty's Theatre, and from 1847 to 1866 he sang nearly every season at Covent Garden. His large repertory included Papageno, Gioachino Rossini's Figaro, Iago and William Tell, and Verdi's Don Carlo (*Ernani*); in 1853 he became the first London Rigoletto.

In many ways, Ronconi was the prototype of the 'modern', Verdian baritone. As the *Musical World* (11 September 1847) said: 'His voice is not particularly melodious, nor is his intonation strictly true…nevertheless…its power is immense, and its extent extraordinary for a barytone. In *forte* passages its volume fills the house like a thunder-peal; and in passionate phrases, when the artist comes out with an upper G, or sometimes an A, with all his power, the effect is quite electrical'. It was clearly this unprecedented power in the highest register that Verdi exploited so thoroughly, and that became a model for many baritones of the next generation. Ronconi was married to the soprano Elguerra Giannoni; his brother Sebastiano (*b* Venice, May 1814; *d* Milan, 6 Feb 1900) was a baritone who made his début at Lucca in 1836 and had a successful career in Europe and the USA.

H.F. Chorley: *Thirty Years' Musical Recollections* (London, 1862/*R*, abridged 2/1926/*R* by E. Newman)
T. Kaufman: 'Giorgio Ronconi', *Donizetti Society Journal*, v (1984), 169–206 [incl. chronology of his opera appearances]

Elizabeth Forbes (with Roger Parker)

Roocroft, Amanda

(*b* Coppull, Lancs., 9 Feb 1966). English soprano. She studied with Barbara Robotham at the RNCM and won the Kathleen Ferrier Prize in 1988. In 1990 she made her operatic début as Sophie in *Der Rosenkavalier* with the WNO at Cardiff. The following year brought débuts at Glyndebourne (Fiordiligi in *Così fan tutte*) and Covent Garden (Pamina in *Die Zauberflöte*). In 1993 she began an association with the Staatsoper in Munich, where she was enthusiastically welcomed and which has seen some of her best work. The operas of G.F. Handel and W.A. Mozart remained central to her repertory, but she expanded it to include Vincenzo Bellini (*I Capuleti e i Montecchi*), Giuseppe Verdi (*Simon Boccanegra* and *Otello*) and Giacomo Puccini (*La bohème*). Recitals in leading European cities and concerts with leading orchestras enhanced a reputation which grew rapidly in these years. She was also promoted strongly by her record company, arousing expectations she could not always fulfil. Her career reached a critical point involving the cancellation of her first Arabella, scheduled for Covent Garden in 1996. She reappeared with success as Kát'á Kabanová at Glyndebourne in 1998, when her pure, bright, firm voice had gained penetration, perhaps with a touch of hardness. Her Kát'á at Covent Garden in 2000 was even more searing, and the same year she was highly acclaimed for her moving portrayal of Jenůfa at Glyndebourne. On recordings she is represented at her best in the *Così fan tutte* of 1992 with John Eliot Gardiner, fresh of tone, technically assured and strongly characterized.

J.B. Steane

Rootering, Jan-Hendrik

(*b* Wedingfeld, 18 March 1950). German bass. After early lessons with his father, the Dutch tenor Hendrikus Rootering, he studied at the Hamburg Conservatory and while there took small parts at the Staatsoper. He made his stage début as Colline at Gelsenkirchen in 1980. After Gelsenkirchen he worked at the Deutsche Oper am Rhein before being engaged by Sawallisch for the Staatsoper in Munich (1982), where he remained an ensemble member until 1988 and has returned frequently since then, notably as Hans Sachs in 1998. He has made guest appearances in all the major houses in Europe and the USA, with a special emphasis on the Metropolitan Opera, where James Levine has cast him in such roles as Sarastro, Don Basilio, Gremin, King Philip and Gurnemanz. His firm, flexible bass, used with innate artistry and a deal of character, has been heard on many recordings, notably as Daland, Heinrich der Vogler (*Lohengrin*) and Fasolt. He is also an accomplished soloist in choral works (including Ludwig van Beethoven's Ninth Symphony and Antonin Dvořák's *Stabat mater* on disc) and a thoughtful interpreter of lieder. In 1994 he was appointed a professor of singing at the Musikhochschule in Munich.

Alan Blyth

Rooy, Anton(ius Maria Josephus) van

(*b* Rotterdam, 1 Jan 1870; *d* Munich, 28 Nov 1932). Dutch bass-baritone. He studied singing in Frankfurt with Julius Stockhausen, and made his début at Bayreuth in 1897, singing Wotan at every festival until 1902, and adding the roles of Hans Sachs in 1899 and the Dutchman in 1901. His gifts were instantly recognized: he appeared at Covent Garden in the leading Wagner roles every year but one from 1898 to 1913, and at the Metropolitan every year but one from 1898 to 1908. Having consented to sing Amfortas in the unauthorized New York *Parsifal* of 1903, he was thenceforth banned at Bayreuth. He also took part in several non-Wagner operas, and in 1907 was John the Baptist in the American première of *Salome*. For over a decade he was the unchallenged leading exponent of all the leading Wagner roles, especially Wotan, Sachs and the Dutchman. Latterly he also sang at Frankfurt. He retired in 1913, and thereafter lived in Munich. Despite primitive studio technique, brief recorded excerpts from his leading roles allow us to glimpse the noble tone and grandeur of declamation that made him a supreme Wagner interpreter.

L. Hevingham-Root: 'The London Red G&Ts of 1902: Anton van Rooy', *Record Collector*, xiii (1960–61), 23–8

Desmond Shawe-Taylor

Röschmann, Dorothea

(*b* Flensburg, 17 June 1967). German soprano. She studied at the Hochschule für Musik und darstellende Kunst in Hamburg, with BARBARA SCHLICK at the Akademie für Alte Musik in Bremen and subsequently in Los Angeles, New York and (with Vera Rozsa) London. She made her professional concert début in 1986 and her operatic début, as Barbarina in *Le nozze di Figaro*, at the Vienna Akademie in 1992. The same year she appeared as Zerlina in Israel, and in 1993 made her début at the Halle Handel Festival as Dorinda in *Orlando*. Röschmann's acclaimed Salzburg Festival début, as W.A. Mozart's Susanna, followed in 1995, and she has since returned to the Festival as Ilia, Servilia (*La clemenza di Tito*) and Pamina. In 1994 she became a company member of the Deutsche Staatsoper, Berlin, where her roles have included Elmira in Reinhard Keiser's *Croesus* (which she has recorded), the title role in Alessandro Scarlatti's *La Griselda*, Ännchen, Nannetta (*Falstaff*), Pamina and Susanna. With the Staatsoper in Munich she has sung parts such as Drusilla (*L'incoronazione di Poppea*), Almirena (*Rinaldo*) and Marzelline, in addition to the light lyric Mozart roles for which she has been widely praised. Röschmann is also much admired in the Baroque concert repertoire, working with such conductors as John Eliot Gardiner, Nikolaus Harnoncourt, Philippe Herreweghe, René Jacobs, Nicholas McGegan and Paul McCreesh. Her clear, silvery tone and graceful phrasing can be heard on numerous recordings, including Bach cantatas, *Messiah*, G.P. Telemann's *Orpheus* and a delightful disc of G.F. Handel's German Arias.

Richard Wigmore

Roselle, Anne [Gyenge, Anna]

(*b* Budapest, 20 March 1894 or 19 April 1890; *d* Philadelphia, ? 21 March 1955). Hungarian soprano. She grew up in the USA. Following her début in Budapest in 1915, she returned to New York, appearing first at the Strand Theatre and then in 1920 at the Metropolitan Opera, where she made her début as Musetta. Her career flourished with Antonio Scotti's touring company and when she joined the Dresden Staatsoper (1925). Her great triumph there was as Turandot in the German première of 1926; she repeated the part at Verona (1928) and with limited success at Covent Garden (1934). Her previous appearance in London had been as Donna Anna in 1929, when her performance gained strength during the course of the opera. A more substantial achievement was her singing of Marie in the first American performance of *Wozzeck* under Leopold Stokowski in 1931 at Philadelphia, where she later returned to teach. Her few recordings include two of Turandot's solos, in which her warm tone suits 'Del primo pianto' very well and 'In questa reggia' hardly at all.

J.B. Steane

Rosing, Vladimir

(*b* St Petersburg, 23 Jan 1890; *d* Los Angeles, 24 Nov 1963). Russian tenor and director. He studied in St Petersburg with Joachim Tartakov and in Paris with JEAN DE RESZKE. In 1912 he made his début in *Yevgeny Onegin* at St Petersburg, and the following year went to London, where in 1915 he directed a Russian and French season at the Stoll Theatre; he introduced *The Queen of Spades* to London, 'working like a veritable Trojan' (*Musical Opinion*, July 1915) in the role of Hermann. He sang with the Carl Rosa Opera Company at Covent Garden in 1921 as Cavaradossi, and in 1923 founded a company which for six years toured the USA giving opera in English. Rosing directed, and Albert Coates conducted, the British Music Drama Opera Company, founded in 1936, and their single season at Covent Garden included the première of Coates's *Pickwick* and the first performance in England of Modest Musorgsky's *The Fair at Sorochintsï*. His production in 1938 of George Lloyd's *The Serf* for the English Opera Company at Covent Garden was admired, but in 1939 he moved to the USA, where he organized the Southern California Opera Association and from 1950 to 1958 was director for the New York City Opera. In concert work his manner was flamboyant and his style exaggerated, but he was a fervent advocate of Russian song, of which he made some pioneering recordings. Rosing was one of the most determined, individualistic and enterprising figures of his day. His voice, though powerful enough, was subject to some rough usage. His insistence on intelligibility in opera was timely and influential.

F. Juynboll: 'Vladimir Rosing', *Record Collector*, xxxvi (1991), 186–203, 331 only

J.B. Steane

Rösler, Endre

(*b* Budapest, 27 Nov 1904; *d* Budapest, 13 Dec 1963). Hungarian tenor. He made his Budapest Opera House début in 1927 as Alfredo (*La traviata*), having studied with FERNANDO DE LUCIA and EDOARDO GARBIN. From the outset he undertook a wide range of roles, both lyric and dramatic, favouring the Mozart repertory above all. His performances were notable not so much for beauty of voice (as a young singer he had contracted an inflammation of the vocal cords that affected his higher register) as for expressive power, great musicality, a keen sense of style, excellent acting ability and versatility in character parts such as Shuysky (*Boris Godunov*), Malatestino (Riccardo Zandonai's *Francesca da Rimini*) and Loge (*Das Rheingold*), perhaps his greatest role. He played Florestan under Arturo Toscanini at Salzburg (1935), later recording the role with the Hungarian State Opera under Otto Klemperer (1948), and appeared several times at the Florence Maggio Musicale and elsewhere. At the end of the 1950s he resigned his leading roles, playing only comprimario and character parts. He was also a leading Hungarian recitalist and concert singer.

Péter P. Várnai/Alan Blyth

Rossi-Lemeni, Nicola

(*b* Istanbul, 6 Nov 1920; *d* Bloomington, IN, 12 March 1991). Italian bass. A pupil of his mother, Xenia Macadon, and of Carnevali-Cusinati, he made his début at La Fenice in 1946 as Varlaam, a role he repeated in 1947 at La Scala, where he continued to appear until 1960. At first he was heard as Boris, Philip II and Mephistopheles (Charles Gounod and Arrigo Boito); he sang in all the major Italian theatres and also at Buenos Aires, San Francisco (American début, as Boris, 1951), Covent Garden (1952, as Boris), the Metropolitan, Chicago and other houses. An interpreter of marked intelligence and sensitivity, he began with a smooth, mellow and well-focussed voice. Later he compensated for his premature vocal decline with over-emphatic phrasing and vigorous declamation. He specialized in modern operas such as Ildebrando Pizzetti's *Assassinio nella cattedrale* (as Becket, including première at La Scala in 1958), *Wozzeck*, Ernest Bloch's *Macbeth* and Benjamin Britten's *Billy Budd* (Italian première, 1965, Florence). His second wife was the soprano VIRGINIA ZEANI. He recorded, among other parts, the title role in Gioachino Rossini's *Mosè in Egitto*, Henry VIII (*Anna Bolena*, with Callas) and Oroveso (*Norma*).

Rodolfo Celletti/Alan Blyth

Rössler, Ernestine

See SCHUMANN-HEINK, ERNESTINE.

Rössl-Majdan, Hilde(gard)

(*b* Moosbirbaum, nr Vienna, 21 Jan 1921). Austrian contralto. She studied in Vienna, making her début in 1950 at the Staatsoper, where she was engaged for more than 20 years. At Salzburg she sang Dryad in *Ariadne auf Naxos* (1954), Lucrezia in *Palestrina* (1958), Annina in *Der Rosenkavalier* and Marcellina in *Le nozze di Figaro* (1960). She had a firm, rich-toned voice and sang a wide repertory that ranged from G.F. Handel and W.A. Mozart to Giuseppe Verdi, Richard Wagner and Johann Strauss. She recorded Eduige (*Rodelinda*) and Czipra (*Der Zigeunerbaron*).

Elizabeth Forbes

Rosvaenge [Roswaenge, Rosenvinge Hansen], Helge

(*b* Copenhagen, 29 Aug 1897; *d* Munich, 19 June 1972). Danish tenor. Engaged at Neustrelitz, he made his début as Don José in 1921. Engagements followed at Altenburg, Basle, Cologne (1927–30) and the Berlin Staatsoper, where he was leading tenor from 1930, being especially distinguished in the Italian repertory; he also sang regularly in Vienna and Munich. He appeared at Salzburg between 1933 and 1939 as Tamino (a role he recorded memorably under Thomas Beecham), Huon (*Oberon*) and Florestan, which he also sang at Covent Garden in 1938. He sang Parsifal at Bayreuth in 1934 and 1936 but otherwise avoided the Wagnerian repertory. After World War II, Rosvaenge divided his time between Berlin and Vienna, continuing to sing until the late 1960s as Calaf, Radames and Manrico. His brilliant, lustrous voice, with its thrilling high register, is preserved on numerous recordings that encompass every aspect of his large repertory. He was able to reproduce in the recording studio the excitement of his live performances, as can be heard in his accounts of Florestan's scena and Hugo Wolf's *Der Feuerreiter*.

J. Dennis: 'Helge Rosvaenge', *Record Collector*, xxiii (1976–7), 140 [with discography]; addns, xxv (1979–80), 120–22

Alan Blyth

Rothenberger, Anneliese

(*b* Mannheim, 19 June 1924). German soprano. She studied in Mannheim with Erika Müller and made her début in 1943 at Koblenz, where she was soon singing such parts as Gilda and the title role in Hans Pfitzner's *Das Christ-Elflein*. From 1946 to 1973 she was a member of the Hamburg Staatsoper, where her roles included Cherubino, Blonde, Oscar, Musetta, Olympia and the three soprano roles of Gottfried von Einem's *Der Prozess* in its first performance in Germany. At the 1952 Edinburgh Festival she sang Regina with the Hamburg company in the British stage première of *Mathis der Maler*. She first appeared at Salzburg in 1954, creating Telemachus in Rolf Liebermann's *Penelope*; she returned to create Agnes in the German version of his *Die Schule der Frauen* (1957) and to sing Zdenka (*Arabella*), Flaminia (Joseph Haydn's *Il mondo della luna*), Sophie and Konstanze. Her many appearances as Sophie included those at Glyndebourne (1959–60); in 1960 she made her Metropolitan début as Zdenka. She sang regularly at Munich and Vienna from the mid-1950s. Her large repertory included W.A. Mozart's Ilia, Susanna and Pamina, Berg's Lulu, Adele (*Die Fledermaus*), and the title role of Heinrich Sutermeister's *Madame Bovary*, which she created in Zürich (1967). Rothenberger had unusual acting ability and a light, well-schooled voice. She made several complete recordings of both opera and, especially, operetta.

Harold Rosenthal/R

Rothier, Léon

(*b* Reims, 26 Dec 1874; *d* New York, 6 Dec 1951). French bass. His early training was as a violinist, but he was persuaded to pursue singing instead. He studied at the Paris Conservatoire (1894–9) with Eugène Charles Antoine Crosti (singing), PAUL LHÉRIE (*opéra comique*) and Léon Melchissedec (opera). He made his début in 1899 as Jupiter in Charles Gounod's *Philémon et Baucis* at the Opéra-Comique, where he remained until 1903; his roles included Zuniga, the King (*Cendrillon*), Don Fernando (*Fidelio*), Maître Ramon (*Mireille*), Colline, and the junk-seller in *Louise*, which he created in 1900. He then sang with the Marseilles (1903–7), Nice (1907–9) and Lyons (1909–10) companies before going to the USA. His Metropolitan début was in 1910 as Gounod's Méphistophélès, and he remained with the company for 30 years. His roles included Ramfis, Pimen, Alvise Badoero, Raimondo, Arkel, the King (*Le roi d'Ys*) and Sparafucile. He sang Bluebeard at the American première of Paul Dukas' *Ariane et Barbe-bleue* (1911) and created Father Time in Albert Wolff's *L'oiseau bleu* (1919) and Major Duquesnois in Deems Taylor's *Peter Ibbetson* (1931). His last appearance was as Jules Massenet's Count des Grieux (1939). He also sang in San Francisco and with the Chicago summer opera at Ravinia Park.

Katherine K. Preston, Elizabeth Forbes

Rothmüller, (Aron) Marko

(*b* Trnjani, nr Prijedor, 31 Dec 1908; *d* Bloomington, IN, 20 Jan 1993). Croatian baritone. He studied in Zagreb and then in Vienna, with Alban Berg, Regina Weiss and Franz Steiner. He made his début at Hamburg-Altona in 1932 as Ottokar (*Der Freischütz*). He returned to Zagreb for two years and in 1935 was engaged by the Zürich Opera, where he sang regularly until 1947, scoring particular successes in Giuseppe Verdi and Richard Wagner and creating Truchsess von Waldburg in *Mathis der Maler* (1938). In 1946 he joined the Vienna Staatsoper, singing there until 1949. Having made his London début in 1939 as Krušina (*The Bartered Bride*) at Covent Garden, in 1947 he sang Rigoletto with the New London Opera Company at the Cambridge Theatre and John the Baptist (*Salome*) during the Vienna Staatsoper's season at Covent Garden. He was a member of the Covent Garden company from 1948 to 1952, singing a wide variety of roles including Amonasro, Rigoletto, Scarpia, Gunther, Tomsky (*The Queen of Spades*) and the title role in *Wozzeck* in its first British stage performance (1952). He appeared with the Glyndebourne company (1949–55) as Guglielmo, Count Almaviva, Don Carlo (*La forza del destino*), Macbeth and Nick Shadow. He made his New York début with the New York City Opera (1948) and later sang at the Metropolitan (1959–65), making his début as Kothner. From 1955 to 1979 he taught at Indiana University, Bloomington.

Rothmüller had a magnetic stage presence and a voice of incisive and individual timbre. He made a few operatic recordings, among them Wolfram's solos and Scarpia's 'Te Deum' as well as a bleak 1944 recording of *Winterreise*. Interested in Jewish music, he wrote *Die Musik der Juden* (Zürich, 1951; Eng. trans., 1953, rev. 2/1967). He composed a number of works, including Sephardi religious songs, a setting of Psalm xv, a Symphony for strings and two string quartets.

D. Shawe-Taylor: 'Marko Rothmüller', *Opera*, ii (1950–51), 169–74
A. Blyth: Obituary, *Opera*, xliv (1993), 426–7

Harold Rosenthal/Alan Blyth

Rounseville, Robert

(*b* Attleboro, MA, 25 March 1914; *d* New York, 6 Aug 1974). American tenor. After studying medicine, he moved to New York in 1937, where he earned his living mainly as a nightclub crooner and vaudevillian. In 1947–8 he studied at the Berkshire Music Center in Lenox, MA, and in 1948 made his professional début, as Pelléas, at New York City Opera. The following year he scored a triumph as Hoffmann (*Les contes d'Hoffmann*), and shortly afterwards took part in a film of the opera. Further roles at the New York City Opera included Alfredo (*La traviata*) and Don José. He created the role of Tom Rakewell in Igor Stravinsky's *The Rake's Progress* at the Venice Festival (1951).

Richard Wigmore

Rousselière, Charles

(*b* Saint-Nazaire, 17 Jan 1875; *d* Joué-lès-Tours, 11 May 1950). French tenor. Originally a blacksmith by trade, he studied with Albert Vaguet at the Paris Conservatoire and made his début at the Opéra as Samson in 1900. The following year he sang in the première of Camille Saint-Saëns's *Les barbares*, and he remained with the company until 1905. Until 1919 he was a favourite at Monte Carlo, where he appeared first in *La damnation de Faust*; premières there included Pietro Mascagni's *Amica*, Saint-Saëns's *L'ancêtre* and Gabriel Fauré's *Pénélope*. His début at the Metropolitan in *Roméo et Juliette* in 1906 coincided with that of GERALDINE FARRAR, who received more attention; his dramatic skill was appreciated but the power of his voice, sometimes strident, suggested that he should turn to more heroic roles. This he did on his return to France, adding Otello, Lohengrin, Siegfried and Parsifal to his repertory. He also appeared in Berlin, Buenos Aires and Milan, and in his later years sang mostly at the Opéra-Comique where in 1913 he created the title role in Gustave Charpentier's *Julien*. His varied repertory is well represented in recordings made between 1903 and 1926: his voice is strong and clearly defined, his style authoritative in declamation and well mannered in more lyrical music.

J.B. Steane

Roux, Michel

(*b* Angoulême, 1 Sept 1924). French baritone. He studied at Bordeaux and Paris, and in 1948 made his début at the Opéra-Comique in *Lakmé*, becoming a company principal there and at the Opéra until 1955. His début at La Scala was in 1953 as Golaud, a role with which he became closely associated and which he recorded that year under Jean Fournet. He sang at leading theatres in France and Italy, and in 1956 made his British début as Count Almaviva at Glyndebourne, where he returned in most years up to 1970, singing Mozart, Debussy and Rossini roles including Raimbaud (*Le comte Ory*), which he recorded with the Glyndebourne company under Vittorio Gui (1957). His American début was at the Chicago Lyric Opera in 1959 as Athanaël (*Thaïs*). Other engagements took him to the Vienna Staatsoper and Deutsche Oper, Berlin, mainly in French and Italian roles, which he sang with intelligent style and often vivid stage character; he later taught in Paris.

Noël Goodwin

Rubini, Giacomo.

See LAURI-VOLPI, GIACOMO.

Rubini, Giovanni Battista

(*b* Romano, nr Bergamo, 7 April 1794; *d* Romano, 3 March 1854). Italian tenor. The son of a horn player, at the age of eight he sang *Salve regina* in a local monastery so beautifully that his father decided to give him a musical education. After four years' training he was able to sing a female role in an opera in Romano. Thereafter he was engaged at the Teatro Riccardi in Bergamo as violinist and chorister. Wishing to devote himself entirely to singing, he left Bergamo in 1813 and spent the next year in Piedmont as chorister in a touring company. He sang Lindoro in *L'italiana in Algeri* at the Teatro S Moisè, Venice, in 1815, and he attracted the attention of Domenico Barbaia, who offered him a long-term contract at the S Carlo. Rubini's Neapolitan début was in 1815 at the Teatro dei Fiorentini, again as Lindoro. He spent ten years in Naples, performing mostly at the smaller houses where comedy prevailed and benefiting from the tuition of ANDREA NOZZARI, a leading tenor at the S Carlo. He appeared in Rome in 1818. In 1824–5 he first sang in Vienna; world fame was in sight, with engagements in Italy and, for the first time, Paris, where he starred in *La Cenerentola*, *Otello* and *La donna del lago*. But it was in the new Romantic style of Vincenzo Bellini and Gaetano Donizetti that he came into his own: he proved a vital influence on Bellini, creating the tenor leads in *Bianca e Gernando* (1826, Naples), *Il pirata* (1827, Milan), *La sonnambula* (1831, Milan) and *I puritani* (1835, Paris). During the composition of *Il pirata* he lodged with the composer, trying out each piece as it was written. Likewise, Bellini refused to commit to paper a note of Arturo's music in *I puritani* until Rubini was available to be consulted. The Donizetti premières in which Rubini was involved include, in Naples, *La lettera anonima* (1822), *Elvida* (1826), *Gianni di Calais* (1828), *Il paria* (1829) and *Il giovedì grasso* (1829) and, more importantly, *Anna Bolena* (1830, Milan) and *Marino Faliero* (1835, Paris).

Rubini first appeared in London in 1831. From then until 1843 he divided each year between Her Majesty's Theatre in the Haymarket, where his parts included Don Giovanni and, on occasion, Don Ottavio, and the Théâtre Italien in Paris where he created the role of Ermanno in Saverio Mercadante's *I briganti* (1836); there from 1839 he yielded his place in the leading quartet to the young GIOVANNI MATTEO MARIO. He sang in both the French (1837) and English (1838) premières of *Lucia di Lammermoor*. He remained no less in demand in concert halls and at provincial festivals (he had sung the tenor of Joseph Haydn's *Creation* as early as 1821 in Naples). He visited St Petersburg in 1843 and was invited by the tsar to become 'Director of Singing for the Empire'; he returned with TAMBURINI and others to give a season of Italian opera, 1843–4. But in 1845 he retired permanently to his villa in Romano, now a Rubini museum. In the course of his career he published a set of six ariettas under the title *L'addio* and a singing manual, *12 lezioni di canto per tenore o soprano*.

During Rubini's career the tenor, traditionally the young hero of *opera buffa*, was assuming the same role in the serious genre. In the new Romantic opera of the 1830s Rubini had at his disposal an intensity of expression that far outshone the cool heroics of the castratos and their female successors. His phenomenally high range, which induced Bellini to include a high *f″* for him in the third act of *I puritani*, must be understood in the context of the convention of his day, when no tenor was expected to sing any note higher than *a′* with full chest resonance. The upper fifth of Rubini's range was in the less expressive falsetto register. In order to avoid ugly changes of timbre and to gather strength for high notes, he had not only to exaggerate differences between loud and soft, but to sing whole numbers in a whispering *pianissimo* instead of allowing his voice to expand naturally and easily. He is also credited with introducing Romantic mannerisms such as the 'sob'. He was neither good-looking nor a good actor; his strength lay in the beauty of his tone and the natural artistry of his phrasing.

B. Brewer: 'Rubini, the King of Tenors', *Opera*, xxx (1979), 326–9

Donizetti Society Journal, iv (1980) [incl. B. Brewer: 'Il cigno di Romano, the King of Tenors: Giovan Battista Rubini, a Performance Study', 116–24; 'Points for the Reconstruction of the Career of G.B. Rubini', 125–59; 'Rubini's Repertory', 160–65; 'Two Nineteenth Century Accounts of Giovan Battista Rubini', 167–79]

Julian Budden

Ruffo, Titta [Titta, Ruffo Cafiero]

(*b* Pisa, 9 June 1877; *d* Florence, 6 July 1953). Italian baritone. He studied briefly with Venceslao

Persichini, Senatore Sparapani and Lelio Casini. In 1898 he made his début at the Teatro Costanzi, Rome, as the Herald in *Lohengrin*, and then sang at Santiago, Chile (1900), and Buenos Aires (1902). He appeared at Covent Garden in 1903 (Enrico Ashton and Gioachino Rossini's Figaro), but did not return, reputedly because of a disagreement with MELBA. He made his La Scala début during the 1903–4 season as Rigoletto, and was then in demand at all the major European houses. In 1908 he sang at the Colón, where he remained a great favourite until he retired (1931). He was also very popular in the USA, where he first sang in 1912 at Philadelphia (Rigoletto); he then appeared frequently with the Chicago-Philadelphia Grand Opera Company in both cities (until 1926). His Metropolitan début (1922) was as Rossini's Figaro, and he remained with the company for eight seasons, singing Don Carlo (*Ernani*), Amonasro, Gérard (*Andrea Chénier*) and Tonio.

Ruffo's voice was notable for its resonance, power, range and the almost tenor-like ring of its top register, for purity and warmth, and for breath control. It also had a characteristically dark, sometimes sombre colour, particularly noticeable in Ambroise Thomas' *Hamlet* and in Giuseppe Verdi. He was a vigorous and exuberant actor, and his singing was correspondingly dramatic and forceful, if occasionally coarse and loud. His enormous success, in operas such as *L'Africaine*, *La Gioconda*, *Pagliacci* and *Il barbiere di Siviglia*, finally brought about a complete change in Italian vocal taste for baritone singing, towards an unpolished, aggressive style, and away from the refined, classical 19th-century tradition. His numerous recordings, all refurbished on CD, give a very fair idea of the range and power of his singing and of his strengths as an interpreter, most notably as Rigoletto (in which some claim he is unsurpassed) and Hamlet.

F.W. Gaisberg: *The Music Goes Round* (New York, 1943; repr. 1946 as *Music on Record*)

A. Wolf: 'Titta Ruffo', *Record Collector*, ii/5 (1947), 69–74 [with discography]

M. de Schauensee: 'Lion of Pisa', *ON*, xxxi/24 (1966–7), 26–7

A. Farkas, ed.: *Titta Ruffo: an Anthology* (Westport, CT, 1984) [with discography by W.R. Moran]

J.B. Steane: 'Titta Ruffo', *Singers of the Century* (London, 1996), 161–5

Rodolfo Celletti/Alan Blyth

Rünger, Gertrude

(*b* Posen [now Poznań], 1899; *d* Berlin, 10 June 1965). German mezzo-soprano and soprano. She sang at Erfurt (1924–7), then for a season at Magdeburg, and from 1928 to 1935 at Vienna, where she took part in some notable revivals such as *Don Carlos* (1931) and *Macbeth* (1933). She returned to Vienna in 1938 after a period in Berlin. Her career also expanded to include the 1933 and 1934 seasons at Covent Garden, 1937 at the Metropolitan and 1938 at La Scala, where she sang Brünnhilde in the *Ring* cycle under Clemens Krauss, and Isolde the following year under Victor De Sabata. At Salzburg she sang Fatima (*Oberon*), the Nurse (*Die Frau ohne Schatten*), Clytemnestra (*Elektra*) and Leonore (*Fidelio*). In London her most admired role was Kundry in which she 'displayed exceptional power in a wide range of dramatic expression'. Her later career included appearances as Electra under Hans Knappertsbusch (1940) and some postwar seasons in Berlin. Her studio recordings are few, but solos from *Don Carlos* and *Macbeth* show fine quality, both vocal and dramatic. Fragments from the Vienna Archive confirm her position among the most impressive singers of her generation.

J.B. Steane

Rydl, Kurt

(*b* Vienna, 8 Oct 1947). Austrian bass. He studied zoology before training at the Hochschule für Musik in Vienna and the Moscow Academy. His stage career began at Linz in 1972. He made his Vienna Staatsoper début in 1976 as Rocco, and sang the same role for his débuts at La Scala, Milan, in 1990 and Covent Garden in 1993. His voluminous black bass is especially suited to malignant characters such as Caspar (*Der Freischütz*), Hagen and Hunding, but he has proved equally successful as Ochs and Kecal (*The Bartered Bride*), and his ability to combine menace and humour makes him a striking Osmin, a role he sang at the Salzburg Festival in 1987–9. Throughout his career Rydl has maintained strong links with the Vienna Staatsoper where his repertory includes the Verdi bass roles. He is also an experienced concert singer. Notable among his many recordings are Sarastro, Rocco, Caspar, Fafner and Daland.

Andrew Clark

Rysanek, Leonie

(*b* Vienna, 14 Nov 1926; *d* Vienna, 7 March 1998). Austrian soprano. She studied at the Vienna Music Academy with ALFRED JERGER and later with Rudolf Grossmann. She made her début at Innsbruck in 1949 as Agathe (*Der Freischütz*) and then sang at Saarbrücken, where her roles included Arabella, Donna Anna, Senta, Sieglinde and Leonora (*La forza*

Leonie Rysanek as Elisabeth in 'Tannhäuser' (Wagner), Bayreuth, 1964

del destino). At the first postwar Bayreuth Festival in 1951 her Sieglinde created a sensation, and the following year she joined the Staatsoper in Munich. Her opulent voice, with its thrilling upper register, and her dramatic temperament were heard and seen to advantage in the title roles of *Die Liebe der Danae, Die ägyptische Helena* and *Salome*, as the Empress in *Die Frau ohne Schatten* and Chrysothemis, and as Lady Macbeth, Turandot, Tosca, Santuzza and Medea.

Rysanek was first heard in London as Danae in the British première of Richard Strauss's opera during the Munich company's season at Covent Garden in 1953; later she appeared there as Chrysothemis, Sieglinde, Tosca and Elsa. She made her American début in 1956 at San Francisco, where she sang Senta and Sieglinde. She returned to Bayreuth as Elsa (1958), Elisabeth (1964) and Kundry (1982). In 1959 she made her début at the Metropolitan, replacing CALLAS as Lady Macbeth. She then appeared there

regularly in the Italian and the German repertories, sharing most of her time between New York and the Vienna Staatsoper, with guest appearances in other leading European houses. In 1986 she celebrated the 30th anniversary of her American début by singing the Kostelnička at San Francisco, and also sang Ortrud at the Metropolitan. Her later roles included Kabanicha, Herodias (*Salome*) and Clytemnestra, which she sang at the Salzburg Festival in 1996, her final stage appearance. She recorded many of her main roles, most notably Sieglinde (under both Wilhelm Furtwängler and Karl Böhm), Lady Macbeth, the Empress and Electra.

P. Dusek and P. Schmidt: *Leonie Rysanek: 40 Jahre Operngeschichte* (Hamburg, 1990)
A. Blyth: 'Leonie Rysanek', *Opera*, xlv (1994), 15–24

Harold Rosenthal/Alan Blyth

S

Sabbatini, Giuseppe

(*b* Rome, 11 May 1957). Italian tenor. At first a double bass player, he studied with Silvana Ferraro and made his début in 1987 at Spoleto as Edgardo (*Lucia di Lammermoor*), then sang Rodolfo at Trieste, returning in 1989 as Carlo/Viscount de Sirval (*Linda di Chamounix*). He has appeared at La Scala and the Vienna Staatsoper, in Paris, Berlin, Hamburg, Zürich, Florence, Parma and Bologna. His roles include Faust, Werther, Lensky and Gabriele Adorno (which he has recorded). He made his Covent Garden début in 1991 as the Duke, then sang Arturo (*I puritani*) in 1992. An effective actor and a fine musician, he has a soft-grained and flexible voice with a strong top register.

Elizabeth Forbes

Sadler-Grün, Friederike.

See GRÜN, FRIEDERIKE (SADLER-).

Saedén, Erik

(*b* Vänersborg, Stockholm, 3 Sept 1924). Swedish baritone. Educated in Stockholm, he joined the Royal Opera there in 1952. He appeared at Bayreuth (1958), Edinburgh (1959 and 1974), Covent Garden (1960), Montreal (1967), Munich and Berlin, where he created the title role in Luigi Dallapiccola's *Ulisse* (1968), but his career was centred on Stockholm, where he sang in the repertory operas of W.A. Mozart, Giuseppe Verdi, Richard Wagner, Richard Strauss and Giacomo Puccini. His roles also included Wozzeck, Nick Shadow, the title role of Dallapiccola's *Il prigioniero*, Yevgeny Onegin, Ferruccio Busoni's Faust, Baron Prus (*The Makropulos Affair*), Mr Gedge (*Albert Herring*) and Tovey (*The Mines of Sulphur*). He created the Mimaroben in Karl-Birger Blomdahl's *Aniara* (1959), Julien in Lars Johan Werle's *Drömmen om Thérèse* (1964) and Saint Phar in Franz Berwald's *Drottningen av Golconda* (1968) and sang in the premières of Hilding Rosenberg's *Hus med dubbel ingång* (1970) and Nekrotzar in György Ligeti's *Le Grand Macabre* (1978). He sang Schigolch in *Lulu* at Covent Garden (1981) and the Royal Father in Jan Sandström's *Slottet det vita* in Stockholm (1987). Although his voice has no special beauty of timbre, his outstanding musicality and

dramatic conviction combine to make him an artist of exceptional interest. CLAES HÅKAN AHNSJÖ and GÖSTA WINBERGH were his pupils.

Elizabeth Forbes

Saint-Christophle [Saint-Christophe], Mlle de

(*d* after 1682). French soprano. She was originally a member of the *musique du roi*, and is recorded as a 'musicienne de Sa Majesté' in Jean-Baptiste Lully's *Ballet des arts* (8 January 1663). She joined Lully's Opéra in 1674 and sang the title role in *Alceste* (1674), Cybele (*Atys*, 1676), Juno (*Isis*, 1677), the Queen (*Psyché*, 1680) and Night (*Le triomphe de l'amour*, 1681). She was occasionally replaced by MARIE VERDIER, who normally took secondary roles. In 1682 Saint-Christophle sang Cassiopeia in Lully's *Persée*, and not long after retired to a convent. She was succeeded by LE ROCHOIS. François and Claude Parfaict described her as 'grande, bien faite, belle et vertueuse', and as having nobility and taste in deportment, gesture and action, in addition to great beauty of voice.

Philip Weller

Saléza, Albert

(*b* Bruges, Pyrénées, 28 Oct 1867; *d* Paris, 26 Nov 1916). French tenor. He studied with LOUIS-HENRI OBIN at the Paris Conservatoire, and made his début at the Opéra-Comique in 1888 as Mylio (Edouard Lalo's *Le roi d'Ys*). He sang first at the Paris Opéra in 1892 as Mathô (Ernest Reyer's *Salammbô*). At Monte Carlo in 1894 he created the role of Eioff in the première of César Franck's posthumous *Hulda* and sang in Hector Berlioz's *La damnation de Faust*. At the Opéra that year he sang in the première of C.E. Lefebvre's *Djelma* and the first Paris performance of Giuseppe Verdi's *Otello*. He made his Covent Garden and Metropolitan débuts in 1898 in Charles Gounod's *Roméo et Juliette*, and sang Rodolfo at the first Metropolitan performance of *La bohème* (1900). His repertory included Siegmund, Tannhäuser, Gounod's Faust, Raoul (*Les Huguenots*), Edgardo (*Lucia di Lammermoor*), John of Leyden (*Le prophète*), Masaniello (*La muette de Portici*) and the Duke (*Rigoletto*). He made a final appearance at the Opéra-Comique in 1910 as Don José. He had a mellow voice with elegant diction and phrasing.

Elizabeth Forbes

Salminen, Matti

(*b* Turku, 7 July 1945). Finnish bass. He studied in Helsinki and made his début there with the Finnish National Opera in 1966. After further study in Rome, he sang Philip II (*Don Carlos*) with the Finnish National Opera in 1969. He was engaged at Cologne (1972–9), and has also sung at most of the other major European opera houses. He sang Ivan Susanin at Wexford (1973), then made his Covent Garden début (1974) as Fasolt and his Bayreuth début (1976) as Hunding, returning as Daland, the Landgrave, Titurel and King Mark. He made his Metropolitan début (1981) as King Mark, and has subsequently appeared there as Sarastro, Rocco, Hagen, Osmin, Daland and Hunding. His repertory also includes Seneca (*L'incoronazione di Poppea*), the Commendatore, Caspar (*Der Freischütz*), Gremin and many Verdi roles. His magnificently resonant voice, huge stature and dramatic flair are particularly effective in the title role of *Boris Godunov*, which he first sang in 1984 at Zürich and has repeated at Barcelona (1986) and other theatres, and as Ivan Khovansky (*Khovanshchina*), which he first sang in Hamburg in 1994. Salminen has recorded many of his Wagner roles (including a noble, eloquent King Mark under Daniel Barenboim), in addition to Seneca, Osmin, the Commendatore, Sarastro, Caspar and the leading bass roles in Aulis Sallinen's *The Horseman* and *Kullervo*.

Elizabeth Forbes

Salvi, Lorenzo

(*b* Ancona, 4 May 1810; *d* Bologna, 16 Jan 1879). Italian tenor. He studied in Naples, making his début in 1830 at S Carlo as Cam in the first performance of Gaetano Donizetti's *Diluvio universale*. At the Teatro Valle, Rome, he created Fernando in *Il furioso all'isola di San Domingo* (1833) and at the Teatro Nuovo, Naples, he sang Nemorino in 1834, and in the first performance of *Betly* (1836). At Genoa he sang Gennaro (*Lucrezia Borgia*), Edgardo and Gioachino Rossini's Otello. He made his début at La Scala in Federico Ricci's *Un duello sotto Richelieu*, created the title role of Gaetano Donizetti's *Gianni di Parigi*, Riccardo in Giuseppe Verdi's first opera *Oberto* (1839) and Edoardo in Verdi's *Un giorno di regno* (1840). At the Teatro Apollo, Rome, he created Olivero in Donizetti's *Adelia* (1841). He was a member of the Italian Opera

in St Petersburg from 1845, and from 1847 to 1849 he sang at Covent Garden, as Edgardo, Nemorino, Almaviva, Don Ramiro, Lindoro (*L'italiana in Algeri*), Ernani, Pollione, Masaniello (Daniel Auber's *La muette de Portici*) and Robert le diable.

Elizabeth Forbes

Salvini-Donatelli, Fanny [Lucchi, Francesca]

(*b* Florence, ?1815; *d* Milan, June 1891). Italian soprano. She made her début at the Teatro di Apollo, Venice, in 1839 in *Il barbiere di Siviglia*. Engaged in Vienna 1842–3, she sang Abigaille in *Nabucco* under Giuseppe Verdi's supervision. She created the role of Violetta in *La traviata* at La Fenice, Venice (6 March 1853), and was blamed indirectly for the work's failure, supposedly because she weighed 'precisely 130 kilograms'. Other Verdi roles included Lady Macbeth, Lucrezia (*I due foscari*) and Elvire (*Ernani*). After engagements throughout Europe, she sang in Paris and at Drury Lane in London in 1858. She retired the following year but made further appearances in 1865. Hector Berlioz and the London critics esteemed her voice, which was expressive, flexible and lyric and which accommodated itself to dramatic roles.

Charles A. Jahant

Sammarco, (Giuseppe) Mario

(*b* Palermo, 13 Dec 1868; *d* Milan, 24 Jan 1930). Italian baritone. He made his début in 1888 at Palermo as Valentin. In 1894 he appeared in Naples at the S Carlo in *La damnation de Faust* and in 1895 at the Teatro Real, Madrid, as Ambroise Thomas' Hamlet, a role he repeated in 1895–6 at La Scala, where he created Gérard in *Andrea Chénier*, returning there in 1902, 1905 and 1913, and singing at Buenos Aires in 1897. His Covent Garden début was in 1904 as Scarpia; in the same year he sang Michonnet at the London première of *Adriana Lecouvreur*. He continued to appear in London until 1914, and again in 1919. He sang at the Manhattan Opera, New York (1907–10), and at Boston, Philadelphia and Chicago (1909–13). He retired from the stage in 1919. Sammarco's voice was clear but resonant, rounded and of extensive range, as his numerous recordings (1902–15) confirm. A stylish singer, he at first specialized in operas such as *La favorite*, *Ernani*, *Rigoletto*, *Un ballo in maschera*, *Hamlet* and *La Gioconda*, but his theatrical ability later led him to prefer *verismo* roles, particularly Tonio, Gérard,

Scarpia, Rafaele (Ermanno Wolf-Ferrari's *I gioielli della Madonna*), and the parts he created in Ruggero Leoncavallo's *Zazà* (Cascart, 1900) and Alberto Franchetti's *Germania* (1902).

J. Freestone: 'Giuseppe Maria [*sic*] Sammarco', *Gramophone*, xxix (1951–2), 96 only [with discography]

Rodolfo Celletti/R

Sampson, Carolyn

(*b* Bedford, 18 May 1974). English soprano. While a music student at Birmingham University she won the Arnold Goldsborough Prize for Baroque performance and sang with the Birmingham Ex Cathedra choir. She began her professional career singing in small choral groups – the Sixteen, the Tallis scholars and Polyphony – and then developed a reputation as one of the finest British sopranos specializing in early repertories, in solo performances with Robert King, Harry Christophers, Trevor Pinnock, Paul McCreesh, Philippe Herreweghe and other Baroque specialists.

In 2000 Sampson made her major operatic début, as Amore in *L'incoronazione di Poppea* for the ENO. She has subsequently returned to the ENO in 2002 (*The Fairy-Queen*), and in 2004, as Pamina and as a memorably sexy Semele (see colour plate 14). Among her other roles are Ninfa (*Orfeo*), Belinda (*Dido and Aeneas*), Asteria in *Tamerlano* (which she sang in Lille, Caen and Bordeaux in the 2004–5 season), Susanna in *Le nozze di Figaro* (which she first sang at the Opéra de Montpellier, 2006) and Adina (*L'elisir d'amore*). Sampson's radiant timbre, graceful phrasing and nimble coloratura technique can be heard in a number of recordings, including C.W. Gluck's *Paride ed Elena*, Claudio Monteverdi's Vespers, G.F. Handel's *Ode for St Cecilia's Day* and a recital of Handel duets with ROBIN BLAZE.

Richard Wigmore

Sanderson, Sibyl

(*b* Sacramento, CA, 7 Dec 1865; *d* Paris, 15 May 1903). American soprano. She studied with SBRIGLIA and MATHILDE MARCHESI in Paris and made her début (under the name of Ada Palmer) as Jules Massenet's Manon at The Hague in 1888. Massenet, impressed by her beauty and her voice with its range of three octaves, wrote the title roles in two operas for her: *Esclarmonde*, in which she made her Paris début at the Opéra-Comique in 1889; and *Thaïs*, in which she made her Opéra début in 1894. She appeared in Brussels (1890–91) and at Covent Garden (1891), where she sang Manon. She created

the title role in Camille Saint-Saëns's *Phryné* (1893, Opéra-Comique) and also sang Gilda and Charles Gounod's Juliet. She sang in St Petersburg, Moscow and New York, making her Metropolitan début in 1895 as Manon opposite JEAN DE RESZKE. She did not have an outstandingly large or beautiful voice, but its phenomenal range compensated for any lack of size and warmth.

O. Thompson: *The American Singer* (New York, 1937), pp. 313
T. Wilkin: 'Sanderson, Sibyl', *Notable American Women*, ed. E.T. James, J.W. James and P.S. Boyer (Cambridge, MA, 1971)

Elizabeth Forbes

Santley, Sir Charles

(*b* Liverpool, 28 Feb 1834; *d* London, 22 Sept 1922). English baritone. Son of William Santley, a music teacher, he was a chorister and an amateur singer before he went to Milan in 1855 to study with Gaetano Nava. He made his début at Pavia in 1857 as Dr Grenvil in *La traviata*, and after appearing in several other small roles returned to England. His first professional English appearance was at St Martin's Hall, London (16 November 1857), singing Adam in Joseph Haydn's *Creation*. In 1858 he studied with the younger Manuel Garcia. Thereafter he sang in many concert and oratorio performances, and on 1 October 1859 made his English stage début, as Hoël in Giacomo Meyerbeer's *Le pardon de Ploërmel*, with the Pyne-Harrison company at Covent Garden. He remained with the company until 1863, creating the Rhineberg in Vincent Wallace's *Lurline* (1860), Clifford in Michael Balfe's *The Puritan's Daughter* (1861), Don Sallustio in William Howard Glover's *Ruy Blas* (1861), Danny Mann in Julius Benedict's *The Lily of Killarney* (1862) and Fabio in Balfe's *The Armourer of Nantes* (1863).

In 1862 Santley sang Count di Luna in *Il trovatore* with the Royal Italian Opera, Covent Garden, and then joined James Mapleson's company at Her Majesty's Theatre, appearing as Count Almaviva in *Le nozze di Figaro* and Nevers in *Les Huguenots*. In 1863 he sang Valentin with huge success in the first performance of *Faust* in England. During the season of 1864–5 he sang in operas by Giuseppe Verdi, Gaetano Donizetti and Meyerbeer at the Liceu, Barcelona, and in 1866 he appeared at La Scala. In London he remained with Mapleson's company until 1870, singing the Dutchman (in Italian) in the first production of a Richard Wagner opera in England. After a season with an English company at the Gaiety Theatre, London, and a year in concert, in 1872 he toured the USA. Having sung there under Carl Rosa, he joined the newly formed Carl Rosa company in 1875, singing W.A. Mozart's Figaro on the opening night of the company's first London season, and creating the role of Claude Melnotte in Frederick Cowen's *Pauline* (1876). After 1877 he was heard only in concert and oratorio, including Charles Gounod's *Rédemption* (1882, Birmingham) and Felix Mendelssohn's *Elijah* (1885, Birmingham). At the Royal Albert Hall on 1 May 1907 he celebrated his jubilee as a singer and later that year was knighted. On 23 May 1911 he made his farewell appearance at Covent Garden, but he emerged from retirement in 1915 to sing at the Mansion House, London, in a concert in aid of Belgian refugees. Although his voice was not naturally beautiful, he sang with great expression and was a particularly dramatic actor.

Santley wrote a number of religious works for the Roman Catholic Church, and was made Commander of St Gregory by Pope Leo XIII in 1887; he also composed several songs under the pseudonym of Ralph Betterton. His writings include *Method of Instruction for a Baritone Voice*, ed. G. Nava (London, c1872); *Student and Singer* (London, 1892, 2/1893); *Santley's Singing Master* (London, c1895); *The Art of Singing and Vocal Declamation* (London, 1908) and *Reminiscences of my Life* (London, 1909/R).

Obituaries: *The Times* (23 Sept 1922); *MT*, lxiii (1922), 806–7

H. Thompson: 'Sir Charles Santley 1834–1922', *MT*, lxiii (1922), 784–92

J. Mewburn Levien: *Sir Charles Santley* (London, 1930)

Harold Rosenthal/George Biddlecombe

Saporiti [Codecasa], Teresa

(*b* 1763; *d* Milan, 17 March 1869). Italian soprano and composer. As a member of Pasquale Bondini's company she sang, with her sister Antonia (*d* 1787) in Leipzig, Dresden and Prague. A report in the *Litteratur und Theater Zeitung* (summer 1782) refers to 'both Demoiselles Saporiti' being engaged for Bondini's company:

> The elder, Antonia, had been a concert singer in Leipzig. She sings the most difficult passages with considerable ease; it is a pity that her voice is somewhat small and that she neglects expression in recitatives. Her younger sister is half a beginner as an actress and singer, and is acclaimed only because of her figure…the younger Demoiselle Saporiti often appears in man's costume and takes over the role of a castrato, which she does poorly and with a bad grace.

W.A. Mozart thought well enough of Saporiti, however, to write elaborate and demanding music for her as Donna Anna in *Don Giovanni* (1787, Prague). She appeared in Venice in P.A. Guglielmi's *Arsace* (1788) and his *Rinaldo* (1789), and in Francesco Bianchi's *Nitteti* at La Scala (1789), and she sang in Bologna, Parma and Modena. In 1795 she was designated *prima buffa assoluta* in a company at St Petersburg, where she achieved a personal success in Domenico Cimarosa's *L'italiana in Londra* and Giovanni Paisiello's *Il barbiere di Siviglia* (1796). She composed two arias, *Dormivo in mezzo al prato* and *Caro mio ben deh senti*, which appeared in a collection by J.-B. Hanglaise, *Journal d'airs … avec accompagnement de guittare* (1796).

Christopher Raeburn

Sarakatsannis, Melanie

(*b* Ann Arbor, 23 April 1964). American soprano. After studying at Indiana University School of Music, she joined the apprentice program of the Santa Fe Opera House and made her major début as Despina for Palm Beach Opera. She has since sung the lighter Mozart roles, including Papagena, Zerlina, Susanna and Pamina, for Santa Fe Opera and other US companies. In later repertory she has been acclaimed as Norina (*Don Pasquale*) and Adina (*L'elisir d'amore*), as Hero (*Béatrice et Bénédict*), Anne Truelove, and in several Verdi and Puccini roles: Gilda, Violetta, Musetta, Magda (*La rondine*) and Lauretta (*Gianni Schicchi*). Sarakatsannis has sung in several world premières, including David Wargo's *A Chekhov Trilogy* (Chautauqua Opera, 1993), David Lang's *Modern Painters* (Santa Fe, 1995) and Tobias Picker's *Emmeline* (Santa Fe, 1996), in which she created the role of Sophie. She repeated the part for her New York City Opera début the following season. In 1999 she made her Carnegie Hall début, in masses by Franz Schubert and Ludwig van Beethoven.

Richard Wigmore

Sari, Ada [Szayer, Jadwiga]

(*b* Wadowice, nr Kraków, 29 June 1886; *d* Ciechocinek, 12 July 1968). Polish soprano. One of the most distinguished coloratura sopranos of her era, she studied singing in Kraków, Vienna and, from 1907 to 1909, with Antonio Rupnicek in Milan. In 1909 she made an acclaimed début as Marguerite (*Faust*) at the Teatro Drammatico Nazionale in Rome. She subsequently sang in many other Italian theatres, including Bologna, Florence, Venice, Naples (in *Le prophète* and *Der Zigeunerbaron*) and

La Scala. She also sang Santuzza in *Cavalleria rusticana* under Pietro Mascagni and Nedda in *Pagliacci* under Ruggero Leoncavallo in Alexandria. From about 1912 she began to concentrate on coloratura repertory. In the spring of 1914 she made an extensive concert tour of Russia with a group of Italian singers, and also performed in Warsaw, Lemberg and Kraków. After the outbreak of World War I she went to Vienna and then to Poland, joining the Lemberg (later Lwów) Opera in 1916 and the Warsaw Opera the following year; there her performances included *Lucia di Lammermoor*, *Les Huguenots* and Konstanze in *Die Entführung aus dem Serail*. In 1923 Sari settled in Milan, where she was engaged by La Scala; that year she sang the Queen of Night under the direction of Arturo Toscanini. During the next decade she gave a series of triumphant concert tours in Europe and North America and regularly visited Poland. In 1934 she moved back to Warsaw, where she sang frequently at the Wielki Theatre. She spent the war years directing an underground opera studio in Warsaw, and after the war she sang with the opera companies in Wrocław and Kraków, as well as giving concerts and broadcasts. She retired in 1947 to devote herself to teaching.

Sari possessed a phenomenal coloratura technique and a large, resonant voice, with an impressively clear timbre. The lightness of her staccato was breathtaking, but she was also capable of great dramatic power. Her gifts, which included a natural stage temperament, were shown to particular advantage in the roles of Rosina, Gilda, Lakmé, Violetta and Lucia. The charm and virtuosity of Sari's singing are evident in her few recordings of individual arias and songs, mostly dating from 1925.

Barbara Chmara-Żaczkiewicz

Sass, Sylvia

(*b* Budapest, 12 July 1951). Hungarian soprano. She studied in Budapest, making her début there in 1971 as Frasquita. She sang Violetta in Sofia (1972) and at Aix-en-Provence (1976); Giselda (*I Lombardi*) in Budapest (1973) and at Covent Garden (1976), having made her British début in 1975 with the Scottish Opera as Desdemona. In 1977 she sang Tosca at the Metropolitan; she has also appeared in Paris, Vienna, Germany, Rio, New Orleans and Toronto. Her roles include Poppaea, Donna Anna, Fiordiligi, Norma, Lady Macbeth, Elisabeth de Valois, Salome, Turandot and the Mother in Zsolt Durkó's *Mózes* (1977), which she created. She has a refined *pianissimo*, but in *forte* passages her tone becomes strident.

Alan Blyth

Sasse [Sax, Saxe, Sass], Marie (Constance)

(*b* Oudenaarde, 26 Jan 1834; *d* Paris, 8 Nov 1907). Belgian soprano. She studied in Ghent, Paris and Milan and made her début at Venice as Gilda in 1852. At the outset of her career she changed her name to Sax, then to Saxe when the instrument maker Adolphe sued her; when he sued again, she reverted to Sasse and was later known as Sass. While working in Paris as a café-concert singer she came to the notice of Léon Carvalho, director of the Théâtre Lyrique, where she appeared as Countess Almaviva in *Figaro* in 1859. In the same year, she sang Eurydice in the historic revival of C.W. Gluck's *Orphée et Eurydice*, in Hector Berlioz's version, with VIARDOT as Orpheus. Engaged at the Paris Opéra from 1860 to 1877, she sang Elisabeth in the revised *Tannhäuser* (1861), and created Sélika in *L'Africaine* (1865) and Elisabeth de Valois in *Don Carlos* (1867). Her repertory also included Valentine (*Les Huguenots*), Alice (*Robert le diable*) and Leonora (*Il trovatore*). At La Scala she created Cecilia in Carlos Gomes's *Il Guarany* (1870) and sang Lucrezia Borgia (1877). She also appeared in Brussels, St Petersburg and Madrid.

Richard Wagner was pleased with her Elisabeth in *Tannhäuser*; Giuseppe Verdi, who disliked her attitude to colleagues at rehearsal, less so with her heroine in *Don Carlos*. When she was recommended for Amneris in *Aida*, he refused. Sasse was married, briefly, to the bass Armand Castelmary; she retired in 1877 and died in poverty. Her memoirs, *Souvenirs d'une artiste*, were published in Paris in 1902.

Ronald Crichton, Elizabeth Forbes

Sättler, Lisbeth.

See RETHBERG, ELISABETH.

Savage, William

(*b* ?London, 1720; *d* London, 27 July 1789). English singer, composer and organist. His teachers included Johann Pepusch and Francesco Geminiani. Although not educated at the Chapel Royal (as claimed by Charles Burney), Savage came to prominence as a boy treble soloist, singing for G.F. Handel's 1735 Covent Garden season in *Athalia* and *Alcina*, the role of Oberto in the latter being specially written for him. He retained a place in Handel's theatre company for the following season, and then took minor roles in *Giustino* (1737) and *Faramondo* (1738). By the time of *Faramondo* his voice was breaking: his character in the opera has no aria and, although his recitatives are written in the treble clef, Savage's name appears against the tenor stave in a coro movement. He sang as a bass in Handel's last London opera season of 1740–41, with roles in *Imeneo* and *Deidamia*, and performed in *L'Allegro* and *Saul*.

In the Covent Garden oratorio season of 1743 he took the part of Manoa in *Samson* and participated in the first London performances of *Messiah*. Burney described his voice as 'a powerful and not unpleasant bass', and the music that Handel wrote for him as a treble was well judged to display his youthful musical talents.

Savage is described as 'Organist of Finchley' in the subscription list to Maurice Greene's *Forty Select Anthems* (1743). On April 1744 he was admitted as a Gentleman-in-ordinary of the Chapel Royal, and on 5 April 1748 he succeeded Charles King as vicar-choral and Master of the Choristers at St Paul's Cathedral. As a teacher Savage influenced London professional musicians of the next generation, many of whom had probably been choristers at St Paul's. In 1777 he retired to Tenterden, Kent; he returned to London in about 1780 and attempted to re-establish himself as a music teacher, but did not regain his former eminence.

Savage was the composer of both vocal and instrumental music. His catches, rounds and canon were no doubt fruits of his membership of the Noblemen and Gentlemen's Catch Club and the Beef Steak Club. If much of his music gives the impression of being practical and tasteful rather than inspired, Savage's works nevertheless include some unusual items: he composed the song *On the very first of May* (1756) to nonsense verses by his wife, and he wrote an interesting Hallelujah (1770), 'An imitation of the singing at the Jews Synagogue on Duke's Place'.

Donald Burrows/R

Sax, Marie.

See SASSE, MARIE.

Sayão, Bidú [Balduina] (de Oliveira)

(*b* Rio de Janeiro, 11 May 1902; *d* Lincolnville, ME, 12 March 1999). Brazilian soprano. She studied with JEAN DE RESZKE in Nice; returning to Rio de Janeiro in 1925 she sang Rosina at the Teatro Municipal in 1926, repeating the role at the Teatro Costanzi, Rome, subsequently appearing at both Paris houses (1931), at the Colón and in Italy. In 1937 she enjoyed a tremendous success as Jules Massenet's Manon on her début at the Metropolitan (1937), initiating a New York career that lasted until 1951 in lyric and coloratura soprano roles

such as Gilda, Rosina, Charles Gounod's Juliet, Mélisande, Violetta, Mimì, Norina, Adina, Zerlina and – perhaps most memorably – Susanna. She exuded feminine charm, warmth and refinement on stage, singing with pure, silvery tone and enlivening soubrette roles without recourse to soubrette mannerisms. She retired from the stage in 1958. In addition to concert appearances (many with Arturo Toscanini), she gave frequent recitals. Her many recordings, which include Zerlina, Susanna, Juliet (with BJÖRLING) and Manon, show the vitality, delicacy and pathos of her readings.

J.A. Léon and A. Ribeiro Guimaries: 'Bidú Sayão', *Record Collector*, xiii (1960–61), 125 [with discography]
L. Rasponi: *The Last Prima Donnas* (New York, 1984), 505–18

Martin Bernheimer/Alan Blyth

Sbriglia, Giovanni

(*b* Naples, 23 June 1829; *d* Paris, 20 Feb 1916). Italian tenor. He studied in Naples and made his début in 1853 at S Carlo. After appearing in various Italian theatres he went to New York (1859–60) and sang at the Academy of Music with ADELINA PATTI in operas including *Lucia di Lammermoor*, *La sonnambula* and *Rigoletto*. In the 1860s he toured North and South America with the Teresa Parodi Opera Company. In 1875 he settled as a teacher in Paris, where his pupils included LILLIAN NORDICA, EDOUARD and JEAN DE RESZKE, SIBYL SANDERSON, POL PLANÇON, ADA ADINI, Paul Landormy, ALEKSANDER MYSZUGA, Stella Stocker and CLARENCE WHITEHILL. He had a light, flexible voice.

Elizabeth Forbes

Scandiuzzi, Roberto

(*b* Treviso, 14 July 1958). Italian bass. He studied at the conservatory in Treviso and made his début at La Scala in 1982 as Bartolo (*Le nozze di Figaro*) with Riccardo Muti. Thereafter he appeared regularly throughout Italy. He first appeared at Covent Garden in 1985 as Raimondo (*Lucia di Lammermoor*), followed by a superb Fiesco, then equally imposing portrayals of Banquo and King Philip II. In 1992 he made his US operatic début at San Francisco as Padre Guardiano, and his Vienna Staatsoper début in the same role. He first sang at the Metropolitan in 1995 as Fiesco. His other roles include Don Giovanni, Rodolfo (*La sonnambula*), Oroveso (which he sang at the Orange Festival in 1999), Gioachino Rossini's Moses, Henry VIII (*Anna Bolena*), Silva (*Ernani*), Zaccaria (*Nabucco*), Attila, Colline, Gremin, Timur and both Charles Gounod's and

Arrigo Boito's Mephistopheles. His concert repertory includes Rossini's *Stabat mater* and Giuseppe Verdi's *Requiem* (with which he made his US début in 1991), both of which he has recorded. His large, sonorous, typically Italianate bass is supported by his equally impressive presence. Notable among his opera recordings are *Don Carlos*, *Simon Boccanegra*, *Aroldo* and *Jérusalem*.

Alan Blyth

Scaria, Emil

(*b* Graz, 18 Sept 1838; *d* Blasewitz, nr Dresden, 22 July 1886). Austrian bass. He studied at the Vienna Conservatory and made his début in 1860 at Budapest as St Bris in *Les Huguenots* with little success. After further study with Manuel Garcia in London, he made a second début at Dessau, and in 1863 he was engaged at Leipzig and in 1865 at Dresden. His repertory in these early years included Dulcamara in *L'elisir d'amore*, Falstaff in Otto Nicolai's *Die lustigen Weiber von Windsor* and Peter the Great in Albert Lortzing's *Zar und Zimmermann*. Although his powerful voice had the dark colouring of a true bass, its enormous range allowed him to sing baritone roles with equal success. From May 1873 until his death Scaria was engaged at the Vienna Hofoper, where he sang Escamillo in the first performance of *Carmen* outside France (1875) and the first Vienna *Ring* cycle (1879). He sang Wotan in the first Berlin *Ring* cycle, given by Angelo Neumann's company at the Viktoria-theater, in May 1881, and also in the first London cycle at Her Majesty's Theatre, again presented by Neumann, in May 1882. During Act 3 of *Die Walküre* in London he suffered a breakdown and loss of memory, and, though he got through *Siegfried* two nights later, his place was taken by REICHMANN in the second and third cycles. After a rest, Scaria was able to sing Gurnemanz in the first performance of *Parsifal* at Bayreuth on 26 July 1882, and to rejoin Neumann's touring Wagner company through Germany, Belgium, the Netherlands and Italy, singing Wotan and Rocco in *Fidelio*. During 1883 he sang King Mark in *Tristan und Isolde* at both Berlin and Vienna, and returned to Bayreuth to sing Gurnemanz and to produce *Parsifal* at the first festival held after Wagner's death. The following year he toured the USA in Wagner concerts with AMALIE MATERNA and HERMANN WINKELMANN, and also sang Gurnemanz in the first concert performance of *Parsifal* in London, at the Royal Albert Hall on 10 November 1884. Early in 1886 he again suffered a mental breakdown and died insane a few months later.

Elizabeth Forbes

Schack [Cziak, Schak, Žák, Ziak], Benedikt (Emanuel)

(*b* Mirotice, 7 Feb 1758; *d* Munich, 10 Dec 1826). Austrian tenor, composer and flautist of Bohemian origin. He acquired a basic musical and general education from his father, a school teacher, and later studied at Staré Sedlo, Svatá Hora and (from 1773) Prague, where he was a chorister at the cathedral. From 1775 he studied medicine, philosophy and singing (with Karl Frieberth) in Vienna; while a student he wrote some Singspiele and oratorios. In 1780 he was appointed Kapellmeister to Prince Heinrich von Schönaich-Carolath in Silesia. After two years of irregular employment, mostly in Bohemia, he joined EMANUEL SCHIKANEDER's travelling theatre company in 1786. The company toured extensively in southern Germany and Austria before settling in Vienna in 1789, where Schack became the principal tenor at the Freihaus-Theater auf der Wieden (1789). His fame as a composer was based on the series of Schikaneder's seven 'Anton' Singspiele, mostly written in collaboration with F.X. Gerl. He was a close friend of W.A. Mozart, who composed (or assisted with) certain numbers for Schack's theatrical scores (notably the duet 'Nun liebes Weibchen' к625/592*a* for *Der Stein der Weisen*). Mozart also wrote piano variations (к613) on Schack's air 'Ein Weib ist das herrlichste Ding auf der Welt' from *Die verdeckten Sachen*. Schack performed a wide variety of roles: the part of Tamino was written for him (it is to be presumed that he also played Tamino's flute solos), and he was the first German-language Don Gonsalvo (Don Ottavio) and Count Almaviva (Vienna, 1792); he also took the soprano part in an impromptu sing-through of the unfinished Requiem at the composer's bedside on the eve of Mozart's death. His wife Elisabeth (née Weinhold) sang the part of the Third Lady in the première of *Die Zauberflöte*.

In 1793 Schack moved to Graz and in 1796 to Munich, where he was a member of the Hoftheater until about 1813, when he lost his voice and was pensioned. His daughter Antonie (1784–1851) was also a member of the Munich company (1800–06). During his last years he wrote mostly sacred music, including a mass 'with additions by Mozart' (кAnh.C1.02/Anh.235*f*). He died before receiving Constanze Nissen's letter (16 February 1826) asking for help with her husband's biography of Mozart; the letter gives an eloquent if politely exaggerated testimony to the friendship of Schack and Mozart: 'I could think of absolutely no one who knew him better or to whom he was more devoted than you…Of great and general interest will be what you can instance of Mozart's few compositions in your operas'. F.L. Schröder commented (May 1791) on Schack as a singer in Paul Wranitzky's *Oberon*: 'Hüon, Schack, a good [*braver*] tenor, but with an Austrian accent and suburban declamation'. Leopold Mozart was more appreciative in a letter to his daughter (26 May 1786): 'He sings excellently, has a beautiful voice, easy and flexible throat, and beautiful method…This man sings really very beautifully'.

Peter Branscombe/R

Schade, Michael

(*b* Geneva, 23 Jan 1965). Canadian tenor of German parentage. He grew up in Gelsenkirchen and, from 1977, in Toronto, where he sang in St Michael's Choir School. After studying medicine at the University of Western Ontario (he initially contemplated a career as a veterinary surgeon), in 1988 he entered the Curtis Institute of Music in Philadelphia and joined the San Francisco Opera's Merola Program for student singers. That year he made his professional opera début, as Jacquino in *Fidelio*, with Pacific Opera Victoria Canada. In 1990, while still a student at Curtis, he won the New York Oratorio Competition, leading to his Carnegie Hall début, in *Messiah*. The following year he made his European début, as the Evangelist in the St John Passion.

Schade's international opera career was launched when he stepped in at short notice as Almaviva (*Il barbiere di Siviglia*) at the Vienna Staatsoper in 1992. His Metropolitan Opera début, as Jaquino (*Fidelio*), followed in 1993. He has subsequently sung in all the major opera houses in Europe (Covent Garden début, in Carl Nielsen's *Maskarade*, 2005) and the USA, admired above all for the grace and lyrical ardour of his Mozart singing. In addition to his Mozart roles – Tamino, Belmonte, Ferrando, Don Ottavio (which he sang to acclaim at Covent Garden in 2007), Gomatz (*Zaide*), Idomeneo and Titus – Schade's repertory includes David (*Die Meistersinger*), Matteo (*Arabella*), which he sang at the Vienna Staatsoper in 2007, Nemorino (*L'elisir d'amore*) and Rinaldo in Joseph Haydn's *Armida* (Salzburg Festival, 2007). An admired recitalist, he appears regularly at the Schubertiade in Schwarzenberg, and has recorded *Die schöne Müllerin* and songs by Ludwig van Beethoven, Franz Schubert, Richard Strauss, Franz Liszt, Gabriel Fauré and Maurice Ravel. His extensive discography also includes Tamino, Titus, Gomatz, David, the title role in Haydn's *Orlando paladino*, *The Creation* and the Bach Passions.

Richard Wigmore

Schäfer, Christine

(*b* Frankfurt, 3 March 1965). German soprano. She studied at the Berlin Hochschule für Musik with Ingrid Figur and took masterclasses with ARLEEN AUGER, also working with DIETRICH FISCHER-DIESKAU and Aribert Reimann (1986–9). Her recital début was at the Berlin Festival in 1988, singing the première of Reimann's *Nachträume*. Schäfer made her stage début as Papagena at the Monnaie in Brussels in 1991, and in 1993 made her US début as Sophie at San Francisco, leading to concert engagements throughout the USA. She created a sensation at the Salzburg Festival in 1995 as Lulu, a role she also sang at Glyndebourne the following year. Among her other roles are Pamina (Salzburg and Brussels), Gilda (1993, Berne), Lucia di Lammermoor (1994, WNO), Zerbinetta (1996, Munich), Konstanze (1997, Salzburg Festival), Zdenka (1997, Houston) and the title role in *Pierrot Lunaire*, which she has sung with Pierre Boulez at the Théâtre du Châtelet and recorded. In 2000 she made her Covent Garden début, as Sophie. She is equally distinguished as a concert artist, notably in J.S. Bach, Joseph Haydn, W.A. Mozart and Gustav Mahler (Fourth Symphony), and recitalist, admired particularly in Franz Schubert, Robert Schumann and Richard Strauss. Reimann has composed a number of songs for her. Her paradoxically cool yet intense voice and style, allied to a natural command of phrasing and verbal enunciation, is highly individual, as can be judged in her recordings of Bach wedding cantatas and of lieder, and as Konstanze and Lulu (on a video from Glyndebourne).

Alan Blyth

Schak, Benedikt.

See SCHACK, BENEDIKT.

Scheidemantel, Karl

(*b* Weimar, 21 Jan 1859; *d* Weimar, 26 June 1923). German baritone. He studied with B. Borchers and Julius Stockhausen, making his début in 1878 as Wolfram in *Tannhäuser* at Weimar, where he was engaged until 1886. He then sang at Dresden until 1911. After a guest appearance in Munich (1882) as Wolfram, he made his London début at Covent Garden in the same role (1884), and that season also sang Pizarro in *Fidelio*, Telramund in *Lohengrin*, Kurwenal in *Tristan und Isolde* and Rucello in Charles Villiers Stanford's *Savonarola*; he returned in 1899 to sing Hans Sachs. He appeared at every Bayreuth festival from 1886 to 1892, alternating as Klingsor and Amfortas in *Parsifal*, and singing Kurwenal,

Hans Sachs and Wolfram, a part he also sang in Vienna (1899) and at La Scala, Milan (1892). A stylish singer with a fine, well-placed voice, he was as successful in Italian as in German roles; at Dresden, he sang Alfio in *Cavalleria rusticana* (1891), David in *L'amico Fritz* (1892) and Scarpia in *Tosca* (1902), all first local performances. He created two Strauss roles, Kunrad in *Feuersnot* (1901) and Faninal in *Der Rosenkavalier*. After his retirement he taught at the Musikhochschule in Weimar until 1920, and then directed the Landesbühnen Sachsen, Dresden-Radebeul, for two years.

Elizabeth Forbes

Schikaneder, Emanuel (Johann Joseph [Baptist])

(*b* Straubing, 1 Sept 1751; *d* Vienna, 21 Sept 1812). Dramatist, theatre director, actor, singer and composer. Educated at the Jesuit Gymnasium at Regensburg, where he was a cathedral chorister, Schikaneder may briefly have been a town musician before he became an actor with F. J. Moser's troupe in 1773 or 1774. In 1774 he danced in a court ballet at Innsbruck, where his Singspiel *Die Lyranten* (of which he wrote both words and music) was performed in 1775 or 1776. The Innsbruck company, then under Andreas Schopf and Theresia Schimann, moved in 1776 to Augsburg, where on 9 February

1777 he married Maria Magdalena (known as Eleonore) Arth (*b* Hermannstadt, 1751; *d* Vienna, 22 June 1821), an actress in the company. In 1777–8 they were in Nuremberg with Moser's company, and in December 1777 Schikaneder made a famous guest appearance as Hamlet at the Munich court theatre, where he was obliged to repeat the final scene as an encore. From January 1778 he was director of the troupe, appearing at Ulm, Stuttgart, Augsburg, Nuremberg, Rothenburg and elsewhere. In 1780 they went to Laibach (now Ljubljana), Klagenfurt and Linz before beginning a lengthy season at Salzburg in September, during which Schikaneder became friendly with the Mozarts. Further travels through Austria included summer seasons at Graz in 1781 and 1782, the winter of 1782–3 in Pressburg (now Bratislava), and a guest appearance in summer 1783 at the Kärntnertortheater, Vienna.

After further visits to Pest and Pressburg, where Joseph II saw him perform in October 1784, Schikaneder was invited to play in Vienna. He and Hubert Kumpf began a three-month season of operas and Singspiele at the Kärntnertor on 5 November. Thereafter, Schikaneder was a member of the Nationaltheater, performing in plays and operas, from 1 April 1785 until 28 February 1786. During this time his own troupe was run by his wife and Johann Friedel, touring in southern Austria until it moved into the Freihaus-Theater auf der Wieden, Vienna, in November 1788. Schikaneder himself, in February 1786, had been granted an imperial licence for the building of a suburban theatre but did not make use of it for 15 years, forming instead a new company specializing in Singspiele and operas, which he took to Salzburg, Augsburg and Memmingen. In February 1787 he took over the Prince of Thurn and Taxis's court theatre at Regensburg. When Johann Friedel died at the end of March 1789, Schikaneder and his wife took over the Freihaus-Theater, bringing from Regensburg the singer-composers BENEDIKT SCHACK and FRANZ XAVER GERL. Schikaneder's reign at the Freihaus began on 12 July 1789 with the first performance of his 'Anton' opera *Der dumme Gärtner*, and from this time dates the beginning of his steady series of plays, opera and Singspiel librettos which were the backbone of the repertory of his theatre (but which were also performed in other theatres, sometimes with new musical scores).

Schikaneder's years of travel had seen the production of more straight plays than operas; in Vienna he placed the emphasis firmly on opera, and commissioned settings of his own texts from W.A. Mozart (*Die Zauberflöte*, in which he created the role of Papageno), F.X. Süssmayr (*Der Spiegel von Arkadien*), Joseph Wölfl (*Der Höllenberg*), Johann Mederitsch and Peter Winter (one act each

Emanuel Schikaneder

of *Babylons Pyramiden*; Winter also set *Das Labyrinth*, a sequel to *Die Zauberflöte*). He also received scores from his theatre Kapellmeister, J.B. Henneberg (*Die Waldmänner*), Jakob Haibel (*Der Tiroler Wastel*) and Ignaz von Seyfried (*Der Löwenbrunn* and *Der Wundermann am Rheinfall*). As the 1790s advanced, Schikaneder began to suffer from increasing financial difficulties as he strove to surpass the achievements of his rivals and of his own greatest successes. In 1799 he handed over the management of the theatre to Bartholomäus Zitterbarth while continuing his artistic direction. Of the 12 greatest successes at the Freihaus, which closed on 12 June 1801, eight – including the first five – were written by Schikaneder himself.

On 13 June 1801 Schikaneder opened the new Theater an der Wien, using the licence he had previously been granted; it was the most lavishly equipped and one of the largest theatres of its age, and has continued in almost unbroken use. It opened with Franz Teyber's setting of Schikaneder's libretto *Alexander*, but a change in public taste and a decline in Schikaneder's standards and powers of judgment were influential in the decision to sell the licence to Zitterbarth after less than a year. Schikaneder continued to supply plays and librettos, and to act, but despite two further periods as artistic director his fortunes were waning. After the sale of the theatre in 1806 Schikaneder left Vienna and took over the Brno Theatre. At Easter 1809 he was back in Vienna, but financial ruin and failing mental health darkened his last years. On his way to Budapest to take up an appointment as director of a new German theatre company in 1812 he became mad, returned to Vienna, and died in penury shortly after; a performance of his play *Die Schweden vor Brünn* was given for his benefit at the Theater in der Leopoldstadt on 18 July 1812 – an uncommon tribute from a rival theatre, albeit one that had successfully staged his plays since the early 1780s and would continue to do so until the 1850s.

Schikaneder was one of the most talented and influential theatre men of his age. Although it is fashionable to decry his plays (of which there are nearly 50) and librettos, they more than satisfied the demands of their day. J.W. von Goethe praised his skill at creating strong dramatic situations, and, though the verse is often trite, the libretto of *Die Zauberflöte* (Johann Gieseke's claims to the authorship of which were proved false by E.R. von Komorzynski and more scientifically by Rommel) is by no means unworthy of Mozart's music. Some of Schikaneder's comedies (the 'Anton' plays, *Der Tiroler Wastel*, *Das abgebrannte Haus*, *Der Fleischhauer von Ödenburg*, *Die Fiaker in Wien*) continued to be much performed for many years and strongly influenced the later development of the

Viennese *Lokalstück* ('local play'). Early in his career Schikaneder composed two, and perhaps several more, theatre scores: it has long been known that the music as well as the text of *Die Lyranten* was his work; and for the production of his Singspiel *Das Urianische Schloss* (1786, Salzburg) at the Theater in der Leopoldstadt in November 1787, a score by him is specifically mentioned by Wenzel Müller in his diary ('Opera by Em: Schikaneder, music, and book').

Peter Branscombe

Schiøtz, Aksel (Hauch)

(*b* Roskilde, 1 Sept 1906; *d* Copenhagen, 19 April 1975). Danish tenor. He studied in Copenhagen and with JOHN FORSELL. He made his stage début in 1939 at the Royal Opera, Copenhagen, as W.A. Mozart's Ferrando; the next year he sang the title role in *Faust* and Sverkel in J.P.E. Hartmann's *Liden Kirsten*. He refused to sing publicly during the German occupation, but gave recitals in secret for the Resistance workers. In 1946 he shared the role of Male Chorus with PETER PEARS in the first performances of *The Rape of Lucretia* at Glyndebourne. In 1950 a brain tumour brought his career to an abrupt halt. With great fortitude, he learnt to speak and sing once more and, for a while, resumed his career, but as a baritone. After retiring he taught in Minnesota, Toronto, Colorado and Copenhagen.

Schiøtz was among the foremost Mozart and lieder singers of the early postwar period as his recordings, particularly of *Dichterliebe* and *Die schöne Müllerin*, show. His tenor voice had a natural silvery quality and he used it with elegance and feeling. He wrote a book on singing, *The Singer and his Art* (New York, 1969).

Alan Blyth

Schipa, Tito [Raffaele Attilio Amadeo]

(*b* Lecce, 2 Jan 1888; *d* New York, 16 Dec 1965). Italian tenor. He was the outstanding *tenore di grazia* of his generation. Having studied with A. Gerunda in Lecce and E. Piccoli in Milan, he made his début in 1910 in *La traviata* at Vercelli, and by the 1915–16 season had reached La Scala in *Prince Igor* and *Manon*. He soon began to specialize in the lighter and more lyrical roles, and became widely recognized as the successor of DE LUCIA, BONCI and ANSELMI. In 1917 he was the first Ruggero in Giacomo Puccini's *La rondine* at Monte Carlo. His beautiful, flexible voice was at its peak during his years in America: in Chicago from 1919 until 1932, and for the three following seasons (and during one later one, in 1941) at the

Metropolitan. During the 1930s he sang regularly at La Scala, and in later years frequently in Rome, concentrating increasingly on a central repertory consisting of the lighter and more graceful Italian roles and on a smaller French group including the romantic heroes of *Lakmé*, *Mignon*, *Manon* and *Werther*.

Schipa's attractive voice, so well produced as to carry with ease in large theatres, was employed with exquisite skill and taste. His plangent tone, refined musical phrasing and clear enunciation, particularly well suited to moods of tenderness, melancholy and nostalgia, are displayed in his numerous recordings, which include a complete performance of Gaetano Donizetti's *Don Pasquale*. He wrote an operetta, *La Principessa Liana*, and several songs.

T. Hutchinson and S. Winstanley: 'Tito Schipa', *Record Collector*, xiii (1960–61), 77–109 [incl. discography]

Desmond Shawe-Taylor/Alan Blyth

Schipper, Emil (Zacharias)

(*b* Vienna, 19 Aug 1882; *d* Vienna, 20 July 1957). Austrian baritone. He studied in Milan, then made his début in 1904 at the Neues Deutsches Theater, Prague, as Telramund. After engagements at Linz, the Vienna Volksoper and the Vienna Hofoper, in 1916 he joined the Munich Hofoper, where he remained until 1922; he then returned to the Vienna Staatsoper until 1938 and was made an Austrian *Kammersänger*. In Munich he sang Meister Florian in the 1920 revised version of Franz Schreker's *Das Spielwerk und die Prinzessin* and Barak in the first performance there of *Die Frau ohne Schatten*. He appeared regularly at Covent Garden (1924–8) as the Dutchman, Kurwenal, Hans Sachs, Wotan, Telramund, John the Baptist and Amonasro, in Chicago (1928–9) and at the Teatro Colón. Schipper sang Agamemnon in *Iphigénie en Aulide* at the 1930 Salzburg Festival and returned there in 1935–6 as Kurwenal. He also made guest appearances in France, the Netherlands, Spain and Belgium. His voice was powerful and dramatic, but he did not always use it with subtlety. He married the mezzo-contralto MARIA OLSZEWSKA, with whom he recorded a notable version of the Wanderer-Erda encounter from the third act of *Siegfried*.

Obituary, *Record News* [Toronto], ii (1957–8), 33–5 [incl. discography]

Harold Rosenthal/Alan Blyth

Schlick, Barbara

(*b* Würzburg, 21 July 1943). German soprano. She studied singing at the conservatory in her home town and later with Hilde Wesselmann in Essen. She started her career as a member of the Adolf Scherbaum Baroque Ensemble in 1966; later she toured with, among others, the Monteverdi Choir of Hamburg under Jürgen Jürgens. From early on she specialized in music of the Baroque and Classical periods and worked with leading specialists such as Reinhard Goebel, Philippe Herreweghe, Ton Koopman, Sigiswald Kuijken and William Christie in virtually all major musical centres of Europe, the USA, Canada and the former USSR. She teaches at the Staatliche Hochschule für Musik in Würzburg, where DOROTHEA RÖSCHMANN was her pupil. Schlick's numerous recordings include all the major choral works by J.S. Bach, many of his cantatas and several Baroque operas, notably G.F. Handel's *Giulio Cesare* and Johann Hasse's *Piramo e Tisbe*. Schlick uses her exceptionally pure and fluent soprano with touching expressiveness and an acute sense of style.

Martin Elste

Schlosser, Max [Karl]

(*b* Amberg, Bavaria, 17 Oct 1835; *d* Utting am Ammersee, 2 Sept 1916). German tenor. After singing in Zürich, St Gallen and Augsburg, in 1868 he was engaged at the Hofoper, Munich, where he remained until 1904. He sang David in the first performance of *Die Meistersinger* (1868) and Mime in the first performance of *Das Rheingold* (1869). He also sang Mime in *Siegfried* at Bayreuth in the first complete *Ring* cycle (1876). In 1882 he accompanied Angelo Neumann's Wagner tour of Europe, singing Mime in the first London performance of the *Ring*. His repertory included Almaviva (*Barbiere*), Tonio (*La fille du régiment*), Lyonel (*Martha*) and Max (*Der Freischütz*). Towards the end of his career he sang baritone roles, including Beckmesser and the Nightwatchman in *Die Meistersinger*, which he sang at his farewell performance in Munich, in his 70th year.

Elizabeth Forbes

Schlusnus, Heinrich

(*b* Braubach, 6 Aug 1888; *d* Frankfurt, 18 June 1952). German baritone. He trained as a postal official but also studied singing in Frankfurt and made a successful début at Hamburg in 1915 as the Herald in *Lohengrin*. He sang at the Nuremberg Stadttheater (1915–17), then at the Berlin Staatsoper (1917–45), becoming their leading Giuseppe Verdi baritone. In 1932 he sang Guy de Montfort at the Berlin première of *Les vêpres siciliennes*, a role particularly suited to his ease of production over an extensive range. He toured extensively, to Amsterdam (1919), Barcelona (1922), Chicago (Wolfram, 1927) and Bayreuth (Amfortas, 1933). His voice, particularly easy in the high register, was steady and smooth, his style economical. Besides excelling in opera he was an outstanding lieder singer. His recordings are extensive.

E. Csan and A. G. Ross: 'A Schlusnus Discography', *Record News* [Toronto], iii (1958–9), 164–81, 196–206, 319–24, 402–5; iv (1959–60), 136–40

S. Smolian: 'Heinrich Schlusnus: a Discography', *British Institute of Recorded Sound: Bulletin*, no.14 (1959), 5–24; nos.15–16 (1960), 16–26

J.B. Steane: 'Heinrich Schlusnus', *Singers of the Century 2* (London, 1998), 88–92

Carl L. Bruun/Alan Blyth

Schmedes, Erik

(*b* Gentofte, nr Copenhagen, 27 Aug 1866; *d* Vienna, 23 March 1931). Danish tenor. He studied in Berlin and Paris before making his baritone début at Wiesbaden in 1891. From 1894 to 1897 he was engaged at Dresden. In 1898 he went to Vienna, where he made his tenor début as Siegfried and remained through the great Mahler years until 1924, singing the heavier dramatic and Wagnerian parts with great success. In 1899 he sang Siegfried and Parsifal at Bayreuth, returning there until 1906, and in 1908–9 he appeared at the Metropolitan. He was the first Viennese Pedro (*Tiefland*), Palestrina (Hans Pfitzner) and Herod. His style was rather declamatory, and he was an excellent actor. He recorded extensively from 1902, including extracts from his Wagner roles. One commentator wrote, with some justice, that his discs are 'numerous and nasty'.

C. Norton Welsh: 'Erik Schmedes', *Record Collector*, xxvii (1981), 23–47 [with discography]

Carl L. Bruun/Alan Blyth

Schmidt, Andreas

(*b* Düsseldorf, 30 July 1960). German baritone. He studied in his home city with Ingeborg Reichelt and in Berlin with DIETRICH FISCHER-DIESKAU, and sang with the chorus of the Düsseldorf Musikverein, of which his father, Hartmut Schmidt, was conductor. Having won first prize in the Deutscher Musikwettbewerb in 1983, he made his operatic début the following year (as Malatesta in *Don Pasquale*) at the Deutsche Oper, Berlin, where he subsequently took part in the premières of Wolfgang Rihm's

Oedipus (1987) and as Ryuji in H.W. Henze's *Das verratene Meer* (1990). An early international appearance was at Covent Garden, as Valentin in 1986; others have been at Aix-en-Provence, Glyndebourne and the Metropolitan, in the Mozart roles – Count Almaviva, Guglielmo, Papageno – in which his cultivated, gently rounded voice production, sensitivity to verbal nuance and quietly distinguished stage presence prove particularly appreciable. Schmidt is also a skilful, sympathetic lieder and oratorio singer, as revealed in recordings ranging from Bach cantatas to Brahms songs, Schubert cycles, and Hugo Wolf's *Italienisches Liederbuch*. As his voice has grown darker and weightier, he has taken on major Wagnerian roles, including Beckmesser (the role of his Bayreuth début in 1996) and Amfortas, which he first sang at Bayreuth in 2000.

Max Loppert

Schmidt, Joseph

(*b* Davidende, 4 March 1904; *d* Gyrembad, nr Zürich, 16 Nov 1942). Romanian tenor. As a boy he sang in the synagogue at Czernowitz (now Chernovtsy, Ukraine), and he remained active as a cantor throughout his professional life. He studied in Vienna, but his future as an operatic tenor was limited by his smallness of stature. Broadcasts and recordings provided the answer: in 1928 he made his radio début in a performance of *Idomeneo* in Berlin, and he quickly became one of the most popular singers in Germany. He also enjoyed success in films, which led to a first tour of the USA in 1936. Germany became closed to him in 1934 and Austria in 1938; he took refuge in Belgium, then Switzerland, where he died in an internment camp. His many recordings preserve a fine voice, well produced except for a certain nasal quality, with an exceptional upper range and a distinctive personality.

L. di Cave: *Mille voci una stella* (Rome, 1985), pp.184–5

J.B. Steane

Schmidt, Trudeliese

(*b* Saarbrücken, 7 Nov 1934). German mezzo-soprano. She began a commercial career before taking up singing studies with Hans Richrath in Saarbrücken, and later in Rome, and made her stage début at the Saarbrücken Stadttheater in 1965. In 1967 she joined the Deutsche Oper am Rhein, Düsseldorf, where she specialized in trouser roles (Cherubino, Octavian, Siébel, Orlofsky) and played Dorabella and Suzuki, making her British début and with Laurenz Hofer in Hanover, and joined the Duisburg opera chorus at the age of 18, later studying with Robert von der Linde in Berlin. He began singing major roles at Brunswick in 1937; after wartime service he resumed his career, singing in Hanover, Berlin and as a member of the Hamburg Staatsoper (1947–56). His Covent Garden début was in 1949 as Rodolfo (with SCHWARZKOPF as Mimì), followed by Alfredo, Pinkerton and Tamino in the same season. During the 1950s he was admired at the Vienna Staatsoper and at the Salzburg Festival, where he played Idomeneus and sang in the 1954 première of Rolf Liebermann's *Penelope*, and in 1959 appeared as Walther at Bayreuth. He recorded this role under Rudolf Kempe, as he did Lohengrin with Wilhelm Schüchter, Bacchus with Herbert von Karajan and Max under Joseph Keilberth. In 1962 he appeared as Alwa in the Viennese stage première of *Lulu*. Later he became popular in operetta, musical films and television, and was acclaimed as a successor to TAUBER. Schock was a lyric tenor with a strong top register, which allowed him to play such heroic roles as Florestan and Lohengrin; his voice was warmer and more flexible than his acting, which benefited from strong direction.

Noël Goodwin

Schöffler, Paul

(*b* Dresden, 15 Sept 1897; *d* Amersham, Bucks., 21 Nov 1977). Austrian bass-baritone of German birth. After studying various aspects of music at the Dresden Conservatory he concentrated on singing, his teachers including Staegemann at Dresden, Ernst Grenzebach at Berlin and MARIO SAMMARCO at Milan. He was a member of the Dresden Staatsoper from 1925 to 1937, where he participated in the première of Ferruccio Busoni's *Doktor Faust* (1925), joining the Vienna Staatsoper in 1937. He was first heard at Covent Garden in 1934 (Donner, Schwanda), and in the following years London heard him as Gunther, Scarpia, Kurwenal, Figaro, Don Giovanni and Jochanaan, and also as the *Rheingold* Wotan. He sang Hans Sachs at Bayreuth in 1943–4 and the Dutchman in 1956, and during the Vienna Staatsoper 1947 London season he was heard as Don Giovanni, Don Alfonso and Pizarro: he returned in 1953 to sing Hans Sachs. He was invited to the Metropolitan, New York, in 1949, and at Salzburg in 1952 he created the role of Jupiter at the first public performance of Richard Strauss's *Die Liebe der Danae*. He was a notable exponent of Paul Hindemith (Cardillac, Mathis), and among the roles he created was Danton in Gottfried von Einem's

Dantons Tòd (Salzburg, 1947). He continued to be associated with small character parts such as the Music Master (*Ariadne auf Naxos*) and Antonio (*Le nozze di Figaro*) when well over 70.

Schöffler's careful musicianship and fine stage presence were supported by a warm, expressive voice which, though not large, could ride the full orchestra easily and without tiring. Although remembered particularly as an opera singer, he appeared frequently and with success as a concert and recital artist.

Peter Branscombe

Scholl, Andreas

(*b* Eltville, 10 Nov 1967). German countertenor. He studied singing at the Schola Cantorum Basiliensis with Richard Levitt and RENÉ JACOBS. His first recital was in Paris in 1993, since when he has been in constant demand, singing with many of the leading early music ensembles. He has worked with, among others, Jacobs, Christophe Coin, William Christie and Philippe Herreweghe, and has appeared at several of the leading international festivals, including Ambronay, Beaune, Glyndebourne (where he sang a memorable Bertarido in *Rodelinda* in 1998 and 1999), the BBC Promenade Concerts and Saintes. Scholl has been widely admired for his liquid, warmly coloured, evenly projected voice and control of line and nuance. His recordings include Claudio Monteverdi's Vespers, Bach cantatas, the B minor Mass and *Christmas Oratorio*, G.F. Handel's *Messiah* and *Solomon*, a disc of Handel operatic arias, English and German Baroque songs, and Antonio Vivaldi's *Stabat mater*, for which he won a Gramophone Award.

Nicholas Anderson

Schöne, Lotte

(*b* Vienna, 15 Dec 1891; *d* Paris, 23 Dec 1977). Austrian soprano, later naturalized French. She studied in Vienna, made her début at the Volksoper in 1915, and sang at the Staatsoper from 1917 to 1926 and at the Salzburg festivals from 1922 to 1935. Hearing her there, Bruno Walter engaged her for the Berlin Städtische Oper, where she remained from 1926 to 1933. In Vienna and Berlin she was especially famous in all the lighter Mozart roles, as Adele in *Die Fledermaus* and Norina in *Don Pasquale*, as Giuseppe Verdi's Gilda and Oscar, and as Richard Strauss's Sophie and Zerbinetta. Among several Puccini roles she excelled as Liù, which she sang with great success at Covent

Left above: 8. Simon Keenlyside in the title role of 'Billy Budd' (Britten), London Coliseum, 2005
Left below: 9. Plácido Domingo in the title role of 'Otello' (Verdi), Vienna State Opera
Above: 10. Jean-Baptiste Faure in the title role of 'Hamlet' (Thomas), by Edouard Manet, 1875/77

11. *Maria Malibran as Desdemona in 'Otello'*
(Rossini), painting by Henri Decaisne

12. *Henriette Sontag by Paul*
Delaroche, 1831

13. Sally Burgess as Judith and Gwynne Howell as Bluebeard in 'Bluebeard's Castle' (Bartók), English National Opera, 1991

14. Ian Bostridge as Jupiter and Carolyn Sampson as Semele in 'Semele' (Handel), English National Opera, London, 2004

15. *Marian Anderson, portrait by Laura Wheeler Waring, 1944*

Garden in 1927. The latter part of her artistic life was disrupted by the coming to power of the Nazis in 1933. Thereafter she made her home in Paris, where her Mélisande was much admired, but she was obliged to go into hiding in southern France during the war. A beautiful woman, Schöne had a charming stage presence, of which her light and well-schooled soprano seemed the natural counterpart. The best of her many recordings are those made in Berlin between 1927 and 1931. They reveal her skills as a lieder interpreter as well as chronicling the charm of her style in operatic roles.

A. Tubeuf: 'Lotte Schoene', *Record Collector*, xx (1971–2), 75–89 [incl. discography]

Desmond Shawe-Taylor/R

Schorr, Friedrich

(*b* Nagyvárad, 2 Sept 1888; *d* Farmington, CT, 14 Aug 1953). Hungarian bass-baritone, naturalized American. He studied with Adolf Robinson, sang some small roles in Chicago in early 1912, and made his true début in Graz on 20 June 1912 as Wotan in *Die Walküre*. After brief engagements in Graz, Prague and Cologne, he came to wider prominence when engaged by the Berlin Staatsoper in 1923. During his seven Berlin years and thereafter, he was to tackle roles from a surprisingly wide repertory, including Richard Strauss's Barak, Giacomo Meyerbeer's Nélusko and Ferruccio Busoni's Doktor Faust; but it was above all in the great Wagnerian bass-baritone parts that he excelled, not only in Berlin, but at Bayreuth (1925–31), at Covent Garden (1925–33), and especially at the Metropolitan (every season from 1924 to 1943), where he also sang Pizarro, Strauss's Orestes and John the Baptist. His Wotan and Hans Sachs long dominated the international operatic scene; he was beyond question the leading exponent of these and of numerous other Wagnerian roles, especially the Dutchman. His voice had majesty and unfailing beauty; he never fell into the notorious 'Bayreuth bark', but maintained a steady legato flow of tone even in declamatory passages. The most important part of his recorded legacy consists of the extensive Wagnerian excerpts made in his prime, in which his impeccable enunciation plays an important part in the impression of authority that he conveys. One can believe in the grandeur of a Wotan whose utterances are so commandingly distinct, and in the poetic sensibility of a Hans Sachs to whom words are of such evident importance.

D. Shawe-Taylor: 'Friedrich Schorr', *Opera*, xvi (1965), 323–7

A. Frankenstein, E.Arnosi and B. Semeonoff: 'Friedrich Schorr', *Record Collector*, xix (1970–71), 243–84 [incl. discography by J. Dennis]

Desmond Shawe-Taylor/R

Schreier, Peter

(*b* Meissen, 29 July 1935). German tenor and conductor. After training in the Dresden Kreuzchor and private study, he joined the Dresden Staatsoper school in 1959, making his début as the First Prisoner in *Fidelio* in 1961. His operatic career soon took him to La Scala and the Metropolitan (Tamino, 1967) in addition to the leading houses in Germany and Austria. After the untimely death of WUNDERLICH in 1966, Schreier was acclaimed as the leading Mozart tenor of the day, his singing notable for its keen line and diction, allied to a suitably ardent manner. His Belmonte, Idamantes, Ferrando and Titus, all stylish, characterful interpretations, are preserved on recordings under Karl Böhm, his Tamino on Colin Davis's *Zauberflöte*. Among his other notable roles were Otto Nicolai's and Giuseppe Verdi's Fenton, Gioachino Rossini's Almaviva, Jules Massenet's Des Grieux, Richard Strauss's Leukippos (*Daphne*) and Dancing-Master (*Ariadne auf Naxos*), both of which he recorded, and, in Richard Wagner, Loge (an interpretation confirming the character as the *Ring*'s sole intellectual), Mime and David: all three, captured on disc, evince his ability to characterize through an acute treatment of tone and text.

At the same time Schreier developed a distinguished career in oratorio and lieder. He was among the most affecting Evangelists of his day in the Bach Passions, a superbly accomplished soloist in the cantatas and an exemplary soloist in the choral works of Joseph Haydn, W.A. Mozart, Ludwig van Beethoven and Felix Mendelssohn. He was the most significant tenor lieder interpreter of his age, probably of any age, his readings noted for his distinctive, slightly reedy tone, fine legato and expressive phrasing drawn from subtle enunciation of the text; yet he never lost a certain simplicity of approach. His finest recordings include Mozart and Beethoven songs, the three cycles of Franz Schubert (shattering versions of *Winterreise* with both Sviatoslav Richter and András Schiff among them), Robert Schumann's *Dichterliebe* and Joseph von Eichendorff *Liederkreis*, and Hugo Wolf's *Italienisches Liederbuch*. Since the 1980s Schreier has appeared frequently as a conductor, especially in Bach, and in the dual capacity of soloist and conductor has recorded the *St Matthew Passion*, B minor Mass and several cantatas. He retired from singing opera in 1999, but has continued to appear as the Evangelist in his own performances of the Bach Passions and in lieder recitals.

A. Blyth, ed.: *Song on Record 1* (London, 1986)

Alan Blyth

Schröder-Devrient

[née Schröder], **Wilhelmine**

(*b* Hamburg, 6 Dec 1804; *d* Coburg, 26 Jan 1860). German soprano. She was the eldest of four children of the baritone Friedrich Schröder (1744–1816), the first German Don Giovanni, and the actress Sophie Schröder, née Bürger (1781–1868). As a child she appeared in ballet in Hamburg, and in Vienna (15 March 1816). In Vienna she further appeared as Aricida in Friedrich Schiller's *Phädra* (13 October 1819) and as Ophelia in *Hamlet* at the Hoftheater, being carefully schooled in movement and diction by her mother. She also studied singing with Giuseppe Mozatti. Her first operatic appearance was at the Kärntnertortheater as Pamina (20 January 1821), when the freshness and confidence of her singing made a great impression. She followed this with Emmeline (Joseph Weigl's *Schweizerfamilie*), Marie (A.-E.-M. Grétry's *Raoul Barbe-Bleue*, in German) and the title role in Conradin Kreutzer's *Cordelia* (1823); she also sang Agathe in *Der Freischütz* on 7 March 1822 with Carl Maria von Weber conducting. However, her greatest triumph, and the perfor-

Wilhelmine Schröder-Devrient in the title role of 'Fidelio' (Beethoven), 1822

mance that laid the foundations of her international fame, was as Leonore in *Fidelio* on 3 November 1822. She first sang in Dresden that year, and in 1823 was given a two-year contract to sing at the Hoftheater: she remained associated with Dresden until 1847. There she also had further singing lessons with the chorus master Aloys Mieksch. She married the actor Carl Devrient (1797–1872); they had four children, but the marriage was dissolved in 1828.

Schröder-Devrient impressed audiences everywhere with the dramatic power of her performances, especially as Donna Anna, Euryanthe, Reiza, Norma, Romeo, Valentine and Desdemona (in Gioachino Rossini's *Otello*). She created the title role in Louis Spohr's *Jessonda* in Kassel in 1823. She had an outstanding success in Berlin in 1828, though she offended Gaspare Spontini by refusing to sing the title role of *La vestale* (she sang it a year later in Dresden). In Weimar in 1830 she sang to J.W. von Goethe, who wrote some lines in her praise. Travelling on to Paris, she triumphed in appearances with Joseph Röckel's German company (Agathe, 6 May; Leonore, 8 May). She returned to sing Italian opera in 1831 and 1832, appearing with MALIBRAN in *Don Giovanni* and *Otello*. In 1832 she also appeared at the King's Theatre in London ten times monthly during May, June and July, in *Fidelio*, *Don Giovanni* and *Macbeth* (by the season's conductor, H.-A.-B. Chelard). In the following season she was heard in *Der Freischütz*, *Die Zauberflöte*, *Euryanthe* and *Otello*, less successfully owing to the rival attractions of the dancers Marie Taglioni and Fanny Elssler. When, on the death of Malibran in 1836, the English press hailed her as the only artist to take Malibran's place, she was encouraged to return to London in 1837, and sing in *Fidelio*, *La sonnambula* and *Norma*. But her English was poor, her health was failing, and she was paid nothing since the company was found to be bankrupt.

From that time a decline in Schröder-Devrient's vocal powers was noticeable. She seemed tired of the stage and prone to mannerisms, including a tendency to drag the tempo and to declaim rather than sing. Many passing love affairs further dispirited her (the *Memoiren einer Sängerin* (Altona, 1861) attributed to her are a pornographic fabrication). Nevertheless, she continued to have successes in Germany, creating Adriano (*Rienzi*), Senta and Venus, in Dresden, and singing C.W. Gluck's Iphigenia (*Aulide*). Her last appearance was at Riga on 17 December 1847. Her second marriage was to a Saxon officer, Von Döring, with whom she visited St Petersburg and Copenhagen, and who embezzled her earnings. The marriage was dissolved, and in 1850 she married a Livonian baron, Von Bock, who took her to his estate at Trikaten. Having returned to Dresden she was arrested for the sympathy she had publicly expressed with the 1848 revolution; she was banned by a Berlin court from returning to Saxony, and also from re-entering Russia. With difficulty her husband succeeded in overturning these sentences. Her last known concerts were in Germany in 1856.

All accounts agree on the dramatic powers of 'The Queen of Tears', as Schröder-Devrient was dubbed when observed actually to be weeping on stage. In an age when few singers matched their vocal prowess with equal dramatic skill, she impressed audiences especially with her interpretation of Leonore. In this role, Ignaz Moscheles preferred her to Malibran, and many reports give details of the dramatic effect of her performance. Ludwig van Beethoven, who had rehearsed her, thanked her personally, and promised to write an opera for her. According to Eduard Genast, whose wife accompanied her, she persuaded Goethe of the merits of Franz Schubert's setting of his *Erlkönig* when a poor performance had previously caused him to dismiss it. Carl Maria von Weber thought her the best of all Agathes, and to have disclosed more in the part than he had believed was there; however, on hearing her sing Leonore in 1822 he discerned the deficiencies that later (1842) disturbed Hector Berlioz, who deplored her exaggerated acting, her vehement declamation and her failures of style. According to Henry Chorley, 'Her voice was a strong soprano… with an inherent expressiveness of tone which made it more attractive on the stage than many a more faultless organ.…Her tones were delivered without any care, save to give them due force. Her execution was bad and heavy'. However, he praised her acting, even though she exaggerated her characterization as time went on. It was Schröder-Devrient who roused the 16-year-old Richard Wagner to his sense of vocation as a dramatic composer, as he recounted in *Mein Leben*. He dedicated *Über Schauspieler und Sänger* to her memory, and in it gave a moving and detailed critical evaluation of her art, observing that she sang 'more with the soul than with the voice'. Robert Schumann wrote *Ich grolle nicht* for her; he called her singing of it 'nobly projected' and declared that she was the only singer who could survive with Franz Liszt as an accompanist. Her vocal deficiencies were partly due to erratic training, initially under her mother and insufficiently pursued under other teachers; as a singing actress who brought new dramatic powers to the art of opera she was influential on the course of German Romantic opera.

John Warrack

Schubert, Richard

(*b* Dessau, 15 Dec 1885; *d* Oberstaufen, 12 Oct 1959). German tenor. He studied with Rudolf von Milde and made his début as a baritone in 1909 at Strasbourg. After further study in Milan and Dresden, he returned in 1911 as a tenor, singing first at Nuremberg and then at Wiesbaden (1913–17), where he concentrated on the Wagnerian repertory. His career was then divided largely between Hamburg and Vienna. He sang in the première of E.W. Korngold's *Die tote Stadt* (1920, Hamburg), and was also closely associated with Richard Strauss in early performances of *Ariadne auf Naxos*, *Die Frau ohne Schatten* and *Die ägyptische Helena*. Abroad he sang in Paris, Buenos Aires and Chicago. He had a wide repertory of lyric and dramatic roles in Italian and French opera, including Rodolfo, Faust, Radames and Otello. His last appearance in Vienna was as Eisenstein in *Die Fledermaus* in 1937, after which he sang and directed the opera at Osnabrück and then retired to teach. His recordings show a vividly expressive and unusually lyrical style in the Wagnerian repertory; in association with his attractive stage presence these qualities gave him a leading position among the German tenors of his time.

J.B. Steane

Schumann, Elisabeth

(*b* Merseburg an der Saale, 13 June 1888; *d* New York, 23 April 1952). German soprano, naturalized American. She studied with Natalie Hänisch, Marie Dietrich and Alma Schadow. She made her début at the Neues Stadt-Theater, Hamburg, as the Shepherd in *Tannhäuser*, in 1909, and she remained a member of the Hamburg company until 1919, when Richard Strauss persuaded her to join the Vienna Staatsoper. There she became a firm favourite and stayed with the company until 1938, when she left Austria shortly after the *Anschluss*.

She was first heard at Covent Garden in 1924, when she had a great success as Sophie in *Der Rosenkavalier*; after that she made many appearances there in this and in Mozartian parts. Her beautifully controlled high soprano of delicate, ringing timbre and of crystalline purity, and her charming stage presence made her a delightful Susanna, Blonde, Zerlina and Despina. Strauss's Sophie has also remained inseparably linked with her name, especially for her delivery of those long, soaring *pianissimo* phrases with which Sophie acknowledges the gift of the rose at the beginning of the second act; it seemed as though the composer must have had just such a quality of voice in mind when writing the part.

Schumann's Eva in *Die Meistersinger*, though the part taxed her strength, was charmingly youthful and lyrical; her Adele in Bruno Walter's revival of *Die Fledermaus* was a delicious essay in flirtatious gaiety. In the recital hall her popularity was even greater, and Strauss was so delighted by her singing of his songs that he toured the USA with her in 1921. Her emotional range as a lieder singer was to some extent restricted by the light weight and silvery tone of her voice; but within her chosen limits, and especially in the more lyrical and playful songs of Franz Schubert, she was inimitable. She was also much admired as a Bach singer.

From 1938 Schumann made her home in New York, where she had sung Sophie and several other parts (including a triumphant Musetta) at the Metropolitan during the single season of 1914–15. In 1945 she reappeared in Britain at the Royal Albert Hall, and in 1947 took part in the first Edinburgh Festival; and she gave many subsequent recitals, besides teaching and singing at the Bryanston Summer School of Music. The passing years dealt lightly with her voice, and to the end it was rare for her to produce a note which was not of beautiful quality. Her many records, especially the famous abridged version of *Der Rosenkavalier* and the long series of lieder by Schubert, Robert Schumann and others, are among the happiest of their kind ever made.

The second of her three marriages was to Karl Alwin (1891–1945), a conductor at the Vienna Staatsoper and pianist, who often accompanied her in recitals and recordings. She wrote a treatise on German song (London, 1948/*R*).

E. Puritz: *The Teaching of Elisabeth Schumann* (London, 1956)

A. Mathis: 'Elisabeth Schumann', *Opera*, xxiv (1973), 672–80, 783–93, 968–79

F. Juynboll and J. Seddon: 'Elisabeth Schumann Discography', *Record Collector*, xxxiii (1988), 55–116

G. Puritz: *Elisabeth Schumann* (London, 1993) [incl. discography]

Desmond Shawe-Taylor

Schumann-Heink [née Rössler; Heink], Ernestine [Tini]

(*b* Lieben, nr Prague, 15 June 1861; *d* Hollywood, CA, 17 Nov 1936). Austrian contralto and mezzo-soprano, naturalized American. Among her teachers was G.B. Lamperti (the younger). She made her opera début at Dresden as Azucena in 1878, and remained there for four seasons. After marriage to Ernst Heink, she obtained an engagement at Hamburg under Pollini, and remained there until 1897, taking part in the company's London season under the young Gustav Mahler in 1892, when she was much applauded as Erda, Fricka, Waltraute and Brangäne. In 1893, having divorced her first husband, she married the actor Paul Schumann, assum-

ing the familiar hyphenated form of her surname. A long and fruitful relationship with Bayreuth began in 1896, when she sang Erda in five cycles of the *Ring*, and lasted until 1914.

Between 1897 and 1901 Schumann-Heink took part in four consecutive Covent Garden seasons, and became a regular member of the Metropolitan company for a similar period (1898–1903), returning subsequently for single seasons only. By then she had begun the series of popular and profitable cross-country American concert tours that occupied much of the rest of her long career and made her into a national legend. In 1909 she returned to Dresden to sing the part of Clytemnestra in the première of *Elektra*. Although she could sing (and very well) virtually anything, her English and American stage career centred on Richard Wagner; and it was as Erda that she bade farewell to the Metropolitan in 1932, still captivating the audience, as the American critic Olin Downes wrote, with 'knowledge and imagination embodied in the tone and in every syllable of the text she delivered so memorably'. These words well describe the effect vividly conveyed by her Erda and Waltraute recordings made less than three years before. Although largely unrepresentative of her serious repertory, her many other recordings, made over a period of 25 years, give a splendid impression of her powers: of her opulent and flexible tones from low D to high B, the amazing fullness and evenness of her shake, her artistic conviction, dramatic temperament and vivid enunciation. Among them should be mentioned the *brindisi* from *Lucrezia Borgia* (several versions, all good), the prison scene from *Le prophète*, 'Parto, parto' from *La clemenza di Tito*, and the duet with CARUSO ('Ai nostri monti') from *Il trovatore*.

M. Lawton: *Schumann-Heink: the Last of the Titans* (New York, 1928; repr. 1977 with discography by W.R. Moran)

J. McPherson: 'Ernestine Schumann-Heink', *Record Collector*, xvii (1966–8), 99–144 [with discography by W.R. Moran], 154–9; xx (1971–2), 165; xxv (1979–80), 75–7

Desmond Shawe-Taylor

Schütz, Françoise Jeanne.

See LITVINNE, FELIA.

Schützendorf, Gustav

(*b* Cologne, 1883; *d* Berlin, 27 April 1937). German baritone. He studied in Cologne and Milan, and made his début in Krefeld in 1905 as Don Giovanni. From 1914 to 1920 he sang with the Munich Hofoper. After two seasons at the Berlin Staatsoper (1920–22) he was engaged by the Metropolitan; he made his début as Faninal in 1922 and remained with the company until 1935, taking a wide range of roles including Beckmesser, Alberich and Klingsor. He sang the Foreman of the Mill in Leoš Janáček's *Jenůfa* (1924), the Chamberlain in Igor Stravinsky's *The Nightingale* (1926) and the Devil in Jaromir Weinberger's *Svanda the Bagpiper* (1931), all American premières. His younger brother, LEO SCHÜTZENDORF, and his elder brothers, Guido (1880–1967), bass, and Alfons (1882–1946), bass-baritone, were opera singers of international stature; Alfons sang Klingsor at Bayreuth (1910–12) and Wotan at Covent Garden (1910). A famous performance of *Die Meistersinger* at Bremen in 1916 featured Guido as Kothner, Alfons as Hans Sachs, Gustav as Pogner and Leo as Beckmesser, the only time all four brothers appeared in the same performance.

Harold Rosenthal/R

Schütizendorf, Leo

(*b* Cologne, 7 May 1886; *d* Berlin, 18 Dec 1931). German bass-baritone, brother of GUSTAV SCHÜTZENDORF. He studied with Alexander d'Arnals in Cologne and made his début at Düsseldorf in 1908. After engagements in Krefeld, Darmstadt, Wiesbaden and Vienna, he joined the Berlin Staatsoper in 1920. In nine years he made 445 appearances in a repertory of 47 roles, including Ochs, Boris, Beckmesser, Faninal, Méphistophélès and Wozzeck, which he created in 1925. In 1929 he sang in *Der Bettelstudent* at the Metropoltheater, Berlin, but as he had not obtained leave from the Staatsoper he was dismissed, an event that contributed to his final breakdown and early death. He was a versatile actor, as much at home in tragic roles as in comic ones.

J. Dennis: 'Leo Schützendorf', *Record Collector*, xvi (1964–6), 229–37 [with discography]

Harold Rosenthal/R

Schwarz, Hanna

(*b* Hamburg, 15 Aug 1943). German mezzo-soprano. She studied at Essen and Hanover, where she made her début as Maddalena in *Rigoletto* in 1970. In Hamburg her roles included Cherubino and Dorabella; at Bayreuth in 1975 she graduated to Rhinemaiden and Valkyrie, appearing as Erda the following year. Her American début (San Francisco, 1977) as Fricka was praised in *Opera* as 'radiant-toned', and at Covent Garden in 1980 her Waltraute was 'stunningly sung'. Thought to be miscast as Carmen in San Francisco and as Charlotte in

Amsterdam, she scored a particular success as Dido in *Les Troyens* at Hamburg in 1983. She has sung parts as diverse as the Princess in *Adriana Lecouvreur* and Prince Orlofsky in *Die Fledermaus*, but has continued to appear regularly at Bayreuth, and her Waltraute was widely considered to be vocally the greatest asset of Covent Garden's *Götterdämmerung* in 1990. Her rich, steady voice has taken well to recording, though the voice alone hardly suggests the attractiveness and animation of her stage appearance. Success in Hamburg as Mephistophilia in the 1995 première of Alfred Schnittke's *Historia von D. Johann Fausten*, and as Herodias in *Salome* at the Metropolitan in 1996, helped to confirm her as one of the leading mezzos of her time, a position strengthened by her work in concert and oratorio.

J.B. Steane

Schwarz, Joseph

(*b* Riga, 10 Oct 1880; *d* Berlin, 10 Nov 1926). German baritone. He studied in Berlin and Vienna, making his début in 1900 as Amonasro at Linz. After appearances in Riga, Graz and St Petersburg, he was engaged at the Vienna Volksoper and then at the Hofoper, where he made his début in 1909 as Luna. In 1915 he became a member of the Berlin Hofoper (later the Staatsoper). He made his American début in 1921 at Chicago as Rigoletto, returning as Iago and Germont; he sang Rigoletto again at the Paris Opéra (1923) and at Covent Garden (1925). His many distinguished recordings reveal a lyrical voice of considerable beauty which he used with innate intelligence to project dramatic intensity. He was generally considered one of the most notable singing actors in the early years of the 20th century.

M. Scott: *The Record of Singing*, ii (London, 1979), 226–8
G. Walter: 'Joseph Schwarz', *Record Collector*, xxvi (1980–81), 215–34 [incl. discography by C.N. Welsh]

Leo Riemens/Alan Blyth

Schwarz, Vera

(*b* Agram [now Zagreb], 10 July 1888; *d* Vienna, 4 Dec 1964). Croatian soprano. She studied in Vienna and made her début in operetta at the Theater an der Wien in 1908. Her clear voice and good looks quickly brought her leading roles such as Rosalinde (*Die Fledermaus*). She graduated to opera, first at Hamburg, then with the Berlin Staatsoper, and in 1921 at Vienna, where she had a great success as Tosca. Known as 'the poor man's JERITZA', she sang in a repertory ranging from Countess Almaviva to Aida, Ariadne, Marietta (*Die tote Stadt*) and even Carmen. In 1927 she sang in the Viennese

première of *Jonny spielt auf* and in the Berlin première of Franz Lehár's *Der Zarewitsch*. This marked
the beginning of a noted partnership with RICHARD
TAUBER in Lehár operettas. In 1938 at short notice
she appeared at Glyndebourne as Lady Macbeth,
where her acting was found 'outstandingly impressive' though her voice sounded tired. She spent the
next ten years in the USA, singing and later teaching, and returned to Europe in 1948 to give classes
at Salzburg and Vienna. Her versatility, as well as a
less than perfect technical control over a fine but
hard-worked voice, is well illustrated on records.

J.B. Steane

Schwarzkopf, (Olga Maria) Elisabeth (Friederike)

(*b* Jarotschin, Posen province, 9 Dec 1915; *d* Schruns,
3 Aug 2006). German soprano. The outstanding lieder singer of the postwar decades and pre-eminent
among women, as was DIETRICH FISCHER-DIESKAU
among men, she was an operatic artist in whom personal beauty, beauty of tone and line, and rare musical
intelligence were combined. She entered the Berlin
Hochschule für Musik in 1934, studying voice with
LULA MYSZ-GMEINER (but for a year only; the celebrated lieder singer wished to make a contralto of
her). In 1938 she joined the Berlin Städtische Oper,
making her début as a flowermaiden and soon graduating from second-soprano roles to Adele, Musetta,
Zerbinetta etc. Recordings from this period show a

rather dark middle voice and a brilliant coloratura
top. She became a pupil of MARIA IVOGÜN, whom
she regarded as her real teacher. Karl Böhm invited
her to join the Vienna Staatsoper, and after the war
it was as a leading member of this troupe that she
made her Covent Garden début (Donna Elvira,
and Marzelline in *Fidelio*) in 1947. Invited to join
the newly founded Covent Garden company, she
remained with it for five seasons, singing not only
in the German repertory (Pamina, Susanna, Eva,
Sophie) but also Violetta, Gilda, Mimì, Butterfly
and Jules Massenet's Manon – all in English. The
voice became a lustrous, powerful lyric soprano,
full-toned, warm and flexible, and her international
reputation grew. At the Salzburg Festival (début in
1947, W.A. Mozart's Susanna) she appeared most
years until 1964; at La Scala (début in the 1948–9
season, Countess Almaviva) most years until 1963;
with the San Francisco Opera (début in 1955,
Marschallin) most years until 1964. Internationally
she was sought as, above all, a peerless Fiordiligi,
Countess Almaviva, Donna Elvira and Marschallin
(Metropolitan début as the last, 1964; Donna Elvira,
1964), but her repertory ranged from Mélisande,
Marguerite and Iole in G.F. Handel's *Hercules*, all at
La Scala, to Mařenka in an English *Bartered Bride* in
San Francisco.

In 1951 Schwarzkopf created the role of Anne
Trulove in Igor Stravinsky's *The Rake's Progress*
in Venice. Although Italian opera played a relatively small part in her career after she left Covent
Garden, one notable exception was her inimitably
merry, dexterous Alice Ford in Giuseppe Verdi's
Falstaff (Milan, Salzburg, Vienna) – happily captured on gramophone records, as was her Bayreuth
Eva of 1951. Schwarzkopf's fame was furthered by
many excellent recordings; in 1953 she married
Walter Legge, artistic director of EMI records,
and the two perfectionists combined to record a
great deal of her theatre repertory and also some
Johann Strauss the younger and Franz Lehár operetta heroines. Richard Strauss's Ariadne, Arabella
(in excerpt) and Countess (*Capriccio*) are among
her best recorded performances. All Schwarzkopf's
interpretation and execution was marked by great
care for detail; the care was often apparent, and
she did not escape charges of overinflection and
artfulness, particularly in later years when the
voice had lost its earlier freedom. She retired from
the stage after singing *Rosenkavalier* in Brussels in
1972. Among Schwarzkopf's many honours were
a Cambridge MusD and Grosses Verdienst-Kreuz
der Bundesrepublik Deutschland. She was made a
DBE in 1992. In 1981 it emerged that Schwarzkopf
had been a member of the Nazi party, certainly by
1940 and possibly earlier. Although she dismissed
her membership as a professional necessity, her

Elisabeth Schwarzkopf in 'Der Rosenkavalier' (Strauss)

SCOTTI, ANTONIO ～ 443

reputation has remained tarnished by what seems to have been an active party membership.

W. Mann: 'Elisabeth Schwarzkopf', *Gramophone Record Review* (1958), no. 56, p. 659 [with discography by F. F. Clough and G. J. Cuming]

W. Legge: 'Her Master's Voice', *ON*, xxxix/22 (1974–5), 9; also in *Opera*, xxvii (1976), 316–24

E. Greenfield: 'Elisabeth Schwarzkopf', *Gramophone*, liv (1976), 555, 751

Andrew Porter/R

Scio [Le Grand], Julie-[Claudine-]Angélique [Mlle Grécy]

(*b* Lille, 1768; *d* Paris, 14 July 1807). French soprano. She made her début in 1786 under the name of Mlle Grécy. After engagements at Montpellier, Avignon and Marseilles, she made her Paris début in 1792 at the Opéra-Comique, later singing at the Opéra. At the Théâtre Feydeau she created the title roles of Luigi Cherubini's *Elisa* (1794), *Médée* (1797), and Constance in *Les deux journées* (1800). In 1798 she also created the title role in *Léonore* by Pierre Gaveaux. She also took part in the premières of works by H.-M. Berton, J.-F. Le Sueur and N.-M. Dalayrac. Married to the violinist Etienne Scio, she was reputed to have been a highly dramatic singing actress. She died of tuberculosis at the height of her career.

Elizabeth Forbes

Scirolo [Sciroletto, Scirolino].

Nickname of GIUSEPPE APRILE.

Sciutti, Graziella

(*b* Turin, 17 April 1927; *d* Geneva, 9 April 2001). Italian soprano. She studied in Rome and made her début as Lucy in *The Telephone* at the 1951 Aix-en-Provence Festival. There she also sang Susanna, Despina and Zerlina and in 1954 created the title role of Henri Sauguet's *Les caprices de Marianne*. That year she made her British début as Rosina at Glyndebourne and sang the Duchess in Giovanni Paisiello's *Don Chisciotte* to reopen the restored Teatrino di Corte in Naples. In 1955 she sang Carolina (*Il matrimonio segreto*) to inaugurate the Piccola Scala. She appeared many times in both the smaller and the larger auditoriums; her parts included the title role in *La Cecchina*, Adèle (*Le comte Ory*), Norina and Paisiello's Nina.

Sciutti made her Covent Garden début as Oscar in 1956 and returned to sing Nannetta, Susanna and Despina. She made her American début at San Francisco in 1961 as Susanna. She sang regularly at Salzburg and in Vienna and also appeared in Paris in Sacha Guitry and Reynaldo Hahn's *Mozart* and as Polly (*Die Dreigroschenoper*). In 1970 she returned to Glyndebourne as Fiorilla and in 1977 she sang in her own production of *La voix humaine* there. Her vivacity, pointed phrasing and clear diction made her an outstanding soubrette singer. Among her recordings are her Mozart roles, Marzelline (in Lorin Maazel's *Fidelio*) and French song. In the 1980s she worked as a director in New York and Chicago.

H. Rosenthal: *Great Singers of Today* (London, 1966)

J.T. Hughes: 'The Art of Graziella Sciutti', *International Classical Record Collector*, ii/8 (1996–7), 37–44

Harold Rosenthal/Alan Blyth

Scotti, Antonio

(*b* Naples, 25 Jan 1866; *d* Naples, 26 Feb 1936). Italian baritone. A pupil of Ester Triffani Paganini, he made his début at the Circolo Filarmonico, Naples, in March 1889 as Cinna in Gaspare Spontini's *La vestale*. The first part of his career, spent in Madrid, South America, Russia and the major Italian cities, ended with his début at La Scala (1898–9). During this period, smooth delivery, variety of colour, a fine legato and facility in the upper register were his chief qualities, together with the elegance of his acting, in a repertory that, as well as the typically 'noble' baritone roles in *Don Giovanni*, *Les Huguenots*, *I puritani*, *La favorite*, *Ernani* and *Don Carlos*, also included Falstaff and Tonio. After his début at Covent Garden (1899) and at the Metropolitan Opera (1899–1900), Scotti's performances were largely confined to London (until 1910, and in 1913–14) and New York, where he sang regularly until 1933, making his farewell appearance as Cim-Fen in Franco Leoni's *L'oracolo*, a role he had created in 1905. His later career coincided with the ascent of the actor over the singer and of the 'character' over the 'noble' baritone roles – Iago, Marcello, Scarpia, Sharpless, as well as Falstaff and Tonio. In this transformation, his voice soon lost its beauty, becoming thick and inflexible; but his already remarkable abilities as singer and actor were further refined, and explained his continuing hold over the New York public. In 1919 he formed, with colleagues from the Metropolitan, the Scotti Grand Opera Company, which for four seasons undertook tours of the USA and Canada.

M.F. Bott: 'On Tour with Scotti, 1921', *Opera*, xxvii (1976), 1101–7

C. Bishop: *Scotti Grand Opera Company* (Santa Monica, CA, 1982)

W. Hogarth: 'Antonio Scotti', *Record Collector*, xxviii (1983–4), 197–206

W. Hogarth and R.T. See: 'A Critical Survey of the Recorded Legacy of Antonio Scotti, Baritone', ibid., 206–27

Rodolfo Celletti/Valeria Pregliasco Gualerzi

Scotto, Renata

(*b* Savona, 24 Feb 1933). Italian soprano. After studying in Milan, she made her début in 1952 at Savona as Violetta, repeating the role at Milan (Teatro Nuovo) in 1953. She first sang at La Scala in 1954 as Walter (*La Wally*), then appeared in Rome and Venice. In 1957 she made her London début (Stoll Theatre) as Mimì, then sang Adina, Violetta and Donna Elvira. The same year she replaced CALLAS as Amina in one performance of *La sonnambula* at Edinburgh for La Scala, with whom she later sang Elvira (*I puritani*), Antonida (*A Life for the Tsar*), Marguerite, Nannetta and Vincenzo Bellini's Giulietta. She made her American début (1960) in Chicago as Mimì and her Covent Garden début (1962) as Butterfly; later roles included Gilda, Manon, Amina and Lady Macbeth. At the Metropolitan (1965–87) Scotto took on heavier roles from 1974, singing Leonora (*Il trovatore*), Luisa Miller, Amelia (*Ballo in maschera*), Hélène (*Les vêpres siciliennes*), Desdemona, Elisabeth de Valois, Manon Lescaut, Musetta, Giorgetta (*Il tabarro*), Angelica, Lauretta, Berthe (*Le prophète*), Adriana Lecouvreur, La Gioconda, Francesca da Rimini and Norma. Her repertory also included *Lucia di Lammermoor*, *Maria di Rohan*, *Anna Bolena* and *La straniera*.

One of the leading Italian *lirico spinto* sopranos of her day, Scotto invested her roles with a rare combination of vocal agility and dramatic power. Pathos, as in the second act of *La traviata* or the last of *La sonnambula* and *Madama Butterfly*, was her particularly strong suit, and few sopranos have encompassed so easily the qualities called for by both Lucia and Butterfly (which she recorded in a classic version under John Barbirolli). Among Scotto's other operatic recordings are eloquent interpretations of Violetta, Gilda and Desdemona.

E. Gara: 'Renata Scotto', *Opera*, xxii (1971), 199–206
R. Scotto and O. Roca: *Scotto: More than a Diva* (New York, 1984)

Alan Blyth

Sedlmair, Sophie

(*b* Hanover, 25 Jan 1857; *d* Hanover, 14 Oct 1939). German soprano. She appeared first in operetta at Leipzig, then was engaged at Mainz, and at Dresden (1880–85). After a season in Amsterdam, appearances at the Thalia Theatre in New York (1887) and a spell in Berlin, she went to Vienna to renew her studies. In 1893 her career as a dramatic soprano began with what amounted to a second début, in *Fidelio* at Danzig. Guest performances at Budapest in 1896 were followed by a ten-year engagement at the Vienna Staatsoper. Her roles included both lyric and dramatic parts: in *Die Walküre*, for instance, she would sing either Brünnhilde or Sieglinde – the latter was said to have been a portrayal of 'magical tenderness'. In her single Covent Garden season (1897) she sang Isolde and the *Siegfried* Brünnhilde in performances with JEAN DE RESZKE; *The Times* recognized her intelligence but thought the voice not quite powerful enough for the house. Her recordings show both the grandeur of the dramatic soprano and the spirited lightness of a singer experienced in operetta, but are marred by her excessive use of portamento.

J. B. Steane

Seefried, Irmgard

(*b* Köngetried, nr Mindelheim, 9 Oct 1919; *d* Vienna, 24 Nov 1988). Austrian soprano of German birth. She received her first music lessons from her father and at the age of 11, three years after her first public appearance, sang Gretel in Engelbert Humperdinck's opera. After study at the Augsburg Conservatory she was engaged by Herbert von Karajan for the Aachen Opera in 1939; while at Aachen she also sang in performances at the cathedral, under Theodor Rehmann. In 1943 she made her début at the Vienna Staatsoper as Eva in *Die Meistersinger* under Karl Böhm, and then remained a member of the company. In 1944 she sang the Composer in the performance of *Ariadne auf Naxos* at Vienna in honour of Richard Strauss's 80th birthday. (Her supreme interpretation of this role is preserved on recordings with Böhm and Karajan.) After the war she began the series of guest appearances that took her to the opera houses and concert halls of Europe and North and South America; she also undertook concert and recital tours of India, Australia, Japan and South Africa. She first sang at Covent Garden with the Vienna Staatsoper in September 1947 (Fiordiligi and Susanna), returned to sing Susanna and Eva with the Covent Garden company in the 1948–9 season, and soon became a regular soloist at such festivals as Salzburg, Edinburgh and Lucerne. In 1964 she and her husband Wolfgang Schneiderhan gave the first performance of H.W. Henze's *Ariosi* at the Edinburgh

Festival, and in 1968 they took part in the first performance of Frank Martin's *Magnificat* (written for and dedicated to them) at Lucerne. Her last stage appearance was in the title role of *Kát'a Kabanová* in Vienna in 1976.

Seefried's combination of a beautiful lyric soprano voice, charm and pleasing stage deportment made her a favourite with audiences, although she sometimes overplayed the soubrette aspects of some of her favourite Mozart and Strauss roles. She was also a gifted, highly individual lieder singer, as can be heard on many recordings.

E. Werba: 'Irmgard Seefried', *Opera*, xvii (1966), 611–14
J. Schumann: 'Irmgard Seefried Discography', *Fono-Forum* (1974), 812, 1227 only
A. Blyth: 'Irmgard Seefried: an Appreciation', *Opera*, xl (1989), 35–6

Peter Branscombe/R

Seidler-Wranitzky, Karoline

(*b* Vienna, 1790; *d* Berlin, 7 Dec 1872). Czech soprano. She was engaged at Berlin where she was admired as Rosina, Susanna and Jessonda, and created Agathe in *Der Freischütz* (1821); contemporary critics praised the power and range of her voice and the grace of her appearance.

Milan Poštolka/Roger Hickman/R

Seiffert, Peter

(*b* Düsseldorf, 4 Jan 1954). German tenor. He studied at the Robert-Schumann-Hochschule with Hans Kast, and made his début in a small role in Aribert Reimann's *Lear* at the Deutsche Oper am Rhein in 1978, followed by appearances there as Baron Kronthal (*Der Wildschütz*). In 1982 he was engaged by the Deutsche Oper, Berlin, where he has sung, among others, Ottavio, Titus, Tamino, Matteo (*Arabella*), Faust, Lohengrin and Huon. Since 1983 he has sung regularly at the Bayerische Staatsoper in Munich. In 1988 he made his Covent Garden début as Parsifal and in 1994 his Salzburg Festival début as Ottavio. In 1996 he was much admired as Walther in his first Bayreuth appearance. He was similarly acclaimed for his Lohengrin in Munich in 1999 and his first Tannhäuser, in Zürich, the same year. Seiffert is also in demand as a concert singer in works such as Felix Mendelssohn's *Lobgesang*, Ludwig van Beethoven's Ninth Symphony and Gustav Mahler's *Das Lied von der Erde*, which he recorded with Simon Rattle. Among his many operatic recordings his management of the difficult roles of Max and Huon stand out, both under Marek Janowski, as does his

Florestan for Nikolaus Harnoncourt, all evincing a firm, rounded, lyric-dramatic voice with a flexibility remarkable in a tenor of his vocal weight.

Alan Blyth

Seinemeyer, Meta

(*b* Berlin, 5 Sept 1895; *d* Dresden, 19 Aug 1929). German soprano. She studied in Berlin, making her début there in 1918 at the Deutsches Opernhaus in *Orphée aux enfers*. She remained there until 1925, singing such roles as Elsa, Elisabeth, Agathe and Countess Almaviva. In 1923–4 she toured the USA with Sol Hurok's German Opera Company, singing Elisabeth and Eva in New York. After a guest appearance as Marguerite at the Dresden Staatsoper, she was engaged there in 1925 by Fritz Busch, and remained there until her death; she created the Duchess of Parma in Ferruccio Busoni's *Doktor Faust* (1925), and sang Maddalena (*Andrea Chénier*), Manon Lescaut and Leonora (*La forza del destino*). She appeared at the Colón, Buenos Aires (1926), the Vienna Staatsoper (1927) and Covent Garden (1929), where she sang Sieglinde, Eva and Elsa a few months before her death from leukaemia. Her many recordings demonstrate her peculiarly intense and highly individual voice, most notably in arias from Giuseppe Verdi's middle-period operas and in duets with the tenor TINO PATTIERA.

J. Dennis: 'Meta Seinemeyer', *Record Collector*, xiv (1961–2), 158–68 [with discography by J.W.C. Hesser]

Leo Riemens/Alan Blyth

Sekar-Rozhansky [Rozhansky], Anton Vladislavovich

(*b* 6/18 May 1863; *d* 28 Jan 1952). Russian tenor. He graduated from the St Petersburg conservatory in 1891 and for the next five years sang at opera houses in Rostov, Kharkiv and Tbilisi. He made a successful début at the Mariinsky Theatre in 1896, but after only two months left St Petersburg for Moscow, joining S.I. Zimin's Private Opera company, where he was principal tenor until 1914. He had a big voice, strongest in the middle register and baritonal in quality: it was said that when he sang in duet with BATTISTINI it was hard to tell which was the baritone. He was criticized for poor diction and intonation, faults offset by his imposing stage presence and brilliant acting. The title role in Nikolay Rimsky-Korsakov's *Sadko* (Moscow 1897) was written for him, as was an interpolated aria for

Guidon in *The Tale of Tsar Saltan* (Moscow, 1900); he also created the part of Lïkov in *The Tsar's Bride* (1899, Moscow). After retiring from the stage he taught at the conservatories in Moscow and Warsaw.

Boris Semeonoff/R

Selva, Antonio

(*b* Padua, 1824; *d* Padua, Sept 1889). Italian bass. He was a struggling 19-year-old member of the chorus at La Fenice, Venice (with some experience of singing leading parts in a minor theatre) when Giuseppe Verdi in an emergency chose him for the important comprimario part of Don Ruy Gomez de Silva in *Ernani* (1844). This was the type of the granitic Verdi bass; he went on to sing other such parts, for instance Zaccaria in *Nabucco*, in leading Italian theatres and at the Théâtre Italien, Paris. At S Carlo he sang Balthazar in *La favorite* (1848) and also created Count Walter – another comprimario part – in *Luisa Miller* (1849). He sang frequently in Madrid between 1864 and 1874.

John Rosselli

Sembach [Semfke], Johannes

(*b* Berlin, 9 March 1881; *d* Bremerhaven, 20 June 1944). German tenor. He studied in Vienna and later with JEAN DE RESZKE in Paris. In 1900 he made his début at the Vienna Staatsoper, and from 1905 to 1913 was principal dramatic tenor at Dresden, where he created Aegisthus in *Elektra* (1909). In 1910 he was admired at Covent Garden as an excellent Loge and Siegmund, adding Parsifal, Lohengrin and Walther in 1914. His *mezza voce* was the subject of special praise, and the lyric beauty of his voice was again noticed when he sang the title role of Adrien Méhul's *Joseph* in its London première. At the Metropolitan he enjoyed a notable success, first as Parsifal (1914), then as Tamino, Florestan and Adolar (Carl Maria von Weber's *Euryanthe*). He showed further versatility in the following seasons, turning from Siegfried to Pylades (*Iphigénie en Tauride*) and in 1920 learning the Wagnerian repertory in English as required in the immediate postwar years. Sembach returned to New York at the Mecca Temple (later the City Center) in 1931 and also made successful appearances in South America. On stage he presented a more credible hero than most Wagnerian tenors and on records his voice is heard as a strong, incisive instrument, often attractively used.

J.B. Steane

Sembrich, Marcella [Kochańska, Prakseda Marcelina]

(*b* Wiśniewczyk, Galicia, 15 Feb 1858; *d* New York, 11 Jan 1935). Polish soprano, later naturalized American. The daughter of a village musician, she had her first instruction in violin and piano with her father and as a child helped support the family by playing both instruments. She was 11 when a well-to-do villager made it possible for her to attend the conservatory at Lemberg (now L'viv), where her principal teacher was Wilhelm Stengel, whom she later married. Stengel took her to Vienna to sing and play for Julius Epstein, who advised her to cultivate her voice; Franz Liszt later endorsed this suggestion. She studied with Viktor von Rokitansky and the younger G.B. Lamperti, and made her début in Athens on 3 June 1877 as Elvira in Vincenzo Bellini's *I puritani*, adopting her mother's maiden name. After further study in the German repertory, with Richard Lewy in Vienna, she appeared in Dresden in 1878 as Lucia di Lammermoor, the same role she later sang for her débuts at Covent Garden (12 June 1880) and the Metropolitan Opera (24 October 1883, the second night of the first season).

Sembrich's success in New York was immediate. After an active season she showed her versatility at a benefit concert at the Metropolitan by performing two movements of a violin concerto by Charles-Auguste de Bériot, a Chopin mazurka for piano, and part of the role of Gioachino Rossini's Rosina. The season had been artistically brilliant but a financial disaster, and Sembrich spent the next years in Europe. Rejoining the Metropolitan company in 1898, she reigned as a favourite until 1909, when she was honoured with a sumptuous farewell gala in which all the principal artists performed in tribute to her. Having already established herself as a lieder singer, making extended tours, she continued to give recitals until 1917, the year of her husband's death. She was by then active as a teacher, heading the voice departments of both the Curtis Institute and the Institute of Musical Art.

Sembrich was one of the greatest sopranos in history. Like PATTI (who became a staunch friend), she combined a dazzling technique with the purest lyricism. Her scale was perfectly matched over a range from c' to f'''. In addition to Lucia, her most popular roles were Violetta, Gilda and Rosina; she was also a leading interpreter of W.A. Mozart and was admired for her Zerlina, Susanna and the Queen of Night. Her repertory also included two Wagner roles, Elsa (*Lohengrin*) and Eva (*Die Meistersinger*), and Giacomo Puccini's Mimì. She was the 'musicians' singer' of her time, and she enjoyed playing chamber music with such friends as the members of the Flonzaley Quartet, or two-piano music, often with Ignacy Paderewski. Her recordings, made late in her career, hardly do her justice, though they give some impression of the limpid quality of her voice and the brilliance of her coloratura. She confessed that she was never at ease before the acoustic recording horn. Personally, Sembrich was all but unique among singers in that she was utterly free of jealousy and beloved by all of her associates. After an engagement with the Metropolitan in San Francisco during the great earthquake of 1906, she delayed her departure for Europe to give a concert in Carnegie Hall, and raised some $10,000 for the benefit of the orchestra and chorus. Her influence as a teacher was far-reaching: her pupils included DUSOLINA GIANNINI, Hulda Lashanska, Queena Mario, Winifred Cecil and Anna Hamlin, and established artists such as ALMA GLUCK and MARIA JERITZA came to her to perfect their art. In the summer months she used to take a class of students to work with her, at first near Lake Placid, New York, and from 1922 at Bolton Landing on Lake George. Her studio there is now open in the summer as a museum of opera.

Obituary, *New York Times* (12 Jan 1935)

H. Goddard Owen: *A Recollection of Marcella Sembrich* (New York, 1950/*R* 1982 with new introduction by P.L. Miller)

H. Goddard Owen: 'A Recollection of Marcella Sembrich', *Record Collector*, xviii/5–6 (1968–9), pp. 99–38 [incl. discography by W.R. Moran; see also xx (1971–2), 165 only]

Philip L. Miller

Sénéchal, Michel

(*b* Tavery, 11 Feb 1927). French tenor. He studied in Paris, making his début in 1950 at La Monnaie (Brussels), where he sang for three seasons. Established at the Paris Opéra and Opéra-Comique, as well as other French theatres, he sang lyric roles such as Ferrando, Don Ottavio, Tamino, Almaviva, Count Ory, Paolino (*Il matrimonio segreto*), Hylas (*Les Troyens*), Georges Brown (*La dame blanche*) and also many character roles. In 1956 he sang Jean-Philippe Rameau's Platée at Aix-en-Provence, scoring a triumph in the travesty role of an elderly nymph, which he repeated at Amsterdam, Brussels and the Opéra-Comique (1977). Other roles in this category included Erice (*Ormindo*), Monsieur Triquet, Scaramuccio (*Ariadne auf Naxos*), Trabuco (*La forza del destino*), Valzacchi, Rodriguez (*Don Quichotte*) and Teapot/Arithmetic (*L'enfant et les sortilèges*). He sang Gonzalve (*L'heure espagnole*) at Glyndebourne (1966); the Brahmin (Albert Roussel's *Padmâvatî*)

at Florence (1971); Don Basilio and Le Dancaïre (*Carmen*) at Salzburg (1972–88), and Don Jerome in the French première of Sergey Prokofiev's *Betrothal in a Monastery* at Strasbourg (1973). Having made his Metropolitan début in 1982 as the four *Contes d'Hoffmann* tenor comics, he returned as Don Basilio and Guillot (*Manon*). In 1985 he created Fabien in Marcel Landowski's *Montségur* at Toulouse and Pope Leo X in Konrad Boehmer's *Docktor Faustus* at the Opéra. Sénéchal's high, smooth, agile voice and unrivalled ability as a character actor commended him to record companies, for whom he recorded many of his comprimario roles with rare style and unstinting enthusiasm. He made a particularly notable contribution to the Jacques Offenbach discography.

Elizabeth Forbes/Alan Blyth

Senesino [Bernardi, Francesco]

(*b* Siena; *d* ?Siena, by 27 Jan 1759). Italian alto castrato. His nickname was derived from his birthplace. He sang operatic roles in many Italian theatres: in Venice, 1707–8 (including operas by G.M. Ruggeri and Giuseppe Boniventi in which he played Rinaldo) and 1713–14 (in Antonio Lotti's *Irene Augusta* and two operas by C.F. Pollarolo), Vicenza (1708, 1714), Bologna in 1709 (in Antonio Caldara's *L'inimico generoso*) and in 1712, Genoa (1709–12), Rome (1711, in Pietro Ottoboni's private theatre), Reggio nell'Emilia (1712–13, 1715, 1717), Ferrara (1712), Brescia (1714), Florence (1715), Naples (1715–17, where he sang in six operas, including Alessandro Scarlatti's *Carlo re d'Alemagna* and *La virtù trionfante*) and Livorno (1717). He was engaged for Dresden from 1 September 1717 at the huge salary of 7000 thaler and the use of a carriage, and sang in Lotti's *Giove in Argo* (1717), *Ascanio* (1718) and *Teofane* (September 1719, singing the role of Ottone). He was dismissed early in 1720 for insubordination at the rehearsals of Johann Heinichen's *Flavio Crispo*, when he refused to sing one of his arias and tore up MATTEO BERSELLI's part. G.F. Handel, who had been instructed to engage Senesino for London, heard him in *Teofane* and opened negotiations; Senesino sent Giuseppe Riva a power of attorney to accept the Royal Academy's offer of a contract for 3000 guineas and he joined the company for its second season in September 1720. He made his début at the King's Theatre on 19 November in Bononcini's *Astarto* and remained a member of the company until June 1728, singing in all 32 operas produced during this period. They included 13 by Handel (see illustration in BERENSTADT, GAETANO), eight

Senesino [Francesco Bernardi]

by Bononcini (including a revival of *Crispo*, singing the title role and the première of *Griselda*, singing Gualtiero, both 1722) and seven by Attilio Ariosti (including *Caio Marzio Coriolano*, 1723, in which he sang the title role). Senesino's success was spectacular from the start; Mrs Pendarves described him in *Astarto* as 'beyond Nicolini both in person and voice', and he was constantly eulogized in newspapers and private letters in such terms as 'beyond all criticism' (of his performance in Handel's *Giulio Cesare*). However, his arrogant temper clashed with that of the imperious Handel as early as 1720, when according to Pablo Rolli the composer earned his resentment by calling him 'a damned fool'.

After the break-up of the Academy in 1728 Senesino is said to have invested his London profits in a fine house in Siena with an inscription over the door that 'the folly of the English had laid the foundation of it'. He sang in Paris in 1728, Venice in 1729 and Turin in 1730. He apparently gave Handel

a cold reception when they met in Italy, but in August 1730 he was re-engaged by Handel and John Jacob Heidegger for the second Academy, this time at a salary of 1400 guineas, and arrived in October as a replacement for BERNACCHI. According to Lord Harcourt, continental judges thought Bernacchi the finer singer and were puzzled by Senesino's English reputation. In the next three years he sang in four new Handel operas and many revivals, and in the first two London seasons of oratorio (1732–3), playing Ahasuerus in *Esther* (in English), Acis, and Barak in *Deborah*. His popularity was almost as great as before, but his increasing antipathy to Handel came into the open in June 1733, when a movement to set up a rival company was inspired by Senesino, Rolli and their partisans among the aristocracy. This became the so-called Opera of the Nobility, which occupied Lincoln's Inn Fields in the following season and the King's Theatre from autumn 1734, with Nicola Porpora as chief composer and Senesino,

FARINELLI, BERTOLLI, MONTAGNANA and later CUZZONI as the leading singers. In three seasons (1733–6) Senesino sang in five operas by Porpora and in operas by Bononcini, Johann Hasse, Handel (*Ottone*), Pietro Sandoni and Francesco Veracini; his last new part was Apollo in Porpora's serenata *La festa d'Imeneo* in May 1736. He was so moved by Farinelli's singing in Hasse's *Artaserse* that he forgot the character he was playing and embraced him on the stage; but 'several masters, and persons of judgment and probity' assured Charles Burney that Senesino made a profounder impression in London than Farinelli or any of his successors. When he left, a song called *The Lady's Lamentation for the Loss of Senesino* haunted the theatre bills for several years.

Senesino sang in Rimini and Turin in 1737, in several operas in Florence in 1737–9 and privately in a duet with the future Empress Maria Theresa. In the summer of 1739 he refused an invitation to Madrid on grounds of age, but was engaged for the winter season in Naples at a salary of 800 doubloons (3693 ducats). Although Charles de Brosses was enchanted by his singing and acting, the public condemned his style as old-fashioned. His last known performances were in Porpora's *Il trionfo di Camilla* at the S Carlo in 1740. A final glimpse of him is caught in March of that year, when Horace Walpole met him returning to Siena in a chaise: 'We thought it a fat old woman; but it spoke in a shrill little pipe, and proved itself to be Senesini'. His porcine features appear in many caricatures by A.M. Zanetti and Marco Ricci in the Cini collection (see illustration) and at Windsor Castle, and in mezzotints by A. van Halcken (1735, after Hudson) and Elisha Kirkall (after Joseph Goupy). An engraved caricature by J. Vanderbank shows Senesino in a scene probably from Ariosti's *Coriolano*. Evidence of his death comes from the diary of the Florentine Nicolo Susier, who on 27 January 1759 noted that the death of 'Antonio [sic] Bernardi detto il Senesino' had been reported from Siena.

Senesino's quality as an artist may be estimated from the series of superb parts Handel composed for him. Of his 20 roles in Handel's operas, 17 were original: Muzio Scevola, Floridante, Ottone, Guido in *Flavio*, Julius Caesar, Andronico in *Tamerlano*, Bertarido in *Rodelinda*, Luceius in *Scipione* and the title roles in *Alessandro, Admeto, Riccardo Primo, Siroe, Tolomeo, Poro, Ezio, Sosarme* and *Orlando*. He also sang Radamisto, Arsace in *Partenope* and Rinaldo, with earlier music supplemented or transposed. His compass in Handel was narrow (*g* to *e″* at its widest, but the *g* appears very rarely, and many of his parts, especially in later years, do not go above *d″*), yet he was equally renowned for brilliant and taxing coloratura in heroic arias and expressive *mezza voce* in slow pieces. Johann Quantz's statement that he

had 'a low *mezzo-soprano* voice, which seldom went higher than *f‴*' probably refers to his earliest years. Although the impresario Francesco Zambeccari wrote slightingly in 1715 of his acting and delivery of recitative, in both respects he was regarded as outstanding in London. John Hawkins said that 'in the pronunciation of recitative [he] had not his fellow in Europe', and Charles Burney quoted the opinion of many who heard him that he was unsurpassed in the accompanied recitatives of *Giulio Cesare* and *Admeto*. According to the same writer his best style was 'pathetic, or majestic', but his 'articulate and voluminous voice' could bring off the most difficult divisions. Perhaps the best all-round judgment is that of Quantz:

He had a powerful, clear, equal and sweet contralto voice, with a perfect intonation and an excellent shake. His manner of singing was masterly and his elocution unrivalled. Though he never loaded Adagios with too many ornaments, yet he delivered the original and essential notes with the utmost refinement. He sang Allegros with great fire, and marked rapid divisions, from the chest, in an articulate and pleasing manner. His countenance was well adapted to the stage, and his action was natural and noble. To these qualities he joined a majestic figure.

His private character by all accounts was very different, marred by touchiness, insolence and an excess of professional vanity. His intrigues were largely responsible for the split with Handel in 1733. Early in 1724 he insulted ANASTASIA ROBINSON at a public rehearsal, 'for which Lord Peterborough publicly and violently caned him behind the scenes'.

Winton Dean

Sens, Genoveffa [Ginetta].

See CIGNA, GINA.

Sereni, Mario

(*b* Perugia, 25 March 1928). Italian baritone. He studied at the Accademia Musicale Chigiana in Siena and the Accademia di S Cecilia in Rome and privately with MARIO BASIOLA. His début was in 1953 at the Florence Maggio Musicale in Adriano Lualdi's *Il diavolo nel campanile*, and he went on to sing in Buenos Aires, Chicago, Mexico City, Milan, Naples, Palermo, Rome, Verona and Vienna. After his Metropolitan Opera début in 1957, as Gérard in *Andrea Chénier*, he became a mainstay of the company, singing over 380 performances of 26 roles. His robust but flexible voice allowed him to span the baritone repertory from the lyric to the dramatic. It can be heard most advantageously in recordings as Germont in CALLAS's Lisbon *La traviata* and as Sharpless in VICTORIA DE LOS ANGELES's second set of *Madama Butterfly*.

Cori Ellison/Alan Blyth

Serra, Luciana

(*b* Genoa, 4 Nov 1946). Italian soprano. She studied at the Genoa Conservatory and with Michele Casato, and made her début at Budapest in 1966 as Eleonora in Domenico Cimarosa's *Il convito* with the Italian Opera Giacosa company. She sang in Teheran, 1969–76, acquiring a repertory of coloratura and other roles including Susanna, Zerlina and the Queen of Night, as well as Adina, Lucia, Norina, Gilda and Violetta. Engagements following her return to Italy included Covent Garden (1980) as Olympia, and La Scala as Lucia; she was also especially admired as Amina. Her American début at Charleston as Violetta was followed by Lakmé with the Chicago Lyric Opera, and she has appeared in South America and South Africa. Her recordings include *I Capuleti e i Montecchi*, *Aureliano in Palmira* and *Fra Diavolo*, as well as the Queen of Night under Colin Davis (1985) and Norina under Bruno Campanella (1989). Her light, flexible voice serves well in lyric-coloratura music, and is accompanied by a spirited stage personality.

H. Canning: 'Luciana Serra, Covent Garden's Sleepwalker', *Classical Music* (3 July 1982), 11 [interview]

Noël Goodwin

Shalyapin, Fyodor.

See CHALIAPIN, FYODOR.

Sharp, Frederick (Charles)

(*b* Mansfield Woodhouse, Notts., 19 Oct 1911; *d* Tadworth, Surrey, 20 April 1988). English baritone. He studied in London at the RCM. He made his début in 1946 as Junius in *The Rape of Lucretia* at Glyndebourne, where the following year he created Sid in *Albert Herring* for the English Opera Group. He then joined Sadler's Wells Opera, where he remained until 1960, singing a large variety of roles that included Don Giovanni, Germont, Rigoletto, Scarpia, Paolo (*Simon Boccanegra*) and Yevgeny Onegin, his finest and most successful interpretation. Though his voice was not large, it was strongly projected, and he was an actor of fierce intensity.

Elizabeth Forbes

Shelton, Chad

(*b* Orange, TX, 22 Dec 1970). American tenor. He studied at the Louisiana State University and at Yale University's School of Music. He made his major operatic début at Houston in 1998, as Laurie in Mark Adamo's *Little Women*, a role he subsequently repeated for his New York City Opera début, and also recorded. His Australian Opera début was as Belmonte in *Die Entführung*, and his European début as Mitch in the European première of André Previn's *A Streetcar Named Desire* (Strasbourg, 2001). Admired for his warm, lyric timbre and his facility in high, florid writing, Shelton has sung many roles for Houston Grand Opera, including Ferrando (*Così fan tutte*), Charles Gounod's Romeo, Macduff, Alfredo (*La traviata*), Camille (*Die lustige Witwe*), Janek (*The Makropulos Affair*), Vere (*Billy Budd*) and Don José (*Carmen*), a part he first sang in 2006. At Houston he has also created the roles of Ulises in Daniel Catán's *Salsipuedes* (2004), and Niklas in Adamo's *Lystistrata* (2005). In 2005 he sang Tamino in Nancy, and in 2007 made his Opera Pacific début, as Don José.

Richard Wigmore

Sheridan [Burke Sheridan], Margaret

(*b* Castlebar, Co. Mayo, 15 Oct 1889; *d* Dublin, 16 April 1958). Irish soprano. She studied with William Shakespeare at the RAM in London (1909–11) and with Olga Lewenthal, and was much in demand at fashionable musical soirées. In 1916 she went to Rome to continue her studies with Alfredo Martino. Her début was in *La bohème* (Rome, 1918) and in 1919 she appeared at Covent Garden (Mimì, and Iris in the first London performance of Pietro Mascagni's opera). She returned there in 1925 and 1926, and from 1928 to 1930, but sang mostly in Italy at the leading theatres, including La Scala (1922–4). Vocal and other physical problems led to her retirement in 1930. Her voice was pure and colourful, naturally suited to the gentle and sentimental, but also passionate, music of Giacomo Puccini's heroines. A fine actress, she was outstanding as Manon, Cio-Cio-San and also as Madeleine in *Andrea Chénier*.

C. O'Brien, L. Lustig and A. Kelly: 'Margaret Burke Sheridan', *Record Collector*, xxxiii (1988), 187–213
A. Chambers: *La Sheridan: Adorable Diva* (Dublin, 1989) [incl. discography]

Rodolfo Celletti/Valeria Pregliasco Gualerzi

Shicoff, Neil

(*b* New York, 2 June 1949). American tenor. He studied at the Juilliard School, where he sang in Virgil Thomson's *Lord Byron* (1972). In 1975, after making his professional début in Washington DC, as Narraboth (*Salome*), he sang Ernani at Cincinnati and Paco (*La vida breve*) at Santa Fe. He made his Metropolitan début in 1976 as Rinuccio, later singing the Duke of Mantua, Lensky, Jules Massenet's Des Grieux, Werther, Hoffmann, Don Carlos, Faust and Cavaradossi (1991). Since making his Covent Garden début in 1978 as Pinkerton, he has sung Rodolfo (*La bohème*), Macduff, Alfredo, the Duke of Mantua and Hoffmann, one of his finest roles, which he has also sung in other major European houses. He has sung Werther, another favourite role, at Houston, Zürich, Vienna and Aix-en-Provence and made his début at Chicago (1979) as Rodolfo, at San Francisco (1981) as Edgardo (*Lucia*) and at the Paris Opéra (1981) as Charles Gounod's Romeo. His voice, at first essentially lyrical, has strengthened and darkened, enabling him to take on roles such as Don José, which he first sang at Seattle (1987) and performed at Covent Garden in 1994, Rodolfo (*Luisa Miller*) and Riccardo (*Un ballo in maschera*), which he sang at the Deutsche Oper, Berlin, in 1994. Shicoff's recordings include Macduff, the Duke of Mantua (a brilliant, debonair reading under Giuseppe Sinopoli) and Lensky.

G.D. Lipton: 'Playing to Win', *ON*, xlviii/9 (1983–4), 8

Richard Lesueur/Elizabeth Forbes

Shirley, George (Irving)

(*b* Indianapolis, IN, 18 April 1934). American tenor. He studied in Washington and New York, making his stage début in 1959 as Eisenstein at Woodstock, New York. In 1960 he sang Rodolfo at the Teatro Nuovo, Milan, and in 1961 made his New York City Opera and San Francisco débuts in the same role. At Spoleto he sang Herod (1961) and Don José (1962). In 1961 he also sang in Giuseppe Verdi's *Aroldo* (New York) and made his Metropolitan début as Ferrando; later roles there included Don Ottavio, Alfredo, Pinkerton, Romeo and Almaviva. At Santa Fe he sang Alwa in *Lulu* (1963), then Apollo in *Daphne* (1964) and Leandro in H.W. Henze's *König Hirsch* (1965), both American premières. Shirley made his British début at Glyndebourne in 1966 as Tamino, then sang Idomeneus (a role he recorded to acclaim) and Percy (*Anna Bolena*) there. Having made his Covent Garden début in 1967 as Don Ottavio, he returned for David (*Die Meistersinger*), Pelléas and Loge (an unusually sharp study, scornful and cynical), which he repeated in Berlin (1984). He created Romilayu in Leon Kirchner's *Lily* (1977, New York City Opera). He had an individual, bright-toned voice of considerable dramatic power and acted intelligently.

Alan Blyth

Shirley-Quirk, John

(*b* Liverpool, 28 Aug 1931). English bass-baritone. After teaching chemistry at a technical college, and studying with Roy Henderson, he turned to singing professionally and became a member of St Paul's Cathedral choir, 1961–2. He made his operatic début as the Doctor in *Pelléas et Mélisande* at Glyndebourne in 1962. He joined the English Opera Group in 1964 to create the part of the Ferryman in *Curlew River*, and then sang regularly with the company, creating other Britten roles, among them Shadrach in *The Burning Fiery Furnace* (1966), the Father in *The Prodigal Son* (1968) and all seven baritone roles in *Death in Venice* (1973). He was also the first Mr Coyle, a most compassionate study, in *Owen Wingrave* on television in 1971 and at Covent Garden in 1973. With Scottish Opera he sang Count Almaviva, Don Alfonso (also for the Glyndebourne touring company), Mittenhofer (*Elegy for Young Lovers*, 1970, Edinburgh Festival), Yevgeny Onegin and a saturnine Golaud. He made his Metropolitan Opera début in *Death in Venice* in 1974 and in 1977 created Lev in *The Ice Break* at Covent Garden. Shirley-Quirk's wide concert repertory ranged from Bach to Britten, and he was a fine interpreter of Friar Laurence in Hector Berlioz's *Roméo et Juliette* and the solos in Bach's Passions, G.F. Handel's oratorios, Joseph Haydn's *The Creation* and *The Seasons*, Johannes Brahms's *German Requiem*, *The Dream of Gerontius*, *Belshazzar's Feast* and Michael Tippett's *The Vision of St Augustine*. He was also a thoughtful, sympathetic interpreter of lieder, *mélodies* and English song. As his numerous recordings reveal, his work was distinguished by a peculiar intensity of expression, refined phrasing and mellow, well-focussed tone. He was made a CBE in 1975 and in 1982 became an associate artistic director of the Aldeburgh Festival.

Alan Blyth

Shore, Andrew

(*b* Oldham, 30 Sept 1952). English baritone. He studied at the RNCM and the London Opera Centre, then sang with Opera for All and various university groups. With Kent Opera (1981–7) he gave notable performances as Antonio (*Le nozze di Figaro*) and Gioachino Rossini's Bartolo, while for Opera North he has sung such roles as King Dodon (*The Golden Cockerel*), Mr Flint (*Billy Budd*), Gianni Schicchi, Leander (*The Love for Three Oranges*), Varlaam, Don Pasquale, Don Jerome (in the first British staging of Roberto Gerhard's *Duenna*, 1992), Geronimo (*Il matrimonio segreto*) and Wozzeck. Shore's ENO roles have included Doeg in the UK première of Philip Glass's *The Making of the Representative for Planet 8* (1988), King Priam, Don Alfonso, Dulcamara, Gianni Schicchi, Šiškov (*From the House of the Dead*) and Falstaff, which he also sang at Glyndebourne (1990). He made his Covent Garden début (1992) as Trombonok (*Il viaggio a Reims*) and his US début as Dulcamara (*L'elisir d'amore*) in San Diego. He has also appeared with Scottish Opera, the WNO, New Israeli Opera and at the Opéra Bastille, Paris, as the Sacristan in *Tosca*. His other roles include Bottom (*A Midsummer Night's Dream*) and Dr Kolenatý (*The Makropulos Affair*). A superb comedian, with a strong, flexible voice, Shore particularly excels as Falstaff and as Gioachino Rossini's Dr Bartolo, a role he has sung throughout Britain and in Canada and has recorded. He has also been admired for his subtlety and dramatic intensity in tragic parts, above all King Priam and Wozzeck.

Elizabeth Forbes

Shuard, Amy

(*b* London, 19 July 1924; *d* London, 18 April 1975). English soprano. She studied at Trinity College of Music, London, and later with EVA TURNER. After singing Aida, Venus and Giulietta (*Les contes d'Hoffmann*) in Johannesburg, in 1949 she joined the Sadler's Wells Opera, remaining there until 1955, and singing the title role of *Kát'a Kabanová* in the British première in 1951. Her repertory also included Magda Sorel (*The Consul*), Carmen, Eboli, Tàtyana and Tosca. In 1954 she joined Covent Garden Opera, where she distinguished herself first in the Italian repertory as Aida, Turandot (a thrilling portrayal) and Lady Macbeth in the first production there of Giuseppe Verdi's *Macbeth*, then in the German repertory as Sieglinde, Brünnhilde, Kundry and Electra. She sang the title role in *Jenůfa* in the opera's first stage production in Britain in 1956, and the Kostelnička in its 1972 and 1974 revivals. She sang Isolde in Geneva in 1972, and also appeared in Bayreuth, Vienna, Buenos Aires, San Francisco and Milan. Shuard had a bright, gleaming tone and sang with dramatic awareness, as can be heard on a Verdi and Puccini recital recording made under Edward Downes at the height of her career.

H. Rosenthal: 'Amy Shuard', *Opera*, xi (1960), 257–62

Harold Rosenthal/Alan Blyth

Sibiryakov, Lev (Mikhailovich)

(*b* St Petersburg, 1869; *d* Antwerp, Oct 1942). Russian bass. He studied in Milan and made some guest appearances in Italy before returning to Russia,

where he made his début in 1895. Singing first in the provinces, he established himself as a leading bass at the Mariinsky Theatre in St Petersburg, where his roles included Wotan, made remarkable by his ability to 'penetrate any orchestral forte without forcing, becoming an element of the orchestral sound' (Sergei Levik, *Memoirs*). He sang Don Basilio in *Barbiere* (in Russian) with the Boston Opera Company in 1910 and Marcel in *Les Huguenots* at Covent Garden in 1911. Back in Russia, he continued for some years, leaving for Western Europe after the Revolution. In 1932 he sang in *Aida* and *La favorite* at Monte Carlo and made a final appearance in the title role of *Boris Godunov* at Brussels in 1938. At 6' 6" tall and with a voice of proportionate volume, he was often compared with CHALIAPIN. Recordings show a deep-toned voice with an extensive upper range and remarkable control throughout, though for power of vocal characterization he can hardly approach his great contemporary.

J.B. Steane

Siehr, Gustav

(*b* Arnsberg, Westphalia, 17 Sept 1837; *d* Munich, 18 May 1896). German bass. He studied in Berlin, making his début in 1863 at Neustrelitz as Oroveso in Vincenzo Bellini's *Norma*. After singing in Göteborg, Prague and Wiesbaden, in 1881 he was engaged at the Munich Hofoper, where he remained until his death. At Bayreuth he sang Hagen in the first *Ring* cycle (1876), Gurnemanz in *Parsifal* (1882–9) and King Mark in *Tristan und Isolde* (1886). His wide repertory included W.A. Mozart (Sarastro and the Commendatore), Carl Maria von Weber (Caspar in *Der Freischütz*), Giacomo Meyerbeer (Bertram in *Robert le diable*) and other Wagner roles.

Elizabeth Forbes

Siemonn, Mabel.

See GARRISON, MABEL.

Siems, Margarethe

(*b* Breslau [now Wrocław], 30 Dec 1879; *d* Dresden, 13 April 1952). German soprano. She studied with Anna Maria Orgeni, a pupil of PAULINE VIARDOT, and with MATHILDE MARCHESI. She was engaged for the Prague Maifestspiele in 1902, when she sang Marguerite de Valois, and that autumn joined the Neues Deutsches Theater, Prague. In 1908 she became principal dramatic coloratura soprano at Dresden, where she sang until 1920, creating

Chrysothemis (1909) and the Marschallin (1911); she also created Zerbinetta (1912, Stuttgart). In 1913 she made her Covent Garden début as the Marschallin in the first London performance of *Der Rosenkavalier*. Siems was an extraordinarily versatile singer and actress. Her repertory included the coloratura soprano roles of Vincenzo Bellini, Gaetano Donizetti and Giacomo Meyerbeer, as well as the Queen of Night; she successfully undertook the heavier Verdi parts (Leonora, Amelia and Aida) and Wagnerian roles such as Venus and Elisabeth (she often sang both on the same evening), and even Isolde. Richard Strauss considered her the ideal Marschallin, and her portrayal of this role is, partially, preserved on disc. She made a number of other recordings, which show her charming manner and excellent technique.

P. Wilhelm: 'Margarethe Siems', *Record News* [Toronto], ii (1957–8), 421–7 [with discography]

Harold Rosenthal/Alan Blyth

Siepi, Cesare

(*b* Milan, 10 Feb 1923). Italian bass. After private vocal studies, he made his début as Sparafucile at Schio near Vicenza in 1941. The war interrupted a career that he resumed in 1945 in Verona and 1946 at La Scala, singing Zaccaria in *Nabucco* on both occasions. He appeared at Covent Garden during the Scala company's visit in 1950 and that autumn he opened Rudolf Bing's first Metropolitan Opera season as Philip II in *Don Carlos*. A member of the Metropolitan for 24 years, he performed the major *basso cantante* roles of the Italian repertory as well as Méphistophélès in *Faust*, Boris Godunov and Gurnemanz in *Parsifal*. He was especially admired for his Mozart roles, particularly Figaro, and Don Giovanni (which he sang in Salzburg in 1953 under Wilhelm Furtwängler and at Covent Garden in 1962 under Georg Solti). Like his predecessor, EZIO PINZA, he also attempted a Broadway musical comedy (*Bravo, Giovanni!*, 1962) but with little success. With a strikingly handsome physical presence on stage, and a pleasantly warm, pliant, evenly schooled voice, Siepi could always be relied on for musically polished, dramatically striking interpretations that were consistently satisfying if not always of great individuality. He recorded many of his major operatic roles, from Figaro and Don Giovanni to Padre Guardiano, Arrigo Boito's Mefistofele and Baron Archibaldo in *L'amore dei tre re*.

Peter G. Davis

Silja, Anja

(*b* Berlin, 17 April 1940). German soprano. She studied with her grandfather, Egon van Rijn, making her début in 1955 as Rosina at Brunswick, where her roles included Micaëla, Zerbinetta and Leonora (*Il trovatore*). In 1959 she sang the Queen of Night at the Aix-en-Provence Festival. In 1960 Wieland Wagner engaged her for Bayreuth as Senta; during the next seven years (as Elsa, Elisabeth, Eva, Freia and Venus) she became the most controversial singing actress at postwar Bayreuth. Her close personal and professional association with Wieland Wagner continued at Brussels, Cologne, Stuttgart and Frankfurt, where she sang Isolde, Brünnhilde, Leonore, Lulu, Marie (*Wozzeck*), Renata (*The Fiery Angel*), Kát'a, Desdemona, Salome and Electra. The overt sexuality of many of these interpretations, especially of Lulu and Salome, frequently shocked audiences. She made her London début at Sadler's Wells (1963) with the Frankfurt Opera in *Fidelio*, which she also sang at her Covent Garden début in 1967; other Covent Garden roles included Cassandra (*Les Troyens*) and Marie. She made her American début as Salome in San Francisco (1968). At the Metropolitan (1972) she sang Leonore and Salome. Engaged at the Hamburg Staatsoper from 1974 to 1984, she created Luise (Gottfried von Einem's *Kabale und Liebe*) in Vienna (1976). She sang Regan (Aribert Reimann's *Lear*) at San Francisco (1985), Emilia Marty (*The Makropulos Affair*) at Boston (1986), Lady Macbeth (1987) and Grete (*Der ferne Klang*) at Brussels (1988). At Glyndebourne she has sung the Kostelnička in *Jenůfa* (1989, returning in 2000) and Emilia Marty (1995 and 2001), towering interpretations that have been recorded on video. In recent years, too, she has scored notable successes as Herodias and Countess Gershwitz (*Lulu*). She sang Kostelnička at the Met and at La Scala in 2007. Silja is a performer of great magnetism, whose wholehearted stage portrayals are sung in a voice of arresting and individual timbre.

W. Schwinger: 'Anja Silja', *Opera*, xx (1969), 193–8

Harold Rosenthal/Alan Blyth

Sills, Beverly [Silverman, Belle]

(*b* Brooklyn, NY, 25 May 1929; *d* New York, 2 July 2007). American soprano and opera director. Her first singing appearance was at the age of three on commercial radio. When she was 11 she began serious vocal studies with ESTELLE LIEBLING and she made her operatic début as Frasquita with the Philadelphia Civic Grand Opera Company in 1947. For a few years she worked with touring opera companies, gave lieder recitals in the Midwest, and sang with the San Francisco Opera. In 1955 she joined the New York City Opera and became the company's diva; but her full stature was not recognized

Beverly Sills as Pamira in 'Le siège de Corinthe' (Rossini), Metropolitan Opera, New York, 1975

until 1966 when she sang Cleopatra in G.F. Handel's *Giulio Cesare*. Her sensational success in this florid role (which she recorded) led to a series of bel canto revivals at the City Opera, including Gaetano Donizetti's trio of Tudor queens, *Maria Stuarda*, *Anna Bolena* and Elizabeth in *Roberto Devereux*. Appearances in major European opera houses quickly followed, including the Queen of Night at Vienna (1967), Gioachino Rossini's *Le siège de Corinthe* at La Scala (1969) and *Lucia di Lammermoor* at Covent Garden (1970). Her Metropolitan Opera début, as Pamira in a new production of *Le siège de Corinthe*, was in 1975. She was general director of the New York City Opera from 1979 to 1989, and became chairman of the board of Lincoln Center for the Performing Arts in 1993.

Although a singer of secure and often brilliant technical accomplishment, Sills lacked the dramatic weight of a CALLAS or the sheer tonal beauty of CABALLÉ and SUTHERLAND, her principal rivals in this repertory. As a consequence the lighter, less dramatically commanding bel canto roles such as Lucia and Elvira (*I puritani*) seemed more suited to her voice and temperament. An excellent actress with an ingratiating and warm stage personality, she perhaps found her most congenial part in Jules Massenet's Manon, of which she made a delightful recording. In 1980 she received the Presidential Medal of Freedom, and in 1985 a Kennedy Center Honor.

W. Sargeant: 'Beverly Sills', *Divas* (New York, 1973), 77–103

J.B. Steane: *The Grand Tradition* (London, 1974/R), 401–6

R. Jacobson: 'At Long Last!: on the Occasion of her Met Debut Beverly Sills talks with Robert Jacobson', *ON*, xxxix/21 (1974–5), 54

B. Sills: *Bubbles: a Self-Portrait* (New York, 1976, 2/1981 as
Bubbles: an Encore)

B. Sills: *Beverly: an Autobiography* (New York, 1987)

Peter G. Davis

Silveri, Paolo

(*b* Ofena, nr Aquila, 28 Dec 1913). Italian baritone. He studied in Florence and Rome, where he
made his début as a bass in 1939 as Hans Schwarz
(*Meistersinger*). He retrained as a baritone, and in
1944 sang Germont in Rome. He made his London
début at Covent Garden with the S Carlo company in 1946 as Marcello, and then appeared with
the Covent Garden Opera, 1947–9, as Rigoletto,
Escamillo and Boris (in English), returning in 1950
to sing Ford and Iago with the Scala company. In
1948 he appeared at the Edinburgh Festival as
Don Giovanni, returning the following year as
Renato (*Ballo*); from 1950 to 1953 he sang at the
Metropolitan Opera. In 1959 he sang the title role
in Giuseppe Verdi's *Otello* (a tenor part) in Dublin,
but in 1960 reverted to baritone roles. He retired
in 1967. He was gifted with a fine stage presence,
and his virile, resonant voice was especially impressive in Verdi. In his later years he tended to sacrifice
delicacy and precision to mere volume.

Harold Rosenthal/R

Simándy, József

(*b* Budapest, 18 Sept 1916). Hungarian tenor. He
studied with Emilia Posszert, joining the Hungarian
State Opera House chorus in 1940. He made his
début at the Szeged National Theatre in 1946 as
Don José. The following year he returned to the
Budapest Opera, and was its leading heroic tenor
until 1984. Between 1956 and 1960 he was a regular performer in Munich. Although he undertook a wide range of lyric and spinto tenor roles,
Simándy was, in dramatic and vocal character, best
suited to heroic roles, notably Radames, Otello and
Lohengrin. His recordings include the title roles in
Ferenc Erkel's *Bánk bán* and *Hunyadi László*.

Péter P. Várnai

Simionato, Giulietta

(*b* Forlì, 12 May or 15 Dec 1910). Italian mezzo-
soprano. She studied at Rovigo with Ettore Locatello
and Guido Palumbo. She made her début in 1935
in the première of Ildebrando Pizzetti's *Orsèolo* at
Florence and first sang at La Scala in 1939 as Beppe
(*L'amico Fritz*). During the next few years she sang
Cherubino, Rosina, Hänsel, Dorabella and Mignon.

From 1946 she appeared regularly at La Scala,
where her repertory included Charlotte (*Werther*),
Jane Seymour (*Anna Bolena*), Cenerentola, Isabella
(*L'italiana in Algeri*), Carmen, Asteria (*Nerone*) and
Léonor. She made her British début as Cherubino
at the 1947 Edinburgh Festival; she first sang at
Covent Garden in 1953 as Adalgisa, Amneris and
Azucena. In 1954 she sang Romeo (*I Capuleti e
i Montecchi*) in Palermo and made her American
début at Chicago. She sang at Salzburg (1957–63)
as Mistress Quickly, Eboli, Orpheus and Azucena
and at the Metropolitan from 1959 to 1963. In 1962
she sang Valentine at La Scala. She retired in 1966.
Simionato's agile mezzo was secure throughout its
wide range, with a personal and seductive timbre in
its lower register. Among her recordings are notable accounts of Amneris and Azucena. She had an
imposing stage presence, vivacious in comedy, dignified and moving in tragedy.

I. Kolodin: 'Great Artists of our Time: Giulietta Simionato',
HiFi, xi (1959), 37

G. Gualerzi: 'Giulietta Simionato', *Opera*, xv (1964), 87–92

L. Rasponi: *The Last Prima Donnas* (New York, 1982),
377–85

Harold Rosenthal/Alan Blyth

Simon, Ingeborg.

See BORKH, INGE.

Simoneau, Léopold

(*b* Saint-Flavien, Quebec, 3 May 1916; *d* Victoria,
BC, 24 Aug 2006). Canadian tenor. He studied in
Montreal with Salvator Issaurel, and made his début
there in 1941 as Hadji in *Lakmé* with the Variétés
Lyriques. After successful appearances in *Così fan
tutte* and *Die Zauberflöte*, he studied in New York
with PAUL ALTHOUSE. He made his Opéra-Comique
début in 1949, in *Mireille*, and remained in Paris for
five seasons. His reputation as a Mozart specialist,
elegantly lyrical in style, was first established at the
Aix-en-Provence and (from 1951) Glyndebourne
festivals, where he sang Idamantes and Don Ottavio.
He sang in Mozart operas at La Scala (1953), in
London with the Vienna Staatsoper (1954), at the
Teatro Colón, at the Salzburg Festival (1956) and
with the Metropolitan (début 1963 as Don Ottavio).
He made admired recordings of all his major Mozart
roles. Simoneau was Tom in the French première of
The Rake's Progress, at the Opéra-Comique in 1953.
Other roles included C.W. Gluck's Orpheus and
Georges Bizet's Nadir, both of which he recorded.
In 1946 he married the soprano PIERRETTE ALARIE
with whom he often appeared. He played a leading

part in forming the first statutory subsidized opera company in North America, the Opéra du Québec (1971), of which he was initially artistic director. He taught in Quebec, San Francisco, Banff and Victoria, British Columbia, where he founded Canada Opera Piccola in 1982; he was director of the company until 1988. His translation of Reynaldo Hahn's *Du chant* was published in Portland, Oregon, in 1990.

R. Maheu: *Pierrette Alarie, Leopold Simoneau, deux voix, un art* (Montreal, 1988)

Gilles Potvin

Sinclair, John

(*b* nr Edinburgh, 9 Dec 1791; *d* Margate, 23 Sept 1857). Scottish tenor. Having studied music as a child, he joined Campbell of Shawfield's regiment as a clarinettist. He also taught singing in Aberdeen, saving enough money to buy his discharge from the regiment. His first, anonymous, stage appearance was as Captain Cheerly in William Shield's *Lock and Key* at the Haymarket Theatre, 7 September 1810. He was then engaged at Covent Garden, where he appeared on 20 September 1811 as Don Carlos in Richard Brinsley Sheridan and Thomas Linley's *The Duenna*. He remained there for several seasons, creating the tenor roles in Henry Bishop's *Guy Mannering* and *The Slave* (1816), among other works. In April 1819 Sinclair studied in Paris with VALERIANO PELLEGRINI, and subsequently in Milan, with Davide Banderali. He also had some instruction from Gioachino Rossini in Naples in 1821. In 1822 he sang, mostly in Rossini's operas, in Pisa, Bologna, Modena and Florence. In 1823 he was engaged for Venice, and Rossini wrote the part of Idreno in *Semiramide* for him. After singing at Genoa, he returned to England and reappeared at Covent Garden on 19 November 1823 as Prince Orlando in Charles Dibdin's *The Cabinet*, meeting an enthusiastic audience but critical reviews. In 1828–9 he was engaged at the Adelphi, in 1829–30 at Drury Lane. He visited the USA in 1830, and then retired from the stage, becoming director of the Tivoli Gardens, Margate. Sinclair composed a number of songs. In Italy, where he sometimes appeared as Saint-Clair or St-Clair, his technique was said to be remarkable, especially in runs.

W.H. Husk/John Warrack

Sinclair, Monica

(*b* Evercreech, Somerset, 23 March 1925; *d* London, 7 May 2002). English contralto. She studied at the Royal Academy and Royal College of Music in London and joined the Carl Rosa Company in 1948,

making her début as Suzuki in *Madama Butterfly*. This was also her first major role at Covent Garden, where from 1949 to 1967 she was heard in a wide variety of roles including Azucena, Cherubino and Pauline (*The Queen of Spades*). In 1952 she sang Margret in the English stage première of *Wozzeck*, and in 1953 created the role of Frances, Countess of Essex, in Benjamin Britten's *Gloriana*. The following year she created Evadne in William Walton's *Troilus and Cressida*. From 1954 to 1960 she was a favourite at Glyndebourne, especially as Ragonde in *Le comte Ory* and Marcellina in *Le nozze di Figaro*. She was an asset in comic operas and crowned the latter part of her career with appearances at the Metropolitan as the Marquise in *La fille du régiment*. This was with JOAN SUTHERLAND and Richard Bonynge, in whose revivals of Baroque and early-19th-century opera she played a prominent part. She developed exceptional fluency over a wide range, which in combination with her powerful and penetrating tone proved valuable in the productions of *Alcina* at Covent Garden and Venice, in which she sang Bradamante. She also appeared regularly with the Handel Opera Society in London. In 1955 she sang the title role of Jean-Baptiste Lully's *Armide* in Bordeaux, and in the 1960s toured Australia with a company headed by Sutherland. Her recordings include *Alcina* and *La fille du régiment* and some very effective performances as the gorgon-contralto in Gilbert and Sullivan.

J.B. Steane

Singher, Martial (Jean-Paul)

(*b* Oloron Ste Marie, Pyrénées-Atlantiques, 14 Aug 1904; *d* Santa Barbara, CA, 9 March 1990). American baritone of French birth. He studied at the Ecole Normale Supérieure de St Cloud (1925–7) and with ANDRÉ GRESSE at the Paris Conservatoire (1927–30), where he won *premiers prix* in both opera and *opéra-comique* singing. He continued his studies with Juliette Fourestier and in November 1930 made his début in Amsterdam as Orestes in *Iphigénie en Tauride* under Pierre Monteux. He first sang at the Opéra a month later, as Athanaël in *Thaïs*, and remained a principal baritone of that company as well as singing at the Opéra-Comique. At Paris his roles included Richard Wagner's Dutchman, Telramund and Gunther, much Giuseppe Verdi, Ambroise Thomas' Hamlet and Gioachino Rossini's Figaro.

Singher settled in the USA and made his Metropolitan début in 1943 as Dapertutto in *Les contes d'Hoffmann*. He continued as a member of the Metropolitan until 1959, singing Pelléas, Count Almaviva and Figaro in *Figaro*, all four baritone roles in *Hoffmann*, Lescaut in *Manon* and Mercutio in *Roméo et Juliette*, Wolfram and Amfortas. He was the first to sing Maurice Ravel's song cycle *Don Quichotte à Dulcinée* (which he recorded). The lean, clearly focussed, rather dry timbre of his voice was not one of great natural beauty, but he was a fastidious musician and an elegant interpreter, particularly of French music. After he retired from the stage, he was head of the voice department at the Curtis Institute in Philadelphia, then of the voice and opera departments at the Music Academy of the West, Santa Barbara, California (1962–81). Among his pupils were JAMES KING, DONALD GRAMM, JOHN REARDON, LOUIS QUILICO, BENITA VALENTE, JUDITH BLEGEN and JEANNINE ALTMEYER.

Peter G. Davis, Dennis K. McIntire

Sinimberghi, Gino

(*b* Rome, 26 Aug 1913; *d* Rome, 29 Dec 1996). Italian tenor. He studied in Rome and was engaged at the Berlin Staatsoper from 1937 to 1944, then returned to Italy, where he continued to appear until 1968. He sang Ismaele (*Nabucco*) at S Carlo in 1949 with CALLAS; in Rome he sang Grits'ko (*The Fair at Sorochintsï*), Sobinin (*A Life for the Tsar*) and Don Ramiro (*La Cenerentola*), also taking part in the Italian première of Paul Hindemith's *The Long Christmas Dinner* (1962). His other roles included Števa (*Jenůfa*), Herod and Aegisthus. When his originally light, lyrical voice darkened, he became a character tenor of some distinction.

Elizabeth Forbes

Sisout, Georgette-Amélie.

See BRÉJEAN-SILVER, GEORGETTE.

Skovhus, Boje [Bo]

(*b* Århus, 22 May 1962). Danish baritone. After studying at the Copenhagen Opera Academy, he made his début as Don Giovanni at the Vienna Volksoper in 1988. He became an instant favourite in that city, and the role of Giovanni remained central to his repertory, the strong, bright voice being matched by a handsome and athletic stage presence. He first appeared at the Vienna Staatsoper in 1991 and within the next few years became well known in the leading German houses, adding such roles as Wolfram (*Tannhäuser*), Olivier (*Capriccio*), the Count in *Der Wildschütz* and W.A. Mozart's Count Almaviva (which he has recorded with Claudio Abbado). At Cologne in 1993 he sang the title role in *Billy Budd*, introducing himself to a wider audi-

ence that same year in a recording of Benjamin Britten's *War Requiem*. Copenhagen honoured him with a production of Ambroise Thomas' *Hamlet* in 1995. He made his Covent Garden début as Guglielmo in 1997 and his Metropolitan Opera début as Eisenstein (*Die Fledermaus*) in 1998. The same year he was admired for his subtly coloured Wozzeck in Hamburg, his début in the role. In 2000 he sang another new role, Yeletsky in *The Queen of Spades*, at the Lyric Opera of Chicago. As a lieder singer Skovhus impressed strongly with his first Hugo Wolf recordings, but his command of the gentler emotions and of a true legato has sometimes been found defective. His wide concert repertory includes such works as Alexander Zemlinsky's *Lyrische Symphonie* and Luciano Berio's arrangements of songs by Gustav Mahler.

J.B. Steane/R

Slavina, Mariya

(*b* St Petersburg, 24 May/5 June 1858; *d* Paris, 1951). Russian mezzo-soprano. She studied at the St Petersburg Conservatory with Natalia Iretzkaya and Camillo Everardi. In 1879 she made her début as Amneris at the Mariinsky Theatre, St Petersburg, where she later created the roles of Hanna in Nikolay Rimsky-Korsakov's *May Night* (1880), Konchakovna in *Prince Igor* (1890), the Countess in *The Queen of Spades* (1890) and Clytemnestra in S.I. Taneyev's *Oresteia* (1895). Her best role was Carmen, which she introduced to Russian audiences, and she was a notable Olga (*Yevgeny Onegin*), Fidès (*Le prophète*), Ortrud, Fricka and Waltraute. She left Russia at the time of the Revolution and taught singing in Paris.

David Cummings

Slezak, Leo

(*b* Mährisch-Schönberg [now Šumperk], Moravia, 18 Aug 1873; *d* Egern am Tegernsee, Germany, 1 June 1946). Austrian-Czech tenor. Discovered and trained by the well-known baritone and teacher Adolf Robinson, he made a promising début at Brno on 17 March 1896, as Lohengrin. His early career was somewhat chequered; and his Covent Garden début, again as Lohengrin, on 18 May 1900, was ruined by the pandemonium aroused by the war news of the relief of Mafeking in South Africa. By contrast, his career in Vienna, whither he was called by Gustav Mahler in 1901, was brilliant and prolonged; he remained one of the leading tenors of the house until the mid-1920s, and subsequently made occasional guest appearances until a final *Pagliacci* in 1933. During the interim Slezak had become internationally famous, especially after a period of study with JEAN DE RESZKE in 1907. A marked improvement was noted on his reappearance at Covent Garden in 1909, when he sang Otello with robust power and beauty of tone. That autumn he made his first appearance at the Metropolitan Opera as Otello, to still greater acclaim; he remained with the company for four consecutive seasons, singing, among other parts, his main Wagner roles (Tannhäuser, Lohengrin, Walther), Giuseppe Verdi's Manrico and Radames, and P.I. Tchaikovsky's Hermann, and frequently appearing under the direction of Arturo Toscanini and Gustav Mahler. In later years he became well known as an interpreter of lieder, and later still made a new career for himself in 'comic uncle' roles in German and Austrian films. His irrepressible sense of fun comes out in his several autobiographical books; a similar volume by his son, the actor Walter Slezak, called *What Time's the Next Swan?* (New York, 1962), alludes to the tenor's celebrated stage whisper on an occasion when the swan in *Lohengrin* began to move off before he had stepped aboard. Such anecdotes, together with his immense stature and ample girth, might suggest that Slezak was more of a 'character' than a serious artist. But the verdict of the New York critics during his seasons there, as well as numerous recordings made over a period of 30 years, prove the contrary. There were certain flaws in his technique, but at his best he combined great warmth and brilliance of tone with clear enunciation and a most delicate use of *mezza voce*. His lieder recordings are intensely expressive, but verge on the sentimental.

L. Slezak: *Song of Motley: being the Reminiscences of a Hungry Tenor* (London, 1938/R)
J. Dennis: 'Leo Slezak', *Record Collector*, xv (1963–4), 197–235 [with discography by T.G. Kaufman]

Desmond Shawe-Taylor/R

Slobodskaya, Oda

(*b* Vilna [now Vilnius], 28 Nov 1888; *d* London, 29 July 1970). Russian soprano. She studied at the St Petersburg Conservatory and joined the company of the Mariinsky Theatre, where she made her début in 1919 as Lisa in *The Queen of Spades*. During the following years she sang most of the principal soprano parts of the Russian repertory and appeared also as Sieglinde, Marguerite (*Faust*), Elisabeth de Valois and Aida. In 1922 she was invited to sing the part of Parasha in the first performance of Igor Stravinsky's *Mavra* in Paris; and thenceforward she began to make extensive appearances outside Russia. She sang Fevroniya in Nikolay Rimsky-Korsakov's *Legend*

of the Invisible City of Kitezh in Italian at La Scala in 1933, and in 1936 took part in a Russian season at the Teatro Colón, Buenos Aires. In London she sang Venus in *Tannhäuser* (1932, Covent Garden); Natasha in Alexander Dargomïzhsky's *Rusalka*, with CHALIAPIN (1931, Lyceum); Palmyra in Thomas Beecham's production of Frederick Delius's *Koanga* (1935, Covent Garden); and Khivrya in Modest Musorgsky's *Fair at Sorochintsï* at the Savoy and on an English tour, in 1941 and subsequent years. By then Slobodskaya had made her home in England, where she was much in demand by the BBC, both for concert performances of opera (notably as the heroine of Dmitry Shostakovich's *Lady Macbeth of the Mtsensk District*) and for recitals of Russian song. She possessed the imagination and the vivid temperament to convey to an audience ignorant of Russian the precise mood of each song, whether elegiac, boisterous, satirical or childlike. As her many recordings reveal, these rare interpretative powers were matched by a beautiful and ample voice of characteristically Slavonic colour and by a technical mastery which showed itself especially in supple and sustained legato phrasing. Slobodskaya retained her vocal and interpretative powers to an advanced age, making records as late as 1962.

O. Slobodskaya (as told to G. Eves): 'Reminiscences', *Recorded Sound*, xxxv (1969), 495–511 [with discography by H. Barnes and S. Junge]
M. Leonard: *Slobodskaya: a Biography of Oda Slobodskaya* (London, 1979) [with discography]

Desmond Shawe-Taylor

Smirnov, Dmitry (Alekseyevich)

(*b* Moscow, 7/19 Nov 1882; *d* Riga, 27 April 1944). Russian tenor. He studied with EMILIYA PAVLOVSKAYA and apparently in Milan. He made his début as Gigi in the first performance of Michele Esposito's *Camorra* at the Hermitage Theatre, Moscow, in 1903. After a trial début as Sinodal in Anton Rubinstein's *The Demon*, he sang at the Bol'shoy (1904–10), where he created Dante in Serge Rachmaninoff's *Francesca da Rimini* (1906). From 1910 until 1917 he was a member of the Imperial Opera, St Petersburg. He often sang in western Europe (in the Sergey Diaghilev seasons at Paris, and in Monte Carlo, Brussels, Madrid, Barcelona), and appeared at the Metropolitan (1910–12, début as the Duke in *Rigoletto*). In 1911 he sang in *Lakmé* with the Boston Opera Company and toured Latin America. He took part in Thomas Beecham's Drury Lane Russian opera productions in summer 1914. After 1919 he sang widely in Paris, Brussels and London. Besides his large French and Italian repertory, he sang many Russian roles, including Lensky, Grigory (*Boris*), Levko (*May Night*) and Lohengrin. He made approximately 90 recordings, which reveal the peculiar plangency of his tone allied to an instinctive sense of the right style for the music in hand.

J. Stratton: 'Dmitri Smirnoff', *Record Collector*, xiv (1961–2), 245–77 [with discography]

Harold Barnes/Alan Blyth

Smith, Jennifer (Mary)

(*b* Lisbon, 13 July 1945). British soprano. She studied in Lisbon and made her operatic début there as the Voice from Heaven in *Don Carlos* in 1968. In 1971 she moved to London where she had further tuition from Winifred Radford and PIERRE BERNAC. Her roles include W.A. Mozart's Countess Almaviva (1979, WNO) and Amyntas in *Il re pastore* (1987, Lisbon), and Jean-Philippe Rameau's Alphise in the stage première of *Les Boréades* (1982, Aix-en-Provence); she made her American début as Cybele in Jean-Baptiste Lully's *Atys* in New York in 1988. Other parts include C.W. Gluck's Eurydice and Rameau's Folly (*Platée*). She has also appeared with Scottish Opera and Kent Opera, and in 1991 sang the Queen of Night in Toronto and Reine Berthe/La Vieille (Egidio Duni's *La fée Urgèle*) at the Opéra-Comique. In 1998 she sang the title role in Domènech Terradellas's *Artaserse* in Barcelona. Smith is a versatile artist, able on the one hand to bring grandeur and pathos to her interpretations and on the other to sustain light-hearted, comic and mischievous roles, as she has demonstrated in *Platée*. An admired concert singer with a wide repertory, Smith has recorded mainly the Baroque choral and operatic repertory for which she is best known, notably works by Henry Purcell, G.F. Handel, J.S. Bach and Rameau.

Nicholas Anderson

Sobinov, Leonid Vital'yevich

(*b* Yaroslavlý, 26 May/7 June 1872; *d* Riga, 14 Oct 1934). Russian tenor. After embarking on a law career he studied singing in Moscow, where he made his operatic début in small roles with a visiting Italian troupe (1893–4). He sang at the Bol'shoy from 1897, then with private opera companies and at the Moscow and St Petersburg imperial theatres, at La Scala where, in 1904, he sang in a notable revival of *Don Pasquale* (1903–1905, 1911), Monte Carlo and Berlin (1905) and Madrid (1908). He made numerous appearances throughout Russia. He was

much admired for Lensky (*Yevgeny Onegin*), Sinodal (Anton Rubinstein's *Demon*, his Bol'shoy début role), Dubrovsky (in Eduard Nápravník's opera), Vladimir (*Prince Igor*), Berendey (*Snow Maiden*), Levko (*May Night*), Werther, Faust, Romeo, Des Grieux (*Manon*), Ernesto (*Don Pasquale*), the Duke of Mantua, Alfredo (*La traviata*), Lohengrin and Orpheus (C.W. Gluck). Even after he left the stage (1924), he was active at the Bol'shoy in various capacities. He had a profoundly poetic approach to his roles and studied every aspect of them in detail. His attractive stage presence and his even, expressive voice endeared him to a vast public. He made 66 recordings between 1901 and 1910, which reveal a well-placed lyric tenor voice used with the utmost sensitivity; the elegiac quality of his Lensky has been matched by few. Two volumes of his letters, articles, speeches and reminiscences were published, with a discography, in Moscow in 1970.

M. Scott: *The Record of Singing*, i (London, 1977), 217–18

Harold Barnes/Alan Blyth

Söderström(-Olow), (Anna) Elisabeth

(*b* Stockholm, 7 May 1927). Swedish soprano. Trained at the Royal Academy of Music and Opera School in Stockholm, she made her début as W.A. Mozart's Bastienne in the Drottningholm Court Theatre in May 1947. She joined, and remained a member of, the Swedish Royal Opera; she also pursued an international career in a wide variety of roles ranging from Nero in Claudio Monteverdi's *L'incoronazione di Poppea*, through Mozart's Countess Almaviva and Susanna, P.I. Tchaikovsky's Tatyana, Richard Strauss's Octavian, Christine and Marschallin, Claude Debussy's Mélisande, Benjamin Britten's Ellen Orford and Governess, to Leoš Janáček's Jenůfa, Kát'a Kabanová and Emilia Marty. Her recordings of these Janáček roles with Charles Mackerras remain among her finest achievements. She made her Glyndebourne début in 1957, as the Composer in Strauss's *Ariadne auf Naxos*, and remained a favourite there (singing Strauss, Mozart, Beethoven and Tchaikovsky). Her Metropolitan début was as Susanna (1959) and she first appeared at Covent Garden with the Royal Swedish Opera as Daisy Doody in Karl-Birger Blomdahl's *Aniara* (1960); her Australian début was as Emilia Marty (1982, Adelaide). Söderström combined a quick musical intelligence and a vivid and engaging stage personality with a protean voice not especially powerful but well able to express both soubrette mirth and tragic passion. Among her many contemporary roles have been Elisabeth Zimmer in H.W. Henze's *Elegy for Young Lovers* (in the 1961 English language

première at Glyndebourne), Amanda in the première of György Ligeti's *Le Grand Macabre* (1978,
Stockholm) and Juliana Bordereau in the première
of Dominick Argento's *The Aspern Papers* at Dallas in
1988. In 1999 she came out of retirement to sing the
Countess in *The Queen of Spades* at the Metropolitan
Opera. She was also a noted concert singer and
recitalist, and recorded a memorable series of Serge
Rachmaninoff songs with Vladimir Ashkenazy.
From 1993 to 1996 Söderström was artistic director
of the Drottningholm Court Theatre. She has published *I min tonart* (Stockholm, 1978; Eng. trans.,
1979; as *In my own Key*).

Andrew Porter/R

Sontag [Sonntag], Henriette (Gertrud Walpurgis)

(*b* Koblenz, 3 Jan 1806; *d* Mexico City, 17 June
1854). German soprano. The daughter of the actor
Franz Sonntag and the actress and singer Franziska
Sonntag (née Martloff, 1798–1865), and sister of
the actor Karl Sonntag, she first studied with her
mother. Her earliest public appearance was in
Darmstadt aged six in August von Kotzebue's play
Die Beichte (5 March 1811), her first in opera as
Salome in Ferdinand Kauer's *Das Donauweibchen*;
and she continued to appear in juvenile parts,
including some in Prague, where her mother settled after Franz's death in 1814 and was engaged by
Karl Liebich. Though under age, she was accepted
by the conservatory (1815), studying singing with
Anna Czegka, theory with Josef Triebensee and the
piano with Friedrich Pixis. Her juvenile appearances in Prague were an annoyance to the conservatory, and according to one story, she was
expelled in 1821, the year in which she made her
mature début as the princess in Louis Boieldieu's
Jean de Paris. She moved to Vienna in 1822, where
she sang in German and Italian opera and greatly
benefited from the influence of Joséphine Fodor-
Mainvielle. In 1823 Carl Maria von Weber heard
her in Gioachino Rossini's *La donna del lago*: clearly
she had greatly developed, for when he had heard
her in Prague the year previously he had thought
her, 'a pretty girl, but…still very much a beginner,
and rather goose-like', but now he offered her the
title role of *Euryanthe*. On 25 October 1823 she
triumphed; she also sang with great success, and to
the composer's pleasure, in the premières of Ludwig
van Beethoven's Ninth Symphony and *Missa solemnis* (7 and 13 May 1824). After a brief but triumphant season in Leipzig (1825), when she sang in
Der Freischütz and *Euryanthe*, she was engaged for
the Berlin Königstädter Theater, making her début
on 3 August 1825 as Isabella (*L'italiana in Algeri*).

Sontag's international career dates from her
brilliant Paris début at the Théâtre-Italien in 12
roles, initially as Rosina on 15 May 1826. After further German appearances, she returned in January
1828, including Donna Anna and Semiramide in
her repertory. At Weimar, she greatly impressed
J.W. von Goethe, who wrote the poem *Neue Siren*
for his 'fluttering nightingale'; in Berlin, enthusiasm reached the proportions of a *Sontagsfieber*,
much derided by her opponents. Her English début
was also in 1828, as Rosina at the King's Theatre
on 19 April. In London her repertory included
Carolina in *Il matrimonio segreto*; and she herself
contracted a secret marriage with Count Carlo
Rossi, hoping thereby not to compromise his career
in the Sardinian diplomatic service. When the King
of Prussia conferred on her a patent of nobility (as
Von Lauenstein), the obstacle of her low birth was
removed, and she joined her husband openly in
The Hague. But she was obliged to renounce the
stage in 1830, and for some years made only select
private and concert appearances in The Hague,
Frankfurt, St Petersburg, Berlin and other cities
to which her husband was posted. She eventually
returned to the stage when financial difficulties
intervened and when the abdication of the King
of Sardinia ended Rossi's career in 1849. Benjamin
Lumley offered her £6000 for a six months' contract
at Her Majesty's, where she sang Rossini, Gaetano
Donizetti and W.A. Mozart. After an English
tour (1849), she went to Paris, returning to create
Miranda in Fromental Halévy's *La Tempesta* (Her
Majesty's, 8 June 1850) and again singing in Paris
and London in 1851. She renewed her triumphs in
Germany, and in 1852 went with her husband to
America. In 1854 she toured Mexico with an Italian
company, and her last appearance was as Lucrezia
Borgia on 11 June. The following day she was taken
ill with cholera, of which she died.

In spite of the long interruption to her career,
Sontag was one of the most consistently successful and popular German sopranos of the first half
of the 19th century. Of great personal beauty, she
possessed a lively and attractive voice which she
used with great skill: her range was from *a* to *e'''*
and technically she was said to be the equal or superior of any singer of her day, including ANGELICA
CATALANI and her bitter rival MALIBRAN. But she
was essentially a vocalist, a singer of light and brilliant parts which demanded little in the way of dramatic feeling beyond her natural charm of presence.
J.E. Cox gives a description of her 1828 London
appearances:

> Without being deficient in strength, [her voice]
> is not powerful, and its quality is anything rather
> than disagreeable, though not remarkable for

its purity. Its greatest merit consists in its wonderful flexibility. ...Execution is with her everything, expression as nothing...that coolness of temperament which her acting seems to denote has most likely exercised a joint influence in determining the character of her singing. ...She had cultivated the imagination and the fancy to a degree they had never reached before. No singer had ever combined so variously, or executed in the light, brilliant, inventive, fresh and above all in the pleasing manner she attained. In these particulars she stood alone.

However, in the course of an eloquent obituary tribute, Hector Berlioz described her as possessing

the gifts of art and nature: voice, musical feeling, dramatic instinct, style, exquisite taste, passion, reflectiveness, grace, everything and still something more. She sang bagatelles, she played with notes as no Indian juggler has ever juggled with golden balls; but she also sang music, great and immortal music, as musicians sometimes dream of hearing it sung.

On her return to the stage in 1849, Sontag's vocal powers appear to have been undiminished, her artistry more mature; though she had kept her voice fresh in the years of retirement, she had also always refused to sing any part that did not lie easily within her range, declining, for instance, to sing Gaspare Spontini in Berlin. In her final years in America, she benefited from the climate and was able to sing two operas in an evening without fatigue. Her repertory comprised much Rossini (including contralto roles transposed for her), Donizetti especially, Vincenzo Bellini and Mozart: Berlioz gave a vivid and detailed appreciation of her Susanna in the last act of *Figaro*. There is a portrait of her by Paul Delaroche (see colour plate 12).

[J.E. Cox]: *Musical Recollections of the Last Half-Century* (London, 1872)

F. Russell: *Queen of Song: the Life of Henrietta Sontag* (New York, 1964)

John Warrack

Soot, Fritz [Friedrich] (Wilhelm)

(*b* Wellesweiler-Neunkirchen, Saar, 20 Aug 1878; *d* Berlin, 9 June 1965). German tenor. He studied with KARL SCHEIDEMANTEL in Dresden and made his début there in 1908 as Tonio (*La fille du régiment*). While at Dresden he created the Italian Tenor in *Der Rosenkavalier* (1911). He was a member of the Stuttgart Opera (1918–22), then moved to the

Berlin Staatsoper, where his creations included the Drum Major in *Wozzeck* (1925). He was also the first Berlin Laca in *Jenůfa* (1924), Mephistopheles in *Doktor Faust* (1927) and Babinski in *Švanda the Bagpiper* (1929). But it was as a Richard Wagner tenor that he was best known; in 1924 and 1925 he sang Siegmund, Siegfried, Tristan, Erik and Walther at Covent Garden, and later sang Parsifal. His repertory also included Palestrina and Otello. He returned to the Berlin Staatsoper after World War II and continued to sing character roles there until 1952, taking part in the première of Paul Dessau's *Die Verurteilung des Lukullus* (1951).

Harold Rosenthal/R

Sotin, Hans

(*b* Dortmund, 10 Sept 1939). German bass. He studied with Friedrich Wilhelm Hezel and Dieter Jacob. His début was in Essen in 1962, as the Police Inspector in *Der Rosenkavalier*; in 1964 he joined the Hamburg Staatsoper, taking small roles, but soon graduated to virtually all the leading bass roles in the Hamburg repertory, as well as singing Wotan in *Das Rheingold* and *Die Walküre*. He made his Glyndebourne début as Sarastro in 1970, subsequently appearing at the Chicago Lyric Opera (début as the Grand Inquisitor, 1971), the Metropolitan (Sarastro, 1972), Bayreuth (the Landgrave, 1972), the Vienna Staatsoper (King Mark, 1973), Covent Garden (Hunding, 1974) and La Scala (Ochs, 1976). He also sang Pogner, Don Alfonso and van Bett (*Zar und Zimmermann*). Sotin was a distinguished soloist in choral works, notably the *Missa solemnis*, which he recorded. His operatic recordings include the roles of Alfonso, Rocco, King Mark, Pogner and Gurnemanz. His rolling, voluminous tones, his sympathetic stage presence and interpretative independence made him one of the most valuable German basses of his generation.

Martin Bernheimer/R

Souez [née Rains], Ina

(*b* Windsor, CO, 3 June 1903; *d* Santa Monica, CA, 7 Dec 1992). American soprano. She trained at Denver and then in Milan. Her début as Mimì at Ivrea in 1928 led to engagements in Palermo and London, where she sang Liù to EVA TURNER's Turandot in 1929. Her repertory also included *Trovatore*, *Faust*, *Mefistofele* and *Madama Butterfly*, but it was in W.A. Mozart at Glyndebourne that the most enduring part of her reputation was made. She sang Fiordiligi in the opening season of 1934, added Donna Anna in 1936, and appeared regularly in both roles until 1939. She also sang at the

Stockholm Opera and later became a comedy vocalist for Spike Jones and his City Slickers. Her voice, light for Covent Garden, developed a hardness that sometimes limited enjoyment of her work at Glyndebourne, yet hers was probably the greatest personal success there in the early seasons, and her singing of Micaëla in the Covent Garden *Carmen* of 1935 was described as a 'joy to hear'. She recorded both of her prime Mozart roles with Fritz Busch.

J.B. Steane

Souliotis, Elena

(*b* Athens, 25 May 1943; *d* Florence, 4 Dec 2004). Greek soprano. Her family emigrated to Buenos Aires; she studied there and in Milan. Her début was in 1964 as Santuzza (*Cavalleria rusticana*) in Naples, and her American début was at Chicago in 1966 as Helen of Troy in Arrigo Boito's *Mefistofele*. The same year she made her first appearance at La Scala, as Abigaille (*Nabucco*), and in 1968 caused a sensation in the same part at a concert performance in London. Her first appearances at Covent Garden and the Metropolitan were both in 1969 as Lady Macbeth; at Covent Garden, Abigaille and Santuzza followed in 1972 and 1973. Souliotis's career proved short-lived, largely because she lacked the discipline to make the best use of her appreciable resources. On stage she was a vivid though controversial performer. She made a brief comeback as a mezzo in the 1980s.

Alan Blyth

Souzay (Tisserand), Gérard (Marcel)

(*b* Angers, 8 Dec 1918; *d* Antibes, 17 Aug 2004). French baritone. He learnt the tenets of *mélodie* interpretation from his principal teachers, the great exponent of *mélodies*, Pierre Bernac and CLAIRE CROIZA, and studied opera with Vanni Marcoux. He entered the Paris Conservatoire and gave his first recital in 1945. After the war he quickly gained international recognition as a recitalist before he made his opera début in 1960, singing Henry Purcell's Aeneas at the Aix-en-Provence Festival, followed immediately by Claudio Monteverdi's Orfeo at the New York City Opera. Among his most notable subsequent operatic appearances were Golaud at Rome (1962), the Opéra-Comique (1963), Florence (1966) and Wiesbaden (1976); Don Giovanni at the Paris Opéra (1963), Munich (1965) and Lausanne (1967); and Count Almaviva at the Metropolitan and Glyndebourne (1965), where he had to withdraw owing to illness after one performance. He

sang in the British première (concert performance) of Albert Roussel's *Padmâvatî*. His operatic recordings include Jean-Philippe Rameau's Pollux, Hector Berlioz's Méphistophélès, Albert (*Werther*), both Lescaut and the Count des Grieux in *Manon*, Alaouddin (*Padmâvatî*) and in particular Golaud, his finest role.

In *mélodies* he was the heir of Bernac, but he devoted almost as much time to lieder and was acclaimed in Germany as elsewhere for his idiomatic interpretations of Franz Schubert, Robert Schumann and Hugo Wolf, among others. His voice was a warmly expressive high baritone, slender but firm and flexible, an ideal instrument for a singer of such highly developed sensibility; but that very quality sometimes led to a note of preciosity in his interpretations. His recordings of *Die schöne Müllerin* and *Dichterliebe*, and his earlier discs (now on CD) of *mélodies* by Henri Duparc, Gabriel Fauré, Claude Debussy, Maurice Ravel and Francis Poulenc, disclose the best of his art.

J.B. Steane: *The Grand Tradition* (London, 1974/R), 487–90
A. Blyth, ed.: *Song on Record 2* (London, 1988)

Martin Cooper/Alan Blyth

Spani, Hina [Tuñón, Higinia]

(*b* Puán, Buenos Aires, 15 Feb 1896; *d* Buenos Aires, 11 July 1969). Argentine soprano. She studied in Buenos Aires and in Italy, where in 1915 she made her début at La Scala as Anna in Alfredo Catalani's *Loreley*. Returning to Argentina, she performed at the Teatro Colón, notably as Nedda (*Pagliacci*) with CARUSO and RUFFO. After World War I she gained prominence among the lyric sopranos in Italy, while adding to her repertory Richard Wagner's Elsa, Elisabeth and Sieglinde and such dramatic roles in Giuseppe Verdi as Aida and Amelia (*Ballo in maschera*). She reappeared at La Scala as Margherita in *Mefistofele* (1924), sang in France and Spain and toured Australia with NELLIE MELBA and the J.C. Williamson company (1928). In the 1930s she performed in Claudio Monteverdi's *L'incoronazione di Poppea* and *Orfeo*, Jean-Philippe Rameau's *Castor et Pollux* and (at the Colón) Verdi's *Oberto*.

Spani was also a distinguished concert artist and recitalist, with a large and wide-ranging repertory of songs. Her voice had a finely concentrated dramatic power with an exquisite pianissimo, and she was among the most stylish singers of her time.

W. Moran and R. Turró: 'Hina Spani', *Record Collector*, ix (1954), 81–99 [incl. discography]

J.B. Steane

Spence, Toby

(*b* Hertford, 22 May 1969). English tenor. He was a choral scholar at New College, Oxford, and subsequently studied at the GSMD in London. He made his professional operatic début, as Idamante for WNO, in 1995, repeating the role for his Scottish Opera début the following season. In 1996 he also made his Salzburg Festival début, as Marzio in *Mitridate*, and his Covent Garden début, in Giuseppe Verdi's *Alzira*. Spence has returned to Covent Garden as the Simpleton (*Boris Godunov*), Count Almaviva (*Il barbiere di Siviglia*), Ferdinand (in the 2004 world première of Thomas Adès's *The Tempest*) and Váňa Kudrjáš (*Kát'a Kabanová*). At the ENO, where he made his début, as Oronte (*Alcina*) in 1999, his roles have included Almaviva, Narciso (*Il turco in Italia*), Fenton, Ferrando, Tamino and Paris (*La belle Hélène*). He has also sung frequently at the Paris Opéra, in roles such as Calisis (Jean-Philippe Rameau's *Les Boréades*), Oronte and David (*Die Meistersinger*). Spence made his Aix début, as Hyllus (G.F. Handel's *Hercules*) in 2004, and his Santa Fe début, as Tamino, in 2006. In 2005 he was praised for his intensely dramatic performance of the Madwoman in *Curlew River* at the Edinburgh Festival. Spence's distinctive voice – lyrical, yet with an incisive ring to the tone – and intelligent musicianship are heard on recordings including the *St Matthew Passion*, *Messiah*, Calisis, Marzio, Hylas (*Les Troyens*), lieder by Franz Schubert, Robert Schumann and Lisa Lehmann, and Benjamin Britten's *Serenade* and *Les illuminations*. (See colour plate 5.)

Richard Wigmore

Speransky, Nikolay Ivanovich

(*b* 18/30 July 1877; *d* Moscow, 5 March 1952). Russian bass-baritone and opera director. After early musical education in Saratov, he went to study law in Moscow, where he had lessons in singing from Camillo Everardi and MATTIA BATTISTINI and in piano from Serge Rachmaninoff. He made his début in 1901 at the Moscow Private Opera, spent two years at the Tbilisi Opera, and returned to Moscow in 1905 as leading soloist with S.I. Zimin's opera company, where he created the roles of Dodon (*The Golden Cockerel*, 1909) and Suleyman in M.M. Ippolitov-Ivanov's *Izmena* ('The Betrayal', 1910). His repertory spanned a wide range of bass and baritone parts, from the Miller (*Rusalka*) and Kochubey (*Mazepa*) to Escamillo and Amonasro; in *Boris Godunov* he sang Varlaam and Rangoni, as well as the title role. He gave up singing in 1916 and devoted his time to organizing opera and teaching in provincial cities. From 1939 he taught at the Moscow Conservatory.

Boris Semeonoff

Stabile, Mariano

(*b* Palermo, 12 May 1888; *d* Milan, 11 Jan 1968). Italian baritone. He studied in Rome under ANTONIO COTOGNI and made his début in his native Palermo in 1911, as Marcello in *La bohème*. His selection by Arturo Toscanini to sing the title role in Giuseppe Verdi's *Falstaff* for the opening of the 1921–2 season at La Scala, with thorough coaching by both Toscanini and GIUSEPPE DE LUCA, proved to be the turning-point of his career: he scored an enormous success and sang the part nearly 1200 times in the course of 40 years. During his first Covent Garden season, in 1926, he appeared as Falstaff, Iago and Don Giovanni, and later became a notable Gianni Schicchi and Scarpia. He was greatly admired at Glyndebourne as Figaro and as Dr Malatesta in *Don Pasquale*; also as Don Alfonso in the Glyndebourne production of *Così fan tutte* at the 1948 Edinburgh Festival. He repeated some of these parts in London between 1946 and 1949, during the long postwar seasons of Italian opera mounted by the Russian-born impresario Jay Pomeroy at the Cambridge and Stoll theatres.

At the Salzburg Festival he was a noted Falstaff (under Toscanini), Count Almaviva and Figaro (*Barbiere di Siviglia*). Stabile's vocal powers were not exceptional, and his great attainments were the result of a spontaneous dramatic exuberance tempered by a fine sense of style. His enunciation was unusually clear, and his mastery of dramatic inflection and gesture complete. These qualities found full scope in *Don Pasquale* and *Così fan tutte*, and in both these operas his relish of the approaching discomfiture of his victims always delighted the audience. Malatesta's 'Bella siccome un angelo' has been more smoothly vocalized by other singers, but there was something irresistibly comical in the gusto with which Stabile would arouse Don Pasquale's desires by his account of Norina's charms while at the same time holding him at arm's length with imperious gestures of restraint. His Falstaff, an ideal projection of the Fat Knight's geniality, wit and ridiculous ambitions as a lover, is chronicled on disc in both live and studio recordings.

G. Gualerzi: 'Stabile – a Centenary Tribute', *Opera*, xxxix (1988), 1190–94

Desmond Shawe-Taylor/R

Stader, Maria

(*b* Budapest, 5 Nov 1911; *d* Zürich, 27 April 1999). Swiss soprano of Hungarian birth. Orphaned by the First World War, she was taken to Switzerland as a refugee by the International Red Cross. There, she studied singing with Hans Keller and Ilona Durigo.

In 1939 she won the singing prize at the Geneva International Music Competition, and at the end of the war began a career as a concert singer, and also taught at the Zürich Musikakademie. She gave numerous concert tours in the USA, Japan and Africa and sang at the principal festivals. Her fame was based chiefly on her interpretations of W.A. Mozart. Though she rarely appeared in the opera house – she did perform the Queen of Night at Covent Garden in the 1949–50 season – she sang many operatic roles in concerts, and on recordings (mainly with Ferenc Fricsay). Her clean technique and flexible, well-focussed, though not large voice made her much in demand for the concert repertory, from J.S. Bach's Passions to Giuseppe Verdi's Requiem. She gave an indication of her working methods in her book Gesang (Lektion) Arie 'Aus Liebe will mein Heiland sterben': Matthäus-Passion [von] Joh(ann) Seb(astian) Bach (Wie Meister üben, iii, Zürich, 1967; Eng. trans., 1968). She was honoured with the Salzburg Lilli Lehmann Medal (1950), the Mozart silver medal (1956) and the Hans Georg Nägeli Medal of Zürich (1962). She retired from the concert platform in 1969 after a series of farewell concerts. Her autobiography, Nehmt meinen Dank, was published in Munich in 1979.

Jürg Stenzl/R

Stagno, Roberto [Andrioli, Vincenzo]

(b Palermo, 11 Oct 1840; d Genoa, 26 April 1897). Italian tenor. He studied in Milan with Francesco Lamperti, then made his début in 1862 at Lisbon as Rodrigo in Gioachino Rossini's Otello. He appeared at Madrid, Venice, Rome, Naples, Florence and the Metropolitan, where he sang Enzo in the first New York performance of La Gioconda (1883). His repertory included Don Ottavio, Elvino, Pollione, Gennaro (Lucrezia Borgia), Poliuto, Raoul, Robert le diable, Manrico, Radames, Romeo, Faust and Lohengrin. He also sang Giuseppe Verdi's Otello in Buenos Aires (1888). He created Turiddu in Cavalleria rusticana at the Teatro Costanzi, Rome (1890), and sang in the first performance of Umberto Giordano's Mala vita at the Teatro Argentina, Rome (1892). His powerful, flexible voice could encompass a great variety of roles. He was married to the soprano GEMMA BELLINCIONI. Their daughter Bianca Stagno-Bellincioni (1888–1980), also a soprano, sang in Naples, Barcelona, Rome and Lisbon, and appeared at Covent Garden (Bohème and Manon Lescaut) in 1914; she also wrote Roberto Stagno e Gemma Bellincioni, intimi (Florence, 1943/R).

Elizabeth Forbes

Steber, Eleanor

(b Wheeling, WV, 17 July 1916; d Langhorne, PA, 3 Oct 1990). American soprano. After studying privately with PAUL ALTHOUSE and William Whitney, and appearing in Boston in 1936, she won the 1940 Metropolitan Opera Auditions of the Air. This led to her début on 7 December as Sophie, and she remained a leading soprano with the Metropolitan until 1963. As her voice matured, its silvery sheen gave way to greater warmth and breadth, and she began to undertake heavier roles such as the Marschallin, Elsa, Desdemona, Tosca and Donna Anna. She was particularly noted for the suavity and poise of her Mozart heroines – the Countess Almaviva, Fiordiligi, Pamina, Donna Elvira and Konstanze, which she sang at the Metropolitan première of Die Entführung in 1946. She also created the title role in Samuel Barber's Vanessa (1958), sang the title role in the American première of Arabella (Metropolitan, 1955), and Marie in the first Metropolitan Wozzeck (1959). She appeared at the Edinburgh Festival, Bayreuth, Vienna and Florence as well as with numerous American companies; she sang Miss Wingrave in the American première of Benjamin Britten's opera (1973, Santa Fe).

An admired concert singer and recitalist, Steber commissioned and gave the first performance of Barber's Knoxville: Summer of 1915 (1948), which she later recorded; in 1964 she gave three recitals at the Wigmore Hall in London. She also appeared in musical comedy. She was head of the voice department at the Cleveland Institute, 1963–72, and was appointed to the Juilliard School in 1971; in 1975 she established the Eleanor Steber Music Foundation to aid young singers. She made many recordings, including the roles of Countess Almaviva (Metropolitan, 1943), a deeply eloquent Elsa (Bayreuth, 1953) and the title role of Barber's Vanessa. She wrote Eleanor Steber: an Autobiography (Ridgewood, NJ, 1992).

Martin Bernheimer/Alan Blyth

Stefano, Giuseppe di.

See DI STEFANO, GIUSEPPE.

Stehle, Adelina

(b Graz, 30 June 1860; d Milan, 24 Dec 1945). Austrian, later Italian, soprano. She studied in Milan and made her début as Amina at Broni in 1881. In the following years she sang in many of the leading Italian houses before going to La Scala in 1890, where she appeared in several world premières, most notably those of La Wally and Falstaff, both in 1892; in the latter, she sang Nannetta to the Fenton of her husband, EDOARDO GARBIN. In 1892 at the Teatro Dal Verme she was the first Nedda in *Pagliacci*, and in 1895 at La Scala she took the leading soprano roles in two Pietro Mascagni premières, *Guglielmo Ratcliff* and *Silvano*. In 1902 she toured South America and in 1905 was a member of the distinguished Sonzogno company at the Théâtre Sarah Bernhardt in Paris; she also sang in St Petersburg, Berlin and Vienna. Her voice, originally that of a light lyric and coloratura soprano (with Ophelia and Gilda among her roles), developed into a more dramatic instrument, and she was admired as a leading exponent of *verismo* roles such as Adriana Lecouvreur and Umberto Giordano's Fedora. On retirement she became a teacher, her best-known pupil being Giannina Arangi-Lombardi.

J.B. Steane

Stehle, Sophie

(*b* Sigmaringen, 15 May 1838; *d* Schloss Harterode, Hanover, 4 Oct 1921). German soprano. She studied in Augsburg and Munich, where she made her début at the Hofoper in 1860 as Emmeline in Joseph Weigl's *Die Schweizerfamilie*. During the next 14 years she sang a wide variety of roles, including Marguerite, Agathe, Rachel (*La Juive*), Pamina, Amazili (Gaspare Spontini's *Fernand Cortez*), Sélika (*L'Africaine*), Anna (Heinrich Marschner's *Hans Heiling*), Senta, Elisabeth and Elsa. She sang Fricka in the first performance, in Munich, of *Das Rheingold* (1869) and Brünnhilde in *Die Walküre* (1870). She made her farewell in 1874 as Gretchen in Albert Lortzing's *Der Wildschütz*.

Elizabeth Forbes

Stella, Antonietta

(*b* Perugia, 15 March 1929). Italian soprano. She studied in Perugia and Rome, making her début in 1950 at Spoleto as Leonora (*Il trovatore*). In 1951 she sang Leonora (*La forza del destino*) at the Rome Opera and in 1954 appeared at La Scala as Desdemona. In 1955 she made her Covent Garden début as Aida and in 1956 first sang at the Metropolitan, in the same role. She appeared at all the leading European theatres, singing Butterfly, Tosca, Santuzza, Elisabeth de Valois, Violetta and Amelia (*Un ballo in maschera*). She also sang Richard Wagner's Senta, Elisabeth, Elsa and Sieglinde. Her beautiful voice was used with great style.

Elizabeth Forbes

Stepanova, Mariya Matveyevna

(*b* 1811 or 1815; *d* 1903). Russian soprano. Engaged at the Bol'shoy Theatre, St Petersburg (1834–46), she created Antonida in *A Life for the Tsar* (1836) and Lyudmila in *Ruslan and Lyudmila* (1842). She also sang at the Bol'shoy Theatre, Moscow (1846–55), returning to St Petersburg in 1850 (when she was heard as Antonida by the ten-year-old P.I. Tchaikovsky) and in 1852, when she created Kseniya in Anton Rubinstein's first opera *Dmitry Donskoy* (*Kulikovskaya bitva*, 'The Battle of Kulikovo').

Elizabeth Forbes

Stepanova, Yelena Andreyevna

(*b* Moscow, 5/17 May 1891; *d* Moscow, 26 May 1978). Russian soprano. She studied singing with M. Polli. From 1908 she sang in the Bol'shoy chorus until, after a successful début as Antonida (*A Life for the Tsar*), she became a soloist in 1912. Konstantin Stanislavsky, who had great influence on her, prepared her for the roles of Gilda (1919) and Tat'yana (1921); she was also influenced by the conductors Václav Suk, Emil Cooper and Nikolay Golovanov and the director Lossky, as well as by FYODOR CHALIAPIN, LEONID SOBINOV and ANTONINA NEZHDANOVA. Her singing was distinguished by rare clarity, crystalline coloratura and artistic sensitivity. Her Nikolay Rimsky-Korsakov portrayals were fascinating: Marfa (*The Tsar's Bride*), the Snow Maiden, Pannochka-Rusalka (*May Night*) and the Queen of Shemakha (*Golden Cockerel*), among others. Her repertory also included M.I. Glinka's Lyudmila, Violetta, Elsa, Giacomo Meyerbeer's Marguerite de Valois and Lakmé. She left the opera stage in 1944.

I.M. Yampol'sky

Stevens [Steenberg], Risë

(*b* New York, 11 June 1913). American mezzo-soprano of Norwegian origin. She sang with the New York Opera-Comique before becoming a pupil of Anna Schoen-René. Approached by the Metropolitan, she declined and sailed for Europe to study with MARIE GUTHEIL-SCHODER. She then made her formal operatic début in Prague in 1936 as Ambroise Thomas' Mignon; she also sang with the Vienna Staatsoper and in Buenos Aires. Returning to the USA, she made her début with the Metropolitan on tour in Philadelphia in 1938 as Octavian, appearing a month later in New York as Mignon. She remained with the company until 1961 but also sang with other companies (including Glyndebourne in 1939 and, as Cherubino, 1955). Her warm, lyric voice can be heard on studio and off-the-air recordings of her Cherubino, Carmen, Mignon, Delilah and Octavian.

K. Crichton: *Subway to the Met: Risë Stevens' Story* (Garden City, NY, 1959)

J. Hines: 'Risë Stevens', *Great Singers on Great Singing* (Garden City, NY, 1982), 313–22

P. Jackson: *Saturday Afternoons at the Old Met* (New York, 1992)

Max de Schauensee/Alan Blyth

Stewart, Nellie [Eleanor Towzey]

(*b* Sydney, 20 Nov 1858; *d* Sydney, 22 June 1931). Australian soprano and actress. The daughter of Theodosia Yates-Stirling, former chorus mistress at Drury Lane, London, and a singer-actress of great versatility, she made her first stage appearance at the age of five, and followed her mother's example by excelling in both sung and spoken theatre. She sang the leading role in Jacques Offenbach's *La fille du tambour-major* in April 1881 for George Musgrove's management and played Yum-Yum in the Australian première of *The Mikado* in 1885, repeating the role in Melbourne the following year. Her other roles included Marguerite in *Faust*. A descendant of one of David Garrick's leading ladies, she was the most popular operetta and musical comedy performer in Australia before GLADYS MONCRIEFF. She published an autobiography, *My Life's Story* (Sydney, 1923).

Roger Covell

Stewart, Thomas (James)

(*b* San Saba, TX, 29 Aug 1926; *d* Rockville, MD, 24 Sept 2006). American baritone. He studied at the Juilliard School, New York, where he made his début in 1954 as La Roche in the American première of *Capriccio*. He also sang at the New York City Opera and in Chicago. In 1958 he was engaged by the Berlin Deutsche Oper, making his début as Escamillo; he sang the role at Covent Garden in 1960, returning as Gunther, Don Giovanni and the Dutchman. In 1960 he sang Donner, Gunther and Amfortas at Bayreuth, where he appeared regularly until 1975, adding Wotan and Wolfram to his repertory; he also sang Wotan in the Salzburg Easter Festival. He made his Metropolitan début in 1966 as Ford and returned there regularly until 1980, singing Iago, Golaud, John the Baptist, the Hoffmann villains, Wotan and Hans Sachs, which he had first sung at Nuremberg (1971). He sang the title roles in the American premières of *Cardillac* (1967) at Santa Fe and *Lear* (1981) at San Francisco, where he had sung since 1962 as Valentin, Golaud and Yevgeny Onegin. His voice, more lyrical than dramatic, was nevertheless incisive and of sufficient volume to encompass the heroic Wagner roles, as can be heard on his recordings of the Dutchman, Wotan and most notably of Hans Sachs, under Rafael Kubelík. He married the soprano EVELYN LEAR.

Harold Rosenthal/Alan Blyth

Stich-Randall, Teresa

(*b* West Hartford, CT, 24 Dec 1927; *d* Vienna, 17 July 2007). American soprano. She studied at the Hartford School of Music and Columbia University, New York, where she created Gertrude Stein in Virgil Thomson's *The Mother of Us All* (1947) and the title role of Otto Luening's *Evangeline* (1948). In 1949 she sang the High Priestess in Arturo Toscanini's broadcast and recording of *Aida* and in 1950 Nannetta in his *Falstaff*. She made her European début at Florence in 1951 as the Mermaid in *Oberon*. After a season at Basle she was engaged by the Vienna Staatsoper, where her first role was Violetta. From 1953 to 1971 she appeared at the Aix-en-Provence Festival as Fiordiligi, Countess Almaviva, Konstanze, Donna Anna and Pamina. She sang Gilda at Chicago in 1955 and made her Metropolitan début as Fiordiligi in 1961. She took part in the première of Frank Martin's *Le mystère de la Nativité* (1960, Salzburg) and sang throughout Italy, as Richard Strauss's Ariadne and in the W.A. Mozart repertory. She sang Norma at Trier in 1971, the year of her retirement from the stage. In recital and concert she was particularly admired in Bach and G.F. Handel. She had a pure, sweet voice, though her performances were sometimes marred by mannered detail; but at its best her cultivated style won wide praise. Her art is represented by recordings of her Mozart roles from Aix and her Sophie in Herbert von Karajan's first recording of *Der Rosenkavalier*.

Harold Rosenthal/Alan Blyth

Stignani, Ebe

(*b* Naples, 10 July 1903; *d* Imola, 5 Oct 1974). Italian mezzo-soprano. She studied at the Naples Conservatory and made her début at the S Carlo in 1925 as Amneris. In 1926 Arturo Toscanini engaged her for La Scala, where she first appeared as Eboli in *Don Carlos*. In successive seasons at La Scala she added to her repertory all the leading mezzo-soprano parts in Italian opera and a large number of other roles including Delilah, Ortrud, Brangäne and C.W. Gluck's Orpheus. But it was in the tragic characters of Giuseppe Verdi, above all Azucena in *Il trovatore*, that she found the greatest scope and won her greatest successes. At Covent Garden she sang Amneris (1937, 1939 and 1955), and Azucena (1939 and 1952), and Adalgisa to the Norma of MARIA CALLAS (1952 and 1957). She had a voice of rich quality and ample range, extending from f to c'''.

Judged by older standards, neither Stignani's vocalization nor her phrasing was impeccable, yet her singing was always grandiose and authoritative and she brought to the fierce mezzo parts of Verdi (including his Requiem) an intensity and dramatic fire that made her for many years the leading exponent of this music. Stignani's extensive career is well documented on disc: particularly notable are her Eboli and Amneris in sets made during and just after World War II.

H. Rosenthal: 'Ebe Stignani', *Opera*, vi (1952), 334–40
E. Davidson: 'All about Ebe', *ON*, xxxv/21 (1970–71), 28–9

Desmond Shawe-Taylor/R

Stoltz, Rosine [Noël, Victoire]

Rosine Stoltz

(*b* Paris, 13 Jan 1815; *d* Paris, 29 July 1903). French mezzo-soprano. She was discovered at the age of 12 by Alexandre Choron, who took her into his voice class. At 16 she left to perform opera and spoken theatre in Belgium and the Netherlands. In 1836 she appeared as Rachel in Fromental Halévy's *La Juive* opposite ADOLPHE NOURRIT at the Théâtre de la Monnaie in Brussels. Nourrit's admiration probably helped her procure a contract at the Paris Opéra, where she made her début, again as Rachel, in 1837. At the Opéra she created the roles of Ascanio in Hector Berlioz's *Benvenuto Cellini* (1838), Marguerite in Daniel Auber's *Le lac des fées* (1839), Léonor in Gaetano Donizetti's *La favorite* (1840), and Zayda in his *Dom Sébastien* (1843), as well as singing in premières of Halévy's *Guido et Ginevra* (1838), *La reine de Chypre* (1841), *Charles VI* (1843) and *Le lazzarone* (1844). Other roles included Donna Anna, Isolier in Gioachino Rossini's *Le comte Ory*, Desdemona (in his *Otello*), and Valentine in Giacomo Meyerbeer's *Les Huguenots*.

She was a controversial figure at the Opéra, celebrated for the intensity of her acting, but accused of using unfair techniques against her rivals and of profiting from her romantic liaison with the Opéra's director, Léon Pillet. She left the Opéra in 1847 after a scandal that broke out when she lost her temper during a performance of Louis Niedermeyer's *Robert Bruce*. She continued to perform until 1860, appearing in London, the French provinces and South America, and making an unsuccessful comeback attempt at the Opéra in 1854. During this period she may have captured the affections of Charles Baudelaire, who is said to have composed the poem 'Une martyre' in Stoltz's apartments while awaiting her arrival. After retirement she devoted herself to acquiring husbands and aristocratic titles, often by flamboyant means. In old age she turned to composition, publishing a number of songs set to poetry she had written herself, as well as a pamphlet on spiritualism.

Stoltz is remembered today mostly for the role attributed to her in the onset of Donizetti's madness. According to an oft-retold anecdote, Donizetti's mental illness first manifested itself after a rehearsal of *Dom Sébastien*. Stoltz protested violently at having to stand idle on stage during the baritone's *romance* and insisted on cuts; the distraught Donizetti obliged but, the story goes, was never quite the same again. It is now known that Donizetti's illness was a result of long-dormant syphilis, and the tale is revealed as one of those fictions that collect around divas, perhaps in reaction to the influence they can exert during the compositional process.

Stoltz had a range of about two octaves, roughly from a to a'', with excellent low notes and a strong but harsh upper register. She lacked agility and technical control, but her vocal colour and broad palette of timbres were universally praised. In an 1842 letter Donizetti imagined casting her as Hélène in *Le duc d'Albe*, a part he described as 'a role of action, of a type perhaps quite new in the theatre, where women are almost always passive'. The substitute cabaletta he wrote for her in *La favorite* conveys the same forceful image: its jagged contours with sharp shifts between extremes of range, extended passages in the low register and short phrases in a mostly syllabic style create the impression that Donizetti exploited both Stolz's weaknesses and strengths to maximum dramatic effect.

M.A. Smart: 'The Lost Voice of Rosine Stolz', *COJ*, vi (1994), 31–50

Mary Ann Smart

Stolz [Stolzová], Teresa [Teresina, Terezie]

(*b* Elbekosteletz [Kostelec nad Labem], 2 June 1834; *d* Milan, 22 Aug 1902). Bohemian soprano. She was one of a large musical family. Her twin sisters, Francesca (Fanny, Františka, 1826–*c*1903) and Ludmila (Lydia, 1826–*c*1910), both sopranos, became the youthful mistresses (and Ludmila later the wife) of the composer Luigi Ricci, who wrote operas for and fathered a child by each of them. Teresa was trained at the Prague Conservatory; in 1856 she joined Ricci and the twins in Trieste; she had further lessons from Francesco Lamperti in Milan, and in 1857 she made her operatic début in Tbilisi. For some six years she sang in Odessa, Constantinople and often Tbilisi. Her earliest Italian appearances to have been traced were in Turin in autumn 1863. Her successes in Nice (*Il trovatore*, December 1863) and then Granada (*Ernani*, April 1864) led to a *Trovatore* in Spoleto (September 1864), and *Ernani* and *Guillaume Tell* in Bologna. The Bologna performances were conducted by Angelo Mariani, to whom she later became engaged. In 1867 she was chosen for the Italian première of *Don Carlos*, in Bologna, and two years later for the revised *La forza del destino*, at La Scala, Milan; Giuseppe Verdi himself supervised the latter production. In 1872, again at La Scala, Stolz was the first Italian Aida, and in 1874 (and subsequently, during the tour of the work to Paris, London and Vienna) the first soprano of the Verdi Requiem. Verdi's operas had from the start been prominent in her repertory and, both in Italy and abroad, she became a leading and frequent interpreter of his later heroines, from Amelia in *Un ballo in maschera* to Aida. Her last operatic engagement was in St Petersburg (1876–7) and her last public appearance in a performance of the Requiem at La Scala (1879), conducted by Verdi for the benefit of flood victims.

After 1872 her only non-Verdian roles were Alice in *Robert le diable* and Rachel in *La Juive*. She was the Verdian dramatic soprano *par excellence*, powerful and, passionate in utterance but dignified and disciplined in manner, with a voice that

Teresa Stolz in the title role of 'Aida' (Verdi), première performance, La Scala, Milan, 1872

extended securely from *g* to *c'''*. After hearing the Requiem in Paris, Blanche Roosevelt wrote of her thus (*Chicago Times*, June 1875):

Stolz's voice is a pure soprano, with an immense compass and of the most perfectly beautiful quality one ever listened to, from the lowest note to the highest. Her phrasing is the most superb I ever heard and her intonation something faultless. She takes a tone and sustains it until it seems that her respiration is quite exhausted, and then she has only commenced to hold it. The tones are as fine and clearly cut as diamond, and sweet as a silver bell; but the power she gives a high C is something amazing...She opens her mouth slightly when she takes a note, without any perceptible effort, and the tone swells out bigger and fuller, always retaining that exquisite purity of intonation, and the air seems actually heavy with great passionate waves of melody.

Much has been written about the troubled personal relationships between Stolz, Mariani, Verdi and his wife. That Stolz became Verdi's mistress has been both asserted and denied, but there is no doubt that the attentions he paid her between 1872 and 1876 caused pain to Giuseppina Verdi.

Andrew Porter

Stolze, Gerhard

(*b* Dessau, 1 Oct 1926; *d* Garmisch-Partenkirchen, 11 March 1979). German tenor. He studied in Dresden and Berlin, then in 1949 was engaged by the Dresden Staatsoper, where he made his début as Augustin Moser (*Die Meistersinger*). From 1953 to 1961 he was a member of the Berlin Staatsoper. At Bayreuth he took minor roles in 1951, sang David in 1956, and from 1957 to 1969 sang Mime, a role he also recorded with success in both Georg Solti's and Herbert von Karajan's *Ring* cycles and in which he made his Covent Garden début in 1960. He created roles in Werner Egk's *Der Revisor* (1957, Schwetzingen), Heimo Erbse's *Julietta* (1959, Salzburg), Carl Orff's *Oedipus der Tyrann* (1959, Stuttgart), the stage première of Frank Martin's *Le mystère de la Nativité* (1960, Salzburg) and Giselher Klebe's *Jacobowsky und der Oberst* (1965, Hamburg). In 1968 he sang Loge at the Metropolitan. His musical intelligence and dramatic gifts specially suited him to such character roles as Herod, of which he made a notable recording under Solti, the Captain in *Wozzeck*, and Oberon in Benjamin Britten's *A Midsummer Night's Dream*.

Harold Rosenthal/Alan Blyth

Stoppelaer, Michael

(*d* London, 1777, will proved 4 July). Irish tenor and actor. From 1731 Stoppelaer sang leading roles on the London stage in numerous ballad opera afterpieces such as *The Devil to Pay* and Henry Fielding's *The Lottery* and *The Intriguing Chambermaid*. He also sang Orpheus in Fielding's burlesque opera, *Eurydice* He sang Odoardo in the première of G.F. Handel's *Ariodante* (1735). In 1737 JOHN BEARD

took over his roles and for the rest of his long career Stoppelaer was primarily a comic actor singing occasional songs.

Olive Baldwin, Thelma Wilson

Storace, Nancy [Ann Selina; Anna]

(*b* London, 27 Oct 1765; *d* Dulwich, 24 Aug 1817). English soprano, the daughter of Stefano Storace, an Italian double bass player, translator of Italian opera into English and adapter, and sister of the composer Stephen Storace. A vocal prodigy, she appeared in Southampton in 1773 as 'a Child not eight Years old'; her first London concert was at the Haymarket Theatre in April the following year. About this time she began lessons with VENANZIO RAUZZINI, in whose opera *L'ali d'amore*, on 29 February 1776, she created the role of Cupido. She also studied with Antonio Sacchini. In 1778 she followed her brother to Italy. She began her Italian operatic career in 1779 in Florence where she took small roles in *opera seria*. This was followed by appearances in revivals of comic opera (1780–81) in which she took both *prima seria* and *prima buffa* roles. In 1782 she sang in Milan, Turin, Parma, Rome and Venice. The first opera composed for her specifically was one of the most acclaimed of its time, Giuseppe Sarti's *Fra i due litiganti il terzo gode* (1782, Milan).

Her growing celebrity, which MICHAEL KELLY witnessed in Venice where he sang with her, caused

Nancy Storace

the Viennese ambassador to Venice, Count Giacomo Durazzo, to engage her for the newly organized Italian opera in Vienna in 1783. The company's first opera was Antonio Salieri's *La scuola de' gelosi*. Storace sang the Countess, a role she had created at the opera's première in Venice a few weeks earlier. During her first season at the Burgtheater, Storace sang in half of the 14 productions; that year she received the highest salary in the company. On 21 March 1784 she married the composer J.A. Fisher, but he apparently treated her cruelly and they soon parted; she gave birth to a child in early 1785, but it died after only a few months. Her years in Vienna (1783–7) are important for the roles that major composers (Antonio Salieri, Giovanni Paisiello, Vicente Martín y Soler, Salieri, W.A. Mozart) created for her. Her early vocal training and her experience in serious opera in Italy had helped her acquire vocal and dramatic resources that she could integrate into her comic performances; composers responded with roles of stylistic richness and variety. She created the role of Eleanora in Salieri's satire on the opera seria, *Prima la musica e poi le parole* (1786). Her vocal qualities can be inferred from her music in the greatest operas written for her, Mozart's *Le nozze di Figaro* and Martín y Soler's *Una cosa rara* (this latter the greatest popular triumph of Viennese music theatre). Both Susanna (*Figaro*) and Lilla (*Una cosa rara*) exploit her dramatic talents and display her preference for melodies within a limited vocal range (with occasional and modest bravura flourishes) and in *nota e parola* style. Similar vocal writing is found in Mozart's other compositions for Storace, which include a single aria from the aborted *Lo sposo deluso* and the concert aria 'Chi'io mi scordi di te…Non temer amato bene' (for her farewell concert). In Vienna Storace also met Joseph Haydn, in whose oratorio *Il ritorno di Tobia* she sang in 1784.

In February 1787 Storace, her mother, the composer Thomas Attwood and Michael Kelly left for London, where on 24 April she appeared in Paisiello's *Gli schiavi per amore* at the King's Theatre, Haymarket, for which she was provided additional arias by her brother, Domenicho Corri and Joseph Mazzinghi. Stephen wrote that his sister 'has had great opposition from the Italians – who consider it as an infringement on their rights – that any person should be able to sing that was not born in Italy'. After the King's Theatre burnt in 1789 she moved to Drury Lane to join her brother for the 1789–90 season. She launched an extensive career in English opera on 24 November 1789 with her appearance as Adela in her brother's *The Haunted Tower*, for which she received top billing (unusual for a woman on London playbills); its great success was in large measure due to its prima donna and her large-scale italianate piece, 'Be mine tender pas-sion'. Other leading roles in operas by her brother included Margaretta in *No Song, no Supper* (1790), Lilla in *The Siege of Belgrade* (1791) and Fabulina in *The Pirates* (1792). There is reason to think she had a close relationship with the Prince of Wales in the early 1790s, when he, the Duke of Bedford and the Marquis of Salisbury attempted to hire her for their secret court theatre at the Pantheon concert hall in Oxford Street (see Price, 1989, pp.66 ff). She sang at the King's Theatre for a season in 1793.

Storace also took part in the Handel Festival at Westminster Abbey in 1787. Mount Edgcumbe, who heard her at this and subsequent performances at the Abbey, commented that 'in that space, the harsh part of her voice is lost, while its power and clearness filled the whole of it'. In addition to her many appearances in oratorios in London, she also sang in Salisbury in 1787 in a benefit concert for her early teacher Joseph Corfe, and in 1790 she sang in Bath with Rauzzini, the first of several concerts that continued over seven years. She contributed arias to a number of concerts organized by Johann Salomon for Haydn in 1791 and again in 1795. Other oratorio and concert appearances included Salisbury (in 1792 and 1796, the latter another benefit for Corfe), Hereford (1792), Bristol (1793), Manchester (1794) and Liverpool (1794).

After her brother's death in 1796 she left Drury Lane and returned briefly to the King's Theatre before she and her lover, the tenor JOHN BRAHAM, left for a tour of the Continent in 1797. She was present at a rehearsal of Haydn's *The Seasons* in Vienna in 1801. A son, Spencer, was born in London in 1802. Her farewell performance, and that of her friend Kelly, was at Drury Lane in *No Song, no Supper* in 1808. She and Braham parted on acrimonious terms in 1816 and she died a year later.

After her death in 1817 Storace was underpraised by English writers. Charles Burney called her 'a lively and intelligent actress' but said her voice had 'a certain crack and roughness' and 'a deficiency of natural sweetness'. Mount Edgcumbe wrote that she was unfitted for serious opera and was undoubtedly most successful in comic parts: 'In her own particular line…she was unrivalled, being an excellent actress, as well as a masterly singer'. These evaluations suggest that it could not have been her virtuosity or purity of tone that made her voice so compelling to composers but rather that her intelligence, vivacity and charm inspired some of the most vocally and dramatically incisive music of its time.

M. Kelly: *Reminiscences* (London, 1826, 2/1826/R1968 with introduction by A.H. King); ed. R. Fiske (London, 1975)

B. Matthews: 'The Childhood of Nancy Storace', *MT*, cx (1969), 733–5

K. Geiringer and I. Geiringer: 'Stephen and Nancy Storace in Vienna', *Essays on the Music of J.S. Bach and Other Divers Subjects: a Tribute to Gerhard Herz*, ed. R.L. Weaver (Louisville, KY, 1981)

B. Matthews: 'Nancy Storace and the Royal Society of Musicians', *MT*, cxxviii (1987), 325–7

G. Brace: *Anna…Susanna: Anna Storace, Mozart's First Susanna: her Life, Times and Family* (London, 1991)

C. Price: 'Mozart, the Storaces and Opera in London 1787–1790', *Europa im Zeitalter Mozarts*, ed. M. Csáky and W. Pass (Vienna, 1995), 209–13

Patricia Lewy Gidwitz, Betty Matthews

Storchio, Rosina [Rosa]

(*b* Venice, 19 May 1872; *d* Milan, 24 July 1945). Italian soprano. A pupil at the Milan Conservatory, she made her début there in 1892 at the Teatro Dal Verme as Micaëla in *Carmen*. After further study with Alberto Giovannini she appeared at La Scala in 1895 as Sophie in *Werther*; at Venice in 1897 she took part in the first performance of Ruggero Leoncavallo's *La bohème*. The best years of her career began when she sang the title role in the première of *Zazà*, also by Leoncavallo (1900, Milan, Teatro Lirico), and continued with the successes she obtained at La Scala as Gaetano Donizetti's Linda (1902), Stefana in the first performance of Umberto Giordano's *Siberia* (1903), Norina (1904) and Violetta (1906). She also created the title role of *Madama Butterfly* (1904) at La Scala, and returned there occasionally until 1918. She was very popular in Spain, singing frequently at Barcelona and Madrid between 1898 and 1923, and in Buenos Aires (1904–14). In 1921 she appeared at the Manhattan Opera House, New York, and in Chicago. Among her notable parts were Mimì, Jules Massenet's Manon, and the title role in Pietro Mascagni's *Lodoletta*, which she sang at the first performance (1917, Rome). Her voice was not large, but flexible, pure and sweet; at the height of the popularity for *verismo* opera she personified the lyrical, refined, gentle school of singing. Her plaintive and fragile Cio-Cio-San was typical of this approach, in contrast to the more lively and dramatic style of KRUSCENISKI and DESTINN. But in other roles, such as Violetta or Manon, her acute sensitivity led her to depict the characters with passionate and touching impulsiveness. After her retirement in 1922 she taught singing and devoted herself to charitable works. (For another illustration see ZENATELLO, GIOVANNI.)

T. Hutchinson: 'Rosina Storchio', *Record Collector*, xii (1958–60), 52–60 [with discography]

R. Celletti and K. Hardwick: 'Rosina Storchio', *Record News* [Toronto], iv (1959–60), 429–36

Rodolfo Celletti/R

Rosina Storchio as Cio-Cio-San in the première of 'Madama Butterfly' (Puccini), La Scala, Milan, 1904

Stracciari, Riccardo

(*b* Casalecchio di Reno, nr Bologna, 26 June 1875; *d* Rome, 10 Oct 1955). Italian baritone. After studying briefly at the Bologna Conservatory he sang in the chorus in operetta (1894), then continued his studies with Umberto Masetti at Bologna. He made his début in Firenze in 1898 in Lorenzo Perosi's oratorio *La resurrezione di Lazzaro*; his solo operatic début followed a few days later in *La bohème* at the Teatro Duse in Bologna. In the 1900–01 and 1902–3 seasons he appeared at Lisbon, then at La Scala (1904–6, 1908–9), Covent Garden (1905), the Metropolitan (1906–8), the Paris Opéra (1909), the Real, Madrid (1909–11), and other leading theatres. He then sang mostly in Italy (especially Rome), Spain and Argentina, though from 1917 to 1919 he was a member of the Chicago Opera Association. His vocal decline can be dated from 1928, but though he devoted himself to teaching, first in Naples (1926), then later in Milan and Rome (BORIS CHRISTOFF and PAOLO SILVERI were among his pupils), he did not leave the stage until 1942, and in 1944 appeared again in *La traviata* at the Teatro Lirico, Milan. Stracciari's mellow, velvety voice, coloured and resonant over its whole range, with an extended and penetrating upper register, made him, between 1905 and 1915, the rival of TITTA RUFFO and PASQUALE AMATO. His repertory included all the great baritone roles and among the dramatic parts he preferred those in *Il trovatore*, *Rigoletto* and *Aida*. But, thanks to a technique characteristic of the best traditions of the 19th century, he excelled in works which allowed him to display his courtly enunciation, smooth singing, elegant phrasing and musical delicacy: *La favorite*, *Ernani* and above all *La traviata*, in which he played the heavy father with exceptional, gripping effect. He was also a noted Figaro in *Il barbiere di Siviglia*, a role that well displayed his brilliant high notes and which, like Rigoletto, he recorded in 1929. But his voice is heard at its freest and finest in the recordings he made for Fonotipia (1904–15) and Columbia (1917–25).

M. de Schauensee: 'Fourteen Hundred Times Figaro: a Visit with Riccardo Stracciari', *ON*, xix/7 (1954–5), 8–9
R. Celletti and K. Hardwick: 'Riccardo Stracciari', *Record News* [Toronto], iii (1958–9), 75–82 [with discography by F.A. Armstrong]
L. Di Cave and others: 'Riccardo Stracciari', *Record Collector*, xxx (1985), 3–53 [with discography]

Rodolfo Celletti/R

Strada del Pò, Anna Maria

(*b* Bergamo; *fl* 1719–41). Italian soprano. She sang in four operas in Venice in 1720–21, the first of them Antonio Vivaldi's *La verità in cimento*, then in Milan in 1721, Livorno in 1722 and Lucca in 1724. She appeared at the S Bartolomeo, Naples (1724–6), in Leonardo Vinci's *Eraclea* and *Astianatte*, Nicola Porpora's *Semiramide*, Leonardo Leo's *Zenobia in Palmira* and two operas by Bernardo Porta. While in Naples she married Aurelio del Pò, who for a time managed the theatre and signed the dedication of a number of librettos in 1721–5. He is said to have married Strada because he owed her 2000 ducats and could find no other means of satisfying her.

In 1729 G.F. Handel engaged Strada for London, where she made her début as Adelaida in *Lotario* and was the leading soprano in all his operas and oratorios until 1737. She sang more major Handel parts than any other singer, appearing in at least 24 operas, the opera-ballet *Terpsicore* and many other works, and was the only member of his company who did not go over to the Opera of the Nobility in 1733. Handel composed many roles for her: Adelaida in *Lotario* (1729), Partenope (1730), Cleofide in *Poro* (1731), Fulvia in *Ezio* and Elmira in *Sosarme* (1732), Angelica in *Orlando* (1733), Arianna and Erato in *Terpsicore* (1734), Ginevra in *Ariodante* and Alcina (1735), Atalanta and Meleager in *Atalanta* (1736) and Thusnelda in *Arminio*,

Ariadne in *Giustino* and Berenice (1737). She sang in 11 Handel revivals, taking eight roles composed for CUZZONI and one for FAUSTINA BORDONI; nearly all were modified or included new or adapted arias. She also appeared in a number of pasticcios under Handel and in his revival of Attilio Ariosti's *Coriolano* (1732). She refused to sing for Giovanni Bononcini in 1732. In 1738 she left London for Breda; she sang in Naples in 1739–41 and in Turin and Vicenza in 1741 before retiring to Bergamo.

Charles Burney attributed Strada's success largely to Handel, calling her:

a singer formed by himself, and modelled on his own melodies. She came hither a coarse and aukward singer with improvable talents, and he at last polished her into reputation and favour…Strada's personal charms did not assist her much in conciliating parties, or disposing the eye to augment the pleasures of the ear; for she had so little of a Venus in her appearance, that she was usually called the *Pig*. However, by degrees she subdued all their prejudices, and sung herself into favour.

These prejudices are attested by Paolo Rolli and Mrs Pendarves ('her person *very bad* and she makes *frightful mouths*'), though she was clearly no negligible artist. Rolli called her 'a copy of Faustina with a better voice and better intonation, but without her charm and brio', and quoted Handel as saying that

she sings better than the two who have left us, because one of them [Faustina] never pleased him at all and he would like to forget the other [Cuzzoni]. The truth is that she has a penetrating thread of a soprano voice which delights the ear, but oh how far removed from Cuzzona!

She was famous for her shake, and seems to have combined something of Faustina's dramatic flair with the seductive warbling for which Cuzzoni was renowned. Her parts point to a wide range in emotional and expressive power as well as in compass (*c'* to *c'''*, later (1737) *d'* to *b''*).

Winton Dean

Stratas, Teresa [Strataki, Anastasia]

(*b* Toronto, 26 May 1938). Canadian soprano of Greek descent. She studied with IRENE JESSNER and made her début in Toronto with the Canadian Opera in 1958 as Mimì (also the role of her 1961 Covent Garden début). Having won the 1959 Metropolitan Opera Auditions of the Air, she made her début at the Metropolitan that October as Poussette (*Manon*). Her regular appearances in New York included those as Sardula (Gian Carlo Menotti's *Le dernier sauvage*), Lisa (*The Queen of Spades*), Liù, Nedda, Micaëla, Zerlina, Cherubino, Despina and Hänsel. In 1961 she created the title role in Peggy Glanville-Hicks's *Nausicaa* at the Athens Festival (1961). She appeared regularly as a guest in Munich, Hamburg and Paris, and also performed at Salzburg and the Bol'shoy. Her repertory included Giuseppe Verdi's Joan of Arc, Violetta, Tatyana, Mélisande and Lulu, which she sang at the opera's first complete performance and recording (1979, Paris). She sang Violetta to DOMINGO's Alfredo in Franco Zeffirelli's film (1983), appeared on Broadway in *Rags* in 1986, and took the role of Marie Antoinette in the 1991 première at the Metropolitan of John Corigliano's *The Ghosts of Versailles*, which was recorded on video. Her other filmed roles include Nedda and Salome. Stratas had a lyric-dramatic voice of individuality and a keen sense of the stage. Deep involvement in her roles distinguished all her appearances. During the 1980s Stratas travelled to Calcutta and worked with Mother Teresa in an orphanage and in the Home for the Dying. In the 1990s she again took time off from her career to work in a Romanian orphanage. In addition to her operatic career, she has recorded the Jerome Kern musical, *Show Boat*, and two albums of the songs of Kurt Weill.

Harold Rosenthal/Alan Blyth

Stravinsky, Fyodor Ignat'yevich

(*b* Rechitskiy, Minsk province, 8/20 June 1843; *d* St Petersburg, 21 Nov/4 Dec 1902). Russian bass of Polish descent, father of Igor Stravinsky. He attended the *gimnaziya* (grammar school) at Nezhin, and then studied law. While a student, he sang with great success in public concerts and eventually decided to make a career as a singer. He entered the St Petersburg Conservatory in 1869, where, from September 1871, he studied with Camillo Everardi. In 1873, the year in which he graduated, Stravinsky's performance as Don Basilio in a student production of *Il barbiere di Siviglia* attracted the attention of the critics. He was engaged to sing at the opera theatre in Kiev and made his public début as Count Rodolpho in *La sonnambula* on 22 August/3 September 1873. He remained in Kiev until 1876, when he became one of the principal basses at the Mariinsky Theatre in St Petersburg, appearing there regularly until the year of his death. Stravinsky possessed a many-sided dramatic talent, and played both serious and comic roles with great mastery. He made a total of 1235 appearances in 64 different roles. He was particularly successful in Russian opera, creating the roles of Varlaam in *Boris Godunov* (Nikolay Rimsky-Korsakov wrote the drinking scene in *Sadko* especially for Stravinsky after seeing him as Varlaam or, as some

writers claim, as Skula in Aleksandr Borodin's *Prince Igor*, another role he created), the Village Head in Rimsky-Korsakov's *May Night*, Mstivoy in his *Mlada* and Panas in his *Christmas Eve*, Andrey Dubrovsky in Eduard Nápravník's *Dubrovsky*, and Ivan the Terrible in Anton Rubinstein's *Kupets Kalashnikov*. He was noted, too, for his portrayals of Holofernes in A.N. Serov's *Judith*, the Miller in A.S. Dargomïzhsky's *Rusalka*, and Rangoni in *Boris Godunov*. V.V. Stasov considered that in the role of Farlaf (in M.I. Glinka's *Ruslan and Lyudmila*) Stravinsky was the 'worthy successor to Osip Petrov'. P.I. Tchaikovsky was a great admirer of Stravinsky, and asked that he should play the comparatively small part of Orlik in his opera *Mazepa*, since this part in particular required a 'good artist'. Stravinsky sang in three other Tchaikovsky premières, creating the roles of His Highness in *Vakula the Smith*, Dunois in *The Maid of Orleans* and Mamïrov in *The Enchantress*.

An intelligent and inspired performer, Stravinsky scorned the purely routine and superficial approach to his art and made a thorough psychological study of each character he portrayed, jotting down ideas for his interpretation in a notebook which he always carried. He took an interest in every aspect of stagecraft, and was an authority on make-up and costume design. Although his voice was said to be not intrinsically beautiful, especially in his last years, it was powerful and of a wide range (over two octaves). He strove to achieve evenness of tone, flexibility and variety of colour, so that he could use his voice to both musical and dramatic ends with equal success. He was an excellent concert singer; ballads such as Glinka's *Nochnoy smotr* ('The Night Review') and Modest Musorgsky's *Polkovodets* ('The Field Marshal') were ideally suited to his histrionic gifts. FYODOR CHALIAPIN acknowledged Stravinsky's supremacy in the 1890s, and learnt much from him. Stravinsky was a bibliophile whose library numbered over 7000 volumes, and a collector of pictures. His son alleged that he had an uncontrollable temper, and was a somewhat distant and unpredictable parent. But Igor had no doubts about his father's 'brilliant' dramatic gifts as an actor and his 'virtuosic' singing, commenting on the 'nobility' of his interpretations. For most of his last year he was semi-paralysed, and he died from cancer of the spine.

Jennifer Spencer/Edward Garden

Streich, Rita

(*b* Barnaul, Siberia, 18 Dec 1920; *d* Vienna, 20 March 1987). German soprano. She studied with WILLI DOMGRAF-FASSBÄNDER, MARIA IVOGÜN and ERNA BERGER, making her début at Aussig (now Ústí nad Labem) in 1943 as Zerbinetta. From 1946 to 1951 she sang at the Berlin Staatsoper in such roles as Zerlina, Blonde, Gilda, Sophie and Olympia. In 1951 she joined the Berlin Städtische Oper, extending her repertory to include the Queen of Night and Konstanze. She was engaged at the Vienna Staatsoper in 1953 and made her London début with that company at the Royal Festival Hall in 1954 as Zerlina and Susanna. She made her American début at San Francisco in 1957 as Sophie and sang Zerbinetta in the first performance there of *Ariadne auf Naxos* and at her Glyndebourne début in 1958. She also appeared at Salzburg, where she created the title role of Heimo Erbse's *Julietta* (1959), Aix-en-Provence and Bayreuth, where she sang the Woodbird (1952). Her clear, bright voice and keen musicianship can be heard in recordings of her Mozart roles, Sophie, Zerbinetta (under Herbert von Karajan) and Aennchen, and also on her many recordings of lieder, to which she devoted the latter years of her career.

L. Rasponi: *The Last Prima Donnas* (New York, 1975), 519–24

Harold Rosenthal/Alan Blyth

Streit, Kurt (Martin)

(*b* Itazuke, Japan, 14 Oct 1959). American tenor. After studying with Marilyn Tyler at the University of New Mexico (1980–84), he made his first European appearance at Hamburg in 1987; the relationship with the Hamburg company (1987–91) brought him, *inter alia*, leading roles in a Gluck double bill, *Le cinesi* and *Echo et Narcisse*, which was recorded at Schwetzingen. But it is as a Mozart tenor – light, gentle and romantic of tone, capable of proud utterance – that he swiftly rose to international prominence. He made his Glyndebourne début as Belmonte in 1988, and sang the part to acclaim at Covent Garden in 2001. He has been heard and seen to particular advantage as Tamino, a role that has taken him to many of the world's leading stages. Among his other roles are Ramiro (*La Cenerentola*), Ernesto (*Don Pasquale*), Richard Strauss's Flamand and Benjamin Britten's Lysander and Quint. Streit's recordings include *Die Entführung*, two sets of *Così fan tutte* (under Daniel Barenboim and Simon Rattle), *Die Zauberflöte* and *The Yeoman of the Guard*.

Max Loppert

Strepponi, Giuseppina
[Clelia Maria Josepha]

(*b* Lodi, 8 Sept 1815; *d* Sant'Agata, nr Busseto, 14 Nov 1897). Italian soprano, second wife of Giuseppe Verdi. She was the eldest daughter of Feliciano Strepponi (1797–1832), organist of Monza

Cathedral and composer of several operas, of which *Ullà di Bassora* enjoyed some success at La Scala in 1831. She studied the piano and singing at the Milan Conservatory, winning the first prize for bel canto in her final year. She made her début at Adria in Luigi Ricci's *Chiara di Rosembergh* in December 1834; her first triumph was in Gioachino Rossini's *Matilde di Shabran* in Trieste in spring 1835. In the same year she appeared in Vienna as Adalgisa in *Norma* and as the heroine of *La sonnambula*, which became one of her most famous roles. She often appeared with the tenor NAPOLEONE MORIANI and the baritone GIORGIO RONCONI. She was now the breadwinner of her family: her unremitting activity, combined with liaisons which resulted in three illegitimate children, considerably shortened her career. During the late 1830s, however, she aroused fanatical enthusiasm; Gaetano Donizetti wrote his *Adelia* (1841, Rome) for her.

Strepponi made her début at La Scala in 1839. In 1842 she created the role of Abigaille (*Nabucco*), but by then her powers were in decline. Apart from a disastrous season in Palermo in 1845, she thereafter appeared only sporadically (mostly in operas by Verdi) until her retirement in February 1846. In October that year she moved to Paris as a singing teacher. Verdi joined her there the following summer; from then on her history is that of his life-partner, though they were not legally married until 1859. Strepponi was described as having a 'limpid, penetrating, smooth voice, seemly action, a lovely figure; and to Nature's liberal endowments she adds an excellent technique'; her 'deep inner feeling' was also praised. She interpreted Donizetti's Lucia, Bianca in Saverio Mercadante's *Il giuramento* and most of Vincenzo Bellini's heroines especially well. She was equally at home in comedy, as Adina in *L'elisir d'amore* and Sandrina in Luigi Ricci's *Un'avventura di Scaramuccia*. Yet the most famous of all the roles she created, Verdi's Abigaille, was probably the one least suited to her vocal means. Although she was highly talented, she never sang outside Italy after 1835.

Julian Budden

Struckmann, Falk

(*b* Heilbronn, 23 Jan 1958). German baritone. He studied at the Musikhochschule in Stuttgart, and was then engaged (1985–9) at the Kiel Opera, from where he graduated to the Basle Opera, achieving a particular success as Duke Bluebeard. At Antwerp as Scarpia (1991), at the Théâtre de la Monnaie, Brussels, as Donner (1991) and as the Dutchman at Munich (1992), he announced his arrival as a Heldenbariton of note. Daniel Barenboim's advocacy at the Berlin Staatsoper from 1992, when the conductor engaged him as Amfortas in a new staging of *Parsifal* (recorded for CD and video), helped his career to take wing. His further parts at Berlin under Barenboim have included Wotan/the Wanderer, Orestes (recorded), Wozzeck, Pizarro, Telramund (recorded) and eventually Hans Sachs (1998). Struckmann made his Bayreuth début with the same conductor, as Kurwenal, in 1993 (an interpretation preserved on video), and followed that with Donner, Gunther and Amfortas. His first Jochanaan was at Leipzig in a Nikolaus Lehnhoff staging in the 1994–5 season. He first appeared at La Scala as the Wanderer (1997), and made his début at the Metropolitan as Wozzeck in 1998. He possesses a voice of dramatic weight which he uses with vigour, not to say vehemence, to convey presence and character.

J. Breiholz: 'All in the Music', *ON*, lxi/11 (1996–7), 16–18

Alan Blyth

Studer, Cheryl

(*b* Midland, MI, 24 Oct 1955). American soprano. She studied at the Berkshire Music Center at Tanglewood before winning third prize at the Metropolitan Competition for Young Singers in 1978. After further study in Vienna she worked with HANS HOTTER in Munich before joining the Staatsoper there in 1980, singing, among other roles, Mařenka (*The Bartered Bride*), Euryanthe, Daphne, Irene (*Rienzi*), Sieglinde and the Empress (*Die Frau ohne Schatten*). From 1982 to 1984 she was an ensemble member at the Deutsche Oper, Berlin, where she added Violetta and Desdemona to her repertory. In 1984 she made her American début in Chicago, as Micaëla, which was also the role of her first Metropolitan appearance in 1988. Studer made her Bayreuth début in 1985 as Elisabeth (*Tannhäuser*), immediately proclaiming her outstanding gifts as a lyric-dramatic soprano of the first rank, not least with her ringing high B at the end of Elisabeth's Greeting. She appeared again at Bayreuth, as Elsa, in 1987. She made her Covent Garden début as Elisabeth in 1987 and returned for Elsa in 1988, singing both roles to critical acclaim. At La Scala she sang Sieglinde and the Empress (1987), Mathilde in *Guillaume Tell* (1988), Odabella in *Attila* (1989) and Hélène in *Les vêpres siciliennes* (1989) to arresting effect. She made her Vienna Staatsoper début as Chrysothemis, another role she has recorded. Studer's repertory also includes Countess Almaviva, W.A. Mozart's Electra, Pamina, Gaetano Donizetti's Lucia, Gilda and Aida; more recently she has undertaken the Marschallin (which

she first sang at the Salzburg Festival in 1995 and performed at the Vienna Staatsoper in the 2000–01 season), Ariadne and Senta, with which she returned to Bayreuth in 1998 and 1999. In 2000 she was an acclaimed Arabella at the Zürich Opera, and appeared as Sieglinde at Bayreuth. Her singing is distinguished by full, vibrant tone, controlled, warm phrasing and eloquent expression, heard to best advantage on her recordings of *Les vêpres siciliennes*, *La traviata*, *Die Walküre* (with Bernard Haitink), *Salome* (with Giuseppe Sinopoli) and, above all, *Die Frau ohne Schatten* (with Wolfgang Sawallisch). She has also sung with distinction in concert and song, her performances and recording of Richard Strauss's *Vier letzte Lieder* being particularly admired.

A. Blyth: 'Cheryl Studer', *Opera*, xlv (1994), 656–63

Alan Blyth

Stümer, Heinrich [Carl]

(*b* Frödenwald, Prussia, 1789; *d* Berlin, 27 Sept 1856). German tenor. He studied in Berlin, making his debut there in 1811 as Belmonte at the Hofoper, where he was engaged for 20 years. His repertory included Florestan, Belmonte, Almaviva and Max (*Der Freischütz*), which he created at the Berlin Schauspielhaus in 1821; he was particularly renowned for his singing of C.W. Gluck's Pylades, Achilles, Admetus, Renaud (*Armide*) and Orpheus. Friedrich Wilhelm Jähns was his pupil.

Elizabeth Forbes

Stutzmann, Natalie

(*b* Suresne, 6 May 1965). French contralto. She studied at the Nantes Conservatoire and then at the Ecole Nationale in Paris (1983–7) with MICHEL SÉNÉCHAL and Lou Bruder. She made her concert début in 1985 in J.S. Bach's *Magnificat* at the Salle Pleyel in Paris and her recital début at Nantes in 1986. She sang in Henry Barraud's opera *Tête d'or* in Paris (1985) and in Albéric Magnard's *Guercoeur* with Michel Plasson (1986, Toulouse), which was also her first major recording. In 1989 her recording of the title role in G.F. Handel's *Amadigi*, with Marc Minkowski, was praised for its incisiveness and dramatic commitment. She has become an accomplished recitalist, and in both concerts and recordings of lieder and *mélodies* her dark-grained, expressive singing, with its true contralto depth and richness, has provoked wide admiration. Stutzmann has also sung, in firm, unaffected manner (if at times with too much vibrato for some tastes), the alto solos in many performances and recordings of Baroque repertory, including several concerts in John Eliot Gardiner's Bach Pilgrimage in 2000.

Alan Blyth

Summers, Jonathan

(*b* Melbourne, 2 Oct 1946). Australian baritone. He studied in Melbourne and with OTAKAR KRAUS in London, making his début in 1975 as Rigoletto with Kent Opera. In 1976 he sang Falstaff for Glyndebourne Touring Opera and in 1977 made his Covent Garden début as Kilian (*Der Freischütz*); there he has since sung Sonora (*La fanciulla del West*), the Herald (*Lohengrin*), Balstrode, Sharpless, Malatesta, Figaro (Gioachino Rossini and W.A. Mozart), Albert (*Werther*), Marcello, Demetrius, Papageno, Paolo (*Simon Boccanegra*), Faninal, Animal Tamer (*Lulu*) and Ford. For the ENO he has sung Tonio, Posa, Rigoletto, Yevgeny Onegin, Boccanegra, Renato (*Ballo*), Macbeth (1990) and Rodrigo (1992). He has sung with Opera North and Scottish Opera, in Paris, Geneva, Brussels, Sydney, San Diego, Florence and at the Metropolitan, where he made his début in 1988 as Marcello. His repertory includes C.W. Gluck's Orestes and Hercules, Luna, Germont, Nabucco, Gérard, the four villains (*Les contes d'Hoffmann*) and the Traveller (*Death in Venice*). A powerful actor, he has an expressive, keenly focussed voice well suited to Giuseppe Verdi.

Elizabeth Forbes

Supervia [Supervía], Conchita

(*b* Barcelona, 9 Dec 1895; *d* London, 30 March 1936). Spanish mezzo-soprano. She can have had little musical training when at the age of 14 she made her operatic début in minor roles with a touring Spanish company at the Teatro Colón, Buenos Aires. In November 1911, not yet 16, she was chosen as the Octavian of the Rome première of *Der Rosenkavalier*; in the 1915–16 season she appeared in Chicago as Charlotte, Mignon and Carmen, and during the 1920s sang widely in Spain, and at La Scala (Octavian, Cherubino, Humperdinck's Hänsel and Maurice Ravel's Concepcion) and elsewhere in Italy. Her international fame began with her assumption of the brilliant Rossini mezzo parts in *L'italiana in Algeri*, *La Cenerentola* and *Il barbiere*; these roles, together with that of Carmen, formed the centre of her stage repertory during the last decade of her life, and brought her to Covent Garden in 1934 and 1935. By then Supervia had married an Englishman, Ben Rubenstein, and settled in London, becoming very popular also on the concert platform. She died after childbirth when her career was at its height.

Supervia possessed exceptional gifts of musicianship and temperament. Her rich and vibrant mezzo attained a high degree of flexibility. Few singers conveyed so keen a pleasure in the sheer act of singing; and her enunciation, in several languages, was extremely vivid. These virtues, combined with a mischievous sense of humour and a delightful stage and platform personality, made her a superb interpreter of Rossini and Georges Bizet, as of Manuel de Falla, Enrique Granados and Spanish folksong. Her numerous discs, though sometimes adding an untruthfully strident quality to her louder tones, convey well the vivacity, charm and intimacy of her singing.

H.M. Barnes and V. Girard: 'Conchita Supervia', *Record Collector*, vi (1951), 54–71 [with discography]

D. Shawe-Taylor: 'Conchita Supervia (1895–1936)', *Opera*, xi (1960), 16–23

I. Newton: 'Conchita Supervia', *Recorded Sound*, no.52 (1973), 205–29 [with discography by H.M. Barnes, D. Cattanach, V. Girard and others]

J.B. Steane: *Singers of the Century*, ii (London, 1998), 12–17

Desmond Shawe-Taylor

Suthaus, (Heinrich) Ludwig

(*b* Cologne, 12 Dec 1906; *d* Berlin, 7 Sept 1971). German tenor. He studied in Cologne and made his début at Aachen in 1928 as Walther. Engagements followed at Essen (1931–3), Stuttgart (1933–41), the Berlin Staatsoper (1941–8) and then the Berlin Städtische (later Deutsche) Oper (to 1965). He first sang at Bayreuth in 1943 as Walther, a performance which was recorded; he returned in 1944 in the same role and in 1956–7 as Loge and Siegmund. He sang Tristan at Covent Garden in 1953, the year of his American début as Aegisthus (*Elektra*) at San Francisco, where he also sang Tristan, Siegmund and Erik. At Vienna, where he first appeared in 1948, his roles included Florestan, Otello and Hermann (*The Queen of Spades*). In 1949 he sang the Emperor in *Die Frau ohne Schatten* at the Teatro Colón and the next year sang Števa Buryja in the first South American production of *Jenůfa*. His large repertory also included Rienzi, Bacchus, Pedro (*Tiefland*), Samson, the title role in *Sadko*, which he sang at the German premiere in Berlin (1947), and the Drum Major (*Wozzeck*). Suthaus appeared at La Scala as Siegfried (*Götterdämmerung*) in 1954 and Siegmund in 1958. Among the most notable of his recordings of these are his Siegmund, Siegfried and Tristan under Wilhelm Furtwängler. Suthaus's voice was a true Heldentenor, which he used with intelligence and fervour in his Wagner roles.

Harold Rosenthal/Alan Blyth/R

Sutherland, Dame Joan

(*b* Sydney, 7 Nov 1926). Australian soprano. Her mother taught her until she was 19 when she trained formally in Sydney with John and Aida Dickens. She sang in concerts, oratorios and broadcasts throughout Australia and in August 1947 made a significant concert début in Sydney as Henry Purcell's Dido. In 1951 she sang the title role in Eugene Goossens's *Judith* at the NSW Conservatorium. The same year, having won Australia's most prestigious vocal competition, she went to London and studied with CLIVE CAREY at the Opera School of the RCM. She then joined the Covent Garden company, where she immediately made her mark at her début on 28 October 1952, as the First Lady in *Die Zauberflöte*.

At Covent Garden, Sutherland sang a diversity of roles during the 1950s with increasing dramatic and vocal confidence. These included Amelia (*Un ballo in maschera*), Aida, Frasquita and Micaëla (*Carmen*), several parts in the *Ring* cycle, Agathe, the soprano parts in *Les contes d'Hoffmann* and Eva. She created the role of Jenifer in Michael Tippett's *The Midsummer Marriage* (1955) and sang Madame Lidoine in the British première of Francis Poulenc's *Dialogues des Carmélites* (1958). In 1956 she made her Glyndebourne début as Countess Almaviva in *Figaro*, and added a notable Elvira (*I puritani*) in 1960.

Dame Joan Sutherland in 'La Sonnambula' (Bellini)

Her greatest talent, developed and encouraged by Richard Bonynge, whom she married in 1954, lay in Italian bel canto opera of the 18th and 19th centuries. She was a thrillingly agile and eloquent Alcina for the Handel Opera Society in 1957, the year she sang Gilda and Desdemona, both moving portrayals, at Covent Garden. In 1958 she made her North American début as Donna Anna at the Vancouver Festival, recording the role under Carlo Maria Giulini the following year. But international recognition of her full vocal stature came with her sensational appearance at Covent Garden, on 17 February 1959, in the title role of *Lucia di Lammermoor*, produced by Franco Zeffirelli. In Venice, after a performance of *Alcina*, she was hailed as 'La Stupenda', and it was in that role that she made her American début, in Dallas, on 16 November 1960. Her débuts as Lucia at the Paris Opéra (25 April 1960), La Scala (14 May 1961) and the Metropolitan (26 November 1961) were all highly acclaimed. Her two recordings of the part capture her special qualities of pathos and coloratura brilliance. In 1965 she took her own company to Australia, with Bonynge as musical director.

With a beautiful, soft-grained voice of great range, power and flexibility, Sutherland could deliver fiendishly difficult coloratura with exceptional agility, clarity and mellifluous warmth. She had a vocal range

from *g* to *e′′′*, and was blessed with an exquisitely even trill. On the debit side, she was frequently criticized for swallowing the vowels and blurring the consonants, a failure evident on many of her recordings.

From the early 1960s onwards Sutherland enjoyed huge success in all the major international opera houses, extending her repertory to include the Bellini roles of Amina (1960), Beatrice di Tenda (1961) and Norma (1963), and reviving Gioachino Rossini's *Semiramide* (1962) and Gaetano Donizetti's *La fille du régiment* (1966, in which her spirited performance, which she also recorded, was long admired), *Maria Stuarda* (1971), *Lucrezia Borgia* (1972) and *Anna Bolena* (1984). Her lively championship of the early-19th-century Italian repertory did much to bring it back into favour.

To her Verdi roles she added Violetta (1960), Leonora in *Il trovatore* (1975) and Amalia in *I masnadieri* (1980). She was an accomplished Handelian (Cleopatra in *Giulio Cesare* was one of her outstanding roles) and also distinguished herself in the French repertory with Marguerite de Valois in *Les Huguenots* (1962), Marguerite in *Faust* (1965), *Lakmé* (1967) and Jules Massenet's *Esclarmonde* (1974).

Sutherland's recorded repertory includes an early two-disc set entitled 'The Art of the Prima Donna', which catches her tone and technique in their absolute prime, and most of her major roles. In addition to Lucia these include Alcina, Semiramide, Amina, Mary Stuart, Gilda, Violetta, Marguerite de Valois, the four roles in *Les contes d'Hoffman* and Turandot, a part she never sang on stage. While her recordings reveal an intermittent failure to distinguish, by vocal means alone, one character from another, they eloquently enshrine the range and extent of her achievement. In 1979 she was made a DBE. She retired in 1990 (when her farewell performance in Sydney was as Marguerite de Valois) and in 1991 was awarded the Order of Merit.

N. Major: *Joan Sutherland* (London, 1987, 2/1994) [with discography and catalogue of performances]

J. Sutherland: *A Prima Donna's Progress: the Autobiography of Joan Sutherland* (London, 1997)

Norma Major/Alan Blyth

Svanholm, Set (Karl Viktor)

(*b* Västerås, 2 Sept 1904; *d* Saltsjö-Duvnäs, nr Stockholm, 4 Oct 1964). Swedish tenor. At first a church organist and singer, in 1929 he became a pupil of JOHN FORSELL at the Stockholm Conservatory opera school. In 1930 he had made his début with the Swedish Royal Opera in the baritone roles of Silvio and Gioachino Rossini's Figaro, and in 1937 he was engaged by the company. In 1936 he had made his tenor début as Radames (*Aida*), and he subsequently took on such heavy tenor parts as Otello, Siegmund, Parsifal and Tristan. He sang at Salzburg and Vienna (1938), Berlin, Budapest and Milan (1941–2) and Bayreuth (1942). In Sweden his repertory included Manrico (*Il trovatore*), Canio (*Pagliacci*), Florestan, Bacchus (*Ariadne auf Naxos*), Idomeneus, Tristan and the *Ring* tenor roles; in 1946 he sang Peter Grimes in the Swedish première of Benjamin Britten's opera. In the same year he visited North and South America, singing Siegfried at the Metropolitan. At Covent Garden he sang regularly from 1948 to 1957, notably as Lohengrin and Siegfried. His performances were admired for intelligence, musicianship and stamina, as his recordings as Siegfried, Tristan and Loge (in Georg Solti's *Ring*) confirm. His recordings included the first complete version of *Götterdämmerung*, with FLAGSTAD and Norwegian forces, issued in 1956. He was director of the Swedish Royal Opera from 1956 to 1963 and introduced several contemporary operas, among them *The Turn of the Screw*, *Mathis der Maler* and *The Rake's Progress*.

H. Rosenthal: 'Set Svanholm', *Opera*, vi (1955), 357–62

Carl L. Bruun/Alan Blyth/R

Svéd, Sándor [Sved, Alexander]

(*b* Budapest, 28 May 1906; *d* Budapest, 9 June 1979). Hungarian baritone. He studied the violin in Budapest and singing in Milan with SAMMARCO and STRACCIARI, whose example undoubtedly helped form his strong voice and forceful style. He made his début at Budapest as Luna in 1928, but his fame derives from his period at the Vienna Staatsoper, 1935–9, where he was soon entrusted with the heroic roles in the Italian repertory, his Amonasro in *Aida* in 1938 under Victor De Sabata being particularly admired. Bruno Walter esteemed him enough to cast him as Onegin, Lysiart (*Euryanthe*), Posa and Escamillo, while he also made his mark as Wolfram in *Tannhäuser* under Wilhelm Furtwängler. Later he added Sachs to his Wagner repertory, recording two of his monologues. From 1936 he made an equally powerful impression at Covent Garden where he undertook Rigoletto, Amonasro and Scarpia. Despite the size of his voice, his singing was nimble enough to undertake Gioachino Rossini's Figaro. He made his Metropolitan début in 1940 as Renato (*Un ballo in maschera*) and remained there until 1950. In Florence he performed Boccanegra and Guillaume Tell (whose aria he recorded). Svéd sang the latter role again near the end of his stage career, at the Vienna Volksoper in 1958. He also sang lieder, recording some suitably dark-hued songs in 1940. The vibrant depth of his tone can be heard on a representative selection of arias from his Verdi roles recorded between 1936 and 1947.

P. Jackson: *Saturday Afternoons at the Old Met* (New York, 1992), 236ff

Alan Blyth

Svendén, Birgitta

(*b* Porjus, 26 March 1952). Swedish mezzo-soprano. She studied at the Opera School in Stockholm and made her début at the Royal Opera there in 1981 as Olga (*Yevgeny Onegin*). After singing Flosshilde at Bayreuth in 1983, she added most of the Wagner mezzo roles to her repertory, making her débuts at the Metropolitan Opera in 1989, and Covent Garden in 1990, both as Erda, a role she has also recorded. Her Strauss roles include Octavian, Clairon (*Capriccio*) and Gaea (*Daphne*). In 1995 she was appointed a Singer of the Swedish Court. Svendén's performances are distinguished by her even, well-proportioned voice and natural stage intelligence.

Andrew Clark

Svennsson, Birgit.

See NILSSON, BIRGIT.

Sweet, Sharon

(*b* New York, 16 Aug 1951). American soprano. Prevented by an injury from becoming a concert pianist, she turned to singing, studying first in Philadelphia with MARGARET HARSHAW and then in New York with Marinka Gurewich. In the course of five years she gave some 150 auditions in the United States without being engaged, her weight and figure counting against her; but in 1985 she sang Aida in a concert performance in Munich and launched her stage career the following season as Elisabeth in *Tannhäuser* at Dortmund. She made her operatic débuts in Berlin and at the Paris Opéra in 1987, and in 1988 sang in a concert performance of *Norma* in Brussels. Sweet returned to the USA in 1989, singing Aida in San Francisco. At the Metropolitan in 1992 she appeared as Lina in the first performances there of Giuseppe Verdi's *Stiffelio*, returning in later seasons as Aida. This was also the role of her début in 1995 at Covent Garden, where she later sang an admired Turandot. Her Italian début took place in the Arena at Verona in Giuseppe Verdi's *Requiem* conducted by Lorin Maazel. Sweet's concert repertory also includes the *Missa solemnis*, *Gurrelieder* and the *War Requiem*. In 1993 she toured for the first time in a series of song recitals. With powerful tones at her command, she has usually been engaged for the more heroic roles in opera, although recordings such as those of Agathe's arias in *Der Freischütz* show her ability to soften the volume and sweeten the expression.

J.B. Steane

Swenson, Ruth Ann

(*b* New York, 25 Aug 1959). American soprano. She made her professional début at San Francisco in 1983 as Despina, and has returned there for roles including Pamina, Gilda, Dorinda (*Orlando*), Nannetta and Inès (*L'Africaine*), the latter an enchanting performance recorded on video. Her European début was also as Despina (1985, Geneva). She has subsequently sung Eurydice (C.W. Gluck's *Orphée et Eurydice*) at the Théâtre des Champs-Elysées, Paris, Susanna at the Opéra-Bastille, a Young Girl (*Moses und Aron*) at Salzburg and Konstanze at the Staatsoper in Munich. After appearances in Canada and in Chicago (début as Nannetta, 1988), she made her Metropolitan début in 1991 as Zerlina, and has returned to the Metropolitan for roles such as Rosina, Gilda, Charles Gounod's Juliet, Lucia,

Adina and Zerbinetta. In 1996 she sang a delightful Semele in her first appearance at Covent Garden. Her Violetta in Chicago in 1999 was admired both for its virtuosity and its poignancy. Swenson is as adept in French repertory as in Italian. She sang Manon to acclaim in San Francisco in 1998 and has made a notable recording of Juliet in Gounod's opera. Her voice is full, warm and capable of remarkable feats of flexibility.

Alan Blyth

Sylvan, Sanford

(*b* New York, 19 Dec 1953). American bass-baritone. He studied at the Juilliard School, the Manhattan School of Music and subsequently with PHYLLIS CURTIN at the Tanglewood Music Center summer workshops. His major début was at the New England Bach Festival in 1980, since when he has appeared in recitals with pianist David Breitman throughout the USA (including Carnegie Hall) and in Europe (including the Wigmore Hall). He is also a noted oratorio singer, especially in Bach. In opera he has been been especially acclaimed as W.A. Mozart's Figaro and Don Alfonso, and as Leporello, a role he has sung at Glyndebourne (1994) and at the New York City Opera. In 2004 he sang his first Wotan in *Die Walküre*, in an abridged New York production by Christopher Alden, and in 2005 he made his Glimmerglass Opera début, as Don Alfonso.

Sylvan has also won plaudits for his commanding characterisations in contemporary opera. Notable world premières include the role of Chou En-Lai in John Adams's *Nixon in China* (1987, Houston), the title role in the same composer's *The Death of Klinghoffer* (La Monnaie, 1991), and operas by Philip Glass (*The Juniper Tree*, 1984) and John Harbison. He has since sung the two Adams operas throughout the world, and recorded them. He also premièred and recorded Adams's setting for baritone and chamber orchestra of Walt Whitman's *The Wound-Dresser* (1989), a work specially composed for him. In 2000 he gave the first performance, with Breitman, of Jorge Martin's song cycle *The Glass Hammer* at Carnegie Hall. Among Sylvan's other recordings are Michael Tippett's *Ice Break*, Harbison's *Words from Paterson*, American songs and *mélodies* by Gabriel Fauré.

Richard Wigmore

Sylvester, Michael (Lane)

(*b* Noblesville, IN, 21 Aug 1951). American tenor. He studied at Indiana University with MARGARET

Harshaw, made his professional début in Giuseppe Verdi's Requiem (1975) and became a resident artist with the Indianapolis Opera in 1979. In 1987 he made his European début in Stuttgart as Pinkerton and sang Pollione (*Norma*) at the Paris Opéra and Rodolfo (*La bohème*) for the New York City Opera. He has appeared widely in Europe, and made his La Scala début as Pinkerton in 1990. His other roles include Radames, Florestan, Lohengrin, Bacchus, Don José and Samson, the role of his Covent Garden début in 1991. The same year he made his Metropolitan début as Rodolfo (*Luisa Miller*), followed by Don Carlos, which he has also recorded. In 1992 he sang Foresto (*Attila*) in Geneva, and made his début at San Francisco as Cavaradossi, returning in 1993 for Calaf, which he repeated in Santiago, Houston, Buenos Aires and at the Metropolitan. A powerful actor, Sylvester has a strong, bright-toned voice, with an authentic italianate ring, heard to particular advantage in a role such as Verdi's Gabriele Adorno (*Simon Boccanegra*), which he has sung at Covent Garden, the Metropolitan and in Chicago.

ELIZABETH FORBES

Szayer, Jadwiga.

See SARI, ADA.

Székely, Mihály

(*b* Jászberény, 8 May 1901; *d* Budapest, 22 March 1963). Hungarian bass. He studied with Géza László and made his début at the Budapest Municipal Theatre in 1923 as the Hermit (*Der Freischütz*). He joined the Hungarian State Opera the same year and was soon singing leading bass roles such as Cardinal Brogni (*La Juive*), Charles Gounod's Méphistophélès (*Faust*), Sarastro and King Mark. He also worked with the Hungarian composer and pianist Júlia Hajdú. An international career developed after World War II: his Metropolitan début (1947) was as Hunding, after which he sang many Wagner and other bass roles in New York until 1949. At Glyndebourne, from 1957 to 1961, his Sarastro, Osmin, Bartolo (*Figaro*) and Rocco were greatly admired. He played Boris Godunov in Paris (1957), and Béla Bartók's Bluebeard throughout Europe, partly transposed for his bass range by the composer (he successfully recorded the part). Székely was a major figure in the history of Hungarian opera, with a voice of intrinsic beauty and wide range (his lowest notes were of particularly powerful 'black' timbre) and outstanding acting ability. In addition to those already mentioned, his Philip II (*Don Carlos*), Fiesco (*Simon Boccanegra*), Dosifey (*Khovanshchina*) and Khan Konchak (*Prince Igor*) were all memorable portrayals.

PÉTER P. VÁRNAI/R

T

Tacchinardi, Nicola [Niccolò]

(*b* Livorno, 3 Sept 1772; *d* Florence, 14 March 1859). Italian tenor, father of FANNY TACCHINARDI-PERSIANI. After playing the cello in the orchestra of the Teatro della Pergola, Florence, he studied singing, appearing in various Italian cities in 1804. In spring 1805 he made his début at La Scala in Ferdinando Paer's *Griselda* and FARINELLI's *Odoardo e Carlotta* for the celebration of Napoleon I's coronation as king of Italy; during Carnival 1805–6 he sang at the Teatro Carcano, Milan, in Francesco Gnecco's *Le nozze di Lauretta*. He then established himself in Rome, Bergamo, Bologna (summer 1809) and Turin (Carnival 1810–11); his greatest successes were in Rome, at the Teatro Valle (1806–7) and the Teatro Argentina (1809–10) in Francesco Morlacchi's *Le danaidi*, Giuseppe Nicolini's *Traiano in Dacia* and Niccolò Zingarelli's *La distruzione di Gerusalemme*. His performance of the last-named at the Paris Odéon on 4 May 1811 brought him tumultuous applause; he remained in Paris until 1814 at the Théâtre Italien, singing in Paer's *Didone*, *Don Giovanni* (with the title role transposed), Domenico Cimarosa's *Gli Orazi ed i Curiazi* and Vincenzo Pucitta's *Adolfo e Chiara*, and, most successfully, in Giovanni Paisiello's *La molinara*. He sang in Spain, 1815–17, and in Vienna in 1816. In 1818–19 he sang at the Teatro Argentina and elsewhere in Italy, in Nicolini's *Cesare nelle Gallie* and Gioachino Rossini's *Ciro in Babilonia* and *Aureliano in Palmira*. In April 1820 he sang Rossini's *Otello* (which became his warhorse) at the Teatro del Giglio, Lucca, and in 1820–21 appeared in *Il barbiere di Siviglia* and *La donna del lago*.

Tacchinardi was made principal singer of the grand ducal chapel in Florence in 1822, but was free to continue his operatic career; he appeared again in Vienna (1823), Barcelona (1826) and throughout Italy (1827–8); in 1825 he sang at the Teatro Ducale, Parma, in *Il crociato in Egitto*, which Giacomo Meyerbeer composed for him. He retired from the stage in 1831. He wrote an essay on contemporary opera in Italy (*Dell'opera in musica sul teatro italiano e de' suoi difetti*, Florence, 2/1833). Short and stocky, though with a noble, expressive face, Tacchinardi had a voice that was mellow, powerful, extensive in compass and almost baritone in colouring. His technique was masterly, especially with regard to breathing, phrasing, agility in vocal flourishes and ease in passing from chest to head voice. A marble bust of him by Antonio Canova is in the Museo Teatrale alla Scala in Milan.

Francesco Bussi

Tacchinardi-Persiani [née Tacchinardi], Fanny

(*b* Rome, 4 Oct 1812; *d* Neuilly-sur-Seine, 3 May 1867). Italian soprano, daughter of NICOLA TACCHINARDI and wife of the composer Giuseppe Persiani. She made her début in Livorno in 1832 in the title role of Giuseppe Fournier-Gorre's *Francesca da Rimini*. Singing in *Tancredi*, *La gazza ladra*, *Il pirata* and *L'elisir d'amore* (Carnival 1832–3, Venice) and in *L'elisir*, *Beatrice di Tenda* and *La sonnambula* (summer 1833, Milan), she made a deep impression as an interpreter of Vincenzo Bellini and particularly of Gaetano Donizetti, who wrote for her the title roles of *Rosmonda d'Inghilterra* (1834, Florence), *Lucia di Lammermoor* (1835, Naples) and *Pia de' Tolomei* (1837, Venice). She triumphed further in 1834 at the Teatro del Fondo, Naples, in Valentino Fioravanti's *Le cantatrici villane* and again in *L'elisir* and *Beatrice*, and in 1836 at the Teatro Comunale, Bologna, in Persiani's *Ines de Castro*; her frequent appearances in her husband's operas contributed to their success.

She first sang in Paris at the Théâtre Italien in autumn 1837 in *La sonnambula* and *Lucia*, and distinguished herself as Carolina in *Il matrimonio segreto*. She remained there for 13 years, appearing also in *Le nozze di Figaro*, *Don Giovanni* (as Zerlina), *Il barbiere di Siviglia*, *Linda di Chamounix* (1842) and her husband's *Il fantasma*. She sang in London almost every year between 1838 and 1849, first at the King's Theatre (where she made her début in *La sonnambula*) and later at Covent Garden, appearing in, among other operas, *Lucia* with GIOVANNI BATTISTA RUBINI. She also appeared in Vienna (1837, 1844) in *Torquato Tasso*, *Lucrezia Borgia*, *I due Foscari* and *Ernani*, in the Netherlands (1850) and at the Italian Opera in St Petersburg (1850–52), where in her last performances she showed signs of decline with a 'hoarseness' which, according to F.-J. Fétis, had been noticeable in London in 1843.

Called 'la piccola Pasta', she had a small and delicate voice that was sweet, polished, distinct by virtue of good placement, and had a compass of *b* to *f'''*. Her technique was almost impeccable, with an extraordinary agility in embellishing. A lack of fullness of tone and passion was compensated for by exceptional bel canto purity and near-instrumental virtuosity. Tacchinardi-Persiani's ethereal presence and fragile build fitted her for identification with her roles of the early Romantic 'amorosa angelicata'. She was less effective in comic roles (in which she nevertheless triumphed) than as a dejected, tremulous heroine of a gloomy Romantic tragedy.

T. Kaufman: 'Giuseppe and Fanny Persiani', *Donizetti Society Journal*, vi (1988), 123–51 [incl. chronology of operatic appearances]

Francesco Bussi

Taddei, Giuseppe

(*b* Genoa, 26 June 1916). Italian baritone. He studied in Rome and made his début there in 1936 as the Herald in *Lohengrin*. He sang regularly in Rome, where his repertory included Alberich, Germont and Rivière (Luigi Dallapiccola's *Volo di notte*), until he was conscripted into the army in 1942. Engaged in 1946 for two seasons at the Vienna Staatsoper, he scored particular successes in Verdi roles. In 1947 he sang Scarpia and Rigoletto at the Cambridge Theatre, London, and in 1948 W.A. Mozart's Figaro at the Salzburg Festival. At La Scala (1948–61) his roles included Pizarro, Malatesta, the four villains in *Les contes d'Hoffmann* and parts in operas by Nino Sanzogno and Ferrari Trecate. Elsewhere in Italy he sang (in Italian) Hans Sachs, Gunther, Wolfram and the Dutchman. Later he specialized in Mozart, singing Papageno, Figaro and Leporello. He appeared at Covent Garden between 1960 and 1967 as Macbeth, Rigoletto, Iago and Scarpia and also sang in San Francisco, Chicago and at the Bregenz Festival (1968, 1969, 1971) as Falstaff, Dulcamara and Sulpice (*La fille du régiment*). Taddei had a warm, subtly coloured voice and intelligently inflected diction, and was successful in both comic and dramatic roles. He made notable recordings, some with Cetra, of his Verdi roles as well as his Figaro, Guglielmo, Dulcamara and Scarpia.

Harold Rosenthal/Alan Blyth

Tagliabue, Carlo

(*b* Mariano Comense, 13 Jan 1898; *d* Monza, 5 April 1978). Italian baritone. He studied with Gennai and Guidotti and made his début at Lodi in 1922 as Amonasro. After appearances at provincial theatres and in Florence, Palermo and the Verona Arena he was engaged at La Scala, where he sang regularly from 1930 to 1953. As well as the Italian repertory, his roles included Telramund, Wolfram, Gunther and Kurwenal. At the Teatro Reale dell'Opera, Rome, he created Basilio in Ottorino Respighi's *La fiamma* (1934), and he sang Scedeur in the first performances at La Scala of Ildebrando Pizzetti's *Lo straniero*. He sang at the Teatro Colón (1934), at the Metropolitan (1937–9), where he made his début as Amonasro, and in San Francisco (1938). He made his Covent Garden début in 1938 as Rigoletto and returned in 1946 as Germont with the S Carlo company. In 1953 he sang Don Carlo (*La forza del destino*) at the Stoll Theatre. He continued to sing until 1960. His pupils included RAFFAELE ARIÈ and ANGELO GOBBATO. Tagliabue's resonant, well-produced baritone was ideally suited to Verdi roles, as can be heard in his Don Carlo from a wartime recording of *La forza del destino*.

Harold Rosenthal/Alan Blyth/R

Tagliavini, Ferruccio

(*b* Reggio nell'Emilia, 14 Aug 1913; *d* Reggio nell' Emilia, 29 Jan 1995). Italian tenor. He studied in Parma with Italo Brancucci and in Florence with AMEDEO BASSI. He made his début in October 1939 in Florence as Rodolfo in *La bohème* and first sang at La Scala, as Gioachino Rossini's Almaviva, in 1942. By the end of World War II he had established himself as one of the leading tenors of the Italian stage; he then appeared successfully at the Metropolitan (1947–54 and 1961–2). During the visit of the La Scala company to Covent Garden in 1950, he sang Nemorino in *L'elisir d'amore*, revealing his vocal achievements as well as a considerable talent as a comic actor. He made further appearances in London as Cavaradossi (1955–6, Covent Garden) and as Nadir in *Les pêcheurs de perles* (1958, Drury Lane). He retired from the stage in 1966.

Essentially a *tenore di grazia*, Tagliavini excelled in the bel canto operas of Vincenzo Bellini and Gaetano Donizetti and in the title role of Pietro Mascagni's *L'amico Fritz*, which he recorded under the composer's direction, with his wife, the soprano PIA TASSINARI, as Suzel. Many regarded him as the successor of TITO SCHIPA; Tagliavini's style, however, was less dependable. He could spin out a sustained note until it became a mere thread of tone, and he sang florid passages more accurately than was usual in the postwar period; but he also relied on abrupt transitions between *fortissimo* and *pianissimo* to the neglect of the intermediate shades, and in later years permitted his louder tones to develop a harsh quality. His art is best represented in his early Cetra discs, which have been reissued on CD.

H. Sanguinetti and C. Williams: 'Ferruccio Tagliavini', *Record Collector*, xxix (1984), 197–240 [with discography]
A. Blyth: Obituary, *Opera*, xlvi (1995), 408–9

Desmond Shawe-Taylor/R

Tajo, Italo

(*b* Pinerolo, Piedmont, 25 April 1915; *d* Cincinnati, 28 March 1993). Italian bass. He studied in Turin and in 1935 made his début there as Fafner in *Das Rheingold* under Fritz Busch. Busch took him to Glyndebourne that summer as a chorus member and understudy: Tajo sang Bartolo's 'La vendetta' in the first Glyndebourne recording of *Le nozze di Figaro* because NORMAN ALLIN was not available. During the war he sang at the Rome Opera in a variety of roles, including the Doctor in the Italian première of *Wozzeck* (1942), and at La Scala, where he returned in the first postwar season (1946) as Don Magnifico and Ochs, and where he continued to appear until 1956. At the 1947 Edinburgh Festival he sang Figaro and Banquo with the Glyndebourne company, then appeared in London at the Cambridge Theatre (1947–8), as Don Basilio, Leporello and Don Pasquale, and at Covent Garden with the Scala company in 1950 when, as Dulcamara, he revealed his outstanding gifts as a *buffo* artist. He made his American début in Chicago as Ramfis (1946), and sang at San Francisco (1948–56) and the Metropolitan (1948–50). In Italy Tajo created roles in operas by Valentino Bucchi, G.F. Malipiero, Luigi Nono, Luciano Berio, Adriano Lualdi and Vieri Tosatti; he sang Samuel in the first performance at La Scala of Darius Milhaud's *David* (1955), and took part in the Italian premières of *Troilus and Cressida* (1956) and *The Nose* (1964). He continued to make occasional appearances in the USA as the Sacristan and Benoit and in other character roles until the late 1980s. Tajo's voice, though not large, had a distinctive timbre. He made a notable recording of Mozart concert arias.

C. Faria: 'Old Pros: Tajo and Barbieri', *ON*, xli/16 (1976–7), 9–13
A. Blyth: Obituary, *Opera*, xl (1993), 661

Harold Rosenthal/Alan Blyth

Talazac, Jean-Alexandre

(*b* Bordeaux, 6 May 1851; *d* Chatou, Paris, 26 Dec 1896). French tenor. He studied at the Paris Conservatoire, then in 1878 was engaged by the Opéra-Comique, singing Selim in Ernest Reyer's *La statue* and also in Daniel Auber's *Haydée*. He created the title roles of Léo Delibes' *Jean de Nivelle* (1880) and Jacques Offenbach's *Les contes d'Hoffmann* (1881); Gérald in *Lakmé* (1883), Des Grieux in *Manon* (1884) and Mylio in Edouard Lalo's *Le roi d'Ys* (1888). He also sang Tamino, Adrien Méhul's Joseph, Alfredo (*La traviata*) and, at the Eden-Théâtre, Samson in the first staged performance in Paris of Camille Saint-Saëns's *Samson et Dalila* (1890). At Monte Carlo (1883–9) he sang Faust, Wilhelm Meister, Fernand (*La favorite*), Gaetano Donizetti's Edgardo, Noureddin (Félicien David's *Lalla-Roukh*) and A.-E.-M. Grétry's Richard the Lionheart. He appeared in Lisbon (1887) as Raoul and at Covent Garden (1889) as Alfredo, Faust and Nadir (*Les pêcheurs de perles*). His voice was of great brilliance and purity.

Elizabeth Forbes

Talvela, Martti (Olavi)

(*b* Hiitola, 4 Feb 1935; *d* Juva, 22 July 1989). Finnish bass. Perhaps the outstanding Finnish singer of the postwar period, he was originally a schoolteacher by profession. He entered the Lahti Academy of Music in 1958, continued his studies in Stockholm where he was taught by CARL-MARTIN OEHMAN, and made his début at the Swedish Royal Opera there in 1961, as Sparafucile; shortly afterwards, an audition with Wieland Wagner resulted in his being engaged as Titurel at the 1962 Bayreuth Festival (the year he joined the Deutsche Oper, Berlin). A voice of immense size and wide range, capable of thundering grandeur and great gentleness, allied to a giant's physique and an impressive stage presence, won him international fame in Modest Musorgsky, Giuseppe Verdi and all the principal Wagner bass roles. He was Boris Godunov in New York's first 'original version' of the opera, at the Metropolitan (1974). His first Gurnemanz at Covent Garden in 1973 was remarkable for its natural nobility; he is also remembered there for notable appearances as Dosifey (*Khovanshchina*) and Hunding. Talvela was the inaugural director of the Savonlinna Festival (1972–9), the first opera under his aegis being, in 1973, *Die Zauberflöte*, in which he was Sarastro. In 1975 he created (and later recorded) Paavo Ruotsalainen in Joonas Kokkonen's *The Last Temptations* at Savonlinna, repeating the role in London the following year. Along with Boris Godunov and Sarastro, both of which he recorded, this was accounted among Talvela's most majestic and compelling interpretations. His many other recordings include Sibelius and Kilpinen songs (of which he was a devoted advocate), Joseph Haydn's *The Seasons*, Verdi's Requiem, King Mark and the Grand Inquisitor (*Don Carlos*). Shortly before his death he was appointed general director of the Finnish National Opera. He was commemorated by the Finnish composer Leif Segerstam in *Monumental Thoughts: Martti Talvela in memoriam* (1989).

J. Hines: *Great Singers on Great Singing* (Garden City, NY, 1982), 331–7

A. Blyth: Obituary, *Opera*, xl (1989), 1067–8

Max Loppert

Tamagno, Francesco

(*b* Turin, 28 Dec 1850; *d* Varese, 31 Aug 1905). Italian tenor. A pupil of Carlo Pedrotti in Turin, he began his career in the chorus of the Teatro Regio, also singing small roles such as Nearco in Gaetano Donizetti's *Poliuto* (1872). After further study, in 1874 he sang Riccardo (*Un ballo in maschera*) at Palermo and in 1875, Poliuto and Edgardo (*Lucia di Lammermoor*) at La Fenice, Venice. He first appeared at La Scala in 1877 as Vasco da Gama (Giacomo Meyerbeer's *L'Africaine*), then created the title role of Giuseppe Verdi's *Don Carlos* (1878), and sang Alim in Jules Massenet's *Le roi de Lahore* and Fabiano in the first performance of Carlos Gomes's *Maria Tudor* (1879); he created the role of Azaele in Amilcare Ponchielli's *Il figliuol prodigo* (1880), then sang Ernani, and Gabriele Adorno in the first performance of the revised version of *Simon Boccanegra* (1881); he sang Raoul in *Les Huguenots* and John of Leyden in *Le prophète* (1884), created Didier in Ponchielli's *Marion Delorme* (1885), then sang Radames in *Aida* (1886).

His greatest triumph came on 5 February 1887, when he created Verdi's Othello; he repeated the role in the first London performance of *Otello* (Lyceum Theatre) in July 1889, at Chicago (where he had made his American début a few days previously as Arnold in *Guillaume Tell*) in January 1890, at the Metropolitan in March 1890 and at Nice in 1891. He appeared in Giacomo Puccini's *Edgar* at Madrid (1892) and in the first performance of Ruggero Leoncavallo's *I Medici* at the Teatro Dal Verme, Milan (1893). He returned to the Metropolitan for the 1894–5 season, and made his Covent Garden début in 1895 as Othello. After creating the role of Helion in Isidore de Lara's *Messaline* at Monte Carlo in 1899, he sang it at La Scala and at Covent Garden, where he returned for a final season in 1901. Tamagno's heroic voice, with its brazen, trumpet-like top notes, was heard to best advantage

in Verdi roles, especially Othello, which displayed the magnificent strength and security of its upper register. He was a forceful, convincing actor, and though not a subtle artist, he brought great vocal and dramatic excitement to all his performances.

M. Corsi: *Francesco Tamagno* (Milan, 1937/*R* with discography)

Elizabeth Forbes

Tamberlik [Tamberlick], Enrico

(*b* Rome, 16 March 1820; *d* Paris, 13 March 1889). Italian tenor. He studied in Rome, Naples and Bologna. At the age of 18 he sang Gennaro in a semi-private performance of *Lucrezia Borgia*, but his official début, under the name of Danieli, was in 1841 at the Teatro del Fondo, Naples, as Tebaldo (*I Capuleti e i Montecchi*). At the S Carlo in 1843 he appeared (as Tamberlik) in Otto Nicolai's *Il templario*. He made his London début in 1850 as Masaniello at Covent Garden, where he appeared regularly until 1864, singing Gioachino Rossini's Otello, Arnold (*Guillaume Tell*), Florestan, Max, Pollione, Zampa, Ernani, Robert le diable, John of Leyden, Charles Gounod's Faust, Hugo (Louis Spohr's *Faust*) and Alphonse (*La favorite*), a baritone role. He also sang the title role of *Benvenuto Cellini* (1853) and Manrico in *Il trovatore* (1855), both British premières.

Tamberlik sang at St Petersburg, creating Don Alvaro in *La forza del destino* (1862). He also appeared at Buenos Aires, Paris, Madrid and Moscow; in 1881, when over 60, he toured the Spanish provinces as Arturo (*I puritani*), Poliuto, Ernani, Manrico, the Duke and Faust. His robust voice, with its ringing top notes (including a top C sung in full chest voice), was marked by a fast vibrato, but his musicianship and handsome, exciting stage presence made him a superb interpreter of heroic roles.

Elizabeth Forbes

Tamburini, Antonio

(*b* Faenza, 28 March 1800; *d* Nice, 8 Nov 1876). Italian baritone. He made his début at Cento in 1818 in Pietro Generali's *La contessa di Colle Erboso*, and then sang in Piacenza, Naples, Livorno and Turin. In 1822 he appeared at La Scala in Gioachino Rossini's *Matilde di Shabran*, Saverio Mercadante's *Il posto abbandonato* and the first performance of Gaetano Donizetti's *Chiara e Serafina*. After singing in Trieste and Vienna, he took part in the première of Donizetti's *L'ajo nell'imbarazzo* at Rome (1824). Engaged in Palermo (1825–6), he appeared in Rossini's *L'italiana in Algeri*, *Il barbiere di Siviglia*, *Aureliano in Palmira*, *L'inganno felice* and *Tancredi* and Mercadante's *Elisa e Claudio*. In 1826 he sang in the first performance of Donizetti's *Alahor di Granata*.

At La Scala he created Ernesto in Vincenzo Bellini's *Il pirata* (1827), repeating it in Vienna. He sang in Bellini's *Bianca e Fernando* and in the first performance of Donizetti's *Alina, regina di Golconda* at Genoa (1828). He took part in the premières of Donizetti's *Gianni di Calais* (1828), *Imelda de' Lambertazzi* (1830), *Francesca di Foix* (1831), *La romanziera* (1831) and *Fausta* (1832) in Naples. He created Valdeburgo in Bellini's *La straniera* at La Scala (1829), a part he repeated in Naples (1830) and at the King's Theatre, London (1832).

In 1832 Tamburini appeared for the first time at the Théâtre Italien, Paris, singing Dandini (*La Cenerentola*), Assur (*Semiramide*), the title role of *Mosè in Egitto* and Valdeburgo. For a decade he sang alternately in London and Paris; his repertory included W.A. Mozart's Don Giovanni and Count Almaviva, and roles in Rossini's *La gazza ladra*, *Otello*, *La donna del lago*, *Le siège de Corinthe* and *Guillaume Tell*. He created Riccardo in Bellini's *I puritani* and Ismaele in Donizetti's *Marino Faliero* (both 1835, Paris) and also sang in *Lucia di Lammermoor*, *Parisina*, *Roberto Devereux* and *Lucrezia Borgia*. He sang in the first Paris performance of Donizetti's *Linda di Chamounix* (1842) and created Malatesta in *Don Pasquale* (1843). After an absence from London of five years, he sang Assur at the opening of the Royal Italian Opera at Covent Garden (1847). He retired in 1855. His voice, unusually flexible for a baritone, was rich and solid throughout its range.

As is clear from much of the music created for him, Tamburini's compass extended unusually low for a baritone; he would today probably be classed as a bass-baritone. His talent was essentially lyrical, a far cry from the higher, more intense 'Verdian' baritones of the next generation. Henry Chorley wrote in his *Thirty Years' Musical Recollections* (1862): 'He was a singularly handsome man; his voice was rich, sweet, extensive and equal – ranging from F to f', two perfect octaves – and in every part of it entirely under control. His execution has never been exceeded. ...No one since himself has so thoroughly combined grandeur, accent, florid embellishment and solidity.'

Elizabeth Forbes

Tappy, Eric

(*b* Lausanne, 19 May 1931). Swiss tenor. He studied at the Geneva Conservatoire with Fernando Carpi (1951–8), at the Salzburg Mozarteum with Ernst Reichert, in Hilversum with Eva Liebenberg, and in Paris with Nadia Boulanger. He made his début in 1959 at Strasbourg as the Evangelist in the *St Matthew Passion* and later that season appeared in Zürich in Darius Milhaud's *Les malheurs d'Orphée* under Paul Sacher. His musicianship and intelligence commended him to Frank Martin and Ernest Ansermet, and under the latter he sang in the first performances of Martin's *Le mystère de la Nativité* (1959) and *Monsieur de Pourceaugnac* (1963). Tappy's first operatic appearance was in the title role of Jean-Philippe Rameau's *Zoroastre* at the Paris Opéra-Comique in 1964, during the bicentenary commemorations of Rameau's death. In 1966 he created Léon in Darius Milhaud's *La mère coupable* at Geneva. In the same year he sang Claudio Monteverdi's Orpheus at Herrenhausen, and the following year he played Nero in *L'incoronazione di Poppea* at Hanover. From 1963 he appeared regularly at the Grand Théâtre, Geneva, distinguishing himself especially in the W.A. Mozart repertory. He made his Covent Garden début in 1974 in the title role of Mozart's *La clemenza di Tito*, and the same year made his American début as Don Ottavio in San Francisco. His operatic repertory also included Schoenberg's Aaron, Pelléas, Idomeneus and Lysander (*A Midsummer Night's Dream*). His concert repertory included choral works of J.S. Bach, Hector Berlioz, G.F. Handel, Joseph Haydn, Mozart, Heinrich Schütz and Igor Stravinsky, as well as lesser-known music by André Campra, Giacomo Carissimi, Luigi Nono, Alessandro Scarlatti and Antonio Vivaldi. Tappy made many recordings of concert and operatic repertory; his Orpheus (Claudio Monteverdi) and his account of the tenor part in Colin Davis's second recording of *L'enfance du Christ* are perhaps the most notable. With Louis Erlo he was director of The Opéra Studio, attached to the Lyons Opéra as a training school for young singers. His pupils included the Belgian tenor GUY DE MEY and the French soprano CATHERINE DUBOSC.

Harold Rosenthal/R

Tashko-Koço, Tefta

(*b* El Faiyûm, Egypt, 2 Nov 1910; *d* Tirana, 28 or 29 Dec 1947). Albanian soprano. She studied in Montpellier and Paris (1927–35), where her teachers included André Gresse, and returned to Albania in 1935; later she studied in Italy. She gave numerous recitals throughout Albania, even in remote villages. Her combination of a classical opera repertory with Albanian folksong arrangements (and later partisan songs) endeared her to a popular audience, for many of whom she provided the first contact with foreign art-music. She appeared in Rome, Bari and other Italian cities, and in November 1945 sang Rosina and Mimì at the Belgrade Opera. In 1946 she organized singing classes at the newly-founded Jordan Misja, Albania's first teaching institution for music. Her repertory leaned towards coloratura arias. Her perfect intonation and rich, clear, sweet tone were combined with a keen sense of style, natural charm and beauty and great will-power.

George Leotsakos

Taskin, (Emile-)Alexandre

(*b* Paris, 18 March 1853; *d* Paris, 5 Oct 1897). French baritone. He studied in Paris, making his début in 1875 at Amiens as Roland in Fromental Halévy's *Les mousquetaires de la reine*. Engaged by the Opéra-Comique, Paris, from 1878 to 1894, he sang in the first performance of Léo Delibes' *Jean de Nivelle* (1880); he created Lindorf, Coppelius and Dr Miracle in *Les contes d'Hoffmann* (1881), Lescaut in *Manon* (1884), Falstaff in Ambroise Thomas' *Songe d'une nuit d'été* (1886) and Phorcas in *Esclarmonde* (1889). He also sang Count Almaviva (*Le nozze di Figaro*), Escamillo, Ourrias (*Mireille*), Sulpice (*La fille du régiment*), Jupiter (Charles Gounod's *Philémon et Baucis*) and Lothario in the 1000th performance of *Mignon* at the Opéra-Comique (1894).

Elizabeth Forbes

Tassinari, Pia (Domenica)

(*b* Modigliana, 15 Sept 1903; *d* Faenza, 15 May 1995). Italian soprano, later mezzo-soprano. She studied in Bologna with CESARE VEZZANI and in Milan, making her début in 1927 as Mimì at Casale Monferrato. In 1932 she appeared at La Scala in the première of Antonio Veretti's *Il favorito del re*, and in the 1936 season she sang Elsa and Margherita and created Lucia in Riccardo Zandonai's *La farsa amorosa*. After World War II she extended her career to the Americas, but continued to appear at La Scala until 1956. At the Metropolitan in 1947 she sang Tosca to the Cavaradossi of her husband, FERRUCCIO TAGLIAVINI, but her voice was by then considered too worn. From 1952 she sang principally in mezzo roles such as Carmen and Charlotte, giving her last stage performance, as Carmen, in Philadelphia in 1962. Her best solo recordings are those of the 1930s, fresh of tone and generous without being excessive in emotion. She was also an excellent Alice Ford in the first

recording of *Falstaff* (1930); and as a mezzo she sang an effective Ulrica in *Un ballo in maschera* (1954).

J.B. Steane

Tate, Maggie.

See TEYTE, MAGGIE.

Tauber [Taube], Maria Anna [Marianne]

(*fl* 1777–9). Austrian soprano. A member of the Esterházy opera company, she probably sang the role of Markesinn Bellavita in the first performance of Maximilian Ulbrich's *Frühling und Liebe* (Vienna, 8 February 1778), appearing on the playbill as 'Mlle Tauber'. She was probably also the 'Mlle Teuberin' referred to by Baron von Gebler in a letter of the same date. She was not related to THERESE TEYBER, who sang in the same performance.

Tauber, Richard

(*b* Linz, 16 May 1891; *d* London, 8 Jan 1948). Austrian tenor, naturalized British. He was the illegitimate son of the actor and theatre director Richard Anton Tauber. After study at Freiburg, he first appeared in opera at Chemnitz (2 March 1913) as Tamino in *Die Zauberflöte*. He was at once engaged by the Dresden Opera, where he sang all the leading lyrical tenor roles. By 1919 he was well known throughout the German-speaking countries, and he soon became extremely popular at the Munich and Salzburg Mozart festivals, most notably as Belmonte, Ottavio and Tamino. It was to lighter music, however, that he owed his world fame. He appeared with increasing frequency in the operettas of Franz Lehár and others, charming thousands by his true tenor quality, sympathetic and somewhat 'nutty' in timbre, and by the grace and variety of his vocal inflections. His association with Lehár was enormously beneficial to the latter's career. England succumbed in 1931, when Lehár's *Das Land des Lächelns* repeated its widespread success at Drury Lane. When Covent Garden first heard him he was no longer at his very best; in 1938 he sang Tamino and Belmonte, in 1939 Don Ottavio, and Hans in the German version of *The Bartered Bride*. After the war, however, he surprised even his warmest admirers by the excellence of his Don Ottavio in 1947 in a single performance of *Don Giovanni* with the visiting Vienna Staatsoper. Tauber's first marriage was dissolved, and he married the actress Diana Napier in 1936. He wrote three operettas, music for films, and various songs. He also appeared in several films, including in 1936 a British film of *Pagliacci*. Tauber's successful career is chronicled on numerous recordings. The earlier ones prove what a sterling artist he was in a wide variety of operatic roles. His later recordings include, besides lieder, many operetta numbers and popular songs, in which he evinces an innate gift for turning dross into gold. In 1950 the Anglo-Austrian Music Society inaugurated in his memory the Richard Tauber Prize for young singers.

D.N. Tauber: *Richard Tauber* (London, 1949)

D.N. Tauber: *My Heart and I* (London, 1959)

J. Dennis, G.O. and L.E. Abell: 'Richard Tauber', *Record Collector*, xviii (1968–9), 171–272; xix (1970–71), 81–6

C. Castle and D.N.Tauber: *This was Richard Tauber* (London, 1971)

Desmond Shawe-Taylor/R

Tear, Robert

(*b* Barry, 8 March 1939). Welsh tenor. He was a choral scholar at King's College, Cambridge, and made his operatic début in 1963 as the Male Chorus (*The Rape of Lucretia*) with the English Opera Group, for which he created Meshach (*The Burning Fiery Furnace*, 1966), Younger Son (*The Prodigal Son*, 1968), and the title role in Gordon Crosse's *Grace of Todd* (1969). He sang Jaquino for the WNO and Alfredo and Belmonte for Scottish Opera. At Covent Garden he created Dov in *The Knot Garden* (1970), the Deserter in *We Come to the River* (1976) and Rimbaud in John Tavener's *Thérèse* (1976). Tear's many other roles there, revealing his

Renata Tebaldi in the title role of 'Tosca' (Puccini)

versatility and his gifts as a vivid character actor, included Lensky, Paris (*King Priam*), Prince Vasily Golitsïn, Matteo (*Arabella*), Jack (*The Midsummer Marriage*), Froh, Loge (which he also sang in Paris and Munich), Spalanzi, Tom Rakewell, Admetus (*Alceste*), Captain Vere, Peter Grimes, David (*Die Meistersinger*), Jupiter (*Semele*), Prince Shuysky (also in Paris and Brussels), Herod (also in Geneva and with the WNO), Monostatos, the Emperor Altoum (also in Los Angeles), Don Basilio, G.F. Handel's Samson, the Director (British première of Luciano Berio's *Un re in ascolto*, 1989) and Capito (British première of *Mathis der Maler*, 1995). He sang the Painter/Negro in *Lulu* (première of the three-act version, 1979, Paris), Eumaeus in *Il ritorno d'Ulisse* (1985, Salzburg), and Aschenbach in *Death in Venice* (1989, Glyndebourne tour). In 1991 he created the title role of Krzystof Penderecki's *Ubu Rex* at Munich. He continued to sing character parts into his sixties. In concerts he was admired in choral works ranging from Claudio Monteverdi, Henry Purcell, G.F. Handel and J.S. Bach to Benjamin Britten's *War Requiem* and Michael Tippett's *A Mask of Time* (taking part in the première, 1984); his recital repertory was similarly varied, and he was a notable exponent of English song. Tear's keen mind and clear, highly distinctive voice has illuminated all his work, as can be heard on his numerous recordings. He was made a CBE in 1984. His writings include *Tear Here* (London, 1990) and *Singer Beware* (London, 1995).

Alan Blyth

Tebaldi, Renata

(*b* Pesaro, 1 Feb 1922; *d* San Marino, 19 Dec 2004). Italian soprano. She studied at the Conservatorio di Musica A. Boito, Parma, with CARMEN MELIS and made her début in 1944 as Elena in Arrigo Boito's *Mefistofele* at Rovigo. In 1946 she took part in the reopening concert at La Scala, under Arturo Toscanini, and subsequently sang Mimì and Eva in the rebuilt theatre's first winter season (1946–7). She sang regularly at La Scala from 1949 to 1954; her roles included Maddalena (*Andrea Chénier*), Adriana Lecouvreur, Tosca, Desdemona and the title role of Alfredo Catalani's *La Wally*. She also made frequent appearances at S Carlo, Naples, and in South America, where she was compared with CLAUDIA MUZIO, especially for her interpretation of Violetta.

She made her London début at Covent Garden as Desdemona, on the opening night of the Scala company's London season in 1950, and returned to London in 1955 to sing Tosca (see illustration on page 487). Her American début was in San Francisco in 1950 as Aida. She also sang in Chicago,

and became a member of the Metropolitan in 1955, remaining with the company for nearly 20 years. Besides the usual *lirico spinto* repertory, she sang such rarely heard roles as Gaspare Spontini's Olympia, Pamyre in Gioachino Rossini's *Le siège de Corinthe*, Cleopatra in G.F. Handel's *Giulio Cesare* and the title role of Giuseppe Verdi's *Giovanna d'Arco*. Tebaldi possessed one of the most beautiful Italian voices of the 20th century; her *mezza voce* singing was a joy to hear. She relied more on her rich, impeccably produced tone and inborn sense of style than on her acting ability to convey character and feeling. She made many recordings, most notably as Aida, Desdemona, Mimì, Tosca, Maddalena, Wally and, perhaps best of all, as Leonora in a live recording of *La forza del destino* under Dimitri Mitropoulos and on a video from Naples (1958).

F.F. Clough and G.J. Cuming: 'Renata Tebaldi Discography', *Gramophone Record Review*, new ser. (1957), no.46, p.789

E. Forbes: 'Tebaldi: Wonderful Memories', *Opera*, xlii (1991), 883–5

P. O'Connor: 'Tebaldi: Giving and Receiving', *Opera*, xlvii (1996), 492–6

J.B. Steane: 'Renata Tebaldi', *Singers of the Century* (London, 1998), 161–5

Harold Rosenthal/Alan Blyth

Te Kanawa, Dame Kiri

(*b* Gisborne, 6 March 1944). New Zealand soprano. Winner of many prizes in New Zealand and Australia, she later studied at the London Opera Centre with Vera Rozsa. In 1969 her singing of Elena in *La donna del lago* at the Camden Festival marked her as a singer of exceptional promise, and this was confirmed with her first major role at Covent Garden, W.A. Mozart's Countess Almaviva (1971). In the same year she repeated the role at the Lyons Opéra and in her American début at Santa Fe. Further roles at Covent Garden have included Amelia (*Simon Boccanegra*), Donna Elvira, Violetta, Desdemona, Marguerite, Mimì, Fiordiligi, Manon Lescaut, Arabella and the Marschallin. She made her Metropolitan début at three hours' notice as Desdemona in 1974; she has reappeared there regularly. She sang at Glyndebourne in 1973, with further débuts in Paris (1975), Milan and Sydney (1978), Salzburg (1979) and Vienna (1980). In 1982 she gave her only stage performances as Tosca in Paris. In 1980 she added Elisabeth de Valois in *Don Carlos* to her repertory at Chicago, and in 1991 the Countess in *Capriccio*, sung first at Covent Garden and with greater success at Glyndebourne and the Metropolitan in 1998.

Dame Kiri Te Kanawa as Donna Elvira in 'Don Giovanni' (Mozart), Royal Opera House, Covent Garden, 1973

Te Kanawa has also given song recitals in most major cities and appeared with leading orchestras in works such as Richard Strauss's *Vier letzte Lieder*. Her many recordings include most of her principal operatic roles and concert repertory, together with musicals such as *West Side Story* with Leonard Bernstein conducting. She was made DBE in 1982, the year after she sang at the wedding of Prince Charles and Lady Diana Spencer, and has been invested with the Order of Australia (1990) and of New Zealand (1995). Her 'Opera in the Outback' concert was a spectacular and imaginative contribution to the Australian bicentennial celebrations of 1988.

Te Kanawa's voice, vibrant but mellow, ample but unforced, impressed from the first with its freshness and warmth. Less remarkable are her interpretative powers, though her stage presence has both beauty and dignity. Her recordings sometimes lack animation, yet many are unsurpassed as examples of the lyric soprano's art.

E. Forbes: 'Kiri te Kanawa', *Opera*, xxxii (1981), 679–85

D. Fingleton: *Kiri te Kanawa* (London, 1983)

A. Simpson and P. Downes: *Southern Voices: International Opera Singers of New Zealand* (Auckland, 1992), 218–31

G. Jenkins and S. D'Antal: *Kiri: Her Unsung Story* (London, 1998)

J.B. Steane: *Singers of the Century*, ii (London, 1998), 181–5

J.B. Steane

Temple, Richard [Cobb, Richard Barker]

(*b* London, 2 March 1847; *d* London, 19 Oct 1912). English bass-baritone. Following several amateur singing appearances, he made his professional début as Rodolfo in *La sonnambula* in the inaugural production at the Crystal Palace Theatre, London (31 May 1869). He was first engaged by Richard D'Oyly Carte to play Sir Marmaduke Pointdextre in Gilbert and Sullivan's *The Sorcerer* (1877). For the next decade he was intimately identified with D'Oyly Carte's opera company, appearing in the principal bass-baritone roles from *HMS Pinafore* (1878) to *The Yeomen of the Guard* (1888). He then withdrew from the stage, but returned several years later in operatic roles at Covent Garden and several West End theatres; he later appeared in musical comedy.

Temple's voice was of a higher calibre than was usual in comic opera, and he was praised for the dignity and versatility of his acting, particularly for his 'suave and oily Mikado' (E. MacGeorge). In 1910 he was appointed to the RCM, where he directed many student productions. In about 1902–3 he recorded several light operatic numbers for the Gramophone and Typewriter Company.

Frederic Woodbridge Wilson

Tenducci, Giusto Ferdinando

(*b* Siena, *c*1735; *d* Genoa, 25 Jan 1790). Italian soprano castrato and composer. He made his début in Cagliari in 1750, during the wedding festivities of the Duke of Savoy. After appearing both in minor roles and in comic opera in Milan, Naples, Venice, Dresden and Munich, in 1758 he went to London, where he spent two seasons at the King's Theatre and sang in Gioacchino Cocchi's *Ciro riconosciuto* as secondo uomo. His extravagant living led to a short spell in a debtors' prison in 1760, but in 1762 he created Arbaces in Thomas Arne's *Artaxerxes*, subsequently appearing in the première of J.C. Bach's *Adriano in Siria* (1765). He visited Dublin in 1765 and the following year (despite some scandal) married Dora Maunsell, the daughter of a Dublin lawyer. Her relations were outraged; Tenducci was jailed and his wife kidnapped, though Casanova claimed the couple had two children. Tenducci spent a year or more in Edinburgh before returning in 1770 to London, where he sang in a pasticcio of C.W. Gluck's *Orfeo* and was responsible for popularizing the aria 'Che farò senza Euridice'. Impressed with 'Scotch' songs, he persuaded his friend J.C. Bach to arrange some for insertion into English operas, a practice which was then widely adopted by other composers, notably Thomas Linley in *The Duenna*. Tenducci left England and returned to Italy until 1776 (repeating *Orfeo* in Florence), and then appeared in London (1777–85), Paris (1777) and Dublin (1783–4). Tobias Smollett described his voice as particularly lyrical and the *ABCDario Musico* (Bath, 1780) compared him with Gioacchino Conti; he was widely known as another SENESINO. He adapted several operas, but none was very successful; his singing tutor *Instruction of Mr Tenducci to his Scholars* (London, 1782) is of more lasting value.

D. Tenducci: *A True and Genuine Narrative of Mr and Mrs Tenducci* (London, 1768)

Roger Fiske, Dale E. Monson

Terfel, Bryn

(*b* Pwllheli, 9 Nov 1965). Welsh bass-baritone. Brought up in a village in North Wales where singing in chapel and elsewhere was part of the culture, he went on to study at the GSM in London with Rudolf Piernay. With a voice exceptionally mature for his age, he won the GSM's gold medal in 1989, having the previous year won the Kathleen Ferrier Memorial Award. In 1989 he also won the Lieder Prize in the Cardiff Singer of the World Competition, which led to auditions with important conductors and impresarios. He made his operatic début as Guglielmo with the WNO in 1990, later singing W.A. Mozart's Figaro for the company. His international operatic career began in 1991 when he sang the Speaker (*Die Zauberflöte*) at Théâtre de la Monnaie in Brussels. That year he also had great success with his hearty, extrovert Figaro for the ENO, and made his US début with Santa Fe Opera, also as Figaro. In 1992 he appeared both at the Salzburg Easter Festival, singing the role of the Spirit Messenger in *Die Frau ohne Schatten*, and at the main Salzburg Festival, as Jokanaan in *Salome*, and also made his Covent Garden début, as Masetto. Over the following two years he sang Figaro to acclaim at the Théâtre du Châtelet in Paris, the Vienna Staatsoper, in Lisbon and at the Metropolitan Opera. He also sang the role at La Scala in 1997. Terfel's other roles have included Donner, Wolfram (*Tannhäuser*), which he sang at the Metropolitan Opera in 1997, Nick Shadow and Balstrode (*Peter Grimes*). In 1999 he sang his first Falstaff, a spontaneous, richly drawn interpretation, at the Lyric Opera of Chicago; at the end of the year he appeared in the same role in the inaugural production at the newly refurbished Royal Opera House.

Terfel has also developed a flourishing career as a recitalist. With an acute feeling for language (he is bilingual in Welsh and English), he has been particularly successful in lieder, both in German-speaking countries and elsewhere. His vivid, magnetic personality, matching his imposing stature, is ideally suited to the demands of recital work, and the dramatic point of songs has always been a vital element in his interpretations.

Terfel's rapid emergence as an international star has owed much to his careful use of the voice. In his early career he concentrated on Mozart rather than weightier Verdi or Wagner roles, even though the dark, highly individual timbre and magnificent resonance of his voice pointed towards that repertory. More than once he cancelled projected performances when he found the demands of a role excessive, as with the title role in Alban Berg's *Wozzeck*, planned for the 1997 Salzburg Festival. Shrewdly analytical in his interpretations as well as in his vocal technique, Terfel has the rare gift of translating intensive preparation into spontaneous expression, as can be heard on his many recordings, among them Jokanaan (his début role on disc), Mozart's Figaro, Don Giovanni and Leporello, *Elijah*, *Belshazzar's Feast* and discs of Schubert and Schumann lieder and English song.

E. Greenfield: 'I could have Sung all Night', *Gramophone*, lxxiii/Aug (1995), 15–17
J.B. Steane: *Singers of the Century*, ii (London, 1998)

Edward Greenfield/R

Ternina [Trnina], Milka

(*b* Doljnji, Moslavina, 19 Dec 1863; *d* Zagreb, 18 May 1941). Croatian soprano. She studied in Zagreb with Ida Winterberg and at the Vienna Conservatory with Josef Gänzbacher and, while still a student, made her début in 1882 at Zagreb as Amelia in *Un ballo in maschera*. In the following year she was engaged at Leipzig, where she sang Elisabeth in *Tannhäuser*. After performances at Graz and Bremen, in 1889 she made guest appearances in Munich as Valentine in *Les Huguenots*, Amelia and Elisabeth, and in 1890 she inaugurated her engagement as a member of the company singing Leonore in *Fidelio*. She made her Covent Garden début as Isolde on 3 June 1898, later appearing as Sieglinde in *Die Walküre*, Brünnhilde in *Siegfried* and *Götterdämmerung* and as Leonore. In 1899 she sang Kundry in *Parsifal* at Bayreuth, and returning to Covent Garden the following year, she sang both Elsa and Ortrud in *Lohengrin* and Tosca in the first London performance of Puccini's opera (12 July 1900). She made her American début at Boston in 1896, singing Brünnhilde and Isolde with the Damrosch Opera Company, and first appeared at the Metropolitan, New York, in 1900 as Elisabeth. Her later Metropolitan roles included Tosca, which she sang at the American première of the opera (1901), and Kundry (1903) in the first staged performance of *Parsifal* outside Bayreuth. In 1906 she made her Covent Garden farewell as Elisabeth on 28 May, and her final stage appearance at Munich on 19 August, as Sieglinde. She had a superb voice whose 'overwhelming plentitude of warm, mellow tone' (*New York Times*) was heard to best advantage in the great Wagner roles, while her dramatic gifts were magnificently displayed in such parts as Leonore and Tosca. After her retirement, she taught singing, first at the Institute of Musical Art, New York, and then in Zagreb, where ZINKA MILANOV was among her pupils.

Elizabeth Forbes

Terrell, Lella.

See CUBERLI, LELLA.

Teschemacher, Margarete

(*b* Cologne, 3 March 1903; *d* Bad Wiessee, 19 May 1959). German soprano. She studied in Cologne, where she made her début in 1923 as Ruth in *Die toten Augen*. Her first great success came the following year as Micaëla, also at Cologne. Engagements followed at Aachen (1925–7), Dortmund (1927–8), Mannheim (1928–31), Stuttgart (1931–4), Dresden (1935–46) and Düsseldorf (1947–52). At Dresden she created the title role in Richard Strauss's *Daphne* (1938) and Miranda in Heinrich Sutermeister's *Die Zauberinsel* (1942); she was also the first Dresden Countess in *Capriccio* (1944). She sang Pamina and Elsa at Covent Garden in 1931 and Countess Almaviva and Donna Elvira during the Dresden Staatsoper's visit to London in 1936. In 1934 she appeared at the Teatro Colón, as Arabella, Senta, Sieglinde and Mařenka. Teschemacher's roles also included Jenůfa, Minnie, Kundry, and Riccardo Zandonai's Francesca da Rimini. Her warm lyric-dramatic voice can be heard on several recordings most notably as Eva on Karl Böhm's 1938 version of the third act of *Die Meistersinger*, and also in 1944 as Frasquita in Hugo Wolf's rarely performed *Der Corregidor*.

Harold Rosenthal/Alan Blyth/R

Tesi (Tramontini), Vittoria
['La Moretta', 'La Fiorentina']

(*b* Florence, 13 Feb 1700; *d* Vienna, 9 May 1775). Italian contralto. She received her first instruction from Francesco Redi in Florence and from Campeggi in Bologna. (An alleged meeting with G.F. Handel in Florence, in connection with the performance there of his opera *Rodrigo* in 1707, rests on a confusion between Tesi and Vittoria Tarquini.) She first appeared as an opera singer in 1716, in Parma (Alessandro Scarlatti's *Dafni*) and Bologna. In the 1718–19 season she was in Venice as *virtuosa di camera* to Prince Antonio of Parma. By 1719 she was in Dresden, where she sang in Antonio Lotti's *Giove in Argo* for the opening of the new opera house on 3 September, and ten days later appeared as Matilda in his *Teofane*, thereby numbering (along with the singers LAURENTI, DURASTANTI, Santa Stella Lotti and the castrato SENESINO) among the most prominent performers in the musical festivities surrounding the marriage of the Saxon electoral prince to the Archduchess Maria Josepha. With the dissolution of the Italian Opera, Tèsi left Dresden to return to Italy; in Carnival 1721 she sang in Florence and from there travelled until 1747, visiting all the great theatres of Italy between Naples, Venice and Milan, with a guest appearance in Madrid (1739–40) and perhaps a trip to Frankfurt, 1741–2, for the emperor's coronation. Her career reached a peak at the opening of the Teatro S Carlo in Naples (1737, with Domenico Sarri's *Achille in Sciro*) and again ten years later when she appeared there with CAFFARELLI, GIOACCHINO CONTI, Giovanni Manzuoli and others in Ranieri de' Calzabigi's serenata *Il sogno d'Olimpia*, with music by Giuseppe de Majo.

On 14 May 1748 she appeared in Vienna (as *virtuosa di camera della Sacra Cesarea Reale Maestà*), taking the title role in C.W. Gluck's setting of Pietro Metastasio's *Semiramide riconosciuta*. Details of who arranged her appearance there remain uncertain; Gluck had met her in Venice in 1744, when she sang the title role in his *Ipermestra*, but Metastasio had also known her previously, although he had no high opinion of her abilities (calling her a 'grandissima nullità') until her appearance in *Semiramide* convinced him to the contrary. Further successful stage appearances in Vienna included the title roles in Niccolò Jommelli's settings of Metastasio's *Achille in Sciro* and *Didone abbandonata* (1749) and her later appearance as Lisinga in Metastasio's *Le cinesi*, set by Gluck for the famous Schlosshof festival of 24 September 1754. In the early 1750s she began her retirement from the stage. She was not engaged for the 1751–2 season in Naples because of her age; Metastasio, who shortly before had found her 'rejuvenated by 20 years', mentioned in autumn 1751 that Tèsi was 'costume director' for the Vienna court theatre. After retiring from the stage Tèsi devoted herself to the education of younger talent with considerable success; among her pupils were Caterina Gabrielli, ANNA LUCIA DE AMICIS and ELISABETH TEYBER. In Vienna she enjoyed the special patronage of Maria Theresa and of Prince Joseph Friedrich of Hildburghausen, in whose palace (the present Palais Auersperg) she resided. Among those who met her there were Casanova (1753) and Leopold and W.A. Mozart (13 December 1762). She held the honorary title *virtuosa della corte imperiale* until the end of her life, and her husband was an honorary *consigliere del commercio*. Two years before her death Ange and Sarah Goudar, apostrophizing her personality and achievement, called her 'perhaps the first actress who recited well while singing badly'. Many of her contemporaries, including Johann Quantz, Francesco Mancini, Metastasio, C.D. von Dittersdorf and Charles Burney, found her incomparable in expression and stage bearing, and to Ernst Gerber (1792) she was one of the greatest singers of the century.

A Faustini Tèsi, who combined the names of the famous singers FAUSTINA BORDONI and Vittoria Tèsi, may possibly be related to the latter; she was active from 1765 at various Italian theatres, including Venice (1765), Piacenza (1775) and Naples (1777). Karl von Zinzendorf in 1778 mentioned 'cette Tèsi vieille et laide' in Trieste.

Gerhard Croll

Tess(arolo) [Tèssi, Tèssaroli], **Giulia**

(*b* Milan, 9 or 19 Feb 1889; *d* Milan, 17 March 1976). Italian soprano and director. She studied in Verona and made her début as a mezzo-soprano at Prato in 1904; in 1909 she sang Mignon at La Fenice, Venice. After appearances in Prague, Vienna, St Petersburg and other centres as Adalgisa, Léonor (*La favorite*), Amneris and Charlotte, she became a soprano and a leading exponent of the *verismo* repertory. She created Jael in Ildebrando Pizzetti's *Dèbora e Jaéle* at La Scala (1922) and continued to appear in Milan until 1936 in roles that included Salome, Electra and Orsola in the première of Ermanno Wolf-Ferrari's *Il campiello*. She was the first Italian Composer in *Ariadne auf Naxos* (1925, Turin), and sang the title role in the Italian première of Arthur Honegger's *Judith* (1937, Naples). She left the stage in 1940 and worked as a director in Florence, Bologna and Milan, then returned to sing Orsola in her own production of *Il campiello* in Cagliari (1949) and Palermo (1950).

Harold Rosenthal/R

Tetrazzini, Luisa [Luigia]

(*b* Florence, 29 June 1871; *d* Milan, 28 April 1940). Italian soprano. She studied at the Istituto Musicale of her native city and with her elder sister Eva (1862–1938), who was herself a soprano. In 1890 Luisa made a surprise début at the Teatro Pagliano in Florence, as Inès in *L'africaine*. She next sang in Rome, and toured with growing success throughout Italy, adding to her repertory all the more famous roles for coloratura soprano; she also made a reputation abroad, notably in St Petersburg, Madrid, Buenos Aires and Mexico. Her Covent Garden début in 1907, as Violetta, caused a sensation, and she returned to London for every summer season from 1908 to 1912, singing also Lucia, Gilda, Rosina, Amina, Lakmé, Leïla in

Luisa Tetrazzini,
signed photograph

Les pêcheurs de perles and Marguerite de Valois in *Les Huguenots*. Immediately after her London début she was engaged by Hammerstein for his Manhattan Opera House, where, in 1908, she repeated her London triumph, again in the role of Violetta. In three consecutive seasons there, in 1911–12 at the Metropolitan and 1911–12 and 1912–13 in Chicago, she appeared in most of her London roles, as well as in several others, including Mathilde (*Guillaume Tell*), Vincenzo Bellini's Elvira, Gaetano Donizetti's Linda, Adina and Marie (*La fille du régiment*) and Ambroise Thomas' Ophélie and Philine. These pre-

war years were the climax of her career. Thereafter, she made numerous lucrative concert tours, appearing for the last time in New York in 1931, and in London in 1934.

Tetrazzini possessed technical gifts of the highest order, and could dazzle audiences with the ease and agility of her chromatic scales, both ascending and descending, and with her staccato, trills and florid effects of every kind, especially above the staff. A slightly pallid quality in the lower-middle register was felt to impair the absolute consistency of her tone, which was otherwise of a warm, clarinet-like beauty. Her cantilena was shapely, spontaneous and flowing. Between 1908 and 1914, the years of her prime, Tetrazzini recorded extensively. Her records of such pieces as 'Una voce poco fa', the Polonaise from *Mignon* or 'Ah! non giunge' from *La sonnambula*, rank among the most brilliant ever made; while her skill and taste in the delivery of a simple melody show to admiration in her account of Sir Paolo Tosti's *Aprile*. Her writings include *My Life of Song* (London, 1921/R) and *How to Sing* (New York, 1923); repr. as *The Art of Singing* (New York, 1975).

J.B. Richards: 'Luisa Tetrazzini', *Record Collector*, iv (1949), 123–39 [with discography by P.H. Wade]

D. Shawe-Taylor: 'A Gallery of Great Singers: Luisa Tetrazzini', *Opera*, xiv (1963), 593–9

Desmond Shawe-Taylor

Te Wiata, Inia

(*b* Otaki, 10 June 1915; *d* London, 26 June 1971). New Zealand bass. In 1947 he obtained a government scholarship to study in London, under Charles Kennedy Scott and Sir Steuart Wilson and at the Joan Cross Opera School. He was appointed to the resident company at Covent Garden, making his début as the Speaker in *Die Zauberflöte* in 1951. For the next three years he sang a wide range of roles there, creating Dansker in *Billy Budd* (1951) and the ballad-singer in *Gloriana* (1953). After three years he began a freelance career, making frequent guest appearances at Covent Garden as well as with Sadler's Wells, Scottish Opera and other companies. He also took leading roles in a number of musicals. He returned to New Zealand several times for concerts and for two highly successful engagements with the New Zealand Opera Company, as Porgy (1965) and Osmin (1968–9). In 1969 he sang at Covent Garden the dual roles of the Ghost and the Player King in the première of Humphrey Searle's *Hamlet* and the following year, along with the title roles in *Boris Godunov*, *Don Carlos* and *Falstaff*, he sang Schomberg in the London, Berlin and Munich premières of Richard Rodney Bennett's *Victory*. He was taken ill during rehearsals of *Boris* at Covent Garden in 1971 and died soon after.

B. Te Wiata: *Most Happy Fella – a Biography of Inia Te Wiata* (Wellington, 1976)

A. Simpson and P. Downes: *Southern Voices: International Opera Singers of New Zealand* (Auckland, 1992), 64–75

Peter Downes

Teyber, Elisabeth

(*b* Vienna, bap. 16 Sept 1744; *d* Vienna, 9 May 1816). Soprano, sister of THERESE TEYBER. After study with J.A. Hasse and VITTORIA TESI she made her career mainly in Italy, following a series of Vienna performances in the 1760s, including the production of Hasse's *Partenope* in 1767 (Leopold Mozart was not particularly impressed by her – see his letter of 29 September 1767; but Hasse's opinion was more favourable). She then sang with great success in Italy, appearing at Naples, Bologna, Milan and Turin. She married a Marchese Venier but was widowed early. She is said to have sung in Russia in the 1770s but to have been obliged for health reasons to return to Italy, and was not able to resume singing there until 1784. It is by no means certain that she appeared in Vienna again in 1788, as is sometimes stated, or even that she gave a solitary guest appearance there ten years earlier, on 8 September 1778. On this date Maximilian Ulbrich's *Frühling und Liebe* was given for the first time. The playbill includes 'Mlle. Teyberinn' (i.e. Therese Teyber) as Fiametta, and 'Mlle. Tauber' in the role of her stepmother, Markesinn Bellavita. It seems almost certain that this 'Mlle. Tauber' was in fact not Elisabeth Teyber but the unrelated MARIA ANNA (or MARIANNE) TAUBER (or 'Taube'), a soprano of the Esterházy company who in March of that year had impressed the Emperor Joseph II in Joseph Starzer's oratorio *La passione di Gesù Cristo*, but was less successful in subsequent appearances and left Vienna at the end of September.

Peter Branscombe

Teyber, Therese

(*b* Vienna, bap. 15 Oct 1760; *d* Vienna, 15 April 1830). Austrian soprano, sister of ELISABETH TEYBER. She was a pupil of Giuseppe Bonno and VITTORIA TESI. She made her début at the Vienna court theatre on 8 September 1778 as Fiametta in Maximilian Ulbrich's *Frühling und Liebe*. (A letter of 8 February 1778 by Baron von Gebler mentions a 'Mlle Teuberin, until now at Prince Esterházy's Opera' among future attractions, but this doubtless refers to MARIA ANNA TAUBER, who had probably already been engaged to sing in Joseph Starzer's *La passione di Gesù Cristo* in March, and who also sang in *Frühling und Liebe* in September; she is the only singer in the Esterházy records with that or a similar name. This information is corroborated by the *Wiener Diarium* of 1778, no.87.) Teyber was a popular portrayer of young lovers and artless girls, and in the early 1780s she also appeared in the concerts of the Tonkünstler-Sozietät. Her last appearance at one of these concerts seems to have been in March 1784, when she sang Sara in Joseph Haydn's *Il ritorno di Tobia* (her sister Barbara had sung this part in the first performances in 1775). She created the role of Blonde in *Die Entführung aus dem Serail* on 16 July 1782 and appeared with success in many other operas and Singspiele; contemporary reviews praised the charm of her acting ('the best of the women') and singing, though one critic accused her of letting her tongue run away with her in dialogue. In her early years with the court theatre she was one of the lower-paid singers (in 1783 she drew 800 florins, less than a quarter of the salary of NANCY STORACE). In autumn/winter 1785–6 she married the tenor Ferdinand Arnold, who had also sung in *Frühling und Liebe* in 1778; he rejoined the court opera company on 1 September 1785. The Arnolds are reported to have performed together with much success at Hamburg, Berlin, Warsaw and Riga, though the chronology of these appearances is confused. It seems reasonable to assume that it was Therese (and not, as is often stated, Elisabeth Teyber) who replaced LUISA LASCHI as Zerlina in the later Viennese performances of *Don Giovanni* in 1788. Therese is certainly the 'Mad:selle Täuber' ('Teyber') referred to in W.A. Mozart's letters of 29 March and 12 April 1783; they took part in each other's benefit concerts that Lent. Therese Teyber occurs in the court exchequer records of 1792 (the year after her retirement) as 'Arnoldin vormalige Sängerin' with a pension of 466·40 florins.

Peter Branscombe

Teyte [Tate], **Dame** [Margaret] **Maggie**

(*b* Wolverhampton, 17 April 1888; *d* London, 26 May 1976). English soprano. She studied in London, then with JEAN DE RESZKE in Paris. Her first public appearances were in a Mozart Festival organized in 1906 by Reynaldo Hahn and LILLI LEHMANN. In the following year she appeared at Monte Carlo, notably as Zerlina, and in various roles at the Opéra-Comique in Paris. Her big chance came in 1908, when Claude Debussy selected her to succeed MARY GARDEN in the role of Mélisande; besides coaching her, he accompanied her in recitals of his songs, and from that time French song in general, and Debussy in particular, played a prominent part in her career. On her return to England she sang Mélisande and many other roles, including Cherubino, Blonde, Butterfly, Marguerite and Jacques Offenbach's Antonia, with the Beecham Opera Company and in later years with its successor, the British National Opera Company; In 1919 she created the role of Lady Mary in *Monsieur Beaucaire* by André Messager. With the British National Opera Company she was the first Princess in Gustav Holst's *The Perfect Fool* at Covent Garden in 1923.

Teyte sang for three consecutive seasons (1911–14) with the Chicago Opera Company,

Maggie Teyte as Lady Mary Carlisle in the première of 'Monsieur Beaucaire' (Messager), Prince of Wales Theatre, Birmingham, England, 1919

both in Chicago and in Philadelphia and New York. Among her parts with this company was the title role of Jules Massenet's *Cendrillon*, with Mary Garden as Prince Charming. At Boston, where she was a member of the Opera Company from 1914 to 1917, her Mimì and Nedda were specially admired; but her Mélisande was not heard in the USA until the late 1940s (in concert in 1947 and with the New York City Opera the following year). In England, between the wars, she appeared a good deal in operetta and musical comedy (*Monsieur Beaucaire*, *A Little Dutch Girl*, *Tantivy Towers*) and was even in some danger of being regarded as a lightweight artist, when, in 1937, her career received a fresh impetus. The occasion was a commissioned record album of Debussy songs, with Alfred Cortot as pianist, followed in 1940 by a second album of French song from Hector Berlioz to Debussy. During the next eight years she made many further records of Gabriel Fauré and other French songs with Gerald Moore, and her London recitals became notable events. She created the role of Glycère in Paul Hillemacher's *Circé*. In 1951 she appeared at the Mermaid

Theatre as Henry Purcell's Belinda to the Dido of KIRSTEN FLAGSTAD; and in 1955 she made a final concert appearance at the Royal Festival Hall. The exquisite purity and perfect placement of her tone, together with her spontaneity and distinction as an interpreter, secured for her a unique position, which was recognized when she was made a Chevalier of the Légion d'Honneur in 1957 and DBE in 1958. Her voice recorded ideally, and her discs of the French repertory set a standard, as can be confirmed on numerous CD transfers.

D. Tron: 'Maggie Teyte', *Record Collector*, ix (1954), 129–38 [with discography by J. Dennis]

M. Teyte: *Star on the Door* (London, 1958) [with discography by D. Tron]

D. Shawe-Taylor: Obituary, *The Times* (28 May 1976)

G. O'Connor: 'Maggie Teyte and Beecham', *Opera*, xxx (1979), 312–17

G. O'Connor: *The Pursuit of Perfection: a Life of Maggie Teyte* (London, 1979)

Desmond Shawe-Taylor

Thebom, Blanche

(*b* Monessen, PA, 19 Sept 1918). American mezzo-soprano of Swedish parentage. In New York she studied with MARGARET MATZENAUER and EDYTH WALKER. She made her first appearance with the Metropolitan on tour in Philadelphia as Brangäne in 1944 and her New York début with the company as Fricka in *Die Walküre* in the same year; she remained with the Metropolitan until the 1966–7 season, singing much Richard Wagner as well as Marina, Herodias, Orlofsky and Amneris. In 1950 she sang Dorabella at Glyndebourne, and in 1957 she had considerable success at Covent Garden as Dido in the first English professional staged performance of *Les Troyens*. Other roles included Azucena and Carmen. In 1967–8 she was artistic director of the Atlanta Opera Company. At the University of Arkansas, Little Rock, Thebom created an opera theatre programme for students and professionals that ran from 1973–79. Thebom had a wide-ranging mezzo-soprano of generally fine quality, not a great voice, but one capable of most pleasing effect, confirmed by souvenirs of her Dorabella, Eboli and Brangäne on disc. Her article 'Singing or Acting?' was published in *Opera News*, xxix/21 (1964–5), 9–11, and details of her Metropolitan broadcasts can be found in P. Jackson: *Sign-off for the Old Met* (New York, 1997).

Max De Schauensee/Alan Blyth/R

Thévenard, Gabriel-Vincent

(*b* Orléans or Paris, 10 Aug 1669; *d* Paris, 24 Aug 1741). French singer. He went to Paris in 1690 and was a pupil of André Destouches, who wrote several roles for him including Hylas in *Issé* (1698) and Amadis in *Amadis de Grèce* (1699). A member of the Académie Royale de Musique, he performed for over 30 years in some 80 *tragédies* and ballets, including premières of works by André Campra, Pascal Collasse, Henry Desmarets and Marin Marais, as well as revivals of works by Jean-Baptiste Lully. He frequently portrayed the role of a king, god or a grand priest (his *basse-taille* range was approximately G to e') and was admired for the character and nobility which he imparted, and particularly for his ability to declaim recitative in a speech-like manner. He excelled at tragic roles in which, especially in the works of Destouches, he often performed an emotional lament as a monologue. His duets with FRANÇOISE JOURNET, famous for her portrayal of tender roles, were much appreciated (such as 'Que j'éprouve un supplice horrible', the duet for Peleus and Alcyone in Marais' *Alcione*, 1706).

Mary Cyr

Thill, Georges

(*b* Paris, 14 Dec 1897; *d* Paris, 17 Oct 1984). French tenor. After two years' study at the Paris Conservatoire, and two more in Naples with FERNANDO DE LUCIA, he sang Don José and other roles at the Opéra-Comique before making his début as Nicias in *Thaïs* in 1924 at the Opéra. There he stayed for 16 years, graduating from the lighter French repertory, including Marouf, Jean (*Hérodiade*), Roland (*Esclaramonde*), Raoul (*Les Huguenots*), to Admetus (*Alceste*) and Aeneas (*Les Troyens à Carthage*) Walther, Lohengrin, Parsifal, Tannhäuser, Arnold (*Guillaume Tell*), and later Samson. At La Scala and Verona he sang Calaf; Buenos Aires invited him for Don Carlos, Calaf and Arrigo Boito's Faust. He also sang at the Metropolitan Opera in 1931 and 1932, where his first role, Romeo, was followed by Radames, Charles Gounod's Faust and Sadko; in Vienna, and at Covent Garden where he made his début in 1928 as Samson, returning as Don José (1937). He bade farewell to the stage at the Opéra-Comique as Canio, as late as 1953. With his brilliant, robust tone, his spirited phrasing and aristocratic enunciation, Thill was the most distinguished French heroic tenor of his time. His recordings of such roles as Admetus, Werther and Gounod's Roméo set standards and kept alive a tradition of singing which would otherwise have vanished. He also appeared in several films, the most interesting of which is Abel Gance's *Louise* with Grace Moore (1938).

R. Mancini: *Georges Thill* (Paris, 1966) [with discography]
D. Shawe-Taylor: 'A Gallery of Great Singers, 16: Georges Thill (1897–1984)', *Opera*, xxxvi (1985), 741–7

André Tubeuf/R

Thoma, Therese.

See VOGL, THERESE.

Thomas, David

(*b* Orpington, Kent, 26 Feb 1943). English bass. He studied at King's College, Cambridge, where he was a choral scholar, and quickly established himself in the Baroque and Classical repertory, initially as an ensemble and oratorio singer. He made his British operatic début in 1981 with Kent Opera, as Pluto in Claudio Monteverdi's *Il ballo delle ingrate*, and his American début in 1988 at Los Angeles as the Devil in Stefano Landi's *Sant'Alessio*. Thomas has performed throughout the world with many of the leading period instrument ensembles in opera and choral works, including Chiaroscuro and the Consort of Musicke, and has made several tours with the soprano EMMA KIRKBY and the lutenist Anthony Rooley. His numerous recordings include Jean-Philippe Rameau's *Zaïs* (1979), Henry Purcell's *Dido and Aeneas* (1981 and 1992) and *The Fairy-Queen* (1982), Claudio Monteverdi's *Orfeo* (1983) and *Il ritorno d'Ulisse in patria* (1993), and G.F. Handel's *Orlando* (1991) and *Almira* (1995), and many Baroque choral works. His singing is distinguished by a strongly projected, uncommonly wide-ranging voice, deployed with minimal vibrato, and a keen sense of characterization.

Nicholas Anderson

Thomas, Jess (Floyd)

(*b* Hot Springs, SD, 4 Aug 1927; *d* San Francisco, 11 Oct 1993). American tenor. After studying psychology at Stanford University, he was encouraged by his singing teacher, Otto Schulman, to pursue an operatic career. He made his début in 1957 at San Francisco and then went to Germany, where he sang at the Karlsruhe Opera for three years. At that time his roles included Tamino, Alfredo, Manrico, Don José, Calaf and Lensky. He soon began to make guest appearances with larger German companies, and in 1961 Wieland Wagner cast him as

Parsifal in Bayreuth and Radames in Berlin. He returned to the USA and made his Metropolitan début in 1962 as Walther (the role of his Covent Garden début in 1969). He then began to concentrate on the heavy Wagnerian roles such as Siegfried, which he sang in the Bayreuth centenary *Ring* in 1976 and Tristan, which he sang at the Metropolitan and at Covent Garden. Some listeners have felt that the strain of these challenges robbed his voice of freshness and ease; nevertheless, his intelligence and histrionic credibility remained uncommon assets. Other roles included Samson, Florestan, Bacchus and the Emperor in *Die Frau ohne Schatten*; he also sang Caesar in the première of Samuel Barber's *Antony and Cleopatra* for the opening of the new Metropolitan Opera House at Lincoln Center in 1966. He recorded many of his Wagner roles, including Siegfried, Lohengrin and Parsifal (in the notable 1962 recording under Hans Knappertsbusch).

A. Blyth: Obituary, *Opera*, xliv (1993), 1415–16

Martin Bernheimer/R

Thomas, John Charles

(*b* Meyersdale, VA, 6 Sept 1891; *d* Apple Valley, CA, 13 Dec 1960). American baritone. He studied in Baltimore and, after singing in musical comedy and Gilbert and Sullivan, made his operatic début in 1924 at Washington, DC, as Amonasro. Engaged at La Monnaie, he made his début there in 1925 as Herod (*Hérodiade*) and sang Amfortas, Hamlet, Escamillo, Zurga, and Orpheus in the première of Darius Milhaud's *Les malheurs d'Orphée* (1926). He made his Covent Garden début in 1928 as Valentin, also singing Amonasro. In 1930 he sang John the Baptist at San Francisco and Tonio in Chicago, where he later sang Falstaff (1940). He made his Metropolitan début in 1934 as Giorgio Germont, and remained with the company until 1943, also singing Gioachino Rossini's Figaro, Athanaël (*Thaïs*) and Scarpia. In 1943 he returned to San Francisco as Tonio and Rigoletto. His recordings display a voice of great power and intensity.

Richard Lesueur/Elizabeth Forbes

Thorborg, Kerstin

(*b* Venjan, 19 May 1896; *d* Hedemora, Dalarna, 12 April 1970). Swedish mezzo-soprano. She studied in Stockholm, and sang small roles at the Royal Opera in 1923, graduating to principal roles in 1924 as Ortrud. With the company until 1930, she also made appearances elsewhere, notably as Amneris in Göteborg to FLAGSTAD's Aida, in Dresden (Waltraute, 1929) and in Prague. She was engaged at the Städtische Oper, Berlin (1932–5), and the Vienna Staatsoper (1935–8); her roles at Salzburg (1935–7) included Brangäne, Magdalene and Donna Mercedes in *Der Corregidor*. From 1936 to 1939 she made annual appearances at Covent Garden in the Wagner mezzo roles and was greatly acclaimed; Ernest Newman, after her Kundry, described her as 'the greatest Wagnerian actress of the present day'. Also in 1936 she began a Metropolitan Opera career (début as Fricka in *Die Walküre*) which lasted 15 years. Although her rich and ample tones were most admired in Wagner, her repertory also included C.W. Gluck's Orpheus, Marina, Ulrica, Richard Strauss's Herodias and Clytemnestra, and Delilah. She was also an accomplished concert artist. Her operatic career is well documented both on commercial discs and off-the-air recordings from the Metropolitan and elsewhere, most significantly her Fricka and Brangäne. Of her concert performances, live recordings of *Das Lied von der Erde* with Bruno Walter (1936, Vienna) and the Verdi Requiem with Arturo Toscanini (1938, London) represent her grave, involving interpretations at their best.

E.H. Palatsky: 'Goddess in Retirement', *ON*, xxvii/16 (1962–3), 32–3

A. Frankenstein: 'Kerstin Thorborg', *Record Collector*, xxiv (1978), 197–214 [incl. discography]

Carl L. Bruun/Alan Blyth

Thornton, Edna

(*b* Bradford, 1875; *d* Worthing, 15 July 1964). English contralto. She was a pupil of CHARLES SANTLEY and made her début in the musical comedy *Ib and Little Christina* at Daly's Theatre, London, in 1899. At Covent Garden she first appeared in 1905, singing with CARUSO in *Un ballo in maschera* and *Rigoletto*. She took part in the English première of Alberto Franchetti's *Germania* in 1907, and the following year made an impression as Erda in the first *Ring* cycle given in English under Hans Richter. In one performance of *Götterdämmerung* she undertook three roles: First Norn, Waltraute and Flosshilde. Other roles in the pre-war seasons included Brangäne (*Tristan und Isolde*), Geneviève (*Pelléas et Mélisande*) and Giulietta (*Les contes d'Hoffmann*). She sang with the Beecham company at Drury Lane and the Aldwych, and was later a mainstay of the British National Opera Company, singing a wide range of parts including Amneris and Azucena, Delilah and Marfa (*Khovanshchina*). After

tours in Canada, Australia and New Zealand with the Quinlan Company in 1924 she retired to teach. 'Regal' was a favourite word of critics to describe her acting and bearing on stage, while records confirm that she had an exceptionally strong, resourceful contralto voice to match.

J.B. Steane

Tibaldi, Giuseppe (Luigi)

(*b* Bologna, 22 Jan 1729; *d* *c*1790). Italian tenor and composer. He studied singing with Domenico Zanardi and composition with G.B. Martini. In 1747 he was admitted to the Accademia Filarmonica as a singer and in 1750 as a composer; he served as *principe* in 1759, 1777 and 1783. In 1751 he succeeded Giuseppe Alberti as *maestro di cappella* at S Giovanni in Monte of Bologna, but after a few years decided to devote himself entirely to a career as an operatic tenor, becoming one of the few leading opera singers who had a disciplined training in counterpoint. He sang in the most important European opera houses, taking leading roles in the premières of C.W. Gluck's *Alceste* (Vienna, 1767) and W.A. Mozart's *Ascanio in Alba* (Milan, 1771). His 19 letters to Martini (unpublished), written between 1750 and 1775, are a valuable source of information about Italian opera at the time. His few extant compositions (all unpublished) are sacred pieces dating from the time of his study with Martini, except for a later set of *Duetti notturni* for two sopranos and continuo (unpublished).

His son, Ferdinando Tibaldi (*c*1750–1785), was also a singer and composer.

Howard Brofsky

Tibbett [Tibbet], Lawrence

(*b* Bakersfield, CA, 16 Nov 1896; *d* New York, 15 July 1960). American baritone. After beginning his career as an actor and as a singer in church and light operas, he studied with Joseph Dupuy and Basil Ruysdael in Los Angeles and with Frank La Forge and Ignaz Zitomirsky in New York, which led to his Metropolitan début as Lewicki in *Boris Godunov* (1923). A week later he sang Valentin in *Faust*, but recognition did not come until 1925 when he sang Ford in *Falstaff*, eclipsing ANTONIO SCOTTI in the title role; he eventually succeeded Scotti in the leading Italian roles and remained a principal with the company for 27 seasons, noted, in his prime, for his legato and vivid acting. He sang in the premières of Deems Taylor's *The King's Henchman* (1927) and *Peter Ibbetson* (1931), Louis Gruenberg's *The Emperor Jones* (1933), Howard Hanson's *Merry Mount* (1934)

Lawrence Tibbett as Iago in 'Otello' (Verdi)

and J.L. Seymour's *In the Pasha's Garden* (1935). He also took part in the first Metropolitan performances of *Jonny spielt auf*, *Peter Grimes*, Richard Hageman's *Caponsacchi*, *Simon Boccanegra* and *Khovanshchina* (in which he made his last Metropolitan appearance in 1950, as Ivan). He also sang in San Francisco, Chicago, Paris, Vienna and Prague, and at Covent Garden created the title role in Eugene Goossens's *Don Juan de Mañara* (1937). His dark, pliant voice and matinée-idol appearance made him popular in films as well as light opera, and he was a significant force in early American radio. In 1950 he appeared on Broadway in *The Barrier*, and his last stage role was in the musical comedy *Fanny* (1956). He is perhaps best represented by his *Otello* recordings, which reveal him as an Iago of sly wit, his ample fervour in the 'Credo' counterbalanced by a silken

pianissimo in 'Era la notte'. He also sang Germont in the live 1935 Metropolitan recording of *La traviata* with ROSA PONSELLE. Tibbett published an autobiography, *The Glory Road* (Brattleboro, VT, 1933/R).

R. Whelan: 'Lawrence Tibbet Discography', *Record News* [Toronto], v (1960–61), 165–70

A. Farkas: *Lawrence Tibbet, Singing Actor* (Portland, OR, 1989) [with discography by W.R. Moran]

Martin Bernheimer/R

Tichatschek, Joseph (Aloys)
[Ticháček, Josef]

(*b* Ober-Weckelsdorf [now Teplice, nr Broumov], 11 July 1807; *d* Blasewitz, nr Dresden, 18 Jan 1886).

Bohemian tenor. He had his first music lessons from his father, Václav Ticháček, and sang in the choir at the Broumov Gymnasium. In 1827 he was sent to study medicine in Vienna, where he had singing lessons from GIUSEPPE CICCIMARRA, and in 1830 he joined the chorus of the Kärntnertortheater. He soon progressed to comprimario parts, and made his début as a principal in Graz in 1837. He sang in Vienna that year, and also made his Dresden début on 11 August 1837 in the title role of Daniel Auber's *Gustavus III*; the following year he was appointed to the Dresden Hofoper. With WILHELMINE SCHRÖDER-DEVRIENT, from whose friendship and advice he greatly benefited, and the baritone ANTON MITTERWURZER, Tichatschek helped the Dresden Opera set new standards of singing. In 1841 he sang at the Drury Lane Theatre (as Adolar, Tamino and Robert le diable), as well as in Manchester and Liverpool. He was pensioned in 1861 but continued to make appearances until 1870, his voice being remarkably well preserved. His repertory included the principal tenor parts of *Idomeneo*, *Die Zauberflöte*, *Fernand Cortez*, *I Capuleti*, *La muette de Portici* and *La dame blanche*. His range included lyric tenor and *Spieltenor* parts, but he was also the prototype of the Wagner *Heldentenor*, creating the title roles of *Rienzi* (20 October 1842) and *Tannhäuser* (19 October 1845).

All opinions agree on the beauty and brilliance of Tichatschek's voice. Sincerus (Siegmund Schmeider) praised his range of expression, even production, intonation and enunciation, although he had reservations about his coloratura. In 1840 Otto Nicolai called him the greatest German tenor, and Peter Cornelius was deeply moved by his Lohengrin in 1867 (although King Ludwig II of Bavaria was in the same year distressed by his unromantic appearance in the part). Hector Berlioz described him in the role of Rienzi as 'brilliant and irresistible…elegant, impassioned, heroic, his fine voice and great lustrous eyes marvellously effective'. Franz Liszt thought he would be ideal for the role of Cellini and, in a letter to Richard Wagner dated 20 February 1849, described him as 'an admirable artist and a charming comrade and friend'. Wagner, while also liking Tichatschek and admiring his singing ('a brisk and lively nature, a glorious voice and great musical talent'), found him childish and unable to portray 'the dark, gloomy, demonic strain in Rienzi's character'. Tichatschek's simple devotion to his voice, his appearance and his costumes were exclusive of any fuller dramatic perception, and he horrified Wagner at the première of *Tannhäuser* by addressing his outburst in praise of Venus with great passion to Elisabeth.

John Warrack

Tinsley, Pauline (Cecilia)

(*b* Wigan, 23 Nov 1928). English soprano. She studied in Manchester at the Northern School of Music and in London, making her début in 1961 as Desdemona (Gioachino Rossini's *Otello*) at St Pancras Town Hall, London, where she also sang Amalia (*I masnadieri*), Elvira (*Ernani*), Gulnara (*Il corsaro*) and Irene (*Rienzi*). For the WNO (1962–72) she sang Elsa, Susanna, Lady Macbeth, Sinaïde, Donna Elvira, Abigail, Aida and Turandot. At Sadler's Wells (1963–74) she sang Gilda, the Queen of the Night, Fiordiligi, Countess Almaviva, Leonora (*La forza del destino*), Leonore (*Fidelio*, both versions) and Elizabeth (*Maria Stuarda*), which she had already sung for the New York City Opera. At Santa Fe she sang Anne Boleyn (1971) and Senta. She made her Covent Garden debut in 1965 as Overseer (*Elektra*) returning as Amelia (*Un ballo in maschera*), Santuzza, Mother Marie (*Dialogues des Carmélites*) and Lady Billows, which she also sang in St Louis and Rome, at Reggio Emilia and at Glyndebourne. Returning to the WNO (1975–81) she sang the Kostelnička; Electra, a role she repeated at San Diego, Mannheim, Düsseldorf, Basle and Amsterdam; the Dyer's Wife, which she also sang at La Scala and Barcelona (1986); and Tosca. She created Candace (Stephen Paulus's *The Village Singer*, 1979, St Louis). Later roles included Isolde, Ortrud, Kundry, Brünnhilde (*Die Walküre*), the Witch (*Königskinder*) at Wexford, Fortune-Teller (*The Fiery Angel*) at Geneva, Fata Morgana for Opera North, Mother/Witch (*Hänsel und Gretel*) and Kabanicha (*Kát'a Kabanová*) for the ENO. She was an idiosyncratic actress with a flexible voice, brilliant in tone, of great stamina and penetration.

E Forbes: 'Pauline Tinsley', *Opera*, xxxiii (1982), 258–67

Alan Blyth

Titta, Ruffo Cafiero.

See RUFFO, TITTA.

Toczyska, Stefania

(*b* Grudziądz, 19 Feb 1943). Polish mezzo-soprano. She studied at the Gdańsk Conservatory and made her début with the Baltic State Opera, as Carmen, in 1973. After winning prizes in several vocal competitions she embarked on an international career, singing Amneris in Basle in 1977 and making her Vienna Staatsoper début as Preziosilla (*La forza del destino*) the following year. Toczyska has appeared in most of the world's leading opera houses, in such roles as Laura Adorno (*La Gioconda*), which she sang at San Francisco in 1985, Marfa in *Khovanshchina* (the role of her Metropolitan début, 1987), Pauline (*The Queen of Spades*), Rosina, Carmen, Azucena and Amneris, which she first sang at San Francisco in 1981 (with PAVAROTTI and MARGARET PRICE) and subsequently performed at Covent Garden (1983 and 1984). She is also admired as a concert singer (notably in Giuseppe Verdi's Requiem, which she has recorded), and performs a wide range of Polish music, from Fryderyk Chopin to Krzystof Penderecki. Although not always perfectly steady, her voice is ample and highly expressive, as can be heard on her vivid recordings of Vanya (*A Life for the Tsar*), Azucena and Pauline.

Barbara Chmara-Żaczkiewicz

Tomeoni [Tomeoni Dutillieu], Irene

(*b* 1763; *d* Vienna, 12 Oct 1830). Italian soprano. One of her earliest public performances was in Genoa in 1781. She was married to the French composer Pierre Dutillieu, whom she met in Florence in about 1781. In 1787 she went to Naples and sang there almost exclusively during the next three years in comic operas by Domenico Cimarosa, P.A. Guglielmi, Pasquale Anfossi, Giuseppe Sarti and others. In spring 1791 she succeeded ADRIANA FERRARESE as *prima buffa* of the Italian opera troupe in Vienna, making her début as Dorinda in Guglielmi's *La bella pescatrice* (a role she had created in Naples in 1789). She sang in Vienna throughout most of the following decade and a half, specializing in sentimental and cheerful heroines and creating, among others, the title role of Guglielmi's *La pastorella nobile* (1788) and the roles of Carolina in Cimarosa's *Il matrimonio segreto* (1792) and Mrs Ford in Antonio Salieri's *Falstaff* (1799). In 1796–7 she returned to Naples for an engagement at the Fiorentini; after her husband's death in 1798 she also toured in Germany (1809–10). The couple were financially secure, for at her death she left a villa at Penzig, outside Vienna (where, according to Carlo Schmidl, she had briefly operated her own theatre in 1807), and two houses in the city, as well as 2169 florins.

Tomeoni was not a singer of outstanding virtuosity. In writing for her, composers avoided coloratura and rarely exceeded an octave in range. She was noted for the simplicity of her singing, her ingenuous charm and her playfulness.

James L. Jackman/John A. Rice

Tomlinson, John

(*b* Oswaldtwistle, Lancs., 22 Sept 1946). English bass. After studying at Manchester, he began his career with Glyndebourne Touring Opera as Colline in 1972, and as Leporello and Seneca for Kent Opera. He studied further with OTAKAR KRAUS in London, and sang Reede in Alexander Goehr's *Arden Must Die* (New Opera Company, 1974).He joined the ENO in 1975 and sang a large repertory including Talbot (*Maria Stuarda*), King Mark, Fasolt, Pogner, Bluebeard, Charles Gounod's Méphistophélès (to arresting effect in Ian Judge's staging), Baron Ochs (a subtle, detailed portrayal in Jonathan Miller's production), Gioachino Rossini's Moses, Sparafucile, the Padre Guardiano, and Fiesco. He made his Covent Garden début in 1979 as Colline, and has subsequently sung there Figaro, Leporello, the Commendatore, Don Basilio, Timur and, unforgettably, the Green Knight in the première of Harrison Birtwistle's *Gawain* (1991), which he also recorded. Other successes at Covent Garden include astonishingly vivid portrayals of Claggart and King Fisher, Hans Sachs (in a revival of *Die Meistersinger* in 1987) and Wotan, both vocally imposing (if occasionally strained) and acted with tremendous panache. For Opera North he was praised as Boris Godunov (a role which he later sang for the ENO), Attila and Philip II. At Bayreuth he was a massively powerful, anguished Wotan in Harry Kupfer's controversial staging (recorded on both audio and video discs). Tomlinson has also appeared in his Wagner roles at the Berlin Staatsoper and at Munich. He is a noted oratorio singer, particularly in G.F. Handel. His other recordings include *Messiah*, the title role in *Hercules*, Don Alfonso, Titurel and Béla Bartók's Bluebeard and *Cantata profana*. The individuality and authority of his acting is never in doubt: it is supported by a magnificently resonant voice, used unflinchingly if not always with complete control. (See colour plate 7.)

H. Finch: 'John Tomlinson', *Opera*, xli (1990), 770–77

Alan Blyth

Tomowa-Sintow, Anna

(*b* Stara Zagora, 22 Sept 1941). Bulgarian soprano. Her mother was an opera chorus singer and she was involved in opera from an early age as Butterfly's child. Her studies were at the Sofia Conservatory with Gyorgy Zlatew-Tscherkin; she then sang small roles at Leipzig, where she made her main début as Abigaille in 1967. She built her repertory mainly on Italian roles, and in 1972 became a member of the Berlin Staatsoper. The next year she was engaged at Salzburg for the première of Carl Orff's *De temporum fine comoedia* under Herbert von Karajan, who helped promote her international career and developed her Mozart and Strauss repertory. She made her American début at San Francisco as Donna Anna in 1974, and played the same role at the Metropolitan in 1978, following débuts at Covent Garden as Fiordiligi (1975) and at the Vienna Staatsoper as Countess Almaviva (1977). In 1989 she sang in *Yevgeny Onegin* at the Lyric Opera of Chicago. She returned to Covent Garden in 1990 as Yaroslavna (*Prince Igor*). Her beautifully moulded spinto soprano with its creamy tone has also been heard to advantage in roles such as the Empress (*Die Frau ohne Schatten*) and Countess Madeleine in *Capriccio*; she is also a splendid, forceful Tosca. In 2000 she appeared once more at Covent Garden, as the Marschallin, giving an interpretation of great sincerity and inwardness and singing with virutally undiminished lustre. Tomowa-Sintow's many distinguished opera recordings include Donna Anna, Countess Almaviva, the Marschallin and Elsa, all under Karajan, Ariadne under James Levine (1987) and Heliane in E.W. Korngold's *Das Wunder der Heliane*. She is also an admired concert singer and has recorded (with Karajan) such works as Ludwig van Beethoven's Ninth Symphony and *Missa solemnis* and Johannes Brahms's *German Requiem*.

T. Lanier: 'Divided Loyalty', *ON*, xlix/11 (1984–5), 17–19
H. Rosenthal: 'Anna Tomowa-Sintow', *Opera*, xxxviii (1987), 250–53

Noël Goodwin

Tourel [Davidovich], Jennie

(*b* Vitebsk, Belarus, 9/22 June 1900; *d* New York, 23 Nov 1973). American mezzo-soprano. A refugee with her family from the Revolution, she eventually settled in Paris, where she studied with Reynaldo Hahn and Anna El Tour (in later years Tourel denied that her stage name was chosen as an anagram of her teacher's). She made her American début at the Chicago Civic Opera in Ernest Moret's *Lorenzaccio* (1930) and subsequently sang at the Opéra-Comique in Paris as Carmen (1933) and, later, Cherubino and Charlotte (*Werther*). Her career at the Metropolitan was brief: she made her début as Mignon in 1937 and appeared for a few seasons in the 1940s as Rosina, Adalgisa and Carmen. She became an American citizen in 1946.

Tourel's career was dominated by international appearances in recital and concert, and as an interpreter of French music she was considered virtually without rival. Her other specialities included the Italian coloratura mezzo-soprano repertory and the music of Leonard Bernstein, with whom she became closely associated. She gave the first performances of many songs by Francis Poulenc and Paul Hindemith (notably the revised *Marienleben* cycle, 1949). In 1951, in Venice, she created Baba

the Turk in *The Rake's Progress*. She taught at the Juilliard School and at the Aspen Music School. Her reputation, supported by many recordings, rests on her enormous versatility, both musical and linguistic, her stylistic elegance, her sensitivity to textual nuance and tone colour, and a remarkable technique.

E. Burns: 'Teacher Tourel', *ON*, xxxiv/27 (1969–70), 20
A. Hughes: Obituary, *New York Times* (25 Nov 1973)
R. Offergeld: 'Some Notes on the Future of Jennie Tourel', *Stereo Review*, xxxv/5 (1975), 78
P.L. Miller: 'Recorded Tributes to Jennie Tourel and Richard Tucker', *Association for Recorded Sound Collections Journal*, viii/1 (1976), 43

Martin Bernheimer/R

Tozzi, Giorgio [George]

(*b* Chicago, 8 Jan 1923). American bass-baritone. After vocal study with ROSA RAISA, Giacomo Rimini and John Daggett Howell, he made his professional début as Tarquinius in the Broadway production of *The Rape of Lucretia* (1948). He studied further in Milan with Giullo Lorandi, and made the transition from baritone to bass. His Italian début was in 1950 as Rodolfo in *La sonnambula* at the Teatro Nuovo. His La Scala début followed in 1953 (in Alfredo Catalani's *La Wally*), and in 1955 he made his Metropolitan début as Alvise (*La Gioconda*). He then appeared with remarkable success in Salzburg, San Francisco, Florence, Frankfurt, Munich and Lisbon. His notable roles included Philip II, Boris, Don Giovanni and Hans Sachs. He created the Doctor in Samuel Barber's *Vanessa* at the Metropolitan in 1958, and took part in the celebrated La Scala revival of *Les Huguenots* with CORELLI, SUTHERLAND and SIMIONATO in 1962. He has also been active in musical comedy, touring frequently in *South Pacific* and dubbing the lead role in the film version. He has taught at Juilliard, and he joined the music faculty at the Indiana University in 1991, and was awarded the rank of Distinguished Professor there in 2001. At his best, Tozzi was an imposing figure on the stage and a singer of uncommon versatility, warmth and intelligence.

Martin Bernheimer/R

Traubel, Helen (Francesca)

(*b* St Louis, 20 June 1899; *d* Santa Monica, CA, 28 July 1972). American soprano. From the age of 13 she studied singing with Vetta Karst. She made her concert début in 1923 in St Louis, but refused an offer to sing at the Metropolitan in 1926, returning instead to St Louis for further study. Her

Metropolitan début was in Walter Damrosch's *The Man without a Country* (1937); but her first important role was Sieglinde (1939), which initiated her career as the foremost American Wagnerian since NORDICA, with whom she was frequently compared. When KIRSTEN FLAGSTAD left the Metropolitan in 1941, Traubel became her successor, as Brünnhilde, Elisabeth, Elsa, Kundry and, above all, Isolde. Her statuesque presence, vocal grandeur and expressive warmth made her unrivalled in Wagner until Flagstad's return. The two sopranos shared the *Ring* cycles for one season (1951), and Traubel added the Marschallin to her rather limited repertory. In 1953 she left the Metropolitan after a disagreement with Rudolf Bing over her appearances in night-clubs. At the time, despite some loss of freedom at the top, her voice was virtually unimpaired. Thereafter she concentrated on films and television, and appeared in a Broadway show, *Pipe Dream* (1955). Although she sang in South America, Mexico and very briefly in London, Traubel remained essentially an American phenomenon. Her Wagner recordings, including a complete *Lohengrin* recorded at a Metropolitan performance in 1950, display the strength and security of her singing. Her papers are held in the special collections of the Music Division of the Library of Congress, Washington, DC.

H. Traubel: *St Louis Woman* (New York, 1959)

Martin Bernheimer

Treigle, Norman

(*b* New Orleans, 6 March 1927; *d* New Orleans, 16 Feb 1975). American bass-baritone. He studied at the Loyola University College of Music in New Orleans and with the contralto Elizabeth Wood. After a brief career in New Orleans, where he made his stage début in 1947, he joined the New York City Opera in 1953, singing Colline in *La bohème*. In 1954 he created the role of Grandpa Moss in Aaron Copland's *The Tender Land*. For the next 20 years he was a mainstay of that company, singing the major bass-baritone roles of the standard repertory. With a vivid, even flamboyant stage personality, he achieved his greatest successes in such parts as Mephistopheles (Arrigo Boito and Charles Gounod), Boris, Don Giovanni, Reverend Olin Blitch (Carlisle Floyd's *Susannah*), and G.F. Handel's Julius Caesar. In 1966 he sang in *Don Giovanni* with the Baltimore Opera Company, and also sang with the Central City Opera in Chicago.

In 1973 he left the City Opera to broaden his international activities with appearances in Hamburg, London (Covent Garden, *Faust*, 1973) and Milan. A singer who often sacrificed musical

fidelity to a broad theatrical effect, he resembled CHALIAPIN in many respects but vocally was less generously endowed. His voice was well schooled and serviceable but limited by its dry, throaty and occasionally raspy timbre.

Peter G. Davis

Treptow, Günther (Otto Walther)

(*b* Berlin, 22 Oct 1907; *d* Berlin, 28 March 1981). German tenor. He studied in Berlin, where he made his début at the Deutsche Oper in 1936 as the Italian Singer in *Der Rosenkavalier*. Despite being on the 'forbidden' list of non-Aryan musicians (his grandmother was Jewish), he managed to remain a member of the company until 1942, by which time he was singing such parts as Florestan, Pedro (*Tiefland*), Max and Otello. In 1942 he joined the Staatsoper in Munich, where he was heard chiefly in the Wagner repertory. After the war he returned to Berlin, first to the Staatsoper and then to the Deutsche Oper, where he created La Rocca in H.W. Henze's *Der junge Lord* (1965). He made regular guest appearances in Vienna. He sang Siegmund at Bayreuth in 1951 and 1952; Siegmund, Florestan and Tristan at the Metropolitan, 1951; and Siegfried at Covent Garden in 1953. His repertory included Adolar (*Euryanthe*), Tannhäuser and Parsifal. Treptow's dramatic intensity compensated for his occasional lapses in technique. His true Heldentenor voice can be heard in his recordings of Walther (*Die Meistersinger*) and Tristan, both under Hans Knappertsbusch, and as Siegmund in Wilhelm Furtwängler's live recording of *Die Walküre* at La Scala.

Harold Rosenthal/Alan Blyth

Tribou, Denis-François

(*b* c1695; *d* Paris, 14 Jan 1761). French *haute-contre*. He made his début at the Paris Opéra as the Sun in the 1721–2 revival of Jean-Baptiste Lully's *Phaëton*, and during the same run was promoted to sing the title role in place of Louis Muraire. He created the title role in Henry Desmarets' *Renaud* (1722) and in Lully revivals sang Attis (1725), Bellerophon (1728), Amadis (1731, to the rapturously received Oriane of CATHERINE-NICOLE LEMAURE) and Mercury (*Isis*, 1732), before creating Ammon in Michel Pignolet de Montéclair's *Jephté* (1732). In 1734 he took Pylades (Desmarets and André Campra's *Iphigénie en Tauride*) while the role of a Triton was sung by the young JÉLYOTTE, whose meteoric rise to prominence overtook the end of Tribou's career. Yet Tribou created Tacmas in *Les Indes galantes*, Castor in *Castor et Pollux*

(1737) and sang Perseus in 1737, before retiring in 1741 to become a theorist in the *musique de la chambre du roi*.

Philip Weller

Trombetta, Teresa.

See BELLOC-GIORGI, TERESA.

Troszel [Troschel], Wilhelm

(*b* Warsaw, 26 Aug 1823; *d* Warsaw, 2 March 1887). Polish bass. Son of the piano maker Wilhelm Troszel of Warsaw, he studied with August Freyer and others. He made his début at Warsaw on 17 April 1843 as Rodolphe in Daniel Auber's *Le lac des fées* and sang at the Warsaw Opera until 1865. Particularly noted for his interpretations of bass roles in operas by Adam Minchejmer, I.F. Dobrzyński and Stanisław Moniuszko (creating the roles of Stolnik in *Halka*, 1858, and Zbigniew in *The Haunted Manor*, 1865), and in German and Italian operas, he was also a fine recital singer. After retiring from concert and operatic work in 1866, Troszel devoted himself to composition and teaching. He wrote a tutor, *Szkoła do śpiewu na głos sopranowy i mezzosopranowy* (*Singing tutor for sopranos and mezzosopranos*, Warsaw, 1860), and a book of vocal exercises for women's voices (Warsaw, n.d.), as well as composing over 50 songs and some church music.

Irena Poniatowska

Troyanos, Tatiana

(*b* New York, 12 Sept 1938; *d* New York, 21 Aug 1993). American mezzo-soprano. She studied at the Juilliard School with Hans J. Heinz, making her début in 1963 as Hippolyta in the New York première of Benjamin Britten's *A Midsummer Night's Dream* with the City Opera. After two seasons with the company, during which she sang Marina, Igor Stravinsky's Jocasta, Cherubino and Carmen, in 1965 she made her European début as Preziosilla at Hamburg, where she remained for ten years; her roles there included Elisetta (*Il matrimonio segreto*), Dorabella and Baba the Turk, and she created Jeanne in Krzystof Penderecki's *The Devils of Loudun* (1969). She sang the Composer at the Aix-en-Provence (1966), Munich and Edinburgh festivals, and Octavian at Salzburg, Covent Garden and the Metropolitan (where she made her début in 1976). Her other roles included Dido (Henry Purcell and Hector Berlioz), G.F. Handel's Ariodante (which she sang at the inauguration of the Kennedy Center, Washington, in 1971), Sesto, Charlotte, Poppaea, Adalgisa (in which she made her La Scala début

in 1977), Romeo (*I Capuleti*), Eboli, Geschwitz, Santuzza and Brangäne. Troyanos had a warm, flexible voice and an intensely dramatic stage presence. Her recordings include Purcell's Dido, Adalgisa, the Composer and, most notably, Carmen.

M. Mayer: 'Tatiana Troyanos', *Opera*, xxxvi (1985), 268–72
M. Mayer and A. Blyth: 'Tatiana Troyanos, 1938–1993', *Opera*, xliv (1993), 1179–9 [obituary]

Harold Rosenthal/Alan Blyth

Tucci, Gabriella

(*b* Rome, 4 Aug 1929). Italian soprano. After studying at the Rome Conservatory, she continued her vocal training with Leonardo Filoni, whom she later married. In 1951 she made her début in *La forza del destino* opposite GIGLI. She sang throughout Italy (her La Scala début was as Mimì in 1959), and made guest appearances internationally, notably at the Teatro Colón and the Bol'shoy Theatre. She made her London début at the Adelphi Theatre as Mimì in December 1959 and first appeared at Covent Garden in the next year, as Aida and Tosca. Her American début, in San Francisco, was as Maddalena (*Andrea Chénier*) in 1959; the following October, as Butterfly, she began a close association with the Metropolitan which lasted until 1973. Her repertory included most of the standard Italian spinto roles, and she also successfully undertook the challenge of such florid parts as Elcia (*Mosè in Egitto*), Luisa Miller and Elvira (*I puritani*), as well as Mozart, Gluck and Gounod roles. Tucci was an uneven singer, but her best performances were notable for communicative warmth, taste and lustrous tone. A poignant actress, she was especially effective in the final acts of *Otello*, as discs of a performance in Japan corroborate, and *La traviata*. She was also a sympathetic and dramatically convincing Leonora (*Il trovatore*), a role she recorded with Thomas Schippers.

Martin Bernheimer/R

Tucker, Richard [Ticker, Reuben]

(*b* Brooklyn, NY, 28 Aug 1913; *d* Kalamazoo, MI, 8 Jan 1975). American tenor. He studied with PAUL ALTHOUSE and, after a spell in business, made his stage début as Alfredo with the Salmaggi Opera, New York, in 1943. In 1949 he received the accolade of being invited to sing in Arturo Toscanini's recorded broadcast of *Aida*. He made his European début in 1947 at the Verona Arena as Enzo to CALLAS's La Gioconda (her Italian début) and later appeared in London, Vienna, Milan and Florence. America in general and the Metropolitan in particular, however, remained the focal point of his extraordinary career, which spanned three decades of leading roles. Tucker's singing was never notable for finesse, and his acting, though energetic, remained primitive. But he had few peers in the projection of Italianate passions, or in fervour, ease, evenness and vocal security. He gave more than 600 performances in 30 leading roles at the Metropolitan, first lyric and later dramatic, beginning with *La Gioconda* in 1945 and ending with *Pagliacci* a few weeks before his sudden death. Among the recordings that best reveal his forthright, sturdy style are two versions of *La forza del destino* (one with Callas and one with LEONTYNE PRICE) and *Aida* (with Callas). Tucker was a deeply religious man; his wish to sing Eléazar in *La Juive* at the Metropolitan remained unfulfilled though he did undertake the role elsewhere (1973, New Orleans). He was the brother-in-law of a rival tenor, JAN PEERCE.

J.B. Steane: *The Grand Tradition* (London, 1974/R), 426
J.A. Drake: *Richard Tucker: a Biography* (New York, 1984) [with discography by P.A. Kiser]

Martin Bernheimer/R

Tuczek-Ehrenburg, Leopoldine (Margarethe)

(*b* Vienna, 11 Nov 1821; *d* Baden, nr Vienna, 20 Oct 1883). Soprano, daughter of František Tuček. She studied singing at the Vienna Conservatory from 1828 to 1834 and joined the court opera two years later. In 1841 she moved to Berlin, where she was a leading soprano at the court opera for 20 years, earning the title of royal *Kammersängerin*. She created the role of Mrs Ford in Otto Nicolai's *Die lustigen Weiber von Windsor* (Berlin, 1849).

Adrienne Simpson

Turner, Ann.

See ROBINSON, ANN TURNER.

Turner [Haas], Claramae

(*b* Dinuba, CA, 28 Oct 1920). American contralto. She studied at San Francisco, making her début there in 1942 as the voice of a boy in *L'amore dei tre re*. In 1946, after further study in New York, she created Baba (Madame Flora) in *The Medium* at Columbia University and made her Metropolitan début as Marthe (*Faust*), returning as La Frugola (*Il tabarro*), Zita (*Gianni Schicchi*), the Princess (*Suor Angelica*) and Amneris. At New York City Opera she sang Baba (1952) and took part in the première of

Aaron Copland's *The Tender Land* (1954). Her roles at Chicago (1955–7) included the Matron from Milwaukee (Raffaello de Banfield's *Lord Byron's Love Letter*), Fricka, Azucena and Ulrica. She sang Madame de Croissy in *Dialogues des Carmélites* at San Francisco (1957) and Baroness Grünwiesel in *Der junge Lord* at San Diego (1967), both American premières, and created Diana Orsini in *Bomarzo* at Washington, DC (1967). Her repertory included Delilah, Herodias (*Salome*), Mistress Quickly and Little Buttercup (*HMS Pinafore*). With an opulent voice, fine musicianship and an impressive stage presence, she was equally effective in 19th- and 20th-century operas.

Elizabeth Forbes

Turner, Dame Eva

(*b* Oldham, 10 March 1892; *d* London, 16 June 1990). English soprano. She studied in Bristol, and with Albert Richards Broad. She made her début in 1916 as a Page in *Tannhäuser* with the Carl Rosa Company, with which she remained until 1924, singing such roles as Santuzza, Tosca, Aida, Brünnhilde and Butterfly. In the last role she was heard by Ettore Panizza (Arturo Toscanini's assistant at La Scala), who sent her to Milan to sing for Toscanini. She made her La Scala début as Freia (*Das Rheingold*) in 1924 and soon established herself as a leading dramatic soprano, singing Aida, Leonora (*Il trovatore*) and other roles with an Italian company touring Germany in 1925. In 1926–7 at Brescia she sang her first Turandot, a role with which she was closely associated for the next 20 years, and in which Franco Alfano, who completed the opera after Giacomo Puccini's death, considered her ideal. Her recording of 'In questa reggia', made about 1930, created a 'unique impression of power and mastery'. A more extended souvenir of her interpretations exists in a disc of substantial extracts from this role in a live Covent Garden performance of 1937.

Turner first sang at Covent Garden with the Carl Rosa Company in 1920 and then, when established internationally, between 1928 and 1939 and in 1947–8, as Turandot, Aida, Santuzza, Sieglinde, Isolde, Agathe and Amelia (*Un ballo in maschera*). She also appeared in Chicago, Buenos Aires, Lisbon and elsewhere. From 1950 to 1959 she taught singing at the University of Oklahoma, and from 1959 at the RAM, London (among her pupils were AMY SHUARD, Linda Gray and RITA HUNTER). Her penetrating and powerful soprano and authoritative style were admirably suited to the dramatic soprano roles in Giuseppe Verdi and Richard Wagner. She was created DBE in 1962.

T. English: 'Eva Turner', *Opera*, i/6 (1950), 29–35

J.B. Richards: 'Eva Turner', *Record Collector*, xi (1957), 29–57 [with discography], 71, 183–4, 231–3

I. Cook: 'This is Eva Turner', *ON*, xxiv/4 (1959–60), 7, 30–31

R. Crichton and others: 'Eva Turner, 1892–1990', *Opera*, xli (1990), 920–28 [obituary]

Harold Rosenthal/Alan Blyth/R

Tyrén, Arne

(*b* Stockholm, 27 Feb 1928). Swedish bass. After studying in Stockholm, he made his début in 1955 as Bartolo with the Royal Swedish Opera, of which he was a member for 30 years. He created the commander Chefone in Karl-Birger Blomdahl's *Aniara*, repeating the part at Edinburgh (1959) and Covent Garden (1960), the title role of Blomdahl's *Herr von Hancken* (1965) and Reuterholm in Lars Johan Werle's *Tintomara* (1973). In 1978 he created the role of Astradamors in György Ligeti's *Le Grand Macabre*. He sang frequently at Drottningholm and his repertory included many comic roles, such as Buonafede (*Il mondo della luna*), Don Alfonso, Leporello, Don Magnifico, Don Pasquale, Rocco, Daland, Falstaff and Ochs; but he sang Seneca, Sarastro, Wotan, King Mark, Gurnemanz, the Grand Inquisitor and the four villains (*Les contes d'Hoffmann*) with equal success. A superb actor with a moderate-sized but well-projected voice, he excelled in characterizations such as the Doctor in *Wozzeck* or Kolenatý in *The Makropulos Affair*.

Elizabeth Forbes

U

Ugalde [née Beaucé], Delphine

(*b* Paris, 3 Dec 1829; *d* Paris, 19 July 1910). French soprano. She studied in Paris with CINTI-DAMOREAU and made her début in 1848 at the Opéra-Comique as Angèle in Daniel Auber's *Le domino noir*, a role created by her teacher. In 1851 she sang at Her Majesty's Theatre, London, as Delilah in Auber's *L'enfant prodigue*. In 1858 she sang Leonora (*Il trovatore*) at the Paris Opéra and was then engaged at the Théâtre Lyrique. In 1863 she moved to the Bouffes-Parisiens, where in 1867 she sang in her own operetta, *Halte au moulin*. She retired in 1871. Her daughter, Marguerite Ugalde (1862–1940), was a mezzo-soprano who sang with the Opéra-Comique; in 1881 she created Nicklausse in the company's production of *Les contes d'Hoffmann*.

Elizabeth Forbes

Uhde, Hermann

(*b* Bremen, 20 July 1914; *d* Copenhagen, 10 Oct 1965). German baritone. He studied as a bass at Philipp Kraus's opera school in Bremen, where he made his début as Titurel in *Parsifal* (1936). After some years at Freiburg and Munich he first appeared in baritone roles at The Hague in 1942. A prisoner-of-war from 1944 to 1947, he then sang regularly at Hamburg, Vienna and Munich. He scored a great success at Covent Garden with the Munich company as Mandryka in *Arabella* (1953), and later with the resident company as Gunther and Telramund, roles in which he was generally recognized as unsurpassed in his lifetime. He sang at Bayreuth and Salzburg, and made a particular impression at the Metropolitan Opera with his Wozzeck, sung in English. He created many roles, including Creon in Carl Orff's *Antigonae* (which, like his performance of Richard Wagner's Dutchman, is still impressive on record). He died during a performance of Niels Bentzon's *Faust III*.

A. Williamson: 'Hermann Uhde', *Opera*, xii (1961), 762–9

J.B. Steane

Ulfung, Ragnar (Sigurd)

(*b* Oslo, 28 Feb 1927). Norwegian tenor. He studied at Oslo and Milan, making his stage début in 1952 at Oslo as Magadoff (*The Consul*). He sang Faust at Bergen and in 1955 went to Göteborg, where he sang Jeník, Don Ottavio, the Duke of Mantua, Fra Diavolo and Don José. In 1958 he was engaged at the Royal Opera, Stockholm, where he created the Deaf Mute in Karl-Birger Blomdahl's *Aniara* (1959) and sang Canio, Hoffmann, Alfredo, Cavaradossi, Tom Rakewell, Lensky and Gustavus III, which he also sang in Edinburgh (1959) and on the company's visit to Covent Garden (1960). There he returned as Don Carlos (1963), Mime and Herod, and created the title role in *Taverner* (1972). At Hamburg he sang Turiddu, Erik and Števa in *Jenůfa* (also on the company's visit to New York in 1967) and created Christopher in Lars Johan Werle's *Resan* (1969). He made his San Francisco début as Chuck (Gunther Schuller's *The Visitation*), returning for Riccardo, Valzacchi and Mime, the role of his Metropolitan début (1972). Ulfung's repertory included Fatty (*Aufstieg und Fall der Stadt Mahagonny*), Captain (*Wozzeck*), Loge, Aegisthus (1972, La Scala), Otello (1983, Stockholm) and Jadidja (American première of Krzystof Penderecki's *Die schwarze Maske* at Santa Fe, 1988). A brilliant actor with an incisive voice, he excelled as Herod and Mime. He has also directed many operas, including a *Ring* cycle in Seattle.

N. Benvenga: 'Ragnar Ulfung', *Opera*, xxvi (1975), 837–42

Alan Blyth

Unger, Georg

(*b* Leipzig, 6 March 1837; *d* Leipzig, 2 Feb 1887). German tenor. Having abandoned theological studies, he made a successful début as an opera singer at Leipzig in 1867, which led to further engagements in several German cities. At Mannheim in June 1874, on the recommendation of Ernst Frank, Unger sang to Hans Richter, who was touring Germany auditioning singers for the première of Richard Wagner's *Ring* in 1876. Unger sang from *Tannhäuser* and went to Bayreuth in July 1874 to learn the part of Loge with Richter. Eventually, however, he was given the roles of Froh and Siegfried, although performing both roles proved too demanding and caused Unger to miss performances, and he was replaced as Froh in the second cycle to save his voice for the more taxing role of Siegfried. After his appearance in London at the Wagner Festival of 1877, the composer no longer used him. He returned to Leipzig, where he sang until 1881.

J.A. Fuller Maitland/Christopher Fifield

Unger, Gerhard

(*b* Bad Salzungen, Thuringia, 26 Nov 1916). German tenor. He studied in Eisenach and at the Berlin Hochschule für Musik, and in 1947 was engaged at Weimar, where he sang lyric roles such as Tamino, Alfredo and Pinkerton, and also David, his most popular role at that period of his career, at Bayreuth (1951–2). In 1952 he moved to the Berlin Staatsoper and in 1961 to Stuttgart, where he remained until 1982. A member of the Hamburg Staatsoper (1962–73), he appeared at the Vienna Staatsoper, La Scala, the Paris Opéra, the Metropolitan and in Salzburg, where in 1961 he sang Pedrillo (*Die Entführung aus dem Serail*), another favourite role, which he repeated over 300 times. In the 1970s and 80s he specialized in character roles, such as the Captain (*Wozzeck*), Skuratov (*From the House of the Dead*), Brighella (*Ariadne auf Naxos*), the Italian Singer (*Der Rosenkavalier*) and, above all, Mime in both *Das Rheingold* and *Siegfried*, which he sang widely in Europe and North and South America. Unger was also admired as a singer of J.S. Bach. His highly placed, bright, clear-toned voice hardly changed as he grew older, so that in 1980 he could still carry conviction as Pedrillo at Bregenz. He recorded many of his roles, including Pedrillo, Monostatos, Brighella, David and Alwa (*Lulu*).

Wolfram Schwinger/Elizabeth Forbes

Uppman, Theodor

(*b* San Jose, CA, 12 Jan 1920; *d* New York, 17 March 2005). American baritone. He received his vocal training at the Curtis Institute, Stanford University and the University of Southern California. He won praise as Pelléas in a concert performance of the opera by the San Francisco SO under Pierre Monteux in 1947, with MAGGIE TEYTE as Mélisande. Uppman's light, high baritone and boyish appearance made him a particularly suitable choice, and he repeated the role in his débuts with the New York City Opera (1948) and the Metropolitan (1953); he also made a speciality of Papageno. In London he sang the title role in the première of Benjamin Britten's *Billy Budd* (1951, Covent Garden), a performance subsequently issued on CD and revealing how apt vocally Uppman was for the role. He repeated the part in Paris and, on television, in the USA. He also created roles in Carlisle Floyd's *The Passion of Jonathan Wade* (1962, New York City

Opera), Heitor Villa-Lobos's *Yerma* (1971, Santa Fe), Thomas Pasatieri's *Black Widow* (1972, Seattle) and Leonard Bernstein's *A Quiet Place* (1983, Houston). Uppman's Metropolitan repertory included Guglielmo, Piquillo (*La Périchole*), Eisenstein (*Die Fledermaus*), Taddeo (*L'italiana in Algeri*), Harlequin (*Ariadne auf Naxos*) and Marcello.

Martin Bernheimer/R

Upshaw, Dawn

(*b* Nashville, TN, 17 July 1960). American soprano. She studied under JAN DEGAETANI, and also with PHYLLIS CURTIN at Tanglewood While still a pupil at the Manhattan School of Music, she took the title role in Paul Hindemith's *Sancta Susanna* (1983), then Echo in *Ariadne auf Naxos* at the Spoleto Festival (1984). She was engaged by the Metropolitan under the Development of Young Artists Program, progressing from small parts to Sophie (*Werther*), Sister Constance of St Denis and Blanche (*Dialogues des Carmélites*), Ilia, Zerlina, Pamina, Susanna, Despina and Gretel. At the Salzburg Festival (from 1987) her roles have included Susanna and the Angel (Olivier Messiaen's *Saint François d'Assise*). She has appeared at the Aix-en-Provence Festival as Despina and Anne Trulove, one of her most vivid parts which, like several of her Mozart roles, she has recorded. Upshaw took the title role in G.F. Handel's *Theodora* at Glyndebourne in 1996, an interpretation recorded on video. Like all her portrayals, this was notable for its intense sincerity and conviction. With her pure, slender tone, frank manner and ease of communication she has had notable success on the recital platform, and has made delightful recordings of lieder, works by American composers and songs from musicals.

Alan Blyth

Urbani, Valentino.

See VALENTINI.

Urlus, Jacques [Jacobus]

(*b* Hergenrath, 9 Jan 1867; *d* Noordwijk aan Zee, 6 June 1935). Dutch tenor. He studied at The Hague Conservatory, with Cornelie van Zanten and others in Amsterdam, and made his operatic début in Utrecht in 1894 as Beppe (*Pagliacci*). He sang with the Netherlands National Opera, 1894–9, then in Leipzig, 1900–14. One by one he mastered the leading Wagnerian parts, for which his robust yet sensitive singing and declamatory gifts well fitted him. He made his London début at Covent Garden in spring 1910 as Tristan during the Thomas Beecham opera season. In 1911 he was called to Bayreuth, where his first part was Siegmund. He sang regularly at the Metropolitan Opera, 1913–17, becoming its foremost Wagnerian tenor. From 1917 onwards he accepted no fixed engagements, but settled in the Netherlands and toured extensively in Europe and the USA. He was also an excellent concert singer. His many recordings, 1903–24, chronicle every facet of his career and confirm his fine-grained voice and innate sense of style. He published an autobiography, *Mijn loopbaan* ('My career'; Amsterdam, 1930).

O. Spengler: *Jacques Urlus* (New York, 1917)
P. and J. Dennis: 'Jacques Urlus', *Record Collector*, xxvi (1980–81), 245–81 [with discography]

Carl L. Bruun/Alan Blyth

Viorica Ursuleac, probably as Suor Angelica

Ursuleac, Viorica

(*b* Czernowitz [Cernăuți, now Chernovtsy], 26 March 1894; *d* Ehrwald, Tyrol, 23 Oct 1985). Romanian soprano. She studied in Vienna and made her début at Agram in 1922 as Charlotte. She sang at Cernăuți, the Vienna Volksoper and the Frankfurt Opera, whose conductor, Clemens Krauss, she later married. In 1930 she moved to Vienna, in 1935 to the Berlin Staatsoper and finally with Krauss to the Staatsoper in Munich (1937–44). She created the leading soprano roles in Richard Strauss's *Arabella* (1933, Dresden), *Friedenstag* (1938, Munich) and *Capriccio* (1942, Munich) and sang the title role in the public dress rehearsal of *Die Liebe der Danae* (1944, Salzburg). She also appeared in *Elektra*, *Der Rosenkavalier*, *Die Frau ohne Schatten*, *Ariadne auf Naxos* and *Die ägyptische Helena*. Strauss dedicated *Friedenstag* jointly to Krauss and Ursuleac, and some of his songs to Ursuleac; in all she sang 506 performances of 12 Strauss roles during her career.

Ursuleac also created the leading soprano roles in Bernhard Sekles's *Die zehn Küsse* (1926, Frankfurt), Ernst Krenek's *Der Diktator* (1928, Wiesbaden) and Eugen d'Albert's *Mister Wu* (1932, Dresden). She appeared regularly at Salzburg, 1930–34 and 1942–3. She made her only Covent Garden appearance in 1934, when she sang in the English premières of *Arabella* and *Švanda the Bagpiper* and as Desdemona. Her repertory of 83 roles also included Senta, Sieglinde, Tosca, Turandot and Elisabeth de Valois. Her recordings of the Marschallin, Ariadne, Arabella and, above all, Maria (from a live performance of *Friedenstag* by the original cast) confirm her lasting reputation as a Strauss interpreter.

I. Cook: 'Viorica Ursuleac, the First Arabella', *ON*, xix/16 (1954–5), 6–8
L. Rasponi: *The Last Prima Donnas* (New York, 1982), 130–39
I. Cook and A. Frankenstein: 'Remembering Viorica Ursuleac', *Opera*, xxxvii (1986), 22–8

Harold Rosenthal/Alan Blyth

Ustinoff, Nicolai.

See GEDDA, NICOLAI.

V

Vaduva, Leontina

(*b* Roşiile, 1 Dec 1960). Romanian soprano. She studied at the Bucharest Conservatory and with ILEANA COTRUBAS, making her début as Manon in Jules Massenet's opera at Toulouse in 1987. For her performances in the same opera at Covent Garden the following year she won the Laurence Olivier Opera Award, and was re-engaged to sing Gilda, Micaëla, Antonia, Charles Gounod's Juliet and Mimì. She has appeared in Buenos Aires, Barcelona, Cologne, Vienna and most leading French houses. Vaduva's voice was found light for the Opéra Bastille in Paris, although the delicacy of her style and the natural charm of her stage presence did much to compensate. At Covent Garden her Mimì was deeply touching and her Juliet matched the Romeo of ROBERTO ALAGNA in highly praised performances of Gounod's opera in 1994. These are roles she has also recorded, a less pure tone obtruding in some of the louder passages, but with much beauty elsewhere and an appealing warmth of expression throughout.

J.B. Steane

Valdengo, Giuseppe

(*b* Turin, 24 May 1914). Italian baritone. After studying in Turin, he made his début in 1936 at Parma as Gioachino Rossini's Figaro, then sang Sharpless at Alessandria. Though engaged at La Scala in 1939, he did not sing there (because of military service) until 1941, when he made his début as Baron Douphol (*La traviata*). In 1946 he performed at the New York City Opera, then in 1947 made his San Francisco début as Valentin, returning as Escamillo, Sharpless, Iago, Amonasro and Rigoletto. At the Metropolitan (1947–54) he sang Tonio, Marcello, Germont, Count Almaviva, Belcore, Ford, Paolo (*Simon Boccanegra*) and Giacomo Puccini's Lescaut. In 1955 he sang Don Giovanni and Raimbaud (*Le comte Ory*) at Glyndebourne, and in 1961 he created the Lawyer in Renzo Rossellini's *Uno sguardo dal ponte* in Rome. His recordings of Iago, Amonasro and Falstaff, deriving from NBC broadcasts (1947–50) conducted by Arturo Toscanini, are vividly and firmly sung, with an even, flexible line. He wrote an autobiography, *Ho cantato con Toscanini* (Como, 1962).

Alan Blyth

Valente, Benita

(*b* Delano, CA, 19 Oct 1934). American soprano. The daughter of Swiss and Italian immigrants, she began vocal studies with Chester Hayden and later worked with LOTTE LEHMANN in Santa Barbara. She attended the Curtis Institute (1955–60), where she was a pupil of MARTIAL SINGHER, and from 1968 studied with MARGARET HARSHAW. In 1960 she won the Metropolitan Opera Auditions and two years later made her début in Freiburg as Pamina, a role which also served for her débuts in Santa Fe, Strasbourg, Zürich and at the Metropolitan Opera (1973). She subsequently appeared at the Metropolitan as Susanna, Countess Almaviva, Nannetta, Ilia, Gilda (on tour) and Almirena in *Rinaldo*. Though best known as an interpreter of W.A. Mozart and G.F. Handel, she has also enjoyed success as Anne Trulove, Antonia, Eurydice, Liù, Marguerite, Mélisande, Mimì and Violetta in Boston, Dallas, Philadelphia, Pittsburgh, San Diego, Washington, DC, and elsewhere. Her European engagements have included *Rinaldo* in Parma and other Italian cities and seasons in Freiburg (1962–3) and Nuremberg (1966–7). Valente is admired for her pure but warm tone, flawless technique, sympathetic presence and impeccable musicianship.

Cori Ellison

Valentini [Urbani, Valentino]

(*b* Udine; *fl* 1690–1722). Italian alto castrato. He was a pupil of PISTOCCHI and later in the service of the Duke of Mantua. His first known appearances were in 1690 in Venice (in Giacomo Perti's *Brenno in Efeso*) and Parma (Bernardo Sabadini's *Il favore degli dei*). He sang at Bologna in 1691 and 1695, Rome in 1694 and Venice in 1695, in two operas by C.F. Pollarolo. In 1697–1700 he was in the service of the Electress of Brandenburg in Berlin, where he sang the title role in *La festa del Himeneo* by Attilo Ariosti and others (1700). In 1703 he was at Mantua in Antonio Caldara's *Gli equivoci del sembiante*. He was the first castrato to sing regularly in London, making his début at Drury Lane in Nicola Haym's version of *Camilla* (1706) and returning in 1707–11 and 1712–14. He sang in many of the early Italian operas in London, most of them pasticcios and some bilingual – *Thomyris* (1707), *Love's Triumph* and *Pirro e Demetrio* (1708),

Clotilda (1709), *Almahide* and *Idaspe fedele* (1710), *Dorinda* (1712, 1714), *Ernelinda* (1713), *Creso* and *Arminio* (1714) – and in the first performances of G.F. Handel's *Rinaldo* (1711, Eustazio), *Il pastor fido* (1712, Silvio), *Teseo* (1713, Aegeus), and probably the title role in *Silla* (1713). He adapted the music of *Love's Triumph* from a pastoral with music by Carlo Cesarini, Francesco Gasparini and perhaps others, adding French-style choruses and dances and commissioning English words from P.A. Motteux, but it was a failure. After leaving London he sang in five operas in Venice (1717–19) and Francesco Conti's *Don Chisciotte* in Hamburg in 1722.

Valentini's Handel parts were restricted in compass (*a* to *e b"*) and not remarkable for inspiration or virtuosity, but his powers seem to have been on the decline. Charles Burney reported that 'his voice was feeble, and his execution moderate', adding of his part in *Teseo* that Valentini 'seems to have been gifted with very limited powers…It seems manifest that Handel was obliged, in writing for this performer, to ride Pegasus with a curb-bridle'. Others who heard him (which Burney never did) described him as a fine actor and 'more chaste in his singing' than Nicolini.

Winton Dean

Valentini-Terrani, Lucia

(*b* Padua, 29 Aug 1948 *d*. Seattle, WA, 22 June 1998). Italian mezzo-soprano. She studied at the Padua and Venice conservatories. Her début was at the Teatro Grande, Brescia, in 1969 as Angelina (*La Cenerentola*), a role that also introduced her at La Scala (1973) and at Covent Garden (1976) with the Scala company in the Jean-Pierre Ponnelle production conducted by Claudio Abbado. She toured with the company to Washington, Moscow and Tokyo, and first sang at the Metropolitan in 1974 as Isabella; she appeared with the Royal Opera at Covent Garden in 1982 as Mistress Quickly in *Falstaff*, conducted by Carlo Maria Giulini. Her rich, firmly focussed tone, buoyant rhythm and control of *fioriture* were heard to particular advantage in Gioachino Rossini; but she also excelled in roles such as Jules Massenet's Dulcinée and Charlotte and Modest Musorgsky's Marina. She appeared often at the Festival della Valle d'Itria, in Martina Franca, Apulia. Frequent engagements at the Rossini Festival, Pesaro, included *La donna del lago* and *Il viaggio a Reims*, both of which are among her recordings, as are roles in *La fedeltà premiata*, *L'italiana in Algeri*, *Aida*, *Don Carlos*, *Nabucco*, Antonio Vivaldi's *Orlando furioso* and Jacques Offenbach's *La Grande-Duchesse de Gérolstein*.

Noël Goodwin/R

Valesi [Vallesi], Giovanni [Walleshauser, Johann Evangelist]

(*b* Unterhattenhofen [now Hattenhofen], Upper Bavaria, 28 April 1735; *d* Munich, 10 Jan 1816). German tenor and singing teacher. A pupil of Placidus Camerloher, he held posts as a court singer in Munich and was a member of the Munich Hofkapelle, 1770–94. He also sang in Amsterdam and Brussels (1755), in Italy (after 1757, when he assumed the name Valesi, and 1770–75) and in Prague, Dresden and Berlin (1777–8). He sang in the first performance of W.A. Mozart's *La finta giardiniera* (1775) in Munich, where he also created the part of the High Priest of Neptune in the first performance of *Idomeneo* (1781). He trained over 200 singers, among them his children Anna (1776–92), Joseph (1778–1807), Magdalena (*b* 1781), Crescentia (*b* 1785) and Thekla (1789–1868), VALENTIN ADAMBERGER and Carl Maria von Weber.

Hans Schmid

Valletti, Cesare

(*b* Rome, 18 Dec 1922; *d* Genoa, 14 May 2000). Italian tenor. After studying privately under TITO SCHIPA he made his début at Bari in 1947 as Alfredo. In 1950 he took part in *Il turco in Italia* at the Teatro Eliseo, Rome, with CALLAS and STABILE; that autumn he sang Fenton (*Falstaff*) with the Scala company at Covent Garden. He sang regularly at La Scala, as Nemorino, Almaviva, Filipeto (*I quatro rusteghi*), Lindoro and other *tenore di grazia* roles. In 1953 he made his American début at San Francisco as Werther, and from 1953 to 1962 sang regularly at the Metropolitan, where he was especially admired as Don Ottavio (a role he also sang at the Salzburg Festival), Des Grieux, Ferrando and Ernesto. He returned to Covent Garden in 1958 to sing Alfredo opposite Callas, a performance which was recorded live. In 1968 he sang Nero (*L'incoronazione di Poppea*) at the Caramoor Festival in Katonah, New York. He also recorded Lindoro, Almaviva, Ernesto and Fenton, all of which display his exemplary, assured tenor technique and refined sense of style.

Harold Rosenthal/Alan Blyth

Vallin, Ninon [Vallin-Pardo, Eugénie]

(*b* Montalieu-Vercieu, 8 Sept 1886; *d* Lyons, 22 Nov 1961). French soprano. She studied in Lyons and made her début in 1912 as Micaëla with the Opéra-Comique, where she continued to sing throughout her career in a repertory that included Mimì, Mignon, Louise, Manon, Carmen, Nedda, Rozenn (*Le roi d'Ys*), Salud (*La vida breve*), Charlotte and St Mary in the French première of Ottorino Respighi's *Maria Egiziaca* (1934). At La Scala (1916–17) she sang Mignon, Ermanno Wolf-Ferrari's Susanna and the Princess (*Marouf*). She first appeared at the Teatro Colón, Buenos Aires, in 1916 as Charles Gounod's Marguerite, returning there regularly for 20 years, and also sang at the Teatro Municipal in Rio de Janeiro, Brazil. In 1920 she made her Opéra début as Thaïs. She appeared at San Francisco (1934), Orange (1935, *La damnation de Faust*), Vichy, and Monte Carlo (1943). Her repertory also included the three *Hoffmann* heroines, as well as Alcestis, Mélisande and Countess Almaviva, which she sang in 1946 at the Opéra-Comique. Vallin was a distinguished interpreter of *mélodies*, as her excellent recordings confirm, including many Reynaldo Hahn songs and arrangements by Joaquín Nin of Spanish folksongs, in both cases with the composer as accompanist. Her many operatic recordings reveal the distinctive flavour of her voice and her inborn sense of style that did not preclude impassioned involvement with the music in hand, all heard at their best in her complete *Werther* with Georges Thill.

H.M. Barnes: 'Vallin, Ninon', *Record Collector,* viii (1953), 53–65 [with discography]

Martin Cooper/Elizabeth Forbes/Alan Blyth

Van Allan, Richard

(*b* Clipstone, Notts., 28 May 1935). English bass. He studied at the Birmingham School of Music with David Franklin and gained early experience with the Opera for All company. He made his début in 1964 in the chorus at Glyndebourne, where he subsequently sang many roles, creating Jowler in Nicholas Maw's *The Rising of the Moon* (1970). He made his Covent Garden début in 1971 as the Mandarin (*Turandot*) and sang frequently with the WNO and the ENO; he also sang at the Paris Opéra, Wexford, Nice, Bordeaux, Boston and the Metropolitan. His repertory included W.A. Mozart's Figaro, Don Giovanni, Leporello, Don Alfonso and Osmin (roles to which he brought real resonance as well as wit) and Giuseppe Verdi's Zaccaria, Banquo, Massimiliano (*I masnadieri*), Silva (*Ernani*), Padre Guardiano, Philip II and Grand Inquisitor, as well as King Henry (*Lohengrin*), Pizarro, Boris, Hector Berlioz's Méphistophélès, Vodník (*Rusalka*), Colline and Ochs, which he first sang at San Diego in 1976. Van Allan's voice was not particularly large but was firmly focussed and intelligently used, while his dramatic gifts were effectively demonstrated in roles such as Claggart (*Billy Budd*),

Collatinus (*The Rape of Lucretia*) and Tiresias, which he created in John Buller's *Bakxai* (1992). Among his recordings are Masetto and Don Alfonso (both with Colin Davis), Wurm (*Luisa Miller*), Trulove (*Rake's Progress*), Sir Walter Raleigh (*Gloriana*) and Hobson (*Peter Grimes*). He became director of the National Opera Studio in 1986.

Elizabeth Forbes

Van Dam, José [Van Damme, Joseph]

(*b* Brussels, 25 Aug 1940). Belgian bass-baritone. He studied in Brussels, making his début in 1960 at Liège as Gioachino Rossini's Don Basilio. From 1961 to 1965 he was engaged at the Paris Opéra and Opéra-Comique, singing minor roles. After two seasons at Geneva, where he sang in the première of Darius Milhaud's *La mère coupable* (1966), he joined the Deutsche Oper, Berlin; his roles there included W.A. Mozart's Figaro, Leporello and Don Alfonso, Giuseppe Verdi's Attila, Prince Igor and Rangoni (*Boris Godunov*). He has appeared at the Salzburg, Aix-en-Provence and Athens festivals. Equally at home in the French, German or Italian opera, he had a repertory ranging from the four villains (*Les contes d'Hoffmann*), Golaud, Balducci (Benvenuto Cellini) and Guillaume Tell to Sarastro, Caspar (*Der Freischütz*), Wozzeck, Amfortas and Boccanegra. A notable Escamillo, he sang the role on his San Francisco (1970), Covent Garden (1973) and Metropolitan (1975) débuts. He created the title role of Olivier Messiaen's *Saint François d'Assise* in Paris (1983). Van Dam possessed one of the smoothest, most resonant bass-baritones of his generation and was also a notably versatile actor. His lithe Don Giovanni and athletic Escamillo early in his career were succeeded by subtle and penetrating portrayals of such tormented souls as Philip II, the Dutchman, Golaud, John the Baptist, Agamemnon (1987), Albéric Magnard's Guercoeur (1988), and George Enescu's Oedipus (1989), all of which he recorded. He was also unsurpassed as Méphistophélès in Hector Berlioz's *La damnation de Faust*, both in concert and on disc. He was less successful as Falstaff and Hans Sachs, while his preoccupation with even, mellifluous tone often created a rather anonymous impression in lieder and *mélodies*.

A. Clark: 'José van Dam', *Opera* (1993), festival issue, 4–14

Elizabeth Forbes/Alan Blyth

Van Dyck [van Dijck], Ernest (Marie Hubert)

(*b* Antwerp, 2 April 1861; *d* Berlaer-lez-Lierre, 31 Aug 1923). Belgian tenor. He studied with Saint-Yves

Bax in Paris, and having sung at the Concerts Lamoureux from 1883, he made his stage début in 1887 at the Eden-Théâtre as Lohengrin. After intensive coaching from Julius Kniese he sang Parsifal at Bayreuth in 1888, returning there in the same role until 1912 and as Lohengrin in 1894. From 1888 to 1900 he was engaged at the Vienna Hofoper, where he appeared in Antonio Smareglia's *Il vassallo di Szigeth* (1889). He first sang Des Grieux in Jules Massenet's *Manon* at Vienna (1890), and he made his London début in that role at Covent Garden (1891), where he also sang Faust and Lohengrin (1891), Tannhäuser, Siegmund and Mathias in Wilhelm Kienzl's *Der Evangelimann* (1897), Loge in *Das Rheingold* (1898) and Tristan (1901). In Vienna he created the title role of Jules Massenet's *Werther* (1892), and took the part of Marcel in Ruggero Leoncavallo's *La bohème* (1898). He made his début at the Paris Opéra as Lohengrin in 1891 and at the Théâtre de la Monnaie, Brussels, in the same part (1894), becoming a regular visitor to the latter house in Wagner and Massenet roles. He made his American début at Chicago on 9 November 1898 as Tannhäuser, and first appeared at the Metropolitan 20 days later in the same role. In 1907 he managed a season of German opera at Covent Garden and also appeared as Tristan and Siegmund. He returned to the Paris Opéra in 1908 as Siegfried in *Götterdämmerung* and finally, in 1914, as Parsifal. After his retirement from the stage he taught singing, first in Paris and later in Brussels. His voice, both powerful and sweet-toned, encompassed not only the heavy Wagnerian tenor roles with ease, but also the more lyrical French repertory, and he was particularly admired as Des Grieux.

Elizabeth Forbes

Vaness, Carol

(*b* San Diego, 27 July 1952). American soprano. She studied at California State University and with David Scott, who changed her vocal orientation from mezzo-soprano to soprano, in which guise she has become one of the foremost American singers of her generation. She made her début in the 1977 spring season of the San Francisco Opera as Vitellia, a role which was to bring her acclaim in many opera houses later in her career, including, in 1979 the New York City Opera, and in which she has displayed to advantage her mezzo-like vibrancy of timbre, near-instrumental evenness of emission across a wide compass and fluent delivery of florid passagework. Outstanding among her other Mozart roles are Donna Anna (notably at Glyndebourne in 1982, a performance she later recorded), Fiordiligi

(*Così fan tutte*), and Electra (*Idomeneo*), the role of her La Scala début in 1990. A statuesque presence, somewhat cool response to words and detachment in matters of characterization lend her best Mozart performances a special classical distinction, a quality which has also made her an impressive exponent of G.F. Handel's Armida (*Rinaldo*), in which role she made her début at the Metropolitan in 1984, Alcina, Cleopatra (*Guilio Cesare*) and Delilah (*Samson*), and of the heroines of C.W. Gluck's *Iphigénie en Tauride* (which she has recorded with Riccardo Muti) and *Alceste*.

Latterly Vaness has begun to focus on the larger-scaled, more dramatic roles of the Italian repertory, including Vincenzo Bellini (Norma), Giuseppe Verdi (Lenora in *Il trovatore* and *La forza del destino*, Violetta, both Amelias), and Giacomo Puccini (Tosca, which she has recorded, also under Muti). Further dramatic roles include Jules Massenet's Manon, Tatyana, which she sang in Toronto (1990), and the title roles of *Anna Bolena* (1991, Seattle) and *Iphigénie en Tauride* (1992, La Scala). As Rosalinde she shows an unexpected flair for comedy. Vaness is also an admired concert singer, and has recorded works such as Ludwig van Beethoven's Ninth Symphony and *Missa solemnis*, and Verdi's Requiem.

E. Forbes: 'Carol Vaness', *Opera*, xl (1989), 418–24

Max Loppert

Vanini [Boschi], Francesca

(*b* Bologna; *d* Venice, 1744). Italian contralto. She was in the service of the court of Mantua. Between 1695 and 1700 she appeared in operas in Bologna, Florence, Venice, Mantua and Parma. She sang in Naples in 1701 and in Antonio Caldara's *Gli equivoci del sembiante* at Casale in 1703, at Genoa in 1703–6 and Vicenza in 1707. Between 1707 and 1709 she appeared with her husband, the bass GIUSEPPE BOSCHI, in 12 operas in Venice (including G.F. Handel's *Agrippina*) and Bologna, often playing male parts. She accompanied him to London (1710–11), singing in Alessandro Scarlatti's *Pirro e Demetrio*, Giovanni Bononcini's *Etearco* and Handel's *Rinaldo* (Goffredo). Her voice was then on the decline (Goffredo is her last known part), but earlier she had been an outstanding artist: P.F. Tosi praised her for following PISTOCCHI's method 'of introducing Graces without transgressing against Time'. Handel's two parts for her, Otho in *Agrippina* and Goffredo, have a limited compass of *g* to e″; the tessitura of the former is exceptionally low.

Winton Dean

Vanni-Marcoux [Marcoux, Vanni; Marcoux, Jean Emile Diogène]

(*b* Turin, 12 June 1877; *d* Paris, 22 Oct 1962). French bass and baritone. His father was French and his mother Italian; the 'Vanni' which he incorporated into his professional name was originally an abbreviation for 'Giovanni'. He made early appearances in Bayonne (début 1889 as Charles Gounod's Friar Laurence) and in Turin as Sparafucile (1894). But neither heredity nor Italian training affected the timbre of his voice, which was always characteristically French. He was engaged in 1905 by Covent Garden, where he made his début as Gioachino Rossini's Don Basilio, and where he returned every summer until 1912 in a wide variety of roles, both baritone and bass. Exceptionally, he tended to gravitate towards the higher range as his career developed, moving for example from the bass role of Arkel in *Pelléas* (1909, London) to the baritone part of Golaud (1914, Paris, 1937, London). At the Théâtre de la Monnaie in Brussels, in the 1907–8 season, he was still predominantly a bass, singing even Hunding and Fafner in the *Ring*; and it was as Gounod's Méphistophélès that he made his début at the Paris Opéra in 1908. Thereafter for nearly 40 years he remained an admired figure in Parisian musical life, mainly at the Opéra, but also at the Opéra-Comique, where he was particularly famous as the Father in *Louise* and in the title role of *Don Quichotte*. His American career centred on Chicago, where he first appeared in 1913 as Scarpia and as Don Quichotte (singing in both operas with MARY GARDEN), and again frequently between 1926 and 1932. He also appeared with Garden in Boston, where their warm interpretation of Tosca caused a sensation. Among his other leading roles were Boris Godunov, Iago (which he studied with MAUREL), Don Giovanni, Athanaël (*Thaïs*), and Boniface (Jules Massenet's *Le jongleur de Notre-Dame*). He was also director of the Grand Théâtre at Bordeaux from 1948 to 1951. Vanni-Marcoux was a splendid actor as well as an accomplished singer, with exemplary enunciation and a voice remarkable for smoothness and finish rather than for sheer power. Among his many excellent records, those of 'Elle ne m'aime pas' from *Don Carlos* and of extracts from *Don Quichotte* are especially treasurable.

D. Shawe-Taylor: 'Vanni Marcoux', *Opera*, xiv (1963), 156–62; rev. in *Recorded Sound*, nos.29–30 (1968), 266–72 [with discography by H. Barnes]

Desmond Shawe-Taylor/R

Van Rooy, Anton.

See ROOY, ANTON VAN.

Van Steenkiste, Julie.

See DORUS-GRAS, JULIE.

Vanzo, Alain (Fernand Albert)

(*b* Monte Carlo, 2 April 1928; *d* Gournay-sur-Marne, nr Paris, 27 June 2002). French tenor. A boy chorister in Monte Carlo, he later continued his musical studies at Aix-les-Bains. After winning a competition for tenors at Cannes in 1954, he made his Paris Opéra début that year as a Pirate in *Oberon*. Following a period of small roles at both Paris houses, in 1956 he undertook the Duke of Mantua at the Opéra and Gérard (*Lakmé*) at the Opéra-Comique, and won renown throughout France and Belgium in French lyric parts – Hector Berlioz's Cellini, Charles Gounod's Faust (a role he sang in Philadelphia in 1984) and Vincent (*Mireille*), Edouard Lalo's Mylio (*Le roi d'Ys*), Jules Massenet's Des Grieux and Werther – and in Gaetano Donizetti, Giuseppe Verdi and Giacomo Puccini. Although he appeared at Covent Garden, as Edgardo (1961) and Rodolfo in *La bohème* (1963), and in Wexford and the USA, it remains surprising that in a time of shortage a French tenor of his elegant, clean style and well-formed vocal timbre should not have received wider international acclaim. His recordings include *Lakmé*, with SUTHERLAND; *Le roi d'Ys*, *Les pêcheurs de perles* and Massenet's *La Navarraise*. After retirement he was active as a singing teacher.

Max Loppert

Varady, Julia

(*b* Oradea, 1 Sept 1941). Romanian soprano, naturalized German. She studied in Bucharest with Arta Florescu, joining the Cluj State Opera at 22. Guest engagements took her to Italy, Frankfurt and Cologne, where she soon became known as a Mozart soprano of passionate intensity, vocal warmth and technical smoothness, as Elvira, Fiordiligi and Vitellia. After two years at Frankfurt, in the 1972–3 season she was engaged at Munich, where her roles included Jacques Offenbach's Antonia, Butterfly, Giorgetta (*Il tabarro*) and Liù; in 1977 she sang the title role in Richard Strauss's *Arabella* there, and in 1978 was included in the cast of the premiere of Aribert Reimann's *Lear*. As C.W. Gluck's Alcestis in the 1974 Scottish Opera production, she was much admired for her ability to marry emotional power and classically serene line in a portrayal of nobility and dignity, unstrained by the high tessitura of Gluck's music. But in spite of her protean artistry, which enabled her to tackle such parts as Senta (a role she sang at Covent Garden in 1992), it is as a Verdi soprano that she revealed the range of her powers; and she undertook such varied roles as Violetta, Leonora in both *Il trovatore* and *La forza del destino*, Elisabeth de Valois, Desdemona, Aida and Abigaille with thrilling magnetism and vocal *slancio*. Varady's recordings include Cecilius in *Lucio Silla*, *Idomeneo* (Electra, a role she sang in Milan in 1984), Vitellia (*La clemenza di Tito*), *Arabella*, *Bluebeard's Castle* (with DIETRICH FISCHER-DIESKAU, who performed this work with her at the Edinburgh Festival in 1984) as well as Giuseppe Verdi and Giacomo Puccini arias. She married Fischer-Dieskau in 1978. She retired from the operatic stage in 1997 but has continued to make recordings, among them a disc of Tchaikovsky arias that reveals her vocal and interpretative powers still at their height.

A. Blyth: 'Julia Varady', *Opera*, x/iii, 1992, pp. 646–51

Max Loppert

Varesi, Felice

(*b* Calais, 1813; *d* Milan, 13 March 1889). Italian baritone. He made his début in 1834 at Varese as Cardenio in Gaetano Donizetti's *Il furioso all'isola di San Domingo*, then for six years sang throughout Italy, mainly in operas by Donizetti. He first appeared at La Scala in 1841 as Publio in Saverio Mercadante's *La vestale*, then sang in Luigi Ricci's *Le nozze di Figaro*, the first performance of Federico Ricci's *Corrado d'Altamura*, Giovanni Pacini's *Saffo* and the first performance of Alessandro Nini's *Odalisa* (1842). He sang Sir Riccardo Forth in *I puritani* at the Teatro Apollo, Rome, in 1842, having sung Sir Giorgio in the same opera five years earlier at Faenza. A frequent visitor to the Kärntnertortheater, Vienna, he created Antonio in *Linda di Chamounix* (1842) there, and also appeared in Donizetti's *Alina, regina di Golconda* (1843), *Roberto Devereux* (1844) and *Maria Padilla* (1847). His first Verdi roles were Carlo in *Ernani* at Padua (1844) and the Doge in *I due Foscari* at Bergamo (1845). He created the title role of Macbeth at Florence in 1847, then sang Francesco in *I masnadieri* (1849) and Alphonse in *La favorite* (1850) at the S Carlo, Naples, and Malatesta in *Don Pasquale* at the Argentina, Rome (1850). He took part in two Verdi premières at La Fenice, Venice, singing Rigoletto (1851) and Giorgio Germont (1853). He appeared in Madrid (1856–7) and made his London début in 1864 at Her Majesty's Theatre as Rigoletto. Varesi was a prototype of the modern dramatic baritone who evolved from the operas of Donizetti and of early and middle-period Verdi. Although he made a powerful Macbeth, Rigoletto was undoubtedly his finest role; his singing of 'Si vendetta' always

aroused enormous enthusiasm and was invariably encored; he neither understood nor liked the part of Germont. His daughter was the singer Elena Boccabadati-Varesi.

Elizabeth Forbes

Vargas, Ramón

(*b* Mexico City, 1960). Mexican tenor. After studying at the Mexico City Conservatory and then in Vienna, he was engaged at the opera houses in Lucerne (1988–90) and Zürich, his roles including Edgardo, Elvino (*La sonnambula*) and Werther. In 1991 he began to appear regularly in Italy, mostly in W.A. Mozart and Gioachino Rossini, gaining a reputation for his light, flexible and sweet-toned singing, a reputation confirmed when he sang a charming Almaviva in a much lauded recording of *Il barbiere di Siviglia* in 1992. He made a successful début at La Scala in 1993 as Fenton, in a performance of *Falstaff* under Riccardo Muti that was committed to disc. At the same time Vargas appeared regularly at his home house in Mexico City and at the Houston Opera (where he sang his first Hoffmann). His roles at Covent Garden include the Duke of Mantua, Alfredo, and Rodolfo, and at the Metropolitan a much admired Edgardo (the role of his début in 1992), the Duke of Mantua, Alfredo and Ramiro (in a new production of *La Cenerentola*, 1997). He took the role of Don Narciso in Riccardo Chailly's award-winning recording (with BARTOLI) of *Il turco in Italia* (1997), adding a highly accomplished Werther to his discography in 1999. In 2000 he was admired for the elegance and touching pathos of his singing as Gustavus III (*Un Ballo in maschera*) in San Francisco. By then Vargas's light, lyric voice had taken on stronger tones without losing quality or flexibility. He has been aptly compared to his mentor, ALFREDO KRAUS.

Alan Blyth

Varnay, Astrid (Ibolyka Maria)

(*b* Stockholm, 25 April 1918; *d* Munich, 4 Sept 2006). American soprano of Swedish birth. Her family emigrated in 1920 to the USA, where she studied with PAUL ALTHOUSE and Hermann Weigert, whom she married. She made her début at the Metropolitan in 1941 as Sieglinde, a last-minute replacement for LOTTE LEHMANN; six days later she replaced HELEN TRAUBEL as Brünnhilde. She also sang Elsa, Elisabeth, and Telea in the première of Gian Carlo Menotti's *The Island God*. In 1948 she sang her first Italian roles (La Gioconda, Aida, Santuzza) in Mexico City and made her

European début at Covent Garden as the *Siegfried* Brünnhilde; she also sang Isolde and returned to London as a powerful Kostelnička. In 1951 she sang Lady Macbeth at the Florence Maggio Musicale and first appeared at Bayreuth, returning every year until 1967, as Brünnhilde, Isolde, Ortrud, Kundry and Senta. In the 1950s and 60s Varnay sang mostly in Munich, Düsseldorf, Berlin, Vienna and Krefeld. In 1959 she created Jocasta in Carl Orff's *Oedipus der Tyrann* at Stuttgart. In 1962 she began to take mezzo roles, including Richard Strauss's Herodias and Clytemnestra, Begbick (*Aufstieg und Fall der Stadt Mahagonny*) at the Metropolitan in 1979 and Claire (*Der Besuch der alten Dame*). Although her vocal technique was imperfect, her intense, passionate singing and committed acting made her a superb Wagnerian soprano, as can be heard in her live recordings of Senta, Ortrud and Brünnhilde from Bayreuth; she also recorded Elektra at the Metropolitan, and sang Clytemnestra in a film of the same opera.

B.W. Wessling: *Astrid Varnay* (Bremen, 1965) [with discography]

R. Jacobson: 'Varnay Revisited', *ON*, xxxix/8 (1974–5), 24–6

A. Varnay: *Fifty-five Years in Five Acts: My Life in Opera* (Boston: Northeastern, 2000)

Harold Rosenthal/R

Vasoli, Pietro

(*fl* Milan, 1812–14). Italian bass. He took part in three premières of Gioachino Rossini operas at La Scala: as Pacuvio in *La pietra del paragone* (1812), as Licinius in *Aureliano in Palmira* (1813) and as Prosdocimo in *Il turco in Italia* (1814). Apart from an unflattering reference by Stendhal, who heard him in 1812, nothing else is known about this 'ex-grenadier of Napoleon's army in Egypt'.

Elizabeth Forbes

Veasey, Josephine

(*b* Peckham, London, 10 July 1930). English mezzo-soprano. She studied with Audrey Langford and in 1949 joined the Covent Garden chorus, returning in 1955, after a spell with Opera for All, to make her solo début as Cherubino. Later roles included Magdalene, Rosina, Marina, Dorabella, Carmen, Waltraute, Fricka, Amneris, Preziosilla, Hector Berlioz's Dido and Cassandra, Eboli, the title role of *Iphigénie en Aulide*, Brangäne, Venus and the Emperor in the première of H.W. Henze's *We Come to the River* (1976). She first appeared at Glyndebourne in 1957 as Zulma (*L'italiana in Algeri*), then sang Cherubino, Clarice (Gioachino Rossini's *La pietra del paragone*), Octavian and Charlotte. She sang Fricka (*Das Rheingold*) at the Salzburg Easter Festival (later recording the role with Herbert von Karajan) and for her Metropolitan début in 1968. Having made her Paris Opéra début in 1969 as Dido, she returned for Kundry in 1973, then sang Eboli in San Francisco. In 1980 she sang Gertrude (*Hamlet*) at Buxton and in 1982 made her final appearance, at Covent Garden, as Herodias. On the concert platform Veasey was a noted soloist in Giuseppe Verdi's Requiem (which she recorded under Leonard Bernstein) and the works of Berlioz. She had a rich, vibrant voice of wide range and dramatic power, highly effective in roles such as Berlioz's Dido, which she recorded for Colin Davis.

A. Blyth: 'Josephine Veasey', *Opera*, xx (1969), 759–63

Alan Blyth

Vécla, Djemma.

See GRANDI, MARGHERITA.

Veličkova, Ljuba.

See WELITSCH, LJUBA.

Verdier, Marie

(*fl* 1675–80). French soprano. The little we know about her career comes from the Parfaict brothers in their manuscript *Histoire de l'Académie royale de musique*. Esteemed for her performances of confidantes and other secondary parts, she created the following roles in Jean-Baptiste Lully's operas: a priestess of Minerva in *Thésée* (1675); Flora in *Atys* (1676); and La Renommée and a syrinx in *Isis* (1677). Durey de Noinville (*Histoire du théâtre de l'Académie royale de musique*, Paris, 1757), in his discussion of her 1676 performance in *Atys*, claimed that Verdier sang in spectacles 'from the age of 15 to the age of about 60'. She left the stage in 1680; in 1698 she was receiving an opera pension of 500 livres. She was described by the Parfaicts as having been a 'rather good actress, tall and thin with chestnut-brown hair and with a delicate temperament'.

James R. Anthony

Vergnet, Edmond(-Alphonse)

(*b* Montpellier, 4 July 1850; *d* Nice, 15 Feb 1904). French tenor. He studied in Paris, making his début at the Opéra in 1874 as Raimbaut (*Robert le diable*). He also sang Faust, Léopold (*La Juive*),

Ruodi (*Guillaume Tell*), Laertes (*Hamlet*), Don Ottavio, Fernand (*La favorite*), Max (*Der Freischütz*), Alim (*Le roi de Lahore*), John of Leyden, Vasco da Gama, Samson and Lohengrin. At the Théâtre de la Monnaie, Brussels, he created John the Baptist in Jules Massenet's *Hérodiade* (1881) and Shahabarim in Ernest Reyer's *Salammbô* (1890). He sang at Covent Garden (1881–2) as Radames, Faust, Belmonte and Wilhelm Meister. In 1883 he created Admetus in Alfredo Catalani's *Dejanice* at La Scala. At Monte Carlo (1884–9) he sang Riccardo (*Ballo*), Fra Diavolo, Raoul, Gaetano Donizetti's Edgardo, the Duke, Gérald (*Lakmé*) and Florestan. He created Zarastra in Massenet's *Le mage* at the Opéra (1891) and Dominique in Alfred Bruneau's *L'attaque du moulin* at the Opéra-Comique (1894).

Elizabeth Forbes

Vermillion, Iris

(*b* Bielefeld, 1960). German mezzo-soprano. She studied with Mechthild Böhme (Detmold) and Judith Beckmann (Hamburg) and was a finalist at the Cardiff Singer of the World competition before making her stage début at Brunswick in 1986 as Zulma (*L'italiana in Algeri*). She joined the Deutsche Oper in Berlin in 1988, and remained there as an ensemble member until 1993. Her roles include Cherubino, Dorabella, Sextus, Judith (*Bluebeard's Castle*), Charlotte (*Werther*), Octavian, the Composer (*Ariadne auf Naxos*) and Clairon (*Capriccio*), which she sang to marked effect at the Salzburg Festival in 1990: she is, like Clairon herself, an accomplished actress. The following year she was Third Lady in the Salzburg Festival *Zauberflöte*, conducted by Georg Solti. More recently she has taken on heavier roles, including Fricka and Waltraute. She is a sought-after soloist in choral works, including Ludwig van Beethoven's Ninth Symphony and *Missa solemnis* (both of which she has recorded), and a discerning interpreter of lieder. In the latter field she has made a speciality on disc of Carl Loewe's songs. Vermillion is also a warm, expressive soloist in *Das Lied von der Erde*, which she has recorded with Giuseppe Sinopoli. Other admired recordings include lieder by Beethoven, Robert Schumann and Alexander Zemlinsky, Magdalene in *Die Meistersinger* (with Solti), Carl Graun's *Cesare e Cleopatra*, and several recordings in Decca's 'Entartete Musik' series.

Alan Blyth/Richard Wigmore

Verni, Andrea

(*b* Rome, *c*1765; *d* Parma, Aug 1822). Italian bass. He made his début about 1790. From 1800 to 1816

he sang at La Scala, where in 1814 he took the part of Don Magnifico in Stefano Pavesi's *Agatina* (a version of the Cinderella story). In 1817 he sang the same role in the first performance of Gioachino Rossini's *La Cenerentola* at the Teatro Valle, Rome. His cousin Pietro Verni created Gilberto in Gaetano Donizetti's *Enrico di Borgogna* (1818) at the Teatro S Luca, Venice, and several other members of his family were also singers.

Elizabeth Forbes

Verrett [Carter], Shirley

(*b* New Orleans, 31 May 1931). American mezzo-soprano, later soprano. She studied in Los Angeles with Anna Fitziu and Hall Johnson. After winning a television talent show in 1955, she attended the Juilliard School. While a student there she sang the solo in Manuel de Falla's *El amor brujo* under Leopold Stokowski and made her professional operatic début, as Lucretia in Yellow Springs, Ohio, in 1957. The following year she played (under the name Shirley Carter) Irina in Kurt Weill's *Lost in the Stars* at the New York City Opera. Concerts and recitals preceded her European début in Nicolas Nabokov's *Der Tod des Gregori Rasputin* (1959, Cologne). In 1962 her remarkable Carmen was first seen at the Spoleto Festival; it was later repeated at the Bol'shoy (1963), the New York City Opera (1964), her La Scala (1966) and Metropolitan Opera (1968) débuts, and Covent Garden (1973), where she had first appeared as Ulrica (*Un ballo in maschera*) in 1966. Her other notable roles include C.W. Gluck's Orpheus (also at Covent Garden) and Iphigenia (Paris, 1984), Gaetano Donizetti's Elizabeth I (*Maria Stuarda*, Edinburgh, 1968) and Léonore (*La favorite*, Dallas, 1971), Giuseppe Verdi's Amneris, Eboli, Azucena, Saint-Saëns's Delilah, and Selika in Giacomo Meyerbeer's *L'africaine* at San Francisco in 1972, and Lady Macbeth in 1986. At the first Metropolitan performance of *Les Troyens* in 1973 she played both Cassandra and – because of CHRISTA LUDWIG's illness – Dido. She later sang Dido at the opening of the Opéra Bastille, Paris in 1990. Other roles at the Metropolitan included Béla Bartók's Judith, Néocles (*Le siège de Corinthe*), and Adalgisa. Having furthered her studies at Tanglewood, she often appeared with the Boston Opera Company. In the late 1970s she began to assume soprano roles at the Metropolitan, most notably Tosca, Norma, Madame Lidoine (*Dialogues des Carmélites*), Aida and Leonore (*Fidelio*), while retaining most of her mezzo ones. In the late 1980s she gave masterclasses at the Accademia Chigiana in Siena. Her voice was richly burnished with an even range of more than two octaves, used with the utmost intelligence. On stage, especially as Delilah, Eboli or Azucena, she fused word, tone and gesture into an unforgettable characterization. She recorded several of her roles, most memorably Orpheus, Lady Macbeth, Ulrica and Eboli. Her large recital repertory included songs by Franz Schubert, Johannes Brahms, Gustav Mahler, Darius Milhaud, Falla and Ned Rorem.

S. Jenkins: 'Shirley Verrett', *Opera*, xxiv (1973), 585–9
J. Hines: 'Shirley Verrett', *Great Singers on Great Singing* (Garden City, NY, 1982), 338–47

Alan Blyth

Veselá, Marie

(*b* Polesony, 7 April 1935). Czech mezzo-soprano. She studied at the Prague Music Academy and made her major stage début, as Ulrica (*Un ballo in maschera*), at the Prague National Theatre in 1967. As a long-standing member of this company she appeared in a wide range of roles, specialising in Giuseppe Verdi (including Amneris and Eboli) and in Czech operas. She was also much in demand as a concert singer. After retiring she became a highly regarded voice teacher in Prague. Veselá's many recordings include Hata in *The Bartered Bride* and the title role in *Jenůfa*.

Richard Wigmore

Vestris [née Bartolozzi], Lucia Elizabeth [Eliza Lucy]

(*b* London, 3 Jan or 2 March 1797; *d* London, 8 Aug 1856). English contralto, actress and theatre manager of Italian descent. From 1813 to 1817 she was married to the French dancer Auguste-Armand Vestris (1788–1825), ballet-master at the King's Theatre, where she made her début (20 July 1815) in the title role of Peter Winter's *Il ratto di Proserpina*; this was highly successful although her acting and singing abilities were limited. Further appearances in 1816 met with less success, her faults becoming more apparent with familiarity. That winter she appeared in Paris at the Théâtre Italien and various other theatres, including the Théâtre Français, where she played Camille in *Les Horaces*. On returning to London, she made her début at Drury Lane Theatre on 19 February 1820. Her success was immediate, and she remained an extraordinary favourite in opera, musical farces and comedies until her retirement in 1854. At the King's Theatre she sang in the English premières of many Gioachino Rossini operas: *La gazza ladra* (as Pippo, 1821), *La donna del lago* (as Malcolm Graeme, 1823), *Ricciardo e Zoraide* (as Zomira, 1823), *Matilde*

di Shabran (as Edoardo, 1823), *Zelmira* (as Emma, 1824) and *Semiramide* (as Arsace, 1824). She sang there again in 1825, and in 1826 created the role of Fatima in *Oberon* at Covent Garden. She also appeared in Dublin (1824–47), but after 1830 she was more important as a theatre manager, leasing the Olympic (1831–8), Covent Garden (1839–42) and the Lyceum (1847–55); at Covent Garden she occasionally mounted fine opera productions in English. She was influential in developing the more naturalistic style of the 1860s and 70s. But Henry Chorley (1862), among others, never quite forgave her for not becoming the greatest English operatic contralto of her age:

> If she had possessed musical patience and energy, she might have queened it, because she possessed (half Italian by birth) one of the most luscious of low voices…great personal beauty, an almost faultless figure, which she adorned with consummate art, and no common stage address. But a less arduous career pleased her better; and so she could not – or perhaps would not – remain on the Italian stage.

H.F. Chorley: Obituary, *The Athenaeum* (17 Aug 1856)
H.F. Chorley: Thirty Years' Musical Recollections (London, 1862, abridged 2/1926 by E. Newman), 155
C.E. Pearce: *Madame Vestris and her Times* (London, c1923)
W.W. Appleton: *Madame Vestris and the London Stage* (New York and London, 1974)

Vezzani, Cesare

(*b* Bastia, Corsica, 8 Aug 1886; *d* Marseilles, 11 Nov 1951). Corsican tenor. Brought up in Toulon, he studied in Paris and made his début at the Opéra-Comique in the title role of A.-E. M. Grétry's *Richard Coeur-de-lion* (1911); his voice impressed more favourably than his artistry. He appeared with the company in *Dinorah*, Camille Erlanger's *La sorcière*, *Manon* and *Carmen*. A disagreement with the management arose in 1914, after which his career was largely confined to the provinces, though he also sang in Brussels, Switzerland and Algiers and continued as principal tenor at Toulon until 1948. He seems to have been one of those whose gifts exceeded his attainments, for recordings (which include a complete *Faust*) show an exceptional voice, heroic and ringing in quality, admirably suited to such operas as Ernest Reyer's *Sigurd* and Giacomo Meyerbeer's *L'Africaine* and *Le prophète*. In the early 1920s PIA TASSINARI and MAFALDA FAVERO studied with Vezzani in Bologna.

J. B. Steane

Viardot [née García], (Michelle Ferdinande) Pauline

(*b* Paris, 18 July 1821; *d* Paris, 18 May 1910). French singer and composer of Spanish origin. She came from a family of singers: her father was the elder MANUEL GARCÍA, her mother María Joaquina Sitches, her brother the younger Manuel Garcia and her sister MARIA MALIBRAN. After the death of her father in 1832, her mother took over her training. Viardot not only inspired composers such as Fryderyk Chopin, Hector Berlioz, Giacomo Meyerbeer, Charles Gounod, Camille Saint-Saëns, Franz Liszt, Richard Wagner and Robert Schumann with her dramatic gifts but also collaborated on the composition of roles created especially for her. She was active as a teacher, continuing the García method. She studied the piano with Meysenberg and Liszt and composition with Antoine Reicha, but concentrated on sing-

ing after Malibran's death in 1836. A year later, when she was 16, she made her singing début in Brussels at a concert given by her brother-in-law, the Belgian violinist Charles-Auguste de Bériot; her range of three octaves and her musical versatility caused a sensation. During her first concert tour, which took her and her brother to Germany in 1838, she performed her own songs, accompanying herself on the piano. She met Clara Wieck and Robert Schumann in Leipzig. (Schumann published one of her songs in his *Neue Zeitschrift für Musik*, and later dedicated his cycle of Heinrich Heine songs op.24 to her.)

Pauline made her operatic début, like her sister, as Desdemona in Gioachino Rossini's *Otello*, in London on 9 May 1839, and appeared in the same role in Paris on 8 October 1839. Her first engagement in Paris was at the Théâtre Italien, where she demonstrated her talent in a variety of parts in operas by Rossini. Alfred de Musset (who said, 'She sings

Pauline Viardot [left] as Valentine and Marietta Alboni [right] as Urbain, in 'Les Huguenots' (Meyerbeer), Royal Opera House Covent Garden, 1848. Lithograph by John Brandard.

as naturally as she breathes'), George Sand, who depicted her as the heroine of her novel *Consuelo* (1842), and Hector Berlioz were soon among her most ardent admirers. The director of the Théâtre Italien was the writer Louis Viardot, whom she married in 1840. 21 years older than his wife, he gave up his post and accompanied her on concert tours throughout Europe in the years that followed. (Their first daughter, Louise, born in 1841, was brought up by Viardot's mother.) The major cities in which Viardot appeared were London, Berlin, Dresden, Vienna and St Petersburg. From 1843 to 1846 she sang with the opera at St Petersburg, where she met the writer Ivan Turgenev. Turgenev fell in love with her, and lived in close proximity to the Viardot family for the rest of his life. She first appeared in St Petersburg as Norma, one of her most famous roles. While there, she sang works by M.I. Glinka and A.S. Dargomïzhsky in Russian as well as the Italian repertory. She not only spoke fluent Spanish, French, Italian, English, German and Russian, but also composed in different national styles. This stylistic versatility enabled her to assist other composers, influencing works such as Meyerbeer's *Le prophète*, Berlioz's *Les Troyens* and *Béatrice et Bénédict*, Gounod's *Sapho* and Jules Massenet's *Marie-Magdeleine*.

At this time Viardot seldom appeared in Paris, where she might experience hostility as the wife of Louis Viardot, a republican and declared opponent of Louis Napoléon. However, the première in 1849 of Meyerbeer's *Le prophète*, in which she created the part of Fidès, was a triumph. Meyerbeer wrote of the singer, then not quite 28 years old: 'I owe a great part of the opera's success to Viardot, who as singer and actress rose to tragic heights such as I have never seen in the theatre before'. Viardot sang Fidès more than 200 times, on all the great European stages. She was famous for this part and especially for C.W. Gluck's Orpheus, to which she brought great dramatic conviction. The part, originally for castrato, was revised for her by Berlioz in a version that in 1859 brought the forgotten opera back to the stage. Viardot's other notable roles were Ludwig van Beethoven's Leonore, Gluck's Alceste and Giuseppe Verdi's Lady Macbeth (although she was unable to bring success to *Macbeth* itself). In 1863, at the age of 42, she retired from the stage and left France for political reasons. With her husband, her three youngest children and Ivan Turgenev she settled in Baden-Baden, where she taught singers from all over the world. She built an art gallery in her garden and a small opera house, where she, her pupils and her children gave concerts and performed their own dramatic works. The librettos were by Turgenev. One of Viardot's operettas, *Le dernier sorcier* (1869), was also performed in an orchestral ver-

sion in Weimar in 1869 and in Riga and Karlsruhe in 1870. Henry Chorley wrote in the *Athenaeum* (12 October 1867): 'It is not possible to conceive anything of its kind more perfect in quaint fantasy, real charm and complete execution'. She also performed piano duets with Clara Schumann and gave private organ concerts. She sang in the première of Johannes Brahms's Alto Rhapsody (Jena, 3 March 1870) during her time in Baden-Baden. The defeat of Napoléon III in the Franco-Prussian war enabled Viardot to return to Paris (she went first to London, where there was a private performance of *Le dernier sorcier* on 11 February 1871). She continued to live there until her death, teaching and composing, among other works, 'salon operettas' such as *Le conte de fées* (1869) and *Cendrillon* (1904), and presiding over a highly regarded musical salon in the rue de Douai until the death of both her husband and Turgenev in 1883, when she moved to the boulevard St Germain.

Her pupils included DÉSIRÉE ARTÔT, AGLAJA ORGENI, MARIANNE BRANDT and Antoinette Sterling. She published a manual on singing, based on the García method, *Une heure d'étude: exercices pour voix de femmes* (Paris, c1880/R); a collection of selected songs and arias, *Ecole classique de chant* (Paris, 1861), with comments on phrasing, accentuation and interpretation; and a critical edition of 50 of Schubert's lieder. These publications and her own compositions and transcriptions are an important source for the understanding of performing practice in the 19th century.

A. FitzLyon: *The Price of Genius: a Life of Pauline Viardot* (London, 1964)

P. Waddington: 'Henry Chorley, Pauline Viardot and Turgenev: a Musical and Literary Friendship', *MQ*, lxvii (1981), 165–92

Beatrix Borchard

Vickers, Jon(athan Stewart)

(*b* Prince Albert, SK, 29 Oct 1926). Canadian tenor. He studied at the Royal Conservatory of Music, Toronto. After appearances in Canada as the Duke, Don José and the Male Chorus in *The Rape of Lucretia* he joined the Covent Garden Opera in 1957, making his début as Gustavus III, but he made his most striking impression as Don José, Aeneas (*Les Troyens*) and Don Carlos in Luchino Visconti's famous staging of Giuseppe Verdi's opera in 1958. The same year he made his Bayreuth début as Siegmund, sang Samson in G.F. Handel's oratorio in Covent Garden, and Jason to CALLAS's Medea in Dallas.

In 1959 Vickers appeared at the Vienna Staatsoper, made his San Francisco début as Radames (which he had added to his repertory the previous year), and sang Parsifal at Covent Garden. He joined the Metropolitan Opera in 1960, making his début as Canio, and sang there for more than 25 years; his roles included Florestan, Saint-Saëns's Samson, Hermann (*Queen of Spades*), Tristan (which he sang in Buenos Aires in 1971), Otello, Alvaro, Laca (*Jenůfa*) and Grimes. At the Salzburg Festival he appeared under Herbert von Karajan as Tristan, Siegmund, Otello and Don José (the last two roles recorded on film). He sang Herod and Pollione at Orange (1974), took the title role in *Benvenuto Cellini* at Boston (1975) and sang Claudio Monteverdi's Nero in Paris (1978). He repeated Handel's Samson at Covent Garden and the Metropolitan for the composer's tercentenary (1985–6). His heroic voice and arresting declamation are preserved on recordings of his Aeneas, Tristan, Siegmund, Radames, Otello, Florestan, Samson, Don José and Peter Grimes; his dramatic presence and committed acting are best seen in the video recording of *Peter Grimes* (Covent Garden, under Colin Davis).

N. Goodwin: 'Jon Vickers', *Opera*, xiii (1962), 233–9

D. Cairns: *Responses* (London, 1973)

J. Ardoin: 'Jon Vickers', *The Tenors*, ed. H.H. Breslin (New York, 1974), 43–82

M. Loppert: 'Jon Vickers on Peter Grimes', *Opera*, xxxv (1984), 835–43

J. Williams: *Jon Vickers: a Hero's Life* (Boston, 1999)

Harold Rosenthal/Alan Blyth

Vieuille, Félix

(*b* Saugeon, 15 Oct 1872; *d* Saugeon, 28 Feb 1953). French bass. After study at the Paris Conservatoire he made his début at Aix-les-Bains in 1897 as Leporello. He became the leading bass with the Opéra-Comique in 1898, his first major role being Arkel in the première of *Pelléas et Mélisande* (1902). He also created the Junk-seller in Gustave Charpentier's *Louise* (1900), sang in the première of Henri Rabaud's *La fille de Roland* (1904) created the Sultan in *Mârouf* (1914), and Bluebeard in *Ariane et Barbe-Bleue* by Paul Dukas (1907). He also sang in the premières of Ernest Bloch's *Macbeth* (1910) and Darius Milhaud's *Le pauvre matelot* (1927). He appeared at the Manhattan Opera House in the 1908–9 season and sang in the Paris premières of Gabriel Fauré's *Pénélope* and Nikolay Rimsky-Korsakov's *Snow Maiden*.

David Cummings

Villabella, Miguel

(*b* Bilbao, 20 Dec 1892; *d* Paris, 28 June 1954). Spanish tenor. His voice was discovered by the French bass-baritone Lucien Fugère, who encouraged him to study in Paris. After making his concert début in 1917 in San Sebastián and his operatic début in 1918 as Cavaradossi in Poitiers, he was engaged by the Opéra-Comique in Paris, in 1920, beginning with minor roles, then graduating to Jules Massenet's Des Grieux, Gérald (*Lakmé*), Don José, Hoffmann, Nadir, Wilhelm Meister (*Mignon*), George Brown (Adrien Boieldieu's *La dame blanche*) and Alfredo (*La traviata*) among others. His successful début at the Paris Opéra, as Pinkerton, came in 1928, and in a career there that lasted until 1935 his roles included the Duke of Mantua, Faust, Roméo, Gioachino Rossini's Count Almaviva and Don Ottavio. In 1928 he also sang in *La dame blanche*, *Manon* and *Lakmé* in Algiers. Apart from further appearances in Brussels and Monte Carlo, Villabella's career was confined to France, mainly because he was so much in demand there on account of the shining clarity and power of his voice. His numerous recordings, testimony to his popularity, include examples of many of his successful roles. His readings compensate in sheer fervour for what they lack in subtlety. He retired in 1940 and taught in Paris.

Alan Blyth

Villarroel, Verónica

(*b* Santiago, 2 Oct 1965). Chilean soprano. After studying at the Juilliard School, New York, with ELLEN FAULL and privately with RENATA SCOTTO, her mentor, she made her stage début as Musetta (to Scotto's Mimì) at the Teatro Municipale, Santiago, in 1986. In 1988 she was winner of the Pavarotti Prize and in 1989 of the Metropolitan Auditions. Villarroel made her European début, as Fiordiligi, in Barcelona in 1990 and her Metropolitan début, as Mimì, in 1991; she has since appeared successfully at the Metropolitan as Violetta, which she has also performed at Covent Garden and elsewhere in the USA and Europe, her sympathetic personality and warm, expressive voice suiting her well for the role. She has performed zarzuelas in various centres with DOMINGO, taking the role of Cecilia alongside him in Carlos Gomes's *Il Guarany* at Bonn in 1994 and subsequently recording the work. Villarroel's repertory also includes Luisa Miller, Charles Gounod's Marguerite and Butterfly.

Alan Blyth

Villazón, Rolando

(*b* Mexico City, 22 Feb 1972). Mexican tenor. At the age of eleven he joined the Espacios Academy for the Performing Arts, where he studied music, acting, contemporary dance and ballet. In 1990 he began to study singing with the baritone Arturo Nieto and in 1992 entered the Conservatorio Nacional de Música, Mexico City, to continue his vocal studies with Enrique Jaso. After winning national competitions in Mexico City and Guanajuato, Villazón became a pupil of Gabriel Mijares. For a time he had considered going into the priesthood. But in 1998, he joined the San Francisco Opera's Merola Opera Program, where he took part in masterclasses with JOAN SUTHERLAND and sang his first major role, Alfredo in *La traviata*. He subsequently became a member of the Pittsburgh Opera's Young Artists Program.

Villazón's European début, as Des Grieux (*Manon*) in Genoa in 1999, launched his international career. He has been equally acclaimed in Italian roles such as Alfredo, Nemorino, the Duke in *Rigoletto* and Don Carlos (which he sang for his Nederlandse Opera début in 2004) and Rodolfo (the role of his 2003 Glyndebourne début), and in nineteenth-century French roles, including Roméo, Faust (which he first sang at the Opéra Bastille in 2003) and Don José. His triumphant débuts at Covent Garden (as a charismatic, athletic Hoffmann) and the Metropolitan Opera (as Alfredo), both in 2004, prompted some critics to hail him as 'the next Domingo'; and though less powerful, his voice has something of the Spaniard's baritonal depth and fine balance of honey and metal, allied to free, ringing top notes. Villazón is also a discerning musician, with a care for refined dynamic shading and shapely legato phrasing, as can be heard on his widely praised recordings of French and Italian arias.

Richard Wigmore

Villeneuve, Louise [Luisa, Luigia]

(*fl*1786–99). Soprano, active in Italy. According to Karl von Zinzendorf's diary (11 July 1789), she was a pupil of J.-G. Noverre's, in which case she was probably the Mlle Villeneuve who was a member of Noverre's ballet company in Vienna from 1771 to 1774. Her first known appearance as a singer was in 1786 in Milan. In 1788 she appeared in Venice and Milan, singing, among other roles, Amore in Vicente Martín y Soler's *L'arbore di Diana*. She sang the same role for her début in Vienna on 27 June 1789, successfully replacing LUISA LASCHI, the acclaimed original Amore, on account of 'her charming appearance, her sensitive and expressive acting and her artful, beautiful singing' (*Wiener Zeitung*, lii, 1789, p.1673). Mozart supplied arias for her in Domenico Cimarosa's *I due baroni* (K578) and Martín's *Il burbero di buon cuore* (K582–3), and wrote for her Dorabella in *Così fan tutte* (26 January 1790), alluding in her Act 2 aria to her role as Amore.

There is no evidence that, as is often stated, she was the sister of ADRIANA FERRARESE, who sang Fiordiligi. After leaving Vienna in spring 1791, she resumed her peripatetic singing career in Italy, performing at least until 1799, when she appeared in Venice.

D. Link: 'Così fan tutte: Dorabella and Amore', *MJb 1991*, 888–94
D. Link: *The National Court Theatre in Mozart's Vienna: Sources and Documents 1783–1792* (Oxford, 1998)

Dorothea Link

Vinay, Ramón

(*b* Chillán, 31 Aug 1912; *d* Puebla, Mexico, 4 Jan 1996). Chilean baritone, later tenor. He studied with José Pierson in Mexico City, where he made his début as Alphonse (*La favorite*) in 1931. For several years he sang baritone roles, including Rigoletto, Luna and Scarpia, and then, after further study with RENÉ MAISON, he made his tenor début in Mexico City in 1943 as Don José, following it in 1944 with Otello. In 1945 Vinay made his New York début at the City Center as Don José and then sang at the Metropolitan (1946–61). He inaugurated the 1947–8 season at La Scala as Otello, a part he also sang at Salzburg (under Wilhelm Furtwängler, 1951) and Covent Garden (in 1950 with La Scala, and, even more memorably, under Rafael Kubelík in 1955). He made his début in Santiago de Chile in 1948, returning in 1967 to sing *Falstaff*, *Carmen* and *La Bohème*. From 1952 to 1957 he sang at Bayreuth, as Tristan, Parsifal, Tannhäuser and Siegmund. In 1962 he resumed baritone roles, singing Telramund at Bayreuth, and also Iago, Falstaff, Scarpia, Dr Bartolo and Dr Schön (*Lulu*). From 1969 to 1971 Vinay was artistic director of the Santiago opera.

In his prime Vinay sang with ease and expressive, dark-grained tone. His artistry, intelligence and musicianship were always in evidence, and his acting was distinguished by pathos and nobility. His Otello was recorded live under Arturo Toscanini (1947) and Furtwängler (1951), and is a remarkable portrayal of a heroic general undone by jealous vulnerability. Equally eloquent are his recordings from Bayreuth, notably his Siegmund and Parsifal under Clemens Krauss and his Tristan under Herbert von Karajan.

H. Rosenthal: 'Ramón Vinay', *Opera*, ix (1958), 335–9

Harold Rosenthal/R

Vincent [van Ijzer-Vincent], Jo(hanna Maria)

(*b* Amsterdam, 6 March 1898; *d* Monte Carlo, 28 Nov 1989). Dutch soprano. She was the daughter of

Jacobus Vincent, carillonneur of the Amsterdam Royal Palace. She studied with Catherina van Rennes and Cornélie van Zanten, and made her début in 1921. She became the leading concert soprano of the Netherlands; her only operatic appearance was in 1939 at Scheveningen as Countess Almaviva. She appeared regularly in concert with Wilhelm Mengelberg in Ludwig van Beethoven, J.S. Bach and Gustav Mahler. Outside the Netherlands she was particularly popular in England during the 1930s. She sang in the first performance of Benjamin Britten's *Spring Symphony* (Amsterdam, 1949), which was recorded. Her other recordings, which include Schubert lieder, oratorio and Mahler's Second Symphony (under Otto Klemperer), show the pure, ethereal quality of her voice.

Leo Riemens

Vishnevskaya, Galina (Pavlovna)

(*b* Leningrad [now St Petersburg], 25 Oct 1926). Russian soprano. She studied privately with Vera Garina in Leningrad, and made her début in operetta in 1944. In 1952 she joined the Bol'shoy Theatre. A versatile and fascinating artist, she was one of the outstanding Russian singers. Her expressive, rich-hued voice of highly individual timbre, her polished technique and strong dramatic talent allowed her to appear in a wide variety of roles. Her notable array of stage portraits included Tat'yana and Lisa, Kupava (*The Snow Maiden*) and Marfa, Aida, Violetta, Tosca, Leonore and the solo part in Francis Poulenc's *La voix humaine*. She gave the first Bol'shoy performances of Katherine in Vissarion Yakovlevich Shebalin's *Ukroshcheniye stroptivoy* ('The Taming of the Shrew', 1957), Natasha in *War and Peace* (1959), Marina in Vano Il'ich Muradeli's *Oktyabr'* ('October', 1964) and Sof'ya in Sergey Prokofiev's *Semyon Kotko* (1970). She first sang at the Metropolitan, as Aida and Butterfly, in 1961, at Covent Garden (Aida) in 1962 and at La Scala (Liù) in 1964. London critics praised her artistry, her warm, liquid tone and excellent legato, and her passionate and intense style, though some found her acting a little exaggerated. She appeared in the film of Dmitry Shostakovich's *Katerina Izmaylova* (1966).

Vishnevskaya often performed songs by Modest Musorgsky, P.I. Tchaikovsky and Shostakovich, usually with the cellist Mstislav Rostropovich, whom she married in 1955, accompanying her on the piano. Shostakovich dedicated his Seven Romances op.127 to her, and she performed in the première of his 14th Symphony, conducted by Rudol'f Barshay in 1969. Benjamin Britten intended the soprano part of his *War Requiem* for her. Although she was prevented by the Soviet authorities from singing in the première, she took part in the subsequent recording conducted by the composer. Britten also composed for her and Rostropovich his Pushkin cycle, *The Poet's Echo*, which they first performed at the Soviet Conservatory, Moscow, in 1965. Together with other Soviet artists, Vishnevskaya and Rostropovich appeared at the Aldeburgh Festival. The French composer Marcel Landowski wrote his *Messe de l'Aurore* and *Un enfant appelle* for Rostropovitch and Vishnevskaya, to whom he also dedicated his opera, *Galina*. Vishnevskaya has also turned to directing (e.g. Nikolay Rimsky-Korsakov's *The Tsar's Bride*, Washington, DC, 1987). She and Rostropovich left the USSR for political reasons in 1974 and eventually settled in the USA. Her memoir is *Galina: a Russian Story* (London, 1984; Russ. orig., Moscow, 1991).

I.M. Yampol'sky/R

Visse, Dominique

(*b* Lisieux, 30 Aug 1955). French countertenor. At the age of 13 he became a chorister at the maîtrise of Notre Dame in Paris. Later he studied the organ and flute at the Versailles Conservatoire. As an instrumentalist he specialized in medieval and Renaissance music, occasionally singing as a countertenor. Between 1976 and 1978 he was a pupil of ALFRED DELLER and RENÉ JACOBS, became acquainted with NIGEL ROGERS, and decided to specialize in singing. In 1978 he founded the Ensemble Clément Janequin and joined the newly formed group Les Arts Florissants under William Christie. In 1980 Visse began to study with Jean Laurens. He made his opera début at Tourcoing in 1982 in *L'incoronazione di Poppea*. He sang Flora in Antonio Vivaldi's *L'incoronazione di Dario* at Grasse (1984); the title role of M.-A. Charpentier's *Actéon* at Edinburgh (1985); Annius in C.W. Gluck's *La clemenza di Tito* at Tourcoing (1987) and at Lausanne (1991). At the Opéra he sang Cupid in *Orphée aux enfers* and Nirenus in *Giulio Cesare* (1987), and at Innsbruck he sang Delfa in Francesco Cavalli's *Giasone* (1988). He created Geronimo in Claude Prey's *Le rouge et le noir* at Aix-en-Provence in 1989, then sang Octavia's Nurse (*L'incoronazione di Poppea*) at Montpellier. His voice has a distinctive clarity which, with a forceful projection and a lively dramatic sense, lends colour and presence to his stage performances. Besides *Poppea* he has recorded Cavalli's *Xerse* and *Giasone*; Charpentier's *Actéon*, *Les arts florissants*, *David et Jonathas* and *Le malade imaginaire*; André Campra's *Tancrède*; Jean-Philippe Rameau's *Anacréon* and Johann Hasse's *Cleofide*. He married the soprano AGNÈS MELLON.

Nicholas Anderson

Vix [Brouwer], Geneviève

(*b* Le Havre, 31 Dec 1879; *d* Paris, 25 Aug 1939). French soprano. After study at the Paris Conservatoire she made her début at the Opéra-Comique in 1906. Her first roles included Louise, Chrysis in Camille Erlanger's *Aphrodite* and the title role in the première of Paul-Lucien Hillemacher's *Circe* (1907). In 1911 she sang Concepcion in the world première of *L'heure espagnole*, and in the same year took the part of Antonia in the first complete performances of *Les contes d'Hoffmann*. 1915 brought her a notable success in Buenos Aires where she appeared as Jean in *Le jongleur de Notre Dame*, which she adapted, as MARY GARDEN had done, for the soprano. She later performed the part in Chicago, and with the Chicago Company on tour at the Lexington Theatre, New York, sang a much-admired Manon. In Madrid in 1922, as Thaïs and Richard Strauss's Salome, an 'adorable nonchalance' combined with her good looks and capricious sense of rhythm to fascinate her audiences. By 1925 her voice was in poor condition, and after some performances of her old roles, such as Louise (Rome) and Concepcion (Monte Carlo), she retired from opera for a brief spell of concert work and then to teach. Deprived of her physical presence, her recordings generally fail to charm the ear though they show something of her power of characterization.

J. B. Steane

Vogl, Heinrich

(*b* Au, Munich, 15 Jan 1845; *d* Munich, 21 April 1900). German tenor and composer. He studied with Franz Lachner and made his début in 1865 as Max in *Der Freischütz* at the Hofoper, Munich, where he was engaged for 35 years. Having already sung Lohengrin (1867) and Tristan (1869), he created the roles of Loge in *Das Rheingold* (22 September 1869) and Siegmund in *Die Walküre* (26 June 1870), and at Bayreuth he sang Loge in the first complete *Ring* cycle (1876). He sang Siegfried in the first Munich performances of *Siegfried* and *Götterdämmerung* (1878), Loge and Siegmund in the first Berlin *Ring* cycle, as well as both Siegfrieds in the second cycle (1881, Viktoriatheater), and Loge and Siegfried in the first London *Ring* cycle (1882, Her Majesty's Theatre) and accompanied the early part of Angelo Neumann's European Wagner tour (1882). He returned to Bayreuth as Tristan and Parsifal (1886), and made his New York début at the Metropolitan Opera as Lohengrin (1890), also singing Tannhäuser, Tristan, Loge, Siegmund and both Siegfrieds during the season. In Munich he sang in Alexander Ritter's *Faule Hans* (1885), *Otello* (1888),

Benvenuto Cellini (1889), Alberto Franchetti's *Asrael* (1892), *Pagliacci* (1893), *Dalibor* (1894), Hector Berlioz's *La prise de Troie* and Peter Cornelius's *Der Cid* (1895). He sang Baldur at the première of his own opera *Der Fremdling* (7 May 1899) and made his last appearance as Canio (17 April 1900), four days before his death. Besides *Der Fremdling*, he published several songs.

Vogl's voice was powerful and his stamina legendary (he sang Loge, Siegmund and both Siegfrieds in some *Ring* cycles on four consecutive days without apparent strain). During his early years at Munich he was said to lack dramatic ability and understanding (Ludwig Nohl); Richard Wagner, who refused to accept him as Walther for the first performance of *Die Meistersinger* in 1868, even referred to him as 'thoroughly incompetent' (letter to King Ludwig, 30 March 1868), and Walther remained the only major Wagnerian tenor role that he never sang. Later in his career he was greatly admired as Siegmund, Siegfried and Tristan, and LILLI LEHMANN wrote that his Loge 'has never since been equalled: he was born for the part'.

In 1868 Vogl married the soprano Therese Thoma, who as THERESE VOGL frequently sang with him.

Elizabeth Forbes

Vogl, Johann Michael

(*b* Ennsdorf, nr Steyr, Upper Austria, 10 Aug 1768; *d* Vienna, 19 Nov 1840). Austrian baritone. While studying languages and philosophy at the Gymnasium in Kremsmünster he appeared in several Singspiele by F.X. Süssmayr, a fellow pupil. The two became close friends and went together to Vienna in 1786. Vogl studied law at the university and began to practise in the city. Persuaded by Süssmayr to join the German opera company he had founded, Vogl made his début at the Vienna Hofoper on 1 May 1795 in P. Wranitzky's *Die gute Mutter*. The combination of his pleasing baritone voice and dramatic and declamatory gifts made him popular with audiences. He excelled as Orestes (*Iphigénie en Tauride*), Count Almaviva and Mikéli (*Les deux journées*), and he created the part of Pizarro in the 1814 revision of *Fidelio*. He also sang the lead in the première of *Die Zwillingsbrüder* in 1820, having used his influence in the Hofoper to obtain for Franz Schubert the commission for the work. He retired from the theatre in 1822. Vogl met Schubert in 1817 and he is remembered today for his friendship and professional relationship with the composer, who found in the singer his ideal interpreter.

Maurice J. E. Brown/R

Vogl [née Thoma], Therese

(*b* Tutzing, 12 Nov 1845; *d* Munich, 29 Sept 1921). German soprano. She studied in Munich, making her début (as Therese Thoma) in 1865 at Karlsruhe as Casilda in Daniel Auber's *La part du diable*. She was engaged at the Munich Hofoper in 1866, and the following year sang Ortrud in *Lohengrin*. In 1868 she married HEINRICH VOGL and the following year she sang Isolde to her husband's Tristan. She created the role of Wellgunde in the *Das Rheingold* (1869), and she was Sieglinde in the first *Die Walküre* in 1870. In 1872 she appeared in Luigi Cherubini's *Médée*. She was engaged to sing Sieglinde in the first complete *Ring* cycle at Bayreuth, but she became pregnant and had to withdraw. She later sang Brünnhilde in the first complete Munich (1878) and London (1882) *Ring* cycles, but she never appeared at Bayreuth. When casting the first performances of *Parsifal*, Richard Wagner considered that the part of Kundry 'needs…a vocal energy which I did not think I could demand of her' (letter to Hermann Levi, 20 May 1882), and consequently neither she nor her husband sang there that year. Though declining vocally, she sang at Munich for another decade and made her farewell performance as Isolde in 1892.

Elizabeth Forbes

Voigt, Deborah

(*b* Chicago, 4 Aug 1960). American soprano. She studied at California State University and then participated in the Merola Programme of the San Francisco Opera, where she eventually began her career in small roles, her operatic début being as the Voice from Heaven in *Don Carlos* (1986). In 1988 she won the Pavarotti Voice Competition, and in 1990 both the Rosa Ponselle Gold Medal and the Verdi Competition in Busseto. Voigt made her London début as Elvira in *Ernani* with the Chelsea Opera Group in 1990. In 1992 she attracted attention in the *Stabat mater* at a Gioachino Rossini 200th anniversary concert in Avery Fisher Hall, New York, and as Chrysothemis at the Metropolitan. Voigt first sang Ariadne in Boston in 1991, and this was the role of her first appearances in Munich and Vienna. Amelia (*Un ballo in maschera*) marked her début at Chicago (1993) and at Covent Garden (1995). Among her other Verdi parts are Aida (which she sang in Verona in 1994 and at the Metropolitan in 1999–2000) and Lady Macbeth, which she first performed in Bologna in 1995. She sang Chrysothemis for her South American début at the Teatro Colón (1995). Other Strauss roles in which she has made her mark include the Empress

in *Die Frau ohne Schatten* (which she sang to great acclaim at the Deutsche Oper, Berlin, in 1998 and at the Vienna Staatsoper the following year) and Helen of Troy (*Die ägyptische Helena*), of which she gave a concert performance with Covent Garden in 1998; she has recorded both of these roles. Her Wagner roles include Elisabeth (which she first sang at San Francisco in 1994), Sieglinde (1996, the Metropolitan), Senta (1996, Vienna) and Elsa (1998, the Metropolitan). She sang her first Salome at the Tanglewood Festival in 2001. Voigt has a voice of generous proportions, easily produced, but her style and acting can lack specificity. Of her recordings, her Rezia (*Oberon*), Cassandra (in Charles Dutoit's set of *Les Troyens*), Chrysothemis, Helen of Troy and a disc of Wagner love duets with DOMINGO best display the range and power of her voice. She has also recorded several non-operatic works, notably Alexander Zemlinsky's *Lyrische Symphonie*, Alban Berg's *Der Wein* (both with Giuseppe Sinopoli) and Arnold Schoenberg's *Gurrelieder*.

Alan Blyth

Völker, Franz

(*b* Neu-Isenburg, 31 March 1899; *d* Darmstadt, 5 Dec 1965). German tenor. Discovered by Clemens Krauss, he studied singing at Frankfurt and in 1926 was engaged at the opera there, making his début as Florestan. In 1931 he moved to Vienna, in 1935 to Berlin, and in 1945 to Munich, where he remained until 1952. He also sang at the festivals at Salzburg (from 1931) and Bayreuth (from 1933). He sang Florestan and Siegmund at Covent Garden in 1934, and returned for Siegmund in 1937. Admired also as Lohengrin, Don Carlos and Radames, he had in his prime the flexibility for lighter, more lyrical roles, such as Ferrando; he appeared with distinction as Max (*Der Freischutz*) and the Emperor (*Die Frau ohne Schatten*) and, late in his career, Otello and Canio.

Peter Branscombe

Von Stade, Frederica

(*b* Somerville, NJ, 1 June 1945). American mezzo-soprano. She studied at the Mannes School, New York, making her début at the Metropolitan in 1970 as the Third Boy in *Die Zauberflöte*; later roles there included Suzuki, Lola (*Cavalleria rusticana*), Stéphano (*Roméo et Juliette*) and Nicklausse. At Santa Fe she sang Cherubino, Zerlina and Mélisande, and created Maria in Heitor Villa-Lobos's *Yerma* (1971). A spirited Cherubino, notably at the Paris Opéra and Glyndebourne (both 1973) and at Salzburg

Frederica von Stade as Cherubino in 'Le nozze di Figaro' (Mozart), Bavarian State Opera

(1974–5), she was also admired as Octavian, notably at the Holland Festival in 1976. In 1983–4 she sang a series of comic roles She made her Covent Garden début in 1975 as Rosina and returned in 1985 as Ellen (*La donna del lago*), a role she sang at Houston in 1981. In 1983–4 she appeared in a French comic series at Carnegie Hall under the conductor, Michael Epstein. Her repertory included W.A. Mozart's Sextus, Idamantes, Dorabella, Cenerentola (of which she made an outstanding video recording from La Scala in 1981), Adalgisa, Charlotte, Claudio Monteverdi's Penelope, Hänsel, the Composer (*Ariadne*), and Mignon. In 1974 she created Nina in Thomas Pasatieri's *The Seagull* at Houston, and in 1988 created Tina in Dominick Argento's *The Aspern Papers* at Dallas. In 2000 she was an admired Hanna (*Die lustige Witwe*) at the Metropolitan. Her musicianship and personal charm are evident in her many recordings, not only of her principal roles (notably Cherubino, Charlotte, Hänsel and Mélisande) but also in *mélodies*, of which she is a gifted interpreter. *Dark Summer* (1989) by the American composer, Christine Berl, was written for von Stade; Dominick Argento also composed

for her the song cycles *Casa Guidi* (1983) and *A Few Words about Chekhov* (1986).

G. Moshvon: 'Frederica Von Stade', *Opera*, xxxi (1980), 31–4

Harold Rosenthal/Alan Blyth/R

Vyvyan, Jennifer (Brigit)

(*b* Broadstairs, 13 March 1925; *d* London, 5 April 1974). English soprano. She studied at the RAM, and with ROY HENDERSON and Fernando Carpi. Her first professional stage engagement was as Jenny Diver in the première of Benjamin Britten's version of *The Beggar's Opera* (1948), and this was followed by Nancy in *Albert Herring* and the Female Chorus in *The Rape of Lucretia*, all with the English Opera Group. In 1951 she created the Matron in Brian Easdale's *The Sleeping Children* at Cheltenham. She came fully into her own in 1952 with a secure and brilliant Konstanze in *Die Entführung aus dem Serail* at Sadler's Wells; the same season she sang Donna Anna in that house. In 1953 she created the role of Penelope Rich in Britten's *Gloriana* at Covent Garden, which she sang many times thereafter; that year, with Glyndebourne at the Edinburgh Festival, she sang Electra in *Idomeneo*. She created the Governess in Britten's *The Turn of the Screw* (1954, Venice), Titania in his *A Midsummer Night's Dream* (1960, Aldeburgh), the Countess de Serindan in Malcolm Williamson's *The Violins of Saint-Jacques* (1966, Sadler's Wells), various roles in his *Lucky-Peter's Journey* (1969, Sadler's Wells) and Mrs Julian in Britten's *Owen Wingrave* (1971, BBC television). Two other Britten roles, Miss Wordsworth and Lady Billows in *Albert Herring*, gave full scope to her comic gifts.

Vyvyan sang in concerts and broadcasts in Europe and the USA, specializing in such choral works as Ludwig van Beethoven's Ninth Symphony, Britten's *Spring Symphony* (which she recorded under the composer) and *War Requiem*, J.S. Bach's Passions and G.F. Handel's oratorios; she gave distinguished performances in Handel's operas, staged and in concert. She sang in the first performance of Arthur Bliss's *The Beatitudes* at Coventry Cathedral in 1962, and was a noted interpreter of British music. Her singing was marked by astonishing flexibility in florid music, secure intonation and subtle phrasing. In opera she always displayed her dramatic gifts in vividly individual portrayals, as can be heard in her superb recordings of the Governess and Mrs Julian.

Alan Blyth

Wächter, Johann Michael

(*b* Rappersdorf, 2 March 1794; *d* Dresden, 26 May 1853). Austrian baritone. He sang in various church choirs in Vienna and made his stage début in 1819 at Graz in the title role of W.A. Mozart's *Don Giovanni*. Engagements at Bratislava, Vienna and Berlin followed; then in 1827 he joined the Dresden Hofoper, where he remained for the rest of his career. His roles included W.A. Mozart's Figaro, Sherasmin (*Oberon*), Mikéli (Luigi Cherubini's *Les deux journées*) and Brian de Bois-Guilbert (Heinrich Marschner's *Der Templer und die Jüdin*), and he sang in three Wagner premières: *Rienzi* (1842, as Orsini), *Der fliegende Holländer* (1843, title role) and *Tannhäuser* (1845, Biterolf). Hector Berlioz, who heard *Der fliegende Holländer* in Dresden, considered Wächter's baritone 'one of the finest I have ever heard, and he uses it like a consummate singer. It is of that rich and vibrant timbre that has such a wonderful power of expression, provided that the artist sings with soul and feeling, which Wächter does to a high degree' (*Mémoires*). His wife, the mezzo Thérèse Wächter-Wittman (*b* Vienna, 31 August 1802), also sang at Dresden; she created Mary in *Der fliegende Holländer*.

Elizabeth Forbes/R

Waechter, Eberhard

(*b* Vienna, 9 July 1929; *d* Vienna, 29 March 1992). Austrian baritone. After study at Vienna University and the Akademie für Musik (piano and theory) he took singing lessons from Elisabeth Rado. His début at the Volksoper in 1953 as Silvio in *Pagliacci* led to his engagement at the Staatsoper in 1955. His career advanced rapidly: a fine Posa in *Don Carlos* at the Staatsoper in 1956 helped to establish him. The same year he enjoyed considerable success as Count Almaviva in *Figaro* at Covent Garden; in 1958 he was heard as Amfortas and Wolfram at Bayreuth, and engagements followed at the principal houses of Europe and the USA, though his Metropolitan début in 1961 as Wolfram was his only appearance there. Although he was not always wise in his choice of parts (in 1964 he was not ready for a role such as Wotan in *Das Rheingold*), Waechter's warm, expressive voice and fine bearing brought him success in such varied roles as Escamillo, Kurwenal, Don Giovanni, Ford and Boccanegra, Scarpia,

Danilo, Mandryka and Wozzeck, and Danton in Gottfried von Einem's *Dantons Tod*. He appeared as Don Giovanni in the set of stamps issued by Austria to commemorate the centenary of the Vienna Staatsoper in 1969. In 1980 he created Joseph in von Einem's controversial *Jesu Hochzeit* in Vienna. By then he was taking on character parts, such as the Music-master (*Ariadne auf Naxos*), Giovanni Morone (*Palestrina*) and Melchior (*Amahl and the Night Visitors*). Waechter was a fine lieder singer, as his recording of *Dichterliebe* confirms. He became director of the Vienna Volksoper in September 1987 and, in addition, four years later was appointed artistic co-director with Joan (Ion) Holender of the Staatsoper, where he was charged with the task of re-establishing the old ensemble system.

Peter Branscombe/R

Wagele, Antonia.

See BERNASCONI, ANTONIA.

Wagner [Jachmann-Wagner], Johanna

(*b* Seelze, nr Hanover, 13 Oct 1826; *d* Würzburg, 16 Oct 1894). Soprano, adopted daughter of Richard Wagner's elder brother, Albert. Through the influence of her uncle, she made her début at Dresden in 1844 as Agathe. She created the role of Elisabeth in *Tannhäuser* (19 October 1845) and also sang in Daniel Auber's *Le maçon*. After studying in Paris with the younger Manuel Garcia (1846–8), she sang in Hamburg (1849) and was then engaged at the Hofoper, Berlin (1850–61), where she took over the part of Fidès in *Le prophète* from PAULINE VIARDOT. In 1852 she was announced to sing at Covent Garden, but a lawsuit brought by Benjamin Lumley, manager of the rival opera company at Her Majesty's Theatre, prevented her from appearing. She eventually made her London début in 1856 at Her Majesty's as Gioachino Rossini's Tancred, Gaetano Donizetti's Lucretia Borgia and as Romeo in Vincenzo Bellini's *I Capuleti e i Montecchi*. That year she sang Elisabeth in the first Berlin performance of *Tannhäuser*, and in 1859 Ortrud in the first Berlin performance of *Lohengrin*. Early in the 1860s she lost her singing voice and appeared for a decade as an actress. Her voice recovered, she sang in Ludwig van Beethoven's Ninth Symphony at the ceremony celebrating the laying of the foundation stone of the Bayreuth Festspielhaus (1872), and in the first complete *Ring* cycle there (1876), as Schwertleite and the First Norn. From 1882 to 1884 she taught singing at the Königliche Musikschule, Munich, and later gave lessons privately. Her voice was powerful throughout its range, clear and bright in the upper register, round and full in the lower; she had a magnificent stage presence as well as considerable dramatic ability. Her husband, Alfred Jachmann, acted as intermediary when Wagner was negotiating his London concerts in 1877.

Elizabeth Forbes

Walker, Edyth

(*b* Hopewell, NY, 27 March 1867; *d* New York, 19 Feb 1950). American soprano and mezzo-soprano. She studied with Aglaia Orgeni in Dresden, made her first appearance at a Gewandhaus concert in Leipzig and her operatic début as Fidès in *Le prophète* at the Berlin Hofoper on 11 November 1894. She was a member of the Vienna Hofoper from 1895 to 1903. On 16 May 1900 she made her Covent Garden début as Amneris and sang Ortrud, Fricka, Erda and Waltraute in the same season. From 1903 (début on 30 November as Amneris) until 1906 she was a member of the Metropolitan Opera. There she began to add soprano roles, including Brünnhilde in *Die Walküre*, to her repertory, and at the Hamburg Opera (1903–12) she appeared regularly both as soprano and mezzo. In 1908 she sang Ortrud and Kundry at Bayreuth and returned, as Isolde, to Covent Garden, where she was accounted one of the greatest Wagnerian artists to have sung there. Under Thomas Beecham, in 1910, she was the first London Electra, winning high praise for both singing and acting; she also appeared as Thirza in Ethel Smyth's *The Wreckers*. From 1912 until 1917 she sang in the Munich Festivals. After her retirement from the stage she taught singing, chiefly privately but also, from 1933 to 1936, at the American Conservatory in Fontainebleau and subsequently in New York, where her pupils included BLANCHE THEBOM. The few published recordings of her voice were made between 1902 and 1908.

Eric Blom/Harold Barnes

Walker, Sarah

(*b* Cheltenham, 11 March 1943). English mezzo-soprano. She studied in London, and after appearing with the Ambrosian singers, made her début in 1970 as Octavia (*L'incoronazione di Poppea*) with Kent Opera, for which she sang Poppaea, Penelope (*Il ritorno d'Ulisse*) and Andromache (*King Priam*). She sang Diana in *Calisto* at Glyndebourne (1970) and Dido in *Les Troyens* for Scottish Opera (1972), for which she later sang Mistress Quickly (1991). For the ENO she has sung Dorabella, Fricka, Mary Stuart, Herodias, the Countess (*The Queen of Spades*), Cornelia (*Giulio Cesare*) Gloriana, and Agave in the première of John Buller's *Bakxai* (1992). In 1979 she made her Covent Garden début as Charlotte (*Werther*), then sang Baba the Turk, Rose Parrowe (*Taverner*), Marcellina, Mrs Sedley and Caroline with the Thick Mane in the British première of Aulis Sallinen's *The King Goes Forth to France* (1987). Other roles include Madame Larina and Filipyevna (*Yevgeny Onegin*). She has sung in Vienna, San Francisco, Chicago, Geneva and Brussels, and at the Metropolitan, where she made her début in 1988 as Cornelia. An intelligent, musical and very dramatic singer, she excels in modern opera. In recital her performances include lieder, mélodies and British song. Recordings include Baba the Turk and Mrs Sedley, all of Gabriel Fauré's songs, and with Roger Vignoles and THOMAS ALLEN, a noted recital programme called *The Sea*. She was appointed CBE in 1991.

Elizabeth Forbes

Walker, Thomas

(*b* London, 5 June 1698; *d* Dublin, 5 June 1744). English singer, actor and author. He acted in London from 1715, specializing in handsome daredevil roles such as Hotspur. Although untrained as a singer, he was given the role of Macheath in *The Beggar's Opera* (1728) during rehearsals, when he was heard singing some of the airs behind the scenes. Walker is depicted as Macheath in William Hogarth's painting of the scene in Newgate Prison (*A Scene from the Beggar's Opera*, c.1728, National Gallery of Art, Washington, DC). W.R. Chetwood wrote that after his success as Macheath he 'follow'd *Bacchus* too ardently, insomuch that his Credit was often drown'd upon the Stage'. He sang in a few other ballad operas and held on to his roles until 1739. His career then collapsed and he died in poverty. His own ballad opera, *The Quaker's Opera*, was performed in 1728.

Oxford DNB (J. Milling)

Olive Baldwin, Thelma Wilson/R

Wallace, Georgette.

See ARBELL, LUCY.

Walt, Deon van der

(*b* Cape Town, 28 July 1958; *d* Paarl, 29 Nov 2005). South African tenor. He studied singing at the University of Stellenbosch, and made his operatic début as Jaquino in 1981 in Cape Town. From 1982 he was attached to a number of opera houses in Europe, principally in Stuttgart and Zürich, where he sang Tonio in *La fille du régiment* (1989). He made his début at Covent Garden in 1985 as Almaviva and at the Vienna Staatsoper in 1989 as Tamino, singing Belmonte at Salzburg the same year. The lyric quality of his voice made him an ideal interpreter of the works of composers such as Gaetano Donizetti, W.A. Mozart and Gioachino Rossini. Although concentrating at first on lighter roles, he had more recently taken on more dramatic roles by Jules Massenet, Giuseppe Verdi, Giacomo Puccini and others. His most significant recordings include *Così fan tutte* and *Fidelio* (under Nikolaus Harnoncourt), *Meistersinger* (as David; Wolfgang Sawallisch) and many lieder recitals.

James May

Waltz, Gustavus

(*fl* 1732–59). English bass of German birth. His first known appearances were in Thomas Arne's English opera season at the Little Theatre in the Haymarket in spring 1732, when he sang in J.F. Lampe's *Amelia* and a pirated production of G.F. Handel's *Acis*

Gustavus Waltz

and Galatea (Polyphemus). The following season (1732–3) he sang in Lampe's *Britannia*, J.C. Smith's *Ulysses* and Arne's *Opera of Operas* at Lincoln's Inn Fields. On 17 March 1733 he took a small part, probably the Chief Priest of Baal, in the first performance of Handel's *Deborah* at the King's Theatre. He accompanied Handel to Oxford in July, singing in the first performances of *Athalia* (Abner), the bilingual *Acis and Galatea* (Polyphemus), probably *Esther* (Haman) and *Deborah* (Abinoam and Priest of Baal), and in anthems at St Mary's church. He then joined Handel's opera company, first at the King's Theatre, later at Covent Garden, until the summer of 1736. He was to have made his Italian début in the pasticcio *Semiramide riconosciuta* on 30 October, but was apparently replaced. He took part in the revivals of *Ottone* (Emireno), *Sosarme* (Altomaro) and *Il pastor fido* (Tirenio), the pasticcios *Caio Fabricio* and *Oreste*, and the first performances of *Arianna in Creta* (Minos), *Il Parnasso in festa* (Mars), *Ariodante* (King of Scotland), *Alcina* (Melisso) and *Atalanta* (Nicander). At his benefit at Hickford's Room on 21 February 1735 he advertised himself as 'Singer in Mr Handel's Operas'. He also repeated his Oxford parts in oratorios, including the first London performances of *Athalia*, and continued to sing in English theatre pieces, among them Lampe's *Opera of Operas* and *Cupid and Psyche*, *The Tempest* and Arne's *Britannia* in 1733–4, and Arne's *Grand Epithalamium* in April 1736, all at Drury Lane. He had another benefit at Hickford's on 7 April 1737.

Waltz rejoined Handel for the oratorio season of 1738–9, singing the title role in the first performance of *Saul* on 16 January, in the première of *Israel in Egypt* on 4 April, and probably in *Jupiter in Argos* on 1 May. He had meanwhile appeared in G.B. Pescetti's *Angelica e Medoro* at Covent Garden on 10 March. His later career was associated with English theatre pieces of the lighter type, chiefly by Lampe and Arne, though he sang occasionally at concerts and in December 1739 in a composite Henry Purcell masque at Covent Garden. He was employed at that theatre in 1739–42 and again in 1749–51, at Drury Lane and the Little Theatre in the Haymarket in 1743–5, and in May and June 1744 at Ruckholt House, Essex, where he sang in William Boyce's *Solomon* and Handel's *Alexander's Feast*. He had a benefit at the Little Theatre in the Haymarket on 19 December 1748. Handel cast him as Charon in the unperformed incidental music to *Alceste* in January 1750. He was the teacher of Isabella Young (later Mrs Scott) and gave a concert with her at the Little Theatre in the Haymarket on 18 March 1751. He was a choral bass at the Foundling Hospital performances of *Messiah* on 15 May 1754, 27 April 1758 and 3 May 1759, on each occasion receiving the minimum fee of 10s. 6d. He may have sung in the chorus of Handel's Covent Garden oratorios at this period.

Waltz is generally recalled for the wrong reasons. Charles Burney and John Hawkins both said he was at one time Handel's cook, which is possible but unverifiable. He may well have known as much counterpoint as C.W. Gluck in 1745: there is a ring of truth about this reported *mot* of Handel's. But Burney's notorious aspersions on Waltz – 'a German, with a coarse figure, and a still coarser voice', 'Waltz had but little voice, and his manner was coarse and unpleasant' – almost certainly do him an injustice. Burney did not hear him until his later years, when he admitted that 'as an actor, [Waltz] had a great deal of humour'. Although he was never in the class of MONTAGNANA, whom he replaced in 1733, some of Handel's parts for Waltz, notably the King in *Ariodante* and Saul, suggest that he commanded not only dramatic power but majesty and pathos, with a good legato and a compass of nearly two octaves (*G* to *f♯′*). A portrait by John Maurice Hauck, engraved by Johann Sebastian Müller, shows Waltz playing the cello with refreshments at his elbow (see illustration).

W.C. Smith: 'Gustavus Waltz: was he Handel's Cook?', *Concerning Handel: his Life and Works* (London, 1948), 165–94

Winton Dean

Ward, David

(*b* Dumbarton, 3 July 1922; *d* Dunedin, New Zealand, 16 July 1983). Scottish bass. He studied at the RCM and later in Munich with HANS HOTTER. In 1952 he joined the chorus of Sadler's Wells Opera and in 1953 sang the Old Bard in *The Immortal Hour* and Count Walter in *Luisa Miller*; he created Hardy (*Nelson*) the following year and from then until 1958 sang a variety of roles with the company including Méphistophélès, Daland and the Dutchman. In 1960 he made his Covent Garden début as Pogner, sang Lord Walton (*I puritani*) at Glyndebourne and made his Bayreuth début as Titurel. At Covent Garden he sang Fasolt, Hunding, Morosus in the English première of *Die schweigsame Frau* (1961), the Wanderer (1962) and Wotan in a complete *Ring* (1964), as well as Arkel, Pope Clement (*Benvenuto Cellini*), Ivan Khovansky, Rocco and Don Basilio. No less distinguished in Giuseppe Verdi, he sang Zaccaria, Philip II and Fiesco. His Boris with Scottish Opera was highly praised. He sang in Italy, Germany and the USA, and in 1967 he sang Wotan in six complete *Ring cycles* in Buenos Aires. To a voice of beautiful quality and range he added a sensitivity and dignity which made his Wotan and King Mark profoundly moving. He was made a CBE in 1972.

A. Jefferson: 'David Ward', *Opera*, xix (1968), 540–45

Harold Rosenthal/R

Warfield, William

(*b* West Helena, AR, 22 Jan 1920; *d* Chicago, 25 Aug 2002). American bass. He studied at the Eastman School of Music and appeared on Broadway, taking part in the première of Marc Blitzstein's *Regina* (1949). He made his recital début at Town Hall, New York, on 19 March 1950, and his first recordings were produced the following year. In 1952–3 he toured Europe as Porgy (with LEONTYNE PRICE, to whom he was then married, as Bess), appearing in London, Vienna and Berlin, among other cities. He also sang Porgy in New York (1961) and at the Vienna Volksoper (1971–2). Other roles included Joe in *Show Boat*. He also toured widely as a soloist. His fine, deep voice was used with great artistry and he was an excellent actor. He taught at the University of Illinois and at Northwestern University. In 1984 he was elected President of the National Association of Negro Musicians.

Elizabeth Forbes/R

Warren [Warenoff], Leonard

(*b* New York, 21 April 1911; *d* New York, 4 March 1960). American baritone. After formal study with Sidney Dietch he entered the Metropolitan Opera Auditions of the Air and won a contract for 1938. Following further study in Italy, he made his stage début with the Metropolitan in 1939, as Paolo in *Simon Boccanegra*; his last complete performance in the house, 21 years later, was as Simon himself.

During his career, which was dominated by New York engagements, Warren won special acclaim in the great Verdi roles and as Barnaba (*La Gioconda*), Scarpia and Tonio. His voice was huge, smooth, superbly controlled and marked by special freedom in the top range (which extended to the tenor's high C). Foreign engagements took him to Rio de Janeiro and Buenos Aires (1942), Mexico City (1948), La Scala (1953) and the USSR (1958). His recorded legacy is an important one, and includes distinguished performances in *Il trovatore*, *Rigoletto*, *La traviata*, *Un ballo in maschera* and *Macbeth*. He was also an accomplished recitalist, as a live recording from Moscow confirms. He died on the stage of the Metropolitan while singing Don Carlo in *La forza del destino*.

P.L. Miller: 'Leonard Warren 1911–1960', Opera, xi (1960), 397

S. Milnes: 'The Warren Legacy', ON, xxxix/18 (1974–5), 26–7

Martin Bernheimer, Dennis K. McIntire

Watkinson, Carolyn

(b Preston, 19 March 1949). English mezzo-soprano. She studied at the RMCM and The Hague Conservatory. In 1978 she sang Phaedra in Jean-Philippe Rameau's *Hippolyte et Aricie* under Jean-Claude Malgoire (English Bach Festival at Covent Garden and Versailles). She has appeared as Nero in *L'incoronazione di Poppea* in Amsterdam and at the 1979 Spoleto Festival. Other Baroque repertory includes roles in G.F. Handel's *Serse*, *Rinaldo*, *Partenope* and *Ariodante*. She appeared in a staged version of *Solomon* at the 1984 Göttingen Festival. Her voice is not large but is admirably focussed throughout its range, and is well suited to such roles as Idamantes (Salzburg), C.W. Gluck's Orpheus, Cherubino and Cenerentola (Glyndebourne Tour and Festival).

David Cummings

Watson [née McLamore], Claire

(b New York, 3 Feb 1927; d Utting am Ammersee, 16 July 1986). American soprano. She studied at the Eastman School of Music, at Tanglewood, and privately with ELISABETH SCHUMANN, and made her début in 1951 at Graz as Desdemona. In 1955 she was engaged at Frankfurt; during her first season she sang 12 new roles, including Countess Almaviva, Pamina, Elisabeth (*Tannhäuser*), Leonora (*La forza del destino*), Aida and Tatyana. In 1957–8 she sang Fiordiligi, Elisabeth de Valois and the Marschallin, in which role she made her Covent Garden (1958) and Glyndebourne (1960) débuts. She appeared regularly in London, where she was admired as Ellen Orford, an unforgettably intense Sieglinde, Eva, and, with the Munich company in 1972, Ariadne and the Countess in *Capriccio*. Her Munich association began in 1958, when she sang Countess Almaviva at the reopening of the Cuvilliéstheater; in 1963 she sang Eva at the inauguration of the rebuilt Nationaltheater, a performance preserved on disc. Watson made guest appearances in Vienna, Berlin, Italy and the USA, where she sang her first Arabella in New Orleans in 1969. The warmth and musicality of her singing and her sincerity illumine her portrait of Ellen Orford in Benjamin Britten's own recording of *Peter Grimes*.

G. Rothon: 'Claire Watson', *Opera*, xxi (1970), 1004

L. Rasponi: 'Claire Watson', *The Last Prima Donnas* (New York, 1982), 394–403

Harold Rosenthal/Alan Blyth

Watson, Janice

(b London, 8 April 1964). English soprano. She studied the flute and singing at the GSMD, and won the Kathleen Ferrier Award in 1987. The following year she made her Covent Garden début, as Wellgunde in *Das Rheingold*. Her WNO début, as Musetta, followed in 1989, and her ENO début, as Rosalinde (*Die Fledermaus*), in 1991. At ENO she was also admired as W.A. Mozart's Pamina and Countess Almaviva. She made a widely praised Vienna Staatsoper début as Ellen Orford in 1999, repeating the role to equal acclaim at Covent Garden in 2004. She first sang at the Metropolitan Opera, as Micaela (*Carmen*), in 2001, and has returned to the Met as Countess Almaviva and Liù.

Since the mid-1990s Watson has added several lyric Strauss and Wagner roles to her repertory, including Arabella (which she sang for her 1997 Santa Fe début), Eva (also at Santa Fe), Ariadne (WNO, 2004), the Marschallin (ENO, 2005) and Elisabeth (*Tannhäuser*), which she sang for her Opera Australia début in 2007. In 2006 she scored a triumph on her La Scala début in the title role of *Kát'a Kabanová* (she had a comparable success with the part at Covent Garden in 2007), and sang a deeply touching Cio-Cio-San for ENO. Watson's dramatic flair and range of colour are revealed on her recordings of Ellen Orford, Helena (*A Midsummer Night's Dream*) and Jenůfa. With her sweet, rounded tone, she is also an admired concert singer, and has recorded works including Haydn masses, Beethoven cantatas and Francis Poulenc's *Gloria*.

Richard Wigmore

Watson, Lillian

(b Harrow, 4 Dec 1947). English soprano. She studied at the GSMD and the London Opera Centre and made her professional opera début, as Miss Wordsworth (*Albert Herring*), at Wexford in 1970. From 1971 to 1974 she was a company member of the WNO, making her début as Papagena. Other important débuts include Covent Garden, as Barbarina. (1971), Glyndebourne Touring Opera, as Despina (1975), Glyndebourne Festival Opera, as Sophie in *Der Rosenkavalier* (1976), the ENO, as a notably sexy and resourceful Susanna (1978), the Salzburg Festival, as Marzelline (1982), and the

Vienna Staatsoper, as Susanna, in 1984. Watson's bright, agile high soprano and delightful stage personality have also been admired in roles such as Bella in *The Midsummer Marriage* (at Covent Garden), Fiakermilli in *Arabella* (Glyndebourne), Benjamin Britten's Titania (the role of her Aix Festival début, 1991), Sharpears in Leoš Janáček's *Cunning Little Vixen*, which she has sung at Covent Garden and recorded with Simon Rattle, and W.A. Mozart's Blonde (Covent Garden, Glyndebourne, Salzburg and Hamburg), which she has recorded with Colin Davis. Watson's other recordings include Zerlina, Frasquita, E.W. Korngold's *Kathrin*, *Israel in Egypt*, Felix Mendelssohn's *Midsummer Night's Dream* and Sidney Jones's *The Geisha*. In 2007 she became a professor at the RAM.

Richard Wigmore

Watts, Helen (Josephine)

(*b* Milford Haven, 7 Dec 1927). Welsh contralto. She studied at the RAM and made her operatic début in 1958 as Didymus in *Theodora* with the Handel Opera Society, for whom she also sang Ino and Juno (*Semele*) as well as Rinaldo, which she repeated at the Komische Oper, Berlin, and at Halle (1961). In 1964 she sang Benjamin Britten's Lucretia (conducted by the composer) on the English Opera Group tour of the USSR. At Covent Garden (1965–71) she sang First Norn, Erda, Sosostris (*The Midsummer Marriage*) and Mrs Sedley. For the WNO (1969–83) her roles were Mistress Quickly, Sosostris, Mrs Sedley and Larina, which she also sang at Lyons in 1984. She sang W.A. Mozart's Pharnaces at Salzburg (1971) and Claudio Monteverdi's Arnalta for Scottish Opera (1973). She recorded Ursula in *Béatrice et Bénédict*. A stylish singer with a firm technique, she had a warm, clear-toned voice, not large but well projected, admirably suited also to her oratorio and lieder work, of which recordings include her eloquent Angel in Adrian Boult's *Dream of Gerontius*. She was made a CBE in 1978.

Helen Simpson/Elizabeth Forbes

Webb, Lizbeth (Lizabeth)

(*b* Reading, 30 Jan 1926). English soprano. The leading ingénue of British musicals in the 1950s, she received her first break as an understudy, taking over the lead in Vivian Ellis and A.P. Herbert's *Big Ben* in 1946, but is best remembered as Lucy Veracity Willow in Ellis and Herbert's next show, *Bless the Bride* (1947). Her two biggest numbers in this were 'This is my lovely day' and 'I was never kissed before', which demonstrated the powerful

soprano voice and graceful stage presence which she had the misfortune to bring to the West End just as the trend towards more energetic American musical theatre imports was taking over. After playing the juvenile lead in Ivor Novello's *Gay's the Word* (1951) she appeared as Sarah Brown in the first London production of Frank Loesser's *Guys and Dolls* (1953), and in 1959 appeared as Giulietta in the television version of Hans May and Eric Maschwitz's *Carissima*. Although she appeared in the title role of *Die lustige Witwe* in 1969, she had in effect retired from the stage before the end of the 1950s, having married the heir to a baronetcy, in true Edwardian style entering the stage as a singer and leaving as a Lady.

Paul Webb

Weber, Aloysia.

See LANGE, ALOYSIA.

Weber, Ludwig

(*b* Vienna, 29 July 1899; *d* Vienna, 9 Dec 1974). Austrian bass. He abandoned projected careers as teacher and artist when he discovered his vocal promise and began to study with Alfred Boruttau in 1919. Having gained experience at the Vienna Volksoper he joined some of the smaller German companies in the mid- and late 1920s. After a successful appearance at the Munich Wagner Festival of 1931 he joined the Bavarian Staatsoper in 1933 and soon began to receive invitations to sing abroad. He was first heard in London in 1936 (Pogner, Gurnemanz, Hunding and Hagen), and in the following years he added Daland, King Mark, Osmin and Rocco to his Covent Garden roles. In 1938 he created the Holsteiner in *Friedenstag* in Munich. He joined the Vienna Staatsoper in 1945 and during its 1947 London season he sang the Commendatore and Rocco. In the following seasons he returned to give further performances of his Wagnerian roles, and to sing Boris Godunov (1950). From 1951 he was a regular singer at the Bayreuth Festival, and he also appeared at Buenos Aires. He had a magnificently rich and solid bass voice and could darken his tones to accommodate the malevolence of Hagen as successfully as he conveyed the suffering and dignity of Mark or Gurnemanz. In W.A. Mozart he commanded the line and agility to be a splendid Sarastro, Osmin and Commendatore, and he also often appeared on the concert platform. He lacked perhaps the boisterous high spirits of the complete Baron Ochs, though he was never less than impressive in this part (and some have compared him with MAYR); his recording of the role, and of his Gurnemanz in the 1951 Bayreuth recording, are still much admired.

D. Brass: 'Ludwig Weber', *Opera*, ii (1950–51), 352–5

Peter Branscombe

Weede [Wiedefeld], Robert

(*b* Baltimore, 22 Feb 1903; *d* Walnut Creek, CA, 9 July 1972). American singer and actor. After studies at the Eastman School of Music and in Milan, he began his stage career at the Radio City Music Hall in 1933 before making his Metropolitan Opera début as Tonio in *Pagliacci* in 1937. He continued to appear on operatic stages, particularly at the Metropolitan and the San Francisco Opera, for four decades. He created the role of the Emperor of Haiti, Jean Jacques Dessalines, in William Grant Still's *Troubled Island* (1949) for the City Center Opera Company (later New York City Opera). He also appeared in concert and recital, and was a soloist on the 'Great Moments in Music' radio programme from 1942 to 1946. It is as Tony, the lead role in Frank Loesser's Broadway musical *The Most Happy Fella* (1956), that Weede is best remembered; he regarded the vocal technique that it required to be equal to that of any opera. He subsequently appeared on Broadway in *Milk and Honey* (1961) and *Cry for Us All* (1970).

One of the finest American baritones of the century, Weede had the ability and flexibility to adapt his voice successfully to both operatic and musical theatre roles without surrendering to the potential trappings of either style, and the high standards which he established have been recognized as signposts for succeeding generations of American singers. With a large, well-trained voice, his diction, articulation and pitch were virtually unequalled. Even in his later years, his voice possessed a strength and quality which have earned him the respect of singers ever since.

William A. Everett, Lee Snook/R

Weidt, Lucie [Lucy]

(*b* Troppau [now Opava], Silesia, 11 May 1876; *d* Vienna, 28 July 1940). Austrian soprano of German birth. She studied with her father, Heinrich Weidt, a minor Kapellmeister and composer, and with Rosa Papier. Most of her career was spent at the Vienna Staatsoper, of which she was a regular member from 1903 to 1926, first in succession to the retiring SOPHIE SEDLMAIR, and soon sharing the major Wagner roles with ANNA BAHR-MILDENBURG. She became a famous Leonore in *Fidelio* and was the first

Viennese Marschallin in *Der Rosenkavalier*; she was also the first to sing the role of Kundry in Milan. She appeared in Munich between 1908 and 1910, for a few Metropolitan performances as Brünnhilde and Elisabeth in the season of 1910–11, and at Buenos Aires in 1912. Janáček much admired her Kostelnička at the Viennese première of *Jenůfa* in 1918. At the première of Richard Strauss's *Die Frau ohne Schatten* (1919, Vienna) she sang the part of the Nurse. Her recordings show a well-trained and strong voice of marked dramatic intensity.

Desmond Shawe-Taylor/R

Weikl, Bernd

(*b* Vienna, 29 July 1942). Austrian baritone. He studied in Mainz and Hanover, where he made his début in 1968 as Ottokar (*Der Freischütz*). He was engaged at Düsseldorf (1970–73) and sang Melot (*Tristan und Isolde*) at Salzburg in 1971. He first appeared at Bayreuth as Wolfram in 1972, and has subsequently sung there Amfortas, the Herald (*Lohengrin*) and Hans Sachs. He made his Covent Garden début (1975) as Gioachino Rossini's Figaro and his Metropolitan début (1977) as Wolfram, returning as Orestes (*Elektra*), John the Baptist and Hans Sachs. He sings regularly in Berlin, Hamburg, Munich and Vienna, where he created Ferdinand in Gottfried von Einem's *Kabale und Liebe* (1976), repeating the part in Florence. Weikl's huge repertory of over 100 roles ranges from Guglielmo, Count Almaviva, Don Giovanni, Belcore, Luna, Posa, Boccanegra and Ford, which he sang at La Scala in 1980, to Onegin, Tomsky, Golaud, Eisenstein and Morone (*Palestrina*). Weikl's powerful voice, warm and resonant, and his dramatic gifts are particularly well displayed in his Wagner and Strauss roles, notably Hans Sachs, the Dutchman, Mandryka, Orestes and John the Baptist. He has recorded many of his operatic roles and such works as *Winterreise* (of which he is a sensitive interpreter), Johannes Brahms's *German Requiem* and Arnold Schoenberg's *Gurrelieder*.

Elizabeth Forbes

Welitsch [Veličkova], Ljuba

(*b* Borissovo, 10 July 1913; *d* Vienna, 31 Aug 1996). Austrian soprano of Bulgarian birth. After studying in Vienna with Lierhammer she made her début at the Sofia Opera in 1936. She appeared at Graz (1937–40), Hamburg (1941–3) and Munich (1943–6), and then joined the Vienna Staatsoper. She first sang in England in autumn 1947 during the Staatsoper visit, dazzling London audiences with the passion, vocal purity and compelling force of her Salome – her most famous role (which she first sang under Richard Strauss in 1944 and also at her Metropolitan début in 1949). She was a renowned Tosca, Aida and Musetta, and enjoyed great success in other such widely differing roles as Donna Anna, Jenůfa, Minnie (*La fanciulla del West*), Nadja (Franz Salmhofer's *Iwan Tarassenko*) and Rosalinde (*Fledermaus*). Her rise to international fame was meteoric but, sadly, ill-health and insufficient care of her voice denied her continued success in her grandest roles, although she still appeared in a number of character parts in Vienna.

Welitsch's was one of the most exciting voices to appear in the years immediately after World War II. Impressive in dramatic utterance and in soft, sustained lyrical passages, she displayed a total dedication to and absorption in every aspect of her roles. Her few recordings, including versions of the closing scene from *Salome*, reveal her remarkable vocal qualities.

Earl of Harewood: 'Ljuba Welitsch', *Opera*, iv (1953), 72–7

Peter Branscombe

Welker, Hartmut

(*b* Velbert, 27 Oct 1941). German bass-baritone. He studied initially for a technical career, but took up singing in 1972. After making his début at Aachen in 1974, he was a member of the ensemble there until 1980, followed by three years at Karlsruhe. Welker made his début at La Scala, Milan, in 1982 as Telramund, at Covent Garden in 1986 as Pizarro and at the Metropolitan Opera in 1990, also as Pizarro. The dark, cutting timbre of his voice, allied to a strong stage presence, has made him an equally demonic Alberich and Caspar (*Der Freischütz*). His recordings include Pizarro, Telramund and lesser-known works such as Franz Schubert's *Fierrabras*, Franz Schmidt's *Notre Dame* and E.W. Korngold's *Wunder der Heliane*.

Andrew Clark

Wendling [née Spurni], Dorothea

(*b* Stuttgart, 21 March 1736; *d* Munich, 20 Aug 1811). German soprano. She was the daughter of two Stuttgart court musicians, the horn player Franz Spurni and Maria Dorothea (née St Pierre), a lutenist. On 9 January 1752 she married the flautist Johann Baptist Wendling. (Her sister-in-law was the soprano ELISABETH WENDLING.) Having made her Paris début with her husband, she was appointed a singer at the Mannheim court in the same year, where her first role was Hermione in Baldassare Galuppi's *Antigona* (17 January 1753). In 1758 she sang the prima donna role in Ignaz Holzbauer's *Nitteti* and for the next 20 years was the most celebrated soprano at Mannheim. Her salary, 1200 florins in 1759, increased to 1500 in 1778. She appeared in serious operas by Niccolò Jommelli, Holzbauer, Niccolò Piccinni and J.C. Bach, singing in the premières of *Temistocle* (1772) and *Lucio Silla* (1775), and took the title roles in Tommaso Traetta's *Sofonisba* (1762) and Gian Francesco de Majo's *Ifigenia in Tauride* (1764). She also sang in the Italian comic operas performed at Mannheim in the 1770s, and appeared in more than 30 roles in 25 years. W.A. Mozart admired her voice and wrote the concert aria к486a/295a for her in 1778. Christoph Wieland, who heard her during rehearsals for Anton Schweitzer's *Rosamunde*, wrote to Sophie La Roche: 'Her style of singing surpasses everything I have ever heard, even the famous Mara'. Wilhelm Heinse and C.F.D. Schubart praised her as one of the most expressive singers of the day, though the latter also mentioned an unfortunate 'warble'. She remained active after the court transferred to Munich in 1778, and created the title roles in Holzbauer's *La morte di Didone* (1779, Mannheim) and J.P. Verazi's *Laodamia* (1780, Oggersheim). She appeared as a guest in Munich, singing Calipso in Franz Paul Grua's *Telemaco* (1780) and Ilia in W.A. Mozart's *Idomeneo* (1781), a role that she created. After she left the stage, she continued to sing in concerts and taught singing in Mannheim and Munich. Her daughter, Elisabeth Augusta, also occasionally performed in comic operas at Mannheim and Schwetzingen.

Paul Corneilson/R

Wendling [née Sarselli], Elisabeth (Augusta)

(*b* Mannheim, 20 Feb 1746; *d* Munich, 10 Jan 1786). German soprano. Her parents, the tenor Pietro Sarselli and his wife Carolina (née Valvasori), were singers at Mannheim. She accompanied Franz Wendling to Italy in 1760 and after her return to Mannheim in 1761 was appointed a court musician. She married Wendling, the violinist and brother of Johann Baptist, on 1 December 1764. Beginning with the role of Cirene in Tommaso Traetta's *Sofonisba* (1762), she was cast in the seconda donna roles at the Hoftheater, singing opposite her sister-in-law, DOROTHEA WENDLING. Her performances at Mannheim included the premières of J.C. Bach's *Temistocle* (1772) and *Lucio Silla* (1775). She accompanied the court to Munich in 1778, and there created her most famous role, Electra in W.A. Mozart's *Idomeneo* (1781). She also sang the title role in

Antonio Salieri's *Semiramide* (1782); her last role was Zelmira in Alessio Prati's *Armida abbandonata* (1785).

Paul Corneilson/R

Wettergren [Pålson-Wettergren], Gertrud

(*b* Eslöv, Malmö, 17 Feb 1897; *d* Stockholm, 26 Nov 1991). Swedish contralto. She studied in Stockholm, and made her début there in 1922 as Cherubino. Engaged at the Stockholm Royal Opera for more than 25 years, she also sang all over Europe and in the USA, making her Metropolitan Opera début in 1935 as Amneris, and her Chicago début the following year as Carmen. First heard at Covent Garden in 1936 as Amneris, she returned in 1939 as Azucena, a performance preserved on disc. Her large repertory included several Wagner roles – Brangäne, Venus, Fricka – as well as Delilah, Mignon, Herodias (*Salome*), Marina (*Boris Godunov*) and Marfa (*Khovanshchina*). She also appeared in many Swedish operas, including Wilhelm Peterson-Berger's *Adils och Elisiv* and *Domedagsprofeterna*, Hilding Rosenberg's *Resa till Amerika*, Kurt Atterberg's *Bäckahästen* and Gunnar de Frumerie's *Singoalla*, in which she created the title role in 1940. She took part in the Swedish première of *Peter Grimes* (1945) and continued to appear in Stockholm until 1952. Her voice, a true contralto, was firm and well projected, while her strong personality made her a fine interpreter of such roles as Carmen or Delilah, whose arias she recorded. She retired in 1949. Her autobiography, *Mitt ödes stjärna* ('My lucky star'), was published in Stockholm in 1949.

Elizabeth Forbes

White, Willard

(*b* St Catherine, Jamaica, 10 Oct 1946). Jamaican bass. After studying in New York, he made his début in 1974 at Washington, DC, as Trulove, then sang with New York City Opera. He made his British début with the WNO in 1976 as Osmin and has since sung Massimiliano (*I masnadieri*), Orestes (*Elektra*), Zaccaria and Boris Godunov. For the ENO he has sung Seneca, Hunding, Achillas (*Giulio Cesare*), Ivan Khovansky (*Khovanshchina*), Boris (*Lady Macbeth of the Mtsensk District*) and the Dutchman. His Glyndebourne roles include the Speaker (*Zauberflöte*), Colline, King of Clubs (*Love for Three Oranges*) and Porgy. At Amsterdam he has sung Oroveso, Banquo, the Forester (*The Cunning Little Vixen*), Prince Gremin, Hector Berlioz's Méphistophélès and Golaud. White made his Covent Garden début in 1980 as Don Diego (*L'Africaine*),

returning for Klingsor, Timur, Fafner and Pizarro; he was also a magnificent Porgy in the first performance of George Gershwin's opera in that theatre (1992). His other roles include Sarastro, Leporello, and Wotan (*Das Rheingold* and *Die Walküre*), which he has sung for Scottish Opera. He took the role of Moses in *Moses und Aron* at Edinburgh (1992) and sang Claggart (*Billy Budd*) in Geneva in 1994. In 2000 he sang in the première of John Adams's nativity oratorio *El Niño* in Paris, later recording the work, and in 2001 made an imposing Marshal Kutuzov in ENO's new production of Sergey Prokofiev's *War and Peace*. Among his recordings are G.F. Handel's Polyphemus, Pluto in Claudio Monteverdi's *Orfeo*, the Ballad Singer (*Gloriana*) and two complete versions of *Porgy and Bess*. A powerful singer with a ripe, resonant voice capable of both mellow lyricism and imposing declamation, he is a superb actor who has played Shakespeare's Othello in the theatre.

M. Loppert: 'Willard White', *Opera*, xl (1989), 18–25

Elizabeth Forbes

Whitefield, Hugh.

See MARTIN, RICCARDO.

Whitehill, Clarence (Eugene)

(*b* Marengo, IA, 5 Nov 1871; *d* New York, 18 Dec 1932). American baritone and bass-baritone. His vocal talent was discovered in Chicago in 1896 by MELBA, who advised him to study in Paris; his teachers there were Giraudet and GIOVANNI SBRIGLIA. He made his début in Brussels in 1898. After performing in Europe and the USA, and further study with Julius Stockhausen in Frankfurt, he undertook engagements in several German cities, studied the Richard Wagner repertory at Bayreuth, appeared there very successfully as Wolfram (1904) and Amfortas (1908), and was also the much applauded Wotan in Hans Richter's English-language Covent Garden *Ring* of 1908 and 1909. In 1904, he sang in the premiere of *Koanga* by Frederick Delius at the Elberfeld Stadtheater. His début with the Metropolitan company (15 November 1909, Brooklyn) as Wolfram, and at the Metropolitan Opera House (25 November 1909) as Amfortas began a long and successful, though not entirely harmonious, association with that house, where his Hans Sachs was particularly admired. His Metropolitan career lasted until 1932, the year of his death. Whitehill was an outstanding singer and artist, notable for beauty of tone and for nobility and dignity of style. The best of his many recordings are the earlier ones, in which he sang his Wagner excerpts in the original German. His 1914 version of Amfortas's Prayer is unsurpassed in its combination of pure line, perfect enunciation and poignant intensity.

F. Williams: 'Clarence Whitehill', *Record Collector*, xxii (1974–5), 221–63 [with discography by W.R. Moran]

Desmond Shawe-Taylor

Wiata, Inia te.

See TE WIATA, INIA.

Widdop, Walter

(*b* Norland, nr Halifax, 19 April 1892; *d* London, 6 Sept 1949). English tenor. He studied with DINH GILLY in London and joined the British National Opera Company in 1923, making his début as Radames at Leeds. He appeared at Covent Garden first as the protagonist in *Siegfried* (1924), his other Wagnerian roles there being Siegmund (1932) and Tristan (1933, 1937, 1938). In 1928 he sang with FRIDA LEIDER in C.W. Gluck's *Armide* and the following year created the role of Bagoas in Eugene Goossens's *Judith*. In 1936 he sang the title role in the British première of Igor Stravinsky's *Oedipus rex*, in a concert performance under Ernest Ansermet. He appeared in in Spain, the Netherlands and Germany; his roles on tour included Tannhäuser and Samson. His operatic repertory included some of the heavier Italian roles, and in oratorio he brought an able technique as well as an ample voice to such music as 'Sound an alarm' in *Judas Maccabaeus*. Making one of his rare postwar appearances, he sang Lohengrin's Farewell at a Promenade concert the night before he died. Records made around 1930 show a firm resonant voice and a virile style, confirming his place among the best heroic tenors of the century.

A.D. Hillier and J. Jarrett: 'Walter Widdop: a Biography and Discography', *Record Advertiser*, iv/2 (1973–4), 2
A. Blyth: 'Koloman von Pataky and Walter Widdop', *Opera*, xl (1989), 288–95 [with discography]

J.B. Steane

Wiedemann, Hermann

(*b* 1879; *d* Vienna, 1 Jan 1944). German baritone. He made his début at Elberfeld in 1904 and sang at Brno and Hamburg until 1914; in 1912 he took part in the première of Ferruccio Busoni's *Die Brautwahl* in Hamburg. He was a member of the Vienna Hofoper

from 1916 (singing in the German-language première of *Jenůfa* in 1918) and appeared at Salzburg until 1941, notably as Faninal, and as Beckmesser in the performances of *Die Meistersinger* conducted by Arturo Toscanini in 1937. At Zoppot (now Sopot), Buenos Aires, Munich and the Berlin Hofoper he was successful as Guglielmo and Alberich, and in Italian opera. His only Covent Garden appearances were in 1913 as Faninal, in the London première of *Der Rosenkavalier*, and in 1938 as Beckmesser.

David Cummings

Wigniolle, Yvonne.

See PRINTEMPS, YVONNE.

Wildbrunn [Wehrenpfennig], Helene

(*b* Vienna, 8 April 1882; *d* Vienna, 10 April 1972). Austrian soprano. She studied with Rosa Papier and Hans Paumgartner in Vienna, where she sang small roles at the Volksoper in 1906. Engaged at Dortmund (1907–14) as a contralto, she sang Ortrud, Fricka, Amneris and Delilah, but at Stuttgart (1914–18) she moved into the soprano repertory, including Leonore, Amelia, Kundry, Isolde and the Marschallin. In 1917, she created the role of Bianca in Alexander Zemlinsky's *Eine florentinische Tragödie* at the Hoftheater, Stuttgart. She was engaged at the Berlin Staatsoper (1918–25), the Vienna Staatsoper (1919–32) and the Berlin Städtische Oper (1926–9), where her Electra was acclaimed by Richard Strauss. She also sang Kundry at La Scala (1922); Brünnhilde, Isolde, Kundry and the Marschallin at Buenos Aires (1922–3); Donna Anna at Salzburg (1925); Leonore at Covent Garden (1927) and Isolde and Brünnhilde (*Die Walküre*) at the Paris Opéra (1928). Recordings of extracts from her major roles show the strength and security of her voice and her dramatic flair.

Leo Riemens/Alan Blyth

Willer, Luise

(*b* Seeshaupt, Bavaria, 1888; *d* Munich, 27 April 1970). German mezzo-soprano. She studied in Munich, where she sang first in the opera chorus. In 1910, on the recommendation of Bruno Walter, she appeared as Annius in *La clemenza di Tito*, and she remained closely associated with the company until her retirement, as Erda in *Siegfried*, in 1955. At Munich, she sang in the première of E.W. Korngold's *Violanta* (1916) as well as in two Hans Pfitzner premières, *Palestrina* (1917) and *Das Herz* (1931). In 1930 she sang Clytemnestra in *Iphigénie en Aulide* at Salzburg, where she reappeared in 1943 as Adelaide in *Arabella*. She also sang widely throughout Germany, and in 1926 and 1931 was at Covent Garden, considered 'extremely fine vocally' as Fricka in *Die Walküre*, her other roles being Brangäne, Erda and Magdalene in *Die Meistersinger*. Her repertory also included Dorabella, Carmen, Azucena and Delilah, and recordings show a good voice skilfully used, with characterful treatment of words.

J.B. Steane

Williams, Harold

(*b* Woollahra, Sydney, 3 Sept 1893; *d* Gordon, Sydney, 5 June 1976). Australian baritone. He came to professional singing after showing outstanding proficiency in sport. After war service in France and Belgium he took lessons with Charles Phillips in London and made that city his base for most of his career. Following his Wigmore Hall début in 1919, he established a reputation primarily as a concert singer in works such as *Elijah*, *The Dream of Gerontius*, *The Kingdom* and Samuel Coleridge-Taylor's *Scenes from 'The Song of Hiawatha'*, being admired particularly for his even and virile tone, incisive enunciation and exemplary phrasing. He sang the principal baritone roles in *Tannhäuser*, *Otello*, *Pagliacci* and other operas at Covent Garden, and sang two bass roles, Boris Godunov and Charles Gounod's Méphistophélès, at Covent Garden and elsewhere. He was one of the 16 soloists for whom Ralph Vaughan Williams wrote his *Serenade to Music* in 1938; he appeared in most Prom seasons from 1921 to 1951, performed as a soloist at the coronations of George VI and Elizabeth II and was associated with the Edinburgh Festival from its beginning in 1947. Williams toured Australia as a soloist in 1929 and 1940–44, taught at the NSW State Conservatorium in Sydney from 1952 (at Eugene Goossens's invitation) and took part, notably as Escamillo, in the postwar Sydney seasons that led to the establishment of a permanent professional opera company. MARGRETA ELKINS was his pupil.

Roger Covell

Wilson, Sir (James) Steuart

(*b* Clifton, 22 July 1889; *d* Petersfield, 18 Dec 1966). English tenor and administrator. He had music lessons from C.B. Rootham at Cambridge University, 1908–11, and in 1911 he sang Ralph Vaughan Williams's *On Wenlock Edge* for the Oxford University Music Club, so pleasing the composer that he wrote his *Four Hymns* for him. War injuries during his army service affected one lung and

permanently damaged his health, but he resumed his singing career in 1918, playing a leading part in the formation of the English Singers. He took further lessons in 1921 from JEAN DE RESZKE, and rapidly went to the forefront of British singers, with special success in *The Dream of Gerontius* and as the Evangelist in the *St Matthew Passion*. He made concert tours in the USA, Canada and Australia, appeared with the British National Opera Company, in W.A. Mozart operas at the Old Vic Theatre, and in the Glastonbury Festival operas by his friend Rutland Boughton. In 1931 he was a leading soloist in the first performance of Sir George Dyson's *The Canterbury Pilgrims* at Winchester. In 1937 he used damages awarded him in a libel action to sponsor the first London production of Boughton's *The Lily Maid*, which he also conducted.

Wilson became well known as a perceptive judge at competitive festivals and, on retiring from active singing, began a new career as an administrator. He taught at the Curtis Institute, Philadelphia (1939–42), and returned to England to become music director for BBC Overseas Services (to 1945), music director of the newly formed Arts Council of Great Britain (from 1945), and in 1948, when he was knighted, director of music for the BBC He moved to Covent Garden as deputy general administrator of the Royal Opera House, 1949–55, and was principal of the Birmingham School of Music, 1957–60, but this was an unhappy episode. From 1954 to 1957 he was president of the International Music Council. With A.H. Fox Strangways, Wilson published numerous translations of lieder; he also made English translations of *The Creation* and Johannes Brahms's *German Requiem*, and contributed many articles to music magazines. On a recording made in 1927 during a performance at the Royal Albert Hall, London, he sings in extracts from *The Dream of Gerontius* conducted by the composer. He also recorded Vaughan Williams's *On Wenlock Edge* and songs by Denis Browne. INIA TE WIATA was his pupil.

M. Stewart: *English Singer* (London, 1970)

Michael Kennedy

Wilson-Johnson, David

(*b* Northampton, 16 Nov 1950). English baritone. He studied at Cambridge and the RAM, where he sang the King in Carl Orff's *Die Kluge*. In 1976 he made his début at Covent Garden in H.W. Henze's *We Come to the River*, returning for roles in *Boris Godunov*, *The Nightingale*, *L'enfant et les sortilèges*, *Die Zauberflöte*, *Madama Butterfly*, *Turandot*, *Werther*, *Roméo et Juliette* and *Billy Budd* and Don Alfonso in *Così fan tutte*; in 1995 he sang the Counsellor and a Fisherman in the première of Alexander Goehr's *Arianna*. He quickly revealed a particular talent for contemporary music and music theatre, singing Choregos in Harrison Birtwistle's *Punch and Judy* (which he sang for his Netherlands Opera début in 1993 and has also recorded), Peter Maxwell Davies's *Eight Songs for a Mad King* in Paris and London (1979) and Blazes in the première of *The Lighthouse* at Edinburgh (1980). Subsequently he has sung Antony in Samuel Barber's *Antony and Cleopatra* (1982, Edinburgh), the title role in the British première of Olivier Messiaen's *St François d'Assise* (1988, Royal Festival Hall), King Fisher in *The Midsummer Marriage* for television, Lev in *The Ice Break* (a role he has recorded) and The Man in Arnold Schoenberg's *Die glückliche Hand*. Wilson-Johnson's other operatic roles include the title role in *Owen Wingrave*, Hobson and Swallow (*Peter Grimes*), Noye in *Noye's Fludde*, Allazim (*Zaide*) and Hector Berlioz's Méphistophélès. He is also a fine singer of oratorios, lieder and English song, and has recorded Bach cantatas, G.F. Handel's *Belshazzar*, Johannes Brahms's *German Requiem* and Franz Schubert's *Winterreise*, in addition to works by, *inter alia*, Hubert Parry, Edward Elgar, William Walton (*Belshazzar's Feast*), Percy Grainger (*Jungle Book*), Igor Stravinsky, Frank Martin and Edmund Rubbra (*Four Medieval Latin Lyrics*). A versatile and intensely musical artist with a robust voice and incisive diction, he brings a vivid sense of character to all his performances.

Elizabeth Forbes

Winbergh, Gösta

(*b* Stockholm, 30 Dec 1943; *d* Vienna, 18 March 2002). Swedish tenor. He studied in Stockholm with ERIK SAEDÉN. After making his début in 1972 at Göteborg as Rodolfo (*La bohème*), he was engaged at the Swedish Royal Opera and gradually developed an international career. He sang at Drottningholm, Aix-en-Provence, Geneva, Salzburg, Florence, San Francisco, Chigago, Houston and Berlin. He sang Belmonte at Glyndebourne (1980), made his Covent Garden début (1982) as Titus, his Metropolitan début (1983) as Don Ottavio, and his Scala début (1985) as Tamino, returning as Idomeneus (1990) and C.W. Gluck's Pylades (1992). His other Mozart roles included Ferrando, and Mithridates, which he sang at Covent Garden (1991). He also sang such parts as Almaviva, Nemorino, the Duke of Mantua, Alfredo, Lensky, Gluck's Admetus and Pylades, David, Faust, Des Grieux (*Manon*) and Sali in *A Village Romeo and Juliet*. (Zürich, 1991). As his light, lyrical voice became more powerful, he

took on heavier Wagner and Strauss roles, including Lohengrin (Zürich, 1991), Walther, which he sang in Berlin and at Covent Garden (1993), the Emperor (*Die Frau ohne Schatten*), Parsifal and Erik, which he sang in Vienna in 1995. Among Winbergh's recordings are several Mozart roles, including a noble, ringing Titus, and an alluring Ernesto in *Don Pasquale*.

Elizabeth Forbes

Windgassen, Wolfgang

(*b* Annemasse, Switzerland, 26 June 1914; *d* Stuttgart, 5 or 8 Sept 1974). German tenor and director. He studied in Stuttgart with his father, the tenor Fritz Windgassen, and Alfons Fischer. In 1941 he made his début at Pforzheim as Don Alvaro (*La forza del destino*). He was a member of the Stuttgart Staatsoper (1945–72), singing first in the Italian repertory and in such parts as Tamino, Max, Hoffmann and Florestan; he then began to prepare Wagnerian roles and in 1950 sang his first Siegmund. In 1951 he sang Parsifal at Bayreuth to acclaim; he appeared there each year until 1970, as Froh, Siegmund, Siegfried, Lohengrin, Tannhäuser, Walther, Erik, Loge and Tristan, establishing himself as the leading postwar Heldentenor. In 1972 he was appointed director of the Stuttgart Staatsoper, where his productions included *Boris Godunov* (1972). He appeared regularly in the Wagnerian repertory at Covent Garden (1955–66). His roles included Adolar (*Euryanthe*), Rienzi, the Emperor (*Die Frau ohne Schatten*) and Otello. He made his American début at the Metropolitan as Siegmund in 1957 and sang Tristan at San Francisco in 1970. Windgassen's musicality and vocal intensity can be heard in his Siegfried on several Bayreuth *Ring* recordings and under Georg Solti, and in his searing Tristan under Karl Böhm.

K. Honolka: 'Wolfgang Windgassen', *Opera*, xiii (1962), 590–95

A. Natan: 'Windgassen, Wolfgang', *Primo uomo* (Basle and Stuttgart, 1963) [with discography]

Harold Rosenthal/Alan Blyth

Winkelmann [Winckelmann], Hermann

(*b* Brunswick, 8 March 1849; *d* Vienna, 18 Jan 1912). German tenor. The son of a piano maker, he studied singing in Paris and Hanover before making his début in *Il trovatore* at Sondershausen in 1875. After appearances at Altenburg, Darmstadt and Leipzig, in 1878 he settled in Hamburg where he took part in the local premières of *Das Rheingold* (as Loge, 1878), *Götterdämmerung*

(1879), Anton Rubinstein's *Néron* (1879) and *Tristan und Isolde* (1882). He sang in London in 1882 with the Hamburg company under Hans Richter at Drury Lane, his roles including Richard Wagner's Lohengrin, Tannhäuser and Tristan. Following Richter's recommendation, Wagner chose Winkelmann to create the role of Parsifal at Bayreuth (26 July 1882). The next year he was engaged by the Vienna Hofoper, where he became the city's first Tristan (on 4 October) and remained a favourite until his retirement in 1906. During this period he continued to sing at Bayreuth, and in 1884 appeared at the Wagner festivals given by Theodore Thomas in New York, Boston, Philadelphia, Cincinnati and Chicago. Apart from Wagner's operas his repertory included C.W. Gluck's *Alceste* and *Armide*, *Fidelio*, Daniel Auber's *La muette de Portici*, Giuseppe Verdi's *Otello*, Heinrich Marschner's *Der Vampyr* and, in 1897, Bedřich Smetana's *Dalibor* under Gustav Mahler's direction. He created the role of Merlin in Karl Goldmark's opera of that name (1886).

Winkelmann was a leading figure in the first generation of Wagner singers, and was coached by the composer. Although he possessed the ample, sonorous voice of a true heroic tenor, his fluid lyrical delivery stood in marked contrast to the declamatory style of many Bayreuth performers during the later era of Cosima Wagner's hegemony.

Wise, Patricia

(*b* Wichita, KS, 31 July 1943). American soprano. She studied in Kansas and New York, making her début in 1966 at Kansas City as Susanna, then joined the New York City Opera and sang the Dying Soul in the US première of Arnold Schoenberg's *Jakobsleiter* at Santa Fe (1968). She made her Covent Garden début as Rosina (1971) and sang her first Zerbinetta at Glyndebourne (1972). She sang regularly in Vienna in such roles as Pamina, Konstanze, Gilda, Zdenka, Sophie, Lucia, Musetta and Juliet; she also appeared at San Francisco, Berlin, La Scala, where she sang Nannetta (1980), and Salzburg, where she sang the Protagonist in the première of Luciano Berio's *Un re in ascolto* (1984). She sang her first Violetta in Minorca in 1991. The great flexibility of voice and security of technique that Wise revealed in such roles as Lucia and Zerbinetta were displayed to even more dazzling effect as Alban Berg's Lulu, which she first sang in Geneva (1985), repeated in Barcelona, Madrid and Paris, and has also recorded. In 1995 she took up a teaching post at Indiana University, Bloomington.

Elizabeth Forbes

Wittich, Marie

(*b* Giessen, 27 May 1868; *d* Dresden, 4 Aug 1931). German soprano. She studied in Würzburg with Otto-Ubridz and reputedly made her début in 1882, at the age of 14, at Magdeburg as Azucena. After engagements at Basle (1883), Düsseldorf and Schwerin (1886), she joined the Dresden Hofoper, where she sang regularly from 1889 to 1914. Her roles included Leonore (*Fidelio*) and Senta; she took part in the première of Ignacy Paderewski's *Manru* (1901) and created Richard Strauss's Salome (1905). She appeared at Bayreuth (1901–9) as Sieglinde, Isolde and Kundry. At Covent Garden (1905–6), where she appeared as Elsa, Elisabeth, Isolde, Sieglinde and Brünnhilde, she failed to justify her considerable German reputation because of ill-health. The power of her voice, vibrant in tone and extremely dramatic in character, allowed her to triumph in roles for which she was physically unsuited, such as Salome.

Harold Rosenthal/R

Wittrisch, Marcel

(*b* Antwerp, 1 Oct 1903; *d* Stuttgart, 3 June 1955). German tenor. Born of German parents, he was brought up in Belgium and studied in Munich, Leipzig and Milan. He made his début in 1925 at Halle in Heinrich Marschner's *Hans Heiling* and joined the company at Brunswick the following year. The Berlin Staatsoper engaged him in 1929 and he remained there as principal lyric tenor until 1944, singing a wide range of roles; he gained a special reputation in W.A. Mozart. At Covent Garden in 1931 his Eisenstein (*Die Fledermaus*) was admired but he was considered somewhat hard and throaty in *Die Zauberflöte*. In the 1930s his repertory widened to include Lohengrin, which he sang at Bayreuth in 1937. After World War II he was heard as Narraboth (*Salome*) in Paris and as Siegmund and Parsifal at Stuttgart, where he continued to appear until his death. He made many concert tours, sang in operetta and films and, above all, made recordings, in which he was often compared to RICHARD TAUBER. Though less individual in style, he was certainly comparable in timbre and less restricted in the upper register.

T. Semrau: 'Marcel Wittrisch', *Record Collector*, xl (1995), 256–322 [with discography]

J.B. Steane

Wixell, Ingvar

(*b* Luleå, 7 May 1931). Swedish baritone. He studied in Stockholm, and made his début there in 1955 as Papageno, remaining a member of the Swedish Royal Opera until 1967. During the company's visit to Covent Garden in 1960 he sang Silvano (*Ballo in maschera*) and Ruggiero (*Alcina*). In 1962 he sang Guglielmo at Glyndebourne and at the Deutsche Oper, Berlin, where he was subsequently engaged. In 1967 he made his US début as Belcore (*L'elisir d'amore*) at San Francisco. In 1971 he first appeared at Bayreuth, as the Herald (*Lohengrin*). His Covent Garden début, as Boccanegra, followed in 1972, and his Metropolitan début, as Rigoletto, in 1973. He was an admired interpreter of most of the major Verdi baritone roles – Amonasro, Don Carlo (*La forza del destino*), Germont, Posa, Renato, Luna and Falstaff (which he sang at Chicago in 1988) – as well as of such parts as Pizarro, Yevgeny Onegin, Mandryka (*Arabella*) and Scarpia, which he sang at Earl's Court, London, in 1991. Wixell's firm, dark-toned voice and powerful stage presence combined to make him a highly dramatic performer. Among his recordings are Count Almaviva, Don Giovanni, Renato and Scarpia, all with Colin Davis.

Elizabeth Forbes

Wixom, Emma.

See NEVADA, EMMA.

Wolff, Fritz

(*b* Munich, 28 Oct 1894; *d* Munich, 18 Jan 1957). German tenor. He studied in Würzburg and made his début as Loge at Bayreuth in 1925, returning regularly until 1941 as Loge, Walther and Parsifal. After engagements in Hagen and Chemnitz, in 1928 he took part in the première of Franz Schreker's *Der singende Teufel* at the Berlin Staatsoper, where he remained until 1943 and, in addition to his Wagner roles, sang the title role in Hans Pfitzner's *Palestrina*. He appeared regularly at Covent Garden (1929–38) in Wagner roles and as Aegisthus (*Elektra*). He also sang in Vienna, Paris, Prague and other European cities, and as Walther in Cleveland (1934–5). His beautiful voice and dignity of bearing admirably suited him to such roles as Lohengrin and Parsifal.

Harold Rosenthal

Wood [née Paton], Mary Anne

(*b* Edinburgh, Oct 1802; *d* Chapelthorpe, nr Wakefield, 21 July 1864). Scottish soprano. As a child she learnt the harp, piano and violin; her singing début was in 1810. She sang in London (1811–13) and Bath (1820), and made her stage début as Susanna in October 1822; in 1824 she sang Agathe in the first English production of *Der Freischütz*. That year she married Lord William Pitt Lennox. In April 1826 she created the role of Reiza in *Oberon*, which established her as a leading singer in London. She divorced Lennox in 1831, and later married the English tenor Joseph Wood. In the midst of her triumphant career in London, they left for the USA; their joint début was in New York (9 September 1833) in Michael Rophino Lacy's *Cinderella* (an adaptation of *La Cenerentola*). On two separate tours, often travelling in small troupes with other singers, they appeared in New York, Boston, Philadelphia and elsewhere (1833–6 and 1840–41), performing a repertory ranging from 18th-century ballad operas to contemporary English adaptations of Italian works. They contributed greatly to a general American interest (begun by Elizabeth Austin) in Italian bel canto melody, in particular by introducing Americans to Vincenzo Bellini's operas (*La sonnambula*, 13 November 1835, and *Norma*, 11 January 1841, both in New York). Mrs Wood, as she was known, was acclaimed as the finest English singer of her day. She had a pure soprano voice that was powerful, sweet-toned, brilliant and of extensive compass (*a* to *d'''/e'''*); she was an effective actress who was renowned for her beauty. In 1843 she and her husband retired to Yorkshire.

Oxford DNB ('Paton, Mary Ann', L.M. Middleton, rev. John Warrack)

'Miss Paton', *Quarterly Musical Magazine and Review*, v (1823), 191–7

J. Wood: *Memoir of Mr. and Mrs. Wood* (New York, 1840)

Katherine K. Preston

Wunderlich, Fritz

(*b* Kusel, Rheinland-Pfalz, 26 Sept 1930; *d* Heidelberg, 17 Sept 1966). German tenor. During his short career Wunderlich was Germany's leading lyric tenor. He studied at the Freiburg Musikhochschule, sang Tamino there in 1954, and was engaged by the Stuttgart Opera in 1955, making his début (apart from some appearances in small parts) in the same role. In 1958 he joined the Frankfurt company, and at the Salzburg Festival in 1959 he sang Henry in Richard Strauss's *Die schweigsame Frau*, conducted by Karl Böhm. In 1960 he joined the Staatsoper in Munich and from 1962 also spent part of the year with the Vienna Staatsoper.

Wunderlich's voice was well formed, clear and firm of timbre; his style was unaffected, manly and sensitive. At the time of his death from a fall, Rodolfo in *La bohème* and Wagnerian roles were on the horizon. His singing of W.A. Mozart was internationally famous: he sang Don Ottavio at Covent Garden in

1965 (his only appearance there), while his ardent, lyrical Tamino and Belmonte can be heard on the recordings with Böhm and Eugen Jochum. In Munich he also undertook such parts as Alfredo and Lensky, and in Vienna the title role in *Palestrina*. He created the role of Tiresias in Carl Orff's *Oedipus der Tyrann* (1959, Stuttgart) and of Christophh in Werner Egk's *Die Verlobung in San Domingo* (1963, Munich). His last appearance was as Tamino during the Stuttgart Opera's visit to the Edinburgh Festival; a Metropolitan début, as Don Ottavio, was planned for October 1966. Wunderlich was also an admired Bach singer, excelling as the Evangelist in both the Passions, and brought a unique sensuousness and youthful fervour to the tenor solos in *Das Lied von der Erde*, as revealed in the famous recording with Otto Klemperer. He came to lieder relatively late in his short career, but was in demand as a recitalist at the Salzburg Festival and elsewhere, and left unaffected, immaculately sung recordings of *Die schöne Müllerin* and *Dichterliebe*.

H. Canning: 'Fritz Wunderlich: Unforgettable, Unforgotten', *Opera*, xli (1990), 1048–55

Andrew Porter/Richard Wigmore

Y

Yakar, Rachel

(*b* Lyons, 3 March 1938). French soprano. She studied at the Paris Conservatoire and with GERMAINE LUBIN, making her début in 1963 at Strasbourg. In 1964 she joined the Deutsche Oper am Rhein, Düsseldorf, which remained her base for over 20 years. She sang Freia and Gerhilde at Bayreuth (1976), Donna Elvira at Glyndebourne (1977), First Lady (*Zauberflöte*) at Salzburg and Claudio Monteverdi's Poppaea in Edinburgh (1978), and made her Covent Garden début as Freia. Her wide repertory included Jean-Philippe Rameau's Aricia, G.F. Handel's Cleopatra, Celia (*Lucio Silla*), Ilia, Fiordiligi, Tatyana, Mimì, Málinka/Etherea/Kunka (*Excursions of Mr Brouček*), and the Marschallin, which she sang at Glyndebourne in 1980. An extremely musical as well as dramatic singer, capable of subtle tone colouring, Yakar was particularly fine in roles such as Mélisande, which she recorded, and Jenůfa. Her other operatic recordings include several Mozart roles, Climène in Jean-Baptiste Lully's *Phaëton* (which she sang in Lyons in 1993), Madame Lidoine in *Dialogues des Carmélites* and Diane in Arthur Honegger's *Les aventures du roi Pausole*. Yakar also had a notable career as a recitalist and concert singer, and has recorded works ranging from J.S. Bach's B minor Mass to *mélodies* by Reynaldo Hahn.

Elizabeth Forbes

Yermolenko-Yuzhina
[Ermolenko-Yushina; Plugovskaya],
Nataliya (Stepanovna)

(*b* Kiev, 1881; *d* after 1924). Russian soprano. She studied in Kiev and Paris and made her début under the name of Yermolenko as Lisa in *The Queen of Spades* at Kiev in 1900. She went to St Petersburg in 1901 and to the Bol'shoy in 1905. There she met the tenor David Yuzhin, whom she married, adding his name to her own professional name. For two seasons both singers joined Sergey Zimin's Private Opera in Moscow. Yermolenko was also among the most admired members of the distinguished company from Russia that performed in Paris in 1908, introducing *Boris Godunov* to the West. From 1915 to 1917 she was with the Mariinsky Theatre opera company, and in 1924 emigrated to Paris, where all traces of her appear to have been lost. She was considered the leading Russian lyric-dramatic soprano of her time, with a repertory that included Brünnhilde, Norma, Violetta and Carmen as well as many Russian operas; among these, one of her greatest successes was in A.N. Serov's *Judith*. Her rare recordings show clearly the impressive volume and quality of her voice and the authority of her style and technique.

J.B. Steane

Yershov [Ershov, Erschoff],
Ivan Vasil'yevich

(*b* Maliy Nesvetay, nr Novocherkassk, 8/20 Nov 1867; *d* Leningrad [now St Petersburg], 21 Nov 1943). Russian tenor. He studied in Moscow and with S.W. Gabel in St Petersburg, where he made his début as Faust in 1893. There followed a period of training in Italy, with performances at Turin and Reggio Emilia. Back in Russia, he sang for a season at Kharkiv, then in 1895 rejoined the Mariinsky at St Petersburg where he remained until 1929. There he became known as 'the Russian TAMAGNO', specializing in heroic parts such as Otello, Florestan and the heroes of Giacomo Meyerbeer's *Les Huguenots* and *Le prophète*, as well as in a comprehensive Wagnerian repertory in which his Tannhäuser was particularly admired. In 1895 he created the role of Vakula in *Christmas Eve* by Nikolay Rimsky-Korsakov, and Orestes in S.I. Taneyev's *Orestaya*. In 1902 he sang Valery in the first performance of Rimsky-Korsakov's *Servilia*, and 1907 he appeared as Grishka Kuter'ma in the première of Rimsky-Korsakov's *Legend of the Invisible City of Kitezh*. In 1911 he created Golitsin in *Khovanshchina*, and in 1926 Truffaldino in the Soviet première of Prokofiev's *Love for three Oranges*. After retirement from opera he continued to sing in concerts and taught at the Leningrad Conservatory until his death. His recordings, rare in original form, show an imaginative artist whose voice was impressive not simply for its volume, range and ringing quality but also for the elegance of its management and its mastery of light and shade.

J.B. Steane

Young.

English family of singers, active in the eighteenth century. Six singers known as 'Miss Young' sang professionally under their maiden names until their marriages and sometimes afterwards. CECILIA, ISABELLA (i) and ESTHER were daughters of Charles Young, organist of All Hallows, Barking. ISABELLA (ii), ELIZABETH and POLLY were daughters of his son Charles, a clerk in the Treasury.

Young [Youngs], (Basil) Alexander

(*b* London, 18 Oct 1920; *d* 5 March 2000). English tenor. He studied at the RCM with Steffan Pollmann and made his début as Scaramuccio (*Ariadne auf Naxos*) at the 1950 Edinburgh Festival. In 1953 he sang Tom Rakewell in the English première of *The Rake's Progress*, a BBC studio production; he recorded his classic reading of this role in 1964 under Igor Stravinsky's direction. He created Charles Darnay in Arthur Benjamin's *A Tale of Two Cities* (1953, BBC) and Philippe in Lennox Berkeley's *A Dinner Engagement* (1954, Aldeburgh), and sang in the British premières of Humphrey Searle's *The Diary of a Madman* (1960, Sadler's Wells) as Poprichin and H.W. Henze's *The Bassarids* (1968, BBC) as Dionysus. He appeared at Covent Garden (1955–70), notably as Matteo (*Arabella*) and Benjamin Britten's Lysander; at Sadler's Wells, where his roles included a highly amusing Count Ory, Almaviva, C.W. Gluck's and Claudio Monteverdi's Orpheus, Belmonte and G.F. Handel's Jupiter and Xerxes; and with the WNO and Scottish Opera, creating Cicero in Iain Hamilton's *The Catiline Conspiracy* (1974, Stirling). He also sang extensively in concert and oratorio, and from 1973 to 1986 was director of singing at the RNCM. Young was a stylish singer with a silvery tenor which he used with innate musicianship, as can be heard in his many recordings of operas and oratorios by Handel.

Harold Rosenthal/Alan Blyth

Young, Cecilia [Mrs Arne]

(*b* London, bap. 7 Feb 1712; *d* London, 6 Oct 1789). English soprano. A pupil of Francesco Geminiani, she sang in concerts from March 1730 and first appeared on stage in English operas by John Frederick Lampe and J.C. Smith in 1732–3. According to Charles Burney, she had 'a good natural voice and a fine shake [and] had been so well taught, that her style of singing was infinitely superior to that of any other English woman of her time'. G.F. Handel chose her for the premières of his *Ariodante* and *Alcina* (both 1735), *Alexander's Feast* (1736) and *Saul* (1739), and for the first London performance of *Athalia*. After marrying Thomas Arne in 1737 she appeared in his

stage works (notably *Comus*, *Rosamond* and *Alfred*) in London and for two seasons in Dublin (1742–4) and performed his songs at Vauxhall Gardens. The marriage proved unhappy and she was often ill, making only occasional appearances after 1746; her last new Arne role was in *Eliza* (1754). In 1748 she went to Dublin with her sister and brother-in-law, the Lampes, to sing in the winter concert season and returned there with Arne in 1755 to perform in his works at Smock Alley Theatre. Here their marriage broke down and Arne went back to London, leaving her in Ireland with her niece POLLY YOUNG, and in 1758 Mrs Delany found her employed as a singing teacher by a charitable Irish family. She returned to London with Polly in 1762 and seems to have made only one more public appearance, at a benefit concert for Polly and her husband, F.H. Barthélemon, in 1774. She was reconciled with Arne shortly before his death in 1778, after which she lived with the Barthélemons. There were suggestions that she could be unreliable and that she drank too much, but Charles Burney, a pupil of Arne's, remembered her with affection, and Charles Dibdin wrote: 'Mrs Arne was deliciously captivating. She knew nothing in singing or in nature but sweetness and simplicity'.

Olive Baldwin and Thelma Wilson

Young, Elizabeth [Mrs Dorman]

(*d* London, 12 April 1773). English contralto. Her aunt was CECILIA YOUNG [Mrs Arne], and Elizabeth went to Dublin with the Arnes in 1755, singing Grideline in Thomas Arne's *Rosamond* at the Smock Alley Theatre. She returned to England with Arne in 1756, and was a shepherdess in his *Eliza* that December. After playing Lucy in *The Beggar's Opera* in June 1758 (billed as making her first appearance on any stage) she sang regularly at Drury Lane until 1772 and in some seasons at Finch's Grotto Gardens. Her lower voice meant she was given male or older women's parts. She created the roles of Agenor in George Rush's *The Royal Shepherd* (1764) and the duenna Ursula in Charles Dibdin's *The Padlock* (1768). She married the violinist Ridley Dorman in 1762.

Olive Baldwin and Thelma Wilson

Young, Esther [Hester] [Mrs Jones]

(*b* London, 14 Feb 1717; *d* London, bur. 6 June 1795). English contralto. She appeared in concerts from 1736 and created the role of Mauxalinda in John Frederick Lampe's *The Dragon of Wantley*. She had other Lampe roles, played Lucy in John Gay's *The Beggar's Opera* for many years and in 1744 sang Juno and Ino in the première of G.F. Handel's *Semele*. It is sometimes stated that she went to Ireland with the Arnes in 1755, but in fact she sang at Covent Garden throughout the 1755–6 season and in every year after that until her retirement in 1776. She married the music seller and publisher Charles Jones on 8 April 1762; by December 1785, a few years after his death, impoverished and seriously ill, she was being cared for with 'unremitting Tenderness' by her sister Mrs Lampe (ISABELLA YOUNG (i)).

Olive Baldwin and Thelma Wilson

Young, Isabella (i) [Mrs Lampe]

(*b* London, ?bap. 3 Jan 1716; *d* London, 5 Jan 1795). English soprano. She had small singing roles at Drury Lane in 1733–4 but otherwise appeared only in concerts until she sang the heroine Margery in John Frederick Lampe's burlesque opera *The Dragon of Wantley* in 1737. In the middle of its long run she married the composer and subsequently created roles in all his stage works, including Thisbe in *Pyramus and Thisbe* (1745). The Lampes went to Dublin in 1748, and she appeared for two seasons at the Smock Alley Theatre and sang in concerts and at the Marlborough Green pleasure gardens. In November 1750 they went to Edinburgh and, according to Charles Burney, were soon 'settled very much to the satisfaction of the patrons of Music in that city'. However, Lampe died there of a fever in July 1751, and she returned to Covent Garden to sing her old roles and some new ones in musical afterpieces. She remained in the company until the 1775–6 season, often singing with her sister ESTHER YOUNG, although in the later years they were only members of the chorus. Her son Charles John Frederick Lampe took over as organist at All Hallows, Barking-by-the-Tower, after the death of his grandfather Charles Young, and her daughter-in-law sang for a time as Mrs Lampe at the pleasure gardens and Sadler's Wells Theatre.

Olive Baldwin and Thelma Wilson

Young, Isabella (ii) [Mrs Scott]

(*d* London, 17 Aug 1791). English mezzo-soprano. She studied with the bass GUSTAVUS WALTZ, first appearing in a concert with him on 18 March 1751, and sang in Thomas Arne's *Alfred*, *Rosamond* and *Eliza* in 1754. She became a distinguished concert and oratorio singer in London and the provincial festivals. She sang for G.F. Handel in the last few years of the composer's life and was Counsel (Truth) in the first performance of *The Triumph of Time and Truth* in March 1757. She was a soloist in the *Messiah* performances at the Foundling Hospital on a number of occasions. After appearing at Drury Lane as Titania in J.C. Smith's opera *The Fairies* (February 1755), she performed there regularly until 1777, singing between the acts, in musical interludes and afterpieces. She created roles in George Rush's English operas *The Royal Shepherd* and *The Capricious Lovers*. After her marriage to the Hon. John Scott (December 1757) she usually sang in concerts and oratorios as Mrs Scott, but on stage she continued to describe herself as Miss Young until 1769.

Olive Baldwin and Thelma Wilson

Young, Polly [Mary, Maria] [Mrs Barthélemon]

(*b* London, 7 July 1749; *d* London, 20 Sept 1799). English soprano, composer and keyboard player. She went with the Arnes to Ireland and impressed audiences in Dublin by singing 'perfectly in Time and Tune' in Thomas Arne's *Eliza* at the age of six. She remained in Ireland with Mrs Arne (CECILIA YOUNG) and in 1758, after hearing her play the harpsichord, Mrs Delany wrote: 'the race of Youngs are *born* songsters and musicians'. She appeared on stage in Dublin, where John O'Keeffe admired her 'charming face and small figure' as Ariel in *The Tempest*. She returned to London to make her Covent Garden début in September 1762, singing and playing between the acts; the *Theatrical Review* commented on the agreeable innocence of her appearance: 'Her performance on the harpsichord, is equal to her excellence in singing'. After two seasons she moved to sing minor roles with the Italian opera company at the King's Theatre, where the violinist and composer François Hippolyte Barthélemon was leader of the orchestra. She married him in December 1766 and afterwards appeared mainly with him, in occasional seasons at the Italian opera, in oratorios and at the pleasure gardens. There were visits to Ireland, and a highly successful tour of the Continent in 1776–7. She sang in her husband's oratorio *Jefte* in Florence and gave concerts before the Queen of Naples and Marie Antoinette, at which their young daughter Cecilia Maria also sang. However, their careers did not flourish after this; in an injudicious letter (*Morning Post*, 2 November 1784) she complained of being refused engagements, styling herself 'an English Woman, of an unblemished reputation'. Joseph Haydn visited the Barthélemons when he was in England, and at a concert in May 1792 he accompanied her in airs by G.F. Handel and Antonio Sacchini.

Olive Baldwin and Thelma Wilson

Z

Zabela(-Vrubel), Nadeshda [Nadezhda]

(*b* Kaunas, 1 April 1868; *d* St Petersburg, 21 June/4 July 1913). Lithuanian soprano. She studied at St Petersburg and made her début in 1893 at Kiev, then sang at Tbilisi and St Petersburg. She was engaged by the Mamontov opera company, Moscow (1897–1904), where she sang in many of the first performances of Nikolay Rimsky-Korsakov's operas, including the part of Marfa in *The Tsar's Bride* (1899); the Swan Princess in *The Tale of Tsar Saltan* (1900) and as the Princess in *Kashchey the Deathless* (1902). An engagement at the Bol'shoy (1904–11) followed. Her roles included Micaëla, Nedda, Desdemona, Marguerite, Elsa and Elisabeth, as well as Tatyana, Rimsky-Korsakov's Volkova (*Sadko*), and Snow Maiden. In 1907 she sang the part of Sirin in the première of that composer's *Legend of the Invisible City of Kitezh* at the Mariinsky Theatre, St Petersburg. In 1908 she sang the Queen of Shemakha's Hymn to the Sun (from *The Golden Cockerel*) in concert; the opera was only partly performed during Rimsky-Korsakov's lifetime. Married to the painter Mikhail Vrubel, a stage designer for the Mamontov company, she had a full, vibrant voice that was particularly suited to Russian music.

Elizabeth Forbes

Zaccaria, Nicola (Angelo)

(*b* Piraeus, 9 March 1923; *d* Athens, 24 July 2007). Greek bass. He studied in Athens, where he made his début in 1949 as Raimondo in *Lucia di Lammermoor*. In 1953 he first sang at La Scala, as Sparafucile (*Rigoletto*). He continued to sing regularly at La Scala in the Italian bass repertory, and took part there in the first Milan performances of Darius Milhaud's *David*, and created the Third Tempter in the première of Ildebrando Pizzetti's *Assassinio nella cattedrale* (1958). He sang at Rome (from 1956) and Vienna, and at Covent Garden in 1957 as Oroveso (*Norma*) and in 1959 as Creon (*Médée*), on both occasions opposite CALLAS. He first sang at the Salzburg Festival in 1957, as Don Fernando in *Fidelio*, and returned as the Monk (*Don Carlos*), the Commendatore and Ferrando (*Il trovatore*). Zaccaria also appeared regularly with the Dallas Civic Opera, where in March 1976 he sang his first King Mark. In 1982 he sang Colline at Macerata. His mellow, well-produced voice, enhanced by his intelligence and discretion, is to be heard in the bass roles of operas recorded by Callas, most notably as Rodolfo (*La sonnambula*), Oroveso, Sparafucile and Colline. He was also a noted soloist in Ludwig van Beethoven's *Missa solemnis* and Giuseppe Verdi's Requiem, both of which he recorded.

Harold Rosenthal/Alan Blyth

Zadek, Hilde

(*b* Bromberg [now Bydgoszcz], 15 Dec 1917). German soprano. A refugee from Nazi Germany in 1934, she went to Palestine and worked as a nurse in Jerusalem; she studied singing there with Rose Pauly and, from 1945, in Zürich with Ria Ginster. Her début as Aida at the Vienna Staatsoper in 1947 began her international career. She sang in the première of *Antigonae* (Carl Orff) at the 1949 Salzburg Festival, and the next year made her British début at the Edinburgh Festival with the Glyndebourne Opera under Thomas Beecham as Ariadne in Richard Strauss's first version of the opera. Later that year she sang at Covent Garden as Aida, Tosca and Lisa in quick succession, and during the early 1950s she was engaged at the Colón, Buenos Aires, the Metropolitan and San Francisco as well as in major European centres. A dark-toned and deeply musical dramatic soprano, she recorded a notable Donna Anna under Rudolf Moralt (1955). From 1967 she taught at the Vienna Music Academy.

Noël Goodwin

Zádor, Deszö [Desider, Desidery]

(*b* Horna Krupa, 8 March 1873; *d* Berlin, 24 April 1931). Hungarian baritone. He studied in Budapest with Adele Passy-Cornet and made his début at Czernowitz (now Chernovtsy) in 1898, as Count Almaviva in *Figaro*. In 1907 he created the part of the Dark Fiddler in *A Villiage Romeo and Juliet* (Berlin, Komische Oper). He sang at Elberfeld, Prague and the Komische Oper, Berlin, until 1911, appearing at Dresden from 1911 to 1916. Between 1906 and 1910 he was heard at Covent Garden as Alberich in the *Ring* cycles conducted by Hans Richter, and as the Father in *Hänsel und Gretel*. He conducted as well as sang at the Budapest National Opera (1916–19) and appeared in North America with the German Opera Company (1922–4). In 1918 he produced the first performance of Béla Bartók's *Bluebeard's Castle* (Budapest, Opera). Further engagements took him to Paris, Milan, Vienna and the Richard Wagner festival at Zoppot (now Sopot). In 1908 he recorded Valentin's music in *Faust*.

David Cummings

Zajick, Dolora

(*b* Salem, OR, 24 March 1952). American mezzo-soprano. She studied at the University of Nevada as a pupil of Theodore Pufferand and then at the Manhattan School of Music with Helen Vanni and Lou Gualtiero. With the Nevada Opera she sang first in the chorus, then in secondary roles such as Kate Pinkerton in *Madama Butterfly*. In 1982 she won third prize at the Tchaikovsky Competition in Moscow, and the following year the Merola Prize in San Francisco. It was there, in 1986, that she made her début in a major role, as Azucena in *Il trovatore*. From this point her career developed successfully in both Europe and America, where she became one of the leading mezzo-sopranos of her generation. Her special field has been the Giuseppe Verdi repertory. Milan, Naples, London and Paris heard her in the *Requiem*, she made her Italian début at the Caracalla Baths, Rome, as Amneris in *Aida* in 1988 (a role she subsequently repeated at Covent Garden), and later that year she appeared at the Metropolitan as Azucena, Amneris and Ulrica (*Un ballo in maschera*). Zajick sang at the Vienna Staatsoper in 1989, and at the Maggio Musicale in Florence in 1990. Other roles have included Adalgisa in *Norma*, Léonor in *La favorite*, P.I. Tchaikovsky's Joan of Arc (sung first in concert version at Carnegie Hall) and Marfa in *Khovanshchina* (1990, San Francisco). In 1998 she won special acclaim for her Eboli in *Don Carlos* at the Paris Opéra and in 2000 scored a similar success as Azucena at the Metropolitan. Her recordings, many of them with James Levine, include the Verdi roles for which she is best known. They show a voice of ample range and power, most remarkable in the full-bodied high notes and the incisive quality of her chest tones. Her singing of the Veil Song in *Don Carlos* shows her to be capable of delicacy, and, in a very different field, her ability to characterize is well brought out by her performance as the witch Ježibaba in a recording of Antonín Dvořák's *Rusalka* under Charles Mackerras.

H. Matheopoulos: *Diva: the New Generation* (London, 1998), 332–54

J.B. Steane

Žák, Benedikt.

See SCHACK, BENEDIKT.

Zamboni, Luigi

(*b* Bologna, 1767; *d* Florence, 28 Feb 1837). Italian bass-baritone. He made his début in 1791 at Bologna in Domenico Cimarosa's *Il fanatico burlato*. He sang in Naples, Venice, Parma, at La Scala and at the Teatro Argentina, Rome, where in 1816 he created Figaro in *Il barbiere di Siviglia*, a role that Gioachino Rossini, whose father was a family friend, had written specially for him. For two seasons from 1829 he directed an Italian company at St Petersburg, performing 19 Rossini operas (and other works) in Italian, with recitatives intact.

Elizabeth Forbes

Zamboni, Maria

(*b* Peschiera, 25 July 1895; *d* Verona, 25 March 1976). Italian soprano. She studied at the Parma Conservatory and in Milan. Following her début in 1921 as Marguerite in *Faust* at Piacenza, she sang in many leading Italian houses, including La Scala from 1924 to 1931, missing only the 1928 season. In 1926 she sang Liù in the première of *Turandot* under Arturo Toscanini, and in 1930 created the part of Maria in Ildebrando Pizzetti's *Lo straniero*. She was also a favourite in South America. Her repertory included the roles of Elsa and Eva, Desdemona, and Manon in the operas of both Jules Massenet and Giacomo Puccini. The latter she recorded complete in 1930. She retired in 1936, shortly after appearing at the S Carlo, Naples, in her original role of Liù and in the title role of Mario Persico's *Morenita*. As heard on records, her vibrato is too prominent for comfort, but she sings with lively temperament and characterizes vividly.

J.B. Steane

Zampieri, Mara

(*b* Padua, 24 May 1941). Italian soprano. She studied in Padua and made her début in 1972 at Pavia as Nedda. After singing at various Italian houses, in 1978 she appeared at La Scala in three Verdi roles: Elisabeth de Valois (*Don Carlos*), Amelia (*Un ballo in maschera*) and Amalia (*I masnadieri*). Having made her British début in 1983 at Newcastle as Tosca, she sang the role at Covent Garden a year later. She has appeared in Zürich, Berlin, Hamburg, Munich, Bonn, Vienna, Frankfurt, Hanover and Lisbon. Her repertory also includes Donizetti's 'Tudor trilogy': Anne Boleyn, Maria Stuart and Elizabeth (*Roberto Devereux*), Norma, Maddalena (*Andrea Chénier*), Riccardo Zandonai's Francesca, Giacomo Puccini's Minnie and Manon Lescaut and Katerina Izmaylova, which she sang at La Scala in 1992. Giuseppe Verdi's

Lady Macbeth (which she has recorded memorably with Giuseppe Sinopoli), Odabella (*Attila*), Elvira (*Ernani*), Leonora (*Il trovatore*), Aida and Amelia (*Simon Boccanegra*) are among her finest roles. The dramatic intensity of Zampieri's performances and the magnetism of her appearance compensate for a slightly raw edge to her tone.

Elizabeth Forbes

Zancanaro, Giorgio

(*b* Verona, 9 May 1939). Italian baritone. He studied in Verona and after winning the 1970 Voci Verdiane competition made his début at the Teatro Nuovo, Milan, as Riccardo (*I puritani*). He appeared at Parma, Bologna, Florence and Venice, then launched an international career singing Luna at Hamburg (1977). He has appeared in Vienna, Munich, Zürich, Paris, Frankfurt and Lisbon. He made his Covent Garden début in 1978 as Miller (*Luisa Miller*), returning as Enrico Ashton, Escamillo, Posa, Gérard (*Andrea Chénier*), Ezio (*Attila*) and Anckarstroem (*Un ballo in maschera*). He sang Ford at La Scala (1981), and made his Metropolitan début (1982) as Anckarstroem, subsequently appearing there as Luna. His repertory also includes Enrico Ashton, Escamillo, Albert (*Werther*), Scarpia and many Verdi roles, notably Nabucco, Macbeth, Ezio (*Attila*), Germont, Posa and Iago, which he sang at Verona in 1994. His many recordings include Luna, Carlo (*La forza del destino*), Germont, Rigoletto, Montfort (*Les vêpres siciliennes*), William Tell (which he performed at La Scala in 1988), and Scarpia. Zancanaro has a powerful voice, particularly strong in the upper register, and though not a particularly subtle artist, he can portray a character on stage with impressive conviction.

Elizabeth Forbes

Zanelli (Morales), Renato

(*b* Valparaiso, 1 April 1892; *d* Santiago, 25 March 1935). Chilean baritone, later tenor. He studied in Santiago as a baritone and made his début there in 1916 as Valentin (*Faust*). He was engaged by the Metropolitan in 1919, making his début as Amonasro. In 1923 he went to Italy and was advised to change his voice to tenor; after a year's intensive study he made his tenor début at Naples as Raoul (*Les Huguenots*), following it with Alfredo (*La traviata*) and other lyric parts. He became a noted exponent of dramatic roles; in 1926 he sang Otello for the first time in Turin, following it with Lohengrin. In 1928 he made his Covent Garden début as Otello, an interpretation of historic power. In the next few

years he became the leading Wagnerian tenor in Italy and sang Tristan, Lohengrin and Siegmund. In 1930 he created the leading tenor role in Ildebrando Pizzetti's *Lo straniero* in Rome. Extracts of his Otello on disc confirm his power in the role; other recordings, made early in his career, show his beauty of tone and line as a baritone.

R. Saavedra and W.R. Moran: 'Renato Zanelli', *Record Collector*, vii (1952), 197–207 [with discography]
J.B. Steane: *Singers of the Century* (London, 1996), 51–5

Harold Rosenthal/Alan Blyth

Zaremba, Eléna

(*b* Moscow, 10 July 1957). Russian mezzo-soprano. Born into a family of singers, she joined the Bol'shoy Opera in 1984 upon graduating from the Gnesin State Institute in Moscow. She made her Western début on the 1989 Bol'shoy tour to La Scala, singing Vanya in *A Life for the Tsar*. Her repertory then was dominated by a typical mixture of Russian roles, ranging from Laura (*The Stone Guest*) and the Innkeeper (*Boris Godunov*) to Olga (*Yevgeny Onegin*) and Amelfa (*The Golden Cockerel*), and Western ones, including Cherubino and Lola (*Cavalleria rusticana*). Her first Western engagement was as Konchakovna (*Prince Igor*) at Covent Garden in 1990 (recorded on video), and other débuts followed: New York (Bol'shoy at the Metropolitan, 1991), Vienna Staatsoper (Ulrica, 1992) and Bregenz (Carmen, 1992). In 1991 she sang in the world première of Nicolas Slonimsky's *Master i Margarita* in Moscow. Since moving to the West, Zaremba has widened her repertory to include such roles as Dalila, which she has sung regularly. She has recorded Richard Wagner's Erda with Christoph von Dohnányi, although most of her recordings, which range from Nikolay Rimsky-Korsakov's *Christmas Eve* to songs by Dmitry Shostakovich, are of Russian music. Her statuesque voice has a contralto-like richness.

John Allison

Zazzerino.

See PERI, JACOPO.

Zbruyeva, Yevgeniya (Ivanova)

(*b* Moscow, 24 or 26 Dec 1867/5 or 7 Jan 1868; *d* Moscow, 20 Oct 1936). Russian contralto. She was the daughter of the singer and composer Pyotr Bulakhov. She graduated from LAVROVSKAYA's class at the Moscow Conservatory in 1893 and joined the Bol'shoy the following year. In 1905 she joined the

Mariinsky Theatre in St Petersburg and taught at the conservatory (1915–17). Zbruyeva's voice was deep, rich and smooth, powerful and beautiful throughout its wide range. Her clear diction, precise intonation and keen, subtle phrasing made her a finished performer. Her great roles were M.I. Glinka's Vanya and Ratmir, and Marfa in *Khovanshchina* (which she sang at the 1911 Mariinsky première), but she was also extraordinarily successful in such character parts as Solokha (Nikolay Rimsky-Korsakov's *Christmas Eve*) and the Innkeeper (*Boris*); she created the role of Alkonost in Rimsky-Korsakov's *Legend of the Invisible City of Kitezh* (1907). Her memoirs are published in the collection *Muzikal'noye nasledstvo* ('Musical heritage', i, Moscow, 1962).

I.M. Yampol'sky

Zeani [Zehan], Virginia

(*b* Solovastru, 21 Oct 1925). Italian soprano of Romanian birth. After studying with LIPKOWSKA in Bucharest and with PERTILE in Milan, she made her début at Bologna in 1948 as Violetta, which she also sang at her London (1953, Stoll Theatre), Vienna (1957), Paris (1957), Metropolitan (1966) and Bol'shoy (1969) débuts and at Covent Garden (1959). She made her Scala début in 1956 as G.F. Handel's Cleopatra opposite NICOLA ROSSI-LEMENI (whom she married) as Julius Caesar. In 1957 she created Blanche in *Dialogues des Carmélites* at La Scala. She participated in important revivals of *Maria di Rohan* (1965, Naples), Gioachino Rossini's *Otello* (1968, Rome) and Giuseppe Verdi's *Alzira* (1970, Rome). Originally a specialist in coloratura parts including Lucia, Elvira (*I puritani*) and Adèle (*Le comte Ory*), she began in 1970 to undertake more dramatic roles, notably Aida, Manon Lescaut, Tosca, Magda Sorel (*The Consul*) and Umberto Giordano's Fedora (1977–8, Barcelona). Zeani had a naturally beautiful voice, and performed with great dramatic conviction; among her recordings she is best represented by her intense, involving Violetta. After retirement from the stage she taught in the USA, at Bloomington, Indiana, and Urbana-Champaign, Illinois.

Harold Rosenthal/Alan Blyth/R

Zednik, Heinz

(*b* Vienna, 21 Feb 1940). Austrian tenor. After studying in Vienna, he made his début in 1964 at Graz as Trabuco (*Forza*). Engaged at the Vienna Staatsoper for more than 30 years, he created Kalb in Gottfried von Einem's *Kabale und Liebe* (1976). He sang David, Mime and Loge at Bayreuth (1970–80) and made

his Metropolitan début in 1981 as Mime and Loge. He sang at Frankfurt, Zürich and Salzburg, where he created the Producer in Luciano Berio's *Un re in ascolto* (1984), repeating it at La Scala (1986). He also took part in the premières of Ernst Krenek's *Kehraus um St Stephan* at the Ronacher, Vienna (1990), and Alfred Schnittke's *Gesualdo* at the Vienna Staatsoper (1995). An excellent character actor with a strong voice, he had a repertory of some 140 roles, ranging from Monostatos, Pedrillo and Jaquino to Vašek, Remendado, Valzacchi, Herod and the Captain (*Wozzeck*). He made many recordings, including Pedrillo, Monostatos, the Captain and such vivid cameos as the Shabby Peasant (*Lady Macbeth of the Mtsensk District*), a Drunken Cossack (*Mazeppa*) and the spoken role of Njegus (*Die lustige Witwe*).

Elizabeth Forbes

Zenatello, Giovanni

(*b* Verona, 22 Feb 1876; *d* New York, 11 Feb 1949). Italian tenor. He studied as a baritone at Verona with Zannoni and made his début at Belluno in 1898 as Silvio in *Pagliacci*; the next year, at the Mercadante, Naples, he sang Canio in the same opera. He continued his studies with F. Moretti in Milan and, after a period in minor theatres, he appeared at Lisbon (1902) and during the 1902–3 season at La Scala (*La damnation de Faust* and *Un ballo in maschera*). He sang at La Scala frequently until 1907, taking the leading tenor roles in many premières there, notably of Umberto Giordano's *Siberia* (1903), *Madama Butterfly* (1904) and Francesco Cilea's *Gloria* (1907). He was often engaged in South America, notably at Buenos Aires (1903, 1905 in the title role of Giacomo Puccini's definitive version of *Edgar*, and 1910), and was first heard at Covent Garden in 1905 as Riccardo, returning until 1909 and again in 1926 (as Otello). He made his New York début in 1907 at the Manhattan Opera House, where he sang regularly until 1910; during the next few years he worked mainly at the Boston Opera (1910–14 and 1915–17). He married the mezzo-soprano MARÍA GAY in 1913. After retiring from the stage in the 1928–9 season he directed a school of singing in New York (among the pupils was LILY PONS), and for several seasons he was manager of the Verona Arena, where he had inaugurated the opera performances as Radames (1913). Among his qualities were a warm and resonant baritonal timbre, and a clear, easily produced top register. A vigorous and passionate interpreter of Don José, Canio and Puccini's Des Grieux, he was also much admired in Giuseppe Verdi (especially as Radames and Otello), although his style sometimes showed the coarsening influence of *verismo*.

Giovanni Zenatello [second from the right] as Faust with, from left, Manfredi as Marthe, Fyodor Chaliapin as Méphistophélès, and Rosina Storchio as Marguerite, in an Italian production of 'Faust' (Gounod), 1904

T. Hutchinson and C.W. Williams: 'Giovanni Zenatello', *Record Collector*, xiv (1961–2), 100–43, 170–71; xv (1963–4), 18–20 [with discography]

Rodolfo Celletti/Valeria Pregliasco Gualerzi/R

Zerr, Anna

(*b* Baden-Baden, 26 July 1822; *d* Winterbach, 14 Dec 1881). German soprano. She studied in Paris and made her début in 1839 in Karlsruhe as Amina (*La sonnambula*). In 1846 she was engaged at the Vienna Hofoper, making her début as Lucia and creating the title role of Friedrich Flotow's *Martha* (1847). Dismissed from Vienna in 1848 for announcing her intention of singing in a concert for Hungarian refugees in London, she sang at Covent Garden as the Queen of Night (1851), Röschen in Louis Spohr's *Faust* and Catherine in Adolphe Jullien's *Pietro il grande* (1852). She retired in 1858.

Elizabeth Forbes

Ziak, Benedikt.

See SCHACK, BENEDIKT.

Žídek, Ivo

(*b* Kravaře, nr Opava, 4 June 1926; *d* 19 May 2003). Czech tenor. He studied in Ostrava, where he made his début as Werther (1944), then joined the Prague Opera in 1948, his roles including Tamino, Don Carlos, Siegmund, Hoffmann, Tom Rakewell and Peter Grimes. Many of his greatest successes were in Leoš Janáček operas, most notably as Gregor in *The Makropulos Affair*, Števa and Laca in *Jenůfa* and Skuratov in *From the House of the Dead*. In 1966 he sang the Inventor in the première of Václav Kašlík's *Krakatit*. He also appeared in Vienna, Wexford, Germany, South America and at the Edinburgh Festival (1964 and 1970 as Dalibor and as Mazal in the British première of Janáček's *The Excursions of Mr Brouček*). Though occasionally reported as sounding strained or coarse, he was widely acclaimed for the commanding style of his acting and the clear-cut intensity of his singing. Recordings include ardent performances as Jeník in *The Bartered Bride*, Števa in *Jenůfa* and Michel in Bohuslav Martinů's *Julietta*. He became Intendant of the Prague National Opera in 1989.

J.B. Steane

Ziesak, Ruth

(*b* Hofheim am Taunus, 9 Feb 1963). German soprano. She studied with CHRISTOPH PRÉGARDIEN at the Musikhochschule in Frankfurt and with Elsa Cavelti. She made her début as Valencienne in *Die lustige Witwe* in Heidelberg in 1988, and then worked at the Deutsche Oper am Rhein (1990–91). Her first international engagement was as Pamina with Georg Solti at the 1991 Salzburg Festival. She later sang the role at La Scala, the Staatsoper in Munich, Dresden's Sächsische Staatsoper and the Vienna Staatsoper. She made her début at the Opéra Bastille in Paris as Susanna in 1993, followed by Sophie in 1998, and first appeared at Covent Garden in 1997 as Ighino (*Palestrina*). Her other roles include Ilia, Aenchen (*Der Freischütz*) and Countess Almaviva, which she sang to acclaim at Glyndebourne and in Zürich in 2003. Ziesak is also an accomplished soloist in concert works; she won first prize at the lieder competition at 's-Hertogenbosch, and following her Viennese recital début in 1991 has gained a reputation as a discerning interpreter of lieder. Among her many recordings, those of Pamina for Georg Solti, Marzelline for Christoph von Dohnányi, Aennchen for Marek Janowski, Gretel for Donald Runnicles, the title role of Robert Schumann's *Genoveva* for Nikolaus Harnoncourt and Hugo Wolf's *Italienisches Liederbuch* reveal her pure tone and fresh, unaffected style.

Alan Blyth/R

Ziliani, Alessandro

(*b* Bussetto, 3 June 1906; *d* Milan, 18 Feb 1977). Italian tenor. He studied with Alfredo Cechi in Milan and in 1928 made his début there at the Dal Verme in *Madama Butterfly*. At Rome he sang in the première of Ermanno Wolf-Ferrari's *La vedova scaltra* (1931) and Pietro Mascagni's *Pinotta* (1932). In that year he also made his début at La Scala, where he continued to appear until 1946. His roles there included Dmitry in *Boris Godunov*, Enzo in *La Gioconda* and Des Grieux in *Manon Lescaut*, in which he was widely considered to be the best of his generation. He made guest appearances at San Francisco in 1938 and travelled extensively in Europe. When Ferruccio Busoni's *Turandot* had its Italian première in 1940 he sang the role of Calaf. He also appeared with MARIA CALLAS in the revival of Gioachino Rossini's *Armida* at the Florence Festival of 1952. In later years he turned to operetta, films and concert work; he then established himself as an agent, promoting, among others, the career of LUCIANO PAVAROTTI. His recordings include the part of Alfredo in the first electrical recording of *La traviata* and display a resonant lyric voice and pleasing style.

J.B. Steane

Zilli, Emma

(*b* Fagnano, Udine, 11 Nov 1864; *d* Havana, Jan 1901). Italian soprano. She made her début in 1887 at Ferrara as Paolina (*Poliuto*) and in 1889 first sang at La Scala as Camille (*Zampa*). There she created Alice Ford in Giuseppe Verdi's *Falstaff* (1893), repeating the role at Covent Garden in the British première of the opera (1894). She also created the title role in Isaac Albéniz's *Pepita Jiménez* (5 Jan 1896, Barcelona). A powerful singing actress, she was partial to such roles as Giacomo Puccini's Manon Lescaut and Fidelia (*Edgar*). She contracted yellow fever while touring South America and died at the height of her career.

Elizabeth Forbes/R

Zítek, Vilém

(*b* Prague, 9 Sept 1890; *d* Prague, 11 Aug 1956). Czech bass. He was apprenticed and worked as a mechanic; at 18 he joined a choral society, then entered František Pivoda's School of Singing as a pupil of Alois Vávra (1909–11). In 1912 he joined the Prague National Theatre, at first in small parts; he also performed in plays and ballets. In the 1920s and 30s he was the company's leading member and was given many opportunities by Otakar Ostrčil, then head of opera, with whom Zítek maintained a close friendship and who greatly valued him as an artist. Zítek studied with Giovanni Binetti in Milan in 1925 and then took short engagements in Turin, Copenhagen, Milan, Stockholm, Paris, Berlin, Florence, Yugoslavia and the USSR. He was the first Czech singer to be made National Artist (1946); his career was cut short by a heart attack in 1947.

Zítek had a sonorous, perfectly controlled voice of wide compass and with rich possibilities of expression and timbre, an outstanding ability as an actor (acquired by studying the great Czech actor, Eduard Vojan) and a highly developed feeling for the heroic. Among the most remarkable of his dramatic roles were Vodník in *Rusalka* (Antonín Dvořák), Kecal in *The Bartered Bride*, the Devil in *The Devil's Wall* and Chrudoš in *Libuše* (by Bedřich Smetana), Boris Godunov, W.A. Mozart's Figaro, Don Giovanni, Pizarro, Don Quichotte and Philip II in *Don Carlos*. He created the role of Sacristan in Leoš Janáček's *The Excursions of Mr Brouček* (1920). His performances were often compared with

CHALIAPIN's, whom as a singing-actor he much resembled.

Alena Němcová/R

Zottmayr, Ludwig

(*b* Amberg, Bavaria, 31 March 1828; *d* Weimar, 16 Oct 1899). German bass-baritone. He made his début in 1855 at Nuremberg and was then engaged at Hamburg, Hanover and, in 1865, at the Munich Hofoper, where he remained until 1880. He sang King Mark in the first performance of *Tristan und Isolde* (1865), and his repertory included W.A. Mozart's Figaro, Don Giovanni, Hans Heiling, William Tell and Luna, as well as bass and baritone Wagner roles.

Elizabeth Forbes

Zschiesche, August

(*b* Berlin, 29 March 1800; *d* Berlin, 7 July 1876). German bass. He sang in the children's chorus of the Berlin Hofoper, then in the regular chorus and in 1819 took on small parts there. After an engagement in Budapest, in 1826 he joined the Königstädtisches Theater, Berlin, making his début as Gaveston (*La dame blanche*). In 1829 he returned to the Hofoper as Mafaru in Peter Winter's *Das unterbrochene Opferfest* and remained there for the rest of his career. He created Falstaff in *Die lustigen Weiber von Windsor* (1849) and sang a wide variety of roles, including Sarastro, Osmin, Rocco, the High Priest in *Fernand Cortez* and Pontifex Maximus in *La vestale*. He retired in 1861, 52 years after his first stage appearance.

Elizabeth Forbes

Zylis-Gara, Teresa

(*b* Landvarov, nr Vilnius, 23 Jan 1935). Polish soprano. She studied at Łódz and made her début in 1957 at Kraków as Halka. After winning the 1960 Munich radio prize she sang at Oberhausen, Dortmund (1962) and Düsseldorf (1965–70). She appeared as Octavian at Glyndebourne (1965), made her Covent Garden début in 1968 as Violetta, then sang Countess Almaviva, Donna Elvira and Desdemona, a role she took to La Scala in 1977. She made her Metropolitan début in 1968 as Donna Elvira; later roles there included Tatyana, Suor Angelica, Fiordiligi, Elsa (*Lohengrin*), Elisabeth (*Tannhäuser*), Marguerite, the Marschallin, Mimì, Tosca, Butterfly and Manon Lescaut. She sang throughout Europe and the USA, her repertory including Adriana Lecouvreur, Amelia (*Un ballo in maschera*), Leonora (*Il trovatore*), Liù, Lisa (*The Queen of Spades*), Maddalena de Coigny, and both the Composer and Ariadne. Zylis-Gara was also admired as a concert singer and recitalist. She was a dignified yet impassioned actress, and had a fresh, lyric voice, notable for its smoothness of production. Among her recordings are a radiant Composer under Rudolf Kempe.

Alan Blyth

Index of Roles

This list of opera roles and the singers who created them is based on the index to The Grove Book of Operas. Singers with biographies in this book are in boldface.

Abbreviations: **a** – alto; **b** – bass; **bb** – bass-baritone; **bt** – baritone; **ct** – countertenor; **hc** – haute-contre; **ms** – mezzo-soprano; **s** – soprano; **sp** – spoken role; **t** – tenor; **tr** – treble

A

Aaron, t, *Mose in Egitto*, Rossini, **Giuseppe Ciccimarra**

Aaron, t, *Moses und Aron (concert performance, 1954)*, Schoenberg, **Helmut Krebs**

Aaron, t, *Moses und Aron (staged performance, 1957)*, Schoenberg, **Helmut Melchert**

Abigaille, s, *Nabucco*, Verdi, **Giuseppina Strepponi**

Abul Hassan Ali Ebn Bekar, bt, *Der Barbier von Bagdad*, Cornelius, **Hans von Milde**

Achillas/Achilla, b, *Giulio Cesare in Egitto*, Handel, **Giuseppe Boschi**

Achilles, t, *Iphigénie en Aulide*, Gluck, **Joseph Legros**

Achilles, t, *King Priam*, Tippett, **Richard Lewis**

Acis, t, *Acis et Galatée*, Lully, **Dumesnil**

Adalberto, s, *Ottone*, Handel, **Gaetano Berenstadt**

Adalgisa, s, *Norma*, Bellini, **Giulia Grisi**

Adam Brant, bt, *Mourning Becomes Electra*, Levy, **Sherrill Milnes**

Adelaida, s, *Lotario*, Handel, **Anna Maria Strada del Pò**

Adelaide, s, *Adelaide di Borgogna*, Rossini, **Elisabetta Manfredini-Guarmani**

Adele, s, *Die Fledermaus*, Strauss, J., Caroline Charles-Hirsch

Adèle, Countess, s, *Le comte Ory*, Rossini, **Laure Cinti-Damoreau**

Adelia, s, *Ugo, conte di Parigi*, Donizetti, **Giulia Grisi**

Adina, s, *L'elisir d'amore*, Donizetti, **Sabine Heinefetter**

Admeto/Admetus, a, *Admeto*, Handel, **Senesino**

Admetus, t, *Alceste*, Guglielmi, **Guglielmo Ettore**

Admetus/Admète/Admeto, hc, *Alceste*, Lully, **Bernard Clédière**

Admetus/Admète/Admeto, t, *Alceste (French version, 1776)*, Gluck, **Joseph Legros**

Admetus/Admète/Admeto, t, *Alceste (Italian version, 1767)*, Gluck, **Giuseppe Tibaldi**

Adolar, Count of, t, *Euryanthe*, Weber, **Anton Haizinger**

Adolfo, s, *Faramondo*, Handel, **Margherita Chimenti**

Adoniram, t, *La reine de Saba*, Gounod, **Louis Guéymard**

Adriana Lecouvreur, s, *Adriana Lecouvreur*, Cilea, **Angelica Pandolfini**

Adriano, ms, *Adriano in Siria*, Pergolesi, **Caffarelli**

Adriano Colonna, ms, *Rienzi*, Wagner, **Wilhelmine Schröder-Devrient**

Aegisthus, t, *Elektra*, Strauss, **Johannes Sembach**

Aeglé, s, *Thésée*, Lully, **Marie Aubry**

Aeneas, t, *Didon*, Desmarets, **Dumesnil**

Aeneas, t, *Les Troyens (1863)*, Berlioz, Jules-Sebastien Monjauze

Aeneas, t, *Les Troyens (1890)*, Berlioz, Alfred Oberlander

Aennchen, ms, *Der Freischütz*, Weber, Johanna Eunicke

Afer, t, *Servilia*, Rimsky-Korsakov, **Andrey Labinsky**

Afra, ms, *La Wally*, Catalani, Adriana Guerrini

Agamemnon, bt, *Iphigénie en Aulide*, Gluck, **Henri Larrivée**

Agamemnon, bt, *La belle Hélène*, Offenbach, Henri Couder

Agathe, s, *Der Freischütz*, Weber, **Karoline Seidler-Wranitzky**

Agave, ms, *The Bassarids*, Henze, **Kerstin Meyer**

Arbace/Arbaces, s, *Catone in Utica*, Leo, **Farinelli**

Arbaces, s, *Artaxerxes*, Arne,
Giusto Ferdinando Tenducci

Arbaces, s, *Gl' amanti generosi*, Mancini,
Maria Maddalena Fratini

Arbaces/Arbace, t, *Idomeneo*, Mozart,
Domenico Panzacchi

Arbates/Arbate, s, *Mitridate*, Mozart,
Pietro Muschietti

Arcabonne, s, *Amadis*, Lully, **Marie Le Rochois**

Arcalaus, b, *Amadis*, Lully, **Jean Dun (i)**

Arcas, b, *Iphigénie en Aulide*, Gluck, Beauvalet

Arcesius, b/bt, *Die toten Augen*, S'Albert,
Friedrich Plaschke

Archibaldo, Baron, b, *L'amore dei tre re*,
Montemezzi, **Nazzareno de Angelis**

Arethusa, s, *Proserpine*, Lully, **Marie
Le Rochois**

Argante, b, *Rinaldo*, Handel, **Giuseppe Boschi**

Argenius, b, *Imeneo*, Handel, **Henry Reinhold**

Ariadne/Ariane, s, *Ariane*, Martinů, **Maria Callas**

Ariadne/Arianna, s, *Arianna in Nasso*, Porpora,
Francesca Cuzzoni

Ariadne/Prima Donna, s, *Ariadne auf Naxos
(1912)*, Strauss, R., **Maria Jeritza**

Ariadne/Prima Donna, s, *Ariadne auf Naxos
(1916)*, Strauss, R., **Maria Jeritza**

Ariandne, s, *Arianna in Creta*, Handel,
Anna Maria Strada del Pò

Ariane, ms, *Ariane et Barbe-bleue*, Dukas,
Georgette Leblanc

Aricie, s, *Hippolyte et Aricie*, Rameau,
Marie Pélissier

Ariodante, ms, *Ariodante*, Handel,
Giovanni Carestini

Ariodate, b, *Serse*, Handel, **Antonio
Montagnana**

Aristaeus/Aristée, t, *The Mask of Orpheus*,
Birtwistle, **Tom McDonnell**

Aristobolo, b, *Berenice*, Handel,
Henry Reinhold

Arkel, King, b, *Pelléas et Mélisande*, Debussy,
Felix Vieuille

Armand des Grieux, t, *Boulevard Solitude*,
Henze, Walter Buckow

Armida, s, *Armida*, Haydn, Matilde Bologna

Armida, s, *Armida*, Rossini, **Isabella Colbran**

Armida, s, *Armida abbandonata*, Jommelli, **Anna
Lucia De Amicis**

Armida, s, *Rinaldo*, Handel, **Elisabetta
Pilotti-Schiavonetti**

Armide, s, *Armide*, Gluck, **Rosalie Levasseur**

Armide, s, *Armide*, Lully, **Marie Le Rochois**

Arminda, s, *La finta giardiniera*, Mozart, Teresa
Manservisi

Armindo, a, *Partenope*, Handel, **Francesca
Bertolli**

Arminius/Arminio, a, *Arminio*, Handel,
Domenico Annibali

Arnold Melcthal, t, *Guillaume Tell*, Rossini,
Adolphe Nourrit

Arrigo, t, *La battaglia di Legnano*, Verdi,
Gaetano Fraschini

Arsace, a, *Berenice*, Handel, **Maria Caterina
Negri**

Arsace, a, *Partenope*, Handel, **Antonio Maria
Bernacchi**

Arsace, s, *Partenope*, Handel, **Antonio Maria
Bernacchi**

Arsace, a, *Semiramide*, Rossini, **Rosa Mariani**

Arsamene, ms, *Serse*, Handel, **Maria Antonia
Marchesini**

Arsinoe, s, *Die toten Augen*, D'Albert,
Grete Merrem-Nikisch

Artabanes, t, *Artaxerxes*, Arne, **John Beard**

Artaxerxes, a, *Gl' amanti generosi*, Mancini,
Elena Garofalina

Artemidoro, t, *La grotta di Trofonio*, Salieri,
Vincenzo Calvesi

Arthur, King, t, *Gawain*, Birtwistle, Richard
Greager

Artidoro, bt, *Gli sposi malcontenti*, Storace,
Stefano Mandini

Arturo, t, *La straniera*, Bellini, **Domenico
Reina**

Arturo Talbo, Lord, t, *I puritani*, Bellini,
Giovanni Battista Rubini

Arvino, t, *I Lombardi*, Verdi, Giovanni Severi

Ascanio, ms, *Benvenuto Cellini*, Berlioz,
Rosine Stoltz

Aschenbach, t, *Death in Venice*, Britten,
Peter Pears

Asdrubale, Count, b, *La pietra del paragone*,
Rossini, **Filippo Galli**

Ashby, b, *La fanciulla del West*, Puccini,
Adam Didur

Asmus Modiger, t, *Das Herz*, Pfitzner,
Fritz Krauss

Aspasia, s, *Mitridate*, Mozart, **Antonio
Bernasconi**

Assur, b, *Semiramide*, Rossini, **Filippo Galli**

Astarco, b, *Andromeda*, Manelli,
Francesco Manelli

Asteria, s, *Nerone*, Boito, Rosa Raisa

Asteria, s, *Tamerlano*, Handel,
Francesca Cuzzoni

Index of Voices

Alto (contralto)
Alboni, Marietta
Anderson, Marian
Belloc-Giorgi, Teresa
Benningsen, Lillian
Bertolli, Francesca
Brambilla, Giuseppina
Brambilla, Marietta
Brandram, Rosina
Butt, Dame Clara
Cahier, Mme Charles
Chookasian, Lili
Deschamps-Jehin Blanche
Desmond, Astra
Dominguez, Oralia
Dotti, Anna Vincenza
Höffgen, Marga
Homer, Louise
Laurenti, Antonia Maria
Madeira, Jean
Malanotte, Adelaide
Marcolini, Marietta
Mariani, Rosa
Matzenauer, Margaret
Merighi, Antonia Margherita
Metzger, Ottilie
Mingardo, Sara
Mysz-Gmeiner, Lula
Negri, Maria Caterina
Offers, Maartje
Onegin, Sigrid
Petrova, Anna Yakovlevna
Podles, Ewa
Powers, Marie
Rappé, Jadwiga
Raveau, Alice
Righetti, Geltrude
Robinson, Anastasia
Rössl-Majdan, Hilde
Schumann-Heink, Ernestine
Sinclair, Monica
Stutzmann, Natalie
Tesi, Vittoria
Thornton, Edna
Turner, Claramae
Vanini, Francesca
Vestris, Lucia Elizabeth
Watts, Helen
Wettergren, Gertrud
Young, Elizabeth
Young, Esther
Zbruyeva, Yevgeniya

Baritone
Agache, Alexandru
Ahlersmeyer, Matthieu
Aldighieri, Gottardo
Allen, Sir Thomas
Amato, Pasquale
Ancona, Mario
Bacquier, Gabriel
Baklanov, Georgy
Bär, Olaf
Barroilhet, Paul
Basiola, Mario
Bassi, Luigi
Bastianini, Ettore
Battistini, Mattia
Baugé, André
Bechi, Gino
Betz, Franz
Bispham, David
Blanc, Ernest
Bouhy, Jacques
Bourdin, Roger
Braun, Victor
Brownlee, John
Bruson, Renato
Burg, Robert
Capecchi, Renato
Cappuccilli, Piero
Carey, Clive
Cartagenova, Gian-Orazio
Cassel, Walter
Chernov, Vladimir
Coates, John
Coletti, Filippo
Colini, Filippo

Welitsch, Ljuba
Wendling, Dorothea
Wendling, Elisabeth
Wildbrunn, Helene
Wise, Patricia
Wittich, Marie
Wood, Mary Anne
Yakar, Rachel
Yermolenko-Yuzhina, Nataliya
Young, Cecilia
Young, Isabella (i)
Young, Polly
Zabela, Nadeshda
Zadek, Hilde
Zamboni, Maria
Zampieri, Mara
Zeani, Virginia
Zerr, Anna
Ziesak, Ruth
Zilli, Emma
Zylis-Gara, Teresa

Tenor
Adamberger, Valentin
Adams, Charles R.
Affré, Agustarello
Agnew, Paul
Ahnsjö, Claes Håkan
Ainsley, John Mark
Alagna, Roberto
Alcaide, Tomáz
Alchevs'ky, Ivan Olexiyovych
Alexander, John
Althouse, Paul
Alva, Luigi
Alvarez, Albert
Álvarez, Marcello
Alvary, Max
Anders, Peter
Anselmi, Giuseppe
Anthony, Charles
Aragall, Giacomo
Araiza, Francisco
Atlantov, Vladimir
Bada, Angelo
Baglioni, Antonio
Barbot, Joseph-Théodore-Désiré
Bassi, Amedeo
Baxevanos, Peter
Beard, John
Beck, Karl
Bergonzi, Carlo
Berthelier, Jean-François

Björling, Jussi
Blachut, Beno
Blake, Rockwell
Blochwitz, Hans Peter
Bonci, Alessandro
Bonfigli, Lorenzo
Bonisolli, Franco
Borgatti, Giuseppe
Borgioli, Dino
Borosini, Antonio
Borosini, Francesco
Bostridge, Ian
Braham, John
Bulakhov, Pavel Petrovich
Burian, Karel
Burrows, Stuart
Calleja, Joseph
Calvesi, Vincenzo
Campanini, Italo
Campora, Giuseppe
Carreras, José
Caruso, Enrico
Cassilly, Richard
Chishko, Oles' Semyonovich
Ciccimarra, Giuseppe
Clark, Graham
Clément, Edmond
Corelli, Franco
Cornelius, Peter
Cortis, Antonio
Cossutta, Carlo
Craig, Charles
Crimi, Giulio
Crook, Howard
Crooks, Richard
Cuénod, Hugues
Cura, José
Curioni, Alberico
Daddi, Francesco
Dalmorès, Charles
Dauer, Johann Ernst
David, Léon
Davide, Giovanni
Davidoff, Aleksandr
Davies, Arthur
Davies, Ryland
Davies, Tudor
De Lucia, Fernando
De Marchi, Emilio
De Mey, Guy
Del Monaco, Mario
Demmer, Joseph
Dermota, Anton
Di Stefano, Giuseppe

List of Operas

A basso porto, Nicola Spinelli
A Kékszakállú herceg vára [Bluebeard's Castle], Béla Bartók
Abesalom da Eteri, Zakhary Petrovich Paliashvili
Abreise, Die, Eugen d'Albert
Abstrakte Oper no.1, Boris Blacher
Abu Hassan, Carl Maria von Weber
Acante et Céphise, Jean-Philippe Rameau
Achille, Ferdinando Paer
Acis and Galatea, George Frideric Handel
Acis et Galatée, Jean-Baptiste Lully
Acis y Galatea, Antonio De Literes
Actéon, Marc-Antoine Charpentier
Ada, Minoru Miki
Adelaide, Antonio Sartorio
Adelaide di Borgogna, Gioachino Rossini
Adelheit von Veltheim, Christian Gottlob Neefe
Adelson e Salvini, Vincenzo Bellini
Ademira, Angelo Tarchi
Adina [Adina, o Il califfo di Bagdad], Gioachino Rossini
Admeto, George Frideric Handel
Adriana Lecouvreur, Francesco Cilea
Adriano in Siria, Pasquale Anfossi
Adriano in Siria, Antonio Caldara
Adriano in Siria, Giovanni Battista Pergolesi
Aeneas i Cartago [Aeneas i Cartago, eller Dido och Aeneas], Joseph Martin Kraus
Affair, The, Felix Werder
Africaine, L', Giacomo Meyer
Agamemnon, Felix Werder
Agesilao, re di Sparta, Gaetano Andreozzi
Agnes von Hohenstaufen, Gaspare Spontini
Agnese, Ferdinando Paer
Agreeable Surprise, The, Samuel Arnold
Agrippina, George Frideric Handel
Ägyptische Helena, Die, Richard Strauss
Aida, Giuseppe Verdi
Aiglon, L', Arthur Honegger and Jacques Ibert
Ajo nell'imbarazzo, L', Gaetano Donizetti
Akhnaten, Philip Glass
Al gran sole carico d'amore, Luigi Nono
Albert Herring, Benjamin Britten

Albion and Albanius, Luis Grabu
Alceste, Christoph Willibald Gluck
Alceste, Pietro Alessandro Guglielmi
Alceste, Jean-Baptiste Lully
Alceste, Anton Schweitzer
Alchymist, Der, Joseph Schuster
Alcide al bivio, Johann Adolf Hasse
Alcide negli orti esperidi, Gian Francesco di Majo
Alcina, George Frideric Handel
Alcyone, Marin Marais
Aleko, Sergey Vasil'yevich Rakhmaninov
Alessandro, George Frideric Handel
Alessandro nelle Indie, Giovanni Pacini
Alessandro Severo, George Frideric Handel
Alessandro Severo, Antonio Lotti
Alessandro Stradella, Friedrich Flotow
Alfonso und Estrella, Franz Schubert
Alfred, Antonín Dvořák
Alina, regina di Golconda, Gaetano Donizetti
Aline, reine de Golconde, Pierre-Alexandre Monsigny
Almahide, John Jacob Heidegger
Almast, Alexander Spendiaryan
Almena, Micheal Arne and Jonathan Battishill
Almira, George Frideric Handel
Alonso e Cora, Francesco Bianchi
Alpenkönig und der Menschenfeind, Der, Wenzel Müller
Alzira, Giuseppe Verdi
Amadigi di Gaula, George Frideric Handel
Amadis, Jean-Baptiste Lully
Amadis de Gaule, Johann Christian Bach
Amadis de Grèce, André Cardinal Destouches
Amahl and the Night Visitors, Gian Carlo Menotti
Amante di tutte, Baldassare Galuppi
Amanti generosi, Gl', Francesco Mancini
Amazone corsara, L' [L'amazone corsara, ovvero L'Alvilda regina de' Goti], Carlo Pallavicino
Ambleto, Francesco Gasparini
Amelia al ballo, Gian Carlo Menotti
Amico Fritz, L', Pietro Mascagni

Amleto, Gaetano Andreozzi

Amleto, Franco Faccio

Amor coniugale, L', Simon Mayr

Amor contrastato, ossia La molinara, L'
    [La molinara], Giovanni Paisiello

Amor vuol sofferenza, Leonardo Leo

Amore artigiano, L', Florian Leopold Gassmann

Amore dei tre re, L', Italo Montemezzi

Amore medico, L', Ermanno Wolf-Ferrari

Amori di Ergasto, Gli, Jakob Greber

*Amour des trois oranges, L' [The Love for Three
    Oranges]*, Sergey Prokofiev

Amour, fléchy par la constance, L', Michel-Richard
    de Lalande

Amours de Ragonde, Les, Jean-Joseph Mouret

Amours déguisés, Les, Thomas-Louis Bourgeois

Amphion, Johann Gottlieb Naumann

Amy Robsart, Isidore de Lara

Anacréon, Jean-Philippe Rameau

Anagilda, Antonio Caldara

Andrea Chénier, Umberto Giordano

Andromaca, Francesco Feo

Andromaca, Leonardo Leo

Andromeda, Francesco Manelli

Andzhelo, César Antonovich Cui

Angélique, Jacques Ibert

Aniara, Karl-Birger Blomdahl

Anima allegra, Franco Vittadini

Anima del filosofo, L', Joseph Haydn

Anna Bolena, Gaetano Donizetti

Anna Karenina, Iain Hamilton

Antigona, Tommaso Traetta

Antigonae, Carl Orff

Antony and Cleopatra, Samuel Barber

Anush, Armen Tigran Tigranyan

Apollo et Hyacinthus, Wolfgang Amadeus
    Mozart

Arabella, Richard Strauss

Arbace, Francesco Bianchi

Arbore di Diana, L', Vicente Martín y Soler

*Arbre enchanté, L' [L'arbre enchanté ou Le tuteur
    dupé]*, Christoph Willibald Gluck

Arcadia in Brenta, L', Baldassare Galuppi

Arden muss sterben [Arden must Die], Alexander
    Goehr

Arden must Die [Arden muss sterben], Alexander
    Goehr

*Argonauti in Colco, Gli [Gli Argonauti in Colco,
    o sia La conquista del vello d'oro]*, Giuseppe
    Gazzaniga

Ariadna [Ariane], Bohuslav Martinů

Ariadne auf Naxos, Georg Benda

Ariadne auf Naxos, Richard Strauss

Ariane [Ariadna], Bohuslav Martinů

Ariane [Ariane ou Le mariage de Bacchus], Robert
    Cambert and Luis Grabu

Ariane et Barbe-bleue, Paul Dukas

Arianna, Claudio Monteverdi

Arianna in Creta, George Frideric Handel

Arianna in Nasso, Nicola Porpora

Ariarate, Angelo Tarchi

Ariodant, Etienne-Nicolas Méhul

Ariodante, George Frideric Handel

Aristo e Temira, Ferdinando Bertoni

Arlecchino [Arlecchino, oder Die Fenster],
    Ferruccio Busoni

Arlesiana, Francesco Cilea

Arme Heinrich, Der, Hans Pfitzner

Armida, Antonín Dvořák

Armida, Joseph Haydn

Armida, Johann Gottlieb Naumann

Armida, Gioachino Rossini

Armida, Antonio Sacchini

Armida, Antonio Salieri

Armida, Tommaso Traetta

Armida abbandonata, Niccolò Jommelli

Armide, Christoph Willibald Gluck

Armide, Jean-Baptiste Lully

Arminio, George Frideric Handel

Aroldo, Giuseppe Verdi

Arsace, Domenico Natale Sarro

Arsinoe, Thomas Clayton

Artaserse, Baldassare Galuppi

Artaserse, Johann Adolf Hasse

Artaserse, Leonardo Vinci

Artaxerxes, Thomas Augustine Arne

Artémis, Alberto Nepomuceno

Arts florissants, Les, Marc-Antoine Charpentier

Ascanio, Camille Saint-Saëns

Ascanio in Alba, Wolfgang Amadeus Mozart

Ashmedai, Josef Tal

Askold's Grave, Alexey Nikolayevich Verstovsky

Aspern Papers, The, Dominick Argento

Asrael, Alberto Franchetti

Assassinio nella cattedrale, Ildebrando Pizzetti

Assedio di Calais, L', Gaetano Donizetti

Assedio di Corinto, L' [Le siège de Corinthe],
    Gioachino Rossini

Astarto, Giovanni Bononcini

Astianatte, Giovanni Bononcini

Astuzie femminili, Le, Domenico Cimarosa

At the Boar's Head, Gustav Holst

Atalanta, George Frideric Handel

Athalie, Johann Abraham Peter Schulz

Atomtod, Giacomo Manzoni

Attaque du moulin L', Alfred Bruneau

Attila, Giuseppe Verdi

Attilio Regolo, Johann Adolf Hasse

Boccaccio, Franz Suppé
Bogatïri, Alexander Porfir'yevich Borodin
Bohdan Khmel'nyts'ky, Kostyantyn Fedorovych Dan'kevych
Bohème, La, Ruggero Leoncavallo
Bohème, La, Giacomo Puccini
Bohemian Girl, The, Michael William Balfe
Bohemios, Amadeo Vives
Bomarzo, Alberto Ginastera
Boor, The, Dominick Argento
Boréades, Les, Jean-Philippe Rameau
Boris Godunov, Modest Petrovich Musorgsky
Boulevard Solitude, Hans Werner Henze
Brandenburgers in Bohemia, The [Braniboři v Čechách], Bedřich Smetana
Braniboři v Čechách [The Brandenburgers in Bohemia], Bedřich Smetana
Bratři Karamazovi, Otakar Jeremiáš
Brautwahl, Die, Ferruccio Busoni
Bravo, Il, Saverio Mercadante
Brenno, Johann Friedrich Reichardt
Brigands, Les, Jacques Offenbach
Briganti, I, Saverio Mercadante
Bruja, La, Ruperto Chapí
Buon soldato Svejk, Il, Guido Turchi
Buona figliuola, La [La Cecchina, ossia La buona figliuola], Niccolò Piccinni
Buona figliuola maritata, La, Niccolò Piccinni
Bürger von Calais, Die, Rudolf Wagner-Régeny
Bürgschaft, Die, Kurt Weill
Burning Fiery Furnace, The, Benjamin Britten

C'est la guerre, Emil Petrovics
Cadi dupé, Le, Christoph Willibald Gluck
Cadmus et Hermione, Jean-Baptiste Lully
Calife de Bagdad, Le [The Caliph of Baghdad], Adrien Boieldieu
Caliph of Baghdad, The [Le Calife de Bagdad], Adrien Boieldieu
Calisto, Francesco Cavalli
Callirhoé, André Cardinal Destouches
Calliroe, Felice Alessandri
Calliroe, Antonio Sacchini
Calto, Francesco Bianchi
Calypso and Telemachus, John Ernest Galliard
Cambiale di matrimonio, La, Gioachino Rossini
Camilla, ossia Il sotterraneo, Ferdinando Paer
Campana sommersa, La, Ottorino Respighi
Campanello di notte, Il, Gaetano Donizetti
Campiello, Il, Ermanno Wolf-Ferrari
Candide, Leonard Bernstein
Cantatrici villane, Le, Valentino Fioravanti

Canterina, La, Joseph Haydn
Cappello di paglia di Firenze, Il, Nino Rota
Capricci di Callot, I, Gian Francesco Malipiero
Capriccio, Richard Strauss
Capuleti e i Montecchi, I, Vincenzo Bellini
Caravane du Caire, La, André-Ernest-Modeste Grétry
Cardillac, Paul Hindemith
Carmen, Georges Bizet
Carmina burana, Carl Orff
Carnaval de Venise, Le, André Campra
Carnevale di Venezia, Il [Il carnevale di Venezia, ossia Le precauzioni], Errico Petrella
Casanova's Homecoming, Dominick Argento
Cascina, La, Giuseppe Scolari
Caserío, El, Jesús Guridi
Castaway, Lennox Berkeley
Castle of Andalusia, The, Samuel Arnold
Castor et Pollux, Jean-Philippe Rameau
Castore e Polluce, Francesco Bianchi
Castore e Polluce, Georg Joseph Vogler
Catarina Cornaro, Königin von Cypern, Franz Paul Lachner
Catena d'Adone, La, Domenico Mazzocchi
Caterina Cornaro, Gaetano Donizetti
Caterina di Guisa, Carlo Coccia
Catiline Conspiracy, The, Iain Hamilton
Catone in Utica, Johann Christian Bach
Catone in Utica, Leonardo Leo
Catone in Utica, Niccolò Piccinni
Catulli carmina, Carl Orff
Cavalieri di Ekebù, I, Riccardo Zandonai
Cavalleria rusticana, Pietro Mascagni
Cavalleria rusticana, Domenico Monleone
Caverne, La, Jean-François Le Sueur
Cecchina, ossia La buona figliuola, La [La buona figliuola], Niccolò Piccinni
Cecilia, Licinio Refice
Célestine, La, Maurice Ohana
Celos aun del aire matan, Juan Hidalgo
Celos hacen estrellas, Los, Juan Hidalgo
Cena delle beffe, La, Umberto Giordano
Cendrillon, Nicolas Isouard
Cendrillon, Jules Massenet
Cenerentola, La [La Cenerentola, ossia La bontà in trionfo], Gioachino Rossini
Čert a Káča [The Devil and Kate], Antonín (Leopold) Dvořák
Čertova stěna [The Devil's Wall], Bedřich Smetana
Chalaça, O, Francisco Mignone
Chalet, Le, Adolphe Adam
Chaplet, The, William Boyce

Charles VI, Fromental Halévy
Charodeyka [The Enchantress], Pyotr Il'yich
Tchaikovsky
Cherevichki, Pyotr Il'yich Tchaikovsky
Chérubin, Jules Massenet
Chi soffre speri [L'Egisto, ovvero Chi soffre speri],
Virgilio Mazzocchi and Marco Marazzoli
Chocolate Soldier, The [Der Tapfere Soldat], Oscar
Straus
Chopin, Giacomo Orefice
Christelflein, Das, Hans Pfitzner
Christmas Carol, A, Thea Musgrave
Christmas Eve [Noch' pered rozhdestvom], Nikolay
Andreyevich Rimsky-Korsakov
Christmas Rose, The, Frank Bridge
Christophe Colomb, Darius Milhaud
*Christophorus [Christophorus, oder Die Vision einer
Oper],* Franz Schreker
Chute de la maison Usher, La, Claude Debussy
Ciboulette, Reynaldo Hahn
Cid, Der, Peter Cornelius
Cid, Le, Jules Massenet
Cidde, Il, Antonio Sacchini
Cifra, La, Antonio Salieri
Cinesi, Le, Christoph Willibald Gluck
Ciottolino, Luigi Ferrari Trecate
*Ciro in Babilonia [Ciro in Babilonia, ossia La caduta
di Baldassare],* Gioachino Rossini
Clarissa, Robin Holloway
Claudine von Villa Bella, Ignaz Von Beecke
Claudine von Villa Bella, Johann Friedrich
Reichardt
*Claudius [Die verdammte Staat-Sucht, oder Der
verführte Claudius],* Reinhard Keiser
Clemenza di Scipione, La, Johann Christian Bach
Clemenza di Tito, La, Wolfgang Amadeus
Mozart
Cleofide, Johann Adolf Hasse
Cleopatra, Pasquale Anfossi
*Cleopatra [Die unglückselige Cleopatra, Königin
von Egypten, oder Die betrogene Staats-Liebe],*
Johann Mattheson
Cloches de Corneville, Les, Robert Planquette
*Coachman of Longjumeau [Le postillon de
Lonjumeau],* Adolphe Adam
Coccodrillo, Il, Valentino Bucchi
Colas Breugnon [Kola Bryun'on: Master iz Klamsi],
Dmitry Borisovich Kabalevsky
Colas et Colinette, ou Le bailli dupé, Joseph
Quesnel
Compadecida, A, José Siqueira
Comte Ory, Le, Gioachino Rossini
Comus, Thomas Augustine Arne

Conchita, Riccardo Zandonai
Consul, The, Gian Carlo Menotti
Contadina astuta, La [Livietta e Tracollo],
Giovanni Battista Pergolesi
Contadina in corte, La, Antonio Sacchini
Conte di Saldagna, Il, Angelo Tarchi
Contes d'Hoffmann, Les, Jacques Offenbach
Contrabbasso, Il, Valentino Bucchi
Contratador de diamantes, O, Francisco
Mignone
Convenienze teatrali, Le, Gaetano Donizetti
Convito, Il, Domenico Cimarosa
Cooper, The, Thomas Augustine Arne
Coq d'or, Le [The Golden Cockerel], Nikolay
Andreyevich Rimsky-Korsakov
Cora och Alonzo, Johann Gottlieb Naumann
Cordovano, Il, Goffredo Petrassi
Coriolanus, Ján Cikker
*Coronatione di Poppea, La [L'incoronazione di
Poppea],* Claudio Monteverdi
Corregidor, Der, Hugo Wolf
Corsaro, Il, Giuseppe Verdi
*Cosa rara, Una [Una cosa rara, o sia Bellezza ed
onestà],* Vicente Martín y Soler
*Così fan tutte [Così fan tutte, ossia La scuola degli
amanti],* Wolfgang Amadeus Mozart
Costanza e Fortezza, Johann Joseph Fux
*Cox and Box [Cox and Box; or the Long-Lost
Brothers],* Arthur Sullivan
Creso, Antonio Sacchini
Crispino e la comare, Luigi Ricci and Federico
Ricci
Crispo, Giovanni Bononcini
Cristoforo Colombo, Alberto Franchetti
Critic, The, Charles Villiers Stanford
Crociato in Egitto, Il, Giacomo Meyer
*Croesus [Der hochmüthige, gestürtzte und wieder
erhabene Croesus],* Reinhard Keiser
Cry of Clytaemnestra, The, John C. Eaton
Csárdásfürstin, Die, Emmerich Kálmán
*Cud mniemany [Cud mniemany, czyli Krakowiacy i
górale],* Jan Stefani
*Cunning Little Vixen, The [Příhody Lišky
Bystroušky],* Leoš Janáček
Cunning Man, The, Charles Burney
Cunning Peasant, The [Šelma sedlák], Antonín
Dvořák
Cupid and Death, Christopher Gibbons
and Matthew Locke
Cupido [Der sich rächende Cupido], Reinhard
Keiser
Curioso indiscreto, Il, Pasquale Anfossi
Curlew River, Benjamin Britten

Cymon, Michael Arne
Cyrano de Bergerac, Franco Alfano
Cythère assiégée, Christoph Willibald Gluck
Czaar und Zimmermann, oder Die zwei [beiden] Peter [Zar und Zimmermann], Albert Lortzing

Dafne, Marco Da Gagliano
Dafni, Giuseppe Mulè
Dafni, Alessandro Scarlatti
Daisi, Zakhary Petrovich Paliashvili
Dal male il bene, Antonio Maria Abbatini and Marco Marazzoli
Dalgerie, James Penberthy
Dalibor, Bedřich Smetana
Dame blanche, La [The White Lady], Adrien Boieldieu
Damnation de Faust, La, Hector Berlioz
Danaïdes, Les, Antonio Salieri
Danton and Robespierre, John C. Eaton
Dantons Tod, Gottfried Von Einem
Daphne, Richard Strauss
Dardanus, Jean-Philippe Rameau
Dardanus, Antonio Sacchini
David et Jonathas, Marc-Antoine Charpentier
Death in Venice, Benjamin Britten
Death of Dido, The, Johann Christoph Pepusch
Dèbora e Jaéle, Ildebrando Pizzetti
Decembrists, The [Dekabristi], Yury Alexandrovich Shaporin
Decision, The, Thea Musgrave
Deidamia, George Frideric Handel
Deirdre, Healey Willan
Déjanire, Camille Saint-Saëns
Dekabristi [The Decembrists], Yury Alexandrovich Shaporin
Demetrio e Polibio, Gioachino Rossini
Democrito corretto, Carl Ditters von Dittersdorf
Demofoonte, Niccolò Jommelli
Demon, The, Anton Grigor'yevich Rubinstein
Déserteur, Le, Pierre-Alexandre Monsigny
Deux aveugles, Les, Jacques Offenbach
Deux journées, Les [The Water Carrier], Luigi Cherubini
Deux petits Savoyards, Les, Nicolas-Marie Dalayrac
Devil and Daniel Webster, The, Douglas Moore
Devil and Kate, The [Čert a Káča], Antonín Dvořák
Devil Take her, The, Arthur Benjamin
Devil's Wall, The [Čertova stěna], Bedřich Smetana
Devils of Loudun, The, Krzysztof Penderecki

Devin du village, Le, Jean-Jacques Rousseau
Diable à quatre, Le [Le diable à quatre, ou La double métamorphose], Christoph Willibald Gluck and Others
Dialogues des Carmélites, Francis Poulenc
Diamant des Geisterkönigs, Der, Joseph Drechsler
Diavolessa, La, Baldassare Galuppi
Diavolo nel campanile, Il, Adriano Lualdi
Dibuk, Il, Lodovico Rocca
Dido and Aeneas, Henry Purcell
Dido, Königin von Carthago, Christoph Graupner
Dido, Queen of Carthage, Stephen Storace
Didon, Henry Desmarets
Didon, Niccolò Piccinni
Didone, Francesco Cavalli
Didone abbandonata, Giuseppe Sarti
Didone abbandonata, Leonardo Vinci
Dimitrij, Antonín (Leopold) Dvořák
Dinner Engagement, A, Lennox Berkeley
Dinorah, Giacomo Meyer
Dioclesian, Henry Purcell
Dirindina, Domenico Scarlatti
Disingannati, I, Antonio Caldara
Dissoluto punito, ossia Il Don Giovanni, Il [Don Giovanni (ii)], Wolfgang Amadeus Mozart
Djamileh, Georges Bizet
Docteur Miracle, Le, Georges Bizet
Doktor Faust, Ferruccio Busoni
Doktor Faust, Ignaz Walter
Doktor Faustus, Giacomo Manzoni
Doktor und Apotheker, Carl Ditters von Dittersdorf
Dolores, La, Tomás Bretón
Dom Sébastien, roi de Portugal, Gaetano Donizetti
Domanda di matrimonio, Una, Luciano Chailly
Domino noir, Le, Daniel-François-Esprit Auber
Don Carlos, Giuseppe Verdi
Don Chisciotte, Vito Frazzi
Don Giovanni [Don Giovanni, o sia Il convitato di pietra; Don Giovanni Tenorio], Giuseppe Gazzaniga
Don Giovanni [Il dissoluto punito, ossia Il Don Giovanni], Wolfgang Amadeus Mozart
Don Pasquale, Gaetano Donizetti
Don Perlimplin, Bruno Maderna
Don Procopio, Georges Bizet
Don Quichotte, Jules Massenet
Don Rodrigo, Alberto Ginastera
Doña Francisquita, Amadeo Vives
Donauweibchen, Das, Ferdinand Kauer
Donna del lago, La, Gioachino Rossini
Donna serpente, La, Alfredo Casella

Grisélidis, Jules Massenet
Grossmüthige Tomyris, Die [Tomyris], Reinhard Keiser
Grotta di Trofonio, La, Antonio Salieri
Guarany, Il, Carlos Gomes
Guercoeur, Albéric Magnard
Guglielmo Ratcliff, Pietro Mascagni
Guglielmo Tell [Guillaume Tell], Gioachino Rossini
Guido et Ginevra [Guido et Ginevra, ou La peste de Florence], Fromental Halévy
Guillaume Tell, André-Ernest-Modeste Grétry
Guillaume Tell [Guglielmo Tell], Gioachino Rossini
Guirlande, La [La guirlande, ou Les fleurs enchantées], Jean-Philippe Rameau
Gunlöd, Peter Cornelius
Günstling, Der [Der Günstling, oder Die letzten Tage des grossen Herrn Fabiano], Rudolf Wagner-Régeny
Günther von Schwarzburg, Ignaz Holzbauer
Guntram, Richard Strauss
Gustaf Wasa, Johann Gottlieb Naumann
Gustave III [Gustave III, ou Le bal masqué], Daniel-François-Esprit Auber
Gute Freund, Der [The Boatswain's Mate], Ethel Smyth
Gwendoline, Emmanuel Chabrier

Halka, Stanisław Moniuszko
Hamlet, Ambroise Thomas
Hans Heiling, Heinrich August Marschner
Hans Sachs, Albert Lortzing
Hänsel und Gretel, Engelbert Humperdinck
Happy End, Kurt Weill
Harmonie der Welt, Die, Paul Hindemith
Harriet, the Woman called 'Moses', Thea Musgrave
Háry János [Háry János kalandozásai Nagyabonytul a Burgváráig], Zoltán Kodály
Haunted Manor, The[Straszny dwór], Stanisław Moniuszko
Haunted Tower, The, Stephen Storace
Häusliche Krieg, Der [Die Verschworenen], Franz Schubert
Heimchen am Herd, Das, Karl Goldmark
Heimkehr aus der Fremde, Die, Felix Mendelssohn
Heimsuchung, Die [The Visitation], Gunther Schuller
Hélène, Camille Saint-Saëns
Help, Help, the Globolinks!, Gian Carlo Menotti
Henry VIII, Camille Saint-Saëns

Hercules, George Frideric Handel
Hérodiade, Jules Massenet
Herz, Das, Hans Pfitzner
Heure espagnole, L', Maurice Ravel
Hieronymus Knicker, Carl Ditters von Dittersdorf
Higglety Pigglety Pop!, Oliver Knussen
Hin und zurück, Paul Hindemith
Hippolyte et Aricie, Jean-Philippe Rameau
Hiroshima no Orufe, Yasushi Akutagawa
HMS Pinafore [HMS Pinafore; or, The Lass that Loved a Sailor], Arthur Sullivan
Hochmüthige, gestürtzte und wieder erhabene Croesus, Der [Croesus], Reinhard Keiser
Hochzeit des Camacho, Die, Felix Mendelssohn
Holzdieb, Der, Heinrich August Marschner
Honzovo království, Otakar Ostrčil
Horaces, Les, Antonio Salieri
Hra o láske a smrti [Das Spiel von Liebe und Tod], Ján Cikker
Hry o Marii, Bohuslav Martinů
Hubička [Kiss, The], Bedřich Smetana
Hugh the Drover [Hugh the Drover, or Love in the Stocks], Ralph Vaughan Williams
Huguenots, Les, Giacomo Meyer
Hulda, César Franck
Hunyadi László, Ferenc Erkel
Hyperion, Bruno Maderna

Ice Break, The, Michael Tippett
Idalma [L'Idalma, overo Chi la dura la Vince], Bernardo Pasquini
Idiota, L', Luciano Chailly
Idoménée, André Campra
Idomeneo, re di Creta, Wolfgang Amadeus Mozart
If I were King [Si j'étais roi], Adolphe Adam
Ifigenia in Tauride, Gian Francesco De Majo
Ifigenia in Tauride, Niccolò Jommelli
Ifigenia in Tauride, Tommaso Traetta
Ile de Merlin, L' [L'île de Merlin, ou Le monde renversé], Christoph Willibald Gluck
Im weissen Rössl, Ralph Benatzky
Imeneo, George Frideric Handel
Immortal Hour, The, Rutland Boughton
Importance of Being Earnest, The [L'importanza di esser Franco], Mario Castelnuovo-Tedesco
Importanza di esser Franco, L' [The Importance of Being Earnest], Mario Castelnuovo-Tedesco
Impresario in angustie, L', Domenico Cimarosa
Incontro improvviso, L', Joseph Haydn
Incoronazione di Poppea, L' [La Coronatione di Poppea], Claudio Monteverdi
Indes galantes, Les, Jean-Philippe Rameau

Marito disperato, Il, Domenico Cimarosa
Marito giocatore e la moglie bacchettona, Il,
  Giuseppe Maria Orlandini
Mariya Styuart, Sergey Mikhaylovich Slonimsky
Marriage [Zhenit'ba], Modest Petrovich
  Musorgsky
Martha [Martha, oder Der Markt zu Richmond],
  Friedrich Flotow
Martyrdom of St. Magnus, The, Peter Maxwell
  Davies
Maruxa, Amadeo Vives
Mary, Queen of Scots, Thea Musgrave
*Masagniello [Masagniello (Masaniello) furioso
  [oder] Die neapolitanische Fischer-Empörung]*,
  Reinhard Keiser
Maschinist Hopkins, Max Brand
Mask of Orpheus, The, Harrison Birtwistle
Maskarade, Carl Nielsen
Masnadieri, I, Giuseppe Verdi
Massimilla Doni, Othmar Schoeck
Master i Margarita, Sergey Mikhaylovich
  Slonimsky
Mathis der Maler, Paul Hindemith
*Matilde di Shabran [Matilde di Shabran, ossia
  Bellezza, e cuor di ferro]*, Gioachino Rossini
Matka, Alois Hába
Matrero, El, Felipe Boero
Matrimonio segreto, Il, Domenico Cimarosa
Matti per amore, Li, Gioacchino Cocchi
Mavra, Igor Stravinsky
May Night [Mayskaya noch'], Nikolay
  Andreyevich Rimsky-Korsakov
Mayskaya noch' [May Night], Nikolay
  Andreyevich Rimsky-Korsakov
Mazepa, Pyotr Il'yich Tchaikovsky
Medea, Georg Benda
Medea, Giovanni Pacini
Medea in Corinto, Simon Mayr
Médecin malgré lui, Le, Charles-François Gounod
Médée, Marc-Antoine Charpentier
Médée, Luigi Cherubini
Médée et Jason, Joseph-François Salomon
Medici, I, Ruggero Leoncavallo
Medium, The, Gian Carlo Menotti
Medonte, re di Epiro, Giuseppe Sarti
Medoro, Francesco Lucio
Mefistofele, Arrigo Boito
Meister und Margarita, Der, York Höller
Meister und Margarita, Der, Rainer Kunad
Meistersinger von Nürnberg, Die, Richard
  Wagner
Mélidore et Phrosine, Etienne-Nicolas Méhul
Mel'nik – koldun, obmanshchik i svat [The Miller],
  Mikhail Matveyevich Sokolovsky

Mercante di Venezia, Il [The Merchant of Venice],
  Mario Castelnuovo-Tedesco
Mercato di Malmantile, Il, Domenico Fischietti
Merchant of Venice, The [Il mercante di Venezia],
  Mario Castelnuovo-Tedesco
Mère coupable, La, Darius Milhaud
Merope, Domènech Miguel Bernabé Terradellas
Merrie England, Edward German
Messaline, Isidore de Lara
Messidor, Alfred Bruneau
Midsummer Marriage, The, Michael Tippett
Midsummer Night's Dream, A, Benjamin Britten
Mignon, Ambroise Thomas
Mikado, The [The Mikado; or, The Town of Titipu],
  Arthur Sullivan
Miller, The [Mel'nik – koldun, obmanshchik i svat],
  Mikhail Matveyevich Sokolovsky
Mines of Sulphur, The, Richard Rodney Bennett
Mirandolina, Bohuslav Martinů
Mireille, Charles-François Gounod
Miser, The [Skupoy], Vasily Alexeyevich
  Pashkevich
Miserly Knight, The [Skupoy rïtsar'], Sergey
  Vasil'yevich Rakhmaninov
Mitridate Eupatore, Alessandro Scarlatti
Mitridate, re di Ponto, Wolfgang Amadeus
  Mozart
Mitternachtstunde, Die, Franz Danzi
Mlada, César Antonovich Cui, Modest
  Petrovich Musorgsky and Nikolay
  Andreyevich Rimsky-Korsakov
  (Acts 2 and 3) and Alexander
  Porfir'Yevich Borodin
Mlada, Nikolay Andreyevich Rimsky-Korsakov
Modista raggiratrice, La, Giovanni Paisiello
Moïse et Pharaon, Gioachino Rossini
*Molinara, La [L'amor contrastato, ossia La
  molinara]*, Giovanni Paisiello
Mona Lisa, Max von Schillings
Mond, Der, Carl Orff
Mondo della luna, Il, Baldassare Galuppi
Mondo della luna, Il, Joseph Haydn
Monsieur Beaucaire, André Messager
Montezuma, Carl Heinrich Graunto
Montezuma, Roger Sessions
Moon and Sixpence, The, John Gardner
Mörder, Hoffnung der Frauen, Paul Hindemith
Morte d'Orfeo, La, Stefano Landi
Morte dell'aria, Goffredo Petrassi
Morte di Cesare, La, Francesco Bianchi
Mosè in Egitto, Gioachino Rossini
Moses und Aron, Arnold Schoenberg
Motezuma, Gian Francesco di Majo
Mother of Us All, The, Virgil Thomson

Motsart i Sal'yeri [Mozart and Salieri], Nikolay
  Andreyevich Rimsky-Korsakov
Mountain Sylph, The, John Barnett
Mourning Becomes Electra, Marvin David Levy
Mozart and Salieri [Motsart i Sal'yeri], Nikolay
  Andreyevich Rimsky-Korsakov
Muette de Portici, La, Daniel-François-Esprit
  Auber
Mulata de Córdoba, La, José Pablo Moncayo
  García
Muzika dlya zhivikh, Giya Alexandrovich Kancheli
Muzio Scevola, Filippo Amadei, Giovanni
  Bononcini and George Frideric Handel
Myortvïye dushi, Rodion Konstantinovich
  Shchedrin

Nabucco, Giuseppe Verdi
Nacht in Venedig, Eine, Johann Strauss
*Nachtlager in Granada, Das [Das Nachtlager von
  Granada]*, Conradin Kreutzer
*Nachtlager von Granada, Das [Das Nachtlager in
  Granada]*, Conradin Kreutzer
Naïs [Naïs, opéra pour la Paix], Jean-Philippe
  Rameau
*Naissance d'Osiris, La [La naissance d'Osiris, ou La
  fête Pamilie]*, Jean-Philippe Rameau
Narciso, Domenico Scarlatti
Narcissa [Narcissa, or The Cost of Empire], Mary
  Carr Moore
Naufrageurs, Les [The Wreckers], Ethel Smyth
Nausicaa, Peggy Glanville-Hicks
Navarraise, La, Jules Massenet
Ne tol'ko lyubov', Rodion Konstantinovich
  Shchedrin
Nélée et Myrthis, Jean-Philippe Rameau
Nelson, Lennox Berkeley
Néron, Anton Grigor'yevich Rubinstein
Nerone, Giuseppe Maria Orlandini
Nerone, Arrigo Boito
Neue Sonntagskind, Das [Das Neusonntagskind],
  Wenzel Müller
Neues vom Tage, Paul Hindemith
Neugierigen Frauen, Die [Le donne curiose],
  Ermanno Wolf-Ferrari
Neusonntagskind, Das [Das neue Sonntagskind],
  Wenzel Müller
Nevěsta messinská, Zdeněk Fibich
New Year, Michael Tippett
Night at the Chinese Opera, A, Judith Weir
Nightingale, The [Solovey; Le rossignol], Igor
  Stravinsky
Nina [Nina, o sia La pazza per amore], Giovanni
  Paisiello

Nina, ou La folle par amour, Nicolas-Marie
  Dalayrac
Nitteti, Nicola Conforto
Nitteti, Giovanni Paisiello
Nitteti, Pasquale Anfossi
Nixon in China, John Adams
Nizhegorodtsï, Eduard Nápravník
No Song, No Supper, Stephen Storace
Noces de Jeannette, Les, Victor Massé
Noch' pered rozhdestvom [Christmas Eve], Nikolay
  Andreyevich Rimsky-Korsakov
Nonne sanglante, La, Charles-François Gounod
Norma, Vincenzo Bellini
Nos [The Nose], Dmitry Shostakovich
Nose, The [Nos], Dmitry Shostakovich
Notte critica, La [Die unruhige Nacht], Florian
  Leopold Gassmann
Nottetempo, Sylvano Bussotti
Noye's Fludde, Benjamin Britten
Nozze di Figaro, Le, Wolfgang Amadeus Mozart
Nozze di Teti e di Peleo, Le, Francesco Cavalli
Nozze istriane, Antonio Smareglia
Nozze, Le, Baldassare Galuppi
Numitore, Giovanni Porta
Nurmahal, oder Das Rosenfest von Kaschmir,
  Gaspare Spontini
Nusch-Nuschi, Das, Paul Hindemith

O escravo [Lo schiavo], Carlos Gomes
Oberon [Oberon, or The Elf King's Oath], Carl
  Maria von Weber
Oberon, König der Elfen, Paul Wranitzky
Oberto, conte di San Bonifacio, Giuseppe Verdi
*Obrucheniye v monastïre [Betrothal in a
  Monastery]*, Sergey Prokofiev
Oca del Cairo, L', Wolfgang Amadeus Mozart
Occasione fa il ladro, L', Gioachino Rossini
Occulist, The [Der Augenarzt], Adalbert
  Gyrowetz
Occurrence at Owl Creek Bridge, An, Thea
  Musgrave
Oceàna, Antonio Smareglia
*Octavia [Die römische Unruhe, oder Die
  edelmühtige Octavia]*, Reinhard Keiser
Odyssee, Die, August Bungert
Oedipe, George Enescu
Oedipe à Colone, Antonio Sacchini
Oedipus, Harry Partch
Oedipus rex, Igor Stravinsky
Ognennïy angel [The Fiery Angel], Sergey
  Prokofiev
Oktyabr', Vano Il'ich Muradeli
Old Maid and the Thief, The, Gian Carlo Menotti
Olimpiade, L', Antonio Caldara

Olimpiade, L', Baldassare Galuppi
Olimpiade, L', Niccolò Jommelli
Olimpiade, L', Leonardo Leo
Olimpiade, L', Giovanni Battista Pergolesi
Olimpie, Gaspare Spontini
Olivo e Pasquale, Gaetano Donizetti
Olympians, The, Arthur Bliss
On ne s'avise jamais de tout, Pierre-Alexandre Monsigny
One Man Show, Nicholas Maw
Opera, Luciano Berio
Opernball, Der, Richard Heuberger
Ophelia of the Nine Mile Beach, James Penberthy
Oprichnik, Pyotr Il'yich Tchaikovsky
Optimisticheskaya tragediya, Alexander Nikolayevich Kholminov
Oreste, George Frideric Handel
Oresteya, Sergey Ivanovich Taneyev
Orfeide, L', Gian Francesco Malipiero
Orfeo [L'Orfeo], Claudio Monteverdi
Orfeo [L'Orfeo], Luigi Rossi
Orfeo [L'Orfeo], Antonio Sartorio
Orfeo ed Euridice, Ferdinando Bertoni
Orfeo ed Euridice [Orphée et Eurydice], Christoph Willibald Gluck
Orione [Orione, o sia Diana vendicata], Johann Christian Bach
Oristeo, Francesco Cavalli
Orlando, George Frideric Handel
Orlando [Orlando furioso], Antonio Vivaldi
Orlando furioso [Orlando], Antonio Vivaldi
Orlando paladino, Joseph Haydn
Orleanskaya deva [The Maid of Orléans], Pyotr Il'yich Tchaikovsky
Ormindo, Francesco Cavalli
Orontea, Antonio Cesti
Orphée aux enfers, Jacques Offenbach
Orphée et Eurydice [Orfeo ed Euridice], Christoph Willibald Gluck
Orpheus, Friedrich Benda
Orpheus og Eurydike, Johann Gottlieb Naumann
Orpheus und Eurydike, Ernst Krenek
Ossian, ou Les bardes, Jean-François Le Sueur
Osud, Leoš Janáček
Otello, Giuseppe Verdi
Otello [Otello, ossia Il moro di Venezia], Gioachino Rossini
Ottone [Ottone, re di Germania], George Frideric Handel
Ottone in villa, Antonio Vivaldi
Our Man in Havana, Malcolm Williamson
Owen Wingrave, Benjamin Britten

P'tites Michu, Les, André Messager
Padlock, The, Charles Dibdin
Padmâvatî, Albert Roussel
Paganini, Franz Lehár
Pagliacci, Ruggero Leoncavallo
Paladins, Les, Jean-Philippe Rameau
Palazzo incantato, Il [Il palazzo incantato, ovvero La guerriera amante], Luigi Rossi
Palestrina, Hans Pfitzner
Palmira, regina di Persia, Antonio Salieri
Pan Voyevoda, Nikolay Andreyevich Rimsky-Korsakov
Pan y toros, Francisco Asenjo Barbieri
Paride ed Elena, Christoph Willibald Gluck
Parisina, Gaetano Donizetti
Parisina, Pietro Mascagni
Parsifal, Richard Wagner
Partenope, George Frideric Handel
Passaggio, Luciano Berio
Passion selon Sade, La, Sylvano Bussotti
Pasterz [King Roger], Karol Szymanowski
Pastor fido, Il, George Frideric Handel
Pastorella nobile, La, Pietro Alessandro Guglielmi
Patience [Patience; or, Bunthorne's Bride!], Arthur Sullivan
Patria, R. Murray Schafer
Paul Bunyan, Benjamin Britten
Paul et Virginie [Paul et Virginie, ou Le temple de la vertu], Jean-François Le Sueur
Pauline, Frederick Hymen Cowen
Pauvre matelot, Le, Darius Milhaud
Pearl Tree, The, Edgar Bainton
Pêcheurs de perles, Les, Georges Bizet
Pêcheurs, Les, François-Joseph Gossec
Pedro Malasarte, Camargo Guarnieri
Peer Gynt, Werner Egk
Peines et les plaisirs de l'amour, Les, Robert Cambert
Peintre amoureux de son modèle, Le, Egidio Duni
Peleus and Thetis, William Boyce
Pelléas et Mélisande, Claude Debussy
Penelope, Domenico Cimarosa
Pénélope, Gabriel Fauré
Penny for a Song, A, Richard Rodney Bennett
Penthesilea, Othmar Schoeck
Pepita Jiménez, Isaac Albéniz
Per Massimiliano Robespierre, Giacomo Manzoni
Perfect Fool, The, Gustav Holst
Périchole, La, Jacques Offenbach
Persée, Jean-Baptiste Lully
Perséphone, Igor Stravinsky
Pescatrici, Le, Ferdinando Bertoni
Pescatrici, Le [Die Fischerinnen], Joseph Haydn

Quiet Flows the Don [Tikhiy Don], Ivan Ivanovich Dzerzhinsky
Quiet Place, A, Leonard Bernstein
Quinto Fabio, Ferdinando Bertoni

Racine, Le, Sylvano Bussotti
Radamisto, George Frideric Handel
Rake's Progress, The, Igor Stravinsky
Rape of Lucretia, The, Benjamin Britten
Rapimento di Cefalo, Il, Giulio Caccini
Rappresentatione di Anima, et di Corpo, Emilio de' Cavalieri
Rattenfänger von Hameln, Der, Viktor Nessler
Ratto della sposa, Il, Pietro Alessandro Guglielmi
Rauchfangkehrer, Der [Der Rauchfangkehrer, oder Die unentbehrlichen Verräther ihrer Herrschaften aus Eigennutz], Antonio Salieri
Raymond and Agnes, Edward Loder
Re Hassan, Giorcio Federico Ghedini
Re in ascolto, Un, Luciano Berio
Re pastore, Il, Wolfgang Amadeus Mozart
Re Teodoro in Venezia, Il, Giovanni Paisiello
Re, Il, Umberto Giordano
Rebecca, Wilfred Josephs
Řecké pašije [The Greek Passion], Bohuslav Martinů
Reconstructie, Louis Andriessen, Reinbert De Leeuw, Misha Mengelberg, Peter Schat and Jan Van Vlijmen
Red Line, The [Punainen viiva], Aulis Sallinen
Reggente, Il, Saverio Mercadante
Regina, Marc Blitzstein
Reine de Chypre, La, Fromental Halévy
Reine de Saba, La, Charles-François Gounod
Renard [Bayka pro lisu, petukha, kota da barana], Igor Stravinsky
Rencontre imprévue, La, Christoph Willibald Gluck
Rendez-vous bourgeois, Les, Nicolas Isouard
Retablo de maese Pedro, El, Manuel de Falla
Revelation in the Courthouse Park, Harry Partch
Revoltosa, La, Ruperto Chapí
Rey que rabió, El, Ruperto Chapí
Rheingold, Das, Richard Wagner
Riccardo Primo [Riccardo Primo, re d'Inghilterra], George Frideric Handel
Ricciardo e Zoraide, Gioachino Rossini
Richard Coeur-de-lion, André-Ernest-Modeste Grétry
Riders to the Sea, Ralph Vaughan Williams
Rienzi, der Letzte der Tribunen, Richard Wagner
Rigoletto, Giuseppe Verdi
Rinaldo, George Frideric Handel

Ring des Nibelungen, Der, Richard Wagner
Rising of the Moon, The, Nicholas Maw
Risurrezione, Franco Alfano
Rita [Rita, ou Le mari battu], Gaetano Donizetti
Rites of Passage, Peter Sculthorpe
Ritorno d'Ulisse in patria, Il, Claudio Monteverdi
Robert le diable, Giacomo Meyerbeer
Roberto Devereux [Roberto Devereux, ossia Il conte di Essex], Gaetano Donizetti
Robin Woman: Shanewis, The [Shanewis], Charles Wakefield Cadman
Robinson Crusoé, Jacques Offenbach
Rodelinda, George Frideric Handel
Rodrigo [Vincer se stesso è la maggior vittoria], George Frideric Handel
Rodrigue et Chimène, Claude Debussy
Rogneda, Alexander Nikolayevich Serov
Roi Arthus, Le, Ernest Chausson
Roi d'Ys, Le, Edouard Lalo
Roi de Lahore, Le, Jules Massenet
Roi et le fermier, Le, Pierre-Alexandre Monsigny
Roi l'a dit, Le, Léo Delibes
Roi malgré lui, Le, Emmanuel Chabrier
Roland, Jean-Baptiste Lully
Roland, Niccolò Piccinni
Roméo et Juliette, Charles-François Gounod
Roméo et Juliette, Daniel Steibelt
Romeo und Julia, Heinrich Sutermeister
Romeo und Julia auf dem Dorfe [A Village Romeo and Juliet], Frederick Delius
Romeo und Julie, Georg Benda
Römische Unruhe, oder Die edelmühtige Octavia, Die [Octavia], Reinhard Keiser
Rondine, La, Giacomo Puccini
Rosa bianca e la rosa rossa, La, Simon Mayr
Rosamond, Thomas Clayton
Rosamunde, Anton Schweitzer
Rosaura, Giacomo Antonio Perti
Rose vom Liebesgarten, Die, Hans Pfitzner
Rosenkavalier, Der, Richard Strauss
Rosina, William Shield
Rossignol, Le [The Nightingale], Igor Stravinsky
Rote Käppchen, Das [Das rote Käppchen, oder Hilft's nicht, so schadt's nicht], Carl Ditters von Dittersdorf
Royal Hunt of the Sun, The, Iain Hamilton
Ruddigore [Ruddigore; Ruddygore; The Witch's Curse], Arthur Sullivan
Ruggiero [Il Ruggiero, ovvero L'eroica gratitudine], Johann Adolf Hasse
Rusalka, Alexander Sergeyevich Dargomïzhsky
Rusalka, Antonín Dvořák
Ruslan and Lyudmila [Ruslan i Lyudmila], Mikhail Ivanovich Glinka

Ruslan i Lyudmila [Ruslan and Lyudmila], Mikhail Ivanovich Glinka
Ruth, Lennox Berkeley
Ruy Blas, Filippo Marchetti

Sacra rappresentazione di Abram e d'Isaac, La, Ildebrando Pizzetti
Sacrifice interromptu, Le [Das Unterbrochene Opferfest], Peter Winter
Sacrifizio interrotto, Il [Das Unterbrochene Opferfest], Peter Winter
Sadko, Nikolay Andreyevich Rimsky-Korsakov
Saffo, Giovanni Pacini
Saint François d'Assise [Scènes franciscains], Olivier Messiaen
Saint of Bleecker Street, The, Gian Carlo Menotti
Sakùntala [La leggenda di Sakùntala], Franco Alfano
Salammbô, Ernest Reyer
Salammbô [Liviyets], Modest Petrovich Musorgsky
Salome, Richard Strauss
Salvator Rosa, Carlos Gomes
Samori, Georg Joseph Vogler
Samson et Dalila, Camille Saint-Saëns
Sancia di Castiglia, Gaetano Donizetti
Sancta Susanna, Paul Hindemith
Sanktpeterburgskiy gostinnïy dvor, Vasily Alexeyevich Pashkevich
Sant' Alessio, Stefano Landi
Sapho, Charles-François Gounod
Sapho, Jules Massenet
Šárka, Zdeněk Fibich
Satyagraha, Philip Glass
Satyricon, Bruno Maderna
Saul og David, Carl Nielsen
Sāvitri, Gustav Holst
Scala di seta, La, Gioachino Rossini
Scanderberg, François Francoeur and François Rebel
Scènes franciscains [Saint François d'Assise], Olivier Messiaen
Schatzgräber, Der, Franz Schreker
Schauspieldirektor, Der, Wolfgang Amadeus Mozart
Schiava liberata, La, Niccolò Jommelli
Schiavo di sua moglie, Lo, Francesco Provenzale
Schiavo, Lo [O escravo], Carlos Gomes
Schmied von Gent, Der, Franz Schreker
Schmuck der Madonna, Der [I gioielli della Madonna], Ermanno Wolf-Ferrari
Schöne Galathee, Die, Franz Suppé
Schöne Schusterinn, Die, Ignaz Umlauf

Schöne und getreue Ariadne, Die, Johann Georg Conradi
Schuhu und die fliegende Prinzessin, Der, Udo Zimmermann
Schwarze Maske, Die, Krzysztof Penderecki
Schweigsame Frau, Die, Richard Strauss
Schweizerfamilie, Die, Joseph Weigl
Schwestern von Prag, Die, Wenzel Müller
Scipione, George Frideric Handel
Scipione affricano, Francesco Cavalli
Scuola de' gelosi, La, Antonio Salieri
Scylla, Theobaldo di Gatti
Scylla et Glaucus, Jean-Marie Leclair
Seal-Woman, The, Granville Bantock
Secret, The, Bedřich Smetana
Seelewig, Sigmund Theophil Staden
Segreto di Susanna, Il, Ermanno Wolf-Ferrari
Seleuco, re di Siria, Francesco Bianchi
Šelma sedlák [The Cunning Peasant], Antonín Dvořák
Selva sin amor, La, Filippo Piccinini and Bernardo Monanni
Sem'ya Tarasa, Dmitry Borisovich Kabalevsky
Semele, John Eccles
Semele, George Frideric Handel
Semiramide, Gioachino Rossini
Semiramide riconosciuta, Nicola Porpora
Semyon Kotko, Sergey Prokofiev
Sentenza, La, Giacomo Manzoni
Serail, Das [Zaide], Wolfgang Amadeus Mozart
Serrana, Alfredo Keil
Serse, George Frideric Handel
Serva padrona, La, Giovanni Battista Pergolesi
Serve rivali, Le [Le due serve rivali], Tommaso Traetta
Servilia [Serviliya], Nikolay Andreyevich Rimsky-Korsakov
Serviliya [Servilia], Nikolay Andreyevich Rimsky-Korsakov
Sevil', Fikret Amirov
Shakh-Senem, Reyngol'd Moritsevich Glier
Shamus O'Brien, Charles Villiers Stanford
Shanewis [The Robin Woman: Shanewis], Charles Wakefield Cadman
Shepherd's Lottery, The, William Boyce
Shurishe Vose [Vosstaniye Vose], Sergey Artem'yevich Balasanian
Shuzenji monogatari, Osamu Shimizu
Si j'étais roi [If I were King], Adolphe Adam
Siberia, Umberto Giordano
Sich rächende Cupido, Der [Cupido], Reinhard Keiser
Sieben Todsünden, Die, Kurt Weill

Tale of Tsar Saltan, The [The Tale of Tsar Saltan, of his Son the Renowned and Mighty Bogatïr Prince Guidon Saltanovich, and of the Beautiful Swan-Princess (Skazka o Tsare Saltane o sïne ego slavnom i moguchem bogatïre knyaze Gvidone Saltanoviche i o prekrasnoy Tsarevne Lebedi], Nikolay Andreyevich Rimsky-Korsakov

Tale of Two Cities, A, Arthur Benjamin

Tambor de granaderos, El, Ruperto Chapí

Tamerlano, George Frideric Handel

Tancia, La [Il potestà di Colognole], Jacopo Melani

Tancrède, André Campra

Tancredi, Gioachino Rossini

Tannhäuser [Tannhäuser und der Sängerkrieg auf Wartburg], Richard Wagner

Tapfere Soldat, Der [The Chocolate Soldier; Der Praliné-Soldat], Oscar Straus

Tarare, Antonio Salieri

Tartuffe, Arthur Benjamin

Taverner, Peter Maxwell Davies

Telemach, der Königssohn aus Ithaka [Der Königssohn aus Ithaka], Franz Anton Hoffmeister

Telemaco [Telemaco, ossia L'isola di Circe], Christoph Willibald Gluck

Telephone, The [The Telephone, or L'amour à trois], Gian Carlo Menotti

Temistocle, Johann Christian Bach

Tempelbrand, Der [Kinkakuji], Toshirō Mayuzumi

Tempest, The, John C. Eaton

Tempest, The [The Tempest, or The Enchanted Island], John Weldon

Tempesta, La, Felice Lattuada

Tempestad, La, Ruperto Chapí

Temple de la Gloire, Le, Jean-Philippe Rameau

Templer und die Jüdin, Der, Heinrich August Marschner

Tempranica, La, Jerónimo Giménez

Tender Land, The, Aaron Copland

Tenor, The, Hugo Weisgall

Teofane, Antonio Lotti

Teraminta, John Stanley

Teseo, George Frideric Handel

Testament de la tante Caroline, Le [Testament Tèty Karoliny], Albert Roussel

Testament Tety Karoliny [Le testament de la tante Caroline], Albert Roussel

Tetide in Sciro, Domenico Scarlatti

Teufelsmühle am Wienerberge, Die, Wenzel Müller

Thaïs, Jules Massenet

Thérèse, Jules Massenet

Thérèse, John Tavener

Thésée, Jean-Baptiste Lully

Thétis et Pélée, Pascal Collasse

Thetis och Pelée, Francesco Antonio Baldassare Uttini

Thomas, Einojuhani Rautavaara

Thomas and Sally [Thomas and Sally, or The Sailor's Return], Thomas Augustine Arne

Thurm zu Babel, Der [Vavilonskoye stolpotvoreniye], Anton Grigor'yevich Rubinstein

Tiefland, Eugen d'Albert

Tigers, The, Havergal Brian

Tigrane [Il Tigrane, o vero L'egual impegno d'amore e di fede], Alessandro Scarlatti

Tikhiy Don [Quiet Flows the Don], Ivan Ivanovich Dzerzhinsky

Timbre d'argent, Le, Camille Saint-Saëns

Tindaridi, I [I tindaridi, o Castore e Polluce], Tommaso Traetta

Tintomara, Lars Johan Werle

Tito, Antonio Cesti

Tito Manlio, Antonio Vivaldi

Tkmuleba Shota Rustavelze, Dimitri Ignat'yevich Arakishvili

Toi [Loving], R. Murray Schafer

Tolomeo, George Frideric Handel

Tom Jones, Edward German

Tom Jones, François-André Danican Philidor

Tomyris [Die grossmüthige Tomyris], Reinhard Keiser

Tonnelier, Le, François-Joseph Gossec and others

Töpfer, Der, Johann André

Torneo notturno, Gian Francesco Malipiero

Torquato Tasso, Gaetano Donizetti

Torvaldo e Dorliska, Gioachino Rossini

Tosca, Giacomo Puccini

Tote Stadt, Die, Erich Wolfgang Korngold

Toten Augen, Die, Eugen d'Albert

Totila, Giovanni Legrenzi

Toussaint [Toussaint, or The Aristocracy of the Skin], David Blake

Trame deluse, Le [Le trame deluse, ossia I raggiri scoperti], Domenico Cimarosa

Transposed Heads, The, Peggy Glanville-Hicks

Traumgörge, Der, Alexander Zemlinsky

Travelling Companion, The, Charles Villiers Stanford

Traviata, La, Giuseppe Verdi

Tre commedie goldoniane, Gian Francesco Malipiero

Treemonisha, Scott Joplin

Trial by Jury, Arthur Sullivan

Trilogia das barcas, Joly Braga Santos

Trionfo dell'onore, Il, Alessandro Scarlatti

Trionfo di Afrodite, Carl Orff

Trionfo di Camilla, regina de' Volsci, Il, Giovanni Bononcini
Trionfo di Clelia, Il, Johann Adolf Hasse
Tristan und Isolde, Richard Wagner
Troia distrutta, Michele Mortellari
Troilus and Cressida, William Walton
Trois fermiers, Les, Nicolas Dezède
Trois souhaits, Les [Trojí přání], Bohuslav Martinů
Trojí přání [Les trois souhaits], Bohuslav Martinů
Trompeter von Säkkingen, Der, Viktor Nessler
Trovatore, Il, Giuseppe Verdi
Troyens, Les, Hector Berlioz
Tsar's Bride, The [Tsarskaya nevesta], Nikolay Andreyevich Rimsky-Korsakov
Tsarskaya nevesta [The Tsar's Bride], Nikolay Andreyevich Rimsky-Korsakov
Turandot, Ferruccio Busoni
Turandot, Giacomo Puccini
Turco in Italia, Il, Gioachino Rossini
Turn of the Screw, The, Benjamin Britten
Tutti in maschera, Carlo Pedrotti
Two Windows, The, Bedřich Smetana
Tyroler Wastel, Der, Jakob Haibel

Uccellatrice, L', Niccolò Jommelli
Ugo conte di Parigi, Gaetano Donizetti
Ukroshcheniye stroptivoy, Vissarion Yakovlevich Shebalin
Ulisse, Luigi Dallapiccola
Ultimo giorno di Pompei, L', Giovanni Pacini
Ulysse, Jean-Féry Rebel
Ulysses, Reinhard Keiser
Ulysses, John Christopher Smith
Undina, Pyotr Il'yich Tchaikovsky
Undine, E. T. A. Hoffmann
Undine, Albert Lortzing
Unglückselige Cleopatra, Königin von Egypten, oder Die betrogene Staats-Liebe, Die [Cleopatra], Johann Mattheson
Uno dei Dieci, Gian Francesco Malipiero
Unruhige Nacht, Die [La notte critica], Florian Leopold Gassmann
Unterbrochene Opferfest, Das [Il sacrifizio interrotto; Le sacrifice interromptu], Peter Winter
Uthal, Etienne-Nicolas Méhul

V buryu, Tikhon Nikolayevich Khrennikov
V studni, Vilém Blodek
Vakula the Smith [Kuznets Vakula], Pyotr Il'yich Tchaikovsky
Valis, Tod Machover

Vampuka, ili Nevesta afrikanskaya, Vladimir Georgiyevich Ehrenberg
Vampyr, Der, Heinrich August Marschner
Vampyr, Der, Peter Joseph Von Lindpaintner
Vanda, Antonín Dvořák
Vanessa, Samuel Barber
Vavilonskoye stolpotvoreniye [Der Thurm zu Babel], Anton Grigor'yevich Rubinstein
Věc Makropulos [The Makropulos Affair], Leoš Janáček
Vedova scaltra, La, Ermanno Wolf-Ferrari
Veitsi, Paavo Heininen
Velikaya druzhba, Vano Il'ich Muradeli
Venere prigioniera, Gian Francesco Malipiero
Vénitienne, La, Michel de La Barre
Ventaglio, Il, Pietro Raimondi
Venus and Adonis, John Blow
Venus and Adonis, Johann Christoph Pepusch
Vêpres siciliennes, Les [I vespri siciliani], Giuseppe Verdi
Vera costanza, La, Pasquale Anfossi
Vera costanza, La, Joseph Haydn
Vera storia, La, Luciano Berio
Verbena de la paloma, La, Tomás Bretón
Verdammte Staat-Sucht, oder Der verführte Claudius, Die [Claudius], Reinhard Keiser
Verlobung in San Domingo, Die, Werner Egk
Véronique, André Messager
Verratene Meer, Das, Hans Werner Henze
Verschwender, Der, Conradin Kreutzer
Verschworenen, Die [Der häusliche Krieg], Franz Schubert
Verurteilung des Lukullus, Die, Paul Dessau
Verwandelten Weiber, Die [Die verwandelten Weiber, oder Der Teufel ist los, erster Theil], Johann Adam Hiller
Veselohra na mostě, Bohuslav Martinů
Vespasiano, Il, Attilio Ariosti
Vespri siciliani, I [Les Vêpres siciliennes], Giuseppe Verdi
Vestale, La, Saverio Mercadante
Vestale, La, Gaspare Spontini
Viaggiatori felici, I, Pasquale Anfossi
Viaggio a Reims, Il [Il viaggio a Reims, ossia L'albergo del giglio d'oro], Gioachino Rossini
Victory, Richard Rodney Bennett
Vida breve, La, Manuel de Falla
Vie parisienne, La, Jacques Offenbach
Vienna Blood [Wiener Blut], Adolf Müller the younger, arranged from the music of Johann Strauss
Vier Grobiane, Die [I quatro rusteghi], Ermanno Wolf-Ferrari
Viimeiset kiusaukset, Joonas Kokkonen

Zar und Zimmermann [Czaar und Zimmermann, oder Die zwei [beiden] Peter], Albert Lortzing

Zarewitsch, Der, Franz Lehár

Zauberflöte, Die, Wolfgang Amadeus Mozart

Zaubergeige, Die, Werner Egk

Zazà, Ruggero Leoncavallo

Zelmira, Gioachino Rossini

Zemira, Francesco Bianchi

Zémire et Azor, André-Ernest-Modeste Grétry

Zemire und Azor, Louis Spohr

Zenobia di Palmira, Pasquale Anfossi

Zenobia, regina de' Palmireni, Tomaso Giovanni Albinoni

Zéphyre, Jean-Philippe Rameau

Zhenit'ba [Marriage], Modest Petrovich Musorgsky

Zhizn' za tsarya [A Life for the Tsar], Mikhail Ivanovich Glinka

Zigeunerbaron, Der, Johann Strauss

Zingara, La, Rinaldo di Capua

Zirkusprinzessin, Die, Emmerich Kálmán

Zite 'ngalera, Li, Leonardo Vinci

Zolotoy petushok [The Golden Cockerel], Nikolay Andreyevich Rimsky-Korsakov

Zolotyy obruch, Borys Mykolayovych Lyatoshyns'ky

Zoraide di Grenata, Gaetano Donizetti

Zoroastre, Jean-Philippe Rameau

Zuzana Vojířová, Jiří Pauer

Zwerg, Der, Alexander Zemlinsky

Zwillingsbrüder, Die, Franz Schubert